The Norton Introduction to

# PHILOSOPHY

# The Norton Introduction to

# PHILOSOPHY

**GIDEON ROSEN**

Princeton University

**ALEX BYRNE**

Massachusetts Institute of Technology

**JOSHUA COHEN**

Apple University

**SEANA VALENTINE SHIFFRIN**

University of California, Los Angeles

W. W. NORTON & COMPANY, INC.

New York • London

W. W. Norton & Company has been independent since its founding in 1923, when William Warder Norton and Mary D. Herter Norton first published lectures delivered at the People's Institute, the adult education division of New York City's Cooper Union. The firm soon expanded its program beyond the Institute, publishing books by celebrated academics from America and abroad. By midcentury, the two major pillars of Norton's publishing program—trade books and college texts—were firmly established. In the 1950s, the Norton family transferred control of the company to its employees, and today—with a staff of four hundred and a comparable number of trade, college, and professional titles published each year—W. W. Norton & Company stands as the largest and oldest publishing house owned wholly by its employees.

Editor: Peter J. Simon
Associate Editor: Quynh Do
Project Editor: Diane Cipollone
Editorial Assistant: Gerra Goff
Managing Editor, College: Marian Johnson
Managing Editor, College Digital Media: Kim Yi
Production Manager: Vanessa Nuttry
Electronic Media Editor: Cliff Landesman
Marketing Manager, Philosophy: Michael Moss
Design Director: Hope Miller Goodell
Permissions Manager: Megan Jackson
Composition: S4Carlisle Publishing Services
Manufacturing: Quad/Graphics-Taunton

Permission to use copyrighted material is included on page 1125.

Library of Congress Cataloging-in-Publication Data
The Norton introduction to philosophy / Gideon Rosen, Princeton University; Alex Byrne, Massachusetts Institute of Technology; Joshua Cohen, Stanford University; Seana Valentine Shiffrin, University of California, Los Angeles.—First Edition.
        pages cm
  Includes bibliographical references and index.
  **ISBN 978-0-393-93220-1 (pbk. : alk. paper)**
  1. Philosophy—Textbooks. I. Rosen, Gideon A., editor. II. Byrne, Alex, 1960- editor. III. Cohen, Joshua, 1951- editor. IV. Shiffrin, Seana Valentine, editor.
  BD21.N67 2015
  100—dc23

                                        2014046330

W. W. Norton & Company, Inc., 500 Fifth Avenue, New York, NY 10110
wwnorton.com

W. W. Norton & Company Ltd., Castle House, 75/76 Wells Street, London W1T 3QT

1 2 3 4 5 6 7 8 9 0

# Contents

## PART I   PHILOSOPHY OF RELIGION

## 1    Does God Exist?    3

# 4　How Can We Know about What We Have Not Observed?    133

# 5    How Can We Know What Causes What?    192

# 6    How Can You Know Your Own Mind, or the Mind of Another Person?    237

# 7    How Can We Know about the External World?    294

## PART III   METAPHYSICS AND THE PHILOSOPHY OF MIND

# 10  What Is Color?    452

# PART IV    FROM METAPHYSICS TO ETHICS

## PART V    ETHICS AND POLITICAL PHILOSOPHY

# 15   Why Do What Is Right?

# 16 How Do We Reason about What Is Right? 744

# 17 Do Your Intentions Matter? 817

# 18   What Is the Right Thing to Do?

# 19  How Can the State Be Justified?  922

# 20  What Is the Value of Liberty?  973

# 21  Does Justice Require Equality?   1010

# Preface

Philosophy is an ancient subject, and an important one. The great philosophers — Plato, Aristotle, Descartes, and Kant, and the rest — have shaped the way people think about the world.

Philosophy is also a peculiar subject. Philosophers focus on fundamental questions: Do we know anything at all? Does the material world exist? Are actions really right or wrong? In everyday life and in every other academic discipline we take the "obvious" answers to these questions for granted. In philosophy we pause over these answers and subject them to exacting scrutiny.

Such scrutiny can be unsettling. What was once familiar seems puzzling. Confident understanding gives way to perplexity. A tempting response to this perplexity is to turn away from the questioning that gives rise to it. In philosophy, we make it our business to face the perplexity head-on, and so to ask whether and how our basic assumptions about knowledge, existence, and morality can be defended.

Because philosophy focuses on fundamental questions of this sort, it can seem to operate at a great distance from life's practical concerns. In *The Clouds*, the great Athenian playwright Aristophanes portrays his contemporary Socrates as a manic babbler who spouts (and sells) manifestly useless nonsense. Such mockery can seem like the right response to people who spend their time puzzling over our basic assumptions about knowledge, existence, and morality, when life constantly confronts us with urgent questions that need answers here and now.

We feel the force of this dismissive stance, especially in those frustrating moments when we struggle to get a grip on the hardest philosophical questions. But we resist it. It is possible to live a life that is both engaged and reflective, focused simultaneously on practical concerns and on the basic assumptions that guide our thoughts and choices. Socrates famously said that "the unexamined life is not worth living," one of the great overstatements in the history of philosophy. It would be better to say that philosophical reflection can inform and enhance the value of any life. Philosophy is rooted in the deep — and deeply practical — human aspiration to live reflectively. In this book, we aim to keep faith with that aspiration and to provide our readers with materials that will help them pursue it for themselves.

* * *

*The Norton Introduction to Philosophy* is designed for use in introductory courses in philosophy and as a resource for readers approaching the subject for the first time. Composing an introductory book for this large field has required numerous editorial decisions. Philosophy does not have a well-defined structure or settled boundaries; nothing is obvious. To explain the shape of the book, we would like to say a few words about our guiding editorial ideas.

We start from the premise that philosophy is best learned and taught from primary sources. The first formulations of great ideas and arguments are not just historically significant. They are rich with nuances that are easily lost as the ideas are distilled and refined by others. More important, to learn how to read a complex and nuanced philosophical text is (to a very significant extent) to learn how to *do* philosophy. The challenge in reading is to approach the text with the right mix of openness and critical scrutiny, and this is the same challenge students face, with respect to their own ideas, as they begin to do philosophy on their own. An introduction to philosophy should expose readers to important philosophical ideas. But it should also help them to read and think like philosophers. The best way to achieve this purpose is to engage with the original texts.

That engagement, however, presents a challenge. The great books in the history of philosophy were not written for contemporary readers; the important works of contemporary philosophy were not written for beginning students. In almost every case, the original texts assume more than anyone new to the subject can be expected to know.

*The Norton Introduction to Philosophy* is designed to address this challenge. The historical and contemporary selections in the book have been supplemented with substantial editorial materials. These are designed to supply relevant background and to focus the reader's attention on central themes. But they are mainly designed to enable readers to approach philosophical texts as philosophers do: to restate the thesis in plain terms; to reconstruct the arguments; to illustrate them with fresh examples; and to engage with the arguments, sympathetically and critically.

These supporting materials are informed by our belief that the largest purpose in reading philosophy is not to learn what other philosophers have thought but to work out what we should think, and thus to live more reflectively.

Most introductions to philosophy draw their materials exclusively from previously published books and articles. We have done something very different. Philosophy is not a collection of settled findings or a canon of established texts. It is a living subject. Contemporary philosophers engage directly with many of the issues that animated their predecessors. But their approaches (and in some cases, their questions) are new, informed by recent developments in the sciences, in other scholarly disciplines, and within philosophy itself. To convey the current vitality of the discipline, we have commissioned 25 essays from contemporary philosophers specifically for inclusion in *The Norton Introduction to Philosophy*. In each case the author was asked to write an essay on an active research problem in his or her field and to present the issue in terms that someone new to the subject can understand. These commissioned essays are not neutral summaries or surveys. They are works of original contemporary philosophy cast in an idiom that any reader of this book will find accessible. Taken together, they paint a vivid (though inevitably partial) picture of what philosophers are doing now. They are:

Alex Byrne, "Skepticism about the Internal World"
David Chalmers, "The Hard Problem of Consciousness"
Stewart Cohen, "Contextualism"
Alan Hájek, "Pascal's Ultimate Gamble"
Ned Hall, "Causation and Correlation"
Elizabeth Harman, "Is It Reasonable to Rely on 'Intuitions' in Ethics?"
Barbara Herman, "Impermissibility and Wrongness"
Rosalind Hursthouse, "Virtue Ethics"
Rae Langton, "Ignorance of Things in Themselves"
David Lyons, "The Utilitarian Justification of the State"
Tim Maudlin, "Science and Metaphysics"
Martha Nussbaum, "Political Equality"
Gideon Rosen, "Numbers and Other Immaterial Objects"
T. M. Scanlon, "When Do Intentions Matter to Permissibility?"
John Simmons, "Rights-Based Justifications for the State"
Galen Strawson, "Free Will"
Sharon Street, "Does Anything Really Matter?"
Judith Jarvis Thomson, "Why Ought We Do What Is Right?"
Michael Tye, "The Puzzle of Transparency"
Jonathan Vogel, "Skepticism and Inference to the Best Explanation"
R. Jay Wallace, "Moral Subjectivism"
Roger White, "The Argument from Cosmological Fine-Tuning"
Timothy Williamson, "Knowledge and Belief"
Jonathan Wolff, "Equality as a Basic Demand of Justice"
Stephen Yablo, "A Thing and its Matter"

In choosing materials for this book, we have been guided to a significant degree by a shared philosophical orientation. We editors are all trained in and identify with the so-called "analytic" tradition in philosophy, the dominant tradition in Anglo-American philosophy since the early twentieth century (and powerfully represented outside the Anglo-American world as well). Analytic philosophy does not have a well-defined method or a distinctive set of topics. Insofar as it is unified at all, it is so by an intellectual style that emphasizes clear, precisely stated theses and explicit arguments. Most of the modern selections we have included, and all of the newly commissioned essays, are in the analytical tradition.

We should also note that while philosophy is an expansive subject of broad human interest, the academic discipline of philosophy suffers from a genuine shortcoming. Though the field is changing, women and people of color have been, and continue to be, underrepresented. Their underrepresentation in this volume is partly a consequence of our decision to stress the historical roots of the subject.

The newly commissioned pieces reflect the current state of the discipline, and so come some way toward correcting this deficiency. We are hopeful that the field will continue to become more inclusive and diverse and that this progress will be reflected in future editions.

## Organization and Readings

*The Norton Introduction to Philosophy* includes 104 selections, more than any other text of its kind. Of these, 79 are drawn from previously published work. These present central arguments and classic formulations of important problems from the most influential works in the history of philosophy, including Plato's *Republic*, Aristotle's *Politics*, Descartes' *Meditations*, Kant's *Groundwork*, and Mill's *Utilitarianism*. Selections from previously published work have been edited for length and lightly annotated to supply definitions of key terms and needed background. Because our aim was to provide a text suitable for a first course in philosophy, we have omitted classic readings that assume substantial acquaintance with the field or are in other ways too challenging for beginners.

We have organized these selections into five major parts: "Philosophy of Religion," "Epistemology," "Metaphysics and the Philosophy of Mind," "From Metaphysics to Ethics," and "Ethics and Political Philosophy." Each part is divided into chapters, each of which is headed by a question. Some of these questions will be familiar to students (e.g., "Does God exist?"); others may be new (e.g., "How Can the State Be Justified?"). We name each chapter with a question in order to emphasize that philosophy is a form of inquiry, and that the first step in any inquiry is to ask the right questions.

We have focused on a selection of central topics in philosophy. To do them justice and to give a sense of competing perspectives, we have had to exclude other rich and exciting parts of the field, including the philosophy of language, aesthetics, the philosophy of physics, feminist philosophy, the philosophy of mathematics, action theory, the philosophy of race, and the philosophy of biology. Work in these areas often presupposes the material covered here, and we are confident that readers of this book will be in a good position to approach these and other important topics after working through the material included here.

That said, we should note that unlike many introductory texts, *The Norton Introduction to Philosophy* devotes substantial space to moral theory, metaethics, and political philosophy. These are areas that have been central to philosophy from its beginnings, but they are not always represented in introductory texts, on the ground that they are specialized subjects that require prior training. We disagree. Philosophical questions about the good life, the structure of morality, and the demands of justice provide a natural and compelling point of entry into philosophy.

To ensure that students read the primary texts as thoughtfully as possible, each chapter opens with an Introduction that frames the questions in accessible and compelling terms and provides essential background about the essays and the arguments presented in them. Each primary text is followed by questions labeled "Test Your Understanding," designed to help students determine whether they have read the text carefully, and by a set of "Notes and Questions," designed to encourage students to analyze the arguments more carefully, to respond to problems raised by the text, to reply on the author's behalf to apparent counterexamples to central claims, and so on. Each chapter then closes with a feature called "Analyzing the Arguments," which prompts to students to bring the readings into dialogue with one another. This closing section also points readers to problems that merit further study and, in many cases, to open questions of current interest.

The volume concludes with an extensive glossary in which technical terms are explained and illustrated, and in which some of the main issues that arise in the interpretation of these technical distinctions are addressed, along with a brief guide to logic and argumentation, and some guidelines for writing a good philosophy paper.

\* \* \*

Despite its long history and despite the intrinsic difficulty of its problems, philosophy is that rare academic field in which it is possible for beginning students not only to learn the discipline but to practice it. Our hope is that this *Norton Introduction to Philosophy* will be especially useful for readers who approach the study of philosophy with a double aim: to understand the ideas of great philosophers past and present and to use those ideas as a resource in their own philosophical investigations.

Gideon Rosen, Princeton University
Alex Byrne, MIT
Joshua Cohen, Apple University
Seana Shiffrin, UCLA
July 2014

# Acknowledgments

Each of us loves philosophy. That common passion drew us together to work on *The Norton Introduction to Philosophy*. It has sustained us through seven years, from conception to publication. Before letting the book go, we want to acknowledge the many people who have helped us complete it.

First things first: we are very grateful to Roby Harrington, Director of the College Department at W. W. Norton, for initiating the project, and to Roby and our editor, Pete Simon, for their philosophical and editorial insights, as well as their patience (and the limits on their patience). We are grateful, too, for the help of the other publishing professionals at Norton—Conor Sullivan and Quynh Do, Associate Editors; Gerra Goff, Editorial Assistant; Diane Cipollone, Project Editor; Megan Jackson, Permissions Manager; Hope Miller Goodell, Associate Design Director; Debra Morton Hoyt, Design Director; Vanessa Nuttry, Production Manager; and Cliff Landesman, Media Editor—who assisted in simplifying the complex process of wrestling this large book to the ground.

We would like to thank Anand Krishnamurthy, Tobey Scharding, and Elyse Meyers for expert assistance in preparing the manuscript, and Robbie Hirsch for invaluable assistance with the glossary and illustrations.

We also wish to thank the many instructors who offered us advice and feedback on early draft chapters. It is our firm hope that this book will be useful to teachers of philosophy everywhere, from the smallest colleges to the largest universities and beyond. The wise counsel of colleagues with widely diverse experience in the classroom has been invaluable in informing our choices at every stage.

Thanks to the philosophers who responded to the publisher's initial survey about the introductory course: Christa Acampora (Hunter College and The Graduate Center, CUNY); Kendrick Adams (University of Arkansas Community College at Hope); David Aiken (University College Roosevelt, The Netherlands); Panos Alexakos (Santa Fe Community College); William Allbritton (Blinn College); Dawn Allen-Herron (University of Alaska Southeast); Torin Alter (University of Alabama); Kenneth Anderson (Oxford College of Emory University); Linda Anthony (Blue Mountain Community College); Mike Austin (Eastern Kentucky University); Karen Bardsley (Morehead State University); Carmine Bell (Pasco-Hernando State College); Joseph Bessing (Lehigh Carbon Community College); Carrie-Ann Biondi (Marymount Manhattan College); Daniel Bonevac

(University of Texas at Austin); Marshell Bradley (Sam Houston State University); Alexandra Bradner (Kenyon College); Girard Brenneman (William Jewell College); Robert Brimlow (St. John Fisher College); Robert Briscoe (Loyola University, New Orleans); Michael Carper (Lindenwood University); Thomas Carroll (Middlesex Community College); Charles Cassini (Barry University); Daniel Christensen (Iowa Western Community College); William Clohesy (University of Northern Iowa); Kevin Coffey (New York University, Abu Dhabi); Charlie Coil (John Brown University); James Coleman (Central Michigan University); Juan Comesaña (University of Arizona); Sam Condic (University of Houston-Downtown); Elizabeth Cooke (Creighton University); Ron Cooper (College of Central Florida); Glen Cosby (Spokane Community College); Olga-Maria Cruz (Bellarmine University); Norman Cubbage (University of Louisville); Mike Cundall (North Carolina A&T State University); Margaret Cuonzo (Long Island University); Elaine Davis (Mississippi Gulf Coast Community College); Douglas Deaver (Santiago Canyon College); David Denby (Tufts University); Christian Diehm (University of Wisconsin-Stevens Point); Jill Dieterle (Eastern Michigan University); Dittmar Dittrich (Loyola University, New Orleans); Tyler Doggett (University of Vermont); Yancy Dominick (Seattle University); Cian Dorr (New York University); Karánn Durland (Austin College); JoAnne Dyson (Front Range Community College); M. Dominic Eggert (Vanderbilt University); Zoe Eisenman (Saint Xavier University); Gary Elkins (Toccoa Falls College); Linda Emmerson (Walla Walla University); Miguel Endara (Azusa Pacific University); Jonathan Evans (University of Indianapolis); Michael Fara (Princeton University); Dean Finley (Ozarks Technical Community College); Michael Fitch (Florida State College); Russell Ford (Elmhurst College); Roger Foster (Borough of Manhattan Community College, CUNY); Craig Fox (California University of Pennsylvania); Jonathan Gainor (Harrisburg Area Community College); Erik Gardner (University of Hawaii: Windward Community College); Bruno Garofalo (West Chester University); Aaron German (Eastern Kentucky University); Caryl Gibbs (Rose State College); Douglas Giles (Elmhurst College); Ron Glass (University of Wisconsin-La Crosse); Steven Godby (Broward College); James Grady (Vanderbilt University); Franz-Peter Griesmaier (University of Wyoming); Kevin Guilfoy (Carroll University); John Gulley (Winston-Salem State University); Dorothy Haney (Marywood University); Robert Hansen; Richard Hanson (University of Wisconsin-Washington Country); Gary Hardcastle (Bloomsburg University); Kate Harkins (Coconino Community College); Maralee Harrell (Carnegie Mellon University); Allan Hazlett (University of Edinburgh); Scott Hendricks (Clark University); Will Heusser (Cypress College); Travis Hicks (Merced College); David Hoekema (Calvin College); Kent Hoeffner (McLennan Community College); Mark Horton (Norwalk Community College); Robert J. Howell (Dedman College, Southern Methodist University); Clark Hutton (Volunteer State Community College); Creed Hyatt (Lehigh Carbon Community College); Debbie Ingle (Rose State College); William Jamison (University of Alaska Anchorage); Scott Jenkins (University of Kansas); Michael Jordan (Iona College); Thomas

Keyes (Our Lady of the Lake University); Hye-Kyung Kim (University of Wisconsin-Green Bay); Boris Kment (Princeton University); Achim Koeddermann (State University of New York, Oneonta); Avery Kolers (University of Louisville); A. J. Kreider (Miami Dade College); Douglas Krueger (Northwest Arkansas Community College); Denny Kuhn (Hillsdale Free Will Baptist College); Safro Kwame (Lincoln University); Jennifer Lackey (Northwestern University); Philip LaFountain (Eastern Nazarene College); Michael Latzer (Gannon University); Stephen Leach (University of Texas-Pan American); Kenneth Locke (Glendale Community College); Jessica E. Logue (University of Portland); Paul Long (Metropolitan Community College-Maple Woods); Shannon Love (Old Dominion University); William Lycan (University of North Carolina); Tim Maddox (Hardin-Simmons University); Adrianne McEvoy (Mansfield University); Michael McGlone (The University at Buffalo, SUNY); Marcia McKelligan (DePauw University); Jon Mandle (The University at Albany, SUNY); Don Merrell (Arkansas State University); Garret Merriam (University of Southern Indiana); Anthony Miccoli (Western State Colorado University); Daniel Milsky (Northeastern Illinois University); Marc Moffett (University of Wyoming); Brad Morris (North Dakota State University); John. G. Moore (Lander University); Mark Moyer (University of Vermont); John Mullen (Bethany College); Jennifer Mulnix (University of Massachusetts, Dartmouth); Daniel Musgrave (New Mexico Military Institute); Vasile Munteanu (College of Southern Nevada); Alan Nichols (Georgia Highlands College); Kathryn Norlock (Trent University); Suzanne Obdrzalek (Claremont McKenna College); Douglas Olena (Evangel University); Barry Padgett (Bellarmine University); David Palmer (Massachusetts Maritime Academy); John Pappas (Saint Joseph's University); Michael Patton (University of Montevallo); Richard Peddicord (Aquinas Institute of Theology); Emile Piscitelli (Northern Virginia Community College); Stephen Pluhacek (Michigan Technological University); Consuelo Preti (The College of New Jersey); David Przekupowski (Northeast Lakeview College); Richard Reilly (Blinn College); Ray Rennard (University of the Pacific); John Rettura (Lackawanna College); Jay Reuscher (Georgetown University); Victoria Rogers (Indiana University-Purdue University Indianapolis); Michael Rosenthal (University of Washington); Chad Russell (University of Mississippi); Nathan Sager (Mesabi Range Community College); Mark Sanders (Three Rivers Community College); John Sarnecki (University of Toledo); James Schaar (University of Minnesota, Crookston); Kevin Scharp (The Ohio State University); Stephen Schmid (University of Wisconsin-Rock County); Edward Schoen (Western Kentucky University); Sally Scholz (Villanova University); Stephen Scholz (St. Augustine's College); Emily Sedgwick (East Los Angeles College); Darin Senestraro (East Los Angeles College); Robert Sessions (Emeritus, Kirkwood Community College); Gail Shaughnessey (Cochise College); Warren Shrader (Indiana University South Bend); Ivana Simic (University of Florida); Jack Simmons (Armstrong Atlantic State University); Thomas Singleton (Spring Hill College); Robert Skipper (St. Mary's University); James Spence (Adrian College); Jeffrey Staudt (Washington State Community

College); Robert Stecker (Central Michigan University); Roderick Stewart (Austin College); Todd Stewart (Illinois State University); Bill Stone (Northeast Mississippi Community College); Andrew Strauss; Kevin Sweeney (University of Tampa); Robert Sweet (Clark State Community College); James Swindler (Illinois State University); Ed Szymanski, Jr. (Valencia Community College); Matthew Tedesco (Beloit College); Carolyn Thomas (University of New Mexico); Debbie Thompson (Ozarks Technica Community College); Katherine Tietge (Ocean County College); Terry Toma (St. Louis Community College at Forest Park); Zev Trachtenberg (University of Oklahoma); Ariela Tubert (University of Puget Sound); Dale Turner (California State Polytechnic University, Pomona); Donald Turner (Hillsdale College); Zach VanderVeen (Vanderbilt University); Andrew Vassar (Northeastern State University); Lorraine M. Victoria (Bucks County Community College); Steven Vogel (Denison University); Russell Waltz (University of North Carolina at Charlotte); Andrea Weisberger (University of North Florida); Scott West (Harford Community College); David White (St. John Fisher College); Glenn Whitehouse (Florida Gulf Coast University); Joel Wilcox (Barry University); Stephen Wilhelm (Metropolitan Community College); Melissa Willmore (Jefferson College); Anita Wilson (Bismarck State College); Marc Wilson (Treasure Valley Community College); Ted Zenzinger (Regis College); and Robert Zeuschner (Pasadena City College).

We also owe a great debt to the philosophers (and philosophically-minded friends) who took the time to read and review early draft chapters. They include Joseph Baltimore (West Virginia University); Yancy Dominick (Seattle University); Craig Duncan (Ithaca College); Heimir Geirsson (Iowa State University); Cody Gilmore (University of California, Davis); Deke Gould (Syracuse University); Christopher Grau (Clemson University); Jeff Foss (University of Victoria); Kevin Harrelson (Ball State University); Claire Horisk (University of Missouri at Chapel Hill); Michael Horton (University of Alabama); Peter Hutcheson (Texas State University); Kristen Intemann (Montana State University); Janine Jones (University of North Carolina at Greensboro); Andrew Melnyk (University of Missouri); Seyed Hossein Mousavian (Princeton University); Catherine Muller (University of Birmingham); Pam Spritzer; William Ramsey (University of Nevada, Las Vegas); Michele Reeves; Sharon Ryan (West Virginia University); Timothy Schroeder (The Ohio State University); Adam Sennet (University of California, Davis); Matthew Silverstein (New York University, Abu Dhabi); Matthew Strawbridge; Matthew Talbert (West Virginia University); James Stacey Taylor (The College of New Jersey); and Andreas Teuber (Brandeis University).

Thank you all.

# Part I

## PHILOSOPHY OF RELIGION

# 1

# Does God Exist?

When a philosopher tells you that he is going to prove that God exists (or that God does not exist) your first thought should be, "Wait! Stop! Before you say another word, tell me as clearly and as plainly as you can what you mean by the word 'God.'" Like most familiar words, the word "God" has many meanings, and each yields a different interpretation of the question "Does God exist?" Here are some of the most important possibilities.

## Some Meanings of "God"

### THE GOD OF SCRIPTURE AND TRADITION

We have ancient books about God and complex religious traditions built around them. One way to use the word "God" is to use it to mean *the figure described in one or another of these traditions*. In this view, when we ask whether God exists, we are asking whether there exists a being who did all or most of the things that God is said to have done in (say) the Hebrew Bible, or the Koran. Atheists who answer "no" regard these stories as myths, as we now regard the Babylonian *Epic of Gilgamesh,* while theists in the relevant tradition regard them as true stories about a real being whom they more or less accurately depict.

### THE GOD OF THE PHILOSOPHERS

Philosophers often use the word "God" to mean *an absolutely perfect being*. Anselm's famous **ontological argument** is not an argument for the historical accuracy of the Christian scriptures. It is an argument for the existence of a being *than which none greater can be thought.* A being of this sort would be perfect in all respects: perfectly powerful (omnipotent), perfectly wise (omniscient), perfectly good (omnibenevolent), and so on. When the word is used in this way, it is a contradiction to say that God is limited in some way. Even if the world was created by an immaterial spirit who loves mankind and ensures that justice is done in the next life, if that being is imperfect in any way, then that being *is not God* when the word is used in Anselm's sense.

### GOD AS FIRST CAUSE; GOD AS DESIGNER

For some writers, the debate over the existence of God is a debate about the origin of the universe. In this view, when we ask whether God exists, we are asking whether the natural world owes its existence to a being that is not simply part of nature. A supernatural creator must presumably be immaterial, since it exists before any material thing exists. If it is to count as a designer, it must presumably be intelligent and very powerful. But it need not be perfect in every way, and it need not play the role in human history that God is said to play in (say) the Bible.

### GOD AS A TRANSCENDENT SOURCE OF "MEANING"

If philosophy could establish the existence of a supernatural cause of the universe, that would be an amazing contribution to metaphysics. But it would not by itself have much religious significance. We can imagine someone saying, "Wow, that's fascinating. But unless this cosmic being plans to interfere with my life, I plan to ignore it. You've given me no reason to take this being into account, or to live my life differently in light of its existence." Some writers use the word "God" to signify a being that no one could sensibly shrug off in this way. On this conception, to say that God exists is to affirm the existence of a being whose existence somehow manages to give meaning, purpose, directions, or limits to human life — a being which, by its very nature, merits something like devotion or obedience or even love.

# Ground Rules in Philosophical Theology

These are rough sketches of some of the many meanings that philosophers have attached to the word "God." Which is the correct meaning? *This is a misguided question.* It's like asking what the word "bat" really means, when we all know that it sometimes means a stick used in sports like baseball, and sometimes a flying rodent of the order Chiroptera. Anselm seeks to establish the existence of God, by which he means a *perfect being.* You can object to his argument in many ways. But you should not object to it by saying, "By 'God' *I* mean the supernatural creator of the universe; Anselm has not proved the existence of a creator, so his argument is no good." When you review the arguments for and against the existence of God,

> Your first job is to figure out what the author means by the words in his or her text.
>
> Your second job is determine what his or her argument is supposed to be.
>
> Your third job is to decide whether the argument establishes its conclusion.

Given these aims, it makes no sense to quibble with the author's terminological choices. You have much more important things to do.

That said, it is possible to abuse the word. Occasionally someone will say, "I'm a religious person; I believe in God," and then go on to explain that she doesn't believe in anything supernatural. "When I say that God exists, I just mean to express my hope for human progress." There is no law against this sort of Humpty Dumptyish use of words. ("'When I use a word,' Humpty Dumpty said—in a rather scornful tone—'it means just what I choose it to mean, neither more nor less.'") But in philosophy this sort of idiosyncratic usage is a recipe for confusion. So avoid it. If you want to express your secular hope for the future of humanity, we have perfectly good words for that already. There is no need to co-opt the language of theology for your purposes.

One last potential source of confusion should be mentioned. It is surprisingly common in discussions of the existence of God for people to say that God is an *idea* or a *concept*. One hears this from atheists who mean to say that God is just a figment of the imagination. But one also hears it from professed theists who seem to think that it makes their position less controversial. This way of speaking is, however, seriously misleading. There may be such a thing as *the idea of God*. In fact there may be many such things: *your* idea of God, *my* idea of God, etc. These ideas are representations in the minds or brains of human beings, and for present purposes, no one denies their existence. In general, it is a grave mistake to confuse your idea of X with X itself. You would never confuse your *idea* of your mother with *your mother*. Your mother is a flesh-and-blood person with hands and feet who existed years before you existed. Your idea of your mother is—well, who knows exactly what it is? But it is obviously nothing like *that*. Similarly, your idea of God did not create the universe. Your idea of God is not omnipotent, even if it is the idea *of* an omnipotent thing. The debate over God's existence is a debate over the existence of a real being with extraordinary attributes. It is not a debate about the existence of an idea.

## A Brief Taxonomy of the Arguments

However we understand the word, everyone agrees that, if God exists, God is invisible, intangible, and undetectable by means of scientific instruments. How then are we to approach the question of God's existence? In this book we set aside arguments that depend on special revelation or on private religious experiences that are not widely shared. These arguments are important. But the main philosophical challenge has always been to ask whether God's existence can be established by philosophical reasoning informed by ordinary experience. This is the project of **natural theology.**

Some arguments proceed **a priori.** The most important is Anselm's ontological argument — one of the strangest and also one of the most difficult arguments in this area. Think of it as a **reductio ad absurdum.** The atheist says, "A perfect being does not exist." But if he says this, he must understand the phrase "a perfect being," and whatever he understands must exist in his understanding, according to Anselm. So the atheist must agree that God exists in the understanding (i.e., in the mind). The only question is whether he exists in reality as well. Anselm then seeks to show that if God exists only in the understanding, God could have been greater than he is. But since God is a perfect being, this is absurd. And so it follows that God must exist both in the understanding *and in reality*. Almost every modern student of this argument rejects it, but there is no consensus about where the error lies. If you reject the argument, your job is not simply to show *that* it is unsound; it is to identify the source of the problem: the false premise, the invalid step. Be advised: this is very slippery material.

The remaining arguments all proceed **a posteriori.** The aim is to show that certain facts of observation and experiment constitute "evidence of things unseen." The **cosmological argument** begins with an observed causal or explanatory sequence in nature, and then argues that this sequence must have an *origin* — a first cause — that is not just another part of nature. Some versions assume that each such sequence must have a beginning in time. But the most sophisticated versions hold that even if the natural universe has always existed, there must still be something outside the world to explain why the world exists, and so to answer the question: "Why is there something rather than nothing?"

The most important arguments in recent natural theology begin with detailed observations drawn from the sciences. The **design argument** begins from the observation that the parts of plants and animals are brilliantly adapted to serve the purposes of the organisms of whose parts they are. Before Darwin, the only serious explanations for this fact were theological, and even after Darwin, some versions of this argument are worth discussing. Darwinian arguments assume the existence of living things; but the first living thing must already have had parts that were adapted to benefit the whole. Thus, some writers argue that the existence of life itself constitutes evidence of God's existence.

There is of course a famous danger in such arguments. At any given stage in the history of science there will be facts that science cannot explain. Given such a gap, a theist can say, "Aha! Science can't explain it. But it must have an explanation. So God exists." The defect in arguments of this form should be clear. Science makes progress. What we cannot explain today, we may well explain tomorrow. So given an ordinary gap in our scientific understanding of nature, the rational response is not to posit a convenient **God of the Gaps,** but rather to acknowledge that for now we just don't know, and perhaps to hope that ordinary science will solve the problem.

The most recent of the arguments for God's existence is crafted to evade this difficulty. The **cosmic fine-tuning argument** begins from a claim about the fundamental constants of nature: certain numbers—like the gravitational constant—that appear in the basic laws of nature. We do not know these laws in detail. But we know a bit about them, and what we know suggests the following: If the fundamental constants had been slightly different from what they are, stars and planets would not have formed and life would never have arisen. This raises a question: Why do the constants have "life-permitting" values? And here (it is claimed) there can be no scientific explanation. The constants are aspects of the *fundamental* laws of nature. But a fundamental law—by definition—cannot be explained. (If it could, it would not be *fundamental*.) So the answer to our question, if there is one, cannot possibly come from science. Proponents of the argument regard the fact of "fine tuning" as a reason to believe that a divine first cause exists. Are they right? The argument is new: unlike the other arguments discussed in this section, it is a creature of the late twentieth century. The science it assumes remains unsettled, and philosophers are not going to settle it from the armchair. The question for you is therefore conditional: *If* the physicists tell us that the fundamental constants of nature appear to be "fine-tuned," what would this show about the existence of God?

# The Case for Atheism

Suppose the arguments for the existence of God are all no good. Would this vindicate the atheist? Not automatically. Our search for extraterrestrial life has so far turned up nothing. But this does not warrant the conclusion that no such life exists, and at this stage, the only reasonable attitude on that question is **agnosticism:** a principled refusal to answer the question given the present state of the evidence. By parity of reasoning, the atheist who wishes to affirm with confidence that there is no God needs a positive argument for this negative conclusion. What is it to be?

The most important argument for atheism is the **argument from evil**. The target is the God of the Philosophers. If there were a perfect being, there would be no unnecessary suffering in the world, since a good God would prevent unnecessary suffering if he could, and an omnipotent God could certainly prevent it. But there *is* unnecessary suffering: think of the animals injured in forest fires who suffer terribly before they die. And so, the argument concludes, there is no God. The argument is as old as theology, though it has been refined over the years. It has occasionally been offered as a knockdown *proof* of atheism. These days, however, it is generally understood as providing *evidence* for atheism—evidence that any defensible form of theism must overcome. A theistic argument that attempts to meet this challenge is called a **theodicy**.

After you have read and discussed these arguments, it will be useful to step back. What have you been discussing? The existence of an invisible spirit—a being whose existence would be of absolutely fundamental importance, both for our understanding of the universe and for the conduct of our lives. How have you been approaching the question? By reading and thinking and talking. Have you made progress? One hopes so. Even if you have not settled the question, you have a clearer sense of what it would take to settle it. Familiar arguments that once seemed compelling may strike you as hopeless; unfamiliar arguments may strike you as promising. This encourages the thought that more work of this sort might bring the issue into sharper focus. Perhaps the most important point to stress is that philosophical progress in this area, as in others, does not always consist in marshaling knockdown arguments that "compel assent" from any rational creature whatsoever, but rather in displaying the available positions and the best arguments for and against them. The questions addressed in this chapter are very old, as the classic selections from Anselm of Canterbury and Thomas Aquinas attest. The selections from William Paley and John Stuart Mill illustrate how they were transformed by the rise of science. The contemporary selections from William Rowe and Roger White show that progress is still being made.

## Anselm of Canterbury (c. 1033–1109)

Anselm is one of the first and most important figures in the history of scholasticism, the effort to supply an explicit philosophical foundation for Christian doctrine that incorporates the insights of Greek philosophy. His *Proslogion*, an extended meditation on the attributes of God, was originally entitled *Fides quaerens intellectum*, or "faith seeking reason."

# THE ONTOLOGICAL ARGUMENT
## from *Proslogion*

# Chapter 2

### THAT GOD TRULY EXISTS

Therefore, Lord, you who grant understanding to faith, grant that, insofar as you know it is useful for me, I may understand that you exist as we believe you exist, and that you are what we believe you to be. Now we believe that you are something than which nothing greater can be thought. So can it be that no such nature exists, since "The fool has said in his heart, 'There is no God'" (Psalm 14:1; 53:1)? But when this same fool hears me say "something than which nothing greater can be thought," he surely understands what he hears; and what he understands exists in his understanding, even if he does not understand that it exists [in reality]. For it is one thing for an object to exist in the understanding and quite another to understand that the object exists [in reality]. When a painter, for example, thinks out in advance what he is going to paint, he has it in his understanding, but he does not yet understand that it exists, since he has not yet painted it. But once he has painted it, he both has it in his understanding and understands that it exists because he has now painted it. So even the fool must admit that something than which nothing greater can be thought exists at least in his understanding, since he understands this when he hears it, and whatever is understood exists in the understanding. And surely that than which a greater cannot be thought cannot exist only in the understanding. For if it exists only in the understanding, it can be thought to exist in reality as well, which is greater. So if that than which a greater cannot be thought exists only in the understanding, then that than which a greater *cannot* be thought is that than which a greater *can* be thought. But that is clearly impossible. Therefore, there is no doubt that something than which a greater cannot be thought exists both in the understanding and in reality.

# Chapter 3

## THAT HE CANNOT BE THOUGHT NOT TO EXIST

This [being] exists so truly that it cannot be thought not to exist. For it is possible to think that something exists that cannot be thought not to exist, and such a being is greater than one that can be thought not to exist. Therefore, if that than which a greater cannot be thought can be thought not to exist, then that than which a greater cannot be thought is *not* that than which a greater cannot be thought; and this is a contradiction. So that than which a greater cannot be thought exists so truly that it cannot be thought not to exist.

## TEST YOUR UNDERSTANDING

1. Anselm identifies God with "something than which nothing greater can be thought." Briefly explain this formulation.

2. "It is one thing for an object to exist in the understanding, and quite another to understand that the object exists [in reality]." Explain this distinction using examples of your own.

## NOTES AND QUESTIONS

1. *Anselm on "existence in the understanding."* Anselm's argument assumes that whenever we think of X, X exists *in our understanding*, or, as we might say, *in our mind*. But that is a peculiar idiom. It suggests that the mind is a place, populated with real things like Barack Obama, and also with shadowy unreal things like the Loch Ness Monster. One way to resist Anselm's argument is to reject this way of speaking. We might concede that when we think of the Loch Ness Monster, an *idea* of the Monster exists in our minds. But we should not confuse our idea of the Monster, which exists in the mind, with the Monster itself, which does not exist at all.

   Some versions of the ontological argument do without this assumption. Say that a *perfection* is a property that any perfect being must possess. When $F$ is a perfection it is always greater (in Anselm's sense) to possess $F$ than to lack it. Now consider the following argument:

   1. God is a perfect being.

   2. So God possesses every perfection.

   3. Existence is a perfection.

   4. Therefore, God exists.

   *Exercise:* Identify the flaws in this argument.

2. *Gaunilo's perfect island.* An eleventh-century monk named Gaunilo presents a famous parody of Anselm's argument from *Proslogion 2*:

   It is said that somewhere in the ocean is an island . . . which has an inestimable wealth of all manner of riches and delicacies [and which] is more excellent than all other countries, which are inhabited by mankind, in the abundance with which it is stored.

   Now if some one should tell me that there is such an island, I should easily understand his words, in which there is no difficulty. But suppose that he went on to say, as if by a logical inference: "You can no longer doubt that this island which is more excellent than all lands exists somewhere, since you have no doubt that it is in your understanding. And since it is more excellent not to be in the understanding alone, but to exist both in the understanding and in reality, for this reason it must exist. For if it does not exist, any land which really exists will be more excellent than it; and so the island already understood by you to be more excellent will not be more excellent."

   How might a proponent of the ontological argument distinguish Anselm's proof from Gaunilo's?

   *Note:* Even if Anselm's argument cannot be distinguished from Gaunilo's parody, it is still important to say *where* these arguments go wrong. The parody may show us that there must be a mistake somewhere, but a satisfying response to Anselm must locate that mistake explicitly.

For Gaunilo's critique and Anselm's reply, see *Philosophy in the Middle Ages,* ed. A. Hyman and J. J. Walsh., (3rd ed., Hackett, 2010).

3. *Two ontological arguments.* The selection presents two independent arguments. The argument of *Proslogion 2* relies on the distinction between *existence in thought* and *existence in reality.* The argument of *Proslogion 3* relies on a rather different distinction between *things that can be thought not to exist* and *things that cannot be thought not to exist.*

What can Anselm mean when he says that God *cannot be thought not to exist*? After all, he says himself that the fool believes in his heart that there is no God. *Hint:* Distinguish the *psychological* claim that no one is capable of denying the existence of God from the *logical* claim that no one can *consistently* or *coherently* deny God's existence.

## Thomas Aquinas (1225–1274)

Aquinas, the "Angelic Doctor," is one of the great figures in the history of Catholic philosophy and theology. His major works, *Summa Theologica* and *Summa contra Gentiles,* seek to provide the rational basis for those aspects of Christian doctrine that can be established without special revelation and to reconcile Christian doctrine as a whole with key insights of Aristotle.

# THE FIVE WAYS
## from *Summa Theologica*

---

# Article 3. Whether God exists.

### Objection 1

It seems that God does not exist; because if one of two contraries be infinite, the other would be altogether destroyed. But the word "God" means that He is infinite goodness. If, therefore, God existed, there would be no evil discoverable; but there is evil in the world. Therefore God does not exist.

### Objection 2

Further, it is superfluous to suppose that what can be accounted for by a few principles has been produced by many. But it seems that everything we see in the world can be accounted for by other principles, supposing God did not exist. For all natural things can be reduced to one principle which is nature; and all voluntary things can be reduced to one principle which is human reason, or will. Therefore there is no need to suppose God's existence.

On the contrary, It is said in the person of God: "I am Who am." (Exodus 3:14)

I answer that, The existence of God can be proved in five ways.

The first and more manifest way is the argument from motion. It is certain, and evident to our senses, that in the world some things are in motion. Now whatever is in motion is put in motion by another, for nothing can be in motion except it is in potentiality to that towards which it is in motion; whereas a thing moves inasmuch as it is in act. For motion is nothing else than the reduction of something from potentiality to actuality.[1] But nothing can be reduced from potentiality to actuality, except by something in a state of actuality. Thus that which is actually hot, as fire, makes wood, which is potentially hot, to be actually hot, and thereby moves and changes it. Now it is not possible that the same thing should be at once in actuality and potentiality in the same respect, but only in different respects. For what is actually hot cannot simultaneously be potentially hot; but it is simultaneously potentially cold. It is therefore impossible that in the same respect and in the same way a thing should be both mover and moved, i.e., that it should move itself. Therefore, whatever is in motion must be put in motion by another. If that by which it is put in motion be itself put in motion, then this also must needs be put in motion by another, and that by another again. But this cannot go on to infinity, because then there would be no first mover, and, consequently, no other mover; seeing that subsequent movers move only inasmuch as they are put in motion by the first mover; as the staff moves only because it is put in motion by the hand. Therefore it is necessary to arrive at a first mover, put in motion by no other; and this everyone understands to be God.

The second way is from the nature of the efficient cause.[2] In the world of sense we find there is an order of efficient causes. There is no case known (neither is it, indeed, possible) in which a thing is found to be the efficient cause of itself; for so it would be prior to itself, which is impossible. Now in efficient causes it is not possible to go on to infinity, because in all efficient causes following in order, the first is the cause of the intermediate cause, and the intermediate is the cause of the ultimate cause, whether the intermediate cause be several, or only one. Now to take away the cause is to take away the effect. Therefore, if there be no first cause among efficient causes, there will be no ultimate, nor any intermediate cause. But if in efficient causes it is possible to go on to infinity, there will be no first efficient cause, neither will there be an ultimate effect, nor any intermediate efficient causes; all of which is plainly false. Therefore it is necessary to admit a first efficient cause, to which everyone gives the name of God.

---

1. Aquinas speaks of "motion" — change of place — and then invokes a general theory of change due to Aristotle. According to this theory, a change occurs when something that is *potentially F* becomes *actually F*, as when something that is potentially hot becomes hot, or something that is potentially in Los Angeles comes to be in Los Angeles.

2. Following Aristotle, Aquinas distinguishes several kinds of cause. The **efficient cause** of an object or event is the thing whose activity brings that object into being, or produces the event in question.

The third way is taken from possibility and necessity, and runs thus. We find in nature things that are possible to be and not to be, since they are found to be generated, and to corrupt, and consequently, they are possible to be and not to be.[3] But it is impossible for these always to exist, for that which is possible not to be at some time is not. Therefore, if everything is possible not to be, then at one time there could have been nothing in existence. Now if this were true, even now there would be nothing in existence, because that which does not exist only begins to exist by something already existing. Therefore, if at one time nothing was in existence, it would have been impossible for anything to have begun to exist; and thus even now nothing would be in existence — which is absurd. Therefore, not all beings are merely possible, but there must exist something the existence of which is necessary. But every necessary thing either has its necessity caused by another, or not. Now it is impossible to go on to infinity in necessary things which have their necessity caused by another, as has been already proved in regard to efficient causes. Therefore we cannot but postulate the existence of some being having of itself its own necessity, and not receiving it from another, but rather causing in others their necessity. This all men speak of as God.

The fourth way is taken from the gradation to be found in things. Among beings there are some more and some less good, true, noble and the like. But "more" and "less" are predicated of different things, according as they resemble in their different ways something which is the maximum, as a thing is said to be hotter according as it more nearly resembles that which is hottest; so that there is something which is truest, something best, something noblest and, consequently, something which is uttermost being; for those things that are greatest in truth are greatest in being, as it is written in [Aristotle's] *Metaphysics,* ii. Now the maximum in any genus is the cause of all in that genus; as fire, which is the maximum heat, is the cause of all hot things. Therefore there must also be something which is to all beings the cause of their being, goodness, and every other perfection; and this we call God.

The fifth way is taken from the governance of the world. We see that things which lack intelligence, such as natural bodies, act for an end, and this is evident from their acting always, or nearly always, in the same way, so as to obtain the best result. Hence it is plain that not fortuitously, but designedly, do they achieve their end. Now whatever lacks intelligence cannot move towards an end, unless it be directed by some being endowed with knowledge and intelligence; as the arrow is shot to its mark by the archer. Therefore some intelligent being exists by whom all natural things are directed to their end; and this being we call God.

---

3. A thing that is "possible to be and not to be" is a contingent being: a thing that exists, but could have failed to exist, or which fails to exist, but could have existed. You are a contingent being, since you exist, but could easily have failed to exist. A thing that exists and could not have failed to exist is a necessary being.

## TEST YOUR UNDERSTANDING

1. In the First Way, Aquinas claims that "whatever is in motion is put in motion by another." Briefly state the argument for this claim.

2. In the Second Way, Aquinas argues for the existence of a "first cause." Say what this means.

3. In the Third Way, Aquinas distinguishes between "things that are possible to be and not to be" (i.e., contingent beings) and necessary beings. Explain the distinction with examples.

## NOTES AND QUESTIONS

1. *Aquinas on the uniqueness of God.* Aquinas's arguments are designed to establish the existence of a being that differs radically from ordinary objects in various important respects. The First Way starts from the fact that ordinary objects are moved and seeks to show that there is at least one object that is not moved. The Second Way starts from the fact that ordinary objects are caused and seeks to show that there is at least one thing that is not caused, and so on. In each case Aquinas writes as if his argument shows something stronger, namely, that *exactly* one being possesses the remarkable property in question, but the argument for this further claim is not explicit.

   *Exercise:* Reconstruct Aquinas's arguments in stages. First produce an argument for the conclusion that there is at least one being with the remarkable property in question. Then try to complete the argument by showing that there can be at most one such being.

   *Note:* Even if these arguments succeed in establishing the existence of a unique first mover, a unique necessary being, and so on, it would require further argument to show that a single being possesses all of these attributes. How do we know that the first mover established by the First Way is also the necessary being established by the Third Way? The Five Ways do not pretend to address this question. Aquinas's arguments for the unity of God are found elsewhere (*Summa Theologica,* part 1, question 11, article 3).

2. *The cosmological argument.* Aquinas's first two Ways are versions of the **cosmological argument,** one simple version of which runs as follows:

   1. Every natural object is caused to exist.

   2. No natural object causes itself to exist.

   3. So given any natural object X, there is a chain of objects leading up to X that contains X's causes, the causes of X's causes, and so on.

   4. This chain must have a first member. Call it G.

   5. G is not caused to exist by something else.

   6. So G is not a natural object.

   7. So there is at least one supernatural object.

This argument has two questionable premises: (1) and (4).

> *Against (1):* There is no reason to believe that every natural object has a cause. It is not contradictory to suppose that a thing might simply pop into existence for no reason; indeed, contemporary physics suggests that this sometimes happens. Nor is it contradictory to suppose that a natural object (say an atom) has always existed.
>
> *Against (4):* There may be good scientific reasons for positing a first event (the "Big Bang"). But the idea of a causal sequence that extends infinitely backwards in time is not absurd: time might have the structure of the number line, infinite in both directions.

A proponent of the argument must either defend these premises or reconfigure the argument so as to avoid them. For a version of the argument that explicitly allows for the possibility of infinite causal chains, see Samuel Clarke, *A Demonstration of the Being and Attributes of God* (1705); for discussion, William Rowe, *The Cosmological Argument* (Princeton, 1975).

## William L. Rowe (born 1931)

Professor emeritus of philosophy at Purdue University, Rowe is a leading figure in the "analytic philosophy of religion," the effort to bring the tools of analytical philosophy to bear on problems in philosophical theology. His *Philosophy of Religion* (Wadsworth, 1978) is an accessible introduction to the subject.

# THE PROBLEM OF EVIL AND SOME VARIETIES OF ATHEISM

This paper is concerned with three interrelated questions. The first is: Is there an argument for atheism based on the existence of evil that may rationally justify someone in being an atheist? To this first question I give an affirmative answer and try to support that answer by setting forth a strong argument for atheism based on the existence of evil. The second question is: How can the theist best defend his position against the argument for atheism based on the existence of evil? In response to this question I try to describe what may be an adequate rational defense for theism against any argument for atheism based on the existence of evil. The final question is: What position should the informed atheist take concerning the rationality of theistic belief? Three different answers an atheist may give to this question serve to distinguish three varieties of atheism: unfriendly atheism, indifferent atheism, and friendly atheism. In the final part of the paper I discuss and defend the position of friendly atheism.

In developing the argument for atheism based on the existence of evil, it will be useful to focus on some particular evil that our world contains in considerable abundance. Intense human and animal suffering, for example, occurs daily and in great plenitude in our world. Such intense suffering is a clear case of evil. Of course, if the intense suffering leads to some greater good, a good we could not have obtained without undergoing the suffering in question, we might conclude that the suffering is justified, but it remains an evil nevertheless. For we must not confuse the intense suffering in and of itself with the good things to which it sometimes leads or of which it may be a necessary part. Intense human or animal suffering is in itself bad, an evil, even though it may sometimes be justified by virtue of being a part of, or leading to, some good which is unobtainable without it. What is evil in itself may sometimes be good as a means because it leads to something that is good in itself. In such a case, while remaining an evil in itself the intense human or animal suffering is, nevertheless, an evil which someone might be morally justified in permitting.

Taking human and animal suffering as a clear instance of evil which occurs with great frequency in our world, the argument for atheism based on evil can be stated as follows:

1. There exist instances of intense suffering which an omnipotent, omniscient being could have prevented without thereby losing some greater good or permitting some evil equally bad or worse.

2. An omniscient, wholly good being would prevent the occurrence of any intense suffering it could, unless it could not do so without thereby losing some greater good or permitting some evil equally bad or worse.

3. There does not exist an omnipotent, omniscient wholly good being.

What are we to say about this argument for atheism, an argument based on the profusion of one sort of evil in our world? The argument is valid; therefore if we have rational grounds for accepting its premises, to that extent we have rational grounds for accepting atheism. Do we, however, have rational grounds for accepting the premises of this argument?

Let's begin with the second premise. Let $s_1$ be an instance of intense human or animal suffering which an omniscient, wholly good being could prevent. We will also suppose that things are such that $s_1$ will occur unless prevented by the omniscient, wholly good (*OG*) being. We might be interested in determining what would be a *sufficient* condition of *OG* failing to prevent $s_1$. But, for our purpose here, we need only try to state a *necessary* condition for *OG* failing to prevent $s_1$. That condition, so it seems to me, is this:

*Either* (i) there is some greater good, *G*, such that *G* is obtainable by *OG* only if *OG* permits $s_1$, *or* (ii) there is some greater good, $G$, such that $G$ is obtainable by $OG$ only if $OG$ permits either $s_1$ or some evil equally bad or worse,

*or* (iii) $s_1$ is such that it is preventable by $OG$ only if $OG$ permits some evil equally bad or worse.

It is important to recognize that (iii) is not included in (i). For losing a good greater than $s_1$ is not the same as permitting an evil greater than $s_1$. And this because the *absence* of a good state of affairs need not itself be an evil state of affairs. It is also important to recognize that $s_1$ might be such that it is preventable by $OG$ *without* losing $G$ (so condition (i) is not satisfied) but also such that if $OG$ did prevent it, $G$ would be lost *unless* $OG$ permitted some evil equal to or worse than $s_1$. If this were so, it does not seem correct to require that $OG$ prevent $s_1$. Thus, condition (ii) takes into account an important possibility not encompassed in condition (i).

Is it true that if an omniscient, wholly good being permits the occurrence of some intense suffering it could have prevented, then either (i) or (ii) or (iii) obtains? It seems to me that it is true. But if it is true then so is premise (2) of the argument for atheism. For that premise merely states in more compact form what we have suggested must be true if an omniscient, wholly good being fails to prevent some intense suffering it could prevent. Premise (2) says that an omniscient, wholly good being would prevent the occurrence of any intense suffering it could, unless it could not do so without thereby losing some greater good or permitting some evil equally bad or worse. This premise (or something not too distant from it) is, I think, held in common by many atheists and nontheists. Of course, there may be disagreement about whether something is good, and whether, if it is good, one would be morally justified in permitting some intense suffering to occur in order to obtain it. Someone might hold, for example, that no good is great enough to justify permitting an innocent child to suffer terribly. Again, someone might hold that the mere fact that a given good outweighs some suffering and would be lost if the suffering were prevented, is not a morally sufficient reason for permitting the suffering. But to hold either of these views is not to deny (2). For (2) claims only that *if* an omniscient, wholly good being permits intense suffering *then* either there is some greater good that would have been lost, or some equally bad or worse evil that would have occurred, had the intense suffering been prevented. (2) does not purport to describe what might be a *sufficient* condition for an omniscient, wholly good being to permit intense suffering, only what is a *necessary* condition. So stated, (2) seems to express a belief that accords with our basic moral principles, principles shared by both theists and nontheists. If we are to fault the argument for atheism, therefore, it seems we must find some fault with its first premise.

Suppose in some distant forest lightning strikes a dead tree, resulting in a forest fire. In the fire a fawn is trapped, horribly burned, and lies in terrible agony for several days before death relieves its suffering. So far as we can see, the fawn's intense suffering is pointless. For there does not appear to be any greater good such that the prevention of the fawn's suffering would require either the loss of that good or the occurrence of an evil equally bad or worse. Nor does there seem to be any equally bad or worse evil so connected to the fawn's suffering that it would have had to occur had the fawn's suffering been prevented. Could an omnipotent, omniscient being have prevented the fawn's apparently pointless suffering? The answer is obvious, as even the theist will insist. An omnipotent, omniscient being could have easily prevented the fawn from being horribly burned, or, given the burning, could have spared the fawn the intense suffering by quickly ending its life, rather than allowing the fawn to lie in terrible agony for several days. Since the fawn's intense suffering was preventable and, so far as we can see, pointless, doesn't it appear that premise (1) of the argument is true, that there do exist instances of intense suffering which an omnipotent, omniscient being could have prevented without thereby losing some greater good or permitting some evil equally bad or worse?

It must be acknowledged that the case of the fawn's apparently pointless suffering does not *prove* that (1) is true.

We cannot know with certainty that instances of suffering of the sort described in (1) do occur in our world. But it is one thing to *know* or *prove* that (1) is true and quite another thing to have *rational grounds* for believing (1) to be true. We are often in the position where in the light of our experience and knowledge it is rational to believe that a certain statement is true, even though we are not in a position to prove or to know with certainty that the statement is true. In the light of our past experience and knowledge it is, for example, very reasonable to believe that neither Goldwater nor McGovern will ever be elected President, but we are scarcely in the position of knowing with certainty that neither will ever be elected President. So, too, with (1), although we cannot know with certainty that it is true, it perhaps can be rationally supported, shown to be a rational belief.

Consider again the case of the fawn's suffering. Is it reasonable to believe that there is some greater good so intimately connected to that suffering that even an omnipotent, omniscient being could not have obtained that good without permitting that suffering or some evil at least as bad? It certainly does not appear reasonable to believe this. Nor does it seem reasonable to believe that there is some evil at least as bad as the fawn's suffering such that an omnipotent being simply could not have prevented it without permitting the fawn's suffering. But even if it should somehow be reasonable to believe either of these things of the fawn's suffering, we must then ask whether it is reasonable to believe either of these things of *all* the instances of seemingly pointless human and animal suffering that occur daily in our world. And surely the answer to this more general question must be no. It seems quite unlikely that *all* the instances of intense suffering occurring daily in our world are intimately related to the occurrence of greater goods or the prevention of evils at least as bad; and even more unlikely, should they somehow all be so related, then an omnipotent, omniscient being could not have achieved at least some of those goods (or prevented some of those evils) without permitting the instances of intense suffering that are supposedly related to them. In the light of our experience and knowledge of the variety and scale of human and animal suffering in our world, the idea that none of this suffering could have been prevented by an omnipotent being without thereby losing a greater good or permitting an evil at least as bad seems an extraordinarily absurd idea, quite beyond our belief. It seems then that although we cannot *prove* that (1) is true, it is, nevertheless, altogether *reasonable* to believe that (1) is true, that (1) is a *rational* belief.

Returning now to our argument for atheism, we've seen that the second premise expresses a basic belief common to many theists and nontheists. We've also seen that our experience and knowledge of the variety and profusion of suffering in our world provides *rational support* for the first premise. Seeing that the conclusion "There does not exist an omnipotent, omniscient, wholly good being" follows from these two premises, it does seem that we have *rational support* for atheism, that it is reasonable for us to believe that the theistic God does not exist.

## II

Can theism be rationally defended against the argument for atheism we have just examined? If it can, how might the theist best respond to that argument? Since the argument from (1) and (2) to (3) is valid, and since the theist, no less than the nontheist, is more than likely committed to (2), it's clear that the theist can reject this atheistic argument only by rejecting its first premise, the premise that states that there are instances of intense suffering which an omnipotent, omniscient being could have prevented without thereby losing some greater good or permitting some evil equally bad or worse. How, then, can the theist best respond to this premise and the considerations advanced in its support?

There are basically three responses a theist can make. First, he might argue not that (1) is false or probably false, but only that the reasoning given in support of it is in some way *defective*. I suppose some theists would be content with this rather modest response to the basic argument for atheism. But given the validity of the basic argument and the theist's likely acceptance of (2), he is thereby committed to the view that (1) is false, not just that we have no good reasons for accepting (1) as true. The second two responses are aimed at showing that it is reasonable to believe that (1) is false. Since the theist is committed to this view 1 shall focus the discussion on these two attempts, attempts which we can distinguish as "the direct attack" and "the indirect attack."

By a direct attack, I mean an attempt to reject (1) by pointing out goods, for example, to which suffering may well be connected, goods which an omnipotent, omniscient being could not achieve without permitting suffering. It is doubtful, however, that the direct attack can succeed. The theist may point out that some suffering leads to moral and spiritual development impossible without suffering. But it's reasonably clear that suffering often occurs in a degree far beyond what is required for character development. The theist may say that some suffering results from free choices of human beings and might be preventable only by preventing some measure of human freedom. But, again, it's clear that much intense suffering occurs not as a result of human free choices.

The general difficulty with this direct attack on premise (1) is twofold. First, it cannot succeed, for the theist does not know what greater goods might be served, or evils prevented, by each instance of intense human or animal suffering. Second, the theist's own religious tradition usually maintains that in this life it is not given to us to know God's purpose in allowing particular instances of suffering. Hence, the direct attack against premise (1) cannot succeed and violates basic beliefs associated with theism.

The best procedure for the theist to follow in rejecting premise (1) is the indirect procedure. This procedure I shall call "the G. E. Moore shift," so-called in honor of the twentieth century philosopher, G. E. Moore, who used it to great effect in dealing with the arguments of the skeptics. Skeptical philosophers such as David Hume have advanced ingenious arguments to prove that no one can know of the existence of any material object. The premises of their arguments employ plausible principles, principles which many philosophers have tried to reject directly, but only with questionable success. Moore's procedure was altogether different. Instead of arguing directly against the premises of the skeptic's arguments, he simply noted that the premises implied, for example, that he (Moore) did not know of the existence of a pencil. Moore then proceeded indirectly against the skeptic's premises by arguing:

I do know that this pencil exists.
If the skeptic's principles are correct I cannot know of the existence of this pencil.
∴ The skeptic's principles (at least one) must be incorrect.

Moore then noted that his argument is just as valid as the skeptic's, that both of their arguments contain the premise "If the skeptic's principles are correct Moore cannot know of the existence of this pencil," and concluded that the only way to choose between the two arguments (Moore's and the skeptic's) is by deciding which of the first premises it is more rational to believe — Moore's premise "I do know that this pencil exists" or the skeptic's premise asserting that his skeptical principles are correct. Moore concluded that his own first premise was the more rational of the two.[1]

Before we see how the theist may apply the G. E. Moore shift to the basic argument for atheism, we should note the general strategy of the shift. We're given an argument: p, q, therefore, r. Instead of arguing directly against p, another argument is constructed — not-r, q, therefore, not-p — which begins with the denial of the conclusion of the first argument, keeps its second premise, and ends with the denial of the first premise as its conclusion.

Compare, for example, these two:

$$
\begin{array}{ll}
\text{I. } p & \text{II. } not\text{-}r \\
\quad q & \quad q \\
\hline
\quad r & \quad not\text{-}p
\end{array}
$$

---

1. See, for example, the two chapters on Hume in G. E. Moore, *Some Main Problems of Philosophy* (George Allen & Unwin, 1953). [Rowe's note.]

It is a truth of logic that if I is valid II must be valid as well. Since the arguments are the same so far as the second premise is concerned, any choice between them must concern their respective first premises. To argue against the first premise (*p*) by constructing the counter argument II is to employ the G. E. Moore shift.

Applying the G. E. Moore shift against the first premise of the basic argument for atheism, the theist can argue as follows:

not-3. There exists an omnipotent, omniscient, wholly good being.

2. An omniscient, wholly good being would prevent the occurrence of any intense suffering it could, unless it could not do so without thereby losing some greater good or permitting some evil equally bad or worse.

therefore,

not-1. It is not the case that there exist instances of intense suffering which an omnipotent, omniscient being could have prevented without thereby losing some greater good or permitting some evil equally bad or worse.

We now have two arguments: the basic argument for atheism from (1) and (2) to (3), and the theist's best response, the argument from (not-3) and (2) to (not-1). What the theist then says about (1) is that he has rational grounds for believing in the existence of the theistic God (not-3), accepts (2) as true, and sees that (not-1) follows from (not-3) and (2). He concludes, therefore, that he has rational grounds for rejecting (1). Having rational grounds for rejecting (1), the theist concludes that the basic argument for atheism is mistaken.

## III

We've had a look at a forceful argument for atheism and what seems to be the theist's best response to that argument. If one is persuaded by the argument for atheism, as I find myself to be, how might one best view the position of the theist? Of course, he will view the theist as having a false belief, just as the theist will view the atheist as having a false belief. But what position should the atheist take concerning the *rationality* of the theist's belief? There are three major positions an atheist might take, positions which we may think of as some varieties of atheism. First, the atheist may believe that no one is rationally justified in believing that the theistic God exists. Let us call this position "unfriendly atheism." Second, the atheist may hold no belief concerning whether any theist is or isn't rationally justified in believing that the theistic God exists. Let us call this view "indifferent atheism." Finally, the atheist may believe that some theists are rationally justified in believing that the theistic God exists. This view we shall call "friendly atheism." In this final part of the paper I propose to discuss and defend the position of friendly atheism.

If no one can be rationally justified in believing a false proposition then friendly atheism is a paradoxical, if not incoherent, position. But surely the truth of a belief is not a necessary condition of someone's being rationally justified in having that belief. So in holding that someone is rationally justified in believing that the theistic God exists, the friendly atheist is not committed to thinking that the theist has a true belief. What he is committed to is that the theist has rational grounds for his belief, a belief the atheist rejects and is convinced he is rationally justified in rejecting. But is this possible? Can someone, like our friendly atheist, hold a belief, be convinced that he is rationally justified in holding that belief, and yet believe that someone else is equally justified in believing the opposite? Surely this is possible. Suppose your friends see you off on a flight to Hawaii. Hours after take-off they learn that your plane has gone down at sea. After a twenty-four hour search, no survivors have been found. Under these circumstances they are rationally justified in believing that you have perished. But it is hardly rational for you to believe this, as you bob up and down in your life vest, wondering why the search planes have failed to spot you. Indeed, to amuse yourself while awaiting your fate, you might very well reflect on the fact that your friends are rationally justified in believing that you are now dead, a proposition you disbelieve and are rationally justified in disbelieving. So, too, perhaps an atheist may be rationally justified in his atheistic belief and yet hold that some theists are rationally justified in believing just the opposite of what he believes.

What sort of grounds might a theist have for believing that God exists? Well, he might endeavor to justify his belief by appealing to one or more of the traditional arguments: Ontological, Cosmological, Teleological, Moral, etc. Second, he might appeal to certain aspects of religious experience, perhaps even his own religious experience. Third, he might try to justify theism as a plausible theory in terms of which we can account for a variety of phenomena. Although an atheist must hold that the theistic God does not exist, can he not also believe, and be justified in so believing, that some of these "justifications of theism" do actually rationally justify some theists in their belief that there exists a supremely good, omnipotent, omniscient being? It seems to me that he can.

If we think of the long history of theistic belief and the special situations in which people are sometimes placed, it is perhaps as absurd to think that no one was ever rationally justified in believing that the theistic God exists as it is to think that no one was ever justified in believing that human beings would never walk on the moon. But in suggesting that friendly atheism is preferable to unfriendly atheism, I don't mean to rest the case on what some human beings might reasonably have believed in the eleventh or thirteenth century. The more interesting question is whether some people in modern society, people who are aware of the usual grounds for belief and disbelief and are acquainted to some degree with modern science, are yet rationally justified in accepting theism. Friendly atheism is a significant position only if it answers this question in the affirmative.

It is not difficult for an atheist to be friendly when he has reason to believe that the theist could not reasonably be expected to be acquainted with the grounds for disbelief that he (the atheist) possesses. For then the atheist may take the view that some theists are rationally justified in holding to theism, but would not be so were they to be acquainted with the grounds for disbelief — those grounds being sufficient to tip the scale in favor of atheism when balanced against the reasons the theist has in support of his belief.

Friendly atheism becomes paradoxical, however, when the atheist contemplates believing that the theist has all the grounds for atheism that he, the atheist, has, and yet is rationally justified in maintaining his theistic belief. But even so excessively friendly a view as this perhaps can be held by the atheist if he also has some reason to think that the grounds for theism are not as telling as the theist is justified in taking them to be.[2]

## TEST YOUR UNDERSTANDING

1. Rowe claims that the suffering of animals is an *evil*. Explain what Rowe means by this word.

2. According to Rowe, while the existence of evil does not *prove* there is no God, it nonetheless provides *rational grounds* for denying God's existence. Explain this distinction and illustrate it with examples drawn from other areas.

3. Does Rowe believe that theists are irrational?

## NOTES AND QUESTIONS

1. The most straightforward response to the Problem of Evil is to argue that the suffering we find in nature is always *necessary* for the realization of some great good. But note how difficult this is. It is sometimes said, for example, that God permits these evils so that we may know the difference between good and evil. But even if we grant that knowledge of good and evil is itself an important good, this is not a satisfactory response. The experience of evil in the world around us may be *one* way for human beings to learn the difference between good and evil. But it is not the only way: after

2. Suppose that I add a long sum of numbers three times and get result $x$. I inform you of this so that you have pretty much the same evidence I have for the claim that the sum of the numbers is $x$. You then use your calculator twice over and arrive at result $y$. You, then, are justified in believing that the sum of the numbers is *not* $x$. However, knowing that your calculator has been damaged and is therefore unreliable, and that you have no reason to think that it is damaged, *I* may reasonably believe not only that the sum of the numbers is $x$, but also that you are justified in believing that the sum is not $x$. Here, is a case, then, where you have all of my evidence for $p$, and yet I can reasonably believe that you are justified in believing not-$p$ — for I have reason to believe that your grounds for not-$p$ are not as telling as you are justified in taking them to be. [Rowe's note.]

all, an omnipotent God could endow us with *innate* knowledge of good and evil. A response to the Problem of Evil must point to some good that God could not *possibly* have secured without permitting the suffering of the innocent or some other comparable evil. Review some of the possibilities and say whether they provide a satisfactory response to the argument.

2. Earlier discussions of the Problem of Evil often focused on evil done by human beings. This left room for what is sometimes called the Free Will Defense:

> The only way for God to prevent all human evil is for him to deprive human beings of free will. But human freedom is a great good, so God is justified in permitting human evil for freedom's sake.

Rowe focuses on the suffering of animals and human beings at the hands of *nature* in order to sidestep this argument. But the argument is worth considering in its own right. Is it true that God could not prevent human evil without depriving human beings of free will? Is free will valuable enough to justify God in permitting the brutality that human beings visit on one another when they exercise it? For discussion, see Alvin Plantinga, *God, Freedom, and Evil* (Eerdmans, 1974).

## William Paley (1743–1805)

Paley was known in his day both for his lucid contributions to theology, of which his *Natural Theology* (1802) is the most famous, and for his *Principles of Moral and Political Philosophy* (1785), which urged the reform of British law according to utilitarian principles.

# THE ARGUMENT FROM DESIGN
### from *Natural Theology*

# Chapter I

### STATE OF THE ARGUMENT

In crossing a heath, suppose I pitched my foot against a *stone*, and were asked how the stone came to be there, I might possibly answer, that, for any thing I knew to the contrary, it had lain there for ever: nor would it perhaps be very easy to shew the absurdity of this answer. But suppose I had found a *watch* upon the ground, and it should be enquired how the watch happened to be in that place,

I should hardly think of the answer which I had before given, that, for any thing I knew, the watch might have always been there. Yet why should not this answer serve for the watch, as well as for the stone? Why is it not as admissible in the second case, as in the first? For this reason, and for no other, viz., that, when we come to inspect the watch, we perceive (what we could not discover in the stone) that its several parts are framed and put together for a purpose, e.g., that they are so formed and adjusted as to produce motion, and that motion so regulated as to point out the hour of the day; that, if the several parts had been differently shaped from what they are, of a different size from what they are, or placed after any other manner, or in any other order, than that in which they are placed, either no motion at all would have been carried on in the machine, or none which would have answered the use, that is now served by it. To reckon up a few of the plainest of these parts, and of their offices, all tending to one result: — We see a cylindrical box containing a coiled elastic spring, which, by its endeavour to relax itself, turns round the box. We next observe a flexible chain (artificially wrought for the sake of flexure) communicating the action of the spring from the box to the fusee. We then find a series of wheels, the teeth of which catch in, and apply to, each other, conducting the motion from the fusee to the balance, and from the balance to the pointer; and at the same time, by the size and shape of those wheels, so regulating that motion, as to terminate in causing an index, by an equable and measured progression, to pass over a given space in a given time. We take notice that the wheels are made of brass, in order to keep them from rust; the springs of steel, no other metal being so elastic; that over the face of the watch there is placed a glass, a material employed in no other part of the work, but, in the room of which, if there had been any other than a transparent substance, the hour could not be seen without opening the case. This mechanism being observed (it requires indeed an examination of the instrument, and perhaps some previous knowledge of the subject, to perceive and understand it; but being once, as we have said, observed and understood), the inference, we think, is inevitable; that the watch must have had a maker; that there must have existed, at some time and at some place or other, an artificer or artificers who formed it for the purpose which we find it actually to answer; who comprehended its construction, and designed its use.

I. Nor would it, I apprehend, weaken the conclusion, that we had never seen a watch made; that we had never known an artist capable of making one; that we were altogether incapable of executing such a piece of workmanship ourselves, or of understanding in what manner it was performed: all this being no more than what is true of some exquisite remains of ancient art, of some lost arts, and, to the generality of mankind, of the more curious productions of modern manufacture. Does one man in a million know how oval frames are turned? Ignorance of this kind exalts our opinion of the unseen and unknown artist's skill, if he be unseen and unknown, but raises no doubt in our minds of the existence and agency of such an artist, at some former time, and in some place or other. . . .

II. Neither, secondly, would it invalidate our conclusion, that the watch sometimes went wrong, or that it seldom went exactly right. The purpose of the machinery, the design, and the designer, might be evident, and in the case supposed would be evident, in whatever way we accounted for the irregularity of the movement, or whether we could account for it or not. It is not necessary that a machine be perfect, in order to shew with what design it was made: still less necessary, where the only question is, whether it were made with any design at all.

III. Nor, thirdly, would it bring any uncertainty into the argument, if there were a few parts of the watch, concerning which we could not discover, or had not yet discovered, in what manner they conduced to the general effect; or even some parts, concerning which we could not ascertain, whether they conduced to that effect in any manner whatever. For, as to the first branch of the case; if, by the loss, or disorder, or decay of the parts in question, the movement of the watch were found in fact to be stopped, or disturbed, or retarded, no doubt would remain in our minds as to the utility or intention of these parts, although we should be unable to investigate the manner according to which, or the connection by which, the ultimate effect depended upon their action or assistance: and the more complex is the machine, the more likely is this obscurity to arise. Then, as to the second thing supposed, namely, that there were parts, which might be spared without prejudice to the movement of the watch, and that we had proved this by experiment, — these superfluous parts, even if we were completely assured that they were such, would not vacate the reasoning which we had instituted concerning other parts. The indication of contrivance remained, with respect to them, nearly as it was before.

IV. Nor, fourthly, would any man in his senses think the existence of the watch, with its various machinery, accounted for, by being told that it was one out of many possible combinations of material forms; that whatever he had found in the place where he found the watch, must have contained some internal configuration or other; and that this configuration might be the structure now exhibited, viz., of the works of a watch, as well as a different structure. . . .

VII. And [he would be] not less surprised to be informed, that the watch in his hand was nothing more than the result of the laws of *metallic* nature. It is a perversion of language to assign any law, as the efficient, operative, cause of any thing. A law presupposes an agent; for it is only the mode, according to which an agent proceeds: it implies a power; for it is the order, according to which that power acts. Without this agent, without this power, which are both distinct from itself, the *law* does nothing; is nothing. . . .

VIII. Neither, lastly, would our observer be driven out of his conclusion, or from his confidence in its truth, by being told that he knew nothing at all about the matter. He knows enough for his argument. He knows the utility of the end: he knows the subserviency and adaptation of the means to the end. These points being known, his ignorance of other points, his doubts concerning other points, affect not the certainty of his reasoning. The consciousness of knowing little, need not beget a distrust of that which he does know.

# Chapter II

## STATE OF THE ARGUMENT CONTINUED

Suppose in the next place, that the person, who found the watch, should, after some time, discover, that, in addition to all the properties which he had hitherto observed in it, it possessed, the unexpected property of producing, in the course of its movement, another watch like itself; (the thing is conceivable;) that it contained within it a mechanism, a system of parts, a mould for instance, or a complex adjustment of laths, files, and other tools, evidently and separately calculated for this purpose; let us enquire, what effect ought such a discovery to have upon his former conclusion?

I.  The first effect would be to increase his admiration of the contrivance, and his conviction of the consummate skill of the contriver. Whether he regarded the object of the contrivance, the distinct apparatus, the intricate, yet in many parts intelligible, mechanism by which it was carried on, he would perceive, in this new observation, nothing but an additional reason for doing what he had already done; for referring the construction of the watch to design, and to supreme art. . . .

II.  He would reflect, that though, the watch before him were, *in some sense,* the maker of the watch, which was fabricated in the course of its movements, yet it was in a very different sense from that, in which a carpenter, for instance, is the maker of a chair; the author of its contrivance, the cause of the relation of its parts to their use. With respect to these, the first watch was no cause at all to the second: in no such sense as this was it the author of the constitution and order, either of the parts which the new watch contained, or of the parts by the aid and instrumentality of which it was produced. We might possibly say, but with great latitude of expression, that a stream of water ground corn: but no latitude of expression would allow us to say, no stretch of conjecture could lead us to think, that the stream of water built the mill, though it were too ancient for us to know who the builder was. Therefore,

III.  Though it be now no longer probable, that the individual watch which our observer had found, was made immediately by the hand of an artificer, yet doth not this alteration in any wise affect the inference, that an artificer had been originally employed and concerned in the production. The argument from design remains as it was. Marks of design and contrivance are no more accounted for now, than they were before. In the same thing, we may ask for the cause of different properties. We may ask for the cause of the colour of a body, of its hardness, of its heat, and these causes may be all different. We are now asking for the cause of that subserviency to a use, that relation to an end, which we have remarked in the watch before us. No answer is given to this question by telling us that a preceding watch produced it. There cannot be design without a designer, contrivance without a contriver; order without choice; arrangement, without any thing capable of arranging; subserviency and relation to a purpose, without that which could intend a purpose; means suitable to an end, and executing their office in accomplishing that end, without the end ever having been contemplated, or the means accommodated to it. Arrangement, disposition of parts, subserviency of means to an end, relation of instruments to an use, imply the presence of intelligence and mind. No one, therefore, can rationally believe, that the insensible, inanimate watch, from which the watch before us issued, was the proper cause of the mechanism we so much admire in it, could be truly said to have constructed the instrument, disposed its parts, assigned their office, determined their order, action, and mutual dependency, combined their several motions into one result, and that also a result connected with the utilities of other beings. All these properties, therefore, are as much unaccounted for, as they were before.

IV. Nor is any thing gained by running the difficulty further back, i.e., by supposing the watch before us to have been produced from another watch, that from a former, and so on indefinitely. Our going back ever so far brings us no nearer to the least degree of satisfaction upon the subject. Contrivance is still unaccounted for. We still want a contriver. A designing mind is neither supplied by this supposition, nor dispensed with. If the difficulty were diminished the further we went back, by going back indefinitely we might exhaust it. And this is the only case to which this sort of reasoning applies. Where there is a tendency, or, as we increase the number of terms, a continual approach towards a limit, *there,* by supposing the number of terms to be what is called infinite, we may conceive the limit to be attained: but where there is no such tendency or approach, nothing is effected by lengthening the series. There is no difference as to the point in question (whatever there may be as to many points), between one series and another; between a series which is finite, and a series which is infinite. A chain, composed of an infinite number of links; can no more support itself, than a chain composed of a finite number of links. . . . The machine, which we are inspecting, demonstrates; by its construction, contrivance and design. Contrivance must have had a contriver; design, a designer; whether the machine immediately proceeded from another machine, or not. . . .

The question is not simply, How came the first watch into existence? which question, it may be pretended, is done away by supposing the series of watches thus produced from one another to have been infinite, and consequently to have had no such *first,* for which it was necessary to provide a cause. This, perhaps, would have been nearly the state of the question, if nothing had been before us but an unorganised, unmechanised, substance, without mark or indication of contrivance. It might be difficult to shew that such substance could not have existed from eternity, either in succession (if it were possible, which I think it is not, for unorganised bodies to spring from one another), or by individual perpetuity. But that is not the question now. To suppose it to be so, is to suppose that it made no difference whether we had found a watch or a stone. As it is, the metaphysics of that question have no place; for, in the watch which we are examining, are seen contrivance, design; an end, a purpose; means for the end, adaptation to the purpose. And the question which irresistibly presses upon our thoughts, is, whence this contrivance and design. The thing required is the intending mind, the adapting hand, the intelligence by which that hand was directed. This question, this demand, is not shaken off, by increasing a number of succession of substances, destitute of these properties; nor the more, by increasing that number to infinity. If it be said, that, upon the supposition of one watch being produced from another in the course of that other's movements, and by means of the mechanism within it, we have a cause for the watch in my hand, viz., the watch from which it proceeded, I deny, that for the design, the contrivance, the suitableness of means to an end, the adaptation of instruments to an use (all which we discover in the watch), we have any cause whatever. It is in vain, therefore, to assign a series of such causes; or to alledge that a series may be carried back to infinity; for I do not admit that we have yet any cause at all of the phenomena, still less any series of causes either finite or infinite. Here is contrivance, but no contriver: proofs of design, but no designer. . . .

The conclusion which the *first* examination of the watch, of its works, construction, and movement suggested, was, that it must have had, for the cause and author of that construction, an artificer, who understood its mechanism, and designed its use. This conclusion is invincible. A *second* examination presents us with a new discovery. The watch is found, in the course of its movement, to produce another watch, similar to itself: and not only so, but we perceive in it a system of organisation, separately calculated for that purpose. What effect would this discovery have, or ought it to have, upon our former inference? What, as hath already been said, but to increase, beyond measure, our admiration of the skill, which had been employed in the formation of such a machine? Or shall it, instead of this, all at once turn us round to an opposite conclusion, viz., that no art or skill whatever has been concerned in the business, although all other evidences of art and skill remain as they were, and this last and supreme piece of art be now added to the rest? Can this be maintained without absurdity? Yet this is atheism.

# Chapter III

## APPLICATION OF THE ARGUMENT

This is atheism: for every indication of contrivance, every manifestation of design, which existed in the watch, exists in the works of nature; with the difference, on the side of nature, of being greater and more, and that in a degree which exceeds all computation. I mean that the contrivances of nature surpass the contrivances of art, in the complexity, subtlety, and curiosity of the mechanism; and still more, if possible, do they go beyond them in number and variety; yet, in a multitude of cases, are not less evidently mechanical, not less evidently contrivances, not less evidently accommodated to their end, or suited to their office, than are the most perfect productions of human ingenuity.

I know no better method of introducing so large a subject, than that of comparing a single thing with a single thing; an eye, for example, with a telescope. As far as the examination of the instrument goes, there is precisely the same proof that the eye was made for vision, as there is that the telescope was made for assisting it. They are made upon the same principles; both being adjusted to the laws by which the transmission and refraction of rays of light are regulated. I speak not of the origin of the laws themselves; but, such laws being fixed, the construction, in both cases, is adapted to them. For instance; these laws require, in order to produce the same effect, that the rays of light, in passing from water into the eye, should be refracted by a more convex surface, than when it passes out of air into the eye. Accordingly we find, that the eye of a fish, in that part of it called the crystalline lense, is much rounder than the eye of terrestrial animals. What plainer manifestation of design can there be than this difference? What could a mathematical instrument maker have done more, to shew his knowledge of his principle, his application of that knowledge, his suiting of his means to his end; I will not say to display the compass or excellency of his skill and art, for in these all comparison is indecorous, but to testify counsel, choice, consideration, purpose?

To some it may appear a difference sufficient to destroy all similitude between the eye and the telescope, that the one is a perceiving organ, the other an unperceiving instrument. The fact is, that they are both instruments. And, as to the mechanism, at least as to mechanism being employed, and even as to the kind of it, this circumstance varies not the analogy at all. For observe, what the constitution of the eye is. It is necessary, in order to produce distinct vision, that an image or picture of the object be formed at the bottom of the eye. Whence this necessity arises, or how the picture is connected with the sensation, or contributes to it, it may be difficult, nay we will confess, if you please, impossible for us to search out. But the present question is not concerned in the enquiry. It may be true, that, in this, and in other instances, we trace mechanical contrivance a certain way; and that then we come to something which is not mechanical, or which is inscrutable. But this affects not the certainty of our investigation, as far as we have gone. The difference between an animal and an automatic statue consists in this, — that, in the animal, we trace the mechanism to a certain point, and then we are stopped; either the mechanism becoming too subtile for our discernment, or something else beside the known laws of mechanism taking place; whereas, in the automaton, for the comparatively few motions of which it is capable, we trace the mechanism throughout. But, up to the limit, the reasoning is as clear and certain in the one case as the other. In the example before us, it is a matter of certainty, because it is a matter which experience and observation demonstrate, that the formation of an image at the bottom of the eye is necessary to perfect vision. The image itself can be shewn. Whatever affects the distinctness of the image, affects the distinctness of the vision. The formation then of such an image being necessary (no matter how) to the sense of sight, and to the exercise of that sense; the apparatus by which it is formed is constructed and put together, not only with infinitely more art, but upon the self-same principles of art, as in the telescope or the camera obscura. The perception arising from the image may be laid out of the question: for the production of the image, these are instruments of the same kind. The end is the same; the means are the same. The purpose in both is alike; the contrivance for accomplishing that purpose is in both alike: The lenses of the telescope, and the humours of the eye bear a complete resemblance to one another, in their figure their position; and in their power over the rays of light, viz., in bringing each pencil to a point at the right distance from the lense; namely, in the eye, at the exact place where the membrane is spread to receive it. How is it possible, under circumstances of such close affinity, and under the operation of equal evidence, to exclude contrivance from the one, yet to acknowledge the proof of contrivance having been employed, as the plainest and clearest of all propositions in the other? . . .

# Chapter V

## APPLICATION OF THE ARGUMENT CONTINUED

Every observation which was made, in our first chapter, concerning the watch, may be repeated with strict propriety concerning the eye; concerning animals; concerning plants; concerning, indeed, all the organized parts of the works of nature. As,

I. When we are enquiring simply after the *existence* of an intelligent Creator, imperfection, inaccuracy, liability to disorder, occasional irregularities, may subsist, in a considerable degree, without inducing any doubt into the question: just as a watch may frequently go wrong, seldom perhaps exactly right, may be faulty in some parts, defective in some, without the smallest ground of suspicion from thence arising, that it was not a watch; not made; or not made for the purpose ascribed to it. When faults are pointed out, and when a question is started concerning the skill of the artist, or the dexterity with which the work is executed, then indeed, in order to defend these qualities from accusation, we must be able, either to expose some intractableness and imperfection in the materials, or point out some invincible difficulty in the execution, into which imperfection and difficulty the matter of complaint may be resolved; or, if we cannot do this, we must adduce such specimens of consummate art and contrivance proceeding from the same hand, as may convince the enquirer of the existence, in the case before him, of impediments like those which we have mentioned, although, what from the nature of the case is very likely to happen, they be unknown and unperceived by him. This we must do in order to vindicate the artist's skill, or, at least, the perfection of it; as we must also judge of his intention; and of the provisions employed in fulfilling that intention, not from an instance in which they fail, but from the great plurality of instances in which they succeed. But, after all, these are different questions from the question of the artist's existence; or, which is the same, whether the thing before be a work of art or not: and the questions ought always to be kept separate in the mind. So likewise it is in the works of nature. Irregularities and imperfections are of little or no weight in the consideration, when that consideration relates simply to the existence of a Creator. When the argument respects his attributes, they are of weight; but are then to be taken in conjunction (the attention is not to rest upon them, but they are to be taken in conjunction) with the unexceptionable evidences which we possess, of skill, power, and benevolence, displayed in other instances, which evidences may, in strength, number, and variety be such, and may so overpower apparent blemishes, as to induce us, upon the most reasonable ground, to believe, that these last ought to be referred to some cause, though we be ignorant of it, other than defect of knowledge or of benevolence in the author. . . .

## TEST YOUR UNDERSTANDING

1. Paley argues that living things are like watches in one crucial respect: both exhibit "contrivance" or "design." Say what this means.

2. "Nor is any thing gained . . . by supposing the watch before us to have been produced from another watch, that from a former, and so on indefinitely. . . . Contrivance is still unaccounted for." State the argument implicit in this passage.

## NOTES AND QUESTIONS

1. *Analogy and inference to the best explanation.* Paley's argument is sometimes taken to be an argument by analogy:

   Living things are like watches.
   Watches are the product of intelligent design.
   Therefore, living things are the product of intelligent design.

   But arguments from analogy are notoriously weak. Consider:

   Living things are like watches.
   Watches are made in factories.
   Therefore, living things are made in factories.

   It is more fruitful to view Paley's argument as an **Inference to the Best Explanation.** Such arguments have the following general form:

   Some remarkable fact F is observed.
   The best (or perhaps the only) explanation for F is hypothesis H.
   Therefore H is (probably) true.

   *Exercise:* Recast Paley's core argument in this form. Then explain why the extended analogy with watches provides important support for the argument.

2. *Paley and Darwin.* Paley argues that the only reasonable explanation for the observed "design" in nature is that living things were made by an intelligent creator. In this form, the argument was undermined by Darwin. Without appeal to supernatural

causes, the theory of evolution by natural selection can explain why living things are well adapted to their environments. (Paley wrote before Darwin, so he cannot be faulted for failing to anticipate this alternative.) For a detailed Darwinian response to Paley, see Richard Dawkins, *The Blind Watchmaker* (W. W. Norton, 1986).

A version of Paley's argument nonetheless survives the Darwinian response. Darwin's theory explains why populations of living things change over time. But it does not explain the emergence of life itself. (This is not an objection to Darwin's theory: it was never meant to explain this process.) Moreover, we can be confident that the first living things exhibited remarkable "order and contrivance." Any creature capable of reproduction needs intricate systems for taking in food from the environment, copying its genetic material, and so on. So consider the first cell. It is like Paley's watch — an intricate contrivance that exhibits "apparent design." Why are *its* parts so brilliantly adapted to its needs? Modern biology has no answer. So Paley might insist: the only available explanation for this fact is intelligent design. It is reasonable to believe the best explanation. So it is reasonable to believe in intelligent design.

*Exercise:* Consider how the atheist might respond to this argument. In doing so, *do not try to invent your own theory of the origin of life.* That would be hopeless speculation and it should not be necessary. Contemporary atheists believe that even in the absence of a positive scientific account of the emergence of life, it is unreasonable to posit an intelligent designer. This sort of atheist must reject at least one premise in this Paley-style argument. Identify the most vulnerable premise and say why it might be reasonable to reject it.

For a modern version of this argument, see Michael Behe, *Darwin's Black Box*, (Free Press, 1996). For a response, see H. Allen Orr, "Darwinism vs. Intelligent Design (Again)" (*Boston Review* December 1996 / January 1997).

## John Stuart Mill (1806–1873)

Born in London, England, Mill was educated by his father, James Mill, a distinguished Scottish philosopher, political theorist, economist, and historian. A utilitarian, empiricist, and important public thinker, Mill was the author of *Utilitarianism, Considerations on Representative Government, Principles of Political Economy, Subjection of Women, System of Logic, The Autobiography of John Stuart Mill,* and, most famously, *On Liberty.* Apart from his writings, Mill worked at the East India Company (1823–58), served as a Member of Parliament (1865–68), and was Lord Rector of the University of St. Andrews (1865–68).

# THEISM

from *Three Essays on Religion*

# Part I

## THE ARGUMENT FROM MARKS OF DESIGN IN NATURE

We now at last reach an argument of a really scientific character, which does not shrink from scientific tests, but claims to be judged by the established canons of Induction. The Design argument is wholly grounded on experience. Certain qualities, it is alleged, are found to be characteristic of such things as are made by an intelligent mind for a purpose. The order of Nature, or some considerable parts of it, exhibit these qualities in a remarkable degree. We are entitled, from this great similarity in the effects, to infer similarity in the cause, and to believe that things which it is beyond the power of man to make, but which resemble the works of man in all but power, must also have been made by Intelligence, armed with a power greater than human.

I have stated this argument in its fullest strength, as it is stated by its most thoroughgoing assertors. A very little consideration, however, suffices to show that though it has some force, its force is very generally overrated. Paley's illustration of a watch puts the case much too strongly.[1] If I found a watch on an apparently desolate island, I should indeed infer that it had been left there by a human being; but the inference would not be from marks of design, but because I already knew by direct experience that watches are made by men. I should draw the inference no less confidently from a foot print, or from any relic however insignificant which experience has taught me to attribute to man: as geologists infer the past existence of animals from coprolites, though no one sees marks of design in a coprolite. The evidence of design in creation can never reach the height of direct induction; it amounts only to the inferior kind of inductive evidence called analogy. Analogy agrees with induction in this, that they both argue that a thing known to resemble another in certain circumstances (call those circumstances A and B) will resemble it in another circumstance (call it C). But the difference is that in induction, A and B are known, by a previous comparison of many instances, to be the very circumstances on which C depends, or with which it is in some way connected. When this has not been ascertained, the argument amounts only to this, that since it is not known with which of the circumstances existing in the known case C is connected, they may as well be A and B as any others; and therefore there is a greater probability of C in cases where we know that A and B exist, than in cases of which we know nothing at all. This argument is of a weight very difficult to estimate at all, and impossible to estimate precisely.

---

1. See Paley, *Natural Theology*, p. 24 of this anthology.

It may be very strong, when the known points of agreement, A and B &c. are numerous and the known points of difference few; or very weak, when the reverse is the case: but it can never be equal in validity to a real induction. The resemblances between some of the arrangements in nature and some of those made by man are considerable, and even as mere resemblances afford a certain presumption of similarity of cause: but how great that presumption is, it is hard to say. All that can be said with certainty is that these likenesses make creation by intelligence considerably more probable than if the likenesses had been less, or than if there has been no likenesses at all.

This mode, however, of stating the case does not do full justice to evidence of Theism. The Design argument is not drawn from mere resemblances in Nature to the works of human intelligence, but from the special character of those resemblances. The circumstances in which it is alleged that the world resembles the works of man are not circumstances taken at random, but are particular instances of a circumstance which experience shows to have a real connection with an intelligent origin, the fact of conspiring to an end. The argument therefore is not one of mere analogy. As mere analogy it has its weight, but it is more than analogy. It surpasses analogy exactly as induction surpasses it. It is an inductive argument.

This, I think, is undeniable, and it remains to test the argument by the logical principles applicable to Induction. For this purpose it will be convenient to handle, not the argument as a whole, but some one of the most impressive cases of it, such as the structure of the eye, or of the ear. It is maintained that the structure of the eye proves a designing mind. . . .

The parts of which the eye is composed, and the collocations which constitute the arrangement of those parts, resemble one another in this very remarkable property, that they all conduce to enabling the animal to see. These things being as they are, the animal sees: if any one of them were different from what it is, the animal, for the most part, would either not see, or would not see equally well. And this is the only marked resemblance that we can trace among the different parts of this structure, beyond the general likeness of composition and organisation which exists among all other parts of the animal. Now the particular combination of organic elements called an eye had, in every instance, a beginning in time and must therefore have been brought together by a cause or causes. The number of instances is immeasurably greater than is, by the principles of inductive logic, required for the exclusion of a random concurrence of independent causes, or speaking technically, for the elimination of chance. We are therefore warranted by the canons of induction in concluding that what brought all these elements together was some cause common to them all; and inasmuch as the elements agree in the single circumstance of conspiring to produce sight, there must be some connection by way of causation between the cause which brought those elements together, and the fact of sight.

This I conceive to be a legitimate inductive inference, and the sum and substance of what Induction can do for Theism. The natural sequel of the argument would be this. Sight, being a fact not precedent but subsequent to the putting together of the organic structure of the eye, can only be connected with the production of that structure in the character of a final, not an efficient cause;[2] that is, it is not Sight itself but an antecedent Idea of it, that must be the efficient cause. But this at once marks the origin as proceeding from an intelligent will.

I regret to say, however, that this latter half of the argument is not so inexpugnable as the former half. Creative forethought is not absolutely the only link by which the origin of the wonderful mechanism of the eye may be connected with the fact of sight. There is another connecting link on which attention has been greatly fixed by recent speculations, and the reality of which cannot be called in question, though its adequacy to account for such truly admirable combinations as some of those in Nature, is still and will probably long remain problematical. This is the principle of "the survival of the fittest."

This principle does not pretend to account for the commencement of sensation or of animal or vegetable life. But assuming the existence of some one or more very low forms of organic life, in which there are no complex adaptations nor any marked appearances of contrivance, and supposing, as experience warrants us in doing, that many small variations from those simple types would be thrown out in all directions, which would be transmissible by inheritance, and of which some would be advantageous to the creature in its struggle for existence and others disadvantageous, the forms which are advantageous would always tend to survive and those which are disadvantageous to perish. And thus there would be a constant though slow general improvement of the type as it branched out into many different varieties, adapting it to different media and modes of existence, until it might possibly, in countless ages, attain to the most advanced examples which now exist.

It must be acknowledged that there is something very startling, and *prima facie* improbable in this hypothetical history of Nature. It would require us, for example, to suppose that the primeval animal of whatever nature it may have been, could not see, and had at most such slight preparation for seeing as might be constituted by some chemical action of light upon its cellular structure. One of the accidental variations which are liable to take place in all organic beings would at some time or other produce a variety that could see, in some imperfect manner, and this peculiarity being transmitted by inheritance, while other variations continued to take place in other directions, a number of races would be produced who, by the power of even imperfect sight, would have a great advantage over all other creatures which could not see and would in time extirpate them from all places, except, perhaps a few very peculiar situations underground. Fresh variations supervening would give rise to races with better and better seeing powers until we might at last reach as extraordinary a combination of structures and functions as are seen in the eye of man and of the more important animals. Of this theory when pushed to this extreme point, all that can now be said is that it is not so absurd as it looks, and that the analogies which have been discovered in experience, favourable to its possibility, far exceed what any one

---

2.  An efficient cause of an event is a prior occurrence that brings that event about. A **final cause** of an event is the purpose for which that event occurs.

could have supposed beforehand. Whether it will ever be possible to say more than this, is at present uncertain. The theory if admitted would be in no way whatever inconsistent with Creation. But it must be acknowledged that it would greatly attenuate the evidence for it.

Leaving this remarkable speculation to whatever fate the progress of discovery may have in store for it, I think it must be allowed that, in the present state of our knowledge, the adaptations in Nature afford a large balance of probability in favour of creation by intelligence. It is equally certain that this is no more than a probability; and that the various other arguments of Natural Theology which we have considered, add nothing to its force. . . .

# Part II

## ATTRIBUTES

The question of the existence of a Deity, in its purely scientific aspect, standing as is shown in the First Part, it is next to be considered, given the indications of a Deity, what *sort* of a Deity do they point to? What attributes are we warranted, by the evidence which Nature affords of a creative mind, in assigning to that mind?

It needs no showing that the power if not the intelligence, must be so far superior to that of Man, as to surpass all human estimate. But from this to Omnipotence and Omniscience there is a wide interval. And the distinction is of immense practical importance.

It is not too much to say that every indication of Design in the Kosmos is so much evidence against the Omnipotence of the Designer. For what is meant by Design? Contrivance: the adaptation of means to an end. But the necessity for contrivance — the need of employing means — is a consequence of the limitation of power. Who would have recourse to means if to attain his end his mere word was sufficient? The very idea of means implies that the means have an efficacy which the direct action of the being who employs them has not. Otherwise they are not means, but an incumbrance. A man does not use machinery to move his arms. If he did, it could only be when paralysis had deprived him of the power of moving them by volition. But if the employment of contrivance is in itself a sign of limited power, how much more so is the careful and skilful choice of contrivances? Can any wisdom be shown in the selection of means, when the means have no efficacy but what is given them by the will of him who employs them, and when his will could have bestowed the same efficacy on any other means? Wisdom and contrivance are shown in overcoming difficulties, and there is no room for them in a Being for whom no difficulties exist. The evidences, therefore, of Natural Theology distinctly imply that the author of the Kosmos worked under limitations; that he was obliged to adapt himself to conditions independent of his will, and to attain his ends by such arrangements as those conditions admitted of.

And this hypothesis agrees with what we have seen to be the tendency of the evidences in another respect. We found that the appearances in Nature point indeed to an origin of the Kosmos, or order in Nature, and indicate that origin to be Design but do not point to any commencement, still less creation, of the two great elements of the Universe, the passive element and the active element, Matter and Force. There is in Nature no reason whatever to suppose that either Matter or Force, or any of their properties, were made by the Being who was the author of the collocations by which the world is adapted to what we consider as its purposes; or that he has power to alter any of those properties. It is only when we consent to entertain this negative supposition that there arises a need for wisdom and contrivance in the order of the universe. The Deity had on this hypothesis to work out his ends by combining materials of a given nature and properties. Out of these materials he had to construct a world in which his designs should be carried into effect through given properties of Matter and Force, working together and fitting into one another. This did require skill and contrivance, and the means by which it is effected are often such as justly excite our wonder and admiration: but exactly because it requires wisdom, it implies limitation of power, or rather the two phrases express different sides of the same fact.

If it be said, that an Omnipotent Creator, though under no necessity of employing contrivances such as man must use, thought fit to do so in order to leave traces by which man might recognize his creative hand, the answer is that this equally supposes a limit to his omnipotence. For if it was his will that men should know that they themselves and the world are his work, he, being omnipotent, had only to will that they should be aware of it. . . .

Omnipotence, therefore, cannot be predicated of the Creator on grounds of natural theology. The fundamental principles of natural religion as deduced from the facts of the universe, negative his omnipotence. They do not, in the same manner, exclude omniscience: if we suppose limitation of power, there is nothing to contradict the supposition of perfect knowledge and absolute wisdom. But neither is there anything to prove it. The knowledge of the powers and properties of things necessary for planning and executing the arrangements of the Kosmos, is no doubt as much in excess of human knowledge as the power implied in creation is in excess of human power. And the skill, the subtlety of contrivance, the ingenuity as it would be called in the case of a human work, is often marvellous. But nothing obliges us to suppose that either the knowledge or the skill is infinite. We are not even compelled to suppose that the contrivances were always the best possible. If we venture to judge them as we judge the works of human artificers, we find abundant defects. The human body, for example, is one of the most striking instances of artful and ingenious contrivance which nature offers, but we may well ask whether so complicated a machine could not have been made to last longer, and not to get so easily and frequently out of order. We may ask why the human race should have been so constituted as to grovel in wretchedness and degradation for countless ages before a small portion of it was enabled to lift itself into the very imperfect state of intelligence, goodness and happiness which we enjoy. The divine power may not have been equal to doing more; the obstacles to a better arrangement of things may have been insuperable. But it is also possible that they were not. The skill of the Demiourgos was sufficient to produce what we see; but we cannot tell that this skill reached the extreme limit of perfection compatible with the material it employed and the forces it had to work with. I know not how we can even satisfy ourselves on grounds of natural theology, that the Creator foresees all the future; that he foreknows all the effects that will issue from his own contrivances. There may be great wisdom without the power of foreseeing and calculating everything: and human workmanship teaches us the possibility that the workman's knowledge of the properties of the things he works on may enable him to make arrangements admirably fitted to produce a given result, while he may have very little power of foreseeing the agencies of another kind which may modify or counteract the operation of the machinery he has made. Perhaps a knowledge of the laws of nature on which organic life depends, not much more perfect than the knowledge which man even now possesses of some other natural laws, would enable man, if he had the same power over the materials and the forces concerned which he has over some of those of inanimate nature, to create organized beings not less wonderful nor less adapted to their conditions of existence than those in Nature. . . .

We now pass to the moral attributes of the Deity, so far as indicated in the Creation; or (stating the problem in the broadest manner) to the question, what indications Nature gives of the purposes of its author. This question bears a very different aspect to us from what it bears to those teachers of Natural Theology who are incumbered with the necessity of admitting the omnipotence of the Creator. We have not to attempt the impossible problem of reconciling infinite benevolence and justice with infinite power in the Creator of such a world as this. The attempt to do so not only involves absolute contradiction in an intellectual point of view but exhibits to excess the revolting spectacle of a jesuitical defence of moral enormities. . . .

At the stage which our argument has reached there is none of this moral perplexity. Grant that creative power was limited by conditions the nature and extent of which are wholly unknown to us, and the goodness and justice of the Creator may be all that the most pious believe; and all in the work that conflicts with those moral attributes may be the fault of the conditions which left to the Creator only a choice of evils.

It is, however, one question whether any given conclusion is consistent with known facts, and another whether there is evidence to prove it: and if we have no means for judging of the design but from the work actually produced, it is a somewhat hazardous speculation to suppose that the work designed was of a different quality from the result realized. Still, though the ground is unsafe we may, with due caution, journey a certain distance on it. Some parts of the order of nature give much more indication of contrivance than others; many, it is not too much to say, give no sign of it at all. The signs of contrivance are most conspicuous in the structure and processes of vegetable and animal life. But for these, it is probable that the appearances in nature would never have seemed to the thinking part of mankind to afford any proofs of a God. But when a God had been inferred from the organization of living beings, other parts of Nature, such as the structure of the solar system, seemed to afford evidences, more or less strong, in confirmation of the belief: granting, then, a design in Nature, we can best hope to be enlightened as to what that design was, by examining it in the parts of Nature in which its traces are the most conspicuous.

To what purpose, then, do the expedients in the construction of animals and vegetables, which excite the admiration of naturalists, appear to tend? There is no blinking the fact that they tend principally to no more exalted object than to make the structure remain in life and working order for a certain time: the individual for a few years, the species or race for a longer but still a limited period. And the similar though less conspicuous marks of creation which are recognized in inorganic Nature, are generally of the same character. The adaptations, for instance, which appear in the solar system consist in placing it under conditions which enable the mutual action of its parts to maintain instead of destroying its stability, and even that only for a time, vast indeed if measured against our short span of animated existence, but which can be perceived even by us to be limited: for even the feeble means which we possess of exploring the past, are believed by those who have examined the subject by the most recent lights, to yield evidence that the solar system was once a vast sphere of nebula or vapour, and is going through a process which in the course of ages will reduce it to a single and not very large mass of solid matter frozen up with more than arctic cold. If the machinery of the system is adapted to keep itself at work only for a time, still less perfect is the adaptation of it for the abode of living beings since it is only adapted to them during the relatively short portion of its total duration which intervenes between the time when each planet was too hot and the time when it became or will become too cold to admit of life under the only conditions in which we have experience of its possibility. Or we should perhaps reverse the statement, and say that organisation and life are only adapted to the conditions of the solar system during a relatively short portion of the system's existence.

The greater part, therefore, of the design of which there is indication in Nature, however wonderful its mechanism, is no evidence of any moral attributes, because the end to which it is directed, and its adaptation to which end is the evidence of its being directed to an end at all, is not a moral end: it is not the good of any sentient creature, it is but the qualified permanence, for a limited period, of the work itself, whether animate or inanimate. The only inference that can be drawn from most of it, respecting the character of the Creator, is that he does not wish his works to perish as soon as created; he wills them to have a certain duration. From this alone nothing can be justly inferred as to the manner in which he is affected towards his animate or rational creatures. . . .

When all these things are considered it is evident that a vast deduction must be made from the evidences of a Creator before they can be counted as evidences of a benevolent purpose: so vast indeed that some may doubt whether after such a deduction there remains any balance. Yet endeavouring to look at the question without partiality or prejudice and without allowing wishes to have any influence over judgement, it does appear that granting the existence of design, there is a preponderance of evidence that the Creator desired the pleasure of his creatures. This is indicated by the fact that pleasure of one description or another is afforded by almost everything, the mere play of the faculties, physical and mental, being a never-ending source of pleasure, and even painful things giving pleasure by the satisfaction of curiosity and the agreeable sense of acquiring knowledge; and also that pleasure, when experienced, seems to result from the normal working of the machinery, while pain usually arises from some external interference with it, and resembles in each particular case the result of an accident. Even in cases when pain results, like pleasure, from the machinery itself, the appearances do not indicate that contrivance was brought into play purposely to produce pain: what is indicated is rather a clumsiness in the contrivance employed for some other purpose. The author of the machinery is no doubt accountable for having made it susceptible of pain; but this may have been a necessary condition of its susceptibility to pleasure; a supposition which avails nothing on the theory of an Omnipotent Creator but is an extremely probable one in the case of a contriver working under the limitation of inexorable laws and indestructible properties of matter. The susceptibility being conceded as a thing which did enter into design, the pain itself usually seems like a thing undesigned; a casual result of the collision of the organism with some outward force to which it was not intended to be exposed, and which, in many cases, provision is even made to hinder it from being exposed to. There is, therefore, much appearance that pleasure is agreeable to the Creator, while there is very little if any appearance that pain is so: and there is a certain amount of justification for inferring, on grounds of Natural Theology alone, that benevolence is one of the attributes of the Creator. But to jump from this to the inference that his sole or chief purposes are those of benevolence, and that the single end and aim of Creation was the happiness of his creatures, is not only not justified by any evidence but is a conclusion in opposition to such evidence as we have. If the motive of the Deity for creating sentient beings was the happiness of the beings he created, his purpose, in our corner of the universe at least, must be pronounced, taking past ages and all countries and races into account, to have been thus far an ignominious failure; and if God had no purpose but our happiness and that of other living creatures it is not credible that he would have called them into existence with the prospect of being so completely baffled. If man had not the power by the exercise of his own energies for the improvement both of himself and of his outward circumstances, to do for himself and other creatures vastly more than God had in the first instance done, the Being who called him into existence would deserve something very different from thanks at his hands. . . .

Such are the indications of Natural Religion in respect to the divine benevolence. If we look for any other of the moral attributes which a certain class of philosophers are accustomed to distinguish from benevolence, as for example Justice, we find a total blank. There is no evidence whatever in Nature for divine justice, whatever standard of justice our ethical opinions, may lead us to recognize. There is no shadow of justice in the general arrangements of Nature; and what imperfect realization it obtains in any human society (a most imperfect realization as yet) is the work of man himself, struggling upwards against immense natural difficulties, into civilization, and making to himself a second nature, far better and more unselfish than he was created with. . . .

These, then, are the net results of Natural Theology on the question of the divine attributes. A Being of great but limited power, how or by what limited we cannot even conjecture; of great, and perhaps unlimited intelligence, but perhaps, also, more narrowly limited than his power: who desires, and pays some regard to, the happiness of his creatures, but who seems to have other motives of action which he cares more for, and who can hardly be supposed to have created the universe for that purpose alone. Such is the Deity whom Natural Religion points to; and any idea of God more captivating than this comes only from human wishes, or from the teaching of either real or imaginary Revelation.

## TEST YOUR UNDERSTANDING

1. Explain Mill's distinction between arguments by "analogy" and "inductive" arguments.

2. What is Mill's ultimate assessment of Paley's argument for the existence of an intelligent designer?

3. Mill argues that "every indication of Design in the Kosmos is so much evidence against the Omnipotence of the Designer." Briefly explain why Mill believes this.

## NOTES AND QUESTIONS

1. Mill's "Theism" represents an early attempt by a scientifically informed philosopher to assess the relative merits of Paley's version of intelligent design and Darwin's alternative explanation for the intricate adaptations found in nature. (*The Origin of Species* was published in 1859; Mill's essay dates from 1868–70.) Mill's assessment of Darwin's theory begins with the observation that "there is something very startling, and *prima facie* improbable in this hypothetical history of Nature" (p. 36), and concludes by noting that while the theory is "not so absurd as it looks," it remains the case that "in the present state of our knowledge, the adaptations in Nature afford a large balance of probability in favour of creation by intelligence" (p. 37).

   In the intervening years, Darwin's theory of evolution has become a cornerstone of modern biology. The theory is no longer speculative: it is brilliantly confirmed by an astonishingly diverse body of evidence. Imagine how Mill might rewrite part I of "Theism" in light of this development within biology.

2. Mill concludes that the evidence of natural theology points to "a Being of great but limited power. . .; of great, and perhaps unlimited intelligence. . .; who desires, and pays some regard to, the happiness of his creatures, but who seems to have other motives of action which he cares more for, and who can hardly be supposed to have created the universe for that purpose alone" (p. 42). Review Mill's arguments for this assessment and imagine how Paley might respond. Paley's detailed arguments for the traditional attributes of God are found in chapters 24–26 of *Natural Theology*.

## Roger White (born 1967)

White is Professor of Philosophy at the Massachusetts Institute of Technology. He specializes in epistemology and the philosophy of science.

# THE ARGUMENT FROM COSMOLOGICAL FINE-TUNING

A high-security combination lock is wired up to nuclear warheads that threaten to destroy the whole world. The bombs will be detonated unless several dials are set to a very precise configuration of values. Miraculously it turns out that the dials are delicately set within the tiny range that deactivates the bombs. Had they differed ever so slightly from their actual positions all life would be gone. Is this just a lucky accident, or might they have been adjusted that way on purpose?

The fanciful story is in certain respects analogous to the view presented by many contemporary physical cosmologists. We are told that our universe is "fine-tuned for life." What is meant is roughly the following. For life to have any chance of evolving the universe must meet certain conditions. It turns out that these conditions are extremely stringent. Had the values of various physical constants differed ever so slightly from their actual values the universe would not have been hospitable to life. It is said that these crucial constants could easily have taken different values. If we were to witness another big bang, the new universe it created would almost certainly be a rather boring one. It might collapse within seconds, or contain nothing but hydrogen, or nothing but black holes. There is only the tiniest chance that the crucial particle masses and force strengths would take the precise values required for life to emerge. While there is room for controversy over the details, the picture sketched here is widely endorsed by experts in the field. Our question is what philosophical implications this might have.

To say that our universe is "fine-tuned" in this sense is not to imply that there is a Fine-Tuner, an intelligent agent who had a hand in setting the values of the physical constants. It is just to say that these constants happen to fall in the narrow range required for life to exist. However, that our universe meets the stringent conditions for life has been taken as the basis for contemporary version of the Argument from Design. There are many ways that such an argument can be developed in detail. I will consider just one way, which focuses on *explanation*. Here is an outline of the argument.

# Fine-Tuning Argument (FTA)

1. If a fact E that we observe stands in need of explanation, and hypothesis H provides a satisfactory explanation of E that is better than any alternative explanation available, then E provides significant evidential support for H.

2. That our universe is hospitable to life stands in need of explanation.

3. That God adjusted the constants in order to allow for life to develop provides a satisfactory explanation for why our universe is life-permitting.

4. There is no comparably satisfying explanation of this fact available.

5. Therefore, that our universe is life-permitting provides significant evidential support for theism.

First, a couple of general points about this argument. The conclusion of this argument is not that there *is* a God, or even that all things considered it is most reasonable to believe that there is. The argument seeks only to establish an evidential connection between certain observed facts and theism. This makes the conclusion somewhat modest while far from trivial. Any assessment of theism will have to consider various considerations for and against. The FTA just focuses on one such consideration. Second, the FTA as presented here concerns the existence of God. Often discussions of cosmological fine-tuning focus on the more modest *design hypothesis*: that some kind of intelligent agent or agents influenced the values of the constants. (Theism is a specific version of the design hypothesis.) It can make sense to frame the issue this way, as the attributes of God according to traditional theism go well beyond what is required to explain the fine-tuning facts. Nevertheless, our focus here is on an argument for the existence of God, and insofar as the data support the existence of a designer they will also support the existence of God, even if much more is involved in an assessment of theism.

Let's consider the premises in turn. Premise 1 states a general principle of evidential support, a version of what is called Inference to the Best Explanation. The idea is a familiar one. Among the myriad facts that a detective is faced with, some stand out and compel her to ask "Why?" The plausibility of her case hinges on how well her hypothesis can explain these various clues. Similarly, we can't *see* electrons the way we do tables and chairs, and we weren't around to observe the origin of species. Why then should we believe in electrons or evolutionary theory? Because they provide the most satisfying explanation of certain striking facts that we do observe.

There is a distinction being appealed to here between facts that *stand in need* of explanation and those that don't. Some situations rightly compel us to ask *why* things are like so. We are compelled because we think there surely is some answer. For others an appropriate response may be, "That's just the way things are." Suppose I spill some soapy water and it splatters in some arbitrary shape on the floor. It need not have landed in the very shape that it did. There are indefinitely many possible puddle shapes that might have been formed. But the fact that it landed in *this* very pattern does not strike us as in special need of explanation. The water had to land in some way, and this is just one of many ways it could have landed. While it is possible that there is more to discover here, nothing about the shape of the puddle compels us to seek further answers. It is a different matter when the soapy water is blown through a wire ring. Now a thin film of liquid forms a perfect sphere. Even without any understanding of chemistry and physics we are compelled to ask why it formed in this way. We have no doubt that there is some deeper explanation for why this occurred than that it just turned out that way. It is scarcely credible to be told, "Well, it had to be in some shape and on this occasion it happened to form a perfect sphere."

It needn't redound to the credit of a hypothesis that it can explain some fact that didn't strike us as needing explanation in the first place. We find some alphabet tiles scattered on the table reading "ANOW AWNVIUUEPOBN VNJSKNVJKEWN AJKFN." Might some undiscovered law of physics determine that they be arranged thus? More plausibly, might someone have arranged them to form a coded message? Perhaps. But their configuration gives us little reason to believe any such hypothesis, as their arrangement doesn't require much of an explanation in the first place. Finding the letters "O THAT THIS TOO TOO SOLID FLESH WOULD MELT THAW AND RESOLVE ITSELF INTO A DEW" is a different matter. It would be crazy to believe that the pieces happen to be arranged in this manner for no reason. Of course in this case the obvious explanation is that someone arranged them in order to spell a line from *Hamlet*. To the extent that this gives a satisfying explanation, we have reason to suppose that it is true.

The last point to note concerning the principle is that the degree of support that a hypothesis enjoys depends on how it compares with alternative explanations. The papers on my desk are not where I left them. Why? They could hardly move around by themselves. Perhaps an intruder was rifling through my stuff. This might well explain it, although it leaves us with the question of how he managed to get into a locked room on the ninth floor when there are no signs of forced entry. I notice the window is slightly ajar. A simpler explanation might be that a gust of wind blew the papers out of place. Only insofar as this provides a satisfying explanation is the case for an intruder diminished. I notice further that my financial documents are all left in one pile. The intruder hypothesis may explain this in a way that the wind cannot. And this might make it the more plausible hypothesis despite its other difficulties.

Does the fact that the universe is suitable for life stand in need of explanation as premise 2 asserts? It is not easy to say in general how we assess whether something needs explanation. In most cases it is just obvious. We don't need to apply some theory to see that spherical soap bubbles and meaningful strings of alphabet tiles require explanation. Rightly or wrongly, the cosmological fine-tuning argument strikes many scientists and philosophers the same way (including many with no sympathy for theism or any design hypothesis). If the fine-tuning of the constants does not strike you this way, then this version of the FTA may have little appeal for you. While there isn't space here for a detailed argument that cosmological fine-tuning does call for an explanation, we can make some suggestive points. First, without some further explanation the fine-tuning of our universe is thought to be extremely *improbable*. If we were to witness a new big bang we should firmly expect it *not* to produce anything like a universe with stable stars and planets and enough of the right elements for life. But while this is part of what makes something call for an explanation, it can't be the whole story. It is highly unlikely that by tossing a handful of alphabet tiles on the table we will see the sequence "ANOW AWNVIUUEPOBN VNJSKNVJKEWN AJKFN," since there are trillions of possible sequences of that length. But this hardly calls for an explanation. Typically those facts that do call for explanation involve some further significant feature that makes them stand out among the alternative possibilities. The spherical soap bubble is a *simple geometrical figure*; most possible shapes of water are irregular splatters. The line from *Hamlet* is *meaningful*; most such sequences are gibberish. Perhaps what makes a universe with *life* stand out is that it is *valuable*, morally and aesthetically. Most of the possible outcomes of a big bang are pretty bleak, just vast lifeless space with some simple atoms floating about. That against all odds we have the vast panoply of living creatures we find here can seem extraordinary.

Before turning to consider possible explanations of fine-tuning, let's briefly consider a common suggestion as to why we shouldn't find it remarkable in the first place. It is sometimes said that we shouldn't be surprised that we find the constants to be fine-tuned for life, since if they weren't we wouldn't be here to observe them. Since we couldn't observe the constants taking other than life-permitting values, there is nothing puzzling about the fact that we find them to be so. The following story illustrates what is unsatisfying about this response. You are standing before a firing squad with fifty rifles aimed in your direction. To your astonishment, as the guns blast each bullet flies close by you, leaving you unharmed. Why did all the bullets miss? Was it just an accident? Surely this cries out for explanation if anything does. It cannot help to be told, "Well, if they hadn't all missed you wouldn't be alive to see it." While this is true, it does nothing to remove the mystery of how the bullets all managed to miss you. Whatever appeal this suggestion has seems to rest on the confusion of thinking that our observations of the fine-tuned constants are somehow *inevitable*, and hence not in need of any further explanation. It was not inevitable that we would observe the constants to be fine-tuned. What was inevitable was just that *if* we were to observe the constants at all, we would find them to be fine-tuned for life. But there was a slim chance that we or anyone else would be around to observe anything at all. That we are here to observe our good fortune remains as puzzling as ever.

If the fine-tuning facts do require explanation, can theism provide a satisfactory explanation, as premise 3 claims? Let's begin by considering the positive case before addressing some objections. We explain phenomena by appeal to the actions of rational agents all the time. Why do the letter tiles spell a line from *Hamlet*? Why were the dials set to the very combination that disabled the nuclear warheads? Why are the financial documents on my desk sitting in one pile? In each case the answer is that an agent brought matters about on purpose. Many such explanations are utterly compelling, as good as any explanation of anything.

Of course in each of the last three cases it is a familiar *human* agent that we have in mind. While everyone must grant that there are overwhelmingly plausible explanations that appeal to human agency, numerous objections have been raised to explanations invoking *divine* agency. We will briefly look at just two of these. First, there is thought to be something suspiciously *too easy* about invoking acts of God to explain some puzzling phenomenon. An omnipotent being can bring about anything. So no matter what we find, we could in principle just point to it and say, "God did that." This gives rise to the suspicion that such appeals are in some sense *empty*. The worry is sometimes expressed in the slogan "Whatever can explain anything explains nothing."

But of course humans are capable of arranging letter tiles in any possible sequence, dials in any configuration, and papers in any order. No matter how we found the letters we could in principle say, "Someone put them like that." This observation does nothing at all to diminish the force of the explanation when the letters form meaningful sentences. The grain of truth behind the emptiness complaint might be illustrated by the following story. We read that some stranger Jane Smith just won the lottery. "Aha," I say. "What are the odds of that, given the millions that bought tickets? I'll bet the lottery was rigged in her favor. That would explain why *she* won out of all those players." One way to see what is silly about my conspiracy theorizing is to note that if Bob Brown or Suzie Jones had won instead, I could just as well have invoked a similar explanation to account for his or her good fortune. But what goes wrong here is not just that I *could* propose such an explanation no matter how the lottery turned out. The problem is that such an explanation is no more or less compelling in the case of Jane Smith's winning than any other. Her having won no more *stands in need* of explanation than any other possible outcome would. And this can only show that it does not require an explanation at all. For it can hardly be that no matter how the lottery turned out we would have reason to suppose that it was rigged. The crucial point is that there is nothing about Jane Smith that I'm aware of that makes *her* having won rather than someone else especially striking. Someone had to win, and it could just as well have been Smith as anyone else. It would be a different matter if she had won the last three lotteries, or if she had just taken a senior position at the lottery commission.

The charge of explanatory emptiness may carry some force if the observed features of the universe are no more in need of explanation than any other possible features, and if we were no less inclined to invoke divine design regardless of how the universe was. But the possible outcomes of a big bang do not equally call for an explanation. If instead of a universe suitable for life the big bang had yielded nothing but a bland lifeless cosmic soup, it would not strike us as in urgent need of explanation. Here it is significant that the existence of living creatures has value in a way that other possible outcomes do not. It is not unlikely that a benevolent, rational being would prefer a universe hospitable to living creatures over, say, one containing nothing but thinly dispersed hydrogen atoms. Note that for the explanation to be compelling it is not necessary that on the basis of theism one could *predict* that the universe will be suitable for life, let alone that there will be creatures much like us. Supposing that a human agent is arranging some letter tiles hardly allows me to predict that they will spell "O THAT THIS TOO TOO SOLID FLESH WOULD MELT THAW AND RE-SOLVE ITSELF INTO A DEW." There are billions of possible sentences that an agent might produce. We can't even be so sure that the letters will form a *meaningful* string. This agent might just shuffle them about in meaningless ways that strike her fancy. Nevertheless, arranging the letters in a meaningful way is a plausible purpose that an agent might have. And that is enough to make a far more satisfying explanation than supposing that they fell in this order by accident. Similarly, if the creation of life is a plausible purpose that a rational agent might have, then theism may provide a satis-factory explanation of the fine-tuning of the constants, one that is far more satisfying than supposing that it just happened by accident.

A second objection notes that when we invoke *human* agency to explain things we understand quite well *how* this might occur, as we understand how humans func-tion. Humans have brains, a nervous system, muscles, and limbs. We understand how such a being can manipulate wooden tiles or fiddle with dials. We haven't the faintest grip on how a being like God can "set" the physical constants to within some range of values. To invoke God, the objection goes, is just to introduce a mystery and not to make any explanatory progress.

We can first note that the explanatory force of our appeal to human agents does not crucially depend on our understanding of human physiology. Long before we had the faintest clue as to how our brains and bodies work, we could understand that human agents were responsible for various phenomena we observed. A short conversation with someone is enough to make it abundantly clear that there is a thinking agent behind the sounds coming out of her mouth. This is just by far the most satisfying explanation of my observations even if I have no idea whether brains even exist let alone how they work or how mental activity is related to a physical body, or anything of the sort. To further evaluate the force of the current objection, it is useful to consider a hypothetical case. David Hume imagined there being a voice booming from the sky for everyone in the world to hear. We can elaborate the story and suppose that we also see the clouds shuffle about to create messages in all the languages on earth. The voice provides us with all sorts of extraordinary information that we can verify to be correct. It gives us a detailed explanation of a cure for cancer. It makes amazingly precise predictions about future events such as the exact time and location of every raindrop over the next week. We are able to converse with the mystery voice, and it appears to reveal knowledge and intelligence orders of magnitude beyond what any human could have. Now I hardly have a better grasp of how an agent might do all of this than I do of how an agent might "fine-tune" the constants to permit life. But this would do little to blunt my conviction that somehow, some kind of agent vastly more powerful and intelligent than any human is behind the voice from the sky. I can perfectly well understand *why* we hear a voice in the sky (some kind of extraordinary agent is speaking) without much understanding of *how* this is achieved. I can similarly understand why the universe is life-permitting (God or some extraordinary agent made it so) without much of a grasp of how this could be done.

Even if theism can provide a satisfying explanation for the fine-tuning facts, the force of the argument will be diminished to the extent that there are plausible rivals. The argument is perhaps most vulnerable at premise 4, which claims that there is no comparably satisfying explanation available. What might an alternative explanation look like?

The most interesting proposal is that our universe is just one of very many universes, one part of a large "multiverse." The constants on which life depends may vary randomly among the universes. Given a large enough number of universes, it is to be expected that at least one such universe will meet the conditions for life. To illustrate, suppose we take a handful of alphabet pieces and drop them on the table. The letters form a string of gibberish. We try it again. Another (different) string of gibberish. We try it again. We repeat the process trillions of trillions of times until eventually we find a line from *Hamlet*. Amazing? Hardly. This sort of thing is bound to happen sometime if you repeat the process enough times. Similarly, the supposition that there have been many random "attempts" at a fine-tuned universe would appear to give a satisfying account of what would otherwise seem extraordinary.

Should we suppose that there are multiple universes? Some argue that the observed fine-tuning of the universe itself provides evidence for the existence of a multiverse, just as others see it as evidence of divine design. There is reason to be dubious of this inference. Suppose we tossed the letter tiles and they spelled out a line from *Hamlet* on the first try. Does our observation give us reason to suppose that these pieces have been tossed on the table many times before by others, or that there are millions of people out there similarly tossing letter tiles? Surely not. Even if such a multi-toss hypothesis were plausible to begin with, the surprising outcome that we have observed does nothing to support the hypothesis further. The crucial point here is that while the occurrence of multiple tosses makes it likely that the letters will land in a meaningful sequence on some occasion, it is no more likely that we will find such a sequence on the one toss that we observe. Similarly with the universes. That there are other universes out there makes it no more likely that we will find the one universe that we observed to be fine-tuned. Putting the matter in terms of explanation, the answer to the question "Why is the universe that we observe fine-tuned?" is not "Because there are lots of other universes." Even if they are out there, these universes have no bearing on what goes on in the universe that we see. So arguably our observations of a fine-tuned universe provide no evidence for the existence of other universes.

There could, however, be independent theoretical grounds to believe in a multiverse. Cosmologists are divided on whether there are such grounds. And even proponents of the multiverse admit that the matter is highly speculative. Still, it is worth considering how the FTA fares in the event that we do have reason to believe in a multiverse, independently of the fine-tuning data. In this case it does seem that the FTA is undermined. However, I would suggest that it is not premise 4 that is threatened in this case but premise 2. The existence of a multiverse does not *explain* but rather *removes the need to explain* the fine-tuning of our universe. Once we suppose there are many universes, it is to be expected that at least one of these will be fine-tuned just by chance. The question of why it is that *this* one, the one that we inhabit, is fine-tuned loses its urgency. Like Jane Smith's winning the lottery, our universe could just as easily be a lucky one as any other, and there is nothing about our particular universe that makes it stand in special need of explanation.

I have hardly scratched the surface of the possible defenses, rebuttals, and replies concerning the premises of this argument, not to mention the other ways we might frame the whole issue. But I hope to have conveyed some of the intuitive force of the puzzle about fine-tuning as an argument for theism. The argument, I would suggest, carries considerable force, although the verdict may ultimately depend on the credibility of the multiverse hypothesis.

## TEST YOUR UNDERSTANDING

1. The cosmological fine-tuning argument begins from the observation that the fundamental laws of nature appear to be "fine-tuned" to permit the existence of life. Say what this means.

2. The argument assumes as a premise that the fine-tuning of the fundamental laws "stands in need of explanation." Explain this claim and say why it matters for White's argument.

## NOTES AND QUESTIONS

1. The worst arguments for the existence of God go like this: "Here is some marvelous fact. Science can't explain it. Therefore God exists." These arguments are bad because science makes progress. At any given stage in the development of science, there will be facts that science cannot explain. But in many of these cases, the explanation will be just around the corner, and even when it isn't, the success of science gives us reason to think that scientific explanation is possible in principle. When we are confronted with a fact that science cannot explain, the rational response is almost always, "Let's wait and see." Why isn't the cosmological fine-tuning argument just another appeal to this **"God of the Gaps"**?

2. The scientific basis for the cosmological fine-tuning argument is controversial. The key premise is a claim about the *fundamental* laws of nature, but we do not know the fundamental laws, so any such claim is at best conjectural. For a review of some of the relevant facts, see Paul Davies, *Cosmic Jackpot: Why Our Universe Is Just Right for Life* (Penguin, 2006).

## ANALYZING THE ARGUMENTS

1. *The attributes of God.* The traditional attributes of God—omniscience, omnipotence, perfect goodness, etc.—cry out for analysis. For some attributes, this is easy. To say that God is omniscient, for example, is to say that for **every true proposition** *p*, God knows that *p* is true. In other cases, the analysis raises interesting questions.

   *Omnipotence.* It is sometimes said that God's omnipotence consists in his ability to do *absolutely anything*. If God were omnipotent in this sense, God could make a triangle with four sides, or a free human being who was incapable of acting badly, or a world in which there is no God; but it is widely assumed that God need not be omnipotent in *that* sense.

   *Exercise:* Provide an account of God's omnipotence that does not have these implications.

   *Perfect goodness.* It is tempting to suppose that a perfectly good being is a being that always chooses the best available option. As applied to God, this **entails** that a perfect God would create the best of all possible worlds. But there is no such thing as the *best* possible world. No matter how excellent the world is—no matter how many happy and flourishing creatures living in harmony with one another it contains—there might have been a better world containing more happy creatures living even happier lives. If this is right, we cannot say that God's perfect goodness consists in his choice to create the best of all possible worlds (since there is no such thing).

   *Exercise:* Provide an account of God's perfect goodness that avoids this problem.

2. *The God of the Philosophers.* The authors of our selections generally agree that there *could* be a perfect being. But it has occasionally been claimed that the idea of such a being is contradictory. Consider the following arguments:

   *The paradox of omnipotence.* A perfect being would be *omnipotent*. But there cannot possibly be an omnipotent being. Suppose that X is omnipotent and ask: Can X create a stone so heavy that she cannot move it? If she cannot create such a stone, then she is not omnipotent, because there is something she cannot do. But if she *can* create such a stone, then again, there is something she cannot do, namely, move the stone in question. So either way, there is something X cannot do. So X is not omnipotent.

   *The paradox of moral perfection and omnipotence.* A perfect being would be both perfectly good and perfectly powerful. But there cannot be a being that combines these attributes. A perfectly good being would be *essentially good*. It would be *impossible for her to sin*. But if X cannot sin, X is not omnipotent. (After all, *you* can sin, and an omnipotent being can do anything you can do.) So if X is perfectly good, X is not omnipotent.

   *The paradox of omniscience and omnipotence.* A perfect being would be both omnipotent and omniscient. But it is impossible for a being to be both omniscient and omnipotent. To see why, suppose that X is both omniscient and omnipotent and suppose that X is on the brink of a decision: she must decide whether to destroy the moon or to leave it alone. If X is omnipotent, then X can choose either option. But if X is omniscient, then she knows exactly what she will do. But if she *knows* now that she will not destroy the moon, then it is settled now that she will not destroy it. And if it is settled now that she will not destroy it, it is not in her power to destroy it. So if X is omniscient, she is not omnipotent.

*Exercise:* Set out these arguments in full and identify a premise that the theist might reject. Then try to strengthen the argument so as to block this response.

3.  *Inference to the best explanation in natural theology.* Proponents of **Natural Theology** maintain that the hypothesis of God's existence provides the best explanation of certain observed facts—the adaptation of organisms to their environments, the fine-tuning of the fundamental constants, etc.—and that belief in God is therefore justified on scientific grounds. But even if the best *available* explanation for some observed fact posits God, this by itself cannot justify belief in God. After all, the best available explanation may be the best of a bad lot, and when it is, we should not accept it. Moreover, there is reason to believe that theological explanations are always *terrible* explanations by scientific standards.

    a.  Unlike serious scientific explanations, the theological explanation is not *testable*. Scientists accept Einstein's theory of gravitation, for example, only because it makes detailed predictions that have been confirmed by experiment. The God hypothesis makes no predictions, so it is not acceptable by scientific standards. (For the claim that a scientific hypothesis must be testable, see K. Popper, *Conjectures and Refutations,* Chapter 11 [Routledge and Kegan Paul, 1963].)

    b.  Unlike serious scientific explanations, the theological explanation is thin. Scientists accept our current theory of quarks and electrons because it provides a *detailed* account of how subatomic particles generate the phenomena we observe. By contrast, the God hypothesis tells us nothing about *how* God does what he is supposed to do, so it is not a serious hypothesis by scientific standards.

    c.  Unlike serious scientific explanations, the theological explanation is *stalled*. Good scientific theories generate progressive research programs. They generate new theoretical questions, the answers to which motivate improvements in the theory: new lines of inquiry are opened up; new phenomena are identified. By contrast, the God hypothesis has not generated any *new* science, and it is unclear how it could. So it is not a serious hypothesis by scientific standards. (See I. Lakatos, "Falsification and the Methodology of Scientific Research Programs," in *Criticism and the Growth of Knowledge,* ed. I. Lakatos and A. Musgrave [Cambridge University Press, 1970].)

*Exercise:* Say how the proponent of Natural Theology might respond to these objections.

4.  *The argument from evil*

    a.  *Is God a murderer?* The Argument from Evil begins from the premise that if there is an omnipotent and omniscient God, he *allows* innocent creatures to suffer and die when he could easily save them. But we can entertain a stronger premise: If there is an omnipotent and omniscient *creator* God, then God *knowingly causes* the slow and painful deaths of innocents and is thus a torturer and a murderer. God may not cause these deaths directly. But if God made the natural world and the laws that govern it, God causes them indirectly, and that is just as bad.

*Exercise:* Say how the theist might respond to this challenge.

b.  *The problem of evil and the virtue of faith.* If there is a God, then God permits (and perhaps even causes) the deaths of millions of children every year from famine and disease. Many theists will grant this point and say, "While we do not understand how a good God could do this, still we have *faith* that God is good." This raises a moral question: Is this sort of faith a virtue? Suppose a powerful dictator did these things, and suppose his subjects insist that even though they cannot comprehend his motives, they nonetheless have faith that he is good. We would not regard *this* faith as a virtue: we would regard it as a pitiable moral failing. Why is faith in the goodness of God any different?

# 2

# Is it Reasonable to Believe without Evidence?

Suppose you have reviewed the arguments for and against the existence of God and found them wanting. Not only do they fail to *prove* that God exists (or that God does not exist): they fail to provide good, solid reasons for belief—reasons of the sort we often get in daily life and in the sciences even when proof is not in the cards. It is always possible that there are better arguments waiting to be discovered. But we don't have them yet, and that raises a question: Can it be reasonable to believe that God exists even though we cannot provide reasons for this belief? We sometimes use the word "faith" to describe a belief that we cannot defend by giving reasons. So we can also put our question like this: Is faith in God's existence ever reasonable?

## The Problem of "Properly Basic" Belief

A negative answer would follow immediately from a general principle:

> You shouldn't hold a belief unless you can support it by citing evidence or giving an argument.

This can sound extremely plausible. When you get caught up in arguments about the existence of God or any other controversial matter, it is easy to feel that if you can't defend your position by providing reasons that your opponent must accept, then you've lost: your position has been shown to be unreasonable. Moreover there are contexts in which the principle clearly applies. It *is* unreasonable to believe that the defendant is guilty of murder or that $835 \times 267 = 222{,}945$ if you can't say anything in support of your opinion. So the only question is whether there are exceptions to the rule — special cases in which it is reasonable to hold a belief even though you can't support it.

Alvin Plantinga calls beliefs of this sort **properly basic**. A belief is basic (for you) if you can't defend it with an argument, and *properly* basic if it is nonetheless reasonable for you to hold it. So we have three questions:

Are there any properly basic beliefs?
If so, what are the conditions under which a belief is properly basic?

And finally:

Does a belief in God satisfy those conditions?

# An Argument for the Existence of Properly Basic Beliefs

A simple argument seems to show that there must be *some* properly basic beliefs. Take anything you believe — e.g., $835 \times 267 = 222{,}945$. (Check the math if you have doubts.) In this case you can give an argument by running through the calculation. But that argument will have premises. For example, the first step in the calculation is $5 \times 7 = 35$. You took this for granted when you did the math; you didn't bother to argue for it. Of course you could provide an argument for this assumption if you were pressed. But when you set out *that* argument you will again find yourself relying on premises that you have not defended. And when you are pressed to defend *those* premises, and the premises upon which *they* depend, and so on, you will eventually reach a premise that you can't defend. Why? Because you are a finite being and no matter how smart you are, you have only a finite number of arguments at your disposal. (*Exercise:* Reconstruct your reasons for believing that $7 \times 5 = 35$ and identify the assumptions that underlie this belief that you cannot prove.) So if you start with any belief you hold and turn the spotlight on the premises that support it, you will eventually arrive at premises that are basic for you.

Now we could say that these basic beliefs are all unreasonable simply because you can't defend them. But then we will be forced to say that *all* of your beliefs are unreasonable. After all, an argument can only support its conclusion if we are justified in accepting its premises. So if there are no properly basic beliefs to get us started, our arguments will never get us anywhere. (Garbage in, garbage out.) This is an ancient argument for radical **skepticism**: the view that it is never reasonable to believe anything. But radical skepticism is very hard to believe. It clearly *is* reasonable for you to believe that 7 times 5 is 35. And that means the argument for skepticism must go wrong somewhere.

## When Is a Belief Properly Basic?

Many philosophers (including Plantinga) take this to show that some of our beliefs must be properly basic. And this leads to one of the great unsolved problems in philosophy: *When* is a belief properly basic? When is it reasonable to believe a proposition we cannot support or defend by argument?

Some philosophers have held that a belief is properly basic only if its denial is somehow unthinkable—absurd, incoherent, self-contradictory. This might explain why some basic principles of logic and mathematics are properly basic. But a belief in God will not count as properly basic on such a view, since the atheist's worldview is not unthinkable. Others have held that a belief is properly basic when it is psychologically impossible for a human being to doubt it. This might explain why our belief in the reality of the external world is properly basic, since no psychologically normal human being can doubt it for very long. It might also explain how beliefs about our own conscious mental states can be properly basic, since no one who is in pain can seriously doubt that he is in pain. But even if this were right it would be no comfort to the theist, since it is obviously possible for human beings to doubt the existence of God.

## Theoretical vs. Practical Reasons for Belief

One important tradition, represented here by Blaise Pascal and William James, approaches this question in a different way. In order to understand the approach, we need a distinction. Suppose you've been invited to interview for a terrific job, and you know two things about your prospects. On the one hand, you're one of five equally qualified candidates, all with the same skills and experience. On the other hand, you've just read a scientific study that shows that *confident* candidates — candidates who firmly believe they will get the job — are somewhat more likely to succeed than candidates who harbor doubts. Given all of this information, what should you believe about your prospects?

Two incompatible arguments suggest themselves:

1. You're one of five equally qualified candidates, so you probably won't get the job. Even if you can somehow work up some confidence — say, by looking in the mirror and repeating, "This job is *mine*. This job is *mine*!" — that would only improve your chances a little bit: from 20 percent to (say) 25 percent. So it is reasonable to believe that you won't get the job.

2. If you believe that you will get the job, you improve your chances, and that's what matters. A rational person does what she can to get what she wants (at least when her goals are permissible and the means are moral, as they are here). Just as it's reasonable to "dress for success" when that will give you an edge over the competition, it's reasonable for you to be confident, since that will also give you an edge. So it's reasonable for you to believe that you will get the job.

These conclusions sound contradictory. How can a single belief be both reasonable and unreasonable?

The answer is that words like "rational" and "reasonable" are ambiguous. When we ask whether a belief is rational, we might be asking whether it is likely to be true given the evidence, or whether it would be reasonable to hold it if one's sole concern were to believe the truth about the issue at hand. A belief that is rational in this sense is said to be **theoretically** or *epistemically* **rational**. Alternatively, and much less commonly, we may be asking whether holding the belief will have good consequences. A belief that is rational in this sense is said to be **practically rational**. These two notions usually coincide. It is almost always beneficial to hold beliefs that are likely to be true given your evidence. But they occasionally come apart, as they do here. And when they do, it makes no sense to ask without qualification, "What is it reasonable to believe?" We must say which sort of rationality we have in mind. In this puzzling case, it is practically rational for you to believe that you will get the job, even though you have no epistemic reasons to believe this.

# The Practical Rationality of Belief in God

Now if the word "rational" is ambiguous, then so is the notion of a properly basic belief. When we ask whether belief in God is properly basic, we could be asking whether an undefended belief in God is *theoretically* rational; but we could also be asking whether such belief is *practically* rational.

Pascal defends a positive answer to the second question. He admits that there are no good theoretical arguments for God's existence. But that does not show that religious belief is irrational in every sense. Pascal assumes that if there is a God, he rewards those who believe with "infinite felicity"—eternal and unsurpassable happiness. He then gives a gambler's argument, analyzed in detail by Alan Hájek. Think of your belief in God as a bet that yields infinite happiness if God exists. How much should you be willing to pay for this bet? Pascal argues that you should be willing to pay any finite amount for a chance to win this infinitely valuable prize, including whatever costs you would incur by believing in God and living a religious life. Pascal concludes that religious belief is practically rational even if the theoretical arguments are inconclusive.

We can think of this is as a partial solution to our problem about properly basic beliefs. According to Pascal, it is *practically* rational to hold a belief that one cannot defend by argument when holding that belief is in your interest. Pascal does not say that such beliefs are theoretically rational. But he does think that a rational *person*—i.e., someone who aims to be both theoretically and practically rational—has no choice but to believe.

William James appeals to our practical interests in a different way. He begins by noting that the question of God's existence is very special. Like many questions, it can't be settled on the basis of the available evidence. But in most cases of this sort, we are under no pressure to form an opinion. (Is the number of stars odd or even? No one needs an answer to that question.) When it comes to the existence of God, however, the question is both *forced* and *momentous*. It is forced because at every moment we must choose either belief or unbelief. (Agnosticism is a form of unbelief.) And it is momentous, James thinks, because *if* God exists, then a belief in God is of enormous value. James disdains Pascal's crass appeal to posthumous rewards and punishments. He thinks that an intellectual connection to God is of profound value *here and now*: every moment one goes without it, one misses out on a great good.

Now an epistemological rule that forbids us from believing without evidence would cut us off from this great good. And for James, that is enough to show that such rules must be rejected. Instead James says (in effect): When you are confronted with a forced and momentous question that you cannot resolve on intellectual grounds, then you may believe *what would best promote your legitimate interests as you understand them*. If you are inclined to take a risk—the risk of being wrong—in order to secure a benefit—intellectual contact with God—then you are free to take that risk. Anyone who says otherwise merely shows "his own preponderant horror of becoming a dupe."

Unlike Pascal, James is arguing that it may be both practically and *theoretically* rational to believe what one cannot prove. All theoretical inquiry, including science, is guided by values, the most important of which are a love of truth and a fear of error. Rationality does not tell us exactly how much weight to give these values. But it allows us to place *more* value on attaining truth than on avoiding error, especially when the truths in question are valuable for other reasons. And for someone who has values of this sort, it can be theoretically rational to believe what he cannot prove in the hope of achieving the benefits—both practical and intellectual—that come with being right.

This view has important implications. Suppose that you and I face a profound moral or religious question that cannot be settled by evidence and argument, and that we arrive at different answers because we have different values: you care more about truth; I care more about avoiding error. James's position entails that we may both be perfectly reasonable *even though neither of us can give the other a reason to change his mind*. There is a powerful tendency to suppose, in the heat of moral or religious debate, that anyone who disagrees with us must be either pigheaded or blind. But if James is right, there is another possibility. Your opponent may be perfectly reasonable, disagreeing with you only because he attaches different weights to the values that guide his intellectual life.

# The Problem Restated

You may reject James's view, but that will not make the problem go away. Every epistemologist owes us an account of when it is rational to believe what we cannot prove. The selections below address this issue as it arises in the philosophy of religion. But as you read through the selections, you should bear this general problem in mind. The epistemology of religious belief is an important topic. But there are no special-purpose rules of religious epistemology. The principles of rationality that govern our beliefs about God also govern our beliefs in other areas. So you can always test a proposed defense of religious faith by extracting the principle that underlies it and applying that principle elsewhere. To repeat a point made earlier, we all know that it is *sometimes* unreasonable to believe what we cannot prove or defend by argument. If Seymour believes that the world will end on New Year's Eve 2035 but can provide no evidence whatsoever for his opinion, then Seymour is not 100 percent rational. The question is whether an ungrounded belief in God is like Seymour's belief in doomsday. And we cannot answer that question without a general principle that tells us when our basic beliefs are rational and when they aren't.

## Blaise Pascal (1623–1662)

Pascal invented the first mechanical calculator and made foundational contributions to physics and mathematics. His main contribution to philosophy — *Pensées* — was published posthumously in 1669 based on scattered fragments found among his papers.

# THE WAGER
## from *Pensées*

Unity when joined to the infinite does not increase it at all, any more than a foot when added to an infinite length. The finite annihilates itself in the presence of the infinite, and becomes a pure nothing. So does our mind when confronted with God, so does our justice before divine justice. Yet the disproportion between our justice and God's is not as great as that between unity and infinity.

The justice of God must be as enormous as his mercy. The justice he shows to the damned is less enormous and should shock us less than the mercy he shows to the elect.

We know that there is an infinite, and we are ignorant of its nature. Similarly, we know it is false that the series of numbers is finite, and it is therefore true that there is an infinite number, but we do not know what it is. It is false that it is even; it is false that it is odd; for by adding a unit the infinite does not change its nature. Yet it is a number, and every number is even or odd — this may be truly understood of every finite number.

Thus we can perfectly well recognize that there is a God, without knowing what he is. . . .

We know the existence and the nature of the finite, since we, like it, are finite and extended.

We know the existence of the infinite and we are ignorant of its nature, since it has extension like us, but does not have limits as we do.

But we do not know either the existence or the nature of God, because he has neither extension nor limits.

But by faith we know his existence, and in glory we shall come to know his nature.

Now I have already shown that one may quite well know the existence of a thing without knowing its nature.

Let us now speak according to our natural lights.

If there is a God, he is infinitely beyond our comprehension, since having neither parts nor limits he bears no relation to us. We are thus incapable of knowing either what he is or if he is. This being so, who will dare undertake to resolve this question? Surely not we, who bear no relation to him.

Who then will blame Christians for not being able to provide reasons for their belief, since they profess a religion for which they cannot provide a rational basis? In proclaiming it to the world they declare that it is "folly," and will you then complain that they do not prove it? If they were to prove it, they would not be keeping their word. This very lack of proof shows they do not lack sense. "Yes; but even if this excuses those who offer their religion in this way and takes away any blame for their putting it forward without reason, it does not excuse those who *accept* it without reason." Let us then examine this point. Let us say: either God is, or he is not. But which side shall we incline towards? Reason cannot settle anything here. There is an infinite chaos which separates us. A game is being played at the far end of this infinite distance: the coin will come down heads or tails. How will you bet? Reason will not enable you to decide either way, or rule out either alternative.

So do not blame those who have made a choice, or say they have chosen a false path, for you know nothing of the matter. "No, but I will blame them for having made not *this* choice but *a* choice; for though the player who chooses heads is no more at fault than the other one, both of them are still at fault. The correct option is not to bet at all."

Yes, but you must bet. It is not voluntary; you are already involved. Which will you choose then? Look: since you must choose, let us see which is the less profitable option. You have two things to lose, the true and the good, and two things to stake, your reason and your will, your knowledge and your happiness. Your nature has two things to avoid, error and wretchedness. Since a choice must necessarily be made, your reason is no more offended by choosing one rather than the other. There is one point settled. But your happiness? Let us weigh up the gain and the loss in choosing heads, that God exists. Let us figure out the two results: if you win, you win everything, and if you lose, you lose nothing. So bet that he exists, without any hesitation. "This is splendid: yes, I must bet, but maybe I am betting too much." Let us see. Since there is an equal chance of gain and loss, if you stood merely to gain merely two lives for one, you could still bet. But suppose you had three lives to gain?

You would have to play (since you must necessarily play), and you would be foolish, since you are forced to play, not to risk your life to gain three lives in a game where there is equal chance of losing and winning. But there is an eternity of life and happiness. This being so, in a game where there were an infinity of chances and only one in your favor, you would still be right to wager one life in order to gain two; and you would be making the wrong choice, given that you were obliged to play, if you refused to bet one life against three in a game where there were an infinity of chances and only one in your favor, if the prize were an infinity of infinitely happy life. But the prize here *is* an infinity of infinitely happy life, one chance of winning against a finite number of chances of losing, and what you are staking is finite. This leaves only one choice open, in any game that involves infinity, where there is not an infinite number of chances of losing to set against the chance of winning. There is nothing to ponder — you must stake everything. When you are forced to play, you would have to be renouncing reason if you were to hang on to life rather than risk it for an infinite gain which is just as likely to come about as a loss which is a loss of nothing.

It is no use saying that it is uncertain whether you will win and certain that you are taking a chance; or that the infinite distance between the certainty of what you are risking and the uncertainty of what you stand to gain makes the finite good which you are certainly risking as great as the infinite gain that is uncertain. This is not how things stand. Every player takes a certain risk in exchange for an uncertain gain; but it is no sin against reason for him to take a certain and finite risk for an uncertain finite gain. It is just not true that there is an infinite distance between the certainty of what is risked and the uncertainty of the gain. There is, in truth, an infinite distance between the certainty of winning and the certainty of losing; but the proportion between the uncertainty of winning and the certainty of what is being risked corresponds to the proportion between the chances of winning and losing. From this it follows that if there are as many chances on one side as on the other, the game is being played for even odds. And hence the certainty of what you are risking is equal to the uncertainty of the possible gain, so far from being infinitely distant from it. There is thus infinite force in the position I am taking, when the stakes are finite in a game where the chances of winning and losing are equal and the prize is infinite.

This result has demonstrative force, and if human beings are capable of any truth, this is it.

"'I confess it, I admit it, but is there not any way at all of seeing what lies behind the game?" Yes, Holy Scripture and the rest. "Yes, but my hands are tied and my mouth is gagged; I am being forced to wager and I am not at liberty. I cannot get free and my constitution is such that I am incapable of believing. So what do you want me to do?'" What you say is true, but you must at least realize that your inability to believe comes from your passions. Since reason moves you to believe, and nevertheless you cannot, your task is not to convince yourself by adding on more proofs of God, but by reducing your passions. Your desired destination is faith, but you do not know the road. You want to cure yourself of unbelief, and you ask for remedies: learn from those who were tied like you and who now wager all they possess. These are people who know the road you would like to follow; they are cured of the malady for which you seek a cure; so follow them and begin as they did — by acting as if they believed, by taking holy water, by having masses said, and so on. In the natural course of events this in itself will make you believe, this will tame you. "But that is just what I fear." Why? What have you to lose? If you want to know why this is the right way, the answer is that it reduces the passions, which are the great obstacles to your progress. . . .

Now what harm will come to you if you make this choice? You will be faithful, honest, humble, grateful, a doer of good works, a good friend, sincere and true. Admittedly you will not dwell amid tainted pleasures, in glory and luxury, but will you not have others?

I tell you that you will be the gainer in this life, and that on every step you take on this path you will see such certainty of gain, and such emptiness of what you hazard, that you will finally know that what you have wagered for is something certain and infinite, and what you have given in exchange is nothing.

## TEST YOUR UNDERSTANDING

1. Pascal likens the decision whether to believe in God to a bet. In an ordinary bet we choose a proposition — e.g., "The Yankees will win the 2018 World Series." Then we specify the payoffs: how much you win if the proposition turns out to be true, and how much you lose if it turns out to be false. Represent Pascal's Wager as a bet in this sense.

2. Suppose you are talking to someone who maintains that it is highly unlikely, though still possible, that God exists. Construct an argument based on Pascal's text to show this person that it is in her interest to believe that God exists.

## NOTES AND QUESTIONS

1. *A crash course in decision theory.* Pascal's argument assumes a (now) widely accepted account of rational choice. The key idea is that a rational agent seeks to maximize the *expected utility* of his choices. Suppose you've been asked to bring the wine to a dinner party and you have two choices: red or white. You don't know what's for dinner, but there are only two possibilities: beef or chicken. Many people have a slight preference for white wine with chicken and a strong preference for red wine with beef. If those are your preferences, we can represent your situation as follows:

|  | They serve chicken | They serve beef |
| --- | --- | --- |
| Bring white | 10 | 2 |
| Bring red | 7 | 10 |

Here the numbers represent (somewhat arbitrarily) the **utility** you attach to the outcome in question: how *good* that outcome is by your lights.

In order to determine what you should do in the situation, you need one more bit of information: how *likely* it is that they will serve chicken as opposed to beef. These probabilities are measured with numbers between 0 and 1. If you attach a probability of 1 to a proposition, you are sure that it is true; if you attach a probability of 0, you are sure that the proposition is false. A probability of 0.5 means that you think it is just as likely to be true as not.

The **expected utility** of bringing white wine is the sum of the utility of bringing white wine if they serve chicken and the utility of bringing white wine if they serve beef, each weighted by the appropriate probability. So suppose first that chicken and beef are equally likely. Then the expected utility of bringing white is $0.5(10) + 0.5(2) = 6$, whereas the expected utility of bringing red is $0.5(7) + 0.5(10) = 8.5$. Since the expected utility of bringing red is higher, that is what you should do. According to this account of rational choice—**standard decision theory**—*a rational agent always acts so as to maximize expected utility.*

But now suppose that in your long experience with your hosts, they have served chicken 90 percent of the time. In that case, the expected utility of bringing white is

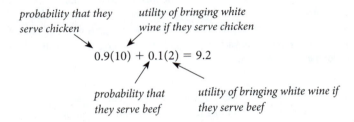

whereas the expected utility of bringing red is

$$0.9(7) + 0.1(10) = 7.3$$

In that case, you should bring white wine, even though you are risking the bad outcome in which you bring white and they serve beef. This makes sense because, although this outcome is bad, it is unlikely. (For a rigorous introduction to decision theory, see R. C. Jeffrey, *The Logic of Decision*, University of Chicago Press, 1983.)

2. *Representing Pascal's Wager as a decision problem.* You have two options—Believe in God or Don't believe—and there are two possibilities: God exists, or God does not exist. In order to represent the Wager as a decision problem, we need to specify the utilities and the probabilities.

   *Probabilities:* Pascal seems to assume that for someone faced with this decision, the probability of God's existence must be ½. This is unwarranted, but it makes no difference. As we will see, so long as the probability of God's existence is not zero, Pascal's argument is unaffected.

   *Utilities:* Pascal assumes that if you believe in God and God exists, your reward is an unending blissful afterlife, the value of which is *infinite*—greater than any finite value. No ordinary finite number can represent an infinite value. So let us suppose that there is an *infinite* number ∞, greater than any finite number. *We must be very careful here.* The "arithmetic" of infinite numbers is a very tricky subject. But in fact we only need one assumption about this infinite number for Pascal's purposes:

For any positive number $n$ between 0 and 1, $n \times \infty = \infty$.

We may then represent the Wager as follows:

|  | God exists | God does not exist |
| --- | --- | --- |
| Believe | ∞ | 17 (or any finite number) |
| Don't believe | 17 (or any finite number) | 17 (or any finite number) |

*Exercise:* Show that given these assumptions, you maximize expected utility by believing in God no matter what probability you attach to God's existence, provided that probability is not 0.

*Exercise:* Vary the finite utilities. Suppose that if God does not exist, then a religious life is somewhat worse than a nonreligious life (since one forgoes certain pleasures). Alternatively, suppose that a religious life is better than a nonreligious one, perhaps for the serenity it brings. Show that these variations all yield the same result: the finite values do not matter, so long as they are finite.

3.  *The Many Gods Objection.* Pascal assumes that there are only two possibilities: Either there exists a God like the Christian God who rewards believers with infinite happiness, or there is no God at all. But in fact there are many other possibilities. For example, there might be a Perverse God who rewards nonbelievers with infinite posthumous happiness (much to their surprise!) while punishing religious believers with posthumous annihilation. This may not be likely, but it is possible. How does Pascal's Wager look if we take this possibility into account? You have two possible acts, Believe and Don't Believe, and there are three possible states of the world relevant to your decision:

|  | Christian God exists | Perverse God exists | No God exists |
| --- | --- | --- | --- |
| Believe | ∞ | 17 | 17 |
| Don't believe | 17 | ∞ | 17 |

*Exercise:* Determine the expected utility of belief and nonbelief on the assumption that there is some non-zero chance that each of these possibilities obtains.

There are, of course, many other possibilities. There might be a Doubly Perverse God who rewards nonbelievers while *punishing* believers with infinite misery. There might be two Gods, A and B, each of whom rewards those who believe in him while punishing those who believe in his rival, and so on. It is useful to explore the implications of these possibilities for Pascal's reasoning.

## Alan Hájek (born 1962)

Hájek is Professor of Philosophy at the Australian National University. He works mainly in probability and decision theory.

# PASCAL'S ULTIMATE GAMBLE

As you enter the casino, a host of gambling games vie for your attention — and cash. The first is especially simple. A coin you know to be fair will be tossed. If it lands heads, you win $1; if it lands tails, you lose $2. Should you play? Let's assume that all you care about here is money — you don't receive an additional benefit from the thrill of gambling, for example — and that you value equally each dollar gained or lost. Then it seems that you *should not play*: while there is an equal probability of losing and of winning, the magnitude of a loss would be greater than that of a win.

Then there is an announcement. It is now Happy Hour, and the game has suddenly changed: now, if the coin lands heads, you win $1; if it lands tails, you lose $1. Obviously this is an *improvement* for you — there is now a way the coin could land (tails) for which your payoff is better than it was before; otherwise, your payoff is the same as before. Moreover, the new game seems *fair* to you — in the long run, you would expect to break even. You could rationally play the game, but also rationally turn it down.

You have just engaged in three little exercises in *decision theory* (their respective upshots being respectively that you *should not play* the first game, that the second game is an *improvement*, and that the second game is *fair*). Decision theory is an account of how probabilities and utilities (payoffs) associated with your various options together determine what it is rational for you to do. Soon we will see in more detail what the theory has to say about these gambles.

In his classic *Pensées*, Pascal contended that in an important sense, there is an ultimate gamble that we all face. We must choose whether to believe in God or not — in his words, whether to "wager that He is" or not. If we found some decisive argument that settled the matter of God's existence either way, then our job would be done: we should simply believe the conclusion of the argument. But this is not our situation according to Pascal: "God is, or He is not. But to which side shall we incline? Reason can decide nothing here."[1] However, he insists, reason *can* decide that we should *wager* that God exists. He presents the problem of whether to wager that God exists as a *decision* problem, and he solves it with the same decision-theoretic machinery that one should deploy when faced with a gamble in a casino. Indeed, he was one of the pioneers of that machinery, and his Wager is described by Hacking as "the first well-understood contribution to decision theory."[2]

---

1. Blaise Pascal, 1910. *Pascal's Pensées*, trans. W. F. Trotter (London: J. M. Dent & Sons Ltd; New York: E. P. Dutton & Co. Inc., 1910).

2. Ian Hacking, *The Emergence of Probability* (Cambridge University Press, 1975).

In short, Pascal maintains that one should wager for God because *it is the best bet*. And how good a bet is it? According to Pascal, *infinitely good*.

# A One-Minute Primer on Decision Theory

To understand the Wager, we will need to understand how to set up a decision problem and two fundamental principles of decision theory. In a decision problem, what you do and what the world does together determine what you get. If the problem is nontrivial, you have a choice of at least two actions, and there are at least two ways that the world could be — "states" — that are relevant to your fate and about which you are uncertain. We may represent this as a matrix, with rows corresponding to your possible actions, and columns corresponding to the states. In each cell of the matrix we have a number, called a *utility*, that represents the degree to which you value the corresponding outcome — think of it as a payoff. For example, the original gamble in the casino confronted you with this decision matrix:

|            | Heads | Tails |
|------------|-------|-------|
| **Play**       | 1     | −2    |
| **Don't play** | 0     | 0     |

Here −2 is the utility of your losing $2, and 0 is the utility of your neither losing nor winning money. The "Happy Hour" decision matrix is:

|            | Heads | Tails |
|------------|-------|-------|
| **Play**       | 1     | −1    |
| **Don't play** | 0     | 0     |

In *decisions under uncertainty* you have to decide solely on the basis of utilities. Suppose you had to choose between playing the original gamble and the Happy Hour gamble, with the same coin toss determining the outcome. But now suppose that you have no idea whether the coin in question is fair. (This ignorance of probabilities makes this a decision under uncertainty.) You could not do worse in the Happy Hour gamble, and you could do better (if the coin lands tails), so it seems you should choose it. This is an instance of *dominance* reasoning. More generally, given two actions $A_1$ and $A_2$, say that $A_1$ dominates $A_2$ if each outcome associated with $A_1$ is at least as good as the corresponding outcome associated with $A_2$, and for at least one state, $A_1$'s outcome is strictly better than $A_2$'s. Dominance reasoning can be captured by the following principle of rationality: *Choose the dominant action if there is one*. Playing the Happy Hour game dominates playing the original game, so by the principle, you should play the Happy Hour game if you have to choose between them.

Now let's return to the opening examples, in which you know that the coin is fair. You thus have more information at your disposal than just the utilities: you also have *probabilities* for the various states. This makes each decision about whether to play or not a *decision under risk* (as opposed to a decision under uncertainty). For such a decision, a simple formula yields a figure of merit for each action, called the *expected utility* of the action: for each state, multiply its probability by the utility of the outcome associated with the action; then add these numbers. The centerpiece of decision theory is the rationality principle: *choose the action of maximal expected utility if there is one.* The games we have described involve flipping a fair coin, so we know that the probability of heads and the probability of tails are both ½. The expected utility of playing the original game is therefore:

$$(½ \times 1) + (½ \times -2) = -½$$

which is less than the expected utility of not playing, 0. So you should not play. The expected utility of the Happy Hour game is

$$(½ \times 1) + (½ \times -1) = 0$$

the same as not playing. This reflects the fairness of the game — you could rationally play it or not. And when faced with a choice between the two games, you should choose the latter.

We now have two tools for solving decision problems. You can use dominance reasoning to solve certain decisions under uncertainty, although when it applies it can tell you only *what* to choose, not *how desirable* your choice is, and in particular not *how much better* it is than some alternative. Decisions under risk allow more nuanced treatment: the expected utilities of the alternative actions are numerical measures of their desirabilities.

## Pascal's Gamble

Pascal presents you with a decision problem: Should you wager that God exists or not? First, we will look to the relevant passage of the *Pensées* to construct the decision problem as he conceived it. Then, we will use these decision-theoretic tools to solve it.

Pascal writes:

> Which will you choose then?. . . . You have two things to lose, the true and the good; and two things to stake, your reason and your will, your knowledge and your happiness; and your nature has two things to shun, error and misery. Your reason is no more shocked in choosing one rather than the other, since you must of necessity choose. . . . But your happiness? Let us weigh the gain and the loss in wagering that God is. . . . If you gain, you gain all; if you lose, you lose nothing. Wager, then, without hesitation that He is.[3]

Your possible actions are to wager that God exists (for short: *wager for God*), and to wager that He doesn't (*wager against God*). There are two possible states: either He

3. All quotes in English are from Blaise Pascal, 1910. *Pascal's Pensées*, trans. W. F. Trotter (London: J. M. Dent & Sons Ltd; New York: E. P. Dutton & Co. Inc., 1910). [Hájek's note.]

exists, or He does not. We are not yet in a position to put numerical values on the utilities of the corresponding outcomes, but Pascal's qualitative characterization of them seems to be captured by the following:

|  | God exists | God does not exist |
|---|---|---|
| **Wager for God** | Gain all | Lose nothing = status quo |
| **Wager against God** | Misery | Status quo |

This is informative enough for us to apply dominance reasoning — wagering for God dominates wagering against God, so it seems that you should wager for God.[4]

At this point Pascal regards himself as having settled the question of *what* to choose. But he imagines an interlocutor replying: "Yes, I must wager; but I may perhaps wager too much." This invites the further question: What is wagering for God worth? So Pascal then goes on to determine *how desirable* that choice is, and in particular how much better it is than wagering against God. This requires a calculation of expected utilities, which in turn require probabilities.

So Pascal immediately makes a probabilistic assumption: "There is an equal risk of gain and of loss." As we would say it nowadays: the probability that God exists is ½. This appears to be a naïve application of the so-called "classical" theory of probability, according to which the probability of an event is equal to the number of outcomes in which the event occurs, divided by the total number of possible outcomes. (Thus, the classical probability that a die lands even is 3/6.) This theory finds its natural home in gambling games, and once again Pascal writes as if he is taking the gambling picture literally. To be sure, from a modern perspective this application of the theory appears particularly strained.[5] But bear with Pascal for now, for as we will see, he will soon relax this assumption.

Expected utilities also require utilities — what are they to be? In a startling move, Pascal makes the unit of utility a *life*:

> if you had only to gain two lives, instead of one, you might still wager . . . and you would be imprudent, when you are forced to play, not to chance your life to gain three at a game where there is an equal risk of loss and gain.

The metaphysics may be questionable, but the decision-theoretic reasoning is impeccable: the first hypothetical gamble has an expected utility of

$$\tfrac{1}{2} \times 2 \text{ lives} = 1 \text{ life}$$

---

4. This is too quick (Alan Hájek, "Blaise and Bayes," in *Probability in the Philosophy of Religion*, eds. Jake Chandler and Victoria Harrison [Oxford University Press, 2011]). Dominance reasoning may fail when the actions and states are not probabilistically independent of each other. This brings in complications that are beyond the scope of this essay. See also Hacking for a discussion of Pascal's dominance reasoning here. (Ian Hacking, "The Logic of Pascal's Wager," *American Philosophical Quarterly* 9/2 (1972): 186–92. Reprinted in *Gambling on God: Essays on Pascal's Wager*, ed. Jeff Jordan (Rowman & Littlefield, 1994). [Hájek's note.]

5. What probability should you give to my next car being blue (all over)? According to the classical theory, the answer is ½. After all, there are two possible outcomes: either it is blue or it is not blue, and in one out of these two outcomes the car is blue. What probability should you give to my next car being red? Again, the classical theory says ½. And so on for each different color. But that's absurd: these outcomes are mutually exclusive (the car can only be one color all over) so they cannot all have probability ½. [Hájek's note.]

so you could rationally stake one life to play it, or not. (Compare the Happy Hour gamble.) The second hypothetical gamble has an expected utility of

$$\frac{1}{2} \times 3 \text{ lives} = 1\frac{1}{2} \text{ lives}$$

so you would be imprudent not to stake one life to play it. But according to Pascal, the *actual* gamble that you face is far more favorable than these:

> But there is here an infinity of an infinitely happy life to gain, a chance of gain against a finite number of chances of loss, and what you stake is finite. It is all divided; wherever the infinite is and there is not an infinity of chances of loss against that of gain, there is no time to hesitate, you must give all. And thus, when one is forced to play, he must renounce reason to preserve his life . . .

Measured in lives, a gamble that pays *infinity* ($\infty$) with probability $\frac{1}{2}$ (and nothing otherwise) has an expected utility in lives of

$$\frac{1}{2} \times \infty = \infty$$

so all the more you would be imprudent not to stake one life to play it.

But notice how the probability $\frac{1}{2}$ plays no special role in this reasoning. We could replace it with any positive probability $p$:[6]

$$p \times \infty = \infty$$

This means that the expected utility of wagering for God is infinite, *no matter how unlikely it is that God exists*, provided the probability of God's existence is greater than 0. And this in turn means that you should be prepared to stake not only one life to play such a gamble, but any finite amount ("what you stake is finite . . . you must give all"). In particular, you should be prepared to stake your reason, which presumably you value only finitely. We now have our answer to the question of what wagering for God is worth: *an infinite amount*. In Pascal's words, "our proposition is of infinite force."

What does giving up your *reason* have to do with all this? That seems to come out of nowhere, but a subsequent passage helps us make sense of it. An imaginary interlocutor grants Pascal his conclusion ("I confess it, I admit it"), but plaintively admits being unable to do what is rationally required:

> "I am forced to wager, and am not free I. . . . am so made that I cannot believe. What, then, would you have me do?"

The problem is that it seems that you cannot believe in God at will. Yet this was supposed to be a *decision problem*, and you can choose only among actions that you

---

6. I assume that $p$ is not infinitesimal — a tiny number that is positive, but smaller than every positive real number. It is striking that Pascal explicitly makes this assumption, albeit in different words ("there is not an infinity of chances of loss against that of gain"). [Hájek's note.]

are capable of performing. Pascal's advice to you is to suppress your passions, which are an obstacle to your belief, and in particular to engage in the practices of those who believe: "taking the holy water, having masses said, etc." In short, *act like a believer*; "this will naturally make you believe, and deaden your acuteness." The phrase that is translated here as "deaden your acuteness" is even more astonishing in French. Its literal meaning is "will make you a beast" — i.e., something devoid of reason. And yet according to Pascal, this is a price worth paying; after all, it's a finite price for an option that has infinite expected utility.

There is some tension within these passages of Pascal's. He began by saying that "if you lose, you lose nothing"; but now he seems to admit that if you lose, you lose *something*, namely your reason. This threatens to undermine his argument that wagering for God *dominates* wagering against God. Yet it seems that in the end this does not matter, for he still has the argument from expected utilities. The utilities associated with wagering against God are finite, and whatever they are, they are swamped in the expected utility calculations by the infinite utility that you may gain by wagering for God — much as the probability that God exists did not matter, beyond its being positive. The expected utilities then apparently carry the day for wagering for God.

There is also some dispute among commentators about what the utility of "misery" is supposed to be. Perhaps Pascal, who was a Catholic, has in mind the doctrine of eternal damnation, in which case this utility may be *negative infinite*? But he writes: "The justice of God must be vast like His compassion. Now justice to the outcast is less vast . . . than mercy towards the elect." This suggests that "misery" is only finitely bad, "less vast" than the infinitude of the reward of salvation.

Let us summarize Pascal's reasoning in modern parlance.

P1. You should choose the action of maximal expected utility if there is one.

P2. The probability $p$ that God exists is positive.

P3. The decision matrix is as follows, where $f1$, $f2$ and $f3$ are finite utilities:

|  | God exists | God does not exist |
| --- | --- | --- |
| Wager for God | $\infty$ | $f_1$ |
| Wager against God | $f_2$ | $f_3$ |

Conclusion 1: Wagering for God has infinite expected utility.

Conclusion 2: You should wager for God.

Conclusion 1 follows from the premises. The expected utility of wagering for God is:

$$(\infty \times p) + f_1 \times (1 - p) = \infty$$

And conclusion 2 seems to follow from conclusion 1 and the premises, since the expected utility of wagering against God is finite:

$$(f_2 \times p) + f_3 \times (1 - p) = some\ finite\ quantity$$

which is less than the infinite expected utility of wagering for God. When philosophers speak of "Pascal's Wager," it is typically a version of this argument that they have in mind.

## Objections

A host of objections to the Wager vie for our attention.[7]

### OBJECTING TO P1

While P1 is enshrined in modern decision theory, it has met with considerable opposition. The Allais, Ellsberg, and St. Petersburg paradoxes, well known to economists, are thought by many to provide counterexamples to it. They all turn on intuitions that other factors may determine choiceworthiness besides expected utilities — for example, the *variance* of the utilities (a measure of how spread out the utilities are). Roughly, high-variance gambles are *risky* in the sense that they may with disturbingly high probabilities yield outcomes far worse than their expected utilities.

Indeed, in the St. Petersburg paradox, getting less than your expected utility is guaranteed. Imagine that you are offered the following gamble: a coin is tossed until it lands heads for the first time. The longer it takes, the better for you: your reward grows exponentially according to the number of tosses up to and including the first heads. Specifically, if it takes a total of $n$ trials for the first heads to appear, you get $2^n$ dollars. Equating utility with dollar amount, the expected utility of the gamble is:

$$\left(2 \times \frac{1}{2}\right) + \left(4 \times \frac{1}{4}\right) + \left(8 \times \frac{1}{8}\right) + \cdots = 1 + 1 + 1 + \cdots = \infty$$

Again, we have an *infinite* expected utility. Yet *every possible amount you could win is finite* ($2, or $4, or $8, or . . .). Thus, it seems that decision theory overvalues the gamble. In fact, most people would not pay more than $50 up front to play the gamble, much less an infinite amount. Offhand, this is a counterexample to P1: if you are like most people, you would prefer $100, say, to this gamble, even though the latter has far greater expected utility.[8] The apparent failure of decision theory's appeal to expected

---

7. See Alan Hájek, "Pascal's Wager," *Stanford Encyclopedia of Philosophy,* ed. Edward Zalta (http://plato .stanford.edu/archives/fall2008/entries/pascal-wager/) for more objections, and more responses to objections, than I can present here. [Hájek's note.]

8. There is a vast literature of replies to the St. Petersburg paradox; Martin (2008) surveys some of it. [Hájek's note.]

utilities here should make us wary of appealing to them in Pascal's Wager. Note that there is an *infinite* discrepancy among the utilities in Pascal's Wager, so the concern that expected utilities are a poor guide to choiceworthiness in high-variance gambles may have particular force.

## OBJECTING TO P2

An atheist may insist that the probability that God exists is 0 — perhaps citing some argument that an omnipotent, omniscient, omnibenevolent being is impossible. This is essentially to disregard entirely the first column of Pascal's decision matrix, so the decision comes down to a comparison of $f_1$, and $f_3$. If "losing your reason" comes at a cost, then it may be that $f_1 < f_3$; or if both are the utility of the "status quo," then $f_1 = f_3$. Either way, you are not required to wager for God after all.

Notice, however, just how strong the atheist's conviction needs to be in order to dispute P2. It will not suffice, for example, to think that the probability that God exists is one in a trillion, or one in a googol, or one in a googolplex — those numbers are positive, and enough to give Pascal's argument a toehold. The atheism required is *absolute*. But many authors believe that this is really an extreme form of *dogmatism*, unwarranted by any evidence that we could ever get, and therefore *irrational*.

At the "[e]nd of this discourse," Pascal goes on to strengthen his claims about the benefits of wagering for God:

> Now, what harm will befall you in taking this side? You will be faithful, humble, grateful, generous, a sincere friend, truthful. Certainly you will not have those poisonous pleasures, glory and luxury; but will you not have others? I will tell you that you will thereby *gain in this life.* [My italics]

Then it surely does follow that you should wager for God (whether or not you are an atheist). But now the problem has only been shifted: many of us will not grant Pascal this strengthened claim — for example, those who value earthly pleasures rather more than Pascal does.[9] One of the great virtues of Pascal's Wager, its neutrality regarding the comparative sizes of $f_1$, $f_2$ and $f_3$, has been lost.

## OBJECTING TO P3

Pascal assumes that we all face the same decision problem. However, perhaps the payoffs are different for different people. Perhaps, for example, there is a predestined infinite reward for the Chosen, whatever they do, and finite utility for the rest, as Mackie suggests. But even granting Pascal this assumption, we may still dispute what that decision problem is.

---

9. Alan Hájek, "Pascal's Wager," *Stanford Encyclopedia of Philosophy,* ed. Edward Zalta (http://plato.stanford .edu/archives/fall2008/entries/pascal-wager/) discusses some more technical objections to P2: the probability of God's existence may be positive but *infinitesimal;* and it may be *imprecise* over an interval that includes 0. [Hájek's note.]

*Disputing the rows.* Perhaps there is more than one way to wager for God, and the rewards that God bestows vary accordingly. Perhaps, for example, God does *not* reward those who wager for Him solely based on the mercenary considerations of the very kind that Pascal advocates, as James suggests. Or perhaps God rewards sincere inquiry rather than blind faith, a possibility mooted by Dawkins.

*Disputing the columns.* Here we come to the most famous objection to Pascal's Wager: the *many Gods objection.* Pascal envisages the God of Christianity. But the same considerations that he adduces apparently apply equally to other Gods. As Diderot writes: "An Imam could reason just as well this way"; and Mackie extends the point to the Anabaptists, Mormons, and the worshippers of Kali or of Odin. Indeed, Cargile generates infinitely many alternative Gods: for each real number $x$, consider the God who prefers contemplating $x$ more than any other activity and who rewards only those who believe in *him.* If Pascal is right that "reason can decide nothing here," then presumably it cannot decide among myriad theistic hypotheses. Perhaps, then, reason itself *requires* us to stay open-minded about all of them, dignifying each of them with at least some probability. But then there are multiple putative routes to infinite expected utility.

In response, some authors argue that the many Gods objection can be mitigated. For example, some of the rival Gods — Kali and Odin among them — do not bestow infinite rewards, so they may be dismissed from our calculations. Among those that do, we arguably should confine our attention to theistic hypotheses that are based on tradition or serious theology (Jordan), or that are in some sense the simplest (Lycan and Schlesinger).

## DENYING THAT THE WAGER IS VALID

Now, grant for the sake of the argument all of Pascal's premises. Does it follow that you should wager for God? Earlier I said that Pascal's conclusion *seems* to follow from his premises, but does it really? No. To see why not, consider a different strategy. Toss a fair coin; if it lands heads, wager for God; if it lands tails, wager against God. What is the expected utility of this strategy? With probability ½, the coin lands heads, and then you will perform an action that has an expected utility of ∞, by Pascal's lights; with probability ½, the coin lands tails, and then you will perform an action that has some finite expected utility. So the expected utility of this strategy is

$$(½ \times \infty) + (½ \times \text{some finite utility}) = \infty$$

But notice how the ½ plays no special role in this reasoning. We could replace it with any positive probability $p$. Sounds familiar? Like a snake eating its own tail, Pascal's assumption of infinite utility for salvation returns to annihilate his own argument! Suppose you wager for God if the winning ticket in a million-ticket lottery is #17; otherwise you wager against God. This strategy has expected utility

$$(1/1000000 \times \infty) + (999999/1000000 \times \text{some finite utility}) = \infty$$

And so it goes: *any* strategy for which you have *some* positive probability of winding up wagering for God has infinite expectation.

But isn't that any strategy whatsoever? For *whatever* you do, there is surely such a probability. Suppose you decide to have a beer. There is *some* positive probability that you will wind up wagering for God by the end of the beer. Multiply that probability by ∞, and you see that having a beer has infinite expected utility. Or suppose you do all you can to *avoid* wagering for God — you *express* your passions, you engage in the practices of those who *disbelieve,* and so on. Still, there is *some* probability that you will fail and wager for God nonetheless. Multiply that probability by ∞ and calculate the expected utility of doing everything in your power to *avoid* belief in God. Not only is Pascal's Wager invalid; it is invalid in the worst possible way. Far from establishing that you should wager for God, it "establishes" that every possible action you may undertake is equally good: everything you might do has infinite expected utility given Pascal's assumptions. "The first well-understood contribution to decision theory"? This looks more like *indecision* theory.[1]

## Pascal's Final Sting in the Tail

It appears that Pascal's Wager runs aground. But perhaps Pascal has the last laugh. I have posed the problem that all actions that you may undertake have infinite expected utility as a problem for his Wager. But perhaps it is a problem for all of us.

The problem arose when we granted for the sake of the argument all of Pascal's premises. Very well then; let's *not* grant those premises. In fact, I invite you to be highly skeptical of each of them. By all means assign tiny probability to each of them. In fact, assign to the conjunction of them as small a probability $p$ as you like, as long as $p$ is positive. Go ahead and assume that there is some *minuscule but positive* probability that you should maximize expected utility *and* that God exists *and* that Pascal's decision matrix is correct. Sounds familiar? In doing so, you assign probability $p$ to things being exactly as Pascal claims they are. But we know what follows: every action you may undertake has expected utility ∞. Why? Because $p$ times ∞ equals ∞. So it isn't just by Pascal's lights that every action you may undertake is equally good. As long as you dignify Pascal's assumptions with at least *some* probability, that staggering conclusion is true by *your* lights as well.

---

1. See Antony Duff, "Pascal's Wager and Infinite Utilities," *Analysis* 46 (1986): 107–9; and Alan Hájek, "Waging War on Pascal's Wager," *Philosophical Review* 112/1 (January 2003): 27–56 for versions of this argument and further refinements. See also George Schlesinger, "A Central Theistic Argument," in *Gambling on God: Essays on Pascal's Wager,* ed. Jeff Jordan (Rowman & Littlefield, 1994) for a tie-breaking principle that one might add to the Wager in response, and Hájek (2003) and (2011) for six reformulations of Pascal's Wager that render it valid. [Hájek's note.]

But what's your alternative? To assign probability *zero* to his premises all being true? (Not one in a trillion; not one in a googol; not one in a googolplex; . . .) That seems like an extreme form of dogmatism, unwarranted by your evidence. To be sure, we have seen various ways of questioning the premises, of arguing against them. By all means question them, argue against them. But can you really justify giving them *no* credence whatsoever, given your evidential situation? That seems like a sin against *theoretical rationality*. You may insist that this sin is preferable to the sin against *practical rationality* to which you are committed if you regard every action you may undertake as equally good. But it is surely a disquieting thought, to say the least, that as far as rationality is concerned, you appear to be a sinner whatever you do.

You may need that beer.[2]

REFERENCES

Maurice Allais, "Le Comportement de l'Homme Rationnel Devant le Risque: Critique des Postulats et Axiomes de l'École Américaine," *Econometrica* 21 (1953): 503–46.

James Cargile, "Pascal's Wager," *Philosophy* 35 (1966): 250–57.

Richard Dawkins, *The God Delusion* (Bantam Books, 2006).

Denis Diderot, *Pensées Philosophiques*, LIX, *Oeuvres*, ed. J. Assézat, vol. I., 1875–77.

D. Ellsberg, "Risk, Ambiguity and the Savage Axioms," *Quarterly Journal of Economics* 25 (1961): 643–69.

William James, "The Will to Believe," in *The Will to Believe and Other Essays in Popular Philosophy* (Dover Publications, 1956).

Jeff Jordan, "The Many Gods Objection," in *Gambling on God: Essays on Pascal's Wager*, ed. Jeff Jordan (Rowman & Littlefield, 1994).

William Lycan and George Schlesinger "You Bet your Life," in *Reason and Responsibility*, 7th ed., ed. Joel Feinberg Wadsworth, 1989). Also in the 8th, 9th, 10th editions; in *Philosophy and the Human Condition*, 2nd ed., ed. Tom Beauchamp et al. (Prentice Hall, 1989); and in *Contemporary Perspectives on Religious Epistemology*, ed. Douglas Geivet and Brendan Sweetmar (Oxford University Press, 1993).

J. L. Mackie, *The Miracle of Theism* (Oxford, 1982).

Robert Martin, "The St. Petersburg Paradox," *Stanford Encyclopedia of Philosophy* (Fall 2008 Edition), ed. Edward N. Zalta <http://plato.stanford.edu/archives/fall2008/entries/paradox-stpetersburg/>.

2. I thank Gideon Rosen for many helpful suggestions. [Hájek's note.]

## TEST YOUR UNDERSTANDING

1. Hájek emphasizes that in assessing the force of Pascal's argument, it does not matter whether the probability of God's existence is ½ or 1/1,000,000. Explain the basis for this claim.

2. Construct an argument, using Hájek's assumptions, for the claim that tying your shoes has *infinite* expected utility.

## NOTES AND QUESTIONS

1. *Two pills*. You are offered a choice between a red pill that will grant you infinite, eternal happiness with a probability of 10% and a blue pill that will grant you the same reward with a probability of 99%. (If the pill doesn't work, it does nothing.) Hájek's principles entail that these options have the same expected utility. (*Exercise:* Explain why.) But intuitively, there is only one rational choice: it would be crazy to take the red pill; you should take the blue one. So consider the following modification of standard decision theory:

   > When faced with several otherwise similar options, each of which might yield a certain infinite payoff, choose the act that has the highest probability of yielding that payoff.

   Does this new theory avoid Hájek's problem? Is it an acceptable theory of rational choice?

## William James (1842–1910)

James was trained as a physician and made important contributions to both philosophy and psychology. His *Principles of Psychology* (1890) established experimental psychology as a scientific discipline in the United States. His contributions to philosophy include *Pragmatism* (1907) and *The Meaning of Truth* (1909).

# THE WILL TO BELIEVE

I have brought with me tonight something like a sermon on justification by faith to read to you, — I mean an essay in justification of faith, a defence of our right to adopt a believing attitude in religious matters, in spite of the fact that our merely logical intellect may not have been coerced. "The Will to Believe," accordingly, is the title of my paper.

## |

Let us give the name of hypothesis to anything that may be proposed to our belief; and just as the electricians speak of live and dead wires, let us speak of any hypothesis as either live or dead. A live hypothesis is one which appeals as a real possibility to him to whom it is proposed. If I ask you to believe in the Mahdi,[1] the notion makes no electric connection with your nature, — it refuses to scintillate with any credibility at all. As an hypothesis it is completely dead. To an Arab, however (even if he be not one of the Mahdi's followers), the hypothesis is among the mind's possibilities: it is alive. This shows that deadness and liveness in an hypothesis are not intrinsic properties, but relations to the individual thinker. They are measured by his willingness to act. The maximum of liveness in an hypothesis means willingness to act irrevocably. Practically, that means belief; but there is some believing tendency wherever there is willingness to act at all.

Next, let us call the decision between two hypotheses an option. Options may be of several kinds. They may be:

- Living or dead;
- Forced or avoidable;
- Momentous or trivial;

and for our purpose we may call an option a genuine option when it is of the forced, living, and momentous kind.

1. A living option is one in which both hypotheses are live ones. If I say to you: "Be a theosophist[2] or be a Mohammedan," it is probably a dead option, because for you neither hypothesis is likely to be alive. But if I say: "Be an agnostic or be Christian," it is otherwise: trained as you are, each hypothesis makes some appeal, however small, to your belief.

2. Next, if I say to you: "Choose between going out with your umbrella or without it," I do not offer you a genuine option, for it is not forced. You can easily avoid it by not going out at all. . . . But if I say, "Either accept this truth or go without it," I put on you a forced option, for there is no standing place outside of the alternative. Every dilemma based on a complete logical disjunction, with no possibility of not choosing, is an option of this forced kind.

1. The redeemer, a descendant of Muhammad whose coming is expected in some branches of Islam.

2. Theosophy is a system of esoteric doctrine associated in James's time with the mystical teachings of Mme. Blavatsky (1831–1891).

3. Finally, if I were Dr. Nansen[3] and proposed to you to join my North Pole expedition, your option would be momentous; for this would probably be your only similar opportunity, and your choice now would either exclude you from the North Pole sort of immortality altogether or put at least the chance of it into your hands. He who refuses to embrace a unique opportunity loses the prize as surely as if he tried and failed. *Per contra*, the option is trivial when the opportunity is not unique, when the stake is insignificant, or when the decision is reversible if it later prove unwise. Such trivial options abound in the scientific life. A chemist finds an hypothesis live enough to spend a year in its verification: he believes in it to that extent. But if his experiments prove inconclusive either way, he is quit for his loss of time, no vital harm being done.

It will facilitate our discussion if we keep all these distinctions well in mind.

## II

The next matter to consider is the actual psychology of human opinion. When we look at certain facts, it seems as if our passional and volitional nature lay at the root of all our convictions. When we look at others, it seems as if they could do nothing when the intellect had once said its say. Let us take the latter facts up first.

Does it not seem preposterous on the very face of it to talk of our opinions being modifiable at will? Can our will either help or hinder our intellect in its perceptions of truth? Can we, by just willing it, believe that Abraham Lincoln's existence is a myth, and that the portraits of him in McClure's Magazine are all of some one else? Can we, by any effort of our will, or by any strength of wish that it were true, believe ourselves well and about when we are roaring with rheumatism in bed, or feel certain that the sum of the two one-dollar bills in our pocket must be a hundred dollars? . . .

In Pascal's *Thoughts* there is a celebrated passage known in literature as Pascal's wager. In it he tries to force us into Christianity by reasoning as if our concern with truth resembled our concern with the stakes in a game of chance. Translated freely his words are these: You must either believe or not believe that God is — which will you do? Your human reason cannot say. A game is going on between you and the nature of things which at the day of judgment will bring out either heads or tails. Weigh what your gains and your losses would be if you should stake all you have on heads, or God's existence: if you win in such case, you gain eternal beatitude; if you lose, you lose nothing at all. If there were an infinity of chances, and only one for God in this wager, still you ought to stake your all on God; for though you surely risk a finite loss by this procedure, any finite loss is reasonable, even a certain one is reasonable,

---

3. The Norwegian explorer Fridtjof Nansen (1861–1930) did not reach the North Pole on his famous journey of 1893, though he did come closer than anyone had come before.

if there is but the possibility of infinite gain. Go, then, and take holy water, and have masses said; belief will come and stupefy your scruples. . . . Why should you not? At bottom, what have you to lose?

You probably feel that when religious faith expresses itself thus, in the language of the gaming-table, it is put to its last trumps. It is evident that unless there be some pre-existing tendency to believe in masses and holy water, the option offered to the will by Pascal is not a living option. Certainly no Turk ever took to masses and holy water on its account; and even to us Protestants these seem such foregone impossibilities that Pascal's logic, invoked for them specifically, leaves us unmoved. . . .

The talk of believing by our volition seems, then, from one point of view, simply silly. From another point of view it is worse than silly, it is vile. When one turns to the magnificent edifice of the physical sciences, and sees how it was reared; what thousands of disinterested moral lives of men lie buried in its mere foundations; what patience and postponement, what choking down of preference, what submission to the icy laws of outer fact are wrought into its very stones and mortar; how absolutely impersonal it stands in its vast augustness, — then how besotted and contemptible seems every little sentimentalist who comes blowing his voluntary smoke-wreaths, and pretending to decide things from out of his private dream! . . .

[As] that delicious *enfant terrible* Clifford[4] writes: "Belief is desecrated when given to unproved and unquestioned statements for the solace and private pleasure of the believer. . . . Whoso would deserve well of his fellows in this matter will guard the purity of his belief with a very fanaticism of jealous care, lest at any time it should rest on an unworthy object, and catch a stain which can never be wiped away. . . . If [a] belief has been accepted on insufficient evidence [even though the belief be true, as Clifford on the same page explains] the pleasure is a stolen one. . . . It is sinful because it is stolen in defiance of our duty to mankind. That duty is to guard ourselves from such beliefs as from a pestilence which may shortly master our own body and then spread to the rest of the town. . . . It is wrong always, everywhere, and for every one, to believe anything upon insufficient evidence."

## III

All this strikes one as healthy. . . . Yet if any one should thereupon assume that intellectual insight is what remains after wish and will and sentimental preference have taken wing, or that pure reason is what then settles our opinions, he would fly quite as directly in the teeth of the facts.

It is only our already dead hypotheses that our willing nature is unable to bring to life again. But what has made them dead for us is for the most part a previous action of our willing nature of an antagonistic kind. When I say "willing nature," I do not mean

4. W. K. Clifford (1845–1879), English mathematician and philosopher, author of "The Ethics of Belief" (1877), a celebrated defense of the view that it is morally wrong to believe without sufficient evidence.

only such deliberate volitions as may have set up habits of belief that we cannot now escape from, — I mean all such factors of belief as fear and hope, prejudice and passion, imitation and partisanship, the circumpressure of our caste and set. As a matter of fact we find ourselves believing, we hardly know how or why. . . . Here in this room, we all of us believe in molecules and the conservation of energy, in democracy and necessary progress, in Protestant Christianity and the duty of fighting for "the doctrine of the immortal Monroe," all for no reasons worthy of the name. . . . Our reason is quite satisfied, in nine hundred and ninety-nine cases out of every thousand of us, if it can find a few arguments that will do to recite in case our credulity is criticised by some one else. Our faith is faith in some one else's faith, and in the greatest matters this is most the case. . . .

As a rule we disbelieve all facts and theories for which we have no use. Clifford's cosmic emotions find no use for Christian feelings. . . . Newman,[5] on the contrary, goes over to Romanism, and finds all sorts of reasons good for staying there, because a priestly system is for him an organic need and delight. This very law which the logicians would impose upon us — if I may give the name of logicians to those who would rule out our willing nature here — is based on nothing but their own natural wish to exclude all elements for which they, in their professional quality of logicians, can find no use. . . .

The state of things is evidently far from simple; and pure insight and logic, whatever they might do ideally, are not the only things that really do produce our creeds.

# IV

Our next duty, having recognized this mixed-up state of affairs, is to ask whether it be simply reprehensible and pathological, or whether, on the contrary, we must treat it as a normal element in making up our minds. The thesis I defend is, briefly stated, this: *Our passional nature not only lawfully may, but must, decide an option between propositions, whenever it is a genuine option that cannot by its* nature be decided on intellectual grounds; for to say, under such *circumstances,* "*Do not decide, but leave the question open," is itself a passional decision, — just like deciding yes or no, — and is attended with the same risk of losing the truth. . . .*

# VII

One more point, small but important, and our preliminaries are done. There are two ways of looking at our duty in the matter of opinion. . . *We must know the truth; and we must avoid error,* — these are our first and great commandments as would-be

---

5. John Henry Newman (1801–1890) converted from Anglicanism to Catholicism and later became a cardinal of the Roman Catholic Church.

knowers; but they are not two ways of stating an identical commandment, they are two separable laws . . . and by choosing between them we may end by coloring differently our whole intellectual life. We may regard the chase for truth as paramount, and the avoidance of error as secondary; or we may, on the other hand, treat the avoidance of error as more imperative, and let truth take its chance. Clifford exhorts us to the latter course. Believe nothing, he tells us, keep your mind in suspense forever, rather than by closing it on insufficient evidence incur the awful risk of believing lies. You, on the other hand, may think that the risk of being in error is a very small matter when compared with the blessings of real knowledge, and be ready to be duped many times in your investigation rather than postpone indefinitely the chance of guessing true. I myself find it impossible to go with Clifford. We must remember that these feelings of our duty about either truth or error are in any case only expressions of our passional life. . . . [H]e who says, "Better go without belief forever than believe a lie!" merely shows his own preponderant private horror of becoming a dupe. . . . For my own part, I have also a horror of being duped; but I can believe that worse things than being duped may happen to a man in this world: so Clifford's exhortation has to my ears a thoroughly fantastic sound. . . . Our errors are surely not such awfully solemn things. In a world where we are so certain to incur them in spite of all our caution, a certain lightness of heart seems healthier than this excessive nervousness on their behalf. . . .

# VIII

And now, after all this introduction, let us go straight at our question. I have said, and now repeat it, that not only as a matter of fact do we find our passional nature influencing us in our opinions, but that there are some options between opinions in which this influence must be regarded both as an inevitable and as a lawful determinant of our choice.

I fear here that some of you my hearers will begin to scent danger. . . . Two first steps of passion you have indeed had to admit as necessary, — we must think so as to avoid dupery, and we must think so as to gain truth; but the surest path to those ideal consummations, you will probably consider, is from now onwards to take no further passional step.

Well, of course, I agree as far as the facts will allow. Wherever the option between losing truth and gaining it is not momentous, we can throw the chance of gaining truth away, and at any rate save ourselves from any chance of believing falsehood, by not making up our minds at all till objective evidence has come. In scientific questions, this is almost always the case; and even in human affairs in general, the need of acting is seldom so urgent that a false belief to act on is better than no belief at all. . . . Let us agree [then] that wherever there is no forced option, the dispassionately judicial intellect with no pet hypothesis, saving us, as it does, from dupery at any rate, ought to be our ideal.

The question next arises: Are there not somewhere forced options in our speculative questions, and can we (as men who may be interested at least as much in positively gaining truth as in merely escaping dupery) always wait with impunity till the coercive evidence shall have arrived?

# IX

Moral questions immediately present themselves as questions whose solution cannot wait for sensible proof. A moral question is a question not of what sensibly exists, but of what is good, or would be good if it did exist. Science can tell us what exists; but to compare the worths, both of what exists and of what does not exist, we must consult not science, but what Pascal calls our heart. Science herself consults her heart when she lays it down that the infinite ascertainment of fact and correction of false belief are the supreme goods for man. Challenge the statement, and science can only repeat it oracularly, or else prove it by showing that such ascertainment and correction bring man all sorts of other goods which man's heart in turn declares. . . .

Turn now from these wide questions of good to a certain class of questions of fact, questions concerning personal relations, states of mind between one man and another. Do you like me or not? — for example. Whether you do or not depends, in countless instances, on whether I meet you half-way, am willing to assume that you must like me, and show you trust and expectation. The previous faith on my part in your liking's existence is in such cases what makes your liking come. But if I stand aloof, and refuse to budge an inch until I have objective evidence, until you shall have done something apt, as the absolutists say, . . . ten to one your liking never comes. . . . The desire for a certain kind of truth here brings about that special truth's existence; and so it is in innumerable cases of other sorts. Who gains promotions, boons, appointments, but the man in whose life they are seen to play the part of live hypotheses, who discounts them, sacrifices other things for their sake before they have come, and takes risks for them in advance? His faith acts on the powers above him as a claim, and creates its own verification.

A social organism of any sort whatever, large or small, is what it is because each member proceeds to his own duty with a trust that the other members will simultaneously do theirs. Wherever a desired result is achieved by the co-operation of many independent persons, its existence as a fact is a pure consequence of the precursive faith in one another of those immediately concerned. A government, an army, a commercial system, a ship, a college, an athletic team, all exist on this condition, without which not only is nothing achieved, but nothing is even attempted. A whole train of passengers (individually brave enough) will be looted by a few highwaymen, simply because the latter can count on one another, while each passenger fears that if he makes a movement of resistance, he will be shot before any one else backs him up. If we believed that the whole car-full would rise at once with us, we should each severally rise, and train-robbing would never even be attempted.

There are, then, cases where a fact cannot come at all unless a preliminary faith exists in its coming. And where faith in a fact can help create the fact, that would be an insane logic which should say that faith running ahead of scientific evidence is the "lowest kind of immorality" into which a thinking being can fall. Yet such is the logic by which our scientific absolutists pretend to regulate our lives!

## X

In truths dependent on our personal action, then, faith based on desire is certainly a lawful and possibly an indispensable thing.

But now, it will be said, these are all childish human cases, and have nothing to do with great cosmic matters, like the question of religious faith. Let us then pass on to that. . . . What then do we now mean by the religious hypothesis? Science says things are; morality says some things are better than other things; and religion says essentially two things.

First, she says that the best things are the more eternal things, the overlapping things, the things in the universe that throw the last stone, so to speak, and say the final word. . . .

The second affirmation of religion is that we are better off even now if we believe her first affirmation to be true.

Now, let us consider what the logical elements of this situation are in case the religious hypothesis in both its branches be really true. . . . So proceeding, we see, first that religion offers itself as a momentous option. We are supposed to gain, even now, by our belief, and to lose by our nonbelief, a certain vital good. Secondly, religion is a forced option, so far as that good goes. We cannot escape the issue by remaining sceptical and waiting for more light, because, although we do avoid error in that way if religion be untrue, we lose the good, if it be true, just as certainly as if we positively chose to disbelieve. . . Scepticism, then, is not avoidance of option; it is option of a certain particular kind of risk. *Better risk loss of truth than chance of error,* — that is your faith-vetoer's exact position. . . . To preach scepticism to us as a duty until "sufficient evidence" for religion be found, is tantamount therefore to telling us, when in presence of the religious hypothesis, that to yield to our fear of its being error is wiser and better than to yield to our hope that it may be true. It is not intellect against all passions, then; it is only intellect with one passion laying down its law. . . . I simply refuse obedience to the scientist's command to imitate his kind of option, in a case where my own stake is important enough to give me the right to choose my own form of risk. If religion be true and the evidence for it be still insufficient, I do not wish, by putting your extinguisher upon my nature, . . . to forfeit my sole chance in life of getting upon the winning side, — that chance depending, of course, on my willingness to run the risk of acting as if my passional need of taking the world religiously might be prophetic and right. . . .

Now, to most of us religion comes in a still further way that makes a veto on our active faith even more illogical. The more perfect and more eternal aspect of the universe is represented in our religions as having personal form. The universe is no longer a mere *It* to us, but a *Thou*, if we are religious; and any relation that may be possible from person to person might be possible here. For instance, although in one sense we are passive portions of the universe, in another we show a curious autonomy, as if we were small active centres on our own account. We feel, too, as if the appeal of religion to us were made to our own active good-will, as if evidence might be forever withheld from us unless we met the hypothesis half-way. . . . This feeling, forced on us we know not whence, that by obstinately believing that there are gods . . . we are doing the universe the deepest service we can, seems part of the living essence of the religious hypothesis. If the hypothesis were true in all its parts, including this one, then pure intellectualism, with its veto on our making willing advances, would be an absurdity; and some participation of our sympathetic nature would be logically required. I, therefore, for one, cannot see my way to accepting the agnostic rules for truth-seeking. . . . I cannot do so for this plain reason, that *a rule of thinking which would absolutely prevent me from acknowledging certain kinds of truth if those kinds of truth were really there, would be an irrational rule. . . .*

I confess I do not see how this logic can be escaped. But sad experience makes me fear that some of you may still shrink from radically saying with me, *in abstracto,* that we have the right to believe at our own risk any hypothesis that is live enough to tempt our will. I suspect, however, that if this is so, it is because you have got away from the abstract logical point of view altogether, and are thinking (perhaps without realizing it) of some particular religious hypothesis which for you is dead. The freedom to "believe what we will" you apply to the case of some patent superstition; and the faith you think of is the faith defined by the schoolboy when he said, "Faith is when you believe something that you know ain't true." I can only repeat that this is misapprehension. *In concreto,* the freedom to believe can only cover living options which the intellect of the individual cannot by itself resolve; and living options never seem absurdities to him who has them to consider. When I look at the religious question as it really puts itself to concrete men, and when I think of all the possibilities which both practically and theoretically it involves, then this command that we shall put a stopper on our heart, instincts, and courage, and wait — acting of course meanwhile more or less as if religion were not true[6] — till doomsday, or till such time as our intellect and senses working together may have raked in evidence enough, — this command, I say, seems to me

---

6. Since belief is measured by action, he who forbids us to believe religion to be true, necessarily also forbids us to act as we should if we did believe it to be true. The whole defence of religious faith hinges upon action. If the action required or inspired by the religious hypothesis is in no way different from that dictated by the naturalistic hypothesis, then religious faith is a pure superfluity, better pruned away, and controversy about its legitimacy is a piece of idle trifling, unworthy of serious minds. I myself believe, of course, that the religious hypothesis gives to the world an expression which specifically determines our reactions, and makes them in a large part unlike what they might be on a purely naturalistic scheme of belief. [James's note.]

the queerest idol ever manufactured in the philosophic cave. Were we scholastic absolutists, there might be more excuse. If we had an infallible intellect with its objective certitudes, we might feel ourselves disloyal to such a perfect organ of knowledge in not trusting to it exclusively, in not waiting for its releasing word. But if we are empiricists, if we believe that no bell in us tolls to let us know for certain when truth is in our grasp, then it seems a piece of idle fantasticality to preach so solemnly our duty of waiting for the bell. Indeed we may wait if we will, — I hope you do not think that I am denying that, — but if we do so, we do so at our peril as much as if we believed. In either case we act, taking our life in our hands. No one of us ought to issue vetoes to the other, nor should we bandy words of abuse. We ought, on the contrary, delicately and profoundly to respect one another's mental freedom: then only shall we bring about the intellectual republic; then only shall we have that spirit of inner tolerance without which all our outer tolerance is soulless, and which is empiricism's glory; then only shall we live and let live, in speculative as well as in practical things.

## TEST YOUR UNDERSTANDING

1. According to James, it is rational to believe a proposition in the absence of evidence when the option is *forced, live,* and *momentous,* and when the question *cannot be resolved on intellectual grounds.* Explain these four conditions with examples.

2. James objects to Clifford's claim that "it is wrong . . . to believe anything upon insufficient evidence" by insisting that "a rule of thinking which would absolutely prevent me from acknowledging certain kinds of truth if those kinds of truth were really there, would be an irrational rule." Explain why James believes that Clifford's rule is irrational.

3. James holds that our intellectual lives are governed by two commandments: "Believe truth!" and "Shun error!" Explain why these are two distinct commandments.

## NOTES AND QUESTIONS

1. *Clifford's moralism.* James's essay is a response to W. K. Clifford's "Ethics of Belief" (1877), the main argument of which may be summarized as follows:

> Human beings are prone to superstition, wishful thinking, prejudice, and other forms of thinking that lead us to believe on insufficient evidence. These tendencies are profoundly damaging. Belief is not a private matter. We act on our beliefs, and our actions affect the lives of other people. Irrational beliefs place other people at risk without justification, and are

therefore morally wrong. Even when an individual belief is harmless, allowing oneself the license to believe without evidence is reckless. Intellectual laziness on your part contributes to intellectual laziness in society, which has manifestly bad effects. So we each have a moral duty to do our part to maintain intellectual standards by believing only what the evidence supports.

James does not respond directly to this moral argument. How should he respond to it? In answering the question, be sure to pose the sharpest version of Clifford's challenge. The religious view James endorses is vague and benign, but consider someone who has read James's essay and who has come to embrace a *violent* religion and the way of life it recommends, not because he has evidence for its truth, but rather as a free choice in the face of a live, forced, and momentous option. Is James committed to saying that this choice is every bit as reasonable as his own?

2. *James's self-refutation argument.* James argues that Clifford's position undermines itself:

> Our passional nature not only lawfully may, but must, decide an option between propositions, whenever it is a genuine option that cannot by its nature be decided on intellectual grounds; for to say, under such circumstances, "Do not decide, but leave the question open," is itself a passional decision — just like deciding yes or no — and is attended with the same risk of losing the truth.

Clifford affirms the moral proposition that it is wrong to believe without evidence. But according to James, this proposition itself is not supported by evidence, and so Clifford is wrong by his own lights in affirming it.

*Exercise:* Present an explicit formulation of this argument and say how Clifford might respond.

3. *James on the value of religious belief.* James holds that if there is a God, then the belief that God exists is of great value to the individual here and now, and not just in the afterlife. But what sort of value might he have in mind? Why are we better off in believing, as James puts it, that "perfection is eternal"?

## Alvin Plantinga (born 1932)

Plantinga, Professor of Philosophy at Calvin College, has been called "America's leading orthodox Protestant philosopher." He is the author of important studies in metaphysics (*The Nature of Necessity,* 1974) and epistemology (*Warrant and Proper Function,* 1993), and numerous contributions to theology and the philosophy of religion.

# IS BELIEF IN GOD PROPERLY BASIC?

Many philosophers have urged the *evidentialist* objection to theistic belief; they have argued that belief in God is irrational or unreasonable or not rationally acceptable or intellectually irresponsible because, as they say, there is insufficient evidence for it. . . . Many other philosophers and theologians — in particular, those in the great tradition of natural theology — have claimed that belief in God is intellectually acceptable, but only because the fact is there is sufficient evidence for it. These two groups unite in holding that theistic belief is rationally acceptable only if there is sufficient evidence for it. More exactly, they hold that a person is rational or reasonable in accepting theistic belief only if she has sufficient evidence for it — only if, that is, she knows or rationally believes some *other* propositions which support the one in question and believes the latter on the basis of the former. . . . The evidentialist objection is rooted in *classical foundationalism*, an enormously popular picture or total way of looking at faith, knowledge, justified belief, rationality and allied topics. This picture has been widely accepted ever since the days of Plato and Aristotle; its near relatives, perhaps, remain the dominant ways of thinking about these topics. We may think of the classical foundationalist as beginning with the observation that some of one's beliefs may be *based upon* others; it may be that there are a pair of propositions $A$ and $B$ such that I believe $A$ *on the basis of B*. Although this relation isn't easy to characterize in a revealing and non-trivial fashion, it is nonetheless familiar. I believe that the word "umbrageous" is spelled u-m-b-r-a-g-e-o-u-s: this belief is based on another belief of mine: the belief that that's how the dictionary says it's spelled. I believe that $72 \times 71 = 5112$. This belief is based upon several other beliefs I hold: that $1 \times 72 = 72$; $7 \times 2 = 14$; $7 \times 7 = 49$; $49 + 1 = 50$; and others. Some of my beliefs, however, I accept but don't accept on the basis of any other beliefs. Call these beliefs *basic*. I believe that $2 + 1 = 3$, for example, and don't believe it on the basis of other propositions. I also believe that I am seated at my desk, and that there is a mild pain in my right knee. These too are basic to me; I don't believe them on the basis of any other propositions. According to the classical foundationalist, some propositions are *properly* or *rightly* basic for a person and some are not. Those that are not, are rationally accepted only on the basis of *evidence*, where the evidence must trace back, ultimately, to what is properly basic. . . .

Now many Reformed thinkers and theologians[1] have rejected *natural theology* (thought of as the attempt to provide proofs or arguments for the existence of God). They have held not merely that the proffered arguments are unsuccessful, but that the whole enterprise is in some way radically misguided. . . . The reformed rejection of

---

1. A Reformed thinker or theologian is one whose intellectual sympathies lie with the Protestant tradition going back to John Calvin (not someone who was formerly a theologian and has since seen the light). [Plantinga's note.]

natural theology is best construed as an inchoate and unfocused rejection of classical foundationalism. What these Reformed thinkers really mean to hold, I think, is that belief in God need not be based on argument or evidence from other propositions at all. They mean to hold that the believer is entirely within his intellectual rights in believing as he does even if he doesn't know of any good theistic argument (deductive or inductive), even if he doesn't believe that there is any such argument, and even if in fact no such argument exists. They hold that it is perfectly rational to accept belief in God without accepting it on the basis of any other beliefs or propositions at all. In a word, they hold that *belief in God is properly basic.* In this paper I shall try to develop and defend this position.

But first we must achieve a deeper understanding of the evidentialist objection. It is important to see that this contention is a *normative* contention. The evidentialist objector holds that one who accepts theistic belief is in some way irrational. . . . Here "rational" and "irrational" are to be taken as normative or evaluative terms; according to the objector, the theist fails to measure up to a standard he ought to conform to. There is a right way and a wrong way with respect to belief as with respect to actions; we have duties, responsibilities, obligations with respect to the former just as with respect to the latter. . . .

This "ethics of the intellect" can be construed variously; many fascinating-issues — issues we must here forebear to enter — arise when we try to state more exactly the various options the evidentialist may mean to adopt. Initially it looks as if he holds that there is a duty or obligation of some sort not to accept without evidence such propositions as that God exists — a duty flouted by the theist who has no evidence. If he has no evidence, then it is his duty to cease believing. But there is an oft remarked difficulty: one's beliefs, for the most part, are not directly under one's control. Most of those who believe in God could not divest themselves of that belief just by trying to do so, just as they could not in that way rid themselves of the belief that the world has existed for a very long time. So perhaps the relevant obligation is not that of divesting myself of theistic belief if I have no evidence (that is beyond my power), but to try to cultivate the sorts of intellectual habits that will tend (we hope) to issue in my accepting as basic only propositions that are properly basic. . . .

[But] perhaps the evidentialist need not speak of duty or obligation here at all. Consider someone who believes that Venus is smaller than Mercury, not because he has evidence of any sort, but because he finds it amusing to hold a belief no one else does — or consider someone who holds this belief on the basis of some outrageously bad argument. Perhaps there isn't any obligation he has failed to meet. Nevertheless his intellectual condition is deficient in some way; or perhaps alternatively there is a commonly achieved excellence he fails to display. And the evidentialist objection to theistic belief, then, might be understood as the claim, not that the theist without evidence has failed to meet an obligation, but that he suffers from a certain sort of intellectual deficiency (so that the proper attitude toward him would be sympathy rather than censure).

These are some of the ways, then, in which the evidentialist objection could be developed; and of course there are still other possibilities. For ease of exposition, let us take the claim deontologically;[2] what I shall say will apply *mutatis mutandis* if we take it one of the other ways. The evidentialist objection, therefore, presupposes some view as to what sorts of propositions are correctly, or rightly, or justifiably taken as basic; it presupposes a view as to what is *properly* basic. And the minimally relevant claim for the evidentialist objector is that belief in God is *not* properly basic. Typically this objection has been rooted in some form of *classical foundationalism*, according to which a proposition *p* is properly basic for a person *S* if and only if *p* is either self-evident or incorrigible for *S* (modern foundationalism) or either self-evident or "evident to the senses" for *S* (ancient and medieval foundationalism) [Elsewhere] I argued that both forms of foundationalism are self-referentially incoherent and must therefore be rejected.

Insofar as the evidentialist objection is rooted in classical foundationalism, it is poorly rooted indeed: and so far as I know, no one has developed and articulated any other reason for supposing that belief in God is not properly basic. Of course it doesn't follow that it *is* properly basic; perhaps the class of properly basic propositions is broader than classical foundationalists think, but still not broad enough to admit belief in God. But why think so? What might be the objections to the Reformed view that belief in God is properly basic?

I've heard it argued that if I have no evidence for the existence of God, then if I accept that proposition, my belief will be groundless, or gratuitous, or arbitrary. I think this is an error; let me explain.

Suppose we consider perceptual beliefs, memory beliefs, and beliefs which ascribe mental states to other persons: such beliefs as

1.  I see a tree,

2.  I had breakfast this morning,

and

3.  That person is angry.

Although beliefs of this sort are typically and properly taken as basic, it would be a mistake to describe them as *groundless*. Upon having experience of a certain sort, I believe that I am perceiving a tree. In the typical case I do not hold this belief on the basis of other beliefs; it is nonetheless not groundless. My having that characteristic sort of experience . . . plays a crucial role in the formation and justification of that belief. We might say this experience, together, perhaps, with other circumstances, is what *justifies* me in holding it; this is the *ground* of my justification, and, by extension, the ground of the belief itself.

---

2. **Deontology** is the theory of duty or obligation.

If I see someone displaying typical pain behavior, I take it that he or she is in pain. Again, I don't take the displayed behavior as *evidence* for that belief; I don't infer that belief from others I hold; I don't accept it on the basis of other beliefs. Still, my perceiving the pain behavior plays a unique role in the formation and justification of that belief; as in the previous case, it forms the ground of my justification for the belief in question. The same holds for memory beliefs. I seem to remember having breakfast this morning; that is, I have an inclination to believe the proposition that I had breakfast, along with a certain past-tinged experience that is familiar to all but hard to describe. . . . In this case as in the others, however, there is a justifying circumstance present, a condition that forms the ground of my justification for accepting the memory belief in question.

In each of these cases, a belief is taken as basic, and in each case properly taken as basic. In each case there is some circumstance or condition that confers justification; there is a circumstance that serves as the *ground* of justification. So in each case there will be some true proposition of the sort

4. In condition *C*, *S* is justified in taking *p* as basic.

Of course *C* will vary with *p*. For a perceptual judgment such as

5. I see a rose-colored-wall before me,

*C* will include my being appeared to in a certain fashion. No doubt *C* will in-clude more. If I'm appeared to in the familiar fashion but know that I'm wearing rose-colored glasses, or that I am suffering from a disease that causes me to be thus appeared to, no matter what the color of the nearby objects, then I'm not justified in taking (5) as basic. . . .

So being appropriately appeared to, in the perceptual case, is not sufficient for justification; some further condition — a condition hard to state in detail — is clearly necessary. The central point, here, however, is that a belief is properly basic only in certain conditions; these conditions are, we might say, the ground of its justification and, by extension, the ground of the belief itself. In this sense, basic beliefs are not, or are not necessarily, *groundless* beliefs.

Now similar things may be said about belief in God. When the Reformers claim that this belief is properly basic, they do not mean to say, of course, that there are no justifying circumstances for it, or that it is in that sense groundless or gratuitous. Quite the contrary. Calvin[3] holds that God "reveals and daily discloses himself to the whole workmanship of the universe," and the divine art "reveals itself in the innumerable and yet distinct and well ordered variety of the heavenly host." God has so created us that we have a tendency or disposition to see his hand in the world about us. More precisely, there is in us a disposition to believe propositions of the sort *this flower was created by God* or *this vast and intricate universe was created by God* when we contemplate the flower or behold the starry heavens or think about the vast reaches of the universe.

3. John Calvin (1509–1564), early Protestant theologian, author of the *Institutes of the Christian Religion.*

Calvin recognizes, at least implicitly, that other sorts of conditions may trigger this disposition. Upon reading the Bible, one may be impressed with a deep sense that God is speaking to him. Upon having done what I know is cheap, or wrong, or wicked, I may feel guilty in God's sight and form the belief *God disapproves of what I've done.* Upon confession and repentance, I may feel forgiven, forming the belief *God forgives me for what I've done.* A person in grave danger may turn to God, asking for his protection and help; and of course he or she then forms the belief that God is indeed able to hear and help if he sees fit. When life is sweet and satisfying, a spontaneous sense of gratitude may well up within the soul; someone in this condition may thank and praise the Lord for his goodness, and will of course form the accompanying belief that indeed the Lord is to be thanked and praised. . . .

Of course none of these beliefs . . . is the simple belief that God exists. What we have instead are such beliefs as

6. God is speaking to me,

7. God has created all this,

8. God disapproves of what I have done,

9. God forgives me,

and

10. God is to be thanked and praised.

These propositions are properly basic in the right circumstances. But it is quite consistent with this to suppose that the proposition *there is such a person as God* is neither properly basic nor taken as basic by those who believe in God. Perhaps what they take as basic are such propositions as (6)–(10), believing in the existence of God on the basis of propositions such as those. From this point of view, it isn't exactly right to say that it is belief in God that is properly basic; more exactly; what are properly basic are such propositions as (6)–(10), each of which self-evidently entails that God exists. It isn't the relatively high level and general proposition *God exists* that is properly basic, but instead propositions detailing some of his attributes or actions. . . .

We may say, speaking loosely, that belief in God is properly basic; strictly speaking, however, it is probably not that proposition but such propositions as (6)–(10) that enjoy that status. But the main point, here, is that belief in God or (6)–(10), are properly basic; to say so, however, is not to deny that there are justifying conditions for these beliefs, or conditions that confer justification on one who accepts them as basic. They are therefore not groundless or gratuitous.

A second objection I've often heard: if belief in God is properly basic, why can't *just any* belief be properly basic? Couldn't we say the same for any bizarre aberration we can think of? What about voodoo or astrology? What about the belief that the Great Pumpkin returns every Halloween? Could I properly take *that* as basic? And if

I can't, why can I properly take belief in God as basic? Suppose I believe that if I flap my arms with sufficient vigor, I can take off and fly about the room; could I defend myself against the charge of irrationality by claiming this belief is basic? If we say that belief in God is properly basic, won't we be committed to holding that just anything, or nearly anything, can properly be taken as basic, thus throwing wide the gates to irrationalism and superstition?

Certainly not. What might lead one to think the Reformed epistemologist is in this kind of trouble? The fact that he rejects the criteria for proper basicality purveyed by classical foundationalism? But why should *that* be thought to commit him to such tolerance of irrationality?. . .

The fact that he rejects the Classical Foundationalist's criterion or proper basicality does not mean that he is committed to supposing just anything is properly basic.

But what then is the problem? Is it that the Reformed epistemologist not only rejects those criteria for proper basicality, but seems in no hurry to produce what he takes to be a better substitute? If he has no such criterion, how can he fairly reject belief in the Great Pumpkin as properly basic?

This objection betrays an important misconception. How do we rightly arrive at or develop criteria for . . . justified belief, or proper basicality? Where do they come from? Must one have such a criterion before one can sensibly make any judgments — positive or negative — about proper basicality? Surely not. Suppose I don't know of a satisfactory substitute for the criteria proposed by classical foundationalism; I am nevertheless entirely within my rights in holding that certain propositions are not properly basic in certain conditions. Some propositions seem self-evident when in fact they are not: that is the lesson of some of the Russell paradoxes.[4] Nevertheless it would be irrational to take as basic the denial of a proposition that seems self-evident to you. Similarly, suppose it seems to you that you see a tree; you would then be irrational in taking as basic the proposition that you don't see a tree, or that there aren't any trees. . . .

And this raises an important question — one Roderick Chisholm has taught us to ask. What is the status of criteria for knowledge, or proper basicality, or justified belief? Typically, these are universal statements. The modern foundationalist's criterion for proper basicality, for example, is doubly universal:

18. For any proposition $A$ and person $S$, $A$ is properly basic for $S$ if and only if $A$ is incorrigible for $S$ or self-evident to $S$.

But how could one know a thing like that? What are its credentials? Clearly enough, (18) isn't self-evident or just obviously true. But if it isn't, how does one arrive at it? What sorts of arguments would be appropriate? Of course a foundationalist might find (18) so appealing, he simply takes it to be true, neither offering argument for it, nor

---

4. Bertrand Russell (1872–1970) showed in 1902 that an apparently evident "axiom" of mathematics was in fact self-contradictory. The axiom states that whenever there exist some things, there exists a class that contains all and only those things as members. Russell was also, incidentally, a famously outspoken atheist.

accepting it on the basis of other things he believes. If he does so, however, his noetic structure will be self-referentially incoherent. (18) itself is neither self-evident nor incorrigible; hence in accepting (18) as basic, the modern foundationalist violates the condition of proper basicality he himself lays down in accepting it. On the other hand, perhaps the foundationalist will try to produce some argument for it from premises that are self-evident or incorrigible: it is exceedingly hard to see, however, what such an argument might be like. And until he has produced such arguments, what shall the rest of us do — we who do not find (18) at all obvious or compelling? How could he use (18) to show us that belief in God, for example, is not properly basic? Why should we believe (18), or pay it any attention?

The fact is, I think, that neither (18) nor any other revealing necessary and sufficient condition for proper basicality follows from clearly self-evident premises by clearly acceptable arguments. And hence the proper way to arrive at such a criterion is, broadly speaking, *inductive*. We must assemble examples of beliefs and conditions such that the former are obviously properly basic in the latter, and examples of beliefs and conditions such that the former are obviously *not* properly basic in the latter. We must then frame hypotheses as to the necessary and sufficient conditions of proper basicality and test these hypotheses by reference to those examples. Under the right conditions, for example, it is clearly rational to believe that you see a human person before you: a being who has thoughts and feelings, who knows and believes things, who makes decisions and acts. It is clear, furthermore, that you are under no obligation to reason to this belief from others you hold; under those conditions that belief is properly basic for you. But then (18) must be mistaken; the belief in question, under those circumstances, is properly basic, though neither self-evident nor incorrigible for you. Similarly, you may seem to remember that you had breakfast this morning, and perhaps you know of no reason to suppose your memory is playing you tricks. If so, you are entirely justified in taking that belief as basic. Of course it isn't properly basic on the criteria offered by classical foundationalists; but that fact counts not against you but against those criteria.

Accordingly, criteria for proper basicality must be reached from below rather than above; they should not be presented as *ex Cathedra*, but argued to and tested by a relevant set of examples. But there is no reason to assume, in advance, that everyone will agree on the examples. The Christian will of course suppose that belief in God is entirely proper and rational; if he doesn't accept this belief on the basis of other propositions, he will conclude that it is basic for him and quite properly so. Followers of Bertrand Russell and Madalyn Murray O'Hair[5] disagree, but how is that relevant? Must my criteria, or those of the Christian community, conform to their examples? Surely not. The Christian community is responsible to *its* set of examples, not to theirs.

Accordingly, the Reformed epistemologist can properly hold that belief in the Great Pumpkin is not properly basic, even though he holds that belief in God is properly basic and even if he has no full-fledged criterion of proper basicality. Of course he is committed to supposing that there is a relevant *difference* between belief

---

5. Madalyn Murray O'Hair (1919–1995), founder of American Atheists.

in God and belief in the Great Pumpkin, if he holds that the former but not the latter is properly basic. But this should prove no great embarrassment; there are plenty of candidates. These candidates are to be found in the neighborhood of the conditions I mentioned in the last section that justify and ground belief in God. Thus, for example, the Reformed epistemologist may concur with Calvin in holding that God has implanted in us a natural tendency to see his hand in the world around us; the same cannot be said for the Great Pumpkin, there being no Great Pumpkin and no natural tendency to accept beliefs about the Great Pumpkin.

By way of conclusion then: being self-evident, or incorrigible, or evident to the senses is not a necessary condition of proper basicality. Furthermore, one who holds that belief in God *is* properly basic is not thereby committed to the idea that belief in God is groundless or gratuitous or without justifying circumstances. And even if he lacks a general criterion of proper basicality, he is not obliged to suppose that just any or nearly any belief — belief in the Great Pumpkin, for example — is properly basic. Like everyone should, he begins with examples; and he may take belief in the Great Pumpkin as a paradigm of irrational basic belief.

## TEST YOUR UNDERSTANDING

1. What is it for a belief to be properly basic?

2. Sketch Plantinga's argument for the claim that *some* beliefs must be properly basic.

3. Plantinga argues that whether a belief is properly basic is not settled by the content of the belief, but also depends on the circumstances in which it is held. Explain the basis for this claim.

4. Plantinga suggests that certain theistic beliefs — like the belief that God is talking to me now — are strongly analogous to perceptual beliefs, like the belief that I am looking at a rose. List three important respects in which such beliefs are similar according to Plantinga.

## NOTES AND QUESTIONS

1. *The Great Pumpkin problem.* Plantinga imagines an objector who says, in effect, "If a belief in God can be properly basic for you, why can't a belief in the Great Pumpkin be properly basic for me?" Let's consider a more sober version of the question. The ancient Greeks believed in many gods: Zeus, Athena, and so on. Let us suppose that some of these beliefs were basic for them. Were these beliefs *properly* basic? Plantinga does not provide a theory of the conditions under which a belief is properly basic for a person. So we cannot answer the question by applying a general criterion. But we can ask: Is there *any* epistemologically relevant respect in which the basic

religious beliefs of the ancient Greeks differed from the basic religious beliefs of a modern Protestant Christian like Plantinga? (Plantinga may say that his beliefs are *true* while theirs were not; but a belief can be properly basic without being true.)

*Exercise:* Try to construct a theory of the conditions of proper basicality that answers this question. For Plantinga's own views, see *Warranted Christian Belief* (Oxford University Press, 2000). Would it be an objection to Plantinga's view if he were forced to say that the Greeks were justified in holding their religious beliefs as basic?

2. *The problem of disagreement.* If I'm looking at a rose in normal conditions, then the belief that I am looking at a rose may be properly basic for me. But if someone comes up to me and says, "I'm sorry but *I* don't see a rose. You must be hallucinating," then I am no longer warranted in taking my belief as basic. I must suspend judgment until I can produce some evidence that my eyes are working properly, or that his are not. This suggests a condition on proper basicality: *A belief is not properly basic for a person when that person is aware of other equally competent, equally informed people who reject it.* If this condition holds, then religious belief in our culture is not properly basic, since everyone is aware of intelligent, thoughtful atheists who deny that God exists.

*Exercise:* Say how Plantinga should respond to this argument.

## ANALYZING THE ARGUMENTS

1. *Belief and the will.* Pascal and James often write as if belief were under our voluntary control. But is it? Take a **proposition** about which you currently have no opinion and no evidence, e.g., the proposition that the number of hairs on your head is even. Now try to believe that proposition. Can you? (You can certainly *say* that you believe it; but can you summon up real *conviction*?) If not, does this show that it is always impossible to believe at will? And if it is impossible to believe at will, does that undermine the practical arguments for religious belief given by Pascal and James? For discussion of the general problem, see Bernard Williams, "Deciding to Believe," in *Problems of the Self* (Cambridge University Press, 1973).

2. *Practical reasons for belief and the value of faith.* Both James and Pascal provide what might be called *self-interested* reasons for believing that God exists. Many people find arguments of this sort unseemly. Faith—religious conviction that is not grounded in compelling evidence—is supposed by many to be a virtue (for which one might be admired) or a gift (for which one might be grateful). Do the defenses of faith in James and Pascal deprive faith of its value?

3. *Drawing the line.* Any philosopher who maintains that it is *sometimes* reasonable to believe in the absence of evidence must immediately concede that it is not *always* permissible to believe what we cannot prove. (*Exercise:* Explain in vivid terms why this "anything goes" principle is unacceptable.) Any such view must therefore provide a principle that specifies the conditions under which evidence and argument are not required. Any such principle must satisfy two conditions: It must be consistent with what we already know— e.g., that many of our scientific beliefs are reasonable, that superstitious beliefs are unreasonable, etc. But it must also be *non-arbitrary*. It must draw a plausible, principled line between the cases in which ungrounded belief is reasonable and the cases in which it is not. This is a notoriously difficult problem. As an exercise, begin the effort to identify such a principle. Make a list of the opinions *you* hold, but cannot defend by means of explicit argument. Determine which of those opinions you regard as reasonable upon reflection. Then try to articulate a principle that draws the line where you have drawn it. Is this principle plausible upon reflection? What does it imply about other cases that were not part of the raw materials from which it was developed? What does it imply about the various cases of religious belief discussed in the selections?

4. *Reasonable vs. unreasonable belief.* The selections all presume a distinction between beliefs that are reasonable or justified and beliefs that are unreasonable or unjustified. Imagine that you are trying to explain this distinction to someone who is unfamiliar with it. Suppose he says, for example, "I don't see why it takes a fancy argument to show that it's OK for me to believe that God exists. It's a free country. I can believe what I like!" This person needs an explanation of the difference between a *legally permissible belief* and a *reasonable belief.* An ideal account will take the form of an explicit definition:

   *A belief is reasonable (warranted, justified) if and only if . . .*

   But even if that is too much to ask, an informal explanation should be possible.

   *Exercise:* Imagine that you are addressing someone who doesn't understand the distinction between a reasonable belief and a belief that one is legally permitted to hold. What is the best way to put her in a position to understand this important contrast?

# Part II

## EPISTEMOLOGY

# 3

# What Is Knowledge?

In 2008, Nicholas Evans, the author of the novel *The Horse Whisperer*, picked some wild mushrooms, sautéed them in butter, and served them to his family. They nearly died. The mushrooms were deadly webcaps, which contain the potentially fatal toxin orellanine. Evans's kidneys failed, and he later received a kidney transplant from his daughter.

Evans did not know that the mushrooms were poisonous. If he had known that, he would never have cooked them. This illustrates one way in which knowledge is valuable. Lack of knowledge can have serious, even fatal, consequences. Sometimes knowledge can save your life.

## Propositional Knowledge, Personal Knowledge, Procedural Knowledge

The kind of knowledge Evans lacked was *propositional* (or *factual*) knowledge, where what follows the verb "to know" is a clause beginning with "that." You know that the Earth is round, and you know that Evans wrote *The Horse Whisperer*. These clauses pick out what philosophers call **propositions**, things that can be *true* or *false*. That the Earth is round is a true proposition; that the Earth is flat is a false proposition. This is why the kind of knowledge reported by a statement like "You know that the Earth is round" is called **propositional knowledge** (and also sometimes *knowledge-that*). This is the topic of the selections that follow, and the main subject matter of the branch of philosophy called **epistemology**—derived from the Greek word for knowledge, *episteme*.

Propositional knowledge is not the only kind of knowledge, as the variety of grammatical constructions using the verb "to know" indicates. For example, in one construction the verb is followed by a noun (or noun phrase) that typically picks out a person or a place. Nicholas Evans knows Scotland: he is quite familiar with that country, having picked mushrooms there. He also knows Robert Redford, the director and star of the movie based on Evans's novel. We could paraphrase these claims by saying that Evans is acquainted with both Scotland and Redford. This sort of knowledge is accordingly called *acquaintance knowledge*, or *personal knowledge*.

Propositional knowledge is not a kind of personal knowledge. Someone can know that Paris is the capital of France without knowing Paris, or France. What about the other way around? Could personal knowledge be a kind of propositional knowledge? That seems doubtful. If you read Michael Callan's lengthy *Robert Redford: The Biography* you will acquire a lot of propositional knowledge about Redford but will not thereby know him. The case that propositional and acquaintance knowledge are quite different can be strengthened by noting that many languages distinguish them using different verbs, where English has only one. In French, for instance, "connaître" is used for acquaintance knowledge, and "savoir" for propositional knowledge.

There are other notable constructions using the verb "to know." For example: Evans knows where Edinburgh is, knows who inspired the main character in *The Horse Whisperer*, and knows which actor directed the movie. These constructions seem to say something about Evans's propositional knowledge. If Evans knows where Edinburgh is, then he knows that it's in Scotland, or south of the Firth of Forth, or some other salient fact about its location, and similarly for the other two examples.

There is another related construction that is less clearly propositional: Evans knows how to cook mushrooms, how to tie his shoes, and how to write best sellers. These are examples of *knowledge-how* or *procedural knowledge*. Is procedural knowledge a kind of propositional knowledge? One might think not, on the ground that reading Julia Child's *Mastering the Art of French Cooking* will give you lots of propositional knowledge about French cooking but is not guaranteed to prevent your soufflés from collapsing. It is a controversial matter whether knowledge-how is a kind of propositional knowledge, although not one taken up in the selections.[1]

## Propositional Knowledge: Belief, Truth, and Justification

Now that we have the relevant kind of knowledge clearly in view, the task is to say something interesting about it. The traditional approach is to try to break knowledge down into its components, as one might study an engine by taking it apart.

One uncontroversial component of propositional knowledge is truth. When Evans picked the deadly webcaps, he believed that they were harmless. Indeed, he presumably took himself to *know* that they were harmless. "I know that these are

---

1. For an argument that knowledge-how is a kind of propositional knowledge, see J. Stanley and T. Williamson, "Knowing How," *Journal of Philosophy* 98 (2001): 411–44.

harmless," we can imagine him saying. But he *didn't* know that the mushrooms were harmless, because they weren't. You can't know what's false: if S (a person) knows p, then p must be true.

Belief is a good candidate for another component of knowledge. If you know that the Earth is round, then you will probably reply "The Earth is round" if asked about its shape, be unconcerned when a ship disappears over the horizon, and so forth. That is, you will give every impression that you *believe* that the Earth is round. Although the belief component is not as uncontroversial as the truth component (the selection by Timothy Williamson discusses one objection), it is widely accepted. So let us assume that if S knows p, then S must believe p.

So far, we have two components of knowledge: truth and belief. If S knows p, then it must be that (i) p is true, and (ii) S believes p. In other words, (i) and (ii) are **necessary conditions** for S to know p.

Necessary conditions need not also be **sufficient conditions**. Having four equal sides is a necessary condition for being a square: it is impossible to be a square without having four equal sides. But it is not a *sufficient* condition: having four equal sides does not guarantee being a square, as some rhomboids (which have four equal sides) are not squares. What about (i) and (ii)? Might they also be, taken together, a sufficient condition for knowledge? And if they are, then knowledge is just the two components of belief and truth added together. That is: S knows p if and only if (i) p is true, and (ii) S believes p.

However, as has been known since Plato's time, belief and truth are not sufficient for knowledge. Suppose someone buys a ticket for the lottery convinced that he will win because his fortune teller told him so, and by a fluke he does. He truly believed that he would win, but he did not *know* that he would win. As Plato puts it, knowledge is not "correct opinion"; as a contemporary philosopher might say, knowledge cannot be "analyzed" as true belief. What might another component of knowledge be?

The lottery winner has no *reasons* or *evidence* for his true belief that he will win. That is, his belief is not *justified*. Conversely, your true belief that the Earth is round is justified—perhaps you read about its shape in a reliable textbook, or a knowledgeable teacher told you that it is round. So this suggests that justification is another component of knowledge. Like the belief component, the justification component is also widely accepted. So let us assume that if S knows p, then S must justifiably believe p.

Now we have three necessary conditions for S to know p. If S knows p, then it must be that (i) p is true, (ii) S believes p, and (iii) S's belief is justified. Might (i), (ii), and (iii) together be sufficient conditions for knowledge? And if they are, then knowledge is just the three components of belief, truth, and justification added together. That is: S knows p if and only if (i) p is true, (ii) S believes p, and (iii) S's belief is justified.

What else could knowledge be? There is no obvious fourth component, so the received view used to be that knowledge simply is justified true belief.

# Gettier's Counterexamples, and the Aftermath

All that changed with the publication in 1963 of Edmund Gettier's "Is Justified True Belief Knowledge?" Gettier presents a series of examples in which someone has a justified true belief, but apparently does not know. These *Gettier cases* are commonly taken to refute the claim that (i), (ii), and (iii) are sufficient for S to know p.

Once you get the idea, Gettier cases are easy to construct. Here is one. Suppose that Evans believes that the mushrooms are harmless because he consulted the authoritative *Field Guide to Edible Mushrooms of Britain and Europe*. Due to a printer's error (most unlikely in a work of this kind), the photograph of deadly webcaps was captioned *Ceps*, a desirable type of edible mushroom. Evans's false belief that the mushrooms are harmless is justified: he knows that past editions of the *Field Guide* were accurate. Evans puts the mushrooms in a bag and takes them back to his kitchen. As far as he knows, these are his only mushrooms. He believes that the mushrooms in the bag are harmless, and that they are in his kitchen. Evans makes a trivial deductive **inference** from the premise that the mushrooms in the bag in his kitchen are harmless, and believes that there are some harmless mushrooms in his kitchen. Since Evans is justified in believing the premise, and the conclusion deductively follows from the premise, he is also justified in believing the conclusion. So Evans's belief that there are some harmless mushrooms in his kitchen is justified. By luck, it is also true: Evans's wife bought some mushrooms from the supermarket yesterday, and put them in the refrigerator. Yet Evans does not *know* that there are some harmless mushrooms in his kitchen.

Gettier's paper immediately created an industry tasked with finding a fourth component of knowledge that, when added to truth, belief, and justification, would result in a sufficient condition. It proved very difficult. Gilbert Harman made one of the more promising attempts. He noticed that a number of Gettier-style cases involve reasoning from a false **premise**: in the example above, Evans reasons from the false premise that the mushrooms in the bag in his kitchen are harmless. This suggests a fourth component of knowledge: (iv) S did not infer p from a false premise. Are (i), (ii), (iii), and (iv) necessary *and* sufficient conditions for knowledge? As Harman points out, there are other examples where someone fails to know p but yet these four components seem to be present. Harman argues that on closer examination these examples involve reasoning from a false premise after all.

Linda Zagzebski argues that all attempts to repair the analysis of knowledge must fail. Suppose a philosopher proposes that knowledge is justified true belief plus something else. This extra ingredient might be thought of as itself composed of two sub-ingredients, justification and some extra factor X (as in Harman's proposal). Or the extra ingredient might be thought of as one unified thing, a special kind of justification that is sometimes called "warrant." Now this addition to true belief—justification + X, or warrant—is typically thought of as compatible with *false* belief. In other words, someone can have a justified belief (+ X) that is false, or someone can have a warranted belief that is false. (This is why truth needs to be added to the analysis of knowledge separately: if justification + X, or warrant, were *sufficient* for truth, then the truth component would be redundant.) Given the assumption that the addition to true belief is not itself sufficient for truth, Zagzebski argues that Gettier cases will inevitably arise.

For this and other reasons many philosophers have become very skeptical that knowledge can be broken down into components. They accept that there are a variety of necessary conditions for S to know p, but they deny that these conditions are also jointly sufficient for S to know p. Prominent among them is Timothy Williamson, who champions a "knowledge-first" approach to epistemology. Knowledge, according to Williamson, cannot be analyzed as justified true belief + some extra factor X; instead, knowledge should be taken as explanatorily fundamental in its own right. Inquiry always proceeds with *some* things being taken for granted, not needing a definition or analysis, and why can't knowledge be one?

Even if knowledge is unanalyzable, that doesn't mean we can't discover anything interesting about it. Indeed, to say that truth, justification, and belief are necessary conditions for knowledge is already to say something interesting. And Williamson finds much more to say.

Many questions about knowledge remain. One is raised by Plato: Why is knowledge better than true belief, or "correct opinion"? If Evans had known that the mushrooms were poisonous, then he wouldn't have cooked them. But he wouldn't have cooked them if he had believed truly that they were poisonous, whether or not he also knew that they were poisonous. Plato suggests a (somewhat metaphorical) answer to that question: knowledge is "tied down" in the mind, whereas true belief has a tendency to "run away and escape." Williamson suggests a way to develop Plato's answer. Suppose Evans has a mere true belief that the mushrooms in his possession are poisonous because some overconfident friend told him that all mushrooms in Scotland are poisonous. Evans might well learn later that his friend is not to be trusted, or that there are many edible mushrooms in Scotland. And if he does, he will give up his belief that the mushrooms are poisonous, and perhaps will take them back to his kitchen and start sautéing. By contrast, if he knows that the mushrooms are poisonous, he is much less likely to change his mind.

## Plato (429–347 BCE)

Plato is one of the most important figures in Western philosophy. He founded the Academy in Athens, which was a major center of learning in Classical Greece, where he taught Aristotle (384–322 BCE). Plato's works typically take the form of dialogues, and nearly all of them feature his teacher Socrates (469–399 BCE).

# MENO

Socrates:  Can you mention any other subject[1] of which those who claim to be teachers not only are not recognized to be teachers of others but are not recognized to have knowledge of it themselves, and are thought to be poor in the very matter which they profess to teach? Or any other subject of which those who are recognized as worthy teachers at one time say it can be taught and at other times that it cannot? Would you say that people who are so confused about a subject can be effective teachers of it?[2]—No, by Zeus;[3] I would not.

S:  If then neither the sophists nor the worthy people themselves are teachers of this subject, clearly there would be no others?—I do not think there are.

S:  If there are no teachers, neither are there pupils?—As you say.

S:  And we agreed that a subject that has neither teachers nor pupils is not teachable?—We have so agreed.

S:  Now there seem to be no teachers of virtue anywhere?—That is so.

S:  If there are no teachers, there are no learners?—That seems so.

S:  Then virtue cannot be taught?

Meno:  Apparently not, if we have investigated this correctly. I certainly wonder, Socrates, whether there are no good men either, or in what way good men come to be.

S:  We are probably poor specimens, you and I, Meno. Gorgias has not adequately educated you, nor Prodicus me.[4] We must then at all costs turn our attention to ourselves and find someone who will in some way make us better. I say this in view of our recent investigation, for it is ridiculous that we failed to see that it is not only under the guidance of knowledge that men succeed in their affairs, and that is perhaps why the knowledge of how good men come to be escapes us.

M:  How do you mean, Socrates?

S:  I mean this: we were right to agree that good men must be beneficent, and that this could not be otherwise. Is that not so?—Yes.

S:  And that they will be beneficent if they give us correct guidance in our affairs. To this too we were right to agree?—Yes.

S:  But that one cannot guide correctly if one does not have knowledge; to this our agreement is likely to be incorrect.—How do you mean?

S:  I will tell you. A man who knew the way to Larissa[5] or anywhere else you like, and went there and guided others would surely lead them well and correctly?—Certainly.

---

1. That is, any subject other than virtue.

2. Text after dash is Meno's response.

3. Chief of the many ancient Greek gods.

4. Gorgias and Prodicus were both Sophists — ancient Greek philosophers and rhetoricians.

5. City in ancient (and present-day) Greece.

S: What if someone had had a correct opinion as to which was the way but had not gone there nor indeed had knowledge of it, would he not also lead correctly? — Certainly.

S: And as long as he has the right opinion about that of which the other has knowledge, he will not be a worse guide than the one who knows, as he has a true opinion, though not knowledge. — In no way worse.

S: So true opinion is in no way a worse guide to correct action than knowledge. It is this that we omitted in our investigation of the nature of virtue, when we said that only knowledge can lead to correct action, for true opinion can do so also. — So it seems.

S: So correct opinion is no less useful than knowledge?

M: Yes, to this extent, Socrates. But the man who has knowledge will always succeed, whereas he who has true opinion will only succeed at times.

S: How do you mean? Will he who has the right opinion not always succeed, as long as his opinion is right?

M: That appears to be so of necessity, and it makes me wonder, Socrates, this being the case, why knowledge is prized far more highly than right opinion, and why they are different.

S: Do you know why you wonder, or shall I tell you? — By all means tell me.

S: It is because you have paid no attention to the statues of Daedalus,[6] but perhaps there are none in Thessaly.[7]

M: What do you have in mind when you say this?

S: That they too run away and escape if one does not tie them down but remain in place if tied down. — So what?

S: To acquire an untied work of Daedalus is not worth much, like acquiring a runaway slave, for it does not remain, but it is worth much if tied down, for his works are very beautiful. What am I thinking of when I say this? True opinions. For true opinions, as long as they remain, are a fine thing and all they do is good, but they are not willing to remain long, and they escape from a man's mind, so that they are not worth much until one ties them down by (giving) an account of the reason why. And that, Meno my friend, is recollection, as we previously agreed. After they are tied down, in the first place they become knowledge, and then they remain in place. That is why knowledge is prized higher than correct opinion, and knowledge differs from correct opinion in being tied down.

M: Yes, by Zeus, Socrates, it seems to be something like that.

S: Indeed, I too speak as one who does not have knowledge but is guessing. However, I certainly do not think I am guessing that right opinion is a different thing than knowledge. If I claim to know anything else — and I would make that claim about few things — I would put this down as one of the things I know. — Rightly so, Socrates.

6. Daedalus: mythological architect, inventor, and craftsman.

7. Thessaly: region of Greece containing the city Larissa.

S: Well then, is it not correct that when true opinion guides the course of every action, it does no worse than knowledge? — I think you are right in this too.

S: Correct opinion is then neither inferior to knowledge nor less useful in directing actions, nor is the man who has it less so than he who has knowledge. — That is so.

S: And we agreed that the good man is beneficent. — Yes.

S: Since then it is not only through knowledge but also through right opinion that men are good, and beneficial to their cities when they are, and neither knowledge nor true opinion come to men by nature but are acquired — or do you think either of these comes by nature? — I do not think so.

S: Then if they do not come by nature, men are not so by nature either. — Surely not.

S: As goodness does not come by nature, we inquired next whether it could be taught. — Yes.

S: We thought it could be taught, if it was knowledge? — Yes.

S: And that it was knowledge if it could be taught? — Quite so.

S: And that if there were teachers of it, it could be taught, but if there were not, it was not teachable? — That is so.

S: And then we agreed that there were no teachers of it? — We did.

S: So we agreed that it was neither teachable nor knowledge? — Quite so.

S: But we certainly agree that virtue is a good thing? — Yes.

S: And that which guides correctly is both useful and good? — Certainly.

S: And that only these two things, true belief and knowledge, guide correctly, and that if a man possesses these he gives correct guidance. The things that turn out right by some chance are not due to human guidance, but where there is correct human guidance it is due to two things, true belief or knowledge. — I think that is so.

S: Now because it cannot be taught, virtue no longer seems to be knowledge? — It seems not.

S: So one of the two good and useful things has been excluded, and knowledge is not the guide in public affairs. — I do not think so.

S: So it is not by some kind of wisdom, or by being wise, that such men lead their cities, those such as Themistocles[8] and those mentioned by Anytus[9] just now? That is the reason why they cannot make others be like themselves, because it is not knowledge which makes them what they are.

M: It is likely to be as you say, Socrates.

S: Therefore, if it is not through knowledge, the only alternative is that it is through right opinion that statesmen follow the right course for their cities. As regards knowledge, they are no different from soothsayers and prophets. They too say many true things when inspired, but they have no knowledge of what they are saying. — That is probably so.

S: And so, Meno, is it right to call divine these men who, without any understanding, are right in much that is of importance in what they say and do? — Certainly.

---

8. Themistocles: Athenian politician and military leader.

9. Anytus: Athenian politician who makes an earlier appearance in the dialogue.

S: We should be right to call divine also those soothsayers and prophets whom we just mentioned, and all the poets, and we should call no less divine and inspired those public men who are no less under the gods' influence and possession, as their speeches lead to success in many important matters, though they have no knowledge of what they are saying. — Quite so.

S: Women too, Meno, call good men divine, and the Spartans,[1] when they eulogize someone, say "This man is divine."

M: And they appear to be right, Socrates, though perhaps Anytus here will be annoyed with you for saying so.

S: I do not mind that; we shall talk to him again, but if we were right in the way in which we spoke and investigated in this whole discussion, virtue would be neither an inborn quality nor taught, but comes to those who possess it as a gift from the gods which is not accompanied by understanding, unless there is someone among our statesmen who can make another into a statesman. If there were one, he could be said to be among the living as Homer said Teiresias was among the dead, namely, that "he alone retained his wits while the others flitted about like shadows."[2] In the same manner such a man would, as far as virtue is concerned, here also be the only true reality compared, as it were, with shadows.

M: I think that is an excellent way to put it, Socrates.

S: It follows from this reasoning, Meno, that virtue appears to be present in those of us who may possess it as a gift from the gods. We shall have clear knowledge of this when, before we investigate how it comes to be present in men, we first try to find out what virtue in itself is. But now the time has come for me to go. You convince your guest friend Anytus here of these very things of which you have yourself been convinced, in order that he may be more amenable. If you succeed, you will also confer a benefit upon the Athenians.

## TEST YOUR UNDERSTANDING

1. The dialogue gives a reason for thinking that correct opinion and knowledge are equally valuable. What is it? According to Socrates, do we think that they are equally valuable?

2. Does Socrates think that the possession of knowledge explains why someone is virtuous?

---

1. Inhabitants of Sparta, a city-state in ancient Greece.

2. Teiresias (or Tiresias): mythical blind prophet; the quotation is from Homer's ancient Greek epic poem *The Odyssey.*

## NOTES AND QUESTIONS

1. The *Meno* is one of Plato's many dialogues featuring his teacher Socrates (469–399 BCE), and mostly concerns the questions of whether virtue can be taught, and what virtue is. The selection is from the end of the *Meno*; earlier in the dialogue Socrates raises the following puzzle:

   > [A] man cannot search either for what he knows or what he does not know.... He cannot search for what he knows — since he knows it, there is no need to search — nor for what he does not know, for he does not know what to look for. (*Meno* 80e)

   *Exercise:* Set out this puzzle more clearly. What is the solution?

2. Plato's main dialogue on knowledge is the *Theaetetus*, in which Socrates, a mathematician Theodorus, and his student Theaetetus discuss the question "What is knowledge?" (The following selection by Gettier refers to this dialogue in note 1, as well as to the *Meno*.) One proposed definition is that knowledge is "true belief with an account" (*Theaetetus* 201d). As Gettier says, this sounds rather like the "justified true belief" analysis of knowledge. After examining this suggestion at some length, Socrates ends up rejecting it. For a discussion of the dialogue and various interpretive controversies, see Timothy Chappell, "Plato on Knowledge in the *Theaetetus*," *Stanford Encyclopedia of Philosophy*, ed. E. Zalta. (<http://plato.stanford.edu/archives/win2012/entries/plato-theaetetus/>).

## Edmund Gettier (born 1927)

Gettier is Emeritus Professor of Philosophy at the University of Massachusetts at Amherst. "Is Justified True Belief Knowledge?" is one of the most widely cited papers in contemporary philosophy.

# IS JUSTIFIED TRUE BELIEF KNOWLEDGE?

Various attempts have been made in recent years to state necessary and sufficient conditions for someone's knowing a given proposition. The attempts have often been such that they can be stated in a form similar to the following:[1]

   a.  S knows that P    *IFF*[2]    (*i*)   P is true,

                                   (*ii*)  S believes that P, and

                                   (*iii*)  S is justified in believing that P.

---

1. Plato seems to be considering some such definition at *Theaetetus* 201, and perhaps accepting one at *Meno* 98. [Gettier's note.] (See p. 105 of this anthology.)

2. **IFF** or **iff**: abbreviation for "if and only if."

For example, Chisholm has held that the following gives the necessary and sufficient conditions for knowledge.[3]

b.  S knows that P          *IFF*          (*i*)  S accepts P,
                                           (*ii*)  S has adequate evidence for P, and
                                           (*iii*)  P is true.

Ayer[4] has stated the necessary and sufficient conditions for knowledge as follows.

c.  S knows that P          *IFF*          (*i*)  P is true,
                                           (*ii*)  S is sure that P is true, and
                                           (*iii*)  S has the right to be sure that P is true,

I shall argue that (a) is false in that the conditions stated therein do not constitute a *sufficient* condition for the truth of the proposition that S knows that P. The same argument will show that (b) and (c) fail if "has adequate evidence for" or "has the right to be sure that" is substituted for "is justified in believing that" throughout.

I shall begin by noting two points. First, in that sense of "justified" in which S's being justified in believing P is a necessary condition of S's knowing that P, it is possible for a person to be justified in believing a proposition that is in fact false. Secondly, for any proposition P, if S is justified in believing P, and P entails[5] Q, and S deduces Q from P and accepts Q as a result of this deduction, then S is justified in believing Q. Keeping these two points in mind, I shall now present two cases in which the conditions stated in (a) are true for some proposition, though it is at the same time false that the person in question knows that proposition.

# Case I

Suppose that Smith and Jones have applied for a certain job. And suppose that Smith has strong evidence for the following conjunctive[6] proposition:

d.  Jones is the man who will get the job, and Jones has ten coins in his pocket.

Smith's evidence for (d) might be that the president of the company assured him that Jones would in the end be selected, and that he, Smith, had counted the coins in Jones's pocket ten minutes ago. Proposition (d) entails:

e.  The man who will get the job has ten coins in his pocket.

---

3. Roderick M. Chisholm (1916–1999) taught at Brown University for many years and made influential contributions to epistemology and other subjects.

4. A. J. Ayer (1910–1989) was one of the leading British philosophers of the last century.

5. **Entails:** logically implies.

6. The conjunction of two sentences "p" and "q" is the sentence "p and q."

Let us suppose that Smith sees the entailment from (d) to (e), and accepts (e) on the grounds of (d), for which he has strong evidence. In this case, Smith is clearly justified in believing that (e) is true.

But imagine, further, that unknown to Smith, he himself, not Jones, will get the job. And, also, unknown to Smith, he himself has ten coins in his pocket. Proposition (e) is then true, though proposition (d), from which Smith inferred (e), is false. In our example, then, all of the following are true: (*i*) (e) is true, (*ii*) Smith believes that (e) is true, and (*iii*) Smith is justified in believing that (e) is true. But it is equally clear that Smith does not *know* that (e) is true; for (e) is true in virtue of the number of coins in Smith's pocket, while Smith does not know how many coins are in Smith's pocket, and bases his belief in (e) on a count of the coins in Jones's pocket, whom he falsely believes to be the man who will get the job.

# Case II

Let us suppose that Smith has strong evidence for the following proposition:

> f.  Jones owns a Ford.

Smith's evidence might be that Jones has at all times in the past within Smith's memory owned a car, and always a Ford, and that Jones has just offered Smith a ride while driving a Ford. Let us imagine, now, that Smith has another friend, Brown, of whose whereabouts he is totally ignorant. Smith selects three place-names quite at random, and constructs the following three propositions:

> g.  Either Jones owns a Ford, or Brown is in Boston;
>
> h.  Either Jones owns a Ford, or Brown is in Barcelona;
>
> i.  Either Jones owns a Ford, or Brown is in Brest-Litovsk.

Each of these propositions is entailed by (f). Imagine that Smith realizes the entailment of each of these propositions he has constructed by (f), and proceeds to accept (g), (h), and (i) on the basis of (f). Smith has correctly inferred (g), (h), and (i) from a proposition for which he has strong evidence. Smith is therefore completely justified in believing each of these three propositions. Smith, of course, has no idea where Brown is.

But imagine now that two further conditions hold. First, Jones does *not* own a Ford, but is at present driving a rented car. And secondly, by the sheerest coincidence, and entirely unknown to Smith, the place mentioned in proposition (h) happens really to be the place where Brown is. If these two conditions hold then Smith does *not* know that (h) is true, even though (*i*) (h) is true, (*ii*) Smith does believe that (h) is true, and (*iii*) Smith is justified in believing that (h) is true.

These two examples show that definition (a) does not state a *sufficient* condition for someone's knowing a given proposition. The same cases, with appropriate changes, will suffice to show that neither definition (b) nor definition (c) do so either.

## TEST YOUR UNDERSTANDING

1. Is Gettier arguing that belief, truth, and justification are not necessary for knowledge?

2. In Gettier's two examples Smith is justified in believing a certain **proposition** P and reasons from P to another proposition Q, which Gettier says Smith does not know. Does Smith know P?

## NOTES AND QUESTIONS

1. Consider the following example, due to Alvin Goldman:

> Henry is driving in the countryside with his son. For the boy's edification Henry identifies various objects on the landscape as they come into view. "That's a cow," says Henry, "That's a tractor," "That's a silo," "That's a barn," etc. Henry has no doubt about the identity of these objects; in particular, he has no doubt that the last-mentioned object is a barn, which indeed it is. Each of the identified objects has features characteristic of its type. Moreover, each object is fully in view, Henry has excellent eyesight, and he has enough time to look at them reasonably carefully, since there is little traffic to distract him.... [Now suppose] that, unknown to Henry, the district he has just entered is full of papier-mâché facsimiles of barns. These facsimiles look from the road exactly like barns, but are really just façades, without back walls or interiors, quite incapable of being used as barns. They are so cleverly constructed that travelers invariably mistake them for barns. Having just entered the district, Henry has not encountered any facsimiles; the object he sees is a genuine barn. But if the object on that site were a facsimile, Henry would mistake it for a barn.[1]

---

1. Alvin Goldman, "Discrimination and Perceptual Knowledge," *Journal of Philosophy* 73 (1976): 771–91, pp. 772–73.

Henry says, pointing at the barn, "That's a barn." What he says is true. Does he *know* that that's a barn? Assuming that he doesn't, how does this case differ from Gettier's two examples?

2. Suppose you have bought a lottery ticket. The odds of your winning are a million to one. The winning ticket has been selected and it's not yours, but the number has not yet been announced on television. You're sure that you've lost. Do you *know* that you've lost? Assuming you don't know that you've lost, how does this case differ from Gettier's two examples?

## Gilbert Harman (born 1938)

Harman is the James S. McDonnell Distinguished University Professor of Philosophy at Princeton University. His books include major studies in the philosophy of mind (*Thought*, 1973), epistemology (*Change in View*, 1986), moral philosophy (*The Nature of Morality*, 1978), and statistical learning theory (*Reliable Reasoning*, 2007, with Sanjeev Kulkarni.)

# EVIDENCE ONE DOES NOT POSSESS
## from *Thought*

Recall[1] that Gettier was able to show that knowledge is not simply justified true belief. From premises one knows to be true one can inductively infer[2] something false and be justified in doing so. One can go on to infer something true from that first conclusion and still be justified. One's second conclusion is true and one is justified in believing it; but one does not know that it is true. Therefore we are led to accept roughly the following principle:

P   Reasoning that essentially involves false conclusions, intermediate or final, cannot give one knowledge.

Many Gettier examples are not obviously accounted for by P, since it is not always evident that there has been any relevant reasoning. . . .

---

1. Harman is referring to Edmund Gettier's paper "Is Justified True Belief Knowledge?" (see p. 108 of this chapter), which gives examples of justified true belief that are not knowledge.

2. An inductive **inference** is one where the premises do not logically imply the conclusion.

# 1. Three Examples

## EXAMPLE (1)

While I am watching him, Tom takes a library book from the shelf and conceals it beneath his coat. Since I am the library detective, I follow him as he walks brazenly past the guard at the front door. Outside I see him take out the book and smile. As I approach he notices me and suddenly runs away. But I am sure that it was Tom, for I know him well. I saw Tom steal a book from the library and that is the testimony I give before the University Judicial Council. After testifying, I leave the hearing room and return to my post in the library. Later that day, Tom's mother testifies that Tom has an identical twin, Buck. Tom, she says, was thousands of miles away at the time of the theft. She hopes that Buck did not do it; but she admits that he has a bad character.

Do I know that Tom stole the book? Let us suppose that I am right. It was Tom that took the book. His mother was lying when she said that Tom was thousands of miles away. I do not know that she was lying, of course, since I do not know anything about her, even that she exists. Nor does anyone at the hearing know that she is lying, although some may suspect that she is. In these circumstances I do not know that Tom stole the book. My knowledge is undermined by evidence I do not possess.

## EXAMPLE (2)

Donald has gone off to Italy. He told you ahead of time that he was going; and you saw him off at the airport. He said he was to stay for the entire summer. That was in June. It is now July. Then you might know that he is in Italy. It is the sort of thing one often claims to know. However, for reasons of his own Donald wants you to believe that he is not in Italy but in California. He writes several letters saying that he has gone to San Francisco and has decided to stay there for the summer. He wants you to think that these letters were written by him in San Francisco, so he sends them to someone he knows there and has that person mail them to you with a San Francisco postmark, one at a time. You have been out of town for a couple of days and have not read any of the letters. You are now standing before the pile of mail that arrived while you were away. Two of the phony letters are in the pile. You are about to open your mail. I ask you, "Do you know where Donald is?" "Yes," you reply, "I know that he is in Italy." You are right about where Donald is and it would seem that your justification for believing that Donald is in Italy makes no reference to letters from San Francisco. But you do not know that Donald is in Italy. Your knowledge is undermined by evidence you do not as yet possess.

## EXAMPLE (3)

A political leader is assassinated. His associates, fearing a coup, decide to pretend that the bullet hit someone else. On nationwide television they announce that an assassination attempt has failed to kill the leader but has killed a secret service man by mistake. However, before the announcement is made, an enterprising reporter on the scene telephones the real story to his newspaper, which has included the story in its final edition. Jill buys a copy of that paper and reads the story of the assassination. What she reads is true and so are her assumptions about how the story came to be in the paper. The reporter, whose by-line appears, saw the assassination and dictated his report, which is now printed just as he dictated it. Jill has a justified true belief and, it would seem, all her intermediate conclusions are true. But she does not know that the political leader has been assassinated. For everyone else has heard about the televised announcement. They may also have seen the story in the paper and, perhaps, do not know what to believe; and it is highly implausible that Jill should know simply because she lacks evidence everyone else has. Jill does not know. Her knowledge is undermined by evidence she does not possess.

These examples pose a problem for my strategy. They are Gettier examples and my strategy is to make assumptions about inference that will account for Gettier examples by means of principle *P*. But these particular examples appear to bring in considerations that have nothing to do with conclusions essential to the inference on which belief is based.

Some readers may have trouble evaluating these examples. Like other Gettier examples, these require attention to subtle facts about ordinary usage; it is easy to miss subtle differences if, as in the present instance, it is very difficult to formulate a theory that would account for these differences. We must compare what it would be natural to say about these cases if there were no additional evidence one does not possess (no testimony from Tom's mother, no letters from San Francisco, and no televised announcement) with what it would be natural to say about the cases in which there is the additional evidence one does not possess. We must take care not to adopt a very skeptical attitude nor become too lenient about what is to count as knowledge. If we become skeptically inclined, we will deny there is knowledge in either case. If we become too lenient, we will allow that there is knowledge in both cases. It is tempting to go in one or the other of these directions, toward skepticism or leniency, because it proves so difficult to see what general principles are involved that would mark the difference. But at least some difference between the cases is revealed by the fact that we are *more inclined* to say that there is knowledge in the examples where there is no undermining evidence a person does not possess than in the examples where there is such evidence. The problem, then, is to account for this difference in our inclination to ascribe knowledge to someone.

# 2. Evidence against What One Knows

If I had known about Tom's mother's testimony, I would not have been justified in thinking that it was Tom I saw steal the book. Once you read the letters from Donald in which he says he is in San Francisco, you are no longer justified in thinking that he is in Italy. If Jill knew about the television announcement, she would not be justified in believing that the political leader has been assassinated. This suggests that we can account for the preceding examples by means of the following principle.

> One knows only if there is no evidence such that if one knew about the evidence one would not be justified in believing one's conclusion.

However, by modifying the three examples it can be shown that this principle is too strong.

Suppose that Tom's mother was known to the Judicial Council as a pathological liar. Everyone at the hearing realizes that Buck, Tom's supposed twin, is a figment of her imagination. When she testifies no one believes her. Back at my post in the library, I still know nothing of Tom's mother or her testimony. In such a case, my knowledge would not be undermined by her testimony; but if I were told only that she had just testified that Tom has a twin brother and was himself thousands of miles away from the scene of the crime at the time the book was stolen, I would no longer be justified in believing as I now do that Tom stole the book. Here I know even though there is evidence which, if I knew about it, would cause me not to be justified in believing my conclusion.

Suppose that Donald had changed his mind and never mailed the letters to San Francisco. Then those letters no longer undermine your knowledge. But it is very difficult to see what principle accounts for this fact. How can letters in the pile on the table in front of you undermine your knowledge while the same letters in a pile in front of Donald do not? If you knew that Donald had written letters to you saying that he was in San Francisco, you would not be justified in believing that he was still in Italy. But that fact by itself does not undermine your present knowledge that he is in Italy.

Suppose that as the political leader's associates are about to make their announcement, a saboteur cuts the wire leading to the television transmitter. The announcement is therefore heard only by those in the studio, all of whom are parties to the deception. Jill reads the real story in the newspaper as before. Now, she does come to know that the political leader has been assassinated. But if she had known that it had been announced that he was not assassinated, she would not have been justified in believing that he has, simply on the basis of the newspaper story. Here, a cut wire makes the difference between evidence that undermines knowledge and evidence that does not undermine knowledge.

We can know that $h$ even though there is evidence $e$ that we do not know about such that, if we did know about $e$, we would not be justified in believing $h$. If we know that $h$, it does not follow that we know that there is not any evidence like $e$. This can seem paradoxical, for it can seem obvious that, if we know that *h*, we know that any evidence against *h* can only be misleading. So, later if we get that evidence we ought to be able to know enough to disregard it.

A more explicit version of this interesting paradox goes like this. "If I know that *h* is true, I know that any evidence against *h* is evidence against something that is true; so I know that such evidence is misleading. But I should disregard evidence that I know is misleading. So, once I know that *h* is true, I am in a position to disregard any future evidence that seems to tell against *h*." This is paradoxical, because I am never in a position simply to disregard any future evidence even though I do know a great many different things.

A skeptic might appeal to this paradox in order to argue that, since we are never in a position to disregard any further evidence, we never know anything. Some philosophers would turn the argument around to say that, since we often know things, we are often in a position to disregard further evidence. But both of these responses go wrong in accepting the paradoxical argument in the first place.

I can know that Tom stole a book from the library without being able automatically to disregard evidence to the contrary. You can know that Donald is in Italy without having the right to ignore whatever further evidence may turn up. Jill may know that the political leader has been assassinated even though she would cease to know this if told that there was an announcement that only a secret service agent had been shot.

The argument for paradox overlooks the way actually having evidence can make a difference. Since I now know that Tom stole the book, I now know that any evidence that appears to indicate something else is misleading. That does not warrant me in simply disregarding any further evidence, since getting that further evidence can change what I know. In particular, after I get such further evidence I may no longer know that it is misleading. For having the new evidence can make it true that I no longer know that Tom stole the book; if I no longer know that, I no longer know that the new evidence is misleading.

Therefore, we cannot account for the problems posed by evidence one does not possess by appeal to the principle, which I now repeat:

> One knows only if there is no evidence such that if one knew about the evidence one would not be justified in believing one's conclusion.

For one can know even though such evidence exists.

## 3. A Result Concerning Inference

When does evidence one doesn't have keep one from having knowledge? I have described three cases, each in two versions, in which there is misleading evidence one does not possess. In the first version of each case the misleading evidence undermines someone's knowledge. In the second version it does not. What makes the difference?

My strategy is to account for Gettier examples by means of principle *P*. . . . I want to use the examples in order to learn something more about inference, in particular about what other conclusions are essential to the inference that Tom stole the book, that Donald is in Italy, or that the political leader has been assassinated.

It is not plausible that the relevant inferences should contain essential intermediate conclusions that refer explicitly to Tom's mother, to letters from San Francisco, or to special television programs. For it is very likely that there is an infinite number of ways a particular inference might be undermined by misleading evidence one does not possess. If there must be a separate essential conclusion ruling out each of these ways, inferences would have to be infinitely inclusive — and that is implausible.

Therefore it would seem that the relevant inferences must rule out undermining evidence one does not possess by means of a single conclusion, essential to the inference, that characterizes all such evidence. But how might this be done? It is not at all clear what distinguishes evidence that undermines knowledge from evidence that does not. How is my inference to involve an essential conclusion that rules out Tom's mother's testifying a certain way before a believing audience but does not rule out (simply) her testifying in that way? Or that rules out the existence of letters of a particular sort in the mail on your table but not simply the existence of those letters? Or that rules out a widely heard announcement of a certain sort without simply ruling out the announcement?

Since I am unable to formulate criteria that would distinguish among these cases, I will simply *label* cases of the first kind "undermining evidence one does not possess." Then we can say this: one knows only if there is no undermining evidence one does not possess. If there is such evidence, one does not know. However, these remarks are completely trivial.

It is somewhat less trivial to use the same label to formulate a principle concerned with inference.

Q  One may infer a conclusion only if one also infers that there is no undermining evidence one does not possess.

There is of course an obscurity in principle *Q*; but the principle is not as trivial as the remarks of the last paragraph, since the label "undermining evidence one does not possess" has been explained in terms of knowledge, whereas this is a principle concerning inference.

If we take principle *Q*, concerning inference, to be basic, we can use principle *P* to account for the differences between the two versions of each of the three examples described above. In each case an inference involves essentially the claim that there is no undermining evidence one does not possess. Since this claim is false in the first version of each case and true in the second, principle *P* implies that there can be knowledge only in the second version of each case.

So there is, according to my strategy, some reason to think that there is a principle concerning inference like principle *Q*. That raises the question of whether there is any independent reason to accept such a principle; and reflection on good scientific practice suggests a positive answer. It is a commonplace that a scientist should base his conclusions on all the evidence. Furthermore, he should not rest content with the evidence he happens to have but should try to make sure he is not overlooking any relevant evidence. A good scientist will not accept a conclusion unless he has some reason to think that there is no as yet undiscovered evidence which would undermine his conclusion. Otherwise he would not be warranted in making his inference. So good scientific practice reflects the acceptance of something like principle Q, which is the independent confirmation we wanted for the existence of this principle.

Notice that the scientist must accept something like principle Q, with its reference to "undermining evidence one does not possess." For example, he cannot accept the following principle,

> One may infer a conclusion only if one also infers that there is no evidence at all such that if he knew that evidence he could not accept his conclusion.

There will always be a true proposition such that if he learned that the proposition was true (and learned nothing else) he would not be warranted in accepting his conclusion. If *h* is his conclusion, and if *k* is a true proposition saying what ticket will win the grand prize in the next New Jersey State Lottery, then *either k or not h* is such a proposition. If he were to learn that it is true that *either k or not h* (and learned nothing else), *not h* would become probable since (given what he knows) *k* is antecedently very improbable. So he could no longer reasonably infer that *h* is true.

There must be a certain kind of evidence such that the scientist infers there is no as yet undiscovered evidence of that kind against *h*. Principle Q says that the relevant kind is what I have been labeling "undermining evidence one does not possess." Principle Q is confirmed by the fact that good scientific practice involves some such principle and by the fact that principle Q together with principle P accounts for the three Gettier examples I have been discussing.

## TEST YOUR UNDERSTANDING

1. Harman says that in his first example, he does not know that Tom stole the book. Does Harman think his lack of knowledge can be solely explained by principle *P*?

2. Does Harman think that you know a **proposition** p only if there is no evidence e such that if you knew e, you would not be justified in believing p?

## NOTES AND QUESTIONS

1. Harman tries to explain why there is no knowledge in his three examples by invoking principle *P* and principle *Q*. Explain and assess Harman's proposed explanation.

2.  Consider Alvin Goldman's Barn example (see the "Notes and Questions" to Gettier, "Is Justified True Belief Knowledge?"). Assume that (i) it is a case of justified true belief without knowledge, (ii) it is a case of *non-inferential belief* (that is, Henry does not believe that the object before him is a barn by **inference** from other things he believes). Given these assumptions, explain why Harman's theory fails to account for Henry's lack of knowledge. Suppose Harman replied by denying (ii). Is there another example with the same structure for which a similar reply is implausible?

## Linda Trinkaus Zagzebski (born 1946)

Zagzebski holds the Kingfisher College Chair of Philosophy of Religion and Ethics at the University of Oklahoma. She has made many contributions to epistemology and the philosophy of religion; her books include *Virtues of the Mind* (1996) and *Divine Motivation Theory* (2004).

# THE INESCAPABILITY OF GETTIER PROBLEMS

Gettier problems arise in the theory of knowledge when it is only by chance that a justified true belief is true. Since the belief might easily have been false in these cases, it is normally concluded that they are not instances of knowledge.[1] The moral drawn in the thirty years since Gettier published his famous paper is that either justified true belief (JTB) is not sufficient for knowledge, in which case knowledge must have an "extra" component in addition to JTB, or else justification must be reconceived to *make it* sufficient for knowledge. I shall argue that given the common and reasonable assumption that the relation between justification and truth is close but not inviolable, it is not possible for either move to avoid Gettier counter-examples. What is more, it makes no difference if the component of knowledge in addition to true belief is identified as something other than justification, e.g., warrant or well-foundedness. I conclude that Gettier problems are inescapable for virtually every analysis of knowledge which at least maintains that knowledge is true belief plus something else.

Notice first that Gettier problems arise for both internalist and externalist notions of justification. On internalist theories the grounds for justification are accessible to the consciousness of the believer, and Gettier problems arise when there is nothing wrong with the internally accessible aspects of the cognitive situation, but there is a mishap in something inaccessible to the believer. Since justification does not guarantee truth, it is possible for there to be a break in the connection between justification and truth, but for that connection to be regained by chance.

---

1.  See Edmund Gettier, "Is Justified True Belief Knowledge?," p. 108 of this chapter.

The original "Smith owns a Ford or Brown is in Barcelona" case is an example of this sort. Here we are to imagine that Smith comes to you bragging about his new Ford, shows you the car and the bill of sale, and generally gives you lots of evidence that he owns a Ford. Basing what you think on the evidence, you believe the proposition "Smith owns a Ford," and from that you infer its disjunction[2] with "Brown is in Barcelona," where Brown is an acquaintance and you have no reason at all to think he is in Barcelona. It turns out that Smith is lying and owns no Ford, but Brown is by chance in Barcelona. Your belief "Smith owns a Ford or Brown is in Barcelona" is true and justified, but it is hardly the case that you know it.

In this case the problem arises because in spite of the fact that you have done everything to reach the truth from your point of view and everything that anyone could expect of you, your efforts do not lead you to the truth. It is mere bad luck that you are the unwitting victim of Smith's lies, and only an accident that a procedure that usually leads you to the truth leads you to believe the falsehood "Smith owns a Ford." The fact that you end up with a true belief anyway is due to a second accidental feature of the situation — a feature that has nothing to do with your cognitive activity. What generates the problem for JTB, then, is that an accident of bad luck is cancelled out by an accident of good luck. The right goal is reached, but only by chance.

Internalist theories are not the only ones afflicted with Gettier problems, contrary to a recent claim made by Alvin Plantinga.[3] Consider how the problem arises for reliabilism. In this group of theories believers are justified when their beliefs are formed in a reliable, or truth-conducive, manner. On this account also there is no guarantee that justified beliefs are true, and a breakdown in the connection between a reliable belief-forming process and the truth is possible. When that happens, even if you manage to hit on the truth anyway, you do not have knowledge.

The well-known fake barn case[4] can be described as an example of this sort. Here we are to imagine that you are driving through a region in which, unknown to you, the inhabitants have erected three barn façades for each real barn in an effort to make themselves look more prosperous. Your eyesight is normal and reliable enough in ordinary circumstances to spot a barn from the road. But in this case the fake barns are indistinguishable from the real barns at such a distance. As you look at a real barn you form the belief "That's a fine barn." The belief is true and justified, but is not knowledge.

As in the first case, the problem arises because of the combination of two accidental features of the cognitive situation. It is only an accident that visual faculties normally reliable in this sort of situation are not reliable in this particular situation; and it is another accident that you happened to be looking at a real barn and hit on the truth anyway. Again the problem arises because an accident of bad luck is cancelled out by an accident of good luck.

Gettier problems cannot be avoided by Alvin Plantinga's new theory either. Plantinga calls the property that in sufficient quantity converts true belief into knowledge "warrant" rather than "justification." On his proposal warrant is the

---

2. The disjunction of two sentences "p" and "q" is the sentence "p or q."

3. Alvin Plantinga, *Warrant and Proper Function* (Oxford University Press, 1993), p. 48. [Zagzebski's note.]

4. See "Notes and Questions" to Gettier, "Is Justified True Belief Knowledge?," p. 111 of this chapter.

property a belief *B* has for believer *S* when *B* is produced in *S* by *S*'s faculties working properly in the appropriate environment, according to a design plan successfully aimed at truth. But Plantinga does not maintain that every warranted belief is true any more than reliabilists maintain that every reliably formed belief is true or internalists maintain that every internally justified belief is true. Let us see if we can form a Gettier case for Plantinga's theory parallel to the other two cases we have considered. To do so we need to look for a situation in which *S*'s faculties are working the way they were designed to in the appropriate environment, but *S* unluckily has a false belief. We can then add a second accident which makes the belief true after all.

Suppose that Mary has very good eyesight, but it is not perfect. It is good enough to allow her to identify her husband sitting in his usual chair in the living room from a distance of fifteen feet in somewhat dim light (the degree of dimness can easily be specified). She has made such an identification in these circumstances many times. Each time her faculties have been working properly and the environment has been appropriate for the faculties. There is nothing at all unusual about either her faculties or the environment in these cases. Her faculties may not be functioning perfectly, but they are functioning well enough, so that if she goes on to form the belief "My husband is sitting in the living room," that belief has enough warrant to constitute knowledge when true and we can assume that it is almost always true.

The belief is *almost* always true, we say. That is because warrant in the degree necessary for knowledge does not guarantee truth, according to Plantinga. If it *did* guarantee truth, of course, the component of truth in the analysis of knowledge would be superfluous. Knowledge would simply be warranted belief. So it is possible for Mary to make a mistake even though her faculties are functioning properly enough for knowledge and the environment is normal for the faculties. Let us look at one such case.

Suppose Mary simply misidentifies the chair-sitter who is, let us suppose, her husband's brother. Her faculties may be working as well as they normally do when the belief is true and when we do not hesitate to say it is warranted in a degree sufficient for knowledge. It is not a question of their suddenly becoming defective, or at any rate, more defective than usual, nor is there a mismatch between her faculties and the environment. No one is dressing up as her husband to fool her, or anything like that, so the environment is not abnormal as the fake barn case is abnormal. Her degree of warrant is as high as it usually is when she correctly identifies her husband since even in those cases it is true that she *might* have misidentified the chair-sitter if it had been her husband's brother instead. Of course, she usually has no reason to suspect that it *is* her husband's brother and we can imagine that she has no reason to suspect so in this case either. Maybe she knows that her husband's brother looks a lot like him, but she has no reason to believe that he is in the vicinity, and, in fact, has strong reason to believe he has gone to Australia. So in the case we are considering, when Mary forms the false belief, her belief is as warranted as her beliefs normally are in these circumstances. In spite of well-functioning faculties and a benign environment, she just makes a mistake.

Now, of course, *something* has gone wrong here, and that something is probably in Mary rather than in the environment. It may even be correct to say that there is a minor defect in her faculties; perhaps she is not perfectly attentive or she is a little too hasty in forming her belief. But she is no less attentive and no more hasty than she usually is in such cases and usually it does not matter. People do not have to be perfectly attentive and perfectly cautious and have perfect vision to have beliefs sufficiently warranted for knowledge on Plantinga's theory. And this is not a *mistake* in Plantinga's theory. It would surely be unreasonable of him to expect perfectly functioning faculties in a perfectly attuned environment as his criteria for the warrant needed for knowledge. So Mary's defect need not be sufficient to bring her degree of warrant down below that needed for knowledge on Plantinga's account.

We can now easily emend the case as a Gettier example. Mary's husband could be sitting on the other side of the room, unseen by her. In that case her belief "My husband is sitting in the living room" is true and has sufficient warrant for knowledge on Plantinga's account, but she does not have knowledge. . . .

The three examples we have considered suggest a general rule for the generation of Gettier cases. It really does not matter how the *particular* element of knowledge in addition to true belief is analyzed. As long as there is a small degree of independence between this other element and the truth, we can construct Gettier cases by using the following procedure: start with a case of justified (or warranted) false belief. Make the element of justification (warrant) strong enough for knowledge, but make the belief false. The falsity of the belief will not be due to any systematically describable element in the situation, for if it were, such a feature could be used in the analysis of the components of knowledge other than true belief, and then truth would be entailed by the other components of knowledge, contrary to the hypothesis. The falsity of the belief is therefore due to some element of luck. Now emend the case by adding another element of luck, only this time an element which makes the belief true after all. The second element must be independent of the element of warrant so that the degree of warrant is unchanged. The situation might be described as one element of luck counteracting another. We now have a case in which the belief is justified (warranted) in a sense strong enough for knowledge, the belief is true, but it is not knowledge. The conclusion is that as long as the concept of knowledge closely connects the justification component and the truth component, but permits *some* degree of independence between them, justified true belief will never be sufficient for knowledge. . . .

It appears, then, that no account of knowledge as true belief plus something else can withstand Gettier objections as long as there is a small degree of independence between truth and the other conditions of knowledge. What are our alternatives? . . . [O]ne way to solve the problem is to give up the independence between the justification condition and the truth condition. Justification would be defined in such a way that no false belief can satisfy it. Since Gettier cases are based on situations in which the belief is true, but it might just as well have been false, all such cases would be excluded from the class of justified (warranted) beliefs. On this approach the element of truth in the account of knowledge is superfluous and knowledge is simply justified (warranted) belief. "S is justified in believing *p*" entails *p*. Few philosophers have supported this view.

So Gettier problems can be avoided if there is no degree of independence at all between truth and justification. A second way to avoid them is to go to the opposite extreme and to make the justification condition and the truth condition almost completely independent. It could still be the case that justification puts the subject in the best position available for getting the truth, but if the best position is not very good, most justified beliefs will be false. Perhaps most justified scientific hypotheses since the world began have been false. Perhaps Plato, Spinoza, Kant and Hegel were justified in believing their metaphysical theories, but most of their theories (at least) were false.[5] Still, if one of them is true, some theorists might be willing to call it knowledge. On this approach the element of luck permitted in the state of knowledge is so great that alleged counter-examples based on luck do not count against it. From this viewpoint, Gettier cases would simply be accepted as cases of knowledge. After all, if knowledge is mostly luck anyway, there will be nothing bothersome about a case in which the truth is acquired by luck.

Perhaps neither of these alternatives will appeal to most philosophers, who find the idea that there is a small but real degree of independence between justification and the acquisition of truth just too attractive to give up. A third reaction to the problem, then, is to accept the fact that no "true belief + x" account of knowledge will be sufficient, but that it will always be necessary to add the element of luck to the analysis. So knowledge is true belief + x + luck. This approach recognizes the fact that the concept we substitute for "x" ought to be one that has a strong general connection with the acquisition of truth, but that an inviolable connection would be unreasonable. On the other hand, it also recognizes the fact that we are much less forgiving with the concept of knowledge itself. The connection between justification or whatever it is we substitute for "x" and truth must exist in each and every particular case of knowledge. The notion of knowledge requires success, both in reaching the goal of truth, and in reaching it via the right cognitive path. The notion of justification or warrant is less stringent, requiring only that the right path is one that is *usually* successful at getting the truth. It is this difference between the notion of knowledge and the notion of justification that is responsible for Gettier problems.

Almost every contemporary theory of justification or warrant aims only to give the conditions for putting the believer in the best position for getting the truth. The best position is assumed to be very good, but imperfect, for such is life. Properly functioning faculties need not be working perfectly, but only well enough; reliable belief-producing mechanisms need not be perfectly reliable, only reliable enough; evidence for a belief need not support it conclusively, but only well enough; and so on. As long as the truth is never assured by the conditions which make the state justified, there will be situations in which a false belief is justified. I have argued that with this common, in fact, almost universal assumption, Gettier cases will never go away.

---

5. The Greek philosopher Plato (429–347 BCE), the Dutch philosopher Baruch Spinoza (1632–1677), the German philosopher Immanuel Kant (1724–1804), and the German philosopher Georg Wilhelm Friedrich Hegel (1770–1831) each had striking and controversial views about the nature of reality.

## TEST YOUR UNDERSTANDING

1. In Gettier's original cases, Zagzebski says, "an accident of bad luck is cancelled out by an accident of good luck." Explain what she means.

2. Does Plantinga think that knowledge is warranted belief?

3. Zagzebski gives a general recipe for the "generation of Gettier cases." Explain this recipe in your own words.

## NOTES AND QUESTIONS

1. What is Plantinga's analysis of knowledge? Does the analysis (or some elaboration of it) correctly predict that Gettier's original examples are not cases of knowledge? Explain and assess Zagzebski's alleged counterexample to Plantinga's analysis. If the counterexample works, can the theory be repaired to avoid it?

2. For an exhaustive survey of various attempts to analyze knowledge see Jonathan Jenkins Ichikawa and Matthias Steup, "The Analysis of Knowledge," *Stanford Encyclopedia of Philosophy*, ed. Edward Zalta (http://plato.stanford.edu/archives/fall2013/entries/knowledge-analysis/).

## Timothy Williamson (born 1958)

Williamson is Wykeham Professor of Logic at the University of Oxford, and is known for bringing formal methods to bear on traditional philosophical problems. He is the author of many influential books and papers, including *Vagueness* (1994), *Knowledge and Its Limits* (2000), *The Philosophy of Philosophy* (2007), and *Modal Logic as Metaphysics* (2013).

# KNOWLEDGE AND BELIEF

The most striking difference between knowledge and belief is that although there is false belief there cannot be false knowledge. People once believed that the Earth was flat. They believed falsely, because the Earth was not flat. They did not *know* that the Earth was flat, because knowing that the Earth was flat would have required the Earth to be flat. They *believed* that they knew that the Earth was flat, but that was another of their false beliefs.

We can make the same point about a disagreement without even taking sides. Suppose that Mary believes that there is life on other planets while John believes that there is no life on other planets. We do not know which of them is right, but we know that there are only two possibilities. Either there *is* life on other planets, in which case Mary believes truly while John believes falsely, so John has belief without knowledge, or there is *no* life on other planets, in which case Mary believes falsely while John believes truly, so Mary has belief without knowledge. Either way, one of them falsely believes that something is the case without knowing that it is the case, even if we cannot tell which of them it is.

Belief does not imply knowledge. What about the other way round: does knowledge imply belief? It seems obvious that you could not know that the Earth is round without believing that the Earth is round. However, there are some tricky cases. Suppose that many years ago Kerry read a good history of China, but has forgotten all about doing so. Now she enters a quiz. Some of the questions turn out to be on Chinese history, of which Kerry believes herself to be totally ignorant. Nevertheless, answers pop into her head. She regards them as random guesses, but nevertheless tries them out, since she has nothing better. They are all correct. In fact, her answers were caused by memory traces derived from the book. One hypothesis is that Kerry unconsciously knows those truths about Chinese history, because she remembers them, although she does not believe them. If so, knowledge does not imply belief. But that hypothesis has problems. Consider Terry, who also read a history of China many years ago and has forgotten all about doing so. When Terry enters the quiz, answers about Chinese history pop into his head too, and he tries them out too, for want of anything better, despite regarding them as random guesses. In fact, Terry's answers too are caused by memory traces derived from a book. However, all Terry's answers are wrong, because his book was a bad one, full of mistakes. The hypothesis that Terry unconsciously knows those falsehoods about Chinese history does not work, since false knowledge is impossible. If Kerry unconsciously knows the right answers, Terry unconsciously *believes* the wrong answers. But then, since Kerry is no less sincere than Terry, Kerry also unconsciously believes the right answers. Thus Kerry is not a convincing example of knowledge without belief. She may instead be an example of unconscious knowledge and belief without conscious knowledge or belief. That knowledge implies belief is a good working hypothesis.

The upshot so far is that knowledge implies true belief. But true belief does not imply knowledge. If Larry believes that the name of the capital of California starts with "S," he believes truly, since the capital is Sacramento. But if that belief rests only on his irrational belief that the capital is San Francisco, Larry does not *know* that the name of the capital begins with "S." Similarly, although either John or Mary has a true belief as to whether there is life on other planets, perhaps neither of them *knows* whether there is life on other planets, because neither of them has sufficient evidence for their belief.

Many philosophers have reacted to such examples by asking: what must be added to true belief to get knowledge? At one time a popular answer was: justification, in the sense of blameless belief. The idea was that Larry's true belief that the name of the capital begins with "S" does not amount to knowledge because he deserves blame for irrationally believing that the name of the capital begins with "S"; his belief, although it happens to be true, is not justified. However, we can imagine a slightly different story, in which Barry is the victim of a massive hoax, so that he has strong misleading evidence that San Francisco is the capital. For example, that is what his high school teacher tells the class, everyone whom he asks confirms that it is, his classmates hack into his computer so that he cannot access websites that say differently, and so on. Barry's beliefs that San Francisco is the capital and that the name of the capital begins with "S" *are* blameless, and in that sense justified. Thus Barry has a justified true belief that the name of the capital begins with "S," but he still does not *know* that the name of the capital begins with "S." For he does not know that San Francisco is the capital, since that is false, and beliefs based on ignorance do not constitute knowledge. In a famous article, "Is Justified True Belief Knowledge?," the philosopher Edmund Gettier used such examples to make just this point, that justified true belief is not always knowledge.

Gettier's 1963 article acted as a challenge to philosophers to find the "missing ingredient" that added to true belief would make knowledge. Many proposals have their supporters, but in each case they are greatly outnumbered by opponents. In effect, the aim is to find a solution to the equation:

$$\text{knowledge} = \text{true belief} + \text{X}$$

Typically, when someone proposes such an X, other philosophers soon find examples of knowledge without true belief + X, or of true belief + X without knowledge, either of which suffices to refute the equation. Although no argument refutes all such proposals at one shot, their track record looks increasingly poor. Rather than examine in detail various attempts to solve the equation, let us take a step back and consider the presupposition that it has a solution.

An analogy: Crimson is a specific type of red. Just as all knowledge is true belief but not all true belief is knowledge, so all crimson is red but not all red is crimson. Now consider the equation:

$$\text{crimson} = \text{red} + \text{Y}$$

We have no reason to expect this equation to have a useful solution. It asks for a property Y such that the crimson things are exactly those red things that have Y. The only natural suggestion is: Y = crimson. Crimson is indeed equivalent to red that is crimson, but as an account of crimson that is blatantly circular (all it tells us is that crimson implies red). Similarly, knowledge is indeed equivalent to true belief that is knowledge, but as an account of knowledge that is blatantly circular (all it tells us is that knowledge implies true belief). The attempt to analyse crimson as red plus other elements is wrongheaded. Why should the attempt to analyse knowledge as true belief plus other elements do better? Why should we try to explain knowledge in terms of belief rather than belief in terms of knowledge? What should we take as our starting point? In philosophy, as in the rest of life, where you start makes a big difference to where you end up.

There are specific reasons why philosophers have regarded belief as "simpler" or "more basic" than knowledge, and therefore as a better starting-point for explanation. One reason is that, until recently, the dominant conception of mind was an *internalist* one. According to internalism, what mental states you are in is completely determined by what is going on internally to you, which for present purposes we can understand as: inside your head. Although an event outside your head can *cause* you to be in a specific mental state, as when a glass breaking causes you to have a corresponding experience, it does so by causing other events to occur in your head, and internalists say that the events in your head completely determine that you are having the experience, irrespective of what is going on outside your head. For them, any difference between two situations in your mental state implies a difference in what is going on in your head. Belief seems to fit this account much better than knowledge does. In one situation, a pilot knows that he is flying above the Atlantic. In another situation, without realizing it the pilot was put in a perfect flight simulator back at the airport and falsely believes that he is flying above the Atlantic; therefore the pilot does not know that he is flying above the Atlantic. Thus the two situations differ in what the pilot knows. They do not seem to differ in what he believes. In both situations, he *believes* that he is flying above the Atlantic. By hypothesis, what is going on in the pilot's head is also the same in the two situations, in the sense that exactly the same microscopic descriptions apply. Consequently, his knowledge violates the internalist principle "No difference in mental state without a difference in the head," while his belief seems not to. The internalist diagnosis is that knowledge, unlike belief, is not a "pure" mental state. Rather, for internalists, knowing that one is flying above the Atlantic is a *mixture* of mental states such as believing that one is flying above the Atlantic with non-mental conditions, typically on the external environment, such as that one really is flying above the Atlantic. On that view, it is very natural to try to analyse knowledge into components such as belief and truth and perverse to try to analyse belief into components such as knowledge.

However, further reflection suggests that not even belief really fits the internalist model. Imagine a third situation, a perfect duplicate of the first except for being on a different planet, exactly like Earth but billions of miles from it. The Atlantic is not on that other planet — it is on Earth. Rather, the people on that planet have another ocean exactly like the Atlantic. They even spell its name "Atlantic," but that is *their* name for it. When *we* use the name "Atlantic," we refer to the ocean on Earth, not to the one on the other planet. Does the extraterrestrial pilot believe that he is flying above the Atlantic? If so, his belief is false, because he is not flying above the Atlantic; he is flying above another ocean billions of miles from the Atlantic. But he is no more mistaken about his position by billions of miles than the terrestrial pilot is (the one who really is flying above the Atlantic). Both of them know where they are. Thus the extraterrestrial pilot does *not* believe that he is flying above the Atlantic. In fact, neither pilot has any beliefs about the other's ocean at all, because he has no idea that there is any such ocean. Thus they differ in their beliefs, even though what is going on in their heads is exactly similar. More specifically, they differ in the *content* of their beliefs: the content of the terrestrial pilot's belief is that he is flying the Atlantic; the extraterrestrial pilot also has a belief, but its content is different, because it is about a different ocean. More generally, the contents of mental states are *world-involving* in the sense that they essentially involve relations to things out there in the world, such as oceans.

Far from being "impurities," relations to the external environment are the point of the mental. With minds, we can get what we need by adjusting our behaviour to what we know of a complex, changing environment. We perceive our surroundings and intentionally act on them. Thinking mediates between perception and action. Emotions too involve relations to the external environment. To treat the person whom you love or hate as inessential to your emotion is to forget that love and hate are essentially relations, not undirected qualities of feeling. Since mental states have this sort of world-involving function, no wonder they have world-involving contents. To abstract away from relations to the world in search of pure mind is like peeling layer after layer away in search of pure onion.

Belief is world-involving in its content. Knowledge is world-involving not only in its content but also in the way in which the knower is related to that content. Whether the pilot knows or merely believes that he is flying above the Atlantic depends in part on whether he *is* flying above the Atlantic. Given what was just said about the nature of mind, this extra dimension of world-involvingness in knowledge may make it more central to mind than belief is, not less.

When things go as they should with our cognitive faculties, such as perception and memory, we get knowledge. When something goes wrong, we get mere belief. "Knowledge" is a success term; "belief" is neutral between success and failure. The relation between believing and knowing resembles that between trying to be something and being it by intention. If you believe that you are popular, you may or may not *be* popular. Similarly, if you try to be popular, you may or may not *be* popular. But if you know that you are popular, you *are* popular. Similarly, if you are popular by intention, you *are* popular. Cases in which you believe truly that you are popular without knowing that you are popular correspond to cases in which you try to be popular and are popular, but not by intention — for example, you may be popular *despite* your embarrassing attempts to be popular. Just as it would be perverse to investigate the phenomenon of trying to be something without special reference to the phenomenon of being something by intention (the case when action goes well), so it is perverse to investigate the phenomenon of believing something without special reference to the phenomenon of knowing something (the case when cognition goes well). Malfunctioning must be understood in relation to good functioning. Misremembering must be understood in relation to remembering, misperceiving in relation to perceiving, and so on. All this suggests a knowledge-first methodology.

Defenders of a belief-first methodology may reply that once we start giving detailed causal explanations, success terms like "knowledge" are no longer useful, because they are irrelevant to a step-by-step analysis of a causal process. In explaining how an automobile engine works, at some point you have to specify the actual physical processes involved, and their effects do not depend on whether they are classified as functioning or malfunctioning. Similarly, they say, whether you drink from the glass does not depend on whether you *know* that it contains water; you will drink from it as long as you *believe* that it contains water (and desire water), whether or not your belief constitutes knowledge or is true. However, this simple picture faces several problems.

First, explanations of action in terms of mental states typically involve a time lag between the mental states and the completion of the action, during which feedback can occur. For example, a reporter decides to interview a politician involved in a scandal; she drives to his house and knocks on the door. The mental states "immediately behind" an action at a given instant, such as moving her hand a fraction closer to the door, are typically just those concerned with the execution of that stage of the action plan.

The connection with the original reasoning that gave the action its point — "I want more embarrassing details for this story, and he can supply them, so I'll interview him" — is less direct. Once you have worked out an action plan, you need not keep referring back to the reasons for adopting it in the first place. When we seek to explain human action, our aim is typically to understand it in terms of the earlier reasoning that gave the action its point, so there is a time lag between the reasoning and the completion of the action. That allows for the difference between knowledge and mere belief to make a causal difference to whether the action is completed. For example, how the reporter reacts if her knock at the door is not answered may depend on whether she started with knowledge or mere true belief that the politician was at home. If she knew he was at home, she is likely to be more persistent, and so more likely to get the interview. If she merely had a true belief, she is likely to give up more easily.

Second, what *reasons* are available to you to act on depends on what you know, not on what you believe. If you know that the glass contains water, you may drink from it *because it contains water*. Your knowledge makes the fact that the glass contains water available to you as a reason to act on. If you believed falsely that the glass contained water, my explanation "You drank from the glass because it contained water" is automatically false. In cases of mere belief, we might say "You drank from the glass because *you believed that* it contained water." However, such a fact about your beliefs is not normally a reason on which you act, in the way in which you act on the fact that the glass contains water when you know. For the premise of your reasoning is normally something like "The glass contains water," not "I believe that the glass contains water." You are thirsty, so you think about the water, not about your beliefs. Moreover, the fact that *you believed that* the glass contained water is not what made drinking from it a good thing to do; what made it a good thing to do is the fact that the glass *did* contain water. Water quenches thirst; beliefs do not. A reason for drinking from the glass is a fact that makes drinking from it a good thing to do. But to act on a fact you must be aware of that fact, which is to know the fact. You need knowledge; not even blameless true belief is enough. For example, if your blameless true belief that the glass contained water were based on your blameless false belief that you could see the water, when it was a trick opaque glass with water in it, the fact that the glass contained water would be outside your awareness, since you lacked knowledge. Thus in order to act on a reason, you must *know* the fact that is the reason. For acting on reasons, what matters is knowledge, not belief.

But then how are we to explain the actions of the agent who has mere belief? The agent who merely believes acts *as if* on known facts. They are in a state that resembles knowledge in its immediate effect on action. If you did not know that the glass contained water, you were not in a position to act on the fact that it contained water (even if there was such a fact), but you could act as if on the fact that it contained water, if you believed that it contained water. Thus the central case is reason-giving explanation, in which we explain why an agent did something by citing facts known to the agent that made it a good thing to do, but the central case is surrounded by a mass of somewhat similar cases that deviate from it more or less because things went more or less wrong, in one way or another. That the agent has mere belief rather than knowledge is one common deviation. Another is that the agent merely tried to do something, but did not succeed. These defective cases do not fit the original pattern, but we can nevertheless understand them as deviations from it.

Mere belief is to be understood as a deviation from knowledge. To believe is to be in a mental state similar to knowing in its immediate effects on action, but which differs from knowing in other respects. To work with such an account is to understand belief in terms of knowledge, rather than knowledge in terms of belief.

Mental life is a bewildering complex of interacting processes. The key to understanding the nature of these processes is to focus on what happens when things go right. For that, we need the notions of knowing and doing. Having seen the point of these processes, we must then go on to understand all the ways in which things can go more or less wrong. For that, we need the notions of believing and trying.[1]

## TEST YOUR UNDERSTANDING

1. Williamson claims that there is no reason to suppose that the equation "crimson = red + Y" has "a useful solution." What does he mean? What is this analogy supposed to show?

2. Does Williamson endorse an "internalist" conception of mind?

## NOTES AND QUESTIONS

1. Consider the following principle:

    *Knowledge-Internalism*: Necessarily, if the brains of two people, S and S*, are internally exactly the same (i.e., same neurons, connected in the same way, firing in the same pattern, etc.) then if S knows P so does S*.

    Explain how Williamson's first example of the two pilots shows that Knowledge-Internalism is false.

2. Consider a similar principle for belief:

    *Belief-Internalism*: Necessarily, if the brains of two people, S and S*, are internally exactly the same (i.e., same neurons, connected in the same way, firing in the same pattern, etc.) then if S believes P so does S*.

    Williamson's second pilot example is supposed to show that Belief-Internalism is false. How? Is this argument just as convincing as the one against Knowledge-Internalism?

3. Williamson discusses a potential counterexample to the claim that knowledge requires believing. How does he respond to this counterexample? Is his response convincing?

4. For more on Williamson's "knowledge-first" approach, see chapter 1 of *Contemporary Debates in Epistemology*, ed. M. Steup, J. Turri, and E. Sosa (Wiley-Blackwell, 2013).

---

1. The knowledge-first approach advocated in this essay is developed at greater length in Timothy Williamson, *Knowledge and its Limits* (Oxford University Press, 2000). [Williamson's note.]

## ANALYZING THE ARGUMENTS

1. Knowing that this is the road to Larissa is better, somehow, than not knowing but truly believing that this is the road to Larissa. Why? Does Williamson's discussion of the connections between knowledge, action, and reason help to suggest an answer? Is knowledge also better than not knowing but truly believing on the basis of excellent evidence that this is the road to Larissa?

2. Consider the following *simple causal analysis* of knowledge:

   S knows p **iff** (*i*) p is true, and (*ii*) p causes S to believe p.

   For example, suppose you look out of the window. It's raining, and this fact causes you to believe that it's raining—you believe that it's raining because it's raining. So, according to the simple causal analysis, you know that it's raining, which seems to be the right result. Does the simple causal analysis correctly predict that Gettier's original examples are not cases of knowledge? Give some convincing objections to the simple causal analysis. *Hint:* A case described in the "Notes and Questions" to Gettier's paper is a counterexample.

3. Often, if someone knows p, they can give reasons or evidence in support of p. For instance: "Bob's office light is on and he said he was coming into work today; that's my reason for believing that he's in his office." That might suggest that a **necessary condition** for knowing p is being able to give reasons or evidence in support of p. Give some examples to show that this suggestion is implausible. (You may find it helpful to look at the discussion of "properly basic beliefs" in the introduction to chapter 2, "Is It Reasonable to Believe without Evidence?")

4. Consider the following analysis of knowledge (simplified from Robert Nozick, *Philosophical Explanations*, Oxford University Press, 1981, chapter 3):

   S knows p **iff** (*i*) p is true, (*ii*) S believes p, and (*iii*) if p had been false S wouldn't have believed p.

   Explain why this analysis seems to get the right result in Gettier's two cases.

5. Saul Kripke objected to Nozick's analysis as follows (using the example given in the "Notes and Questions" to Gettier's paper):

   > [Consider] Henry and the barn. Suppose . . . there is a real barn in the field Henry looks at, while unbeknownst to Henry counterfeit barns abound in the area, and but for the building of this real barn a counterfeit would surely have been built in its place. Henry naively judges that there is a real barn in the field, but the third condition is not satisfied (though the others are); had there been no genuine barn there, the counterfeit there in its place would have taken Henry in. So, according to Nozick's theory, Henry does not know that there is a barn in the field.
   >
   > So far so good, but now let us suppose that the barn is red. Suppose further that any counterfeit erected in its place would have been green. (We can suppose, if we wish, that for some chemical reason the cardboard in the counterfeit barns cannot be painted red. Alternatively, those who erected counterfeit barns definitely preferred green ones, or even definitely preferred a green one in this

particular location.) Now consider Henry's true belief (thus satisfying the first two conditions) that there is a (genuine) red barn in the field. Now the third condition is satisfied. If there had not been a red barn in the field, then there would have been a green counterfeit, and Henry would not have believed that there was a red barn in the field. . . .[1]

How do you think Kripke's objection continues? *Hint:* The objection is related to the following plausible "closure" principle: if p entails q, and you know p, then you are in a position to know q. (Gettier appeals to a similar principle for justification in "Is Justified True Belief Knowledge?")

6. Can the barn example be modified so that Nozick's theory wrongly predicts that Henry does know that there is a barn in the field? *Hint:* The counterfeit barns are made of papier-mâché, and (let's suppose) cannot be erected in fields that are especially boggy.

1. Saul Kripke, *Philosophical Troubles* (Oxford University Press, 2011), pp. 185–86.

# 4

# How Can We Know about What We Have Not Observed?

You're reading a book and it's getting dark, so you flip the switch and the lights come on. This sudden illumination does not surprise you. You knew in advance that the lights would come on when you flipped the switch.

How did you know this? You did not know it **a priori**, independently of experience, in the way you know the truths of mathematics.[1] Someone who had never seen a light switch or anything like it could not possibly have known what would happen when you flipped the switch. So your knowledge in this case must be **empirical**: it must somehow derive from your experience.

This is obvious, but it is also puzzling. After all, your knowledge that the lights would come on was knowledge of the *future*. It concerned an event—the illumination of the room—that you had not yet experienced. But how can experience provide us with information about the future? This is a special case of a more general problem. Experience by itself provides us with knowledge of the present. In conjunction with memory it provides us with knowledge of the past, or more precisely, with those aspects of the past that we happen to have observed. This does not include the future, obviously. But it also does not include those aspects of the past and present that we have not managed to inspect. *And yet we know a great deal about these things.* You know that there are people in Siberia right now, that the book in front of you will not explode when you turn the page, that dinosaurs once roamed the Earth, and so on. All of this knowledge must be grounded

---

1. Sensory experience is certainly *useful* in mathematics. When you add up a column of numbers with pencil and paper, your knowledge of the conclusion is based in part on your visual experience of the figures you've written down. But this sort of experience is not strictly necessary: you could, in principle, perform the calculations "in your head." If this is true in general, it shows that while much of our mathematical knowledge may be empirical, the truths of mathematics are nonetheless *knowable* a priori.

in experience. But it is not the *direct* upshot of experience. And that sets our question: How can experience provide us with knowledge of things we have not experienced?

# The Problem of Induction

Before we try to answer the question, we need to clarify it. We have framed the question as a question about knowledge. But as we will see as the discussion unfolds, there is a powerful tendency to back off from claims to "knowledge" when one is pressed—to say, "OK, fine. Maybe I don't really *know* anything about the future." So it is important to emphasize that the problem is not really a problem about knowledge or certainty. The crucial starting point is the observation that our beliefs about the unobserved are not all on a par. If you believe that tomorrow's lottery numbers will be 4, 8, 15, 16, 23, and 34 because these numbers came to you in a dream, your belief may be real enough, but it is *totally unwarranted*. (Even if it's true, it's just a lucky guess.) Your belief that the sun will rise tomorrow, or the scientist's belief that there will be a solar eclipse on April 30, 2041, is very different: these beliefs are **justified**. They may even amount to knowledge when all goes well. Now when we ask how experience can provide us with "knowledge" of the unobserved, we are asking an epistemological question that is best put as follows: How can experience *justify* beliefs about things we have not seen? How can our observations make it *rational* for us to form beliefs about the unobserved? This is the most general statement of the **problem of induction.**

# Enumerative Induction

Let's consider what ought to be a simple case. You've been sent to an uncharted planet to investigate the wildlife. You step out of your spaceship and before long you spot a bright blue beast in the middle distance. Careful scientist that you are, you write this down:

*Saw an animal. It was blue.*

Your turn over a rock and find a bluish worm, so you write:

*Animal 2. Also blue.*

This continues:

*Animal 163. Blue.*
*Animal 164. Blue again.*

So far this is just a record of your observations, and if you are cautious, you will stick with claims of this sort for some time. But eventually, when you have collected many observations, you will make a leap:

*Therefore, the next animal I encounter will be blue.*

In fact you may infer a stronger claim:

*Therefore all (or most) of the animals on this planet are blue.*

At this point you have relied on your experience as a source of information about the unobserved.

The general form of this transition seems to be this:

Premise:          In a large sample, all observed *F*s are *G*.
Conclusion:    Therefore all *F*s are *G* (or at least, the next *F* we encounter will be *G*).

This form of argument is sometimes called **enumerative induction**. There is little doubt that we often seem to reason in this way. More importantly, we think that reasoning in this way is often justified. Enumerative induction is not just something that we quirky human beings happen to do: it is a rational procedure, or so we think. So this is a preliminary solution to our problem: experience justifies beliefs about the unobserved when those beliefs are supported by enumerative induction.

# Hume's Problem

This brings us to the first great puzzle in the theory of inductive reasoning. Begin by noting that the inference from

In a large sample, all observed *F*s are *G*.

to

All *F*s are *G*.

is patently **invalid**: the premise does not guarantee the truth of the conclusion. No matter how many blue animals you have inspected, there is no contradiction in supposing that the animals you have *not* inspected are all pink, or purple, or some random hodgepodge of colors. But how can an invalid argument justify its conclusion? If there is nothing more to inductive reasoning, it seems bogus.

Of course we can turn these inductive arguments into valid deductive arguments by supplying a missing premise:

UN:                    If all observed *F*s are *G*, then all *F*s are *G*.

Following John Stuart Mill, this is sometimes called the principle of the **uniformity of nature** (see Mill, *A System of Logic*, book 2, chapter 3). You may never have formulated it explicitly. But it would seem that whenever you go in for a bit of inductive reasoning, you take this principle or something like it for granted.

If we include UN as a premise, your inductive inferences will be valid.

Data:            All observed *F*s are *G*.
UN:              If all observed *F*s are *G*, then all *F*s are *G*.
Generalization:  Therefore all *F*s are *G*.

But note: if *this* is the general form of inductive reasoning, our conclusions are justified only if we are justified in accepting UN. (This is an instance of a general rule: An argument justifies its conclusion only if the premises of the argument are independently justified.) And there's the rub. A famous argument due to David Hume appears to show that however natural this assumption may be, we can have no rational justification whatsoever for believing it.

Note first that UN is not a **necessary truth**. We can easily imagine situations in which it is false — situations in which your experience is not a representative sample of the rest of nature. From this it follows, Hume thinks, that UN cannot be justified a priori, since a priori reasoning can only disclose necessary truths like the truths of mathematics.

Note second that UN is itself a claim about the unobserved. It says that the unobserved things resemble the observed things in certain ways. And this means that UN cannot be justified directly by experience. We cannot *see* that things we have not seen resemble the things we have seen.

Note third that UN cannot possibly be justified by induction. If UN is a *premise* in every inductive argument, then any attempt to support UN by induction will be circular.

But these are the only ways to justify a belief, Hume thinks. And if that is so, it follows immediately that *UN cannot be justified*. We accept this principle instinctively, and thank goodness we do: we would be paralyzed without it. Unfortunately, we have no reason to believe that it is true.

Let us be perfectly clear about what is at stake here. Science and common sense would be useless if they did not supply us with information about the unobserved. But all of our reasoning about the unobserved appears to presuppose UN or something like it. So if this presupposition cannot be justified, our scientific and commonsensical beliefs about the unobserved are totally unwarranted. It is not just that we cannot be *certain* about these things. If Hume's argument is sound, we have *no reason whatsoever* to believe that the sun will rise tomorrow, or that the lights will come on when we flip the switch, or that smoking causes cancer, because every argument for these conclusions involves a premise that we have no reason to accept. This result is absurd, so there must be some mistake in Hume's argument. The challenge is to find it.

# Responses

The most straightforward response would be to provide an explicit justification for UN. You should try this. It is a profoundly instructive exercise. However, most modern philosophers take another tack. We were led to posit UN when we noticed that without it, our inductive inferences would be invalid. But why is that a problem? Valid inferences are infallible; when the premises are true, the conclusion *must* be true. But why shouldn't there be *good* inferences — inferences that justify their conclusions — that are also fallible? Consider the scientist who has examined thousands of animals on that distant planet and found every one of them to be blue. The evidence does not *guarantee* that the next animal she encounters will be blue. But surely the evidence *all by itself* makes it reasonable for her to believe this proposition. An inference of this sort — deductively invalid but cogent nonetheless — is called a **non-demonstrative inference.** If there can be cogent non-demonstrative inferences, Hume's problem as we have framed it disappears.

If we take this approach, we immediately face two problems. The first is to provide some explicit rules for distinguishing the good non-demonstrative arguments from the bad ones. There are plenty of bad arguments that fit the crude form given above, e.g.,

*So far, I have not died.*
*Therefore I will never die.*

So we need a better account of what distinguishes the good inductive arguments from the rest. But even if we had a formal test for sorting the inductive arguments into two categories — "good" and "bad" — there would still be a further question: Why is it *rational* to believe the conclusion of the "good" arguments, given that it is always perfectly possible for the premises to be true and the conclusion false?

P. F. Strawson argues that there are many forms of cogent inductive reasoning, and that there need be no simple account of what they all have in common. We as a society (or as a species) have adopted rules for reasoning: standards we bring to bear whenever we say that so-and-so is being unreasonable (superstitious, biased, incautious, insane). We cannot easily articulate those rules. We have mastered them implicitly, in much the same sense in which we have mastered the grammatical rules of English. It would be useful to make those standards explicit if we can. But even before we have done this, we can bring our tacit mastery of these rules to bear in order to judge whether an argument conforms to them. Now suppose we ask the larger question: "How do we know that our standards for assessing inductive arguments are the *right* ones? How do we know that an argument that is *cogent-by-our-standards* is really *cogent*?" According to Strawson, this is a silly question. To be a cogent argument—an argument that justifies its conclusion—*just is* to be an argument that meets our standards for cogency. There is no higher standard against which our shared standards might be measured.

# The New Riddle of Induction

It is natural to assume that inductive reasoning must be governed by formal rules, analogous to the formal rules that govern deductive reasoning. In 1947 Nelson Goodman *proved* that this is not so. Real proofs are rare in philosophy, so this is a remarkable achievement. Goodman's paper shows that *for every good inductive argument, there is a bad inductive argument with exactly the same form.* Deduction is not like this. In many cases a valid deductive argument will have a form every instance of which is valid. For example,

> All cats are animals.
> Fred is a cat.
> Therefore Fred is an animal.

is of the valid form

> All $F$s are $G$.
> $X$ is $F$.
> Therefore $X$ is $G$.

But now suppose we are given a cogent inductive argument, say:

> In a large sample, every emerald we have examined has been green.
> Therefore the next emerald we examine will be green.

We can extract a form from the argument by replacing the special-purpose words like "emerald" with schematic letters.

> In a large sample, every $F$ is $G$.
> Therefore the next $F$ will be $G$.

Goodman's argument shows that whenever we do this, there will always be instances of resulting schema that are *clearly* no good.

Goodman's argument has a striking implication. You might have thought that it should be possible in principle to program a computer to reason inductively: to take the data derived from observation as input and spit out the conclusions that are supported by that data. Goodman—writing in 1947—does not mention computers. But his result entails that there is no general-purpose algorithm that will do this. Any mechanical system that learns from experience, as many now do, must include not just a formal rule, but also some sort of *substantive constraint* on the language in which the data is represented—in effect, a constraint on what sorts of *words* can be substituted for *F* and *G* in the formal schema above. The *new* riddle of induction is the problem of explaining how this line is to be drawn.

# Induction and Inference to the Best Explanation

It is an established scientific fact that the diversity of living things on Earth is the result of a long process of evolution driven mainly by natural selection. This is a fact about the unobserved. The theory of evolution tells a story about the diversification of life in the distant past, almost all of which took place before human beings were on the scene. How do we know what we know about the history of life on Earth? Not by direct observation, clearly. *And not by enumerative induction either.* It's not as if we have *observed* the emergence of new species in many cases, noticed that it is always driven by natural selection, and concluded that the unobserved cases must resemble the observed ones in this respect. This shows that there must be some way of arriving at knowledge of the unobserved that is not a matter of enumerative induction.

Gilbert Harman calls it *Inference to the Best Explanation* (IBE). The idea is familiar from detective stories: we collect clues; we formulate hypotheses that would explain why the evidence is as it is; we notice that one candidate explanation is clearly better than the others, and eventually we conclude that the best explanation of our observations is (probably) true. Harman argues that enumerative induction is really a special case of IBE. When we notice that every observed emerald is green, and conclude that all emeralds are green, we are in effect arguing as follows:

> All observed emeralds are green.
> The best explanation of this fact is that all emeralds are green.
> Therefore (by IBE) probably all emeralds are green.

If this is correct, the old problem of induction dissolves. But of course new problems arise. There is the descriptive problem of saying what it means for one explanation to be "better" than another, and there is a justificatory problem of saying why it's reasonable to believe the best explanation. To get a feel for the justificatory problem, note that just as induction seems to presuppose the uniformity of nature, IBE seems to presuppose that nature is "simple"—that the simplest, most plausible story about the evidence yields a correct account of the universe as a whole. This is not a necessary truth. We can imagine badly behaved worlds in which the unobserved parts of the universe are messier and more complicated than our observations would lead us to suspect. If we live in one of those worlds IBE will lead us astray. The justificatory problem for IBE is to say why we're justified in assuming that our world is simple or well behaved. And here we face a problem exactly analogous to Hume's problem for induction. We cannot know this a priori, since this is not a necessary truth. We can't know it by observation, since the claim is a claim about the unobserved part of the universe. And we can't know it by IBE, since any IBE argument for this conclusion would be circular. Harman does not address the justificatory question, but it is very much worth addressing. (For discussion, see Peter Lipton, *Inference to the Best Explanation*, Routledge, 1991.)

## Science without Induction

Karl Popper maintains that Hume's original problem has no solution and concludes that science never provides us with positive grounds for believing hypotheses about the unobserved. On Popper's alternative conception, the aim of science is to subject hypotheses to stringent tests and to exclude theories that fail to pass them. At any given stage in the history of science, we are not entitled to say that our theories are true or even probable. All we can say is that our best theories have survived countless efforts at refutation.

The main question for this approach is to explain how we can be justified in *relying* on scientific theories when we make practical decisions. Suppose you're an engineer reviewing plans for a new bridge. You've been asked to say whether the bridge will be able to withstand the load it will have to bear, so you employ your best battle-tested theory for the purpose. Your theory tells you that the bridge will do its job, and you report these results to the planning board that is about to authorize construction. One of the board members asks you a question: "You used a theory to derive your predictions about this bridge. Do you believe the theory you used?" If you are a Popperian you should say, "No. All I know is that it has not been refuted yet." The challenge for Popper is to say how a theoretically informed decision about the future can be rational if we have no rational *beliefs* about the future.

## The Staggering Fact

You have existed for a brief time, and your experience has been confined to a tiny corner of an unfathomably vast universe. And yet you know (or think you know) a great deal about this universe. This staggering fact yields two questions that must be addressed together: "How do we reason about what we have not observed?" and "How, if at all, can this reasoning be justified?" The selections that follow seek to untangle the knots that arise as we think through these questions.

## David Hume (1711–1776)

Hume was a Scottish philosopher, essayist, and historian, and a central figure in Western philosophy. His *Treatise of Human Nature* (1739), *An Enquiry Concerning Human Understanding* (1748), and *An Enquiry Concerning the Principles of Morals* (1751) have been very influential. (The two *Enquiries* revise material in the *Treatise.*) Many contemporary philosophical discussions in epistemology, metaphysics, and ethics are reactions to Hume's theories and arguments. Hume's *Dialogues Concerning Natural Religion* (published posthumously in 1779) is a classic attack on "design arguments" for the existence of God.

# SCEPTICAL DOUBTS CONCERNING THE OPERATIONS OF THE UNDERSTANDING

from *An Enquiry Concerning Human Understanding*, Section IV

PART I

All the objects of human reason or enquiry may naturally be divided into two kinds, to wit, Relations of Ideas, and Matters of Fact. Of the first kind are the sciences of Geometry, Algebra, and Arithmetic; and in short, every affirmation which is either intuitively or demonstratively certain.[1] That the square of the hypothenuse is equal to the square of the two sides, is a proposition which expresses a relation between these figures. That three times five is equal to the half of thirty, expresses a relation between these numbers. Propositions of this kind are discoverable by the mere operation of thought, without dependence on what is anywhere existent in the universe. Though there never were a circle or triangle in nature, the truths demonstrated by Euclid would for ever retain their certainty and evidence.

---

1. A proposition is **intuitively certain** (or *self-evident*) if any fully rational being who understands it is in a position to know that it is true without further reasoning. An example might be: If $x$ is greater than $y$, then $y$ is less than $x$. A proposition is **demonstratively certain** when it can be derived from intuitively certain premises by a sequence of steps, each of which is clearly valid. Hume assumes that the truths of mathematics are all either intuitively or demonstratively certain.

Matters of fact, which are the second objects of human reason, are not ascertained in the same manner; nor is our evidence of their truth, however great, of a like nature with the foregoing. The contrary of every matter of fact is still possible; because it can never imply a contradiction, and is conceived by the mind with the same facility and distinctness, as if ever so conformable to reality. That the sun will not rise tomorrow is no less intelligible a proposition, and implies no more contradiction than the affirmation, that it will rise. We should in vain, therefore, attempt to demonstrate its falsehood. Were it demonstratively false, it would imply a contradiction, and could never be distinctly conceived by the mind.

It may, therefore, be a subject worthy of curiosity, to enquire what is the nature of that evidence which assures us of any real existence and matter of fact, beyond the present testimony of our senses, or the records of our memory. This part of philosophy, it is observable, has been little cultivated, either by the ancients or moderns; and therefore our doubts and errors, in the prosecution of so important an enquiry, may be the more excusable. . . . They may even prove useful, by exciting curiosity, and destroying that implicit faith and security, which is the bane of all reasoning and free enquiry. The discovery of defects in the common philosophy, if any such there be, will not, I presume, be a discouragement, but rather an incitement, as is usual, to attempt something more full and satisfactory than has yet been proposed to the public.

All reasonings concerning matter of fact seem to be founded on the relation of Cause and Effect. By means of that relation alone we can go beyond the evidence of our memory and senses. If you were to ask a man, why he believes any matter of fact, which is absent; for instance, that his friend is in the country, or in France; he would give you a reason; and this reason would be some other fact; as a letter received from him, or the knowledge of his former resolutions and promises. A man finding a watch or any other machine in a desert island, would conclude that there had once been men in that island. All our reasonings concerning fact are of the same nature. And here it is constantly supposed that there is a connexion between the present fact and that which is inferred from it. Were there nothing to bind them together, the inference would be entirely precarious. The hearing of an articulate voice and rational discourse in the dark assures us of the presence of some person: Why? because these are the effects of the human make and fabric, and closely connected with it. If we anatomize all the other reasonings of this nature, we shall find that they are founded on the relation of cause and effect, and that this relation is either near or remote, direct or collateral. Heat and light are collateral effects of fire, and the one effect may justly be inferred from the other.

If we would satisfy ourselves, therefore, concerning the nature of that evidence, which assures us of matters of fact, we must enquire how we arrive at the knowledge of cause and effect.

I shall venture to affirm, as a general proposition, which admits of no exception, that the knowledge of this relation is not, in any instance, attained by reasonings a priori; but arises entirely from experience, when we find that any particular objects are constantly conjoined with each other. Let an object be presented to a man of ever so strong natural reason and abilities; if that object be entirely new to him, he will not be able, by the most accurate examination of its sensible qualities, to discover any of its causes or effects.

Adam, though his rational faculties be supposed, at the very first, entirely perfect, could not have inferred from the fluidity and transparency of water that it would suffocate him, or from the light and warmth of fire that it would consume him. No object ever discovers, by the qualities which appear to the senses, either the causes which produced it, or the effects which will arise from it; nor can our reason, unassisted by experience, ever draw any inference concerning real existence and matter of fact.

This proposition, that causes and effects are discoverable, not by reason but by experience, will readily be admitted with regard to such objects, as we remember to have once been altogether unknown to us. . . . Present two smooth pieces of marble to a man who has no tincture of natural philosophy; he will never discover that they will adhere together in such a manner as to require great force to separate them in a direct line, while they make so small a resistance to a lateral pressure. . . . [N]or does any man imagine that the explosion of gunpowder, or the attraction of a loadstone, could ever be discovered by arguments a priori. . . .

But the same truth may not appear, at first sight, to have the same evidence with regard to events, which have become familiar to us from our first appearance in the world, which bear a close analogy to the whole course of nature, and which are supposed to depend on the simple qualities of objects, without any secret structure of parts. We are apt to imagine that we could discover these effects by the mere operation of our reason, without experience. We fancy, that were we brought on a sudden into this world, we could at first have inferred that one billiard-ball would communicate motion to another upon impulse; and that we needed not to have waited for the event, in order to pronounce with certainty concerning it. Such is the influence of custom, that, where it is strongest, it not only covers our natural ignorance, but even conceals itself, and seems not to take place, merely because it is found in the highest degree.

But to convince us that all the laws of nature, and all the operations of bodies without exception, are known only by experience, the following reflections may, perhaps, suffice. Were any object presented to us, and were we required to pronounce concerning the effect, which will result from it, without consulting past observation; after what manner, I beseech you, must the mind proceed in this operation? It must invent or imagine some event, which it ascribes to the object as its effect; and it is plain that this invention must be entirely arbitrary. The mind can never possibly find the effect in the supposed cause, by the most accurate scrutiny and examination. For the effect is totally different from the cause, and consequently can never be discovered in it. Motion in the second billiard-ball is a quite distinct event from motion in the first; nor is there anything in the one to suggest the smallest hint of the other. A stone or piece of metal raised into the air, and left without any support, immediately falls: but to consider the matter a priori, is there anything we discover in this situation which can beget the idea of a downward, rather than an upward, or any other motion, in the stone or metal?

And as the first imagination or invention of a particular effect, in all natural operations, is arbitrary, where we consult not experience; so must we also esteem the supposed tie or connexion between the cause and effect, which binds them together, and renders it impossible that any other effect could result from the operation of that cause. When I see, for instance, a billiard-ball moving in a straight line towards another; even suppose motion in the second ball should by accident be suggested to me, as the result of their contact or impulse; may I not conceive, that a hundred different events might as well follow from that cause? May not both these balls remain at absolute rest? May not the first ball return in a straight line, or leap off from the second in any line or direction? All these suppositions are consistent and conceivable. Why then should we give the preference to one, which is no more consistent or conceivable than the rest? All our reasonings a priori will never be able to show us any foundation for this preference.

In a word, then, every effect is a distinct event from its cause. It could not, therefore, be discovered in the cause, and the first invention or conception of it, a priori, must be entirely arbitrary. And even after it is suggested, the conjunction of it with the cause must appear equally arbitrary; since there are always many other effects, which, to reason, must seem fully as consistent and natural. In vain, therefore, should we pretend to determine any single event, or infer any cause or effect, without the assistance of observation and experience. . . .

Nor is geometry, when taken into the assistance of natural philosophy, ever able to remedy this defect, or lead us into the knowledge of ultimate causes, by all that accuracy of reasoning for which it is so justly celebrated. Every part of mixed mathematics[2] proceeds upon the supposition that certain laws are established by nature in her operations; and abstract reasonings are employed, either to assist experience in the discovery of these laws, or to determine their influence in particular instances, where it depends upon any precise degree of distance and quantity. Thus, it is a law of motion, discovered by experience, that the moment or force of any body in motion is in the compound ratio or proportion of its solid contents and its velocity;[3] and consequently, that a small force may remove the greatest obstacle or raise the greatest weight, if, by any contrivance or machinery, we can increase the velocity of that force, so as to make it an overmatch for its antagonist. Geometry assists us in the application of this law, by giving us the just dimensions of all the parts and figures which can enter into any species of machine; but still the discovery of the law itself is owing merely to experience, and all the abstract reasonings in the world could never lead us one step towards the knowledge of it.

## PART II

When it is asked, What is the nature of all our reasonings concerning matter of fact? the proper answer seems to be, that they are founded on the relation of cause and effect. When again it is asked, What is the foundation of all our reasonings and conclusions concerning that relation? it may be replied in one word, Experience. But if

---

2. Now called "applied" mathematics: the use of mathematics in physics, engineering, and other sciences.

3. Hume conflates two laws of Newtonian physics: *force = mass × acceleration; momentum = mass × velocity.*

we still carry on our sifting humour, and ask, What is the foundation of all conclusions from experience? this implies a new question, which may be of more difficult solution and explication. . . .

I shall content myself, in this section, with an easy task, and shall pretend only to give a negative answer to the question here proposed. I say then, that, even after we have experience of the operations of cause and effect, our conclusions from that experience are not founded on reasoning, or any process of the understanding. This answer we must endeavour both to explain and to defend.

It must certainly be allowed, that nature has kept us at a great distance from all her secrets, and has afforded us only the knowledge of a few superficial qualities of objects; while she conceals from us those powers and principles on which the influence of those objects entirely depends. . . . But notwithstanding this ignorance of natural powers and principles, we always presume, when we see like sensible qualities, that they have like secret powers, and expect that effects, similar to those which we have experienced, will follow from them. If a body of like colour and consistence with that bread, which we have formerly eaten, be presented to us, we make no scruple of repeating the experiment, and foresee, with certainty, like nourishment and support. Now this is a process of the mind or thought, of which I would willingly know the foundation. It is allowed on all hands that there is no known connexion between the sensible qualities and the secret powers; and consequently, that the mind is not led to form such a conclusion concerning their constant and regular conjunction, by anything which it knows of their nature. As to past Experience, it can be allowed to give direct and certain information of those precise objects only, and that precise period of time, which fell under its cognizance: but why this experience should be extended to future times, and to other objects, which for aught we know, may be only in appearance similar; this is the main question on which I would insist. The bread, which I formerly ate, nourished me; that is, a body of such sensible qualities was, at that time, endued with such secret powers: but does it follow, that other bread must also nourish me at another time, and that like sensible qualities must always be attended with like secret powers? The consequence seems nowise necessary. At least, it must be acknowledged that there is here a consequence drawn by the mind; that there is a certain step taken; a process of thought, and an inference, which wants to be explained. These two propositions are far from being the same, *I have found that such an object has always been attended with such an effect, and I foresee, that other objects, which are, in appearance, similar, will be attended with similar effects.* I shall allow, if you please, that the one proposition may justly be inferred from the other: I know, in fact, that it always is inferred. But if you insist that the inference is made by a chain of reasoning, I desire you to produce that reasoning. The connexion between these propositions is not intuitive. There is required a medium, which may enable the mind to draw such an inference, if indeed it be drawn by reasoning and argument. What that medium is, I must confess, passes my comprehension; and it is incumbent on those to produce it, who assert that it really exists, and is the origin of all our conclusions concerning matter of fact.

This negative argument must certainly, in process of time, become altogether convincing, if many penetrating and able philosophers shall turn their enquiries this way and no one be ever able to discover any connecting proposition or intermediate step, which supports the understanding in this conclusion. But as the question is yet new, every reader may not trust so far to his own penetration, as to conclude, because an argument escapes his enquiry, that therefore it does not really exist. For this reason it may be requisite to venture upon a more difficult task; and enumerating all the branches of human knowledge, endeavour to show that none of them can afford such an argument.

All reasonings may be divided into two kinds, namely, demonstrative reasoning, or that concerning relations of ideas, and moral reasoning, or that concerning matter of fact and existence. That there are no demonstrative arguments in the case seems evident; since it implies no contradiction that the course of nature may change, and that an object, seemingly like those which we have experienced, may be attended with different or contrary effects. May I not clearly and distinctly conceive that a body, falling from the clouds, and which, in all other respects, resembles snow, has yet the taste of salt or feeling of fire? Is there any more intelligible proposition than to affirm, that all the trees will flourish in December and January, and decay in May and June? Now whatever is intelligible, and can be distinctly conceived, implies no contradiction, and can never be proved false by any demonstrative argument or abstract reasoning a priori.

If we be, therefore, engaged by arguments to put trust in past experience, and make it the standard of our future judgment, these arguments must be probable only, or such as regard matter of fact and real existence according to the division above mentioned. But that there is no argument of this kind, must appear, if our explication of that species of reasoning be admitted as solid and satisfactory. We have said that all arguments concerning existence are founded on the relation of cause and effect; that our knowledge of that relation is derived entirely from experience; and that all our experimental conclusions proceed upon the supposition that the future will be conformable to the past. To endeavour, therefore, the proof of this last supposition by probable arguments, or arguments regarding existence, must be evidently going in a circle, and taking that for granted, which is the very point in question....

Should it be said that, from a number of uniform experiments, we *infer* a connexion between the sensible qualities and the secret powers; this, I must confess, seems the same difficulty, couched in different terms. The question still recurs, on what process of argument this *inference* is founded? Where is the medium, the interposing ideas, which join propositions so very wide of each other? It is confessed that the colour, consistence, and other sensible qualities of bread appear not, of themselves, to have any connexion with the secret powers of nourishment and support. For otherwise we could infer these secret powers from the first appearance of these sensible qualities, without the aid of experience; contrary to the sentiment of all philosophers, and contrary to plain matter of fact. Here, then, is our natural state of ignorance with regard to the powers and influence of all objects. How is this remedied by experience? It only shows us a number of uniform effects, resulting from certain objects, and teaches us that those particular objects, at that particular time, were endowed with such powers and forces. When a new object, endowed with similar sensible qualities, is produced, we expect similar powers and forces, and look for a like effect. From a body of like colour and consistence with bread we expect like nourishment and support. But this surely is a step or progress of the mind, which wants to be explained. When a man says, *I have found, in all past instances, such sensible qualities conjoined with such secret powers*: And when he says, *Similar sensible qualities will always be conjoined with similar secret powers*; he is not guilty of a tautology, nor are these propositions in any respect the same. You say that the one proposition is an inference from the other. But you must confess that the inference is not intuitive; neither is it demonstrative: Of what nature is it, then? To say it is experimental, is begging the question. For all inferences from experience suppose, as their foundation, that the future will resemble the past, and that similar powers will be conjoined with similar sensible qualities. If there be any suspicion that the course of nature may change, and that the past may be no rule for the future, all experience becomes useless, and can give rise to no inference or conclusion. It is impossible, therefore, that any arguments from experience can prove this resemblance of the past to the future; since all these arguments are founded on the supposition of that resemblance. Let the course of things be allowed hitherto over so regular; that alone, without some new argument or inference, proves not that, for the future, it will continue so.... My practice, you say, refutes my doubts. But you mistake the purport of my question. As an agent, I am quite satisfied in the point; but as a philosopher, who has some share of curiosity, I will not say scepticism, I want to learn the foundation of this inference. No reading, no enquiry has yet been able to remove my difficulty, or give me satisfaction in a matter of such importance. Can I do better than propose the difficulty to the public, even though, perhaps, I have small hopes of obtaining a solution? ...

It is certain that the most ignorant and stupid peasants — nay infants, nay even brute beasts — improve by experience, and learn the qualities of natural objects, by observing the effects which result from them. When a child has felt the sensation of pain from touching the flame of a candle, he will be careful not to put his hand near any candle; but will expect a similar effect from a cause which is similar in its sensible qualities and appearance. If you assert, therefore, that the understanding of the child is led into this conclusion by any process of argument or ratiocination, I may justly require you to produce that argument; nor have you any pretence to refuse so equitable a demand. You cannot say that the argument is abstruse, and may possibly escape your enquiry; since you confess that it is obvious to the capacity of a mere infant. If you hesitate, therefore, a moment, or if, after reflection, you produce any intricate or profound argument, you, in a manner, give up the question, and confess that it is not reasoning which engages us to suppose the past resembling the future, and to expect similar effects from causes which are, to appearance, similar. This is the proposition which I intended to enforce in the present section.

# SCEPTICAL SOLUTION OF THESE DOUBTS

from *An Enquiry Concerning Human Understanding*, Section V

## PART I

Suppose a person, though endowed with the strongest faculties of reason and reflection, to be brought on a sudden into this world; he would, indeed, immediately observe a continual succession of objects, and one event following another; but he would not be able to discover anything farther. He would not, at first, by any reasoning, be able to reach the idea of cause and effect; since the particular powers, by which all natural operations are performed, never appear to the senses; nor is it reasonable to conclude, merely because one event, in one instance, precedes another, that therefore the one is the cause, the other the effect. Their conjunction may be arbitrary and casual. There may be no reason to infer the existence of one from the appearance of the other. And in a word, such a person, without more experience, could never employ his conjecture or reasoning concerning any matter of fact, or be assured of anything beyond what was immediately present to his memory and senses.

Suppose, again, that he has acquired more experience, and has lived so long in the world as to have observed familiar objects or events to be constantly conjoined together; what is the consequence of this experience? He immediately infers the existence of one object from the appearance of the other. Yet he has not, by all his experience, acquired any idea or knowledge of the secret power by which the one object produces the other; nor is it by any process of reasoning, he is engaged to draw this inference. But still he finds himself determined to draw it: and though he should be convinced that his understanding has no part in the operation, he would nevertheless continue in the same course of thinking. There is some other principle which determines him to form such a conclusion.

This principle is Custom[4] or Habit. For wherever the repetition of any particular act or operation produces a propensity to renew the same act or operation, without being impelled by any reasoning or process of the understanding, we always say, that this propensity is the effect of Custom. By employing that word, we pretend not to have given the ultimate reason of such a propensity. We only point out a principle of human nature, which is universally acknowledged, and which is well known by its effects.... And it is certain we here advance a very intelligible proposition at least, if not a true one, when we assert that, after the constant conjunction of two objects — heat and flame, for instance, weight and solidity — we are determined by custom alone to expect the one from the appearance of the other. This hypothesis seems even the only one which explains the difficulty, why we draw, from a thousand instances, an inference which we are not able to draw from one instance, that is, in no respect, different

---

4. In Hume's English, a "custom" need not be a *social* custom, a way of doing things that differs from time to time and place to place. A custom is *any* acquired habit of the mind that does not result from reasoning.

from them. Reason is incapable of any such variation. The conclusions which it draws from considering one circle are the same which it would form upon surveying all the circles in the universe. But no man, having seen only one body move after being impelled by another, could infer that every other body will move after a like impulse. All inferences from experience, therefore, are effects of custom, not of reasoning.

Custom, then, is the great guide of human life. It is that principle alone which renders our experience useful to us, and makes us expect, for the future, a similar train of events with those which have appeared in the past. Without the influence of custom, we should be entirely ignorant of every matter of fact beyond what is immediately present to the memory and senses. We should never know how to adjust means to ends, or to employ our natural powers in the production of any effect. There would be an end at once of all action, as well as of the chief part of speculation. . . .

What, then, is the conclusion of the whole matter? A simple one; though, it must be confessed, pretty remote from the common theories of philosophy. All belief of matter of fact or real existence is derived merely from some object, present to the memory or senses, and a customary conjunction between that and some other object. Or in other words; having found, in many instances, that any two kinds of objects — flame and heat, snow and cold — have always been conjoined together; if flame or snow be presented anew to the senses, the mind is carried by custom to expect heat or cold, and to believe that such a quality does exist, and will discover itself upon a nearer approach. This belief is the necessary result of placing the mind in such circumstances. It is an operation of the soul, when we are so situated, as unavoidable as to feel the passion of love, when we receive benefits; or hatred, when we meet with injuries. All these operations are a species of natural instincts, which no reasoning or process of the thought and understanding is able either to produce or to prevent.

## TEST YOUR UNDERSTANDING

1. Explain Hume's distinction between "relations of ideas" and "matters of fact" using your own examples.

2. Say why "The future will resemble the past" is a "matter of fact" claim.

3. Explain Hume's claim that "all inferences from experience . . . are effects of custom, not reasoning."

4. Does Hume claim that these "inferences from experience" are irrational?

## NOTES AND QUESTIONS

1. *Illustrating Hume's theory.* Hume gives a general account of how we come by our beliefs about unobserved "matters of fact," but most of his examples concern a special case: beliefs about the future. Choose an example that does not fit this mold — a belief

about some past or present matter of fact that you have not personally observed. Give a Humean account of how you came by this opinion and assess the merits of this account.

2. *Cause and effect.* Hume claims that all of our reasoning concerning (unobserved) matters of fact is "founded on the relation of cause and effect." But this is puzzling. People living near the ocean have always known that high tide is followed by low tide at certain intervals. These people experience a regularity and come to expect it to persist into the future, and this would appear to be a clear example of the sort of reasoning Hume seeks to understand. But over the centuries most of these people have had no idea what *causes* the tides. That is a scientific discovery (due to Isaac Newton). So is Hume just wrong to say that reasoning about the unobserved always involves reasoning about causes? Hume's theory of causation is developed in section VII of *An Enquiry Concerning Human Understanding*, "Of the Idea of Necessary Connexion," excerpted in chapter 5 of this volume.

3. *A reconstruction of Hume's skeptical argument.* There are many ways to extract a detailed, explicit argument from Hume's text. Consider the following possibility:

   1. A "matter of fact" claim about the future is justified only if it is supported by an inductive argument, e.g., an argument of the form

      | Data: | In a large sample, all observed $F$s are $G$. |
      | UN: | If, in a large sample, all observed $F$s have been $G$, then in the future, all $F$s will be $G$. |
      | Generalization: | Therefore, in the future, all $F$s will be $G$. |

   2. An inductive argument of this form justifies its conclusion only if we are independently justified in accepting UN (the uniformity of nature).

   3. UN is a "matter of fact" claim about the future.

   4. So UN is justified only if it is supported by an inductive argument.

   5. But UN is a premise in every inductive argument.

   6. So any inductive argument for UN would be circular.

   7. Circular arguments never justify their conclusions.

   8. So UN cannot be justified.

   9. So inductive arguments never justify their conclusions.

   10. So matter of fact claims about the future are never justified.

   Does Hume accept the conclusion of this argument? If not, which premises or transitions would he reject?

   *Exercise:* Never mind what Hume thinks. Is this a cogent argument? If not, choose one vulnerable premise or transition and say why it is mistaken. If so, defend the argument against a challenge to it.

## P. F. Strawson (1919–2006)

Until his retirement in 1987, Strawson was the Waynflete Professor of Metaphysical Philosophy at the University of Oxford. His influential writings include seminal contributions to the philosophy of language ("On Referring," 1950), metaphysics (*Individuals*, 1959), and the interpretation of Kant's philosophy (*The Bounds of Sense*, 1966).

# THE "JUSTIFICATION" OF INDUCTION
## from *Introduction to Logical Theory*

7. What reason have we to place reliance on inductive procedures? Why should we suppose that the accumulation of instances of *A*s which are *B*s, however various the conditions in which they are observed, gives any good reason for expecting the next *A* we encounter to be a *B*? It is our habit to form expectations in this way; but can the habit be rationally justified? When this doubt has entered our minds it may be difficult to free ourselves from it. For the doubt has its source in a confusion; and some attempts to resolve the doubt preserve the confusion; and other attempts to show that the doubt is senseless seem altogether too facile. The root-confusion is easily described; but simply to describe it seems an inadequate remedy against it. So the doubt must be examined again and again, in the light of different attempts to remove it. . . .

Suppose that a man is brought up to regard formal logic as the study of the science and art of reasoning. He observes that all inductive processes are, by deductive standards, invalid; the premises never entail the conclusions. Now inductive processes are notoriously important in the formation of beliefs and expectations about everything which lies beyond the observation of available witnesses. But an *invalid* argument is an *unsound* argument; an *unsound* argument is one in which *no good reason* is produced for accepting the conclusion. So if inductive processes are invalid, if all the arguments we should produce, if challenged, in support of our beliefs about what lies beyond the observation of available witnesses are unsound, then we have no good reason for any of these beliefs. This conclusion is repugnant. So there arises the demand for a justification, not of this or that particular belief which goes beyond what is entailed by our evidence, but a justification of induction in general. And when the demand arises in this way it is, in effect, the demand that induction shall be shown to be really a kind of deduction; for nothing less will satisfy the doubter when this is the route to his doubts.

Tracing this, the most common route to the general doubt about the reasonableness of induction, shows how the doubt seems to escape the absurdity of a demand that induction in general shall be justified by inductive standards. The demand is that induction should be shown to be a rational process; and this turns out to be the demand that one kind of reasoning should be shown to be another and different kind. Put thus crudely, the demand seems to escape one absurdity only to fall into another. Of course, inductive arguments are not deductively valid; if they were, they would be deductive arguments. Inductive reasoning must be assessed, for soundness, by inductive standards. Nevertheless, fantastic as the wish for induction to be deduction may seem, it is only in terms of it that we can understand some of the attempts that have been made to justify induction.

8. The first kind of attempt I shall consider might he called the search for the supreme premise of inductions. In its primitive form it is quite a crude attempt; and I shall make it cruder by caricature. We have already seen that for a particular inductive step, such as "The kettle has been on the fire for ten minutes, so it will be boiling by now," we can substitute a deductive argument by introducing a generalization (e.g., "A kettle always boils within ten minutes of being put on the fire") as an additional premise. This manoeuvre shifted the emphasis of the problem of inductive support on to the question of how we established such generalizations as these, which rested on grounds by which they were not entailed. But suppose the manoeuvre could be repeated. Suppose we could find one supremely general proposition, which taken in conjunction with the evidence for any accepted generalization of science or daily life (or at least of science) would entail that generalization. Then, so long as the status of the supreme generalization could be satisfactorily explained, we could regard all sound inductions to unqualified general conclusions as, at bottom, valid deductions. The justification would be found, for at least these cases. The most obvious difficulty in this suggestion is that of formulating the supreme general proposition in such a way that it shall be precise enough to yield the desired entailments, and yet not obviously false or arbitrary. Consider, for example, the formula: "For all $f$, $g$, wherever $n$ cases of $f \cdot g$,[1] and no cases of $f \cdot \frown g$,[2] are observed, then all cases of $f$ are cases of $g$." To turn it into a sentence, we have only to replace "$n$" by some number. But what number? If we take the value of "$n$" to be 1 or 20 or 500, the resulting statement is obviously false. Moreover, the choice of any number would seem quite arbitrary; there is no privileged number of favourable instances which we take as decisive in establishing a generalization. If, on the other hand, we phrase the proposition vaguely enough to escape these objections — if, for example, we phrase it as "Nature is uniform" — then it becomes too vague to provide the desired entailments. . . .

Even if these difficulties could be met, the question of the status of the supreme premise would remain. How, if a non-necessary proposition, could it be established? The appeal to experience, to inductive support, is clearly barred on pain of circularity. If, on the other hand, it were a necessary truth and possessed, in conjunction with the evidence for a generalization, the required logical power to entail the generalization, . . . then the evidence would entail the generalization independently, and the problem would not arise: a conclusion unbearably paradoxical.

9. I shall next consider a more sophisticated kind of attempt to justify induction: more sophisticated both in its interpretation of this aim and in the method adopted to achieve it. The aim envisaged is that of proving that the probability of a generalization, whether universal or proportional, increases with the number of instances for which it is found to hold. . . .

---

1. "$f \cdot g$" = "$f$ and $g$"
2. "$f \cdot \frown g$" = "$f$ and not $g$"

I state the argument as simply as possible; but; even so, it will be necessary to introduce and explain some new terms. Suppose we had a collection of objects of different kinds, some with some characteristics and some with others. Suppose, for example, we had a bag containing 100 balls, of which 70 were white and 30 black. Let us call such a collection of objects a *population*; and let us call the way it is made up (e.g., in the case imagined, of 70 white and 30 black balls) the *constitution* of the population. From such a population it would be possible to take *samples* of various sizes. For example, we might take from our bag a sample of 30 balls. Suppose each ball in the bag had an individual number. Then the collection of balls numbered 10 to 39 inclusive would be one sample of the given size; the collection of balls numbered 11 to 40 inclusive would be another and different sample of the same size; the collection of balls numbered 2, 4, 6, 8 . . . 58, 60 would be another such sample; and so on. Each possible collection of 30 balls is a different sample of the same size. Some different samples of the same size will have the same constitutions as one another; others will have different constitutions. Thus there will be only one sample made up of 30 black balls. There will be many different samples which share the constitution: 20 white and 10 black. It would be a simple matter of mathematics to work out the number of possible samples of the given size which had any one possible constitution. Let us say that a sample *matches* the population if, allowing for the difference between them in size, the constitution of the sample corresponds, within certain limits, to that of the population. For example, we might say that any possible sample consisting of, say, 21 white and 9 black balls matched the constitution (70 white and 30 black) of the population, whereas a sample consisting of 20 white and 10 black balls did not. Now it is a proposition of pure mathematics that, given any population, the proportion of possible samples, all of the same size, which match the population, increases with the size of the sample. . . .

Conclusions about the ratio of a subset of equally possible chances to the whole set of those chances may be expressed by the use of the word "probability." Thus of the 52 possible samples of one card from a population constituted like an orthodox pack, 16 are court-cards or aces. This fact we allow ourselves to express (under the conditions, inductively established, of equipossibility of draws) by saying that the probability of drawing a court-card or an ace was $\frac{4}{13}$. If we express the proposition referred to at the end of the last paragraph by means of this use of "probability" we shall obtain the result: The probability of a sample matching a given population increases with the size of the sample. It is tempting to try to derive from this result a general justification of the inductive procedure: which will not, indeed, show that any given inductive conclusion is entailed by the evidence for it, taken in conjunction with some universal premise, but will show that the multiplication of favourable instances of a generalization entails a proportionate increase in its probability. For, since matching is a symmetrical relation,[3] it might seem a simple deductive step to move from

---

3. A **relation** R is *symmetric* if and only if, whenever x bears R to y, y also bears R to x. For example, marriage is a symmetric relation, since whenever x is married to y, y is also married to x. Love, on the other hand, is not symmetric, since there can be cases in which x loves y, but y does not love x.

I. The probability of a sample matching a given population increases with the size of the sample.

to

II. The probability of a population matching a given sample increases with the size of the sample.

II might seem to provide a guarantee that the greater the number of cases for which a generalization is observed to hold, the greater is its probability; since in increasing the number of cases we increase the size of the sample from whatever population forms the subject of our generalization. Thus pure mathematics might seem to provide the sought-for proof that the evidence for a generalization really does get stronger, the more favourable instances of it we find.

The argument is ingenious enough to be worthy of respect; but it fails of its purpose, and misrepresents the inductive situation. Our situation is not in the least like that of a man drawing a sample from a given, i.e., fixed and limited, population from which the drawing of any mathematically possible sample is equiprobable with that of any other. Our only datum is the sample. No limit is fixed beforehand to the diversity, and the possibilities of change, of the "population" from which it is drawn: or, better, to the multiplicity and variousness of different populations, each with different constitutions, any one of which might replace the present one before we make the next draw. Nor is there any *a priori* guarantee that different mathematically possible samples are equally likely to be drawn. If we have or can obtain any assurance on these points, then it is assurance derived inductively from our data, and cannot therefore be assumed at the outset of an argument designed to justify induction. So II, regarded as a justification of induction founded on purely mathematical considerations, is a fraud. . . .

10. Let us turn from attempts to justify induction to attempts to show that the demand for a justification is mistaken. We have seen already that what lies behind such a demand is often the absurd wish that induction should be shown to be some kind of deduction — and this wish is clearly traceable in the two attempts at justification which we have examined. What other sense could we give to the demand? Sometimes it is expressed in the form of a request for proof that induction is a *reasonable* or *rational* procedure, that we have *good grounds* for placing reliance upon it. Consider the uses of the phrases "good grounds," "justification," "reasonable," &c. Often we say such things as "He has *every justification* for believing that *p*"; "I have *very good reasons* for believing it"; "There are *good grounds* for the view that *q*"; "There is *good evidence* that *r*." We often talk, in such ways as these, of justification, good grounds or reasons or evidence for certain beliefs. Suppose such a belief were one expressible in the form "Every case of *f* is a cause of *g*." And suppose someone were asked what he meant by saying that he had good grounds or reasons for holding it. I think it would be felt to be a satisfactory answer if he replied: "Well, in all my wide and varied experience I've come across innumerable cases of *f* and never a case of *f* which wasn't a case of *g*." In saying this, he is clearly claiming to have *inductive* support, *inductive* evidence, of a certain kind, for his belief; and he

is also giving a perfectly proper answer to the question, what he meant by saying that he had ample justification, good grounds, good reasons for his belief. It is an analytic proposition that it is reasonable to have a degree of belief in a statement which is proportional to the strength of the evidence in its favour; and it is an analytic proposition, though not a proposition of mathematics, that, other things being equal, the evidence for a generalization is strong in proportion as the number of favourable instances, and the variety of circumstances in which they have been found, is great. So to ask whether it is reasonable to place reliance on inductive procedures is like asking whether it is reasonable to proportion the degree of one's convictions to the strength of the evidence. Doing this is what "being reasonable" *means* in such a context.

As for the other form in which the doubt may be expressed, viz., "Is induction a justified, or justifiable, procedure?," it emerges in a still less favourable light. No sense has been given to it, though it is easy to see why it seems to have a sense. For it is generally proper to inquire *of a particular belief,* whether its adoption is justified; and, in asking this, we are asking whether there is good, bad, or any, evidence for it. In applying or withholding the epithets "justified," "well founded," &c., in the case of specific beliefs, we are appealing to, and applying, inductive standards. But to what standards are we appealing when we ask whether the application of inductive standards is justified or well grounded? If we cannot answer, then no sense has been given to the question. Compare it with the question: Is the law legal? It makes perfectly good sense to inquire of a particular action, of an administrative regulation, or even, in the case of some states, of a particular enactment of the legislature, whether or not it is legal. The question is answered by an appeal to a legal system, by the application of a set of legal (or constitutional) rules or standards. But it makes no sense to inquire in general whether the law of the land, the legal system as a whole, is or is not legal. For to what legal standards are we appealing? . . .

11. It seems, however, that this way of showing the request for a general justification of induction to be absurd is sometimes insufficient to allay the worry that produces it. And to point out that "forming rational opinions about the unobserved on the evidence available" and "assessing the evidence by inductive standards" are phrases which describe the same thing, is more apt to produce irritation than relief. The point is felt to be "merely a verbal" one; and though the point of this protest is itself hard to see, it is clear that something more is required. So the question must be pursued further. First, I want to point out that there is something a little odd about talking of "the inductive method," or even "the inductive policy," as if it were just one possible method among others of arguing from the observed to the unobserved, from the available evidence to the facts in question. If one asked a meteorologist what method or methods he used to forecast the weather, one would be surprised if he answered: "Oh, just the inductive method." If one asked a doctor by what means he diagnosed a certain disease, the answer "By induction" would be felt as an impatient evasion, a joke, or a rebuke. The answer one hopes for is an account of the tests made, the signs taken account of, the rules and recipes and

general laws applied. When such a specific method of prediction or diagnosis is in question, one can ask whether the method is justified in practice; and here again one is asking whether its employment is inductively justified, whether it commonly gives correct results. This question would normally seem an admissible one. One might be tempted to conclude that, while there are many different specific methods of prediction, diagnosis, &c., appropriate to different subjects of inquiry, all such methods could properly be called "inductive" in the sense that their employment rested on inductive support; and that, hence, the phrase "non-inductive method of finding out about what lies deductively beyond the evidence" was a description without meaning, a phrase to which no sense had been given; so that there could be no question of justifying our selection of one method, called "the inductive," of doing this.

However, someone might object: "Surely it is possible, though it might be foolish, to use methods utterly different from accredited scientific ones. Suppose a man, whenever he wanted to form an opinion about what lay beyond his observation or the observation of available witnesses, simply shut his eyes, asked himself the appropriate question, and accepted the first answer that came into his head. Wouldn't this be a non-inductive method?" Well, let us suppose this. The man is asked: "Do you usually get the right answer by your method?" He might answer: "You've mentioned one of its drawbacks; I never do get the right answer; but it's an extremely easy method." One might then be inclined to think that it was not a method of finding things out at all. But suppose he answered: "Yes, it's usually (always) the right answer." Then we might be willing to call it a method of finding out, though a strange one. But, then, by the very fact of its success, it would be an inductively supported method. For each application of the method would be an application of the general rule, "The first answer that comes into my head is generally (always) the right one"; and for the truth of this generalization there would be the inductive evidence of a long run of favourable instances with no unfavourable ones (if it were "always"), or of a sustained high proportion of successes to trials (if it were "generally").

So every successful method or recipe for finding out about the unobserved must be one which has inductive support; for to say that a recipe is successful is to say that it has been repeatedly applied with success; and repeated successful application of a recipe constitutes just what we mean by inductive evidence in its favour. Pointing out this fact must not be confused with saying that "the inductive method" is justified by its success, justified because it works. This is a mistake, and an important one. I am not seeking to "justify the inductive method," for no meaning has been given to this phrase. *A fortiori*, I am not saying that induction is justified by its success in finding out about the unobserved. I am saying, rather, that any successsful method of finding out about the unobserved is necessarily justified by induction. This is an analytic proposition. The phrase "successful method of finding things out which has no inductive support" is self-contradictory. Having, or acquiring, inductive support is a necessary condition of the success of a method.

Why point this out at all? First, it may have a certain, therapeutic force, a power to reassure. Second, it may counteract the tendency to think of "the inductive method" as something on a par with specific methods of diagnosis or prediction and therefore, like them, standing in need of (inductive) justification.

12. There is one further confusion, perhaps the most powerful of all in producing the doubts, questions, and spurious solutions discussed in this Part. We may approach it by considering the claim that induction is justified by its success in practice. The phrase "success of induction" is by no means clear and perhaps embodies the confusion of induction with some specific method of prediction, &c., appropriate to some particular line of inquiry. But, whatever the phrase may mean, the claim has an obviously circular look. Presumably the suggestion is that we should argue from the past "successes of induction" to the continuance of those successes in the future; from the fact that it has worked hitherto to the conclusion that it will continue to work. Since an argument of this kind is plainly inductive, it will not serve as a justification of induction. One cannot establish a principle of argument by an argument which uses that principle. But let us go a little deeper. The argument rests the justification of induction on a matter of fact (its "past successes"). This is characteristic of nearly all attempts to find a justification. The desired premise of Section 8 [p. 152] was to be some fact about the constitution of the universe which, even if it could not be used as a suppressed premise to give inductive arguments a deductive turn, was at any rate a "presupposition of the validity of induction." Even the mathematical argument of Section 9 [pp. 153–54] required buttressing with some large assumption about the makeup of the world. I think the source of this general desire to find out some fact about the constitution of the universe which will "justify induction" or "show it to be a rational policy" is the confusion, the running together, of two fundamentally different questions: to one of which the answer is a matter of non-linguistic fact, while to the other it is a matter of meanings.

There is nothing self-contradictory in supposing that all the uniformities in the course of things that we have hitherto observed and come to count on should cease to operate to-morrow; that all our familiar recipes should let us down, and that we should be unable to frame new ones because such regularities as there were were too complex for us to make out. (We may assume that even the expectation that all of us, in such circumstances, would perish, were falsified by someone surviving to observe the new chaos in which, roughly speaking, nothing foreseeable happens.) Of course, we do not believe that this will happen. We believe, on the contrary, that our inductively supported expectation-rules, though some of them will have, no doubt, to be dropped or modified, will continue, on the whole, to serve us fairly well; and that we shall generally be able to replace the rules we abandon with others similarly arrived at. We might give a sense to the phrase "success of induction" by calling this vague belief the belief that induction will continue to be successful. It is certainly a factual belief, not a necessary truth; a belief, one may say, about the constitution of the universe. We might express it as follows, choosing a phraseology which will serve the better to expose the confusion I wish to expose:

I.  (The universe is such that) induction will continue to be successful.

I is very vague: it amounts to saying that there are, and will continue to be, natural uniformities and regularities which exhibit a humanly manageable degree of
simplicity. But, though it is vague, certain definite things can be said about it. (1) It
is not a necessary, but a contingent, statement; for chaos is not a self-contradictory
concept. (2) We have good inductive reasons for believing it, good inductive evidence
for it. We believe that some of our recipes will continue to hold good because they
have held good for so long. We believe that we shall be able to frame new and useful
ones, because we have been able to do so repeatedly in the past. Of course, it would
be absurd to try to use I to "justify induction," to show that it is a reasonable policy;
because I is a conclusion inductively supported.

Consider now the fundamentally different statement:

II. Induction is rational (reasonable).

We have already seen that the rationality of induction, unlike its "successful-
ness," is not a fact about the constitution of the world. It is a matter of what we
mean by the word "rational" in its application to any procedure for forming opinions about what lies outside our observations or that of available witnesses. For
to have good reasons for any such opinion is to have good inductive support for
it. The chaotic universe just envisaged, therefore, is not one in which induction
would cease to be rational; it is simply one in which it would be impossible to form
rational expectations to the effect that specific things would happen. It might be
said that in such a universe it would at least be rational to refrain from forming
specific expectations, to expect nothing but irregularities. Just so. But this is itself a
higher-order induction: where irregularity is the rule, expect further irregularities.
Learning not to count on things is as much learning an inductive lesson as learning
what things to count on.

So it is a contingent, factual matter that it is sometimes possible to form rational
opinions concerning what specifically happened or will happen in given circumstances (I); it is a non-contingent, *a priori* matter that the only ways of doing this
must be inductive ways (II). What people have done is to run together, to conflate,
the question to which I is [an] answer and the quite different question to which II is
an answer; producing the muddled and senseless questions: "Is the universe such that
inductive procedures are rational?" or "What must the universe be like in order for
inductive procedures to be rational?" It is the attempt to answer these confused questions which leads to statements like "The uniformity of nature is a presupposition of
the validity of induction." The statement that nature is uniform might be taken to be a
vague way of expressing what we expressed by I; and certainly this fact is a condition
of, for it is identical with, the likewise contingent fact that we are, and shall continue
to be, able to form rational opinions, of the kind we are most anxious to form, about
the unobserved. But neither this fact about the world, nor any other, is a condition of
the necessary truth that, if it is possible to form rational opinions of this kind, these
will be inductively supported opinions.

## TEST YOUR UNDERSTANDING

1. "Of course, inductive arguments are not deductively valid; if they were, they would be deductive arguments. Inductive reasoning must be assessed, for soundness, by inductive standards." Explain what Strawson means by this.

2. Explain Strawson's point in the following passage:

   > To ask whether it is reasonable to place reliance on inductive procedures is like asking whether it is reasonable to proportion the degree of one's convictions to the strength of one's evidence. Doing this is what "being reasonable" means in this context.


## NOTES AND QUESTIONS

1. *Strawson's appeal to "analyticity."* Strawson's account depends crucially on the notion of an analytic proposition (or statement). This concept is a descendant of Hume's notion of a "relation of ideas." It is sometimes explained by saying that an **analytic** statement is one that is true *simply in virtue of the meanings of the words that make it up*. Putative examples include "All bachelors are unmarried," "Red is a color," "If *x* is taller than *y*, then *y* is shorter than *x*," and so on. The crucial feature of analytic statements, for Strawson, is that they cannot meaningfully be called into question. Anyone who doubts that bachelors are unmarried and asks for a justification of this statement shows that he doesn't know what the English word "bachelor" means. Similarly, Strawson suggests, anyone who doubts the rationality of induction shows that he does not know what the word "rational" means. The notion of analyticity played a central role in twentieth-century philosophy. It was famously attacked by W. V. Quine in "Two Dogmas of Empiricism" (in *From a Logical Point of View*, Harvard University Press, 1960) and defended by Grice and Strawson in "In Defense of a Dogma" (*Philosophical Review* 65/2 [Apr., 1956]).

   *Exercise:* Assess Strawson's claim that

   > It is an analytic proposition that it is reasonable to have a degree of belief in a statement which is proportional to the strength of the evidence in its favour; and it is an analytic proposition . . . that, other things being equal, the evidence for a generalization is strong in proportion as the number of favourable instances, and the variety of circumstances in which they have been found, is great. So to ask whether it is reasonable to place reliance on inductive procedures is like asking whether it is reasonable to proportion the degree of one's convictions to the strength of one's evidence. Doing this is what "being reasonable" means in this context.

   In order to do this, try to describe a rational, competent speaker of English who has genuine doubts about the reasonableness of induction.

2. *Alternative inductive practices.* Suppose we come upon a tribe that forms beliefs about the future more or less as we do, with this exception: when they have an especially important question that they cannot answer by ordinary means, they kill a chicken and inspect its entrails for clues. (They have an elaborate set of rules for deriving predictions from the entrails of birds.) We want to know whether they are reasonable in following this method. They don't speak English, but their language has a word, "gleeb," that we have translated with our word "rational" (The translation works perfectly in every other context.) So we ask them, "Why is it *gleeb* to make predictions by inspecting the entrails of birds?" And they say, "We've read our Strawson, so we know that your question is misguided. Doing this is what *'being gleeb'* means in this context."

*Exercise:* Explain the problem this case raises for Strawson's justification of induction and say how Strawson might reply.

## Karl Popper (1902–1994)

Popper was born in Austria, trained as a psychologist, and spent most of his career at the London School of Economics. His influential contributions to the philosophy of science include *The Logic of Scientific Discovery* (1934) and *Conjectures and Refutations* (1963). *The Open Society and Its Enemies* (1945), published in the immediate aftermath of World War II, is an effort to identify the sources of totalitarianism in the history of Western thought.

# THE PROBLEM OF INDUCTION
## from *Replies to My Critics*

H ume's problem of induction has almost always been badly formulated by what may be called the philosophical tradition. I will first give a few of these bad formulations, which I shall call the *traditional formulations of the problem of induction.* I shall soon replace them, however, by what I regard as better formulations.

I

Typical examples of formulations of the problem of induction that are both traditional and bad are the following.

What is the justification for the belief that the future will resemble the past? What is the justification of so-called *inductive inferences?*

By an inductive inference is here meant an inference from repeatedly *observed instances* to some as yet *unobserved instances.* It is of comparatively minor significance whether such an inference from the observed to the unobserved is, from the point of view of time, predictive or retrodictive; whether we infer that the sun will rise tomorrow or that it did rise 100,000 years ago. Of course, from a pragmatic point of view, one might say that it is the predictive type of inference which is the more important. No doubt usually it is.

There are various philosophers other than I who also regard as misconceived this traditional problem of induction. Some say that it is misconceived because no justification is needed for inductive inference; no more in fact than for deductive inference. Inductive inference is inductively valid just as deductive inference is deductively valid. I think it was Professor Strawson who was the first to say this.

I am of a different opinion. I hold with Hume that there simply is no such logical entity as an inductive inference; or, that all so-called inductive inferences are logically invalid — and even *inductively* invalid, to put it more sharply. We have many examples of deductively valid inferences, and even some partial criteria of deductive validity; but no example of an inductively valid inference exists And I hold, incidentally, that this result can be found in Hume, even though Hume, at the same time, and in sharp contrast to myself, *believed in the psychological power of induction*; not as a valid procedure, but as a procedure which animals and men successfully make use of, as a matter of fact and of biological necessity.

I take it as an important task, in replying to my critics, to make clear, even at the cost of some repetition, where I agree and where I disagree with Hume.

I agree with Hume's opinion that induction is invalid and in no sense justified. Consequently neither Hume nor I can accept the traditional formulations which uncritically ask for the justification of induction; such a request is uncritical because it is blind to the possibility that induction is invalid *in every sense,* and therefore *unjustifiable*.

I disagree with Hume's opinion (the opinion incidentally of almost all philosophers) that induction is a fact and in any case needed. I hold that neither animals nor men use any procedure like induction, or any argument based on the repetition of instances. The belief that we use induction is simply a mistake. It is a kind of optical illusion.

What we do use is a method of trial and of the elimination of error; however misleadingly this method may look like induction, its logical structure, if we examine it closely, totally differs from that of induction. Moreover, it is a method which does not give rise to any of the difficulties connected with the problem of induction.

Thus it is not because induction can manage without justification that I am opposed to the traditional problem; on the contrary, it would urgently need justification. But the need cannot be satisfied. Induction simply does not exist, and the opposite view is a straightforward mistake.

## II

There are many ways to present my own noninductivist point of view. Perhaps the simplest is this. I will try to show that the whole apparatus of induction becomes unnecessary once we admit the general fallibility of human knowledge or, as I like to call it, *the conjectural character of human knowledge*.

Let me point this out first for the best kind of human knowledge we have; that is, for scientific knowledge. I assert that scientific knowledge is essentially conjectural or hypothetical.

Take as an example classical Newtonian mechanics. There never was a more successful theory. If repeated observational success could establish a theory, it would have established Newton's theory. Yet Newton's theory was superseded in the field of astronomy by Einstein's theory, and in the atomic field by quantum theory. And almost all physicists think now that Newtonian classical mechanics is no more than a marvellous conjecture, a strangely successful hypothesis, and a staggeringly good approximation to the truth.

I can now formulate my central thesis, which is this. Once we fully realize the implications of the conjectural character of human knowledge, then the problem of induction changes its character completely: there is no need any longer to be disturbed by Hume's negative results, since there is no need any longer to ascribe to human knowledge a *validity* derived from repeated observations. Human knowledge possesses no such validity. On the other hand, we can explain all our achievements in terms of the method of trial and the elimination of error. To put it in a nutshell, our conjectures are our trial balloons, and we test them by criticizing them and by trying to replace them — by trying to show that there can be better or worse conjectures, and that they can be improved upon. The place of the problem of induction is usurped by the problem of the comparative goodness or badness of the rival conjectures or theories that have been proposed. . . .

# IV

Hume's two problems of induction — the logical problem and the psychological problem — can best be presented, I think, against the background of the commonsense theory of induction. This theory is very simple. Since all knowledge is supposed to be the result of past observation, so especially is all expectational knowledge such as that the sun will rise tomorrow, or that all men are bound to die, or that bread nourishes. All this has to be the result of past observation.

It is to Hume's undying merit that he dared to challenge the commonsense view of induction, even though he never doubted that it must be largely true. He believed that induction by repetition was logically untenable — that rationally, or logically, *no amount* of observed instances can have the slightest bearing upon unobserved instances. This is Hume's negative solution of the problem of induction, a solution which I fully endorse.

But Hume held, at the same time, that although induction was rationally invalid, it was a psychological fact, and that we all relied on it.

Thus Hume's two problems of induction were:

(a) The logical problem:

*Are we rationally justified in reasoning from repeated instances of which we have had experience to instances of which we have had no experience?*

Hume's unrelenting answer is: No, we are not justified, however great the number of repetitions may be. And he added that it did not make the slightest difference if, in this problem, we ask for the justification not of *certain* belief, but of *probable* belief. Instances of which we have had experience do not allow us to reason or argue about the *probability* of instances of which we have had no experience, any more than to the *certainty* of such instances.

(b) The following psychological question:

*How is it that nevertheless all reasonable people expect and believe that instances of which they have had no experience will conform to those of which they have had experience?* Or in other words, why do we all have *expectations*, and why do we hold on to them with such great *confidence*, or such strong belief?

Hume's answer to this psychological problem of induction was:

*Because of "custom or habit"; or in other words because of the irrational but irresistible power of the law of association.* We are *conditioned by repetition;* a conditioning mechanism without which, Hume says, we could hardly survive.

My own view is that Hume's answer to the logical problem is right and that his answer to the psychological problem is, in spite of its persuasiveness, quite mistaken.

# V

The answers given by Hume to the logical and psychological problems of induction lead immediately to an irrationalist conclusion. According to Hume, all our knowledge, and especially all our scientific knowledge, is just irrational habit or custom, and it is rationally totally indefensible.

Hume himself thought of this as a form of scepticism; but it was rather, as Bertrand Russell pointed out, an unintended surrender to irrationalism. It is an amazing fact that a peerless critical genius, one of the most rational minds of all ages, not only came to disbelieve in reason, but became a champion of unreason, of irrationalism.

Nobody has felt this paradox more strongly than Bertrand Russell, an admirer and, in many respects, even a late disciple of Hume. Thus in the Hume chapter in his *History of Western Philosophy,* published in 1946, Russell says about Hume's treatment of induction: "Hume's philosophy . . . represents the bankruptcy of eighteenth-century reasonableness" and, "It is therefore important to discover whether there is any answer to Hume within a philosophy that is wholly or mainly *empirical.* If not, *there is no intellectual difference between sanity and insanity.* The lunatic who believes that he is a poached egg is to be condemned solely on the ground that he is in a minority. . . ."

Russell goes on to assert that if induction (or the principle of induction) is rejected, "every attempt to arrive at general scientific laws from particular observations is fallacious, and Hume's scepticism is inescapable for an empiricist."

And Russell sums up his view of the situation created by the clash between Hume's two answers; by the following dramatic remark:

*"The growth of unreason throughout the nineteenth century and what has passed of the twentieth* is a natural sequel to Hume's destruction of empiricism."[1]

This last quotation of Russell's goes *perhaps* too far. I do not wish to overdramatize the situation; and although I sometimes feel that Russell is right in his emphasis, at other moments I doubt it.

Yet the following quotation from Professor Strawson seems to me to support Russell's grave opinion: "[If] . . . there is a problem of induction, and . . . Hume posed it, it must be added that he solved it . . . [;] our acceptance of the 'basic canons' [of induction] . . . is forced upon us by Nature. . . . Reason is, and ought to be the slave of the passions."[2]

However this may be, I assert that I have an answer to Hume's psychological problem which completely removes the clash between the logic and the psychology of knowledge; and with it, it removes all of Hume's and Strawson's reasoning against reason.

# VI

My own way of avoiding Hume's irrationalist consequences is very simple. I solve the psychological problem of induction (and also such formulations as the pragmatic problem) in a manner which satisfies the following *"principle of the primacy of the logical solution,"* or, more briefly, the *"principle of transference."* The principle runs like this: the solution of the logical problem of induction, far from clashing with those of the psychological or pragmatic problems, can, with some care, be directly transferred to them. As a result, there is no clash, and there are no irrationalist consequences.

The logical problem of induction itself needs some reformulation to start with.

First, it must be formulated in terms not only of "instances" (as by Hume) but of universal regularities or laws. Regularities or laws are presupposed by Hume's own term "instance"; for an instance is an instance *of* something — *of* a regularity or *of* a law. (Or, rather, it is an instance of many regularities or many laws.)

Secondly, we must widen the scope of reasoning from instances to laws so that we can take heed also of counterinstances.

In this way, we arrive at a reformulation of Hume's *logical problem of induction* along the following lines:

*Are we rationally justified in reasoning from instances or from counterinstances of which we have had experience to the truth or falsity of the corresponding laws, or to instances of which we have had no experience?*

---

1. The three quotations are from Bertrand Russell, *A History of Western Philosophy* (George Allen & Unwin, 1946), pp. 698f.; new ed. (1961), pp. 645–47. (Italics mine.) [Popper's note.]

2. See p. 21 of P. F. Strawson, "On Justifying Induction", *Philosophical Studies,* 9 (1958), 20f. See also Hume, *Treatise,* Book II, Part III, section III (Selby-Bigge ed., p. 415): "Reason is, and ought only to be the slave of the passions. . . ." [Popper's note.]

This is a purely logical problem. It is essentially merely a slight extension of Hume's logical problem of induction formulated here earlier, in subsection IV.

The answer to this problem is: as implied by Hume, we certainly are not justified in reasoning from an instance to the truth of the corresponding law. But to this negative result a second result, equally negative, may be added: we *are* justified in reasoning from a counterinstance to the *falsity* of the corresponding universal law (that is, of any law of which it is a counterinstance). Or in other words, from a purely logical point of view, *the* acceptance of *one* counterinstance to "All swans are white" implies the falsity of the law "All swans are white" — that law, that is, whose counterinstance we accepted. Induction is logically invalid; but refutation or falsification is a logically valid way of arguing from a single counterinstance to — or, rather, against — the corresponding law.

This shows that I continue to agree with Hume's negative logical result; but I extend it.

This logical situation is completely independent of any question of whether we would, in practice, accept a single counterinstance — for example, a solitary black swan — in refutation of a so far highly successful law. I do not suggest that we would necessarily be so easily satisfied; we might well suspect that the black specimen before us was not a swan. And in practice, anyway, we would be most reluctant to accept an isolated counterinstance. But this is a different question (though one which I have dealt with extensively). Logic forces us to reject even the most successful law the moment we accept one single counterinstance.

Thus we can say: Hume was right in his negative result that there can be no logically valid positive argument leading in the inductive direction. But there is a further negative result; there are logically valid negative arguments leading in the inductive direction: *a counterinstance may disprove a law.*

# VII

Hume's negative result establishes for good that all our universal laws or theories remain forever guesses, conjectures, hypotheses. But my own negative result concerning the force of counterinstances by no means rules out the possibility of a positive theory of how, by purely rational arguments, we can *prefer* some competing conjectures to others.

In fact, we can erect a fairly elaborate *logical theory of preference* — preference from the point of view of the search for truth.

To put it in a nutshell, Russell's desperate remark that if with Hume we reject all positive induction, "there is no intellectual difference between sanity and insanity" is mistaken. For the rejection of induction does not prevent us from preferring, say, Newton's theory to Kepler's[3] or Einstein's theory to Newton's: during our rational critical discussion of these theories we *may* have accepted the existence of counterexamples to Kepler's theory which do not refute Newton's, and of counterexamples to Newton's which do not refute Einstein's. Given the acceptance of these

---

3. Johannes Kepler (1571–1630) identified three laws of planetary motion, all of which can be explained (at least approximately) by Newton's much more general theory of gravitation.

counterexamples we can say that Kepler's and Newton's theories are certainly false; whilst Einstein's may be true or it may be false: that we don't know. Thus there may exist *purely intellectual* preferences for one or the other of these theories; and we are very far from having to say with Russell that all the difference between science and lunacy disappears. Admittedly, Hume's argument still stands, and therefore the difference between a scientist and a lunatic is not that the first bases his theories securely upon observations while the second does not, or anything like that. Nevertheless we may now see that there *may be* a difference: it *may be* that the lunatic's theory is easily refutable by observation, while the scientist's theory has withstood severe tests.

What the scientist's and the lunatic's theories have in common is that both belong to *conjectural knowledge*. But some conjectures are much better than others; and this is a sufficient answer to Russell, and it is sufficient to avoid radical scepticism. For since it is possible for some conjectures to be *preferable* to others, it is also possible for our conjectural knowledge to improve, and to *grow*. (Of course, it is possible that a theory that is preferred to another at one time may fall out of favour at a later time so that the other is now preferred to it. But, on the other hand, this may not happen.)

We may *prefer* some competing theories to others on purely rational grounds. It is important that we are clear what the principles of preference or selection are.

In the first place they are governed by the idea of truth. We want, if at all possible, theories which are true, and for this reason we try to eliminate the false ones.

But we want more than this. We want new and interesting truth. We are thus led to the idea of *the growth of informative content*[4] and especially of *truth content*. That is, we are led to the following *principle of preference:* a theory with a great informative content is on the whole more interesting, even before it has been tested, than a theory with little content. Admittedly, we may have to abandon the theory with the greater content, or as I also call it, the bolder theory, if it does not stand up to tests. But even in this case we may have learned more from it than from a theory with little content, for falsifying tests can sometimes *reveal new and unexpected facts and problems*.

Thus our logical analysis leads us direct to a theory of method, and especially to the following methodological rule: try out, and aim at, bold theories, with great informative content; and then let these bold theories compete, by discussing them critically and by testing them severely....

---

4. The "informative content" of a theory, for Popper, is a measure of how strong or opinionated the theory is. For technical purposes, Popper identifies the informative content of a theory with the set of statements incompatible with that theory. Strong, informative theories are incompatible with many statements; weaker, less informative theories are incompatible with fewer statements. For example, the theory that the moon is a physical object is incompatible with statements like "The moon is a god" or "The moon is an illusion," whereas the theory that the moon is *made of cheese* is incompatible with all of these statements and many more, for example: "The moon is made of chocolate." The latter theory is thus more informative than the former. (As the example shows, a false theory can have more "informative content" than a true one.) For discussion, see Karl Popper, *Unended Quest: An intellectual Autobiography* (Routledge, 1992), p. 24.

## 14. THE PSYCHOLOGICAL AND PRAGMATIC PROBLEMS OF INDUCTION

My *solution* of the logical problem of induction was that we may have *preferences* for certain of the competing conjectures; that is, for those which are highly informative and which so far have stood up to eliminative criticism. These preferred conjectures are the result of selection, of the struggle for survival of the hypotheses under the strain of *criticism, which is artificially intensified selection pressure.*

The same holds for the psychological problem of induction. Here too we are faced with competing hypotheses, which may perhaps be called beliefs, and some of them are eliminated, while others survive, anyway for the time being. Animals are often eliminated along with their beliefs; or else they survive with them. Men frequently outlive their beliefs; but for as long as the beliefs survive (often a very short time), they form the (momentary or lasting) *basis of action.*

My central thesis is that this Darwinian procedure of the selection of beliefs and actions can in no sense be described as irrational. In no way does it clash with the rational solution of the logical problem of induction. Rather, it is just the transference of the logical solution to the psychological field. (This does not mean, of course, that we never suffer from what are called "irrational beliefs.")

Thus with an application of the principle of transference to Hume's psychological problem Hume's irrationalist conclusions disappear.

In talking of preference I have so far discussed only the theoretician's preference — if he has any; and why it will be for the "better," that is, more testable, theory, and for the better tested one. Of course, the theoretician may not have *any* preference: he may be discouraged by Hume's, and my, "sceptical" solution to Hume's logical problem; he may say that, if he cannot *make sure* of finding the true theory among the competing theories, he is not interested in any method like the one described — not even if the method makes it reasonably certain that, *if* a true theory should be among the theories proposed, it will be among the surviving, the preferred, the corroborated ones. Yet a more sanguine or more dedicated or more curious "pure" theoretician may well be encouraged, by our analysis, to propose again and again new competing theories in the hope that one of them may be true — even if we shall never be able to make sure of any one that it is true.

Thus the pure theoretician has more than one way of action open to him; and he will choose a method such as the method of trial and the elimination of error only if his curiosity exceeds his disappointment at the unavoidable uncertainty and incompleteness of all our endeavours.

It is different with him *qua* man of practical action. For a man of practical action has always to *choose* between some more or less definite alternatives, since even *inaction is a kind of action.*

But every action presupposes a set of expectations, that is, of theories about the world. Which theory shall the man of action choose? Is there such a thing as a *rational choice?*

This leads us to the *pragmatic problems of induction,* which to start with, we might formulate thus:

a. Upon which theory should we rely for practical action, from a rational point of view?

b. Which theory should we prefer for practical action, from a rational point of view?

My answer to (a) is: from a rational point of view, we should not "rely" on any theory, for no theory has been shown to be true, or can be shown to be true (or "reliable").

My answer to (b) is: we should *prefer* the best tested theory as a basis for action.

In other words, there is no "absolute reliance"; but since we *have* to choose, it will be "rational" to choose the best tested theory. This will be "rational" in the most obvious sense of the word known to me: the best tested theory is the one which, in the light of our *critical discussion,* appears to be the best so far; and I do not know of anything more "rational" than a well-conducted critical discussion.

Since this point appears not to have got home I shall try to restate it here in a slightly new way, suggested to me by David Miller. Let us forget momentarily about what theories we "use" or "choose" or "base our practical actions on," and consider only the resulting *proposal* or *decision* (to do *X;* not to do *X;* to do nothing; or so on). Such a proposal can, we hope, be rationally criticized; and if we are rational agents we will want it to survive, if possible, the most testing criticism we can muster. *But such criticism will freely make use of the best tested scientific theories in our possession.* Consequently any proposal that ignores these theories (where they are relevant, I need hardly add) will collapse under criticism. Should any proposal remain, it will be rational to adopt it.

This seems to me all far from tautological. Indeed, it might well be challenged by challenging the italicized sentence in the last paragraph. Why, it might be asked, does rational criticism make use of the best tested although highly unreliable theories? The answer, however, is exactly the same as before. Deciding to criticize a practical proposal from the standpoint of modern medicine (rather than, say, in phrenological terms) is itself a kind of "practical" decision (anyway it may have practical consequences). Thus the rational decision is always: adopt critical methods that have themselves withstood severe criticism.

There is, of course, an infinite regress here. But it is transparently harmless.

Now I do not particularly want to deny (or, for that matter, assert) that, in choosing the best tested theory as a basis for action, we "rely" on it, in some sense of the word. It may therefore even be described as the *most* "reliable" theory available, in some sense of this term. Yet this is not to say that it is "reliable." It is "unreliable" at least in the sense that we shall always do well, even in practical action, to foresee the possibility that something may go wrong with it and with our expectations.

But it is not merely this trivial caution which we must derive from our negative reply to the pragmatic problem (a). Rather, it is of the utmost importance for the understanding of the whole problem, and especially of what I have called the traditional problem, that in spite of the "rationality" of choosing the best tested theory as a basis of action, this choice is *not* "rational" in the sense that it is based upon *good reasons in favour* of the expectation that it will in practice be a successful choice: *there can be no good reasons* in this sense, and this is precisely Hume's result. On the contrary, even if our physical theories should be true, it is perfectly possible that the world as we know it, with all its pragmatically relevant regularities, may completely disintegrate in the next second. This should be obvious to anybody today; but I said so before Hiroshima: there are infinitely many possible causes of local, partial, or total disaster.

From a pragmatic point of view, however, most of these possibilities are obviously not worth bothering about because we cannot *do* anything about them: they are beyond the realm of action. (I do not, of course, include atomic war among those disasters which are beyond the realm of human action, although most of us think just in this way since we cannot do more about it than about an act of God.)

All this would hold even if we could be certain that our physical and biological theories were true. But we do not know it. On the contrary, we have very good reason to suspect even the best of them; and this adds, of course, further infinities to the infinite possibilities of catastrophe.

It is this kind of consideration which makes Hume's and my own negative reply so important. For we can now see very clearly why we must beware lest our theory of knowledge proves too much. More precisely, *no theory of knowledge should attempt to explain why we are successful in our attempts to explain things.*

Even if we assume that we have been successful — that our physical theories are true — we can learn from our cosmology how infinitely improbable this success is: our theories tell us that the world is almost completely empty, and that empty space is filled with chaotic radiation. And almost all places which are not empty are occupied either by chaotic dust, or by gases, or by very hot stars — all in conditions which seem to make the application of any physical method of acquiring knowledge impossible.

There are many worlds, possible and actual worlds, in which a search for knowledge and for regularities would fail. And even in the world as we actually know it from the sciences, the occurrence of conditions under which life, and a search for knowledge, could arise — and succeed — seems to be almost infinitely improbable. Moreover, it seems that if ever such conditions should appear, they would be bound to disappear again, after a time which, cosmologically speaking, is very short.

It is in this sense that induction is inductively invalid, as I said above. That is to say, any strong positive reply to Hume's logical problem (say, the thesis that induction is valid) would be paradoxical. For, on the one hand, if induction is the method of science, then modern cosmology is at least roughly correct (I do not dispute this); and on the other, modern cosmology teaches us that to generalize from observations taken, for the most part, in our incredibly idiosyncratic region of the universe would almost always be quite invalid. Thus if induction is "inductively valid" it will almost always lead to false conclusions; and therefore it is inductively invalid.

## TEST YOUR UNDERSTANDING

1. Where does Popper agree with Hume? Where does he disagree?

2. Explain Popper's claim (in section III) that "the place of the problem of induction is usurped by the problem of the comparative goodness or badness of the rival conjectures or theories that have been proposed."

3. Explain Popper's claim that "we should *prefer* the best tested theory as a basis for action."

## NOTES AND QUESTIONS

1. *Popper's philosophy of science.* Popper is famous for posing the **demarcation problem**: What distinguishes genuine science from pseudoscience? His solution, in a nutshell, is to insist that genuine science traffics in *falsifiable* conjectures and devotes itself to seeking to refute new hypotheses as they are proposed. Many philosophers and scientists accept some version of this idea, but go on to add that when a hypothesis has survived repeated efforts to falsify it, it is thereby *confirmed* (to some high degree). Popper denies this. A theory that has survived rigorous efforts to falsify it may be *better* than its untested rivals; but it is not *more probable* or more *likely to be true*. Scientists are justified in *focusing their attention* on well-tested theories, and in using such theories for practical purposes. But they are not justified in *believing* that their theories are true. Popper takes Hume's skeptical arguments to have established this conclusion. Popper's views are developed in *Conjectures and Refutations* (Routledge and Kegan Paul, 1963). For an accessible presentation, see David Miller, *Critical Rationalism: A Restatement and Defense* (Open Court, 1998).

2. Suppose that we notice that in our experience, litmus paper turns red when dipped in acid. We then formulate two hypotheses:

    Litmus paper always turns red when dipped in acid.

    Litmus paper always turns red when dipped in acid before December 31, 2025, at which point it will begin to turn blue.

We then conduct further experiments designed to test these hypotheses, and both survive. We are now asked to place a bet on an experiment that will be run on New Year's Day, 2026. Does Popper's view entail that these hypotheses are equally good, and that it would therefore be perfectly rational to rely on either one in making our decision? Explain why this is a problem for Popper's theory and imagine how he might respond.

## Nelson Goodman (1906–1998)

Goodman was a central figure in the development of analytic philosophy in America. His books include *Fact, Fiction, and Forecast* (1955), a landmark study in epistemology and the philosophy of language, *Languages of Art* (1968), and *Ways of Worldmaking* (1978), which defends the bold thesis that there are many worlds, all equally real and all made by *us*.

# THE NEW RIDDLE OF INDUCTION
### from *Fact, Fiction, and Forecast*

# 1. The Old Problem of Induction

What is commonly thought of as the Problem of Induction has been solved, or dissolved; and we face new problems that are not as yet very widely understood. To approach them, I shall have to run as quickly as possible over some very familiar ground.

The problem of the validity of judgments about future or unknown cases arises, as Hume pointed out, because such judgments are neither reports of experience nor logical consequences of it. Predictions, of course, pertain to what has not yet been observed. And they cannot be logically inferred from what has been observed; for what *has* happened imposes no logical restrictions on what *will* happen. . . .

Hume's answer to the question how predictions are related to past experience is refreshingly non-cosmic. When an event of one kind frequently follows upon an event of another kind in experience, a habit is formed that leads the mind, when confronted with a new event of the first kind, to pass to the idea of an event of the second kind. The idea of necessary connection arises from the felt impulse of the mind in making this transition.

Now if we strip this account of all extraneous features, the central point is that to the question "Why one prediction rather than another?" Hume answers that the elect prediction is one that accords with a past regularity, because this regularity has established a habit. Thus among alternative statements about a future moment, one statement is distinguished by its consonance with habit and thus with regularities observed in the past. Prediction according to any other alternative is errant.

How satisfactory is this answer? The heaviest criticism has taken the righteous position that Hume's account at best pertains only to the source of predictions, not their legitimacy; that he sets forth the circumstances under which we make given predictions — and in this sense explains why we make them — but leaves untouched the question of our license for making them. To trace origins, runs the old complaint, is not to establish validity: the real question is not why a prediction is in fact made but how it can be justified. . . .

All this seems to me quite wrong. I think Hume grasped the central question and considered his answer to be passably effective. And I think his answer is reasonable and relevant, even if it is not entirely satisfactory. . . .

I suppose that the problem of justifying induction has called forth as much fruitless discussion as has any halfway respectable problem of modern philosophy. The typical writer begins by insisting that some way of justifying predictions must be found; proceeds to argue that for this purpose we need some resounding universal law of the Uniformity of Nature[1] and then inquires how this universal principle itself can be justified. At this point, if he is tired, he concludes that the principle must be accepted as an indispensable assumption; or if he is energetic and ingenious, he goes on to devise some subtle justification for it. Such an invention, however, seldom satisfies anyone else; and the easier course of accepting an unsubstantiated and even dubious assumption much more sweeping than any actual predictions we make seems an odd and expensive way of justifying them.

## 2. Dissolution of the Old Problem

Understandably, then, more critical thinkers have suspected that there might be something awry with the problem we are trying to solve. Come to think of it, what precisely would constitute the justification we seek? If the problem is to explain how we know that certain predictions will turn out to be correct, the sufficient answer is that we don't know any such thing. If the problem is to *find* some way of distinguishing antecedently between true and false predictions, we are asking for prevision rather than for philosophical explanation. Nor does it help matters much to say that we are merely trying to show that or why certain predictions are *probable*. Often it is said that while we cannot tell in advance whether a prediction concerning a given throw of a die is true, we can decide whether the prediction is a probable one. But if this means determining how the prediction is related to actual frequency distributions of future throws of the die, surely there is no way of knowing or proving this in advance. On the other hand, if the judgment that the prediction is probable has nothing to do with subsequent occurrences, then the question remains in what sense a probable prediction is any better justified than an improbable one.

Now obviously the genuine problem cannot be one of attaining unattainable knowledge or of accounting for knowledge that we do not in fact have. A better understanding of our problem can be gained by looking for a moment at what is involved in justifying non-inductive inferences. How do we justify a *deduction*? Plainly, by showing that it conforms to the general rules of deductive inference. An argument that so conforms is justified or valid, even if its conclusion happens

---

1. Many philosophers have supposed that inductive arguments are really *deductive* arguments with an unstated premise to the effect that the future will resemble the past. The simplest statement of this principle is this: If all observed *F*s are *G*s, then all *F*s are *G*s. The problem of induction in this tradition is to *justify* our acceptance of this principle. But there is a more serious problem. As stated, the principle is clearly false. (All observed emeralds have been observed; but there are many emeralds that have not been observed.) The more serious problem is to *state* a version of the principle that stands a chance of being true.

to be false. An argument that violates a rule is fallacious even if its conclusion happens to be true. To justify a deductive conclusion therefore requires no knowledge of the facts it pertains to. Moreover, when a deductive argument has been shown to conform to the rules of logical inference, we usually consider it justified without going on to ask what justifies the rules. Analogously, the basic task in justifying an inductive inference is to show that it conforms to the general rules of *in*duction. Once we have recognized this, we have gone a long way towards clarifying our problem.

Yet, of course, the rules themselves must eventually be justified. The validity of a deduction depends not upon conformity to any purely arbitrary rules we may contrive, but upon conformity to valid rules. When we speak of *the* rules of inference we mean the valid rules — or better, *some* valid rules, since there may be alternative sets of equally valid rules. But how is the validity of rules to be determined? Here again we encounter philosophers who insist that these rules follow from some self-evident axiom, and others who try to show that the rules are grounded in the very nature of the human mind. I think the answer lies much nearer the surface. Principles of deductive inference are justified by their conformity with accepted deductive practice. Their validity depends upon accordance with the particular deductive inferences we actually make and sanction. If a rule yields inacceptable inferences, we drop it as invalid. Justification of general rules thus derives from judgments rejecting or accepting particular deductive inferences.

This looks flagrantly circular. I have said that deductive inferences are justified by their conformity to valid general rules, and that general rules are justified by their conformity to valid inferences. But this circle is a virtuous one. The point is that rules and particular inferences alike are justified by being brought into agreement with each other. *A rule is amended if it yields an inference we are unwilling to accept; an inference is rejected if it violates a rule we are unwilling to amend.* The process of justification is the delicate one of making mutual adjustments between rules and accepted inferences; and in the agreement achieved lies the only justification needed for either.

All this applies equally well to induction. An inductive inference, too, is justified by conformity to general rules, and a general rule by conformity to accepted inductive inferences. Predictions are justified if they conform to valid canons of induction; and the canons are valid if they accurately codify accepted inductive practice.

A result of such analysis is that we can stop plaguing ourselves with certain spurious questions about induction. We no longer demand an explanation for guarantees that we do not have, or seek keys to knowledge that we cannot obtain. It dawns upon us that the traditional smug insistence upon a hard-and-fast line between justifying induction and describing ordinary inductive practice distorts the problem. . . .

This clears the air but leaves a lot to be done. As principles of *de*ductive inference, we have the familiar and highly developed laws of logic; but there are available no such precisely stated and well-recognized principles of inductive inference. . . .

# 3. The Constructive Task of Confirmation Theory

The task of formulating rules that define the difference between valid and invalid inductive inferences is much like the task of defining any term with an established usage. If we set out to define the term "tree," we try to compose out of already understood words an expression that will apply to the familiar objects that standard usage calls trees, and that will not apply to objects that standard usage refuses to call trees. A proposal that plainly violates either condition is rejected; while a definition that meets these tests may be adopted and used to decide cases that are not already settled by actual usage. Thus the interplay we observed between rules of induction and particular inductive inferences is simply an instance of this characteristic dual adjustment between definition and usage, whereby the usage informs the definition, which in turn guides extension of the usage.

Of course this adjustment is a more complex matter than I have indicated. Sometimes, in the interest of convenience or theoretical utility, we deliberately permit a definition to run counter to clear mandates of common usage. We accept a definition of "fish" that excludes whales. Similarly we may decide to deny the term "valid induction" to some inductive inferences that are commonly considered valid, or apply the term to others not usually so considered. A definition may modify as well as extend ordinary usage.

Some pioneer work on the problem of defining confirmation or valid induction has been done by Professor Hempel.[2] Let me remind you briefly of a few of his results. Just as deductive logic is concerned primarily with a relation between statements — namely the consequence relation — that is independent of their truth or falsity, so inductive logic as Hempel conceives it is concerned primarily with a comparable relation of confirmation between statements. Thus the problem is to define the relation that obtains between any statement $S_1$ and another $S_2$ if and only if $S_1$ may properly be said to confirm $S_2$ in any degree.

With the question so stated, the first step seems obvious. Does not induction proceed in just the opposite direction from deduction? Surely some of the evidence-statements that inductively support a general hypothesis are consequences of it. Since the consequence relation is already well defined by deductive logic, will we not be on firm ground in saying that confirmation embraces the converse relation?[3] The laws of deduction in reverse will then be among the laws of induction.

Let's see where this leads us. We naturally assume further that whatever confirms a given statement confirms also whatever follows from that statement. But if we combine this assumption with our proposed principle, we get the embarrassing result that every statement confirms every other. Surprising as it may be that such innocent

---

2.  Carl G. Hempel (1905–1997), philosopher of science. The work Goodman discusses is presented in Hempel's "Studies in the Logic of Confirmation," in his *Aspects of Scientific Explanation* (Free Press, 1965).

3.  Given any **relation** *R*, the *converse* of *R* is that relation in which *b* stands to *a* if and only if *a* bears *R* to *b*. For example, the converse of *taller than,* is *shorter than*; the converse of *loves* is *is loved by*, etc.

beginnings lead to such an intolerable conclusion, the proof is very easy. Start with any statement $S_1$. It is a consequence of, and so by our present criterion confirms, the conjunction of $S_1$ and any statement whatsoever — call it $S_2$. But the confirmed conjunction, $S_1 \cdot S_2$[4] of course has $S_2$ as a consequence. Thus every statement confirms all statements.

The fault lies in careless formulation of our first proposal. While some statements that confirm a general hypothesis are consequences of it, not all its consequences confirm it. . . . Consider the heterogeneous conjunction:

8497 is a prime number and the other side of the moon is flat and Elizabeth the First was crowned on a Tuesday.

To show that any one of the three component statements is true is to support the conjunction by reducing the net undetermined claim. But support of this kind is not confirmation; for establishment of one component endows the whole statement with no credibility that is transmitted to other component statements. Confirmation of a hypothesis occurs only when an instance imparts to the hypothesis some credibility that is conveyed to other instances. . . .

Our formula thus needs tightening. This is readily accomplished, as Hempel points out, if we observe that a hypothesis is genuinely confirmed only by a statement that is an instance of it in the special sense of entailing not the hypothesis itself but its relativization or restriction to the class of entities mentioned by that statement. The relativization of a general hypothesis to a class results from restricting the range of its . . . quantifiers to the members of that class. Less technically, what the hypothesis says of all things the evidence statement says of one thing. . . . This obviously covers the confirmation of the conductivity of all copper by the conductivity of a given piece; and it excludes confirmation of our heterogeneous conjunction by any of its components. And, when taken together with the principle that what confirms a statement confirms all its consequences, this criterion does not yield the untoward conclusion that every statement confirms every other.[5]

New difficulties promptly appear from other directions, however. One is the infamous paradox of the ravens. The statement that a given object, say this piece of paper, is neither black nor a raven confirms the hypothesis that all non-black things are non-ravens. But this hypothesis is logically equivalent to the hypothesis that

---

4. The dot means "and."

5. A *general hypothesis* is a statement of the form "All Fs are Gs." **Quantifiers** are expressions like "all," "every," "some," and "at least one." To *relativize* a general hypothesis to a class is to consider a restricted version of that hypothesis that applies only to members of that class. So for example, if we start with the hypothesis:

All bats are blind.

we can relativize it to the class of *North American animals* by restricting the initial quantifier as follows:

All bats *in North America* are blind.

The proposal under discussion holds that the *instances of* a general hypothesis of the form "All Fs are Gs" are statements of the form "All Fs that are *H* are also *G*," or "The Fs that are *H* are also *G*." For example, the statement "The bats *in this cave* are blind" would count as an instance of "All bats are blind." According to Hempel, a statement *confirms* a generalization only when it is an instance of that generalization in this sense.

all ravens are black. Hence we arrive at the unexpected conclusion that the statement that a given object is neither black nor a raven confirms the hypothesis that all ravens are black. The prospect of being able to investigate ornithological theories without going out in the rain is so attractive that we know there must be a catch in it. The trouble this time, however, lies not in faulty definition, but in tacit and illicit reference to evidence not stated in our example. Taken by itself, the statement that the given object is neither black nor a raven confirms the hypothesis that everything that is not a raven is not black as well as the hypothesis that everything that is not black is not a raven. We tend to ignore the former hypothesis because we know it to be false from abundant other evidence — from all the familiar things that are not ravens but are black. But we are required to assume that no such evidence is available. Under this circumstance, even a much stronger hypothesis is also obviously confirmed: that nothing is either black or a raven. In the light of this confirmation of the hypothesis that there are no ravens, it is no longer surprising that under the artificial restrictions of the example, the hypothesis that all ravens are black is also confirmed. And the prospects for indoor ornithology vanish when we notice that under these same conditions, the contrary hypothesis that no ravens are black is equally well confirmed. . . .

No one supposes that the task of confirmation-theory has been completed. But the few steps I have reviewed — chosen partly for their bearing on what is to follow — show how things move along once the problem of definition displaces the problem of justification. Important and long-unnoticed questions are brought to light and answered; and we are encouraged to expect that the many remaining questions will in time yield to similar treatment.

But our satisfaction is shortlived. New and serious trouble begins to appear.

# 4. The New Riddle of Induction

Confirmation of a hypothesis by an instance depends rather heavily upon features of the hypothesis other than its syntactical form. That a given piece of copper conducts electricity increases the credibility of statements asserting that other pieces of copper conduct electricity, and thus confirms the hypothesis that all copper conducts electricity. But the fact that a given man now in this room is a third son does not increase the credibility of statements asserting that other men now in this room are third sons, and so does not confirm the hypothesis that all men now in this room are third sons. Yet in both cases our hypothesis is a generalization of the evidence statement. The difference is that in the former case the hypothesis is a *lawlike* statement; while in the latter case, the hypothesis is a merely contingent or accidental generality. Only a statement that is *lawlike* — regardless of its truth or falsity or its scientific importance — is capable of receiving confirmation from an instance of it; accidental statements are not. Plainly, then, we must look for a way of distinguishing lawlike from accidental statements.

So long as what seems to be needed is merely a way of excluding a few odd and unwanted cases that are inadvertently admitted by our definition of confirmation, the problem may not seem very hard or very pressing. We fully expect that minor defects will be found in our definition and that the necessary refinements will have to be worked out patiently one after another. But some further examples will show that our present difficulty is of a much graver kind.

Suppose that all emeralds examined before a certain time $t$ are green. At time $t$, then, our observations support the hypothesis that all emeralds are green; and this is in accord with our definition of confirmation. Our evidence statements assert that emerald $a$ is green, that emerald $b$ is green, and so on; and each confirms the general hypothesis that all emeralds are green. So far, so good.

Now let me introduce another predicate[6] less familiar than "green." It is the predicate "grue" and it applies to all things examined before $t$ just in case they are green but to other things just in case they are blue. Then at time $t$ we have, for each evidence statement asserting that a given emerald is green, a parallel evidence statement asserting that that emerald is grue. And the statements that emerald $a$ is grue, that emerald $b$ is grue, and so on, will each confirm the general hypothesis that all emeralds are grue. Thus according to our definition, the prediction that all emeralds subsequently examined will be green and the prediction that all will be grue are alike confirmed by evidence statements describing the same observations. But if an emerald subsequently examined is grue, it is blue and hence not green. Thus although we are well aware which of the two incompatible predictions is genuinely confirmed, they are equally well confirmed according to our present definition. Moreover, it is clear that if we simply choose an appropriate predicate, then on the basis of these same observations we shall have equal confirmation, by our definition, for any prediction whatever about other emeralds — or indeed about anything else. As in our earlier example, only the predictions subsumed under lawlike hypotheses are genuinely confirmed; but we have no criterion as yet for determining lawlikeness. And now we see that without some such criterion, our definition not merely includes a few unwanted cases, but is so completely ineffectual that it virtually excludes nothing. . . .

Nevertheless, the difficulty is often slighted because on the surface there seem to be easy ways of dealing with it. Sometimes, for example, the problem is thought to be much like the paradox of the ravens. We are here again, it is pointed out, making tacit and illegitimate use of information outside the stated evidence: the information, for example, that different samples of one material are usually alike in conductivity, and the information that different men in a lecture audience are usually not alike in the number of their older brothers. But while it is true that such information is being smuggled in, this does not by itself settle the matter as it settles the matter of the ravens. There the point was that when the smuggled information is forthrightly

---

6. A **predicate** is a linguistic expression that combines with a proper name (or a sequence of proper names) to yield a complete sentence. So, for example, "… is tall" and "… loves …" are predicates, since they yield complete sentences when the blanks are filled in by names. Sometimes we omit the copula (the linking verb) and say that "tall" by itself qualifies as a predicate.

declared, its effect upon the confirmation of the hypothesis in question is immediately and properly registered by the definition we are using. On the other hand, if to our initial evidence we add statements concerning the conductivity of pieces of other materials or concerning the number of older brothers of members of other lecture audiences, this will not in the least affect the confirmation, according to our definition, of the hypothesis concerning copper or of that concerning this lecture audience. Since our definition is insensitive to the bearing upon hypotheses of evidence so related to them, even when the evidence is fully declared, the difficulty about accidental hypotheses cannot be explained away on the ground that such evidence is being surreptitiously taken into account. . . .

The most popular way of attacking the problem takes its cue from the fact that accidental hypotheses seem typically to involve some spatial or temporal restriction, or reference to some particular individual. They seem to concern the people in some particular room, or the objects on some particular person's desk; while lawlike hypotheses characteristically concern all ravens or all pieces of copper whatsoever. Complete generality is thus very often supposed to be a sufficient condition of lawlikeness; but to define this complete generality is by no means easy. Merely to require that the hypothesis contain no term naming, describing, or indicating a particular thing or location will obviously not be enough. The troublesome hypothesis that all emeralds are grue contains no such term; and where such a term does occur, as in hypotheses about men in *this room,* it can be suppressed in favor of some predicate (short or long, new or old) that contains no such term but applies only to exactly the same things. One might think, then, of excluding not only hypotheses that actually contain terms for specific individuals but also all hypotheses that are equivalent to others that do contain such terms. But, as we have just seen, to exclude only hypotheses of which *all* equivalents contain such terms is to exclude nothing. On the other hand, to exclude all hypotheses that have *some* equivalent containing such a term is to exclude everything; for even the hypothesis

All grass is green.

has as an equivalent:

All grass in London or elsewhere is green.

The next step, therefore, has been to consider ruling out predicates of certain kinds. A syntactically universal hypothesis is lawlike, the proposal runs, if its predicates are "purely qualitative" or "non-positional." This will obviously accomplish nothing if a purely qualitative predicate is then conceived either as one that is equivalent to some expression free of terms for specific individuals, or as one that is equivalent to no expression that contains such a term; for this only raises again the difficulties just pointed out. The claim appears to be rather that at least in the case of a simple enough predicate we can readily determine by direct inspection of its meaning whether or not it is purely qualitative. But even aside from obscurities in the notion of "the meaning" of a predicate, this claim seems to me wrong. I simply do not know how to tell whether a predicate is qualitative or positional, except perhaps by completely begging the question at issue and asking whether the predicate is "well-behaved" — that is whether simple syntactically universal hypotheses applying it are lawlike.

This statement will not go unprotested. "Consider," it will be argued, "the predicates 'blue' and 'green' and the predicate 'grue' introduced earlier, and also the predicate 'bleen' that applies to emeralds examined before time *t* just in case they are blue and to other emeralds just in case they are green. Surely it is clear," the argument runs, "that the first two are purely qualitative and the second two are not; for the meaning of each of the latter two plainly involves reference to a specific temporal position." To this I reply that indeed I do recognize the first two as well-behaved predicates admissible in lawlike hypotheses, and the second two as ill-behaved predicates. But the argument that the former but not the latter are purely qualitative seems to me quite unsound. True enough, if we start with "blue" and "green," then "grue" and "bleen" will be explained in terms of "blue" and "green" and a temporal term. But equally truly, if we start with "grue" and "bleen," then "blue" and "green" will be explained in terms of "grue" and "bleen" and a temporal term; "green," for example, applies to emeralds examined before time *t* just in case they are grue, and to other emeralds just in case they are bleen. Thus qualitativeness is an entirely relative matter and does not by itself establish any dichotomy of predicates. . . .

We have so far neither any answer nor any promising clue to an answer to the question what distinguishes lawlike or confirmable hypotheses from accidental or non-confirmable ones; and what may at first have seemed a minor technical difficulty has taken on the stature of a major obstacle to the development of a satisfactory theory of confirmation. It is this problem that I call the new riddle of induction.

## 5. The Pervasive Problem of Projection

At the beginning of this lecture, I expressed the opinion that the problem of induction is still unsolved, but that the difficulties that face us today are not the old ones; and I have tried to outline the changes that have taken place. The problem of justifying induction has been displaced by the problem of defining confirmation, and our work upon this has left us with the residual problem of distinguishing between confirmable and non-confirmable hypotheses. . . .

The vast amount of effort expended on the problem of induction in modern times has thus altered our afflictions but hardly relieved them. The original difficulty about induction arose from the recognition that anything may follow upon anything. Then, in attempting to define confirmation in terms of the converse of the consequence relation, we found ourselves with the distressingly similar difficulty that our definition would make any statement confirm any other. And now, after modifying our definition drastically, we still get the old devastating result that any statement will confirm any statement. Until we find a way of exercising some control over the hypotheses to be admitted, our definition makes no distinction whatsoever between valid and invalid inductive inferences.

The real inadequacy of Hume's account lay not in his descriptive approach but in the imprecision of his description. Regularities in experience, according to him, give rise to habits of expectation; and thus it is predictions conforming to past regularities that are normal or valid. But Hume overlooks the fact that some regularities do and some do not establish such habits; that predictions based on some regularities are valid while predictions based on other regularities are not. Every word you have heard me say has occurred prior to the final sentence of this lecture; but that does not, I hope, create any expectation that every word you will hear me say will be prior to that sentence. Again, consider our case of emeralds. All those examined before time *t* are green; and this leads us to expect, and confirms the prediction, that the next one will be green. But also, all those examined are grue; and this does not lead us to expect, and does not confirm the prediction, that the next one will be grue. Regularity in greenness confirms the prediction of further cases; regularity in grueness does not. To say that valid predictions are those based on past regularities, without being able to say *which* regularities, is thus quite pointless. Regularities are where you find them, and you can find them anywhere. As we have seen, Hume's failure to recognize and deal with this problem has been shared even by his most recent successors.

## TEST YOUR UNDERSTANDING

1. Explain Goodman's claim that principles of inductive reasoning are justified when they "accurately codify accepted inductive practice."

2. Restate Goodman's definition of "grue" and illustrate it with examples.

3. Explain Goodman's claim that "lawlike or projectable hypotheses cannot be distinguished on any merely syntactic grounds or even on the ground that such hypotheses are purely general in meaning." Say why this claim is important.

## NOTES AND QUESTIONS

1. *Goodman's coherentism.* Philosophers often suppose that when a particular case of reasoning is justified, it is justified because it conforms to a general rule that is independently justified. This is analogous to a similar claim in ethics, namely, that when an action is morally right, that is because it is permitted by moral rules that can be established prior to any examination of particular cases. One of Goodman's most radical proposals is that this conception of justification must be rejected. At any given stage, we have a large stock of examples of good inferences, or morally good actions, and any number of provisional rules that we accept. When we are challenged

to justify some particular inference or action, we may reply by showing that it conforms to previously accepted rules. But when we face a question about the status of a *rule*, we can assess it by asking how well it coheres with concrete *examples* of good reasoning or good conduct. This conception of justification has been influential. For its application in ethics, see John Rawls, "Outline of a Decision Procedure for Ethics," *Philosophical Review* 60, 2 (1951).

2. *Goodman's "theorem."* Goodman's paper contains the materials for a proof of the following proposition:

> All purely formal inductive rules are inconsistent, in the sense that they yield incompatible predictions when applied to any body of evidence.

Consider a simple inductive rule:

> All observed *F*s have been *G*.
> Therefore, the next *F* we examine will be *G*.

Now suppose that as of December 31, 2015, we have examined a million emeralds from all over the world and found them all to be green. (Suppose that emeralds are identified by a chemical test, and not by their color.) Tomorrow morning a new emerald — call it Bob — will be brought to light and examined. Our question is: What color will Bob be?

We have the following instance of the simple rule:

> All observed emeralds have been green.
> Therefore, Bob will be green.

So the simple rule tells us to predict that Bob will be green.

Now we follow Goodman's lead and define a new word:

> *x* is *gred* if and only if *x* has been examined before 2016 and *x* is green, or *x* has not been examined before 2016 and *x* is red.

(Stop here and practice using the word. Give yourself examples of green things that are gred, green things that are not gred, and so on.) That gives us another instance of the simple rule:

> All observed emeralds have been gred.
> Therefore Bob will be gred.

The premise here is true. (If that's not obvious, check the definition of "gred" and confirm it.) So the simple rule tells us that Bob will be gred. But we know that Bob will not be examined before 2016. So when we describe the evidence in this way, the simple rule tells us to predict that Bob will be *red*! (If that's not obvious, check the definition one more time.)

So we have two instances of the simple rule. They have exactly the same form. They both have true premises. But they yield *incompatible* conclusions. And any rule that does that is no good.

*Exercise:* Show that whenever the simple rule applies, it can be made to yield any prediction you like about the next case given a suitable choice of vocabulary.

*Exercise:* Goodman asserts that his argument will apply to any purely formal rule of induction. Consider the following more sophisticated rule and show that it falls to Goodman's argument as well:

If the ratio of *F*s to *G*s in a large random sample is r, then in the population as a whole, the ratio of *F*s to *G*s is (roughly) r.

3. *Solving the "new riddle".* A solution to the "new riddle" will take the form of a restriction on vocabulary suitable for inductive reasoning. "Green" is clearly **projectable** — suitable for induction — since we are familiar with many good inductive arguments about the colors of objects. Goodman's invented word *grue* is not projectable. The challenge is to provided a principled way of drawing the distinction. Goodman considers some possibilities in his essay, but there are many others. For a sampling of proposals, see D. Stalker, ed., *Grue! The New Riddle of Induction* (Open Court, 1994).

*Exercise:* Invent a test for projectability — a rule of the form

A predicate "F" is suitable for inductive reasoning if and only if . . .

Then assess your test using Goodman's methodology. Does your rule exclude any of the good inductive inferences we already accept? Does it ratify any of the bad inductive inferences we would ordinarily reject?

## Gilbert Harman (born 1938)

Harman is the James S. McDonnell Distinguished University Professor of Philosophy at Princeton University. His books include major studies in the philosophy of mind (*Thought*, 1973), epistemology (*Change in View*, 1986), moral philosophy (*The Nature of Morality*, 1978), and statistical learning theory (*Reliable Reasoning*, 2007, with Sanjeev Kulkarni.)

# THE INFERENCE TO THE BEST EXPLANATION

I wish to argue that enumerative induction should not be considered a warranted form of nondeductive inference in its own right.[1] I claim that, in cases where it appears that a warranted inference is an instance of enumerative induction, the inference should be described as a special case of another sort of inference, which I shall call "the inference to the best explanation."

---

1. Enumerative induction infers from observed regularity to universal regularity or at least to regularity in the next instance. [Harman's note.]

The form of my argument in the first part of this paper is as follows: I argue that even if one accepts enumerative induction as one form of nondeductive inference, one will have to allow for the existence of "the inference to the best explanation." Then I argue that all warranted inferences which may be described as instances of enumerative induction must also be described as instances of the inference to the best explanation.

So, on my view, either (a) enumerative induction is not always warranted or (b) enumerative induction is always warranted but is an uninteresting special case of the more general inference to the best explanation. Whether my view should be expressed as (a) or (b) will depend upon a particular interpretation of "enumerative induction."

In the second part of this paper, I attempt to show how taking the inference to the best explanation (rather than enumerative induction) to be the basic form of nondeductive inference enables one to account for an interesting feature of our use of the word "know." This provides an additional reason for describing our inferences as instances of the inference to the best explanation rather than as instances of enumerative induction.

|

"The inference to the best explanation" corresponds approximately to what others have called "abduction," "the method of hypothesis," "hypothetic inference," "the method of elimination," "eliminative induction," and "theoretical inference." I prefer my own terminology because I believe that it avoids most of the misleading suggestions of the alternative terminologies.

In making this inference one infers, from the fact that a certain hypothesis would explain the evidence, to the truth of that hypothesis. In general, there will be several hypotheses which might explain the evidence, so one must be able to reject all such alternative hypotheses before one is warranted in making the inference. Thus one infers, from the premise that a given hypothesis would provide a "better" explanation for the evidence than would any other hypothesis, to the conclusion that the given hypothesis is true.

There is, of course, a problem about how one is to judge that one hypothesis is sufficiently better than another hypothesis. Presumably such a judgment will be based on considerations such as which hypothesis is simpler, which is more plausible, which explains more, which is less *ad hoc*, and so forth. I do not wish to deny that there is a problem about explaining the exact nature of these considerations; I will not, however, say anything more about this problem.

Uses of the inference to the best explanation are manifold. When a detective puts the evidence together and decides that it *must* have been the butler, he is reasoning that no other explanation which accounts for all the facts is plausible enough or simple enough to be accepted. When a scientist infers the existence of atoms and subatomic particles, he is inferring the truth of an explanation for various data which he wishes to account for. These seem the obvious cases; but there are many others. When we infer that a witness is telling the truth, our inference goes as follows: (i) we infer that he says what he does because he believes it; (ii) we infer that he believes what he does because he actually did witness the situation which he describes. That is, our confidence in his testimony is based on our conclusion about the most plausible explanation for that testimony. Our confidence fails if we come to think there is some other possible explanation for his testimony (if, for example, he stands to gain a great deal from our believing him). Or, to take a different sort of example, when we infer from a person's behavior to some fact about his mental experience, we are inferring that the latter fact explains better than some other explanation what he does.

It seems to me that these examples of inference (and, of course, many other similar examples) are easily described as instances of the inference to the best explanation. I do not see, however, how such examples may be described as instances of enumerative induction. It may seem plausible (at least prima facie) that the inference from scattered evidence to the proposition that the butler did it may be described as a complicated use of enumerative induction; but it is difficult to see just how one would go about filling in the details of such an inference. Similar remarks hold for the inference from testimony to the truth of that testimony. But whatever one thinks about these two cases, the inference from experimental data to the theory of subatomic particles certainly does not seem to be describable as an instance of enumerative induction. The same seems to be true for most inferences about other people's mental experiences.

I do not pretend to have a conclusive proof that such inferences cannot be made out to be complicated uses of enumerative induction. But I do think that the burden of proof here shifts to the shoulders of those who would defend induction in this matter, and I am confident that any attempt to account for these inferences as inductions will fail. Therefore, I assert that even if one permits himself the use of enumerative induction, he will still need to avail himself of at least one other form of nondeductive inference.

As I shall now try to show, however, the opposite does not hold. If one permits himself the use of the inference to the best explanation, one will not still need to use enumerative induction (as a separate form of inference). Enumerative induction, as a separate form of nondeductive inference, is superfluous. All cases in which one appears to be using it may also be seen as cases in which one is making an inference to the best explanation.

Enumerative induction is supposed to be a kind of inference that exemplifies the following form. From the fact that all observed $A$'s are $B$'s we may infer that all $A$'s are $B$'s (or we may infer that at least the next $A$ will probably be a $B$). Now, in practice we always know more about a situation than that all observed $A$'s are $B$'s, and before we make the inference, it is good inductive practice for us to consider the total evidence. Sometimes, in the light of the total evidence, we are warranted in making our induction, at other times not. So we must ask ourselves the following question: under what conditions is one permitted to make an inductive inference?

I think it is fair to say that, if we turn to inductive logic and its logicians for an answer to this question, we shall be disappointed. If, however, we think of the inference as an inference to the best explanation, we can explain when a person is and when he is not warranted in making the inference from "All observed *A*'s are *B*'s" to "All *A*'s are *B*'s." The answer is that one is warranted in making this inference whenever the hypothesis that all *A*'s are *B*'s is (in the light of all the evidence) a better, simpler, more plausible (and so forth) hypothesis than is the hypothesis, say, that someone is biasing the observed sample in order to make us think that all *A*'s are *B*'s. On the other hand, as soon as the total evidence makes some other, competing hypothesis plausible, one may not infer from the past correlation in the observed sample to a complete correlation in the total population.

The inference from "All observed *A*'s are *B*'s" to "The next observed *A* will be *B*" may be handled in the same way. Here, one must compare the hypothesis that the next *A* will be different from the preceding *A*'s with the hypothesis that the next *A* will be similar to preceding *A*'s. As long as the hypothesis that the next *A* will be similar is a better hypothesis in the light of all the evidence, the supposed induction is warranted. But if there is no reason to rule out a change, then the induction is unwarranted.

I conclude that inferences which appear to be applications of enumerative induction are better described as instances of the inference to the best explanation. My argument has been (1) that there are many inferences which cannot be made out to be applications of enumerative induction but (2) that we can account for when it is proper to make inferences which appear to be applications of enumerative induction, if we describe these inferences as instances of the inference to the best explanation.

## II

I now wish to give a further reason for describing our inferences as instances of the inference to the best explanation rather than enumerative inductions. Describing our inference as enumerative induction disguises the fact that our inference makes use of certain lemmas, whereas, as I show below, describing the inference as one to the best explanation exposes these lemmas. These intermediate lemmas play a part in the analysis of knowledge based on inference. Therefore, if we are to understand such knowledge, we must describe our inference as inference to the best explanation.

Let me begin by mentioning a fact about the analysis of "know" which is often overlooked.[2] It is now generally acknowledged by epistemologists that, if a person is to know, his belief must be both true and warranted. We shall assume that we are now speaking of a belief which is based on a (warranted) inference.[3] In this case, it is not sufficient for knowledge that the person's final belief be true. If these intermediate

---

2. But see Edmund L. Gettier, "Is Justified True Belief Knowledge?," *Analysis* 23 (1963): 121–23 and Clark, "Knowledge and Grounds: A Comment on Mr. Gettier's Paper," *Analysis* 24 (1963); 46–48. [Harman's note.] (See chapter 3 of this anthology.)

3. Cf. "How Belief Is Based on Inference," *Journal of Philosophy* 61 (1964): 353–60. [Harman's note.]

propositions are warranted but false, then the person cannot be correctly descibed as *knowing* the conclusion. I will refer to this necessary condition of knowledge as "the condition that the lemmas be true."

To illustrate this condition, suppose I read on the philosophy department bulletin board that Stuart Hampshire is to read a paper at Princeton tonight. Suppose further that this warrants my believing that Hampshire will read a paper at Princeton tonight. From this belief, we may suppose I infer that Hampshire will read a paper (somewhere) tonight. This belief is also warranted. Now suppose that, unknown to me, tonight's meeting was called off several weeks ago, although no one has thought to remove the announcement from the bulletin board. My belief that Hampshire will read a paper at Princeton tonight is false. It follows that I do not know whether or not Hampshire will read a paper (somewhere) tonight, even if I am right in believing that he will. Even if I am accidentally right (because Hampshire has accepted an invitation to read a paper at N.Y.U.), I do not know that Hampshire will read a paper tonight. The condition that the lemmas be true has not been met in this case.

I will now make use of the condition that the lemmas be true in order to give a new reason for describing the inferences on which belief is based as instances of the inference to the best explanation rather than of enumerative induction. I will take two different sorts of knowledge (knowledge from authority and knowledge of mental experiences of other people) and show how our ordinary judgment of when there is and when there is not knowledge is to be accounted for in terms of our belief that the inference involved must make use of certain lemmas. Then I will argue that the use of these lemmas can be understood only if the inference is in each case described as the inference to the best explanation.

First, consider what lemmas are used in obtaining knowledge from an authority. Let us imagine that the authority in question either is a person who is an expert in his field or is an authoritative reference book. It is obvious that much of our knowledge is based on authority in this sense. When an expert tells us something about a certain subject, or when we read about the subject, we are often warranted in believing that what we are told or what we read is correct. Now one condition that must be satisfied if our belief is to count as knowledge is that our belief must be true. A second condition is this: what we are told or what we read cannot be there by mistake. That is, the speaker must not have made a slip of the tongue which affects the sense. Our belief must not be based on reading a misprint. Even if the slip of the tongue or the misprint has changed a falsehood into truth, by accident, we still cannot get knowledge from it. This indicates that the inference which we make from testimony to truth must contain as a lemma the proposition that the utterance is there because it is believed and not because of a slip of the tongue or typewriter. Thus our account of this inference must show the role played by such a lemma.

My other example involves knowledge of mental experience gained from observing behavior. Suppose we come to know that another person's hand hurts by seeing how he jerks it away from a hot stove which he has accidentally touched. It is easy to see that our inference here (from behavior to pain) involves as lemma the proposition that the pain is responsible for the sudden withdrawal of the hand. (We do not know the hand hurts, even if we are right about the pain being there, if in fact there is some alternative explanation for the withdrawal.) Therefore, in accounting for the inference here, we will want to explain the role of this lemma in the inference.

My claim is this: if we describe the inferences in the examples as instances of the inference to the best explanation, then we easily see how lemmas such as those described above are an essential part of the inference. On the other hand, if we describe the inferences as instances of enumerative induction, then we obscure the role of such lemmas. When the inferences are described as basically inductive, we are led to think that the lemmas are, in principle, eliminable. They are not so eliminable. If we are to account properly for our use of the word "know," we must remember that these inferences are instances of the inference to the best explanation.

In both examples, the role of the lemmas in our inference is explained only if we remember that we must infer an explanation of the data. In the first example we infer that the best explanation for our reading or hearing what we do is given by the hypothesis that the testimony is the result of expert belief expressed without slip of tongue or typewriter. From this intermediate lemma we infer the truth of the testimony. Again, in making the inference from behavior to pain, we infer the intermediate lemma that the best explanation for the observed behavior is given by the hypothesis that this behavior results from the agent's suddenly being in pain.

If in the first example we think of ourselves as using enumerative induction, then it seems in principle possible to state all the relevant evidence in statements about the correlation between (on the one hand) testimony of a certain type of person about a certain subject matter, where this testimony is given in a certain manner, and (on the other hand) the truth of that testimony. Our inference appears to be completely described by saying that we infer from the correlation between testimony and truth in the past to the correlation in the present case. But, as we have seen, this is not a satisfactory account of the inference which actually does back up our knowledge, since this account cannot explain the essential relevance of whether or not there is a slip of the tongue or a misprint. Similarly, if the inference used in going from behavior to pain is thought of as enumerative induction, it would again seem that getting evidence is in principle just a matter of finding correlations between behavior and pain. But this description leaves out the essential part played by the lemma whereby the inferred mental experience must figure in the explanation for the observed behavior.

If we think of the inferences which back up our knowledge as inferences to the best explanation, then we shall easily understand the role of lemmas in these inferences. If we think of our knowledge as based on enumerative induction (and we forget that induction is a special case of the inference to the best explanation), then we will think that inference is solely a matter of finding correlations which we may project into the future, and we will be at a loss to explain the relevance of the intermediate lemmas. If we are adequately to describe the inferences on which our knowledge rests, we must think of them as instances of the inference to the best explanation.

I have argued that enumerative induction should not be considered a warranted form of inference in its own right. I have used two arguments: (a) we can best account for when it is proper to make inferences which appear to be applications of enumerative induction by describing these inferences as instances of the inference to the best explanation; and (b) we can best account for certain necessary conditions of one's having knowledge (for example, which is knowledge from authority or which is knowledge of another's mental experience gained through observing his behavior) if we explain these conditions in terms of the condition that the lemmas be true and if we think of the inference on which knowledge is based as the inference to the best explanation rather than as enumerative induction.

## TEST YOUR UNDERSTANDING

1. Give an example of enumerative induction and recast it as an example of Inference to the Best Explanation (IBE).

2. Give an instance of IBE that cannot be recast as a case of enumerative induction.

## NOTES AND QUESTIONS

1. *What makes one explanation "better" than another?* Harman notes that a complete characterization of IBE will need an account of what makes one explanation "better" than another, but he does not pursue the issue. Consider a simple example. You hear scratching noises in the kitchen late at night. You notice that your cheese is starting to disappear. And you conclude that you have a mouse in your kitchen. Of course there are other hypotheses consistent with your evidence. Maybe your roommates are playing a trick on you; maybe you have a cheese-loving iguana in your kitchen. But in an ordinary case it would be unreasonable to accept any of these hypotheses.

   *Exercise:* Say why the "mouse hypothesis" is a better explanation of the evidence than these alternatives. Try to develop a general account of what makes one explanation better than another. Then assess your account.

2. *Formulating IBE.* The simplest formulation of IBE would be this:

   > Certain facts $F_1, F_2 \ldots$ have been established.
   > The best explanation for these facts is $H$.
   > Therefore, $H$ is (probably) true.

   But this is clearly much too crude. Consider:

   i. We know that life emerged on earth about 4.5 billion years ago. We have a hypothesis about how this happened—the so-called *RNA world* hypothesis—that explains the known facts better than its rivals. But the explanation is still quite weak by scientific standards, and no one thinks that it would be reasonable to accept it on the basis of the evidence we now possess. It is the best explanation we've got, but it is not nearly good enough to merit acceptance in its present form.

ii. Detectives are investigating a crime and they have two suspects. The hypothesis that Mustard is the culprit explains the evidence brilliantly; but so does the hypothesis that Plum did it. Suppose the Mustard hypothesis is slightly better: a smudged fingerprint left at the scene is a slightly better fit to Mustard, but could easily have come from Plum. It would be unreasonable to conclude on this basis that Mustard did it, even though this is the best explanation of the evidence.

So here is a better formulation of IBE:

Certain facts have been established.
The best explanation for these facts is $H$.
$H$ is a very good explanation of the facts.
$H$ is a substantially better explanation than any of its rivals.
Therefore, $H$ is (probably) true.

*Exercise:* Show that this is still not an adequate formulation of the rule we actually follow and consider how it might be improved. Hint: Think of a case in which scientists have developed an excellent hypothesis but have not tested it.

## ANALYZING THE ARGUMENTS

1. *Bootstrapping and the "inductive" justification of induction.* Consider the following argument.

   Hume argued that no inductive argument could show that the future will resemble the past, since every inductive argument includes this assumption as a premise. But Hume was wrong about the last point: As Strawson has shown, inductive arguments of the form

   All observed *F*s have been *G*.

   Therefore, in the future, *F*s will be *G*.

   can be cogent as they stand, without a further premise connecting the premise to the conclusion. They are not *deductively* valid; but they are good arguments all the same.

   But if this is right, then we can justify the assumption that Hume regarded as unjustifiable. After all, we have engaged in a great many inductive inferences in the past, and almost all of them have been successful. (We tend to remember the spectacular failures; but they are actually very rare.) So we know this:

   In (almost) all observed cases, the future has resembled the past.

   And from this we may conclude, *by induction*, that

   In the future, the future will resemble the past.

   But this is just to say that we can provide an inductive argument for the conclusion that in the future, induction will be reliable.

   Note that this argument does not literally beg the question: it does not include its conclusion as a premise. And yet one is tempted to say: "This argument shows nothing, since it *presupposes* what it seeks to prove." Assess the argument in light of this challenge.

2. *The counterinductivists.* You encounter a tribe who do not reason as we do. Their senses and their memories are every bit as good as ours, but when they notice that all observed emeralds have been green, they conclude that the next emerald they encounter will *not* be green. In general, they follow a rule of *counterinduction*.

   All observed *F*s have been *G*.

   Therefore, the next *F* we examine will not be *G*.

   You are deep in conversation with a counterinductivist when you are told that a new emerald has just come to light. The two of you are asked to predict its color. You say that it will be green; the counterinductivist says the opposite. You point out that the examined emeralds have all been green. The counterinductivist says, "I know. That gives us reason to think that this one will be different." You say, "But induction has almost always worked in the past." The counterinductivist says. "Precisely. That gives us reason to think that it will fail in this case." You say, "But your track record is terrible; almost all of your predictions have been wrong!" And the counterinductivist replies: "Exactly. That gives us reason to believe that this time we'll be right!"

   *Exercise:* Is the counterinductivist irrational (despite his maddening consistency)? If so, say why. If not, say why not.

3. *Evolutionary epistemology and the justification of induction.* Hume is surely right that we have an innate tendency to form expectations about the future on the basis of regularities in our experience. This tendency can be shaped by education and training, but there can be no doubt that it has a biological basis. Hume declined to speculate about the origin of this tendency, but after Darwin a plausible hypothesis suggests itself. As W. V. Quine put it, "Creatures inveterately wrong in their inductions have a pathetic but praiseworthy tendency to die before reproducing their kind."[1] The plausible speculation is that the biological basis for inductive reasoning is the result of evolution by natural selection.

   *Exercise:* Suppose this is right. Does it provide the basis for a justification of induction?

4. *Inference to the Best Explanation.* By the middle of the nineteenth century scientists had accumulated abundant evidence to suggest that the Earth is much older than a literal reading of the Bible would suggest. In 1857, in an effort to reconcile biblical literalism with this body of evidence, the British naturalist Philip Henry Gosse proposed the *Omphalos Hypothesis.* According to his proposal, the Earth is in fact quite young—as the Bible suggests—but was created by God with all of the traces of a (fictional) distant past in place. Gosse gave what he thought were good theological reasons for this elaborate ruse on God's part.[2]

   Gosse's theory fits the observed facts perfectly. It also explains them. (Why are the apparently ancient fossils in place? Because God put them there!) So why isn't Gosse's theory a *good* explanation of the facts? Consider Gould's (Popperian) answer:

   > [W]hat is so desperately wrong with Omphalos? Only this really (and perhaps paradoxically): that we can devise no way to find out whether it is wrong—or for that matter, right. Omphalos is the classic example of an utterly untestable notion, for the world will look exactly the same in all its intricate detail whether fossils and strata are prochronic [signs of a fictitious past] or products of an extended history. . . .
   >
   > Science is a procedure for testing and rejecting hypotheses, not a compendium of certain knowledge. Claims that can be proved incorrect lie within its domain . . . But theories that cannot be tested in principle are not part of science. . . . [W]e reject Omphalos as useless, not wrong.[3]

   Is this persuasive?

   *Exercise:* Assess the following response to Gould's argument:

   > Gould says that good scientific theories are testable, and that Omphalos is not. But compare a standard scientific account of the distant past, T, with its Omphalos version, T*: the claim God made the world 6,000 years ago so as to give the appearance that T is true. These theories make exactly the same predictions about future excavations and experiments. So any test that would refute T would also refute T*. So if T is testable, as Gould claims, then T* must be testable as well.

1. W. V. Quine "Natural Kinds," in *Ontological Relativity and Other Essays* (Columbia University Press, 1969).

2. For an account of Gosse's theory, see Stephen Jay Gould, "Adam's Navel," in *The Flamingo's Smile: Reflections in Natural History* (W. W. Norton, 1985).

3. Gould, "Adam's Navel," pp. 110–11.

# 5

# How Can We Know
# What Causes What?

The natural world is a vast mosaic of **events** spread out in space and time. Everything that happens — the Big Bang, the American Revolution, your birth — has a place in this mosaic, which is to say that every event stands in various spatial and temporal relations to every other.

Now suppose a rock hits a window and the window breaks. Here we have two events: the collision of the rock with the window and the shattering of the glass. They occur one after the other, in immediate spatial proximity. When we see the collision, we certainly see this much. On the basis of ordinary experience we can know that *first* the rock hit the window and *then* the window broke.

But as we ordinarily think, there is more to the story. The collision did not just *precede* the shattering. The collision *caused* the shattering. This appears to be a further fact. But what does it come to, and how do we know it?

Begin by noting there is nothing at all special about this case. Causation is everywhere. You stub your toe and you feel pain. This is not just a coincidence. The stubbing causes the pain. You smoke and you get lung cancer. Sometimes this *is* a coincidence. But sometimes it's not: sometimes the smoking — a series of events spread out over many years — causes the cancer. The static you hear when your radio is not tuned to a broadcast station has many causes, but some of it is the causal residue of the Big Bang.

Given any event, we can in principle trace out its causes looking backward and its effects looking forward. The result is a complex network binding the past and present to the future. Without this network, all of nature would be "loose and separate," in Hume's phrase, just one thing after another. With this network in place, these bits of the universe are connected. As David Hume also put it, causation is (or appears to be) the "cement of the universe."

It is hard to overstate the importance of causation and causal reasoning. Our practical lives are devoted in large part to preventing bad things from happening and to seeing to it that good things happen. But we can only control what happens if we understand the causal connections between our actions here and now and what will happen down the road. Our moral and legal lives are devoted in part to assigning responsibility—praise and blame, punishment and reward. But we are only responsible for what we cause (or fail to cause), so this part of life presumes that we can often know what causes what. Our intellectual lives are devoted in large part to understanding why things happen. But to understand a natural phenomenon or an historical event almost always involves knowing something about what caused it. Philosophers have occasionally suggested that causation is an illusion—that everything in nature really is loose and separate—and they may be right. But as these illustrations show, this is a profoundly revisionary doctrine, wildly at odds with some our most firmly held beliefs. If nothing ever causes anything, then our moral, practical, and intellectual lives are founded on an illusion.

## Two Questions about Causation

Causation raises two connected questions for philosophers.

> *The analytic question*: What is it for one event to cause another? When we say that the collision of the rock with the window caused the shattering, what exactly are we saying? To answer this question is to provide an **analysis** of causation: a completion of the sentence

> Event *C* causes event *E* if and only if . . .

in which the word "cause" and its close cousins ("make," "produce") do not occur on the right-hand side.

> *The **epistemological** question*: How can we know when one event causes another? Can we *observe* causal connections between events? If not, how can our commonsensical and scientific beliefs about causation be **justified**?

## Hume's Account

Modern discussions of causation begin with David Hume's famous discussion of the topic. Hume begins with the epistemological question, and here he makes three important claims. The first is that our knowledge of causation is **empirical** knowledge. We cannot know the causes or effects of an event **a priori**. Consider a curious scientist who has no experience whatsoever with toadstools—someone who has never seen a toadstool, never read about toadstools, never taken a class on the behavior of toadstools—but who is somehow capable of *thinking* about toadstools. This scientist can focus as intensely as she likes on her *idea* of a toadstool, but she will never be able to determine their causal history or their causal powers just by thinking.

Hume's second claim is that our knowledge of causation cannot be derived simply by inspecting the cause on its own. Let our scientist have a good look at a single toadstool. Let her take it apart, examine it under the microscope, and so on. Now ask her about its causal powers. Is it poisonous (to human beings)? If she has never seen a person eat a toadstool and has no other relevant experience, she will have no way of knowing. (You can examine the toadstool and determine its chemical composition; and that might tell you that it is poisonous to human beings; but that is only because you have prior experience of what the relevant chemicals do to human beings. Inspection of the cause *by itself*, without such background knowledge, can never yield knowledge of causal powers.)

Hume's third (and most controversial) claim is that causal information cannot be gleaned by observing a single *pair* of events. Suppose our scientist sees Bob eat a toadstool and then turn green. One possibility is that the toadstool caused the illness. Another is that the conjunction of events was a coincidence. A third is that the toadstool actually worked as an antidote to a more serious illness. Let our scientist inspect this particular *pair* of events at her leisure, replaying the video as often as she likes. If this is her only source of information, she will find nothing to favor one hypothesis over the others.

How then do we arrive at our knowledge of causes? (If the knowledge is empirical, but it doesn't come from looking at the cause alone, or from looking at the cause and effect together, where does it come from?) According to Hume, it always takes experience of many cases. We see *A* followed by *B*. So far this tells us nothing. But then we seen another event rather like *A* followed by an event rather like *B*—and then another, and then another. Eventually we come to *expect* a *B*-like event whenever we witness an *A*-like event. After our scientist has seen many people sicken after eating toadstools, she will come to expect the next person who eats a toadstool to sicken. At this point she has accepted a general causal law: *Toadstools make people sick*. When she sees Bob eat a toadstool and turn green, she applies this law to his case and concludes that Bob's ingestion of the fungus caused his illness.

So far this is just a psychological story about how we arrive at our causal judgments. But it suggests an epistemological account of how those judgments can be justified. According to this account, when a causal judgment about a single case is backed up by a causal law, which is in turn supported by abundant evidence from past conjunctions of events, the causal judgment is **warranted**. The judgment may concern a single case. "Bob turned green because he ate that toadstool." But the evidence that supports it inevitably concerns a *pattern* in the data spread out over many observations.

For Hume this answer to the epistemological question sheds light on the analytic question. If causation were some sort of glue connecting one event to another, it would be unclear why we cannot detect it by examining an isolated pair of events. Can you imagine a device—a "causation detector"—that distinguishes cause-effect pairs from coincidences just by examining the events in question very closely, without looking beyond them? Hume thinks not, and so concludes that causation is not a relation that holds between events considered in isolation.

Rather, when we say that Bob's ingestion of the toadstool caused his illness, we are really saying that that these events conform to regularity. A simple version of this Humean analysis runs as follows:

> C causes E if and only if E follows C and *in general*, every C-like event is followed by an E-like event.

According to this theory, known as the **regularity theory of causation**, causation *is* constant conjunction. We may imagine that events are bound together by hidden glue, but that is an illusion, which Hume endeavors to explain. When we experience a pattern in nature, we come to expect an E-like event whenever we observe a C-like event. This *feeling* of expectation is in fact wholly subjective. And yet we mistake it for the perception of some further quality in the events themselves — some "necessary connexion," as Hume puts it. Once we correct for this mistake we will see that causation is nothing "in the objects" beyond constant conjunction.

# The Simple Regularity Theory Is too Simple

This is an elegant view, but it is clearly wrong as stated. Suppose we note (simplifying the real facts) that whenever the barometer falls precipitously it rains soon afterwards. We might notice this without being tempted to conclude that the falling barometer caused the rain. And even if we were tempted by this conclusion, we would be wrong. Here we have correlation — constant conjunction — without causation. The main question for Hume's theory and every theory like it is whether it can be modified so as to distinguish genuine causation from mere correlation. *This distinction is of the first importance.* After all, if we want to prevent the rainstorm, we must prevent its causes. But it will do no good to destroy the barometer. Knowledge of correlations can be valuable. But knowledge of real causal relations is vastly more valuable. A theory that cannot draw this line is inadequate.

# Alternatives to the Regularity Theory

One response is to reject the regularity theory altogether, and to insist that causation is, after all, a relation between cause and effect considered in isolation. Hume rejects this view because he thinks that if it were correct, causation would be observable in isolated cases. But this is too quick. Things have many features that we cannot observe: a piece of chalk is made of atoms, but you can't know this just by looking. So a philosopher might say that the causal relation between events C and E is a real *but unobservable* feature of the events taken by themselves. It is a "theoretical relation" in the same sense in which atoms are theoretical entities. Just as we posit atoms in order to explain the observable behavior of matter, so we posit causal relations in order to explain observable phenomena. On this view, when we see the rock break the window, all we really *see* is the sequence:

> *rock hits window; window breaks*

We then *infer* that these events stand in a further, invisible causal relation.

This view raises a host of questions: How exactly does positing this invisible causal glue help us to *explain* the things we see? Would the observable world be detectably different if the causal relations were absent? Can we imagine a "Hume World," as it is sometimes called, in which the pattern of events is just as it is, but the causal relations are subtracted, so that nothing really causes anything? If so, what reason do we have for thinking that our world is not a Hume World?

A more intriguing possibility is to maintain, *contra* Hume, that causation *is* observable in single cases. Susanna Siegel defends a version of this position. Her central thesis is that ordinary visual experience often tells us that one event has caused another. Many philosophers assume that visual experience by itself tells us very little: we see the shapes and colors and movements of things; but we don't literally *see* that the thing lying on the couch is a *dog*, or that the man weeping in the corner is *sad*. If we instantly *judge* that the thing is a dog, or that the man is sad, that is because we *infer* these conclusions—very quickly and unconsciously—from the shapes and colors that we see. Siegel rejects this narrow view of sensory experience. She thinks that we can literally *see* that a dog is on the couch: no inference needed. Of course it can be very hard for a theorist—a psychologist or a philosopher—to distinguish what we literally *see* from what we quickly and unconsciously infer. (Suppose you're at a party with John, and then turn around and notice that he's no longer there. Can you literally see that John has left the room? Or is that something you infer, quickly and unconsciously, from what you see?) So Siegel describes a method for drawing this line and applies it to the case of causation. The upshot, she argues, is that visual experience tells us about the causal relations among events in the same sense in which it tells us about shapes and colors. If this is right, then we don't need to *infer* these causal facts. We simply see them.

It must be stressed that Siegel does not claim that our causal experiences are always accurate. There can be illusions of causation: magicians make a living by producing them. It is even conceivable that all of our causal experiences are illusory. Her point is modest, and yet quite bold: *if there are real causal relations between events, then it is possible in principle for us to see them*. Her account of causal experience would have to be supplemented by a metaphysical account of the nature of the causal relation in order for it to constitute a complete alternative to Hume's theory.

# Causal Inference in the Sciences

Even if some causal connections are directly observable, it is clear that many of them are not. If you take an aspirin and your headache goes away, there is a real question whether the pill relieved your pain, and no one thinks that we can always settle these questions "just by looking." So everyone needs an account of how we arrive at this sort of causal knowledge, and since our best source of such knowledge is the sciences, we naturally turn to them for illumination.

The gold standard for causal inference in the sciences is the controlled experiment. The best possible evidence that aspirin cures headaches is a large experiment in which we assemble two groups of people with headaches, identical in every respect, and give aspirin to one group—the test group—but not the other—the control group. If the headaches disappear more quickly in the test group, that is excellent evidence for our hypothesis. Of course real experiments are much more complicated than this. But we can raise the philosophical questions by reflecting on this simple case. What is causation that controlled experiments should furnish knowledge of it? John Stuart Mill was among the first philosophers to address this question. Mill accepts a version of Hume's regularity theory, so his focus is almost entirely epistemological. As Hume tells the story, we are relatively passive in arriving at our causal judgments: we allow the world of experience to wash over us, notice some regularities, and form habits of expectation which we then express by saying "this caused that." But Mill knows that scientists are *active* in arriving at causal knowledge, and he wants to know how and why this sort of experimental activity does its job.

Alas, controlled experiments are not always possible. If we want to know whether smoking causes cancer, we cannot begin with two matched groups and then instruct one of them to smoke for thirty years. This is both impractical and seriously unethical. In such cases, we may have no choice but to extract our causal information from observed statistics—patterns we simply *find*, but which do not result from controlled experiments that we create. This is possible, and much of our most valuable causal information in medicine and elsewhere is gleaned in this way. Philosophers have had relatively little to say about this topic, which has become increasingly important as mathematicians, statisticians, computer scientists, and software engineers seek new methods for extracting causal information from massive data sets. The essay by Ned Hall is designed to serve as an introduction to these timely issues.

## David Hume (1711–1776)

Hume was a Scottish philosopher, essayist, and historian, and a central figure in Western philosophy. His *Treatise of Human Nature* (1739), *An Enquiry Concerning Human Understanding* (1748), and *An Enquiry Concerning the Principles of Morals* (1751) have been very influential. (The two *Enquiries* revise material in the *Treatise*.) Many contemporary philosophical discussions in epistemology, metaphysics, and ethics are reactions to Hume's theories and arguments. Hume's *Dialogues Concerning Natural Religion* (published posthumously in 1779) is a classic attack on "design arguments" for the existence of God.

# OF THE IDEA OF NECESSARY CONNEXION
from *An Enquiry Concerning Human Understanding*

## Part I

. . . There are no ideas, which occur in metaphysics, more obscure and uncertain, than those of *power, force, energy* or *necessary connexion,* of which it is every moment necessary for us to treat in all our disquisitions. We shall, therefore, endeavour, in this section, to fix, if possible, the precise meaning of these terms, and thereby remove some part of that obscurity, which is so much complained of in this species of philosophy.

It seems a proposition, which will not admit of much dispute, that all our ideas are nothing but copies of our impressions, or, in other words, that it is impossible for us to *think* of anything, which we have not antecedently *felt*, either by our external or internal senses. I have endeavoured to explain and prove this proposition, and have expressed my hopes, that, by a proper application of it, men may reach a greater clearness and precision in philosophical reasonings, than what they have hitherto been able to attain. Complex ideas may, perhaps, be well known by definition, which is nothing but an enumeration of those parts or simple ideas, that compose them. But when we have pushed up definitions to the most simple ideas, and find still some ambiguity and obscurity; what resource are we then possessed of? By what invention can we throw light upon these ideas, and render them altogether precise and determinate to our intellectual view? Produce the impressions or original sentiments, from which the ideas are copied. These impressions are all strong and sensible. They admit not of ambiguity. They are not only placed in a full light themselves, but may throw light on their correspondent ideas, which lie in obscurity. And by this means, we may, perhaps, attain a new microscope or species of optics, by which, in the moral sciences, the most minute, and most simple ideas may be so enlarged as to fall readily under our apprehension, and be equally known with the grossest and most sensible ideas, that can be the object of our enquiry.

To be fully acquainted, therefore, with the idea of power or necessary connexion, let us examine its impression; and in order to find the impression with greater certainty, let us search for it in all the sources, from which it may possibly be derived.

When we look about us towards external objects, and consider the operation of causes, we are never able, in a single instance, to discover any power or necessary connexion; any quality, which binds the effect to the cause, and renders the one an infallible consequence of the other. We only find, that the one does actually, in fact, follow the other. The impulse of one billiard-ball is attended with motion in the second. This is the whole that appears to the *outward* senses. The mind feels no sentiment or *inward* impression from this succession of objects: Consequently, there is not, in any single, particular instance of cause and effect, any thing which can suggest the idea of power or necessary connexion.

From the first appearance of an object, we never can conjecture what effect will result from it. But were the power or energy of any cause discoverable by the mind, we could foresee the effect, even without experience; and might, at first, pronounce with certainty concerning it, by the mere dint of thought and reasoning.

In reality, there is no part of matter, that does ever, by its sensible qualities, discover any power or energy, or give us ground to imagine, that it could produce any thing, or be followed by any other object, which we could denominate its effect. Solidity, extension, motion; these qualities are all complete in themselves, and never point out any other event which may result from them. The scenes of the universe are continually shifting, and one object follows another in an uninterrupted succession; but the power or force, which actuates the whole machine, is entirely concealed from us, and never discovers itself in any of the sensible qualities of body. We know, that, in fact, heat is a constant attendant of flame; but what is the connexion between them, we have no room so much as to conjecture or imagine. It is impossible, therefore, that the idea of power can be derived from the contemplation of bodies, in single instances of their operation; because no bodies ever discover any power, which can be the original of this idea.

Since, therefore, external objects as they appear to the senses, give us no idea of power or necessary connexion, by their operation in particular instances, let us see, whether this idea be derived from reflection on the operations of our own minds, and be copied from any internal impression. It may be said, that we are every moment conscious of internal power; while we feel, that, by the simple command of our will, we can move the organs of our body, or direct the faculties of our mind. An act of volition produces motion in our limbs, or raises a new idea in our imagination. This influence of the will we know by consciousness. Hence we acquire the idea of power or energy; and are certain, that we ourselves and all other intelligent beings are possessed of power. This idea, then, is an idea of reflection, since it arises from reflecting on the operations of our own mind, and on the command which is exercised by will, both over the organs of the body and faculties of the soul.

We shall proceed to examine this pretension; and first with regard to the influence of volition over the organs of the body. This influence, we may observe, is a fact, which, like all other natural events, can be known only by experience, and can never be foreseen from any apparent energy or power in the cause, which connects it with the effect, and renders the one an infallible consequence of the other. The motion of our body follows upon the command of our will. Of this we are every moment conscious. But the means, by which this is effected; the energy, by which the will performs so extraordinary an operation; of this we are so far from being immediately conscious, that it must for ever escape our most diligent enquiry.

For *first*; is there any principle in all nature more mysterious than the union of soul with body; by which a supposed spiritual substance acquires such an influence over a material one, that the most refined thought is able to actuate the grossest matter? Were we empowered, by a secret wish, to remove mountains, or control the planets in their orbit; this extensive authority would not be more extraordinary, nor more beyond our comprehension. But if by consciousness we perceived any power or energy in the will, we must know this power; we must know its connexion with the effect; we must know the secret union of soul and body, and the nature of both these substances; by which the one is able to operate, in so many instances, upon the other.

*Secondly,* We are not able to move all the organs of the body with a like authority; though we cannot assign any reason besides experience, for so remarkable a difference between one and the other. Why has the will an influence over the tongue and fingers, not over the heart or liver? This question would never embarrass us, were we conscious of a power in the former case, not in the latter. We should then perceive, independent of experience, why the authority of will over the organs of the body is circumscribed within such particular limits. Being in that case fully acquainted with the power or force, by which it operates, we should also know, why its influence reaches precisely to such boundaries, and no farther.

A man, suddenly struck with a palsy in the leg or arm, or who had newly lost those members, frequently endeavours, at first, to move them, and employ them in their usual offices. Here he is as much conscious of power to command such limbs, as a man in perfect health is conscious of power to actuate any member which remains in its natural state and condition. But consciousness never deceives. Consequently, neither in the one case nor in the other, are we ever conscious of any power. We learn the influence of our will from experience alone. And experience only teaches us, how one event constantly follows another; without instructing us in the secret connexion, which binds them together, and renders them inseparable.

*Thirdly,* We learn from anatomy, that the immediate object of power in voluntary motion, is not the member itself which is moved, but certain muscles, and nerves, and animal spirits,[1] and, perhaps, something still more minute and more unknown, through which the motion is successively propagated, ere it reach the member itself whose motion is the immediate object of volition. Can there be a more certain proof, that the power, by which this whole operation is performed, so far from being directly and fully known by an inward sentiment or consciousness, is, to the last degree, mysterious and unintelligible? Here the mind wills a certain event: Immediately another event, unknown to ourselves, and totally different from the one intended, is produced: This event produces another, equally unknown: Till at last; through a long succession, the desired event is produced. But if the original power were felt, it must be known: Were it known, its effect must also be known; since all power is relative to its effect. And *vice versa,* if the effect be not known, the power cannot be known nor felt. How indeed can we be conscious of a power to move our limbs, when we have no such power; but only that to move certain animal spirits, which, though they produce at last the motion of our limbs, yet operate in such a manner as is wholly beyond our comprehension?

We may, therefore, conclude from the whole, I hope, without any temerity, though with assurance; that our idea of power is not copied from any sentiment

---

1. A term for the substance supposed in the eighteenth century and earlier to flow in the nerves, transmitting information to and from the brain.

or consciousness of power within ourselves, when we give rise to animal motion, or apply our limbs to their proper use and office. That their motion follows the command of the will is a matter of common experience, like other natural events: But the power or energy by which this is effected, like that in other natural events, is unknown and inconceivable.

Shall we then assert, that we are conscious of a power or energy in our own minds, when, by an act or command of our will, we raise up a new idea, fix the mind to the contemplation of it, turn it on all sides, and at last dismiss it for some other idea, when we think that we have surveyed it with sufficient accuracy? I believe the same arguments will prove, that even this command of the will gives us no real idea of force or energy. . . .

# Part II

But to hasten to a conclusion of this argument, which is already drawn out to too great a length: We have sought in vain for an idea of power or necessary connexion in all the sources from which we could suppose it to be derived. It appears that, in single instances of the operation of bodies, we never can, by our utmost scrutiny, discover any thing but one event following another; without being able to comprehend any force or power by which the cause operates, or any connexion between it and its supposed effect. The same difficulty occurs in contemplating the operations of mind on body — where we observe the motion of the latter to follow upon the volition of the former, but are not able to observe or conceive the tie which binds together the motion and volition, or the energy by which the mind produces this effect. The authority of the will over its own faculties and ideas is not a whit more comprehensible: So that, upon the whole, there appears not, throughout all nature, any one instance of connexion which is conceivable by us. All events seem entirely loose and separate. One event follows another; but we never can observe any tie between them. They seem *conjoined,* but never *connected.* And as we can have no idea of any thing which never appeared to our outward sense or inward sentiment, the necessary conclusion *seems* to be that we have no idea of connexion or power at all, and that these words are absolutely without any meaning, when employed either in philosophical reasonings or common life.

But there still remains one method of avoiding this conclusion, and one source which we have not yet examined. When any natural object or event is presented, it is impossible for us, by any sagacity or penetration, to discover, or even conjecture, without experience, what event will result from it, or to carry our foresight beyond that object which is immediately present to the memory and senses. Even after one instance or experiment, where we have observed a particular event to follow upon another, we are not entitled to form a general rule, or foretell what will happen in like cases; it being justly esteemed an unpardonable temerity to judge of the whole course of nature from one single experiment, however accurate or certain. But when one particular species of event has always, in all instances, been conjoined with another, we make no longer any scruple of foretelling one upon the appearance of the other, and of employing that reasoning, which can alone assure us of any matter of fact or existence. We then call the one object, *Cause*; the other, *Effect*. We suppose that there is some connexion between them; some power in the one, by which it infallibly produces the other, and operates with the greatest certainty and strongest necessity.

It appears, then, that this idea of a necessary connexion among events arises from a number of similar instances which occur of the constant conjunction of these events; nor can that idea ever be suggested by any one of these instances, surveyed in all possible lights and positions. But there is nothing in a number of instances, different from every single instance, which is supposed to be exactly similar; except only, that after a repetition of similar instances, the mind is carried by habit, upon the appearance of one event, to expect its usual attendant, and to believe that it will exist. This connexion, therefore, which we *feel* in the mind, this customary transition of the imagination from one object to its usual attendant, is the sentiment or impression from which we form the idea of power or necessary connexion. Nothing farther is in the case. Contemplate the subject on all sides; you will never find any other origin of that idea. This is the sole difference between one instance, from which we can never receive the idea of connexion, and a number of similar instances, by which it is suggested. The first time a man saw the communication of motion by impulse, as by the shock of two billiard balls, he could not pronounce that the one event was *connected:* but only that it was *conjoined* with the other. After he has observed several instances of this nature, he then pronounces them to be *connected.* What alteration has happened to give rise to this new idea of *connexion*? Nothing but that he now *feels* these events to be *connected* in his imagination, and can readily foretell the existence of one from the appearance of the other. When we say, therefore, that one object is connected with another, we mean only that they have acquired a connexion in our thought, and give rise to this inference, by which they become proofs of each other's existence: A conclusion which is somewhat extraordinary, but which seems founded on sufficient evidence. Nor will its evidence be weakened by any general diffidence of the understanding, or sceptical suspicion concerning every conclusion which is new and extraordinary. No conclusions can be more agreeable to scepticism than such as make discoveries concerning the weakness and narrow limits of human reason and capacity.

And what stronger instance can be produced of the surprising ignorance and weakness of the understanding than the present? For surely, if there be any relation among objects which it imports to us to know perfectly, it is that of cause and effect. On this are founded all our reasonings concerning matter of fact or existence. By means of it alone we attain any assurance concerning objects which are removed from the present testimony of our memory and senses. The only immediate utility of all sciences, is to teach us, how to control and regulate future events by their causes. Our thoughts and enquiries are, therefore, every moment, employed about this relation: Yet so imperfect are the ideas which we form concerning it, that it is impossible to give any just definition of cause, except what is drawn from something extraneous and foreign to it. Similar objects are always conjoined with similar. Of this we have experience. Suitably to this experience, therefore, we may define a cause to be *an object, followed by another, and where all the objects similar to the first are followed by objects similar to the second.* Or in other words *where, if the first object had not been, the second never had existed.* The appearance of a cause always conveys the mind, by a customary transition, to the idea of the effect. Of this also we have experience. We may, therefore, suitably to this experience, form another definition of cause, and call it, *an object followed by another, and whose appearance always conveys the thought to that other.* But though both these definitions be drawn from circumstances foreign to the cause, we cannot remedy this inconvenience, or attain any more perfect definition, which may point out that circumstance in the cause, which gives it a connexion with its effect. We have no idea of this connexion, nor even any distinct notion what it is we desire to know, when we endeavour at a conception of it. We say, for instance, that the vibration of this string is the cause of this particular sound. But what do we mean by that affirmation? We either mean *that this vibration is followed by this sound, and that all similar vibrations have been followed by similar sounds:* Or, *that this vibration is followed by this sound, and that upon the appearance of one the mind anticipates the senses, and forms immediately an idea of the other.* We may consider the relation of cause and effect in either of these two lights; but beyond these, we have no idea of it.

To recapitulate, therefore, the reasonings of this section: Every idea is copied from some preceding impression or sentiment; and where we cannot find any impression, we may be certain that there is no idea. In all single instances of the operation of bodies or minds, there is nothing that produces any impression, nor consequently can suggest any idea, of power or necessary connexion. But when many uniform instances appear, and the same object is always followed by the same event; we then begin to entertain the notion of cause and connexion. We then *feel* a new sentiment or impression, to wit, a customary connexion in the thought or imagination between one object and its usual attendant; and this sentiment is the original of that idea which we seek for. For as this idea arises from a number of similar instances, and not from any single instance, it must arise from that circumstance, in which the number of instances differ from every individual instance. But this customary connexion or transition of the imagination is the only circumstance in which they differ. In every other particular they are alike. The first instance which we saw of motion communicated by the shock of two billiard balls (to return to this obvious illustration) is exactly similar to any instance that may, at present, occur to us; except only, that we could not, at first, *infer* one event from the other; which we are enabled to do at present, after so long a course of uniform experience. I know not whether the reader will readily apprehend this reasoning. I am afraid that, should I multiply words about it, or throw it into a greater variety of lights, it would only become more obscure and intricate. In all abstract reasonings there is one point of view which, if we can happily hit, we shall go farther towards illustrating the subject than by all the eloquence and copious expression in the world. This point of view we should endeavour to reach, and reserve the flowers of rhetoric for subjects which are more adapted to them.

## TEST YOUR UNDERSTANDING

1.  Restate Hume's argument that our idea of cause does not derive from sensory experience.

2.  Restate Hume's positive account of the origin of our idea of causation.

3.  Hume gives two (or perhaps three) definitions of causation:

    > We may define a cause to be [i] *an object, followed by another, and where all objects similar to the first are followed by objects similar to the second.* Or in other words [ii] *where, if the first had not been, the second never had existed....*
    >
    > We may ... form another definition of cause and call it, [iii] *an object followed by another, and whose appearance always conveys the thought to that other.*

    Restate these definitions in the standard format:

    *C* causes *E* if and only if . . .

## NOTES AND QUESTIONS

1.  *Stating the regularity theory.* Hume's writing on causation is the principle source for the **regularity theory of causation**, the simplest version of which runs as follows:

    > An individual event *C* causes an individual event *E* iff every *C*-like event is followed by an *E*-like event.

    This simple theory faces a number of well-known difficulties.

    > *The problem of spurious correlations.* Consider two synchronized clocks both set to chime at 12:00. Here is a perfectly good regularity: Whenever clock *A* reads "12:00," clock *B* chimes. But the display on clock *A* doesn't cause clock *B* to chime.
    >
    > *The problem of unique events.* Let *A* and *B* be two unique events, each unlike anything that has happened before or since: e.g., a pink flash in the sky followed by the birth of a three-headed calf. We then have a perfectly good "regularity": pink flashes in the sky are always followed by the birth of a three-headed calf. So the simple theory implies that the flash caused the birth. But that's ridiculous. The sequence could be a coincidence.
    >
    > *The problem of imperfect regularities.* Suppose we observe the following regularity: In 92 cases out of 100, people who ingest cyanide die immediately afterward. Now suppose that Jones ingests some cyanide and dies. It is highly likely that the cyanide caused his death. But the regularity seems to entail the opposite, since there is no perfect regularity linking the ingestion of cyanide with death.

    *Exercise:* Discuss how the regularity theory might be modified in light of these examples.

2. *The nature of necessary connection.* According to Hume, our ordinary idea of causation involves *necessary connection.* When we say that C caused E, we imply that C somehow *forced E to happen,* or that *E had to happen* given that C occurred.

Hume traces the origin of this idea to our subjective experience of expectation. When we expect E to occur after contemplating or imagining C, this anticipation feels a certain way. This feeling does not represent an objective feature of the events in question. It's just a feeling — an *impression,* in Hume's vocabulary — much like the pain you feel when you prick your finger.

With this in mind, consider four competing interpretations of Hume's theory of causation.

**Reductionism.** When we judge that *C made E happen,* we are simply judging that C preceded E, and that E-like events are always preceded by C-like events. Causation is *nothing over and above* constant conjunction. (We do also have the feeling Hume describes. But that feeling is not part of our judgments about causation.)

**Error theory.** When we judge that *C made E happen,* we make a mistake. We treat a subjective feeling of expectation as if it were an indication of some invisible objective glue connecting C and E. But there is no such glue, so our judgment is false.

**Subjectivism.** When we judge that *C made E happen,* we are making an objective claim — that C-like events are always followed by E-like events. But we are also making a *psychological* claim to the effect that creatures like us are disposed to anticipate an E-like event when we witness C-like events. This latter claim is partly about us; it is not a claim about invisible objective glue. And yet this psychological claim may be perfectly correct, so there need be no error in our causal judgments.

**Expressivism.** When we judge that *C made E happen,* we are making an objective claim about C and E, while at the same time *expressing* or *giving voice to* our feeling of expectation. To express a feeling is not to describe it. There is a difference between saying "Ouch" and asserting "I am in pain." Unlike descriptions of our feelings, an *expression* of feeling can't be correct or incorrect. Our causal judgments thus have both a descriptive aspect (Es follow Cs, etc.), which may be true, and an expressive aspect, which is not in the business of being true or false. So there need be no error in our causal judgments.

*Exercise:* Does Hume's text favor one of these interpretations? Which is the best, most defensible version of Hume's theory? Hume's discussion of necessary connection in the *Treatise of Human Nature* (book I, part III, chapter 14) is highly relevant to this topic. For a provocative scholarly discussion, see Galen Strawson, *The Secret Connexion* (Oxford University Press, 1992).

## Susanna Siegel (born 1970)

Siegel is the Edgar Pierce Professor of Philosophy at Harvard University. Many of the themes in the essay below are developed in her 2010 book, *The Contents of Visual Experience* (Harvard University Press).

# THE VISUAL EXPERIENCE OF CAUSATION

## I. The Causal Thesis

The central thesis defended in this paper is this:

*Causal thesis.* Some visual experiences represent causal relations.

What is a causal relation? The relations of pushing, pulling, lifting, stopping, moving, supporting, hanging from, and preventing something from happening might naturally be considered modes of causation: they are specific ways of causing something else to happen. There also seems to be a more general relation which these relations exemplify—causation itself. . . . The causal thesis should be interpreted as saying that visual experiences represent either the more general relation, or one of its specific modes.

What is it for a visual experience to represent a causal relation? The notion of representing a property in experience derives from the notion of representing that such and such is the case in experience. If experience represents that such and such is the case, then if such and such did not obtain, the experience would be inaccurate. For instance, if your visual experience represents that the square before you is red, then it will be inaccurate if there is a square before you that is not red. None of this is a definition of what it is for experience to represent that such and such is the case, but it is a start. To finish it, what is needed is an account specifying which accuracy-conditions are the ones at issue. Here the main constraint is that the accuracy-conditions are supposed to reflect the phenomenal character[1] of the experience, so that a statement of the accuracy-conditions of the experience would characterize the subject *S*'s experience, from *S*'s point of view.

One reason to think that visual experiences are assessable for accuracy is that we regularly classify some of them as "veridical" or "illusory." A straightforward account of this is that they are *correct* when they are veridical, and *incorrect* when they are illusory. . . .

Once it is granted that visual experiences have accuracy-conditions, it is a short step to defining what it is for experiences to represent a property. In the visual experiences of the sort at issue, the properties that are experientially represented are the properties that the objects *S* sees appear to *S* to have. For instance, ordinary objects appear to have colour and shape properties, and the causal thesis says that they can appear to stand in causal relations as well. If the causal thesis is true, causal relations are represented in experience in the same way as colour and shape properties are.

---

1. Two experiences have the same **phenomenal character** if and only if they are *subjectively indistinguishable* in every respect, i.e., if they *feel* exactly the same to the subject of the experience. If you see a red ball on the table in front of you and then *hallucinate* exactly the same scene, in such a way that you could not in principle tell the difference between the two experiences, then the experiences have the same phenomenological character, even though they clearly differ in other ways.

To maximize the interest of the causal thesis, it will be useful to make two stipulations about the kind of mental state that can count as an experiential representation of a property. First, since no one doubts that we form beliefs about the causal relations between things, beliefs will not count as experiential representations (if they did, then the causal thesis would be true just in virtue of the fact that people believe that one thing caused something else to happen). Secondly, some philosophers think of experiences as a conjunction of judgements and sensations. In the case of the experiences to be discussed here, this view categorizes them as conjunctions of judgements that one thing has caused another thing to happen, where the judgement itself is not systematically or intrinsically related to any phenomenal character; and a sensation which is intrinsically phenomenal, but is not systematically or intrinsically related to any representation of causation, judgemental or otherwise. On such a view, experiential representations of causation are structured much as Thomas Reid[2] supposed perceptions to be: the sensational and the representational aspects can vary independently. I shall interpret the notion of an experiential representation in such a way that the causal thesis would not be made true by such a conjunction of states. . . .

## II. Michotte's Results

In the 1960s Michotte[3] published the results of about 150 experiments which showed that adults are inclined to describe scenes of launching and entraining in causal terms. In launching, object *a* moves toward a stationary object *b*, makes contact with it, and *b* then without delay begins to move in the same direction as *a* while *a* stops. Entraining is the same except that *a* moves along with *b*. It will be useful to keep these vividly in mind for the subsequent discussion.[4]

Michotte's experiments were attempts to isolate the exact parameters of motion that elicited such descriptions from adults. In some of the experiments the "objects" were lights or shadows projected on a screen, in others they were ordinary hefty objects such as wooden balls, and some experiments combined both. Subjects knew that no actual causal relations were operative in many of the situations they saw (such as where a shadow "launches" a ball or *vice versa*), but that did not influence their descriptions. This led Michotte to posit a representation of causality which was something other than a belief about what was happening in the environment. He called it an "impression of causation." Michotte's results

2. Thomas Reid (1710–1796), Scottish philosopher best known for his defense of common sense against the skeptical arguments of Hume and others. For Reid's account of perceptual experience, see his *Essays on the Intellectual Powers of Man*, Essay II, chapter 5.

3. Albert Michotte (1881–1965), Belgian experimental psychologist.

4. Readers are encouraged to view these at http://research.yale.edu/perception/causality/capture-launch Alone.mov and http://research.yale.edu/perception/causality/entraining.mov. [Siegel's note.]

establish that adults regularly describe launching and entraining in causal terms, saying things like "The red square moved the blue one along," or "The ball pushed the shadow."

What, if anything, do Michotte's results establish about the contents of the visual experiences their subjects report? In general, how people report what they see is a poor guide to the contents of their visual experience. People may use different expressions to describe a scene that looks the same — for instance, two people might try to guess how large or how far away something is, and differ in how good they are at making such estimations. Taking their reports as a guide would force us to conclude that tables (say) look as if they are of different sizes and at different distances from each subject, when in fact there might be no such differences at all. So if Michotte's results tell us anything about the contents of his subjects' visual experiences, this will not be because we can simply read the contents off their reports. In general, one cannot do that.

Michotte's results do not by themselves entail the causal thesis. At best, they entail it when combined with further theoretical assumptions about the relation between experience, beliefs and reports. Suppose in a case of launching the "launching" object (sometimes called the "motor object") is a ball, and the "launched" object is a patch of light. Adults know that hefty objects cannot cause patches of light to move. Suppose also that we take the following substantive assumption as a rough guide to the contents of experience: these are the contents of what one would believe if one relied on what one knows about the relata.[5] Then we should probably say that the contents of experience are roughly that there is a certain pattern of continuous motion between the ball and the "moving" patch of light. If we changed the substantive assumption so that the guide to the contents of experience is instead what one would believe if one bracketed what one knows about the nature of the relata then we might get a different result — that the ball causes the patch of light to move. Either way, we get a verdict that bears on the causal thesis only when Michotte's results are combined with substantive theoretical assumptions linking reports to background beliefs and contents of experience.

Furthermore, Michotte's results are compatible with the claim that the visual experiences reported in his experiments (and others like them) merely represent the input-conditions that elicit the causal reports, as opposed to representing causation (or a kinetic mode of causation) itself. The input-conditions are the specific spatiotemporal pattern of continuous motion that elicits the reports. These conditions are features of the world that obtain (we may assume) independently of the subjects' having any experiences. When we ask what contents experiences have, we are asking how experiences present things to the subject. We are asking, roughly, how a specific pattern of motion looks. Michotte's results are compatible with the claim that the subjects' experiences have contents which exactly match this pattern of motion. It is

---

5. The relata of a **relation** are the items that stand in that relation to one another. So if Alice is taller than Bob, we have a relation — *taller than* — and two relata: Alice and Bob.

this pattern that elicits the causal descriptions, even when people know that there is no actual causation. Moreover, there are also cases of actual causation, such as heat causing water to boil, or pressure on a button making a light go on, that do not elicit the causal descriptions, as well as cases without actual causation that do elicit it. So an opponent of the causal thesis might say that the natural conclusion to draw is that Michotte's subjects represent the spatiotemporal pattern of continuous motion, rather than causation. . . .

## III. How to Defend the Causal Thesis

If the causal thesis is true, then some visual experiences represent causal relations. One candidate for illustrating the causal thesis is experiences of certain static scenes. Suppose there is a cat sitting on a loose mesh hammock, forming a sitting-cat-shaped dip in the hammock's surface. The causal thesis allows that your experience of seeing the cat represents that the cat is pulling the hammock downwards. If the causal thesis is false, then your experience can represent that the part of the net directly under the cat is closer to the ground than the rest of it, but not that the cat is pressing on it. The opponent of the causal thesis holds that experience simply remains neutral on whether any force is being continuously exerted in such a case.

The descriptions of these static experiences championed by an opponent of the causal thesis do not strike me as phenomenologically apt. But the phenomenological aptitude of a proposed content for visual experience can be hard to judge when we are given only a single case. Given only a single case, it can be difficult to discern what the phenomenal character of the visual experience is, hence hard to discern which contents most adequately reflect it. How, then, might we proceed if we want to know whether the causal thesis is true?

One way to proceed is to focus on a pair of cases that fairly obviously differ phenomenologically. At this stage, what is important is that people who may ultimately disagree about what, if anything, is represented in experience would agree that these are cases that differ phenomenally. All that introspection is relied upon to do is to recognize a phenomenal contrast, without taking any stand on whether it is also a difference in what is represented, let alone on what the representational difference, if there is one, may be. Once we have such a phenomenal contrast in hand, the following method is available for reaching a reasoned verdict about whether the contrasting experiences represent causal relations. The method is to reason about the best explanation of the phenomenal difference, ruling out some hypotheses and making the case for others. This method is general: it can in principle be used with respect to any property or relation that is putatively represented in experience. How successful it is may vary from case to case, depending on the properties or relations in question, and on the sort of considerations that are available for assessing alternatives. . . .

# IV. Causal Unity in Experience

In defending the causal thesis, I shall discuss pairs of experiences which differ phenomenally. These pairs will bring into focus a specific and familiar kind of unity in experience. Suppose you are playing catch indoors. A throw falls short and the ball lands in a potted plant, with its momentum absorbed all at once by the soil. You see it land, and just after that, the lights go out. The ball's landing in the plant does not cause the lights to go out, and I shall suppose that you do not believe that it does. Nevertheless it may seem to you that the ball's landing somehow caused the lights to go out. This is the first case. In the second case, you likewise see the ball land and the lights go out. But this case is unlike the first: you do not have any feeling that the ball's landing *caused* the lights to go out. Your visual experience represents the ball's trajectory and landing, and it also represents the lights going out, but so far as your visual experience is concerned, these events merely occur in quick succession.

It seems plain that there can be a phenomenal difference between two such experiences. This provides a starting-point for the method described above. But in this case, a bit more can be said at the outset about the phenomenal contrast to be explained. This contrast seems to have something to do with the connection between events: the difference stems from how the lights' going off seems to you to be related to the landing of the ball. The successive events seem to be unified in experience in a way that is not merely temporal.

There are also cases of a similar sort of experienced unity involving simultaneous events. Suppose you draw open the curtain from a window and let in some light. Here there is one event, the uncovering of the window, that occurs simultaneously with another event, the increased illumination of the room. These events occur simultaneously. They can also, let us assume, be experienced as occurring simultaneously. Contrast this with a case in which you draw open a curtain that does not block out any light in the first place (perhaps because it is translucent). Just as you uncover the window, the sun comes out from behind a dark cloud, causing the room to lighten progressively as the curtain is drawn open. Here we have a very similar event of uncovering the window, coupled with an event of the room gradually lightening, and (we can suppose) these events have and are experienced as having the same duration. But it seems that there could none the less be a phenomenal difference between the two experiences, with respect to how the window's uncovering and the room's illumination are experienced as related to one another. I am taking this to be an intuition. In this application of the method for investigating whether a certain content is a content of visual experience, I am taking the *explanandum*[6] to be not merely a phenomenal contrast, but more specifically a contrast with respect to whether the events in question seem to be unified — leaving open, at the outset, just what kind of unity those events seem to have.

---

6. "Explanandum": that which is to be explained.

In what way might the events seem to be unified? A natural suggestion is that in the one case there is an experiential representation of causation, whereas in the other case there is not. If so, then in the ball case one of the experiences represents the ball-landing and the lights' going off as causally unified, and in the curtain case one of the experiences represents that the uncovering of the window lets in the light. The main merit of the causal thesis is that it provides a plausible account of the phenomenal difference between each pair.

To defend the causal thesis properly, what is needed is reason to think that this is the best account of the phenomenal contrast. . . .

# V. Non-Causal Contents

One might think that the phenomenal difference between the two cases in each pair (the ball and the curtain) is a difference exclusively in non-causal contents. The central question about this proposal is whether the contents of the experiences in question could be exhausted by non-causal contents. . . .

[Consider the suggestion] that visual experience represents the events in question as unified, without representing them as causally unified. What kind of unity might this be? Perhaps there is a kind of unity analogous to the kind discussed by Husserl[7] in connection with the experience of the passage of time. Suppose you hear a series of five sounds: the clink of a cup against a saucer, the groan of an accelerating bus, a creak from a chair, a snippet of a loud voice, and the honk of a car's horn. Compare this auditory experience with hearing five notes of a melody. We experience the notes of the melody as unified in a way in which we need not experience the five sounds as unified, even if at each moment we remember the sounds from the previous moments. Husserl observed that such remembering does not suffice to make us experience any remembered series of motley sounds as integrated, as we hear the notes of a melody to be integrated. Rather, when we hear the sounds as a melody, the previous ones remain present to us in a distinctive way even after they have ceased. Husserl had a special term, "retention," for this way of remaining present to us. In the case of the melody, the previous notes are "retained," whereas in the motley series they are not, and that is what makes it the case that we hear the notes as a melody, but not the motley sounds.

There seems to be a phenomenal difference between these two experiences, one which stems not just from the different qualities of the individual sounds, but from the way in which the sounds seem to be related to one another in each experience. One might think that analogously, the ball's landing in the plant seems in the first case to be unified with the lights' going out, while it does not seem like that in the second case. The general idea seems to be that the events somehow belong together

---

7. Edmund Husserl (1859–1938), German philosopher and founder of phenomenology, an approach to philosophy that emphasizes the careful description of the structures and objects of conscious experience.

as a unit — perhaps in something like the way in which the *Gestalt* psychologists[8] thought that the geese in a flock appear to be a unit.

As stated, this proposal is not a very specific one. Moreover, it does not make clear what accuracy-conditions it is positing. Likewise, in the case of retention, it is difficult to say how the world has to be in order for experiences of retention to be accurate. It is clearly not enough that the notes of the melody occur in succession. The opponent of the causal thesis I have been considering draws an analogy between retention, on the one hand, and a kind of unity that can be visually represented in the case of the ball or the curtain, on the other, where the unity experiences have exclusively non-causal contents. This raises the question of which contents these are. A proposal which we can assess needs to say, at a minimum, how things in the world have to be in order for the experience to be accurate.

Returning to the case of the ball landing in the plant and appearing to turn off the lights, I shall suppose that the ball's landing does not really turn off the light. So the proponent of the causal thesis (if in agreement that this experience illustrates the thesis) predicts that the experience is falsidical, because it represents two events as causally related when they are not. What does the opponent predict about the experience? Is it veridical because the events really are unified in the way in which experience presents them as being (and there is no other illusion), or is it falsidical because the events only appear to be "unified"? Similar questions apply to the experience of seeing the light coming on at 6 a.m. and then hearing the neighbour's whirring coffee grinder. There does not seem to be any obvious relation that events in the world can have when such experiences are veridical but lack when they are falsidical. This suggests to me that the analogy with Husserlian retention should not be taken to suggest that there is non-causal unity content in the curtain and ball cases. The lesson of the analogy should just be that there is a special kind of temporal relation that one can experience events as having, and that sometimes such events also seem to be causally related, but at other times they do not. . . .

## VI. Two-Component Views

. . . I now turn to another alternative to the causal thesis, which chalks up the unity phenomenology to a cognitive element, such as a disposition to form a causal belief.

According to the simplest version of this view, experience proper consists of a state without causal content — perhaps a state with exclusively non-causal contents, or perhaps a raw feel with no contents at all. But, this position says, when two events seem to be unified in a visual experience, in addition S is disposed to form a causal

---

8. The Gestalt psychologists — notably, Kurt Koffka, Wolfgang Köhler, and Max Wertheimer — sought to identify the principles that underlie the structural aspects of sense perception, most famously our capacity to experience objects as figures emerging from a ground and to experience clusters of objects as falling into groups.

belief (as it might be, a belief that uncovering the window let in the light). According to a different version of the view, experiences are identified with a sensory-cognitive complex, rather than with the sensory component alone. Either way, there are two components in the vicinity of the experiences in the ball and the curtain cases: the sensory component, and a disposition to form a causal belief. . . .

Whichever state or pair of states is identified with experiences, the crucial question is what exactly makes *S* disposed to form a causal belief. Here is a crucial difference between the Michotte cases and the case of the ball and the light. In Michotte's cases, an impression of causation is inevitable. It is easy to imagine a version of the ball case, however, where one did not feel that the ball landing in the plant and light going off were unified. One might just experience this as a succession of events that are not unified as they are in the initial example. Indeed, the two-component view is committed to allowing such cases, since each component could in principle be had without the other. But if the sensory component can be had without *S*'s being disposed to form a causal belief, then it is doubtful that the sensory component is what gives *S* that disposition. The two-component view, then, seems to lack a good account of why in the ball case *S* is disposed to form a causal belief. . . .

I have argued that the causal thesis is a good explanation of the unity experienced in the ball and the curtain cases. There are of course alternative explanations, and I have not addressed every possibility. One alternative I have set aside is that there might be no contents involved in the experiences in question at all. But if there are, then the options seem to fall exhaustively into two broad categories: there are non-causal contents, and there are combinations of cognitive causal contents with sensory component lacking causal contents. I have tried to address the main considerations surrounding each of these alternatives.

## TEST YOUR UNDERSTANDING

1. Siegel's thesis is that visual experiences sometimes *represent* causal relations. Putting causation to the side, briefly explain what it means for an experience to *represent* some feature or relation.

2. Siegel gives a test for determining when a feature is represented in visual experience. Describe the test and present a case that illustrates its application.

## NOTES AND QUESTIONS

1. **Representational content *and* phenomenal character.** Earlier writers sometimes assume that sense experience is simply a matter of brute sensation. A mere sensation, like a pain or a tickle, cannot be accurate or inaccurate. We may *draw conclusions* from our awareness of our sensations, and these conclusions may be inaccurate. But the sensation itself simply happens. Siegel rejects this view: for her, to have

a visual experience is to represent the external environment as being a certain way. So your visual experience right now might *represent a situation in which you are holding a book in your hands,* and the experience would be accurate if and only if a situation of this sort actually obtains.

The central challenge for this view is to distinguish the representational content of an experience itself from the content of the various beliefs that we typically form very quickly and unconsciously when we have that experience. When you see a friend and instantly judge, "There goes Charlie," does your visual experience *itself* represent the fact that Charlie is on the scene? Or does it represent the fact that a person with a certain appearance is on the scene, from which you quickly infer that Charlie has arrived? This is a very difficult question, not just in practice, but also in principle. What sort of evidence can we use to isolate the representational content of *the experience itself?*

Siegel's proposed method is as follows: when we can find two very similar experiences that differ phenomenologically—that feel different to the subject—the best explanation for this difference is often that there is some subtle feature of the environment represented by one but not the other.

*Exercise:* Apply this method in other cases. Does Siegel's test suggest that visual experience represents

    a. the fact that Fido is a *dog*?
    b. the fact that Jones is *sad*?
    c. the fact that the cup is *about to fall off the table*?

Siegel's theory of perceptual experience is developed in her book *The Contents of Visual Experience* (Oxford University Press, 2010).

2. *Implications for the epistemology of causation.* Siegel's paper does not present an account of how our causal beliefs can be justified, or of the nature of causation. But it is clearly relevant to both questions. Consider the following package of views:

    *Siegel's thesis*: Visual experience sometimes represents causal relations between events.

    *Epistemological thesis*: If your experience represents things as being thus-and-so, and you have no special reason to distrust your experience, then you are justified in believing that things are thus-and-so. For example, if your visual experience represents a red tomato on the table, and you have no reason to distrust your experience, then you are justified in believing that there is a red tomato on the table.

    *Metaphysical thesis*: Causation is a simple relation between pairs of events, on a par with, but distinct from, spatial proximity and temporal succession. We cannot say, in more basic terms, what it is for $C$ to cause $E$, just as we cannot say, in more basic terms, what it is for $C$ to precede $E$.

*Exercise:* Give a fresh example of a causal claim and explain how it might be justified by experience according to this theoretical approach. Then assess the merits of the approach.

## John Stuart Mill (1806–1873)

Born in London, England, Mill was educated by his father, James Mill, a distinguished Scottish philosopher, political theorist, economist, and historian. A utilitarian, empiricist, and important public thinker, Mill was author of *Utilitarianism, Considerations on Representative Government, Principles of Political Economy, Subjection of Women, System of Logic, The Autobiography of John Stuart Mill,* and, most famously, *On Liberty.* Apart from his writings, Mill worked at the East India Company (1823–58), served as a Member of Parliament (1865–68), and was Lord Rector of the University of St. Andrews (1865–68).

# THE METHOD OF DIFFERENCE
### from *System of Logic*

The law of causation, the recognition of which is the main pillar of inductive science, is but the familiar truth that invariability of succession is found by observation to obtain between every fact in nature and some other fact which has preceded it, independently of all considerations respecting the ultimate mode of production of phenomena and of every other question regarding the nature of "things in themselves."

# Chapter V: Of the Law of Universal Causation

### 3. THE CAUSE OF A PHENOMENON IS THE ASSEMBLAGE OF ITS CONDITIONS

It is seldom, if ever, between a consequent and a single antecedent, that this invariable sequence subsists.[1] It is usually between a consequent and the sum of several antecedents; the concurrence of all of them being requisite to produce, that is, to be certain of being followed by, the consequent. In such cases it is very common to single out one only of the antecedents under the denomination of cause, calling the others merely conditions. Thus, if a person eats of a particular dish and dies in consequence, that is, would not have died if he had not eaten of it, people would be apt to say that eating

---

1. "Antecedent" and "consequent" here refer to *events* or *states*. The antecedent is an event or state that precedes the consequent in time. If lightning is always followed by thunder, then *lightning* is the antecedent and *thunder* the consequent. (These words are sometimes used in other ways. In a **conditional** statement of the form "if *p* then *q*," the sentence *p* is often called the *antecedent* and *q* the *consequent*. Mill is not using the words in this way.)

of that dish was the cause of his death. There needs not, however, be any invariable connection between eating of the dish and death; but there certainly is, among the circumstances which took place, some combination or other on which death is invariably consequent, as, for instance; the act of eating of the dish, combined with a particular bodily constitution, a particular state of present health, and perhaps even a certain state of the atmosphere; the whole of which circumstances perhaps constituted in this particular case the *conditions* of the phenomenon, or, in other words, the set of antecedents which determined it and but for which it would not have happened. The real cause is the whole of these antecedents, and we have, philosophically speaking, no right to give the name of cause to one of them, exclusively of the others. What, in the case we have supposed, disguises the incorrectness of the expression is this: that the various conditions, except the single one of eating the food, were not *events* (that is, instantaneous changes or successions of instantaneous change) but *states*, possessing more or less of permanency, and might, therefore, have preceded the effect by an indefinite length of duration, for want of the event which was requisite to complete the required concurrence of conditions, while as soon as that event, eating the food, occurs, no other cause is waited for, but the effect begins immediately to take place; and hence the appearance is presented of a more immediate and close connection between the effect and that one antecedent than between the effect and the remaining conditions. But though we may think proper to give the name of cause to that one condition the fulfillment of which completes the tale and brings about the effect without further delay, this condition has really no closer relation to the effect than any of the other conditions has. All the conditions were equally indispensable to the production of the consequent, and the statement of the cause is incomplete unless in some shape or other we introduce them all. . . .

If we do not, when aiming at accuracy, enumerate all the conditions, it is only because some of them will in most cases be understood without being expressed, or because for the purpose in view they may without detriment be overlooked. For example, when we say the cause of a man's death was that his foot slipped in climbing a ladder, we omit as a thing unnecessary to be stated the circumstance of his weight, though quite as indispensable a condition of the effect which took place. . . . When the decision of a legislative assembly has been determined by the casting vote of the chairman, we sometimes say that this one person was the cause of all the effects which resulted from the enactment. Yet we do not really suppose that his single vote contributed more to the result than that of any other person who voted in the affirmative. . . .

The cause, then, philosophically speaking, is the sum total of the conditions, positive and negative taken together, the whole of the contingencies of every description, which being realized, the consequent invariably follows. . . .

## 4. THE CAUSE IS NOT THE INVARIABLE ANTECEDENT, BUT THE *UNCONDITIONAL* INVARIABLE ANTECEDENT

It now remains to advert to a distinction which is of first-rate importance both for clearing up the notion of cause and for obviating a very specious objection often made against the view which we have taken of the subject.

When we define the cause of anything . . . to be "the antecedent which it invariably follows," we do not use this phrase as exactly synonymous with "the antecedent which it invariably *has* followed in our past experience." Such, a mode of conceiving causation would be liable to the objection very plausibly urged by Dr. Reid[2] namely, that according to this doctrine night must be the cause of day and day the cause of night, since these phenomena have invariably succeeded one another from the beginning of the world. But it is necessary to our using the word cause that we should believe not only that the antecedent always *has* been followed by the consequent, but that, as long as the present constitution of things[3] endures, it always *will* be so. And this would not be true of day and night. We do not believe that night will be followed by day under all imaginable circumstances, but only that it will be so *provided* the sun rises above the horizon. If the sun ceased to rise, which, for aught we know, may be perfectly compatible with the general laws of matter, night would be, or might be, eternal. On the other hand, if the sun is above the horizon, his light not extinct, and no opaque body between us and him, we believe firmly that, unless a change takes place in the properties of matter, this combination of antecedents will be followed by the consequent, day; that, if the combination of antecedents could be indefinitely prolonged, it would be always day; and that, if the same combination had always existed, it would always have been day, quite independently of night as a previous condition. Therefore is it that we do not call night the cause, nor even a condition, of day. The existence of the sun (or some such luminous body) and there being no opaque medium in a straight line between that body and the part of the earth where we are situated are the sole conditions, and the union of these, without the addition of any superfluous circumstance, constitutes the cause. This is what writers mean when they say that the notion of cause involves the idea of necessity. If there be any meaning which confessedly belongs to the term necessity, it is *unconditionalness*. That which is necessary, that which *must* be, means that which will be whatever supposition we may make in regard to all other things. The succession of day and night evidently is not necessary in this sense. It is conditional on the occurrence of other antecedents. That which will be followed by a given consequent when, and only when, some third circumstance also exists is not the cause, even though no case should ever have occurred in which the phenomenon took place without it. . . .

---

2. Thomas Reid (1710–1796), Scottish philosopher. His discussion of causation, including this famous objection to Hume's theory, is found in his *Essays on the Active Powers of the Human Mind* (1768).

3. I mean by this expression the ultimate laws of nature (whatever they may be) as distinguished from the derivative laws and from the collocations. The diurnal revolution of the earth (for example) is not a part of the constitution of things, because nothing can be so called which might possibly be terminated or altered by natural causes. [Mill's note.]

We may define, therefore, the cause of a phenomenon to be the antecedent, or the concurrence of antecedents, on which it is invariably and *unconditionally* consequent. . . .

# Chapter VII: Of Observation and Experiment

## 1. THE FIRST STEP OF INDUCTIVE INQUIRY IS A MENTAL ANALYSIS OF COMPLEX PHENOMENA INTO THEIR ELEMENTS

It results from the preceding exposition that the process of ascertaining what consequents, in nature, are invariably connected with what antecedents, or, in other words, what phenomena are related to each other as causes and effects, is in some sort a process of analysis. . . . If the whole prior state of the entire universe could again recur, it would again be followed by the present state.[4] The question is how to resolve this complex uniformity into the simpler uniformities which compose it and assign to each portion of the vast antecedent the portion of the consequent which is attendant on it.

This operation, which we have called analytical inasmuch as it is the resolution of a complex whole into the component elements, is more than a merely mental analysis. No mere contemplation of the phenomena and partition of them by the intellect alone will of itself accomplish the end we have now in view. Nevertheless, such a mental partition is an indispensable first step. The order of nature, as perceived at a first glance, presents at every instant a chaos followed by another chaos. We must decompose each chaos into single facts. We must learn to see in the chaotic antecedent a multitude of distinct antecedents, in the chaotic consequent a multitude of distinct consequents. This, supposing it done, will not of itself tell us on which of the antecedents each consequent is invariably attendant. To determine that point, we must endeavor to effect a separation of the facts from one another not in our minds only, but in nature. The mental analysis, however, must take place first. . . .

## 2. THE NEXT IS AN ACTUAL SEPARATION OF THOSE ELEMENTS

The different antecedents and consequents being, then, supposed to be, so far as the case requires, ascertained and discriminated from one another, we are to inquire which is connected with which. In every instance which comes under our observation, there are many antecedents and many consequents. If those antecedents could not be severed from one another except in thought or if those consequents never were found apart, it would be impossible for us to distinguish (*a posteriori*, at least)

---

4. This is a substantive assumption, amounting to a form of **determinism**. Mill assumes that the laws of nature have the following feature: Given a complete, fully detailed specification of the state of the universe at any one time, the laws of nature fix the state of the universe at any future time. To say this is to say that the laws of nature leave no room for chance or randomness.

the real laws, or to assign to any cause its effect, or to any effect its cause. To do so we must be able to meet with some of the antecedents apart from the rest and observe what follows from them, or some of the consequents and observe by what they are preceded. We must, in short, follow the Baconian[5] rule of *varying the circumstances*. This is, indeed, only the first rule of physical inquiry and not, as some have thought, the sole rule, but it is the foundation of all the rest.

For the purpose of varying the circumstances, we may have recourse (according to a distinction commonly made) either to observation or to experiment; we may either *find* an instance in nature suited to our purposes or, by an artificial arrangement of circumstances, *make* one. The value of the instance depends on what it is in itself, not on the mode in which it is obtained; its employment for the purposes of induction depends on the same principles in the one case and in the other, as the uses of money are the same whether it is inherited or acquired. There is, in short, no difference in kind, no real logical distinction, between the two processes of investigation. There are, however, practical distinctions to which it is of considerable importance to advert.

# Chapter VIII: Of the Four Methods of Experimental Inquiry

## 1. METHOD OF AGREEMENT

The simplest and most obvious modes of singling out from among the circumstances which precede or follow a phenomenon those with which it is really connected by an invariable law are two in number. One is by comparing together different instances in which the phenomenon occurs. The other is by comparing instances in which the phenomenon does occur with instances in other respects similar in which it does not. These two methods may be respectively denominated the method of agreement and the method of difference. . . .

We shall denote antecedents by the large letters of the alphabet and the consequents corresponding to them by the small. Let A, then, be an agent or cause, and let the object of our inquiry be to ascertain what are the effects of this cause. If we can either find or produce the agent A in such varieties of circumstances that the different cases have no circumstance in common except A, then whatever effect we find to be produced in all our trials is indicated as the effect of A. Suppose, for example, that A is tried along with B and C and that the effect is *a b c;* and suppose that A is next tried with D and E, but without B and C, and that the effect is *a d e*. Then we may reason thus: *b* and *c* are not effects of A, for they were not produced by it in the second experiment; nor are *d* and *e*, for they were not produced in the first. Whatever is

---

5. Francis Bacon (1561–1626) was an English philosopher, statesman, and jurist. Bacon's *Novum Organum Scientiarum* (1620) was an early attempt to describe and promote what has since come to be called the "scientific method."

really the effect of A must have been produced in both instances; now this condition is fulfilled by no circumstance except *a*. The phenomenon *a* cannot have been the effect of B or C, since it was produced where they were not; nor of D or E, since it was produced where they were not. Therefore, it is the effect of A.

For example, let the antecedent A be the contact of an alkaline substance and an oil. This combination being tried under several varieties of circumstances, resembling each other in nothing else, the results agree in the production of a greasy and detersive or saponaceous substance; it is, therefore, concluded that the combination of an oil and an alkali causes the production of a soap. It is thus we inquire by the method of agreement into the effect of a given cause.

In a similar manner we may inquire into the cause of a given effect. Let *a* be the effect. Here . . . we have only the resource of observation without experiment; we cannot take a phenomenon of which we know not the origin and try to find its mode of production by producing it; if we succeeded in such a random trial, it could only be by accident. But if we can observe *a* in two different combinations, *a b c* and *a d e*, and if we know or can discover that the antecedent circumstances in these cases respectively were A B C and A D E, we may conclude, by a reasoning similar to that in the preceding example that A is the antecedent connected with the consequent *a* by a law of causation. . . .

For example, let the effect *a* be crystallization. We compare instances in which bodies are known to assume crystalline structure but which have no other point of agreement, and we find them to have one and, as far as we can observe, only one, antecedent in common: the deposition of a solid matter from a liquid state, either a state of fusion or of solution. We conclude, therefore, that the solidification of a substance from a liquid state is an invariable antecedent of its crystallization.

In this example we may go further and say it is not only the invariable antecedent but the cause, or, at least, the proximate event which completes the cause. For in this case we are able, after detecting the antecedent A, to produce it artificially and, by finding that *a* follows it, verify the result of our induction. The importance of thus reversing the proof was strikingly manifested when, by keeping *a* phial of water charged with siliceous particles undisturbed for years, a chemist succeeded in obtaining crystals of quartz, and in the equally interesting experiment in which Sir James Hall produced artificial marble by the cooling of its materials from fusion under immense pressure; two admirable examples of the light which may be thrown upon the most secret processes of Nature by well-contrived interrogation of her.

But if we cannot artificially produce the phenomenon A, the conclusion that it is the cause of *a* remains subject to very considerable doubt. Though an invariable, it may not be the unconditional antecedent of *a*, but may precede it as day precedes night or night day. This uncertainty arises from the impossibility of assuring ourselves that A is the *only* immediate antecedent common to both the instances. If we could be certain of having ascertained all the invariable antecedents, we might be sure that the unconditional invariable antecedent, or cause, must be found somewhere among them. Unfortunately, it is hardly ever possible to ascertain the antecedents unless the phenomenon is one which we can produce artificially. . . .

The mode of discovering and proving laws of nature which we have now examined proceeds on the following axiom: whatever circumstances can be excluded without prejudice to the phenomenon, or can be absent notwithstanding its presence, is not connected with it in the way of causation. The causal circumstances being thus eliminated, if only one remains, that one is the cause which we are in search of; if more than one, they either are, or contain among them, the cause; and so, *mutatis mutandis*, of the effect. As this method proceeds by comparing different instances to ascertain in what they agree, I have termed it the method of agreement, and we may adopt as its regulating principle the following canon:

FIRST CANON

> If two or more instances of the phenomenon under investigation have only one circumstance in common, the circumstance in which alone all the instances agree is the cause (or effect) of the give phenomenon.

Quitting for the present the method of agreement, to which we shall almost immediately return, we proceed to a still more potent instrument of the investigation of nature, the method of difference.

## 2. METHOD OF DIFFERENCE

In the method of agreement, we endeavored to obtain instances which agreed in the given circumstance but differed in every other: in the present method we require, on the contrary, two instances resembling one another in every other respect, but differing in the presence or absence of the phenomenon we wish to study. If our object be to discover the effects of an agent A, we must procure A in some set of ascertained circumstances, as A B C, and having noted the effects produced, compare them with the effect of the remaining circumstances B C, when A is absent. If the effect of A B C is *a b c*, and the effect of B C *b c*, it is evident that the effect of A is *a*. So again, if we begin at the other end and desire to investigate the cause of an effect *a*, we must select an instance, as *a b c*, in which the effect occurs, and in which the antecedents were A B C, and we must look out for another instance in which the remaining circumstances, *b c*, occur without *a*. If the antecedents, in that instance, are B C, we know that the cause of *a* must be A — either A alone; or A in conjunction with some of the other circumstances present.

It is scarcely necessary to give examples of a logical process to which we owe almost all the inductive conclusions we draw in daily life. When a man is shot through the heart, it is by this method we know that it was the gunshot which killed him, for he was in the fullness of life immediately before, all circumstances being the same except the wound.

The axioms implied in this method are evidently the following: whatever antecedent cannot be excluded without preventing the phenomenon is the cause, or a condition, of that phenomenon; whatever consequent can be excluded, with no other difference in the antecedents than the absence of a particular one, is the effect of that one. Instead of comparing different instances of a phenomenon to discover in what they agree, this method compares an instance of its occurrence with an instance of its non-occurrence to discover in what they differ. The canon which is the regulating principle of the method of difference may be expressed as follows:

SECOND CANON

If an instance in which the phenomenon under investigation occurs and an instance in which it does not occur have every circumstance in common save one, that one occurring only in the former, the circumstance in which alone the two instances differ, is the effect, or the cause, or an indispensable part of the cause, of the phenomenon.

## TEST YOUR UNDERSTANDING

1. You strike a match and the match lights. What, according to Mill, caused the match to light?

2. Give examples to illustrate the method of agreement and the method of difference.

## NOTES AND QUESTIONS

1. *Mill's definition of cause.* Mill's definition of causation is designed to save Hume's theory from an objection due to Thomas Reid. According to Hume, C causes E when every C-like event is followed by an E-like event. Reid notes that taken literally, this implies that night causes day, since every period of daylight is preceded by a period of nighttime darkness. (See Reid's *Essays on the Active Powers of the Human Mind* [1768], Essay IV, chapter 9.) But that's absurd: the daylight is caused by the sun, or more exactly, by the fact that there is an unobstructed line between the sun and our position on the surface of the Earth. Mill responds by modifying Hume's account:

We may define . . . the cause of a phenomenon to be the antecedent . . . on which it is invariably and unconditionally consequent.

Here is Mill's idea. It is true that daylight is always preceded by a period of darkness. But there are **physically possible** circumstances—circumstances compatible with the laws of nature—in which this is not so, e.g., circumstances in which the Earth turns on its axis once per year, and thus always shows the same face to the sun. So the fact that day is always preceded by night, though invariable, is *conditional* on the fact that these circumstances do not obtain. Mill's definition thus implies that this sequence is not a causal sequence, meeting Reid's objection.

*A* positive statement of Mill's definition might run as follows:

> *C* causes *E* if and only if it follows from the *fundamental laws of nature* by them-
> selves, without further assumptions, that every *C*-like event is followed by an
> *E*-like event.

(This is supported by Mill's footnote 3 and the text surrounding it.) Is this an adequate
definition?

2. *Mill's determinism.* In discussions of causation it is important to distinguish causation
   itself — a relation between events — from what is sometimes called the *principle of
   causality* or *causal* **determinism**: the thesis that absolutely every event is determined
   by prior causes. Before the twentieth century almost every writer on the subject held
   that with the possible exception of free human choices, every natural event is causally
   determined. As Mill puts it:

   > If the whole prior state of the entire universe could again recur, it would again
   > be followed by the present state.

   It is important to appreciate that this is a big, substantive assumption. It amounts
   to the claim that the fundamental laws of nature leave no room for randomness or
   chance. This was a plausible assumption in the nineteenth century, but modern physics is very different and somewhat unsettled on this point. So philosophers can no
   longer assume the principle of causality in their work.

   To see that Mill's methods presuppose determinism, consider an application of
   the method of differences. Suppose we arrange a pair of experiments as follows. In
   condition 1, circumstances *A*, *B*, and *C* are present, and some result *a* follows. In condition 2, *B* and *C* are present but *A* is not, and *a* does not follow. The method of differences instructs us to conclude from this experiment that *A* is either the cause or an
   indispensable part of the cause of *a*. But that assumes that *a* had a cause. It is possible,
   given just these results, that if we were to run the first experiment again, *a* would *not*
   result. There could be a fundamental law of nature that says: When *B* and *C* are present, *a* follows 50 precent of the time.

   *Exercise:* Discuss the prospects for a modified version of Mill's theory that allows for the
   possibility of indeterminism.

## Ned Hall (born 1966)

Hall, Professor of Philosophy at Harvard University, works at the intersection of epistemology, metaphysics, and the philosophy of science. His theory of causation is developed
in *Causation: A User's Guide* (Oxford University Press, 2013), coauthored with L. A. Paul.

# CAUSATION AND CORRELATION

## Introduction

You've heard it a thousand times: Don't confuse correlation with causation. Even if you don't quite know what correlation and causation are, you know roughly what this means. Every day, when the hands on the town clock both point to 12, the bell rings. These events are tightly correlated. Yet neither event causes the other: Correlation, without causation. Jones kills Smith in a hideously original way, the likes of which the police have never seen before. There is no doubt that Jones caused Smith's death. But the killing does not conform to some general pattern: Causation, without correlation.

Yet *something* connects these two notions. Often (though not always) we derive our understanding of some causal structure from close examination of statistical patterns—correlations. It was known in the 1940s that there was a rough correlation between smoking and lung cancer. But this crude finding was not enough to establish a causal link. That took a much more careful examination of detailed patterns in the data. We want to know how this works. If causation is not correlation, how can a detailed inquiry into correlational patterns provide us with information about causal relationships?

This is an epistemological question. We observe patterns of correlation. We do not observe causal relations. (We cannot tell "just by looking" that smoking causes cancer.) We want to know the nature of the inference that takes us from facts about correlations to facts about causation. We want to know this in part because we are curious about the source of our knowledge of causation, and in part because we want to know how to avoid the many pitfalls that arise in science and in daily life when we try to identify the causes of things. To telegraph my answer, I will suggest that causal inference is a form of what philosophers have called *inference to the best explanation*. We observe correlations. We ask, What pattern of causal relationships would best explain those correlations? And when we have found one explanation that is clearly superior to the rest, we accept it on the basis of our evidence. The pitfalls of causal inference arise because too often we ignore explanations that we should take very seriously.

To make sense of this, we first need to say more about how these two terms—"causation" and "correlation"—are to be understood.

## Causation and Dependence

Coming up with a definition of "causation" that will satisfy everyone is likely impossible. We need something, though; so we'll settle for an account of what *causal structure* is that is almost certainly in the right ballpark, and that is clear enough for our purposes: We will take causal structure to consist in *dependency structure*.[1] Suppose that what goes on in one region of space and time R2 depends, systematically, on what goes on in some earlier region R1: had conditions in R1 differed in such-and-such ways, conditions in R2 would have differed in such-and-such corresponding ways. Example: Suzy throws a rock at time 1, and at time 2 (a few seconds later), the rock strikes a window, breaking it. The breaking *depends* on the throw: for if, instead, she had stood idle, the window would *not* have broken; and if she had thrown a little less vigorously, the window would merely have cracked; and so on. The pattern of dependency connecting her throw with the breaking *just is* a simple example of what we are calling "causal structure."

Thinking of causal structure as *dependency* structure clarifies a number of issues. Here are two.

Typically, the object of our study causally depends on *many* factors (even if, as in the case of Suzy and the broken window, one of these factors stands out as specially salient). When one factor depends on several other factors, it is sometimes — but not always, or even often — possible to measure their relative importance. Suppose you have some boxes, each with a light on top, and blue and red knobs on the sides. Each knob has ten settings. Turn the knobs, and the intensity with which the light shines changes. Let $y$ be the light's intensity, $x$ the setting of the blue knob (1 through 10), and $z$ the setting of the red knob (1 through 10). Assume that these boxes all work in the same way, and consider two possible ways that $y$'s dependency on $x$ and $z$ might be captured as a function.

First way: $y = 10x + z$. Then, if you have, say, one box for which $x = 1$ and $z = 1$, and another for which $x = 3$ and $z = 4$, you can quite correctly say that, of the 23-unit difference in the value of $y$ between the boxes, 20 units of it is due to the difference in $x$, and only 3 units to the difference in $z$.

Second way: $y = x^z$. Then, if you have, again, one box for which $x = 1$ and $z = 1$, and another for which $x = 3$ and $z = 4$, you can't say *anything* meaningful about "how much" of the 80-unit difference in the value of $y$ between the boxes is due to the difference in $x$, and how much to the difference in $z$. Only if the dependence is cleanly "additive," as it is in the first example, will these sorts of judgments make sense. We'll draw on this point later on.

Next, causal dependencies can exist at many different *scales*. The tides depend on the moon. My ongoing state of health depends on my diet. The action of a particular cell depends on the presence of certain enzymes within it. And so on. It's a good idea, when asking what sorts of conclusions about causal structure you can draw from a certain set of data, to have clearly in mind the scale that you are interested in. For, when the data are *statistical* in nature, there is danger of a very specific kind of confusion. I will illustrate by example.

Suppose there is a large population of people in their fifties. Some have lung cancer, some don't; some smoked heavily in their youths, some not at all. Suppose it's

---

1. For much more on the relation betweeen causal structure and dependency structure, see the articles in John Collins, Ned Hall, and L. A. Paul, eds., *Causation and Counterfactuals* (MIT Press, 2004). [Hall's note.]

true that, had *none* of these people smoked, the present incidence of cancer would have been much lower. Then we can truthfully say that, within this population at least, *smoking causes lung cancer.*

But this claim is ambiguous. On the one hand, it might be a claim about *the population as a whole*, considered as a kind of unit. It is a truth about this very population — this thing — that if the incidence of early smoking in *it* had been zero, then the incidence of later lung cancer in *it* would have been much lower than in fact it is. Thinking of the population as an entity in its own right, there are dependency facts that pertain to it, and this is one of them. On the other hand, it might be a generalization about the dependency structure pertaining to *each member* of the population. Understood this second way, it is unhelpfully vague: for it is clearly *not* the universal claim that every member of the population is such that if he or she had not smoked, he or she would not have contracted lung cancer. That's much too strong a claim, given our data. (Mightn't a few members of the population be immune to the effects of smoking?) Better to take it to mean something roughly like this: In a reasonably significant percentage of this population, one's probability for contracting cancer depends on smoking to a reasonably high degree.

Here's the upshot: The claim that "smoking causes lung cancer" can mean something relatively sharp, when it is understood as a claim about a population as a whole; or it can mean something rather squishier, when it is understood as a generalization about the members of the population.

## Correlation: What It Is

Correlation is a *statistical* concept: it only makes sense to speak of "correlation" when you have already settled on some (large, preferably) population of entities as the place where the correlation is to be found. What these entities are is wide open. They might be people, or distinct stages in the life of a single person, or rocks, or experiments, etc. For our purposes, let us borrow from an earlier example and suppose that they are boxes, all of which have a light on top and a certain number of knobs and switches on their sides.

Next, we choose *characteristics* of our entities, where each characteristic can have one of a number of distinct *values*. Let one such characteristic be the setting $x$ of the single blue knob on each box (1 through 10). Let another be the behavior $y$ of the light on the top of each box: this light can be off, or on, shining with a variable intensity. Then for each box, we can record two pieces of *data*: $x$ and $y$.

A *correlation* between two such characteristics is just a systematic relationship between the values of those characteristics across the members of our population. We might discover, for example, that $y$ is a simple linear function of $x$. But we might also discover something more complicated, e.g., that in every case, $y = (x - 5)^2$, or something less systematic, e.g., that in 75% of cases, $y = 2x$, while in the remaining 25% of cases $y$ is highly variable, but always more than $8x$.

# Correlational Data versus Data from a Controlled Experiment

Knowledge of correlations can evidently be used purely as a basis for prediction — in which case it really doesn't matter whether a given correlation has its source in some interesting underlying causal structure, or in mere chance. Suppose I know this, concerning my large population of boxes: as $x$ goes up, $y$ tends to go up as well. Then, from the information that the knob setting on *this* box is 0, and the knob setting on *that* box is 9, I can conclude (not for certain, but with a high degree of confidence) that the light on *that* box is shining more brightly than the light on *this* box. I can draw this conclusion, even if I firmly believe that the correlation between $x$ and $y$ holds purely as a fluke.

Here, though, we are interested in how information about correlations can be used (or misused) as a guide to *causal structure*. The first point to emphasize is that, compared to the kind of data one can get from a *controlled experiment*, correlational information is a lousy guide to causal structure.

Suppose you have one of our boxes before you. You're interested in knowing how it works — how the behavior of the light depends on the settings of the various knobs and switches. Consider two strategies for investigation. The first is to run a series of exhaustive controlled experiments: set the knobs and switches to every possible configuration in turn, and see what happens. The second is to simply observe the box as it is, and then observe a large number of other boxes that are superficially like it, and perform a bunch of statistical analyses to look for correlations between the behavior of the lights and the settings of the knobs and switches.

It would be completely idiotic to choose the second strategy over the first.

Unless. Maybe there are obstacles that stand in the way of controlled experiment. Maybe the box is fragile, so that after experimenting on it just a few times, it's likely to break. Or maybe the internal construction of the box is not stable, but will change over time in a way that will make later data irrelevant to the question of what causal dependencies *currently* govern it. Or maybe you are simply unable to manipulate certain of the knobs and switches. Or maybe you have good reason to suspect that there are hidden knobs and switches that influence the behavior of the lights — but you have no idea where these are or how they are set. Pile up enough of these obstacles, and the ideal of a controlled experiment on the box will be a pipe dream. (Exercise: Think of real-world examples in which these sorts of obstacles are present; you should easily be able to come up with dozens.) In that case, it may be that the best that you can do is to collect correlational data about the population of boxes to which your target box belongs.

# Four Questions

What might you hope to learn, about causal structure, from correlational data? That will depend on the answers to four questions:

1.  What question about causal structure are you asking?

2.  What assumptions are you entitled to make about the structure of your population?

3.  How are the data gathered?

4.  How strong are the correlations manifested in the data?

Take these in turn.

1. *What question about causal structure are you asking?*

You might be interested just in the causal characteristics of the given target box: how (if at all) the behavior of *its* lights depends on the settings of *its* knobs and switches. But you might also be interested in the corresponding causal characteristics of other boxes — perhaps, all of them. Finally, you might be interested in *population-scale* causal structure: for example, how does *average light intensity* across the population depend on the *average* setting of the blue knobs? The individual-scale/population-scale distinction will matter a great deal shortly, for we'll see that correlational data is a much better guide to population-scale causal structure than it is to individual-scale causal structure. But for now, let's assume that you're interested in the individual scale: you want to know how the boxes themselves work, and are particularly interested in the box before you.

2. *What assumptions are you entitled to make about the structure of your population?*

One assumption in particular stands out: you had better have good reason to believe that the target box is *similar in its causal characteristics to the other boxes in the population*. Remember that the behavior of these other boxes is serving as *proxy* for the thing you can't accomplish: namely, proper controlled experiment on the box of interest. And these proxies will be adequate only to the extent that the boxes are similar to one another in causal structure. Now, the data from the other boxes may itself lend some support to the hypothesis that the target box is causally like them: suppose, for example, that a large number of the other boxes have their knobs and switches set in exactly the same way as your target box, and the behavior of their lights is identical to its. That will provide some grounds for thinking that all these boxes are causally alike. But those grounds get wobbly, if your target box looks quite different from the others, comes from a different factory, is 30 years older than any of the other boxes, etc. So it's important to have some *independent* reason to think that your target box is, in its causal characteristics, representative of the population from which you are drawing correlational data.

3. *How are the data gathered?*

This question is critical. Suppose that you have only been able to identify one causal characteristic upon which the behavior of your box's light might depend: the setting of the blue knob. You're confident that there are other knobs and switches that matter, but you haven't been able to find them. So all you can do, when examining your population, is to record the setting of the blue knob for each box, and check for correlations between this setting and the behavior of the light. You've discovered something striking: across the population, light intensity $y$ never differs more than negligibly from a simple function of knob setting $x$: $y = 10x$. May you conclude that — not only for your target box, but for each other box as well — $y$ *depends* on $x$ in this way?

Not without ruling out other explanations. Many correlations are due to chance (though the stronger the correlation, the less likely this is). Or maybe there *is* causal dependence, but in the contrary direction: the setting of the knob depends, somehow, on the intensity of the light. Setting these possibilities aside, two more interesting ones remain.

Perhaps, unbeknownst to you, your population of boxes has been *selected* from some larger population, via a mechanism that itself guarantees the correlation. Your mischievous lab assistant has decided to trick you into thinking that light intensity depends on knob setting. She's collected a huge sample of boxes. She destroys those (the vast majority) in which $y$ differs significantly from $10x$. She shows you the rest.

This possibility is not, alas, fanciful. Suppose you're a pharmaceutical company. You have lots of money to fund studies testing the effects of one of your drugs on a given disease. But the money comes with strings attached: you have control over whether a study gets published. So what's your best strategy (best, that is, given the aim of maximizing profit)? Publish only those studies that "show" a "statistically significant" beneficial effect. Finance enough studies, and you're almost guaranteed — just by chance alone! — that some of them will say what you want them to.

Finally, it might be that what explains the correlation is that the setting of the knob and the intensity of the light both depend on some *third* factor — a "confounding variable." Perhaps some internal mechanism determines the setting of the blue knob as a function of the setting of some other, unknown knob; and it is this *other* knob that controls the light's intensity. In this case, too, the inference from correlation to causation goes badly astray.

Real-world examples are legion. As ice cream consumption goes up, so do deaths by drowning; what is going on? Does eating ice cream make people poorer swimmers? No: *hot weather* induces people to eat more ice cream, *and* to swim more often.

How might you guard against these last two pitfalls (selection effects, and confounding)? There is one really effective way. But it requires that you be able to do more than just passively *observe* the boxes: you must *intervene directly* on the settings of their knobs, and then see what change, if any, follows in the behavior of the light.

Now, if the question you're asking concerns the causal structure of just the one target box, and you can intervene on its knob as many times as you like, then there is no *point* to gathering correlational data: just perform this limited controlled experiment, instead. But there are plenty of real-world situations where you can intervene only *once*, or where the underlying dependencies will not remain *constant* from intervention to intervention. (Think of testing a medical treatment: you only get *one shot*, with each patient.)

Let's suppose our boxes are like that: we can intervene on each one now, and see what happens; but we can't intervene again.

What does such an intervention get us? It guarantees that correlation won't result merely from the process of selection. And it guarantees that the knob settings do not depend on any *other*, unknown factor — which, in turn, allows us to rule out the possibility that an observed correlation between $x$ and $y$ results from a "common cause."

Well, *almost*: there is one more loophole to plug. Suppose that you yourself decide how to set the knob on each box. *Something* influences your decision in each case, even if you are not consciously aware of it. How can you be sure that these influences don't *also* affect light intensity, *independently* of the knob setting? Granted, in the present case that skeptical worry seems pretty wild; but in real-world cases it isn't. You're a doctor, deciding which patients to give the real drug to, and which the placebo: are you sure that this choice won't depend at all on what you know about each patient? Best to nip this skeptical worry in the bud, by letting a *random process* determine the intervention on each box — e.g., by letting the roll of a fair, ten-sided die determine your choice for each knob setting. (Hence: "randomized controlled trial.")

4. *How strong are the correlations manifested in the data?*

You've set up a proper randomized controlled trial on your boxes: you randomly divide the population into 10 subgroups, and within each subgroup intervene directly to set the knob at one of the ten possible values. Then our final question concerns the quality of the data you gather. We'll consider four possibilities — and what each one does and does not tell you about causal structure.

## Possible Inferences to Causation

### FIRST POSSIBILITY: PERFECT CORRELATION BETWEEN X AND Y

You've hit the jackpot: whenever two boxes have their knobs set to the same value, the lights are shining with *exactly* the same intensity. Then you may infer — fallibly, but with a high degree of confidence — that in each individual case, the intensity of the light depends on the setting of the knob, in a way that you can read off the data.

But don't overreach. Restricting attention *just* to your sampled population, differences in light intensity are almost certainly due solely to differences in knob setting. But suppose you have good reason to believe that all other factors that might influence the light's intensity are *identical* across all the boxes. Then for all you know, maybe it's only in populations *just like this one* that $y$ depends so cleanly on $x$. More generally, you should conclude only that for any two boxes whose settings for the other parameters lie in the range "sampled" by your population, differences in light intensity depend solely on differences in knob setting.

This is not just being fussy. Here's a real-world example where this point matters. People afflicted with phenylketonuria can't process the amino acid phenylalanine. Unless they follow an extremely careful diet, phenylalanine builds up in their bodies to quite horrible effect. A statistical study might well lead us to conclude that possessing this trait *dooms* someone to die: for when we sample a population known to vary extremely widely with respect to other potentially causally relevant factors, we find that the sickness and death characteristic of this disease is *perfectly correlated* with whether one has the trait. (That's because we weren't smart enough to include, in our sampled population, anyone who followed the careful diet.) But viewing phenylketonuria as an unavoidable death sentence on the basis of such data would be a tragic mistake.

## SECOND POSSIBILITY: STRONG BUT IMPERFECT CORRELATION

This time, the correlation between $x$ and $y$ is extremely good, but not perfect. As before, you may conclude that there is substantial dependence of light intensity on knob setting, with the same caveats. But one additional cautionary remark is needed. For you might be tempted to dismiss the deviation from *perfect* correlation as due to "mere noise": in *every* box, you think, $y$ depends almost entirely on $x$, with some small amount of dependence on myriad little influences remaining. Sure, that's *one* explanation for the data. But here's another:

Unbeknownst to you, each box features, in addition to its blue knob, ten switches and an additional, red knob. Let $z$ be the setting of this knob. If—but only if—all ten switches are in the "on" position, then $y = z$. But if even one of the switches is in the "off" position, then $y = x$. In a large population, where each switch is equally likely to be *on* or *off*, an easy calculation shows that the correlation between $x$ and $y$ (as measured in the standard way) will be close to 1. But in no good sense is the deviation from perfect correlation due to "noise": it's rather that there is a tiny chance that the light intensity will be controlled by the red knob instead of the blue knob, and this chance is occasionally realized.

## THIRD POSSIBILITY: WEAK CORRELATION

Let's suppose now that the correlation between light intensity and knob setting is weak (but not zero). The weaker it is, the more seriously you have to take the possibility that it's there due only to chance; but let's set that worry aside. Assuming it's *not* just due to chance, what does it tell us about causal structure?

Not much. We can conclude that in at least some of the boxes, $y$ depends partially, and somehow, on $x$. We can't conclude much more than that. In particular, we absolutely *cannot* treat the strength of the correlation as measuring the *degree* of dependence of $y$ on $x$. Sure, *maybe y* depends on $x$ to a small extent, in every case. But maybe $y$ depends on $x$ a great deal, in a small number of cases—and not at all, in the rest. For that matter, maybe the way that $x$ interacts with other influences on $y$ robs the question of $x$'s "degree" of influence of any meaning (cf. §1). You just can't tell. And why would you expect to be able to? After all, what's going on here is really quite simple: when the correlation between $x$ and $y$ is weak, the correlational data places correspondingly weak constraints on *the nature of the causal hypotheses that can plausibly explain it.*

## FOURTH POSSIBILITY: NO CORRELATION

Suppose, finally, that in each subpopulation of boxes, distinguished by their value for $x$, the distribution of light intensity is *the same*. Then, alas, you're quite at sea. Of course you can make some *negative* judgments: e.g., $y$ does not depend solely on $x$, in each case. But you *can't* infer the stronger claim that in each case, there is no dependence of $y$ on $x$. There could be scads of dependence — but dependence that works in different ways, in different kinds of boxes, where these differences in construction cancel each other out, at the statistical level.

Example: In the population as a whole, half the lights are shining with intensity 10, and half are off (intensity 0). The boxes come in two types. In type-1 boxes, $y = 10$ if $x > 5$, but $y = 0$ if $x \leq 5$. Type-2 boxes work in exactly the reverse manner. Then within *each* subpopulation, half the lights are shining with intensity 10, and half are off. There is no correlation between light intensity and knob setting. Yet it's true of *every* box that its light's intensity depends on the setting of its blue knob.

This example reminds us how important it is to have independent evidence that your population is causally homogeneous. So suppose that you know that it *is*. *Then* you may reasonably infer that there is no dependence of light intensity on knob setting. But just as in the case of perfect correlation, there is a danger of overreach. For all we know, light intensity depends on lots of factors. All that we can be sure of, just on the basis of the observed lack of correlation, is that within whatever range of values of these other parameters happens to be sampled by our population, difference in knob setting makes no difference to light intensity. We can't draw any conclusions about the possible importance of knob setting, in *different* circumstances. Suppose, to illustrate, that you're testing a certain cancer treatment, to see whether it can extend the lives of your patients. It doesn't: there is no correlation between longevity, and whether or not the treatment is administered. That could be because the drug simply has no relevant biochemical impact whatsoever on the cancer. But it could also be because it has nasty side effects: and were you somehow able to *inhibit* these side effects, the drug would in fact *cure* the cancer. You would surely like to know which of these hypotheses obtain. But the correlational data alone won't tell you.

## A SOUND, POPULATION-SCALE INFERENCE

So far, our discussion has reinforced our claim that correlational data is a poor substitute for data from a controlled experiment. But there is one kind of inference you can make from data drawn from a randomized trial that is high quality. And that is because, in a certain clear sense, a randomized trial *just is* a properly controlled experiment — *on a population*.

Suppose that, among all those boxes whose knobs were set to 1, the average light intensity was 3. By contrast, among all those boxes whose knobs were set to 10, the average intensity was 8. Then, *given the way the experiment was conducted*, you are entitled to infer two dependency facts about the population as a whole: if the knobs on *all* the boxes had been set to 1, the average intensity across the population would very likely have been very close to 3; and if all the boxes' knobs had been set to 10, the average intensity would very likely have been very close to 8. In short, your data unambiguously tells you about a certain *population-scale dependency structure*. And it does this quite regardless of how strong the correlation is between knob setting and light intensity.

Why is this? Well, you *randomly selected* those boxes whose knobs were to be set to 1, etc. So the statistical distribution of *other* causally relevant factors, within each subpopulation, is, with very high probability, going to be close to the same. (The larger your subpopulations, the higher the probability.) But the average intensity in each subpopulation is just going to be determined by the knob setting, together with this distribution of other factors.

Here is a way to make the point perfectly explicit. Suppose you have before you 10 boxes, and you know that they are identical, with respect to every causal factor other than the setting of their knobs. Suppose you can manipulate these knob set-tings. Then, by setting the knob of each of the 10 boxes to a different setting, you will be able to infer exactly how — given the disposition of the other causally relevant factors — light intensity depends on knob setting. That just is a controlled experi-ment. *But this is precisely what we are doing, at the scale of the populations themselves, when we use a random procedure to subdivide our population into 10 subgroups.* We know that one population-scale variable — namely, the statistical distribution of the *other* factors on which light intensity depends — is identical (or near enough), across our subpopulations. In each subpopulation, we set the variable of interest $x$ to a dif-ferent value. We see what population-scale effect this has, and so can infer exactly how population-scale features concerning light intensity depend on population-scale features concerning knob setting.

Notice, finally, that if our study is *not* a randomized controlled study — if we just happen to find 10 subpopulations, distinguished by the settings of the given knob — then this inference is *worthless*; for the design of our experiment gives us no reason whatsoever to think that these 10 subpopulations — considered now as entities in their own right — are causally alike with respect to the factors other than knob setting.

## Conclusion

There is a simple piece of advice for anyone who's in the business of drawing con-clusions about the way the world is based on observational evidence. (That would be all of us.) When you gather some data, and you find yourself strongly attracted to a certain hypothesis as being the best explanation of it, STOP. Force yourself to conduct the exercise of canvassing, as thoroughly and systematically as you can, the space of *alternative* explanations. For only then can you form a proper judgment about whether the data in fact *supports* the hypothesis you like. The error of ignoring this advice is ubiquitous, both in everyday life and in scientific contexts. Too often, "inference to the best explanation" becomes "inference to the only explanation I hap-pened to think of."

That's really all that's going on, when people hastily infer causation from correlation.[2] They have some evidence: variable $x$ is correlated with variable $y$. They wonder what could *explain* this evidence. They note that the hypothesis that $x$ causes $y$ could do so — and conveniently forget the wealth of rivals that ought to be ruled out, before leaping to this conclusion.

As a psychological matter, thinking of causation in terms of dependence helps to guard against this mistake. That is because it is *much* easier, when thinking directly in terms of structures of dependency, to recognize how rich is the range of explanatory hypotheses concerning how one factor might depend on some others; similarly, it is much easier to avoid the crude mistakes we can fall into when we characterize causation as coming in "degrees," or when we elide the distinction between population-scale and individual-scale causal structure. By contrast, our ordinary ways of talking about "causation" sometimes seem positively to *encourage* wooly-headedness. In sum, then, I find myself oddly sympathetic to Russell's famous remark, that "The law of causality, I believe, like much that passes muster among philosophers, is a relic of a bygone age, surviving, like the monarchy, only because it is erroneously supposed to do no harm." It's just that I think that the monarchy should be reformed, not abolished.

## TEST YOUR UNDERSTANDING

1.  Give an example of your own to illustrate the distinction between causation and mere correlation.

2.  For Hall, the aim of causal inquiry is to identify the *dependency structure* exhibited by the system we are studying. Say what this means.

## NOTES AND QUESTIONS

1.  *Causal inference and Inference to the Best Explanation.* Hall claims causal reasoning is an instance of Inference to the Best Explanation. (See Gilbert Harman, "The Inference to the Best Explanation," reprinted in chapter 4 of this volume.) The general form of such reasoning is as follows:

    1.  Some facts $E$ are observed.

    2.  The best explanation of $E$ is H.

    3.  $H$ is a good explanation of $E$ (and not just the best of a bad lot).

    4.  Therefore, $H$ is (probably) true.

    Choose an example of causal reasoning and represent it as an argument of this form.
    Hall's views on causation are developed in L. A. Paul and Ned Hall, *Causation: A User's Guide* (Oxford University Press, 2013).

---

2.  I'm indebted to Alex Byrne for this point. [Hall's note.]

## ANALYZING THE ARGUMENTS

1.  *The counterfactual theory.* Hume remarks in passing that "we may define a cause to be an object, followed by another . . . where, if the first had not been, the second never had existed." This is the inspiration for what has come to be called the *counterfactual theory of causation.* A **counterfactual conditional** is a statement of the form "If it had been that *p*, it would have been that *q*." The simplest version of the counterfactual theory is this:

    > *C* caused *E* if and only if *C* and *E* both occurred, and if *C* had not occurred, *E* would not have occurred.

    This account seems to cover many cases. When we say that the rock broke the window, it is natural to understand the claim as follows: If the rock had not collided with the window, the window would not have broken. The account also explains a number of important features of causation:

    a.  It explains why the causal facts are not readily observable. If the causal facts are facts about what *would have happened* had things been different, then they are not facts about how things *actually are.* And it is not surprising that we cannot readily detect such facts by means of the senses.

    b.  It explains why causal information is so valuable. If we want to know whether the doctor is responsible for the patient's death, it may be crucial to know whether the patient would have died if the doctor had given him some other medication. If we want to know which pill the doctor ought to give the patient now, it may be crucial to know what *would* happen if the doctor *were* to prescribe such and such a pill. So for practical purposes, the information we often need is information about **counterfactual dependence**, and according to the counterfactual theory, causal information just is information of this sort.

    Unfortunately, this simple version of the theory faces a number of difficulties:

    > *Preemption.* Jones and Smith throw rocks at a bottle. Jones's rock gets there first and smashes the bottle, but Smith's rock would have smashed the bottle if Jones's rock hadn't gotten there first. Intuitively, Jones broke the bottle. But according to the counterfactual theory, this is equivalent to the claim that if Jones had not thrown his rock, the bottle would not have broken. And that claim is false.

    > *Overdetermination.* Jones and Smith throw rocks at a bottle and the two rocks arrive simultaneously. Intuitively, Jones and Smith both broke the bottle. (They are certainly both responsible for breaking the bottle.) But according to the counterfactual theory, neither of them caused the bottle to break.

    *Exercise (very difficult):* Modify the counterfactual theory so as to avoid these results.

    The most important modern defender of the counterfactual theory is David Lewis ("Causation," in his *Philosophical Papers, vol. 2,* Cambridge University Press, 1986). For later developments, see J. Collins, N. Hall and L. A. Paul, eds., *Causation and Counterfactuals* (MIT Press, 2004).

2.  *The probabilistic theory.* Before the twentieth century, most philosophical discussions of causation assumed that the laws of nature are deterministic, and in particular, that the occurrence of a cause *guarantees* or *necessitates* the occurrence of the effect.

More recent discussions allow for the possibility that $C$ may cause $E$ even though $C$ can occur without $E$ and vice versa. This probabilistic turn suggests an analysis of causation:

> $C$ causes $E$ if and only if $C$ and $E$ both occur and the probability of $E$ given $C$ was greater than the probability of $E$ given *not-C*.

Suppose we learn by analyzing the statistics that the probability of contracting lung cancer if you smoke is much higher than the probability of contracting lung cancer if you do not smoke. Now suppose that Brown, a smoker, contracts lung cancer. The statistics suggest that the probability that Brown would get cancer given that she's a smoker was much higher than it would have been if Brown had not been a smoker. And if that's right it follows automatically, given the probabilistic analysis, that Brown's smoking caused her cancer (or better, that it contributed causally to her cancer).

*Question:* Is this is an adequate analysis of causation? Can you think of a counterexample?

For discussion, see C. Hitchcock, "Do All and Only Causes Raise the Probabilities of their Effects?" (in Collins, Hall, and Paul, *Causation and Counterfactuals*).

3. *The hardest puzzle about causation.* Questions of causation arise constantly in the law. The crime of murder, for example, is typically defined to involve the intentional killing of a human being, where it is understood that to "kill" a person is to cause the person's death. With this in mind, consider the following case:

> Rocky is about to cross a long stretch of desert, so he fills three canteens with water. Boris wants Rocky dead, so when Rocky isn't looking, he poisons the water in the third canteen in the hope that Rocky will eventually drink from it and die. Natasha also wants Rocky dead, but she is unaware of what Boris has done. Later that evening, she sneaks into Rocky's tent and pokes small holes in the third canteen in the hope that the water will leak out and that Rocky will eventually die of thirst. The next morning Rocky sets out, and after walking for a week, reaches for his third canteen, which is now empty. It's too late for Rocky to turn back, so he presses on, dying of thirst several days later.
> Boris and Natasha are charged with murder. Boris says: "But your honor, I didn't kill him! I admit that I *tried* to kill him by poisoning his water. But he never drank the poison. So how can you say that I caused his death?" Natasha says, "I didn't kill him either. If I hadn't emptied the canteen, he would have died instantly from the poison several days earlier. If anything, I *prolonged* his life. So how can you say that I caused his death?"

*Question:* Who killed Rocky?

4. Many of the most important essays on causation are collected in E. Sosa and M. Tooley, eds., *Causation* (Oxford University Press, 1993). Some of the most significant recent insights into causal inference are due to statisticians. See for example, Judea Pearl, *Causality: Models, Reasoning, and Inference* (Cambridge University Press, 2000).

# 6

# How Can You Know Your Own Mind, or the Mind of Another Person?

Does your mother love you? Does your friend believe that you're the one who drank the last of the milk and didn't replace it? Does the well-built man who is waving his fist in your face want your iPhone, or does he just want directions to the nearest nail salon? Imagine what life would be like if you couldn't answer these sorts of questions. If people in general didn't have huge swaths of knowledge about the mental lives of others, human society would not exist.

What about knowledge of your own mind, or *self-knowledge*, as philosophers often call it: is that important too, or is it like knowledge of baseball batting averages — trivial knowledge that isn't of much use in daily life? Suppose that your instructor has announced that a philosophy quiz will be held tomorrow. Failing the quiz will mean a poor final grade, at best. There's still time to drop the class. Should you drop it, or take the exam? Your career prospects may hang on the correct answer to this question. To give it your best shot, you need some knowledge of your own mind — specifically, you need to know what you know and don't know about philosophy.

Here's another example to illustrate the importance of knowledge of your own mind. Suppose you meet some strangers while backpacking. If they believe you want food, then they'll give you some. Similarly for water: if they believe you want water, then they'll give you some. But what will make them believe these things? Merely seeing you won't do it: you don't look obviously undernourished or dehydrated, and a typical backpacker on this trail carries enough food and water. In practice, the only way to get them to believe that you want food (or water) is to say "I want food!" (or "I want water!"). (Ideally you should be a little more polite.) Suppose, in fact, you have run out of supplies, are hungry and want food; you have had plenty to drink and don't want water. You know that if you want food, you should say so. You also know that if you want water, you should say so. So what should you do? Say you want food? Say you want water? Say nothing? If you *don't know* that you want food, you don't know what to do.

Knowledge of others' minds and of our own minds could hardly be more fundamental to our lives. But how do we obtain such knowledge? What is the relation between knowledge of one's own mind and knowledge of others' minds? These are the topics of the readings in this chapter.

# The Traditional "Problem of Other Minds"

Here is a line of thought that can seem very plausible:

> How do I know that you have a mind? Well, I can't observe your mind directly, as I can observe the movement of your legs, or the color of your hair. What I can observe directly is the behavior of your body in a variety of circumstances—your arm waving, your eyes widening, and so forth. Somehow I have to get from this behavioral evidence to a conclusion about your inner mental life—that you feel pain, want pizza, and so on. How can I connect your behavior with your mental life? Well, I have *myself* as an example. I know that certain things cause me to feel pain, and that my feeling pain causes me to behave in a certain way; similarly with wanting pizza and other mental states. That is, I have amassed a large amount of evidence of the form: circumstances C cause *me* to be in mental state M, and this in turn causes *me* to behave in manner B. I now see that *you* are in circumstances C, and *you* are behaving in manner B. That's pretty good evidence that you are in mental state M.

According to the argument, you and I are similar in relevant respects; that's why this is called the "argument by analogy" for other minds.[1] A classic expression of the argument by analogy is this passage by the nineteenth-century British philosopher John Stuart Mill:

> I conclude that other human beings have feelings like me, because, first, they have bodies like me, which I know, in my own case, to be the antecedent condition of feelings; and because, secondly, they exhibit the acts, and other outward signs, which in my own case I know by experience to be caused by feelings. I am conscious in myself of a series of facts connected by an uniform sequence, of which the beginning is modifications of my body, the middle is feelings, the end is outward demeanor. In the case of other human beings I have the evidence of my senses for the first and last links of the series, but not for the intermediate

---

1. William Paley's argument for the existence of God is sometimes taken to be an argument by analogy: see p. 32 of this anthology.

link. I find, however, that the sequence between the first and last is as regular and constant in those other cases as it is in mine. In my own case I know that the first link produces the last through the intermediate link, and could not produce it without. Experience, therefore, obliges me to conclude that there must be an intermediate link; which must either be the same in others as in myself, or a different one: I must either believe them to be alive, or to be automatons: and by believing them to be alive, that is, by supposing the link to be of the same nature as in the case of which I have experience, and which is in all other respects similar, I bring other human beings, as phenomena, under the same generalizations which I know by experience to be the true theory of my own existence.[2]

There are two frequently made objections to the argument by analogy. First, the argument is on shaky ground because the evidence about the links between bodily "modifications" (for example, the stubbing of a toe), "feelings" (for example, pain), and "outward demeanor" (for example, hopping up and down) all concern *one case*—my own. The sample size $n = 1$, so isn't the argument at best very speculative?

We can illustrate this with—appropriately—an analogy. Suppose I have a closed box. When a button is pushed on one side, a light on the other side flashes on. I open up my box and find that the mechanism involves a strange beetle who, when it hears the click of the pushed button, runs to an electrical circuit inside the box and flips a switch, causing the outside light to flash. I now see that you also have a closed box. Superficially, it looks the same as mine on the outside, and exhibits the same response to button-pushing—a light briefly turns on. I can't see inside your box. Should I conclude "by analogy" that your box has a beetle inside it too? That sounds no better than an educated guess: even if there is a beetle in your box, I can't *know* that there is on the basis of such weak evidence. Maybe there's no beetle in your box and the button is connected directly to the circuit. Or maybe there's a team of ants who get the job done—how can I rule out these rival possibilities?

The second objection points to a *disanalogy* between the argument by analogy and the beetle in the box example. In principle, I could open up your box and observe what's inside, and thus independently check my conclusion. But (one might think) I *can't* observe your own mental life—if I could, there would be no need for the argument by analogy. And this is a limitation that holds of *necessity*—it make no sense to say that I can perceive your thoughts, feel your pains, or peek at your intentions. And how can the argument by analogy be any good if it's absolutely impossible for me to check that the conclusion is correct? Alec Hyslop and Frank Jackson try to rebut both objections to the argument by analogy.

There is another, much more subtle, objection to the argument by analogy, or more precisely to the motivation for taking it to be important. The conclusion of the argument is about your unobservable mind. The premises include *facts about minds*, specifically about *my* mind. Why is this? Often we can know about unobservable Xs on the basis of premises that aren't themselves about Xs. For example, physicists

2. J. S. Mill, *An Examination of Sir William Hamilton's Philosophy* (1889), quoted in Norman Malcolm, "Knowledge of Other Minds," in his *Knowledge and Certainty* (Prentice-Hall, 1963), pp. 130–31. Selections from Mill's other writings are in chapters 1, 5, 16, and 20 of this anthology.

discovered in the nineteenth century that matter was composed of atoms without ever observing a single atom. The atomic hypothesis provided an elegant explanation of a range of phenomena, including the ratios in which elements combine to form compounds, and that's why the physicists accepted it. Why can't I know about your mind in a similar fashion, by reasoning that the hypothesis that you are in such-and-such mental states provides the best explanation of your behavior? (This would be an "inference to the best explanation": see Harman, "The Inference to the Best Explanation," in chapter 4 of this anthology.) Presumably a proponent of the argument by analogy thinks that premises about my mind are essential if I am to know about your mind, but why? Why do I need to know about my own mental life in order to know about yours? Why is *self*-knowledge needed for *other*-knowledge?

A tempting answer is that it is needed because we only *understand* what mental states are from our own case. Bodily sensations are the most persuasive example. In order to know what pain is, for example, arguably I need to know that *this* (clutching my painful knee) is pain. If I didn't have that special first-person knowledge of my own pain, I wouldn't really understand the word "pain," and couldn't even entertain the hypothesis that *you* are in pain. And if I can't so much as entertain that hypothesis, there is no question of my knowing it.

Ludwig Wittgenstein was one of the most important philosophers of the last century, and in his posthumously published *Philosophical Investigations* (Blackwell, 1953) he suggests that this is mistaken:

> If one has to imagine someone else's pain on the model of one's own, this is none too easy a thing to do: for I have to imagine pain which I do not feel on the model of the pain which I do feel. That is, what I have to do is not simply to make a transition in imagination from one place of pain to another. As, from pain in the hand to pain in the arm. For I am not to imagine that I feel pain in some region of his body. (Which would also be possible.) (§302)

Why, exactly, does Wittgenstein think that there is a difficulty in imagining "someone else's pain on the model of one's own"? Saul Kripke offers an interpretation and defense of Wittgenstein's complaint. If Wittgenstein (as interpreted by Kripke) is right, then the traditional problem of other minds is relatively superficial — the profound problem is explaining how *my* pain could help me understand what the hypothesis that *you* are in pain could possibly amount to.

# Knowledge of Other Minds without Self-Knowledge

At the very least, the idea that you need to know about your own mind in order to know about others' minds should not be assumed uncritically. And if that assumption is given up, then other options come into view. We have already seen one, that you know about others' minds on the basis of an "inference to the best explanation" of their behavior. A closely related idea, widely discussed in the psychological literature, is that we implicitly possess a theory of psychology and its relation to behavior (often called a *theory of mind*) and that we apply that theory to gain knowledge of others' minds.[3]

The traditional problem of other minds makes another assumption that should not be taken for granted, namely that the minds of others are "unobservable." Supposedly, all I can strictly and literally perceive is the condition of your body, your head nodding, your face flushing, and so on. But is that right? Suppose that two people are having a heated conversation, right in front of you. If asked to describe what you observed, you would naturally use psychological vocabulary: she *insulted* him, he got *upset*, she *felt embarrassed, he walked off in a huff*, and so on. It would be quite contrived to describe what you observed using some austere vocabulary of "bodily movements," purged of all traces of psychology. So what's wrong with saying the natural thing? As Maurice Merleau-Ponty puts it in "Man Seen from the Outside," "I could not imagine the malice and cruelty which I discern in my opponent's looks separated from his gestures, speech, and body. None of this takes place in some other-worldly realm, in some shrine located beyond the body of the angry man." (Gilbert Ryle defends a similar view in his 1949 book *The Concept of Mind*, from which the selection by Ryle is taken.)

## Self-Knowledge

So far we have discussed the view that we have knowledge of other minds by (a) an analogical inference, and briefly touched on the alternative suggestions that such knowledge involves, (b) an inference to the best explanation, (c) the use of an implicit theory of mind, and (d) perception. (Some versions of these last three views may well be compatible.) What about knowledge of our *own* minds?

3. This view is called the "theory-theory." It is not easy to explain the sense in which we are said to "implicitly possess" a theory of mind: the principles of that theory are not generally supposed to be ones that ordinary people would recognize as correct. Similarly, the principles posited by linguists to explain our ability to produce grammatical sentences of English and other natural languages are taken to be equally unfamilar. Sometimes this is put by saying that these psychological or linguistic principles are "tacitly known." If so-called tacit knowledge really is a kind of *knowledge*, then the theory-theory does take my knowledge of *your* mind to depend on my knowledge of *minds*. Unlike the knowledge at work in the argument by analogy, however, this knowledge is not knowledge of *my* mind.

The theory-theory is usually opposed to a view called the "simulation theory." The basic idea of the simulation theory is something like this: I know about your mental life by imagining how *I* would think or feel in *your* circumstances. As with the theory-theory, it is a complicated matter to state the theory in a relatively precise and clear way. For an introduction to this debate, and an argument for the theory-theory over the simulation theory, see Shaun Nichols and Stephen Stich, *Mindreading* (Oxford University Press, 2003).

Knowledge of one's own mind seems as immediate and direct as knowledge of objects in one's environment. And of course we get knowledge of our environment by perception—we know that this tomato is red by seeing it. So one very natural (and popular) idea is that self-knowledge is a variety of *perceptual* knowledge, in many respects like our perceptual knowledge of our environment. "The *Perception of the Operations of our own Minds* within us," according to the seventeenth-century English philosopher John Locke, "is very like [the perception of "External Material things"], and might properly enough be call'd internal Sense" (*Essay Concerning Human Understanding*, II.1.iv).[4] D. M. Armstrong defends such an *inner-sense theory.* As he sums it up in his 1968 book *A Materialist Theory of the Mind* (from which the selection is taken):

> Kant suggested the correct way of thinking about introspection when he spoke of the awareness of our own mental states as the operation of "inner sense."[5] He took sense-perception as the model of introspection. By sense-perception we become aware of current physical happenings in our environment and our body. By inner sense we become aware of current happenings in our own mind. (p. 95)

Gilbert Ryle attacks this idea, or at least an extreme version of it, on which "[i]nner perception . . . sets a standard of veridical perception, which sense perception can never emulate." In its place he proposes the simplest possible replacement. No special faculty is needed, because our knowledge of our own minds is achieved simply by applying our ability to know the minds of others to ourselves: "The sorts of things that I can find out about myself are the same as the sorts of things that I can find out about other people, and *the methods of finding them out are much the same*" (emphasis added).

Finally, there is yet another assumption behind the traditional problem of other minds that can be questioned. The traditional problem takes knowledge of one's own mind for granted—that the argument by analogy appeals to my knowledge of *my* mind is not taken to be problematic. Why is knowledge of *other* minds taken to be problematic? Because there are (it is said) powerful considerations in favor of **skepticism** *about other minds*, the view that we can't have knowledge of another's mind. Similarly, perceptual knowledge of one's environment is typically taken to be problematic because there are (it is said) powerful considerations in favor of *skepticism about the external world*, the view that we can't have knowledge of our environment. (See chapter 7 of this anthology.) Alex Byrne argues that the really troubling sort of skepticism is not skepticism about the external

---

4. A selection from Locke's *Essay* is in chapter 10 of this anthology, and a selection from another of Locke's works is in chapter 20.

5. Armstrong is referring to Kant's *Critique of Pure Reason* (1781). A selection from Kant's *Groundwork for the Metaphysics of Morals* is in chapter 16 of this anthology.

world (or, he would presumably add, other minds), but rather *skepticism about the internal world,* the view that we can't have knowledge of our own minds. On Byrne's view, the case for skepticism about the internal world is *stronger* than the case for skepticism about the external world, so, far from being unproblematic, self-knowledge turns out to be the most problematic of all.

## Alec Hyslop (born 1938)

Hyslop is an Honorary Research Associate at La Trobe University, specializing in epistemology, aesthetics, and moral psychology, and is the author of *Other Minds* (1995).

## Frank Cameron Jackson (born 1943)

Jackson is an Australian philosopher who has made many contributions to philosophy of mind and language, metaphysics, and ethics. His books include *Perception: A Representative Theory* (1977), *Conditionals* (1987), and *From Metaphysics to Ethics: A Defense of Conceptual Analysis* (1997). He is Distinguished Professor at the Australian National University and Visiting Professor of Philosophy at Princeton University.

# THE ANALOGICAL INFERENCE
# TO OTHER MINDS

The argument by analogy for other minds (AA) has been widely supposed to involve *conceptual* confusion. It has also been widely supposed to be, simply, a bad inductive argument.[1] In this paper we shall be concerned to defend AA from the latter charge.

AA has been held to be a bad inductive argument because, (i) it proceeds from *one* case, and (ii) it has, of *logical necessity,* an uncheckable conclusion. . . . We shall call objections to AA which turn on the fact that AA has an uncheckable conclusion, A-type. We shall call objections which turn on the fact . . . that AA proceeds from one case, B-type. Of course, not all objections to AA *qua*[2] inductive argument can be unequivocally classified as A-type or B-type. Such objections that we consider below have been classified according to their general character.

---

1. An inductive argument is one whose premises do not logically imply the conclusion.
2. As (Latin).

|

In this section we criticize a representative selection of A-type objections.[3] But before doing this we argue that a reply to A-type objections, sufficiently widely discussed to be called "the standard reply," misses the point at issue.

The standard reply to the objection that AA is an analogical argument from the observable to the logically unobservable is that there are perfectly acceptable analogical arguments having just this characteristic; namely, analogical arguments from the present to the past.

The crucial error in this reply is that an advocate of AA cannot allow that the past is unobservable in the sense in which he holds that other minds are unobservable, because the sample class from which AA constructs the inductive generalization to other minds *itself contains past events*; namely, *remembered* correlations between behavior and mental states. Therefore, when it is said, as it so often is, that AA proceeds from what we are (directly) aware of, this must be understood as "what we are, or remember having been, aware of." But it is true of any past event that it is logically possible that we should remember being aware of it, thus a defender of AA must allow that we may be aware of the past in the relevant sense of "aware."

## CRITICISM OF A-TYPE OBJECTIONS

The various A-type objections that we shall consider have in common the claim that

(P) No analogical (inductive) argument which proceeds from observed facts to conclusions about what cannot, logically, be observed is a good analogical argument.

The differences between them lie in the reasons, if any, offered in support of the principle (P) embodied in this claim.

Two points of clarification need to be made about (P). The first is that, as the mental states of others are, strictly speaking, not unobservable (they are observable by others), (P) should be read as prohibiting a particular person's arguing analogically from what *he* as propounder can observe to what *he* as propounder cannot observe. We shall follow the usual practice of keeping this implicit, rather than making it explicit, in our discussion.

The second point of clarification concerns the relevant sense in which AA is an argument to what cannot be observed. It is commonly asserted that what generates the problem of other minds is the impossibility of being *directly aware* of the mental states of others. This is a mistake. First, it is not at all clear that it is impossible to be directly aware of another's mental state. Secondly, and more importantly, being

---

3. Six, in the original paper. Four are included in this selection.

directly aware of someone else's pain would not, in itself, tell me that that person was in pain, because I should still require grounds for supposing that what I was aware of *was* someone else's pain (as well as my own). These grounds would have to lie in that person's behavior (or brain states, etc.). Therefore, the relevant sense in which AA is an argument to what cannot be observed is that it is an argument to what cannot be *directly known.* However, nothing in what follows turns on the precise sense in which others' mental states cannot be directly checked, verified, observed, or whatever.

## Objection A1

The first A-type objection that we consider consists, in effect, of the bald assertion that AA violates (P). Thus, it is urged that AA is a bad argument because it purports to establish, on analogical grounds, conclusions about items, namely the mental states of others, which cannot be directly observed.

Clearly A1 is a good objection only if one is entitled to assert (P) without offering specific reasons for (P); that is, it is a good objection only if (P) is, in some sense, self-evident. We shall argue, against A1, (i) that not only is (P) not self-evident, but that, in the absence of positive reasons, (P) should be taken to be false. . . .

(i) It is clear for two reasons that (P) is not self-evident. First, the fact that an inductive argument from premises $X$ to conclusion $Y$ violates (P) shows, *in itself,* only that $Y$ is such that evidence for it additional to $X$ of a direct kind cannot be obtained. Now to say that $Y$ is such that certain kinds of additional evidence for it cannot be obtained is to say something which, on the face of it, is quite different from saying that $X$ does not support $Y$. Therefore, no claim that the former implies the latter can be regarded as self-evident.

Secondly, there are perfectly acceptable inductive arguments which, while not violating (P), violate a principle sufficiently close to (P) for the onus of proof to lie with a defender of (P). Here is an example of such an argument.

Helium, like all the elements, has a characteristic spectrum. The nature of this spectrum was determined by experiments carried out, of course, *on earth.* It was then observed (actually, it was remembered) that light from the sun displayed this spectrum (along with hundreds of others), and from this it was inferred that helium was present on the sun. Now the argument just outlined is an argument which proceeds from the fact that certain observed samples of helium on earth have a certain spectrum, to the conclusion that the helium on the sun, which has not been observed, also has this spectrum. Moreover, it is an argument from the observed to the *unobservable,* for it is *impossible* to observe the helium on the sun. Now, of course, this impossibility is empirical, not logical, so there is a difference between the argument for helium on the sun and AA. At the same time, it seems clear that this difference is not *obviously* relevant, therefore the onus of proof lies with an advocate of (P); that is, (P) is not self-evident. Indeed, the helium argument shows not just that (P) is not self-evident, but that (P) should be taken as false in the absence of positive reasons for (P). . . .

*Objection A3*

The most familiar A-type objection to AA turns on the claim that any acceptable analogical argument must rest on an *independently* established correlation, and that, because AA violates (P), there is no appropriate independently established correlation for AA to rest on.

Despite the widespread acceptance of this kind of objection; it is hard to see any force in it. It is just false that "there could be no way of establishing the necessary correlation between the overt moves and their hidden causal counterparts," because one can establish a correlation in one's own case. It may be replied that a correlation in one's own case between behavior and mental states could only entitle one to argue analogically about one's own mind, and that to argue analogically to the minds of others it is necessary to establish a correlation between the behavior of others and the mental states of others. This reply is, however, quite unacceptable; because it amounts to the claim that if *x* is inferred from *y* then *x* must on at least one occasion have been directly observed to be present when *y* was present. We could not, that is, infer to a party in a shuttered house unless we had on at least one occasion observed directly a party in *that* house, even though we had observed a score of parties in a score of houses other than the house in question.

At this point a modification of A3 might be suggested, *viz.*, to construe A3 so that it turns on the fact that while in normal cases conclusions arrived at analogically can be independently checked, in the case of the analogical inference to other minds no conclusion reached by the use of this method of inference can ever be independently (directly) checked. In short, the modified objection is that AA is a method of inference whose use has never, and can never, be shown to be successful.

Our reply to the modification follows Hampshire[4] in "The Analogy of Feeling" where he says

> ... each one of us is constantly able to compare the results of this type of inference [AA] with what he knows to be true directly and non-inferentially; each one of us is in a position to make this testing comparison, whenever he is the designated subject of a statement about feelings and sensations [made by another on analogical grounds].[5]

Malcolm,[6] of course, and his view is widely accepted, thinks Hampshire guilty of an *ignoratio elenchi* (presumably he meant to say *petitio principii*),[7] arguing that "... the reasoning that he [Hampshire] describes involves the assumption that other human figures *do* have thoughts and sensations; for they are assumed to *make*

---

4. Stuart Hampshire (1914–2004), British philosopher.

5. S. Hampshire, "The Analogy of Feeling," *Mind* 61 (1952): 1–12 (see p.4). [Hyslop and Jackson's note.]

6. Norman Malcolm (1911–1990), American philosopher.

7. "*Ignoratio elenchi*": literally, "ignorance of refutation" (Latin). Used to label reasoning to an irrelevant conclusion. "*Petitio principii*": literally, "request for the principle" (Latin). Used to label reasoning that assumes what is supposed to be proved (also known as "begging the question").

*inferences* about me from *observations* of my behaviour,"[8] and, obviously, a defender of AA is not entitled to make this assumption. Now it is not clear whether Hampshire's argument, as he formulates it, makes this assumption; but it *is* clear that it need not make this assumption, because it does not depend on the assumption that other human figures are minded. The argument is hypothetical in character; it is that *if* other human figures make inferences about my mind on the basis of observing my behavior, *then* those inferences, involving analogical reasoning, can be directly tested.

A more extreme modification of A3 is sometimes put in terms of the impossibility of knowing that the method of inference involved in AA is reliable; that is, is a method which regularly yields true conclusions. Thus V. Chappell's[9] imaginary sceptic demands that the method of inference be known to be perfectly reliable, where ". . . to know that a method of inference from $x$ to $y$ is perfectly reliable is to know that $x$ occurs whenever $y$ occurs."[1]

This version of A3 fails for two reasons. First, the objection depends on an illegitimate identification of a sound inductive method of inference with a perfectly reliable method of inference. The whole point about good inductive arguments, as opposed to valid deductive arguments, is that their premises may be true when their conclusions are false. Secondly, and more importantly, since any defender of AA does, of course, believe that his method of inference is very probably, though not necessarily, perfectly reliable; this version of A3 is a *petitio principii*. Just because a defender of AA thinks AA is a good inductive argument, he holds that we do know that the method of inference in question is perfectly reliable. The objector can only hold that we do not know with high probability that the method of inference is perfectly reliable, *if* he assumes that AA is not a good argument, which is to beg the question at issue.

## Objection A4

This is that because AA violates (P), the *observational* evidence, as far as an advocate of AA is concerned, is simply that others do not have minds.

As Alexander[2] puts it:

> In spite of the fact that similar behaviour to that I exhibit, accompanied by my experiences, is exhibited by everyone else unaccompanied, as far as I can observe, by experiences — in spite of the fact, that is, that I observe more samples of purposive behaviour *without* experiences than I do samples of such behaviour with experiences — I am yet content to conclude that all those samples are really accompanied by experiences, when I should, on the evidence, it seems, conclude that I am unusual.[3]

8. N. Malcolm, "Knowledge of Other Minds," in V. Chappell (ed.), *The Philosophy of Mind* (Prentice-Hall, 1962), pp. 151–59 (see p. 153). [Hyslop and Jackson's note.]

9. Vere Chappell (1930–), American philosopher.

1. V. Chappell (ed.), *The Philosophy of Mind* (Prentice-Hall, 1962), p. 3. [Hyslop and Jackson's note.]

2. Peter Alexander (1917–2006), British philosopher.

3. P. Alexander, "Other People's Experiences," *Proceedings of the Aristotelian Society*, vol. 5 (1950/51), pp. 24–46 (see pp. 43–44). Alexander is considering, without definitely endorsing, this objection. [Hyslop and Jackson's note.]

Now it is, of course, true that when we fail to observe that something is the case this can generally be taken as counter-evidence to the claim that it is the case. Nevertheless, as Plantinga[4] points out:

> There is a difference, in general, between failing to observe the presence of A's and observing the absence of A's (observing that no A's are present).[5]

And where it is impossible to observe the absence of A's then the consequent failure to observe the presence of A's is in no way counter-evidence to the presence of A's. Therefore, since it is not possible to observe the absence of mental states in the case of another human figure, our failure to observe their presence is not counter-evidence to there being such mental states.

### Objection A6

The last A-type objection we consider is that put forward Sydney Shoemaker.[6] He says:

> It has often been suggested, of course, that one can discover empirical correlations between *one's own* psychological states and facts about one's own body and behaviour, and that one's knowledge of these correlations can provide a basis for inductive inferences from the bodily and behavioural states of others to assertions about their psychological states. . . . But even if one could discover this, one could have no grounds for supposing that the correlations that hold in one's own case hold in the case of other persons as well.[7]

Shoemaker's reason for holding that "one could have no grounds for supposing that the correlations that hold in one's own case hold in the case of other persons as well" is that anyone who employs AA presumably holds that behavioral and psychological states are only contingently related; and, therefore, that it is contingent that the relation which holds in one's own case holds in the case of others. But, if this is contingent, the analogical arguer can have no ground for supposing it to be the case, because the only empirical evidence he has concerns the relation in his own case. He has not, for example, independently established a correlation between the relationship between physical and psychological in his own case and the relationship in another's case, to sustain the generalization that the relationship is the same in all cases.

Shoemaker's objection raises issues in inductive logic which are beyond the scope of this paper. We shall content ourselves with pointing out that *if* A6 is successful, then *no analogical arguments whatever are successful*; because what Shoemaker says

---

4. Alvin Plantinga (1932–), American philosopher.

5. A. Plantinga, *God and Other Minds* (Cornell University Press, 1967), p. 248. [Hyslop and Jackson's note.]

6. (1931–), American philosopher.

7. S. Shoemaker, *Self-Knowledge and Self-Identity* (Cornell University Press, 1963), p.168. [Hyslop and Jackson's note.]

about AA can be said about *any* analogical argument concerning the unobserved. Whenever one argues inductively from all observed As having been Bs to the unobserved As being Bs, it will be true both that it is contingent that the unobserved As are like the observed As (otherwise the argument would be deductive, not inductive), and that there is no independently established correlation between observed As and unobserved As to sustain the generalization that observed As and unobserved As are alike (otherwise the unobserved As would be observed, not unobserved).

## II

We now turn to B-type objections to AA. Before criticizing them we shall argue, as we did concerning A-type objections, that a reply to B-type objections sufficiently widely discussed to be called "the standard reply," fails.

The standard reply is a reply to the objection to AA that it is a wild generalization from one case, and is, in effect, that the objection commits the *fallacy of equivocation.*[8]

If "one case" means just one occasion of a mental state being correlated with a physical state, then the objection is simply based on a false premise. It is not true that AA is based on one case in this sense. It is based on the multitude of correlations between mental and physical that one has observed in one's own case. On the other hand, so the standard reply goes, if "one case" just refers to the fact that the multitude of correlations between mental and physical are all in one's own case, then the objection is merely drawing attention to the fact that the members of the sample on which AA is based have a common property; namely, of being correlations in one's own case. And it is quite generally the case that analogical arguments proceed from samples having common properties. For example, in the helium argument discussed before, all the samples of helium were on earth.

It seems to us that this standard reply is quite mistaken. Despite the fact that there is a multitude of correlations in one's own case between mental and physical goings on, there is an important sense in which AA is an analogical argument from only one case, rather than an analogical argument from a number of cases having a common property. Two rather different considerations show that AA must be taken as an argument from one case.

The first turns on the point that it is just false that *every*, rather than most or many, instances of, for example, pain behavior on one's own part are accompanied by a pain of one's own. This means that if we regarded AA as proceeding from the many instances of mental-physical correlation in one's own case, the only conclusion that could be obtained would be: Many instances of behavioral states are associated with mental states. Now this conclusion is just not the conclusion we want AA to yield, because it is consistent with certain human bodies which behave just as one's own

---

8. Reasoning that breaks down because an expression is used in different senses.

does, not having *any* associated mental states. The conclusion we want AA to yield is that for *every* body which behaves much as one's own does, it is true that many instances of its behavioral states are associated with mental states.

The second consideration arises from the fact that we believe that for each living human body there is at least one person such that the behavioral states of that body are accompanied by the mental states of that person. . . . The only analogical argument that could show this would be one generalizing from the fact that for one's own body there is at least one person (oneself) such that the behavioral states of that body are accompanied by the mental states of that person. Now this is, and must be, an inductive generalization from *one* case; therefore, if the analogical argument for other minds is to establish that for each living body there is at least one person whose mental states correspond to the behavior of that body, the argument must be regarded as an analogical argument from one case.

## CRITICISM OF B-TYPE OBJECTIONS

If our comments on the standard reply are correct, then AA is an analogical argument from one case. This is the point on which the major objection we consider below turns; however, we first consider an objection sometimes confused with this objection.

### Objection BI

This is that the ratio of examined to unexamined instances is not high enough. Don Locke[9] complains that "[AA] proceeds from the smallest possible basis to the largest possible conclusion; it argues from one solitary instance to, perhaps, an infinity of cases."[1]

This objection involves a misunderstanding about the nature of AA, in that it involves treating AA as a species of *statistical* argument.[2] In fact, as the following argument shows, the soundness of AA is independent of the ratio of examined to unexamined cases.

Suppose I use AA in an attempt to establish that just one other person has a mind, then no complaint can be made about the ratio of examined to unexamined cases because this ratio will be very much higher than in the vast majority of cases of inductive generalization. But, clearly, this one other might be *any* other. Therefore, if it is reasonable to use AA to show that one other person has a mind, then, for any other person, it is reasonable to use AA to show that he has a mind; provided, of course, that he is behaviorally sufficiently like myself. The reason why the ratio of examined

9. New Zealand philosopher (1938–).

1. D. Locke, *Myself and Others* (Oxford, 1968), p. 49. [Hyslop and Jackson's note.]

2. An argument that a population has a certain feature based on a random sample from that population. For example, if we randomly take ten balls from a bag of twenty, and find that all ten are red, we may argue on statistical grounds that most of the balls in the bag are red.

to unexamined cases is irrelevant to the soundness of an analogical argument is that the soundness of an analogical argument depends on the relevant analogy between the examined and the unexamined cases. If the analogy between the examined cases and some given unexamined case is sufficient to sustain the inference, then, by parity of reasoning, in *any* unexamined case where the analogy holds, regardless of how many of these there are, we are entitled to make the inference in question.

## Objection B2

The last B-type objection that we consider is that put by Norman Malcolm. He says ". . . this [AA] would be very *weak* inductive reasoning, based as it is on the observation of a single instance."[3] This objection is distinct from B1 because it turns, not on the ratio of examined cases to unexamined cases being low, but on the fact that there is only one examined case. As such, it is *prima facie* a good objection because it is indisputable that we often require arguments from analogy to be based on more than one instance. (However, this objection should not be confused with the objection: "How do I know that it is not my individual peculiarity to feel angry when I frown?"[4] One may enquire of any inductive base, how do I know that it is not a peculiarity of the sampled cases to be as they are? Since it can be raised against *any* analogical argument it is not an objection to AA as such.)

Although we often demand that an analogical argument be based on more than one instance, nevertheless there are analogical arguments which we take to establish their conclusions with very high probability which proceed from only one examined case. Our reply to B2 will be to argue that AA is of the latter kind. Our argument will proceed via a discussion of an analogical argument which, as it stands, requires to be based on more than one instance.

Suppose I drop an egg on the floor and it breaks. Am I entitled to infer that the next egg dropped will break? Obviously, we should all be happier with such an inference if it were based on a number of cases of eggs that had been dropped and had broken. Why should we be happier? Because we should have a statistically more significant sample? Surely not, because the total number of eggs there are is so large that a few more cases will not yield any significant increase in the percentage of eggs tested. Surely the answer is that if we carry out more tests we rule out the possibility of the breaking in the case of the tested eggs being due to something other than their being dropped. What appears to follow from this is that if we know, somehow or other, that the first egg broke just because it was dropped, then the additional tests would not have been necessary. We shall put this point more generally. Suppose that we are arguing from the fact that $x_1, \ldots x_n$ are both $F$ and $G$, and that $y$ is $F$, to the conclusion that $y$ is $G$. When do we need $n$ to be large? The suggestion we are making is that we need $n$ to be large just when (i) a large sample will provide us with information about the (causal) relation between an $x$ being $F$ and being $G$, (ii) this

---

3. Malcolm, "Knowledge of Other Minds," p. 152. [Hyslop and Jackson's note.]

4. J. Day, *Inductive Probability* (Routledge & Kegan Paul, 1961), p. 64. [Hyslop and Jackson's note.]

information is necessary for the inference to $y$ being $G$, and (iii) we do not already have this information. The important point is (iii). If we already have the required information the sample need not be large.

We can now apply this suggestion to show that AA does not need to proceed from more than one case. In the one case from which AA proceeds we know, without appeal to a larger sample, that the possession of a mind is the operative cause of the displaying of behavior of the kind which in others is then the basis for supposing that they have minds. I know in my own case that my body behaves as it does because I have a mind; and I know this independently of what I know about the minds of others, because I would know this even if I were the only person in existence. However, the information that, in the sampled case (my own), a mind is the operative cause is all that a larger sample could give me relevant to the inference from the behavior of another to the mind of another. Therefore, as I already have the only relevant information a larger sample could yield, a larger sample is unnecessary. To ask where does this information come from would be beside the point. We have it, and we have it, as noted, independently of our knowledge of other minds, and so, there is no circularity in using this information to support AA.

In our view what has bedeviled discussion of B2 is the feeling that the important point arising from the fact that AA is based on just one case is that one is left without direct evidence against this one case being unique. But what good, if it were possible, would enlarging the sample on which AA is based do? It would provide direct evidence that one's own case was not unique, of course, but how would this help? One would still have no direct evidence that the sampled cases were not unique. It is a necessary truth that no analogical argument, no matter how large its sample, provides direct evidence that its sample is not unique. Therefore, sample size must have some other role to play in analogical arguments. We have tried to argue that its role is to provide certain causal information, and that this role is not needed in the case of AA because we already have this information.

In arguing this, we are not denying that the possibility of the sample being unique raises a serious problem. "How does one know that the cause in the sample case is the cause in the unsampled cases?" is a perfectly reasonable question. But, as we have in effect already noted, it is a question that can be raised against *any* analogical argument. The fact is that we know that the cause of certain behavior in our own case is mental. To suppose, in the absence of any plausible alternative cause, that the operative cause in the case of others is different would be to indulge in a fantastic piece of *a priori* speculation.[5] Why would this be fantastic? Perhaps Occam's Razor[6] and the undoubted *predictive* power of the other minds hypothesis provide part of the answer to this question; but, at any rate, the answer to this question will be the answer to the problem of induction for it will tell us when it is reasonable to suppose that a sample is like a population, and, fortunately, the problem of induction has not been the problem with which this paper has been concerned.

---

5. Speculation based only on claims knowable independently of experience.

6. A methodological principle of parsimony in theorizing, often rendered as "Do not multiply entities beyond necessity." Named after the English philosopher William of Occam (or Ockham) (c. 1287–1347).

The problem this paper has been concerned with is whether, given that there are some sound analogical arguments, there is any good reasons for denying that AA *qua* analogical argument is such an analogical argument. We conclude that there is not.

## TEST YOUR UNDERSTANDING

1. What is the example of helium on the sun supposed to show about principle (P)?

2. Do Hyslop and Jackson think that a good analogical argument for the conclusion that another person is in pain is a **valid** argument?

3. One general objection to the analogical argument is that it proceeds just from one case, one's own. A reply to this objection is that it can't be right because then we wouldn't know that there's helium on the sun. For we know that there's helium on the basis of a similar analogical argument from "one case," the behavior of helium on Earth. What do Hyslop and Jackson think about this reply?

## NOTES AND QUESTIONS

1. One (relatively) modest project is to find evidence that establishes that other people are in various mental states, like feeling pain, believing that it's raining, wanting pizza, and so forth. A more ambitious project is to find out how *ordinary people* know that others feel pain, believe that it's raining, want pizza, and so forth. Explain, using examples, why the success of the modest project doesn't guarantee the success of the ambitious project. Suppose that one can establish the existence of other minds by an analogical inference, and thus that the modest project succeeds. Are there any reasons for doubting that ordinary people know about others' minds by an analogical inference?

2. For surveys of the problem of other minds, see Alec Hyslop, "Other Minds," *Stanford Encyclopedia of Philosophy*, ed. Edward Zalta (http://plato.stanford.edu/archives/fall2010/entries/other-minds/), and Anita Avramides, *Other Minds* (Routledge, 2001).

## Saul Kripke (born 1940)

Kripke is Distinguished Professor of Philosophy at the City University of New York. He previously taught at Princeton University, where he gave a series of lectures that became *Naming and Necessity* (1980), one of the most influential books in philosophy in the twentieth century.

# WITTGENSTEIN[1] AND OTHER MINDS
## from *Wittgenstein on Rules and Private Language*

Traditional philosophy of mind had argued, in its "problem of other minds," that given that I know what it means for *me* to feel a tickle, I can raise the sceptical question whether others ever feel the same as I do, or even whether there are conscious minds behind their bodies at all. The problem is one of the epistemic *justification* of our "belief" that other minds exist "behind the bodies" and that their sensations are similar to our own. For that matter, we might equally well ask whether stones, chairs, tables, and the like think and feel; it is assumed that the hypothesis that they do think and feel makes perfect sense. A few philosophers — solipsists — doubt or positively deny that any body other than one ("my body") has a mind "back of" it. Some others — panpsychists — ascribe minds to all material objects. Yet others — Cartesians[2] — believe that there are minds behind human bodies, but not those of animals, let alone inanimate bodies. Perhaps the most common position ascribes minds to both human and animal bodies, but not to inanimate bodies. All presuppose without argument that we begin with an antecedently understood general concept of a given material object's "having," or not having, a mind; there is a problem as to which objects in fact have minds and why they should be thought to have (or lack) them. In contrast, Wittgenstein seems to believe that the very *meaningfulness* of the ascription of sensations to others is questionable if, following the traditional model, we attempt to extrapolate it from our own case. On the traditional model in question, Wittgenstein seems to be saying, it is doubtful that we could *have* any "belief" in other minds, and their sensations, that ought to be justified. . . .

Let me attempt to give the reader a feeling for the difficulty, and for its historical roots. According to Descartes, the one entity of whose existence I may be certain, even in the midst of doubts of the existence of the external world, is myself.[3] I may doubt the existence of bodies (including my own), or, even assuming that there are bodies, that there ever are minds "behind" them; but I cannot doubt the existence of my own mind. Hume's[4] reaction to this is notorious: "There are some philosophers, who imagine we are intimately conscious of what we call our *self*; that we feel its existence and its continuance in existence; and are certain, beyond the evidence of a demonstration, both of its perfect identity and simplicity. The strongest sensation, the most violent passion, say they, instead of distracting us from this view, only fix it the more intensely, and make us consider their influence on *self* either by their pain

---

1. The Austrian philosopher Ludwig Wittgenstein (1889–1951) was one of the major figures in twentieth-century philosophy.

2. Those holding similar views to the French philosopher René Descartes (1596–1650).

3. See Descartes, Meditation II, in chapter 8 of this anthology.

4. Scottish philosopher David Hume (1711–1776); the quotation following is from Hume's most famous work, *A Treatise of Human Nature* (1740). Selections from the *Treatise* are in chapters 7, 15, and 17 of this anthology.

or pleasure. To attempt a farther proof of this were to weaken its evidence; since no proof can be derived from any fact of which we are so intimately conscious; nor is there any thing, of which we can be certain, if we doubt of this. Unluckily all these positive assertions are contrary to that very experience, which is pleaded for them, nor have we any idea of *self*, after the manner it is here explain'd. . . . For my part, when I enter most intimately into what I call *myself*, I always stumble on some particular impression or other, of heat or cold, light or shade, love or hatred, pain or pleasure. I never can catch *myself* at any time without a perception, and never can observe any thing but the perception. . . . If any one, upon serious and unprejudic'd reflection, thinks he has a different notion of *himself*, I must confess I can reason no longer with him. All I can allow him is, that he may be in the right as well as I, and that we are essentially different in this particular. He may, perhaps, perceive something simple and continu'd, which he calls *himself*; tho' I am certain there is no such principle in me."

So: where Descartes would have said that I am certain that "I have a tickle," the only thing Hume is aware of is the tickle itself. The self — the Cartesian ego — is an entity which is wholly mysterious. We are aware of no such entity that "has" the tickle, "has" the headache, the visual perception, and the rest; we are aware only of the tickle, the headache, the visual perception, itself. Any direct influences from Hume to Wittgenstein are difficult to substantiate; but the Humean thoughts here sketched continued through much of the philosophical tradition, and it is very easy to find the idea in the *Tractatus*.[5] In 5.631 of that work, Wittgenstein says, "There is no such thing as the subject that thinks or entertains ideas. If I wrote a book called *The World as I found it* . . . it alone could *not* be mentioned in that book." Continuing in 5.632–5.633, he explains: "The subject does not belong to the world: rather, it is a limit of the world. Where *in* the world is a metaphysical subject to be found? You will say that this is exactly like the case of the eye and the visual field. But really you do *not* see the eye. And nothing *in the visual field* allows you to infer that it is seen by an eye." . . .

Wittgenstein returned to this theme in several of his writings, lectures, and discussions of the late 1920s and early 1930s, during the period usually regarded as transitional between the "early" philosophy of the *Tractatus* and the "late" philosophy of the *Investigations*.[6] In his account of Wittgenstein's Cambridge lectures in 1930–3, Moore reports that Wittgenstein "said that 'just as no (physical) eye is involved in seeing, so no Ego is involved in thinking or in having toothache'; and he quotes, with apparent approval, Lichtenberg's saying 'Instead of "I think" we ought to say "It thinks"' ('it' being used, as he said, as 'Es' is used in 'Es blitzet'); and by saying this he meant, I think, something similar to what he said of the 'eye of the visual field' when he said that it is not anything which is *in* the visual field."[7] In *Philosophical*

---

5. Wittgenstein's *Tractatus Logico-Philosophicus* was published in 1921.

6. *Philosophical Investigations*, published posthumously in 1953.

7. "Moore": British philosopher G. E. Moore (1873–1958). "Lichtenberg": German physicist and satirist Georg Christoph Lichtenberg (1742–1799). "Es blitzet": literally, it flashes (German, i.e., there is lightning).

*Remarks*,[8] §58, Wittgenstein imagines a language in which "I have a toothache" is replaced by "There is toothache," and, following Lichtenberg; "I am thinking" becomes "It is thinking."

Now the basic problem in extending talk of sensations from to "myself" to "others" ought to be manifest. Supposedly, if I concentrate on a particular toothache or tickle, note its qualitative character, and abstract from particular features of time and place, I can form a concept that will determine when a toothache or tickle comes again. . . . How am I supposed to extend this notion to the sensations of "others"? What is this supposed to mean? If I see ducks in Central Park, I can imagine things which are "like these" — here, still *ducks* — except that they are *not* in Central Park. I can similarly "abstract" even from *essential* properties[9] of these particular ducks to entities like these but lacking the properties in question — ducks of different parentage and biological origin, ducks born in a different century, and so on. . . . But what can be meant by something "just like this toothache, only it is not I, but someone else, who has it"? In what ways is this supposed to be similar to the paradigmatic toothache on which I concentrate my attention, and in what ways dissimilar? We are supposed to imagine another entity, similar to "me" — another "soul," "mind" or "self" — that "has" a toothache *just like* this toothache, except that it (he? she?) "has" it, just as "I have" this one. All this makes little sense, given the Humean critique of the notion of the self that Wittgenstein accepts. I have no idea of a "self" in my own case, let alone a generic concept of a "self" that in addition to "me" includes "others." Nor do I have any idea of "having" as a relation between such a "self" and the toothache. Supposedly, by concentrating my attention on one or more particular toothaches, I can form the concept of toothache, enabling me thereby to recognize at later times when "there is a toothache" or "it toothaches" (as in, "it is raining") on the basis of the "phenomenological quality" of toothaches. Although we have expressed this in the Lichtenbergian terminology Wittgenstein commends, "it toothaches" means what we naively would have expressed by "I have a toothache." The concept is supposed to be formed by concentrating on a particular toothache: when something just like this recurs, then "it toothaches" again. What are we supposed to abstract from this situation to form the concept of an event which is like the given paradigm case of "it toothaches," except that the toothache is not "mine," but "someone else's"? I have no concept of a "self" nor of "having" to enable me to make the appropriate abstraction from the original paradigm. The formulation "it toothaches" makes this quite clear: consider the total situation, and ask what I am to abstract if I wish to remove "myself."

I think that it is at least in part because of this kind of consideration that Wittgenstein was so much concerned with the appeal of solipsism, and of the behavioristic idea that to say of someone else that he has a toothache is simply to make a statement about his behavior. When he considers the adoption of

---

8. Published in 1964.

9. An essential **property** of an object is a property that the object could not have lacked; an object's non-essential properties are its *accidental* properties, those properties that it could have lacked.

Lichtenberg's subjectless sensation language, attributions of sensations to others give way to expressions like "The body A is behaving similarly to the way X behaves when it pains," where "X" is a name for what I would ordinarily call "my body." This is a crude behaviorist ersatz for imagining the sensations of others on the model of my own: attributing a sensation to A in no way says that something is happening that resembles what happens when I am in pain (or, rather, when it pains). The attraction, for Wittgenstein, of this combination of solipsism and behaviorism, was never free of a certain discontent with it. Nevertheless, during the most verificationist[1] phase of his transitional period, Wittgenstein felt that it is hard to avoid the conclusion that since behavior is our sole method of verifying attributions of sensations to others, the behaviorist formulation is all that I can mean when I make such an attribution (see *Philosophical Remarks*, §§64–5).

The point comes into sharp relief when we consider many customary formulations of the problem of other minds. How do I know, it is said, that other bodies "have" "minds" like my own? It is assumed that I know from my own case *what* a "mind" is, and what it is for a "body" to "have" it. But the immediate point of the Hume–Lichtenberg criticism of the notion of the self is that I have no such idea in my own case that can be generalized to other bodies. I *do* have an idea, from my own case, of what it is like for there "to be pain," but I have no idea what it would be like for there to be a pain "just like this, except that it belongs to a mind other than my own."...

§350[2] questions whether we know what it means to say that "someone else has pain" on the basis of my own case. At the end, the example given is that of a *stove*: do we know what it means to say of a stove that it is in pain? As we said above, the traditional view assumes, without supposing the need of any further justification, that we have a general concept of an arbitrary material object "having" sensations, or, rather, "having" a "mind" that in turn is the "bearer" of the sensations. (The physical object "has" sensations in a derivative sense, if it "has" a "mind" that "has" the sensations.) Now: are we so sure that we understand all this? As we have emphasized, we have no idea what a "mind" is. And do we know what relation is to hold between a "mind" and a physical object that constitutes "having"? Suppose a given chair "has" a "mind." Then there are many "minds" in the universe, only one of which a given chair "has." What relationship is that "mind" supposed to have to the chair, that another "mind" does not? Why is this "mind," rather than that one, the one the chair "has"? (Of course I don't mean: what is the (causal) *explanation* why in fact the chair "has" this "mind" rather than that? I mean: what relation is supposed to hold between the chair and one mind, rather than another, that *constitutes* its having this mind, rather than that?) For that matter, why is it the chair as a whole, rather than just its back, or its legs, that is related to the given mind?

---

1. Verificationism is the view that the meaning of a sentence consists in its method of verification — the ways in which one could find out that the sentence is true. Verificationism was a core commitment of the early-twentieth-century movement known as *logical positivism*, which drew inspiration from Wittgenstein's *Tractatus Logico-Philosophicus*.

2. Of the *Investigations*. All subsequent section-number references are to this book.

(Why not another physical object altogether?) Under what circumstances would it be the back of the chair, rather than the whole chair, that "has" a given "mind" and hence thinks and feels? (This is not the question: how would we *verify* that the relation holds, but rather, under what circumstances would it hold?) Often discussions of the problem of other minds, of panpsychism, and so on, simply ignore these questions, supposing, without further ado, that the notion of a given body "having" a given "mind" is self-evident. Wittgenstein simply wishes to question whether we really have such a clear idea what this means: he is raising intuitive questions. See, e.g., §361 ("The chair is thinking to itself: . . . WHERE? In one of its parts? Or outside its body; in the air around it? Or not *anywhere* at all? But then what is the difference between the chair's saying anything to itself and another one's doing so, next to it?. . .") or §283 ("Can we say of the stone that it has a soul [or: a mind] and *that* is what has the pain? What has a soul [or: mind], or pain, to do with a stone?").

It is possible to make various attempts to understand the idea of an object — even an inanimate one — "having" a "mind" or a sensation without invoking the notions of "minds" and "having" themselves. I might, for example, imagine that the physical object I call "my body" turns to stone while my thoughts, or my pains, go on (see §283). This could be expressed in Lichtenberg's jargon: There is thinking, or pain, even while such-and-such an object turns to stone. But: "if that has happened, in what sense will the *stone* have the thoughts or the pains? In what sense will they be ascribable to the stone?" Suppose I were thinking, for example, of the proof that $\pi$ is irrational, and my body turned to stone while I was still thinking of this proof. Well: what relation would my thoughts of this proof have to the stone? In what sense is the stone still "my body," not just "formerly my body"? What difference is there between this case and the case where after "my body" turned to stone, "my mind switched bodies" — perhaps to *another* stone? Suppose for the moment that after I turn to stone I think only about mathematics. In general, what could connect a thought about mathematics with one physical object rather than another? In the case where my body turns to stone, the only connection is that the stone *is* what my body *has become*. In abstraction from such a prior history, the connection between the thought and the physical object is even harder to spell out: yet if there is a connection, it must be a connection that exists *now*, independently of an imagined prior history.

Actually, in §283 Wittgenstein is concerned with the connection of a pain, a sensation, with the stone. Now if we forget for a moment that sensations are ascribed to a "mind" that a physical object "has," and if we think simply of the connection between the sensation and the physical object without worrying about the intermediate links, then in some cases we may still be able to make sense of the connection between a given sensation and a given physical object, even an inert one such as a stone. Pains, for example, are *located*. They are located in the causal sense that damage or injury to a certain area produces the pain. In another causal sense, relief applied to a certain area may alleviate or eliminate the pain. They are also located in the more primitive, non-causal sense in which I *feel* a pain as "in my foot," "in my arm," and the like. Very often these senses coincide, but not always — certainly there is no conceptual reason why they must coincide. But: what if they all coincide, and, by all three tests, a certain pain is "located" in a certain position in a stone? As I understand Wittgenstein, he deals with this particular question in §302 where someone else's body, not a stone, is in question. Assuming that I can imagine that a pain is "located" in another body, does that give a sense to the idea that "someone else" might be in pain? Recall the Lichtenbergian terminology: if "there is pain," perhaps "there is pain in the stone," or "there is pain in that arm," where the arm in question is not my arm. Why isn't this just to imagine that *I* feel pain, only "in" the arm of another body, or even in a stone? Remember that "there is pain" means "I have pain," with the mysterious subject suppressed: so it would seem that to imagine "pain in that arm" is to imagine that *I* have pain in the arm of another body (in the way a person who has lost his arm can feel a pain in the area where his arm once was). There is no concept here of *another* "self" who feels the pain in the stone, or in the other body. It is for this reason that the experiment of ignoring the other "mind," and trying to imagine a direct connection between the sensation and the body, fails. To repeat some of what was quoted in §302: "If one has to imagine someone else's pain on the model of one's own, this is none too easy a thing to do. . . what I have to do is not simply to make a transition in imagination from one place of pain to another. As, from . . . the hand to . . . the arm. For I am not to imagine that I feel pain in some region of his body. (Which would also be possible.)" In the Lichtenbergian jargon, "there is pain" *always* means that *I* feel pain.

Even if we ignore the Lichtenbergian terminology, the problem can be restated: What is the difference between the case where *I* have a pain in another body, and where that pain in the other body is "someone else's" pain and not mine? It would seem that this difference can be expressed only by a direct attack on the problems we have just now been trying to evade: what is a mind, what is it for it to "have" a sensation, what is it for a body to "have" a mind? The attempt to bypass these intermediaries and deal directly with the connection of the sensation and the physical object fails, precisely because I cannot then define what it means for "another mind" to have the sensation in a given physical object, as opposed to "my" having it there. Wittgenstein insists that the possibility that one person might have a sensation in the body of another is perfectly intelligible, even if it never occurs: "Pain behavior can point to a painful place—but the subject of pain is the person who gives it expression" (§302). . . .

In sum, any attempt to imagine a direct connection between a sensation and a physical object without mentioning a "self" or "mind" leads me simply to imagine that *I* have a sensation located elsewhere. So we are compelled to contemplate the original mystery: What is a "mind," what is it for a "mind" to "have" a sensation, what is it for a body to "have" a "mind"? Here the argument of Hume and Lichtenberg, and the other considerations we have mentioned, say that we have no such notions. As Wittgenstein puts the question in §283, speaking of the ascription of sensations to other bodies: "One has to say it of a body, or, if you like, of a soul [mind] which some body *has*. And how can a body *have* a soul [mind]?"

## TEST YOUR UNDERSTANDING

1. Wittgenstein (as interpreted by Kripke) thinks that the traditional problem of other minds rests on a false assumption. Set out the traditional problem, making every assumption explicit. What assumption does Wittgenstein think is false?

2. Descartes was confident that he was thinking. What, according to Wittgenstein (as interpreted by Kripke), should he have been sure of instead?

## NOTES AND QUESTIONS

1. If it makes no sense to attribute *a sensation like this* (here I attend to my aching tooth) to "another mind," perhaps statements like "Griffin has a toothache" and "Sabine has a toothache" *don't* characterize Griffin and Sabine as having sensations *like this*, because then they would be nonsense, and surely statements like this are not nonsense. Indeed, they are sometimes true. Here is an alternative: while first-person statements like "I have a toothache" report the existence of a sensation *like this*, these third-person statements say nothing about sensations, and instead just characterize Griffin's and Sabine's outward behavior. On this view (which Kripke mentions), there is a radical difference in meaning between "I have a toothache" and "Griffin has a toothache": the first statement concerns a sensation; the second statement concerns Griffin's behavior.

   *Exercise:* First motivate this view, drawing on the considerations raised by Kripke. Then criticize it.

2. The selection is taken from Kripke's book *Wittgenstein on Rules and Private Language*, which is mostly concerned with Wittgenstein's views on linguistic meaning, as they appear in his *Philosophical Investigations* (Blackwell, 1953). The interpretation of Wittgenstein that Kripke advances in the book is controversial, but the arguments that Kripke attributes to Wittgenstein are of great interest in their own right, and for this reason the book is regarded as a contemporary classic. It is quite accessible, and relatively short. For an introduction to the *Philosophical Investigations*, see Marie McGinn, *The Routledge Guidebook to Wittgenstein's Philosophical Investigations* (Routledge, 2013).

## Maurice Merleau-Ponty (1908–1961)

Merleau-Ponty was Chair of Philosophy at the Collège de France in Paris from 1952 until his death. Influenced by the German philosopher Edmund Husserl (1859–1938), Merleau-Ponty's major work is *The Phenomenology of Perception* (1945), which criticizes Cartesian dualism and emphasizes the importance of embodiment to our experience of the world.

# MAN SEEN FROM THE OUTSIDE
from *The World of Perception*

[In previous lectures] we have tried to look at space and the things which inhabit it, both animate and inanimate, through the eyes of perception and to forget what we find "entirely natural" about them simply because they have been familiar to us for too long; we have endeavoured to consider them as they are experienced naïvely. We must now try to do the same with respect to human beings themselves. Over the last thirty or more centuries, many things have undoubtedly been said about human beings. Yet these were often the products of reflection. What I mean by this is that Descartes,[1] when he wanted to know what man is, set about subjecting the ideas which occurred to him to critical examination. One example would be the idea of mind and body. He purified these ideas; he rid them of all trace of obscurity and confusion. Whereas most people understand spirit to be something like very subtle matter, or smoke, or breath (consistent, in this regard, with primitive peoples), Descartes showed admirably that spirit is something altogether different. He demonstrated that its nature is quite other, for smoke and breath are, in their way, things — even if very subtle ones — whereas spirit is not a thing at all, does not occupy space, is not spread over a certain extension as all things are, but on the contrary is entirely compact and indivisible — a being — the essence of which is none other than to commune with, collect and know itself. This gave rise to the concepts of pure spirit and pure matter, or things. Yet it is clear that I can only find and, so to speak, touch this absolutely pure spirit in myself. Other human beings are never pure spirit for me: I only know them through their glances, their gestures, their speech — in other words, through their bodies. Of course *another human being* is certainly more than simply a body to me: rather, this other is a body animated by all manner of intentions, the origin of numerous actions and words. These I remember and they go to make up my sketch of their moral character. Yet I cannot detach someone from their silhouette, the tone of their voice and its accent. If I see them for even a moment, I can reconnect with them instantaneously and far more thoroughly than if I were to go through a list of everything I know about them from experience or hearsay. Another person, for us, is a spirit which haunts a body and we seem to see a whole host of possibilities contained within this body when it appears before us; the body is the very presence of these possibilities. So the process of looking at human beings from the outside — that is, at other people — leads us to reassess a number of distinctions which once seemed to hold good such as that between mind and body.

---

1. René Descartes (1596–1650), French philosopher, scientist, and mathematician; a central figure in Western philosophy.

Let us see what becomes of this distinction by examining a particular case. Imagine that I am in the presence of someone who, for one reason or another, is extremely annoyed with me. My interlocutor gets angry and I notice that he is expressing his anger by speaking aggressively, by gesticulating and shouting. But where is this anger? People will say that it is in the mind of my interlocutor. What this means is not entirely clear. For I could not imagine the malice and cruelty which I discern in my opponent's looks separated from his gestures, speech and body. None of this takes place in some other-worldly realm, in some shrine located beyond the body of the angry man. It really is here, in this room and in this part of the room, that the anger breaks forth. It is in the space between him and me that it unfolds. I would accept that the sense in which the place of my opponent's anger is on his face is not the same as that in which, in a moment, tears may come streaming from his eyes or a grimace may harden on his mouth. Yet anger inhabits him and it blossoms on the surface of his pale or purple cheeks, his blood-shot eyes and wheezing voice. . . . And if, for one moment, I step out of my own viewpoint as an external observer of this anger and try to remember what it is like for me when I am angry, I am forced to admit that it is no different. When I reflect on my own anger, I do not come across any element that might be separated or, so to speak, unstuck, from my own body. When I recall being angry at Paul, it does not strike me that this anger was in my mind or among my thoughts but rather, that it lay entirely between me who was doing the shouting and that odious Paul who just sat there calmly and listened with an ironic air. My anger is nothing less than an attempt to destroy Paul, one which will remain verbal if I am a pacifist and even courteous, if I am polite. The location of my anger, however, is in the space we both share — in which we exchange arguments instead of blows — and not in me. It is only afterwards, when I reflect on what anger is and remark that it involves a certain (negative) evaluation of another person, that I come to the following conclusion. Anger is, after all, a thought; to be angry is to think that the other person is odious and this thought, like all others, cannot — as Descartes has shown — reside in any piece of matter and therefore must belong to the mind. I may very well think in such terms but as soon as I turn back to the real experience of anger, which was the spur to my reflections, I am forced to acknowledge that this anger does not lie beyond my body, directing it from without, but rather that in some inexplicable sense it is bound up with my body.

There is something of everything in Descartes, as in the work of all great philosophers. And so it is that he who draws an absolute distinction between mind and body also manages to say that the soul is not simply like the pilot of a ship, the commander-in-chief of the body, but rather that it is very closely united to the body, so much so that it suffers with it, as is clear to me when I say that I have toothache.[2]

---

2. See Descartes, *Meditation VI*, p. 361 of this anthology.

Yet this union of mind and body can barely be spoken of, according to Descartes; it can only be experienced in everyday life. As far as Descartes is concerned, whatever the facts of the matter may be — and even if we live what he himself calls a true *mélange*[3] of mind and body — this does not take away my right to distinguish absolutely between parts that are united in my experience. I can still posit, by rights, an absolute distinction between mind and body which is denied by the fact of their union. I can still define man without reference to the immediate structure of his being and as he appears to himself in reflection: as thought which is somehow strangely joined to a bodily apparatus without either the mechanics of the body or the transparency of thought being compromised by their being mixed together in this way. It could be said that even Descartes' most faithful disciples have always asked themselves exactly how it is that our reflection, which concerns the human being as given, can free itself from the conditions to which it appears to have been subject at the outset.

When they address this issue, today's psychologists emphasise the fact that we do not start out in life immersed in our own self-consciousness (or even in that of things) but rather from the experience of other people. I never become aware of my own existence until I have already made contact with others; my reflection always brings me back to myself, yet for all that it owes much to my contacts with other people. An infant of a few months is already very good at differentiating between goodwill, anger and fear on the face of another person, at a stage when he could not have learned the physical signs of these emotions by examining his own body. This is because the body of the other and its various movements appear to the infant to have been invested from the outset with an emotional significance; this is because the infant learns to know mind as visible behaviour just as much as in familiarity with its own mind. The adult himself will discover in his own life what his culture, education, books and tradition have taught him to find there. The contact I make with myself is always mediated by a particular culture, or at least by a language that we have received from without and which guides us in our self-knowledge. So while ultimately the notion of a pure self, the mind, devoid of instruments and history, may well be useful as a critical ideal to set in opposition to the notion of a mere influx of ideas from the surrounding environment, such a self only develops into a free agent by way of the instrument of language and by taking part in the life of the world.

This leaves us with a very different view of the human being and humanity from the one with which we began. Humanity is not an aggregate of individuals, a community of thinkers, each of whom is guaranteed from the outset to be able to reach agreement with the others because all participate in the same thinking essence. Nor, of course, is it a single Being in which the multiplicity of individuals are dissolved and into which these individuals are destined to be reabsorbed. As a matter of principle, humanity is precarious: each person can only believe what

---

3. Mixture, blend (French).

he recognises to be true internally and, at the same time, nobody thinks or makes up his mind without already being caught up in certain relationships with others, which leads him to opt for a particular set of opinions. Everyone is alone and yet nobody can do without other people, not just because they are useful (which is not in dispute here) but also when it comes to happiness. There is no way of living with others which takes away the burden of being myself, which allows me to not have an opinion; there is no "inner" life that is not a first attempt to relate to another person. In this ambiguous position, which has been forced on us because we have a body and a history (both personally and collectively), we can never know complete rest. We are continually obliged to work on our differences, to explain things we have said that have not been properly understood, to reveal what is hidden within us and to perceive other people. Reason does not lie behind us, nor is that where the meeting of minds takes place: rather, both stand before us waiting to be inherited. Yet we are no more able to reach them definitively than we are to give up on them.

It is understandable that our species, charged as it is with a task that will never and can never be completed, and at which it has not necessarily been called to succeed, even in relative terms, should find this situation both cause for anxiety and a spur to courage. In fact, these are one and the same thing. For anxiety is vigilance, it is the will to judge, to know what one is doing and what there is on offer. If there is no such thing as benign fate, then neither is there such a thing as its malign opposite. Courage consists in being reliant on oneself and others to the extent that, irrespective of differences in physical and social circumstance, all manifest in their behaviour and their relationships that very same spark which makes us recognise them, which makes us crave their assent or their criticism, the spark which means we share a common fate. It is simply that this modern form of humanism has lost the dogmatic tone of earlier centuries. We should no longer pride ourselves in being a community of pure spirits; let us look instead at the real relationships between people in our societies. For the most part, these are master–slave relationships. We should not find excuses for ourselves in our good intentions; let us see what becomes of these once they have escaped from inside us. There is something healthy about this unfamiliar gaze we are suggesting should be brought to bear on our species. Voltaire[4] once imagined, in *Micromégas*, that a giant from another planet was confronted with our customs. These could only seem derisory to an intelligence higher than our own. Our era is destined to judge itself not from on high, which is mean and bitter, but in a certain sense from below. Kafka[5] imagines a man who has metamorphosed into a strange insect and who looks at his family through the eyes of such an insect. Kafka also imagines a dog that investigates the human world which it rubs up

---

4. The pen-name of François-Marie Arouet (1694–1778), a French writer and philosopher; "Micromégas" is one of his short stories.

5. Franz Kafka (1883–1924), Austro-Hungarian novelist and short story writer; the two works mentioned are his novella *The Metamorphosis* and short story "Investigations of a Dog."

against. He describes societies trapped in the carapace of customs which they themselves have adopted. In our day, Maurice Blanchot[6] describes a city held fast in the grip of its laws: everyone is so compliant that all lose the sense of their difference and that of others. To look at human beings from the outside is what makes the mind self-critical and keeps it sane. But the aim should not be to suggest that all is absurd, as Voltaire did. It is much more a question of implying, as Kafka does, that human life is always under threat and of using humour to prepare the ground for those rare and precious moments at which human beings come to recognise, to find, one another.

## TEST YOUR UNDERSTANDING

1. Does Merleau-Ponty think that while I cannot separate the anger of *another* person from his behavior, *my* anger is a condition of an indivisible pure spirit?

2. Does Merleau-Ponty disagree with the view that "The mind is the commander-in-chief of the body"? Does Descartes?

## NOTES AND QUESTIONS

1. Towards the end of the selection Merleau-Ponty writes that "[t]his leaves us with a very different view of the human being and humanity from the one with which we began." What are these two views? Explain and evaluate Merleau-Ponty's argument for the superiority of the "very different view."

2. For a defense of the idea that we can perceive that others are in mental states (e.g., that Sabine is angry) without inference from their behavior, see Chapter 5 of Quassim Cassam, *The Possibility of Knowledge* (Oxford University Press, 2007).

## D. M. Armstrong (1926–2014)

Armstrong was Challis Professor of Philosophy at the University of Sydney, retiring in 1991. He is known for his many contributions to philosophy of mind and metaphysics, including *A Materialist Theory of the Mind* (1968), *Universals and Scientific Realism* (1978), *What Is a Law of Nature?* (1983), and *Sketch for a Systematic Metaphysics* (2010).

---

6. (1907–2003) French novelist and literary critic; the work mentioned is his novel *The Most High*.

# INTROSPECTION
from *A Materialist Theory of the Mind*

## I. Recapitulation[1]

In sense-perception we become aware of current happenings in the physical world. . . . .
In introspection, on the contrary, we become aware of current happenings in our own
mind. . . . Nevertheless, introspection may properly be compared to sense-perception,
and Kant's description of introspection as "inner sense"[2] is perfectly justified.

The possession of language may alter, and make more sophisticated, our
perceptions. But perception is not logically dependent on language for its
existence, as is shown by the fact that animals and young children can perceive
although they cannot speak. In the same way, there seems no reason to think
that introspection is logically dependent on language. That is to say, introspection
does not logically demand the making of introspective reports, or having the
power of making introspective reports. It seems plausible to say that animals
and young children do not merely have pains, but are aware of having pains. It
seems perfectly possible that they not merely have desires, perceptions and mental
images, but that they are aware of having such things. If so, they have the power
of introspection, although they lack the power to make introspective reports.
Incidentally, this is compatible with the view that there is a close empirical[3]
connection between the possession of any extensive introspective ability, and the
power to use language.

In the case of perception, we must distinguish between the perceiving, which is
a mental event, and the thing perceived, which is something physical. In the case
of introspection we must similarly distinguish between the introspecting and the
thing introspected. Confusion is all the more easy in the latter case because *both* are
mental states of the same mind. Nevertheless, although they are both mental states, it
is impossible that the introspecting and the thing introspected should be one and the
same mental state. A mental state cannot be aware of itself, any more than a man can
eat himself up. The introspection may itself be the object of a further introspective
awareness, and so on, but, since the capacity of the mind is finite, the chain of
introspective awareness of introspections must terminate in an introspection that is
not an object of introspective awareness.

---

1. This section summarizes Armstrong's views on perception, defended in earlier chapters of *A Materialist Theory of the Mind*.

2. In his *Critique of Pure Reason*, the German philosopher Immanuel Kant (1724–1804) writes that "inner sense. . . . [is] the intuition of ourselves and of our inner state" (A33/B49).

3. Here: contingent, i.e., could have been otherwise. N.B. there are other uses of "**empirical**."

If we make the materialist[4] identification of mental states with material states of the brain, we can say that introspection is a self-scanning process in the brain. The scanning operation may itself be scanned, and so on, but we must in the end reach an unscanned scanner. However, the unscanned scanner is not a logically unscannable scanner, for it is always possible to imagine a further scanning operation. Although the series logically must end somewhere, it need not have ended at the particular place it did end.

The distinction between the introspecting and the introspected state casts light on the much-lamented "systematic elusiveness of the subject."[5] The "elusiveness" of that mental state which is an awareness of some other state of affairs, physical or mental, is a mere logical elusiveness, the consequence of the fact that the awareness of something logically cannot also be an awareness of that awareness.

In the case of most forms of sense-perception we say that we perceive *with* certain parts of the body. These parts of the body we call sense-organs. The full concept of a sense-organ involves both (i) that perceptions of a certain characteristic range arise as a causal result of the stimulation of these parts of the body; (ii) that certain alterations in these parts of the body are under the direct control of the will, alterations which enable us to perceive different features of the environment. . . . The so-called proprioceptors, stimulation of which gives rise to bodily perception, are not *organs* in the fullest sense because their operation is not under the direct control of the will. In bodily perception there is nothing we perceive *with*.

Bodily perception has the further peculiarity that its object — our own body — is private to each perceiver. If each of us were confined to bodily sense, there would be no overlap between our sense-fields, in the way that there is overlap in the case of the other senses. This privacy is purely empirical, and we can imagine having the same direct perceptual access to states of other people's bodies that we now have to our own.

These two features of bodily perception make it an appropriate model for introspection conceived of as "inner sense." In the first place, when we are aware of happenings in our own minds, there is nothing that we are aware *with*. (If there were an organ involved it would be something whose operation was under the direct control of our will. This, in turn, would demand a power of gaining direct awareness of the different states of this "introspective organ." At some point there would have to be a direct awareness that did not involve the use of an organ.) In the second place, our introspective awareness is confined to our own minds. It was argued elsewhere that it is only an empirical fact that our direct awareness of mental states is confined to our own mind. We could conceive of a power of acquiring non-verbal non-inferential knowledge of current states of the minds of others. This would be a direct awareness, or perception, of the minds of others. Indeed, when people speak of "telepathy" it often seems to be this they have in mind.

---

4. **Materialism** (or **physicalism**) is the view that the mind — and the world in general — is wholly physical.

5. Famously noticed by the Scottish philosopher David Hume (1711–1776): see Kripke's quotation from Hume in the reading earlier in this chapter (pp. 254–55).

When we perceive, there are many (indeed innumerable) features of our environment that we do not perceive. In the same way, when we are aware of our own current mental states, there are mental states and features of mental states of which we are unaware. These are mental states or features of mental states of which we are unconscious. Unconscious mental states stand to conscious mental states, in the realm of our own mind, as unperceived states of affairs stand to perceived states of affairs in the physical realm. In between the unperceived and the perceived there are those things which are just perceived, or are marginally perceived. In the case of introspective awareness there is a similar twilight zone.

Perception may be erroneous. Contrary to what might be called the Cartesian tradition, it is equally possible for introspection to be erroneous.[6] This does not mean that introspective awareness may not *in fact* regularly satisfy the conditions for *knowledge*.

Eccentric cases apart, perception, considered as a mental event, is the acquiring of information or misinformation about our environment. It is not an "acquaintance" with objects, or a "searchlight" that makes contact with them, but is simply the getting of beliefs. Exactly the same must be said of introspection. It is the getting of information or misinformation about the current state of our mind.

It is the burden of this book that a mental state is a state of the person apt for the bringing about of certain bodily behaviour. So when I acquire by introspection the information that, for example, I am sad now or that I have a certain sort of perception now, this information is information about certain of my behaviour-producing or potentially behaviour-producing states. Now if introspection is conceived of as "acquaintance" with mental states, or a searchlight that makes contact with them, it is difficult to see how all it can yield is information of such highly abstract nature about inner causes or potential inner causes. But if introspection as well as perception is conceived of as a mere flow of information or beliefs, then there is no difficulty.

We can even find an analogy for the sort of information acquired in introspection in the tactual perception of pressure upon our body. In such tactual perception we may be aware of no more than that something we know not what is pressing, with greater or lesser force, upon us. "Pressing with greater or lesser force" here seems to mean no more than a greater or lesser aptness for producing a certain sort of effect: either the distortion or motion of our flesh.

The only further topic to be recapitulated is that concerning the biological value of introspection. We argued that without introspection there could be no purposive mental activity. As we have seen, purposive physical behaviour logically demands perception. For unless we can become apprised of the situation as it develops, so that this awareness can react back upon the cause that initiates and sustains purposive behaviour, there will be no possibility of the adjustment of behaviour to circumstances that is an essential part of such behaviour. And it is by perception that we become apprised of the situation as it develops.

---

6. "Cartesian": relating to the French philosopher René Descartes (1596–1650). Armstrong argues for this claim in an earlier chapter of *A Materialist Theory of the Mind.*

If there are to be purposive trains of mental activity, then there must equally be some means by which we become apprised of our current mental state. Only so can we adjust mental behaviour to mental circumstances. For instance, if we are doing a calculation "in our head" we will need to become aware of the current stage in the mental calculation that we have reached. Only if we do become so aware will we know what to do next. So there must be a way of becoming aware of our current mental state, which means that there must be introspection. The biological value of purposive mental activity is, of course, obvious. It permits of a far more sophisticated response to stimuli if we can "think before we act." But such thinking must be purposive thinking to be of real value.

This does not imply that purposive mental activity demands a highly self-conscious introspective scrutiny. Something far less may be, and normally is, all that is required. But without information of some sort about the current state of our mind, purposive trains of mental activity would be impossible. . . .

## III. Introspection and Behaviour

We have argued that introspection is the acquiring of information (or misinformation) about our own current mental states. These mental states will be, *qua*[7] mental states, states of the person apt in their various ways for the production of certain sorts of physical behaviour. So introspection will be the acquiring of information about current states of ourselves apt for the production of certain behaviour. But, of course, introspective awareness of mental states is itself a (distinct) mental state (more precisely, it is a mental event). So it, too, must be an aptness for certain behaviour: a certain sort of selection-behaviour towards ourselves. Now since the concept of a mental state is such a complex one, as compared to simpler concepts like "red" or "round," it will be advisable to spell out in more detail the sort of behaviour a person would have to exhibit to convince us that he had the capacity for introspective discriminations. This is the business of this section.

It may be helpful to consider an imaginary model first. What behaviour would convince us that a person could acquire a *non-inferential* knowledge[8] that certain substances, such as untoughened glass, were brittle simply by putting their fingers in contact with the substance?

It will not be enough that the person was able to discriminate in a systematic way between material that is brittle, and material that is not brittle. Such behaviour will show that the perceiver can make a distinction between two sorts of material, a distinction that is in fact the distinction between being brittle and not being brittle. But does the perceiver perceive the distinction *as* the distinction between being brittle and not being brittle? The successful sorting does not demonstrate this.

---

7. As (Latin).

8. *Inferential* knowledge is the result of **reasoning**, as when one comes to know that Smith killed Jones by reasoning from the fact that Jones's blood was found on Smith's hand. Knowledge that is not inferential is *non-inferential*.

What must be added? In the first place, the perceiver must be able to discriminate between those occurrences which constitute the manifestation of the disposition of brittleness and those which do not. For instance, a number of samples of material are struck sharply. Some break up, shatter or fly apart. Some do not. The perceiver must demonstrate that he can discriminate between the first sort of performance and the second sort.

This addition, although necessary, is clearly insufficient. The perceiver has still got to demonstrate that he understands the link between the first sort of discrimination (where nothing actually happens to the samples of material) and the occurrence or non-occurrence on other occasions of breaking, shattering or flying apart as a result of being struck. What sort of behaviour will demonstrate understanding of this link?

The answer is that the behaviour must have as its *objective* the actualization of the disposition or the prevention of the actualization of the disposition. Suppose the perceiver is rewarded when samples of material do not break, but punished when they do break. Suppose, after touching samples of material, the perceiver sorts them into two groups which are in fact the group of the brittle and the group of the non-brittle materials. Suppose furthermore that he treats objects in the two groups differently. The first group are handled very carefully, that is to say they are handled in a way that is, as an objective matter of physical fact, not conducive to their breaking. The other group are handled in a quite normal way, that; is to say, a way that would as an objective matter of physical fact be conducive to their breaking if, contrary to the facts, they had been brittle. Does not such behaviour show that the perceiver perceives the connection between the original tactual discrimination and the brittleness or lack of brittleness of the samples? The perceiver has shown a capacity to link the original discrimination with later easy breaking and absence of easy breaking.

Let us now use this case as a model (over-simple and over-schematic perhaps) to unfold the behaviour that will betoken the making of non-inferential introspective discriminations. Let us take as our example the non-inferential awareness that we are angry.

We must in the first place exhibit a capacity to behave towards ourselves in a systematically different way when we are angry and when we are not angry. (Such behaviour, of course, must be something more than the behaviour the anger itself expresses itself in, if it does express itself. For this would allow no distinction between a mere angry state, and *being aware* that one was in an angry state.) To take a quite artificial example, we might exhibit the behaviour of pressing a button that lighted up a red light, when, and only when, we are angry.

(It is clear, incidentally, that the teaching and learning of such discriminations will be a rather tricky business in the case of anger that is not expressed in angry behaviour. Nevertheless, even if there are (empirical) difficulties in *checking* on whether discrimination has been successful, we can still have the possibility that it *is* successful and that in fact we light up the red light when and only when we are angry.)

This behaviour so far only shows that we can discriminate between the cases where we are in fact angry, and the cases where we are not. It does not show that we are aware of the distinction *as* a distinction between being angry and not being angry. What further capacities for behaviour must we exhibit?

In the next place, we must have the capacity to discriminate systematically between angry behaviour and non-angry behaviour in ourselves and others. When I say "angry behaviour" here I do not mean behaviour that actually springs from anger, I mean angry *behaviour*. There can be angry behaviour that has not sprung from anger, and some behaviour brought about by anger is not what we would call *angry* behaviour. But there are certain typical sets of behaviours which occur when we are angry. (The relation of anger to its expression is more complicated than the relation of brittleness to its manifestations.) We must have the capacity to discriminate this sort of behaviour from other behaviour.

Finally, we must exhibit the capacity to link the original discrimination with angry behaviour. We must show ourselves capable of behaviour having as its *objective* the aiding or the inhibiting of the expression of anger. Suppose, for instance, we exhibit the following behaviour. After picking out those cases which are in fact cases where we are angry, we take action that has an inhibiting effect on anger but no similar effect on other mental states. We put our heads in cold water, or address soothing words to ourselves. We take no such action in the other cases. Have we not shown that the original introspective awareness was an awareness *of anger*?

No doubt what I have said here is oversimplified. But I think it has shown that there is no difficulty in principle in giving an account of the introspective acquiring of information about our own mental states as an acquiring of a capacity for certain sorts of discriminative behaviour. The parallel between perception and introspection is therefore maintained.

## IV. Mental States and the Mind

One final topic remains to be discussed. The account given in the last section would seem to be adequate for no more than an awareness of a current happening apt for the production of a certain sort of behaviour in a certain body. (If it is asked "What body?," the answer is that the awareness is itself an acquiring of a capacity for discriminative behaviour by a certain body, and that the discriminative behaviour is directed towards that selfsame body.)

Now if we consider a statement such as "I am angry now" (taken as a purely descriptive remark), it seems to say more than is involved in the introspective awareness. For does not the use of the word "I" here imply (among other things) that the current happening apt for the production of a certain sort of behaviour belongs to an organised set of happenings — a mind — all of which are happenings apt for the production of behaviour in the same body? The analysis of the last section does not do justice to this implication.

One might try to brush aside this difficulty by arguing that what is *meant* by "a mind" is simply that group of happenings which are apt for the production of certain sorts of behaviour in a particular body. Unfortunately, however, this does not seem to be correct. For we can perfectly well understand the suggestion that something which is not *our* mind should have a capacity to bring about certain behaviour by our body of the sort that betokens mind. The notion of such "possession" of our body seems a perfectly intelligible one, even if we think that in fact it never occurs.

What, then, does constitute the unity of the group of happenings that constitute a single mind? We are back at the problem that proved Hume's downfall.[9] . . .

I do not see any way to solve the problem except to say that the group of happenings constitute a single mind because they are all states of, processes in or events in, a single *substance*.[1] Resemblance, causal relationship and memory are all of them important. Unless there were extensive relations of this sort between the different mental states that qualify the one substance we should not talk of the substance as "a mind." But the concept of a mind is the concept of a substance.

In taking the mind to be a substance, then, the Cartesian Dualists[2] show a true understanding of the formal features of the concept of mind. Their view that the mind is a *spiritual* substance is, however, a further theory about the nature of this substance, and, while it is an intelligible theory, it is a singularly empty one. For it seems that we can only characterize the spiritual (except for its *temporal* characteristics) as "that which is not spatial." Modern materialism is able to put forward a much more plausible (and much more easily falsified) theory: the view that the mind is the brain. Mental states, processes and events are physical states of the brain, physical processes in the brain or physical events in the brain. . . .

But we must however grant Hume that the existence of the mind is not something that is given to unaided introspection. All that "inner sense" reveals is the occurrence of individual mental happenings. This is the difficulty from which this section started. I suggest that the solution is that the notion of "a mind" is a *theoretical* concept: something that is *postulated* to link together all the individual happenings of which introspection makes us aware. In speaking of minds, perhaps even in using the word "I" in the course of introspective reports, we go beyond what is introspectively observed. Ordinary language here embodies a certain theory. The particular *nature* of this substance is a *further* theoretical question, but when ordinary language speaks of "minds" it postulates *some* sort of substance.

The position, then, is this. Introspection makes us aware of a series of happenings apt for the production of certain sorts of behaviour in the one body. In a being without language, it may be presumed that introspection goes no further than this. Beings with language go on to form the notion that all these states are states of a single substance. This postulated substance is called "the mind." Once the notion of

---

9. In his *Treatise of Human Nature*, Hume argues that "what we call a *mind*, . . . is nothing but a heap or collection of different perceptions, united together by certain relations" (Book 1, part 4, sec. 2). When discussing this view later in the Appendix to the *Treatise*, he writes that "I find myself involv'd in such a labyrinth, that, I must confess, I neither know how to correct my former opinions, nor how to render them consistent." See also note 5 above.

1. Philosophical term dating back to the Ancient Greek philosopher Aristotle (384–322 BCE). In the use of the term here, a **substance** is a particular object or individual (a rock, a horse, an atom, a banana . . .); **properties** (hardness, yellowness, . . .) are not substances.

2. Those who follow Descartes in taking mind and body to be distinct (non-identical) things, i.e., substances.

"the mind" is introduced, there can be further speculation about its particular nature. (Just as, once the notion of the gene is introduced, there can be further speculation about *its* particular nature.) There is no absolute necessity for such a postulation of a single substance in the observed facts: it is simply a natural postulate to make. And sometimes, particularly in the case of primitive persons, a mental state, of which we become introspectively aware may seem so alien to the other members of the "bundle" that we may form the hypothesis that it is not a state of the same substance of which the other members are states. "It is not I, but something alien." Such an hypothesis is perfectly intelligible, even if it is not true, and even if it is a mark of maturity to recognize that everything we become aware of by introspection is part of the *one* mind: our own.

A *person* is something that has both body and mind. It will be seen, then, that when in the past we have spoken of a mental state as a state of a *person* apt for the production of certain sorts of behaviour we already presuppose the existence of *minds*. To that extent, this account of a mental state goes beyond the bare deliverances of introspection, and puts forward a *theory* about the objects of introspective awareness. But provided it is clear that we are doing so, there seems to be no objection to this procedure.

## TEST YOUR UNDERSTANDING

1. In what respects are introspection and proprioception similar, according to Armstrong?

2. Does Armstrong think that introspection is immune to error?

3. Armstrong is not a **dualist** like Descartes; rather, he is a **physicalist** or **materialist** like J.J.C. Smart (see chapter 8 of this anthology for Descartes and Smart). Nonetheless, he agrees with the Cartesian dualist on one important point. What is it?

## NOTES AND QUESTIONS

1. For a defense of an Armstrong-style account of self-knowledge, see chapter 4 of Shaun Nichols and Stephen Stich, *Mindreading* (Oxford University Press, 2003). For a critical discussion of the inner sense theory, see chapter 5 of Brie Gertler, *Self-Knowledge* (Routledge, 2011), and section 2.2 of Gertler, "Self-Knowledge," *Stanford Encyclopedia of Philosophy*, ed. Edward Zalta (http://plato.stanford.edu/archives/spr2011/entries/self-knowledge/).

## Gilbert Ryle (1900–1976)

Ryle was an English philosopher who spent his entire career at the University of Oxford, where he was elected Waynflete Professor of Metaphysical Philosophy in 1945. His most influential work is *The Concept of Mind* (1949), a sustained attack on Cartesian dualism and a defense of a more behaviorist approach.

# SELF-KNOWLEDGE
## from *The Concept of Mind*

# (1) Foreword

A natural counterpart to the theory that minds constitute a world other than "the physical world" is the theory that there exist ways of discovering the contents of this other world which are counterparts to our ways of discovering the contents of the physical world. In sense perception we ascertain what exists and happens in space; so what exists or happens in the mind must also be ascertained in perception, but perception of a different and refined sort, one not requiring the functioning of gross bodily organs.

More than this, it has been thought necessary to show that minds possess powers of apprehending their own states and operations superior to those they possess of apprehending facts of the external world. If I am to know, believe, guess or even wonder anything about the things and happenings that are outside me, I must, it has been supposed, enjoy constant and mistake-proof apprehension of these selfsame cognitive operations of mine.

It is often held therefore (1) that a mind cannot help being constantly aware of all the supposed occupants of its private stage, and (2) that it can also deliberately scrutinise by a species of non-sensuous perception at least some of its own states and operations. Moreover both this constant awareness (generally called "consciousness"), and this non-sensuous inner perception (generally called "introspection") have been supposed to be exempt from error. A mind has a twofold Privileged Access to its own doings, which makes its self-knowledge superior in quality, as well as prior in genesis, to its grasp of other things. I may doubt the evidence of my senses but not the deliverances of consciousness or introspection.

One limitation has always been conceded to the mind's power of finding mental states and operations, namely that while I can have direct knowledge of my own states and operations, I cannot have it of yours. I am conscious of all my own feelings, volitions, emotions and thinkings, and I introspectively scrutinise some of them. But I cannot introspectively observe, or be conscious of, the workings of your mind. I can satisfy myself that you have a mind at all only by complex and frail inferences from what your body does.

This theory of the twofold Privileged Access has won so strong a hold on the thoughts of philosophers, psychologists and many laymen that it is now often thought to be enough to say, on behalf of the dogma of the mind as a second theatre, that its consciousness and introspection discover the scenes enacted in it. On the view for which I am arguing consciousness and introspection cannot be what they are officially described as being, since their supposed objects are myths; but champions of the dogma of the ghost in the machine[1] tend to argue that the imputed objects of consciousness and introspection cannot be myths, since we are conscious of them and can introspectively observe them. The reality of these objects is guaranteed by the venerable credentials of these supposed ways of finding them.

In this chapter, then, I try to show that the official theories of consciousness and introspection are logical muddles. But I am not, of course, trying to establish that we do not or cannot know what there is to know about ourselves. On the contrary, I shall try to show how we attain such knowledge, but only after I have proved that this knowledge is not attained by consciousness or introspection, as these supposed Privileged Accesses are normally described. Lest any reader feels despondency at the thought of being deprived of his twofold Privileged Access to his supposed inner self, I may add the consolatory undertaking that on the account of self-knowledge that I shall give, knowledge of what there is to be known about other people is restored to approximate parity with self-knowledge. The sorts of things that I can find out about myself are the same as the sorts of things that I can find out about other people, and the methods of finding them out are much the same. A residual difference in the supplies of the requisite data makes some differences in degree between what I can know about myself and what I can know about you, but these differences are not all in favour of self-knowledge. In certain quite important respects it is easier for me to find out what I want to know about you than it is for me to find out the same sorts of things about myself. In certain other important respects it is harder. But in principle, as distinct from practice, John Doe's ways of finding out about John Doe are the same as John Doe's ways of finding out about Richard Roe. To drop the hope of Privileged Access is also to drop the fear of epistemological isolationism; we lose the bitters with the sweets of Solipsism.[2] ...

# (2) Consciousness

... Working with the notion of the mind as a second theatre, the episodes enacted in which enjoy the supposed status of "the mental" and correspondingly lack the supposed status of "the physical," thinkers of many sorts have laid it down as the cardinal positive property of these episodes that, when they occur, they occur consciously. The states and operations of a mind are states and operations of which it is necessarily aware, in some sense of "aware," and this awareness is incapable of being delusive. The things that a mind does or experiences are self-intimating, and this is supposed to be a feature which characterises these acts and feelings not just sometimes but always. It is part of the definition of their being mental that their occurrence entails

---

1. "The dogma of the ghost in the machine" is Ryle's pejorative term for Descartes's view that the mind and the body are distinct things. See Ryle, "Descartes' Myth," chapter 8 of this anthology.

2. The view that oneself is the only thing that exists (or that is the only thing that can be known to exist).

that they are self-intimating. If I think, hope, remember, will, regret, hear a noise, or feel a pain, I must, *ipso facto*,[3] know that I do so. Even if I dream that I see a dragon, I must be apprised of my dragon-seeing, though, it is often conceded, I may not know that I am dreaming. . . .

[T]o relapse perforce into simile, it is supposed that mental processes are phosphorescent, like tropical sea-water, which makes itself visible by the light which it itself emits. Or, to use another simile, mental processes are "overheard" by the mind whose processes they are, somewhat as a speaker overhears the words he is himself uttering. . . .

The radical objection to the theory that minds must know what they are about, because mental happenings are by definition conscious, or metaphorically self-luminous, is that there are no such happenings; there are no occurrences taking place in a second-status world, since there is no such status and no such world and consequently no need for special modes of acquainting ourselves with the denizens of such a world. But there are also other objections which do not depend for their acceptance upon the rejection of the dogma of the ghost in the machine.

First, and this is not intended to be more than a persuasive argument, no one who is uncommitted to a philosophical theory ever tries to vindicate any of his assertions of fact by saying that he found it out "from consciousness," or "as a direct deliverance of consciousness," or "from immediate awareness." He will back up some of his assertions of fact by saying that he himself sees, hears, feels, smells or tastes so and so; he will back up other such statements, somewhat more tentatively, by saying that he remembers seeing, hearing, feeling, smelling or tasting it. But if asked whether he really knows, believes, infers, fears, remembers or smells something, he never replies "Oh yes, certainly I do, for I am conscious and even vividly conscious of doing so." Yet just such a reply should, according to the doctrine, be his final appeal. . . .

Next, there is no contradiction in asserting that someone might fail to recognise his frame of mind for what it is; indeed, it is notorious that people constantly do so. They mistakenly suppose themselves to know things which are actually false; they deceive themselves about their own motives; they are surprised to notice the clock stopping ticking, without their having, as they think, been aware that it had been ticking; they do not know that they are dreaming, when they are dreaming, and sometimes they are not sure that they are not dreaming, when they are awake; and they deny, in good faith, that they are irritated or excited, when they are flustered in one or other of those ways. If consciousness was what it is described as being, it would be logically impossible for such failures and mistakes in recognition to take place.

Finally, even though the self-intimation supposed to be inherent in any mental state or process is not described as requiring a separate act of attention, or as constituting a separate cognitive operation, still what I am conscious of in a process of inferring, say, is different from what the inferring is an apprehension of. My consciousness is of a process of inferring, but my inferring is, perhaps, of a geometrical conclusion from geometrical premisses. The verbal expression of my inference might be, "because this is

---

3. By that very fact (Latin).

an equilateral triangle, therefore each angle is 60 degrees," but the verbal expression of what I am conscious of might be "Here I am deducing such and such from so and so." But, if so, then it would seem to make sense to ask whether, according to the doctrine, I am not also conscious of being conscious of inferring, that is, in a position to say "Here I am spotting the fact that here I am deducing such and such from so and so." And then there would be no stopping-place; there would have to be an infinite number of onion-skins of consciousness embedding any mental state or process whatsoever. If this conclusion is rejected, then it will have to be allowed that some elements in mental processes are not themselves things we can be conscious of, namely those elements which constitute the supposed outermost self-intimations of mental processes; and then "conscious" could no longer be retained as part of the definition of "mental."

The argument, then, that mental events are authentic, because the deliverances of consciousness are direct and unimpeachable testimony to their existence, must be rejected. So must the partly parallel argument from the findings of introspection.

# (3) Introspection

"Introspection" is a term of art and one for which little use is found in the self-descriptions of untheoretical people. More use is found for the adjective "introspective," which is ordinarily used in an innocuous sense to signify that someone pays more heed than usual to theoretical and practical problems about his own character, abilities, deficiencies and oddities; there is often the extra suggestion that the person is abnormally anxious about these matters.

The technical term "introspection" has been used to denote a supposed species of perception. It was supposed that much as a person may at a particular moment be listening to a flute, savouring a wine, or regarding a waterfall, so he may be "regarding," in a non-optical sense, some current mental state or process of his own. The state or process is being deliberately and attentively scrutinised and so can be listed among the objects of his observation. On the other hand, introspection is described as being unlike sense observation in important respects. Things looked at, or listened to, are public objects, in principle observable by any suitably placed observer, whereas only the owner of a mental state or process is supposed to be able introspectively to scrutinise it. Sense perception, again, involves the functioning of bodily organs, such as the eyes, the ears, or the tongue, whereas introspection involves the functioning of no bodily organ. Lastly, sense perception is never exempt from the possibility of dullness or even of illusion, whereas, anyhow according to the bolder theories, a person's power of observing his mental processes is always perfect; he may not have learned how to exploit his power, or how to arrange or discriminate its findings, but he is immune from any counterparts to deafness, astigmatism, colour-blindness, dazzle or *muscae volitantes.*[4] Inner perception, on these theories, sets a standard of veridical perception, which sense perception can never emulate.

---

4. Literally, "flying flies" (Latin); "floaters" in the eye.

The findings of introspection are reputed to differ in one way at least from the supposed deliverances of consciousness; introspection is an attentive operation and one which is only occasionally performed, whereas consciousness is supposed to be a constant element of all mental processes and one of which the revelations do not require to be receipted in special acts of attention. Moreover we introspect with the intention of finding the answers to particular problems, whereas we are conscious, whether we wish it or not; everyone is constantly conscious, while awake, but only those people introspect who are from time to time interested in what is going on in their minds.

It would be admitted that only people with a special training ever speak of "introspecting," but in such phrases as "he caught himself wondering how to do so and so," or "when I catch myself getting into a panic, I do such and such," the plain man is expressing at least part of what is meant by the word.

Now supposing (which it is the negative object of this book to deny) that there did exist events of the postulated ghostly status, there would still be objections to the initially plausible assumption that there also exists a species of perception capable of having any of these events for its proprietary objects. For one thing, the occurence of such an act of inner perception would require that the observer could attend to two things at the same time. He would, for example, be both resolving to get up early and concomitantly observing his act of resolving; attending to the programme of rising betimes and perceptually attending to his attending to this programme. This objection is not, perhaps, logically fatal, since it might be argued that some people can, anyhow after practice, combine attention to the control of a car with attention to the conversation. The fact that we speak of undivided attention suggests that the division of attention is a possibility, though some people would describe the division of attention as a rapid to-and-fro switch of attention, rather than as a synchronous distribution of it. But many people who begin by being confident that they do introspect, as introspection is officially described, become dubious that they do so, when they are satisfied that they would have to be attending twice at once in order to do it. They are more sure that they do not attend twice at once than that they do introspect. . . .

When psychologists were less cautious than they have since become, they used to maintain that introspection was the main source of empirical information about the workings of minds.[5] They were not unnaturally embarrassed to discover that the empirical facts reported by one psychologist sometimes conflicted with those reported by another. They reproached one another, often justly, with having professed to find by introspection just those mental phenomena which their preconceived theories had led them to expect to find. There still occur disputes which should be finally soluble by introspection, if the joint theories of the inner life and inner perception were true. Theorists dispute, for example, whether there are activities of conscience distinct from those of intellect and distinct from habitual deferences to taboos. Why do they not look and see? Or, if they do so, why do their reports not tally? . . . Why do we argue about the existence of these processes, when the question ought to be as easily decidable as the question whether or not there is a smell of onions in the larder?

---

5. An allusion to the beginnings of experimental psychology in the late nineteenth century.

There is one last objection to be made against the claims for introspection, that made by Hume.[6] There are some states of mind which cannot be coolly scrutinised, since the fact that we are in those states involves that we are not cool, or the fact that we are cool involves that we are not in those states. No one could introspectively scrutinise the state of panic or fury, since the dispassionateness exercised in scientific observation is, by the definition of "panic" and "fury," not the state of mind of the victim of those turbulences. Similarly, since a convulsion of merriment is not the state of mind of the sober experimentalist, the enjoyment of a joke is also not an introspectible happening. States of mind such as these more or less violent agitations can be examined only in retrospect. Yet nothing disastrous follows from this restriction. We are not shorter of information about panic or amusement than about other states of mind. If retrospection can give us the data we need for our knowledge of some states of mind, there is no reason why it should not do so for all. And this is just what seems to be suggested by the popular phrase "to catch oneself doing so and so." We catch, as we pursue and overtake, what is already running away from us. I catch myself daydreaming about a mountain walk after, perhaps very shortly after, I have begun the daydream; or I catch myself humming a particular air only when the first few notes have already been hummed. Retrospection, prompt or delayed, is a genuine process and one which is exempt from the troubles ensuing from the assumption of multiply divided attention; it is also exempt from the troubles ensuing from the assumption that violent agitations could be the objects of cool, contemporary scrutiny.

Part, then, of what people have in mind, when they speak familiarly of introspecting, is this authentic process of retrospection. But there is nothing intrinsically ghostly about the objects of retrospection. In the same way that I can catch myself daydreaming, I can catch myself scratching; in the same way that I can catch myself engaged in a piece of silent soliloquy, I can catch myself saying something aloud. . . .

The fact that retrospection is autobiographical does not imply that it gives us a Privileged Access to facts of a special status. But of course it does give us a mass of data contributory to our appreciations of our own conduct and qualities of mind. A diary is not a chronicle of ghostly episodes, but it is a valuable source of information about the diarist's character, wits and career.

# (4) Self-Knowledge without Privileged Access

. . . The questions "What knowledge can a person get of the workings of his own mind?" and "How does he get it?" by their very wording suggest absurd answers. They suggest that, for a person to know that he is lazy, or has done a sum carefully, he must have taken a peep into a windowless chamber, illuminated by a

---

6. The Scottish philosopher David Hume (1711–1776).

very peculiar sort of light, and one to which only he has access. And when the question is construed in this sort of way, the parallel questions, "What knowledge can one person get of the workings of another mind?" and "How does he get it?" by their very wording seem to preclude any answer at all; for they suggest that one person could only know that another person was lazy, or had done a sum carefully, by peering into another secret chamber to which, *ex hypothesi*,[7] he has no access.

In fact the problem is not one of this sort. It is simply the methodological question, how we establish, and how we apply, certain sorts of law-like propositions[8] about the overt and the silent behaviour of persons. I come to appreciate the skill and tactics of a chess-player by watching him and others playing chess, and I learn that a certain pupil of mine is lazy, ambitious and witty by following his work, noticing his excuses, listening to his conversation and comparing his performances with those of others. Nor does it make any important difference if I happen myself to be that pupil. I can indeed then listen to more of his conversations, as I am the addressee of his unspoken soliloquies; I notice more of his excuses, as I am never absent, when they are made. On the other hand, my comparison of his performances with those of others is more difficult, since the examiner is himself taking the examination, which makes neutrality hard to preserve and precludes the demeanour of the candidate, when under interrogation, from being in good view. . . .

I discover my or your motives in much, though not quite, the same way as I discover my or your abilities. The big practical difference is that I cannot put the subject through his paces in my inquiries into his inclinations as I can in my inquiries into his competences. To discover how conceited or patriotic you are, I must still observe your conduct, remarks, demeanour and tones of voice, but I cannot subject you to examination-tests or experiments which you recognise as such. You would have a special motive for responding to such experiments in a particular way. From mere conceit, perhaps, you would try to behave self-effacingly, or from mere modesty you might try to behave conceitedly. None the less, ordinary day to day observation normally serves swiftly to settle such questions. To be conceited is to tend to boast of one's own excellences, to pity or ridicule the deficiencies of others, to daydream about imaginary triumphs, to reminisce about actual triumphs, to weary quickly of conversations which reflect unfavourably upon oneself, to lavish one's society upon distinguished persons and to economise in association with the undistinguished. The tests of whether a person is conceited are the actions he takes and the reactions he manifests in such circumstances. Not many anecdotes, sneers or sycophancies are required from the subject for the ordinary observer to make up his mind, unless the candidate and the examiner happen to be identical. . . .

---

7. By hypothesis (Latin).

8. True generalizations like the "laws" found in the physical sciences.

Of course an agent can, from time to time, if he is prompted to do so, announce to himself or the world "Hallo, here I am whistling 'Home Sweet Home.'" His ability to do so is part of what is meant by saying that he is in that particular frame of mind that we call "being alive to what he is doing." But not only is his actually making such announcements not entailed by the fact that he is concentrating on whistling this tune, but his concentration would be broken each time he produced such a commentary. . . .

Now in almost the same way as a person may be, in this sense, alive to what he is doing, he may be alive to what someone else is doing. In the serial operation of listening to a sentence or a lecture delivered by someone else, the listener, like the speaker, does not altogether forget, yet nor does he have constantly to recall the earlier parts of the talk, and he is in some degree prepared for the parts still to come, though he does not have to tell himself how he expects the sentence or lecture to go on. Certainly his frame of mind is considerably different from that of the speaker, since the speaker is, sometimes, creative or inventive, while the listener is passive and receptive; the listener may be frequently surprised to find the speaker saying something, while the speaker is only seldom surprised; the listener may find it hard to keep track of the course taken by the sentences and arguments, while the speaker can do this quite easily. While the speaker intends to say certain fairly specific things, his hearer can anticipate only roughly what sorts of topics are going to be discussed.

But the differences are differences of degree, not of kind. The superiority of the speaker's knowledge of what he is doing over that of the listener does not indicate that he has Privileged Access to facts of a type inevitably inaccessible to the listener, but only that he is in a very good position to know what the listener is often in a very poor position to know. The turns taken by a man's conversation do not startle or perplex his wife as much as they had surprised and puzzled his fiancée, nor do close colleagues have to explain themselves to each other as much as they have to explain themselves to their new pupils. . . .

A person's knowledge about himself and others may be distributed between many roughly distinguishable grades yielding correspondingly numerous roughly distinguishable senses of "knowledge." He may be aware that he is whistling "Tipperary" and not know that he is whistling it in order to give the appearance of a sang-froid which he does not feel.[9] Or, again, he may be aware that he is shamming sang-froid without knowing that the tremors which he is trying to hide derive from the agitation of a guilty conscience. He may know that he has an uneasy conscience and not know that this issues from some specific repression. But in none of the senses in which we ordinarily consider whether a person does or does not know something about himself, is the postulate of a Privileged Access necessary or helpful for the explanation of how he has achieved, or might have achieved, this knowledge. There are respects in which it is easier for me

9. "Tipperary": a popular song. "Sang-froid": literally, "cold blood" (French); composure.

to get such knowledge about myself than to get it about someone else; there are other respects in which it is harder. But these differences of facility do not derive from, or lead to, a difference in kind between a person's knowledge about himself and his knowledge about other people. No metaphysical Iron Curtain[1] exists compelling us to be for ever absolute strangers to one another, though ordinary circumstances, together with some deliberate management, serve to maintain a reasonable aloofness. Similarly no metaphysical looking-glass exists compelling us to be for ever completely disclosed and explained to ourselves, though from the everyday conduct of our sociable and unsociable lives we learn to be reasonably conversant with ourselves.

## TEST YOUR UNDERSTANDING

1. Does Ryle think that you are always in a better position to know what mental states you are in than someone else is?

2. Does Ryle think it is possible

    (i)  to be in a mental state and not know that you are?

    (ii) to be mistaken about what mental state you are in?

## NOTES AND QUESTIONS

1. According to Ryle (p. 275 of this anthology), "in principle, as distinct from practice, John Doe's ways of finding out about John Doe are the same as John Doe's ways of finding out about Richard Roe." Does Ryle make a good case for this claim?

2. Contemporary accounts of self-knowledge with a strong Rylean flavor include Peter Carruthers, *The Opacity of Mind* (Oxford, 2011), and Alison Gopnik, "How We Know Our Own Minds: The Illusion of First-Person Knowledge of Intentionality," *Behavioral and Brain Sciences* 16 (1993): 29–113.

## Alex Byrne (born 1960)

Byrne is Professor of Philosophy at the Massachusetts Institute of Technology. He works mainly in philosophy of mind and epistemology.

1. The post–World War II division between Eastern and Western Europe that disappeared with the end of the Cold War in 1991; the phrase is due to Winston Churchill, the wartime British prime minister.

# SKEPTICISM ABOUT THE INTERNAL WORLD[1]

## 1. Introduction

You know much about your own mental or psychological life. Perhaps there is some of it that you can only know after years of therapy, but it's easy to know, for example, that you have a headache, that you want water, that you believe that it's raining, and that you see a cat.

Epistemologists (philosophers who study knowledge) have generally concentrated on knowledge of another sort, namely knowledge about your environment that you gain through perception — knowledge that there is water in the glass, that it's raining, that the cat is on the mat, and so on. The chief reason for this focus on "external world" knowledge is the threat of skepticism. There is, it is often said, an apparently compelling argument for "skepticism about the external world," the alarming claim that we do not know anything about our environment. According to the skeptic about the external world, we may know many things about our mental lives, but as to whether there is beer in the fridge, or whether the fridge exists at all, we are irremediably ignorant. Because many philosophers think the skeptic's case is hard to answer, they conclude that there is something deeply puzzling about our knowledge of our environment.

I shall argue that this is all back to front. The real puzzle is not how we know about our environment, but how we know about our own minds. The argument for skepticism about the external world has an obvious weak point, but the argument for skepticism about our own minds — skepticism about the "internal world" — is much more difficult to dismiss.

Let us start by discussing a standard argument for skepticism about the external world. Once we have seen how this is not very convincing, we will be in a position to mount a parallel and potentially more powerful argument for skepticism about the internal world.

## 2. Skepticism about the External World

In his *First Meditation*,[2] Descartes considers the possibility that he is not, as he seems to be, sitting by a fire and holding a piece of paper, but instead is in bed enjoying an especially vivid dream. He "sees plainly," he says, "that there are never any sure signs by means of which being awake can be distinguished from being asleep." Accordingly, he (provisionally) concludes that he does not know that he is awake and sitting by the fire.

---

1. This essay is dedicated to the memory of Fred Dretske. [Byrne's note.]

2. See p. 299 of this anthology.

What goes for Descartes goes for the rest of us, of course. If he is right, I do not know that I am sitting in a chair, balancing a laptop on my knees. And — it is easy to think — he *is* right. After all, if I were vividly dreaming that I am sitting in a chair, things would *seem just the same* as they do when I really am sitting in a chair.

## 2.1 THE EXTERNAL WORLD SKEPTICAL ARGUMENT EXAMINED

Descartes is not very explicit about why there are no "sure signs" that indicate that he is awake and sitting by the fire, rather than in bed fast asleep. For some assistance, let us turn to a passage from Barry Stroud's classic book *The Significance of Philosophical Scepticism*,[3] in which Stroud draws some lessons from the *First Meditation*:

> If we are in the predicament Descartes finds himself in at the end of his *First Meditation* we cannot tell by means of the senses whether we are dreaming or not; all the sensory experiences we are having are *compatible with* our merely dreaming. . . . Our knowledge is in that way *confined to our sensory experiences*. . . . There seems to be *no way of going beyond them* to know that the world around us really is this way rather than that. (p. 31, my italics)

To see the significance of the italicized phrases, imagine a detective investigating a murder. Mr. Boddy has been found stabbed in the library with a chef's knife, and Colonel Mustard and Professor Plum are the two suspects. Both men wanted Boddy dead, and both lack alibis for the night of the crime. A witness says he saw a tall man with a mustache enter the library, clutching a large knife. And that's it — the witness cannot be more helpful, there are no fingerprints or incriminating blood stains, nothing. The detective's problem is that *both* Mustard and Plum are tall and mustached. She might sum up her predicament as follows: "The witness's testimony and my other evidence are *compatible with* the hypothesis that Mustard is the murderer, and the rival hypothesis that Plum is the murderer. There *seems to be no way of going beyond this evidence* to know that one hypothesis is correct; my evidence, in other words, does not favor one hypothesis over the other. My knowledge is therefore *confined to my evidence*: I know that the murderer is tall and mustached, and used a chef's knife, but that is all."

So the quotation from Stroud suggests the following argument for skepticism about the external world. In general — the argument begins — our evidence for claims or hypotheses about the external world consists in facts about our sensory experiences. For example, your evidence for the hypothesis that you are sitting in a chair is that you seem to see the arms of the chair, seem to feel the pressure of the chair against your back, and so on. This evidence is compatible with other hypotheses, for instance the hypothesis that you are lying in bed vividly dreaming that you are sitting

---

3. B. Stroud, *The Significance of Philosophical Scepticism* (Oxford University Press, 1984). [Byrne's note.]

in a chair. And there seems to be no way of going beyond this evidence to know that one hypothesis is correct. Your evidence, in other words, does not favor the *sitting hypothesis* over the *dreaming hypothesis*, and so you do not know that the sitting hypothesis is true.

It will be useful to set out the argument with numbered premises and a conclusion:

P1.  If you know that the sitting hypothesis is true, you know this solely on the basis of your evidence about your sensory experiences.

P2.  This evidence does not favor the sitting hypothesis over the dreaming hypothesis, and so does not allow you to know that the sitting hypothesis is true.

Hence:

C.  You do not know that the sitting hypothesis is true; that is, you do not know that you are sitting in a chair.

Obviously this argument generalizes from you to others, and from claims about sitting in a chair to other sorts of external world claims. If it is sound, then everyone is completely ignorant about their environment. Setting aside the issue of whether this is faithful to Descartes's intentions, it is certainly one of the standard arguments for skepticism about the external world.

Since the argument is valid, the only way to avoid the conclusion is to deny one of the premises. And in fact, one premise looks highly suspicious on closer examination, namely P1.[4]

According to P1, if you know that you are sitting in a chair, that knowledge is based on your evidence about your sensory experiences. Now if someone knows a hypothesis H on the basis of her evidence E, this implies that she has concluded or inferred H from E, which in turn implies that she knew E. For example, if part of the detective's evidence is that no fingerprints were found at the scene, and she knows that the murderer wore gloves on that basis, then the detective must have known that no fingerprints were found at the scene. If the scene was fingerprint-free, but for some reason the detective was ignorant of this piece of evidence, then she couldn't have used it as a basis on which to extend her knowledge. As we might put it, if the detective didn't know that no fingerprints were found, this piece of evidence was not part of *her* evidence.[5]

Now consider certain non-human animals, for instance dogs. They have sensory experiences (or so we may suppose) but there is not much reason to think that they *know* that they have sensory experiences. Knowledge of one's own mind requires a sophistication that dogs appear to lack. So if a dog knows that there is a rabbit behind

4. P2 might also be called into question: see Vogel, "Skepticism and Inference to the Best Explanation," [Byrne's note.] (See p. 328 of this anthology.)

5. For a difficult but rewarding discussion of evidence and its relation to knowledge, see T. Williamson, *Knowledge and Its Limits* (Oxford University Press, 2000), chap. 9. [Byrne's note.]

a tree by using its eyes, it is not on the basis of evidence about its sensory experiences. And if evidence about sensory experiences is not needed for a *dog* to have environmental knowledge, it isn't needed for *us* to have environmental knowledge either. You could know that you are sitting in a chair without appealing to evidence about your sensory experiences, and presumably you do. Hence P1 is false.

Not surprisingly, proponents of the argument will have replies to this objection, which we cannot examine here. But whether or not those replies succeed in rescuing P1, at the very least that premise should not strike us as initially plausible. Let us see if the parallel argument for internal world skepticism is any better.

## 3. Skepticism about the Internal World[6]

Let us start with an example. Suppose you are facing a cat asleep on a mat, the light is good, your visual system is working perfectly, and so on. Then, by using your eyes, you can come to know that the cat is asleep on the mat (or so we think). *What* you know—that the cat is asleep on the mat—has nothing to do with you or your perceptual state. The cat would have been peacefully sleeping whether or not you had been around to notice that fact.

Here is a second fact; that *you see* the cat. It is important to realize that this is a very different sort of fact than the first. This fact, unlike the first, *is* about you and your perceptual state. You know the first fact, that the cat is asleep on a mat, by using your eyes. How do you know the second fact, that you *see* the cat? That is not an easy question to answer.

But here is a clue. Suppose I ask you a question that is *not* about you, or your perceptual state: "Is a cat here?" You may answer by attending to the scene before your eyes: "Yes, there's a cat, asleep on the mat." Now suppose I ask you a question that *is* about you and your perceptual state: "Do you see a cat?" Is your way of answering that second question much different from the way you answered the first question? That is, don't you answer the second question *also* by *looking*? And looking is, apparently, *all* you need to do. If there's a cat right there, then you don't need any further information to answer confidently "Yes, I do see a cat."

Since this point is absolutely crucial for what follows, we should dwell on it for a moment. Consider the following example. You are reading a newspaper story about last night's baseball game, in which the Red Sox came back in the bottom of the ninth to squeak out a victory over the Yankees. If the story is sufficiently interesting, the newspaper itself will fade into the background: you will be preoccupied with the message, not the medium. If I ask you "Were the bases loaded?" you will not be thinking about the newspaper font or the color of the page. But of course you can always shift

---

6. The classic presentation of internal world skepticism is in F. Dretske, "How Do You Know You Are Not a Zombie?," in *Privileged Access: Philosophical Accounts of Self-Knowledge*, ed. B. Gertler (Ashgate, 2003), to which this section is much indebted. [Byrne's note.]

your attention back from the message (the details of the game) to the medium (the newspaper). And indeed you must, if I ask you "Is the story printed in two columns?" or "Are you reading about the game in a newspaper?" In order to answer those questions, you have to turn your attention from the home run with the bases loaded to something quite different — paper and ink, held in your hands. In other words, you can't know *that you are reading about the game* just by attending to *the game*.

The point is that the newspaper example is *not* a good model for how you know you see something. That is, if I ask you "Do you see a cat?" you do *not* have to attend to something that is analogous to the newspaper (perhaps a "sensory experience" or a "visual sensation"). When you read about the Red Sox, you don't just find facts about baseball, you also find the newspaper. But when you open your eyes, your seeing is in a way invisible. What you initially find is the *world*, not your *seeing* of the world.[7]

This suggests that in order to know *that* you see, you must somehow reach that conclusion from *what* you see. In other words, the evidence you use to find out that you see something is simply evidence about *your visual environment*, your environment as revealed to you by your sense of sight. That evidence includes facts about the cat (for example, that it is black and furry), and facts about the cat's spatial relation to you (for example, that you are facing it).

Now if someone claims to know hypothesis H on the basis of evidence E, one can challenge whether E really is good enough evidence for H by formulating a rival hypothesis H* that seems to be equally well supported by E. This happens all the time in science and everyday life, and was the basic idea of the external world skeptical argument, using the dreaming hypothesis as the alternative. But what hypothesis should we oppose to the *seeing hypothesis*, that you see a cat?

For maximum vividness and generality we can make the alternative hypothesis as radical as can be. Consider the hypothesis that you do not have a mind at all. Outwardly you look and behave just as a minded person does, but really all is dark within: you do not see anything, think or believe or want or feel anything, and so on. So, in particular, you do not see the cat, despite its being (say) a few feet away in front of you in broad daylight. Call this the *mindless hypothesis*.

Now your evidence about your visual environment — that the cat is black and furry, that you are facing it a few feet away in broad daylight, and other similar pieces of evidence — are compatible with both the seeing hypothesis and the rival mindless hypothesis. Offhand, it is not clear at all why this evidence favors the seeing hypothesis over the mindless hypothesis. Compare our earlier discussion of external world skepticism: if you agree that your evidence about your sensory experiences doesn't favor the sitting hypothesis over the dreaming hypothesis, then the parallel move for internal world skepticism should seem hard to resist. And if the evidence you have for the seeing hypothesis doesn't favor it over the mindless hypothesis, you don't know that the seeing hypothesis is true — you don't know that you see a cat.

---

7. For a much earlier version of the newspaper example, used to argue for (something close to) the *opposite* conclusion, see C. D. Broad, *Scientific Thought* (Kegan Paul, Trench Trubner & Co., 1927), p. 247. [Byrne's note.]

We can now set out our parallel argument with numbered premises and a conclusion:

P1*.   If you know that the seeing hypothesis is true, you know this solely on the basis of your evidence about your environment.

P2*.   This evidence does not favor the seeing hypothesis over the mindless hypothesis, and so does not allow you to know that the seeing hypothesis is true.

Hence:

C*.    You do not know that the seeing hypothesis is true; that is, you do not know that you see a cat.

Notice that P1* seems more secure than P1. P1* was defended by reflection on how we actually go about discovering that we see things like cats, and is immune to the animals objection. If P1 is defensible at all, its defense is less straightforward.

So far, so good, but how is the argument supposed to generalize to *all* mental states? It is fairly easy to see how the argument of the previous section generalizes — that's why it amounts to an argument for skepticism about *the external world*, rather than merely for skepticism about *sitting*. P1 seems no less plausible if we replace "the sitting hypothesis" by "the hypothesis that it's raining," or "the hypothesis that the earth is round," and so on. But now consider various other hypotheses about your mental life, say:

The *believing* hypothesis: that you believe that the cat is asleep on the mat
The *liking* hypothesis: that you like chocolate
The *feeling* hypothesis: that you feel a twinge in your elbow

Are the corresponding versions of P1* at all plausible? Perhaps surprisingly, a case can be made that they are. Take the believing hypothesis first. On the face of it, your way of answering the question "Do you *believe* that the cat is asleep on the mat?" (a question about your own mind) is not much different from your way of answering the very different question "Is the cat asleep on the mat?" In both cases you consider the cat, its state of wakefulness, and its relation to the mat, not your own mind. Once you have good evidence that the cat *is* asleep on the mat, then that is *all* you need to conclude that you *believe* that the cat is asleep on the mat.[8]

Now take the liking hypothesis. Why do you think you like chocolate? Isn't the answer something about *the chocolate*? You like chocolate because it *tastes good*. That is a fact about the chocolate, not about you. When you savor a piece of chocolate

---

8. For an in-depth examination of this idea, see R. Moran, *Authority and Estrangement* (Princeton University Press, 2001). [Byrne's note.]

on your tongue, your sensory systems are detecting features of the chocolate, in particular its agreeable sweet taste. On the basis of this evidence *about the chocolate* you conclude that *you like* it.

Finally, the feeling hypothesis. Surely here the corresponding version of P1* is obviously wrong! Well, that's right, if the "environment" is taken to be the environment *external* to your body, but there is no reason to adopt such a narrow construal. Your body is as much a part of your physical environment as the cat and the piece of chocolate. So consider the question "Do you feel a twinge in your elbow?" How do you go about answering it? By examining your own mind, wherever that is? No, by examining *the elbow*, of course. If there is the sort of disturbance in the elbow that has the character of a twinge (rather than a dull ache, for example), then you will answer "Yes, I do feel a twinge in my elbow."[9]

Of course this is only a sketch of an argument for a fully general skepticism about the internal world. But let's assume that the details can be filled out. Does the argument face any obvious objections?

# 4. Two Objections

It is easy enough to feel the pull of the skeptic's claim that you can't rule out the hypothesis that you are dreaming. Many books and movies trade on this idea. It is considerably harder to see the force of skepticism about the *internal* world — the claim that you don't know that you have a mind might understandably strike you as too absurd to be worth discussing. Still, philosophy does not progress by dismissing arguments for absurd conclusions, but by carefully explaining where they go awry.

Let us consider two objections. Seeing why neither works will help clarify the skeptical argument, and indicate that diagnosing its flaws is no easy matter.

The first objection is that something must have gone badly wrong with the argument because the mindless hypothesis is incoherent. According to the mindless hypothesis, the objection runs, it *seems* to you that you have a mental life. It seems to you that you see, believe, desire, and so forth — even though you do not. But if it seems to you that such-and-such, then you are *not* mindless, because seemings *are* mental states. If it seems to you that you see a cat, then you might not be seeing a cat, but you certainly have a mind.

This objection rests on a simple confusion. If you find it tempting, then you have failed to grasp just how outlandish the mindless hypothesis really is. According to the mindless hypothesis, it does *not* seem to you that you see a

---

9. It is clear that the corresponding version of P2* is plausible for the *believing* hypothesis: how could the evidence that the cat is on the mat favor the believing hypothesis over the mindless hypothesis? The cat would be on the mat whether you believed it or not. Exercise: are the corresponding versions of P2* as plausible for the liking and feeling hypotheses? (See also the paper by Dretske cited in note 6, pp. 4–6.) [Byrne's note.]

cat, for exactly the reason given in the objection. If the mindless hypothesis is right, you do not perceive, believe, or desire, and *neither does it seem to you that you see, believe, or desire*. The mindless hypothesis is not incoherent — at least, not in the way the first objection claims. So it is not misleadingly named: in the mindless scenario you are facing the cat with your eyes open, yet you seem to see nothing.

The second objection also rests on a confusion, but this time it is more subtle. Return to the argument for external world skepticism, and the skeptic's claim that your knowledge is confined to evidence about your sensory experiences: there is no way of "going beyond" this evidence to know what the external world is like. If the argument for internal world skepticism is parallel, the internal world skeptic should presumably say something similar — namely, your knowledge is confined to *evidence about your environment*: there is no way of going beyond this evidence to know what the *internal* world is like. But wait — if the skeptic concedes that you *know* something, then the mindless hypothesis is false! (You can't know something if you don't have a mind.)

All that is quite correct, but it does not affect the argument. The skeptic is *not* arguing that the mindless hypothesis is *true*, but rather that *you do not know that it is false*. If it is false, then you do have a mind, and in particular you know various things about your environment. But, according to the skeptic, that is *all* you know — you can't "go beyond" this evidence to know what your mental life is like.

The second objection does highlight one difference between external and internal world skepticism. The external world skeptic will allow that you have knowledge of some evidence (namely, evidence about your sensory experiences) if the dreaming hypothesis is true. In contrast, the internal world skeptic will *not* allow that you have *any* knowledge if the mindless hypothesis is true. That difference does not spoil the parallel between the two arguments, however.

The point of this article is not to convince you that you don't know anything about your own mind. Rather, the point is to highlight the problem of self-knowledge. We surely know a lot about our own minds — yet it is obscure how this is possible. Our knowledge of *cats* is quite well understood; our knowledge that we *see* cats, on the other hand, remains a mystery.

## TEST YOUR UNDERSTANDING

1.  Does Byrne think that in order to answer the question "What do you see?" there is no need to turn your attention to your sensory experience?

2.  Does the skeptic about the external world argue that you don't have a hand? Does the skeptic about the internal world argue that you don't see a hand? If they aren't arguing for these conclusions, what conclusions are they arguing for instead?

## NOTES AND QUESTIONS

1.  If we say that a zombie is a creature who looks like and behaves similarly to a normal human being, but who has no mind at all, then Byrne's "mindless hypothesis" can be put as follows: you are a zombie. Consider the following suggestion:

    > It is true that besides seeing objects in the world you see these objects from a point of view. There is a perspective we have on the world, a "boundary," if you will, between things we see and things we don't see. And of the things we see, there are parts (surfaces) we see and parts (surfaces) we don't see. This partition determines a point of view that changes as we move around. Since zombies don't have points of view, it may be thought that this is our way of knowing we are not zombies. Although everything we see exists in the world of a zombie, what doesn't exist in the world of a zombie is this egocentric partition, this boundary, between things (and surfaces) we see and things (and surfaces) we don't see, and the fact that there is, for us, this point of view, this perspective, is what tells us we are not zombies.[1]

    Is this a way in which one could come to know that Byrne's "seeing hypothesis" is true, and so that the mindless hypothesis is false?

2.  Some philosophers have attempted to explain how one can know of one's mental states (or at least some of them) by attending to one's environment — for instance, how one can know that one *sees* a cat by attending to *the cat*. This is called the *transparency* view. The transparency view comes in many different varieties; a recent defense of one version is Jordi Fernández, *Transparent Minds: A Study of Self-Knowledge* (Oxford University Press, 2013). For criticisms of this approach, see chapter 6 of Brie Gertler, *Self-Knowledge* (Routledge, 2011), and section 2.3 of Brie Gertler, "Self-Knowledge," *Stanford Encyclopedia of Philosophy*, ed. Edward Zalta (http://plato.stanford.edu/archives/spr2011/entries/self-knowledge/).

---

1. Fred Dretske, "How Do You Know You Are Not a Zombie?," in Brie Gertler (ed.), *Privileged Access: Philosophical Accounts of Self-Knowledge* (Ashgate, 2003), p. 2.

## ANALYZING THE ARGUMENTS

1. Here is one version of an analogical argument for the existence of other minds:

   P1. I have a mind and a body.

   P2. Others have bodies.

   C. Others have minds.

   This argument is not very persuasive. Why not? How should the analogical argument for the existence of other minds be set out so that it is as persuasive as possible?

2. Suppose you are wondering whether I have a mind, and if so what my mental life is like. Is the fact that I am biologically similar to you an important piece of evidence? Is the fact that I appear to speak a language you can understand an important piece of evidence? Is the fact that I move around and interact with my environment in a similar way to you an important piece of evidence? In addressing these questions, use a variety of examples in which some of these features are absent: languageless chimpanzees, talking space aliens, immobile computers, etc.

3. Search on the Internet for "Heider and Simmel video. " You should find a short (1: 40) video showing two triangles and a circle moving in and around a box with a door. (This video was used in a series of famous experiments reported in Fritz Heider and Marianne Simmel, "An Experimental Study of Apparent Behavior," *American Journal of Psychology* 57: 243–59, 1944.)

   Watch the video and write a paragraph describing what you saw. If you're like most of the subjects studied by Heider and Simmel, you will have described what you saw using psychological vocabulary. Does this support the view that we can directly observe what others are thinking, feeling, and intentionally doing, so that no "argument by analogy" is needed?

4. How well do we know our own minds? Is it significantly easier to know our own minds than it is to know the minds of others? Are there cases where it's easier to know someone else's mind than one's own? In answering these questions, consider a wide range of examples: perception (vision, audition), sensation (pain, dizzyness), emotion (anger, disgust, pride), mood (depression, anxiety), imagining, believing, wanting, hoping, and so on.

5. Consider the following four principles. For all subjects S:

   i-b. If S is in pain, S believes she is in pain.

   i-k. If S is in pain, S knows she is in pain.

   ii-b. If S believes she is in pain, S is in pain.

   ii-k. If S knows she is in pain, S is in pain.

Assume that knowing p **entails** believing p. Does i-b entail i-k? Does i-b entail ii-b? Does i-b entail ii-k? Answer similar questions for the other possibilities. Three of these principles are controversial; one is uncontroversial. Which is the uncontroversial one? Formulate similar principles for the mental state of *believing that it's raining*. Are they as plausible? A creature (say, a dog) might have beliefs but not have the conceptual capacity to think about its mental life. If that's right, some of the four principles are false. Which ones? Can you amend the false principles to avoid this problem?

6. In his *Essay Concerning Human Understanding* (1689), John Locke describes a case in which

> by the different Structure of our Organs, it were so ordered, That *the same Object should produce in several Men's Minds different* Ideas at the same time; [for example] if the *Idea*, that a *Violet* produced in one Man's Mind by his Eyes, were the same that a *Marigold* produces in another Man's, and *vice versâ*. (book 2, chapter 32, section 15)

Locke is imagining a situation like this: ripe tomatoes, strawberries, and Elmo look to me the way grass, guacamole, and Kermit the Frog do to you, and vice versa. This is a so-called *inverted spectrum scenario*. Do you know that I am not spectrum-inverted with respect to you? Suppose you ask me how tomatoes look to me, and I reply "They look red." You might think that helps, because presumably I know how tomatoes look to me and am perfectly capable to communicating that piece of knowledge to you. And if you know that tomatoes look red to me, since you know that tomatoes look red to you, you know that they look red to both of us. On the other hand, you might think that this linguistic evidence shows nothing, because if we *were* spectrum-inverted, I would have replied in the same way. This is because if we were spectrum-inverted, you would have come to associate the word "red" with the "reddish" sensations tomatoes produce in you, and I would have come to associate the word "red" with the "greenish" sensations tomatoes produce in me, with the result that we use the word similarly. Does linguistic evidence help? Could there be behavioral evidence of any other kind that would count against the spectrum inversion hypothesis? Could neuroscience somehow settle the question?

# 7

# How Can We Know about the External World?

You know that the Earth is round, that penguins inhabit Antarctica, that trees shed their leaves in the fall, that you have a heart, and so on and so on. In other words, you know a lot about the "external world," including your own body.[1] That much is obvious.

Or is it? Consider the hypothesis that your entire life has been a remarkably vivid dream. Not only have you been dreaming the whole time, but the Earth never existed. No penguins, trees, nothing like that. In fact, you don't even have a heart. You are a heartless android, lying comatose in a robot junkyard on a planet orbiting the star Kepler-11. "From the inside" things seem exactly the same to you: you seem to see this page, you seem to remember that penguins inhabit Antarctica, and so on, even though there is no page, and no Antarctica. So how can you know that this "Android Hypothesis" is false? That question can seem very difficult to answer, which suggests that you *can't* know that the android hypothesis is false.

This claim of ignorance might not seem so bad by itself, but once it is conceded, it is difficult to stop ignorance from spreading much more widely. Take, for example, one thing that you apparently know, namely that penguins inhabit Antarctica. Now the claim that penguins inhabit Antarctica straightforwardly **entails** that the Android Hypothesis is false. If penguins inhabit Antarctica, you are *not* a dreaming android who lives in a penguin-free world. So, *if* you know that penguins inhabit Antarctica, you can perform an elementary logical inference, and come to know that the Android Hypothesis is false. So, if you *can't* know that the Android Hypothesis is false, you don't know that penguins inhabit Antarctica. By the same **argument**, neither do you know that the Earth is round, that trees shed

---

1. This kind of knowledge is called **propositional** or **factual** knowledge. See the introduction to chapter 3, "What Is Knowledge?"

their leaves in the fall, and so on. In short, if you can't know that the Android Hypothesis is false, you are completely ignorant about the external world—that is, *external world* **skepticism** is true. (A *skeptic* about some subject matter M is someone who denies that we have knowledge about M.)

Still, you might wonder whether even external world skepticism is worth worrying about. Suppose you're offered a choice between going on a roller coaster ride and entering the roller coaster simulator. The simulator is perfect: as far as excitement goes, it's just as good as the real thing, although you aren't really rattling down a narrow track at 100 mph. The choice doesn't seem to matter much (actually, you might even prefer the simulator on the grounds that it's much safer). Here virtual reality is no worse than reality itself. Isn't that true in general? Why care whether you're a dreaming android? The thrills and spills of life would be the same in any case.

But this reaction is overly complacent. The dreaming android has no friends, has no mother who loves it, and has never accomplished anything—vividly dreaming that you are acing your final exams is not a way of doing well in school. Having friends, to say nothing of a mother who loves you, is a valuable thing. (Imagine discovering that someone whom you thought a faithful friend was just pretending.) So if you are a dreaming android, you are in a very unfortunate predicament—friendless, unloved, and unaccomplished. You should want to be reassured that you are *not* in this predicament. That is, you should want to *know* that you have friends, are loved, and so forth. If external world skepticism is true, reassurance that your life is not an empty sham is forever beyond your reach.

The readings in this chapter respond to the threat of skepticism about the external world. (One exception, as we'll see below, is the essay by Rae Langton.) Before getting to the many different responses, it will help to set out the argument for the skeptical conclusion more precisely. And in the course of doing that, we will see how the argument is a particular instance of a general form of skeptical argument.

# A General Skeptical Argument

Let a *skeptical hypothesis* be a hypothesis according to which the world is different from how you take it to be. We have already seen one skeptical hypothesis, according to which you are a dreaming android and the Earth never existed. There are other similar skeptical hypotheses, the most famous of which is René Descartes's *Demon Hypothesis*, that "some malicious demon of the utmost power and cunning has employed all his energies in order to deceive me." The contemporary version of the Demon Hypothesis is the *Brain in a Vat Hypothesis*, that you are a brain kept alive in a vat by some evil scientist and stimulated so that "from the inside" things seem exactly as if you see this page, and so on.

These hypotheses are *global* skeptical hypotheses—if they are true, almost *nothing* you take yourself to know about the external world is true. But skeptical hypotheses can be more modest. Indeed, in an everyday situation in which you wonder whether you really are right to think that you left your laptop at home, you are entertaining a very modest skeptical hypothesis—that the world is very similar to the way you take it to be, except that your laptop is not at home. Philosophers have devised many other skeptical hypotheses that are intermediate in strength between global skeptical hypotheses and very modest skeptical hypotheses like the one just mentioned.

For instance, there is the *No Other Minds Hypothesis*, according to which you are the only creature with a mind—everyone else behaves just *as if* they believe, feel, and perceive, but they are actually entirely mindless. (See Saul Kripke's "Wittgenstein and Other Minds," in chapter 6.) And there is the *Unexpected Future Hypothesis*, according to which the future is radically different from the past—if this hypothesis is true, bread will not nourish tomorrow, the sun will not rise tomorrow, and so on. (See the introduction to chapter 4, "How Can We Know About What We Have Not Observed?")

Now take a skeptical hypothesis SH, and any claim p that entails that SH is false. We can argue that you don't know p as follows:

1. If you know p, you can know that SH is false.

2. You can't know that SH is false.

So:

3. You don't know p.

For example, suppose you think (p) that your bike is where you left it, padlocked to a bike rack. Let SH be the modest skeptical hypothesis that your bike has been stolen. The claim p (your bike is where you left it) entails that SH (your bike has been stolen) is false, in other words that your bike has not been stolen. So we can argue that you don't know that your bike is where you left it as follows:

1†. If you know that your bike is where you left it, you can know that your bike has not been stolen.

2†. You can't know that your bike has not been stolen.

So:

3†. You don't know that your bike is where you left it.

This form of argument—If p then q, it is not the case that q, so it is not the case that P—is called **modus tollens**.

Let us look more carefully at **premise** 1. Suppose you know that all fish have gills and that Wanda is a fish. Now the statement that all fish have gills and Wanda is a fish entails that Wanda has gills. So you are now in a position to draw the conclusion that Wanda has gills from what you already know. And if you go ahead and do that, it seems very plausible that you will end up *knowing* that Wanda has gills. In general, one way to extend our knowledge is to trace out the **logical consequences** of what we already know: this happens whenever someone proves a theorem in mathematics, for example. Put more precisely: if p entails (or logically implies) q, and you know p, then you are in a position to know q. This is (one version of) a principle called **Closure**.

Given Closure, premise 1 of the skeptical argument is true. Closure is difficult to deny, and the argument is **valid**, so when faced with a skeptical argument of this form you have two options: deny premise 2, or accept the conclusion.[2]

We can generate an argument for external world skepticism by letting SH be a global skeptical hypothesis, for instance Descartes's Demon Hypothesis, and letting p be any claim about the external world that entails that the Demon Hypothesis is false, say, that the Earth is round:

1*. If you know that the Earth is round, you can know that the Demon Hypothesis is false.

2*. You can't know that the Demon Hypothesis is false.

So:

3*. You don't know that the Earth is round.

Again, assuming Closure, there are two options: deny premise 2* or accept 3*, the skeptical conclusion.

# Responses to External World Skepticism

The readings from David Hume, George Edward Moore, Stewart Cohen, and Jonathan Vogel offer contrasting responses to external world skepticism.

According to Hume, our senses provide scant evidence for hypotheses about the external world. In a paragraph omitted from the selection he writes: "'Tis impossible . . . that from the existence or any of the qualities of [perceptions], we can ever form any conclusion concerning the existence of [objects]." So Hume is a (rare) example of a real-life skeptic: he accepts the conclusion of the skeptical argument. His main concern is not so much to defend skepticism (which he

---

2. In fact, despite the plausibility of Closure, some philosophers deny it. A notable example is Robert Nozick: see his *Philosophical Explanations* (Harvard University Press, 1981), chapter 3. But none of the contributors to this chapter deny it. See "Analyzing the Arguments" at the end of this chapter.

thinks is pretty much unassailable) but rather to give a psychological explanation for why we think that there is an external world of familiar tables, chairs, penguins, and so on, even though we have no good reason for doing so.

Vogel, in effect, directly replies to Hume. While Hume thinks that our senses can't show us that we are not brains in vats, or deceived by an evil demon, Vogel thinks otherwise, and so denies the second premise. Vogel argues that the "real world hypothesis"—that the Earth is round, you have a head, are reading this book, and so on—provides a much better explanation of your "sensory experiences" (or, in Hume's terminology, "perceptions") than any global skeptical hypothesis. So you have a good reason to believe the real world hypothesis by an "inference to the best explanation."[3]

Moore is principally concerned to deny the conclusion of the skeptical argument, rather than to explain which premise is false. He tries to turn the tables on the skeptic by offering what he claims is a *proof* of the existence of things like tables and books. For example: here is a book (Moore holds up a copy of this book), here is another book (Moore holds up a copy his own famous book on ethics, *Principia Ethica*), therefore books exist. Of course, the skeptic will not grant that this is a proof, on the grounds that Moore does not know the premises. But, as Moore points out, in ordinary life we take arguments of this sort "as absolutely conclusive proofs of certain conclusions." For instance, we allow that someone can prove that there are at least three misprints on a page from the premises "There's one misprint here, another there, and another here." And if we really can prove such things, we must have knowledge about the external world. Why isn't the skeptic just being unreasonable in rejecting Moore's proof?

Cohen's "contextualist" response to the skeptical argument can be hard to understand at first. In order to explain it, we need to note a crucial fact, that sometimes the same sentence can be used to make different claims on different occasions. Pronouns are a simple example. Suppose Tim utters the sentence "I am hungry." Then he is making a claim about Tim, specifically that Tim is hungry. Suppose, on the other hand, that another person, Tilly, utters the very same sentence, "I am hungry." Then she is making a claim about Tilly, specifically that Tilly is hungry. Tilly is not saying that Tim is hungry, nor vice versa. Different claims, same sentence.

Here is a less obvious example. Suppose I hand you a piece of ordinary chocolate and say (perhaps as a joke) "Chocolate is poisonous." What I said was false. Suppose, on the other hand, you are about to feed the chocolate to your dog. "Wait," I say, "chocolate is poisonous!" What I said was true. (A few ounces of dark chocolate can make a small dog quite sick.) Again, different claims, same sentence. We could spell out my two claims as follows: the first claim is that chocolate is poisonous *to humans* (false), and the second claim is that chocolate is poisonous *to dogs* (true).

---

3. For more on this kind of inference see Gilbert Harman, "The Inference to the Best Explanation," p. 182 of this anthology.

This at least opens the possibility that something similar holds for sentences like "George knows that he has hands"—that is, that a sentence ascribing knowledge can be used to make different claims on different occasions. Cohen argues (with some reservations) that this is correct, and that it shows us what's wrong—and what's right!—with the skeptical argument. In an ordinary conversational situation (or "context"), if you say "I know that the Earth is round" you make a *true* claim. But in a context in which skeptical possibilities have been made salient (for instance in a philosophy class on skepticism), if you say "I know that the Earth is round" you make a *false* claim. So there is a sense in which the skeptical argument succeeds, and a sense in which it doesn't. "You don't know that the Earth is round" and "You can't know that the Demon Hypothesis is false" are *false* relative to an ordinary context, but they are *true* relative to some extraordinary contexts.

# Kantian Skepticism

Rae Langton's essay defends a limited but nonetheless fascinating form of skepticism, which she finds suggested by the work of the German philosopher Immanuel Kant (1724–1804). This Kantian skepticism (or "Kantian humility," as Langton calls it) is not external world skepticism. As both Moore and Langton note, Kant thought we had plenty of knowledge about the external world.

However, in his *Critique of Pure Reason*, Kant argues for another kind of skepticism: as he put it, we have no knowledge of "things in themselves." What did he mean by that? Langton offers an answer, and a defense of a kind of skepticism that she thinks is at least in the spirit of Kant's actual view. According to Langton, the physical sciences can only penetrate so far into reality: there is a layer further down that is in principle beyond their reach. If that is right, then although we can know that there are books, and that we have friends, ignorance of the fundamental nature of the world is part of the human condition.

## René Descartes (1596–1650)

Descartes was a French philosopher, mathematician, and scientist. He made important early contributions to mathematical physics, invented the Cartesian coordinate system familiar from high-school geometry, and is widely regarded as "the founder of modern philosophy." The *Meditations on First Philosophy* (1641) is his most famous book; his other major works include *Principles of Philosophy* (1644) and *The Passions of the Soul* (1649).

# MEDITATION I: WHAT CAN BE CALLED INTO DOUBT

### from *Meditations on First Philosophy*

Some years ago I was struck by the large number of falsehoods that I had accepted as true in my childhood, and by the highly doubtful nature of the whole edifice that I had subsequently based on them. I realized that it was necessary, once in the course of my life, to demolish everything completely and start again right from the foundations if I wanted to establish anything at all in the sciences that was stable and likely to last. But the task looked an enormous one, and I began to wait until I should reach a mature enough age to ensure that no subsequent time of life would be more suitable for tackling such inquiries. This led me to put the project off for so long that I would now be to blame if by pondering over it any further I wasted the time still left for carrying it out. So today I have expressly rid my mind of all worries and arranged for myself a clear stretch of free time. I am here quite alone, and at last I will devote myself sincerely and without reservation to the general demolition of my opinions.

But to accomplish this, it will not be necessary for me to show that all my opinions are false, which is something I could perhaps never manage. Reason now leads me to think that I should hold back my assent from opinions which are not completely certain and indubitable just as carefully as I do from those which are patently false. So, for the purpose of rejecting all my opinions, it will be enough if I find in each of them at least some reason for doubt. And to do this I will not need to run through them all individually, which would be an endless task. Once the foundations of a building are undermined, anything built on them collapses of its own accord; so I will go straight for the basic principles on which all my former beliefs rested.

Whatever I have up till now accepted as most true I have acquired either from the senses or through the senses. But from time to time I have found that the senses deceive, and it is prudent never to trust completely those who have deceived us even once.

Yet although the senses occasionally deceive us with respect to objects which are very small or in the distance, there are many other beliefs about which doubt is quite impossible, even though they are derived from the senses — for example, that I am here, sitting by the fire, wearing a winter dressing-gown, holding this piece of paper in my hands, and so on. Again, how could it be denied that these hands or this whole body are mine? Unless perhaps I were to liken myself to madmen, whose brains are so damaged by the persistent vapours of melancholia that they firmly maintain they are kings when they are paupers, or say they are dressed in purple when they are naked, or that their heads are made of earthenware, or that they are pumpkins, or made of glass. But such people are insane, and I would be thought equally mad if I took anything from them as a model for myself.

A brilliant piece of reasoning! As if I were not a man who sleeps at night, and regularly has all the same experiences while asleep as madmen do when awake — indeed sometimes even more improbable ones. How often, asleep at night, am I convinced of just such familiar events — that I am here in my dressing-gown, sitting by the fire — when in fact I am lying undressed in bed! Yet at the moment my eyes are certainly wide awake when I look at this piece of paper; I shake my head and it is not asleep; as I stretch out and feel my hand I do so deliberately, and I know what I am doing. All this would not happen with such distinctness to someone asleep. Indeed! As if I did not remember other occasions when I have been tricked by exactly similar thoughts while asleep! As I think about this more carefully, I see plainly that there are never any sure signs by means of which being awake can be distinguished from being asleep. The result is that I begin to feel dazed, and this very feeling only reinforces the notion that I may be asleep.

Suppose then that I am dreaming, and that these particulars — that my eyes are open, that I am moving my head and stretching out my hands — are not true. Perhaps, indeed, I do not even have such hands or such a body at all. Nonetheless, it must surely be admitted that the visions which come in sleep are like paintings, which must have been fashioned in the likeness of things that are real, and hence that at least these general kinds of things — eyes, head, hands and the body as a whole — are things which are not imaginary but are real and exist. For even when painters try to create sirens and satyrs with the most extraordinary bodies, they cannot give them natures which are new in all respects; they simply jumble up the limbs of different animals. Or if perhaps they manage to think up something so new that nothing remotely similar has ever been seen before — something which is therefore completely fictitious and unreal — at least the colours used in the composition must be real. By similar reasoning, although these general kinds of things — eyes, head, hands and so on — could be imaginary, it must at least be admitted that certain other even simpler and more universal things are real. These are as it were the real colours from which we form all the images of things, whether true or false, that occur in our thought.

This class appears to include corporeal nature in general, and its extension; the shape of extended things; the quantity, or size and number of these things; the place in which they may exist, the time through which they may endure, and so on.

So a reasonable conclusion from this might be that physics, astronomy, medicine, and all other disciplines which depend on the study of composite things, are doubtful; while arithmetic, geometry and other subjects of this kind, which deal only with the simplest and most general things, regardless of whether they really exist in nature or not, contain something certain and indubitable. For whether I am awake or asleep, two and three added together are five, and a square has no more than four sides. It seems impossible that such transparent truths should incur any suspicion of being false.

And yet firmly rooted in my mind is the long-standing opinion that there is an omnipotent God who made me the kind of creature that I am. How do I know that he has not brought it about that there is no earth, no sky, no extended thing, no shape, no size, no place, while at the same time ensuring that all these things appear to me to exist just as they do now? What is more, since I sometimes believe that others go astray in cases where they think they have the most perfect knowledge, may I not similarly go wrong every time I add two and three or count the sides of a square, or in some even simpler matter, if that is imaginable? But perhaps God would not have allowed me to be deceived in this way, since he is said to be supremely good. But if it were inconsistent with his goodness to have created me such that I am deceived all the time, it would seem equally foreign to his goodness to allow me to be deceived even occasionally; yet this last assertion cannot be made.

Perhaps there may be some who would prefer to deny the existence of so powerful a God rather than believe that everything else is uncertain. Let us not argue with them, but grant them that everything said about God is a fiction. According to their supposition, then, I have arrived at my present state by fate or chance or a continuous chain of events, or by some other means; yet since deception and error seem to be imperfections, the less powerful they make my original cause, the more likely it is that I am so imperfect as to be deceived all the time. I have no answer to these arguments, but am finally compelled to admit that there is not one of my former beliefs about which a doubt may not properly be raised; and this is not a flippant or ill-considered conclusion, but is based on powerful and well thought-out reasons. So in future I must withhold my assent from these former beliefs just as carefully as I would from obvious falsehoods, if I want to discover any certainty.

But it is not enough merely to have noticed this; I must make an effort to remember it. My habitual opinions keep coming back, and, despite my wishes, they capture my belief, which is as it were bound over to them as a result of long occupation and the law of custom. I shall never get out of the habit of confidently assenting to these opinions, so long as I suppose them to be what in fact they are, namely highly probable opinions — opinions which, despite the fact that they are in a sense doubtful, as has just been shown, it is still much more reasonable to believe than to deny. In view of this, I think it will be a good plan to turn my will in completely the opposite direction and deceive myself, by pretending for a time that these former opinions are utterly false and imaginary. I shall do this until the weight of preconceived opinion is counter-balanced and the distorting influence of habit no longer prevents my judgement from perceiving things correctly. In the meantime, I know that no danger or error will result from my plan, and that I cannot possibly go too far in my distrustful attitude. This is because the task now in hand does not involve action but merely the acquisition of knowledge.

I will suppose therefore that not God, who is supremely good and the source of truth, but rather some malicious demon of the utmost power and cunning has employed all his energies in order to deceive me. I shall think that the sky, the air, the earth, colours, shapes, sounds and all external things are merely the delusions of dreams which he has devised to ensnare my judgement. I shall consider myself as not having hands or eyes, or flesh, or blood or senses, but as falsely believing that I have all these things. I shall stubbornly and firmly persist in this meditation; and, even if it is not in my power to know any truth, I shall at least do what is in my power, that is, resolutely guard against assenting to any falsehoods, so that the deceiver, however powerful and cunning he may be, will be unable to impose on me in the slightest degree. But this is an arduous undertaking, and a kind of laziness brings me back to normal life. I am like a prisoner who is enjoying an imaginary freedom while asleep; as he begins to suspect that he is asleep, he dreads being woken up, and goes along with the pleasant illusion as long as he can. In the same way, I happily slide back into my old opinions and dread being shaken out of them, for fear that my peaceful sleep may be followed by hard labour when I wake, and that I shall have to toil not in the light, but amid the inextricable darkness of the problems I have now raised.

## TEST YOUR UNDERSTANDING

1.  Why does Descartes switch from considering the hypothesis that he might be dreaming to considering the hypothesis that a malicious demon is deceiving him?

2.  Do the (provisional) conclusions of *Meditation I* include:

    (i)  A demon has deceived Descartes into believing that he has hands?

    (ii) Descartes doesn't know that he has hands?

## NOTES AND QUESTIONS

1.  Descartes claims he "regularly has all the same experiences while asleep as madmen do when awake." Suppose your dreams aren't quite as vivid as Descartes's: you only dream in faint shades of gray, and you only dream about dragons. Does that mean that you should not be worried by the thought that you don't know you are not dreaming?

2.  The *Meditations* has this ambitious subtitle: "Wherein are demonstrated the Existence of God and the Distinction of Soul from Body." Descartes attempts to "demonstrate" (i.e., prove) the existence of God in two parts of the *Meditations*. He gives one argument for the existence of God in *Meditation III* and another in *Meditation V*. The first argument is, briefly, that the only cause of Descartes's idea of God could be God Himself. (This is often classified as a **cosmological argument**.) The second argument is a version of Anselm's **ontological argument** (see chapter 1 of this anthology). In Descartes's version, the argument purports to derive the existence of God from the premise that the "clear and distinct" idea of God is that of a "supremely perfect being" whose existence is part of its nature.

    According to Descartes, the existence of God provides a way out of the skeptical predicament of *Meditation I*, because God would not radically deceive us.

    For Descartes's attempt to demonstrate the distinction between soul and body, see the selections from *Meditations II* and *VI* (see chapter 8 of this anthology).

3.  Skepticism deriving from the considerations of *Meditation I* is called *Cartesian skepticism*. Skeptical ideas were also prevalent in antiquity, associated with philosophers such as Pyrrho (c. 365–275 BCE) and Arcesilaus (c. 316–241 BCE). The relationship between ancient

skepticism and the later Cartesian kind is controversial. For more on ancient skepticism, see Katja Vogt, "Ancient Skepticism," *Stanford Encyclopedia of Philosophy*, ed. Edward Zalta (http://plato.stanford.edu/archives/win2011/entries/skepticism-ancient/).

## David Hume (1711–1776)

Hume was a Scottish philosopher, essayist, and historian, and a central figure in Western philosophy. His *Treatise of Human Nature* (1739), *An Enquiry Concerning Human Understanding* (1748), and *An Enquiry Concerning the Principles of Morals* (1751) have been very influential. (The two *Enquiries* revise material in the *Treatise*.) Many contemporary philosophical discussions in epistemology, metaphysics, and ethics are reactions to Hume's theories and arguments. Hume's *Dialogues Concerning Natural Religion* (published posthumously in 1779) is a classic attack on "design arguments" for the existence of God.

# OF SCEPTICISM WITH REGARD TO THE SENSES
## From *A Treatise of Human Nature*

Thus the sceptic still continues to reason and believe, even tho' he asserts, that he cannot defend his reason by reason; and by the same rule he must assent to the principle concerning the existence of body, tho' he cannot pretend by any arguments of philosophy to maintain its veracity. Nature has not left this to his choice, and has doubtless esteem'd it an affair of too great importance to be trusted to our uncertain reasonings and speculations. We may well ask, *What causes induce us to believe in the existence of body?* but 'tis in vain to ask, *Whether there be body or not?* That is a point, which we must take for granted in all our reasonings.

The subject, then, of our present enquiry is concerning the *causes* which induce us to believe in the existence of body: And my reasonings on this head I shall begin with a distinction, which at first sight may seem superfluous, but which will contribute very much to the perfect understanding of what follows. We ought to examine apart those two questions, which are commonly confounded together, *viz.* Why we attribute a CONTINU'D existence to objects, even when they are not present to the senses; and why we suppose them to have an existence DISTINCT from the mind and perception. . . . These two questions concerning the continu'd and distinct existence of body are intimately connected together. For if the objects of our senses continue to exist, even when they are not perceiv'd, their existence is of course independent of and distinct from the perception; and *vice versa*, if their existence be independent of the perception and distinct from it, they must continue to exist, even tho' they be not perceiv'd. But tho' the decision of the one question decides the other; yet that we may the more easily discover the principles of human nature, from whence the decision arises, we shall carry along with us this distinction, and shall consider, whether it be the *senses, reason,* or the *imagination,* that produces the opinion of a *continu'd* or of a *distinct* existence. These are the only questions, that are intelligible on the present subject. . . .

To begin with the SENSES, 'tis evident these faculties are incapable of giving rise to the notion of the *continu'd* existence of their objects, after they no longer appear to the senses. For that is a contradiction in terms, and supposes that the senses continue to operate, even after they have ceas'd all manner of operation. These faculties, therefore, if they have any influence in the present case, must produce the opinion of a distinct, not of a continu'd existence; and in order to that, must present their impressions either as images and representations, or as these very distinct and external existences.

That our senses offer not their impressions as the images of something *distinct,* or *independent,* and *external,* is evident; because they convey to us nothing but a single perception, and never give us the least intimation of any thing beyond. A single perception can never produce the idea of a double existence, but by some inference either of the reason or imagination. . . .

If our senses, therefore, suggest any idea of distinct existences, they must convey the impressions as those very existences, by a kind of fallacy and illusion. Upon this head we may observe, that all sensations are felt by the mind, such as they really are, and that when we doubt, whether they present themselves as distinct objects, or as mere impressions, the difficulty is not concerning their nature, but concerning their relations and situation. Now if the senses presented our impressions as external to, and independent of ourselves, both the objects and ourselves must be obvious to our senses, otherwise they cou'd not be compar'd by these faculties. The difficulty, then, is how far we are *ourselves* the objects of our senses.

'Tis certain there is no question in philosophy more abstruse than that concerning identity, and the nature of the uniting principle, which constitutes a person. So far from being able by our senses merely to determine this question, we must have recourse to the most profound metaphysics to give a satisfactory answer to it; and in common life 'tis evident these ideas of self and person are never very fix'd nor determinate. 'Tis absurd, therefore, to imagine the senses can ever distinguish betwixt[1] ourselves and external objects. . . .

The senses give us no notion of continu'd existence, because they cannot operate beyond the extent, in which they really operate. They as little produce the opinion of a distinct existence, because they neither can offer it to the mind as represented, nor as original. To offer it as represented, they must present both an object and an image. To make it appear as original, they must convey a falsehood . . . and even in that case they do not, nor is it possible they shou'd, deceive us. We may, therefore, conclude with certainty, that the opinion of a continu'd and of a distinct existence never arises from the senses.

---

1. Between.

To confirm this we may observe, that there are three different kinds of impressions convey'd by the senses. The first are those of the figure,[2] bulk,[3] motion and solidity of bodies. The second those of colours, tastes, smells, sounds, heat and cold. The third are the pains and pleasures, that arise from the application of objects to our bodies, as by the cutting of our flesh with steel, and such like. Both philosophers and the vulgar[4] suppose the first of these to have a distinct continu'd existence. The vulgar only regard the second as on the same footing. Both philosophers and the vulgar, again, esteem the third to be merely perceptions; and consequently interrupted and dependent beings.

Now 'tis evident, that, whatever may be our philosophical opinion, colours, sounds, heat and cold, as far as appears to the senses, exist after the same manner with motion and solidity, and that the difference we make betwixt them in this respect, arises not from the mere perception. So strong is the prejudice for the distinct continu'd existence of the former qualities, that when the contrary opinion is advanc'd by modem philosophers, people imagine they can almost refute it from their feeling and experience, and that their very senses contradict this philosophy. 'Tis also evident, that colours, sounds, etc. are originally on the same footing with the pain that arises from steel, and pleasure that proceeds from a fire; and that the difference betwixt them is founded neither on perception nor reason, but on the imagination. For as they are confest to be, both of them, nothing but perceptions arising from the particular configurations and motions of the parts of body, wherein possibly can their difference consist? Upon the whole, then, we may conclude, that as far as the senses are judges, all perceptions are the same in the manner of their existence.

We may also observe in this instance of sounds and colours, that we can attribute a distinct continu'd existence to objects without ever consulting REASON, or weighing our opinions by any philosophical principles. And indeed, whatever convincing arguments philosophers may fancy they can produce to establish the belief of objects independent of the mind, 'tis obvious these arguments are known but to very few, and that 'tis not by them, that children, peasants, and the greatest part of mankind are induc'd to attribute objects to some impressions, and deny them to others. Accordingly we find, that all the conclusions, which the vulgar form on this head, are directly contrary to those, which are confirm'd by philosophy. For philosophy informs us, that every thing, which appears to the mind, is nothing but a perception, and is interrupted, and dependent on the mind; whereas the vulgar confound perceptions and objects, and attribute a distinct continu'd existence to the very things they feel or see. This sentiment, then, as it is entirely unreasonable, must proceed from some other faculty than the understanding. . . . So that upon the whole our reason neither does, nor is it possible it ever shou'd, upon any supposition, give us an assurance of the continu'd and distinct existence of body. That opinion must be entirely owing to the IMAGINATION: which must now be the subject of our enquiry.

2. Shape.

3. Size.

4. Ordinary people, non-philosophers.

Since all impressions are internal and perishing existences, and appear as such, the notion of their distinct and continu'd existence must arise from a concurrence of some of their qualities with the qualities of the imagination; and since this notion does not extend to all of them, it must arise from certain qualities peculiar to some impressions. 'Twill therefore be easy for us to discover these qualities by a comparison of the impressions, to which we attribute a distinct and continu'd existence, with those, which we regard as internal and perishing.

We may observe, then, that 'tis neither upon account of the involuntariness of certain impressions, as is commonly suppos'd, nor of their superior force and violence, that we attribute to them a reality, and continu'd existence, which we refuse to others, that are voluntary or feeble. For 'tis evident our pains and pleasures, our passions and affections, which we never suppose to have any existence beyond our perception, operate with greater violence, and are equally involuntary, as the impressions of figure and extension, colour and sound, which we suppose to be permanent beings. The heat of a fire, when moderate, is suppos'd to exist in the fire; but the pain, which it causes upon a near approach, is not taken to have any being except in the perception.

These vulgar opinions, then, being rejected, we must search for some other hypothesis, by which we may discover those peculiar qualities in our impressions, which makes us attribute to them a distinct and continu'd existence.

After a little examination, we shall find, that all those objects, to which we attribute a continu'd existence, have a peculiar *constancy*, which distinguishes them from the impressions, whose existence depends upon our perception. Those mountains, and houses, and trees, which lie at present under my eye, have always appear'd to me in the same order; and when I lose sight of them by shutting my eyes or turning my head, I soon after find them return upon me without the least alteration. My bed and table, my books and papers, present themselves in the same uniform manner, and change not upon account of any interruption in my seeing or perceiving them. This is the case with all the impressions, whose objects are suppos'd to have an external existence; and is the case with no other impressions, whether gentle or violent, voluntary or involuntary.

This constancy, however, is not so perfect as not to admit of very considerable exceptions. Bodies often change their position and qualities, and after a little absence or interruption may become hardly knowable. But here 'tis observable, that even in these changes they preserve a *coherence*, and have a regular dependence on each other; which is the foundation of a kind of reasoning from causation, and produces the opinion of their continu'd existence. When I return to my chamber[5] after an hour's absence, I find not my fire in the same situation, in which I left it: But then I am accustom'd in other instances to see a like alteration produc'd in a like time, whether I am present or absent, near or remote. This coherence, therefore, in their changes is one of the characteristics of external objects, as well as their constancy.

Having found that the opinion of the continu'd existence of body depends on the COHERENCE and CONSTANCY of certain impressions, I now proceed to examine after what manner these qualities give rise to so extraordinary an opinion. To begin

---

5. Private room.

with the coherence; we may observe, that tho' those internal impressions, which we regard as fleeting and perishing, have also a certain coherence or regularity in their appearances, yet 'tis of somewhat a different nature, from that which we discover in bodies. Our passions[6] are found by experience to have a mutual connexion with and dependence on each other; but on no occasion is it necessary to suppose, that they have existed and operated, when they were not perceiv'd, in order to preserve the same dependence and connexion, of which we have had experience. The case is not the same with relation to external objects. Those require a continu'd existence, or otherwise lose, in a great measure, the regularity of their operation. I am here seated in my chamber with my face to the fire; and all the objects, that strike my senses, are contain'd in a few yards around me. My memory, indeed, informs me of the existence of many objects; but then this information extends not beyond their past existence, nor do either my senses or memory give any testimony to the continuance of their being. When therefore I am thus seated, and revolve over these thoughts, I hear on a sudden a noise as of a door turning upon its hinges; and a little after see a porter, who advances towards me. This gives occasion to many new reflexions and reasonings. First, I never have observ'd, that this noise cou'd proceed from any thing but the motion of a door; and therefore conclude, that the present phenomenon is a contradiction to all past experience, unless the door, which I remember on t'other side the chamber, be still in being. Again, I have always found, that a human body was possest of a quality, which I call gravity, and which hinders it from mounting in the air, as this porter must have done to arrive at my chamber, unless the stairs I remember be not annihilated by my absence. But this is not all. I receive a letter, which upon opening it I perceive by the hand-writing and subscription to have come from a friend, who says he is two hundred leagues[7] distant. 'Tis evident I can never account for this phenomenon, conformable to my experience in other instances, without spreading out in my mind the whole sea and continent between us, and supposing the effects and continu'd existence of posts[8] and ferries, according to my memory and observation. To consider these phaenomena of the porter and letter in a certain light, they are contradictions to common experience, and may be regarded as objections to those maxims, which we form concerning the connexions of causes and effects. I am accustom'd to hear such a sound, and see such an object in motion at the same time. I have not receiv'd in this particular instance both these perceptions. These observations are contrary, unless I suppose that the door still remains, and that it was open'd without my perceiving it: And this supposition, which was at first entirely arbitrary and hypothetical, acquires a force and evidence by its being the only one, upon which I can reconcile these contradictions. There is scarce a moment of my life, wherein there is not a similar instance presented to me, and I have not occasion to suppose the continu'd existence of objects, in order to connect their past and present appearances, and give them such an union with each other, as I have found by experience to be

6. Desires, emotions, and feelings.

7. One league is approximately three miles.

8. Vehicles used to carry mail.

suitable to their particular natures and circumstances. Here then I am naturally led to regard the world, as something real and durable, and as preserving its existence, even when it is no longer present to my perception. . . .

Objects have a certain coherence even as they appear to our senses; but this coherence is much greater and more uniform, if we suppose the objects to have a continu'd existence; and as the mind is once in the train of observing an uniformity among objects, it naturally continues, till it renders the uniformity as compleat as possible. The simple supposition of their continu'd existence suffices for this purpose, and gives us a notion of a much greater regularity among objects, than what they have when we look no farther than our senses.

But whatever force we may ascribe to this principle, I am afraid 'tis too weak to support alone so vast an edifice, as is that of the continu'd existence of all external bodies; and that we must join the *constancy* of their appearance to the *coherence,* in order to give a satisfactory account of that opinion. . . .

'Tis indeed evident, that as the vulgar *suppose* their perceptions to be their only objects, and at the same time *believe* the continu'd existence of matter, we must account for the origin of the belief upon that supposition. Now upon that supposition, 'tis a false opinion that any of our objects, or perceptions, are identically the same after an interruption; and consequently the opinion of their identity can never arise from reason, but must arise from the imagination. The imagination is seduc'd into such an opinion only by means of the resemblance of certain perceptions; since we find they are only our resembling perceptions, which we have a propension[9] to suppose the same. This propension to bestow an identity on our resembling perceptions, produces the fiction of a continu'd existence; since that fiction, as well as the identity, is really false, as is acknowledg'd by all philosophers, and has no other effect than to remedy the interruption of our perceptions, which is the only circumstance that is contrary to their identity. In the last place this propension causes belief by means of the present impressions of the memory; since without the remembrance of former sensations, 'tis plain we never shou'd have any belief of the continu'd existence of body. . . .

But tho' we are led after this manner, by the natural propensity of the imagination, to ascribe a continu'd existence to those sensible objects or perceptions, which we find to resemble each other in their interrupted appearance; yet a very little reflection and philosophy is sufficient to make us perceive the fallacy of that opinion. I have already observ'd, that there is an intimate connexion betwixt those two principles, of a *continu'd* and of a *distinct* or *independent* existence, and that we no sooner establish the one than the other follows, as a necessary consequence. 'Tis the opinion of a continu'd existence, which first takes place, and without much study or reflection draws the other along with it, wherever the mind follows its first and most natural tendency. But when we compare experiments, and reason a little upon them, we quickly perceive, that the doctrine of the independent existence of our sensible perceptions is contrary to the plainest experience. This leads us backward upon our

9. Propensity.

footsteps to perceive our error in attributing a continu'd existence to our perceptions, and is the origin of many very curious opinions, which we shall here endeavour to account for.

'Twill first be proper to observe a few of those experiments, which convince us, that our perceptions are not possest of any independent existence. When we press one eye with a finger, we immediately perceive all the objects to become double, and one half of them to be remov'd from their common and natural position. But as we do not attribute a continu'd existence to both these perceptions, and as they are both of the same nature, we clearly perceive, that all our perceptions are dependent on our organs, and the disposition of our nerves and animal spirits. This opinion is confirm'd by the seeming increase and diminution of objects, according to their distance; by the apparent alterations in their figure; by the changes in their colour and other qualities from our sickness and distempers;[1] and by an infinite number of other experiments of the same kind; from all which we learn, that our sensible perceptions are not possest of any distinct or independent existence.

The natural consequence of this reasoning shou'd be, that our perceptions have no more a continu'd than an independent existence; and indeed philosophers have so far run into this opinion, that they change their system, and distinguish, (as we shall do for the future) betwixt perceptions and objects, of which the former are suppos'd to be interrupted, and perishing, and different at every different return; the latter to be uninterrupted, and to preserve a continu'd existence and identity. But however philosophical this new system may be esteem'd, I assert that 'tis only a palliative remedy, and that it contains all the difficulties of the vulgar system, with some others, that are peculiar to itself. There are no principles either of the understanding or fancy, which lead us directly to embrace this opinion of the double existence of perceptions and objects, nor can we arrive at it but by passing thro' the common hypothesis of the identity and continuance of our interrupted perceptions. Were we not first persuaded, that our perceptions are our only objects, and continue to exist even when they no longer make their appearance to the senses, we shou'd never be led to think, that our perceptions and objects are different, and that our objects alone preserve a continu'd existence. . . .

There is a great difference betwixt such opinions as we form after a calm and profound reflection, and such as we embrace by a kind of instinct or natural impulse, on account of their suitableness and conformity to the mind. If these opinions become contrary, 'tis not difficult to foresee which of them will have the advantage. As long as our attention is bent upon the subject, the philosophical and study'd principle may prevail; but the moment we relax our thoughts, nature will display herself, and draw us back to our former opinion. Nay she has sometimes such an influence, that she can stop our progress, even in the midst of our most profound reflections, and keep us from running on with all the consequences of any philosophical opinion. Thus tho' we clearly perceive the dependence and interruption of our perceptions, we stop short in our career, and never upon that account reject the notion of an independent

---

1. Illnesses.

and continu'd existence. That opinion has taken such deep root in the imagination, that 'tis impossible ever to eradicate it, nor will any strain'd metaphysical conviction of the dependence of our perceptions be sufficient for that purpose.

But tho' our natural and obvious principles here prevail above our study'd reflections, 'tis certain there must be some struggle and opposition in the case; at least so long as these reflections retain any force or vivacity. In order to set ourselves at ease in this particular, we contrive a new hypothesis, which seems to comprehend both these principles of reason and imagination. This hypothesis is the philosophical one of the double existence of perceptions and objects; which pleases our reason, in allowing, that our dependent perceptions are interrupted and different; and at the same time is agreeable to the imagination, in attributing a continu'd existence to something else, which we call *objects*. This philosophical system, therefore, is the monstrous offspring of two principles, which are contrary to each other, which are both at once embrac'd by the mind, and which are unable mutually to destroy each other. The imagination tells us, that our resembling perceptions have a continu'd and uninterrupted existence, and are not annihilated by their absence. Reflection tells us, that even our resembling perceptions are interrupted in their existence, and different from each other. The contradiction betwixt these opinions we elude by a new fiction, which is conformable to the hypotheses both of reflection and fancy, by ascribing these contrary qualities to different existences; the *interruption* to perceptions, and the *continuance* to objects. Nature is obstinate, and will not quit the field, however strongly attack'd by reason; and at the same time reason is so clear in the point, that there is no possibility of disguising her. Not being able to reconcile these two enemies, we endeavour to set ourselves at ease as much as possible, by successively granting to each whatever it demands, and by feigning a double existence, where each may find something, that has all the conditions it desires. Were we fully convinc'd, that our resembling perceptions are continu'd, and identical, and independent, we shou'd never run into this opinion of a double existence; since we shou'd find satisfaction in our first supposition, and wou'd not look beyond. Again, were we fully convinc'd, that our perceptions are dependent, and interrupted, and different, we shou'd be as little inclin'd to embrace the opinion of a double existence; since in that case we shou'd clearly perceive the error of our first supposition of a continu'd existence, and wou'd never regard it any farther. 'Tis therefore from the intermediate situation of the mind, that this opinion arises, and from such an adherence to these two contrary principles, as makes us seek some pretext to justify our receiving both; which happily at last is found in the system of a double existence.

Another advantage of this philosophical system is its similarity to the vulgar one; by which means we can humour our reason for a moment, when it becomes trouble-some and solicitous,[2] and yet upon its least negligence or inattention, can easily return to our vulgar and natural notions. Accordingly we find, that philosophers neglect not this advantage; but immediately upon leaving their closets, mingle with the rest of mankind in those exploded opinions, that our perceptions are our only objects, and continue identically and uninterruptedly the same in all their interrupted appearances.

2. Anxious.

## TEST YOUR UNDERSTANDING

1. This book exists when you are not seeing it. Given this, does Hume think that you sometimes see this book?

2. Hume examines whether it is the "senses, reason, or imagination" that explains why we believe in the continued and distinct existence of the objects that are present to our senses. Which one is it, according to Hume?

3. According to Hume, when "the vulgar" (i.e., ordinary people) see a thing X, they typically make a mistake about X. What is that mistake?

4. "This philosophical system, therefore, is the monstrous offspring of two principles, which are contrary to each other, which are both at once embrac'd by the mind, and which are unable mutually to destroy each other." What is "this philosophical system"? What are the "two principles"?

## NOTES AND QUESTIONS

1. Hume argues that the phenomenon of double vision shows that "our perceptions are not possest of any independent existence." What does Hume mean by "perception"? What does it mean to say that something has no "independent existence"? Set out Hume's argument in the form of premises and conclusion. Is the argument convincing?

2. What does Hume mean by "continued existence" and "distinct existence"? What connection does Hume find between the two? What is his explanation of how the "coherence" and "constancy" of "certain impressions" give rise to our belief in the continued existence of tomatoes, trees, tables, and so on? Is his proposed explanation correct?

3. The selection omits parts of Hume's complicated psychological explanation of "what causes induce us to believe in the existence of body." For discussion of this, see Barry Stroud, *Hume* (Routledge, 1981), chapter 5, and Harold Noonan, *Hume* (Oneworld, 2007), chapter 4.

## George Edward Moore (1873–1958)

Moore was an English philosopher who taught at the University of Cambridge for most of his career. He was a central figure in analytic philosophy, a philosophical tradition that dominated academic philosophy in Britain, the United States and Australia in the twentieth century. Moore wrote a seminal book on ethics, *Principia Ethica* (1903), and a number of classic articles on philosophy of mind and epistemology.

# PROOF OF AN EXTERNAL WORLD

In the Preface to the second edition of Kant's *Critique of Pure Reason*[1] some words occur, which, in Professor Kemp Smith's translation, are rendered as follows:

> It still remains a scandal to philosophy . . . that the existence of things outside of us . . . must be accepted merely on *faith,* and that, if anyone thinks good to doubt their existence, we are unable to counter his doubts by any satisfactory proof.

It seems clear from these words that Kant thought it a matter of some importance to give a proof of "the existence of things outside of us" or perhaps rather (for it seems to me possible that the force of the German words is better rendered in this way) of "the existence of *the* things outside of us"; for had he not thought it important that a proof should be given, he would scarcely have called it a "scandal" that no proof had been given. And it seems clear also that he thought that the giving of such a proof was a task which fell properly within the province of philosophy; for, if it did not, the fact that no proof had been given could not possibly be a scandal to *philosophy.*

Now, even if Kant was mistaken in both of these two opinions, there seems to me to be no doubt whatever that it is a matter of some importance and also a matter which falls properly within the province of philosophy, to discuss the question what sort of proof, if any, can be given of "the existence of things outside of us." And to discuss this question was my object when I began to write the present lecture. But I may say at once that, as you will find, I have only, at most, succeeded in saying a very small part of what ought to be said about it.

The words "it . . . remains a scandal to philosophy . . . that we are unable . . ." would, taken strictly, imply that, at the moment at which he wrote them, Kant himself was unable to produce a satisfactory proof of the point in question. But I think it is unquestionable that Kant himself did not think that he personally was at the time unable to produce such a proof. On the contrary, in the immediately preceding sentence, he has declared that he has, in the second edition of his *Critique,* to which he is now writing the Preface, given a "rigorous proof" of this very thing; and has added that he believes this proof of his to be the only possible proof. . . .

If, therefore, it were certain that the proof of the point in question given by Kant in the second edition is a satisfactory proof, it would be certain that at least one satisfactory proof can be given; and all that would remain of the question which I said I proposed to discuss would be, firstly, the question as to what *sort* of a proof this of Kant's is, and secondly the question whether (contrary to Kant's own opinion) there may not perhaps be other proofs, of the same or of a different sort, which are also satisfactory. But I think

---

1. The most famous of the German philosopher Immanuel Kant's (1724–1804) three "Critiques": the other two are the *Critique of Practical Reason* (about ethics) and the *Critique of Judgment* (about aesthetics).

it is by no means certain that Kant's proof is satisfactory. I think it is by no means certain that he did succeed in removing once for all the state of affairs which he considered to be a scandal to philosophy. And I think, therefore, that the question whether it is possible to give *any* satisfactory proof of the point in question still deserves discussion.

But what is the point in question? I think it must be owned that the expression "things outside of us" is rather an odd expression, and an expression the meaning of which is certainly not perfectly clear. It would have sounded less odd if, instead of "things outside of us" I had said "external things," and perhaps also the meaning of this expression would have seemed to be clearer; and I think we make the meaning of "external things" clearer still if we explain that this phrase has been regularly used by philosophers as short for "things external to *our minds*." The fact is that there has been a long philosophical tradition, in accordance with which the three expressions "external things," "things external to *us*," and "things external to *our minds*" have been used as equivalent to one another, and have, each of them, been used as if they needed no explanation. The origin of this usage I do not know. It occurs already in Descartes; and since he uses the expressions as if they needed no explanation, they had presumably been used with the same meaning before. Of the three, it seems to me that the expression "external to *our minds*" is the clearest, since it at least makes clear that what is meant is not "external to *our bodies*"; whereas both the other expressions might be taken to mean this: and indeed there has been a good deal of confusion, even among philosophers, as to the relation of the two conceptions "external things" and "things external to *our bodies*." But even the expression "things external to our minds" seems to me to be far from perfectly clear.[2] . . .

It seems to me that, so far from its being true, as Kant declares to be his opinion, that there is only one possible proof of the existence of things outside of us, namely the one which he has given, I can now give a large number of different proofs, each of which is a perfectly rigorous proof; and that at many other times I have been in a position to give many others. I can prove now, for instance, that two human hands exist. How? By holding up my two hands, and saying, as I make a certain gesture with the right hand, "Here is one hand," and adding, as I make a certain gesture with the left, "and here is another." And if, by doing this, I have proved *ipso facto*[3] the existence of external things, you will all see that I can also do it now in numbers of other ways: there is no need to multiply examples.

But did I prove just now that two human hands were then in existence? I do want to insist that I did; that the proof which I gave was a perfectly rigorous one; and that it is perhaps impossible to give a better or more rigorous proof of anything whatever. Of course, it would not have been a proof unless three conditions were satisfied; namely (1) unless the premiss which I adduced as proof of the conclusion was different from the conclusion I adduced it to prove; (2) unless the premiss which

---

2. Moore then spends many pages investigating what this expression might mean. He finally concludes that to say that some thing is "external to our minds" is to say that "there is no contradiction in supposing [it] to exist at a time when [we] are having no experiences."

3. By that very fact (Latin).

I adduced was something which I *knew* to be the case, and not merely something which I believed but which was by no means certain, or something which, though in fact true, I did not know to be so; and (3) unless the conclusion did really follow from the premiss. But all these three conditions were in fact satisfied by my proof. (1) The premiss which I adduced in proof was quite certainly different from the conclusion, for the conclusion was merely "Two human hands exist at this moment"; but the premiss was something far more specific than this — something which I expressed by showing you my hands, making certain gestures, and saying the words "Here is one hand, and here is another." It is quite obvious that the two were different, because it is quite obvious that the conclusion might have been true, even if the premiss had been false. In asserting the premiss I was asserting much more than I was asserting in asserting the conclusion. (2) I certainly did at the moment *know* that which I expressed by the combination of certain gestures with saying the words "There is one hand and here is another." I *knew* that there was one hand in the place indicated by combining a certain gesture with my first utterance of "here" and that there was another in the different place indicated by combining a certain gesture with my second utterance of "here." How absurd it would be to suggest that I did not know it, but only believed it, and that perhaps it was not the case! You might as well suggest that I do not know that I am now standing up and talking — that perhaps after all I'm not, and that it's not quite certain that I am! And finally (3) it is quite certain that the conclusion did follow from the premiss. This is as certain as it is that if there is one hand here and another here *now*, then it follows that there are two hands in existence *now*.

My proof, then, of the existence of things outside of us did satisfy three of the conditions necessary for a rigorous proof. Are there any other conditions necessary for a rigorous proof, such that perhaps it did not satisfy one of them? Perhaps there may be; I do not know; but I do want to emphasize that, so far as I can see, we all of us do constantly take proofs of this sort as absolutely conclusive proofs of certain conclusions — as finally settling certain questions, as to which we were previously in doubt. Suppose, for instance, it were a question whether there were as many as three misprints on a certain page in a certain book. A says there are, B is inclined to doubt it. How could A prove that he is right? Surely he *could* prove it by taking the book, turning to the page, and pointing to three separate places on it, saying "There's one misprint here, another here, and another here": surely that is a method by which it *might* be proved! Of course, A would not have proved, by doing this, that there were at least three misprints on the page in question, unless it was certain that there was a misprint in each of the places to which he pointed. But to say that he *might* prove it in this way, is to say that it *might* be certain that there was. And if such a thing as that could ever be certain, then assuredly it was certain just now that there was one hand in one of the two places I indicated and another in the other.

I did, then, just now, give a proof that there were *then* external objects; and obviously, if I did, I could then have given many other proofs of the same sort that there were external objects *then*, and could now give many proofs of the same sort that there are external objects *now*.

But, if what I am asked to do is to prove that external objects have existed *in the past*, then I can give many different proofs of this also, but proofs which are in important respects of a different *sort* from those just given. And I want to emphasize that, when Kant says it is a scandal not to be able to give a proof of the existence of external objects, a proof of their existence in the past would certainly *help* to remove the scandal of which he is speaking. He says that, if it occurs to anyone to question their existence, we ought to be able to confront him with a satisfactory proof. But by a person who questions their existence, he certainly means not merely a person who questions whether any exist at the moment of speaking, but a person who questions whether any have *ever* existed; and a proof that some have existed in the past would certainly therefore be relevant to *part* of what such a person is questioning. How then can I prove that there have been external objects in the past? Here is one proof. I can say: "I held up two hands above this desk not very long ago; therefore two hands existed not very long ago; therefore at least two external objects have existed at some time in the past, Q.E.D."[4] This is a perfectly good proof, provided I *know* what is asserted in the premiss. But I *do* know that I held up two hands above this desk not very long ago. As a matter of fact, in this case you all know it too. There's no doubt whatever that I did. Therefore I have given a perfectly conclusive proof that external objects have existed in the past; and you will all see at once that, if this is a conclusive proof, I could have given many others of the same sort, and could now give many others. But it is also quite obvious that this sort of proof differs in important respects from the sort of proof I gave just now that there were two hands existing *then*.

I have, then, given two conclusive proofs of the existence of external objects. The first was a proof that two human hands existed at the time when I gave the proof; the second was a proof that two human hands had existed at a time previous to that at which I gave the proof. These proofs were of a different sort in important respects. And I pointed out that I could have given, then, many other conclusive proofs of both sorts. It is also obvious that I could give many others of both sorts now. So that, if these are the sort of proof that is wanted, nothing is easier than to prove the existence of external objects.

But now I am perfectly well aware that, in spite of all that I have said, many philosophers will still feel that I have not given any satisfactory proof of the point in question. And I want briefly, in conclusion, to say something as to why this dissatisfaction with my proofs should be felt.

One reason why, is, I think, this. Some people understand "proof of an external world" as including a proof of things which I haven't attempted to prove and haven't proved. It is not quite easy to say *what* it is that they want proved — what it is that is such that unless they got a proof of it, they would not say that they had a proof of the existence of external things; but I can make an approach to explaining what they want by saying that if I had proved the propositions which I used as *premisses* in my two proofs, then they would perhaps admit that I had proved the existence of external things, but, in the absence of such a proof (which, of course, I have neither

---

4. *Quod erat demonstrandum,* Latin for "which was to be demonstrated."

given nor attempted to give), they will say that I have not given what they mean by a proof of the existence of external things. In other words, they want a proof of what I assert *now* when I hold up my hands and say "Here's one hand and here's another"; and, in the other case, they want a proof of what I assert *now* when I say "I did hold up two hands above this desk just now." Of course, what they really want is not merely a proof of these two propositions, but something like a general statement as to how *any* propositions of this sort may be proved. This, of course, I haven't given; and I do not believe it can be given: if this is what is meant by proof of the existence of external things, I do not believe that any proof of the existence of external things is possible. Of course, in some cases what might be called a proof of propositions which seem like these can be got. If one of you suspected that one of my hands was artificial he might be said to get a proof of my proposition "Here's one hand, and here's another," by coming up and examining the suspected hand close up, perhaps touching and pressing it, and so establishing that it really was a human hand. But I do not believe that any proof is possible in nearly all cases. How am I to prove now that "Here's one hand, and here's another"? I do not believe I can do it. In order to do it, I should need to prove for one thing, as Descartes pointed out, that I am not now dreaming.[5] But how can I prove that I am not? I have, no doubt, conclusive reasons for asserting that I am not now dreaming; I have conclusive evidence that I am awake: but that is a very different thing from being able to prove it. I could not tell you what all my evidence is; and I should require to do this at least, in order to give you a proof.

But another reason why some people would feel dissatisfied with my proofs is, I think, not merely that they want a proof of something which I haven't proved, but that they think that, if I cannot give such extra proofs, then the proofs that I have given are not conclusive proofs at all. And this, I think, is a definite mistake. They would say: "If you cannot prove your premiss that here is one hand and here is another, then you do not know it. But you yourself have admitted that, if you did not know it, then your proof was not conclusive. Therefore your proof was not, as you say it was, a conclusive proof." This view that, if I cannot prove such things as these, I do not know them, is, I think, the view that Kant was expressing in the sentence which I quoted at the beginning of this lecture, when he implies that so long as we have no proof of the existence of external things, their existence must be accepted merely on *faith*. He means to say, I think, that if I cannot prove that there is a hand here, I must accept it merely as a matter of faith — I cannot know it. Such a view, though it has been very common among philosophers, can, I think, be shown to be wrong — though shown only by the use of premisses which are not known to be true, unless we do know of the existence of external things. I can know things, which I cannot prove; and among things which I certainly did know, even if (as I think) I could not prove them, were the premisses of my two proofs. I should say, therefore, that those, if any, who are dissatisfied with these proofs merely on the ground that I did not know their premisses, have no good reason for their dissatisfaction.

5. See Descartes's *Meditation I* earlier in this chapter.

## TEST YOUR UNDERSTANDING

1. Does Moore think that one has proved a conclusion from some premises only if one knows the premises?

2. Does Moore think that one has proved a conclusion from some premises only if one is able to prove the premises?

3. Why does Moore think that the premises of his proofs are different from their conclusions?

4. "It is snowing, therefore it is snowing" is a valid **argument** (see the "Guide to Logic and Argumentation" in the back of this anthology). Suppose I know that it is snowing, and argue from the premise that it is snowing to the conclusion that it is snowing. Does Moore think I have proved that it is snowing?

## NOTES AND QUESTIONS

1. Consider the following argument:

   P1. I am wide awake.

   P2. If I am wide awake, then I am not dreaming.

   C. I am not dreaming.

   Can you use this argument to prove that you are not dreaming? If not, why not? Moore says he can't prove that he is "not now dreaming." Are his reasons persuasive?

## Stewart Cohen (born 1952)

Cohen is Professor of Philosophy at the University of Arizona, the editor of the journal *Philosophical Studies*, and the author of many influential articles on epistemology.

# CONTEXTUALISM

## 1. Skeptical Paradoxes

We take ourselves to know a great deal about the world around us. But if we begin to think reflectively about what we know, we can find ourselves involved in paradox. Consider a mundane example. Suppose someone asks me if I know where my car is. Because I remember having parked my car in lot 2, I would not hesitate to answer that I do know where my car is. Suppose I am also asked whether I know that my car has not been stolen. Though I think that this has probably not happened, I would have to admit that I do not know it has not happened. A paradox arises because it is hard to see how I could know that my car is parked in lot 2 unless I know it has not been stolen. This latter thought derives from the intuitively compelling idea that is sometimes called the "deductive closure principle for knowledge":

> If I know P and that P entails Q, then I know (or at least, am in a position to know) Q.

Because my car's being in lot 2 entails that it has not been stolen (and removed from lot 2), it follows by this principle that I know that my car is in lot 2 only if I know it has not been stolen.

These considerations leave us with three propositions, each of which seems difficult to deny:

(1) I know my car is parked in lot 2.

(2) I do not know that my car has not been stolen.

(3) If I know my car is parked in lot 2, then I know my car has not been stolen.

A paradox arises because these propositions form an inconsistent triad. That is to say, it is impossible for all three of them to be true. This means that although each proposition seems compelling, we must give up at least one of them. A skeptic about knowledge would argue that we should deny (1). According to the skeptic, the truth of (2) and (3) gives us good reason to deny (1).

We can construct analogous arguments against almost any claim to know. For example, I do not know that I will be in Europe tomorrow, because I do not know the plane I am traveling on will not crash. And I do not know I will never be a multimillionaire, because I do not know I will never win the lottery. This way of viewing matters leads to the conclusion that we fail to know many of the things we take ourselves to know. Such a view about what we know is called "skepticism."

If we wish to avoid this skeptical result, we have two options. First we can argue that (2) is false. But this position seems hard to sustain. While I have some statistical evidence that my car has not been stolen, that does not seem sufficient for me to *know* that my car has not been stolen.

The other option for avoiding the skeptical result is to deny (3). Denying (3) would mean denying the deductive closure principle for knowledge. But it seems very puzzling how this principle could be false. How could I know one proposition, know that it entails a second proposition, yet fail (to at least be in a position) to know the second proposition? In the case we have been considering, how could I know that my car is parked in lot 2, if I do not know that it has not been stolen?

None of these options for responding to the inconsistent triad seems palatable. Of course, this just underscores that we are confronting a paradox.

The hypothesis that my car has been stolen threatens my knowledge of a very limited set of propositions, e.g., my car is parked in lot 2, my car is where I left it, etc. A more radical skepticism threatens when we consider what are sometimes called "global skeptical hypotheses." Global skeptical hypotheses threaten all or at least most of our claims to know things about the world around us. Consider the hypothesis that I am in the matrix, or that I am a brain-in-a-vat being stimulated to have the very sensory experiences I am now having. Do I know these skeptical hypotheses are false? If I am a brain-in-a-vat, I would be having exactly the same experiences I am now having. This means that there is nothing I can point to as evidence that I am not a brain-in-a-vat. How then could I ever know that I am not a brain-in-a-vat? But if I do not know I am not a brain-in-a-vat, then it looks as if I know nothing about the world. If I do not know I am not a brain-in-a-vat, then I do not even know that I have a hand. This follows from the deductive closure principle for knowledge because my having a hand entails that I am not a brain-in-a-vat.

The skeptical doubts engendered by global skeptical hypotheses result in the same kind of skeptical paradox that arises in the car theft case:

(4) I know I have a hand.

(5) I do not know I am not a brain-in-a-vat.

(6) If I know I have a hand, then I do not know I am not a brain-in-a-vat.

Again, it seems hard to deny either (5) or (6), and so the truth of (4) is threatened. But the paradox based on the global skeptical hypothesis threatens all of our knowledge. We can substitute any empirical proposition for the proposition that I have a hand, and the same paradox will arise. This makes it hard to see how we can know anything about the world around us.

# 2. Contextualism

The skeptical paradoxes we have considered raise the issue of exactly what it takes to know that a certain proposition P is true. Almost everyone agrees that in order to know P, one must have good evidence to believe P, i.e., evidence that is sufficient to make one justified in believing P. But how justified in believing P does one have to be in order to know P? We can see how this issue might arise by considering a hypothetical case:

Mary and John are at the L.A. airport contemplating taking a certain flight to New York. They want to know whether the flight has a layover in Chicago. They overhear someone ask a passenger Smith if he knows whether the flight stops in Chicago. Smith looks at the flight itinerary he got from the travel agent and responds, "Yes I know — it does stop in Chicago." It turns out that Mary and

John have a very important business contact they have to make at the Chicago airport. Mary says, "How reliable is that itinerary? It could contain a misprint. They could have changed the schedule at the last minute. Smith does not know the plane stops in Chicago." John agrees with Mary and they decide to check with the airline agent.[1]

In this case, Smith claims to know that the flight stops in Chicago, but Mary and John deny that Smith knows this. Mary and John seem to be using a stricter standard than Smith for how good one's reasons have to be in order to know something. Invariantism is the view that the standards for knowing are always the same for everyone. Therefore, the invariant must answer the question: Whose standard for knowing is correct — Smith's or John and Mary's? We can consider several competing answers:

1. Mary and John's stricter standard is too strong, i.e., Smith's standard is correct and so Smith can know the flight stops in Chicago (on the basis of consulting the itinerary).

Can this answer be defended? If the weaker standard is correct, then John and Mary are using the word "know" incorrectly. But then what would be the correct way for them to describe their situation? Certainly they are being prudent in refusing to rely on the itinerary. They have a very important meeting in Chicago. Yet if Smith knows on the basis of the itinerary that the flight stops in Chicago, what should they have said — "Okay, Smith knows that the flight stops in Chicago, but still, we need to check further"? It is difficult to make sense of such a claim. Moreover, if what is printed in the itinerary is good enough evidence for Smith to know, then it is good enough evidence for John and Mary to know. So if the weaker standard is correct, then Mary should have said, "Okay, *we* know the plane stops in Chicago, but still, we need to check further." Again it is hard to make sense of such a claim.

Perhaps then the correct answer is:

2. John and Mary are right and so Smith's standard is too weak. (Smith cannot know, but John and Mary can know — after checking further with the agent.)

This is a natural response to this case as I have described it. But this contrasts with the standards we typically use for knowledge ascriptions. In everyday contexts, we readily ascribe knowledge to someone on the basis of written information contained in sources like flight itineraries. If we deny that Smith knows, then we have to hold that many of our everyday knowledge ascriptions that we thought are true, are in fact false. Moreover, we could describe a case where even Mary and John's standard does not seem strict enough: If someone's life were at stake, we might not even be willing to ascribe knowledge on the basis of the testimony of the airline agent. We might insist on checking with the pilot. This suggests a third alternative.

1. S. Cohen, "Contextualism, Skepticism, and the Structure of Reasons," *Philosophical Perspectives* 13 (1999): 57–89. [Cohen's note.]

3.  Both Smith's standard and Mary and John's standard are too weak.

Like the skeptical paradoxes we considered about, this option leads to skepticism regarding a great deal of what we ordinarily claim to know.

None of the answers to our question we have considered seems satisfactory. Perhaps we need to reexamine some of the assumptions we have been making about knowledge. One such assumption is the invariantist assumption that the standards for knowing are always the same for everyone. If we ask how much one must be justified in believing a proposition in order to know that proposition, the invariantist answers that the amount is always the same. Particular invariantists may disagree on what the invariant standards are. While we tend to assume that the invariant standards for knowing allow us to have lots of knowledge, a skeptical invariantist may hold that the invariant standards are high enough to prevent us from knowing anything.

Contextualism is the denial of invariantism. According to contextualism, the standards for knowing, i.e., the standards for how justified one must be in believing P in order to know P, depend on the context. But what is the context? While "context" is used by philosophers in different ways, the relevant notion for our purposes is the context of ascription (also sometimes called "context of use"). Suppose I say, "You know that Paris is the capital of France." Here I am ascribing knowledge to you, i.e., asserting that you know something. According to contextualism, it is the context of the person ascribing knowledge that determines the standard of justification required for knowledge. As the ascriber of knowledge, certain facts about my situation determine the standard your justification must meet, in order for me to truly say, "You know that Paris is the capital of France." According to contextualism, if someone else were to ascribe knowledge to you, then facts about his or her context would determine the standard your justification must meet in order for him or her to truly say, "You know Paris is the capital of France." So what separates contextualism from invariantism is the claim that in different contexts, different standards for knowing apply. In some contexts, the standards will be stronger, and in other contexts, the standards will be weaker.

Sometimes I may ascribe knowledge to myself, as in the case where I say, "I know my car is parked in lot 2." Again, because I am doing the ascribing (in this case to myself) it is my context that determines the standard for knowing. Were you to say of me, "He does not know his car is parked in lot 2," then because you are the one ascribing knowledge to me, the relevant standard would be determined by your context.

Recall our question concerning the case of John and Mary. Which standard is the correct one for evaluating whether they know the plane stops in Chicago — Smith's weaker standard, or John and Mary's stronger standard? According to contextualism, neither standard is simply correct or incorrect. Because the standards for knowledge ascriptions can vary across contexts, each claim, Smith's as well as Mary's, can be correct in the context in which it was made. When Smith says, "I know the plane stops in Chicago," what he says is true given the weaker standard operating in his context. When Mary says "Smith does not know the plane stops in Chicago," what she says is true given the stricter standard operating in her context. And crucially, according to contextualism, there is no context-independent correct standard.

Fundamentally, contextualism is a semantic thesis, that is, a thesis about the meaning of the word "know" and its cognates. It says that "know" is context-sensitive. Consider a paradigm of context-sensitivity, the word "I". Depending on the context of use, it refers to different individuals. So when I say "I am cold," "I" refers to me, and when you say "I am not cold," "I" refers to you. Even though the form of the sentence you use to make your assertion is the denial of the form of the sentence I use to make my assertion, we are not disagreeing.

Many words are thought to be context-sensitive in this way. Suppose someone from Colorado says that a certain road is flat while someone from Kansas says that same road is not flat. Are they disagreeing? They need not be if the standards for flatness depend on the context of the person saying that the road is flat. People from Kansas will tend to have stricter standards for how flat a road has to be in order for it to be flat than will people from Colorado. So the person from Colorado and the person from Kansas are actually saying different things about the road. The person from Colorado is saying the road is flat relative to weak standards, and the person from Kansas is saying the road if flat relative to stricter standards. Although they may appear to be disagreeing, each could be saying something true.

According to contextualism, "know" (and its cognates) is context-sensitive in just this way. Like "flat", we can think of different uses of "know" as involving different standards. These standards govern how justified one has to be in order to know. In some contexts, stricter standards will be in effect, and in other contexts, weaker standards will be in effect. This means that contextualism has the following striking feature: Holding fixed subject S, the proposition P, and time t, it will be possible for one ascriber to say "S knows P at t," and for another to say "S does not know P at t," and for both ascriptions to be true. This can happen because the subject's level of justification may meet the standard of one context, but fall short of the standard of the other context.

# 3. Contextualism and Skeptical Paradoxes

Consider again the skeptical paradoxes with which we began. A successful resolution of these paradoxes must do more than argue that one of the propositions comprised by the paradox is false. This would leave us with the question of why it seems intuitively true. A successful resolution of the paradox must not only deny one proposition from the inconsistent triad, it must explain why we mistakenly thought the proposition was true.

This is just what contextualism purports to do. According to contextualism, the sentences that express the inconsistent triad are not true or false independent of a particular context. Rather, each will be true at some contexts and false at others. According to contextualism, the paradox results from our shifting contexts as we consider the different members of the inconsistent triad. I start off at an everyday context at which my justification is strong enough for (1) to be true. At that context, my justification is strong enough for (2) to be false, as well. But when I actually consider (2), I shift to a context governed by stricter standards. My justification fails to meet the strict standards of this new context. So at this strict context, (2) is true and (1) is false. So according to contextualism, at ordinary contexts (1) is true and (2) is false, and at stricter contexts, (1) is false and (2) is true. And there is no context at which both (1) and (2) are true. So (3) remains true at every context.

In this way, contextualism can explain why each proposition of the triad seems true, while still holding that at every context, at least one member of the triad is false. Although (1) is false at stricter contexts, its intuitive appeal results from our considering it at an ordinary context. And although (2) is false at ordinary contexts, the appeal of (2) results from our considering it at a stricter context. The fact that (3) is true at every context reflects the status of the closure principle as a fundamental principle about knowledge.

Contextualism can use the same strategy for skeptical paradoxes involving global skeptical hypotheses:

(4) I know I have a hand.

(5) I do not know I am not a brain-in-a-vat.

(6) If I know I have a hand, then I do not know I am not a brain-in-a-vat.

According to contextualism, at everyday contexts (4) is true and (5) is false. At stricter contexts, (4) is false and (5) is true. And (6) is true at every context.

In the case of global skeptical hypotheses, an issue remains as to how I can know they are false even relative to everyday standards.

# 4. The Mechanism of Context Shifting

We have seen that contextualism holds that different contexts of ascription can have different standards for the truth of sentences containing "know" and its cognates. In particular we have seen that certain contexts have standards that are stricter than the standards of typical or ordinary contexts. What explains why some contexts have stricter standards? While contextualist theories differ on details, a common thread is that the salience of error possibilities in a context tends to drive up the standards. Consider again the case of John and Mary at the airport. When, in response to a normal query, Smith consults his flight itinerary and says, "I know the plane stops in Chicago," intuitively what he says is true. As we noted earlier, we readily allow that we can come to know things on the basis of written information contained in things like flight itineraries. But when we consider the situation of John and Mary, intuitively they speak truly when they say, "Smith does not know the plane stops in Chicago." We can appeal to the mechanism of salience to explain the shift. Because it is very important to John and Mary whether the plane stops in Chicago, error possibilities become salient to them. It is very natural for John and Mary to think about the possibility that the itinerary contains a misprint, that the route has changed, etc. Because these error possibilities are salient, the standards rise so that when Mary says, "Smith does not know the plane stops in Chicago," what she says is true.

We can also explain how the skeptical paradox arises by appealing to the salience of error possibilities. We normally allow that we can express mundane truths by saying things like "I know my car is parked in lot 2." Given closure, if I know my car is parked in lot 2, then I know, or at least am in a position to know, that my car has not been stolen. But when we actually consider (2), the possibility that my car has been stolen becomes salient. This raises the standards to the point where "I know my car has not been stolen" and "I know my car is parked in lot 2" are false. So we end up evaluating sentence (2) of the skeptical paradox at a higher standard than the standard at which we initially evaluated sentence (1). Once we are in the high standards context, sentence (1) will be false. But common sense can reassert itself and lead us to shift back to a context where (1) is true and (2) is false. Positing these kinds of contextual shifts explains why we often vacillate between skepticism and common sense.

## 5. Semantic Blindness

According to contextualism, skeptical paradoxes arise because we mistakenly think that certain knowledge ascriptions conflict. For example, we mistakenly think that my utterance "I do not know my car is parked in lot 2" made in a high standards context conflicts with my utterance "I know my car is parked in lot 2" made in an every-day low standards context. Similarly, in the airport case, we mistakenly think Mary's utterance of "Smith does not know the plane stops in Chicago" conflicts with Smith's utterance of "I know the plane stops in Chicago." Thus the contextualist is committed to the view that although sentences of the form "S knows P" are context-sensitive, competent speakers are unaware of this fact. Although their knowledge ascriptions track shifts in context, these speakers are unaware that this is occurring. This phenomenon has come to be called "semantic blindness."[2]

Some philosophers find this semantic blindness thesis to be implausible.[3] If "know" is context-sensitive, competent speakers should be aware of it. What can the contextualist say in defense of the semantic blindness thesis? First of all we can note that semantic blindness exists for other terms in natural language. Consider "flat." By pointing out that microscopic deviations from perfect flatness exist in all physical surfaces, one can get competent speakers to deny that any physical surface is flat.[4] Should we worry that all along we have been speaking falsely when we have called things "flat"? A little reflection will convince most that ascriptions of flatness

---

2. J. Hawthorne, *Knowledge and Lotteries* (Oxford University Press, 2004). [Cohen's note.]

3. S. Schiffer, "Contextualist Solutions to Skepticism," *Proceedings of the Aristotelian Society* 96 (1996): 317–33. [Cohen's note.]

4. P. Unger, *Ignorance: A Case for Scepticism* (Oxford University Press, 1975). [Cohen's note.]

are relative to context-sensitive standards. Flatness comes in degrees, and how flat a surface must be in order to count as flat *simpliciter*[5] depends on the context. When we are in the kind of strict context induced by the previous considerations, an utterance of "Nothing is flat" can be true. But the truth of this utterance does not conflict with an utterance of the form "X is flat" made at an everyday context.

When we are in the grip of "flatness skepticism," we are inclined to deny the truth of our previous utterances of the form "X is flat." That is to say, we mistakenly think our utterance of "Nothing is flat" conflicts with our (and others') previous utterances of the form "X is flat." And this is exactly the same kind of mistake the contextualist attributes to us regarding "knows." So it appears that competent speakers can be blind to the context-sensitivity of a term in their own language. This lends credibility to the contextualist's claim that competent speakers are semantically blind with respect to "know."

There is, however, an important disanalogy between our semantic blindness with respect to "know" and our semantic blindness with respect to "flat." As we noted, contextualist theories of flatness ascriptions gain easy acceptance for most people. But contextualist theories of knowledge do not. So the claim that ascriptions of knowledge are context-sensitive requires positing a much higher degree of semantic blindness than does the claim that ascriptions of flatness are context-sensitive. This is a theoretical cost for the contextualist. For one wonders whether it is plausible to attribute such a high degree of semantic blindness to competent speakers.

Whether or not contextualism can provide an adequate treatment of the skeptical paradoxes will depend in part on whether the semantic blindness problem can be handled.

## TEST YOUR UNDERSTANDING

1. Here are three claims about Cohen's example of Mary, John, and Smith. Which one(s) does Cohen agree with?

   (i)   Smith knows that the plane stops in Chicago and Mary doesn't.

   (ii)  When Smith says "I know that the plane stops in Chicago" and Mary says "Smith doesn't know that the plane stops in Chicago," they are disagreeing, in the sense that they can't both be speaking truly.

   (iii) Both Smith and Mary are speaking truly, and so are not disagreeing.

2. In the philosophy lecture on skepticism, when the instructor has just argued that you can't know you have a hand because you don't know that you're not a (handless) brain in a vat, you raise your hand and protest, "But I do know that I have a hand!" Does Cohen think that you spoke truly?

3. Suppose you wake up in the hospital after an operation for severe frostbite. Beforehand, the surgeons were debating whether they would have to amputate your hands and your feet. When you wake, you can't see or feel your feet. You

5. Simply (Latin).

wave your intact right hand in front of your face. "Phew!" you say, "I don't know whether I have feet, but at least I know that I have a hand!" Does Cohen think you spoke truly?

## NOTES AND QUESTIONS

1. What is "semantic blindness"? Explain why the contextualist solution to skepticism requires attributing "a high degree of semantic blindness to competent speakers." Why is this a problem for the contextualist? Is this problem serious, or does the contextualist have a plausible reply?

2. Consider the following two cases, due to Keith DeRose:

   *Bank Case A.* My wife and I are driving home on a Friday afternoon. We plan to stop at the bank on the way home to deposit our paychecks. But as we drive past the bank, we notice that the lines inside are very long, as they often are on Friday afternoons. Although we generally like to deposit our paychecks as soon as possible, it is not especially important in this case that they be deposited right away, so I suggest that we drive straight home and deposit our paychecks on Saturday morning. My wife says, "Maybe the bank won't be open tomorrow. Lots of banks are closed on Saturdays." I reply, "No, I know it'll be open. I was just there two weeks ago on Saturday. It's open until noon."

   *Bank Case B.* My wife and I drive past the bank on a Friday afternoon, as in Case A, and notice the long lines. I again suggest that we deposit our paychecks on Saturday morning, explaining that I was at the bank on Saturday morning only two weeks ago and discovered that it was open until noon. But in this case, we have just written a very large and very important check. If our paychecks are not deposited into our checking account before Monday morning, the important check we wrote will bounce, leaving us in a very bad situation. And, of course, the bank is not open on Sunday. My wife reminds me of these facts. She then says, "Banks do change their hours. Do you know the bank will be open tomorrow?" Remaining as confident as I was before that the bank will be open then, still, I reply, "Well, no. I'd better go in and make sure."[1]

   It might seem that DeRose is correct in Case A when he says "I know [the bank] will be open [tomorrow]" and that he is *also* correct in Case B when he replies "No" to his wife's question "Do you know the bank will be open?" Explain how this might be held to support contextualism, and how a contextualist would describe the two cases. How might a non-contextualist describe the two cases? Which is the more plausible description?

---

1. Keith DeRose, "Contextualism and Knowledge Attributions," *Philosophy and Phenomenological Research* 52 (1992): 913.

3. For more on contextualism pro and con, see chapter 3 of *Contemporary Debates in Epistemology*, ed. Matthias Steup, John Turri, and Ernest Sosa (Wiley-Blackwell, 2013). A different theory of knowledge motivated by the same sorts of examples discussed by Cohen is in Jason Stanley, *Knowledge and Practical Interests* (Oxford University Press, 2008), which also contains a detailed critique of contextualism.

## Jonathan Vogel (born 1954)

Vogel is Professor of Philosophy at Amherst College, and has made many contributions to skepticism and related topics in epistemology.

# SKEPTICISM AND INFERENCE TO THE BEST EXPLANATION

More than two thousand years ago, the philosopher Zhuangzi posed the question, how can a man know that he is a man, rather than a butterfly dreaming that he is a man? Later, René Descartes asked how he could be sure that his sensory experience wasn't caused by an evil demon, who was bent on deceiving him.[1] And, today, you might consider the possibility that, instead of your really seeing this book, your brain is being stimulated by a computer to make it appear to you, falsely, that you're seeing a book. What reason do you have for thinking that this isn't happening to you now?

Thoughts like these raise one of the oldest and deepest problems in philosophy, the problem of skepticism about the external world. Skepticism is the sweeping and unsettling doctrine that we have no knowledge of the world around us. It presents a philosophical problem because it is supported by a simple, formidable line of thought, known as the *deceiver argument*:

1. Your sensory experiences could come about through ordinary perception, so that most of what you believe about the world is true. But your sensory experiences could also be caused deceptively, so that what you believe about the world is entirely false.

---

1. According to tradition, Zhuangzi (Chinese, fourth century BCE) is the author of the influential treatise which bears his name. René Descartes (French, 1596–1650) is often viewed as the founder of modern philosophy in the West. His best known work is *Meditations on First Philosophy* (1641), where Descartes raises the possibility that an evil demon is deceiving him (see the selection from the *Meditations* earlier in this chapter). Other selections from the *Meditations* are in chapter 8 of this anthology.

2. You have no reason at all to believe that your sensory experiences arise in one way rather than the other.

3. Therefore, you have no knowledge of the world around you.[2]

But, of course you do have knowledge of the world. There must be something wrong with the deceiver argument. What, though? Premise (1) seems extremely plausible.[3] So, if the deceiver argument fails, either premise (2) must false, or else the conclusion (3) doesn't really follow from premise (2).

I think the conclusion does follow from premise (2), by way of a general principle about knowledge called the underdetermination principle. This principle says that if you are faced with two (or more) mutually exclusive hypotheses, and the information available to you gives you no reason to believe one rather than the other, then you don't know that either hypothesis is the case. For example, consider the claim that there is water on Mars. It might be that water formed there long ago and remains to this day. However, Mars is smaller than the Earth and has a very different surface and atmosphere. Maybe the Martian water, if any, was lost over the ages. In the absence of any information one way or the other — say, evidence provided by telescopes or by probes sent to Mars — a scientist who maintained or denied the presence of water on Mars would just be guessing. She wouldn't know that her hypothesis is true, precisely because she has no information which favors that hypothesis over its competitor. This is an illustration of how the underdetermination principle governs what counts as knowledge.[4]

---

2. There are subtle but significant questions about exactly how the argument ought to proceed, but I'm setting those aside. See Jonathan Vogel, "Skeptical Arguments," *Philosophical Issues* 14 (2004): 426–55. [Vogel's note.]

3. Some philosophers have rejected premise (1). J. L. Austin, *Sense and Sensibilia* (Oxford University Press, 1962), may have held such a view, and nowadays John McDowell, "Criteria, Defeasibility, and Knowledge," *Proceedings of the British Academy* 68 (1982): 455–79, and Timothy Williamson, *Knowledge and Its Limits* (Oxford University Press, 2000), might be read as denying premise (1), too. Another response regards the whole argument as somehow misconceived, perhaps because it involves hidden presuppositions about knowledge we needn't accept or ought to reject. See the classic writings of Ludwig Wittgenstein, *On Certainty*, ed. G.E.M. Anscombe and G. H. Von Wright (Blackwell, 1975), and J. L. Austin, "Other Minds," *Proceedings of the Aristotelian Society*, supplementary vol. 20 (1946): 148–87, and more recently Michael Williams, *Unnatural Doubts: Epistemological Realism and the Basis of Scepticism* (Blackwell, 1992), and Alex Byrne, "How Hard Are the Skeptical Paradoxes?," *Noûs* 38 (2004): 299–325. [Vogel's note.]

4. In my opinion, the underdetermination principle is perfectly correct. However, some philosophers have developed sophisticated views about knowledge which are inconsistent with it. *Relevant alternatives theorists* hold that, to know a proposition, a person may need to have reasons to reject some competitors to it, but she doesn't need to have reasons to reject *all* the competitors, in every case. Thus, the underdetermination principle doesn't hold in full generality, and the conclusion of the deceiver argument doesn't follow from premise (2) after all. Certain *reliabilist* theories of knowledge go further than the relevant alternatives theory. They deny that there is any fundamental connection between knowing a proposition and having reasons to believe that proposition (and to reject its competitors). In particular, advocates of these accounts hold that we can know propositions about the world, whether we have reasons to reject skeptical hypotheses or not. Thus they, too, will deny that the conclusion of the deceiver argument is supported by premise (2). I've offered various criticisms of the relevant alternatives and reliabilist approaches. See Jonathan Vogel, "The New Relevant Alternatives Theory," *Philosophical Perspectives* 13 (1999): 155–80; Jonathan Vogel, "Reliabilism Leveled," *Journal of Philosophy* 97 (2000): 602–23; Jonathan Vogel, "Externalism Resisted," *Philosophical Studies* 131 (2006): 729–42; and Jonathan Vogel, "Subjunctivitis," *Philosophical Studies* 134 (2006): 73–88. [Vogel's note.]

This principle matters for our purposes as follows. The deceiver argument confronts you with two competing hypotheses. One is that the world is the way it appears to be, the other is that you are the victim of massive sensory deception. If premise (2) is true, you have no reason to favor the first over the second, or vice versa. It then follows by the underdetermination principle that you don't know that either hypothesis is true. In particular, you may believe that the world is the way it appears to be, but you don't know that it is. So, premise (2) leads to the conclusion, given the underdetermination principle.

Since premise (2) does support the conclusion, the only way to escape the deceiver argument is to deny premise (2). If premise (2) is false, then skepticism is incorrect because we really do possess some reason for believing that we aren't victims of sensory deception, after all. Contemporary philosophers have advanced three principal proposals as to what such a reason might be. One is the *Moorean* view.[5] The Moorean maintains that a sensory experience has a distinctive character or content, and, other things being equal, your having such an experience justifies you in holding a corresponding belief. For instance, suppose you seem to see a tree. The experience you have makes you justified in believing that there is a tree before you. But if there really is a tree before you, it can't be that you're deceived by a nefarious computer when you seem to see a tree.[6] So, according to the Moorean, your sensory experience gives you reason to believe that there is a tree before you, which in turn gives you a reason to believe that you're not deceived by a computer when you seem to see a tree before you. The same goes for any other sensory experience you may have. In general, your sensory experience gives you a reason to believe that you're not deceived by a computer, and premise (2) of the skeptical argument is false.

The Moorean approach is simple and decisive, but it strikes many as unsatisfactory. The trouble can be brought out by an analogy. Suppose you use the gas gauge in your car to tell you how much gas is in the fuel tank. You take a look, and determine that the tank is half full. But surely, you can't then infer that, because the gauge says that the tank is half full, the gauge must be reading correctly! The Moorean seems to be up to something just as dubious. You can't use a particular sensory experience to establish that the experience itself isn't deceptive, any more than you can use a gauge to establish that the gauge itself isn't deceptive (i.e., to establish that it is reading correctly).

One reaction to this situation is to think that experience can't give you *any* reason for believing that you're not deceived by a computer. If you do have some basis for this belief, the basis can't be experience; your belief must be justified non-experientially or *a priori*. This is a second strategy for denying premise (2) of the deceiver argument. However, what is being suggested is somewhat hard to fathom. If you have non-experiential grounds for thinking that your sensory experience isn't deceptive, it

---

5. Named for the British philosopher G. E. Moore. A classic statement of Moore's view is his "Proof of an External World," *Proceedings of the British Academy* 25 (1939): 273–300 [see earlier in this chapter]. For a more recent version, see James Pryor, "The Skeptic and the Dogmatist," *Noûs* 34 (2000): 517–49. [Vogel's note.]

6. To be more explicit: If the computer is deceiving you, then there is no tree before you. But, then, if there is a tree before you, the computer isn't deceiving you. [Vogel's note.]

seems that the source of those grounds would have to be reason. But how could reasoning — just thinking about things — establish whether your sensory experience is caused by a computer or not? In the face of such worries, some philosophers maintain that believing that one's sensory experience isn't generally deceptive is simply part of what it is to *be rational*.[7] But what would make that so? And how is this different from just coming up with something nice to say ("it's rational") about an assumption that we make blindly and without any reason whatsoever?

These remarks about the Moorean and *a priori* replies to the deceiver argument leave a great deal unsaid. But let's move on, and consider a third sort of reply, which I'll call *explanationism*.[8] The idea behind this approach is that very often we are justified in adopting hypotheses because they do a good job of explaining the data we have. Here is an illustration. Suppose that a patient, Roger, goes to see his physician, Dr. G. Roger is sneezing, he has moist eyes, and his condition recurs at a certain time of the year. Roger's having an allergy explains these symptoms. There are other possible explanations. It could be that Roger has had a series of colds over the years, or that he has a chronic respiratory infection that lies dormant for much of the time. But if Roger's having an allergy explains his symptoms extremely well, and his having any of these other conditions would explain his symptoms much less well, then Dr. G has good reason to reject those other diagnoses. Dr. G would be in a position to conclude that Roger's symptoms are due to an allergy. Dr. G's arriving at a diagnosis in this way is an example of what is known as *inference to the best explanation*. In general, if one hypothesis provides a significantly better explanation of the available evidence than its competitors do, that is a reason to accept the explanation and to reject the competitors.

This point carries over to the deceiver argument as follows. One explanation for the occurrence of your sensory experiences is that the world is actually the way you think it is and you're perceiving it properly. For example, we normally suppose that you have a visual experience of the ocean, because you are seeing the ocean. Similarly, you have a visual experience of sand dunes, because you are really seeing sand dunes, and so on. Call the collection of your ordinary beliefs about the world the "real world hypothesis." Skepticism emerges as a problem because there are alternative explanations of how your sensory experiences as a body come about. Call these "skeptical hypotheses." If the real world hypothesis explains the occurrence of your sensory experiences as a body better than skeptical hypotheses do, then, by inference to the best explanation, you have good reason to accept the real world hypothesis and to reject the skeptical alternatives. This outcome contradicts premise (2) of the deceiver argument, which says that you have no reason to believe one thing rather than the other. We see that premise (2) is false, and that the deceiver argument as a whole is no good.

---

7. Wittgenstein (1975) [see note 3] wrote: "The reasonable man does not have certain doubts" (Remark 220, p. 29e). [Vogel's note.]

8. Other philosophers have offered explanationist approaches to skepticism that differ from the one presented here. See, for example, Laurence BonJour, *The Structure of Empirical Knowledge* (Harvard University Press, 1985), and Christopher Peacocke, *The Realm of Reason* (Oxford University Press, 2006). [Vogel's note.]

In my view, inference to the best explanation provides a refutation of the deceiver argument along the lines just set out. But to make this response to skepticism work, a proponent has to show why and how the real world hypothesis offers better explanations than the skeptical hypotheses do. There are some significant obstacles in the way. For one thing, there is no philosophical consensus about what an explanation is, or about the details of what makes one explanation superior to another. Another difficulty is that skeptical hypotheses can be formulated in importantly different ways. These issues can't be fully resolved here, but it's possible nonetheless to take some significant steps toward formulating an explanationist response to skepticism. I'll proceed by examining two diametrically different kinds of skeptical hypothesis. One is reticent and minimal, and we'll find that it is too impoverished to be acceptable. The other is more explicit and elaborate. It turns out that this fully developed version fails to match the real world hypothesis in explanatory merit, as well.

At bottom, the concern raised by skepticism is that our sensory experiences are caused *unveridically*, i.e., in such a way that they don't correctly reflect the way the world really is. Consider some particular experience you have, such as your seeing this page now (hereafter, P). On the one hand, the real world hypothesis furnishes what seems like a perfectly adequate explanation of how P comes about (there is a page in front of you, your eyes are open, there is light shining on the page and so you see it). Now, suppose that the skeptic offers, as an alternative, the following *minimal skeptical hypothesis*: Your experiences are caused unveridically (i.e., caused deceptively by something other than what you think). That's it. The minimal skeptical hypothesis is incompatible with the real world hypothesis. In particular, the minimal skeptical hypothesis and the real world hypothesis differ as to what the cause of your experience P is. But the minimal skeptical hypothesis says little or nothing about why you have P or how P comes about. In fact, it hardly explains the occurrence of P at all. Explanations that are defective in this way are called *ad hoc* explanations.

To get a feel for what's wrong with ad hoc explanations, you may recall the example of Dr. G diagnosing Roger's symptoms. Dr. G considers various hypotheses about the cause of Roger's symptoms (it's an allergy, a series of colds, or an ongoing respiratory infection). Roger's having an allergy explains his symptoms better than the other possibilities do, so Dr. G concludes that Roger does, indeed, have an allergy. Now imagine that someone else, Mr. S, comes along and says to Dr. G: "You don't really have a reason to think Roger suffers from an allergy. There's a competing explanation that's just as good, which you have no reason to reject. That competing explanation is: Something other than an allergy (don't ask me what) is causing Roger's symptoms." Taken verbatim, Mr. S's suggestion does little or nothing to explain why or how Roger's symptoms have come about. Dr. G would be foolish to set aside her diagnosis that Roger has an allergy, if all that Mr. S can offer as an alternative is the bare suggestion that Roger's symptoms are due to something other than an allergy. Similarly, you have no reason to set aside your belief that you are seeing the page of a book, if the competing hypothesis is just the bare claim that your experience of the page is caused by something else.

The upshot is that our ordinary beliefs about the world provide a rich and comprehensive explanation of why we have the experiences we do, and the minimal skeptical hypothesis falls short by comparison. If a skeptical hypothesis is going to keep up with the real world hypothesis, it will have to go into more detail than the minimal skeptical hypothesis does as to how our experiences arise. But it's possible to overshoot in this direction, too. As a general matter, we want hypotheses that say enough to get the explanatory job done, and no more. Some hypotheses are defective because they say too little, but others are defective because they say too much.

Here is an example of this second failing. You believe that the Earth is round. The fact that the Earth is round explains why someone traveling in the same direction eventually gets back to the same spot, why the Earth appears as a disk from the surface of the Moon, and so on. However, there are people who belong to an organization called the "Flat Earth Society," and they believe that the Earth isn't really round at all. To explain why travelers can get back to the same spot by apparently going in the same direction, Flat Earthers have to claim that compasses and other navigational devices systematically mislead us. We think we're going in the same direction, but we're really not. To explain why pictures from the Moon show the Earth as a disk, Flat Earthers say that there was a conspiracy to preserve the conviction that the Earth is round, and the Moon landings and pictures were all faked. The Flat Earth story is just too complicated to be believable. A much simpler and better explanation of everything is that the Earth really is round. This point generalizes. Other things being equal, a simpler, more economical explanatory hypothesis is better than a less simple, unnecessarily complicated one.

Now, we've seen that some hypotheses of massive sensory deception, like the minimal skeptical hypothesis, don't serve the skeptic's purposes. The skeptic needs to advance a hypothesis of massive sensory deception that will match exactly the explanatory success of the real world hypothesis. Could there be such a skeptical hypothesis, and if so, what would it look like? Consider what I'll call the *isomorphic skeptical hypothesis.*[9] Imagine a computer that simulates the world item by item, feature by feature. For example, suppose you have the experience of seeing a cat eating. The computer has a file for a cat, and an entry in the file which says that it is eating. This file, rather than a real cat, causes you to have a visual experience like that of a real cat eating. Next, suppose you have the experience of the cat's stopping eating and grooming itself. The ordinary explanation of why you have this experience is, of course, that you are seeing a real cat that has stopped eating and is now grooming itself. But, according to the isomorphic skeptical hypothesis, what's going on instead is that the computer's cat file has been updated. The entry for eating has been deleted, and has been replaced by an entry for grooming, which causes the corresponding experience in you. Overall, the isomorphic skeptical hypothesis denies that your experience is caused by everyday objects with familiar properties. Your experience is caused instead by computer files with electronic properties, such that the files mimic exactly everyday objects with familiar properties. The isomorphic skeptical hypothesis

9. "Isomorphic" means "similar in structure."

is supposed to match the real world hypothesis explanation for explanation. If it does, then the real world hypothesis is no better than the isomorphic skeptical hypothesis from an explanatory point of view, and explanatory considerations give us no basis for accepting the real world hypothesis rather than the skeptical alternative.

However, it is doubtful that the isomorphic skeptical hypothesis is truly the equal of the real world hypothesis in explanatory terms. Here is the basic thought, setting aside some important points: The real world hypothesis ascribes various familiar properties to ordinary objects. For example, if you have an experience as of seeing a round peg, you ascribe the property of being round to an object, namely a peg. According to the real world hypothesis, the round peg behaves like something that is round (it looks round to you, it fits into a round hole, and so forth). Moreover, it appears that very little needs to be said to explain why a round thing like the peg behaves as it does. The peg behaves like a round thing *because it is round*. By contrast, on the side of the isomorphic skeptical hypothesis, something that *isn't* round is supposed to behave as though it were round. The isomorphic skeptical hypothesis can't explain such behavior the way the real world hypothesis does; the computer file doesn't behave like a round thing because it is round. Some *further, more complicated* explanation needs to be given as to why the computer file behaves systematically as though it were a round thing.[1] In this way, the explanatory apparatus of the isomorphic skeptical hypothesis turns out to be more complicated than that of the real world hypothesis, after all.

The claim here is that the difference between the real world hypothesis and the isomorphic skeptical hypothesis is comparable to the difference between the "round Earth hypothesis" and the "flat Earth hypothesis." On the round Earth hypothesis, the Earth's really being round explains why it behaves as though it's round (e.g., why you're able to get back to the same spot by going in what is apparently one direction). On the flat Earth hypothesis, the Earth behaves in various respects as though it were round (e.g., you're able to get back to the same spot by going in what is apparently one direction), but the flat Earth hypothesis doesn't explain this behavior by ascribing roundness to the Earth. Instead, that hypothesis needs to be loaded up with some additional rigamarole to account for why the Earth behaves as though round when it's not (e.g., why compasses and other navigational devices systematically mislead us, and so forth). Ultimately, just as you are entitled to reject the flat Earth hypothesis because of its explanatory deficiencies, so, too, you are entitled to reject the isomorphic skeptical hypothesis in light of its similar explanatory shortcomings.

Let's sum up. The deceiver argument is philosophically a stroke of brilliance, which seems to make skepticism about the external world inevitable. However, there are in principle two ways out of trouble. We may deny that the argument's conclusion follows from premise (2), or we may deny the truth of premise (2). The

---

1. The same point applies to other properties besides roundness, of course. There is more to say about exactly why the isomorphic skeptical hypothesis turns out to be more complicated than the real world hypothesis. See Jonathan Vogel, "Cartesian Skepticism and Inference to the Best Explanation," *Journal of Philosophy* 87 (November 1990): 658–66, and Jonathan Vogel, "The Refutation of Skepticism," in *Contemporary Debates in Epistemology*, ed. Matthias Steup and Ernest Sosa (Blackwell, 2005). [Vogel's note.]

first maneuver doesn't work. The conclusion does follow from premise (2), by way of the underdetermination principle. However, the second path lies open. The real world hypothesis provides better explanations than skeptical hypotheses do. The explanatory superiority of the real world hypothesis gives you reason to believe it, and to reject its skeptical competitors. Thus, premise (2) of the deceiver argument is wrong, and the argument as a whole fails. Explanationism gives us the answer to the problem of skepticism about the external world.

## TEST YOUR UNDERSTANDING

1. Does Vogel think that the problem with the deceiver argument is that the underdetermination principle needs to be assumed in order to derive the conclusion?

2. Vogel discusses two failings an explanatory hypothesis may have. What are they?

## NOTES AND QUESTIONS

1. There is arguably a disanalogy between Vogel's example of Dr. G and ordinary cases of knowledge by perception, say knowing that there is a book on the table by vision. Suppose Dr. G knows that Roger has an allergy because this hypothesis best explains Roger's symptoms. Then this involves fairly sophisticated reasoning by Dr. G from her evidence that Roger is sneezing, that Roger has moist eyes, etc. If knowing by vision that there is a book on the table is similar, presumably it also involves sophisticated reasoning. Is this plausible? How do you think Vogel would respond to this worry?

2. For another example of this kind of response to the skeptic, see Laurence BonJour, "A Version of Internalist Foundationalism," in L. BonJour and E. Sosa, *Epistemic Justification: Internalism vs. Externalism, Foundations vs. Virtues* (Blackwell, 2003).

   A general discussion of "inference to the best explanation" is in Gilbert Harman, "The Inference to the Best Explanation," in chapter 4 of this anthology. See also the "Notes and Questions" to Paley, "The Argument from Design," in chapter 1 of this anthology.

## Rae Langton (born 1961)

Langton is Professor of Philosophy at the University of Cambridge, and has made influential contributions to the history of philosophy, ethics, metaphysics, and feminist philosophy. She is the author of *Kantian Humility* (2001) and *Sexual Solipsism* (2009).

# IGNORANCE OF THINGS IN THEMSELVES

## 1. Skepticism and Humility

Many philosophers have wanted to tell us that things may not be quite as they seem: many have wanted to divide appearance from reality. Democritus wrote in the fifth century BCE:

> by convention sweet and by convention bitter, by convention hot, by convention cold, by convention color; but in reality atoms and void.[1]

Plato argued for a different division: the imperfect, changeable things we see around us are mere appearance, and reality is an independent realm of perfect, invisible, eternal forms. Much later, Descartes wondered whether the familiar world of stoves and dressing gowns, streets and people, might turn out to be mere appearance — not because it is less real than the realm of atoms, or Forms, but because, for all we know, the stoves and dressing gowns, streets and people, don't exist at all.[2] Perhaps I am dreaming, or deceived by an Evil Demon, who interferes with my mind (like that evil neuroscientist of science-fiction!), so that what appears to me is nothing like what's really there.

That Demon still haunts the halls of philosophy, despite Descartes's own efforts to banish him. The mere possibility of his deceptive machinations persuades some philosophers that, even if there is actually no Demon, and appearance captures reality very nicely, we nevertheless can't be quite *sure* that it does. This means we don't know what we thought we knew. We confront skepticism. We don't have knowledge of "the external world." We are ignorant of "things in themselves," in some sense of that phrase: we lack knowledge of things independent of our minds.

Kant described skepticism as a scandal, and in 1781 he published his *Critique of Pure Reason* to set the scandal to rest.[3] The *Critique* is a brilliant but formidably difficult work. In it, Kant aims to show that skepticism is wrong because, roughly, we could not have thoughts at all, unless we had thoughts about things. Perhaps he was trying to say that appearance just *is* reality: for provided we are thinking at all, we can't be wholly ignorant of things.

---

1. Trans. C.C.W. Taylor, *The Atomists: Leucippus and Democritus. Fragments, A Text and Translation with a Commentary*, (University of Toronto Press, 1999), cited by Sylvia Berryman, "Democritus," *Stanford Encyclopedia of Philosophy*. [Langton's note.]

2. René Descartes, *Meditations on First Philosophy* (1641), trans. John Cottingham (Cambridge University Press, 1986). [See the selection from the *Meditations* earlier in this chapter. Other selections from the *Meditations* are in chapter 8 of this anthology.] [Langton's note.]

3. Immanuel Kant, *Critique of Pure Reason*, trans. Norman Kemp Smith (Macmillan, 1929). [Langton's note.]

Whether Kant set skepticism to rest is one question. Whether he was really trying to, is another. For Kant said something else as well, famously and often. Although we have knowledge of things, these things are only "phenomena," and "we have no knowledge of things in themselves." Are those the words of someone offering a cure for skepticism? The skeptic says we have knowledge only of appearances: Kant says we have knowledge only of phenomena. The skeptic says we have no knowledge of things independent of our minds: Kant says we have no knowledge of things "in themselves." Appearance is not reality after all. It looks like Kant is saying just what the skeptic says — doesn't it?

Evidently it depends what Kant means by "things in themselves." If "things in themselves" means things independent of our minds, then being ignorant of them is a way of being a skeptic. Instead of having a cure for skepticism, Kant has the disease. To be sure, Kant's proposal relieves the symptoms: he offers a wealth of arguments about the very special knowledge we have of objects — but they are *phenomenal* objects, mere appearances. What a disappointment, if we were hoping for knowledge of reality, of things independent of our minds. What consolation is it to learn that we have special knowledge, if it's knowledge of mere appearance? Kant's subtle arguments about the conditions of our thought look irrelevant, if they deny knowledge of reality, and land us in skepticism again.

What, though, if Kant means something quite different by "things in themselves"? Then ignorance of "things in themselves" needn't be skepticism. Knowledge of phenomena needn't restrict us to knowledge of mind-dependent appearance. That is exactly the idea we're going to pursue here. We won't go into Kant's famous arguments against skepticism — about how we can't think, unless we think about objects. We're going to look instead at what "ignorance of things in themselves" amounts to. We'll take seriously the possibility that you and I, right now, are ignorant of things in themselves, just as Kant said — and that we can welcome this conclusion, without thereby welcoming skepticism.

The key idea is this. The phrase "things in themselves" does not mean "things independent of our minds." It means "the way things are independently" — that is, independently of their relations not just to our minds, but to *anything else* at all.

We are often interested in the relations one thing bears to another. Sometimes the relevant relations are spatial: the tennis ball flew over the net, and over the white line. Sometimes the relevant relations are biological: Jane is Jim's cousin, and Joan's granddaughter. But when we talk about the relations a thing has to other things, we tend to assume there is something *more* to the thing than those relations. There is more to Jane than being Jim's cousin and Joan's granddaughter. There is more to the tennis ball than its passage over the net, and over the white line. Now, Kant sometimes uses the word "phenomenon" to mean, quite generally, an object "in a relation" to some other object. And he sometimes talks about this assumption that there must be something more to an object than its relations to other things:

> The understanding, when it entitles an object in a relation mere phenomenon, at the same time forms, apart from that relation, a representation of an *object in itself.* (B306, emphasis added)

He also says:

> Concepts of relation presuppose things which are absolutely [i.e., independently] given, and without these are impossible. (A284/B340)

This absolute or independent thing, which isn't exhausted by its relations to other things, is something to which we can give the name "substance," which just means an independent thing that has an independent, or intrinsic, nature.

> Substances in general must have some intrinsic nature, which is therefore free from all external relations. (A274/B330)

Putting this all together, the idea that there is a thing "in itself" turns out to be the idea that there is something to an object over and above its relations to other things: something more to you than being the son or daughter of A, the cousin of B, the grandchild of C; something more to the tennis ball than its spatial relations to nets and lines on a tennis court. A thing that has relations to something else must have something more to it than that: it must have some intrinsic nature, independent of those relations. It is this something else, this something more, that is the thing "in itself."

If we take this idea at face value, it promises to solve the difficulty we face. Ignorance of things "in themselves" is not skepticism. It doesn't rule out knowledge of things independent of our minds. It rules out knowledge only of a thing's non-relational, intrinsic properties.

We can know a lot! Appearance *is* reality: things as they appear to us are things as they really are. But something is still ruled out: namely, knowledge of how things are independent of their relations to other things. Appearance is reality, but it's not *all* of reality. We can know a lot about the world, but we can't know everything about it: we can't know its independent, *intrinsic* nature.

To say we can know a lot about something, but not everything, is not skepticism, but a kind of epistemic modesty — so let's call it "humility." And since it is at the center of Kant's philosophy (or so I'm arguing), let's call it "Kantian humility."[4] In what follows, I'm going to say why Kant believed it. And then I'll say why you, too, should believe it.

## 2. Humility in Kant

I've suggested that Kant's distinction between "phenomena" and "things in themselves" is a contrast not between "appearance" and "reality," but between extrinsic and intrinsic aspects of something. On this usage, if we say a tennis ball fell over the

---

4. Rae Langton, *Kantian Humility: Our Ignorance of Things in Themselves* (Oxford University Press, 1998; 2001). [Langton's note.]

white line, we ascribe to it a relational, hence "phenomenal," property; whereas if we say it is spherical, we ascribe to it an intrinsic property, which concerns the tennis ball as it is "in itself." Let's summarize the distinction this way.

*Distinction:* "Things in themselves" are things that have intrinsic properties; "phenomena" are their extrinsic, or relational, properties.

Against this backdrop, ignorance of things in themselves is not skepticism, but ignorance of certain properties — intrinsic properties:

*Humility:* We have no knowledge of the intrinsic properties of things.

This could be construed as the idea that we have no knowledge of *any* of the intrinsic properties of things, and that (I think) is the idea we should ascribe to Kant. Admittedly, it sounds odd. If an intrinsic property is a property something has independent of its relations to other things, then many of those seem perfectly accessible to us: for example, the sphericality of the tennis ball. But Kant himself seemed to think we lack knowledge of any intrinsic properties: we do have knowledge of certain physical properties of things, such as their shape, and their powers of attraction and impenetrability; but he thinks these are not intrinsic, as the following passages illustrate.

> The *Intrinsic* and *Extrinsic*. In an object of pure understanding the intrinsic is only that which has no relation whatsoever (so far as its existence is concerned) to anything different from itself. It is quite otherwise with a *substantia phaenomenon* [phenomenal substance] in space; its intrinsic properties are nothing but relations, and it itself is entirely made up of mere relations. We are acquainted with substance in space only through forces which are active in this and that space, either drawing other objects (attraction) or preventing their penetration (repulsion and impenetrability). We are not acquainted with any other properties constituting the concept of the substance which appears in space and which we call matter. As object of pure understanding, on the other hand, every substance must have intrinsic properties and powers which concern its inner reality. (A265/B321)
>
> Substances in general must have some intrinsic nature, which is therefore free from all external relations.... But what is intrinsic to the state of a substance cannot consist in place, shape, contact, or motion (these determinations being all external relations). (A274/B330)
>
> All that we know in matter is merely relations (what we call its intrinsic properties are intrinsic only in a comparative sense), but among these relations some are ... enduring, and through these we are given a determinate object.... It is certainly startling to hear that a thing is to be taken as consisting wholly of relations. Such a thing is, however, mere appearance. (A285/B341)

Kant thinks the physical world is made up of matter, "phenomenal substance," but that matter somehow "consists wholly of relations." He is drawing on a dynamical account of matter (further developed in his works on physical theory) according to which matter is constituted by forces. He has a proto-*field theory*, which had an important historical role to play, influencing scientists who went on to develop field theory proper in the nineteenth century.[5] And familiar physical properties — shape, impenetrability, attractive power — count, for him, as extrinsic or relational properties.

Whether that is the right way to classify them depends on how we understand the intrinsic/relational distinction. We have said, loosely, that an intrinsic property is one that doesn't depend on relations to anything else. Some philosophers have tried to make this more precise by saying a property is intrinsic just in case it is compatible with *isolation* — i.e., it does not imply the existence of another wholly distinct object.[6] On this way of thinking, a tennis ball's sphericality will be intrinsic: a tennis ball can be spherical and be the only thing in the universe. And the tennis ball's bounciness will also be intrinsic. After all, a tennis ball can be *bouncy* and be the only thing in the universe, although, to be sure, it will not bounce unless there is something else for it to bounce off! On the face of things, shape properties like sphericality, and dispositional properties like bounciness, are intrinsic: something could have them, and exist all on its own.

If Kant nonetheless describes them as relational, perhaps he has a different conception of intrinsicness in mind. Perhaps he thinks a thing's shape properties are relational because they depend on a relation to the *parts* of the thing. For example, the sphericality of the tennis ball depends on how the parts making up its surface are equidistant from its center. Perhaps he thinks dispositional properties are relational because they depend on how something *would* relate to other things if they were there. For example, whether something is bouncy depends on what it *would* do in relation to something else — if, say, it were dropped on the ground, or thwacked against a tennis racket.

Some metaphysicians like to ponder the distinction between intrinsic and relational properties, but we needn't settle it here. All we need is that Kant denies us knowledge of any intrinsic properties, in some defensible sense of "intrinsic," and that this is what he means by denying us knowledge of "things in themselves."

Why does Kant deny us knowledge of intrinsic properties? The answer, I suggest, has two parts. First, he thinks, as many philosophers do, that our knowledge is "receptive": our minds need to be causally affected by something, if we are to have knowledge of it.

> The receptivity of our mind, its power of receiving representations in so far as it is affected in any way, is called 'sensibility' [. . . .] Our nature is such that our intuition can never be other than sensible, that is, it contains only the way in which we are affected by objects. (A51/B75)

---

5. According to Faraday's biographer: see L. P. Williams, *Michael Faraday: A Biography* (Chapman and Hall, 1965). [Langton's note.]

6. For some efforts to define "intrinsic" see, e.g., Rae Langton and David Lewis, "Defining Intrinsic," *Philosophy and Phenomenological Research* 58 (1998): 333–45; I. L. Humberstone, "Intrinsic/Extrinsic," *Synthèse* 108 (1996): 205–67. The "isolation" test has many difficulties which I won't go into here. [Langton's note.]

Our knowledge of things is receptive, "sensible": we gain knowledge only through being affected by objects.

> *Receptivity:* Human knowledge depends on sensibility, and sensibility is receptive: we can have knowledge of an object only in so far as it affects us.

This simple fact about our knowledge, he seems to think, dooms us to ignorance of things in themselves.

> Properties that belong to things as they are in themselves can never be given to us through the senses. (A36/B52)
>
> It is not that through sensibility we are acquainted in a merely confused way with the nature of things as they are in themselves; we are not acquainted with that nature in any way at all. (A44/B62)

Why should the "receptivity" of knowledge imply ignorance of things in themselves? Many philosophers have wondered about this on Kant's behalf, and some have criticized him roundly on the topic. P. F. Strawson wrote:

> knowledge through perception of things . . . as they are in themselves is impossible. For the only perceptions which could yield us any knowledge at all of such things must be the outcome of our being affected by those things; and for this reason such knowledge can be knowledge only of those things as they appear . . . and not of those things as they . . . are in themselves. The above is a fundamental and unargued complex premise of the *Critique*.[7]

Is Kant really taking this for granted, as a "fundamental and unargued complex premise"? Perhaps not. Perhaps he has good reason to connect receptivity to ignorance — but a reason that has gone unnoticed.

Here is a simple suggestion. According to receptivity, we have knowledge only of what affects us. But things "as they are in themselves" *do not affect us*: the intrinsic properties of things do not affect us. If Kant believed this, then that, together with his commitment to receptivity about knowledge, would certainly explain why we are ignorant of things in themselves.

A case can be made that this is just what Kant believes. I confess that, as a matter of interpretation, it is controversial. Here is not the place to do it justice. It involves detailed investigative work of a kind we historians of philosophy find strangely thrilling, although we're aware not everyone shares our enthusiasm. But here at least are two small gestures in this direction. In an early philosophical treatise Kant argues that

> a substance never has the power through its own intrinsic properties to determine others different from itself, as has been proven.[8]

---

7. P. F. Strawson, *The Bounds of Sense* (Methuen, 1966), p. 250. [Langton's note.]

8. Kant, *Principiorum primorum cognitionis metaphysicae nova dilucidatio* (1755), Ak. vol. 1, 415. English translation (here amended) from "A New Exposition of the First Principles of Metaphysical Knowledge," in *Kant's Latin Writings: Translations, Commentaries and Notes,* ed. L.W. Beck et al. (P. Lang, 1986). [Langton's note.]

According to Kant, the causal powers of a substance are something over and above its intrinsic properties. At this stage of his thinking he believes that they require an additional act of creation on God's part — an act which is "obviously arbitrary on God's part." He took this idea about the insufficiency of intrinsic properties for causal power to imply not only the contingency of causal power, but the inertia of intrinsic properties. The idea returns in the *Critique of Pure Reason*:

> when everything is merely intrinsic . . . the state of one substance cannot stand in any active connection whatsoever with the state of another. (A274/B330)[9]

Receptivity requires that if we are to have knowledge of something, we have to be in active causal connection with it: but we're not in active causal connection with a thing's intrinsic properties. Receptivity means we can be acquainted with the causal powers of things, the ways they relate to each other and to ourselves: but however deeply we explore this causal nexus, we cannot reach the things in themselves.

## 3. Why We Are Ignorant of Things in Themselves

Kant said we are ignorant of things in themselves: ignorant of the intrinsic properties of things. The picture I have painted on his behalf is, I hope, appealing, in certain respects: Kantian humility does not, at least, condemn us to skepticism. But the picture will not appeal to everyone. Kant's conclusion seems too strong: we have no knowledge of *any* of the intrinsic properties of things. His reasons invoke a seemingly idiosyncratic conception of intrinsicness: a tennis ball's sphericality and bounce are not among its intrinsic properties. And they invoke a seemingly implausible causal thesis: intrinsic properties are causally inert. So however this interpretation succeeds as a way to understand Kant, it is unlikely to succeed in reaching a wider audience.

But wait. There is a conclusion very similar to Kant's that is significantly closer to home. Kant says we are ignorant of the intrinsic properties of things: and he is *right*, though not for quite the reasons we have been looking at. And if he is right, of course, then *you* too should believe we are ignorant of things in themselves.

Imagine that a detective is investigating a murder case. She puts together the clues. The murderer had a key, since no windows were broken. He was known to the dog, since there was no barking. He had size ten shoes — there are his footprints. More and more of the picture begins to be filled out. He wore gloves, since there were no fingerprints. He had a tame parakeet — there are green feathers on the rug. The detective learns a lot about the murderer. Does she know who he is? She knows who the murderer is in relation to other things — houses, shoes, parakeets, and so on. She knows that the murderer is *whoever fits this role*. But does she, so to speak,

---

9. The context is a discussion of Kant's predecessor, Gottfried Leibniz, who denied causal interaction between substances. [Langton's note.]

know the murderer *in himself*? Is there something more to the murderer than being a possessor of keys, parakeets, and shoes? Of course. There must, in the end, be more to something or someone than their merely relational properties, as Kant pointed out. And ultimately, let us hope, the detective finds herself in a position to identify the person who exists independently of these relations to other things: "Aha! There is one person who fits this role. There is one person who is known to the dog, wears size ten shoes, has a tame parakeet, could have a key, and that person is . . . Pirate Pete!" Then she knows who the murderer is. Then she knows who fits the role: she knows, so to speak, the murderer "in himself."

Some philosophers have suggested we are in a situation rather like that of the detective. An important recent attempt to show this is that of David Lewis, whose "Ramseyan Humility" explicitly claims inspiration from "Kantian" humility.[1] We are trying to find out, not about a murderer, but about the fundamental features of the world. We put our best theorists on the job, and they tell us a lot. Suppose we want to find out about our tennis ball. They tell us that a tennis ball is whatever fits this sort of profile: it's something that can be hit across a net with a tennis racket, something that has a specific degree of resistance and elasticity, something that is readily visible to human eyes in normal conditions, something that will roll smoothly downwards when placed on a slope. These relational descriptions, suitably filled out, give us a story about the role something must fit if it's to be a tennis ball. They capture the relational or (if you like) "phenomenal" aspect of the tennis ball. Is there something more to the tennis ball than this relational role? Of course there must be, just as there is something more to Pirate Pete than his relations to keys and parakeets.

And our theorists can tell us about this "something more." They tell us not only that the tennis ball can land over the white line, not only that it is spherical and bouncy, but that it is made of rubber and felt, which in turn are made of very tiny parts called molecules, which in turn are made up of tinier parts, called atoms, which in turn are made up of still tinier parts, called protons, neutrons, and electrons — and more, with names too peculiar to recount here. Our experts give detailed descriptions of the tiny parts something must have, and their particular arrangements, if that something is to fit the "tennis ball" role. They are giving us a splendid account of what the tennis ball is, "in itself." What more could there be to know about what the tennis ball is, "in itself"?

We certainly know a lot about the tennis ball. In Kant's terms, we know a lot about the tennis ball as "phenomenon" — how it relates to tennis rackets, nets, and players. And yes: we also know a lot about the tennis ball "as it is in itself," what its parts are made of and how they are arranged. But now shift the question: what exactly do we know about those tiny parts of the tennis ball?

---

1. David Lewis, "Ramseyan Humility," in *Conceptual Analysis and Philosophical Naturalism*, ed. Robert Nola and David Braddon-Mitchell (MIT Press, 2009). This section is in turn inspired by Lewis's argument, though it is very far from doing him justice. There have been many attempts to respond, but see, e.g., Jonathan Schaffer, "Quidditistic Knowledge," *Philosophical Studies* 123 (2005): 1–32; Anne Whittle, "On an Argument for Humility," *Philosophical Studies* 130 (2006): 461–97. [Langton's note.]

Take the electron, for example. Our story about the electron has something in common with the detective's story about the murderer. It captures a complicated relational profile. An electron is whatever it is that fits a distinctive role, whatever it is that fits the "electron" pattern of relating to other things. An electron is the thing that repels other things we call "electrons," attracts other things we call "protons." It's the thing that, in company with lots of other electrons, makes the light bulb go on, makes your hair stand on end on a cold, dry day, and so on. The physicist will have a more detailed story, but it will nevertheless be a story that has this relational form. "Electron" refers to whatever fits the physicist's relational "electron" role, just as "the murderer" refers to whoever fits the detective's relational "murderer" role.

The detective discovers who the murderer is, "in himself" as we put it, when she discovers who fits the relational "murderer" role: namely Pirate Pete. The physicist discovers what the electron is when she discovers what fits the relational "electron" role: namely . . . what? Here the analogy with the detective breaks down. The detective is able to find out who the murderer is, apart from the story about how the murderer relates to keys, shoes, parakeets. But the physicist is unable to find out what the electron is, apart from the story about how the electron relates to protons, hair, and light bulbs. For the detective, there is something more to say. For the physicist, there is nothing more to say. The electron is, to borrow a phrase from Kant, merely a "something = x" about which we can say nothing, or rather nothing *more* than what's given in our relational description. The upshot: we know the electron as "phenomenon," so to speak, but we don't know the electron "as it is in itself."

Here is another way to bring out the point. Suppose, inconveniently, more than one person fits the role given by the detective's list of clues: suppose Pirate Pete, Pirate Percy, and Pirate Peggy all have keys, parakeets, large shoes, and so on. Then although the detective knows a lot, she still doesn't know who the murderer is. That, or something like it, is the situation we face with the electron. Consider the thing, whatever it is, that fits the electron role. We are supposing its intrinsic properties are not inert (we are leaving that part of Kant behind), but are the causal grounds of its power to repel other electrons, attract protons, and so on. We are, indirectly, in causal contact with those intrinsic properties — but, receptivity notwithstanding, that is still not enough for us to know what those intrinsic properties are. Why not? Suppose we give a name to the intrinsic property responsible for this complex causal profile: let's call it "negative charge," or "NC" for short. Now let's draw on Kant's insight about the contingency of causal power, which is shared, in some form, by many philosophers today (including Lewis). This contingency means that NC *could have been* associated with a completely different relational, causal profile; and a different intrinsic property — call it NC* — *could have been* associated with the electron's relational, causal profile. But now ask: is the electron's intrinsic property NC, or NC*? We don't know, any more than the detective knows whether the murderer is Pirate Pete or Pirate Percy. So we are faced with humility again.

*Humility*: we have no knowledge of the most fundamental intrinsic properties of things.

This is admittedly a modified version of humility: the conclusion is less drastic than Kant's. We are not denied knowledge of all intrinsic properties: the tennis ball is spherical, and is made of rubber and felt, which in turn are constituted by molecules, elements, and subatomic particles. We know a lot about the intrinsic nature of the tennis ball.

But we do lack knowledge of things in themselves. Kant was right to say it, and we need to accept it. It's not so bad. It's not skepticism. It is what it is. We face the sad fact that we know less than we thought: there are some intrinsic properties of which we shall forever be ignorant. And, sadly, they are the most fundamental properties of all.


## TEST YOUR UNDERSTANDING

1. Kant said we are ignorant of "things in themselves." On Langton's interpretation, Kant meant that we are ignorant of the "intrinsic properties" of things. As she notes, the property of being spherical is often counted as an "intrinsic property." Does this mean that, according to Kant, we don't know whether tennis balls are spherical?

2. The argument for Kant's version of humility appeals to the premise that the intrinsic properties of things do not affect us. Does the argument for Langton's version of humility appeal to this premise too?

3. According to Langton, will physicists eventually discover all the fundamental properties of elementary particles like electrons and neutrinos?


## NOTES AND QUESTIONS

1. Set out the **argument** for the version of humility endorsed by Langton in the form of premises and conclusion. Is the argument **valid**? If not, what premises need to be added so that the argument is valid?

2. Now that you have a valid argument for humility, is it also **sound**?

3. Langton mentions David Lewis's defense of "Ramseyan humility" in note 10, and defends it herself in the last section of her article. For a more detailed comparison of Ramseyan and Kantian humility, and a connection with "contextualism" (the thesis defended in the selection by Cohen), see Langton, "Elusive Knowledge of Things in Themselves," *Australasian Journal of Philosophy* 82 (2004): 129–36.

## ANALYZING THE ARGUMENTS

1.  Hume, Moore, Cohen, and Vogel offer very different responses to the skeptic about the external world. Compare and contrast their views.

2.  Even though Hume finds the case for skepticism compelling, he admits that it is difficult or impossible to be a skeptic once one stops thinking about philosophy and turns to finding a good place for lunch or paying one's library fines. At the end of "Of Scepticism with Regard to the Senses" he writes (in a paragraph omitted from the selection):

    > This sceptical doubt, both with respect to reason and the senses, is a malady, which can never be radically cur'd, but must return upon us every moment, however we may chase it away, and sometimes may seem entirely free from it. 'Tis impossible upon any system to defend either our understanding or senses; and we but expose them farther when we endeavour to justify them in that manner. As the sceptical doubt arises naturally from a profound and intense reflection on those subjects, it always increases, the farther we carry our reflections, whether in opposition or conformity to it. Carelessness and inattention alone can afford us any remedy. For this reason I rely entirely upon them; and take it for granted, whatever may be the reader's opinion at this present moment, that an hour hence he will be persuaded there is both an external and internal world.

    Indeed, if Hume were able to fully live his skepticism, why did he bother writing a book? If you don't know that there are any books, and readers to read them, the ambition to write a book is as pointless as the ambition to meet Bigfoot.

    Does this show that there is something badly wrong with skepticism? The fact that skepticism can seem plausible in the classroom and absurd outside might be thought to support Cohen's position. Explain why. Does it really support Cohen's position? How do you think Moore and Vogel would explain the appeal of skepticism?

3.  *Defining Closure.* Consider this statement of Closure:

    Closure$_1$: If p entails q, and you know p, then you know q.

    There is a simple objection to Closure$_1$ that motivates the following revised version of Closure (the one used in the introduction to this section):

    Closure$_2$: If p entails q, and you know p, then you are in a position to know q.

    What is that objection? *Hint*: Sometimes someone can *come to know* a truth q of which she was previously ignorant by proving or deducing q from some premises.

4.  *Counterexamples to Closure.* Suppose you are at the zoo, looking at a black-and-white-striped animal in a cage marked "Common Zebra, *Equus quagga*." The animal is indeed a zebra. Explain why one might think the following argument provides a **counterexample** to Closure:

    1-z.  This is a zebra.

    2-z.  If this is a zebra, it is not a mule cleverly disguised by the zoo authorities to look exactly like a zebra.

3-z. This is not a mule cleverly disguised by the zoo authorities to look exactly like a zebra.[2]

Now do the same for the following argument:

1-h. I have a hand.

2-h. If I have a hand, I am not a handless brain-in-a-vat.

3-h. I am not a handless brain-in-a-vat.

Does either one of these arguments provide a genuine counterexample to Closure? Assuming that Closure is true, can you explain why someone might be tempted by either one of these arguments into thinking that it's false? For discussion of the case for and against Closure, see Fred Dretske and John Hawthorne, "Is Knowledge Closed under Known Entailment?" in *Contemporary Debates in Epistemology*, ed. M. Steup, J. Turri, and E. Sosa (Wiley-Blackwell, 2013).

5. Consider the following account of knowledge (simplified from Robert Nozick, *Philosophical Explanations*, Harvard University Press, 1981, chapter 3):

S knows p **iff** (i) p is true, (ii) S believes p, and (iii) if p had been false S wouldn't have believed p.

Nozick thought that it was an advantage of his account that it had the following two features:

(i)   You can know that you have a hand.

(ii)  You cannot know that you are not a handless brain-in-a-vat.

Because of (i), the account agrees with common sense. Because of (ii), the account also concedes something to the skeptic. Explain why Nozick's account has these two features, and why Nozick must deny Closure.

---

2. This example is from Fred Dretske, "Epistemic Operators," *Journal of Philosophy* 67 (1970): 1007–23.

# Part III

# METAPHYSICS AND THE PHILOSOPHY OF MIND

# 8

# Is Mind Material?

A chunk of ice is transparent and slippery. Physics and chemistry can explain why it has these properties. The chunk of ice is composed of $H_2O$ molecules arranged in a repeating hexagonal pattern. It is transparent because $H_2O$ molecules do not absorb (much) light in the visible spectrum. It is slippery because friction on the ice breaks the chemical bonds that hold the $H_2O$ molecules together, creating a thin lubricating layer of $H_2O$ in its liquid state—water, in other words.

Admittedly, the explanation for its transparency is incomplete. Snowballs are composed of small chunks of ice, so why aren't they transparent? And the explanation of why ice is slippery is actually controversial—other explanations have been proposed. Still, no one doubts that the slipperiness of ice, and indeed *all* of the characteristic properties of ice, can in principle be completely explained in terms of its chemical or physical makeup. In this sense, a chunk of ice is a wholly material or physical thing: it is "nothing but" $H_2O$ molecules bound together in a certain crystalline form.

As far as objects in our environment go, a chunk of ice is pretty simple. A rock is considerably more complex. Still, there's every reason to think that rocks are wholly physical things, in the sense that our ice cube is. A lump of granite is hard, dense, and radioactive. No geologist would dispute that these and other characteristic properties of granite can be completely explained in terms of its physical or chemical makeup.

What about living things? Let's start with something relatively simple, a virus. A virus basically consists of some genetic material inside a protective structure made from protein. The genetic material and the proteins themselves are incredibly complex molecules. But again, virology proceeds (extremely successfully) on the assumption that a virus is a wholly material thing, "nothing but" a complex molecular structure.

Viruses are not cellular organisms, and for that reason are sometimes not counted as living things. So what about a single-celled organism, say a bacterium? Is this where the explanatory limits of biochemistry are apparent? Not according to modern bacteriology which, just like virology, supposes that its objects of study are wholly material. The theory known as *vitalism*, according to which a special "vital spirit" is needed to explain life, is no longer regarded as credible.

How could it make a difference if we multiply the number of cells? If single-celled organisms are wholly material, aren't multicellular organisms wholly material too? And if they are, *we* are wholly material things.

We certainly have many properties that can be explained in terms of our physical or chemical makeup. Suppose, for example, that Adam has a body temperature of 98°F and that Eve is digesting a bagel. Although the regulation of body temperature and digestion are far from easy to explain, it seems a very safe bet that complete explanations of these phenomena need not appeal to anything more than the physical and chemical makeup of organisms.

What about our *psychological* or **mental states**, though? Tom thinks it's time for lunch, Dick has a headache, and Harriet hears her phone ring. Are thinking, feeling, and perceiving "nothing but" physical states of organisms? To take a particularly vivid example, imagine having a throbbing headache. Could this be "nothing but" having a certain pattern of neural activity in your brain?

There is an intuitive difficulty here, which the German philosopher and mathematician Gottfried Wilhelm Leibniz captured in 1714 with the following thought experiment:

> Suppose that there be a machine, the structure of which produces thinking, feeling, and perceiving; imagine this machine enlarged but preserving the same proportions, so that you could enter it as if it were a mill. This being supposed, you might visit its inside; but what would you observe there? Nothing but parts which push and move each other, and never anything that could explain perception.[1]

It doesn't affect the force of the example if we imagine, not a machine with parts that push and move each other, but a brain with parts that interact by sending and receiving chemical and electrical signals. Imagine the brain enlarged so you can walk through it, each neuron and glial cell (the two sorts of cells in the brain) being clearly visible, as they might be in a model seen in a science museum. Admittedly, walking around the brain might take some time (the number of neurons is of the order of 100 billion, and the number of glial cells is even greater). But could you find anything among this tangle of biological wiring that could explain the occurrence of a headache?

Contrast digestion. Imagine the stomach and intestines enlarged, so you can see the chemical processes at work. Taking a submarine trip through the body, as in the 1966 movie *Fantastic Voyage*, you see particles of chewed bagel being broken down by enzymes and gastric acid, and so on. There doesn't seem to be much of a problem in supposing that what you are seeing *just is* digestion.

There appears to be a deep puzzle, then, about how to fit the mind into the material world. This is called the **mind-body problem**, and is the topic of the selections that follow. You will find them easier to understand if you have a basic grasp of the four main theories of mind, which are explained in the remainder of this introduction.

1. Leibniz, *Monadology*, trans. P. Schrecher and A. M. Schrecher (Bobbs-Merrill, 1965), sec. 17.

# Behaviorism

Lieutenant Commander Data, a character in *Star Trek: The Next Generation*, is an android — a robot who looks and behaves like a human being. Even though Data's innards are quite different from ours, the other Star Trek characters simply assume without argument that he has a mental life. They are quite sure that Data thinks that his home planet is Omicron Theta, wants to understand humans better, and can see objects that are before his eyes. Could they be completely and utterly wrong? Might Data actually be as mindless as a robotic vacuum cleaner?

If you think that Data's behavior *guarantees* that he has a mental life, then you are some sort of *behaviorist*. According to **behaviorism**, to have a mind, or to be in such-and-such mental states, *just is* to behave in certain ways or, more precisely, to be *disposed* or *inclined* to behave in certain ways.

Our bodily movements can presumably be explained in terms of our physical and chemical makeup. Your hand goes up because muscle fibers contract; muscle fibers contract because signals reach them via nerves; the signals themselves are produced by activity in your motor cortex; and so on. At no point in this chain of explanations do we need to assume that you are more than a purely physical thing. Accordingly, if our mental life is just a matter of our behavior, then there is no puzzle about how a purely material object can have a mind.

But is behaviorism correct? Suppose Data's behavior is controlled remotely via wireless links by the alien Romulans. These diabolical puppeteers ensure that Data behaves exactly *as if* he had a mind. No one on the Starship *Enterprise* knows that this is going on. As before, they are all convinced that Data has beliefs, desires, intentions, perceptions, and so forth. If behaviorism is true, they are right. Are they?

Consider another example, this time drawn from real life. In 1995 the French journalist Jean-Dominique Bauby suffered a stroke which left him almost completely paralyzed — he could move his left eyelid, but little else. Despite his almost total paralysis he was able to communicate by blinking. Using this method, he managed to write a memoir, *The Diving Bell and the Butterfly*, later made into a movie of the same name. If Bauby had lost the use of his left eyelid, becoming completely paralyzed, that would not have made his rich mental life vanish. We may further imagine that Bauby becomes completely resigned to his behavior-free condition, and begins to enjoy being alone with his own thoughts. He has now lost even any disposition or inclination to behave: if his paralysis were cured, he wouldn't speak or move at all. Yet surely his mental life continues on.

These examples suggest that complex behavior, although it may be excellent *evidence* of a mental life, is not *what it is* to have a mind. And isn't this just common sense? Mental states are inner states of a creature that *cause and explain* behavior, or tendencies to behave. Bauby has the mental causes, but without their typical behavioral effects. And Data, when he is controlled by the Romulan puppet masters, has the typical behavioral effects without the mental causes.

# The Identity Theory

If thinking, perceiving, and feeling are inner states that cause behavior, then we might expect that science (in particular neuroscience) will tell us what they are. Suppose the desire for water causes you to turn on the faucet on Monday, and causes you to got to the store for a bottle of spring water on Tuesday. Suppose that neuroscience tells us that neural firing pattern W caused you to turn on the faucet on Monday, and go to the store on Tuesday. Enough evidence of this sort might support the view that desiring water *just is* having a brain in neural firing pattern W. We can put this in terms of *property identity*. Here is one **property** (feature, attribute) you had on Monday and Tuesday: the property of desiring water. Here is another property you had on Monday and Tuesday: the property of having a brain in neural firing pattern W. And here is a hypothesis: the first property and the second property are *the very same property*. If that's right, the property of having a brain in neural firing pattern W is not really "another" property: it is *identical to* the property of desiring water. This is an illustration of the **identity theory**, or (as in the selection by J.J.C. Smart) the *brain process thesis*, or (as in the selection by Hilary Putnam) the *brain-state theory*. Science discovers property identities all the time; for instance the property of being table salt has turned out to be identical to the property of being sodium chloride.

The selection by Smart, published in 1959, is one of the earliest defenses of the identity theory. Smart concentrates on what might be thought to be the hardest case for a materialist theory of the mind, bodily sensations (such as a headache).[2] To have a sensation, Smart argues, is simply to have a certain physical process occurring in one's brain, nothing more.

One worry about the identity theory, raised by Putnam, is that it is too narrow in scope. Let's go back to Data. As portrayed on *Star Trek*, Data has a "positronic brain," not a biological brain. He has no neurons, thus he cannot have a brain in neural firing pattern W. So if desiring water just is to have a brain in neural firing pattern W, Data cannot desire water. In general, if the identity theory is correct, Data cannot have a mental life at all, simply because he doesn't have a biological brain. Is that plausible?

---

2. Conscious states like *being in pain* or *seeing green* are often supposed to be especially resistant to physical explanation. For more on this, see the introduction to chapter 9, "What Is Consciousness?"

# Functionalism

Data himself supplies our final materialist theory of mind, **functionalism**. Data's positronic brain is some kind of computer, programmed with software that (in the *Star Trek* fiction) results in a mind. Computer hardware can be made out of almost anything. The first programmable computer, as designed by the English mathematician Charles Babbage in the 1830s but never built, was entirely mechanical. Computers could be made from water pipes and valves, or (as they actually are made now) out of minute electronic circuits printed on silicon chips. The problem with the identity theory, one might think, is that it ties mental states too tightly to *hardware* — in particular, our biological hardware.

But perhaps mental states are more a matter of *software*: what matters is that the right program is running, not whether it is running on a Mac, or a clockwork computer, or a biological brain. Put more generally: mental states are identical to *functional states*. Functional states are those that perform a certain *function*, for instance the function of causing a certain piece of information to be stored for subsequent use in a long calculation. And functions in general (whether or not they can involve computation) can be implemented in a variety of "hardware." For example, a bottle opener is something that performs the function of opening bottles. Bottle openers can be made from different materials, and work in different ways: they can be made of steel or aluminum, and they can magnetically lift up the bottle cap, or lever it off. Putnam was one of the first to attempt to work through some of the details of a functionalist theory of mind, or (in Putnam's terminology) the *functional-state theory*.

Functionalism — specifically the version that holds that the brain is some kind of computer — is probably the dominant theory of mind in philosophy and cognitive science today. Yet it is not without objectors, and the philosopher John Searle is prominent among them. His famous "Chinese room argument" is supposed to show that running a computer program, no matter how complicated, is not a **sufficient condition** for having a mind.

# Dualism

If behaviorism, the identity theory, and functionalism all face serious problems, that suggests that the mind is not material after all, a position known as **dualism**. Dualism has a long history, going back to Plato, and the selection by René Descartes is a classic defense of it. Descartes argues that he is "simply a thinking, non-extended thing," somehow connected to his physical body. But the connection could be broken: Descartes is "really distinct" from his body, and he could "exist without it." The selection by Gilbert Ryle gives a series of objections to dualism or, as he disparagingly calls it, "the dogma of the ghost in the machine." The selection is from Ryle's influential book *The Concept of Mind*, published in 1949, which sets out his own sophisticated behaviorist theory.

## René Descartes (1596–1650)

Descartes was a French philosopher, mathematician, and scientist. He made important early contributions to mathematical physics, invented the Cartesian coordinate system familiar from high-school geometry, and is widely regarded as "the founder of modern philosophy." The *Meditations on First Philosophy* (1641) is his most famous book; his other major works include *Principles of Philosophy* (1644) and *The Passions of the Soul* (1649).

# MEDITATION II: THE NATURE OF THE HUMAN MIND, AND HOW IT IS BETTER KNOWN THAN THE BODY

### from *Meditations on First Philosophy*

So serious are the doubts into which I have been thrown as a result of yesterday's meditation[1] that I can neither put them out of my mind nor see any way of resolving them. It feels as if I have fallen unexpectedly into a deep whirlpool which tumbles me around so that I can neither stand on the bottom nor swim up to the top. Nevertheless I will make an effort and once more attempt the same path which I started on yesterday. Anything which admits of the slightest doubt I will set aside just as if I had found it to be wholly false; and I will proceed in this way until I recognize something certain, or, if nothing else, until I at least recognize for certain that there is no certainty. Archimedes[2] used to demand just one firm and immovable point in order to shift the entire earth; so I too can hope for great things if I manage to find just one thing, however slight, that is certain and unshakeable.

I will suppose then, that everything I see is spurious. I will believe that my memory tells me lies, and that none of the things that it reports ever happened. I have no senses. Body, shape, extension, movement and place are chimeras. So what remains true? Perhaps just the one fact that nothing is certain.

Yet apart from everything I have just listed, how do I know that there is not something else which does not allow even the slightest occasion for doubt? Is there not a God, or whatever I may call him, who puts into me the thoughts I am now having? But why do I think this, since I myself may perhaps be the author of these thoughts? In that case am not I, at least, something? But I have just said that I have no senses and no body. This is the sticking point: what follows from this? Am I not so bound up with a body and with senses that I cannot exist without them? But I have convinced myself that there is absolutely nothing in the world, no sky, no earth, no minds, no bodies. Does it now follow that I too do not exist? No: if I convinced myself of something then I certainly existed. But there is a deceiver of supreme power and cunning

---

1. *Meditation I*: see chapter 7 of this volume.

2. Ancient Greek scientist and mathematician (c. 287 BCE–c. 212 BCE).

who is deliberately and constantly deceiving me. In that case I too undoubtedly exist, if he is deceiving me; and let him deceive me as much as he can, he will never bring it about that I am nothing so long as I think that I am something. So after considering everything very thoroughly, I must finally conclude that this proposition, *I am, I exist,* is necessarily true whenever it is put forward by me or conceived in my mind.

But I do not yet have a sufficient understanding of what this "I" is, that now necessarily exists. So I must be on my guard against carelessly taking something else to be this "I," and so making a mistake in the very item of knowledge that I maintain is the most certain and evident of all. I will therefore go back and meditate on what I originally believed myself to be, before I embarked on this present train of thought. I will then subtract anything capable of being weakened, even minimally, by the arguments now introduced, so that what is left at the end may be exactly and only what is certain and unshakeable.

What then did I formerly think I was? A man. But what is a man? Shall I say "a rational animal"? No; for then I should have to inquire what an animal is, what rationality is, and in this way one question would lead me down the slope to other harder ones, and I do not now have the time to waste on subtleties of this kind. Instead I propose to concentrate on what came into my thoughts spontaneously and quite naturally whenever I used to consider what I was. Well, the first thought to come to mind was that I had a face, hands, arms and the whole mechanical structure of limbs which can be seen in a corpse, and which I called the body. The next thought was that I was nourished, that I moved about, and that I engaged in sense-perception and thinking; and these actions I attributed to the soul. But as to the nature of this soul, either I did not think about this or else I imagined it to be something tenuous, like a wind or fire or ether, which permeated my more solid parts. As to the body, however, I had no doubts about it, but thought I knew its nature distinctly. If I had tried to describe the mental conception I had of it, I would have expressed it as follows: by a body I understand whatever has a determinable shape and a definable location and can occupy a space in such a way as to exclude any other body; it can be perceived by touch, sight, hearing, taste or smell, and can be moved in various ways, not by itself but by whatever else comes into contact with it. For, according to my judgement, the power of self-movement, like the power of sensation or of thought, was quite foreign to the nature of a body; indeed, it was a source of wonder to me that certain bodies were found to contain faculties of this kind.

But what shall I now say that I am, when I am supposing that there is some supremely powerful and, if it is permissible to say so, malicious deceiver, who is deliberately trying to trick me in every way he can? Can I now assert that I possess even the most insignificant of all the attributes which I have just said belong to the nature of a body? I scrutinize them, think about them, go over them again, but nothing suggests itself; it is tiresome and pointless to go through the list once more. But what about the attributes I assigned to the soul? Nutrition or movement? Since now I do not have a body, these are mere fabrications. Sense-perception? This surely does not occur without a body, and besides, when asleep I have appeared to perceive through the senses many things which I afterwards realized I did not perceive through the senses at all. Thinking? At last I have discovered it — thought; this alone is inseparable from me. I am, I exist — that is certain. But for how long? For as long as I am thinking. For it could be that were I totally to cease from thinking, I should totally cease to exist. At present I am not admitting anything except what is necessarily true. I am, then, in the strict sense only a thing that thinks; that is, I am a mind, or intelligence, or intellect, or reason — words whose meaning I have been ignorant of until now. But for all that I am a thing which is real and which truly exists. But what kind of a thing? As I have just said — a thinking thing.

What else am I? I will use my imagination. I am not that structure of limbs which is called a human body. I am not even some thin vapour which permeates the limbs — a wind, fire, air, breath, or whatever I depict in my imagination; for these are things which I have supposed to be nothing. Let this supposition stand; for all that I am still something. And yet may it not perhaps be the case that these very things which I am supposing to be nothing, because they are unknown to me, are in reality identical with the "I" of which I am aware? I do not know, and for the moment I shall not argue the point, since I can make judgements only about things which are known to me. I know that I exist; the question is, what is this "I" that I know? If the "I" is understood strictly as we have been taking it, then it is quite certain that knowledge of it does not depend on things of whose existence I am as yet unaware; so it cannot depend on any of the things which I invent in my imagination. And this very word "invent" shows me my mistake. It would indeed be a case of fictitious invention if I used my imagination to establish that I was something or other; for imagining is simply contemplating the shape or image of a corporeal thing. Yet now I know for certain both that I exist and at the same time that all such images and, in general, everything relating to the nature of body, could be mere dreams. . . . Once this point has been grasped, to say "I will use my imagination to get to know more distinctly what I am" would seem to be as silly as saying "I am now awake, and see some truth; but since my vision is not yet clear enough, I will deliberately fall asleep so that my dreams may provide a truer and clearer representation." I thus realize that none of the things that the imagination enables me to grasp is at all relevant to this knowledge of myself which I possess, and that the mind must therefore be most carefully diverted from such things if it is to perceive its own nature as distinctly as possible.

But what then am I? A thing that thinks. What is that? A thing that doubts, understands, affirms, denies, is willing, is unwilling, and also imagines and has sensory perceptions.

This is a considerable list, if everything on it belongs to me. But does it? Is it not one and the same "I" who is now doubting almost everything, who nonetheless understands some things, who affirms that this one thing is true, denies everything else, desires to know more, is unwilling to be deceived, imagines many things even involuntarily, and is aware of many things which apparently come from the senses? Are not all these things just as true as the fact that I exist, even if I am asleep all the time, and even if he who created me is doing all he can to deceive me? Which of all these activities is distinct from my thinking? Which of them can be said to be separate from myself? The fact that it is I who am doubting and understanding and willing is so evident that I see no way of making it any clearer. But it is also the case that the "I" who imagines is the same "I." For even if, as I have supposed, none of the objects of imagination are real, the power of imagination is something which really exists and is part of my thinking. Lastly, it is also the same "I" who has sensory perceptions, or is aware of bodily things as it were through the senses. For example, I am now seeing light, hearing a noise, feeling heat. But I am asleep, so all this is false. Yet I certainly *seem* to see, to hear, and to be warmed. This cannot be false; what is called "having a sensory perception" is strictly just this, and in this restricted sense of the term it is simply thinking.

From all this I am beginning to have a rather better understanding of what I am. But it still appears — and I cannot stop thinking this — that the corporeal things of which images are formed in my thought, and which the senses investigate, are known with much more distinctness than this puzzling "I" which cannot be pictured in the imagination. And yet it is surely surprising that I should have a more distinct grasp of things which I realize are doubtful, unknown and foreign to me, than I have of that which is true and known — my own self. But I see what it is: my mind enjoys wandering off and will not yet submit to being restrained within the bounds of truth. Very well then; just this once let us give it a completely free rein, so that after a while, when it is time to tighten the reins, it may more readily submit to being curbed.

Let us consider the things which people commonly think they understand most distinctly of all; that is, the bodies which we touch and see. I do not mean bodies in general — for general perceptions are apt to be somewhat more confused — but one particular body. Let us take, for example, this piece of wax. It has just been taken from the honeycomb; it has not yet quite lost the taste of the honey; it retains some of the scent of the flowers from which it was gathered; its colour, shape and size are plain to see; it is hard, cold and can be handled without difficulty; if you rap it with your knuckle it makes a sound. In short, it has everything which appears necessary to enable a body to be known as distinctly as possible. But even as I speak, I put the wax by the fire, and look: the residual taste is eliminated, the smell goes away, the colour changes, the shape is lost, the size increases; it becomes liquid and hot; you can hardly touch it, and if you strike it, it no longer makes a sound. But does the same wax remain? It must be admitted that it does; no one denies it, no one thinks otherwise. So what was it in the wax that I understood with such distinctness? Evidently none of the features which I arrived at by means of the senses; for whatever came under taste, smell, sight, touch or hearing has now altered — yet the wax remains.

Perhaps the answer lies in the thought which now comes to my mind; namely, the wax was not after all the sweetness of the honey, or the fragrance of the flowers, or the whiteness, or the shape, or the sound, but was rather a body which presented itself to me in these various forms a little while ago, but which now exhibits different ones. But what exactly is it that I am now imagining? Let us concentrate, take away everything which does not belong to the wax, and see what is left; merely something extended, flexible and changeable. But what is meant here by "flexible" and "changeable"? Is it what I picture in my imagination: that this piece of wax is capable of changing from a round shape to a square shape, or from a square shape to a triangular shape? Not at all; for I can grasp that the wax is capable of countless changes of this kind, yet I am unable to run through this immeasurable number of changes in my imagination, from which it follows that it is not the faculty of imagination that gives me my grasp of the wax as flexible and changeable. And what is meant by "extended"? Is the extension of the wax also unknown? For it increases if the wax melts, increases again if it boils, and is greater still if the heat is increased. I would not be making a correct judgement about the nature of wax unless I believed it capable of being extended in many more different ways than I will ever encompass in my imagination. I must therefore admit that the nature of this piece of wax is in no way revealed by my imagination, but is perceived by the mind alone. (I am speaking of this particular piece of wax; the point is even clearer with regard to wax in general.) But what is this wax which is perceived by the mind alone? It is of course the same wax which I see, which I touch, which I picture in my imagination, in short the same wax which I thought it to be from the start. And yet, and here is the point, the perception I have of it is a case not of vision or touch or imagination — nor has it ever been, despite previous appearances — but of purely mental scrutiny; and this can be imperfect and confused, as it was before, or clear and distinct as it is now, depending on how carefully I concentrate on what the wax consists in.

But as I reach this conclusion I am amazed at how . . . prone to error my mind is. For although I am thinking about these matters within myself, silently and without speaking, nonetheless the actual words bring me up short, and I am almost tricked by ordinary ways of talking. We say that we see the wax itself, if it is there before us, not that we judge it to be there from its colour or shape; and this might lead me to conclude without more ado that knowledge of the wax comes from what the eye sees, and not from the scrutiny of the mind alone. But then if I look out of the window and see men crossing the square, as I just happen to have done, I normally say that I see the men themselves, just as I say that I see the wax. Yet do I see any more than hats and coats which could conceal autom-atons? I *judge* that they are men. And so something which I thought I was seeing with my eyes is in fact grasped solely by the faculty of judgement which is in my mind.

However, one who wants to achieve knowledge above the ordinary level should feel ashamed at having taken ordinary ways of talking as a basis for doubt. So let us proceed, and consider on which occasion my perception of the nature of the wax was more perfect and evident. Was it when I first looked at it, and believed I knew it by my external senses, or at least by what they call the "common" sense[3] — that is, the power of imagination? Or is my knowledge more perfect now, after a more careful investigation of the nature of the wax and of the means by which it is known? Any doubt on this issue would clearly be foolish; for what distinctness was there in my earlier perception? Was there anything in it which an animal could not possess? But when I distinguish the wax from its outward forms — take the clothes off, as it were, and consider it naked — then although my judge-ment may still contain errors, at least my perception now requires a human mind.

But what am I to say about this mind, or about myself? (So far, remember, I am not admitting that there is anything else in me except a mind.) What, I ask, is this "I" which seems to perceive the wax so distinctly? Surely my awareness of my own self is not merely much truer and more certain than my awareness of the wax, but also much more distinct and evident. For if I judge that the wax exists from the fact that I see it, clearly this same fact entails much more evidently that I myself also exist. It is possible that what I see is not really the wax; it is possible that I do not even have eyes with which to see anything. But when I see, or think I see (I am not here distinguishing the

3. The supposed faculty which integrates the data from the five specialized senses (the notion goes back ultimately to Aristotle). [Translator's note.]

two), it is simply not possible that I who am now thinking am not something. By the same token, if I judge that the wax exists from the fact that I touch it, the same result follows, namely that I exist. If I judge that it exists from the fact that I imagine it, or for any other reason, exactly the same thing follows. And the result that I have grasped in the case of the wax may be applied to everything else located outside me. Moreover, if my perception of the wax seemed more distinct after it was established not just by sight or touch but by many other considerations, it must be admitted that I now know myself even more distinctly. This is because every consideration whatsoever which contributes to my perception of the wax, or of any other body, cannot but establish even more effectively the nature of my own mind. But besides this, there is so much else in the mind itself which can serve to make my knowledge of it more distinct, that it scarcely seems worth going through the contributions made by considering bodily things.

I see that without any effort I have now finally got back to where I wanted. I now know that even bodies are not strictly perceived by the senses or the faculty of imagination but by the intellect alone, and that this perception derives not from their being touched or seen but from their being understood; and in view of this I know plainly that I can achieve an easier and more evident perception of my own mind than of anything else. But since the habit of holding on to old opinions cannot be set aside so quickly, I should like to stop here and meditate for some time on this new knowledge I have gained, so as to fix it more deeply in my memory.

# MEDITATION VI: . . . THE REAL DISTINCTION BETWEEN MIND AND BODY
## from *Meditations on First Philosophy*

But now,[4] when I am beginning to achieve a better knowledge of myself and the author of my being, although I do not think I should heedlessly accept everything I seem to have acquired from the senses, neither do I think that everything should be called into doubt.

First, I know that everything which I clearly and distinctly understand is capable of being created by God so as to correspond exactly with my understanding of it. Hence the fact that I can clearly and distinctly understand one thing apart from another is enough to make me certain that the two things are distinct, since they are capable of being separated, at least by God. The question of what kind of power is required to bring about such a separation does not affect the judgement that the two things are distinct. Thus, simply by knowing that I exist and seeing at the same time that absolutely nothing else belongs to my nature or essence except that I am a thinking thing, I can infer correctly that my essence consists solely in the fact that

---

4. Descartes has just reviewed the reasons he earlier gave for doubting his "confident belief in the truth of the things perceived by the senses."

I am a thinking thing. It is true that I may have (or, to anticipate, that I certainly have) a body that is very closely joined to me. But nevertheless, on the one hand I have a clear and distinct idea of myself, in so far as I am simply a thinking, non-extended thing; and on the other hand I have a distinct idea of body, in so far as this is simply an extended, non-thinking thing. And accordingly, it is certain that I am really distinct from my body, and can exist without it. . . .

There is nothing that my own nature teaches me more vividly than that I have a body, and that when I feel pain there is something wrong with the body, and that when I am hungry or thirsty the body needs food and drink, and so on. So I should not doubt that there is some truth in this.

Nature also teaches me, by these sensations of pain, hunger, thirst and so on, that I am not merely present in my body as a sailor is present in a ship, but that I am very closely joined and, as it were, intermingled with it, so that I and the body form a unit. If this were not so, I, who am nothing but a thinking thing, would not feel pain when the body was hurt, but would perceive the damage purely by the intellect, just as a sailor perceives by sight if anything in his ship is broken. Similarly, when the body needed food or drink, I should have an explicit understanding of the fact, instead of having confused sensations of hunger and thirst. For these sensations of hunger, thirst, pain and so on are nothing but confused modes of thinking which arise from the union and, as it were, intermingling of the mind with the body. . . .

There is a great difference between the mind and the body, inasmuch as the body is by its very nature always divisible, while the mind is utterly indivisible. For when I consider the mind, or myself in so far as I am merely a thinking thing, I am unable to distinguish any parts within myself; I understand myself to be something quite single and complete. Although the whole mind seems to be united to the whole body, I recognize that if a foot or arm or any other part of the body is cut off, nothing has thereby been taken away from the mind. As for the faculties of willing, of understanding, of sensory perception and so on, these cannot be termed parts of the mind, since it is one and the same mind that wills, and understands and has sensory perceptions. By contrast, there is no corporeal or extended thing that I can think of which in my thought I cannot easily divide into parts; and this very fact makes me understand that it is divisible. This one argument would be enough to show me that the mind is completely different from the body, even if I did not already know as much from other considerations.

My next observation is that the mind is not immediately affected by all parts of the body, but only by the brain, or perhaps just by one small part of the brain, namely the part which is said to contain the "common" sense.[5] Every time this part of the brain is in a given state, it presents the same signals to the mind, even though the other parts of the body may be in a different condition at the time. This is established by countless observations, which there is no need to review here.

---

5. The pineal gland, according to Descartes. This small gland is near the center of the brain and produces the hormone melatonin.

## TEST YOUR UNDERSTANDING

1. Explain, with examples, how Descartes is using the expression "thinking."

2. Does Descartes think that it is easier to know what bodies (like pieces of wax) are than it is to know what his mind is?

3. According to Descartes, are he and his body:

   (i)   joined as a sailor is to a ship?

   (ii)  related as a fog is to a ship when the fog permeates every part of the ship?

   (iii) related so they form a third thing, a unit composed of Descartes and his body?

4. According to Richard Watson's *Cogito, Ergo Sum: The Life of René Descartes* (Godine, 2007, p. 173), Descartes was short in height, perhaps a little over five feet. Speaking strictly, would Descartes have agreed? Explain your answer.

## NOTES AND QUESTIONS

1. The example of the piece of wax is supposed to show that "bodies are not strictly perceived by the senses or the faculty of imagination but by the intellect alone" (*Meditation II*). Set out Descartes's **argument** for this in the form of premises and conclusion, and evaluate it.[1]

2. You may have noticed that Descartes's famous phrase "I think, therefore I am" (in Latin "Cogito, ergo sum") does not occur in the selection. (It is in Descartes's *Discourse on Method* [1637] and *Principles of Philosophy* [1644]; the *Meditations* was published in 1641.) Instead, Descartes writes in *Meditation II* that "this proposition, *I am, I exist*, is necessarily true whenever it is put forward by me or conceived in my mind." That raises the question whether the difference in formulation in the *Meditations* is significant. For discussion, see Wilson, *Descartes*, chapter 2.

## Gilbert Ryle (1900–1976)

Ryle was an English philosopher who spent his entire career at the University of Oxford, where he was elected Waynflete Professor of Metaphysical Philosophy in 1945. His most influential work is *The Concept of Mind* (1949), a sustained attack on Cartesian dualism and a defense of a more behaviorist approach.

---

1. For a discussion of the wax example, see chapter 2 of Margaret Wilson, *Descartes* (Routledge, 1993).

# DESCARTES' MYTH
from *The Concept of Mind*

## 1. The Official Doctrine

There is a doctrine about the nature and place of minds which is so prevalent among theorists and even among laymen that it deserves to be described as the official theory. Most philosophers, psychologists and religious teachers subscribe, with minor reservations, to its main articles and, although they admit certain theoretical difficulties in it, they tend to assume that these can be overcome without serious modifications being made to the architecture of the theory. It will be argued here that the central principles of the doctrine are unsound and conflict with the whole body of what we know about minds when we are not speculating about them.

The official doctrine, which hails chiefly from Descartes,[1] is something like this. With the doubtful exceptions of idiots and infants in arms every human being has both a body and a mind. Some would prefer to say that every human being is both a body and a mind. His body and his mind are ordinarily harnessed together, but after the death of the body his mind may continue to exist and function.

Human bodies are in space and are subject to the mechanical laws which govern all other bodies in space. Bodily processes and states can be inspected by external observers. So a man's bodily life is as much a public affair as are the lives of animals and reptiles and even as the careers of trees, crystals and planets.

But minds are not in space, nor are their operations subject to mechanical laws. The workings of one mind are not witnessable by other observers; its career is private. Only I can take direct cognisance of the states and processes of my own mind. A person therefore lives through two collateral histories, one consisting of what happens in and to his body, the other consisting of what happens in and to his mind. The first is public, the second private. The events in the first history are events in the physical world, those in the second are events in the mental world.

It has been disputed whether a person does or can directly monitor all or only some of the episodes of his own private history; but, according to the official doctrine, of at least some of these episodes he has direct and unchallengeable cognisance. In consciousness, self-consciousness and introspection he is directly and authentically apprised of the present states and operations of his mind. He may have great or small uncertainties about concurrent and adjacent episodes in the physical world, but he can have none about at least part of what is momentarily occupying his mind.

It is customary to express this bifurcation of his two lives and of his two worlds by saying that the things and events which belong to the physical world, including his own body, are external, while the workings of his own mind are internal. This antithesis of outer and inner is of course meant to be construed as a metaphor, since minds, not being

---

1. René Descartes (1596–1650). See *Meditations II* and *VI* in this chapter.

in space, could not be described as being spatially inside anything else, or as having things going on spatially inside themselves. But relapses from this good intention are common and theorists are found speculating how stimuli, the physical sources of which are yards or miles outside a person's skin, can generate mental responses inside his skull, or how decisions framed inside his cranium can set going movements of his extremities.

Even when "inner" and "outer" are construed as metaphors, the problem how a person's mind and body influence one another is notoriously charged with theoretical difficulties. What the mind wills, the legs, arms and the tongue execute; what affects the ear and the eye has something to do with what the mind perceives; grimaces and smiles betray the mind's moods and bodily castigations lead, it is hoped, to moral improvement. But the actual transactions between the episodes of the private history and those of the public history remain mysterious, since by definition they can belong to neither series. They could not be reported among the happenings described in a person's autobiography of his inner life, but nor could they be reported among those described in some one else's biography of that person's overt career. They can be inspected neither by introspection nor by laboratory experiment. They are theoretical shuttlecocks which are forever being bandied from the physiologist back to the psychologist and from the psychologist back to the physiologist.

Underlying this partly metaphorical representation of the bifurcation of a person's two lives there is a seemingly more profound and philosophical assumption. It is assumed that there are two different kinds of existence or status. What exists or happens may have the status of physical existence, or it may have the status of mental existence. Somewhat as the faces of coins are either heads or tails, or somewhat as living creatures are either male or female, so, it is supposed, some existing is physical existing, other existing is mental existing. It is a necessary feature of what has physical existence that it is in space and time; it is a necessary feature of what has mental existence that it is in time but not in space. What has physical existence is composed of matter, or else is a function of matter; what has mental existence consists of consciousness, or else is a function of consciousness.

There is thus a polar opposition between mind and matter, an opposition which is often brought out as follows. Material objects are situated in a common field, known as "space," and what happens to one body in one part of space is mechanically connected with what happens to other bodies in other parts of space. But mental happenings occur in insulated fields, known as "minds," and there is, apart maybe from telepathy, no direct causal connection between what happens in one mind and what happens in another. Only through the medium of the public physical world can the mind of one person make a difference to the mind of another. The mind is its own place and in his inner life each of us lives the life of a ghostly Robinson Crusoe.[2] People can see, hear and jolt one another's bodies, but they are irremediably blind and deaf to the workings of one another's minds and inoperative upon them.

What sort of knowledge can be secured of the workings of a mind? On the one side, according to the official theory, a person has direct knowledge of the best imaginable

2. The title character of Daniel Defoe's novel *Robinson Crusoe* (1719), in which Crusoe is stranded on an island for 28 years.

kind of the workings of his own mind. Mental states and processes are (or are normally) conscious states and processes, and the consciousness which irradiates them can engender no illusions and leaves the door open for no doubts. A person's present thinkings, feelings and willings, his perceivings, rememberings and imaginings are intrinsically "phosphorescent"; their existence and their nature are inevitably betrayed to their owner. The inner life is a stream of consciousness of such a sort that it would be absurd to suggest that the mind whose life is that stream might be unaware of what is passing down it.

True, the evidence adduced recently by Freud[3] seems to show that there exist channels tributary to this stream, which run hidden from their owner. People are actuated by impulses the existence of which they vigorously disavow; some of their thoughts differ from the thoughts which they acknowledge; and some of the actions which they think they will to perform they do not really will. They are thoroughly gulled by some of their own hypocrisies and they successfully ignore facts about their mental lives which on the official theory ought to be patent to them. Holders of the official theory tend, however, to maintain that anyhow in normal circumstances a person must be directly and authentically seized of the present state and workings of his own mind.

Besides being currently supplied with these alleged immediate data of consciousness, a person is also generally supposed to be able to exercise from time to time a special kind of perception, namely inner perception, or introspection. He can take a (non-optical) "look" at what is passing in his mind. Not only can he view and scrutinize a flower through his sense of sight and listen to and discriminate the notes of a bell through his sense of hearing; he can also reflectively or introspectively watch, without any bodily organ of sense, the current episodes of his inner life. This self-observation is also commonly supposed to be immune from illusion, confusion or doubt. A mind's reports of its own affairs have a certainty superior to the best that is possessed by its reports of matters in the physical world. Sense-perceptions can, but consciousness and introspection cannot, be mistaken or confused.

On the other side, one person has no direct access of any sort to the events of the inner life of another. He cannot do better than make problematic inferences from the observed behaviour of the other person's body to the states of mind which, by analogy from his own conduct, he supposes to be signalised by that behaviour. Direct access to the workings of a mind is the privilege of that mind itself; in default of such privileged access, the workings of one mind are inevitably occult[4] to everyone else. For the supposed arguments from bodily movements similar to their own to mental workings similar to their own would lack any possibility of observational corroboration. Not unnaturally, therefore, an adherent of the official theory finds it difficult to resist this consequence of his premises, that he has no good reason to believe that there do exist minds other than his own. Even if he prefers to believe that to other human bodies there are harnessed minds not unlike his own, he cannot claim to be able to discover their individual characteristics, or the particular things that they undergo and do. Absolute solitude is on this showing the ineluctable destiny of the soul. Only our bodies can meet. . . .

---

3. Sigmund Freud (1856–1939), Austrian neurologist and founder of psychoanalysis.

4. Hidden.

# 2. The Absurdity of the Official Doctrine

Such in outline is the official theory. I shall often speak of it, with deliberate abusiveness, as "the dogma of the Ghost in the Machine." I hope to prove that it is entirely false, and false not in detail but in principle. It is not merely an assemblage of particular mistakes. It is one big mistake and a mistake of a special kind. It is, namely, a category-mistake. It represents the facts of mental life as if they belonged to one logical type or category (or range of types or categories), when they actually belong to another. The dogma is therefore a philosopher's myth. In attempting to explode the myth I shall probably be taken to be denying well-known facts about the mental life of human beings, and my plea that I aim at doing nothing more than rectify the logic of mental-conduct concepts will probably be disallowed as mere subterfuge.

I must first indicate what is meant by the phrase "category-mistake." This I do in a series of illustrations.

A foreigner visiting Oxford or Cambridge for the first time is shown a number of colleges, libraries, playing fields, museums, scientific departments and administrative offices. He then asks "But where is the University? I have seen where the members of the Colleges live, where the Registrar works, where the scientists experiment and the rest. But I have not yet seen the University in which reside and work the members of your University." It has then to be explained to him that the University is not another collateral institution, some ulterior counterpart to the colleges, laboratories and offices which he has seen. The University is just the way in which all that he has already seen is organized. When they are seen and when their co-ordination is understood, the University has been seen. His mistake lay in his innocent assumption that it was correct to speak of Christ Church, the Bodleian Library, the Ashmolean Museum *and* the University,[5] to speak, that is, as if "the University" stood for an extra member of the class of which these other units are members. He was mistakenly allocating the University to the same category as that to which the other institutions belong. . . .

The theoretically interesting category-mistakes are those made by people who are perfectly competent to apply concepts, at least in the situations with which they are familiar, but are still liable in their abstract thinking to allocate those concepts to logical types to which they do not belong. An instance of a mistake of this sort would be the following story. A student of politics has learned the main differences between the British, the French and the American Constitutions, and has learned also the differences and connections between the Cabinet, Parliament, the various Ministries, the Judicature and the Church of England. But he still becomes embarrassed when asked questions about the connections between the Church of England, the Home Office[6] and the British Constitution. For while the Church and the Home Office are institutions, the British Constitution is not another institution in the same sense of that noun.

---

5. Christ Church is a college of the University of Oxford; the Bodleian Library and the Ashmolean Museum are also part of the university.

6. Government department of the United Kingdom, similar to the U.S. State Department but also responsible for domestic security and immigration.

So inter-institutional relations which can be asserted or denied to hold between the Church and the Home Office cannot be asserted or denied to hold between either of them and the British Constitution. "The British Constitution" is not a term of the same logical type as "the Home Office" and "the Church of England." In a partially similar way, John Doe may be a relative, a friend, an enemy or a stranger to Richard Roe; but he cannot be any of these things to the Average Taxpayer. He knows how to talk sense in certain sorts of discussions about the Average Taxpayer, but he is baffled to say why he could not come across him in the street as he can come across Richard Roe.

It is pertinent to our main subject to notice that, so long as the student of politics continues to think of the British Constitution as a counterpart to the other institutions, he will tend to describe it as a mysteriously occult institution; and so long as John Doe continues to think of the Average Taxpayer as a fellow-citizen, he will tend to think of him as an elusive insubstantial man, a ghost who is everywhere yet nowhere.

My destructive purpose is to show that a family of radical category-mistakes is the source of the double-life theory. The representation of a person as a ghost mysteriously ensconced in a machine derives from this argument. Because, as is true, a person's thinking, feeling and purposive doing cannot be described solely in the idioms of physics, chemistry and physiology, therefore they must be described in counterpart idioms. As the human body is a complex organised unit, so the human mind must be another complex organised unit, though one made of a different sort of stuff and with a different sort of structure. Or, again, as the human body, like any other parcel of matter, is a field of causes and effects, so the mind must be another field of causes and effects, though not (Heaven be praised) mechanical causes and effects.

# 3. The Origin of the Category-Mistake

One of the chief intellectual origins of what I have yet to prove to be the Cartesian category-mistake seems to be this. When Galileo[7] showed that his methods of scientific discovery were competent to provide a mechanical theory which should cover every occupant of space, Descartes found in himself two conflicting motives. As a man of scientific genius he could not but endorse the claims of mechanics, yet as a religious and moral man he could not accept, as Hobbes[8] accepted, the discouraging rider to those claims, namely that human nature differs only in degree of complexity from clockwork. The mental could not be just a variety of the mechanical.

He and subsequent philosophers naturally but erroneously availed themselves of the following escape-route. Since mental-conduct words are not to be construed as signifying the occurrence of mechanical processes, they must be construed as signifying the occurrence of non-mechanical processes; since mechanical laws explain movements in space as the effects of other movements in space, other laws must explain some of the non-spatial workings of minds as the effects of other non-spatial workings of minds. The difference between the human behaviours which we describe

---

7. Galileo Galilei (1564–1642), Italian physicist and astronomer.

8. Thomas Hobbes (1588–1679), English philosopher.

as intelligent and those which we describe as unintelligent must be a difference in their causation; so, while some movements of human tongues and limbs are the effects of mechanical causes, others must be the effects of non-mechanical causes, i.e. some issue from movements of particles of matter, others from workings of the mind.

The differences between the physical and the mental were thus represented as differences inside the common framework of the categories of "thing," "stuff," "attribute," "state," "process," "change," "cause" and "effect." Minds are things, but different sorts of things from bodies; mental processes are causes and effects, but different sorts of causes and effects from bodily movements. And so on. Somewhat as the foreigner expected the University to be an extra edifice, rather like a college but also considerably different, so the repudiators of mechanism represented minds as extra centres of causal processes, rather like machines but also considerably different from them. Their theory was a para-mechanical hypothesis.

That this assumption was at the heart of the doctrine is shown by the fact that there was from the beginning felt to be a major theoretical difficulty in explaining how minds can influence and be influenced by bodies. How can a mental process, such as willing, cause spatial movements like the movements of the tongue? How can a physical change in the optic nerve have among its effects a mind's perception of a flash of light? This notorious crux by itself shows the logical mould into which Descartes pressed his theory of the mind. It was the self-same mould into which he and Galileo set their mechanics. Still unwittingly adhering to the grammar of mechanics, he tried to avert disaster by describing minds in what was merely an obverse vocabulary. The workings of minds had to be described by the mere negatives of the specific descriptions given to bodies; they are not in space, they are not motions, they are not modifications of matter, they are not accessible to public observation. Minds are not bits of clockwork, they are just bits of not-clockwork.

As thus represented, minds are not merely ghosts harnessed to machines, they are themselves just spectral machines. Though the human body is an engine, it is not quite an ordinary engine, since some of its workings are governed by another engine inside it — this interior governor-engine being one of a very special sort. It is invisible, inaudible and it has no size or weight. It cannot be taken to bits and the laws it obeys are not those known to ordinary engineers. Nothing is known of how it governs the bodily engine. . . .

It is an historical curiosity that it was not noticed that the entire argument was broken-backed. Theorists correctly assumed that any sane man could already recognise the differences between, say, rational and non-rational utterances or between purposive and automatic behaviour. Else there would have been nothing requiring to be salved from mechanism. Yet the explanation given presupposed that one person could in principle never recognise the difference between the rational and the irrational utterances issuing from other human bodies, since he could never get access to the postulated immaterial causes of some of their utterances. Save for the doubtful exception of himself, he could never tell the difference between a man and a Robot. It would have to be conceded, for example, that, for all that we can tell, the inner lives of persons who are classed as idiots or lunatics are as rational as those of anyone else. Perhaps only their overt behaviour is disappointing; that is to say, perhaps "idiots" are not really idiotic, or "lunatics" lunatic. Perhaps, too, some of those who are classed as sane are really idiots. According to the theory, external observers could never know how the overt behaviour of others is correlated with their mental powers and processes and so they could never know or even plausibly conjecture whether their applications of mental-conduct concepts to these other people were correct or incorrect. It would then be hazardous or impossible for a man to claim sanity or logical consistency even for himself, since he would be debarred from comparing his own performances with those of others. In short, our characterisations of persons and their performances as intelligent, prudent and virtuous or as stupid, hypocritical and cowardly could never have been made, so the problem of providing a special causal hypothesis to serve as the basis of such diagnoses would never have arisen. The question, "How do persons differ from machines?" arose just because everyone already knew how to apply mental-conduct concepts before the new causal hypothesis was introduced. This causal hypothesis could not therefore be the source of the criteria used in those applications. Nor, of course, has the causal hypothesis in any degree improved our handling of those criteria. We still distinguish good from bad arithmetic, politic from impolitic conduct and fertile from infertile imaginations in the ways in which Descartes himself distinguished them before and after he speculated how the applicability of these criteria was compatible with the principle of mechanical causation.

He had mistaken the logic of his problem. Instead of asking by what criteria intelligent behaviour is actually distinguished from non-intelligent behaviour, he asked "Given that the principle of mechanical causation does not tell us the difference, what other causal principle will tell it us?" He realised that the problem was not one of mechanics and assumed that it must therefore be one of some counterpart to mechanics. Not unnaturally psychology is often cast for just this role. . . .

# 4. Historical Note

It would not be true to say that the official theory derives solely from Descartes' theories, or even from a more widespread anxiety about the implications of seventeenth century mechanics. . . . Descartes was reformulating already prevalent theological doctrines of the soul in the new syntax of Galileo. . . .

It would also not be true to say that the two-worlds myth did no theoretical good. Myths often do a lot of theoretical good, while they are still new. One benefit bestowed by the para-mechanical myth was that it partly superannuated the then prevalent para-political myth. Minds and their Faculties had previously been described by analogies with political superiors and political subordinates. The idioms used were those of ruling, obeying, collaborating and rebelling. They survived and still survive in many ethical and some epistemological discussions. As, in physics, the new myth of occult Forces was a scientific improvement on the old myth of Final Causes,[9] so, in anthropological and psychological theory, the new myth of hidden operations, impulses and agencies was an improvement on the old myth of dictations, deferences and disobediences.

9. Ends or purposes: the final cause of studying is knowledge (or good grades, or admission to medical school, etc.). One of the four types of cause distinguished by the Greek philosopher Aristotle (384–322 BCE), supposed to be central to scientific explanations.

## TEST YOUR UNDERSTANDING

1. According to Ryle, why did the Cartesian category-mistake arise?

   (i) Because theorists assumed that the mind was a complicated physical machine, whose workings were not predictable by Galileo's mechanics.

   (ii) Because theorists took the mind to be like the Average Taxpayer.

   (iii) Because it reconciled the view that the mind is not physical with the view that the mind is a sort of machine.

   (iv) Because it was a consequence of Galileo's theory of spectral machines.

2. Is it a category-mistake to think that you have never met the Average Taxpayer?

3. Does Ryle think the human mind is a complicated physical machine?

## NOTES AND QUESTIONS

1. There are many mistakes that aren't category mistakes. So it is possible to hold that Cartesian dualism is a mistake without thinking that it is "a mistake of a special kind . . . namely, a category-mistake." Does Ryle give good reasons for thinking that Cartesian dualism is a mistake of this "special kind"?

2. Ryle is usually taken to be some kind of behaviorist, although this interpretation is not straightforward. See Julia Tanney, "Gilbert Ryle," *Stanford Encyclopedia of Philosophy*, ed. Edward Zalta (http://plato.stanford.edu/archives/win2009/entries/ryle/).

## J.J.C. Smart (1920–2012)

Smart was an Australian philosopher known for his contributions to the philosophy of mind, metaphysics, and ethics. His books include *Philosophy and Scientific Realism* (1963), *Utilitarianism: For and Against* (with Bernard Williams; 1973), and *Essays Metaphysical and Moral* (1987).

# SENSATIONS AND BRAIN PROCESSES

Suppose that I report that I have at this moment a roundish, blurry-edged after-image which is yellowish towards its edge and is orange towards its centre. What is it that I am reporting? One answer to this question might be that I am not reporting anything, that when I say that it looks to me as though there is a roundish yellowy orange patch of light on the wall I am expressing some sort of *temptation*, the temptation to say that there *is* a roundish yellowy orange patch on the wall (though I may know that there is not such a patch on the wall). . . . Similarly, when I "report" a pain, I am not really reporting anything (or, if you like, I am reporting in a queer sense of "reporting"), but am doing a sophisticated sort of wince. . . . I prefer most of the time to discuss an after-image rather than a pain, because the word "pain" brings in something which is irrelevant to my purpose: the notion of "distress." I think that "he is in pain" entails "he is in distress," that is, that he is in a certain agitation-condition. Similarly, to say "I am in pain" may be to do more than "replace pain behavior": it may be partly to report something, though this something is quite nonmysterious, being an agitation-condition, and so susceptible of behavioristic analysis.[1] The suggestion I wish if possible to avoid is a different one, namely that "I am in pain" is a genuine report, and that what it reports is an irreducibly psychical something. And similarly the suggestion I wish to resist is also that to say "I have a yellowish orange after-image" is to report something irreducibly psychical.

Why do I wish to resist this suggestion? Mainly because of Occam's razor.[2] It seems to me that science is increasingly giving us a viewpoint whereby organisms are able to be seen as physico-chemical mechanisms: it seems that even the behavior of man himself will one day be explicable in mechanistic terms. There does seem to be, so far as science is concerned, nothing in the world but increasingly complex arrangements of physical constituents. All except for one place: in consciousness. That is, for a full description of what is going on in a man you would have to mention not only the physical processes in his tissue, glands, nervous system, and so forth, but also his states of consciousness: his visual, auditory, and tactual sensations, his aches and pains. That these should be *correlated* with brain processes does not help, for to say that they are *correlated* is to say that they are something "over and above." You cannot correlate something with itself. You correlate footprints with burglars, but not Bill Sikes the burglar with Bill Sikes the burglar. So sensations, states of consciousness, do seem to be the one sort of thing left outside the physicalist picture, and for various reasons I just cannot believe that this can be so. That everything should be explicable in terms of physics (together of course with descriptions of the ways in which the parts are put together — roughly, biology is to physics as radio-engineering is to electro-magnetism) except the occurrence of sensations seems to me to be frankly unbelievable. Such sensations would be "nomological danglers," to use Feigl's expression.[3] It is not often realized how odd would be the laws whereby these nomological danglers would dangle. It is sometimes asked, "Why can't there be psycho-physical laws which are of a novel sort, just as the laws of electricity and magnetism were novelties from the standpoint of Newtonian mechanics?" Certainly we are pretty sure in the future to come

1. Behaviorism is the view that to have a mind is simply to behave (or to be disposed or inclined to behave) in various ways.

2. A methodological principle of parsimony in theorizing, often rendered as "Do not multiply entities beyond necessity." Named after the English philosopher William of Occam (or Ockham) (c. 1287–1347).

3. "Nomological": relating to laws of nature. Herbert Feigl (1902–1988) was an Austrian philosopher of science.

across new ultimate laws of a novel type, but I expect them to relate simple constitu-ents: for example, whatever ultimate particles are then in vogue. I cannot believe that ultimate laws of nature could relate simple constituents to configurations consisting of perhaps billions of neurons (and goodness knows how many billion billions of ultimate particles) all put together for all the world as though their main purpose in life was to be a negative feedback mechanism of a complicated sort. Such ultimate laws would be like nothing so far known in science. They have a queer "smell" to them. I am just unable to believe in the nomological danglers themselves, or in the laws whereby they would dangle. If any philosophical arguments seemed to compel us to believe in such things, I would suspect a catch in the argument. In any case it is the object of this paper to show that there are no philosophical arguments which compel us to be dualists.[4] . . .

Why should not sensations just be brain processes of a certain sort? There are, of course, well-known (as well as lesser-known) philosophical objections to the view that reports of sensations are reports of brain processes, but I shall try to argue that these arguments are by no means as cogent as is commonly thought to be the case.

Let me first try to state more accurately the thesis that sensations are brain pro-cesses. It is not the thesis that, for example; "after-image" or "ache" means the same as "brain process of sort $X$" (where "$X$" is replaced by a description of a certain sort of brain process). It is that, in so far as "after-image" or "ache" is a report of a process, it is a report of a process that *happens to be* a brain process. It follows that the thesis does not claim that sensation statements can be *translated* into statements about brain processes. Nor does it claim that the logic of a sensation statement is the same as that of a brain-process statement. All it claims is that in so far as a sensation statement is a report of something, that something is in fact a brain process. Sensations are nothing over and above brain processes. Nations are nothing "over and above" citizens, but this does not prevent the logic of nation statements being very different from the logic of citizen statements, nor does it insure the translatability of nation statements into citizen statements. (I do not, however, wish to assert that the relation of sensa-tion statements to brain-process statements is very like that of nation statements to citizen statements. Nations do not just *happen to be* nothing over and above citizens, for example. I bring in the "nations" example merely to make a negative point: that the fact that the logic of A-statements is different from that of B-statements does not insure that A's are anything over and above B's.)

*Remarks on identity.* When I say that a sensation is a brain process or that light-ning is an electric discharge, I am using "is" in the sense of strict identity. (Just as in the — in this case necessary — proposition "7 is identical with the smallest prime number greater than 5.") When I say that a sensation is a brain process or that light-ning is an electric discharge I do not mean just that the sensation is somehow spa-tially or temporally continuous with the brain process or that the lightning is just spatially or temporally continuous with the discharge. . . . I wish to make it clear that the brain-process doctrine asserts identity in the *strict* sense.

---

4. Those who believe, following the French philosopher René Descartes (1596–1650), that the mind and the body are distinct things.

I shall now discuss various possible objections to the view that the processes reported in sensation statements are in fact processes in the brain. Most of us have met some of these objections in our first year as philosophy students. All the more reason to take a good look at them. Others of the objections will be more recondite and subtle.

*Objection 1.*[5] Any illiterate peasant can talk perfectly well about his after-images, or how things look or feel to him, or about his aches and pains, and yet he may know nothing whatever about neurophysiology. A man may, like Aristotle, believe that the brain is an organ for cooling the body without any impairment of his ability to make true statements about his sensations. Hence the things we are talking about when we describe our sensations cannot be processes in the brain.

*Reply.* You might as well say that a nation of slug-abeds, who never saw the morning star or knew of its existence, or who had never thought of the expression "the Morning Star," but who used the expression "the Evening Star" perfectly well, could not use this expression to refer to the same entity as we refer to (and describe as) "the Morning Star."[6]

You may object that the Morning Star is in a sense not the very same thing as the Evening Star, but only something spatiotemporally continuous with it. That is, you may say that the Morning Star is not the Evening Star in the strict sense of "identity" that I distinguished earlier. I can perhaps forestall this objection by considering the slug-abeds to be New Zealanders and the early risers to be Englishmen. Then the thing the New Zealanders describe as "the Morning Star" could be the very same thing (in the strict sense) as the Englishmen describe as "the Evening Star." And yet they could be ignorant of this fact.

There is, however, a more plausible example. Consider lightning. Modern physical science tells us that lightning is a certain kind of electrical discharge due to ionization of clouds of water-vapor in the atmosphere. This, it is now believed, is what the true nature of lightning is. Note that there are not two things: a flash of lightning and an electrical discharge. There is one thing, a flash of lightning, which is described scientifically as an electrical discharge to the earth from a cloud of ionized water-molecules. The case is not at all like that of explaining a footprint by reference to a burglar. We say that what lightning really is, what its true nature as revealed by science is, is an electric discharge. (It is not the true nature of a footprint to be a burglar.)

To forestall irrelevant objections, I should like to make it clear that by "lightning" I mean the publicly observable physical object, lightning, not a visual sense-datum[7] of lightning. I say that the publicly observable physical object lightning is in fact the electric discharge, not just a correlate of it. The sense-datum, or at least the having of the sense-datum, the "look" of lightning, may well in my view be a correlate of the electric discharge. For in my view it is a brain state *caused* by the lightning. But we

5. Smart discusses eight objections, two of which are omitted from this selection.

6. The Morning Star and the Evening Star are both the planet Venus.

7. A sense datum (plural *data*) is an object that (according to some philosophers) one is aware of when one sees a physical object and that (unlike the physical object) always is as it appears to be.

should no more confuse sensations of lightning with lightning than we confuse sensations of a table with the table.

In short, the reply to Objection 1 is that there can be contingent statements of the form "A is identical with B," and a person may well know that something is an A without knowing that it is a B. An illiterate peasant might well be able to talk about his sensations without knowing about his brain processes, just as he can talk about lightning though he knows nothing of electricity.

*Objection 2.* It is only a contingent fact (if it is a fact) that when we have a certain kind of sensation there is a certain kind of process in our brain. Indeed it is possible, though perhaps in the highest degree unlikely, that our present physiological theories will be as out of date as the ancient theory connecting mental processes with goings on in the heart. It follows that when we report a sensation we are not reporting a brain-process.

*Reply.* The objection certainly proves that when we say "I have an after-image" we cannot *mean* something of the form "I have such and such a brain process." But this does not show that what we report (having an after-image) is not *in fact* a brain process. "I see lightning" does not *mean* "I see an electric discharge." Indeed, it is logically possible (though highly unlikely) that the electrical discharge account of lightning might one day be given up. Again, "I see the Evening Star" does not *mean* the same as "I see the Morning Star," and yet "the Evening Star and the Morning Star are one and the same thing" is a contingent proposition. Possibly Objection 2 derives some of its apparent strength from a "Fido" — Fido theory of meaning.[8] If the meaning of an expression were what the expression named, then of course it *would* follow from the fact that "sensation" and "brain process" have different meanings that they cannot name one and the same thing.

*Objection 3.* Even if Objections 1 and 2 do not prove that sensations are something over and above brain processes, they do prove that the qualities of sensations are something over and above the qualities of brain processes. That is, it may be possible to get out of asserting the existence of irreducibly psychic processes, but not out of asserting the existence of irreducibly psychic *properties*. For suppose we identify the Morning Star with the Evening Star. Then there must be some properties which logically imply that of being the Morning Star, and quite distinct properties which entail that of being the Evening Star. Again, there must be some properties (for example, that of being a yellow flash) which are logically distinct from those in the physicalist story. . . .

Now how do I get over [this] objection that a sensation can be identified with a brain process only if it has some [irreducibly psychic] property . . . whereby one-half of the identification may be, so to speak, pinned down?[9]

8. The theory (given this derogatory label by the English philosopher Gilbert Ryle [1900–1976]) that the meaning of an expression is the thing it refers to. Thus the meaning of the name 'Fido' is the dog, Fido.

9. In a true identity statement like "The Morning Star = the Evening Star," the object in question, namely Venus, has two properties corresponding to the different ways Venus is identified or picked out by the two expressions "the Morning Star" and "the Evening Star." These two properties of Venus are *being the brightest object in the morning sky,* and *being the brightest object in the evening sky.* Objection 3 is that if an identity statement like "This pain sensation = such-and-such brain process" is true, then the property corresponding to the way the noun phrase "this pain sensation" identifies or picks out the thing it refers to cannot be a neurophysiological property, and must instead be an irreducibly mental one.

My suggestion is as follows. When a person says, "I see a yellowish-orange after-image," he is saying something like this: "*There is something going on which is like what is going on when* I have my eyes open, am awake, and there is an orange illuminated in good light in front of me, that is, when I really see an orange." ... Notice that the italicized words, namely "there is something going on which is like what is going on when," are all quasi-logical or topic-neutral words. This explains why the ancient Greek peasant's reports about his sensations can be neutral between dualistic metaphysics or my materialistic metaphysics. It explains how sensations can be brain processes and yet how those who report them need know nothing about brain processes. For he reports them only very abstractly as "something going on which is like what is going on when ..." Similarly, a person may say "someone is in the room," thus reporting truly that the doctor is in the room, even though he has never heard of doctors. (There are not two people in the room: "someone" *and* the doctor.) This account of sensation statements also explains the singular elusiveness of "raw feels"[1] — why no one seems to be able to pin any properties on them. Raw feels, in my view, are colorless for the very same reason that *something* is colorless. This does not mean that sensations do not have properties, for if they are brain processes they certainly have properties. It only means that in speaking of them as being like or unlike one another we need not know or mention these properties.

This, then, is how I would reply to Objection 3. The strength of my reply depends on the possibility of our being able to report that one thing is like another without being able to state the respect in which it is like. I am not sure whether this is so or not, and that is why I regard Objection 3 as the strongest with which I have to deal.

*Objection 4.* The after-image is not in physical space. The brain process is. So the after-image is not a brain process.

*Reply.* This is an *ignoratio elenchi*.[2] I am not arguing that the after-image is a brain process, but that the experience of having an after-image is a brain process. It is the *experience* which is reported in the introspective report. Similarly, if it is objected that the after-image is yellowy-orange but that a surgeon looking into your brain would see nothing yellowy-orange, my reply is that it is the experience of seeing yellowy-orange that is being described, and this experience is not a yellow-orange something. So to say that a brain-process cannot be yellowy-orange is not to say that a brain-process cannot in fact be the experience of having a yellowy-orange after-image. There is, in a sense, no such thing as an after-image or a sense-datum, though there is such a thing as the experience of having an image, and this experience is described indirectly in material object language, not in phenomenal language, for there is no such thing. We describe the experience by saying, in effect, that it is like the experience we have when, for example, we really see a yellowy-orange patch on the wall. Trees and wallpaper can be green, but not the experience of seeing or imagining a tree or wallpaper. (Or if they are described as green or yellow this can only be in a derived sense.)

---

1. Sensations.

2. Literally, "ignorance of refutation" (Latin). Used to label reasoning to an irrelevant conclusion.

*Objection 5.* It would make sense to say of a molecular movement in the brain that it is swift or slow, straight or circular, but it makes no sense to say this of the experience of seeing something yellow.

*Reply.* So far we have not given sense to talk of experiences as swift or slow, straight or circular. But I am not claiming that "experience" and "brain process" mean the same or even that they have the same logic. "Somebody" and "the doctor" do not have the same logic, but this does not lead us to suppose that talking about somebody telephoning is talking about someone over and above, say, the doctor. The ordinary man when he reports an experience is reporting that something is going on, but he leaves it open as to what sort of thing is going on, whether in a material solid medium, or perhaps in some sort of gaseous medium, or even perhaps in some sort of nonspatial medium (if this makes sense). All that I am saying is that "experience" and "brain process" may in fact refer to the same thing, and if so we may easily adopt a convention (which is not a change in our present rules for the use of experience words but an addition to them) whereby it would make sense to talk of an experience in terms appropriate to physical processes. . . .

*Objection 7.* I can imagine myself turned to stone and yet having images, aches, pains, and so on.

*Reply.* I can imagine that the electrical theory of lightning is false, that lightning is some sort of purely optical phenomenon. I can imagine that lightning is not an electrical discharge. I can imagine that the Evening Star is not the Morning Star. But it is. All the objection shows is that "experience" and "brain process" do not have the same meaning. It does not show that an experience is not in fact a brain process.

This objection is perhaps much the same as one which can be summed up by the slogan: "What can be composed of nothing cannot be composed of anything." The argument goes as follows: on the brain process thesis the identity between the brain process and the experience is a contingent one. So it is logically possible that there should be no brain process, and no process of any other sort, either (no heart process, no kidney process, no liver process). There would be the experience but no "corresponding" physiological process with which we might be able to identify it empirically.

I suspect that the objector is thinking of the experience as a ghostly entity. So it is composed of something, not of nothing, after all. On his view it is composed of ghost stuff, and on mine it is composed of brain stuff. Perhaps the counter-reply will be that the experience is simple and uncompounded, and so it is not composed of anything after all. This seems to be a quibble, for, if it were taken seriously, the remark "What can be composed of nothing cannot be composed of anything" could be recast as an a priori argument against Democritus and atomism and for Descartes and infinite divisibility.[3] And it seems odd that a question of this sort could be settled a priori. We must therefore construe the word "composed" in a very weak sense, which would allow us to say that even an indivisible atom is composed of something (namely,

---

3. "A priori argument": an argument proceeding from premises that are knowable independently of experience. "Democritus and atomism . . .": according to the Ancient Greek philosopher Democritus (c. 460–370 BCE), physical objects are composed of tiny indivisible particles ("atoms"); Descartes held the opposing position, that physical objects are infinitely divisible.

itself). The dualist cannot really say that an experience can be composed of nothing. For he holds that experiences are something over and above material processes, that is, that they are a sort of ghost stuff. (Or perhaps ripples in an underlying ghost stuff.) I say that the dualist's hypothesis is a perfectly intelligible one. But I say that experiences are not to be identified with ghost stuff but with brain stuff. This is another hypothesis, and in my view a very plausible one. The present argument cannot knock it down a priori. . . .

I have now considered a number of objections to the brain-process thesis. I wish now to conclude by some remarks on the logical status of the thesis itself. U. T. Place[4] seems to hold that it is a straight-out scientific hypothesis. If so, he is partly right and partly wrong. If the issue is between (say) a brain-process thesis and a heart thesis, or a liver thesis, or a kidney thesis, then the issue is a purely empirical one, and the verdict is overwhelmingly in favor of the brain. The right sorts of things don't go on in the heart, liver, or kidney, nor do these organs possess the right sort of complexity of structure. On the other hand, if the issue is between a brain-or-heart-or-liver-or-kidney thesis (that is, some form of materialism) on the one hand and epiphenomenalism[5] on the other hand, then the issue is not an empirical one. For there is no conceivable experiment which could decide between materialism and epiphenomenalism. This latter issue is not like the average straight-out empirical issue in science, but like the issue between the nineteenth-century English naturalist Philip Gosse and the orthodox geologists and paleontologists of his day. According to Gosse, the earth was created about 4000 B.C. exactly as described in *Genesis,* with twisted rock strata, "evidence" of erosion, and so forth, and all sorts of fossils, all in their appropriate strata, just as if the usual evolutionist story had been true. Clearly this theory is in a sense irrefutable: no evidence can possibly tell against it. Let us ignore the theological setting in which Philip Gosse's hypothesis had been placed, thus ruling out objections of a theological kind, such as "what a queer God who would go to such elaborate lengths to deceive us." Let us suppose that it is held that the universe just began in 4004 B.C. with the initial conditions just everywhere as they were in 4004 B.C., and in particular that our own planet began with sediment in the rivers, eroded cliffs, fossils in the rocks, and so on. No scientist would ever entertain this as a serious hypothesis, consistent though it is with all possible evidence. The hypothesis offends against the principles of parsimony and simplicity. There would be far too many brute and inexplicable facts. Why are pterodactyl bones just as they are? No explanation in terms of the evolution of pterodactyls from earlier forms of life would any longer be possible. We would have millions of facts about the world as it was in 4004 B.C. that just have to be *accepted.*

The issue between the brain-process theory and epiphenomenalism seems to be of the above sort. (Assuming that a behavioristic reduction of introspective reports is not possible.) If it be agreed that there are no cogent philosophical

---

4. U. T. Place (1924–2000), British philosopher and psychologist, who published a famous paper defending the brain-process thesis in 1956.

5. "Epiphenomenalism": the view that the mental does not causally affect anything physical.

arguments which force us into accepting dualism, and if the brain-process theory and dualism are equally consistent with the facts, then the principles of parsimony and simplicity seem to me to decide overwhelmingly in favor of the brain-process theory. As I pointed out earlier, dualism involves a large number of irreducible psychophysical laws (whereby the "nomological danglers" dangle) of a queer sort, that just have to be taken on trust, and are just as difficult to swallow as the irreducible facts about the paleontology of the earth with which we are faced on Philip Gosse's theory.

## TEST YOUR UNDERSTANDING

1. According to Smart, is a statement such as "I am in pain" not a genuine report of an irreducibly psychical fact but instead a sophisticated sort of wince?

2. Is Smart arguing that after-images are brain processes?

3. Does Smart think that experiments have shown epiphenomenalism to be false?

4. Are "identical twins" strictly identical? If not, in what sense are identical twins identical?

## NOTES AND QUESTIONS

1. Explain, using examples that are not about the mind or the brain, the difference between saying that sensations are (identical to) brain processes, and saying that sensations are (merely) correlated with brain processes. Explain and assess Smart's main motivation for the thesis that sensations are brain processes.

2. For a lengthy defense of the identity theory, see Christopher Hill, *Sensations: A Defense of Type Materialism* (Cambridge University Press, 1991).

## Hilary Putnam (born 1926)

Putnam is Cogan University Professor Emeritus at Harvard University, and has written widely on almost every area of philosophy, making seminal contributions to philosophy of mathematics, philosophy of science, philosophy of language, epistemology, metaphysics, and philosophy of mind. His books include *Reason, Truth, and History* (1981) and *The Threefold Cord: Mind, Body, and World* (1999). Many of his classic papers are collected in three volumes published by Cambridge University Press in 1975 and 1983.

# THE NATURE OF MENTAL STATES

The typical concerns of the Philosopher of Mind might be represented by three questions: (1) How do we know that other people have pains? (2) Are pains brain states? (3) What is the analysis of the concept *pain*? I do not wish to discuss questions (1) and (3) in this chapter. I shall say something about question (2).

## 1. Identity Questions

... Many philosophers believe that the statement "pain is a brain state" violates some rules or norms of English. But the arguments offered are hardly convincing. For example, if the fact that I can know that I am in pain without knowing that I am in brain state $S$ shows that pain cannot be brain state $S$, then, by exactly the same argument, the fact that I can know that the stove is hot without knowing that the mean molecular kinetic energy is high (or even that molecules exist) shows that it is *false* that temperature is mean molecular kinetic energy, physics to the contrary. In fact, all that immediately follows from the fact that I can know that I am in pain without knowing that I am in brain state $S$ is that the concept of pain is not the same concept as the concept of being in brain state $S$. But either pain, or the state of being in pain, or some pain, or some pain state, might still be brain state $S$. After all, the concept of temperature is not the same concept as the concept of mean molecular kinetic energy. But temperature is mean molecular kinetic energy.

Some philosophers maintain that both "pain is a brain state" and "pain states are brain states" are unintelligible. The answer is to explain to these philosophers, as well as we can, given the vagueness of all scientific methodology, what sorts of considerations lead one to make an empirical reduction (i.e. to say such things as "water is $H_2O$," "light is electro-magnetic radiation," "temperature is mean molecular kinetic energy"). If, without giving reasons, [such a philosopher] still maintains in the face of such examples that one cannot imagine parallel circumstances for the use of "pains are brain states" (or, perhaps, "pain states are brain states") one has grounds to regard him as perverse. ...

Again, other philosophers have contended that all the predictions that can be derived from the conjunction of neurophysiological laws with such statements as "pain states are such-and-such brain states" can equally well be derived from the conjunction of the same neurophysiological laws with "being in pain is correlated with such-and-such brain states," and hence (*sic!*)[1] there can be no methodological grounds for saying that pains (or pain states) *are* brain states, as opposed to saying that they are *correlated* (invariantly) with brain states. This argument, too, would show that

---

1. Thus (Latin). Used to indicate that quoted or reported material is erroneous; Putnam is thus disputing the "hence."

light is only correlated with electromagnetic radiation. The mistake is in ignoring the fact that, although the theories in question may indeed lead to the same predictions, they open and exclude different *questions*. "Light is invariantly correlated with electromagnetic radiation" would leave open the questions "What is the light then, if it isn't the same as the electromagnetic radiation?" and "What makes the light accompany the electromagnetic radiation?" — questions which are excluded by saying that the light *is* the electromagnetic radiation. Similarly, the purpose of saying that pains are brain states is precisely to exclude from empirical meaningfulness the questions "What is the pain, then, if it isn't the same as the brain state?" and "What makes the pain accompany the brain state?" If there are grounds to suggest that these questions represent, so to speak, the wrong way to look at the matter, then those grounds are grounds for a theoretical identification of pains with brain states.

If all arguments to the contrary are unconvincing, shall we then conclude that it is meaningful (and perhaps true) to say either that pains are brain states or that pain states are brain states?

(1) It is perfectly meaningful (violates no "rule of English," involves no "extension of usage") to say "pains are brain states."

(2) It is not meaningful (involves a "changing of meaning" or "an extension of usage," etc.) to say "pains are brain states."

My own position is not expressed by either (1) or (2). It seems to me that the notions "change of meaning" and "extension of usage" are simply so ill defined that one cannot in fact say *either* (1) or (2). I see no reason to believe that either the linguist, or the man-on-the-street, or the philosopher possesses today a notion of "change of meaning" applicable to such cases as the one we have been discussing. The *job* for which the notion of change of meaning was developed in the history of the language was just a *much* cruder job than this one.

But, if we don't assert either (1) or (2) — in other words, if we regard the "change of meaning" issue as a pseudo-issue in this case — then how are we to discuss the question with which we started? "Is pain a brain state?"

The answer is to allow statements of the form "pain is *A*," where "pain" and "*A*" are in no sense synonyms, and to see whether any such statement can be found which might be acceptable on empirical and methodological grounds. This is what we shall now proceed to do.

## 2. Is Pain a Brain State?

We shall discuss "Is pain a brain state?" then. And we have agreed to waive the "change of meaning" issue.

Since I am discussing not what the concept of pain comes to, but what pain is, in a sense of "is" which requires empirical theory-construction (or, at least, empirical speculation), I shall not apologize for advancing an empirical hypothesis. Indeed, my strategy will be to argue that pain is *not* a brain state, not on *a priori* grounds,[2] but on the grounds that another hypothesis is more plausible. The detailed development and verification of my hypothesis would be just as Utopian a task as the detailed development and verification of the brain-state hypothesis. But the putting-forward, not of detailed and scientifically "finished" hypotheses, but of schemata for hypotheses, has long been a function of philosophy. I shall, in short, argue that pain is not a brain state, in the sense of a physical-chemical state of the brain (or even the whole nervous system), but another *kind* of state entirely. I propose the hypothesis that pain, or the state of being in pain, is a functional state of a whole organism.

To explain this it is necessary to introduce some technical notions. In previous papers I have explained the notion of a Turing Machine[3] and discussed the use of this notion as a model for an organism. The notion of a Probabilistic Automaton is defined similarly to a Turing Machine, except that the transitions between "states" are allowed to be with various probabilities rather than being "deterministic." (Of course, a Turing Machine is simply a special kind of Probabilistic Automaton, one with transition probabilities 0, 1. I shall assume the notion of a Probabilistic Automaton has been generalized to allow for "sensory inputs" and "motor outputs" — that is, the Machine Table specifies, for every possible combination of a "state" and a complete set of "sensory inputs," an "instruction" which determines the probability of the next "state," and also the probabilities of the "motor outputs." (This replaces the idea of the Machine as printing on a tape.) I shall also assume that the physical realization of the sense organs responsible for the various inputs, and of the motor organs, is specified, but that the "states" and the "inputs" themselves are, as usual, specified *only* "implicitly" — i.e. by the set of transition probabilities given by the Machine Table.

Since an empirically given system can simultaneously be a "physical realization" of many different Probabilistic Automata, I introduce the notion of a *Description* of a system. A Description of $S$ where $S$ is a system, is any true statement to the effect that $S$ possesses distinct states $S_1, S_2 \ldots S_n$ which are related to one another and to the motor outputs and sensory inputs by the transition probabilities given in such-and-such a Machine Table. The Machine Table mentioned in the Description will then be called the Functional Organization of $S$ relative to that Description, and the $S_i$ such that $S$ is in state $S_i$ at a given time will be called the Total State of $S$ (at the time) relative to that Description. It should be noted that knowing the Total State of a system relative to a Description involves knowing a good deal about how the system is likely to "behave," given various combinations of sensory inputs, but does *not* involve knowing the physical realization of the $S_i$ as, e.g. physical-chemical states of the brain. The $S_i$, to repeat, are specified only *implicitly* by the Description — i.e., specified *only* by the set of transition probabilities given in the Machine Table.

2. Grounds knowable independently of experience.

3. A simple form of hypothetical computer, devised by the English mathematician Alan Turing (1912–1954). At any time, a Turing machine is in one of a finite number of states, and it changes state over time according to rules specified by its Machine Table. Turing machines are often pictured as printing and erasing symbols on a tape.

The hypothesis that "being in pain is a functional state of the organism" may now be spelled out more exactly as follows:

(1) All organisms capable of feeling pain are Probabilistic Automata.

(2) Every organism capable of feeling pain possesses at least one Description of a certain kind (i.e., being capable of feeling pain *is* possessing an appropriate kind of Functional Organization).

(3) No organism capable of feeling pain possesses a decomposition into parts which separately possess Descriptions of the kind referred to in (2).

(4) For every Description of the kind referred to in (2), there exists a subset of the sensory inputs such that an organism with that Description is in pain when and only when some of its sensory inputs are in that subset.

This hypothesis is admittedly vague, though surely no vaguer than the brain-state hypothesis in its present form. For example, one would like to know more about the kind of Functional Organization that an organism must have to be capable of feeling pain, and more about the marks that distinguish the subset of the sensory inputs referred to in (4). With respect to the first question, one can probably say that the Functional Organization must include something that resembles a "preference function"[4] . . . and something that resembles an "inductive logic" (i.e., the Machine must be able to "learn from experience"). . . . In addition, it seems natural to require that the Machine possess "pain sensors," i.e. sensory organs which normally signal damage to the Machine's body, or dangerous temperatures, pressures, etc., which transmit a special subset of the inputs, the subset referred to in (4). Finally, and with respect to the second question, we would want to require at least that the inputs in the distinguished subset have a high disvalue on the Machine's preference function or ordering. . . . The purpose of condition (3) is to rule out such "organisms" (if they can count as such) as swarms of bees as single pain-feelers. The condition (1) is, obviously, redundant, and is only introduced for expository reasons. (It is, in fact, empty, since everything is a Probabilistic Automaton under *some* Description.)

I contend, in passing, that this hypothesis, in spite of its admitted vagueness, is far *less* vague than the "physical-chemical state" hypothesis is today, and far more susceptible to investigation of both a mathematical and an empirical kind. Indeed, to investigate this hypothesis is just to attempt to produce "mechanical" models of organisms — and isn't this, in a sense, just what psychology is about? The difficult step, of course, will be to pass from models to *specific* organisms to a *normal form* for the psychological description of organisms — for this is what is required to make (2) and (4) precise. But this too seems to be an inevitable part of the program of psychology.

I shall now compare the hypothesis just advanced with the hypothesis that pain is a brain state. . . .

---

4. Function from options — possible courses of action facing an agent — to real numbers that represents the agent's preferences between options.

# 3. Functional State versus Brain State

It may, perhaps, be asked if I am not somewhat unfair in taking the brain-state theorist to be talking about *physical-chemical* states of the brain. But (a) these are the only sorts of states ever mentioned by brain-state theorists. (b) The brain-state theorist usually mentions (with a certain pride, slightly reminiscent of the Village Atheist[5]) the incompatibility of his hypothesis with all forms of dualism[6] and mentalism. This is natural if physical-chemical states of the brain are what is at issue. However, functional states of whole systems are something quite different. In particular, the functional-state hypothesis is *not* incompatible with dualism! Although it goes without saying that the hypothesis is "mechanistic" in its inspiration, it is a slightly remarkable fact that a system consisting of a body and a "soul," if such things there be, can perfectly well be a Probabilistic Automaton. (c) One argument advanced by Smart[7] is that the brain-state theory assumes only "physical" properties, and Smart finds "non-physical" properties unintelligible. The Total States and the "inputs" defined above are, of course, neither mental nor physical *per se,* and I cannot imagine a functionalist advancing this argument. (d) If the brain-state theorist does mean (or at least allow) states other than physical-chemical states, then his hypothesis is completely empty, at least until he specifies *what* sort of "states" he *does* mean.

Taking the brain-state hypothesis in this way, then, what reasons are there to prefer the functional-state hypothesis over the brain-state hypothesis? Consider what the brain-state theorist has to do to make good his claims. He has to specify a physical-chemical state such that *any* organism (not just a mammal) is in pain if and only if (a) it possesses a brain of a suitable physical-chemical structure; and (b) its brain is in that physical-chemical state. This means that the physical-chemical state in question must be a possible state of a mammalian brain, a reptilian brain, a mollusc's brain (octopuses are mollusca, and certainly feel pain), etc. At the same time, it must *not* be a possible (physically possible) state of the brain of any physically possible creature that cannot feel pain. Even if such a state can be found, it must be nomologically certain[8] that it will also be a state of the brain of any extraterrestrial life that may be found that will be capable of feeling pain before we can even entertain the supposition that it may *be* pain.

It is not altogether impossible that such a state will be found. Even though octopus and mammal are examples of parallel (rather than sequential) evolution, for example, virtually identical structures (physically speaking) have evolved in the eye of the octopus and in the eye of the mammal, notwithstanding the fact that this organ has evolved from different kinds of cells in the two cases. Thus it is at least possible that parallel evolution, all over the universe, might *always* lead to *one and the same* physical "correlate" of pain. But this is certainly an ambitious hypothesis.

---

5. Lone atheist in a community of religious believers.

6. The view, associated with the French philosopher René Descartes (1596–1650), that the mind and the body are distinct things.

7. J.J.C. Smart (1920–2012), Australian philosopher; he defends his "brain-state theory" in "Sensations and Brain Processes" (earlier in this chapter).

8. "Nomological": relating to laws of nature; "nomologically certain": certain, given laws of nature.

Finally, the hypothesis becomes still more ambitious when we realize that the brain-state theorist is not just saying that *pain* is a brain state; he is, of course, concerned to maintain that *every* psychological state is a brain state. Thus if we can find even one psychological predicate which can clearly be applied to both a mammal and an octopus (say "hungry"), but whose physical-chemical "correlate" is different in the two cases, the brain-state theory has collapsed. It seems to me overwhelmingly probable that we can do this. Granted, in such a case the brain-state theorist can save himself by *ad hoc* assumptions (e.g., defining the disjunction of two states to be a single "physical-chemical state"), but this does not have to be taken seriously.

Turning now to the considerations *for* the functional-state theory, let us begin with the fact that we identify organisms as in pain, or hungry, or angry, or in heat, etc., on the basis of their *behavior*. But it is a truism that similarities in the behavior of two systems are at least a reason to suspect similarities in the functional organization of the two systems, and a much *weaker* reason to suspect similarities in the actual physical details. Moreover, we expect the various psychological states — at least the basic ones, such as hunger, thirst, aggression, etc. — to have more or less similar "transition probabilities" (within wide and ill defined limits, to be sure) with each other and with behavior in the case of different species, because this is an artifact of the way in which we identify these states. Thus, we would not count an animal as *thirsty* if its "unsatiated" behavior did not seem to be directed toward drinking and was not followed by "satiation for liquid." Thus any animal that we count as capable of these various states will at least *seem* to have a certain rough kind of functional organization. And, as already remarked, if the program of finding psychological laws that are not species-specific — i.e., of finding a normal form for psychological theories of different species — ever succeeds, then it will bring in its wake a delineation of the kind of functional organization that is necessary and sufficient for a given psychological state, as well as a precise definition of the notion "psychological state." In contrast, the brain-state theorist has to hope for the eventual development of neurophysiological laws that are species-independent, which seems much less reasonable than the hope that psychological laws (of a sufficiently general kind) may be species-independent, or, still weaker, that a species-independent *form* can be found in which psychological laws can be written. . . .

# 5. Methodological Considerations

So far we have considered only what might be called the "empirical" reasons for saying that being in pain is a functional state, rather than a brain state . . . ; namely, that it seems more likely that the functional state we described is invariantly "correlated" with pain, species-independently, than that there is . . . a physical-chemical state of the brain (must an organism have a *brain* to feel pain? perhaps some ganglia will do) . . . so correlated. If this is correct, then it follows that the identification we proposed is at least a candidate for consideration. What of methodological considerations?

The methodological considerations are roughly similar in all cases of reduction, so no surprises need be expected here. First, identification of psychological states with functional states means that the laws of psychology can be derived from statements of the form "such-and-such organisms have such-and-such Descriptions" together with the identification statements ("being in pain is such-and-such a functional state," etc.). Secondly, the presence of the functional state (i.e., of inputs which play the role we have described in the Functional Organization of the organism) is not merely "correlated with" but actually explains the pain behavior on the part of the organism. Thirdly, the identification serves to exclude questions which (if a naturalistic view is correct) represent an altogether wrong way of looking at the matter, e.g., "What *is* pain if it isn't either the brain state or the functional state?" and "What causes the pain to be always accompanied by this sort of functional state?" In short, the identification is to be tentatively accepted as a theory which leads to both fruitful predictions and to fruitful *questions,* and which serves to discourage fruitless and empirically senseless questions, where by "empirically senseless" I mean "senseless" not merely from the standpoint of verification, but from the standpoint of what there in fact *is.*

## TEST YOUR UNDERSTANDING

1. Does Putnam think that the statement "Pain is a brain state" is meaningless?

2. Suppose that there are Martians ("extraterrestrial life") capable of feeling pain. According to the "brain-state theory," what must there be in common between a Martian in pain and a human in pain?

3. Presumably we find out that others are in pain because we observe them behaving in a certain way (saying "Ow!," holding their foot, etc.). Why does Putnam think this is a piece of evidence for the functional-state theory?

## NOTES AND QUESTIONS

1. The brain-state theory is incompatible with dualism but, Putnam says, "the functional-state hypothesis is *not* incompatible with dualism!" Why does Putnam think that the functional-state hypothesis and dualism are compatible? Does this mean that Putnam himself is a dualist? If the functional-state hypothesis is right, how (if at all) is neuroscience relevant to understanding what it is to be in pain?

2. A short explanation of functionalism together with a discussion of some standard objections is in Ned Block, "Functionalism" (www.nyu.edu/gsas/dept/philo/faculty/block/papers/functionalism.html). For more details see Block, "The Mind as the Software of the Brain" (www.nyu.edu/gsas/dept/philo/faculty/block/papers/msb.html).

## John Searle (born 1932)

Searle is Slusser Professor of Philosophy at the University of California, Berkeley, where he has taught since 1959. He has made many important contributions to the philosophy of language, philosophy of mind, and philosophy of social science. His books include *Speech Acts* (1969), *Intentionality* (1983), *The Rediscovery of the Mind* (1992), and *The Construction of Social Reality* (1995).

# CAN COMPUTERS THINK?
## from *Minds, Brains, and Science*

In the previous chapter, I provided at least the outlines of a solution to the so-called "mind-body problem." Though we do not know in detail how the brain functions, we do know enough to have an idea of the general relationships between brain processes and mental processes. Mental processes are caused by the behaviour of elements of the brain. At the same time, they are realised in the structure that is made up of those elements. I think this answer is consistent with the standard biological approaches to biological phenomena. Indeed, it is a kind of commonsense answer to the question, given what we know about how the world works. However, it is very much a minority point of view. The prevailing view in philosophy, psychology, and artificial intelligence is one which emphasises the analogies between the functioning of the human brain and the functioning of digital computers. According to the most extreme version of this view, the brain is just a digital computer and the mind is just a computer program. One could summarise this view — I call it "strong artificial intelligence," or "strong AI" — by saying that the mind is to the brain, as the program is to the computer hardware.

This view has the consequence that there is nothing essentially biological about the human mind. The brain just happens to be one of an indefinitely large number of different kinds of hardware computers that could sustain the programs which make up human intelligence. On this view, any physical system whatever that had the right program with the right inputs and outputs would have a mind in exactly the same sense that you and I have minds. So, for example, if you made a computer out of old beer cans powered by windmills; if it had the right program, it would have to have a mind. And the point is not that for all we know it might have thoughts and feelings, but rather that it must have thoughts and feelings, because that is all there is to having thoughts and feelings: implementing the right program.

Most people who hold this view think we have not yet designed programs which are minds. But there is pretty much general agreement among them that it's only a matter of time until computer scientists and workers in artificial intelligence design the appropriate hardware and programs which will be the equivalent of human brains and minds. These will be artificial brains and minds which are in every way the equivalent of human brains and minds. . . .

Unlike most philosophical theses, [this view is] reasonably clear, and it admits of a simple and decisive refutation. It is this refutation that I am going to undertake in this chapter.

The nature of the refutation has nothing whatever to do with any particular stage of computer technology. It is important to emphasise this point because the temptation is always to think that the solution to our problems must wait on some as yet uncreated technological wonder. But in fact, the nature of the refutation is completely independent of any state of technology. It has to do with the very definition of a digital computer, with what a digital computer is.

It is essential to our conception of a digital computer that its operations can be specified purely formally; that is, we specify the steps in the operation of the computer in terms of abstract symbols — sequences of zeroes and ones printed on a tape, for example. A typical computer "rule" will determine that when a machine is in a certain state and it has a certain symbol on its tape, then it will perform a certain operation such as erasing the symbol or printing another symbol and then enter another state such as moving the tape one square to the left. But the symbols have no meaning; they have no semantic content; they are not about anything. They have to be specified purely in terms of their formal or syntactical structure. The zeroes and ones, for example, are just numerals; they don't even stand for numbers. Indeed, it is this feature of digital computers that makes them so powerful. One and the same type of hardware, if it is appropriately designed, can be used to run an indefinite range of different programs. And one and the same program can be run on an indefinite range of different types of hardwares.

But this feature of programs, that they are defined purely formally or syntactically, is fatal to the view that mental processes and program processes are identical. And the reason can be stated quite simply. There is more to having a mind than having formal or syntactical processes. Our internal mental states, by definition, have certain sorts of contents. If I am thinking about Kansas City or wishing that I had a cold beer to drink or wondering if there will be a fall in interest rates, in each case my mental state has a certain mental content in addition to whatever formal features it might have. That is, even if my thoughts occur to me in strings of symbols, there must be more to the thought than the abstract strings, because strings by themselves can't have any meaning. If my thoughts are to be *about* anything, then the strings must have a *meaning* which makes the thoughts about those things. In a word, the mind has more than a syntax, it has a semantics. The reason that no computer program can ever be a mind is simply that a computer program is only syntactical, and minds are more than syntactical. Minds are semantical, in the sense that they have more than a formal structure, they have a content.

To illustrate this point I have designed a certain thought-experiment. Imagine that a bunch of computer programmers have written a program that will enable a computer to simulate the understanding of Chinese. So, for example, if the computer is given a question in Chinese, it will match the question against its memory, or data base, and produce appropriate answers to the questions in Chinese. Suppose for the sake of argument that the computer's answers are as good as those of a native Chinese speaker. Now then, does the computer, on the basis of this, understand Chinese, does it literally understand Chinese, in the way that Chinese speakers understand Chinese? Well, imagine that you are locked in a room, and in this room are several baskets full of Chinese symbols. Imagine that you (like me) do not understand a word of Chinese, but that you are given a rule book in English for manipulating these Chinese symbols. The rules specify the manipulations of the symbols purely formally, in terms of their syntax, not their semantics. So the rule might say: "Take a squiggle-squiggle sign out of basket number one and put it next to a squoggle-squoggle sign from basket number two." Now suppose that some other Chinese symbols are passed into the room, and that you are given further rules for passing back Chinese symbols out of the room. Suppose that unknown to you the symbols passed into the room are called "questions" by the people outside the room, and the symbols you pass back out of the room are called "answers to the questions." Suppose, furthermore, that the programmers are so good at designing the programs and that you are so good at manipulating the symbols, that very soon your answers are indistinguishable from those of a native Chinese speaker. There you are locked in your room shuffling your Chinese symbols and passing out Chinese symbols in response to incoming Chinese symbols. On the basis of the situation as I have described it, there is no way you could learn any Chinese simply by manipulating these formal symbols.

Now the point of the story is simply this: by virtue of implementing a formal computer program from the point of view of an outside observer, you behave exactly as if you understood Chinese, but all the same you don't understand a word of Chinese. But if going through the appropriate computer program for understanding Chinese is not enough to give *you* an understanding of Chinese, then it is not enough to give *any other digital computer* an understanding of Chinese. And again, the reason for this can be stated quite simply. If you don't understand Chinese, then no other computer could understand Chinese because no digital computer, just by virtue of running a program, has anything that you don't have. All that the computer has, as you have, is a formal program for manipulating uninterpreted Chinese symbols. To repeat, a computer has a syntax, but no semantics. The whole point of the parable of the Chinese room is to remind us of a fact that we knew all along. Understanding a language, or indeed, having mental states at all, involves more than just having a bunch of formal symbols. It involves having an interpretation, or a meaning attached to those symbols. And a digital computer, as defined, cannot have more than just formal symbols because the operation of the computer, as I said earlier, is defined in terms of its ability to implement programs. And these programs are purely formally specifiable — that is, they have no semantic content.

We can see the force of this argument if we contrast what it is like to be asked and to answer questions in English, and to be asked and to answer questions in some language where we have no knowledge of any of the meanings of the words. Imagine that in the Chinese room you are also given questions in English about such things as your age or your life history, and that you answer these questions. What is the difference between the Chinese case and the English case? Well again, if like me you understand no Chinese and you do understand English, then the difference is obvious. You understand the questions in English because they are expressed in symbols whose meanings are known to you. Similarly, when you give the answers in English you are producing symbols which are meaningful to you. But in the case of the Chinese, you have none of that. In the case of the Chinese, you simply manipulate formal symbols according to a computer program, and you attach no meaning to any of the elements.

Various replies have been suggested to this argument by workers in artificial intelligence and in psychology, as well as philosophy. They all have something in common; they are all inadequate. And there is an obvious reason why they have to be inadequate, since the argument rests on a very simple logical truth, namely, syntax alone is not sufficient for semantics, and digital computers insofar as they are computers have, by definition, a syntax alone.

I want to make this clear by considering a couple of the arguments that are often presented against me.

Some people attempt to answer the Chinese room example by saying that the whole system understands Chinese. The idea here is that though I, the person in the room manipulating the symbols, do not understand Chinese, I am just the central processing unit of the computer system. They argue that it is the whole system, including the room, the baskets full of symbols and the ledgers containing the programs and perhaps other items as well, taken as a totality, that understands Chinese. But this is subject to exactly the same objection I made before. There is no way that the system can get from the syntax to the semantics. I, as the central processing unit, have no way of figuring out what any of these symbols means; but then neither does the whole system.

Another common response is to imagine that we put the Chinese understanding program inside a robot. If the robot moved around and interacted causally with the world, wouldn't that be enough to guarantee that it understood Chinese? Once again the inexorability of the semantics-syntax distinction overcomes this manoeuvre. As long as we suppose that the robot has only a computer for a brain then, even though it might behave exactly as if it understood Chinese, it would still have no way of getting from the syntax to the semantics of Chinese. You can see this if you imagine that I am the computer. Inside a room in the robot's skull I shuffle symbols without knowing that some of them come in to me from television cameras attached to the robot's head and others go out to move the robot's arms and legs. As long as all I have is a formal computer program, I have no way of attaching any meaning to any of the symbols. And the fact that the robot is engaged in causal interactions with the outside world won't help me to attach any meaning to the symbols unless I have some way of finding out about that fact. Suppose the robot picks up a hamburger and this triggers the symbol for hamburger to come into the room. As long as all I have is the symbol with no knowledge of its causes or how it got there, I have no way of knowing what it means. The causal interactions between the robot and the rest of the world are irrelevant unless those causal interactions are represented in some mind or other. But there is no way they can be if all that the so-called mind consists of is a set of purely formal, syntactical operations.

It is important to see exactly what is claimed and what is not claimed by my argument. Suppose we ask the question that I mentioned at the beginning: "Could a machine think?" Well, in one sense, of course, we are all machines. We can construe the stuff inside our heads as a meat machine. And of course, we can all think. So, in one sense of "machine," namely that sense in which a machine is just a physical system which is capable of performing certain kinds of operations, in that sense, we are all machines, and we can think. So, trivially, there are machines that can think. But that wasn't the question that bothered us. So let's try a different formulation of it. Could an artefact think? Could a man-made machine think? Well, once again, it depends on the kind of artefact. Suppose we designed a machine that was molecule-for-molecule indistinguishable from a human being. Well then, if you can duplicate the causes, you can presumably duplicate the effects. So once again, the answer to that question is, in principle at least, trivially yes. If you could build a machine that had the same structure as a human being, then presumably that machine would be able to think. Indeed, it would be a surrogate human being. Well, let's try again.

The question isn't: "Can a machine think?" or: "Can an artefact think?" The question is: "Can a digital computer think?" But once again we have to be very careful in how we interpret the question. From a mathematical point of view, anything whatever can be described as if it were a digital computer. And that's because it can be described as instantiating or implementing a computer program. In an utterly trivial sense, the pen that is on the desk in front of me can be described as a digital computer. It just happens to have a very boring computer program. The program says: "Stay there." Now since in this sense, anything whatever is a digital computer, because anything whatever can be described as implementing a computer program, then once again, our question gets a trivial answer. Of course our brains are digital computers, since they implement any number of computer programs. And of course our brains can think. So once again, there is a trivial answer to the question. But that wasn't really the question we were trying to ask. The question we wanted to ask is this: "Can a digital computer, as defined, think?" That is to say: "Is instantiating or implementing the right computer program with the right inputs and outputs, sufficient for, or constitutive of, thinking?" And to this question, unlike its predecessors, the answer is clearly "no." And it is "no" for the reason that we have spelled out, namely, the computer program is defined purely syntactically. But thinking is more than just a matter of manipulating meaningless symbols, it involves meaningful semantic contents. These semantic contents are what we mean by "meaning."

It is important to emphasise again that we are not talking about a particular stage of computer technology. The argument has nothing to do with the forthcoming, amazing advances in computer science. It has nothing to do with the distinction between serial and parallel processes, or with the size of programs, or the speed of computer operations, or with computers that can interact causally with their environment, or even with the invention of robots. Technological progress is always grossly exaggerated, but even subtracting the exaggeration, the development of computers has been quite remarkable, and we can reasonably expect that even more remarkable progress will be made in the future. No doubt we will be much better able to simulate human behaviour on computers than we can at present, and certainly much better than we have been able to in the past. The point I am making is that if we are talking about having mental states, having a mind, all of these simulations are simply irrelevant. It doesn't matter how good the technology is, or how rapid the calculations made by the computer are. If it really is a computer, its operations have to be defined syntactically, whereas consciousness, thoughts, feelings, emotions, and all the rest of it involve more than a syntax. Those features, by definition, the computer is unable to *duplicate* however powerful may be its ability to *simulate*. The key distinction here is between duplication and simulation. And no simulation by itself ever constitutes duplication.

. . . There is a puzzling question in this discussion though, and that is: "Why would anybody ever have thought that computers could think or have feelings and emotions and all the rest of it?" After all, we can do computer simulations of any process whatever that can be given a formal description. So, we can do a computer simulation of the flow of money in the British economy, or the pattern of power distribution in the Labour party.[1] We can do computer simulation of rain storms in the home counties,[2] or warehouse fires in East London. Now, in each of these cases, nobody supposes that the computer simulation is actually the real thing; no one supposes that a computer simulation of a storm will leave us all wet, or a computer simulation of a fire is likely to burn the house down. Why on earth would anyone in his right mind suppose a computer simulation of mental processes actually had mental processes? I don't really know the answer to that, since the idea seems to me, to put it frankly, quite crazy from the start. But I can make a couple of speculations.

First of all, where the mind is concerned, a lot of people are still tempted to some sort of behaviourism.[3] They think if a system behaves as if it understood Chinese, then it really must understand Chinese. But we have already refuted this form of behaviourism with the Chinese room argument. Another assumption made by many people is that the mind is not a part of the biological world, it is not a part of the world of nature. The strong artificial intelligence view relies on that in its conception that the mind is purely formal; that somehow or other, it cannot be treated as a concrete product of biological processes like any other biological product. There is in these discussions, in short, a kind of residual dualism.[4] AI partisans believe that the mind is more than a part of the natural biological world; they believe that the mind is purely formally specifiable. The paradox of this is that the AI literature is filled with fulminations against some view called

---

1. One of the main political parties in the United Kingdom.

2. Counties in England surrounding London.

3. The view that to have a mind is simply to behave (or to be disposed or inclined to behave) in various ways.

4. The view, associated with the French philosopher René Descartes (1596–1650), that the mind and the body are distinct things.

"dualism." But in fact, the whole thesis of strong AI rests on a kind of dualism. It rests on a rejection of the idea that the mind is just a natural biological phenomenon in the world like any other.

## TEST YOUR UNDERSTANDING

1. Does Searle think that there is some sense in which we are machines?

2. Does Searle think our brains don't run computer programs?

3. Does Searle think of himself as a dualist?

4. Does Searle think that the proponents of strong AI assume that the mind is a part of the natural biological world?

## NOTES AND QUESTIONS

1. Let us grant that when you are manipulating the symbols in the Chinese room you do not understand Chinese. One reply Searle considers (sometimes called the "Systems Reply") is that "the whole system understands Chinese." One might argue that the whole system does not understand Chinese because you are a part of the system and you don't understand Chinese, but this would be a fallacy. Things can be true of a whole that are not true of its parts: you are a philosophy student, and your liver is part of you, but that doesn't imply that your liver is a philosophy student. What is Searle's response to the Systems Reply? Does he avoid the fallacy just mentioned?

2. Some of the standard objections to the Chinese room argument are in Ned Block, "The Mind as the Software of the Brain," sec. 4 (www.nyu.edu/gsas/dept/philo/faculty/block/papers/msb.html). The original article in which the Chinese room argument appeared is in Searle's article "Minds, Brains, and Program" (*Behavioral and Brain Sciences* 3: 417–57 [1980], http://cogprints.org/7150/1/10.1.1.83.5248.pdf). Searle talks about the Chinese room argument in a 1987 clip from the BBC television program *Horizon*: search on the Internet for "Searle Chinese room BBC Horizon."

## ANALYZING THE ARGUMENTS

1.  Consider this passage, excerpted from Raymond M. Smullyan's "An Unfortunate Dualist," in his *This Book Needs No Title* (Prentice-Hall, 1980):

    > Once upon a time there was a dualist. He believed that mind and matter are separate substances. Just how they interacted he did not pretend to know—this was one of the "mysteries" of life. But he was sure they were quite separate substances.
    >
    > This dualist, unfortunately, led an unbearably painful life—not because of his philosophical beliefs, but for quite different reasons. . . . He longed for nothing more than to die. But he was deterred from suicide by such reasons as . . . he did not want to hurt other people by his death. . . . So our poor dualist was quite desperate.
    >
    > Then came the discovery of the miracle drug! Its effect on the taker was to annihilate the soul or mind entirely but to leave the body functioning exactly as before. Absolutely no observable change came over the taker; the body continued to act just as if it still had a soul. Not the closest friend or observer could possibly know that the taker had taken the drug, unless the taker informed him. . . . [O]ur dualist was, of course, delighted! Now he could annihilate himself (his soul, that is) in a way not subject to any of the foregoing objections. And so, for the first time in years, he went to bed with a light heart, saying: "Tomorrow morning I will go down to the drugstore and get the drug. My days of suffering are over at last!" With these thoughts, he fell peacefully asleep.
    >
    > Now at this point a curious thing happened. A friend of the dualist who knew about this drug, and who knew of the sufferings of the dualist, decided to put him out of his misery. So in the middle of the night, while the dualist was fast asleep, the friend quietly stole into the house and injected the drug into his veins. The next morning the body of the dualist awoke—without any soul indeed—and the first thing it did was to go to the drugstore to get the drug. He took it home and, before taking it, said, "Now I shall be released." So he took it and then waited the time interval in which it was supposed to work. At the end of the interval he angrily exclaimed: "Damn it, this stuff hasn't helped at all! I still obviously have a soul and am suffering as much as ever!"
    >
    > Doesn't all this suggest that perhaps there might be something just a little wrong with dualism?

    Does it? What is Smullyan's argument against dualism? How might a dualist respond?

2.  Here is one very simple behaviorist theory of belief:

    S believes that p **iff** S would answer "Yes" if S were asked "Is it true that p?"

    (To get a specific consequence of this theory, replace the letter "S" by the name of any person and replace the letter "p" by any declarative sentence of English.)

    (i)   Why does the theory have the consequence that a monolingual Spanish speaker does not believe that snow is white?

    (ii)  Why does the theory have the consequence that some ordinary cases of lying are impossible?

(iii) Can you repair the theory so that it at least avoids these two problems? It is certain that your repaired theory has *other* problems—what are some of them?

3. In "Troubles with Functionalism" (*Minnesota Studies in the Philosophy of Science* 9 (1978): 261–325), Ned Block presents the following "prima facie **counterexample**" to functionalism (specifically to "machine functionalism," the sort of functionalist theory defended by Putnam):

> Suppose we convert the government of China to functionalism, and we convince its officials to realize a human mind for an hour. We provide each of the billion people in China (I chose China because it has a billion inhabitants) with a specially designed two-way radio that connects them in the appropriate way to other persons and to [an] artificial body. . . .
>
> The system of a billion people communicating with one another plus satellites plays the role of an external "brain" connected to the artificial body by radio. There is nothing absurd about a person being connected to his brain by radio. Perhaps the day will come when our brains will be periodically removed for cleaning and repairs. Imagine that this is done initially by treating neurons attaching the brain to the body with a chemical that allows them to stretch like rubber bands, thereby assuring that no brain-body connections are disrupted. Soon clever businessmen discover that they can attract more customers by replacing the stretched neurons with radio links so that brains can be cleaned without inconveniencing the customer by immobilizing his body.
>
> It is not at all obvious that the China-body system is physically impossible. It could be functionally equivalent to you for a short time, say an hour. . . .
>
> Of course, there are signals the system would respond to what you would not respond to—for example, massive radio interference or a flood of the Yangtze River. Such events might cause a malfunction, scotching the simulation, just as a bomb in a computer can make it fail to realize the machine table it was built to realize. But just as the computer *without* the bomb *can* realize the machine table, the system consisting of the people and artificial body can realize the machine table so long as there are no catastrophic interferences, e.g., floods, etc. . . .
>
> Objection: The Chinese system would work too slowly. The kind of events and processes with which we normally have contact would pass by far too quickly for the system to detect them. Thus, we would be unable to converse with it, play bridge with it, etc.
>
> Reply: It is hard to see why the system's time scale should matter. Is it really contradictory or nonsensical to suppose we could meet a race of intelligent beings with whom we could communicate only by devices such as time-lapse photography? When we observe these creatures, they seem almost inanimate. But when we view the time-lapse movies, we see them conversing with one another. Indeed, we find they are saying that the only way they can make any sense of us is by viewing movies greatly slowed down. To take time scale as all important seems crudely behavioristic.
>
> What makes the homunculi-headed system . . . just described a prima facie counterexample to (machine) functionalism is that there is prima facie doubt whether it has any mental states at all—especially whether it has what philosophers have variously called "qualitative states," "raw feels," or "immediate phenomenological qualities." (You ask: What is it that philosophers have called qualitative states? I answer, only half in jest: As Louis Armstrong said

when asked what jazz is, "If you got to ask, you ain't never gonna get to know.")
In Nagel's terms [see "What Is It Like to Be a Bat?," in chapter 9 of this anthology],
there is a prima facie doubt whether there is anything which it is like to be the
homunculi-headed system.

Is this a counterexample to functionalism? Block thinks that it is a more credible
counterexample to a functionalist theory of "qualitative states," like *being in pain or
seeing blue*, than it is to a functionalist theory of other mental states, like *believing
that Mars has two moons* or *intending to apply to law school*. Is he right about that?
If he is, that suggests that a better theory of mind would be some *combination* of the
theories discussed in this chapter. What theories, and in what combination?

# 9

# What Is Consciousness?

Pinch the skin on the back of your hand—the harder the better. As a result, an electrical signal will travel through nerve fibers in your hand to your spinal cord; the signal is then relayed to your brain, where more electrical activity takes place. So far, all we have is something of interest to neuroscientists or physicians—your nervous system is activated in a complicated way. But of course there's something else going on that is of very great interest to you—you are *in pain*. Surely there could hardly be a better example of *two very different things*! And yet, are they *really* two things? Isn't the sensible scientific view that—somehow—being in pain is *nothing more than* having a complicated pattern of physical events occur in your brain?

The experience of pain is a paradigm example of *consciousness*. Why is consciousness supposed to present an acute difficulty for **materialism**, the view that everything is wholly material or physical? More generally: what is special about consciousness, compared to other mental phenomena? The readings in this section grapple with these questions.

## Varieties of Consciousness

Philosophers have distinguished a number of different (although related) kinds of consciousness. A review of some of these will help us to home in on the kind of consciousness that—as Thomas Nagel claims in "What Is It Like to Be a Bat?"—"makes the mind-body problem really intractable."

The first kind of consciousness is illustrated by statements of the following sort: Sam is conscious of the burning toast, Shannon is conscious of being watched. Here "conscious of" means "aware of": Sam is aware of the burning toast, Shannon is aware of being watched. So this first kind of consciousness is *awareness*.

The second kind of consciousness is *self*-consciousness. This kind of consciousness is related to, but is not quite the same as, the ordinary sense of "self-conscious": if Sam feels self-conscious about his odd socks, then he feels embarrassed about his odd socks. To feel embarrassed about his socks he must be aware of the socks, and moreover know or believe that the socks are *his*. Embarrassment is a self-regarding emotion. So self-consciousness in the ordinary sense requires Sam to be aware of himself, and *awareness of oneself* is self-consciousness as philosophers understand it. To put it another way, Sam is self-conscious in the philosophical sense if he can think thoughts *about himself*, thoughts that he would report using "I," the first-person pronoun.[1]

The third kind of consciousness is the opposite of "unconsciousness" in the ordinary sense. Shannon falls off her bike and becomes unconscious, entirely unresponsive to her surroundings. Later she opens her eyes and "regains consciousness." To say that someone is conscious in this sense simply means that she is awake and alert. This kind of consciousness is sometimes called *creature* consciousness or *agent* consciousness.

We haven't yet got to the really puzzling kind of consciousness. To introduce it, first find something colored — something blue, say — and place it before you. Now pinch the back of your hand again. You are now in two **mental states**:

(i)    seeing blue,

(ii)   feeling pain.

At the same time, no preparation was needed to ensure that you are also in these two mental states:

(iii)  believing that Norton has published an introduction to philosophy,

(iv)  hoping to do well in your classes.

Probably you have believed for at least a few weeks that Norton has published an introduction to philosophy and have hoped to do well in your classes for much longer. In any case, the important point is that you have believed that Norton has published an introduction to philosophy, and hoped to do well in your classes, during times when you were not thinking about philosophy books, or school, at all. In fact, when you were asleep last night you believed that Norton has published an introduction to philosophy, and hoped to do well in school. And you are not unusual in this respect. Your classmate Sidney, say, is in a deep, dreamless sleep. Standing by her bedside, we can point to her and truly say: "She believes that Norton has published an introduction to philosophy, and hopes to do well in school."

Bearing all that in mind, isn't there a striking difference between (i) and (ii), on the one hand, and (iii) and (iv), on the other? Seeing blue and feeling pain make

---

1. Interestingly, some cases of awareness of oneself are not cases of self-consciousness. Suppose you see yourself on the security monitor in a store, but you don't recognize the person *as* yourself. You are aware *of* yourself, but this is not a case of self-consciousness.

a difference to your *conscious experience*, while believing that Norton has published an introduction to philosophy and hoping to do well in your classes do not. Put another way, just after you followed the instruction for (i) and (ii), there was a change in *how things seemed or felt.* Put yet another way, there was *something it was like* for you to see blue, and there was *something it was like* for you to feel pain. But although you also believed that Norton was the publisher, and hoped to do well in school, this did *not* make a difference to your conscious experience. What was it like for you to believe that Norton has published an introduction to philosophy, or hope to do well in school? It wasn't like *anything*, presumably.

In this sense, seeing blue and feeling pain are *conscious* mental states: there is something it's like to see blue, and something it's like to feel pain.[2] Believing and hoping, by contrast, are arguably never conscious in the same sense. Believing that the Earth is round is a perfectly good mental state, but there's nothing it's like to be in it.

This kind of consciousness, which in the first instance is a **property** of mental states, has a number of names in philosophy of mind. Thomas Nagel simply calls it *consciousness*. David Chalmers calls it *experience*. We shall use the term introduced by the philosopher Ned Block, **phenomenal consciousness**.

Seeing blue, and feeling pain, are (at least typically) phenomenally conscious states. But they differ in phenomenally conscious respects. What it's like to see blue, and what it's like to feel pain, are different. Similarly, what it's like to see blue is different from what it's like to see red. When philosophers talk about how these states differ with respect to what it's like to be in them, they often use the term **qualia** (as in the titles of Frank Jackson's two essays; the singular is *quale*) or *phenomenal character* (Michael Tye) or the *subjective character of experience* (Nagel).

# The Explanatory Gap

Consider the bodily process of digestion. Very plausibly, it can be fully explained in terms of physical and chemical processes. We can be confident that digestion can be fully explained even if we don't know all the complicated details. Mental phenomena, however, present an apparent contrast, as the German philosopher Gottfried Wilhelm Leibniz argued with a famous thought experiment (mentioned in the introduction to chapter 8). Supposing the brain, in Leibniz's words, "enlarged but preserving the same proportions, so that you could enter it as if it were a mill," you would not observe anything there, he says, that could explain thinking, feeling, and perceiving.

But perhaps Leibniz's pessimism is too hasty. Consider your belief that the Earth is round. At a first pass, to believe that the Earth is round is to store the

---

2. This should really be put more cautiously: *typically* they are conscious mental states. In typical cases, there is something it's like to see blue, and something it's like to feel pain.

information that the Earth is round in a way that makes it available to control action in certain ways. So, for example, if you tick the "Earth is round" box on the astronomy multiple-choice exam, or form a lump of clay into a ball when making a model of the Earth, the information that the Earth is round—presumably stored in your brain—is making a contribution to bringing those actions about. And it doesn't seem so mysterious that a physical thing could store information and use it to govern its behavior. After all, aren't computers actual examples? Moreover, perhaps the brain *is* some kind of computer, running mental software. (See the introduction to chapter 8.) Admittedly, some philosophers think that this idea is flat wrong: John Searle (see "Can Computers Think?" in chapter 8) is a notable example. But many think it's at least along the right lines, in which case there seems to be a very real prospect of explaining our mental lives in computational terms. And since computers can certainly be built out of biochemical materials, a computational explanation of the mind is in effect a materialist explanation of the mind.

Leibniz's thought experiment, on this view, is misleading. In order to understand how a computer works you need to zoom *out*, and see how everything is wired together, not zoom *in* to a few transistors on a chip. Similarly, zooming in to small groups of neurons (as in Leibniz's thought experiment) is not going to reveal how the brain can generate thought, but that's because it's at the wrong scale.

This sort of strategy might deal with the *cognitive* aspects of mind—roughly, the storage, manipulation, and use of information. But what about the *phenomenal* aspects of mind—that is, *phenomenal consciousness*? The mind-as-computer idea might find a place for believing and hoping in a purely material universe, but what about seeing blue and feeling pain? Here many philosophers (and cognitive scientists) think that pessimism is warranted. Why do certain physical states give rise to phenomenal consciousness? We don't know, and according to the pessimists we have no idea how to find out the answer. Physical phenomena are very well suited to explaining digestion, and perhaps also can explain believing and hoping. But they seem quite ill suited to explain phenomenal consciousness. As the philosopher Joseph Levine puts it, there is an *explanatory gap* between the physical world and phenomenal consciousness.[3] This is what David Chalmers calls the **hard problem**.

# Dualism

There might be an explanation of consciousness in entirely physical terms even though we don't know what it is. The science of the mind has only made really serious progress in the last fifty years or so, and perhaps another millennium of neuroscience combined with new ways of thinking both about the mind and the physical world will bring us complete enlightenment. Nagel expresses some sympathy with this position. Some other philosophers are less sanguine.

---

3. See Levine's "Materialism and Qualia: The Explanatory Gap," *Pacific Philosophical Quarterly* 64 (1983): 354–61.

Although a satisfactory physical explanation of phenomenal consciousness is out there to be found, they think, human beings are just not smart enough to find it.[4]

Alternatively, one might argue that the explanatory gap is a sign that phenomenal consciousness *cannot* be given a complete explanation in physical terms, and so **physicalism** or **materialism** is false. On this view, consciousness is an *additional* ingredient in nature, over and above the ingredients recognized by physics and chemistry. This is a version of **dualism** (see the introduction to chapter 8). In their essays, David Chalmers and Frank Jackson both argue for dualism.

Chalmers's argument turns on the claim that there could have been **zombies**: creatures physically exactly the same as ourselves, living in the same sort of physical world, but who lack phenomenal consciousness. Zombies, being physically the same as ourselves, give every impression of having mental lives that are also the same as ours. Perhaps zombies have beliefs, hopes, and intentions, like us. Perhaps they also see things. But, by stipulation, there is nothing it's like to be a zombie. When a zombie looks at a ripe cranberry in good light, and says (as we might) "That's red," all is dark within. If zombies see cranberries, there is nothing it's like for them to do so. If physicalists are right in thinking that the mind (including phenomenal consciousness) is wholly physical, then once a physical system has reached a certain level of complexity, phenomenal consciousness is inevitable. But if zombies could have existed, phenomenal consciousness is *not* inevitable, and so physicalism is false.

Jackson's essay "Epiphenomenal Qualia" sets out his **knowledge argument** against physicalism. His most vivid and famous thought experiment in that essay concerns Mary, a brilliant scientist who knows every physical fact about colors and color vision, but who has been locked in a black and white room since birth. She has never seen anything chromatically colored. According to Jackson, if physicalism is true, then Mary knows everything about color experiences when she is imprisoned. But, he thinks, she clearly does not know everything: when she is released and sees something red for the first time she will learn something—in particular, she will come to know a fact about qualia. (Jackson later changed his mind. In "Postscript on Qualia" he explains why.)

Patricia Smith Churchland argues that Jackson's argument, and also Nagel's, fail for multiple reasons. If you read Churchland's essay, you may well suspect that she is similarly unimpressed by Chalmers's argument—which indeed she is.[5]

## The Transparency of Consciousness

Once the notion of phenomenal consciousness has been explained, you might think that it is the most obvious and striking thing in the world. Michael Tye argues that, on the contrary, phenomenal consciousness is extremely elusive.

4. For an argument for this conclusion, see Colin McGinn, "Can We Solve the Mind-Body Problem?," *Mind* 98 (1989): 349–66. For related views, see "Analyzing the Arguments," p. 449.

5. See Patricia Smith Churchland, "The Hornswoggle Problem," reprinted in Jonathan Shear (ed.), *Explaining Consciousness: The Hard Problem* (MIT, 1999).

Look at something blue again and put yourself into the phenomenally conscious state of seeing blue. There is something it's like to see blue; in other words, the state of seeing blue has a distinctive quale, or phenomenal character. Try and attend to that phenomenal character, a property of a mental state, not a property of anything in the scene before your eyes. According to Tye, you can't do it. You just end up attending to blue, which is a property of objects like sapphires and the petals of forget-me-nots, not a property of a mental state.

Here's another way of putting the point. Imagine Frank Jackson's Mary seeing a red apple for the first time. Will she be struck by the novel phenomenal character or qualia of her mental state, or the redness of the apple? The redness of the apple! Her eyes will widen with astonishment, she will pick up the apple and examine it more closely, and so on. What has grabbed her attention is something remarkable *in her environment*, not in her mind.

As Tye sums up the problem,

> The conclusion to which we seem driven is that the phenomenal character of your visual experience, as you view the apple, is *hidden* from you, as is your visual experience. You are *blind* to these things. For you, it is as if they aren't there. They are, as it were, transparent to you. You "see" right through them when you try to attend to them and you end up focusing on things outside you. But surely this cannot be right. Your visual experience is an inherently conscious thing. . . . Something has gone terribly wrong.

What has gone wrong? Tye's essay attempts to answer that question.

## Thomas Nagel (born 1937)

Nagel is Emeritus University Professor of Philosophy and Law at New York University. He has made influential contributions to ethics, political philosophy, epistemology, and philosophy of mind. His books include *The Possibility of Altruism* (1970), *The View from Nowhere* (1986), *Equality and Partiality* (1991), and *Mind and Cosmos* (2012).

# WHAT IS IT LIKE TO BE A BAT?

Consciousness is what makes the mind-body problem really intractable. Perhaps that is why current discussions of the problem give it little attention or get it obviously wrong. The recent wave of reductionist euphoria has produced several analyses of mental phenomena and mental concepts designed to explain the possibility of some variety of materialism, psychophysical identification, or reduction.[1] But the problems dealt with are those common to this type of reduction and other types, and what makes the mind-body problem unique, and unlike the water-$H_2O$ problem or the Turing machine[2]–IBM machine problem or the lightning–electrical discharge problem or the gene-DNA problem or the oak tree–hydrocarbon problem, is ignored.

Every reductionist has his favorite analogy from modem science. It is most unlikely that any of these unrelated examples of successful reduction will shed light on the relation of mind to brain. But philosophers share the general human weakness for explanations of what is incomprehensible in terms suited for what is familiar and well understood, though entirely different. This has led to the acceptance of implausible accounts of the mental largely because they would permit familiar kinds of reduction. I shall try to explain why the usual examples do not help us to understand the relation between mind and body — why, indeed, we have at present no conception of what an explanation of the physical nature of a mental phenomenon would be. Without consciousness the mind-body problem would be much less interesting. With consciousness it seems hopeless. The most important and characteristic feature of conscious mental phenomena is very poorly understood. Most reductionist theories do not even try to explain it. And careful examination will show that no currently available concept of reduction is applicable to it. Perhaps a new theoretical form can be devised for the purpose, but such a solution, if it exists, lies in the distant intellectual future.

Conscious experience is a widespread phenomenon. It occurs at many levels of animal life, though we cannot be sure of its presence in the simpler organisms, and it is very difficult to say in general what provides evidence of it. (Some extremists have been prepared to deny it even of mammals other than man.) No doubt it occurs in countless forms totally unimaginable to us, on other planets in other solar systems throughout the universe. But no matter how the form may vary, the fact that an organism has conscious experience *at all* means, basically, that there is something it is like to *be* that organism. There may be further implications about the form of the experience; there may even (though I doubt it) be implications about the behavior of the organism. But fundamentally an organism has conscious mental states if and only if there is something that it is to *be* that organism — something it is like *for* the organism.

We may call this the subjective character of experience. It is not captured by any of the familiar, recently devised reductive analyses of the mental, for all of them are logically compatible with its absence. It is not analyzable in terms of any explanatory

---

1. "The recent wave. . .": recent in 1974, as exemplified by J.J.C. Smart's 1959 paper "Sensations and Brain Processes" (in chapter 8 of this anthology). "Materialism": the view that the mind — and the world in general — is wholly physical; also known as *physicalism*. "Psychophysical identification": the materialist identification of mental states with physical states (in particular brain states: see again Smart, "Sensations and Brain Processes"). "Reduction": Nagel cites some examples of scientific reduction in the next sentence: the reduction of water to $H_2O$, the reduction of genes to certain regions of DNA, and so on. Roughly put, to say that A can be reduced to B is to say that A is nothing over and above B.

2. A simple form of hypothetical computer, devised by the English mathematician Alan Turing (1912–1954).

system of functional states, or intentional states,[3] since these could be ascribed to robots or automata that behaved like people though they experienced nothing. It is not analyzable in terms of the causal role of experiences in relation to typical human behavior — for similar reasons. I do not deny that conscious mental states and events cause behavior, nor that they may be given functional characterizations. I deny only that this kind of thing exhausts their analysis. Any reductionist program has to be based on an analysis of what is to be reduced. If the analysis leaves something out, the problem will be falsely posed. It is useless to base the defense of materialism on any analysis of mental phenomena that fails to deal explicitly with their subjective character. For there is no reason to suppose that a reduction which seems plausible when no attempt is made to account for consciousness can be extended to include consciousness. Without some idea, therefore, of what the subjective character of experience is, we cannot know what is required of physicalist theory.

While an account of the physical basis of mind must explain many things, this appears to be the most difficult. It is impossible to exclude the phenomenological features of experience from a reduction in the same way that one excludes the phenomenal features of an ordinary substance from a physical or chemical reduction of it — namely, by explaining them as effects on the minds of human observers. If physicalism is to be defended, the phenomenological features must themselves be given a physical account. But when we examine their subjective character it seems that such a result is impossible. The reason is that every subjective phenomenon is essentially connected with a single point of view, and it seems inevitable that an objective, physical theory will abandon that point of view.

Let me first try to state the issue somewhat more fully than by referring to the relation between the subjective and the objective, or between the *pour-soi* and the *en-soi*.[4] This is far from easy. Facts about what it is like to be an *X* are very peculiar, so peculiar that some may be inclined to doubt their reality, or the significance of claims about them. To illustrate the connection between subjectivity and a point of view, and to make evident the importance of subjective features, it will help to explore the matter in relation to an example that brings out clearly the divergence between the two types of conception, subjective and objective.

I assume we all believe that bats have experience. After all, they are mammals, and there is no more doubt that they have experience than that mice or pigeons or whales have experience. I have chosen bats instead of wasps or flounders because if one travels too far down the phylogenetic tree, people gradually shed their faith that there is experience there at all. Bats, although more closely related to us than those other species, nevertheless present a range of activity and a sensory apparatus so different

---

3. "Functional states": states of a system definable in terms of causal relations between the system's inputs, outputs, and other states: computers and washing machines, for example, have many complex functional states. "Intentional states": mental states which are about, or directed on, something else; the state of *believing that Nagel is a philosopher* is about or directed on Nagel, and is thus an intentional state.

4. "*Pour-soi*": for-itself; "*en-soi*": in-itself (French). This terminology is from the French philosopher Jean-Paul Sartre's *Being and Nothingness* (1943).

from ours that the problem I want to pose is exceptionally vivid (though it certainly could be raised with other species). Even without the benefit of philosophical reflection, anyone who has spent some time in an enclosed space with an excited bat knows what it is to encounter a fundamentally *alien* form of life.

I have said that the essence of the belief that bats have experience is that there is something that it is like to be a bat. Now we know that most bats (the microchiroptera, to be precise) perceive the external world primarily by sonar, or echolocation, detecting the reflections, from objects within range, of their own rapid, subtly modulated, high-frequency shrieks. Their brains are designed to correlate the outgoing impulses with the subsequent echoes, and the information thus acquired enables bats to make precise discriminations of distance, size, shape, motion, and texture comparable to those we make by vision. But bat sonar, though clearly a form of perception, is not similar in its operation to any sense that we possess, and there is no reason to suppose that it is subjectively like anything we can experience or imagine. This appears to create difficulties for the notion of what it is like to be a bat. We must consider whether any method will permit us to extrapolate to the inner life of the bat from our own case, and if not, what alternative methods there may be for understanding the notion.

Our own experience provides the basic material for our imagination, whose range is therefore limited. It will not help to try to imagine that one has webbing on one's arms, which enables one to fly around at dusk and dawn catching insects in one's mouth; that one has very poor vision, and perceives the surrounding world by a system of reflected high-frequency sound signals; and that one spends the day hanging upside down by one's feet in an attic. In so far as I can imagine this (which is not very far), it tells me only what it would be like for *me* to behave as a bat behaves. But that is not the question. I want to know what it is like for a *bat* to be a bat. Yet if I try to imagine this, I am restricted to the resources of my own mind, and those resources are inadequate to the task. I cannot perform it either by imagining additions to my present experience, or by imagining segments gradually subtracted from it, or by imagining some combination of additions, subtractions, and modifications.

To the extent that I could look and behave like a wasp or a bat without changing my fundamental structure, my experiences would not be anything like the experiences of those animals. On the other hand, it is doubtful that any meaning can be attached to the supposition that I should possess the internal neurophysiological constitution of a bat. Even if I could by gradual degrees be transformed into a bat, nothing in my present constitution enables me to imagine what the experiences of such a future stage of myself thus metamorphosed would be like. The best evidence would come from the experiences of bats, if we only knew what they were like.

So if extrapolation from our own case is involved in the idea of what it is like to be a bat, the extrapolation must be incompletable. We cannot form more than a schematic conception of what it *is* like. For example, we may ascribe general *types* of experience on the basis of the animal's structure and behavior. Thus we describe bat sonar as a form of three-dimensional forward perception; we believe that bats feel some versions of pain, fear, hunger, and lust, and that they have other, more familiar types of perception besides sonar. But we believe that these experiences also have in each case a specific subjective character, which it is beyond our ability to conceive. And if there's conscious life elsewhere in the universe, it is likely that some of it will not be describable even in the most general experiential terms available to us. (The problem is not confined to exotic cases, however, for it exists between one person and another. The subjective character of the experience of a person deaf and blind from birth is not accessible to me, for example, nor presumably is mine to him. This does not prevent us each from believing that the other's experience has such a subjective character.)

If anyone is inclined to deny that we can believe in the existence of facts like this whose exact nature we cannot possibly conceive, he should reflect that in contemplating the bats we are in much the same position that intelligent bats or Martians would occupy if they tried to form a conception of what it was like to be us. The structure of their own minds might make it impossible for them to succeed, but we know they would be wrong to conclude that there is not anything precise that it is like to be us: that only certain general types of mental state could be ascribed to us (perhaps perception and appetite would be concepts common to us both; perhaps not). We know they would be wrong to draw such a skeptical conclusion because we know what it is like to be us. And we know that while it includes an enormous amount of variation and complexity, and while we do not possess the vocabulary to describe it adequately, its subjective character is highly specific, and in some respects describable in terms that can be understood only by creatures like us. The fact that we cannot expect ever to accommodate in our language a detailed description of Martian or bat phenomenology should not lead us to dismiss as meaningless the claim that bats and Martians have experiences fully comparable in richness of detail to our own. It would be fine if someone were to develop concepts and a theory that enabled us to think about those things; but such an understanding may be permanently denied to us by the limits of our nature. And to deny the reality or logical significance of what we can never describe or understand is the crudest form of cognitive dissonance. . . .

Reflection on what it is like to be a bat seems to lead us, therefore, to the conclusion that there are facts that do not consist in the truth of propositions expressible in a human language. We can be compelled to recognize the existence of such facts without being able to state or comprehend them.

I shall not pursue this subject, however. Its bearing on the topic before us (namely, the mind-body problem) is that it enables us to make a general observation about the subjective character of experience. Whatever may be the status of facts about what it is like to be a human being, or a bat, or a Martian, these appear to be facts that embody a particular point of view.

I am not adverting here to the alleged privacy of experience to its possessor. The point of view in question is not one accessible only to a single individual. Rather it is a *type*. It is often possible to take up a point of view other than one's own, so the comprehension of such facts is not limited to one's own case. There is a sense in which phenomenological facts are perfectly objective: one person can know or say of another what the quality of the other's experience is. They are subjective, however, in the sense that even this objective ascription of experience is possible only for someone sufficiently similar to the object of ascription to be able to adopt his point of view — to understand the ascription in the first person as well as in the third, so to speak. The more different from oneself the other experiencer is, the less success one can expect with this enterprise. In our own case we occupy the relevant point of view, but we will have as much difficulty understanding our own experience properly if we approach it from another point of view as we would if we tried to understand the experience of another species without taking up *its* point of view.

This bears directly on the mind-body problem. For if the facts of experience — facts about what it is like *for* the experiencing organism — are accessible only from one point of view, then it is a mystery how the true character of experiences could be revealed in the physical operation of that organism. The latter is a domain of objective facts *par excellence* — the kind that can be observed and understood from many points of view and by individuals with differing perceptual systems. There are no comparable imaginative obstacles to the acquisition of knowledge about bat neurophysiology by human scientists, and intelligent bats or Martians might learn more about the human brain than we ever will.

This is not by itself an argument against reduction. A Martian scientist with no understanding of visual perception could understand the rainbow, or lightning, or clouds as physical phenomena, though he would never be able to understand the human concepts of rainbow, lightning, or cloud, or the place these things occupy in our phenomenal world. The objective nature of the things picked out by these concepts could be apprehended by him because, although the concepts themselves are connected with a particular point of view and a particular visual phenomenology, the things apprehended from that point of view are not: they are observable from the point of view but external to it; hence they can be comprehended from other points of view also, either by the same organisms or by others. Lightning has an objective character that is not exhausted by its visual appearance, and this can be investigated by a Martian without vision. To be precise, it has a *more* objective character than is revealed in its visual appearance. In speaking of the move from subjective to objective characterization, I wish to remain noncommittal about the existence of an end point, the completely objective intrinsic nature of the thing, which one might or might not be able to reach. It may be more accurate to think of objectivity as a direction in which the understanding can travel. And in understanding a phenomenon like lightning, it is legitimate to go as far away as one can from a strictly human viewpoint.

In the case of experience, on the other hand, the connection with a particular point of view seems much closer. It is difficult to understand what could be meant by the *objective* character of an experience, apart from the particular point of view from which its subject apprehends it. After all, what would be left of what it was like to be a bat if one removed the viewpoint of the bat? But if experience does not have, in addition to its subjective character, an objective nature that can be apprehended from many different points of view, then how can it be supposed that a Martian investigating my brain might be observing physical processes which were my mental processes (as he might observe physical processes which were bolts of lightning), only from a different point of view? How, for that matter, could a human physiologist observe them from another point of view?

We appear to be faced with a general difficulty about psychophysical reduction. In other areas the process of reduction is a move in the direction of greater objectivity, toward a more accurate view of the real nature of things. This is accomplished by reducing our dependence on individual or species-specific points of view toward the object of investigation. We describe it not in terms of the impressions it makes on our senses, but in terms of its more general effects and of properties detectable by means other than the human senses. The less it depends on a specifically human viewpoint, the more objective is our description. It is possible to follow this path because although the concepts and ideas we employ in thinking about the external world are initially applied from a point of view that involves our perceptual apparatus, they are used by us to refer to things beyond themselves — toward which we *have* the phenomenal point of view. Therefore we can abandon it in favor of another, and still be thinking about the same things.

Experience itself however, does not seem to fit the pattern. The idea of moving from appearance to reality seems to make no sense here. What is the analogue in this case to pursuing a more objective understanding of the same phenomena by abandoning the initial subjective viewpoint toward them in favour of another that is more objective but concerns the same thing? Certainly it *appears* unlikely that we will get closer to the real nature of human experience by leaving behind the particularity of our human point of view and striving for a description in terms accessible to beings that could not imagine what it was like to be us. If the subjective character of experience is fully comprehensible only from one point of view, then any shift to greater objectivity — that is, less attachment to a specific viewpoint — does not take us nearer to the real nature of the phenomenon: it takes us farther away from it.

In a sense, the seeds of this objection to the reducibility of experience are already detectable in successful cases of reduction; for in discovering sound to be, in reality, a wave phenomenon in air or other media, we leave behind one viewpoint to take up another, and the auditory, human or animal viewpoint that we leave behind remains unreduced. Members of radically different species may both understand the same physical events in objective terms, and this does not require that they understand the phenomenal forms in which those events appear to the senses of members of the other species. Thus it is a condition of their referring to a common reality that their more particular viewpoints are not part of the common reality that they both apprehend. The reduction can succeed only if the species-specific viewpoint is omitted from what is to be reduced.

But while we are right to leave this point of view aside in seeking a fuller understanding of the external world, we cannot ignore it permanently, since it is the essence of the internal world, and not merely a point of view on it. Most of the neobehaviorism of recent philosophical psychology results from the effort to substitute an objective concept of mind for the real thing, in order to have nothing left over which cannot be reduced.[5] If we acknowledge that a physical theory of mind must account for the subjective character of experience, we must admit that no presently available conception gives us a clue how this could be done. The problem is unique. If mental processes are indeed physical processes, then there is something it is like, intrinsically, to undergo certain physical processes. What it is for such a thing to be the case remains a mystery.

What moral should be drawn from these reflections, and what should be done next? It would be a mistake to conclude that physicalism must be false. Nothing is proved by the inadequacy of physicalist hypotheses that assume a faulty objective analysis of mind. It would be truer to say that physicalism is a position we cannot understand because we do not at present have any conception of how it might be true. Perhaps it will be thought unreasonable to require such a conception as a condition of understanding. After all, it might be said, the meaning of physicalism is clear enough: mental states are states of the body; mental events are physical events. We do not know *which* physical states and events they are, but that should not prevent us from understanding the hypothesis. What could be clearer than the words "is" and "are"?

But I believe it is precisely this apparent clarity of the word "is" that is deceptive. Usually, when we are told that *X* is *Y* we know *how* it is supposed to be true, but that depends on a conceptual or theoretical background and is not conveyed by the "is" alone. We know how both "*X*" and "*Y*" refer, and the kinds of things to which they refer, and we have a rough idea how the two referential paths might converge on a single thing, be it an object, a person, a process, an event, or whatever. But when the two terms of the identification are very disparate it may not be so clear how it could be true. We may not have even a rough idea of how the two referential paths could converge, or what kind of things they might converge on, and a theoretical framework may have to be supplied to enable us to understand this. Without the framework, an air of mysticism surrounds the identification.

This explains the magical flavor of popular presentations of fundamental scientific discoveries, given out as propositions to which one must subscribe without really understanding them. For example, people are now told at an early age that all matter is really energy. But despite the fact that they know what "is" means, most of them never form a conception of what makes this claim true, because they lack the theoretical background.

At the present time the status of physicalism is similar to that which the hypothesis that matter is energy would have had if uttered by a pre-Socratic philosopher. We do not have the beginnings of a conception of how it might be true. In order to understand the hypothesis that a mental event is a physical event, we require more than an understanding of the word "is." The idea of how a mental and a physical term might refer to the same thing is lacking, and the usual analogies with theoretical identification in other fields fail to supply it. They fail because if we construe the

---

5. *Behaviorism* identifies mental states with dispositions to behave. The main successor to behaviorism was *functionalism*, which identifies mental states with functional states (see note 3 above). The relevant functional states are often partly specified in terms of the organism's behavior, and this is why Nagel labels recent theories as "neobehaviorism."

reference of mental terms to physical events on the usual model, we either get a reappearance of separate subjective events as the effects through which mental reference to physical events is secured, or else we get a false account of how mental terms refer (for example, a causal behaviorist one).

Strangely enough, we may have evidence for the truth of something we cannot really understand. Suppose a caterpillar is locked in a sterile safe by someone unfamiliar with insect metamorphosis, and weeks later the safe is reopened, revealing a butterfly. If the person knows that the safe has been shut the whole time, he has reason to believe that the butterfly is or was once the caterpillar, without having any idea in what sense this might be so. (One possibility is that the caterpillar contained a tiny winged parasite that devoured it and grew into the butterfly.)

It is conceivable that we are in such a position with regard to physicalism. . . .

I should like to close with a speculative proposal. It may be possible to approach the gap between subjective and objective from another direction. Setting aside temporarily the relation between the mind and the brain, we can pursue a more objective understanding of the mental in its own right. At present we are completely unequipped to think about the subjective character of experience without relying on the imagination — without taking up the point of view of the experiential subject. This should be regarded as a challenge to form new concepts and devise a new method — an objective phenomenology not dependent on empathy or the imagination. Though presumably it would not capture everything, its goal would be to describe, at least in part, the subjective character of experiences in a form comprehensible to beings incapable of having those experiences.

We would have to develop such a phenomenology to describe the sonar experiences of bats; but it would also be possible to begin with humans. One might try, for example, to develop concepts that could be used to explain to a person blind from birth what it was like to see. One would reach a blank wall eventually, but it should be possible to devise a method of expressing in objective terms much more than we can at present, and with much greater precision. The loose intermodal analogies — for example, "Red is like the sound of a trumpet" — which crop up in discussions of this subject are of little use. That should be clear to anyone who has both heard a trumpet and seen red. But structural features of perception might be more accessible to objective description, even though something would be left out. And concepts alternative to those we learn in the first person may enable us to arrive at a kind of understanding even of our own experience which is denied us by the very ease of description and lack of distance that subjective concepts afford.

Apart from its own interest, a phenomenology that is in this sense objective may permit questions about the physical[6] basis of experience to assume a more intelligible

6. I have not defined the term "physical." Obviously it does not apply just to what can be described by the concepts of contemporary physics, since we expect further developments. Some may think there is nothing to prevent mental phenomena from eventually being recognized as physical in their own right. But whatever else may be said of the physical, it has to be objective. So if our idea of the physical ever expands to include mental phenomena, it will have to assign them an objective character — whether or not this is done by analyzing them in terms of other phenomena already regarded as physical. It seems to me more likely, however, that mental-physical relations will eventually be expressed in a theory whose fundamental terms cannot be placed clearly in either category. [Nagel's note.]

form. Aspects of subjective experience that admitted this kind of objective description might be better candidates for objective explanations of a more familiar sort. But whether or not this guess is correct, it seems unlikely that any physical theory of mind can be contemplated until more thought has been given to the general problem of subjective and objective. Otherwise we cannot even pose the mind-body problem without sidestepping it.

## TEST YOUR UNDERSTANDING

1. Does Nagel think that we completely understand the hypothesis that mental events are physical events?

2. Does Nagel think that acting like a bat would enable you to know what it's like to be one?

3. Does Nagel argue that physicalism is false?

4. Does Nagel think there may be facts we could never know?

5. According to Nagel, "we appear to be faced with a general difficulty about psychophysical reduction." What is that difficulty?

## NOTES AND QUESTIONS

1. Nagel contrasts the scientific study of lightning with the scientific study of consciousness. "Lightning has an objective character that is not exhausted by its visual appearance, and this can be investigated by a Martian without vision." He argues that consciousness ("experience") is quite unlike lightning in this respect: "Experience itself . . . does not fit the pattern. The idea of moving from appearance to reality seems to make no sense here." Reconstruct Nagel's **argument** in the form of premises and conclusion. Assess the argument. Is it **valid**? Is it **sound**?

2. Can we know what it's like to be a bat? For some reasons for optimism (together with a detailed discussion of the complexities of bat echolocation) see Kathleen Akins, "What Is It Like to Be Boring and Myopic?" in B. Dahlbom, ed., *Dennett and His Critics* (Blackwell, 1993).

3. Nagel summarizes his current view of the mind-body problem in chapter 3 of his *Mind and Cosmos* (Oxford, 2012).

## Frank Jackson (born 1943)

Jackson is an Australian philosopher who has made many contributions to philosophy of mind and language, metaphysics, and ethics. His books include *Perception: A Representative Theory* (1977), *Conditionals* (1987), and *From Metaphysics to Ethics: A Defense of Conceptual Analysis* (1997). He is Distinguished Professor at the Australian National University and Visiting Professor of Philosophy at Princeton University.

# EPIPHENOMENAL QUALIA[1]

It is undeniable that the physical, chemical and biological sciences have provided a great deal of information about the world we live in and about ourselves. I will use the label "physical information" for this kind of information, and also for information that automatically comes along with it. For example, if a medical scientist tells me enough about the processes that go on in my nervous system, and about how they relate to happenings in the world around me, to what has happened in the past and is likely to happen in the future, to what happens to other similar and dissimilar organisms, and the like, he or she tells me — if I am clever enough to fit it together appropriately — about what is often called the functional role of those states in me (and in organisms in general in similar cases). This information, and its kin, I also label "physical."

I do not mean these sketchy remarks to constitute a definition of "physical information," and of the correlative notions of physical property, process, and so on, but to indicate what I have in mind here. It is well known that there are problems with giving a precise definition of these notions, and so of the thesis of Physicalism that all (correct) information is physical information. But — unlike some — I take the question of definition to cut across the central problems I want to discuss in this paper.

I am what is sometimes known as a "qualia freak." I think that there are certain features of the bodily sensations especially, but also of certain perceptual experiences, which no amount of purely physical information includes. Tell me everything physical there is to tell about what is going on in a living brain, the kind of states, their functional role, their relation to what goes on at other times and in other brains, and so on and so forth, and be I as clever as can be in fitting it all together, you won't have told me about the hurtfulness of pains, the itchiness of itches, pangs of jealousy, or about the characteristic experience of tasting a lemon, smelling a rose, hearing a loud noise or seeing the sky.

There are many qualia freaks, and some of them say that their rejection of Physicalism is an unargued intuition. I think that they are being unfair to themselves.

---

1. "Epiphenomenal": lacking causal power (here: the power to causally affect anything physical). "Qualia": qualities of mental states that specify their subjective character, or phenomenology. See the third paragraph of the reading for some examples.

They have the following argument. Nothing you could tell of a physical sort captures the smell of a rose, for instance. Therefore, Physicalism is false. By our lights this is a perfectly good argument. It is obviously not to the point to question its validity, and the premise is intuitively obviously true both to them and to me.

I must, however, admit that it is weak from a polemical point of view. There are, unfortunately for us, many who do not find the premise intuitively obvious. The task then is to present an argument whose premises are obvious to all, or at least to as many as possible. This I try to do in §1 with what I will call "the Knowledge argument." In §2 I contrast the Knowledge argument with the Modal argument and in §3 with the "What is it like to be" argument. In §4 I tackle the question of the causal role of qualia. The major factor in stopping people from admitting qualia is the belief that they would have to be given a causal role with respect to the physical world and especially the brain; and it is hard to do this without sounding like someone who believes in fairies. I seek in §4 to turn this objection by arguing that the view that qualia are epiphenomenal is a perfectly possible one.

## 1. The Knowledge Argument for Qualia

People vary considerably in their ability to discriminate colours. Suppose that in an experiment to catalogue this variation Fred is discovered. Fred has better colour vision than anyone else on record; he makes every discrimination that anyone has ever made, and moreover he makes one that we cannot even begin to make. Show him a batch of ripe tomatoes and he sorts them into two roughly equal groups and does so with complete consistency. That is, if you blindfold him, shuffle the tomatoes up, and then remove the blindfold and ask him to sort them out again, he sorts them into exactly the same two groups.

We ask Fred how he does it. He explains that all ripe tomatoes do not look the same colour to him, and in fact that this is true of a great many objects that we classify together as red. He sees two colours where we see one, and he has in consequence developed for his own use two words "$red_1$" and "$red_2$" to mark the difference. Perhaps he tells us that he has often tried to teach the difference between $red_1$ and $red_2$ to his friends but has got nowhere and has concluded that the rest of the world is $red_1$-$red_2$ colour-blind — or perhaps he has had partial success with his children, it doesn't matter. In any case he explains to us that it would be quite wrong to think that because "red" appears in both "$red_1$" and "$red_2$," that the two colours are shades of the one colour. He only uses the common term "red" to fit more easily into our restricted usage. To him $red_1$ and $red_2$ are as different from each other and all the other colours as yellow is from blue. And his discriminatory behaviour bears this out: he sorts $red_1$ from $red_2$ tomatoes with the greatest of ease in a wide variety of viewing circumstances. Moreover, an investigation of the physiological basis of Fred's exceptional ability reveals that Fred's optical system is able to separate out two groups of wavelengths in the red spectrum as sharply as we are able to sort out yellow from blue.

I think that we should admit that Fred can see, really see, at least one more colour than we can; red$_1$ is a different colour from red$_2$. We are to Fred as a totally red-green colour-blind person is to us. H. G. Wells' story "The Country of the Blind" is about a sighted person in a totally blind community. This person never manages to convince them that he can see, that he has an extra sense. They ridicule this sense as quite inconceivable, and treat his capacity to avoid falling into ditches, to win fights and so on as precisely that capacity and nothing more. We would be making their mistake if we refused to allow that Fred can see one more colour than we can.

What kind of experience does Fred have when he sees red$_1$ and red$_2$? What is the new colour or colours like? We would dearly like to know but do not; and it seems that no amount of physical information about Fred's brain and optical system tells us. We find out perhaps that Fred's cones respond differentially to certain light waves in the red section of the spectrum that make no difference to ours (or perhaps he has an extra cone) and that this leads in Fred to a wider range of those brain states responsible for visual discriminatory behaviour. But none of this tells us what we really want to know about his colour experience. There is something about it we don't know. But we know, we may suppose, everything about Fred's body, his behaviour and dispositions to behaviour and about his internal physiology, and everything about his history and relation to others that can be given in physical accounts of persons. We have all the physical information. Therefore, knowing all this is *not* knowing everything about Fred. It follows that Physicalism leaves something out.

To reinforce this conclusion, imagine that as a result of our investigations into the internal workings of Fred we find out how to make everyone's physiology like Fred's in the relevant respects; or perhaps Fred donates his body to science and on his death we are able to transplant his optical system into someone else — again the fine detail doesn't matter. The important point is that such a happening would create enormous interest. People would say, "At last we will know what it is like to see the extra colour, at last we will know how Fred has differed from us in the way he has struggled to tell us about for so long." Then it cannot be that we knew all along all about Fred. But *ex hypothesi*[2] we did know all along everything about Fred that features in the physicalist scheme; hence the physicalist scheme leaves something out.

Put it this way. *After* the operation, we will know *more* about Fred and especially about his colour experiences. But beforehand we had all the physical information we could desire about his body and brain, and indeed everything that has ever featured in physicalist accounts of mind and consciousness. Hence there is more to know than all that. Hence Physicalism is incomplete.

Fred and the new colour(s) are of course essentially rhetorical devices. The same point can be made with normal people and familiar colours. Mary is a brilliant scientist who is, for whatever reason, forced to investigate the world from a black and white room *via* a black and white television monitor. She specialises in the neurophysiology of vision and acquires, let us suppose, all the physical information there is to obtain about

---

2. By hypothesis (Latin).

what goes on when we see ripe tomatoes, or the sky, and use terms like "red," "blue," and so on. She discovers, for example, just which wave-length combinations from the sky stimulate the retina, and exactly how this produces *via* the central nervous system the contraction of the vocal chords and expulsion of air from the lungs that results in the uttering of the sentence "The sky is blue." (It can hardly be denied that it is in principle possible to obtain all this physical information from black and white television, otherwise the Open University[3] would *of necessity* need to use colour television.)

What will happen when Mary is released from her black and white room or is given a colour television monitor? Will she *learn* anything or not? It seems just obvious that she will learn something about the world and our visual experience of it. But then it is inescapable that her previous knowledge was incomplete. But she had *all* the physical information. *Ergo*[4] there is more to have than that, and Physicalism is false.

Clearly the same style of Knowledge argument could be deployed for taste, hearing, the bodily sensations and generally speaking for the various mental states which are said to have (as it is variously put) raw feels, phenomenal features or qualia. The conclusion in each case is that the qualia are left out of the physicalist story. And the polemical strength of the Knowledge argument is that it is so hard to deny the central claim that one can have all the physical information without having all the information there is to have.

## 2. The Modal Argument

By the Modal Argument I mean an argument of the following style. Sceptics about other minds are not making a mistake in deductive logic, whatever else may be wrong with their position. No amount of physical information about another *logically entails* that he or she is conscious or feels anything at all. Consequently there is a possible world with organisms exactly like us in every physical respect (and remember that includes functional states, physical history, *et al.*) but which differ from us profoundly in that they have no conscious mental life at all. But then what is it that we have and they lack? Not anything physical *ex hypothesi*. In all physical regards we and they are exactly alike. Consequently there is more to us than the purely physical. Thus Physicalism is false. . . .

The trouble . . . with the Modal argument is that it rests on a disputable modal intuition. Disputable because it is disputed. Some sincerely deny that there can be physical replicas of us in other possible worlds which nevertheless lack consciousness. Moreover, at least one person who once had the intuition now has doubts.

Head-counting may seem a poor approach to a discussion of the Modal argument. But frequently we can do no better when modal intuitions are in question, and remember our initial goal was to find the argument with the greatest polemical utility.

3. U.K. distance-learning university.

4. Therefore (Latin).

Of course, *qua*[5] protagonists of the Knowledge argument we may well accept the modal intuition in question; but this will be a *consequence* of our already having an argument to the conclusion that qualia are left out of the physicalist story, not our ground for that conclusion. Moreover, the matter is complicated by the possibility that the connection between matters physical and qualia is like that sometimes held to obtain between aesthetic qualities and natural ones. Two possible worlds which agree in all "natural" respects (including the experiences of sentient creatures) must agree in all aesthetic qualities also, but it is plausibly held that the aesthetic qualities cannot be reduced to the natural.

## 3. The "What Is It Like To Be" Argument

In "What is it like to be a bat?" Thomas Nagel argues that no amount of physical information can tell us what it is like to be a bat, and indeed that we, human beings, cannot imagine what it is like to be a bat.[6] His reason is that what this is like can only be understood from a bat's point of view, which is not our point of view and is not something capturable in physical terms which are essentially terms understandable equally from many points of view.

It is important to distinguish this argument from the Knowledge argument. When I complained that all the physical knowledge about Fred was not enough to tell us what his special colour experience was like, I was not complaining that we weren't finding out what it is like to *be* Fred. I was complaining that there is something *about* his experience, a property of it, of which we were left ignorant. And if and when we come to know what this property is we still will not know what it is like *to be* Fred, but we will know more *about* him. No amount of knowledge about Fred, be it physical or not, amounts to knowledge "from the inside" concerning Fred. We are not Fred. There is thus a whole set of items of knowledge expressed by forms of words like "that it is *I myself* who is . . ." which Fred has and we simply cannot have because we are not him.

When Fred sees the colour he alone can see, one thing he knows is the way his experience of it differs from his experience of seeing red and so on, *another* is that he himself is seeing it. Physicalist and qualia freaks alike should acknowledge that no amount of information of whatever kind that *others* have *about* Fred amounts to knowledge of the second. My complaint though concerned the first and was that the special quality of his experience is certainly a fact about it, and one which Physicalism leaves out because no amount of physical information told us what it is.

Nagel speaks as if the problem he is raising is one of extrapolating from knowledge of one experience to another, of imagining what an unfamiliar experience would be like on the basis of familiar ones. In terms of Hume's example, from knowledge of some shades of blue we can work out what it would be like to see other shades of

5. As (Latin).

6. See Nagel's "What Is it Like to be a Bat" earlier in this chapter.

blue.[7] Nagel argues that the trouble with bats *et al.* is that they are too unlike us. It is hard to see an objection to Physicalism here. Physicalism makes no special claims about the imaginative or extrapolative powers of human beings, and it is hard to see why it need do so.

Anyway, our Knowledge argument makes no assumptions on this point. If Physicalism were true, enough physical information about Fred would obviate any need to extrapolate or to perform special feats of imagination or understanding in order to know all about his special colour experience. *The information would already be in our possession.* But it clearly isn't. That was the nub of the argument.

## 4. The Bogey of Epiphenomenalism

Is there any really *good* reason for refusing to countenance the idea that qualia are causally impotent with respect to the physical world? I will argue for the answer no, but in doing this I will say nothing about two views associated with the classical epiphenomenalist position. The first is that mental *states* are inefficacious with respect to the physical world. All I will be concerned to defend is that it is possible to hold that certain *properties* of certain mental states, namely those I've called qualia, are such that their possession or absence makes no difference to the physical world. The second is that the mental is *totally* causally inefficacious. For all I will say it may be that you have to hold that the instantiation of *qualia* makes a difference to *other mental states* though not to anything physical. Indeed general considerations to do with how you could come to be aware of the instantiation of qualia suggest such a position.

Three reasons are standardly given for holding that a quale like the hurtfulness of a pain must be causally efficacious in the physical world, and so, for instance, that its instantiation must sometimes make a difference to what happens in the brain. None, I will argue, has any real force. (I am much indebted to Alec Hyslop[8] and John Lucas[9] for convincing me of this.)

(i) It is supposed to be just obvious that the hurtfulness of pain is partly responsible for the subject seeking to avoid pain, saying "It hurts" and so on. But, to reverse Hume, anything can fail to cause anything.[1] No matter how often *B* follows *A*, and no matter how initially obvious the causality of the connection seems, the hypothesis

---

7. The Scottish philosopher David Hume (1711–1776) considered the example of a person "who enjoyed his sight for thirty years" and who became "perfectly well acquainted with colours of all kinds, excepting one particular shade of blue" (*Treatise of Human Nature*, l.1.i).

8. Alec Hyslop (1938–), Australian philosopher; see "The Analogical Inference to Other Minds" in chapter 6 of this anthology.

9. John Lucas (1929–), British philosopher.

1. According to David Hume, "there are no objects, which by the mere survey, without consulting experience, we can determine to be the causes of any other. . . . Any thing may produce anything" (*Treatise of Human Nature*, l.3.xv).

that *A* causes *B* can be overturned by an over-arching theory which shows the two as distinct effects of a common underlying causal process.

To the untutored the image on the screen of Lee Marvin's fist moving[2] from left to right immediately followed by the image of John Wayne's head moving in the same general direction looks as causal as anything. And of course throughout countless Westerns images similar to the first are followed by images similar to the second. All this counts for precisely nothing when we know the over-arching theory concerning how the relevant images are both effects of an underlying causal process involving the projector and the film. The epiphenomenalist can say exactly the same about the connection between, for example, hurtfulness and behaviour. It is simply a consequence of the fact that certain happenings in the brain cause both.

(ii) The second objection relates to Darwin's Theory of Evolution. According to natural selection the traits that evolve over time are those conducive to physical survival. We may assume that qualia evolved over time — we have them, the earliest forms of life do not — and so we should expect qualia to be conducive to survival. The objection is that they could hardly help us to survive if they do nothing to the physical world.

The appeal of this argument is undeniable, but there is a good reply to it. Polar bears have particularly thick, warm coats. The Theory of Evolution explains this (we suppose) by pointing out that having a thick, warm coat is conducive to survival in the Arctic. But having a thick coat goes along with having a heavy coat, and having a heavy coat is *not* conducive to survival. It slows the animal down.

Does this mean that we have refuted Darwin because we have found an evolved trait — having a heavy coat — which is not conducive to survival? Clearly not. Having a heavy coat is an unavoidable concomitant of having a warm coat (in the context, modern insulation was not available), and the advantages for survival of having a warm coat outweighed the disadvantages of having a heavy one. The point is that all we can extract from Darwin's theory is that we should expect any evolved characteristic to be *either* conducive to survival *or* a by-product of one that is so conducive. The epiphenomenalist holds that qualia fall into the latter category. They are a by-product of certain brain processes that are highly conducive to survival.

(iii) The third objection is based on a point about how we come to know about other minds. We know about other minds by knowing about other behaviour, at least in part. The nature of the inference is a matter of some controversy, but it is not a matter of controversy that it proceeds from behaviour. That is why we think that stones do not feel and dogs do feel. But, runs the objection, how can a person's behaviour provide any reason for believing he has qualia like mine, or indeed any qualia at all, unless this behaviour can be regarded as the *outcome* of the qualia. Man Friday's[3] footprint was evidence of Man Friday because footprints are causal outcomes of feet attached to people. And an epiphenomenalist cannot regard behaviour, or indeed anything physical, as an outcome of qualia.

---

2. The American actors Lee Marvin (1924–1987) and John Wayne (1907–1979) appeared in three movies together in the early 1960s.

3. A character in the novel *Robinson Crusoe* (1719) by the English writer Daniel Defoe (1659–1731).

But consider my reading in *The Times* that Spurs[4] won. This provides excellent evidence that *The Telegraph* has also reported that Spurs won, despite the fact that (I trust) *The Telegraph* does not get the results from *The Times*. They each send their own reporters to the game. *The Telegraph's* report is in no sense an outcome of *The Times'*, but the latter provides good evidence for the former nevertheless.

The reasoning involved can be reconstructed thus. I read in *The Times* that Spurs won. This gives me reason to think that Spurs won because I know that Spurs' winning is the most likely candidate to be what caused the report in *The Times*. But I also know that Spurs' winning would have had many effects, including almost certainly a report in *The Telegraph*.

I am arguing from one effect back to its cause and out again to another effect. The fact that neither effect causes the other is irrelevant. Now the epiphenomenalist allows that qualia are effects of what goes on in the brain. Qualia cause nothing physical but are caused by something physical. Hence the epiphenomenalist can argue from the behaviour of others to the qualia of others by arguing from the behaviour of others back to its causes in the brains of others and out again to their qualia.

You may well feel for one reason or another that this is a more dubious chain of reasoning than its model in the case of newspaper reports. You are right. The problem of other minds is a major philosophical problem, the problem of other newspaper reports is not. But there is no special problem of Epiphenomenalism as opposed to, say, Interactionism[5] here.

There is a very understandable response to the three replies I have just made. "All right, there is no knockdown refutation of the existence of epiphenomenal qualia. But the fact remains that they are an excrescence. They *do* nothing, they *explain* nothing, they serve merely to soothe the intuitions of dualists,[6] and it is left a total mystery how they fit into the world view of science. In short we do not and cannot understand the how and why of them."

This is perfectly true; but is no objection to qualia, for it rests on an overly optimistic view of the human animal, and its powers. We are the products of Evolution. We understand and sense what we need to understand and sense in order to survive. Epiphenomenal qualia are totally irrelevant to survival. At no stage of our evolution did natural selection favour those who could make sense of how they are caused and the laws governing them, or in fact why they exist at all. And that is why we can't.

It is not sufficiently appreciated that Physicalism is an extremely optimistic view of our powers. If it is true, we have, in very broad outline admittedly, a grasp of our place in the scheme of things. Certain matters of sheer complexity defeat us — there are an awful lot of neurons — but in principle we have it all. But consider the antecedent probability that everything in the Universe be of a kind that is relevant in some

---

4. Tottenham Hotspur, London football (soccer) team.

5. The view that the mental has physical effects and vice versa.

6. Those who hold that the mind and body are distinct things, or that mental properties are distinct from physical properties.

way or other to the survival of *homo sapiens*. It is very low surely. But then one must admit that it is very likely that there is a part of the whole scheme of things, maybe a big part, which no amount of evolution will ever bring us near to knowledge about or understanding. For the simple reason that such knowledge and understanding is irrelevant to survival.

Physicalists typically emphasise that we are a part of nature on their view, which is fair enough. But if we are a part of nature, we are as nature has left us after however many years of evolution it is, and each step in that evolutionary progression has been a matter of chance constrained just by the need to preserve or increase survival value. The wonder is that we understand as much as we do, and there is no wonder that there should be matters which fall quite outside our comprehension. Perhaps exactly how epiphenomenal qualia fit into the scheme of things is one such.

This may seem an unduly pessimistic view of our capacity to articulate a truly comprehensive picture of our world and our place in it. But suppose we discovered living on the bottom of the deepest oceans a sort of sea slug which manifested intelligence. Perhaps survival in the conditions required rational powers. Despite their intelligence, these sea slugs have only a very restricted conception of the world by comparison with ours, the explanation for this being the nature of their immediate environment. Nevertheless they have developed sciences which work surprisingly well in these restricted terms. They also have philosophers, called slugists. Some call themselves tough-minded slugists, others confess to being soft-minded slugists.

The tough-minded slugists hold that the restricted terms (or ones pretty like them which may be introduced as their sciences progress) suffice in principle to describe everything without remainder. These tough-minded slugists admit in moments of weakness to a feeling that their theory leaves something out. They resist this feeling and their opponents, the soft-minded slugists, by pointing out — absolutely correctly — that no slugist has ever succeeded in spelling out how this mysterious residue fits into the highly successful view that their sciences have and are developing of how their world works.

Our sea slugs don't exist, but they might. And there might also exist super beings which stand to us as we stand to the sea slugs. We cannot adopt the perspective of these super beings, because we are not them, but the possibility of such a perspective is, I think, an antidote to excessive optimism.

## TEST YOUR UNDERSTANDING

1. Does Jackson think the heavy coat of the polar bear is epiphenomenal?

2. Does Jackson think it is a mystery how epiphenomenal qualia fit into the world as described by science?

3. Is it a premise of the knowledge argument that the brilliant imprisoned scientist Mary does not know what it's like to be a normal person living in a multicolored environment?

## NOTES AND QUESTIONS

1. What, according to Jackson, are "qualia"? What, according to Jackson, does it mean to say that qualia are "epiphenomenal"? Evaluate the three objections to the claim that qualia are epiphenomenal discussed by Jackson in section IV. Does Jackson succeed in rebutting them? Are qualia epiphenomenal?

2. Set out the "modal argument" (pp. 415–16) in the form of premises and conclusion so that the **argument** is **valid**. How would Jackson object to the argument as you have set it out? Is the objection convincing?

3. Different authors use the term "qualia" differently. For a short explanation of the various senses of the term, see Michael Tye, "Qualia," *Stanford Encyclopedia of Philosophy*, ed. Edward Zalta (http://plato.stanford.edu/archives/fall2013/entries/qualia/), section 1.

4. Jackson's knowledge argument is still hotly debated. For some interesting essays and a helpful editorial introduction, see Peter Ludlow, Yujin Nagasawa, and Daniel Stoljar (eds.), *There's Something about Mary* (MIT Press, 2004).

# POSTSCRIPT ON QUALIA

I now think that . . . the sensory side of psychology. . . . can be deduced in principle from enough about the physical nature of our world despite the manifest appearance to the contrary that the knowledge argument[1] trades on. This is why I now think that the knowledge argument fails.

Why do I think that the sensory side of psychology, as it is constituted in our world, is deducible in principle from enough about the world's physical nature? Our knowledge of the sensory side of psychology has a causal source. Seeing red and feeling pain impact on us, leaving a memory trace which sustains our knowledge of what it is like to see red and feel pain on the many occasions where we are neither seeing red nor feeling pain. This is why it was always a mistake to say that someone could not know what seeing red and feeling pain is like unless they had actually experienced them: false "memory" traces are enough. This places a constraint on our best opinion about the nature of our sensory states: we had better not have opinions about their nature which cannot be justified by what we know about the causal origin of those opinions. Now the precise connection between causal origin and rational opinion is complex, but for present purposes the following rough maxim will serve: do not have opinions that outrun what is required by the best theory of these opinions' causal origins. Often it will be uncertain what the best theory is, or the question of what it is will be too close to the question under discussion for the maxim to be of much use. But in the case of sensory states, the maxim has obvious bite. We know that our

---

1. Set out and endorsed in the preceding reading, Jackson's "Epiphenomenal Qualia."

knowledge of what it is like to see red and feel pain has purely physical causes. We know, for example, that Mary's transition from not knowing what it is like to see red to knowing what it is like to see red will have a causal explanation in purely physical terms. (Dualist interactionism[2] is false.) It follows, by the maxim, that what she learns had better not outrun how things are physically.

Towards the end of "Epiphenomenal Qualia," I point out that a report in one newspaper may be good evidence for a similar report in another newspaper without its being the case that one report causes the other. This is true but, I now think, does not blunt the force of the argument just rehearsed. As noted in "Epiphenomenal Qualia" the reason we are entitled to hold that the reports are similar depends on our knowing *inter alia*[3] that they have a common cause, namely, the event being reported on. But we know this only because of the way reports in newspapers in general impact on us. The fundamental point remains that our entitlement comes back to causal impacts of the right kinds.

I now think that the puzzle posed by the knowledge argument is to explain why we have such a strong intuition that Mary learns something about how things are that outruns what can be deduced from the physical account of how things are. I suggest that the answer is the strikingly atypical nature of the way she acquires certain relational and functional information. Suppose that you want to know on landing in Chicago if the weather is typical for this time of year. A good deal of collecting and bringing together of information is required. The same goes for information about functional roles. To know that a certain way of driving is dangerous, or that a certain drug slows the progression of AIDS, requires bringing together information from disparate sources. However, the most plausible approach for physicalists[4] to sensory experience sees it as a striking exception to the rule that acquiring this kind of information requires collation. The most plausible view for physicalists is that sensory experience is putative information about certain highly relational and functional properties of goings on inside us. As it is often put nowadays, its very nature is representational: it represents *inter alia* certain highly relational and functional facts about what is happening to us. If this is right — and I have nothing to add to the detailed arguments by those physicalists who came to the position decades ahead of me — sensory experience is a quite unusually "quick and easy" way of acquiring highly relational and functional information. (And evolutionary considerations tell us why we might have acquired this ability to access quickly and easily certain sorts of highly relational and functional information.) Sensory experience is in this regard like the way we acquire information about intrinsic properties[5] — typically, we get the information that something is

---

2. The view, associated with the French philosopher René Descartes (1596–1650), that the mind and the body are distinct things that causally affect each other.

3. Among other things (Latin).

4. Those who think that the mind — and the world in general — is wholly physical.

5. Properties that an object has independently of its relation to other things. Being the second-largest object in the room (Jackson's example) is not an intrinsic property because whether an object is the second-largest in the room depends on what other objects are in the room.

round more quickly and easily than the information that it is the second largest object in the room. In consequence, sensory experience presents itself to us as if it were the acquisition of information about intrinsic nature. But, very obviously, it is not information about intrinsic *physical* nature, so the information Mary acquires presents itself to us as if it were information about something more than the physical. This is, I now think, the source of the strong but mistaken intuition that Mary learns something new about how things are on her release.

I still think though that we should take seriously the possibility that we know little about the intrinsic nature of our world, that we mostly know its causal *cum*[6] relational nature as revealed by the physical sciences. I hope and believe (on Occamist grounds) that this kind of "Kantian" scepticism is mistaken,[7] but I think that the reflections at the end of "Epiphenomenal Qualia" have to be taken seriously. But even if a large part of the intrinsic nature of our world is beyond our epistemic reach, the nature we know about supervenes on the mostly functional *cum* relational nature that the physical sciences tell us about. The considerations at the end of "Epiphenomenal Qualia" can be no reason to hold that Mary learns something new about how things are on her release, but rather that there may (*may*) be a lot about fundamental nature that we and she can never know.

## TEST YOUR UNDERSTANDING

1. Does Jackson think that imprisoned Mary learns nothing new on her release?

2. Does Jackson think that imprisoned Mary could know everything about the physical nature of our world?

## NOTES AND QUESTIONS

1. Where does Jackson think that the knowledge argument goes wrong? Is he right? What is his explanation of our "strong intuition" that Mary learns something when she sees a ripe tomato for the first time? Is it convincing?

2. Jackson elaborates on his diagnosis of why the knowledge argument fails in "Mind and Illusion," reprinted in Peter Ludlow, Yujin Nagasawa, and Daniel Stoljar (eds.), *There's Something about Mary* (MIT Press, 2004).

6. Together with (Latin).

7. "On Occamist grounds": by a methodological principle of parsimony in theorizing ("Occam's Razor"), associated with the English philosopher William of Occam (or Ockham) (c. 1287?–1347). "'Kantian' scepticism": the German philosopher Immanuel Kant (1724–1804) held that we could have no knowledge of (in his phrase) "things in themselves."

## Patricia Smith Churchland (born 1943)

Churchland is Emeritus Professor of Philosophy at the University of California, San Diego. She is known for her work connecting neuroscience and traditional philosophical topics such as consciousness, the self, free will, and ethics. Among other books, she is the author of *Brain-Wise: Studies in Neurophilosophy* (2002) and *Touching a Nerve: The Self as Brain* (2013).

## ARE MENTAL STATES IRREDUCIBLE TO NEUROBIOLOGICAL STATES?
### from *Neurophilosophy*

## Knowing from the Inside/Having a Point of View

For Nagel (1974),[1] there is something special about having an introspective capacity — a capacity to know one's thoughts, feelings, and sensations from the inside, as it were. One's experiences have a certain unmistakable phenomenological character, such as the felt quality of pain or the perceived character of red. One therefore has a subjective point of view. It is the *qualia* or qualitative character of experiences, sensations, feelings, and so forth, to which we have introspective access, and it is this that, in Nagel's view, is not reducible to neural states. These mental states resist reduction because introspective access to them has an essentially different character, yielding essentially different information, than does external access via neuroscience. The argument does exert a powerful attraction, but as stated it is still teasingly vague. In order to see exactly how it works, it is necessary to set out a more precise version.

(A)
(1) The qualia of my sensations are knowable to me by introspection.
(2) The properties of my brain states are *not* knowable to me by introspection.
Therefore:
(3) The qualia of my sensations ≠ the properties of my brain states.

A second argument, complementary to the first, seems also in play:

(B)
(1) The properties of my brain states are knowable by the various external senses.
(2) The qualia of my sensations are *not* knowable by the various external senses.
Therefore:
(3) The qualia of my sensations ≠ the properties of my brain states.

---

1. See "What Is It Like to Be a Bat?" earlier in this chapter.

The general form of the argument seems to be this:

(1) *a* is *F*
(2) *b* is not *F*
Therefore:
(3) *a* ≠ *b*

Leibniz's law says that *a* = *b* if and only if *a* and *b* have every property in common. So if a = *b*, then if *a* is red, *b* is red, if *a* weighs ten pounds, then *b* weighs ten pounds, and so forth. If *a* is red and *b* is not, then *a* ≠ *b*. Assuming their premises are true, arguments (A) and (B) appear to establish the nonidentity of brain states and mental states. But are their premises true?

Let us begin with argument (A). There is no quarrel with the first premise (the qualia of my sensations are known-to-me-by-introspection), especially since qualia are defined as those sensory qualities known by introspection, and in any case I have no wish to deny introspective awareness of sensations. In contrast, the second premise (the properties of my brain states are *not* known-to-me-by-introspection) looks decidedly troublesome. Its first problem is that it begs the very question at issue — that is, the question of whether or not mental states are identical to brain states. This is easy to see when we ask what the justification is for thinking that premise true.

The point is this: *if in fact* mental states are identical to brain states, then when I introspect a mental state, I do introspect the brain state with which it is identical. Needless to say, I may not *describe* my mental state as a brain state, but whether I do depends on what information I have about the brain, not upon whether the mental state really is identical to some brain state. The identity can be a fact about the world independently of my knowledge that it is a fact about the world. Similarly, when Jones swallows an aspirin, he thereby swallows acetylsalicylic acid, whether or not he thinks of himself thus; when Oedipus kissed Jocasta, he kissed his mother, whether or not he thought of himself thus. In short, identities may obtain even when we have not discovered that they do. The problem with the second premise is that the only justification for denying that introspective awareness of sensations *could be* introspective awareness of brain states derives from the assumption that mental states are not identical with brain states. And that is precisely what the argument is supposed to prove. Hence the charge of begging the question. (Although I have used (A) as an illustration, the same kind of criticism applies equally to (B).)

Other problems with these arguments are more subtle. One difficulty is best brought out by constructing an argument analogous to (A) or (B) with respect to the character of the properties under discussion and comparing the arguments for adequacy. Consider the following arguments:

(C)
(1) Smith believes Hitler to be a mass murderer.
(2) Smith does not believe Adolf Schicklgruber to be a mass murderer.

Therefore:

(3)  Adolf Schicklgruber ≠ Adolf Hitler.

As it happens, however, Adolf Schicklgruber = Adolf Hitler, so the argument cannot be right.

Or consider another instance of the general argument form where the property taking the place of *F* is a complex property concerning what John believes or knows:

(D)

(1)  Aspirin is *known by John to be a pain reliever*.

(2)  Acetylsalicylic acid is *not* known by John to be a pain reliever.

Therefore:

(3)  Aspirin ≠ acetylsalicylic acid.

And one final example more closely analogous to the arguments at issue:

(E)

(1)  Temperature is *directly apprehendable by me as a feature of material objects*.

(2)  Mean molecular kinetic energy is *not* directly apprehendable by me as a feature of material objects.

Therefore:

(3)  Temperature ≠ mean molecular kinetic energy.

These arguments fail because being-recognized-as-a-something or being-believed-to-be-a-something is not a genuine feature of the object itself, but rather is a feature of the object *as apprehended under some description or other* or *as thought about in some manner*. Having a certain mass is a property of the object, but being-thought-by-Smith-to-have-a-certain-mass is not a genuine property of the object. Such queer properties are sometimes called "intentional properties" to reflect their thought-mediated dependency. Notice that in (B) the property is being-knowable-by-the-various-external-senses, and in (A) the property is being-known-by-me-by-introspection. Both are sterling examples of thought-dependent properties.

Now the arguments (c) through (E) are fallacious because they treat intentional properties as though they were genuine properties of the objects, and a mistake of this type is called the *intentional fallacy*. It is evident that the arguments designed to demonstrate the nonidentity of qualia and brain states are analogous to arguments (c) through (E). Consequently, they are equally fallacious, and the nonidentity of mental states and brain states cannot be considered established by arguments such as (A) and (B).

The last difficulty with the arguments is better seen in a slightly different and more compelling version of the argument for the nonidentity of mental states and brain states, which I present and discuss below.

# Knowing Our Sensations: Jackson's Argument

The strategy of this second argument once again involves showing that differences between knowing our states via introspection and knowing via nonintrospective means are of such a nature as to constitute grounds for denying the reducibility of psychology to neuroscience. In order to clarify those differences, Frank Jackson (1982)[2] has constructed the following thought-experiment. Suppose that Mary is a neuroscientist who has lived her entire life in a room carefully controlled to display no colors, but only shades of white, gray, and black. Her information about the outside world is transmitted to her by means of a black-and-white television. Suppose further that one way or another she comes to know everything there is to know about the brain and how it works. That is, she comes to understand a completed neuroscience that, among other things, explains the nature of thinking, feeling, and perception, including the perception of colors. (This is all wildly unlikely, of course, but just suppose.)

Now for the argument: despite her knowing everything there is to know about the brain and about the visual system, there would still be something Mary would not know that her cohorts with a more regular childhood would, namely, the nature of the experience of seeing a red tomato. Granted, she knows all about the neural states at work when someone sees a red tomato—after all, she has the utopian neuroscience at hand. What she would not know is *what it is like to see red*—what it is like to have that specific experience. Conclusion: her utopian neuroscience leaves something out. This omission implies that there is something in psychology that is not captured by neuroscience, which in turn implies that psychology cannot be reduced to neuroscience.

More formally and with some simplifications, the argument is this:

(F)
(1) Mary knows everything there is to know about brain states and their properties.
(2) It is not the case that Mary knows everything there is to know about sensations and their properties.
Therefore:
(3) Sensations and their properties ≠ brain states and their properties.

The argument is very interesting, and it gives an unusually clean line to the intuition that mental states are essentially private and have an irreducibly phenomenological character. Nonetheless I am not convinced, and I shall try to explain why.

First, I suspect that the intentional fallacy, which caused problems for arguments (A) and (B), likewise haunts the premises of argument (F). That aside, there are perhaps more revealing criticisms to be made. Paul M. Churchland (1985) and David Lewis (1983) have independently argued that "knows about" is used in different

2. See "Epiphenomenal Qualia" earlier in this chapter.

senses in the two premises. As they see it, one sense involves the manipulation of concepts, as when one knows about electromagnetic radiation and can use the concept "electromagnetic radiation" by having been tutored in the theory. The other sense involves a prelinguistic apprehension, as when one knows about electromagnetic radiation by having had one's retina stimulated in the light of day, though one cannot use the expression "electromagnetic radiation." The latter sense may involve innate dispositions to make certain discriminations, for example. If the first premise uses "knows about" in the first sense and the second uses it in the second sense, then the argument founders on the fallacy of equivocation.

The important point is this: if there are two (at least) modes of knowing about the world, then it is entirely possible that what one knows about via one method is identical to what one knows about via a different method. Pregnancy is something one can know about by acquiring the relevant theory from a medical text or by being pregnant. What a childless obstetrician knows about is the very same process as the process known by a pregnant but untutored woman. They both know about pregnancy. By parity of reasoning, the object of Mary's knowledge when she knows the neurophysiology of seeing red might well be the very same state as the state known by her tomato-picking cohort. Just as the obstetrician does not become pregnant by knowing all about pregnancy, so Mary does not have the sensation of redness by knowing all about the neurophysiology of perceiving and experiencing red. Clearly it is no argument in support of nonidentity to say that Mary's knowledge fails to cause the sensation of redness. Whyever suppose that it should?

There is a further reservation about this argument. With the first premise I take no issue, since we are asked to adopt it simply for the sake of argument. The second premise, in contrast, is supposed to be accepted because it is highly credible or perhaps dead obvious. Now although it does have a first blush plausibility, it is the premise on which the argument stands or falls, and closer scrutiny is required.

On a second look, its obviousness dissolves into contentiousness, because the premise asks me to be confident about something that is too far beyond the limits of what I know and understand. How can I assess what Mary will know and understand if she knows *everything* there is to know about the brain? Everything is a lot, and it means, in all likelihood, that Mary has a radically different and deeper understanding of the brain than anything barely conceivable in our wildest flights of fancy.

One might say well, if Mary knew everything about *existing* neuroscience, she would not know what it was like to experience red, and knowing *absolutely* everything will just be more of the same. That is an assumption to which the property dualist is not entitled to help himself. For to know everything about the brain might well be qualitatively different, and it might be to possess a theory that would permit exactly what the premise says it will not. First, utopian neuroscience will probably look as much like existing neuroscience as modern physics looks like Aristotelian physics. So it will not be just more of the same. Second, all one need imagine is that Mary internalizes the theory in the way an engineer has internalized Newtonian physics, and she routinely makes introspective judgments about her own states using its concepts and principles. Like the engineer who does not have to make an effort but "sees" the world in a Newtonian manner, we may consider that Mary "sees" her internal world via the utopian neuroscience. Such a neuroscience might even tell her how to be very efficient at internalizing theories. It is, after all, the premise tells us, a *complete* neuroscience.

Intuitions and imaginability are, notoriously, a function of what we believe, and when we are very ignorant, our intuitions will be correspondingly naive. Gedanken-experiments[3] are the stuff of theoretical science, but when their venue is so surpassing distant from established science that the pivotal intuition is not uncontroversially better than its opposite, then their utility in deciding issues is questionable.

Moreover, intuitions opposite to those funding premise (2) are not only readily available, they can even be fleshed out a bit. How can I be reasonably sure that Mary would not know what a red tomato looks like? Here is a test. Present her with her first red object, and see whether she can recognize it as a red object. Given that she is supposed to know absolutely *everything* there is to know about the nervous system, perhaps she could, by introspective use of her utopian neuroscience, tell that she has, say, a gamma state in her O patterns, which she knows from her utopian neuroscience is identical to having a red sensation. Thus, she might recognize redness on that basis.

The telling point is this: whether or not she can recognize redness is clearly an empirical question, and I do not see how in our ignorance we can confidently insist that she must fail. Short of begging the question, there is no a priori reason why this is impossible. For all I know, she might even be able to produce red in her imagination if she knows what brain states are relevant. One cannot be confident that such an exercise of the imagination must be empirically impossible. To insist that our make-believe Mary could not make introspective judgments using her neuroscience *because* mental qualia are not identical to brain states would, obviously, route the argument round in a circle.

How could an alchemist assess what he could and could not know if he knew everything about substances? How could a monk living in the Middle Ages assess what he could and could not know if he knew everything there was to know about biology? He might insist, for example, that even if you knew everything there was to know about biology, you still would not know the nature of the vital spirit. Well, we still do not have a complete biology, but even so we know more than this hypothetical monk thought we could. We know (a) that there is no such thing as vital spirit, and (b) that DNA is the "secret" of life — it is what all living things on the planet share.

The central point of this reply to Jackson has been that he needs independent evidence for premise (2), since it is palpably not self-evident. It cannot be defended on a priori grounds, since its truth is an empirical question, and it cannot be defended on empirical grounds, since given the data so far, as good a case can be made for the negation of premise (2) as for premise (2) itself. I do not see, therefore, how it can be defended.

---

3. Thought experiments ("Gedanke" is German for "thought").

REFERENCES

Churchland, Paul M. (1985). "Reduction, Qualia, and the Direct Introspection of Brain States."
    *Journal of Philosophy* 82: 8–28.
Jackson, Frank (1982). "Epiphenomenal Qualia." *Philosophical Quarterly* 32: 127–36.
Lewis, David (1983). Postscript to "Mad Pain and Martian Pain." In *Philosophical Papers,* vol. I,
    122–30. Oxford University Press.
Nagel, Thomas (1974). "What Is It Like to Be a Bat?" *Philosophical Review* 83: 435–50.

## TEST YOUR UNDERSTANDING

1.  Suppose the "general form" of **arguments** (A) and (B) is:

    1.  $a$ is $F$

    2.  $b$ is not $F$

    Therefore:

    3.  $a \neq b$

    Given this assumption, does Churchland think (A) and (B) are **valid**?

2.  Give your own example of an argument that commits the "intentional fallacy."

3.  Churchland suggests that argument (F) commits a "fallacy of equivocation." Using an example of your own (not connected with the knowledge argument), explain what Churchland means.

4.  Jackson asks: "What will happen when Mary is released from her black and white room?" What is Churchland's reply?

## NOTES AND QUESTIONS

1.  Evaluate Churchland's criticisms of Nagel's argument, as she interprets it. Is her interpretation correct, or is Nagel's argument different?

2.  Evaluate Churchland's criticisms of Jackson's argument, as she interprets it. Is her interpretation correct, or is Jackson's argument different?

3.  For Jackson's reply to similar criticisms (offered by Paul Churchland in "Reduction, Qualia, and the Direct Introspection of Brain States," *Journal of Philosophy* 82 [1985]: 8–28), see his "What Mary Didn't Know," *Journal of Philosophy* 83 (1986): 291–95.

4.  The selection by Churchland is entirely critical; for an introduction to her positive views about the mind and the brain, see her *Touching a Nerve: The Self as Brain* (Norton, 2013).

## David Chalmers (born 1966)

Chalmers is an Australian philosopher specializing in philosophy of mind, known in particular for his influential book *The Conscious Mind* (1996), which set out more rigorous forms of traditional arguments for the view that the mind is not wholly material. He is Professor of Philosophy at New York University and Distinguished Professor of Philosophy at the Australian National University, and is also the author of *The Character of Consciousness* (2010) and *Constructing the World* (2012).

# THE HARD PROBLEM OF CONSCIOUSNESS[1]

## 1. Introduction

Why does physical processing in the brain give rise to a conscious inner life: consciousness of shapes, colors, sounds, emotions, and a stream of conscious thought, all experienced from the first-person point of view? This is perhaps the most baffling problem in the science of the mind. All sorts of mental phenomena have yielded to scientific investigation in recent years, but consciousness has stubbornly resisted. Many have tried to explain it, but the explanations always seem to fall short of the target. Some have been led to suppose that the problem is intractable, and that no good explanation can be given.

In this paper, I first isolate the truly hard part of the problem, separating it from more tractable parts and giving an account of why it is so difficult to explain. In the second half of the paper, I argue that if we move to a new kind of explanation that does not try to reduce consciousness to something it is not, a naturalistic account of consciousness can be given.

## 2. The Easy Problems and the Hard Problem

There is not just one problem of consciousness. "Consciousness" is an ambiguous term, referring to many different phenomena. Each of these phenomena needs to be explained, but some are easier to explain than others. At the start, it is useful to divide the associated problems of consciousness into "hard" and "easy" problems. The easy problems of consciousness are those that seem directly susceptible to the standard methods of cognitive science, whereby a phenomenon is explained in terms of computational or neural mechanisms. The hard problems are those that seem to resist those methods.

1. The arguments in this paper are presented in greater depth in David Chalmers, *The Conscious Mind* (Oxford University Press, 1996). [Chalmers's note.]

The easy problems of consciousness include those of explaining the following phenomena:

the ability to discriminate, categorize, and react to environmental stimuli;
the integration of information by a cognitive system;
the reportability of mental states;
the ability of a system to access its own internal states;
the focus of attention;
the deliberate control of behavior;
the difference between wakefulness and sleep.

All of these phenomena are associated with the notion of consciousness. For example, one sometimes says that a mental state is conscious when it is verbally reportable, or when it is internally accessible. Sometimes a system is said to be conscious of some information when it has the ability to react on the basis of that information, or, more strongly, when it attends to that information, or when it can integrate that information and exploit it in the sophisticated control of behavior. We sometimes say that an action is conscious precisely when it is deliberate. Often, we say that an organism is conscious as another way of saying that it is awake.

There is no real issue about whether *these* phenomena can be explained scientifically. All of them are straightforwardly vulnerable to explanation in terms of computational or neural mechanisms. To explain access and reportability, for example, we need only specify the mechanism by which information about internal states is retrieved and made available for verbal report. To explain the integration of information, we need only exhibit mechanisms by which information is brought together and exploited by later processes. For an account of sleep and wakefulness, an appropriate neurophysiological account of the processes responsible for organisms' contrasting behavior in those states will suffice. In each case, an appropriate cognitive or neurophysiological model can clearly do the explanatory work.

If these phenomena were all there was to consciousness, then consciousness would not be much of a problem. Although we do not yet have anything close to a complete explanation of these phenomena, we have a clear idea of how we might go about explaining them. This is why I call these problems the easy problems. Of course, "easy" is a relative term. Getting the details right will probably take a century or two of difficult empirical work. Still, there is every reason to believe that the methods of cognitive science and neuroscience will succeed.

The really hard problem of consciousness is the problem of *experience*. When we think and perceive, there is a whir of information-processing, but there is also a subjective aspect. As Nagel[2] has put it, there is *something it is like* to be a conscious organism. This subjective aspect is experience. When we see, for example, we *experience* visual sensations: the felt quality of redness, the experience of dark and light,

2. Thomas Nagel, "What Is It Like to Be a Bat?" *Philosophical Review* 83 (1974): 435–50, excerpted earlier in this chapter.

the quality of depth in a visual field. Other experiences go along with perception in different modalities: the sound of a clarinet, the smell of mothballs. Then there are bodily sensations, from pains to orgasms; mental images that are conjured up internally; the felt quality of emotion, and the experience of a stream of conscious thought. What unites all of these states is that there is something it is like to be in them. All of them are states of experience.

It is undeniable that some organisms are subjects of experience. But the question of how it is that these systems are subjects of experience is perplexing. Why is it that when our cognitive systems engage in visual and auditory information-processing, we have visual or auditory experience: the quality of deep blue, the sensation of middle C? How can we explain why there is something it is like to entertain a mental image, or to experience an emotion? It is widely agreed that experience arises from a physical basis, but we have no good explanation of why and how it so arises. Why should physical processing give rise to a rich inner life at all? It seems objectively unreasonable that it should, and yet it does.

If any problem qualifies as *the* problem of consciousness, it is this one. In this central sense of "consciousness," an organism is conscious if there is something it is like to be that organism, and a mental state is conscious if there is something it is like to be in that state. Sometimes terms such as "phenomenal consciousness" and "qualia" are also used here, but I find it more natural to speak of "conscious experience" or simply "experience."

# 3. Functional Explanation

Why are the easy problems easy, and why is the hard problem hard? The easy problems are easy precisely because they concern the explanation of cognitive *abilities* and *functions*. To explain a cognitive function, we need only specify a mechanism that can perform the function. The methods of cognitive science are well-suited for this sort of explanation, and so are well-suited to the easy problems of consciousness. By contrast, the hard problem is hard precisely because it is not a problem about the performance of functions. The problem persists even when the performance of all the relevant functions is explained. (Here "function" is not used in the narrow sense of something that a system is designed to do, but in the broader sense of any causal role in the production of behavior that a system might perform.)

To explain reportability, for instance, is just to explain how a system could perform the function of producing reports on internal states. To explain internal access, we need to explain how a system could be appropriately affected by its internal states and use information about those states in directing later processes. To explain integration and control, we need to explain how a system's central processes can bring information contents together and use them in the facilitation of various behaviors. These are all problems about the explanation of functions.

How do we explain the performance of a function? By specifying a *mechanism* that performs the function. Here, neurophysiological and cognitive modeling are perfect for the task. If we want a detailed low-level explanation, we can specify the neural mechanism that is responsible for the function. If we want a more abstract explanation, we can specify a mechanism in computational terms. Either way, a full and satisfying explanation will result. Once we have specified the neural or computational mechanism that performs the function of verbal report, for example, the bulk of our work in explaining reportability is over.

Throughout the higher-level sciences, reductive explanation — explanation that explains a high-level phenomenon wholly in terms of lower-level phenomena — works in just this way. To explain the gene, for instance, we needed to specify the mechanism that stores and transmits hereditary information from one generation to the next. It turns out that DNA performs this function; once we explain how the function is performed, we have explained the gene. To explain life, we ultimately need to explain how a system can reproduce, adapt to its environment, metabolize, and so on. All of these are questions about the performance of functions, and so are well-suited to reductive explanation.

The same holds for most problems in cognitive science. To explain learning, we need to explain the way in which a system's behavioral capacities are modified in light of environmental information, and the way in which new information can be brought to bear in adapting a system's actions to its environment. If we show how a neural or computational mechanism does the job, we have explained learning. We can say the same for other cognitive phenomena, such as perception, memory, and language. Sometimes the relevant functions need to be characterized quite subtly, but it is clear that insofar as cognitive science explains these phenomena at all, it does so by explaining the performance of functions.

When it comes to conscious experience, this sort of explanation fails. What makes the hard problem hard and almost unique is that it goes *beyond* problems about the performance of functions. To see this, note that even when we have explained the performance of all the cognitive and behavioral functions in the vicinity of experience — perceptual discrimination, categorization, internal access, verbal report — there may still remain a further unanswered question: *Why is the performance of these functions accompanied by experience?* A simple explanation of the functions leaves this question open.

There is no analogous further question in the explanation of genes, or of life, or of learning. If someone says "I can see that you have explained how DNA stores and transmits hereditary information from one generation to the next, but you have not explained how it is a *gene*," then they are making a conceptual mistake. All it means to be a gene is to be an entity that performs the relevant storage and transmission function. But if someone says "I can see that you have explained how information is discriminated, integrated, and reported, but you have not explained how it is *experienced*," they are not making a conceptual mistake. This is a nontrivial further question.

This further question is the key question in the problem of consciousness. Why doesn't all this information-processing go on "in the dark," free of any inner feel? Why is it that when electromagnetic waveforms impinge on a retina and are discriminated and categorized by a visual system, this discrimination and categorization is experienced as a sensation of vivid red? We know that conscious experience *does* arise when these functions are performed, but the very fact that it arises is the central mystery. There is an *explanatory gap* (a term due to Levine[3]) between the functions and experience, and we need an explanatory bridge to cross it. A mere account of the functions stays on one side of the gap, so the materials for the bridge must be found elsewhere.

This is not to say that experience *has* no function. Perhaps it will turn out to play an important cognitive role. But for any role it might play, there will be more to the explanation of experience than a simple explanation of the function. Perhaps it will even turn out that in the course of explaining a function, we will be led to the key insight that allows an explanation of experience. If this happens, though, the discovery will be an *extra* explanatory reward. There is no cognitive function such that we can say in advance that explanation of that function will *automatically* explain experience.

To explain experience, we need a new approach. The usual explanatory methods of cognitive science and neuroscience do not suffice. These methods have been developed precisely to explain the performance of cognitive functions, and they do a good job of it. But as these methods stand, they are *only* equipped to explain the performance of functions. When it comes to the hard problem, the standard approach has nothing to say.

# 4. Zombies and the Explanatory Gap

The hard problem of consciousness arises for any physical explanation of consciousness. For any physical process we specify there will be an unanswered question: why should this process give rise to experience?

One way to see this point is via a philosophical thought-experiment: that of a philosophical zombie. A philosophical zombie is a being that is atom-for-atom identical to a conscious being such as you and me, but it is not conscious. Unlike the zombies found in Hollywood movies, philosophical zombies look just like a normal humans from the outside, and their behavior is indistinguishable from that of a conscious being. But on the inside, all is dark. There is nothing it is like to be a zombie.

There is little reason to think that philosophical zombies really exist. But what matters for our purposes is simply that the idea is coherent. There is no internal contradiction in the idea of a zombie, the way that there is an internal contradiction in the idea of a round square. I may believe that you are not a zombie, but I cannot rule out the hypothesis that you are a zombie by a priori reasoning alone.

The hard problem of consciousness might then be put as the problem: why are we not zombies? In our world, in fact, there is consciousness. But everything in physics

3. Joseph Levine, "Materialism and Qualia: The Explanatory Gap," *Pacific Philosophical Quarterly* 64 (1983): 354–61.

and in neuroscience seems to be compatible with the hypothesis that we are zombies. If that is right, then physics and neuroscience alone cannot explain why we are not zombies. More generally, it appears that no purely physical explanation can explain why we are not zombies. If so, no purely physical explanation can solve the hard problem of consciousness.

We can even use this sort of reasoning to generate an argument against materialism, the thesis that our world is wholly physical. To explain materialism, we can use the metaphor of God creating the world. If materialism is true, then God simply needed to create microphysical entities such as atoms and fields, and arrange them in the right way: then everything else, such as cells and organisms and tables, followed automatically.

But zombies suggest that materialism must be false. To see this, note that because there is no contradiction in the idea of a zombie, it seems that it would be within God's powers to create a zombie world: a world that is physically identical to ours, but without consciousness. If this is right, then even after God ensured that all the physical truths about our world obtained, the truths about consciousness did not automatically follow. After creating everything in physics, God had to do more work to put consciousness into the world. This suggests that consciousness is something over and above the physical, and that materialism is false.

Of course God here is a metaphor, but the idea can also be put in terms of the philosophers' idea of a possible world. For example, there may be no antigravity machines in the actual world, but there is no contradiction in the idea (one can tell coherent science fiction about antigravity), so there is at least a possible world in which there is antigravity. Likewise, even if there are no zombies in the actual world, there is at least a possible world in which there are zombies. And if there is a possible world in which there are physical processes just like those in our world but no consciousness, then consciousness does not follow from those processes with absolute necessity. It follows that materialism is false.

We might put the underlying problem as follows. Physical explanation is ultimately cast entirely in terms of microphysical structure and dynamics. This sort of explanation is well-suited to explaining macroscopic structure and dynamics. For problems such as the problem of learning or the problem of life, this is good enough, as in these cases macroscopic structure and dynamics were all that needed explaining. But we have seen that in the case of consciousness, structure and dynamics is not all that needs explaining: we also need to explain why macroscopic structure and dynamics is accompanied by consciousness. And here, physical explanation has nothing to say: structure and dynamics adds up only to more structure and dynamics. So consciousness cannot be wholly explained in physical terms.

If all this is right, then although consciousness may be associated with physical processing in systems such as brains, it is not reducible to that processing. Any *reductive* explanation of consciousness, in purely physical terms, must fail. No matter what sort of physical processes we might invoke, we find an explanatory gap between those processes and consciousness.

# 5. Nonreductive Explanation

At this point some are tempted to give up, holding that we will never have a theory of conscious experience. I think this pessimism is premature. This is not the place to give up; it is the place where things get interesting. When simple methods of explanation are ruled out, we need to investigate the alternatives. Given that reductive explanation fails, *nonreductive* explanation is the natural choice.

Although a remarkable number of phenomena have turned out to be explicable wholly in terms of entities simpler than themselves, this is not universal. In physics, it occasionally happens that an entity has to be taken as *fundamental*. Fundamental entities are not explained in terms of anything simpler. Instead, one takes them as basic, and gives a theory of how they relate to everything else in the world. For example, in the nineteenth century it turned out that electromagnetic processes could not be explained in terms of the wholly mechanical processes that previous physical theories appealed to, so Maxwell[4] and others introduced electromagnetic charge and electromagnetic forces as new fundamental components of a physical theory. To explain electromagnetism, the ontology of physics had to be expanded. New basic properties and basic laws were needed to give a satisfactory account of the phenomena.

Other features that physical theory takes as fundamental include mass and space-time. No attempt is made to explain these features in terms of anything simpler. But this does not rule out the possibility of a theory of mass or of space-time. There is an intricate theory of how these features interrelate, and of the basic laws they enter into. These basic principles are used to explain many familiar phenomena concerning mass, space, and time at a higher level.

I suggest that a theory of consciousness should take experience as fundamental. We know that a theory of consciousness requires the addition of *something* fundamental to our ontology, as everything in physical theory is compatible with the absence of consciousness. We might add some entirely new nonphysical feature, from which experience can be derived, but it is hard to see what such a feature would be like. More likely, we will take experience itself as a fundamental feature of the world, alongside mass, charge, and space-time. If we take experience as fundamental, then we can go about the business of constructing a theory of experience.

Where there is a fundamental property, there are fundamental laws. A nonreductive theory of experience will add new principles to the furniture of the basic laws of nature. These basic principles will ultimately carry the explanatory burden in a theory of consciousness. Just as we explain familiar high-level phenomena involving mass in terms of more basic principles involving mass and other entities, we might

---

4. James Clerk Maxwell (1831–1879), Scottish physicist.

explain familiar phenomena involving experience in terms of more basic principles involving experience and other entities.

In particular, a nonreductive theory of experience will specify basic principles telling us how experience depends on physical features of the world. These *psychophysical* principles will not interfere with physical laws, as it seems that physical laws already form a closed system. Rather, they will be a supplement to a physical theory. A physical theory gives a theory of physical processes, and a psychophysical theory tells us how those processes give rise to experience. We know that experience depends on physical processes, but we also know that this dependence cannot be derived from physical laws alone. The new basic principles postulated by a nonreductive theory give us the extra ingredient that we need to build an explanatory bridge.

Of course, by taking experience as fundamental, there is a sense in which this approach does not tell us why there is experience in the first place. But this is the same for any fundamental theory. Nothing in physics tells us why there is matter in the first place, but we do not count this against theories of matter. Certain features of the world need to be taken as fundamental by any scientific theory. A theory of matter can still explain all sorts of facts about matter, by showing how they are consequences of the basic laws. The same goes for a theory of experience.

This position qualifies as a variety of dualism, the view that the mind is not wholly physical, as it postulates basic mental properties over and above the properties invoked by physics. But it is a version of dualism that is entirely compatible with the scientific view of the world. Nothing in this approach contradicts anything in physical theory; we simply need to add further *bridging* principles to explain how experience arises from physical processes. There is nothing particularly spiritual or mystical about this theory — its overall shape is like that of a physical theory, with a few fundamental properties connected by fundamental laws. It expands the class of primitive properties, to be sure, but Maxwell did the same thing. Indeed, the overall structure of this position is entirely naturalistic, allowing that ultimately the universe comes down to a network of basic entities obeying simple laws, and allowing that there may ultimately be a theory of consciousness cast in terms of such laws. If the position is to have a name, a good choice might be *naturalistic dualism*.

# 6. Conclusion

Most existing theories of consciousness either deny the phenomenon, explain something else, or elevate the problem to an eternal mystery. I hope to have shown that it is possible to make progress on the problem even while taking it seriously. To make further progress, we will need further investigation, more refined theories, and more careful analysis. The hard problem is a hard problem, but there is no reason to believe that it will remain permanently unsolved.

## TEST YOUR UNDERSTANDING

1. Does Chalmers think that explaining the performance of all cognitive and behavioral functions leaves consciousness unexplained?

2. Does Chalmers think that we will never be able to explain how consciousness arises from physical processes?

## NOTES AND QUESTIONS

1. According to Chalmers, "zombies suggest that materialism must be false." What are "zombies"? What does Chalmers mean by "materialism"? Reconstruct Chalmers's zombie **argument** for the falsity of materialism in the form of premises and conclusion. Assess the argument. Is it **valid**? Is it **sound**?

2. Chalmers defends naturalistic dualism at greater length in *The Conscious Mind* (Oxford University Press, 1996), much of which is accessible to the general reader. Chalmers surveys the main positions on the mind-body problem in "Consciousness and Its Place in Nature," reprinted in his book *The Character of Consciousness* (Oxford University Press, 2010). A collection of critical work on Chalmers is Jonathan Shear (ed.), *Explaining Consciousness: The Hard Problem* (MIT, 1999).

3. For more on zombies, see Robert Kirk, "Zombies," *Stanford Encyclopedia of Philosophy*, ed. Edward Zalta (http://plato.stanford.edu/archives/sum2012/entries/zombies/).

## Michael Tye (born 1950)

Tye is Professor of Philosophy at the University of Texas at Austin, specializing in the philosophy of mind. He is the author of many influential books and articles, including *Ten Problems of Consciousness* (1995), *Consciousness Revisited: Materialism without Phenomenal Concepts* (2009), and (with Mark Sainsbury) *Seven Puzzles of Thought (and How to Solve Them): An Originalist Theory of Concepts* (2012).

# THE PUZZLE OF TRANSPARENCY

Sit, facing a red apple in good light. In front of you is a particular thing — an apple. You see the apple. In doing so, you have a visual experience caused by the apple — an experience as of a red, round, bulgy shape before you. That visual experience is also a particular thing, but unlike the apple it is mental. There is, then, or so it is standardly assumed, the external thing (the apple), an internal thing (the experience), and a causal relationship between the two.

Your experience, being an experience, has a *phenomenology*. There is something it is *like* for you subjectively in seeing the apple. What it is like for you is different from what it is like for you to see a banana or an orange in good light. What it is like for you, as you see the apple, is *radically* different from what it is like for you to undergo certain other experiences. Think, for example, of the experience of sharp pain caused by accidentally stepping on a thumbtack. What it is like to undergo an experience is sometimes called the "phenomenal character" of that experience. One natural way to think of the phenomenal character of an experience is as a quality of the experience.

Since what it is like to see a red, round shape has something in common subjectively with what it is like to see a red, square shape, it is also natural to suppose that in many cases, the overall phenomenal character of an experience is made up of a number of different subjective qualities. The subjective qualities of which the overall phenomenal character of the experience is composed are often called "qualia." There is, then, the external thing (the apple) and its qualities, and there is also the internal thing (the experience) and its phenomenal character (or qualia). Whether the experience has further qualities not connected to its phenomenal character, as the apple has further qualities not accessible to your eyes (for example, its weight or cost), is something on which we need take no stand for present purposes.

Now I want you to attend carefully to the apple you are viewing. As you do so, you will likely notice some variations of color that had not stood out before; or you may notice an irregularity in the shape. Next, place a banana to the left of the apple, some distance away but still visible to you from your viewing position, and look again. You can choose to attend to the apple or to the banana or to both. You can switch your attention from one to the other. When you do this, you can attend to the color of the apple or the shape of the banana, for example.

Now I want you to switch your attention from the apple to your visual experience of it. Are you able to do so easily? As easily as you can switch your attention from the apple to the banana? If you think you can, do you notice any new quality of the experience? If these questions puzzle you, well and good. For reasons that will become clear shortly, they *should* puzzle you.

I am not asking you here to fixate your eyes upon your experience in the way that you can fixate your eyes on the apple and then on the banana. Obviously, an experience, being a mental entity, is not the sort of thing upon which you can train your eyes.[1]

I am not asking you to do these things because even in the visual case I take it that attention is not the same as eye fixation. To appreciate what I am getting at here, fixate your eyes upon the plus sign in the center of figure 1. As you continue to fixate your eyes on the plus sign and also to focus mentally upon it, you can tell which rectangles are grey and which are black. However, you cannot tell which rectangles have longer vertical sides. To find that out, you need to switch your attention, that is, your mental

---

1. Of course, if experiences are brain states then they can be viewed through cerebroscopes while the experiences are occurring. But this is not relevant to the points being made here. [Tye's note.]

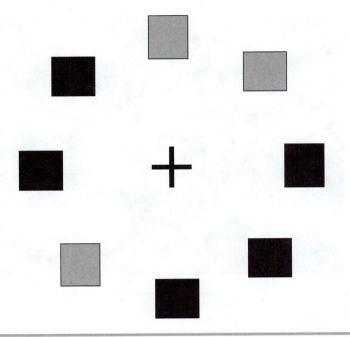

**Figure 1**

focus. As you vary your mental focus, you can attend to the rectangles, one by one, while still fixating on the plus sign, and as you do so, you can determine which have longer vertical sides. Attending to something typically (perhaps always) reveals new qualities of the thing or at least qualities you experience the thing as having, qualities of which you were not aware beforehand.

Returning to the apple and your experience of it, I can only say that in my own case I find that I cannot switch my attention from the apple to my visual experience. Indeed, I find that I cannot attend to my visual experience at all. Moreover, I cannot attend to any of its qualities.[2] When I try to follow the instructions given above in my own case, my very strong belief is that *nothing at all* changes except perhaps that, in trying to do what is asked, I come to notice new qualities of the *apple* of which I was not aware before.

What does this show? Well, if you accept the claims of the previous paragraph in your own case (and I think that they are very hard to deny, though not everyone agrees[3]), at a minimum they should make you extremely puzzled. If you cannot attend to your

2. The first philosopher to comment upon this phenomenon was G. E. Moore, "The Refutation of Idealism," *Philosophical Studies* (Routledge and Kegan Paul, 1922). He remarked, "When we try to introspect the sensation of blue, all we can see is the blue. The other element is as if it were diaphanous." See also Gilbert Harman, "The Intrinsic Quality of Experience," *Philosophical Perspectives* 4 (1990): 31–52. [Tye's note.]

3. See Ned Block, "Inverted Earth," *Philosophical Perspectives* 4 (1990): 53–79; and Ned Block, "Mental Paint," in Martin Hahn and B. Ramberg (eds.), *Reflections and Replies: Essays on the Philosophy of Tyler Burge* (MIT Press, 2003). [Tye's note.]

**Figure 2**

visual experience, then there is an inherently conscious thing — namely, your experience — that is not accessible to your attention. Further, if you cannot attend to any of your visual experience's qualities, then the phenomenal character of your experience is something to which you cannot attend either. How can that be?

To appreciate why this should be puzzling, look at figure 2 and fixate your eyes on the man resting on an elbow at the bottom in the middle. I predict that, as you do so, you will be unable to mentally focus upon the writing implement or the notebook or the beard of the man leaning in on the far left. For you, it will be as if these items are not there, and likewise for their qualities, for example, their shapes. Because you are unable to attend to these things as you fixate on the man in the middle, they are hidden from you. You are blind to them.

Here is another example. Fixate on the plus sign in figure 3. As you do so, you won't be able to focus upon or attend to the fifth vertical bar away from the plus sign. If you think otherwise, tell me how many bars there are on the right without moving your fixation point. I predict that you won't be able to do so. The reason is straightforward: it is not the case that each and every bar on the right is clearly and individually marked out in the phenomenology of your experience. The fifth bar is one of the bars not so marked out. It is effectively hidden from you, given your fixation point. That's why you can't count the bars. This is not to say that *the bars* (plural) are hidden from you. Obviously, they aren't. You are certainly conscious of the bars. But there are individual bars of which you are not conscious. (Compare: you can weigh a bunch of marbles without weighing each marble. Having weighed the marbles, you may still have no precise idea of how much the fifth marble in the bunch weighs.)

**Figure 3**

The conclusion to which we seem driven is that the phenomenal character of your visual experience, as you view the apple, is *hidden* from you, as is your visual experience. You are *blind* to these things. For you, it is as if they aren't there. They are, as it were, transparent to you. You "see" right through them when you try to attend to them and you end up focusing on things outside you. But surely this cannot be right. Your visual experience is an inherently conscious thing. Its phenomenal character — what it is like for you subjectively — is inherently conscious. How can these things be hidden from you? If you cannot attend to the phenomenal character of your visual experience, then it no more contributes to your subjective, conscious life than do the shapes of some of the figures on the left of the picture in figure 2 as you fixate on the pensive man in the middle. In that case, its presence (or absence) is simply irrelevant to your consciousness.

Something has gone terribly wrong. But what exactly? One reaction is to say that the above considerations show that the phenomenal character of a visual experience isn't a quality at all. Instead it is something else, something that isn't hidden. Well, what is it then?

One proposal is that it is a *representational content* that the experience has. This jargon needs a little explanation. If I have an experience as of a red, round thing before me, my experience is accurate if there is a red, round thing before me and inaccurate otherwise. So we may say that my experience has *accuracy conditions*: it is accurate in the condition in which there is a red, round thing before me, and inaccurate in all other conditions. And in having accuracy conditions, it has representational content — for present purposes, the jargon of "representational content" is just another way of talking about "accuracy conditions." My experience represents the world as being a certain way, namely as containing a red, round thing in front of me. Philosophers have often supposed that the phenomenology of an experience is something entirely distinct from its representational content. But in recent work a number of philosophers have argued that the phenomenology cannot be pulled apart from the content.[4]

Here is an illustration of this view. Consider a visual experience as of a red, round thing in front of you and a second visual experience as of a yellow, square thing in front of you. Obviously, what it is like for you subjectively to undergo the first

---

4. See, e.g., Alex Byrne, "Intentionalism Defended," *Philosophical Review* 110 (2001): 49–90; Fred Dretske, *Naturalizing the Mind* (Bradford Books: MIT Press, 1995); and Michael Tye, *Ten Problems of Consciousness* (MIT Press, 1995). [Tye's note.]

experience is different from what it is like for you subjectively to undergo the second. Correspondingly, there is a difference in accuracy conditions: the first experience is accurate under different circumstances than the second. Now consider a third, later visual experience having exactly the same accuracy conditions as the first. Could there be any difference in what it is like for you to undergo that experience and what it is like for you to undergo the first? Many philosophers hold that it is clear that there could be no such difference: the phenomenal character of the one experience would *have* to be the same as the phenomenal character of the other. Why should this be?

A simple explanation is that the phenomenal character of an experience just *is* its representational content. This proposal, which is usually labeled "strong representationalism," is problematic in a number of respects. To mention one: some experiences do not seem to have any representational content (for example, an undirected feeling of anger).

Let us put this worry to one side. Does strong representationalism solve the puzzle of transparency? I have come to think that it does not.[5] If the phenomenal character of your experience, as you view the apple, is the same as the representational content of your experience, and thus not a quality of your experience, it is still something different from any of the apple's perceived qualities. So, you ought to be able to switch your attention from the redness of the apple to the phenomenal character of your experience just as you can switch your attention from the color of the apple to its shape. You ought to be able to focus your attention upon this additional thing. But you can't. Once again, then, the phenomenal character of your experience is hidden from you. That's absurd.

It might be replied that the situation here is like that which obtains when I hear you utter certain words — "Snow is white," say. I hear the words and I have an auditory experience of certain auditory qualities (for example, pitch and loudness). I can focus my attention on the sounds and their auditory qualities or I can focus my attention on the meaning of the sentence, on its representational content. Why not suppose that things are like that in the case of your seeing an apple?

The answer is that in the visual case (a) the bearer of the representational content is the experience itself and (b) the qualities experienced are not qualities of that bearer but rather qualities of the thing experienced, namely the apple. The experience isn't red and round; the apple is. Furthermore, even though the representational content is something the experience possesses, it is not separable from the qualities experienced (redness, roundness, etc.) in the way that the meaning of the sentence "Snow is white" is separable from the auditory qualities of loudness and pitch. In the case of your visual experience, the qualities experienced are involved in, or at any rate, play a role in specifying the representational content. Not so in the auditory example. "Snow is white" is true if and only if snow is white. The accuracy conditions for this sentence, and thus its representational content, have nothing to do with the auditory qualities belonging to a particular utterance of that sentence.

It might now be said that the very fact that the perceived qualities of the apple enter into, or are involved in, the representational content of the visual experience is

---

5. See Michael Tye, *Consciousness Revisited* (MIT Press, 2009). [Tye's note.]

what makes it so difficult to prise apart the content and the qualities when it comes to focusing attention. When you focus your attention on the phenomenal character of your experience, inevitably you also focus your attention on the redness and roundness of the apple (since they are involved in the content, which just is the phenomenal character on the view I am considering). That is why it seems to you that you can't focus on the phenomenal character of your experience alone. This proposal also might be held to explain why you can't switch your attention from the redness of the apple to the phenomenal character of your experience in the same way that you can switch your attention from the redness of the apple to the yellowness of the banana. The redness of the apple does not involve the yellowness of the banana, but the phenomenal character of your experience does involve redness.

Again I am unpersuaded. Even if the representational content of your experience has redness as a component, why can't you focus on the former without focusing on the latter? Consider the two crowds of balls in figure 4 below.[6] You can certainly focus your attention on the upper crowd rather than the lower one. But in doing so, you need not be focusing your attention on each particular ball in that crowd as well. Indeed, it seems impossible to focus your attention simultaneously on each ball. This is one reason why if the crowds are presented one after the other rather than simultaneously, it is very likely that you will fail to notice any difference in them (though they do differ in a ball). To change examples, just as you can weigh a bunch of marbles without weighing any particular marble or think of a department at your university without thinking of any member of that department in particular, so you can attend to a complex thing without attending to any particular component part of that thing. We're still in deep trouble.

So what is the way out? At one level, the answer seems obvious. We must hold that the phenomenal character of your experience, as you view the apple, is one and the same as the complex of qualities you experience the apple as having. That is why you cannot switch your attention from the apple's qualities to the phenomenal character of your experience. That is why you cannot focus on the phenomenal character apart from those qualities. The trouble is that the phenomenal character of your experience, what it is like for you subjectively, is now out there in the world beyond your head where the qualities of the apple are! You *confront* it when you see the apple. Since phenomenal character is mental if anything is, that means that mental items are out there in the world.[7]

That may seem totally crazy. The apple has the relevant complex of qualities even when no one is viewing it. But it surely does not then have the phenomenal character of a visual experience.

This is true. But the natural reply, it seems to me, is to say that the complex of qualities is the phenomenal character of your visual experience only if it meets

---

6. The example is from Fred Dretske, "What We See: the Texture of Conscious Experience," in B. Nanay (ed.), *Perceiving the World: New Essays on Perception* (Oxford University Press, 2010). [Tye's note.]

7. What if you are hallucinating? I would say that you are still confronted by a certain complex of qualities, a complex you *take* to belong to something before you when in reality nothing before you has the relevant qualities. [Tye's note.]

Crowd A of balls

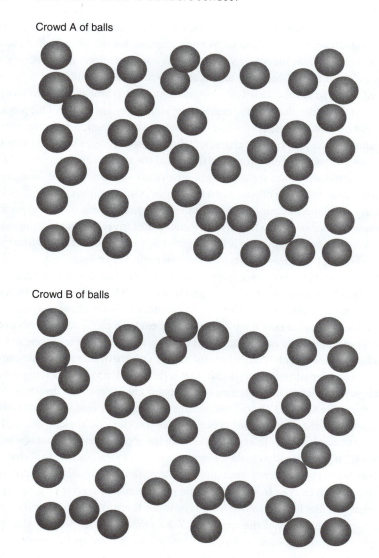

Crowd B of balls

**Figure 4**

certain further conditions, where these conditions rule out the apple's having a visual phenomenal character when no one is seeing it. Still, what are these conditions?

That, in my view, is a really tough question. One part of the answer, I believe, is that the relevant complex of qualities must be *represented* by an internal state meeting certain further conditions. However, we had better not say that these further conditions involve the internal state's having a phenomenal character or circularity threatens (that is to say, our account of phenomenal character will itself appeal to phenomenal character and so no progress will have been made).

On this proposal, the complex of qualities you confront in seeing the apple would not be a phenomenal character if it did not bear an appropriate relation to a mind. Thus in a world without minds there is no phenomenology, just as in a world without bifocals there is no inventor of bifocals.

Philosophers often suppose that there is nothing incoherent in the idea that there are creatures who are just like normal human beings physically but who lack experiences. Such creatures are often called "zombies" in philosophy, but philosophical zombies should not be confused with Hollywood zombies. Philosophical zombies are supposed to behave just as normal human beings do (being just the same physically). Thus, unlike Hollywood zombies, they do not keep going if you chop off their heads. Nor do they come out only at night and eat the flesh of others. Philosophers often claim that the idea of a (philosophical) zombie is not like the idea of a square circle. Unlike the latter idea, there is no internal inconsistency in the former idea. According to these philosophers, even though in reality there are no zombies, we can easily make sense of the *idea* that there are zombies. We simply imagine or conceive of there being creatures who are like us in their physical makeup right down to the last detail but for whom on the inside all is dark, as it were. If zombies really are conceivable, an interesting question now arises. What is the difference between you and your zombie duplicate, as he views the apple from the same viewpoint as you? It cannot be in the qualities the two of you confront: for both of you, the same complex of qualities is represented as belonging to the apple. The difference, it seems to me, is that your zombie twin *mistakenly* believes that *that* (pointing at the complex of qualities he confronts) is what it is like for him to *experience* the apple. In reality, for your zombie replica, there is no experience: the complex of qualities is not a phenomenal character.[8]

So, that is the puzzle of transparency. If you are not yet puzzled by it, you should be!

## TEST YOUR UNDERSTANDING

1. Suppose you are looking at a banana. In Tye's terminology, you are having a "visual experience of the banana." According to Tye, can you attend to:

    a. the banana?

    b. qualities of the banana (for example, its color and shape)?

    c. your experience of the banana?

    d. qualities of your experience of the banana?

8. One further issue that now arises is how it is you know that you are not yourself a zombie. See here Fred Dretske, "How Do You Know You Are Not a Zombie?," in B. Gertler (ed.), *Privileged Access: Philosophical Accounts of Self-Knowledge* (Ashgate, 2003); and Michael Tye, *Consciousness Revisited*. [Tye's note.]

## NOTES AND QUESTIONS

1. What is "strong representationalism," and why does Tye think it fails to solve the puzzle of transparency? What is Tye's solution? The solution, he says, "may seem totally crazy." Does Tye succeed in explaining why it isn't?

2. In note 2 Tye refers to Gilbert Harman's paper, "The Intrinsic Quality of Experience," (*Philosophical Perspectives* 4: 31–52), which is frequently cited as the main contemporary source for the idea that experience is "transparent." Here is the relevant passage from that paper:

> When Eloise sees a tree before her, the colors she experiences are all experienced as features of the tree and its surroundings. None of them are experienced as intrinsic features of her experience. Nor does she experience any features of anything as intrinsic features of her experiences. And that is true of you too. There is nothing special about Eloise's visual experience. When you see a tree, you do not experience any features as intrinsic features of your experience. Look at a tree and try to turn your attention to intrinsic features of your visual experience. I predict you will find that the only features there to turn your attention to will be features of the presented tree. (p. 39)

Not everyone agrees with Tye and Harman that experience is transparent. For the dissenting view, see Amy Kind, "What's So Transparent about Transparency?" *Philosophical Studies* 115 (2003): 225–44.

3. The "transparency of experience" can be used to motivate the "transparency view" of self-knowledge — see "Notes and Questions" to Alex Byrne, "Skepticism about the Internal World," in chapter 6 of this anthology.

## ANALYZING THE ARGUMENTS

1. Jackson (in "Epiphenomenal Qualia") and Chalmers both argue against physicalism. (You may take the thesis Jackson calls "physicalism" to be the same as the one Chalmers calls "materialism.") Jackson, in his subsequent article "Postscript on Qualia," argues for physicalism essentially on the ground that we should not "have opinions that outrun what is required by the best theory of those opinions' causal origins." What does he mean by this? If physicalism is true, where do the knowledge argument and the zombie argument go wrong? If physicalism is false, what's the flaw in Jackson's later argument for it?

2. Jackson distinguishes the knowledge argument from Nagel's argument in "What Is It Like to Be a Bat?" What is Nagel's argument, according to Jackson? Evaluate his criticism of the argument. Sometimes Philosopher A will (unintentionally) slightly distort Philosopher B's argument and so end up criticizing a different argument, not the one B intended. Is this what is going on here, or is Jackson's interpretation of Nagel's argument correct? If it isn't, explain how Nagel's argument differs from the knowledge argument.

3. According to Tye, "The conclusion to which we seem driven is that the phenomenal character of your visual experience, as you view the apple, is *hidden* from you, as is your visual experience. You are *blind* to these things. For you, it is as if they aren't there. They are, as it were, transparent to you." (He later takes it back about phenomenal character, but the point about the experience remains.)

   It seems that Nagel would dispute this passage, and deny that your experience is transparent. In "What Is It Like to Be a Bat?" he writes that you "apprehend" your experience, and in a paragraph omitted from this reading he wonders if it "make[s] sense . . . to ask what my experiences are really like, as opposed to how they appear to me." If you "apprehend" your experience or if experiences "appear" to you, then presumably they are not transparent. Tye would say, rather, that it is only the *apple* that one apprehends, and that appears, say, red and round.

   Are there passages from Jackson ("Epiphenomenal Qualia") and Chalmers that suggest they too would deny that your visual experience of an apple is transparent? Is Tye right in supposing that experiences are transparent? Assuming he is, does this affect the arguments of Nagel, Jackson, and Chalmers?

4. One of Churchland's objections to Jackson's knowledge argument is this:

   > How can I assess what Mary will know and understand if she knows *everything* there is to know about the brain? Everything is a lot and it means, in all likelihood, that Mary has a radically different and deeper understanding of the brain than anything barely conceivable in our wildest flights of fancy.

   Here are three version of this objection:

   a. We have no idea whether someone who knew *everything* that *current neuroscience* tells us about the brain would know what it's like to see red.

b. Granted, someone whose knowledge was limited by *current* neuroscience wouldn't know what it's like to see red, but we have no idea whether someone who knew everything that *complete neuroscience* (neuroscience that human scientists could not improve any further) tells us about the brain would know what it's like to see red.

c. Granted, someone whose knowledge was limited by *complete neuroscience* would not know what it's like to see red, but *this is no reason for denying that consciousness is entirely physical*. Why should our physical theories, even the ones that we cannot improve any further, tell the *whole physical story* about the universe? Maybe there are physical aspects of the universe (and in particular, of our brains) that our best physical theories are going to leave out. And we have no idea whether someone who knew about these hidden physical aspects of our brains would know what it's like to see red.

Which version of the objection is the one (or is closest to the one) Churchland is endorsing? Are any of these three versions plausible?

In support of (c), one might appeal to a conclusion argued for in Rae Langton's "Ignorance of Things in Themselves" (chapter 7 of this anthology):

*Humility*: We have no knowledge of the most fundamental intrinsic properties of things.

If humility is right, then science — even our best science — will never tell us about the fundamental properties of physical things. In particular, it will never tell us about the fundamental properties of brains, neurons, and so on. And if those fundamental properties are physical, then perhaps (c) is the right response to the knowledge argument. Imprisoned Mary is ignorant of crucial facts — knowledge of which would enable her to know what it's like to see red — but these crucial facts concern fundamental *physical* properties, which are out of reach of our best science.

For more on this sort of view, see the discussion of "Type F monism" in David Chalmers, "Consciousness and Its Place in Nature," reprinted in *The Character of Consciousness* (Oxford University Press, 2010), and Galen Strawson, "Real Materialism," in *Real Materialism* (Oxford University Press, 2008). For a lengthy defense of the weaker claim that either (b) or (c) is right, see Daniel Stoljar, *Ignorance and Imagination* (Oxford University Press, 2006).

5. What is physicalism (or materialism)? "Physicalism" is a piece of technical jargon, and so its meaning needs to be carefully explained. Physicalism should be a thesis that:

(a) is a clear expression of the vague and intuitive thought that the world is "wholly physical";

(b) is not obviously false;

(c) is not obviously true.

*Exercise:* Why are (b) and (c) needed?

According to René Descartes, in addition to spatially extended things like tables and rocks, the world also contains unextended minds or souls (see *Meditations* II and VI in chapter 8 of this anthology). And Descartes's theory, *Cartesian dualism*, is certainly not a physicalist theory. That suggests that we could define physicalism simply as follows:

Physicalism$_1$: Cartesian dualism is false.

*Exercise:* Explain why this definition won't work.

Suppose we define a "physical **property**" as follows: P is a physical property **iff** current physics says that some things have P. So: *having mass* is a physical property because current physics says that protons have mass; *being negatively charged* is a physical property because current physics says that electrons are negatively charged. (Combinations of physical properties can themselves be counted as physical properties, so *having mass or being negatively charged* and *having mass and being negatively charged* both count as physical properties.) Consider:

Physicalism$_2$: everything has physical properties.

*Exercise:* Explain why this definition won't work. (More than one reason could be given.)

Let a *non-physical* property be a property that is not a physical property in the sense explained above. Consider:

Physicalism$_3$: nothing has non-physical properties.

*Exercise:* Explain why this definition won't work either. (Again, more than one reason could be given.)

Defining physicalism properly is not an easy matter. For an introduction to the way physicalism is usually defined in the contemporary literature, see Daniel Stoljar, "Physicalism," *Stanford Encyclopedia of Philosophy,* ed. Edward Zalta (http://plato.stanford.edu/archives/fall2009/entries/physicalism/), sections 1–3.

# 10

# What Is Color?

Start with what seems to be an obvious fact: perception tells us a lot about objects in our environment — rocks, smart phones, cats, lemons, etc. By seeing lemons, you can discover that they are yellow, egg-shaped, and have a dimpled texture. Similarly, by tasting a slice of lemon, you can discover that lemons are sour.

That is not to say that perception always gets things right, that appearances always match reality. Take, for example, figure 1. The top line looks longer than

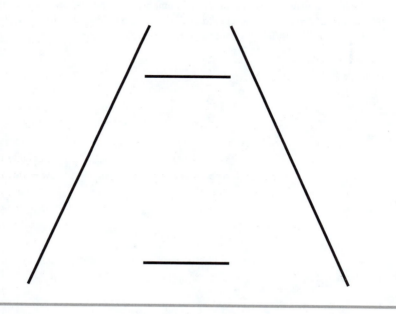

**Figure 1**

the bottom line, but you can easily check that in fact they are the same length. (This is called the *Ponzo illusion*, after its discoverer, the Italian psychologist Mario Ponzo.) Here the appearance of lines of different lengths does not match reality.

It would be a mistake to conclude from the fact that *sometimes* ordinary perception leads us to error that it *always* leads us to error, or anyway is not to be trusted. *The New York Times* sometimes gets the facts wrong, but this is not a good reason for thinking that it always gets the facts wrong, or is not a credible source of news. Still, the phenomenon of perceptual illusions at least raises the question of whether illusions might be much more widespread than we commonly think.

Consider the lemon again, and in particular its apparent color. Why does the lemon look yellow? Presumably because it affects light in a certain way—the lemon absorbs light of some frequencies and reflects the rest. But wait—this is an explanation of why the lemon *looks yellow* that doesn't appeal to the fact that it *is* yellow. And if we don't need to appeal to the fact that the lemon is yellow in order to explain why it looks yellow, why suppose that there is any such fact in the first place? A simpler hypothesis is that the lemon has *no color at all*.

There's nothing special about lemons, of course, and this line of thought quickly leads to the conclusion that color perception is *always* illusory. Physical objects are entirely colorless: blood spots look red, but they aren't red (or any other color); sapphires look blue, but they aren't blue (or any other color); snowballs look white, but they aren't white (or any other color); etc.

The view that no physical objects are colored, that the appearance of a colored world does not match reality, is sometimes called color **eliminativism**. (It is so-called because according to the color eliminativist the colors should be "eliminated" from an accurate description of physical objects.) We can distinguish similar theses for other perceptual qualities: *taste* eliminativism, *shape* eliminativism, *odor* eliminativism, and so on.

In fact, color eliminativism—as well as other kinds of eliminativism, like taste and odor eliminativism—has proved remarkably popular among both scientists and philosophers. The ancient Greek philosopher Democritus (c. 460–370 BCE) is famously reported as saying: "By convention, sweet; by convention, bitter; by convention, hot; by convention, cold; by convention, color; but in reality, atoms and void" (Democritus, frag. 9). "By convention, sweet," "by convention, color," and so on, are usually interpreted to imply that sugar cubes are *not* sweet, and lemons are *not* yellow — we merely have a conventional practice of calling them "sweet" and "yellow." The Italian physicist Galileo (1564–1642) wrote that "tastes, odors, colors, and so on are no more than mere names so far as the object in which we place them is concerned, and that they reside only in the consciousness."[1] Galileo was tried and convicted by the Catholic Church for proclaiming that the Earth went around the Sun; his equally heretical view that cardinals' robes are not red apparently went unpunished.

---

1. "The Assayer," in *Discoveries and Opinions of Galileo*, trans. Stilman Drake (Doubleday, 1957), p. 274.

Many contemporary scientists and philosophers join Democritus and Galileo in their subscription to color eliminativism. Open a textbook on perception and you may well read that colors are not "in objects" but are instead "constructed by the brain." The philosopher C. L. Hardin flatly denies in his book *Color for Philosophers* "that anything is colored."[2]

# The Argument from Science

We have already touched on one reason that might be given for these extraordinary claims—that the apparent colors of things can be explained in terms of the way they reflect light, which seems to make the hypothesis that they really are colored unnecessary. This is a compressed version of a historically influential argument, called the *argument from science*. Let us unpack it more carefully.

Ordinary perception is not our only source of knowledge about lemons, smart phones, and the rest. Science also tells us a lot about them—that lemons and smart phones are composed of atoms, for instance. And sometimes ordinary perception and science conflict, in the sense that they can't both be right. We have already seen a very simple example of this, namely the Ponzo illusion. According to ordinary perception, the lines are of different lengths. This conflicts with the results of a scientific investigation—of the cheap and easy sort that only needs a ruler. And in this kind of conflict between science and perception, the sensible verdict is usually in favor of science. Perception is wrong, and science is right: the lines are of the same length.

Now return to our lemon. Is there any conflict between what ordinary perception and science tell us about the lemon? In particular, can we in good conscience accept both the scientific account of lemons and the deliverances of perception about their color?

Here is the "argument from science." Suppose you see the lemon in good light, and have normal color vision. The lemon will look yellow to you. What features or **properties** *of the lemon* explain why the lemon looks yellow to you? Well, if the lemon really *is* yellow, this presumably gives an explanation of why it *looks* yellow. Contraposing, if it turns out that yellowness does *not* figure in *any* explanation of why the lemon looks yellow, the lemon *isn't* yellow. But science can explain why the lemon looks yellow *without* supposing that the lemon is yellow, and there is no reason to think these explanations should be supplemented by some *other* explanation that appeals to the fact that the lemon is yellow. Hence lemons are not yellow. Since the argument goes through just as well for tomatoes, grass, sapphires, and the rest, the general conclusion is that no physical objects are colored.

---

2. Hardin, *Color for Philosophers* (Hackett, 1988), p. xxiv.

Let us look in a little more detail at the argument from science. When a lemon is illuminated with light from the visible spectrum, it will absorb some and reflect the rest. Figure 2 shows the *reflectance* of a typical lemon, the amount of light at each wavelength that the lemon reflects. As you can see, the lemon reflects a lot of light in the long wavelength (yellow-orange-red) end of the spectrum, and little light in the short wavelength (blue-violet) end. (As you can also see, it is *not* true that a yellow-looking object is one that exclusively reflects yellow light.)

Any object that has this reflectance curve will affect the photoreceptors in the eye in such a way as to make the lemon look yellow in ordinary viewing conditions. (The converse is not true. Many different reflectance curves will result in the appearance of yellow, a phenomenon known as *metamerism*.) So one explanation of why the lemon looks yellow is that it has a reflectance curve of the sort shown in figure 2. And the lemon has this particular sort of reflectance curve because its skin contains certain quantities of pigments called *carotenoids*, which gives us another explanation of why it looks yellow.

Summing up, the features of the lemon that explain why it looks yellow to you are (a) its reflectance curve (more generally, the ways in which it changes the light), and (b) the pigments in its skin (more generally, its physical composition).

Now consider another case entirely. We drop a wine glass, and it breaks. What features of glass explain why it did that? One answer appeals to the complicated molecular structure of glass. But there is another explanation which is a lot easier to give, namely that the wine glass broke *because it was fragile*. And what is fragility? It is a **disposition** (or power, or tendency), namely the disposition

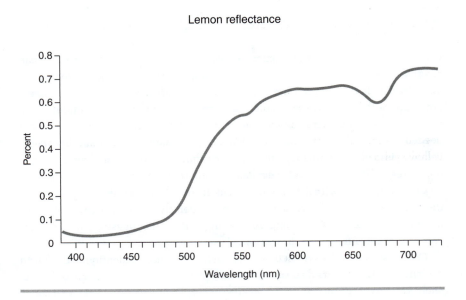

Lemon reflectance

**Figure 2**

to break when struck. So we can put this alternative explanation as follows: the wine glass broke because it has a disposition to break when struck. Perhaps that explanation is not quite as deep or satisfying as an explanation in terms of the molecular structure of the glass, but it seems to be a perfectly genuine explanation nonetheless.

Back to our lemon—is there is an explanation of why it looks yellow to you that is analogous to the dispositional explanation of why the glass broke? There is: the lemon looks yellow to you because it has a disposition to look yellow to people with normal color vision. This is an example of a **secondary quality**, in John Locke's terminology, a disposition "to produce various sensations in us." (Size and shape are examples of what Locke calls **primary qualities**.) Again, perhaps this explanation in terms of the lemon's disposition to look yellow is not as deep as an explanation in terms of its reflectance, but a superficial explanation is still an explanation.

We have, then, one more explanatory feature to add to our list: the features of the lemon that explain why it looks yellow to you are (a) its reflectance curve (more generally, the ways in which the lemon changes the light), and (b) the pigments in its skin (more generally, the lemon's physical composition), *and* (c) its disposition to look yellow.

Should we add to this list a *fourth* explainer, namely (d) the lemon's yellowness? That would seem to multiply explanations unnecessarily. Explanations (a), (b), and (c) fit together as a unified and apparently complete explanatory package. The hypothesis that lemons *are* yellow is entirely gratuitous—we can explain everything that needs to be explained without it. Or so concludes the argument from science.

## Resisting the Argument

How can the argument from science be resisted? On closer examination, we can see that it relies on a tacit assumption that none of the properties of the lemon cited by the three explanations (a), (b), and (c) *is identical to yellowness itself*. For suppose that yellowness simply *is* a certain way of changing the light. Then of course it would be a mistake to conclude that the fourth explainer (d) was not needed, because the first explainer (a) *is* the fourth explainer. Put another way, if yellowness is identical to a certain way of changing the light, then there are really only *three* explainers—one of them has two different names.

*Color physicalists* resist the argument from science either by identifying the fourth explainer (d) with (a), or else by identifying it with (b). This view is defended by D. M. Armstrong. According to the color physicalist, colors are identical to certain *physical* properties.

*Color dispositionalists* resist the argument from science by identifying the fourth explainer (d) with (c), its disposition to *look* yellow. This view is also called the *secondary quality theory of color*, following Locke's explanation of a "secondary quality" as a power or disposition to produce sensory effects in perceivers. Dispositionalism or the secondary quality theory may not be Locke's own view, but it takes a lot of its inspiration from the selection from Locke's *Essay Concerning Human Understanding*. Dispositionalism is elaborated and developed by Colin McGinn.

Color eliminativists, of course, accept the conclusion of the argument from science: according to them, physical objects are not colored. Eliminativism is represented by C. L. Hardin, who raises a number of objections to both physicalism and dispositionalism.

(*Color primitivists*, whose views are not defended in these selections, resist the argument by denying that the "fourth explainer" needs to be identified with either (a) or (b) or (c). According to primitivists, lemons are yellow, even though yellowness is neither a physical property nor a disposition to look yellow. For a discussion of this view, see Alex Byrne and David R. Hilbert, "Color Primitivism," *Erkenntnis* 66 [2007]: 73–105.)

# Terminological Warning: "Secondary Qualities"

As you read the selections, you might notice that the terminology of "secondary qualities" is not used consistently, and this can be confusing. Armstrong explains "secondary quality" by means of a list: "colour, sound, taste, smell, heat and cold." Thus, on Armstrong's usage, a secondary quality simply is a quality or property on that list. So, as Armstrong uses "secondary quality," it is not controversial that redness is a secondary quality.

However, on Locke's usage, secondary qualities are "Powers to produce various Sensations in us." So to say that redness is a secondary quality in this sense *is* to state a disputable philosophical position, namely dispositionalism. As McGinn puts it, on this Lockean understanding of "secondary quality," "it is thus a substantive question whether (say) colour is a secondary quality." On the Lockean understanding of "secondary quality," color physicalists, like Armstrong, or color eliminativists, like Hardin, think that colors are *not* secondary qualities.

## John Locke (1632–1704)

Locke was an English philosopher and medical doctor. His greatest work is *An Essay Concerning Human Understanding* (1689), which is about the limits of human knowledge. His *Two Treatises of Government* (1689) and *Letter Concerning Toleration* (1689), both published anonymously, made important contributions to political philosophy. The second *Treatise* gives a theory of legitimate government in terms of natural rights and the social contract. Locke's political views influenced the Founders of the United States, in particular Thomas Jefferson.

# SOME FURTHER CONSIDERATIONS CONCERNING OUR SIMPLE IDEAS
## from *An Essay Concerning Human Understanding*

---

# CHAPTER VIII

7. To discover the nature of our *Ideas* the better, and to discourse of them intelligibly, it will be convenient to distinguish them, as they are *Ideas* or Perceptions in our Minds; and as they are modifications[1] of matter in the Bodies that cause such Perceptions in us: that so we *may not* think (as perhaps usually is done) that they are exactly the Images and *Resemblances* of something inherent in the subject; most of those of Sensation being in the Mind no more the likeness of something existing without us, than the Names, that stand for them, are the likeness of our *Ideas*, which yet upon hearing, they are apt to excite in us.

8. Whatsoever the Mind perceives in it self, or is the immediate object of Perception, Thought, or Understanding, that I call *Idea*; and the Power to produce any *Idea* in our mind, I call *Quality* of the Subject wherein that power is. Thus a Snow-ball having the power to produce in us the *Ideas* of *White, Cold*, and *Round*, the Powers to produce those *Ideas* in us, as they are in the Snow-ball, I call *Qualities*; and as they are Sensations, or Perceptions, in our Understandings, I call them *Ideas*: which *Ideas*, if I speak of sometimes, as in the things themselves, I would be understood to mean those Qualities in the Objects which produce them in us.

9. Qualities thus considered in Bodies are, First such as are utterly inseparable from the Body, in what estate soever it be[2]; such as in all the alterations and changes it suffers, all the force can be used upon it, it constantly keeps; and such as Sense constantly finds in every particle of Matter, which has bulk[3] enough to be perceived, and the Mind finds inseparable from every particle of Matter, though less than to make it self singly be perceived by our Senses. *v.g.*[4] Take a grain of Wheat, divide it into two parts, each part has still *Solidity, Extension, Figure,*[5] and *Mobility*; divide it again, and it retains still the same qualities; and so divide it on, till the parts become insensible, they must retain still each of them all those qualities. For division (which is all that a Mill, or Pestle, or any other Body, does upon another, in reducing it to insensible parts) can never take away either Solidity, Extension, Figure, or Mobility from any Body, but only makes two, or more distinct separate masses of Matter,

---

1. States, **properties**.

2. In whatever state it is in.

3. Size.

4. For example (abbreviation of Latin *verbi gratia*).

5. Shape.

of that which was but one before, all which distinct masses, reckon'd as so many distinct Bodies, after division make a certain Number. These I call *original* or *primary Qualities* of Body, which I think we may observe to produce simple *Ideas* in us, *viz.* Solidity, Extension, Figure, Motion, or Rest, and Number.

10. Secondly, Such *Qualities,* which in truth are nothing in the Objects themselves, but Powers to produce various Sensations in us by their *primary Qualities, i.e.* by the Bulk, Figure, Texture, and Motion of their insensible parts, as Colours, Sounds, Tastes, *etc.* These I call *secondary Qualities.* To these might be added a third sort which are allowed to be barely Powers though they are as much real Qualities in the Subject, as those which I to comply with the common way of speaking call *Qualities,* but for distinction *secondary Qualities.* For the power in Fire to produce a new Colour, or consistency in Wax or Clay by its primary Qualities, is as much a quality in Fire, as the power it has to produce in me a new *Idea* or Sensation of warmth or burning, which I felt not before, by the same primary Qualities, *viz.* The Bulk, Texture, and Motion of its insensible parts.

11. The next thing to be consider'd, is how *Bodies* produce *Ideas* in us, and that is manifestly *by impulse,* the only way which we can conceive Bodies operate in.

12. If then external Objects be not united to our Minds, when they produce *Ideas* in it; and yet we perceive *these original Qualities* in such of them as singly fall under our Senses, 'tis evident, that some motion must be thence continued by our Nerves, or animal Spirits, by some parts of our Bodies, to the Brains or the seat of Sensation, there to *produce in our Minds the particular* Ideas *we have of them.* And since the Extension, Figure, Number, and Motion of Bodies of an observable bigness, may be perceived at a distance *by* the sight, 'tis evident some singly imperceptible Bodies must come from them to the Eyes, and thereby convey to the Brain some *Motion,* which produces these *Ideas,* which we have of them in us.

13. After the same manner, that the *Ideas* of these original Qualities are produced in us, we may conceive, that the *Ideas of secondary Qualities* are also *produced, viz. by the operation of insensible particles on our Senses.* For it being manifest, that there are Bodies, and good store of Bodies, each whereof is so small, that we cannot, by any of our Senses, discover either their bulk, figure, or motion, as is evident in the Particles of the Air and Water, and other extremely smaller than those, perhaps, as much smaller than the Particles of Air, or Water, as the Particles of Air or Water, are smaller than Peas or Hail-stones. Let us suppose at present, that the different Motions and Figures, Bulk, and Number of such Particles, affecting the several Organs of our Senses, produce in us those different Sensations, which we have from the Colours and Smells of Bodies, *v.g.* that a Violet, by the impulse of such insensible particles of matter of peculiar figures, and bulks, and in different degrees and modifications of their Motions, causes the *Ideas* of the blue Colour, and sweet Scent of that Flower to be produced in our Minds. It being no more impossible, to conceive, that God should annex such *Ideas* to such Motions, with which they have no similitude; than that he should annex the *Idea* of Pain to the motion of a piece of Steel dividing our Flesh, with which that *Idea* hath no resemblance.

14. What I have said concerning *Colours* and *Smells*, may be understood also of *Tastes* and *Sounds, and other the like sensible Qualities*; which, whatever reality we, by mistake, attribute to them, are in truth nothing in the Objects themselves, but Powers to produce various Sensations in us, and *depend on those primary Qualities, viz*. Bulk, Figure, Texture, and Motion of parts; as I have said.

15. From whence I think it is easy to draw this Observation, That the *Ideas of primary Qualities* of Bodies, *are Resemblances* of them, and their Patterns do really exist in the Bodies themselves; but the *Ideas, produced* in us *by* these *Secondary Qualities, have no resemblance* of them at all. There is nothing like our *Ideas*, existing in the Bodies themselves. They are in the Bodies, we denominate from them, only a Power to produce those Sensations in us: And what is Sweet, Blue, or Warm in *Idea*, is but the certain Bulk, Figure, and Motion of the insensible Parts in the Bodies themselves, which we call so.

16. *Flame* is denominated *Hot* and *Light*; *Snow White* and *Cold*; and *Manna*[6] *White* and *Sweet*, from the *Ideas* they produce in us. Which Qualities are commonly thought to be the same in those Bodies, that those *Ideas* are in us, the one the perfect resemblance of the other, as they are in a Mirror; and it would by most Men be judged very extravagant, if one should say otherwise. And yet he, that will consider, that *the same Fire*, that at one distance *produces* in us the Sensation of *Warmth*, does at a nearer approach, produce in us the far different Sensation of *Pain*, ought to bethink himself, what Reason he has to say, That his *Idea* of *Warmth*, which was produced in him by the Fire, is actually *in the Fire*; and his *Idea* of *Pain*, which the same Fire produced in him the same way, is *not* in the *Fire*. Why is Whiteness and Coldness in Snow, and Pain not, when it produces the one and the other *Idea* in us; and can do neither, but by the Bulk, Figure, Number, and Motion of its solid Parts?

17. The particular *Bulk, Number, Figure, and Motion of the parts of Fire, or Snow, are really in them*, whether any one's Senses perceive them or no: and therefore they may be called *real Qualities*, because they really exist in those Bodies. But *Light, Heat, Whiteness*, or *Coldness, are no more really in them, than Sickness or Pain is in* Manna. Take away the Sensation of them; let not the Eyes see Light, or Colours, nor the Ears hear Sounds; let the Palate not Taste, nor the Nose Smell, and all Colours, Tastes, Odors, and Sounds, as they are such particular *Ideas*, vanish and cease, and are reduced to their Causes, *i.e*. Bulk, Figure, and Motion of Parts.

18. A piece of *Manna* of a sensible Bulk, is able to produce in us the *Idea* of a round or square Figure; and, by being removed from one place to another, the *Idea* of Motion. This *Idea* of Motion represents it, as it really is in the *Manna* moving: A Circle or Square are the same, whether in *Idea* or Existence; in the Mind, or in the *Manna*: And this, both *Motion and Figure are really in the Manna*, whether we take notice of them or no: This every Body is ready to agree to. Besides, *Manna* by the Bulk, Figure, Texture, and Motion of its Parts, has a Power to produce the Sensations of Sickness, and sometimes of acute Pains, or Gripings in us. That these *Ideas of Sickness and Pain are not in the* Manna, but Effects of its Operations on us,

---

6. A laxative derived from sap.

and are no where when we feel them not: This also every one readily agrees to. And yet Men are hardly to be brought to think, that *Sweetness and Whiteness are not really in Manna*; which are but the effects of the operations of *Manna,* by the motion, size, and figure of its Particles on the Eyes and Palate; as the Pain and Sickness caused by *Manna,* are confessedly nothing, but the effects of its operations on the Stomach and Guts, by the size, motion, and figure of its insensible parts; (for by nothing else can a Body operate, as has been proved:) As if it could not operate on the Eyes and Palate, and thereby produce in the Mind particular distinct *Ideas,* which in it self it has not, as well as we allow it can operate on the Guts and Stomach, and thereby produce distinct *Ideas,* which in it self it has not. These *Ideas* being all effects of the operations of *Manna,* on several parts of our Bodies, by the size, figure, number, and motion of its parts, why those produced by the Eyes and Palate, should rather be thought to be really in the *Manna,* than those produced by the Stomach and Guts; or why the Pain and Sickness, *Ideas* that are the effects of *Manna,* should be thought to be no-where, when they are not felt; and yet the Sweetness and Whiteness, effects of the same *Manna,* on other parts of the Body, by ways equally as unknown, should be thought to exist in the *Manna,* when they are not seen nor tasted, would need some Reason to explain.

19. Let us consider the red and white colours in *Porphyre:*[7] Hinder light but from striking on it, and its Colours Vanish; it no longer produces any such *Ideas* in us: Upon the return of Light, it produces these appearances on us again. Can any one think any real alterations are made in the *Porphyre,* by the presence or absence of Light; and that those *Ideas* of whiteness and redness, are really in *Porphyre* in the light, when 'tis plain *it has no colour in the dark*? It has, indeed, such a Configuration of Particles, both Night and Day, as are apt by the Rays of Light rebounding from some parts of that hard Stone, to produce in us the *Idea* of redness, and from others the *Idea* of whiteness: But whiteness or redness are not in it at any time, but such a texture, that hath the power to produce such a sensation in us.

20. Pound an Almond, and the clear white *Colour* will be altered into a dirty one, and the sweet *Taste* into an oily one. What real Alteration can the beating of the Pestle make in any Body, but an Alteration of the *Texture* of it?

21. *Ideas* being thus distinguished and understood, we may be able to give an Account, how the same Water, at the same time, may produce the *Idea* of Cold by one Hand, and of Heat by the other: Whereas it is impossible, that the same Water, if those *Ideas* were really in it, should at the same time be both Hot and Cold. For if we imagine *Warmth,* as it is *in our Hands,* to be *nothing but a certain sort and degree of Motion in the minute Particles of our Nerves, or animal Spirits,* we may understand, how it is possible, that the same Water may at the same time produce the Sensation of Heat in one Hand, and Cold in the other; which yet Figure never does, that never producing the *Idea* of a square by one Hand, which has produced the *Idea* of a Globe by another. But if the Sensation of Heat and Cold, be nothing but the increase or diminution of the motion of the minute Parts of our Bodies, caused by

7. Porphyry, a kind of igneous rock.

the Corpuscles[8] of any other Body, it is easy to be understood, That if that motion be greater in one Hand, than in the other; if a Body be applied to the two Hands, which has in its minute Particles a greater motion, than in those of one of the Hands, and a less, than in those of the other, it will increase the motion of the one Hand, and lessen it in the other, and so cause the different Sensations of Heat and Cold, that depend thereon.

22. I have in what just goes before, been engaged in Physical Enquiries a little farther than, perhaps, I intended. But it being necessary, to make the Nature of Sensation a little understood, and to make the *difference between the Qualities in Bodies, and the* Ideas *produced by them in the Mind,* to be distinctly conceived, without which it were impossible to discourse intelligibly of them; I hope, I shall be pardoned this little Excursion into Natural Philosophy,[9] it being necessary in our present Enquiry, to distinguish the *primary,* and *real Qualities* of Bodies, which are always in them, (*viz.* Solidity, Extension, Figure, Number, and Motion, or Rest; and are sometimes perceived by us, *viz.* when the Bodies they are in, are big enough singly to be discerned) from those *secondary* and *imputed Qualities,* which are but the Powers of several Combinations of those primary ones, when they operate, without being distinctly discerned; whereby we also may come to know what *Ideas* are, and what are not Resemblances of something really existing in the Bodies, we denominate from them.

23. The *Qualities* then that are in *Bodies* rightly considered, are of *Three sorts.*

*First,* The *Bulk, Figure, Number, Situation,* and *Motion, or Rest* of their solid Parts; those are in them, whether we perceive them or no; and when they are of that size, that we can discover them, we have by these an *Idea* of the thing, as it is in it self, as is plain in artificial things. These I call *primary Qualities.*

*Secondly,* The *Power* that is in any Body, *by* Reason of *its* insensible *primary Qualities,* to operate after a peculiar manner on any of our Senses, and thereby *produce in us* the *different Ideas* of several Colours, Sounds, Smells, Tastes, *etc.* These are usually called sensible Qualities.

*Thirdly,* The *Power* that is in any Body, *by* Reason of the particular Constitution of *its primary Qualities, to* make such a *change in the Bulk, Figure, Texture, and Motion of another Body,* as to make it operate on our Senses, differently from what it did before. Thus the Sun has a Power to make Wax white, and Fire to make Lead fluid. These are usually called Powers.

The First of these, as has been said, I think, may be properly called *real Original,* or *primary Qualities,* because they are in the things themselves, whether they are perceived or no: and upon their different Modifications it is, that the secondary Qualities depend.

The other two, are only Powers to act differently upon other things, which Powers result from the different Modifications of those primary Qualities.

---

8. The name given by some seventeenth-century scientists to the particles they thought composed all matter.

9. Natural science.

24. But though *these two later sorts of Qualities are Powers barely,* and nothing but Powers, relating to several other Bodies, and resulting from the different Modifications of the Original Qualities; yet they are generally otherwise thought of. For *the Second sort, viz.* The Powers to produce several *Ideas* in us by our Senses, *are looked upon as real Qualities, in the things* thus affecting us: But *the Third sort are call'd, and esteemed barely Powers. v.g.* the *Idea* of Heat, or Light, which we receive by our Eyes, or touch from the Sun, are commonly thought *real Qualities,* existing in the Sun, and something more than mere Powers in it. But when we consider the Sun, in reference to Wax, which it melts or blanches, we look upon the Whiteness and Softness produced in the Wax, not as Qualities in the Sun, but Effects produced by *Powers* in it: Whereas, if rightly considered, these Qualities of Light and Warmth, which are Perceptions in me when I am warmed, or enlightened by the Sun, are no otherwise in the Sun, than the changes made in the Wax, when it is blanched or melted, are in the Sun. They are all of them equally Powers in the Sun, depending on its primary Qualities; whereby it is able in the one case, so to alter the Bulk, Figure, Texture, or Motion of some of the insensible parts of my Eyes, or Hands, as thereby to produce in me the *Idea* of Light or Heat; and in the other, it is able so to alter the Bulk, Figure, Texture, or Motion of the insensible Parts of the Wax, as to make them fit to produce in me the distinct *Ideas* of White and Fluid.

25. The Reason, *Why the one are ordinarily taken for real Qualities, and the other only for bare Powers,* seems to be, because the *Ideas* we have of distinct Colours, Sounds, *etc.* containing nothing at all in them, of Bulk, Figure, or Motion, we are not apt to think them the Effects of these primary Qualities, which appear not to our Senses to operate in their Production; and with which, they have not any apparent Congruity, or conceivable Connexion. Hence it is, that we are so forward to imagine, that those *Ideas* are the resemblances of something really existing in the Objects themselves: Since Sensation discovers nothing of Bulk, Figure, or Motion of parts in their Production; nor can Reason show, how Bodies by their Bulk, Figure, and Motion, should produce in the Mind the *Ideas* of Blue, or Yellow, *etc.* But in the other Case, in the Operations of Bodies, changing the Qualities one of another, we plainly discover, that the Quality produced, hath commonly no resemblance with any thing in the thing producing it; wherefore we look on it as a bare Effect of Power. For though receiving the *Idea* of Heat, or Light, from the Sun, we are apt to think, 'tis a Perception and Resemblance of such a Quality in the Sun: yet when we see Wax, or a fair Face, receive change of Colour from the Sun, we cannot imagine, that to be the Reception or Resemblance of any thing in the Sun, because we find not those different Colours in the Sun it self. For our Senses, being able to observe a likeness, or unlikeness of sensible Qualities in two different external Objects, we forwardly enough conclude the Production of any sensible Quality in any Subject, to be an Effect of bare Power, and not the Communication of any Quality, which was really in the efficient, when we find no such sensible Quality in the thing that produced it. But our Senses, not being able to discover any unlikeness between the *Idea* produced in us, and the Quality of the Object producing it, we are apt to imagine, that our *Ideas* are resemblances of something in the Objects, and not the Effects of certain Powers, placed in the Modification of their primary Qualities, with which primary Qualities the *Ideas* produced in us have no resemblance.

26. To conclude, beside those before mentioned *primary Qualities* in Bodies, *viz.* Bulk, Figure, Extension, Number, and Motion of their solid Parts; all the rest, whereby we take notice of Bodies, and distinguish them one from another, are nothing else, but several Powers in them, depending on those primary Qualities; whereby they are fitted, either by immediately operating on our Bodies, to produce several different *Ideas* in us; or else by operating on other Bodies, so to change their primary Qualities, as to render them capable of producing *Ideas* in us, different from what before they did. The former of these, I think, may be called *Secondary Qualities, immediately perceivable*: The latter, *Secondary Qualities, mediately perceivable*.

## TEST YOUR UNDERSTANDING

1. In section 10, Locke seems to be saying that colors are "Powers to produce various Sensations in us by their *primary Qualities*." In section 19 he claims that "'tis plain [that Porphyre] *has no colour in the dark*." Explain why these two sections apparently contradict each other.

2. In sections 11–13 Locke tries to explain why physical objects produce "Ideas" in us. What is his explanation?

3. In section 15, Locke distinguishes between our *"Ideas of primary Qualities"* and our *"Ideas of secondary Qualities"* in terms of what they "resemble." What do the former ideas resemble and the latter ideas *not* resemble?

4. In section 23 (see also section 26), Locke distinguishes two sorts of dispositions or "powers." One is the power to "produce Ideas in us." What is the other sort?

5. Section 17 suggests that Locke endorses color eliminativism. Explain why.

## NOTES AND QUESTIONS

1. How does Locke explain (in section 9) what a *primary quality* is? Given his explanation, is he right to conclude that "Solidity, Extension, Figure, or Mobility" are all primary qualities? Is he right to conclude that "Colours, Sounds, Tastes" are *not* primary qualities?

2. In section 25, Locke tries to explain why we are "so forward to imagine" (incorrectly, in his view) that our "Ideas of colour" are "resemblances of something really existing with the Objects." What is his explanation? Is it correct?

3. *Locke on primary and secondary qualities.* The *Essay Concerning Human Understanding* is one of the most important works of philosophy in English. It has four books; the selection from the *Essay* is the primary source of what McGinn (see "Secondary Qualities" later in this chapter) calls the "Lockean tradition" of dispositionalism, in the view that colors are dispositions to produce sensory effects in perceivers.

   **Was Locke a dispositionalist?** It is controversial whether Locke himself thought that colors are dispositions to produce sensory effects in perceivers. There are parts of the text you just read that suggest that he endorses dispositionalism. But there are also parts that suggest that he endorses eliminativism: despite having a disposition or power to produce "Ideas of colour" in us, physical objects are not colored.

For a classic defense of the dispositional interpretation, see Jonathan Bennett, *Locke, Berkeley, Hume* (Oxford University Press, 1971) chapter 4, and his *Learning from Six Philosophers* (Oxford University Press, 2003), chapter 25, section 188. For a nuanced defense of the eliminativist interpretation, see Margaret Wilson, "History of Philosophy in Philosophy Today; and the Case of the Sensible Qualities," *Philosophical Review* 101 (1992): 191–243.

*The distinction between primary and secondary qualities.* Following Armstrong (see the introduction to this chapter), let us stipulate that "secondary qualities" are colors, tastes, odors, etc., and that "primary qualities" are shapes, sizes, motions, etc. What is the point or significance of drawing this distinction between two sorts of properties? Distinctions are cheap: we can draw a distinction between what we can call an "alpha quality" (color, size, motion) and a "beta quality" (taste, odor, shape), but this distinction between alpha and beta qualities is presumably uninteresting and arbitrary. Why isn't the distinction between primary and secondary qualities, explained in Armstrong's manner, equally uninteresting and arbitrary? What do colors, tastes, and odors have in common that shapes, sizes, and motions don't, and vice versa? That is not an easy question to answer; for a discussion, see A. D. Smith, "Of Primary and Secondary Qualities," *Philosophical Review* 99 (1990): 221–54.

The primary-secondary quality distinction was made before Locke, notably by Galileo, Descartes, and the English physicist Robert Boyle (1627–1691). It is usually traced back to the Greek atomist Democritus (c. 460–370 BCE).

The distinction as understood in the seventeenth century was closely connected with what Locke calls the "corpuscularian Hypothesis" (*Essay* IV.iii.16), which is roughly the view that all natural phenomena can be explained by the hypothesis that matter consists of tiny particles ("corpuscles") of varying shape, size, and motion, acting on each other by contact. For an example of the corpuscularian hypothesis at work, see sections 12 and 13 of this reading.

Locke took the corpuscularian hypothesis from Boyle, who was a prominent advocate of it. In the *Essay's* "Epistle to the Reader," Locke modestly writes that "*every one must not hope to be a* Boyle ... *'tis Ambition enough to be employed as an Under-Labourer in clearing the Ground a little, and removing some of the Rubbish, that lies in the way to Knowledge.*"

"*Resemblance.*" According to Locke (sec. 15), our "*Ideas of primary Qualities of Bodies, are Resemblances of them,*" unlike our ideas of secondary qualities. Here Locke follows Descartes, who writes in the *Meditation VI* (in a passage omitted from the chapter 8 reading) that

although I feel heat when I go near a fire and feel pain when I go too near, there is no convincing argument for supposing that there is something which resembles the heat, any more than for supposing that there is something which resembles the pain. There is simply reason to suppose that there is something in the fire, whatever it may eventually turn out to be, which produces in us the feelings of heat or pain.[1]

1. *The Philosophical Writings of Descartes*, vol. II, trans. John Cottingham, Robert Stoothoff, and Dugald Murdoch (Cambridge University Press, 1985), p. 57.

(See also Section 16, where Locke uses Descartes's comparison between heat and pain.)

Since it is not clear how an "idea" (or "sensation") in the mind could literally resemble a quality of a physical object, or the object itself, there is a question about Locke's meaning. Does he really mean "resemblance" literally, as in "This portrait of Locke resembles him"? Or is he using the expression in some special technical way, or just writing sloppily? For a defense of a nonliteral interpretation, see Bennett, *Locke, Berkeley, Hume*, p. 106, and his *Learning from Six Philosophers*, chapter 25, section 193. For a defense of the literal interpretation, see Michael Jacovides, "Locke's Resemblance Theses," *Philosophical Review* 108 (1999): 461–96.

## D. M. Armstrong (1926–2014)

Armstrong was Challis Professor of Philosophy at the University of Sydney, retiring in 1991. He is known for his many contributions to philosophy of mind and metaphysics, including *A Materialist Theory of the Mind* (1968), *Universals and Scientific Realism* (1978), *What Is a Law of Nature?* (1983), and *Sketch for a Systematic Metaphysics* (2010).

# THE SECONDARY QUALITIES
## from *A Materialist Theory of Mind*

# 1. The Problem of the Secondary Qualities[1]

In what we have said so far, it has been assumed that the "secondary qualities" — colour, sound, taste, smell, heat and cold — are objective properties of physical objects or physical processes. We discover the colour of an object, or its taste, in just the same way that we discover its shape or its texture. But, it may be argued, such a naively realistic attitude to these qualities is indeed naive. For modem science finds no room for such properties in its account of the physical world.

Some properties of physical objects and processes are susceptible of logical analysis in terms of other properties. Thus, we might give an analysis of hardness in terms of a disposition in the hard object not to change its shape or break up easily when under pressure. But colour, sound, taste, smell, heat and cold, even if no other

---

1. Some numbered objections in the chapter from which this selection is taken have been omitted.

qualities, seem to resist any such analysis. They seem to be *irreducible* qualities. Any connection that they have with other properties of physical objects seems to be a contingent one.

However, as is well-known, the conception of the secondary qualities as irreducible or unanalysable properties of physical objects or processes has led to the greatest problems. The difficulties have been with us at least since the time of Galileo,[2] and have only become more pressing with every advance in physical knowledge. How are we to fit such irreducible properties into the physical world as it is conceived by physicists? For instance, modern physics pictures an ordinary macroscopic object as an indefinitely large swarm of "fundamental particles" moving in a space that is, despite the numbers of these particles, relatively empty. Only in the densest stars, where matter exists in a "collapsed" state, are the fundamental particles packed in at all closely. Now what can we predicate the secondary qualities of? They surely cannot be predicable of individual "fundamental particles." Are they, then, "emergent" properties of the whole area or surface of the area "occupied" by the particles? Perhaps this is a barely possible line to take, but it is not one that a physicist, or, I think, anyone else, could look upon with much enthusiasm.

In the excellent terminology of Wilfrid Sellars,[3] there is a *prima facie* contradiction between the "manifest image" of the physical world that ordinary perception presents us with, and the "scientific image" of the world that physicists are gradually articulating for us. If the secondary qualities are taken to be irreducible properties of physical objects, they can be fitted into the manifest, but not the scientific, image of the world. . . .

But most philosophers and scientists who have tried to tackle this problem have reached a different conclusion. They have concluded that the irreducible *qualia*[4] cannot really qualify the physical objects they appear to qualify. The *qualia* qualify items in the mind of the perceiver. To say that a physical surface is coloured cannot truly imply anything more than that this surface has the power of producing items having a certain irreducible quality in the mind of a normal perceiver.

But from this conclusion further conclusions follow.

In the first place, Berkeley[5] was surely right in arguing that if the secondary qualities qualify mental items, then the other directly perceived properties are also properties of mental, not physical, objects. Colour and visible extension, for instance, are inextricably bound up with each other. If colour qualifies something mental, so does visible extension. And so we are led to the view

2. Galileo Galilei (1564–1642), Italian astronomer, physicist, and mathematician.

3. (1912–1989), American philosopher.

4. Qualities; singular: "quale" (from Latin, "of what kind").

5. George Berkeley (1685–1753), along with John Locke (1632–1704) and David Hume (1711–1776), one of the three great "British empiricists."

that what we are non-inferentially aware[6] of in perception is never a physical situation but a situation in our own mind: our own current sense-impressions, perhaps. . . .

In the second place, we are back in that bifurcation of mental and physical reality which it is the object of a physicalist[7] doctrine of man to overcome. Man's mind becomes a quite different sort of object from physical objects because it is qualified by, or in some way linked with, qualities that physical science need take no account of. To accept the view that the secondary qualities are irreducible *qualia* of mental items would be to abandon the whole programme of this work.

It is clear, then, that a Materialist account of the mind must offer some new account of the secondary qualities. Therefore, I put forward the view that they are nothing but *physical* properties of physical objects or processes. Colours of surfaces, on this view, will be simply physical properties of those surfaces. And by "physical properties" is meant the sort of properties a physicist would be prepared to attribute to those surfaces, the sort of properties that would figure in the "scientific image" of the world.

Notice that it is a physical surface's *being* red that is being identified with physical properties of that surface, and not that surface's *looking* red. Something looking red is a matter of a person or persons having certain perceptions as a result of the causal action of that surface on their eyes. These perceptions, we have argued, are not themselves red, and so do not necessitate the postulating of any *qualia* at all. The perceptions are acquirings of belief, or "potential belief," that something physical *is* red; or, at a deeper level of analysis, they are acquirings of capacities for selective behaviour towards particular red objects, capacities characteristically brought into existence by the red object. As we may put it, red objects are red, but red sensations are not red, save *per accidens*.[8]

In what follows I will concern myself chiefly with the colours of surfaces. There are other physical things that are coloured, such as transparent cubes of coloured glass. There are also other secondary qualities. But in the case of colours of surfaces various problems for our identification come up in an especially acute form. So I do not think that this concentration of attention will involve any evasion of issues.

I will proceed by considering in turn two sorts of objection to a physicalist account of the secondary qualities: *a priori* objections, and empirical objections.[9]

---

6. Not aware on the basis of any inference or **reasoning**.

7. **Physicalism** (or *materialism* — see below) is the view that the mind — and the world in general — is wholly physical.

8. By accident (Latin).

9. The contrast is roughly between objections that can be made with no assumptions about mechanisms of color vision, the physics of light, and so on ("a priori"), and those that do require such assumptions ("empirical").

# 2. A Priori Objections to Identifying Secondary Qualities with Physical Properties

*Objection 1.* We knew what redness was long before we knew what physical properties are necessary and sufficient for redness of physical surface. So redness is not a physical property of surfaces.

*Reply.* The claim that redness is a purely physical property of surfaces is not intended to be a logical analysis of the concept of red. It is not a necessary truth that redness is a purely physical property of that surface. We have argued in this work that, as a contingent matter of fact, mental states are purely physical states of the central nervous system. In just the same way, it is now being claimed that, as a matter of contingent fact, redness is a purely physical property of surfaces.

*Objection 2.* The secondary qualities of things might be imagined to change completely, although the physical characteristics with which they are correlated did not change at all. (What is being imagined here is a change in quality that everybody *noticed*.) So the secondary qualities cannot be identified with physical characteristics.

*Reply.* The objection depends upon covertly treating the connection between the secondary qualities and physical characteristics as if it were necessary, and not contingent. It is perfectly possible, in the logician's sense of "possible," that the redness of surfaces is not a physical property of the surface. And, if this is so, it is perfectly possible that the redness of a surface should begin to vary independently of the physical properties of the surface. Now to imagine a migration of the secondary qualities is simply to imagine that both these conditions are fulfilled.

Consider a parallel case. It is logically possible that the morning star is not the evening star.[1] And if the morning star is not the evening star, it is also possible that one day the two should appear in the sky side-by-side. But, of course, *given that the morning star is in fact the evening star,* it is not possible that the two should appear in the sky side-by-side. In the same way, it is possible that redness of surface is not a physical property of the surface. If this is so, it is further possible that redness of surface should vary independently of the physical properties of the surface. But, of course, *given that redness of surface is in fact a physical property of that surface,* it is not possible that redness of surface should vary independently of the physical properties of the surface. . . .

It is an intelligible hypothesis that redness is an irreducible property that is quite different from the properties considered by physicists. But, from the standpoint of total science, the most *plausible* answer is that redness is a purely physical property. In this way we solve the difficulties raised in the first section of this chapter.

If properties such as redness are not identified with purely physical properties, then, presumably they will have to be correlated with the physical properties. But every consideration of economy speaks in favour of the identification. If we take

---

1. Both the morning star and the evening star are the planet Venus.

a Realistic view of the entities of physics,[2] then we have the physical properties on our hands in any case. So why not identify the secondary qualities with the physical properties?

*Objection 4.* The attempt we have given to characterize redness as an *unknown* property of certain surfaces and objects, breaks down when we remember that redness is seen to have something in common with blue, green, orange, etc. They are all *colours*. If our eyes became sensitive to ultra-violet and infra-red radiation we might become aware of hitherto unperceived visual qualities. Yet we might recognize at once that they were colours, that is, that they resembled the known colours. How could we do this if perception gave us no acquaintance with the nature of colours? Again, we recognize that the colours resemble and differ from each other in certain complex ways. For instance, red is more like orange than it is like yellow. Does not this imply some acquaintance with the nature of the three colours?

*Reply.* This objection shows that there has been an omission in our account. . . . It is true that we recognize that red, green, blue, orange, etc., have something in common. To be precise, what we recognize is that they are all determinates falling under a common determinable.[3] Calling them all "colours" is a verbal acknowledgement of this recognition. But this does not mean that we have any concrete knowledge of what this determinable, colour, is. We simply recognize that red, green, blue, orange and the other colours are determinates falling under a single determinable, *without having any visual awareness of what that determinable is.* The particular colours are identified as visually detected properties of certain surfaces and objects. We recognize further that these properties are determinates falling under a common determinable. But further than this, perception fails to inform us.

In defence of this view, we may recall the notorious difficulty that philosophers have found in saying what it is that all the colours have in common. Any alternative view of the nature of colours, or other "ranges" of secondary qualities, may be challenged to give an account of the uniting principle of such ranges. I am proposing to solve the problem by saying that, although we perceive that the individual colours, etc., have something in common, we do not perceive what it is.

Now we also recognize further similarities and differences between the colours besides the fact that they are all determinates falling under the one determinable. The perceived relationship between red, orange and yellow is a case in point. On our account, this is interpreted as a recognition that red things are more like orange things than they are like yellow things in a certain respect, unaccompanied by any awareness of what that respect is. . . .

---

2. The view that electrons, photons, charge, mass, and other such "entities of physics" actually exist.

3. A "determinable" is (roughly) a general category; a "determinate" of a given determinable is a more specific category within the more general category of the given determinable. For example, *circularity* is a determinate of the determinable *shape*.

Notice . . . that the fact that colours are recognized to be different determinates falling under a common determinable enables a physicalist theory of colour to give worthy hostages to fortune. If the physical properties connected with the colour of surfaces did not turn out to be determinates falling under a determinable physical property, this would count against this theory of colour.

In the same way, we can predict that the physical properties connected with red, orange and yellow surfaces will be such that in some respect they form a scale, a scale on which the physical property connected with orange is the intermediate member. Such a prediction might be falsified. . . .

# 3. Empirical Objections to Identifying Secondary Qualities with Physical Properties

So much for *a priori* objections to our physicalist doctrine of the secondary qualities. But what actual physical properties of objects are the secondary qualities to be identified with? In the case of the colours, the colour of a surface or the colour of an object such as a piece of amber may be identified with a certain physical constitution of the surface or object such that, when acted upon by sunlight, surfaces or objects having that constitution emit light-waves having certain frequencies. The sound an object emits may simply be identified with the sound-waves it emits. Heat and cold are the mean kinetic energy of the molecules of the hot or cold substance. The exact identification of tastes and smells is still a matter of controversy.

There are, however, still a number of empirical difficulties that can be raised against these identifications. As before, these difficulties centre chiefly around colour.

*Objection 8.* We have suggested that the colour of a surface is to be contingently identified with that physical constitution of surface which emits light-waves of certain frequencies when acted upon by sunlight. Now under sunlight surfaces assume one colour, under other forms of illumination they assume another. What we call a blue surface looks blue in sunlight, but it looks purple under fluorescent light. Yet we say the surface is blue, not purple. Why do we do this? Why is the colour presented in sunlight said to be the *real* colour? What privilege does sunlight confer, beyond the contingent fact that it is, at present, the natural form of illumination in our life?

*Reply.* It seems to me that we must admit that a real change in quality occurs at surfaces that, as we *say,* "appear to change" when conditions of illumination are changed. I can see no ground for saying that such changes are in any way illusory or merely apparent. But it seems that there is room here for two different ways of talking about colours.

In one way of talking, the colour of a surface is determined by, and so can be contingently identified with, the actual nature of the light-waves currently emitted at the surface. In this way of talking, the colour of a surface is constantly changing, really changing, as changes in conditions of illumination occur. Such a way of talking about colours is one that naturally commends itself to those who are concerned with the visual arts.

But in another, more usual, way of talking, colour is determined by the nature of the light-waves emitted under *normal illumination*: ordinary sunlight. It is therefore a *disposition* of surfaces to emit certain sorts of light-waves under certain conditions. And so, like all dispositions, colour, in this way of talking, can be identified with the state that underlies the manifestation of the disposition: certain physical properties of the surface. In this way of talking, of course, colour does not change very easily, and so this idiom is better suited to the demands of ordinary life.

The former way of talking is, however, less anthropomorphic, because it does not depend upon the conditions of illumination that are normal in the human environment. It is also logically the more fundamental, because we can give an analysis of colour in the second sense in terms of colour in the first sense: viz. colour (in the first sense) assumed under normal illumination. It may be noted that it seems natural to identify sound with the sound-waves being emitted. That is to say, our account of sound is parallel to our account of colour *in the first sense*. There is no way of talking about sound corresponding to the second way of talking about colour, for obvious reasons.

These two ways of talking about colours may be compared with two possible ways of talking about tennis-balls. In one way of talking, tennis-balls are, from time to time, very far from being round. For instance, at the moment of being struck by a racquet they suffer great distortions of shape. They are only round under "normal conditions": when they are under no particular pressure. But in another, more usual, way of talking, tennis-balls are never anything but round. If they became elliptical they would be discarded. The factory "makes them round" just as a dyer "dyes the cloth blue." Yet we could give an account of this second, more usual, sense of "round" in terms of the first, less usual, but logically more fundamental sense of "round."

This distinction between different ways of talking about colours enables us to solve Locke's problem about porphyry losing its red colour in the dark.[4] In the first, or unusual, way of talking porphyry *does* lose its red colour in the dark. In the dark, the surface of the porphyry emits no light-waves at all. So, in this way of talking, porphyry is black in the dark. (Black surfaces emit no wave-lengths.) But in the second, or usual, way of talking the porphyry is still red. For restore normal conditions, that is, restore normal illumination, and the porphyry will reflect "red" light-waves. It may be noted in passing that there is nothing here that does anything to show that colour is "subjective," although this is the conclusion that Locke draws from the case.

*Objection 9.* But what of the fact that surfaces, etc., under constant illumination may still appear to have different colours in different surroundings and background conditions? The reply to the previous objection will not suffice here. For there may be no change in the light-waves actually emitted by the surface.

---

4. See section 19 of Locke's "Some Further Considerations Concerning Our Simple Ideas" earlier in this chapter. Porphyry is a kind of igneous rock.

*Reply.* I think we should treat these appearances as mere *appearances*. The sun, or a sodium-vapour lamp, actually *act* on the visible surface, and so it is reasonable to think of them causing different effects at that surface. But the differences in colour exhibited by the same surface placed in different environments are not due, I presume, to the differing causal action of these environments. To some extent, of course, the "differences" are just a matter of different relations to the environment. A dingy white surface placed against an even dingier background really is, and is seen to be, whiter than its background. Placed against a dazzling white background, it really is, and is seen to be, less white than this new background. There is no sensory illusion here. But where there really is change in the "colour presented" because of change of background, we can treat this as a change in the *appearances* presented. An obvious analogy is the illusory distortions of visual size and shape that occur in certain sorts of perceptual situation.

Is colour-blindness a matter of being subject to illusions? This is less clear. Colour-blind persons are unable to make all the colour-discriminations that persons with normal sight can make. But mere failure to perceive something is not illusion. There is no necessity to think that any illusion is involved unless the colour-perceptions of the colour-blind are actually *incompatible* with ordinary perceptions. If, however, a surface looks grey to a colour-blind person but looks blue to normal perceivers, then, since grey and blue are incompatible colours, at least one of the perceivers is subject to illusion. The fact that ordinary perceivers make colour-discriminations where colour-blind persons do not (between blue and grey things, say) will then serve as a *reason* for thinking that it is the colour-blind person who is subject to the illusion. For, *in general,* if X perceives a difference between two sorts of thing, but Y perceives no such difference, then there really is a difference. Perception of differences points strongly to the real existence of such differences, failure to perceive differences points much less strongly to the absence of differences. . . .

*Objection 11.* But, even if certain colour-appearances are written off as mere appearances, is it really possible to find one sort of wave-length emitted by all surfaces of the same colour when illuminated by sunlight? In recent years, Smart[5] has emphasized again and again that a huge and idiosyncratic variety of different combinations of wave-length may all present exactly the same colour to the observer. The simple correlations between colour and emitted wave-length that philosophers hopefully assume to exist simply cannot be found. Is this not a bar to an identification of coloured surfaces with surfaces that emit certain wavelengths under sunlight?

*Reply.* One possibility here is that all these different combinations of wave-lengths may be instances that fall under some general formula. Such a formula would have to be one that did not achieve its generality simply by the use of disjunctions[6] to weld together artificially the diverse cases falling under the formula. Provided that such faking were avoided, the formula could be as complicated as we please. Such a formula could be tested, at least in principle, by making up new combinations of

---

5. J.J.C. Smart (1920–2012), Australian philosopher.

6. The disjunction of two sentences "p" and "q" is the sentence "p or q."

wave-lengths that nevertheless still obeyed the formula. If the surface from which these wave-lengths were emitted exhibited the predicted colour-appearance, the formula would be at least verified. Under these conditions, it might well be conceded that, because of its complexity and idiosyncratic nature, the physical property involved was not one of any great importance in physics. But it would still be a perfectly real, even if ontologically insignificant, physical property. Now I know of no physical considerations about colour that rule out such a possibility. . . .

Here, then, is a sketch of a physicalist account of the secondary qualities. . . . We could say that . . . the view put forward here is a Realistic Reductionism. Realism about the secondary qualities accords with common sense, while Reductionism accords with findings of physical science, thus doing justice to both manifest and scientific images of the world.

## TEST YOUR UNDERSTANDING

1. Summarize Armstrong's view by completing the following sentence.
   According to Armstrong, an object is purple if and only if _____.

2. Armstrong says that "If the physical properties connected with the colour of surfaces did not turn out to be determinates falling under a determinable physical property, this would count against [Armstrong's] theory of colour." Explain what Armstrong means by this, and give a hypothetical example of an empirical discovery that would refute Armstrong's theory.

## NOTES AND QUESTIONS

1. The apparent color of an object depends on the background against which the object is viewed. This effect, called *simultaneous color contrast,* can be quite dramatic. (For examples search the Internet for "simultaneous color contrast.") Suppose an object looks bluish against one background, and greenish against another. Is the object bluish, greenish, both, or neither? How would Armstrong answer this question?

2. Elsewhere in his book *A Materialist Theory of the Mind,* from which this selection is taken, Armstrong argues that "mental processes are purely physical processes in the central nervous system" (p. 2). Armstrong's view that "man is nothing but a material object having none but physical properties" (p. 1) is a special case of his more general view that the universe is wholly material or physical. As Armstrong explains, the fact that some objects are colored is not easy to reconcile with this all-encompassing materialism or physicalism. In this selection he makes a case for reconciliation, arguing that colors are "nothing but physical properties of physical objects or processes."

   Armstrong's *color physicalism,* the view that colors are "nothing but physical properties of physical objects or processes," was inherited from another Australian philosopher, J.J.C. Smart, whose pioneering defense of the **identity theory**, that sensations are identical to brain processes, is excerpted in chapter 8 of this anthology. A short and interesting history of Smart's views about color is in Armstrong, "Smart and the Secondary Qualities," reprinted in A. Byrne and D. R. Hilbert, eds. *Readings on Color*, Vol.1: *The Philosophy of Color* (MIT Press, 1997).

Arguably the most natural physical candidate to be identified with (say) the color yellow is a certain type of reflectance or, as Armstrong puts it, a certain "disposition of surfaces to emit certain sorts of light-waves under certain conditions." This view is called *reflectance physicalism*. For an extended defense of reflectance physicalism, see David R. Hilbert, *Color and Color Perception* (University of Chicago Press, 2002) and Alex Byrne and David R. Hilbert, "Color Realism and Color Science," *Behavioral and Brain Sciences* 26 (2003): 3–21. Like dispositionalism, reflectance physicalism identifies colors with dispositions. But it is not a version of dispositionalism because reflectances are not dispositions to affect *perceivers*, just dispositions to reflect light.

## C. L. Hardin (born 1932)

Hardin is Emeritus Professor of Philosophy at Syracuse University. He is known for his scientifically informed work on color, and in particular for his 1988 book *Color for Philosophers*.

# ARE "SCIENTIFIC" OBJECTS COLOURED?

"In a world of 'scientific' objects, objects characterizable by the vocabulary of physics alone, in a world governed by what we now believe to be the laws of nature, can anything be coloured?" I am here concerned to examine the claims of those physicalists[1] who are disposed to give an affirmative answer to that question. In so doing, I shall restrict my attention to the physics of the present time, helping myself to the rather generous assumption that the vocabulary and laws of physiology need not, in the last analysis, outrun those of physics. The physics of the present day [1984] is assuredly not engraved in stone, but the parts of it which have to do with the sources of electromagnetic radiation and its interaction with animal tissue — the only parts which have any conceivable bearing on colour vision — are unlikely to see significant revision.

What are colours? It seems clear that a proper understanding of colours must proceed from sensory acquaintance: the congenitally blind man cannot have an adequate conception of colour. But it is equally apparent that colours are more than

---

1. Those who believe that the mind — and the world in general — is wholly physical; also known as *materialists*.

simple, ineffable qualia.[2] Hume's missing shade of blue[3] rather effectively makes that point. Our concept of colour involves not only manifest colours, but a whole set of ordering relationships among them. Every colour is specifiable by three dimensions: hue, brightness and saturation. Colours of a given hue may be linearly ordered according to brightness, if saturation is held constant, and according to saturation if brightness is held constant. Holding both brightness and saturation constant, the hues may be ordered in a closed array, the end points of the spectral hues being connected through an array of non-spectral purples.[4] These relationships among colours cannot, of course, be extracted from the bare presentation of a single colour sample any more than its 180° angle sum can be extracted from the bare presentation of a triangle. Nevertheless, it is as much an essential property of a colour that it requires exactly three independent parameters for its specification as it is an essential property of, say, a complex number[5] that it requires exactly two real numbers for its specification.

Are there other essential properties of the colours? To see that there are, consider the following situation. An experimental subject is taught to use a monochromator, a device which permits its operator to select a single wavelength in the band of visible light, which extends from approximately 450 nm to about 700 nm. (One nanometer = one billionth of a metre.) Suppose the subject is asked to find a green which is neither yellow nor blue. Will she be able to understand and execute the instruction? Indeed she will, and a normal subject will select a wavelength around 503 nm. Asked to find a blue which is neither red nor green, she makes a selection at about 475 nm. A yellow which is neither red nor green will be near 590 nm. There is no single wavelength which gives a red free of a yellowish tinge, but an appropriate mixture of two wavelengths from opposite ends of the spectrum will yield such a red. Very well. Now suppose she is asked to find an orange which is neither red nor yellow. What will she do? She will wonder just what is being required of her, for every orange has both red and yellow in it. She will be able to find an orange which has as much red as it has yellow, but this is quite another matter.

Now most colours are visibly composite in hue like orange, rather than visibly simple in hue, like green. In fact, there exist only four hues which have none of their neighbors as constituents: these are called *unique* hues. There exist a unique red, a unique green, a unique yellow and a unique blue. Hues like orange or turquoise are known as *binary* hues. The unique hues are sometimes called "psychological primaries," but the use of "primary" here invites confusion with so called "subtractive" (pigmentary mixing) and "additive" (light mixing) primaries.

---

2. Here, perceptible qualities or properties.

3. The Scottish philosopher David Hume (1711–1776) claimed that someone who has "enjoyed his sight for thirty years, and [who has] become perfectly well acquainted with colours of all kinds, excepting one particular shade of blue" (*A Treatise of Human Nature*, I.1.i), would nonetheless be able to imagine this missing shade. Selections from the *Treatise* are in chapters 7, 15, and 17 of this anthology.

4. A spectral hue is a hue of light of a single wavelength (monochromatic light). "Non-spectral purples": purple hues that are not the color of any monochromatic light.

5. A complex number is specified as the sum $a + bi$, where $a$ and $b$ are real numbers and i is a so-called "imaginary" number whose square is $-1$.

One might suspect that the singling out of four hues as unique is a linguistic artifact: "Surely the spectrum is continuous, and no hue has pride of place over another. That is the natural fact about the hues, so any uniqueness must be a product of culture, embedded in a certain linguistic practice." This objection has a surface plausibility, but it is not supported by the facts. The natural primacy of the four hues has been shown by the results of colour sorting tasks with naive adults, differential learning rates of colour name terms with a group of monolingual New Guinea natives whose own language contains only one chromatic colour name, and colour discriminations by four-month old infants.[6]

A response to this is to say that what has been shown is that the unique hues are singled out by us, but this does not show that they have been singled out by the general order of nature. In a way this objection is on the right track, but in another way it is deeply confused. For what conception do we have of hues except insofar as we experience them? Surely we can have alternate access to hues only through some theoretical account of them. But under what circumstances are we entitled to suppose that a theoretical identification or reduction or whatever is adequate?[7] Only, I submit, if it can model the necessary properties of hues. So we must first ask what the necessary properties of hues are, and then ask whether any independently specifiable set of objects or properties has an analogous structure. If it does, it will be an appropriate candidate for theoretical identification with hues, or as a supervenience base for hues.[8] If it does not, it must be rejected out of hand. Let it be understood that this is a necessary but not a sufficient condition[9] for theoretical reduction, etc. We should expect other constraints to be required.

That the existence of unique hues and their distinction from binary hues is necessary to our concept of colour I suppose to be established by the intelligibility of the instruction, "select a green which is neither yellow nor blue." We know exactly what such a candidate would be, but we do not know what a unique orange would be. By the same token, it is a necessary feature of green and red, yellow and blue that they exclude one another; we do not know what it would be like to find a reddish green or a yellowish blue. That there exist these opponent relations among these pairs of hues is, indeed, a necessary condition for our being able to order the hues in a unique circular array. We may see this by noticing that if there were reddish greens there would exist a resemblance path[1] from red to green which did not go through either yellow or blue. If there were yellowish blues there would be a resemblance path from yellow to blue which did not go through either red or green. The resemblance order would thus fail to be unique.

6. Marc Bornstein, William Kessen, and Sally Weiskopf, "Color Vision and Hue Categorization in Young Human Infants," *Journal of Experimental Psychology: Human Perception and Performance* 2 (1976): 115–29. For the anthropological study, see E. H. Rosch, "Natural Categories," *Cognitive Psychology* 4 (1973): 328–50. [Hardin's note.]

7. "Theoretical identification": identification as part of a scientific theory, e.g., the identification of light with electromagnetic radiation. "Reduction": one example of reduction is the identification just mentioned, which implies that light has been "reduced to" electromagnetic radiation.

8. "Supervenience base for hues": Properties on which hues depend.

9. A **necessary condition** for statement p to be true is a condition that must hold if p is true; a **sufficient condition** is a condition such that p must be true if the condition holds.

1. Path in which adjacent steps are similar, as illustrated by the path from red to yellow that passes through yellowish red, orange, and reddish yellow.

I therefore claim that any system of properties with which the colours can be theoretically identified, or upon which colours can supervene, must have structural analogues to the dimensions of hue, saturation and brightness as well as to the unique hues and opponent relationships. Any theory which does not have an account of these characteristics may be a theory of wavelength discrimination, but it will not be a theory of *colour.*

How, then, might some scientific objects be coloured? There are two types of answers which have been discussed in the philosophical literature. The first of these I shall call objectivism. According to objectivists, colours are either identical with clusters of physical properties or else supervenient[2] upon such property-clusters. The existence of colour instances, says the objectivist, does not depend upon the existence of perceiving animals, although the detection of colours does.

Since it is by virtue of our eyes being stimulated by electromagnetic energy of between 450 nm and 700 nm in wavelength that we typically experience colours, the natural physical candidate for colour is either some characteristic of electromagnetic radiation or some property of the coloured object which is responsible for that energy leaving the surface of the object in the way in which it does. Let us first consider electromagnetic radiation.

Light has properties that may appear to answer to brightness, saturation and hue. It looks plausible to identify brightness with an appropriate function of intensity, hue with determinate wavelength, and saturation with the relative proportion of that wavelength and the broad-band radiation known as "white" light. However, none of these identifications will do. Yellow, for instance, is intrinsically less saturated than green. That is, a 580 nm light will be perceived as less saturated than a 503 nm light even though each stimulus consists of a single wavelength. Brightness can at best be seen as a function of relative rather than absolute intensity. Furthermore, it is also strongly a function of contrast of the target object with its surround. The most problematic of these identifications is of wavelength with hue, for no particular wavelength is such that it and it alone corresponds with a given hue. Unique green, for example, is experienced by most subjects when they are stimulated by monochromatic light of 503 nm. But unique green is equally well evoked by a mixture of 490 nm and 540 nm or, indeed, by indefinitely many other wavelength pairs, none of which need contain 503 nm. Nor is there any relationship between unique hues and single wavelengths, or between binary hues and pairs of wavelengths. Any particular orange can be perceptually produced by a single wavelength or by indefinitely many combinations of wavelengths. There is no wavelength relationship that corresponds to the opponent relationships either. An object may reflect equal amounts of 503 nm (which perceptually evokes unique green) and 650 nm light (which evokes a very slightly yellowish red) without producing a perception of greenish red. Instead, it is a white or gray barely tinged with yellow which is seen.

2. Dependent.

So the properties of light do not match up well with the properties of colours, failing as they do to capture even the essential properties of colour. And when it comes to some of the other properties of colour such as successive contrast and simultaneous contrast, the case is quite hopeless.

What about the properties of the physical objects which cause us, via electromagnetic radiation, to see colours? Except for the interference of light with light, the shaping of the spectrum of light by matter always involves the interaction of radiation with electrons. This fact is not unimportant, but it takes us close to an understanding of the physical roots of colour only in the way that the fact that human violence arises from conflict of interests takes us close to an understanding of the causes of war. Consider, for instance, what it is about blue things that makes all of them blue.

The blue of the sky results from the differential scattering of sunlight from the atmosphere, while the blue of a lake arises from reflection of the sky by the water's surface as well as vibrational transitions of the molecular electrons of the water. The blue of the rainbow, on the other hand, is entirely due to dispersion. The iridescent blue of some beetles is a consequence of evenly-spaced fine ridges on their shells which serve as a diffraction grating, but the iridescent blue of some birds comes about because of interference between layers of their feather structures. Sapphire is blue because of the transference of electrons from iron to titanium, but lapis lazuli is blue because of the vibrational energy characteristics of conjugated bonds. The star Sirius glows bluely because of the average temperature of its atoms and ions. The blue glow of a phosphoric dot on a colour television picture tube results from the stimulated emission of a doped semiconductor. And the blue glow emanating from an electron storage ring comes from the rapid acceleration of free electrons. . . .

Apart from their radiative result,[3] there is nothing that blue things have in common, and we have already seen that there is nothing in the structure of that radiation which could serve as counterparts to the unique hues or the opponence of complementary hues.

I conclude that objectivism fails. It fails because nothing in the domain of objects, properties and processes beyond our skins is both causally connected with our colour experiences and models the essential characteristics of colours. Given the physical world as we understand it, objectivism is necessarily false. This is, of course, not to say that objectivism is false in all possible worlds.

So if a physicist is to find a place for colour in the natural order, he must turn to some form of the doctrine which holds that colours of physical objects are to be understood as dispositions of those objects to affect perceivers in a suitable fashion. We may call that doctrine *subjectivism*. Subjectivism is at least as old as the scientific revolution of the seventeenth century, and has more often been given a dualist[4] rather than a physicalist formulation. It was put neutrally by Keith Campbell: "To be (transiently) red is to have the power to give rise to impressions of red."[5]

3. Production and modification of light.
4. Dualism is the view, associated with the French philosopher René Descartes (1596–1650), that the mind and the body are distinct things.
5. "Colours," in Robert Brown and C. D. Rollins, eds., *Contemporary Philosophy in Australia* (Allen and Unwin, 1969), p. 147. [Hardin's note.]

An obvious question of principle concerns the interpretation of the phrase, "impressions of red." After all, the original project was to find a place for colours in a world of objects characterized by the predicates of physics alone. If that project is to be realized, perceivers must be similarly characterizable. We must then take impressions to be (or to be supervenient upon) physical states of perceivers, as Campbell does but as Newton[6] and many other subjectivists do not. We require physical — here, physiological — states whose structure models the internal relations of colour. Given such states, the relational properties which have them as constituents might then in turn model the colour relations.

Within the last fifteen years there has been a substantial theoretical shift in the understanding of colour vision, brought about in large measure by persuasive neurological evidence which has rehabilitated a version of Hering's opponent process theory.[7] As matters are now understood, there exist excitatory and inhibiting cross-connections between the outputs of the three cone types — call them L (longwave), M (mediumwave) and S (shortwave) receptor outputs respectively. According to a representative version of the theory, the neural code is as follows: $(L + M + S)$ is the code for whiteness, $[(L + S) - M]$ codes red when positive and green when negative, $[(L + M) - S]$ codes yellow when positive, and blue when negative. "Positive" and "negative" must here be taken to represent increases or decreases in neural base rate firings. The theory predicts that at 580 nm, for instance, $[(L + M) - S]$ will be strongly positive and $[(L + S) - M]$ will be zero (i.e., base rate firing), so unique yellow ought to be experienced, which it indeed is. Similarly, at 500 nm $[(L + S) - M]$ will be strongly negative and $[(L + M) - S]$ will be zero, so there will be neither a blue nor a yellow signal, and we should expect unique green. Obviously too, the signal for red and the signal for green cannot be sent down the same channel.

It is plain that we now can account for the distinction between unique and binary hues as well as the red-green and yellow-blue opponent relationships. Several other phenomena, ranging from the colours of afterimages to the marked desaturation of yellow when compared with the other "pure" hues, may likewise be explained. On the other hand, many important colour phenomena, notably simultaneous chromatic contrast and so-called "colour constancy,"[8] cannot be entirely accounted for at this relatively early stage in neural processing. There are several more-or-less equivalent mathematical models for these phenomena but the details of their protoplasmic embodiments in the brain are not yet understood. Nonetheless, the physiological specification of chromatic states has now gone beyond the programmatic stage.

6. Isaac Newton (1643–1727), English physicist and mathematician. Newton's famous experiments with prisms on the color of light are described in his *Opticks* (1704).

7. Ewald Hering (1834–1918), German physiologist and psychologist. "Opponent process theory": theory of color vision according to which color information is processed in three opponent channels: red-green, yellow-blue, and black-white.

8. "Simultaneous chromatic contrast": change in apparent color with a change in the color of the background. "Colour constancy": stability in apparent color across changes in illumination.

It is important to notice that the relational predicates[9] which, on the subjectivist account, assign colours to physical objects, will be significantly more peculiar — not just more complicated — than most philosophers seem to realize. We must, of course, include a characterization of both "normal" observers and "standard" conditions. I have elsewhere suggested how problematic these are, but a couple of points might usefully be made here. Philosophers often assume, for instance, that normal observers are simply those observers who can make larger numbers of wavelengths discriminations than non-normal observers. This rules out the "colourblind" — dichromats and monochromats who require only two coloured lights or one coloured light to match any given hue. But there also exist deviant observers known as anomalous trichromats, many of whom have wavelength discrimination capabilities which are quite as acute as "normal" trichromats. Probably because of deviations from average peak cone responses, the anomalous trichromat's hue responses are shifted with respect to more typical observers. He may, for example, locate unique green at 520 nm. Even among "normals," the perception of unique green may vary from one subject to another by as much as 10 nm on either side of 503 nm. (The location of unique hues for a given observer is, however, precisely repeatable from one observation to another.) These are easily noticeable differences: a 505 nm stimulus may look unique green for Jones, yellowish green for Smith, and bluish green for Adams. What saves the stability of ordinary colour terms is that they are crude. But in precise applications such as industrial colour matching, the variations even among "normals" is serious enough for the Commission International de l'Éclairage[1] to standardize its tests on an artificial "Standard Observer" which, in turn, is useful for comparative colour judgements (sample X matches sample Y) but useless for absolute ones (sample X looks yellowish red). Practical uses aside subject variability poses a serious challenge to the particular subjectivist position we are now considering, for if it is axiomatic that every hue must be determinate, how can we determine without unacceptable arbitrariness that sample X is a unique rather than a yellowish or bluish green? . . .

The problem of specifying normal conditions for viewing the "true" colours of objects is equally vexing. Sunlight is the most usual candidate, for instance, but it is hardly the best condition for viewing fluorescent colours or the colours of stars or bioluminescent fish. Colours interact, so the surround of a colour sample is crucial to its appearance. Furthermore, no single choice of surround will yield all possible colour experiences, e.g. of silver, the browns, or the blacks. In fact, the specification of standard conditions will depend upon our intentions: what do we wish to see? "The thing's true colours" is *not* a useful answer to that question.

There are still other problems in the form of anomalous sources of colour experiences, e.g., the Butterfield encoder, which can transmit colour television pictures using only black-and-white equipment. The subjectivist can no doubt construct his relational colour predicates to handle such odd cases (there aren't very

9. **Predicates** that require two or more noun phrases to make a sentence: "is larger than" is relational; "is square" is *non*-relational.

1. International Commission on Illumination (French).

many of them), but it is not obvious that there is a *right* way to legislate each case, that there is a fact of the matter to which we must attend. Together with the previous considerations, it looks as though the dispositions to which we would connect our colour terms, selected as they are by contexts and interests, will be subjective in a rather robust sense of the word.

In sum, it seems likely that the subjectivist can at least in principle construct a set of relational predicates which will function very much like the non-relational color predicates of ordinary speech. Furthermore, these predicates need involve no basic predicates beyond those of scientific discourse. Whether in so doing the subjectivist captures the sense of "colour" philosophers have in mind when they ask whether, in a world of scientific objects, anything is coloured, I don't know, because it's often not clear to me what they had in mind in the first place. People who wish to say four-square that afterimages are coloured will find the particular version of subjectivism presented here to be quite inadequate. Some hair-shirt physicalists may be prepared to say nothing is coloured, so our ordinary attributions of colours to things are, if taken literally, simply false. But a physicalist who is not prepared to reject our colour attributions *tout court*[2] must embrace subjectivism, warts and all. Since objectivism is false, it's the only game in town.

## TEST YOUR UNDERSTANDING

1.  What is the distinction among *hue, saturation,* and *brightness*? What is the distinction between *unique* and *binary* hues? Green paint can be produced by mixing yellow and blue paint. Orange paint can be produced by mixing yellow and red paint. It might seem to follow that green is, like orange, a binary hue. Explain why it doesn't follow.

2.  Why does Hardin reject the identification of the hue of a light source with its emitting light of a certain wavelength?

## NOTES AND QUESTIONS

1.  Objectivism fails, according to Hardin, because nothing in the physical environment "is both causally connected with our colour experiences and models the essential characteristics of colours." What is his argument?

2.  What are the problems Hardin finds for the dispositionalist's appeal to "normal observers" and "normal conditions"? How might a dispositionalist respond?

2. Without qualification (French).

3. *Hardin's eliminativism.* In his book *Color for Philosophers* (Hackett, 1988) Hardin sums up his view as follows:

> [P]hysical objects are not colored. . . . Colored objects are illusions, but not unfounded illusions. We are normally in chromatic perceptual states, and these are neural states. . . . We are to be eliminativists with respect to color as a property of objects, but reductivists with respect to color experiences. (pp. 111–12)

We are to be "reductivists with respect to color experiences" because, on Hardin's view, color experiences are identical to certain (physical) brain states. Thus Hardin endorses (or at least is sympathetic to) J.J.C. Smart's **identity theory** (see chapter 8 of this anthology).

However, Smart is also a color physicalist—which Hardin is not. (See "Notes and Questions" to Armstrong, "The Secondary Qualities" earlier in this chapter.) Hardin thus illustrates how physicalism about the *mind* is a separate thesis from physicalism about *colors*. There are subtle connections between the two views, but it is important not to confuse them.

## Colin McGinn (born 1950)

McGinn taught at University College London, Oxford, Rutgers, and the University of Miami, and is the author of many books and articles in philosophy of mind, metaphysics, and epistemology. His recent books include *The Mysterious Flame* (2000), *Logical Properties* (2003), *Truth by Analysis* (2011), and *Basic Structures of Reality* (2011).

# SECONDARY QUALITIES
## from *The Subjective View*

According to the Lockean tradition, secondary qualities are defined as those whose instantiation in an object consists in a power or disposition of the object to produce sensory experiences in perceivers of a certain phenomenological character; whereas primary qualities are said not to consist in such dispositions to produce experiences.[1] This is simply a stipulative definition of the distinction, leaving it open whether there are in fact any qualities of objects falling under either characterisation; it is thus a substantive question whether (say) colour is a secondary quality. The Lockean tradition then claims that we can assign familiar perceptible qualities of objects to one or other of the two categories: it claims that colours and tastes and sounds and felt qualities and smells belong to the category of secondary qualities,

---

1. See John Locke, "Some Further Considerations Concerning Our Simple Ideas," earlier in this chapter.

whereas shape and size and weight and motion belong to the category of primary qualities. These lists are not exhaustive, but they indicate the kinds of quality which are to count as secondary or primary in the defined sense. The idea is that we can recognise, of any given perceptible quality, into which category it falls, though we may not be able to supply any non-circular condition which determines whether any arbitrary quality is primary or secondary. For example, it is supposed that we can recognise that red is a secondary quality in the sense defined: for an object to be red is for it to present a certain kind of sensory appearance to perceivers. On the other hand, being cubical is recognised not to consist in such a disposition but in some intrinsic feature of the object. It is this general (and received) account of the distinction and its application that I propose to assume in what follows.

It is sometimes supposed that the dispositional thesis about (say) colour involves a circularity the exposure of which undermines any significant distinction between primary and secondary qualities. The circularity is supposed to be this: to specify which kinds of experience a red object is disposed to produce we need to *use* the word "red" — but then the dispositional analysis of being red in terms of how things visually seem is circular. We need to use the word "red" (i.e., invoke the concept of being red) because how a red object seems is precisely a matter of its looking *red*. Now I think it is true that there is no adequate specification of the relevant kinds of experience save by saying that the object looks red, but I do not think this should undermine our confidence in the primary/secondary distinction as we have defined it. Note, first, that the alleged circularity is of a peculiar kind, since it is not *generally* true that an object's looking Q entails that it is Q; this means that a claim of logical equivalence between "is Q" and "seems Q" will not be trivial, since not all values of "Q" will sustain such an equivalence. Thus shape predicates do not sustain the equivalence while colour predicates do; and this asymmetry is quite independent of whether it is proper to hold that "looks red" actually gives the meaning of "red." What we should claim is that being red *consists in* looking red; this is why the equivalence asserted by the dispositional thesis about red holds — though it is also true that "looks red" is semantically complex, having "red" as a semantically significant constituent. . . .

In the case of "red" and "looks red" it seems to me that the alleged circularity is just what we should expect, because we are explaining the instantiation of a quality in terms of the production of experiences with a certain intentional content — and such experiences necessarily consist in representing the world as having certain qualities.[2] We might say that the "circularity" arises, not because being red is inherently resistant to dispositional analysis, but rather because the analysans[3] is inherently intentional: experiences are distinguished by their representational content, so naturally we shall need to use predicates of the external world in specifying them. The threat of circularity might tempt some to seek a non-intentional characterisation of the relevant kinds of experience, and failure in the search make them doubt the dispositional

2. The "intentional content" (or **representational content**) of a perceptual experience is how the experience presents the perceiver's environment — as containing a red, round tomato, for instance.

3. The expression or **concept** that gives an **analysis** or definition; the expression or concept to be analyzed or defined is the *analysandum*. Here "red" is the analysandum, and "looks red" is the analysans.

thesis; but I think that appreciating the source of the "circularity" should dissuade us from undertaking the search and relieve any anxiety about the security of the dispositional thesis on account of its futility. The essential point is that, according to the dispositional thesis, the ultimate criterion for whether an object has a certain colour or taste (etc.) is how it looks and tastes to perceivers; whereas this is not how we think of qualities like shape and size. It does not compromise the claim that the *esse* of colour is *percipi* that the *percipi* can be specified only by using colour concepts.[4] In future, then, I will allow myself to speak of *analysing* secondary qualities in terms of dispositions to produce sensory experiences, understanding by this the thesis that these experiential facts are *constitutive* of the presence of the quality in question.

Let me now spell out some consequences of accepting the dispositional analysis of such qualities as colour and taste. An immediate consequence is that secondary qualities are subjective in the sense that experience enters into their analysis: to grasp the concept of red it is necessary to know what it is for something to look red, since this latter constitutes the satisfaction condition for an object's being red.[5] In contrast, to grasp what it is for something to be square it is not constitutively necessary to know how square things look or feel, since what it *is* to be square does not involve any such relation to experience. But if grasping colour concepts requires knowledge of certain kinds of experience, and if (as is very plausible) this knowledge is available only to one who enjoys those kinds of experience, then grasp of colour concepts will depend upon the kind of acquaintance with sensory experiences which we have only from the first-person perspective. In other words, colours are subjective in Thomas Nagel's sense: they are accessible only from a particular experiential point of view.[6] Primary qualities, since they are not similarly defined in relation to experience, are not subjective in this sense. A man born blind cannot appreciate what it is for something to be red because he lacks the subjective experiences analytic[7] of being red. Secondary qualities are thus subjective in the way sensations are, even though they are ascribable to external things.

It is only slightly less obvious that the dispositional thesis implies the relativity of secondary qualities; for the question arises, to *which* perceiver or perceivers the red object is disposed to look red. The same things can, of course, look different colours to different perceivers; so we need to ask whose experience fixes the correct application of the colour concepts. In practice there is a considerable measure of coincidence in the sensory appearances which things present to different perceivers, so that the constitutional relativity of colour ascriptions does not normally obtrude itself; but it is easy to describe cases in which this relativity is inescapable. Thus suppose a given range of objects looks systematically red to us and systematically green to Martians, and suppose our and their colour discriminations are equally fine.

---

4. The Irish philosopher George Berkeley (1685–1753) notoriously claimed that "esse est percipi," or "to be is to be perceived" (Latin).

5. The "satisfaction condition" for an object to be red is the condition in which the object is red: according to the dispositional analysis, that condition is *being disposed to look red*.

6. See Nagel's "What Is It Like to Be a Bat?" [p. 402 of this anthology]. [McGinn's note.]

7. Definitional.

Then there will be no choosing between these groups of perceivers in respect of whose experience determines the colour of the objects in question. Or suppose sugar goes from tasting sweet to us to tasting bitter overnight, as a result of suitable changes in our taste receptors. The dispositional thesis tells us that sugar thereby ceases to be sweet and becomes bitter, since what it is to have these qualities just consists in how things taste. Secondary qualities resemble properties like being poisonous or nourishing in this respect: plainly, these properties are relative to some implicit or explicit choice of creature as that with respect to which a substance is declared poisonous or nourishing. This relativity implies that there is no genuine disagreement between us and the Martians when they call an object green which we call red; for all these colour ascriptions assert is that the object looks green to them and red to us. It is thus entirely proper to speak of objects as red with respect to perceiver $x$ and green with respect to perceiver $y$. This is not yet to say that colour predicates contain a suppressed argument-place for a perceiver (or group of perceivers) in logical form,[8] so that they differ *semantically* from the syntactically similar primary quality predicates; it is just to say that what it is for a secondary quality to be instantiated is for a certain relation to obtain between the object and some chosen group of perceivers. It is this relativity that permits differences in the perceived secondary qualities of things not to imply genuine disagreement, whereas perceived differences of primary qualities imply that at least one perceiver is in error. This point of distinction between primary and secondary qualities has the consequence that an inventory of the perceptible qualities of an object must be drawn up differently in respect of the two categories: an object has as many colours as there are different ways it (systematically) looks, but this is not so for shape. There is thus a sense in which an object has (or could have) many contrary colours simultaneously.

It may be objected that the relativity just indicated is incompatible with the fact that we acknowledge a distinction between the real and apparent colour (or taste) of a thing. We do indeed make such a distinction, but it is important to see that it is drawn quite differently from the distinction between real and apparent shape or size. In the latter case, there is an experience-independent criterion for whether the primary quality is instantiated, viz. measurement; but for secondary qualities the distinction is drawn from *within* the realm of appearance, by reference to experiences taken as standard. To suffer an illusion with respect to colour is for your colour experience not to match that of a normal perceiver in normal conditions; and we can easily imagine circumstances in which the standard of normality might shift, so that what was once counted as illusory now counts as veridical. And of course this is what the dispositional thesis leads us to expect. Consider what we should say of a simplified practice of colour ascription in which there is just one perceiver with constant illumination and visual receptivity: in such a case it seems that there is no

8. "Argument-place": the **predicate** "is square" can be combined with *one* noun phrase to form a sentence, and so is said to have one argument-place; "is taller than" needs *two* noun phrases to form a sentence; and so has two argument-places, etc. "Logical form": (roughly) the structure of a sentence that determines its logical properties.

way for a distinction between real and apparent colour to arise, since there is no departure from the standard set by this solitary perceiver's experience. But we can certainly suppose our solitary perceiver to suffer illusions as to the primary qualities of things. We shall not, then, significantly misrepresent the nature of secondary qualities if we stick with the simple equation of having the quality and seeming to have it; just as we do not misrepresent the nature of poisonousness by saying simply that poisonous things are disposed to cause ill-health in animals — even though there are special and essentially untypical circumstances in which they do not. It is a conceptual truth that red things *typically* look red.

If the dispositional thesis is correct, we can also predict that a certain kind of scepticism about secondary qualities is incoherent. It makes sense to suggest that we might be systematically in error about the primary qualities of things — a Cartesian demon[9] may interfere with our sense organs in such a way as to make things seem otherwise than they are. But this is not possible for secondary qualities, since their presence is constituted by how things sensorily seem — the Cartesian demon cannot contrive to make us wrong about the colours and tastes of things. The difference here is that no amount of information gleaned from within experience can logically entail which are the primary qualities of an object, but we *can* deduce from the character of our experience which secondary qualities a thing has. We might say that scepticism is ruled out for secondary qualities because (roughly) phenomenalism[1] is correct for them; but phenomenalism is not similarly correct for primary qualities, and so scepticism can get a foothold. The only kind of scepticism appropriate to secondary qualities would be, in effect, a scepticism about other minds: for if the experiences of others in a perceptual group to which one belongs set the standard for correct ascriptions of colour, then one can only know if one's own experiences are veridical by knowing how other people experience things. However, as we just observed, the community-based criterion of correctness is itself a superficial feature of secondary quality ascriptions, and so no deep-going scepticism afflicts such ascriptions.

A close corollary of the last point is that secondary qualities do not have the distinctive characteristics of natural kinds: in particular, they are not reducible to possibly unknown "internal structures" or "real essences."[2] Colours, for example, are not to be identified with wavelengths of the spectrum. This is simply because the dispositional thesis defines colours in terms of sensory appearances, and so we cannot envisage cases in which the identity of a given colour comes apart from its appearance — there cannot be "fool's red" as there can be fool's gold.[3] In this respect

---

9. "I will suppose therefore that . . . some malicious demon of the utmost power and cunning has employed all his energies in order to deceive me" (Descartes, *Meditation I*; see p. 299 of this anthology).

1. The view that statements about physical objects (e.g., "This table is brown, rectangular, and made of oak") can be analyzed in terms of how those objects would perceptually appear in various circumstances.

2. The contrary view is held by David Armstrong, *A Materialist Theory of the Mind*, chapter 12 [excerpted earlier in this chapter]. [McGinn's note.]

3. Iron pyrite, which looks like gold.

secondary qualities are like sensations. This point can be driven home by giving a variable realisation argument against reductive identification. Suppose we discovered that the physical properties of the surfaces of red-looking objects varied in some fairly radical way but that the variation was compensated for in our visual receptors: we would not then say that the objects varied in colour, contrary to what we had supposed on the basis of their appearance; we would say rather that the property of being red was correlated with no single underlying physical property. That is, we would say that objects look red, and so are red, in virtue of *different* "categorical bases"[4] in those objects — the disposition to produce a given kind of experience has a variable ground. The independence of secondary qualities from their physical ground in the object can be obscured by failing to distinguish two ways in which a quality can be associated with a disposition to produce experiences, which we can call intrinsic and extrinsic. It is true that if an object has a primary quality it will be disposed to produce experiences as of that quality under certain conditions; but this disposition is extrinsic to the quality, in the sense that the type of experience is not constitutive of the object's having the quality — it is merely one causal consequence of it. In the case of secondary qualities, the disposition is intrinsic, in the sense that there is no independent characterisation of what it is to have the quality from which the disposition to produce experiences flows. If we confuse these two ways a quality can be dispositional in respect of experience, we will be inclined to think that the secondary quality disposition must have a categorical basis in the object in just the way the primary quality disposition does — that is, we will suppose there to be a reduction of the disposition to its causal ground in the object. But in the case of secondary qualities, the most we should demand is that for any instantiation of such a quality there should be *some* ground in the object which explains (in conjunction with certain other facts) the perceiver's experience; we should not expect the stronger proposition that there is one such ground for any instantiation of the quality. I suspect that confusion on this point is what makes some people wish to combine a Lockean dispositional thesis about colour with a reduction of colour to physical properties of surfaces; but in fact such a reduction is ruled out once the Lockean thesis is properly understood — colours are *intrinsically* dispositional.

It is often observed that secondary qualities are explanatorily idle, and in two ways. First, these qualities are not ascribed to things as part of the enterprise of explaining the causal interactions of objects with each other: colour and taste do not contribute to the causal powers of things. Primary qualities are precisely the qualities that figure in such explanations; that is why the physical sciences speak of primary qualities, but not secondary qualities, in formulating the laws governing objects. Secondly, secondary qualities do not explain our perception of them; primary qualities are what do that. Both of these features of secondary qualities can be seen to follow directly from the dispositional thesis. The first feature issues from the fact

---

4. A categorical base is a non-dispositional property of an object that explains why it has a certain power or disposition.

that the interactions between objects proceed independently of the experiences of perceivers, and these are definitive of secondary qualities. Objects would behave in the same way if there were no perceivers to constitute their secondary qualities; and varying appearance to different perceivers does not affect the object's causal powers in relation to other objects. The second feature issues from the nature of causal explanation: since being red is analysed as looking red, we cannot explain why something looks red by saying that it is red, for this involves an explanatory circle; it is like explaining why a substance poisoned someone by saying it is poisonous. Such "explanations" may not be entirely vacuous, because they suggest that the cited dispositional property operates similarly in other cases; but we know that something more substantial must be available, if only because we also want to explain why things have these effects in general. Primary qualities are then called in to do the explaining secondary qualities cannot manage themselves. This is why it is strictly wrong to say that a red object is disposed to produce experiences as of its looking red in virtue of its being *red*; the analogous claim about primary qualities, on the other hand, is perfectly correct. . . .

The world as it is presented to us in perception — the manifest image — includes secondary qualities; but the world as described by (physical) science is independent of this or that creature's perceptual peculiarities — it deals only in primary qualities. . . .

It has often been supposed that there is a conflict or disagreement between the common-sense view of objects associated with perception and the scientific view of them. The conflict is held to consist, roughly, in this: that common sense says that objects are coloured while science (or scientifically informed philosophy) tells us that they are not *really* coloured (and similarly for the other secondary qualities). Colour is ascribed to objects in the manifest image, but withheld or denied in the scientific image: common sense supposes colours to be really "out there" qualifying physical objects, whereas science and critical philosophy teach that they are in fact only "in the mind."[5] This alleged conflict has been reacted to in a variety of ways, none of them altogether soothing. Some have concluded that common sense is in radical error, that perception itself is under an illusion as to the location of secondary qualities: science is right to deny that things are really coloured and common sense is simply mistaken in its assertion to the contrary. Some have supposed that common sense and science speak of ontologically distinct worlds, the objects of the former being coloured, the objects of the latter not: neither view is in error about its own world — the only error lies in identifying the objects of each. Others have wished to make common sense veracious by adopting an instrumentalist or fictionalist attitude toward science: common sense describes things as they really are, science merely offers a more or less useful picture of the world abstracted from common sense — science does not properly *deny* that things are coloured, because it does not *purport* to describe reality as it is in itself. Then there are those who opt for a relativist

5. I suppose the idea of this conflict goes back to Locke and beyond; the ancient atomists are often credited with raising the issue, at least in a primitive way. [McGinn's note.]

view of colour-ascription: the conflict is resolved by acknowledging that ascriptions of qualities to objects are always made relatively to some chosen standpoint on the world. Relative to the perceptual standpoint things are really red, but relative to the scientific (or philosophical) standpoint they are not really red: so if we ask "is the pillar box red?" no answer can be given until we specify which standpoint is to serve as standard. And yet others seek to dissolve the disagreement by suggesting that common sense and science are in different lines of business: the purpose of science is theoretical knowledge of the world, but the purpose of common sense and perception is essentially practical; the conflict is resolved by saying that neither side wishes to usurp the role of the other.

My own view is that none of these strange and strained doctrines is needed because there is no real conflict between science and common sense as to whether things are really coloured. Firstly, it is not true that, according to the subjectivist view of colour (etc.), it is incorrect to ascribe colours to things; for they do indeed have the power to produce the appropriate sense-experiences in perceivers. What the scientifically informed view denies is just that objects are *objectively* or *intrinsically* coloured, i.e. that objects have colour in the way they have shape; it denies that possession of colour is an observer-independent condition. Now for there to be a conflict between science and common sense the latter would have to contradict this denial; it would have to hold, not just that things are really (i.e., truly) coloured, but further that they are objectively coloured — that being coloured is *not* observer-dependent. But is there any reason to convict common sense of the belief that secondary qualities have the same observer-independent status as primary qualities? I know of no feature of our ordinary use and understanding of colour words which clearly commits common sense to this mistaken assimilation. . . .

If I were asked to choose between the manifest image and the scientific image on the score of representational superiority, I would answer as follows: there is no clear sense in which one has greater verisimilitude than the other. The objective view does not have the relativity of the subjective view, but it purchases this absoluteness at the cost of removing itself from the perceptual standpoint. There can be no question of selecting one kind of view and abandoning the other: to abandon the subjective view is to abandon the possibility of experience of the world; to abandon the objective view is to abandon the idea of an observer-independent unitary reality. Neither view can serve the purposes of the other, and neither can be construed as setting a standard which the other can be criticised for failing to meet.

## TEST YOUR UNDERSTANDING

1. "[S]uppose sugar goes from tasting sweet to us to tasting bitter overnight, as a result of suitable changes to our taste receptors. The dispositional thesis tells us that sugar thereby ceases to be sweet and becomes bitter. . . ." State the dispositional thesis about taste and explain why it has this consequence.

2. Suppose you say "Tomatoes are red" and one of McGinn's Martians says "Tomatoes are *not* red." According to McGinn, are you and the Martian both right, or both wrong, or is one right and the other wrong? Explain your answer.

3. McGinn acknowledges that there is a distinction between the *real color* of an object and its *apparent color*: sometimes the color an object appears or looks to have is not its real color, the color it actually has. How does McGinn explain this distinction?

4. Why does McGinn think that "there is no real conflict between science and common sense as to whether things really are colored"?

## NOTES AND QUESTIONS

1. Suppose someone says to you that some things (e.g., trees, raspberries, stones) are "brillig" and other things (e.g., bushes, strawberries, bricks) are not. You ask what the word "brillig" means, and she gives you the following definition:

   (B)  x is brillig **iff** x is disposed to look brillig.

   (B) is not a satisfactory explanation of what "brillig" means. Why not? Compare the problem with (B) to the objection that the dispositional thesis about color involves a problematic "circularity." What is this objection, exactly? How does McGinn respond to it? Is his response convincing?

2. *McGinn's dispositionalism.* In his book *The Subjective View*, from which this selection is taken, McGinn lays out the "Lockean tradition" and its consequences, but he doesn't pretend to argue for it, at least not directly. In the introduction to the book he says that "I will not supply a full defence of [Lockean] theses about secondary qualities ... since others have argued convincingly for the key points and I do not anticipate much disagreement with the position I adopt" (p. 2). The Lockean tradition was accepted by many at the time (1983), but what is disputable is whether "others have argued convincingly for the key points." At present the Lockean tradition probably enjoys less support than it once did, and dispositionalism is just one of a number of theories of color that are actively debated in the literature.

## ANALYZING THE ARGUMENTS

1. *The dispositional analysis.* Consider the following dispositional analysis of the color red:

   > (DA$_{\text{RED}}$) x is red if and only if x is disposed to look red to normal perceivers in normal conditions.

   Modify (DA$_{\text{RED}}$) so that it has the consequence that a tomato is red when you see it on the kitchen table, but not red when there is no one in the kitchen.

2. *Martians.* Recall McGinn's example of the Martians: "a given range of objects looks systematically red to us and systematically green to Martians, and . . . our and their colour discriminations are equally fine." According to McGinn, in that situation a tomato would be "red with respect to [us]" and "green with respect to [Martians]."

   Modify (DA$_{\text{RED}}$) above to deliver this result. Hint: Start by changing the left-hand side ("x is red") to read "x is red with respect to a group of perceivers P."

3. *The conditional analysis.* Consider the following example:

   > There might have been a shy but powerfully intuitive chameleon which . . . was green but also would intuit when it was about to be put in a viewing condition and would instantaneously blush bright red as a result. So although . . . the chameleon is green it is not true . . . that were it to be viewed it would look green. It would look bright red. (Mark Johnston, "How to Speak of the Colors," reprinted in A. Byrne and D. R. Hilbert, eds., *Readings on Color,* Vol. 1: *The Philosophy of Color,* MIT Press, 1997, p. 145.)

   That is, the chameleon is green, but if a normal perceiver were to see it in normal conditions it would look red. Now consider the following "conditional analysis" of the color green:

   > (CA$_{\text{GREEN}}$) x is green if and only if a normal observer were to see x in normal conditions, x would look green.

   Explain why Johnston's example makes trouble for the conditional analysis.

   (Compare "The conditional analysis" of what a person could have done, "Analyzing the Arguments" in chapter 13 of this anthology.)

4. Consider the following passage from Jonathan Bennett's *Locke, Berkeley, Hume* (Oxford University Press, 1971):

   > To say that x has a power to produce S in me is to say, among other things, that if x were related to me in a certain way then S would occur in me. (p. 94)

   Explain why this passage suggests that:

   > (DA$_{\text{RED}}$) x is red if and only if x is disposed to look red to normal perceivers in normal conditions,

   is *equivalent* to:

   > (CA$_{\text{RED}}$) x is red if and only if a normal observer were to see x in normal conditions, x would look red.

That is, (DA$_{RED}$) is true if and only if (CA$_{RED}$) is. (Of course if the two analyses *are* equivalent, then the example of the shy but intuitive chameleon also makes trouble for the dispositional analysis.)

5. A *biconditional* is a sentence of the form "p if and only if q." State the relationship of the dispositional analysis to the conditional analysis using a biconditional of the form "The dispositional analysis of the color orange is equivalent to the conditional analysis of the color orange if and only if. . . ."

6. Consider the following example (adapted from Johnston, "How to Speak of the Colors," p. 146): a fragile glass vase is internally packed with a special kind of foam so that it would not break if struck. Assuming that fragility is just the disposition to break when struck, and that the vase remains fragile when packed, explain why this is a counterexample to the conditional analysis of fragility: "x is fragile if and only if x would break if struck." Is it a counterexample to the "if" part of the analysis, or to the "only if" part?

7. *Computer displays (and pointillist paintings).* Suppose that your computer display appears to be a uniform shade of bright yellow all over. If you look at a part of the display with a strong magnifying glass, you will see a pattern of green and red pixels, and no yellow ones at all. Supply the missing premise so that the following **argument** is **valid**:

P1. Parts of the display are green.

P2. _____ .

C. The display is not yellow all over.

The "best answer" will be a general principle, not a specific claim about computer displays in particular.
    Is the missing premise that you have supplied true?

8. Can arguments for color eliminativism be extended to other sorts of eliminativism — taste eliminativism (lemons are not sour, honey is not sweet, etc.), shape eliminativism (lemons are not oval, honeycomb cells are not hexagonal), etc.? If the arguments carry over to some but not all perceptual properties, what is the difference between the perceptual properties that eliminativism applies to and those that it does not? Is the dividing line anywhere near Locke's division between primary and secondary qualities?

9. If you put your hand close to a candle flame, the flame will feel hot. And flames are indeed hot — or so any introductory physics textbook will say. In section 16, Locke appears to argue that the heat you feel is not in fact "in" the flame, any more than the pain you feel when you put your hand even closer to the candle is "in" the flame. What is Locke's argument? Is he denying that flames are hot?

10. Recall Hardin's description of how "a 505 nm stimulus may look unique green for Jones, yellowish green for Smith, and bluish green for Adams." What should we conclude from this fact about variation in color perception among normal perceivers? Can it be turned into an objection to dispositionalism, or color physicalism? Can it be turned into an argument for eliminativism?

# 11

# What Is There?

Every intellectual discipline aims to provide an illuminating taxonomy of the objects it studies. Biology seeks a comprehensive inventory of living things; mineralogy catalogues the rocks; physics supplies an elegant taxonomy of the elementary particles, and so on. Of course in all of these cases the aim is not to list all of the *individual* objects of study. Biology, for example, does not aim to catalogue the individual bugs and birds. The aim is rather to identify the most important *categories* into which those individuals may be grouped, and to explain what distinguishes one category from another.

**Metaphysics** has taxonomical aspirations as well. But since the subject matter of metaphysics is *absolutely everything*, the taxonomy is pitched at a rather lofty level of abstraction. Metaphysics does not care about the distinction between the giant panda and the lesser panda, or even about the distinction between pandas and planets. From the standpoint of the metaphysician, these things are all of a piece: they are all **physical objects**. To get a feel for the sort of contrast that might matter to the metaphysician, consider the difference between Mount Everest (a physical object) and iTunes (a computer program). Mount Everest takes up space; it has a certain weight and chemical composition. In these respects it is no different from a dog or a star. By contrast, it makes no good sense at all to ask how much iTunes weighs, or how much space it occupies, or what it's made of. A computer program and a physical object are *radically* different in kind. That is the sort of difference with which metaphysics is concerned.

Having noted this, we should also note that despite their differences, there is a sense in which iTunes and Mount Everest are rather similar: they are both *objects*. To be sure, iTunes is not a *physical* object. But it is still an object in the following sense: It has **properties**—properties like *being a computer program that is more than 100 lines long*—but it is not itself a property or anything of the sort. Suppose you have three green books on your desk. They may differ in size and shape and literary merit. But they have something in common, or so we might well say. What exactly is this "thing" they have in common? It is not a physical object. (The books do not have any *molecules* in common.) Nor is it some sort of ghostly non-physical object. When a book is green, it possesses a *property*: the property of being green; and *that* (among other things) is something your three green books have in common. This is controversial, but if it is right, reality must contain, in addition to objects like Mount Everest and iTunes, the various properties that these objects possess. And if we go this far, we must go further. Suppose that Fred is Sarah's brother, and that Al is Margaret's brother. There is then a **relation**—namely, *brotherhood*—in which Fred stands to Sarah and Al stands to Margaret. This relation is not an object, nor is it a property. So in addition to objects (both physical and nonphysical) and properties, we must apparently recognize a new category of relations.

## A Preliminary Metaphysical Taxonomy

Let us pause to reflect on what just happened. We began with the sciences, which divide the world up rather finely, distinguishing dogs from cats and protons from neutrons. We then moved easily to a level of abstraction at which these things belong to a single category—the category of physical objects—as distinct from apparently nonphysical objects like computer programs. We then moved (perhaps somewhat less easily) to an even loftier level of abstraction at which physical and nonphysical objects belong to a single category—the category of objects—which we distinguished from other equally abstract categories: properties and relations (sometimes collectively called **universals**). The result is a preliminary taxonomical scheme (fig. 1).

Is this taxonomy complete? Does absolutely everything find a place in it? Consider the Battle of Waterloo. This battle is obviously not a property, and it would be odd to call it an object (physical or otherwise). It is an **event**. How might we incorporate events into our taxonomy? In one crucial respect, events are more like objects than they are like properties. Like Mount Everest and iTunes, the Battle of Waterloo has various properties, but nothing *has* it. But events are also different from objects: they are spread out in time; they don't *exist*; they *occur*. So we might posit a basic contrast between what we might call **particulars**—things that have properties but are not themselves *had*—and universals treating objects and events as two distinct species of particular (fig. 2):

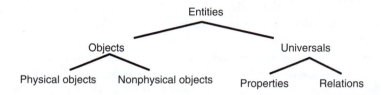

**Figure 1**

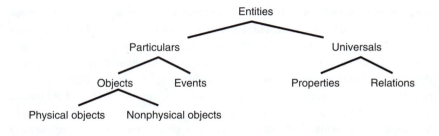

**Figure 2**

Is *this* taxonomy complete? Not obviously. Consider *milk* — not some particular glass of milk, but *milk itself*. (When you say "Milk is delicious" you're not talking about some particular glass of milk; but you are talking about *something*.) It has properties, but it is not a property, so it must be a particular. But is it an object? Is it an event? Or consider *the fact that philosophy is difficult*. Again, this fact would appear to be a particular. But it is neither an object nor an event nor a **stuff** (like milk). So we are not done yet.

# Ontology: The Study of Being

This part of metaphysics is called **ontology**: the study of being. Ontology aims to provide a comprehensive taxonomy in which absolutely everything finds a place, but which discloses order by ranging things into a relatively small number of categories. It is not obvious that this is possible, but even our very cursory reflections should be encouraging. Try this as an exercise: Start with the proposals we have been discussing. Ask yourself what we have left out. Try to range the excluded items into categories at roughly the same level of abstraction as those we have been discussing. Spend an hour at this. You *may* come away with the sense that the task is hopeless — that ontological categories are like species of beetle: whenever you think you've found them all, you find another. But you may also come away with the sense that even if your homemade scheme is not perfectly adequate as it stands, something like this should be possible: it's only a matter of finding the right categories and drawing the lines in the right places.

The selections that follow touch on questions that arise in this part of philosophy. Gideon Rosen's paper argues that any ontological scheme must recognize a category of nonphysical **abstract objects,** taking as its main example the numbers of basic arithmetic. Peter van Inwagen's paper makes a similar point, taking as its main examples fictional characters like Sherlock Holmes. Both papers emphasize an important methodological point. In constructing an ontological system, we begin with what we know best: our commonsensical view of the world as refined by science. Since both science and common sense take arithmetic for granted, any adequate ontological scheme must leave room for numbers. But numbers are not physical objects. So we must reject the otherwise attractive hypothesis that physical objects are the only objects that exist. Of course science and common sense are fallible, so arguments of this sort are not conclusive. But we do not have to wait for a final, settled science in order to begin the search for an ontological scheme. Rather, we should see our metaphysics as a work in progress that evolves as our understanding of the world evolves.

For Tim Maudlin, the chief aim of metaphysics is to present an explicit account of the reality disclosed by physics. If physics itself were fully explicit about these matters, philosophers might have nothing distinctive to contribute. But in fact modern physics leaves a great deal open. The "standard model" of particle physics, based on quantum mechanics, is the best-confirmed scientific theory ever contemplated by human beings. But what does it tell us about the nature of reality? It is a commonplace to say that the world disclosed by quantum mechanics is very strange. But that is misleading. The fact is that it is *unclear* what the world according to quantum mechanics is like. It includes particles, like electrons, that move through space. But how exactly are these related to the space in which they move? Are electrons spread out in a sort of cloud around the nucleus? Are they point-like things that *orbit* the nucleus? Physics itself is muddled on these matters, and for many purposes it need not decide. But the philosopher who wishes to extract an ontological scheme from modern physics must engage these questions, thereby extending and deepening the science that scientists produce.

Stephen Yablo's essay takes up the metaphysics of ordinary physical objects. As we normally think, physical objects exist in space in a distinctive way: there cannot be two physical objects in the same place at the same time. Ordinary experience seems to confirm this. (You can't park two cars in a single parking space, after all. Each car excludes the other from the space it occupies.) But a clever argument seems to show the opposite. Take a lump of clay—call it CLAY—and make a statue—call it STATUE. When you're done, you have a statue occupying a certain region of space. But of course the clay did not disappear when you made your statue. So you also have some clay that occupies the very same region of space. "Big deal," you say. "This is not a case of *two* objects occupying the same place at the same time. The clay and the statue are the same thing. CLAY = STATUE." But not so fast. Suppose you made your statue today with clay that had been sitting around for weeks. We can then argue as follows:

(1) CLAY existed yesterday.

(2) STATUE did not exist yesterday.

(3) Therefore, CLAY ≠ STATUE.

The premises of this argument are extremely plausible. Is the argument valid? The principle that underlies it can be put as follows:

(*) If X differs from Y in some respect, then X ≠ Y.

And again, this seems obvious. How can a thing differ from itself? But if (*) is true, the argument is sound and we have refuted the commonsensical idea that two physical objects cannot occupy the same place at the same time.

Yablo defends a version of this argument. The debate is important for the light it sheds on the category of physical objects. But it also bears on a larger question. Metaphysics is supposed to be a *philosophical* inquiry into the structure of reality. But you might well wonder: how can there be such a thing? Scientists test hypotheses about the structure of reality by conducting experiments. But philosophers don't conduct experiments. Nor do they have a special faculty of extrasensory intuition that allows them to perceive the structure of reality directly. So how is metaphysical inquiry possible? One response is Maudlin's: metaphysics proceeds by interpreting the experimental results produced by scientists. But the debate over the statue and the clay suggests that cannot be the whole story. For note: *there is no science in this debate.* The argument sketched above begins with a *hypothetical* case and appeals to general **a priori** principles like (*). At no point did we rely on observations of real statues. And yet the argument appears to tell us something about real physical objects, namely that it is *possible* for two of them to occupy the same place at the same time. How is a priori metaphysical knowledge of this sort possible? Good question. But let's not get ahead of ourselves. Before we ask how metaphysicians can possibly do what they claim to do, we should take a proper look at what they in fact do. The selections that follow are designed to get you started.

## Peter van Inwagen (born 1942)

Van Inwagen, the John Cardinal O'Hara Professor of Philosophy at the University of Notre Dame, has written widely on topics in metaphysics and the philosophy of religion. Some of his essays in metaphysics are collected in *Ontology, Identity and Modality* (Cambridge University Press, 2002).

# FICTION AND METAPHYSICS

The relations that various novels and stories bear to the questions of metaphysics would be an interesting topic, but it is not the topic of the present article, which is the relevance to metaphysics not of this or that work, but rather of the very existence of such a thing as fiction. We shall see that philosophical reflection on fiction can lead one to certain remarkable metaphysical conclusions. Not surprisingly, the area of metaphysics to which these conclusions pertain is *ontology*. The word, though not the study it represents, is a new one — it is probably a seventeenth-century coinage.

In the present century, the word "ontology" is associated mainly with the names of Heidegger[1] and Quine.[2] I shall be using the word in Quine's sense: as a name for the study that attempts to answer the question, What is there?

Quine's contributions to this study are of central importance for the thesis of this article. These contributions may be divided into two parts: those that belong to ontology proper and those that belong to what we may call meta-ontology. By Quine's "ontology proper," I mean his actual attempt to answer the question, What is there? This attempt is of great intrinsic interest, but it is not relevant to my topic. By Quine's meta-ontology, I mean his famous discussion of what it is to ask what there is and his famous theses about how to approach this question.[3] These theses are the product of a really remarkable effort to think clearly about questions almost no one had thought clearly about, and a proper appreciation of them will liberate one from some very old and very strong illusions about being and existence. Or so many philosophers, including the present author, would say. And yet Quine's meta-ontology, when it is combined with what seem to be some very simple and obvious facts about fiction, yields a result that seems just obviously wrong: that names drawn from works of fic-tion ("Mr. Pickwick" and "Tom Sawyer," for example, as well as proper names of other sorts, such as "Dotheboys Hall" and "Barchester") denote existent objects. The thesis of this article is that this consequence of Quine's meta-ontology does not constitute a *reductio ad absurdum;* rather, Quine's meta-ontology should be retained and this consequence accepted.

I shall first examine Quine's meta-ontology in the abstract, and then in applica-tion to fiction. In the abstract, Quine's meta-ontology may be viewed as comprising four propositions.

(1) Being is the same as existence. That is, to say that things of a certain sort exist and to say that there are things of that sort is to say pretty much the same thing. For example, to say that horses exist is to say there are horses, and to say that there was such a person as Homer is to say that Homer existed. This might seem obvious, but on reflection it can seem less obvious. Suppose I am discussing someone's delusions and I say, "There are a lot of things he believes in that do not exist." On the face of it, I appear to be saying that there are things — the poison in his drink, his uncle's malice, and so on — that do not exist. . . . Perhaps someone who reflects on this example will conclude that it is not obvious that to be is the same as to exist. But whether or not it is obvious, it is true. There *is* no nonexistent poison in the paranoid's drink. . . . In sum, there are no things that do not exist. I cannot argue for this thesis at the length the issues it raises deserve. I will say only this: if you think there are things that do not exist, give me an example of one. The right response to your example will be either, "That does too exist," or "There is no such thing as that."

---

1. Martin Heidegger (1889–1976), German philosopher.

2. W. V. Quine (1908–2000), American philosopher and logician.

3. Quine's meta-ontological views are scattered throughout his writings. A famous systematic exposition of them can be found in "On What There Is" in *From a Logical Point of View* (Harvard University Press, 1953). But this article is far from being a complete statement of Quine's meta-ontology. [Van Inwagen's note.]

(2) Being is univocal. (And, since existence is the same as being, existence is univocal.) Many philosophers have thought that "there is" and "exist" mean one thing when they are applied to material objects, and another when applied to, say, minds, and yet another when applied to (or withheld from) supernatural beings, and one more thing again when applied to abstractions like numbers or possibilities. This is evidently an extremely attractive position. Undergraduates fall effortlessly into it, and it is very hard to convince anyone who subscribes to it that it is false or even that it is not obviously true. But it is false. Perhaps the following consideration will show why it is at least not obviously true. No one would be inclined to suppose that numerals like "six" or "forty-three" mean different things when they are used to count different sorts of objects. The very essence of the applicability of arithmetic is that numbers may count anything: if you have written thirteen epics and I own thirteen cats, then the number of your epics *is* the number of my cats. But existence is closely tied to number. To say that unicorns do not exist is to say something very much like saying that the number of unicorns is zero; to say that horses exist is to say that the number of horses is one or more. And to say that angels or ideas or prime numbers exist is to say that the number of angels, or of ideas, or of prime numbers, is greater than zero. The univocity of number and the intimate connection between numbering and existence should convince us that there is at least very good reason to think that existence is univocal. . . .

(3) The third component of Quine's meta-ontology is difficult to state, even inaccurately, without some discussion of formal logic. There is, in standard contemporary logic, . . . a symbol called the existential quantifier, often written as a reversed sans-serif capital E and pronounced "there exists a" or "there is a" or "for some." Thus, "$\exists x\, x$ is a dog" is read "There is an $x$ such that $x$ is a dog" or "For some $x, x$ is a dog." . . . Quine's third thesis is that this symbol, the existential quantifier, adequately represents that single sense of being or existence that figures in our everyday and our scientific assertions; that this symbol and the rules for using it are best understood as a regimentation of the quotidian "exists" and "there is.". . .

(4) I have said that for Quine ontology is the study that attempts to answer the question, What is there? The fourth component of Quine's meta-ontology gives us a general way of approaching this question. As Quine sees matters, the problem of deciding what to believe about what there is is a very straightforward special case of the problem of deciding what to believe — or, more grandly, a special case of the problem of deciding what theories to accept. To find out what there is, find out what theories to accept. To find out how to find out what there is, find out how to find out what theories to accept. (No easy tasks, to be sure, but ones we are stuck with if we have *any* scientific or epistemological interests.)

Let us suppose I have somehow found out what theories to accept, and let us suppose that, as a result, I accept, say, the General Theory of Relativity, . . . the Chomskian thesis of innate grammar, and the dogma of the Real Presence. (As the items on this list show, we are using "theory" in a broad sense: a theory may be very simple or very complex and to say that one holds a certain theory is not to imply that one is in any way uncertain about the truth of its constituent propositions.) Now that I know what theories I accept, I am in a position to answer the question, What is there? . . .

To find out what there is, once I have found out what theories to accept, I need do no more than find out what my theories say there is. Sometimes this is easy. The theory called *theism,* for example, says that — in fact consists of the assertion that — there is a God. But often matters are not so simple, for a theory may in some sense say of something that it exists without coming right *out* and saying it. For example, one would not normally think of classical mechanics as asserting the existence of numbers, and yet the typical assertions of mechanics are assertions about the relations between sets of numbers. Should I, therefore, just in virtue of accepting the classical description of the motions of physical things in response to impressed forces, also accept the existence of certain nonphysical things, namely the numbers that measure the motions and the forces? This is a tricky question to which Quine's meta-ontology provides an answer: What I must do, in the general case, is to translate my theories into the symbolism of modern formal logic (that flexible and powerful system of symbols that includes "∃"). Then I must examine the sentences of my theories and see which of them begins with an existential quantifier, and these sentences will tell me what there is. For example, if classical gravitational mechanics contains a sentence that begins "∃$x$ $x$ is a number and . . . ," then, in accepting this theory, I commit myself to accepting the existence of at least one number.

Why? Well, to accept a theory is to accept it as *true.* And if a theory contains a sentence that begins "∃$x$ $x$ is a number and . . . ," then that theory is true only if there is at least one number. . . .

So much for Quine's meta-ontology in the abstract. Let us now return to the subject of fiction. What should one say about the ontology of fiction if one accepts Quine's meta-ontology? One's course seems clear: one must first decide what theories about fiction to accept, and then one must translate these theories into the language of formal logic and see what they have to say about what there is.

What are theories about fiction?

Let me back momentarily away from this question and make up a tribe of primitives, as philosophers do when they are dismayed by the complexity of the real world.

Suppose there is a tribe whose members love stories about heroic deeds. The members of this tribe have a word for stories and classify them into three types: histories, lies, and fictions. The "fictions," unlike the histories and like the lies, are products of the imagination; unlike the lies, however, they are not intended to deceive, for, when someone tells a fiction, his audience knows that what is being told them is not a history, and he knows they know, and they know he knows they know, and so on. . . .

If they tell fictions, then, being members of our rather chatty species, they probably talk about fictions. What sorts of things might they say? How deeply might their talk about fictions penetrate their fictions? We may distinguish two "grades of fictional involvement." Here are some one-sentence examples of each grade.

GRADE ONE
"That story we heard last night was hard to follow."
"His new story was even more boring than hers."

"There are some stories I wish would never end."

"I fell asleep during the story."

"His story reminds me of hers."

GRADE TWO

"That story we heard last night had an intricate plot."

"His hero was even more boring than hers."

"When I hear certain stories, I seem to get caught up in the action."

"I fell asleep during the story — how did it end?"

"He has borrowed her device of having a character in one's story tell a story."

We might say that Grade One comprises *holistic* and Grade Two *analytical* story-talk. The former treats stories as unstructured wholes, the latter as things that can be broken down and taken apart *in intellectu*.[4] . . .

Let us turn our attention to the second grade of fictional involvement, to analytical story-talk. Analytical story-talk, if it is highly theoretical, applied to standard texts, informed by knowledge of a literary tradition, and serious in intent, we call *criticism*. (But, of course, not all criticism is analytical story-talk, since there are literary productions — lyric poems, for example — that are not stories.) It will be convenient, however, to call all analytical story-talk criticism. Thus, what we shall call criticism exists even among my primitive tribesmen, and any child of our culture who can talk of plots and characters is capable of it.

A moment ago, I backed away from the question, What are theories about fiction? I am now in a position to answer it: theories about fiction are critical theories in the present sense of the term: theories that treat stories as having an internal structure. Now critical theories, when listened to the way Quine has taught us to listen to theories, tell us something of great metaphysical interest: that there are fictional objects — things like Mr. Pickwick. It is clear that stories themselves do not tell us any such thing. If the members of a certain tribe told fictions but never talked about fictions, or if they talked about fictions but remained within the first grade of fictional involvement, they would never say or do anything that committed them to the thesis that there are fictional objects. Contrary to what G. E. Moore[5] said in a famous symposium, when Dickens wrote, "Mrs. Bardell had fainted in Mr. Pickwick's arms," he was not saying anything about someone called "Mrs. Bardell" or about someone called "Mr. Pickwick."[6] He was not saying anything about them because he was not saying anything about anything. What he was doing was crafting a linguistic object that his readers could, in a certain sense, *pretend* was a record of the doings of — among others — people called "Mrs. Bardell" and "Mr. Pickwick."[7]

4. I.e., in thought.

5. (1873–1958), English philosopher. G. E. Moore's essay "Proof of an External World" appears on p. 313 of this anthology.

6. *Proceedings of the Aristotelian Society*, supp. vol. 12 (1933): 55–70. [Van Inwagen's note.]

7. Here I follow Kendall Walton. See his article, "Fiction, Fiction-making, and Styles of Fictionality," *Philosophy and Literature* 7:1 (April 1983): 78–88. [Van Inwagen's note.]

It is critical theories alone that tell us that there are fictional objects, because it is critical theories alone that contain sentences like these:

> "There are characters in some nineteenth-century novels who are presented with a greater wealth of physical detail than is any character in any eighteenth-century novel."

> "Some characters in novels are closely modeled on actual people, while others are wholly products of the literary imagination, and it is usually impossible to tell which characters fall into which of these categories by textual analysis alone."

> "Since nineteenth-century English novelists were, for the most part, conventional Englishmen, we might expect most novels of the period to contain stereotyped comic Frenchmen or Italians; but very few such characters exist."

Such sentences can be vehicles of objective truth as surely as can the most humdrum sentences about rocks and chemicals and numbers. Therefore, surely, those of us who are interested in the nature of fiction will want to accept theories that contain these sentences — or if not *these* sentences, then others having essentially the same ontological implications. But these sentences, if they are translated in the obvious way into the language of formal logic, will yield sentences that begin "$\exists x\ x$ is a character and. . . ." Therefore, anyone who believes that what these sentences say is literally true and who accepts what seem to be the obvious formal translations of these sentences, accepts the thesis that there are fictional characters. Of course, someone who employs such sentences as these may want to say that his use of them is merely a manner of speaking and that he does not believe that fictional characters *really* have any sort of being. But then we are within our rights if we ask him how he would rewrite or paraphrase such sentences to remove their misleading implications. . . .

Instead of discussing this question, let us raise the question why anyone should want to do this. Why not simply accept the thesis that there are fictional objects. . . . The answer would probably be something like this: "Well, let's look at a particular fictional character — say, Mrs. Gamp.[8] If there was such a person as she, then people in London in the 1840s ought to have been able to look her up and talk to her. But there was no Mrs. Gamp for them to look up — nor was there any Mr. Pecksniff; nor has there ever been any Pickwick or Anna Karenina or Tom Sawyer. In short, there are no fictional characters. Each of these characters, if he or she had any sort of being, would have a certain spatiotemporal location and would display at that location a certain set of properties, a set that could be extracted from various descriptive passages of fiction. But it is obvious that if we could visit the location any of these characters is supposed to occupy, we should find no one in it with the required properties."

This is a real difficulty. Many philosophers who believe in Mrs. Gamp et al. will find it less of a difficulty than does someone who accepts Quine's meta-ontology. Some philosophers think there are things that do not exist, in which category they would place Mrs. Gamp. They will say: "The reason why we could not have found her

---

8. From Charles Dickens's *Martin Chuzzlewit* (1844).

in London in the forties is that she did not *exist*. Of course one cannot 'find' nonexistent things." But this resolution of the difficulty is not open to those who maintain that existence and being are identical, that there is nothing that does not exist. Other philosophers will say: "Mrs. Gamp exists, but she enjoys a mode of existence, *fictional* existence, that is different from yours and mine. That is why we could not have found her." But this resolution of the difficulty is not open to those who maintain that existence is univocal, that existence does not come in types or kinds or styles.

The latter of these proposals is hard to take seriously. To postulate unexplained "modes" of existence is to prefer theft to honest toil. But the former — the proposal to separate being from existence — is worth taking seriously. It seems to be the position that one is driven to if one cannot answer the objection we are considering. Various considerations have been alleged in support of it, but only fiction, in my view, presents us with a really good argument for believing in the nonexistent. Earlier, I recommended a short way with typical attempts to give example of nonexistent things. If someone puts forward, say, Meinong's golden mountain[9] as an example of something nonexistent, one should reply as follows: "There is no golden mountain and therefore you cannot put it forward as an example of *anything*; it is not there to be put forward." But if someone puts forward Mrs. Gamp as an example of a nonexistent thing, one cannot dismiss her so easily. *I* cannot dismiss her at all. For, in my view, she *is* there to be put forward.

What am I to say? Logic leaves only one course open to me. I say Mrs. Gamp exists (in the only sense of "exists" there is); I concede that in London in 1843 there was to be found no fat, old, tippling, umbrella-wielding nurse called "Sarah Gamp," with a husky voice and a moist eye, which she had a remarkable power of turning up, and only showing the white of it. Therefore, I must conclude that Mrs. Gamp had, or has — one's tenses tend to get a bit muddled in discussions of the properties of fictional characters — none of the properties on this list. Nor, in my view, is it strictly true that she is human, made of flesh and blood, or even an inhabitant of the physical world.

Well, what is she then? In philosophical jargon, she is a theoretical entity of literary criticism. Her ontological status may be compared with that of a plot, a rhyme scheme, a narrative passage, or a recurrent pattern of imagery. She is such stuff as they are made on.

"But, look. There must be some sense in which it is true that Mrs. Gamp was fond of gin. If you say that it is false that she was fond of gin — presumably because theoretical entities of criticism cannot be said to drink at all — how will you distinguish between the sense in which it is false that she was fond of gin and the sense in which it is false that she was a teetotaler? If it is false that she was fond of gin, there must be a sense in which it is even more false that she was a teetotaler."

9. The Austrian philosopher Alexius Meinong (1853–1920) developed an elaborate theory of non-existent objects, of which "the golden mountain" — a mythical mountain made entirely of gold — was a prominent example. See A. Meinong, "The Theory of Objects," trans. Isaac Levi, D. B. Terrell, and Roderick Chisholm, in *Realism and the Background of Phenomenology*, ed. Roderick Chisholm (Ridgeview, 1981), pp. 76–117.

This point is right, of course. I am afraid I shall simply meet it by stipulation. I shall simply introduce the word "hold" as a term of art and say that, while Mrs. Gamp does not *have* the property of being fond of gin, she does *hold* it. Being a teetotaler, on the other hand, is a property she neither has *nor* holds. This is not to say that she *has* no properties. I would say that, like everything else, for any given property she has either that property or its negation. Here are some properties she has: being a theoretical entity of criticism; being a satiric villainess; having been created by Dickens; being introduced in Chapter 19 of *Martin Chuzzlewit;* not being a woman; not being made of flesh and blood; holding the property of being a woman.

"But what is this holding?" I cannot define it. I can only give examples. But we all understand it well enough. There is an intimate relation that the main satiric villainess of *Martin Chuzzlewit* bears to the property *being fond of gin.* There is an intimate relation she bears to the property *being introduced in Chapter 19.* The latter, of course, is the relation called *having* in everyday speech; the former is obviously not the same as the latter; I have chosen the name "holding" for it.

We have been calling Mrs. Gamp "she" despite the fact that she does not have the property *being female.* In doing this, we have been following a convention according to which it is usual to talk about fictional characters as if they had the properties they held. This same convention underwrites our use of the "is" of predication in sentences like "Mrs. Gamp is fat." This convention is an obvious and natural one. If authors in laying their stories before the public are, in a certain sense, pretending to have produced histories, then it is not surprising that critics should at least sometimes pretend, in that sense, to be discussing histories. And, of course, if one is pretending to discuss a history, one will use personal pronouns and the "is" of predication.

This, in very broad outline, is a theory about the metaphysical nature of fictional characters: like everything else, they exist; they are theoretical entities of criticism, as are plots, digressions, and asides to the reader; they do not *have* such properties as you and I have, but only "literary" properties like being a villainess or being a minor character, though they bear another sort of relation (which I arbitrarily call "holding") to such properties as you and I have. There is a lot more that would need to be said to give a complete exposition of this theory.[1] My purpose, however, has not been to present a fully developed theory, but to show how fiction presents a problem to the metaphysician and how one metaphysician has attempted to come to grips with it. Let me close by pointing out an advantage of this theory.

Consider the famous question, How many children had Lady Macbeth? One traditional line of thought runs as follows: *Any* definite answer to this question would be wrong. ("None" would be wrong, "One" would be wrong, "Two" would be wrong, and so on.) But, according to the rules of logic that we apply to ordinary, nonfictional beings, some definite answer would have to be right. Therefore, ordinary logic is not applicable to fiction, and a special "logic of fiction" must be devised if we are to know how to evaluate reasoning about fiction. According to the theory proposed above,

---

1. For a fuller development of various aspects of the theory outlined here, see my article "Creatures of Fiction," *American Philosophical Quarterly* 14 (1977): 299–308. [Van Inwagen's note.]

however, no such drastic expedient is forced upon us. We need only point out that: (1) Lady Macbeth *has* the property *having no children,* since she is a theoretical entity of criticism and thus not the sort of thing that could have children, and (2) she *holds* neither this property nor its negation (the property of baving one or more children). The Law of the Excluded Middle requires that, for every property, an object *have* either that property or its negation. But neither this law nor any other principle of logic says anything about what properties an object must *hold.* (A fictional object may hold a logically inconsistent set of properties. Barsetshire,[2] for example, holds an inconsistent set of geographical properties: that is why one cannot draw a coherent map of it.) Therefore, there is no need for a special logic of fiction. Since this article has been an application of Quine's ideas about ontology to a special topic, the ontology of fiction, this is an appropriate point at which to end it. For we have now partly repaid Quine for his service to the ontology of fiction by showing how worries about the need for a special logic of fiction can be prevented from doing a disservice to Quine's philosophy of logic, one central tenet of which is that no subject-matter requires a special logic of its own.

## TEST YOUR UNDERSTANDING

1. Van Inwagen holds that (i) being is the same as existence, and (ii) being is univocal. Explain these claims in your own words.

2. According to van Inwagen, fictional characters "do not *have* such properties as you or I have, but only 'literary' properties like being a villainess or a minor character." Explain and illustrate the claim with a fresh example.

## NOTES AND QUESTIONS

1. Consider two claims one might make in a discussion of *Martin Chuzzlewit.*

    a. Mrs. Gamp is a fictional character.

    b. Mrs. Gamp lived in London in 1843.

   Taken together these seem to entail:

    c. A fictional character lived in London in 1843.

   But that is puzzling. Fictional characters are not flesh-and-blood human beings. They do not literally *live* anywhere at all.

   Van Inwagen responds by distinguishing two ways that an object can possess a property. Mrs. Gamp *has* the property of being a fictional character, whereas she

---

2. The fictional setting for a series of novels by Anthony Trollope.

*holds* (but does not *have*) the property of having lived in London in the 1840s. When van Inwagen insists that fictional characters are not flesh-and-blood human beings, he means that they do not *have* properties like being alive and being human. So that gives us a sense in which (c) is true. We can put the point as follows:

d.  There is an item that *has* the property of being a fictional character, and *holds* the property of having lived in London in 1843.

A theory of this sort must explain what it means for an object to *hold* a property. This is a new, technical notion, and whenever a philosopher introduces an unfamiliar notion, she must explain it. So consider the following proposal: To say that Mrs. Gamp *holds* the property of having lived in London in the 1840s is just to say that

e.  According to Dickens's novel *Martin Chuzzlewit,* Mrs. Gamp lived in London in 1843.

In general,

f.  To say that a fictional character *holds* a property is just to say that *according to a certain fictional story,* the character *has* that property.

This explains an unfamiliar notion in terms of a relatively familiar one. But the proposal raises several questions.

Consider the claim that

g.  Mrs. Gamp was fatter than Sherlock Holmes.

That sounds true; but of course Mrs. Gamp does not *have* the property of being fat; she merely holds it. So (g) must be understood as (h):

h.  Mrs. Gamp holds the property of being fatter than Sherlock Holmes.

But there is no fiction — no novel or story — according to which Mrs. Gamp is fatter than Sherlock Holmes, since there is no story in which both appear as characters.

*Exercise:* Modify the proposed account of what it is for an object to hold a property to accommodate this example.

For further reading, see Amie Thomasson, *Fiction and Metaphysics* (Cambridge University Press, 1999).


## Gideon Rosen (born 1963)

Rosen, Stuart Professor of Philosophy at Princeton University, works in the philosophy of mathematics, metaphysics, and moral philosophy. The argument in the essay below is developed in his book with John P. Burgess, *A Subject with No Object* (Oxford University Press, 1997).

# NUMBERS AND OTHER IMMATERIAL OBJECTS

## 1.

The book in front of you is a physical object. It is located in space — it is there on your desk and not on Mars. It exists in time — it exists now but not a million years ago. It has physical attributes: a certain shape, a certain mass. Most importantly, the book is ultimately composed of smaller objects — quarks, electrons, and other subatomic particles — that can be completely and exhaustively described in the language of basic physics.

Everyday objects are presumably physical objects in this sense: animals and plants, rocks and clouds, cars and computers. So are the exotic objects of the sciences such as viruses and black holes. Our knowledge of these things is of course profoundly limited. We may never be in a position to give a complete description of any of them. Still we know (or think we know) that these things are wholly physical, in the sense that they admit, in principle, of a complete description in the language of an ideal physics.

*Physicalism* is the thesis that every object is a physical object in this sense. It is the thesis that absolutely everything in the universe (or out of it!) is, in fundamental metaphysical respects, rather like the book you are now holding, or the tree outside your window, or an atom, or a black hole: a thing whose nature might be captured by a description in the language of a perfect physics. This definition of physicalism is not entirely satisfactory.[1] A better account would say what it means for a thing to admit of a complete description in such a language.[2] But let us not pause over these subtle matters. We have a fair intuitive idea of what it means for a thing to be a physical object through and through. The question is whether everything is a physical object in this sense.

The first thing to say about physicalism is that it is not obviously true. God is supposed to be a spirit without a body. He may be "everywhere" in some sense, and if so, he exists in space. But God is certainly not composed of matter, and it makes no

---

1. For doubts about this definition, see T. Crane and D. Mellor, "There is No Question of Physicalism," *Mind* 99 (1990): 185–206. For general discussion, see D. Stoljar, "Physicalism," in *Stanford Encyclopedia of Philosophy*, ed. Edward Zalta (http://plato.stanford.edu/archives/fall2008/entries/physicalism/). [Rosen's note.]

2. Here is the rough idea. This book has many properties: it weighs 2 lbs.; it's made mostly of paper; it's about philosophy, etc. Some of these properties are *intrinsic*: they concern the book considered in isolation, without regard for its relations to other things. The intrinsic properties of a thing are the properties it would share with any *perfect duplicate* of it. (Your book *belongs to you*. That's a property it has, but it's not an intrinsic property, since a perfect duplicate of your book might not belong to you.) A thing admits of a complete description in the language of physics if and only if its intrinsic properties are *fully determined by* the physical properties of its parts and their relations to one another. Of course this definition takes the notion of a *physical property* for granted. A complete account would have to explain this idea. [Rosen's note.]

sense to ask how much God weighs or whether he is negatively charged. So if God exists, physicalism is false. Similarly, many philosophers believe that even the most exhaustive physical description of a human being would inevitably leave something out. Consider Jones, who has just stepped on a tack and is now in pain. A complete physical account of his brain and body would be terrifically informative. But according to these philosophers, it would inevitably fail to specify, even implicitly, how it *feels* to be Jones right now. For it seems that there could have been a creature who was like Jones in every physical respect down to the last atom, but who had no conscious mental life at all. If this is possible, then a physical description of Jones would omit a crucial fact. And if that is so, physicalism is false.[3]

These examples may suggest that any serious discussion of physicalism must immediately confront the deepest mysteries in philosophy — the existence of God, the nature of consciousness, etc. But this is not so. Physicalism is false, I claim, and the case against it is straightforward. To see what I have in mind, let's review some elementary facts about . . . arithmetic.

# 2.

*There are two odd numbers between 6 and 10.* You probably knew this already, but even if the question never crossed your mind, you can easily verify the claim right now. (Let's see. 7 is an odd number between 6 and 10; so is 9. Any others? No. Therefore . . .) So let's take this as our starting point and consider the following argument:

1. There are two odd numbers between 6 and 10.

2. Therefore, there are at least two odd numbers.

3. Therefore, there are at least two numbers.

4. Therefore, there are numbers.

The argument has one premise. This was established by informal reflection, though a rigorous proof could easily be given. Each subsequent claim follows logically from the claim above it. The argument thus shows conclusively that anyone who accepts a trivial bit of grade school arithmetic cannot deny that there are numbers.

Now notice: It may be silly to ask how much God weighs, but it's even sillier to ask how much the number 7 weighs, or how fast it's moving, or whether it is round or square or made of carbon. No one ever bothers to ask these questions, but if we take them seriously for a moment, the answers are obvious in every case: the number 7 does

---

3. See D. Chalmers, "The Hard Problem of Consciousness" (p. 431 of this anthology); F. Jackson, "Epiphenomenal Qualia," *Philosophical Quarterly,* 32 (1982); 127–36 (p. 412 of this anthology). [Rosen's note.]

not have a mass; it is not in motion or at rest; it is not made of carbon, etc. But this is just to say that numbers are not physical objects. We thus have a simple refutation of physicalism:

5. There are numbers.

6. Numbers are not physical objects.

7. Therefore physicalism is false.

# 3.

Are you tempted to deny the second premise? If so, you may be confused in an instructive way. The book in front of you contains certain marks shaped like this: 7. If you are reading the Latin translation, it may instead contain marks shaped like this: VII. These marks are physical objects. They are made of ink; they contain carbon. But these marks are not numbers. Suppose I write the numeral "7" on the blackboard and then erase what I have written. I have destroyed the mark I made. Have I destroyed the number 7? Is there now only one odd number between 6 and 10? Surely not. So this particular inscription was not the number 7. But we can run the same argument for every inscription, and this shows that these agglomerations of ink and chalk must be distinguished from the numbers.

We must also distinguish these concrete inscriptions — called *numeral tokens* — from the *numerals* themselves. Suppose I write a list on the board:

6, 7, 125, VII, 7

The list contains five numeral tokens representing three different numbers.[4] But there is also a sense in which the list contains four different numerals: the Arabic numerals "6," "7" and "125," and the Roman numeral "VII." The two instances of the numeral "7" are tokens of the same *numeral type*, just as the two "t's in the word "letter" are tokens of the same *letter* type. The type/token distinction is one of the most important in metaphysics, and it applies in a variety of domains. Jane Austen wrote six novels, but there are millions of copies of those novels. The novels are types; the copies are tokens. Goya's etching *The Sleep of Reason Produces Monsters* is a type; its many physical impressions (the paper and ink copies that hang in museums) are tokens of that type; and so on.[5]

We have said that numeral tokens (at least those of the ink-on-paper variety) are physical objects, and the same goes for the token words and letters on this page, my personal copy of *Northanger Abbey*, etc. But now focus on the types: the Arabic numeral "7," Jane Austen's novel, *Northanger Abbey*. Are *they* physical objects? Where exactly is the numeral "7"? How much does it weigh? What is it made of? Once again, the

4. We count "125" as a single numeral, ignoring the smaller numerals that make it up. [Rosen's note.]
5. For an account of the **type/token** distinction and its significance, see Linda Wetzel, *Types and Tokens: An Essay on Universals* (MIT Press, 2008). [Rosen's note.]

only sensible answers to these silly questions are wholly negative: the numeral type is not really anywhere; it does not have a weight; it is not made of anything. The idea that one might describe a numeral or a novel by means of physical properties like mass or charge is just confused. And so we have another simple argument against physicalism:

8. Types of various sorts exist.

9. These types are not physical objects.

10. Therefore, physicalism is false.

# 4.

These counterexamples to physicalism have something in common. Numbers, numerals, and other types are *abstract objects*. It is sometimes said that abstract objects do not exist in space or time. But this is not strictly correct. *Northanger Abbey* was written in 1798. Before that it did not exist, so there is a sense in which the novel does exist "in time." To choose a rather different example, the *game of chess* is presumably an abstract object. (It is certainly not a physical object.) But the game originated in Persia in the sixth century, later spreading to India and then to Europe, so there is a sense in which the game exists "in space" (which is not to say that it *takes up* space). We get a better characterization if we say that abstract objects are distinguished by their *causal inefficacy*. You can't *interact* with numbers or with types like the letter "t." Abstract objects do not exert forces on other things, and this means that you can't bump into them or bounce photons off of them. In an intuitive and yet elusive sense, abstract objects are incapable of inducing changes in other things. Another argument against physicalism then goes like this:

11. Abstract objects of various sorts exist. (We have seen many examples.)

12. Abstract objects are not physical objects.

13. Therefore, physicalism is false.

# 5.

We have three arguments against physicalism. Each is clearly valid, so the only way to resist them is to reject the premises. Let us focus on the argument from numbers:

5. There are numbers.

6. Numbers are not physical objects.

7. Therefore physicalism is false.

In our discussion, we derived (5) from basic arithmetic by means of an impeccable deductive argument. This means that anyone who wishes to resist the argument must reject basic arithmetic.

Imagine a philosopher who says:

> My attitude towards arithmetic is like the atheist's attitude towards theology. I know what the theory *says*; I just don't believe it. In this case, the theory says that there are infinitely many abstract things called "numbers," 1, 2, 3, etc., which stand in various relations to one another. I reject the theory because in my view these alleged objects do not exist. (I've never seen one. Have you?) Your premise that there are two odd numbers between 6 and 10 is false. It is false because there are no numbers of any sort.

This position is not absurd. There is no contradiction in the claim that there are no numbers. But it is not enough for this philosopher to show that her view is consistent. She must show that we have reason to believe it. The question before us, then, is whether we, given all we know, have reason to reject the arithmetic we learned in school.

This way of framing the issue makes it clear that in this dispute about whether to accept basic arithmetic, the burden lies with the rejectionist. This is a consequence of a general principle. In philosophy as in every intellectual endeavor, we must begin where we are. Whenever we approach a novel question, we bring to bear a vast body of commonsensical and scientific opinion that we do not doubt and which we have seen no reason to doubt. Philosophy and the other intellectual disciplines are in the business of giving us reasons to modify this starting point. The Cartesian idea that we should begin *afresh* in philosophy by setting our received opinions to one side is not just impractical: it is a mistake about the nature of rational inquiry.[6]

Arithmetic is part of our shared starting point in these metaphysical investigations. Before you started reading this essay, you accepted the arithmetic you learned in school without the slightest reservation. And of course you're not the only one. The physicists, engineers, actuaries, and accountants who rely on mathematics in their work may have doubts about certain controversial principles in their fields. But they have no doubt whatsoever that there are two odd numbers between 6 and 10. Perhaps most importantly, the mathematicians who have been studying this topic for millennia have turned up nothing to call our basic mathematical opinions into question.

Needless to say, this is not a conclusive defense of our starting point. Common sense is fallible. So is physics. So is mathematics on rare occasions. The point is rather to insist that any argument against basic arithmetic must be a *skeptical* argument — one that seeks to undermine by philosophical means a body of settled opinion that is fully acceptable both by ordinary standards and by the most exacting scientific standards.[7] How might such an argument proceed?

6. G. Harman, *Change in View* (MIT Press, 1986). [Rosen's note.]

7. Cf. Descartes's argument for skepticism about the senses in *Meditation I*, reprinted on p. 299 of this anthology.

# 6.

One approach begins by noting that physicalism is a wonderfully *simple* theory. It provides an elegant picture of reality according to which absolutely everything falls into a single category. Now other things being equal, a simple theory is likely to be correct. We thus have reason to believe that physicalism is correct. As we have seen, however, physicalism is incompatible with arithmetic. And so, the argument concludes, we should reject basic arithmetic.

Such appeals to simplicity are common in metaphysics, and we need not deny their force. Given two theories that do equal justice to all pertinent evidence and argument, the simpler theory *is* normally to be preferred. (We might ask why this should be. Do we know a priori that the world is a simple place?) In the present context, however, the argument is unpersuasive. After all, we have just argued that physicalism is incompatible with both common sense and settled science, both of which endorse arithmetic. Until we have some positive reason for revising this starting point, we should think: Physicalism is indeed a simple theory. So is the view that there is nothing at all! The trouble with both of these views is that given our starting point, they are *too* simple. We know in advance that there are two odd numbers between 6 and 10. Any theory that says otherwise (without giving us some reason to change our minds) is therefore incompatible with "the facts." We may use simplicity as a tiebreaker when choosing among theories that are consistent with our background knowledge. But when a theory fails to fit the facts, considerations of simplicity are quite irrelevant. (As Einstein is supposed to have said, "Everything should be made as simple as possible, but no simpler.")

# 7.

A more compelling challenge runs as follows.[8] When we asserted our premise that there are two odd numbers between 6 and 10, we implicitly claimed to *know* that there are two odd numbers between 6 and 10. This follows from the general fact that anyone who asserts that p implicitly claims to know that p. (That's why it sounds paradoxical to say: "It's snowing, but I don't know that it's snowing.") In arguing as we have, we have taken it for granted that mathematical knowledge of a certain sort is possible.

But we have also said that mathematics is concerned with abstract entities, and that abstract entities are causally inert. This means that we cannot see them or touch them, since seeing and touching are causal processes. But it also means that we cannot detect them with special instruments, since "detection" is also invariably a causal process. And yet our scientific knowledge of unobservable objects like atoms and black holes always depends on the fact that these objects affect the environment, and ultimately our brains

---

8. See Paul Benacerraf, "Mathematical Truth," *Journal of Philosophy* 70 (1973): 661–79. [Rosen's note.]

and bodies, in characteristic ways. And this suggests a general principle, according to which knowledge *always* requires some causal link between the knower and the objects of his knowledge. This is the core of the so-called *causal theory of knowledge.*[9]

It is easy to see why this might seem plausible. Suppose you're at a conference on extraterrestrial civilizations when Prof. Zipstein stands up and asserts that there is an underground city on the dark side of the moon. You ask him how he knows this. Has he been there? Has he seen photographs? Has he spoken to someone with first-hand knowledge of the place? In response he admits that he has never interacted with the city in any way. You ask again how he knows what he claims to know, and he replies: "Look, I just find these claims intuitively obvious. They strike me as commonsensical, and I've never encountered any positive grounds for doubt."

I think we can agree that even if Zipstein's theory turns out to be correct, as things stand he does not *know* that there is a city on the moon. Moreover, it is natural to support this verdict by saying that Zipstein cannot possibly know what he claims to know because, by his own admission, he has never interacted with the object of his alleged knowledge.

Armed with this principle, the physicalist may go on the offensive:

> You're no better than Zipstein! Your argument begins with a mathematical claim, but by your own admission you've never interacted with the alleged objects of this alleged knowledge. You can't possibly *know* that there are two odd numbers between 6 and 10. And if you don't know this, you have no business asserting it in the context of a serious philosophical discussion.

This is an ingenious challenge. Our case against physicalism turns on examples.[1] The idea was that some claims about numbers and other abstract objects are so well established by scientific standards that it would be unreasonable for a philosopher to deny them without good reasons. The objection we have been discussing, if sound, would show that we are not entitled to our examples. We are entitled to assert a proposition only if we know that it is true. But if the causal theory of knowledge is correct, we don't know anything about abstract objects.

The best response is to reject the causal theory of knowledge. We need not deny that knowledge *sometimes* requires causal interaction. Zipstein really is an ignoramus: he does not know what he claims to know. And perhaps the best way to explain this is to suppose that knowledge of *this sort* — knowledge of contingent features of the physical environment — always requires a causal link. But the causal theory of knowledge is supposed to be a *general* theory, one that applies to mathematical knowledge as well. And yet there is no reason to suppose that mathematical knowledge requires causal interaction with the numbers. This is no part of ordinary

---

9. Alvin Goldman, "A Causal Theory of Knowing," *Journal of Philosophy* 64 (1967): 357–72. [Rosen's note.]

1. Compare G. E. Moore, "Proof of an External World," *Proceedings of the British Academy* 25 (1939): 273–300. [Rosen's note.] (This essay is excepted on p. 312 of this anthology.)

mathematical methodology. Mathematicians don't pretend to observe the numbers or to detect them by means of instruments. Just as arithmetic itself is part of our commonsense starting point, so is the epistemological principle that the usual ways of doing arithmetic (calculation, proof, etc.) are perfectly good ways of arriving at mathematical knowledge. Given this, the causal theory of knowledge looks like a crude over-generalization — a claim about knowledge in general that seems plausible only when we focus on *empirical* knowledge and ignore the mathematical knowledge that we know we have.[2]

This is another application of our master principle. When an ambitious philosophical claim is incompatible with our firm prephilosophical commitments, the reasonable response is to reject the philosophical claim until it can be supported by independent arguments. The causal theory of knowledge is incompatible with the prephilosophical claim that we know quite a bit about arithmetic. There are no compelling independent arguments for the theory. So we should reject it, and with it the indirect defense of physicalism that we have been discussing.

# 8.

The case against physicalism may be summarized as follows:

a. Arithmetic assures us that there are two odd numbers between 6 and 10.

b. Arithmetic is part of our shared starting point. We accept it without reservation, as do the experts who are professionally concerned with such matters.

c. It is rational to affirm our starting point unless there are positive grounds for doubt.

d. There are no good scientific or mathematical reasons for doubting basic arithmetic.

e. Moreover, there are no good *philosophical* grounds for doubt. In particular, the arguments from simplicity and the causal theory of knowledge are unsuccessful.

f. Therefore, it is reasonable to accept the claims of arithmetic, including the claim that there are two odd numbers between 6 and 10.

g. Numbers are not physical objects. Unlike the concrete numeral tokens by means of which we refer to them, they do not possess physical properties like mass and velocity.

h. Therefore, physicalism is false.

2. J. Burgess and G. Rosen, *A Subject with No Object* (Oxford University Press, 1997), 23–41. [Rosen's note.]

Physicalism is a seductive thesis. When first encountered it can seem like the natural expression in metaphysics of a hardheaded scientific worldview, one that rejects ghosts and gods and vital spirits and the like. But when we realize that physicalism entails much more than this — that it entails the rejection of the claim that there are two odd numbers between 6 and 10 — it becomes clear that physicalism is an unwarranted extrapolation from the sensible core of this hardheaded view. In its place, we might consider the weaker claim that every *concrete, causally efficacious* entity is a physical entity wholly composed of objects that admit of a complete description in the language of an ideal physics. Nothing in this essay refutes this view. If there is a version of physicalism worth defending, this is it.

## TEST YOUR UNDERSTANDING

1. Rosen claims that the existence of numbers is incompatible with **physicalism**. Explain the basis for this claim.

2. Give fresh examples to illustrate the distinction between types and tokens.

## NOTES AND QUESTIONS

1. Rosen argues that we are **justified** in believing that numbers exist simply because (a) we already believe basic arithmetic, which **entails** the existence of numbers, and (b) science and (other areas of) mathematics have turned up no reason to doubt these basic claims. But is this enough to show that our arithmetical beliefs are *justified*? Suppose you meet a stranger from a distant land who says:

   > We have the same arithmetic that you have, and we use it exactly as you do. But it never occurred to us to <u>believe</u> in numbers. Arithmetic is just a useful tool. We sometimes <u>pretend</u> that in addition to the real physical objects we find around us, there are infinitely many nonphysical objects — 1, 2, 3, . . . — just as you sometimes pretend that the surface of the Earth is marked by lines of longitude and latitude. But you don't think the lines of longitude and latitude are real, and we don't think that these numbers are real. So why should we believe that arithmetic is more than just a useful fiction?

   How might Rosen respond? Suppose there is no good response. If you cannot provide these strangers with a reason to believe basic arithmetic, are your arithmetical beliefs then unjustified?

2. *Types and tokens.* Rosen's examples of nonphysical abstract entities include *types*, like the numeral "2" (not the *tokens* of this numeral, of which there are many scattered around the world, but the type itself, of which there is only one). We certainly do take

the existence of such things for granted in many contexts; but they are puzzling. The numeral "2," for example, is rounded at the top and flat on the bottom, so it has a shape. But if we ask how big it is, the question obviously has no answer. According to our ordinary ways of thinking, then, the numeral is a thing with a shape but no size! Worse, when we consider the many ways in which tokens of the numeral can differ in shape — 2, 2, 2, — we must conclude that even if the numeral has some sort of shape, it has no *particular* shape.

*Exercise:* Using these materials (or others), construct an argument for the claim that types do not exist. Then imagine how Rosen might respond.

## Stephen Yablo (born 1957)

Yablo is Professor of Philosophy at the Massachusetts Institute of Technology. Some of his papers are collected in *Thoughts* (Oxford University Press, 2009) and *Things* (Oxford University Press, 2010).

# A THING AND ITS MATTER

Here is a small wooden box. I want you to guess its contents, based on the following clues. Clue 1: There is a piece of copper in the box. Clue 2: Everything in the box is the exact same size, shape, weight, and appearance. Clue 3: Everything in the box is in the exact same place. Clue 4: If you were to open the box and inspect its contents, you would say it had one thing in it.

The first clue tells you that the box contains at least a piece of copper, call it Cop. The second suggests that the box contains nothing but pieces of copper, all very similar to Cop. The possibility of several pieces of copper is eliminated by the third clue. Probably, then, the box has just Cop in it. This hypothesis is confirmed by the fourth clue. It looks like the box contains just the one piece of copper.

Now consider another box. The clues this time are different. Clue 1*: The box contains something rare and valuable; and it contains something common and inexpensive. Clue 2*: The box contains something very old along with something relatively new. Clue 3*: The box contains things made in different ways out of different materials. Clue 4*: Experts who have inspected the box's contents tend to agree that it contains more than one thing.

This box has *things* in it — more than one. You might suspect, copper being common, inexpensive, and old, that one of them is our old friend Cop. But Cop has company. There is an unidentified further item X, about which we know mainly that it is rare, valuable, and a relative youngster compared to Cop.

Now I'm going to tell you something that may strike you as ridiculous. The first box, which seemed to contain just the one thing, and the second, which seemed to contain two or more, are in actual fact the same. You have given incompatible answers, then, to a single question, namely, *what is in the box*? Not a very promising start to your career in metaphysics.

Why should this seem ridiculous? Well, clues 1–4 don't sit very well with clues 1*–4*, and that's putting it mildly. The box supposedly contains a thing $X$ which is the same size, shape, weight, and appearance as a certain piece of copper, and is sitting in the exact same place as that piece of copper, but is nevertheless distinct from the piece of copper. How is that possible? What is this mysterious $X$ that's invisible to ordinary mortals (by 4) but reveals itself (by 4*) to the "experts"? Who are these experts, anyway? Since when does expertise give you super-vision?

I hate to brag, but the "experts" here are metaphysicians like me. They're the ones who have thought the hardest about material objects and how to count them. Thinking doesn't improve your eyes, exactly, but it does enable you to see more, by teaching you how to interpret the scene already before you. (Compare the way that musical training lets you hear more, without improving your score on a hearing test.)

The question is, what is this additional item $X$ that, although outwardly indistinguishable from Cop, is seen by (most) metaphysicians as distinct from Cop? You're going to kick yourself when I tell you, because it's something very familiar. The extra thing is a U.S. penny. Call it Pen. Pen is the penny that came into being when, one fine day in 1909, Cop was pressed at the U.S. Mint into a certain familiar shape.

Now everything falls into place. Pen is the same size, shape, weight, and appearance as Cop simply because it is (and always has been, since that day in 1909) *made* of Cop. They are differently constituted because Pen was and is made of Cop, while Cop is *not* made of Cop; a thing is not made of itself. They are differently made because Pen was made in 1909 according to a design by a Lithuanian sculptor named Victor David Brenner. Cop was made billions of years earlier, according to a design by God. Pen is rare owing to the appearance on it of Brenner's initials (VDB). Cop is common because it is a regular old piece of copper. It may perhaps be in a rare condition, the condition of composing a 1909-S VDB penny. But that doesn't make Cop itself rare, any more than being the one piece of copper on Mount Everest would. Pen is valuable because it is rare. A good 1909-S VDB penny is worth several thousand dollars. The amount of copper in Cop can be had for a few cents.

Metaphysicians (not all, but most) think the box contains two (or more) items, I suggested. I should have said that lots of metaphysicians think this. Some deny it: "one-thingers," they're called, or "monists." Monists do not deny that the box contains Pen, or that it contains Cop. It is just that Pen and Cop are the very same item. "They" are like water and $H_2O$, or Ludacris and Chris Bridges.

There are lots of phenomena monists can point to as supporting their view. It is not just that Pen and Cop are so exceedingly similar. If they are really distinct, why would any ordinary person say there's just one thing in the box? If they are really distinct, shouldn't it be possible to pull them apart and send them to their separate corners? Why can't we take Pen to Venice while leaving Cop at home in Colorado? Or, given that this is not possible — Pen and Cop are inseparable — shouldn't the

collector who purchases Pen be asked to pay again for Cop? And yet this never occurs. If we put Pen and Cop on the scale together, we find that they weigh 3.11 grams.
Shouldn't it be 6.22 grams, if there are really two of them?

Of course, there are lots of phenomena that pluralists can point to as well, as we
just saw. Pen is more valuable than Cop, Cop is much older than Pen, they are differently made, and so on. Another seeming difference between them is this. Imagine
that someone is interested in purchasing Cop; they want, let's say, to melt it down and
reshape it into a copper hatpin. Cop would still exist in the hatpin scenario. It would
merely have taken on a different shape. The same cannot be said of Pen, however.
A penny cannot assume the shape of a hat pin. To be melted down and thoroughly
reconfigured would mean the end of Pen's life.

It's a real conundrum, then. The data are genuinely equivocal; they point in two
directions at once. Whatever we ultimately decide about Pen and Cop, we willl have
some explaining to do; we will have to explain away the data appealed to by the other
side. This may sound discouraging, but it in fact suggests a way forward. Our decision ought to be guided by who can best explain away the other side's data. Which is
more puzzling: why we would have guessed "two," when the answer was really "one,"
or why we would have guessed "one," when the true answer was "two"?

To come finally to what I think, I think it is easier to explain why we would *under-
count* than why we would overcount. There is no huge mystery about how someone
could fail to pick up on a super-subtle distinction between otherwise indiscernible
objects (and the distinction between Pen and Cop is nothing if not super-subtle).
This is so unremarkable a failure that we even have a name for it; one falls into an
"understandable confusion."

If there's a similarly familiar term for the opposite mistake, of construing one thing
as two, I don't know what it is. And normally when this happens, there's a perfectly
simple explanation for it: Superman and Clark Kent present such different appearances
and we seem to encounter them on different occasions. Nothing like that is happening with Pen and Cop. They are encountered on the *same* occasions, and are virtually
indiscernible on those occasions. If the pluralist nevertheless sees a difference, that
suggests she is looking past the appearances rather than just acquiescing in them.

The pluralist's error would be an error of *c*ommission; those are harder to explain
away. But maybe not impossible. Sometimes a thing can present different appearances
on the *same* occasion, depending on the perspective we take.

Imagine we are watching a unicyclist from opposite sides of the street. You name
the wheel you see "Lefty," because you are looking from the rider's left; I name the
wheel I see "Righty." If you ask me which way Righty is turning, I will say it is turning
clockwise; if I ask you which way Lefty is turning, you will say it is turning coun-
terclockwise. What's more, both of these answers are correct! I wouldn't dream of
correcting you, nor you me. And yet, Righty and Lefty are one and the same wheel.

How can that be, you ask, when they are spinning in different directions? The one
unbreakable law of metaphysics is "the indiscernibility of identicals," also known as
Leibniz's Law:

(LL)    x is identical to y only if x and y have the same properties.

This seems to imply that Righty cannot be Lefty, after all; for only one of the two is turning clockwise. At this point, in fact, we might begin to wonder how anything can be identical to anything. I am not the Little Steve who used to live in my parents' house in Toronto, for he attended Sheppard Avenue West Public School, while I teach at MIT. Clark Kent is distinct from Superman, because he is a mild-mannered reporter, while Superman is the Caped Crusader.

Now, clearly something has gone wrong here. Lefty really is the same wheel as Righty, Clark Kent really is Superman, and I really am Little Steve. Does this mean there is something wrong with Leibniz's Law?

Not at all; it's just that we were misapplying it. We were assuming that the only reason things would be described differently is that they differ in their properties. But sometimes the different descriptions reflect just a difference in the perspective taken. Righty is turning clockwise *from my vantage point*; but then so is Lefty. Little Steve went to public school *in 1967*, but then so did the author of this article. Clark Kent is in fact a caped superhero; that's just not how we think of him when we think of him as Clark Kent. If these claims sound funny, it's because the two names conjure up alternative lines of sight, ones that it is difficult to maintain at the same time.

This gives the monist a possible comeback. Pen and Cop *seem* different; there is no denying that. But so they would, if the two names conjured up distinct perspectives on one and the same object. Let that putative object be *Pop*. Pop strikes us as rare, the monist says, when we think of it as a 1909-S VDB penny, common when we think of it as a piece of copper. She might add that it's difficult to think of it both ways at once, just as it's difficult to watch a wheel from both sides of the street. But it's the same item either way. Pluralists have been taken in by a trick of perspective.

The monist is not taking issue with Leibniz's Law; she agrees Pen and Cop are distinct *if* they differ in their properties. She simply thinks that their properties are exactly the same. This idea could work in principle, but it has to be handled with care. Otherwise what is to prevent us from saying, of any two things, that they only *seem* different because of our changing perspective on them? Suppose with the monist that Cop = Pen (= Pop). Still, these are *clearly* not identical to the box they (it?) came in.

Ah, but we can imagine a super-monist who holds (ridiculously) that Cop = Box. The monist protests that that can't be right, since Cop is *in* Box, while Box is not in Cop. But this might seem hypocritical. After all, the monist's claim that Cop = Pen was questioned on a similar basis: *that can't be right, since Cop constitutes Pen and not the other way around.* And the monist turned a deaf ear to that objection. To defend herself against the charge of hypocrisy, the monist needs to tell us how it's determined which apparent differences are to be explained away as mere tricks of perspective.

The paradigm here is Righty and Lefty. Offered the choice between "Righty turns clockwise, period" and "Righty turns clockwise when viewed from the right side of the street," the second sounds *better*, in the sense of closer to what we meant all along. Let's say, then, that

> we've got a merely apparent difference when "x is F from perspective P, and y is not F from perspective Q" sounds better — closer to what we meant all along — than "x is F, period, and y is not F, period."

(In the case of relational differences, substitute "x bears R to y" for "x is F," and "y does not bear R to x" for "y is not F.") This helps the monist in her battle with the super-monist, because when we compare

(i) "Pen is in Box from this perspective; however, Box is in Pen from that other one."

to

(ii) "Pen is in Box, period, and Box is not in Pen, period."

the first sounds absolutely ridiculous, while the second sounds absolutely fine. The question is, does it help the monist in her battle with the pluralist? That depends on which we prefer:

(i) "Cop constitutes Pen, judged from this perspective, while Pen does not constitute Cop, judged from that other perspective."

(ii) "Cop constitutes Pen, period, while Pen does not constitute Cop, period."

It appears that (i), far from clarifying the meaning of (ii), is in fact an obscure and unnecessary twist. To that extent, the monist loses her battle with the pluralist over whether Pen and Cop are "really" different or only apparently so.

We have shown, at most, that pluralism is the "intuitive" view — the one that best respects our intuitive judgments on these matters. This is the beginning of the debate, though, not the end. Some monists will insist that they *can* explain away pluralist intuitions. They think they possess a strategy superior to the one set out above. One can't reject this out of hand; every explaining-away strategy has to be considered on its own merits. I don't know, however, of a strategy that does markedly better than the one we have looked at.

A better monistic objection is this. Intuitions are not a good basis for theory-building, anyway. They are commonsensical, to be sure. But that doesn't mean they're reliable. Common sense is the distillate of ancient superstitions and prejudices. Everyday intuitions embody, in Bertrand Russell's phrase, "the metaphysics of the Stone Age." Is this really where we want to turn for guidance about the real, underlying nature of things?

No one has ever won a Nobel Prize for investigations into the commonsense view of pennies and pieces of copper, or missed out on one by making claims that did not fit well with ordinary ways of thinking. (Imagine complaining to Einstein that relativity theory conflicts with "what we all know" about simultaneity.) Nobel Prizes are won by people who pull the curtain aside to reveal truths we had no idea of — truths that, in the popular metaphor, reflect the way things are in themselves.

Let it be that physicists have no use for the distinctions postulated by pluralists. The question is what conclusion to draw from this. It would be one thing if the distinctions were physically untenable. You might indeed have worries on this score. Wouldn't Pen-and-Cop weigh 6.22 grams, rather than 3.11, if they were distinct items? "Distinct" can mean non-identical or it can mean disjoint (non-overlapping).

Pen and Cop would have to be distinct in the second, stronger sense for the prediction to be in order. (It would be "double-counting" to add in the weight of overlapping items twice.) The pluralist maintains only that they are weakly distinct, that is, there are two of them rather than one.

The question is, how much should it bother us if physicists do not postulate a distinction between Pen and Cop? I don't see why it should bother us at all. Neglecting to postulate a thing is not the same as postulating its *non*-existence! Consider an analogy. Wars, fingernails, and cupcakes do not loom large on the physicist's research agenda. This is not taken, even by them, to decide the issue of their reality. Take again Einstein. He was a pacifist. "Nothing will end war," he said, "unless the people themselves refuse to go to war." Why worry yourself about this, if wars are not, in your view, there in the first place? Philosophers can hitch their wagon to science, if they like. But they should not pretend that they are only following the scientist's lead here. Distinctions do not have to be physically fundamental to be fully real.

## TEST YOUR UNDERSTANDING

1. Explain and illustrate Leibniz's Law.

2. Give a fresh example to illustrate the debate over "monism" that Yablo discusses. Construct an explicit argument, based on your example, for the conclusion that two physical objects can be in the same place at the same time.

## NOTES AND QUESTIONS

1. Yablo argues that when we have a rare 1909 penny—PEN—made of a certain piece of copper—COP—then PEN and COP are not literally the same object, even though they exist in exactly the same location. The main arguments are applications of Leibniz's Law:

   > PEN is rare/valuable/less than 200 years old.
   > COP is *not* rare/valuable/less than 200 years old.
   > Therefore, PEN ≠ COP.

   But consider the following **argument** of the same form:

   > Clark Kent wears glasses.
   > Superman does not wear glasses.
   > Therefore, Clark Kent ≠ Superman.

   It's not hard to say where the second argument goes wrong. The argument is **valid**, but one of the premises is false. Superman *does* wear glasses sometimes—when he's dressed up as Clark Kent. The premise is superficially plausible, but as we think about it we can see that it's not strictly true.

Now consider a similar response to Yablo's arguments. Are we sure that COP isn't rare? For an object to be *rare* is for it to be an instance of a kind of which there are relatively few examples. And COP *is* an instance of such a kind: there are very few pieces of copper in the shape of a 1909-S VDB penny. Are we sure that COP is not *valuable*? The value of a thing depends on how much people are willing to pay for it given its condition, and people are willing to pay thousands of dollars for COP so long as it's in the shape of a 1909-S VDB penny. (It would be less valuable if it were melted down; but that doesn't mean that it isn't valuable as it is.)

*Exercise:* Review the arguments Yablo gives for distinguishing the penny from the copper and ask whether they can all be resisted in this way. What is the best argument of this form? Can it be resisted? If so, what does this imply for Yablo's position?

For a sampling of responses to the problem raised in Yablo's paper, see M. Rea, ed., *Material Constitution* (Rowman and Littlefield, 1997).

## Tim Maudlin (born 1958)

Maudlin, Professor of Philosophy at New York University, writes widely on the philosophy of physics and philosophical logic. His account of the relation between science and metaphysics is developed in *The Metaphysics within Physics* (Oxford University Press, 2007).

# SCIENCE AND METAPHYSICS

Metaphysicians seek a general account of what exists. So do scientists. One would therefore expect metaphysics to be continuous with science, and for scientific theories to illuminate metaphysical questions.

The history of ideas bears this out. Early Greeks such as Thales and Heraclitus and Empedocles[1] founded a tradition of inquiry that is both scientific and philosophical. Atomism began as speculation about the nature of the physical world[2] Descartes and Leibniz[3] made important contributions to both physics and metaphysics. Newton[4] described his discipline as "natural philosophy." Kant's theory of space and time[5] was

---

1. Thales (c. 624–546 BCE), Heraclitus (c. 535–475 BCE), and Empedocles (c. 490–430 BCE) were among the first philosophers to seek general principles for the explanation of natural phenomena.

2. Atomism, the view that matter is composed of minute indivisible particles, was first propounded by Leucipus and Democritus in the fifth century BCE.

3. René Descartes (1596–1650) and Gottfried Leibniz (1646–1716) drew no sharp line between their philosophical work and their seminal work in what we now call "physics."

4. Sir Isaac Newton (1643–1727), mathematician and physicist.

5. Immanuel Kant (1724–1804) developed a philosophical account of space and time according to which physical space must conform to the axioms of Euclidean geometry. This is at odds with Einstein's general theory of relativity (1915).

presented as a philosophical theory; but it also speaks to questions addressed by physicists, as shown by the fact that it conflicts directly with the theory of relativity. If philosophy and physics dealt with completely different topics, they could not possibly contradict each other.

Contemporary metaphysics, however, often seems to have lost contact with scientific practice. A widely discussed metaphysical problem is whether a statue is the same thing as the clay it is made of. Another is whether colors have a mind-independent existence in the world. Scientists have produced adequate accounts of both statues and colors insofar as they are objects of scientific inquiry. We know the chemical structure of clay, how it reacts to forces, whether it will retain or lose its shape in various possible circumstances. If none of this information settles whether a statue and its clay are the same or different, we can expect no further help from science. Or again: we have an adequate understanding of how various frequencies of light are reflected from surfaces of things, how the light is focused by the eye on the retina, how the rods and cones of the retina react, and how the input from the optic nerve is processed in the brain to produce the impression of colors.[6] If this scientific account of color vision does not determine whether there are mind-independent colors in the world, then the question seems to have no scientific content. The account as it stands is perfectly adequate for scientific purposes.

These particular examples suggest a dilemma. To the extent that scientific method is able to settle questions, the questions no longer seem to fall in the province of philosophy. And to the extent that science cannot settle them, it is unclear in what sense they are substantive questions about what exists rather than mere haggling over words. If there is a fact about whether a statue and its clay are one or two things, that fact seems to hinge solely on how we use the words "same" and "different" rather than on any features of the statue and clay themselves. Similarly, the dispute about colors no longer appears to be about what there is in the world — there is light that is reflected by objects and goes into eyes, causing neurons to fire — but whether any of the things in the world are properly identified as "colors." No matter how one settles that question, the scientific account of color vision will be unaffected. Science and metaphysics no longer seem to hold problems in common.

This impression, however, is not correct. Science itself raises profound metaphysical questions — questions about the fundamental nature of things — that it cannot settle by experiment or observation. And unlike the question about the statue and the clay, which has no impact on physics, these questions require an answer if we are to have any clear account of the nature of the physical world at all.

For example, one of the primary aims of scientific inquiry is to discover the laws of nature. As the word "discover" suggests, implicit in this quest is the assumption that such laws exist. Experiment and observation can help to determine the mathematical representation of these laws, but leave basic metaphysical questions about them untouched. For example: Do the laws of physics *direct* or *determine* how physical objects behave, or

---

6. This is not to say that we have solved the mind-body problem. But we know under what conditions people will judge colors to be the same or different. [Maudlin's note.]

are they rather only compact summaries of that behavior? In what sense are laws themselves "real"? Different accounts of the nature of law itself yield different answers to this fundamental question. An example can help illustrate the possibilities.

Consider the sequence of numbers 1, 2, 4, 8, 16. It is natural to ask whether there is a pattern to these numbers, and if so what rule is used to generate them. Such a rule would determine what the next number in the sequence should be. The obvious answer is that there is indeed a pattern, and the rule is that each number is twice the preceding. The next number in the sequence, according to this rule, is 32.

But the very same sequence can also be generated by different rules. For example, suppose we randomly put $n$ points on the circumference of a circle and then connect them with straight lines. Into how many parts will the circle be divided? The number of parts goes up in the sequence 1, 2, 4, 8, 16. But when we put the sixth point on the circle the number of parts is 31. For this particular rule, the sequence continues 31, 57, 99 rather than 32, 64, 128. So two different rules can generate the initial sequence 1, 2, 4, 8, 16. If we ask what pattern these numbers exhibit, one answer is that they exhibit many patterns, in that the sequence could have been generated by many different rules. If these particular numbers happen to have been randomly picked out of a hat, then there is no fact at all about which rule was "really" used to generate the pattern. Still, the sequence could be compactly described by several different rules.

We can use this example about the objective reality of a rule used to generate a pattern to understand a parallel debate about the laws of nature. There are regularities in the natural world: things happen in a predicable way. We spontaneously seek rules that generate these regularities. A *realist* about the laws of nature believes that there really is a rule that generates these patterns, a rule that also determines what would have happened in other possible circumstances. A *regularity theorist* has a different view: fundamentally, all that exists is the particular actual set of events. We would like to describe these events compactly, and it is convenient if we can find a simple rule to do so. But it is a mistake, according to this theory, to think that any such rule really plays a role in *producing* the regularity. If two different rules are equally good (i.e., both accurate and equally simple, etc.) at describing the sequence, as our two rules equally describe the sequence 1, 2, 4, 8, 16, then there is no further fact about which is the right one.

The realist and the regularity theorist disagree about what there is. They both accept the collection of actual events, but the realist believes in something more, something that is not an actual event but still plays a role in determining the actual events. So this is a metaphysical debate, a debate about what there is. It is not, however, a question that can be settled by experiment, since experiments only reveal a sequence of actual events. But we must take a stand on this question if we want to know what our scientific theories tell us about the physical world. Are there independently existing laws of nature that generate patterns of events, or only the patterns themselves, which might be described equally well by different rules?

Scientific practice, which includes recording particular events and seeking laws that would generate the observed patterns, is consistent with both realism and the regularity theory. So the debate about how to understand the laws may appear "merely philosophical" or "metaphysical" in the pejorative sense: of no interest to scientists. It may seem to be merely philosophical in another sense as well: although our short sequence of five numbers can be generated by two different simple rules, it is exceedingly implausible that a sequence of hundreds or millions of numbers could be generated by two equally simple but different rules. Since scientists must account for vast quantities of data, the possibility of equally simple laws that would generate that data appears remote. And indeed, arguments between realists and regularity theorists about the laws of nature are more philosophical than scientific. Still, these questions are absolutely central to understanding what science tells us about reality. When physicists tells us that the motions of stars and planets are governed by a *law* of gravitation, what exactly have they told us? Have they said that these motions exhibit regularities that are compactly described by a certain formula? Or have they identified a fact that *lies behind* the observed regularities and explains them? Since the scientists themselves rarely address this further question, science needs philosophy if we are to understand what it is trying to tell us about reality.

These questions about status of the laws of nature may strike the reader as somewhat ghostly. Even if laws have some objective existence beyond the pattern of particular events, they do not exist in the "concrete" way that atoms or planets or mountains do as located and tangible objects.

Can we find a debate about the structure of the physical world that concerns the concrete, material contents of the universe but still cannot be settled by straightforward experimental methods? Indeed we can: such debates occur even in the most familiar parts of physics.

Consider an atom of hydrogen. Scientific inquiry has determined beyond reasonable doubt that an atom of hydrogen consists in a nucleus with one proton, and an electron. But let's ask a more detailed question: what exactly *is* an electron? Or, even more precisely, what is the electron in an atom of hydrogen (in its ground state) *doing*?

Chemistry and physics have discovered much about electrons in atoms. In the ground state, the electron in hydrogen occupies something called a "1s orbital" around the nucleus. Electrons in hydrogen that have been excited into higher energy states, and electrons in larger atoms, can occupy other orbitals. Some electrons in the uranium atom, for example, occupy the more complicated 4f orbital. Chemistry and physics texts contain pictures of these various electron orbitals, such as those in figure 1. But let's ask a question that the physics texts ignore: just what is figure 1 supposed to be a picture *of*?

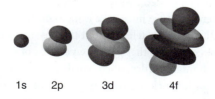

1s     2p     3d     4f

Figure 1  Electron orbitals.

In our humble hydrogen atom, the single electron is in the 1s orbital, whose picture looks like a sphere centered on the nucleus. A more detailed depiction of the orbitals shows them as having varying densities in different places, like a cloud. They do not have sharp edges, but rather fade away outside the illustrated regions. So it appears that physics has discovered something roughly spherical having to do with the electron in the hydrogen atom, and something rather oddly shaped having do with the 4f electrons in uranium. But again: what exactly are these the shapes *of*?

One might think that the term "orbital" answers our question: these are pictures not of electrons but of electron orbits. The old "planetary model" of the atom, which suggests that the electron orbits the nucleus just as the Earth orbits the Sun, would support this idea. If this were accurate, then we could think of these diagrams as analogous to *time-lapse photographs* of the electrons. A planetary orbit is not a physical thing that occupies space: it is rather the collection of locations that a planet occupies throughout a period of time. A simple photograph of our solar system would show the Earth in one particular place relative to the Sun. But a time-lapse photograph taken over the course of a year would indeed reveal the orbit of the Earth to be an ellipse. Perhaps figure 1 should be understood in this way.

Unfortunately, this simple explanation of the electron orbitals is almost certainly incorrect. There are different competing physical accounts of the nature of electrons and orbitals, but the planetary model is not among them. Despite the use of the term "orbital," everyone agrees that the electron in the ground state of hydrogen does not orbit.

We have focused on electron orbitals because physics texts contain diagrams of them. But there is a more fundamental question that arises before one can ask how an electron moves, namely, what is the shape of the electron to begin with?

The physicist John Stewart Bell (1928–1990) introduced a bit of terminology that is useful here. Bell used the term "beable" in order to distinguish those parts of a physical theory that represent real entities from those that are merely mathematical conveniences. "The beables of the theory are those elements which might correspond to elements of reality, to things which exist. Their existence does not depend on 'observation.' Indeed observation and observers must be made out of beables."[7] The beables must include the settings of switches and knobs on experimental equipment, the currents in coils, and the reading of instruments."[8] He further distinguished the *local* beables of a theory as "those which can be assigned to some bounded space-time region."[9] To ask after the local beables of a theory is to ask how, according to the theory, space is populated with real physical stuff. And Bell insisted that these local beables ought to be clearly defined at all scales: if the laboratory equipment has a definite location in space, and it is ultimately composed of electrons and protons and neutrons, then these too must have locations. A precise physical theory should tell us about the locations and shapes of these basic physical items.

---

7. J. S. Bell. *Speakable and Unspeakable in Quantum Mechanics,* 2nd ed. (Cambridge University Press, 2004), p. 174. [Maudlin's note.]

8. Ibid, p. 52. [Maudlin's note.]

9. Ibid, p. 53. [Maudlin's note.]

What sort of local beable is an electron in a hydrogen atom? *Where* exactly is it? Curiously, physics textbooks do not address this question. But without an answer, we have no chance of understanding what figure 1 depicts. Physicists have developed competing approaches to this question.

According to one theory, which we may call the *matter density ontology,* figure 1 is a direct representation of an electron in the ground state: the electron is "smeared out" in the shape of the orbital, with different densities that correspond to the density of the orbital. The electron in the ground state of hydrogen, then, forms a stable sphere surrounding the nucleus. The sphere itself does not change or move, and nothing "orbits."

This account of the electron may seem surprising. Electrons are typically spoken of as much smaller than atoms — indeed, they are typically spoken of as point-like objects, with a precise location and no spatial extent at all. Let us call this alternative account of the electron the *particle ontology.* According to the particle ontology, figure 1 cannot possibly represent an electron in a hydrogen atom at a particular moment. We will soon see what, according to this ontology, figure 1 could represent.

The matter density ontology and the particle ontology are physically different accounts of what an electron is. Since they present distinct understandings of the general nature of material objects, they also qualify as competing metaphysical descriptions. Can the experimental physicist tell which of these is correct?

No experimental consequences can be drawn solely from these ontologies. Any experiment requires interacting with the electron and seeing how a piece of apparatus reacts to that interaction. To make experimental predictions we need to know not only what the theory says an electron is, but also what the theory says about how the electron interacts and moves.

Both the matter density ontology and the particle ontology have been used to make sense of the mathematical formalism called *quantum mechanics.* We do not have the space to go into much detail here, but quantum mechanics employs a novel mathematical object for making predictions called the *wavefunction* of a system. What sort of physical entity — if any — the wavefunction represents is yet another important metaphysical question. Although we will picture the wavefunction as rather like a water wave in the discussion below, this is only possible because we are dealing with single particles. As soon as a system contains more than one particle, the wavefunction of the system cannot be located in physical space-time, and so cannot be regarded as a local beable.

Suppose we fire electrons through a very small hole toward a fluorescent screen. Quantum theory uses a law called *Schrödinger's equation* to specify how the wavefunction of the electrons behaves. The wavefunction spreads out in all directions from the hole like a water wave and eventually reaches the entire surface of the screen. We can define a "density" from the wavefunction, and more of this density will arrive in one part of the screen than another. But when we actually look at the screen, we do not find anything smeared out: we rather find distinct, precise spots, one for each electron shot at the screen. More of these spots accumulate where the density of the wavefunction is greater and fewer where it is less, but each electron appears to reach the screen intact and in a single location.

This phenomenon naturally suggests the particle ontology: the electrons are indeed very small entities that always have a precise location, and each one follows a particular path from the hole to the screen. The role of the wavefunction, on this theory, is to *guide* the particles, to determine where they go. There is a mathematically simple way to specify how the wavefunction guides electrons, and the resulting theory is called the *de–Broglie–Bohm theory*, or the *pilot-wave theory*, or sometimes *Bohmian mechanics* (after David Bohm (1917–1992), who rediscovered the theory some years after it had been discovered and then abandoned by Louis de Broglie (1892–1987). According to this theory, although the wavefunction "spreads out" in going from the hole to the screen, the electron itself does not: it follows a precise trajectory determined by its initial location and the wavefunction.[1]

Bohmian mechanics applied to the hydrogen atom implies that the electron in the atom is not only in a particular place (rather than spread out), but also at rest. So while figure 1 can provide a direct representation of an electron according to the matter density ontology, it cannot represent an electron according to the particle ontology. And since the electron in the ground state does not move according to Bohmian mechanics, figure 1 cannot represent the orbit of an electron either. Rather, what figure 1 represents in this theory is a composite picture of many different hydrogen atoms. If we could determine the exact position of each of the resting electrons, and plot all of these locations on a single piece of paper, we would get the sort of density represented in figure 1.

In the Bohmian picture, each of the electrons shot at the screen starts with a precise location and is guided to the screen by the wavefunction. More electrons get guided along paths where the density derived from the wavefunction is greater, so more spots appear on the screen in those places. Quantum theory only makes probabilistic predictions about where the spots will appear, and according to this theory those probabilities reflect limitations in our knowledge of the exact initial position of the electrons. If we knew exactly where each one started, we could calculate exactly where it would hit the screen.

The way the wavefunction guides the particle is even more striking when there are two holes for the electron to pass through rather than just one. In this case one sees *interference bands* after many particles have gone through: alternating light and dark stripes on the screen. This sort of interference is characteristic of waves, and can be seen for a water wave that passes through a pair of slits in a barrier. Interference of this sort arises because the wave goes through *both* slits, and the waves emanating from each slit interfere constructively or destructively when they reach the screen. But according to the Bohmian ontology, each individual particle goes through only *one* hole, not both. The interference bands form because of the way the wavefunction — which goes through both holes — guides the individual particles. Figure 2 shows various possible paths for particles in the two-slit experiment according to the pilot-wave theory. Notice how the trajectories get bunched up to form the alternating light and dark bands. Every individual electron would follow exactly one of these possible trajectories.

1. A nice presentation of the de–Broglie–Bohm theory can be found in the article "Bohmian Mechanics" by Sheldon Goldstein in the *Stanford Encyclopedia of Philosophy* (http://plato.stanford.edu/entries/qm-bohm/). [Maudlin's note.]

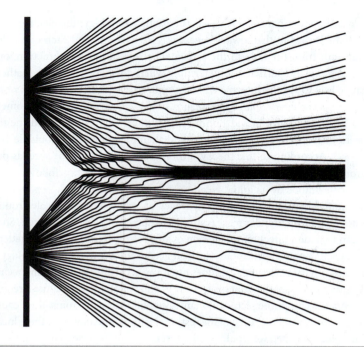

**Figure 2  Particle trajectories for the two-slit experiment.**

What is going on in this experiment according to the mass density ontology? According to that theory, the electron itself — each individual electron — is spread out in space in a way that corresponds to the density derived from the wavefunction. Furthermore, every electron starts out in exactly the same state, since they are all associated with exactly the same sort of initial wavefunction. As the electron travels from the hole toward the screen it becomes more and more diffuse, and when it finally reaches the screen it is spread out over the whole surface of the screen. If there are two holes, then on this picture the matter density of *each* electron goes through *both* holes, the matter density itself spreads out from both holes, and interference bands occur when the spreading matter from the holes overlaps, just as happens with water waves that go through both slits.

But if *the electron itself* has spread out, why do single, discrete, localized spots appear on the screen? At this point, the standard account postulates the "collapse of the wavefunction": a sudden change of the wavefunction from having a density that is spread out all over the screen to having almost all of its density in one location. According to the mass density ontology, when the wavefunction collapses, the matter of the electron suddenly gathers itself together in one place. This collapse is not a deterministic process: two electrons that start with identical wavefunctions can have those wavefunctions collapse in different ways. The probabilities derived from quantum theory, on this view, are founded not in our ignorance of any exact details about the initial state of the system but in a fundamental chanciness in nature. The probability for a collapse to occur in one place rather than another is proportional to the density of the pre-collapse wavefunction, so according to this theory, too, spots will tend to accumulate on the screen where the wavefunction is densest. As a result, the prediction for the distribution of spots will be the same for the matter density ontology as it is for the particle ontology.

The critical question that arises for this sort of theory is why and how the collapses occur. Standard quantum theory associates the collapses with "measurements" or "observations," but as Bell notes, these words are too vague to appear in the statement of any physical law.[2] Occasionally there have been attempts to tie these collapses to the presence of conscious observers, but "conscious observer" is also too vague to be of use in physics: Einstein once asked whether a mouse would be conscious enough to do the job. The most widely discussed *precise* theory with collapses is due to GianCarlo Ghirardi, Alberto Rimini, and Tulio Weber, and is hence known as the GRW theory. In this theory, each fundamental particle has a fixed probability per unit of time of suffering a wavefunction collapse. The GRW theory, using the mass density ontology, gives an account of how observers made out of electrons and protons and neutrons can interact with electrons in the experimental apparatus to yield the sorts of results we see in the laboratory.[3]

So we have two theories that fit the observed facts: according to the particle ontology each individual electron goes from the hole to the screen by a precise path, with different electrons taking different paths and making different spots: according to the GRW theory with the mass density ontology each electron spreads out in just the same way between the hole and the screen, finally gathering together in different places due to the indeterministic collapses happening in different ways. These are clearly quite different metaphysical accounts of the nature of the material world. These theories make very slightly different predictions about the outcomes of possible experiments, but no actual experiment has been able to decide between them, and it is questionable whether any experiment ever will.

Other possible local beables for the electron have been proposed. For example, the GRW dynamics for the wavefunction need not be allied with the mass density ontology. Bell added local beables to the GRW dynamics in a different way:

> It is in the wavefunction that we must find an image of the physical world, and in particular the arrangement of things in ordinary three-dimensional apace. But the wavefunction as a whole lives in a much bigger space, of 3N dimensions. It makes no sense to ask for the amplitude or phase or whatever of the wavefunction at a point in ordinary space. It has neither amplitude nor phase nor anything else until a multitude of points in ordinary three-dimensional space are specified. However, the GRW jumps (which are part of the wavefunction, not something else) are well localized in ordinary space. Indeed, each is centered on a particular

2. See "Against 'Measurement,'" in Bell, *Speakable and Unspeakable*, pp. 213–31. [Maudlin's note.]
3. A clear presentation of the GRW theory can be found in David Albert's *Quantum Mechanics and Experience* (Harvard University Press, 1992), although Albert does not discuss the local beables of the theory. [Maudlin's note.]

space-time point ($x$,t). So we can propose these events as the basis or the "local beables" of the theory. These are the mathematical counterparts in the theory to real events at definite places and times in the real world (as distinct from the many purely mathematical constructions that occur in the working out of physical theories, as distinct from things that may be real but not localized, and as distinct from the "observables" of other formulations of quantum mechanics, for which we have no use here.) A piece of matter is then a galaxy of such events. As a schematic psychophysical parallelism we can suppose that our personal experience is more or less directly of events in particular pieces of matter, our brains, which events are in turn correlated with events in our bodies as a whole, and they in turn with events in the outer world.[4]

This passage should put to rest any notion that metaphysicians and scientists are engaged in fundamentally different pursuits.

Bell's suggestion here differs from both the particle ontology and the mass density ontology. The idea has recently become known as the *flash ontology*. According to the flash ontology, there are no local beables at all — absolutely nothing in physical space — except when a GRW collapse (a "jump") occurs. And when a collapse occurs, there is nothing but a single point event in space-time, a momentary existence at a single point of space. According to the flash ontology, *absolutely nothing* passes in physical space between the hole and the screen. According to the flash ontology, throughout most of its history an electron or proton or neutron is nowhere at all, only "showing up" in space instantaneously when a collapse occurs. According to the flash ontology, there is almost nothing at all locally in space anywhere. But what little there is — the flashes associated with collapse events — would nonetheless present to us a macroscopic image of our familiar world, of tables and cats and screens with spots on them.

In fact, no experiment could decide between GRW with the matter density ontology and GRW with the flash ontology. They make exactly the same predictions about the macroscopically observable outcomes of laboratory experiments even though they give radically different accounts of the fundamental nature of the laboratory apparatus. No experiment can tell them apart even though according to the matter density ontology figure 1 is a direct depiction of the state of a single electron in a hydrogen atom at a given moment, whereas according to the flash ontology figure 1 could at best represent a very, very, very, very long time-lapse photograph (much longer than the history of our universe) of the flashes that occur very seldom in a single hydrogen atom.

As the work of the physicist Bell shows, science *is* metaphysics. It is a quest for a clear and comprehensive account of what exists. But the proprietary methods of science, namely observation and experiment, are not adequate to resolve even the most extreme metaphysical disagreements about the physical world. Since laboratory data are recorded macroscopically, experiments cannot distinguish between

---

4. Bell, *Speakable and Unspeakable*, p. 205. [Maudlin's note.]

theories that make the same macroscopic predictions, even if their accounts of microscopic reality are radically different. We initially worried that metaphysical questions such as the exact microscopic structure of matter, which clearly fall in the purview of science, will also be answered by straightforward scientific means. This worry was unfounded. Subtler arguments of a more philosophical nature must rather be used.

Although we have focused on the quantum-mechanical account of matter, the lessons of this example generalize. Science employs mathematical structures to make predictions, but the exact ontological implications of those structures may not be evident or uncontroversial. The mathematics of the theory of relativity, for example, is clear, but the exact account of space-time structure implicit in the theory is not. We have seen how the very same probabilistic predictions can be understood in terms of very different underlying laws and ontologies. Although empirical science is sometimes presented as built on a solid foundation of observation, and hence as capable of decisively settling questions of what exists by straightforward experimentation, this naïve picture underestimates the subtlety of metaphysical questions even in physics. The underdetermination of fundamental ontology (as well as fundamental law) by observational data is not just a theoretical possibility, as our example with the sequence of numbers suggests, but a practical reality. Far from having become permanently estranged, science and metaphysics are as intimately intertwined as ever.

## TEST YOUR UNDERSTANDING

1. Maudlin says "science itself raises profound metaphysical questions — questions about the fundamental nature of things — that it cannot settle by experiment or observation." Give two examples and explain why they are examples of this phenomenon.

2. Explain the contrast between the *mass density ontology* and the *particle ontology*.

## NOTES AND QUESTIONS

1. Maudlin distinguishes metaphysical disputes that are irrelevant to science — like the dispute over whether colors *really exist* — from metaphysical disputes that arise within science and which we must resolve if we are to understand what science is telling us about reality. As an example of the latter, he cites the debate over whether laws of nature such as the law of gravitation are *mere regularities*, neatly summarized by a mathematical formula, or instead real things that somehow *generate* or *explain* the regularities in nature. Maudlin concedes that this debate "cannot be settled by experiment or observation." How then can it be settled?

According to one widely accepted view, even though metaphysical questions cannot be settled directly by experiment, they can by methods that resemble those of science. In the natural sciences, we come to believe in new unobservable objects — molecules, atoms — when a theory that posits such things permits a detailed explanation of the phenomena we observe. In schematic form:

Certain phenomena are observed.
The best (simplest, most plausible) explanation for these phenomena is a theory according to which $F$s exist.
Therefore $F$s exist.

(See Gilbert Harman, "The Inference to the Best Explanation," on p. 182 of this anthology). Now consider an argument of this form for laws of nature, taken as real things that generate regularities. Let $R$ be a pervasive, regularity in nature: for example, the observed fact that two massive bodies always attract one another with a force proportional to their masses and inversely proportional to the square of their distance. Suppose $R$ is not a special case of some more fundamental regularity. Now consider a metaphysical theory according to which this fact is to be explained by the existence of a *law*, understood as a real thing. The metaphysician may then argue as follows, aping the scientist:

A certain regularity $R$ is observed.
The best explanation for this fact is that there exists a law of nature that entails $R$.
Therefore, probably, such a law exists.

Since nothing explains itself, this law cannot be the regularity or pattern $R$ itself. It must be something distinct from $R$ that somehow makes $R$ happen.

*Exercise:* Are there any important differences between this sort of argument and the scientific arguments for unobservable objects with which you are familiar? If so, do those differences undermine this argument?

# ANALYZING THE ARGUMENTS

1. *Nonexistent objects.* Following W. V. Quine, many contemporary philosophers (including van Inwagen and Rosen) see no significant difference between the following claims:

> *F*s exist.
>
> There are *F*s.
>
> There is at least one *F*.
>
> Some things are *F*.
>
> *F*s are real.

This view demystifies philosophical questions about existence. If a philosopher concedes that fictional characters or numbers exist *in some sense*, she may insist on asking a further question: But do such things *really* exist? Are they *really real*? The Quinean rejects such questions (unless they can be explained in other terms). Once we have conceded that *F*s exist, we have said everything there is to say about the being of *F*s. It remains only to say *what Fs are like*, and how they are related to other things.

But now consider the following little argument.

a. Ponce de León was looking for the Fountain of Youth.

b. Ponce de León was looking for *something*.

c. But the Fountain of Youth does not exist.

d. Therefore, there is something that does not exist.

For the Quinean, this last claim is a contradiction. It might just as well be put as follows:

d*    There exist some things that do not exist.

Some philosophers have concluded that being comes in (at least) two fundamentally different kinds, sometimes called *existence* and *subsistence*. The Fountain of Youth does not exist, but it must have some sort of being, otherwise it would make no sense to say that Ponce de León was looking for *it*.

If we accept this view, we need to say something about the difference between existence and subsistence. What are (merely) subsistent things like? Why can't we see them, touch them, etc.? If we reject this view, we need an account of where the argument goes wrong. Van Inwagen suggests a possibility. Perhaps the mistake lies in line (c). Perhaps the Fountain of Youth, like Mrs. Gamp, exists, but only as an abstract fictional entity. On this view, we have an easy explanation for why Ponce de León never found what he was looking for. Ponce de León was looking for the Fountain of Youth *in Florida*. But this is like looking for the number 27 in London. Abstract entities do not exist in space, so if you look for them in the spatial world you will not find them.

*Question:* Is this a satisfactory response to the problem posed by this argument?

2. *Leibniz's Law.* Many arguments in metaphysics rely on principles that are meant to apply, as a matter of absolute necessity, to absolutely everything. One of the most important examples is Leibniz's Law:

> *LL*: For any entities $X$ and $Y$, $X = Y$ iff $X$ and $Y$ share all of their properties at any given time.

This principle has two components:

> *The Indiscernibility of Identicals*: If $X = Y$, then $X$ and $Y$ share all of their properties at any given time.

> *The Identity of Indiscernibles:* If $X$ and $Y$ share all of their properties at any given time, then $X = Y$.

Yablo's arguments rely only on the first of these principles. (*Exercise:* Check this yourself to verify this reliance.) This principle is almost entirely uncontroversial, but consider the following putative counterexample:

> Mark Twain = Samuel Clemens.

> Mark Twain is famous.

> Samuel Clemens is not famous.

*Exercise:* Say how the defender of the Indiscernibility of Identicals should respond.

The Identity of Indiscernibles has been much more controversial. Consider the following apparent counterexample due to Max Black ("The Identity of Indiscernibles," *Mind* 61 [1952]).

> Imagine a universe that consists only in two iron spheres, $A$ and $B$, each one meter in diameter, orbiting one another endlessly at a distance of 100 kilometers. Suppose the spheres are qualitatively indiscernible: the same shape, size, color, composition, etc. These spheres are not literally identical: $A \neq B$. (There are two of them, after all.) But they have all of their properties in common. Each is round and made of iron; each is 100 km from an iron sphere, floating in otherwise empty space, etc.

*Exercise:* Say how the defender of the Identity of Indiscernibles might respond.

3. *Objects and properties.* All of the essays in this section speak freely both of objects and their properties. Any ontological theory that takes this way of speaking seriously must tell us what sort of thing a property is, and how properties are related to the objects that bear them. Consider, for example, *the property of weighing exactly one kilogram*. The instances of this property are physical objects, e.g., certain rocks. But what is the property itself like? It used to be common to say that properties of this sort exist only *in the mind*. But this implies that nothing had the property of *weighing one kilogram* before minds existed, and yet we know full well that there were rocks that weighed one kilogram before human beings were around to think about them. This suggests that properties, if they exist at all, must be *mind-independent* things.

According to one view—sometimes called *transcendent realism*—properties are abstract entities that do not exist in space. According to another view—sometimes called *immanent realism*—properties literally exist *in* their concrete instances. Both views are strange, and this has led some philosophers to suggest that properties do not exist at all: the rock may indeed weigh one kilogram; but there is no such thing as the *property of weighing one kilogram*. On this view—sometimes called *nominalism*—linguistic expressions like "... weighs one kilogram," though obviously meaningful, do not stand for *entities* of any kind. According to the nominalist, treating these expressions as names of entities leads us on a wild-goose chase, positing objects that do not exist and asking unanswerable questions about what they are like. For a discussion of this ancient debate, see D. M. Armstrong, *Universals: An Opinionated Introduction* (Westview Press, 1989).

4. When a philosopher presents an ontological theory that posits a certain category (type, token, property, law), she aims to provide a clear and explicit account of what it takes for a thing to belong to that category. Sometimes the category cannot be explained in more fundamental terms, so we must explain it by means of examples and informal hints. But this is always second best. One should always aim to provide explicit necessary and sufficient conditions for membership in a category.

*Exercise:* Consider the categories mentioned in the selections:

physical object, abstract entity, fictional character, type, property...

In each case, attempt to produce an explicit account:

*X* is a physical object (etc.) if and only if *X* is ...

*Note:* The philosophical terms you are analyzing may be vague, in which case any precise account will revise our understanding to some degree. That is to be expected. The aim of the exercise is not to conform exactly to ordinary usage or the usage of any particular philosopher. It is to provide a clear and useful account of the category—one that carves reality "at its joints," in Plato's phrase.

# 12

# What Is Personal Identity?

When you die, do you cease to exist? Is death The End? According to many religious traditions, no: bodily death is a mere transition to life in heaven or some other celestial realm, or perhaps to reincarnated life in another body on Earth. And even if death is the end at present, some think that future technology might defeat it. The futurist Ray Kurzweil, for instance, has predicted that by the mid-century we will be able to "upload our knowledge, memories and insights into a computer," allowing us to enjoy a kind of "virtual life" inside a computer-generated virtual reality, somewhat as depicted in the movie *The Matrix*.[1]

Keeping our eyes on the future, suppose that the *Star Trek* fiction of "teletransportation" (or "teleportation") becomes fact. If you step into the transporter, your brain and body are instantly scanned, and the resulting information is beamed to your chosen destination, say Mars. On Mars, the receiving station instantly reconstructs your brain and body from new matter, exactly as it was on Earth.[2] The process of scanning vaporizes the original brain and body, but why should you care? Here you are on Mars, stepping out of the receiving station with a new brain and body that are just as good as the original. If you're afraid of teletransportation, that's like being afraid of flying—you should just try and get over it.

Now consider another scenario. Imagine a perfect 3D photocopier, which can duplicate not just physical objects like stones and tables, but also animals. Would you like another dog, exactly like your beloved Fido, to keep him company? No problem: place Fido on top of the photocopier, press "copy," and a perfect replica of Fido comes out of a chute on the side, barking and wagging his tail. You could even photocopy yourself, getting a perfect "identical twin."

Photocopying yourself would lead to all sorts of practical problems, of course, but being photocopied doesn't harm you in any way. Suppose, though, that the 3D

1. See www.kurzweilai.net/live-forever-uploading-the-human-braincloser-than-you-think. Kurzweil's view in this essay is somewhat similar to Derek Parfit's (see his essay in this chapter).

2. This is not quite how teletransportation works in *Star Trek*, but for our philosophical purposes it's better to think of teletransportation this way.

photocopier develops a fault: it produces a copy just as before, but now destroys the original in the process of scanning it. Would you photocopy yourself now? Surely not — that would be suicide! Perhaps having a replica around after your death to write your term papers and fool your family into thinking you are still alive is some compensation, but nowhere near enough.

Hold on a moment: What's the difference between teletransportation and the malfunctioning 3D photocopier? The product of teletransportation emerges at a great distance from the transporter, unlike the product of 3D photocopying, which emerges right next to the photocopier, but there doesn't seem to be any other significant difference. If so, "teletransportation" is not a means of *transportation* at all. Instead, the misleadingly named "transporter" is a device that destroys the person who steps into it, and creates a replica at the receiving station. Instead of saying "Beam me up, Scotty," it would be more accurate to say "Kill me, Scotty." The person called "James T. Kirk" in this week's episode has not had an eventful life as a Starfleet captain after all! If he stepped out of the transporter chamber on the Starship *Enterprise* yesterday, he is only one day old.

The issues raised above all concern our *survival*: what sorts of changes can we undergo and survive? Can we survive the destruction of our bodies? And does it matter if we don't? These questions are discussed in philosophy under the heading of "personal identity," the topic of the selections that follow.

# Survival and Identity

Personal identity is a special case of a more general topic, the survival (or, as philosophers often say, the **persistence**) of objects over time. It is useful to have a little background in this more general topic when discussing the specific issue of our survival over time.

Commonsense opinion holds that inorganic things (e.g., rocks, laptops, and planets), and plants and animals, typically come into existence at some time, and cease to exist at a later time. For example, a certain cottage might come into existence when enough beams and bricks are assembled, and cease to exist a century later, when it is demolished to make room for a McMansion. A mighty oak tree began life as a tiny green shoot, or perhaps an acorn, and will end its existence when it is sawn into planks.

The cottage and the oak survive a variety of events throughout their careers. The house survives a flood, say. That is, the house existed before the flood and also existed after the flood. We can put this in terms of "identity": the house existed before the flood and something existed after the flood that was *identical* to the house.

Explaining what survival amounts to in terms of **identity** helps to clarify the notion, but it is potentially confusing. Suppose your house burns down and you build "an identical house" in its place. That is not a situation in which your house *survives*—it's a situation in which your house is destroyed and a replica is built in its place. Although your original house and the replica are "identical" in the sense that they are very *similar*, there is another sense in which they are *not* identical. There are *two* houses in the story, and in the "numerical" (or "strict") sense of "identity" *two* things are *never* identical. We have the strict or numerical sense in mind when we say that Lady Gaga and Stefani Germanotta are identical: we don't just mean that Gaga and Germanotta are *similar*, like your smartphone and your friend's smartphone. Gaga and Germanotta are not *two* at all. "They" are one and the same person, with two different names ("Lady Gaga" and "Stefani Germanotta"). Similarly, when we say "$3^2 = 9$," we are not saying that $3^2$ and 9 are *two* numbers. We are instead speaking about *one* number with *two* names ("$3^2$" and "9"). Survival, then, should be defined in terms of strict or numerical identity. When we ask whether you will survive some event, our question is best understood as follows: Will there be someone around after the event who is numerically identical to *you*?

Houses can survive repainting and the addition of a porch; they cannot survive being reduced to ashes or having their parts scattered all at once. But what if the parts of your house are scattered and replaced over a long period of time? Imagine that your ancient family home has been lovingly repaired over the years so that now not a single brick or beam from the original construction remains—the crumbling bricks and rotted beams have been slowly replaced with period bricks and beams from architectural salvage. Has the original house survived? Not an easy question, but it's unlikely to keep you up at night. Sentiment or pure theoretical curiosity aside, it doesn't much matter whether this is (numerically) identical to the house your grandfather lived in, as opposed to one just like it that is built on the same spot. But from your point of view, there is at least one thing whose genuine survival seems to matter a great deal, namely *you*. Suppose you are told that your body will undergo some ordeal—brain surgery or teletransportation or physical death and resurrection—and that there will be someone around afterwards who is like you in many ways. You might reasonably say: "That's all very well, but will that person be *me*?" A theory of personal identity is designed to shed light on this question.

# A "Criterion of Personal Identity"

The philosophical literature on personal identity is often structured around a search for a **"criterion of personal identity."** This is an idea that can be difficult to understand, so it is worth spending some effort getting clear about it.

Suppose someone—call him or her "Casey"—exists at a certain time, say on Monday. Consider someone who exists the following Friday—call him or her "Drew." What would *absolutely guarantee* that Casey and Drew are numerically identical? In other words: what are **sufficient conditions** for Casey and Drew to be numerically identical? For example, suppose that Casey looks a lot like Drew: same hair color, same eyes, etc. Does that guarantee that Casey = Drew?

Now let's ask a different question: what *must be the case*, given that Casey and Drew are numerically identical? In other words: what are **necessary conditions** for Casey and Drew to be numerically identical? For example, given that Casey = Drew, must it be the case that Casey and Drew look alike?

We can write out these two suggestions for, respectively, a necessary condition and a sufficient condition a little more formally. First, the sufficient condition:

It must be the case that: *if* Casey on Monday looks like Drew on Friday, then Casey, who exists on Monday = Drew, who exists on Friday.

Second, the necessary condition:

It must be the case that: Casey, who exists on Monday = Drew, who exists on Friday, *only if* Casey on Monday looks like Drew on Friday.

If we generalize these two theses to all people and all times, and combine them together, we get a thesis stating necessary *and* sufficient conditions for personal identity, which we can express as follows:

*The Physical Appearance Criterion*: It must be the case that: A, who exists at $t_1$ = B, who exists at $t_2$, *if and only if* A at $t_1$ physically resembles B at $t_2$.

This is a *criterion of personal identity*. In general, a criterion of personal identity is a statement of the following form (leaving the "It must be the case that" implicit, and abbreviating "if and only if" as "**iff**"):

A, who exists at $t_1$ = B, who exists at time $t_2$, iff _____.

The Physical Appearance Criterion has the right form, but it is obviously wrong. Sameness of appearance is not *sufficient* for numerical identity: "identical twins" may look alike, but they are not literally one and the same person. Nor is sameness of appearance *necessary* for numerical identity. Drew on Friday may look very different from Casey on Monday; but if Casey underwent cosmetic surgery on Tuesday, they may be the same person nonetheless.

The challenge is to fill in the blank so as to render the resulting statement *true*. Of course there's an easy way to do that. Just replace the blank with "A = B"! Although the resulting statement is undeniably true, it's of absolutely no help in answering questions about our survival—whether we can survive bodily death, for instance. What we want is an *informative* replacement for the blank—one that does not presuppose the notion of identity that we are trying to understand. We should not assume that there *is* such a replacement, but that has certainly not stopped philosophers from trying.

One suggestion that might occur to you on reading Descartes's *Meditation II* (see p. 356 of this anthology) is this:

> *The Soul Criterion*: A, who exists at $t_1$ = B, who exists at $t_2$, iff A's immaterial soul at $t_1$ = B's immaterial soul at $t_2$.

The Soul Criterion highlights something important about a criterion of personal identity. A criterion of personal identity is supposed to state *how things must be* if (and only if) A = B. It need not be an account of *how we tell* that A (say, someone we met last week) is identical to B (someone before us right now). We can often tell that A = B because A's physical appearance is the same as B's. But the corresponding criterion of identity, based on "same physical appearance" is mistaken. Conversely, it is no strike against the Soul Criterion that we do not find out that A = B by discovering that A has the same immaterial soul as B.

The Soul Criterion is defended in the selection by Richard Swinburne (who also emphasizes the point started in the previous paragraph). An obvious objection to the Soul Criterion is that the existence of immaterial souls is extremely controversial: if there are such things, you won't be learning about them in Psychology 101. In the selection by John Locke, you can find a subtler objection.

While the existence of our souls is debatable, the existence of our bodies seems plain enough. So a natural replacement for the Soul Criterion is this:

> *The Bodily Criterion*: A, who exists at $t_1$ = B, who exists at $t_2$, iff A's body at $t_1$ = B's body at $t_2$.

Is this right? Imagine that you swap brains with someone else—call him or her "Emerson." (The selection by Swinburne discusses an example of this sort.) Emerson's brain is transplanted into your body, and your brain is transplanted into Emerson's. Suppose that medical technology is sufficiently well advanced so that after the operation there are two people, alive and well: one with Emerson's old body, and one with yours. Where are *you*? Where your original body is, or where Emerson's body is?

Many people think that in cases of this sort, you follow your brain and not your body. So perhaps a better suggestion is:

> *The Brain Criterion*: A, who exists at $t_1$ = B, who exists at $t_2$, iff A's brain at $t_1$ = B's brain at $t_2$.

But again, there are objections. Imagine that you have some brain disease that will eventually destroy all your brain cells if left unchecked. Suppose that medical technology has advanced to the point where we can gradually replace each brain cell with a prosthetic artificial cell (a tiny device containing a silicon chip). At the end of the process, your brain has completely vanished, replaced by a prosthetic brain. If the artificial cells are sufficiently good, won't you still be around, thankful that the new technology has saved your life? But if you can survive the loss of your original brain, then the Brain Criterion is incorrect.

A quite different idea, proposed by Locke, is that our survival does not consist in the survival of a *thing*, like a soul, body, or brain, but rather in *psychological connections* across time. And Locke had a specific suggestion for what sorts of psychological connections are important, namely those provided by memory. "[A]s far as this consciousness can be extended backwards to any past action or thought," he writes in his *Essay Concerning Human Understanding*, "so far reaches the identity of that person." (See Locke's essay, p. 544 of this chapter, section 9.) This suggests the following:

> *The Memory Criterion*: A, who exists at $t_1$ = B, who exists at $t_2$, iff B can remember at $t_2$ (some of) the experiences of A at $t_1$.

The Memory Criterion implies that amnesia—perfect and total amnesia—amounts to death, and this may seem implausible. Faced with a grim choice between death and amnesia, a self-interested person might well choose amnesia as the lesser of two evils. "At least I'll still be around to start again," he might think. His friends and family might have a similar thought. And if this is right, then the Memory Criterion is unacceptable.

Many philosophers have tried to develop Locke's basic idea in a way that avoids this objection, among others. The most famous "Neo-Lockean" theory of personal identity comes from Derek Parfit, in his 1984 book *Reasons and Persons*. In the selection from that book given in this chapter, Parfit argues for a "Psychological Criterion" of personal identity—one that emphasizes various forms of psychological continuity over time, not just memory. But he also argues, astonishingly, that "personal identity is not what matters." According to Parfit, granted that the Psychological Criterion is correct, in some circumstances your survival should be of *no* concern to you! Compare the case in which the teletransporter functions properly and the case in which it malfunctions, creating *two* duplicates of the original body instead of one. In the latter case, Parfit argues, the original person does not survive. But from the point of view of the person himself, this case is not relevantly different from the case in which the machine works properly. In both cases, there is someone around after the event who is psychologically (though not physically) continuous with the original. The only difference is the *number* of such people. Parfit argues that no one should care very much about this numerical fact, and hence that no one should care very much about whether *he* will exist in the future. All that matters is that people will exist in the future who are psychologically continuous with us as we now are. Since genuine identity and psychological continuity normally go together in our experience, we confuse them and mistakenly think that personal identity is what matters when we worry about our own survival. According to Parfit, a correct account of the nature of personal identity can disabuse us of this error.

As the reader will have noticed, philosophical discussions of personal identity often invoke wild science fiction thought experiments. We are asked to imagine a bizarre scenario involving brain swapping or teletransportation and to consult our "intuitions" about survival and identity. It is not hard to see why this method should be necessary. A philosophical theory of personal identity is meant to apply to every *possible* case. So we must consider far-out cases in order to assess our theories. And yet the method has its pitfalls. The problem is not that our judgments about far-out cases are uncertain, though that may be so. As Bernard Williams argues in his essay in this chapter, the problem is that a single case may elicit different intuitions when presented in different ways. In particular, cases that appear to refute the "bodily" criterion of personal identity can be reformulated so as to confirm it. If this is right, then the method of cases must be deployed with care. It is not useless, but it is fallible. As all of the authors in this chapter stress, the method must be supplemented by reflection on the deepest question in the area: "Why exactly does it *matter* whether I survive, and what could personal identity be that it should matter in this way?"

## John Locke (1632–1704)

Locke was an English philosopher and medical doctor. His greatest work is *An Essay Concerning Human Understanding* (1689), which is about the limits of human knowledge. His *Two Treatises of Government* (1689) and *Letter Concerning Toleration* (1689), both published anonymously, made important contributions to political philosophy. The second *Treatise* gives a theory of legitimate government in terms of natural rights and the social contract. Locke's political views influenced the Founders of the United States, in particular Thomas Jefferson.

# OF IDENTITY AND DIVERSITY
## from *An Essay Concerning Human Understanding*

3. Let us suppose an atom . . . existing in a determined time and place; it is evident, that, considered in any instant of its existence, it is in that instant the same with itself. For, being at that instant what it is, and nothing else, it is the same, and so must continue as long as its existence is continued. In like manner, if two or more atoms be joined together into the same mass, every one of those atoms will be the same, by the foregoing rule: and whilst they exist united together, the mass, consisting of the same atoms, must be the same mass, or the same body, let the parts be ever so differently jumbled. But if one of these atoms be taken away, or one new one added, it is no longer the same mass or the same body. In the state of living creatures, their identity depends not on a mass of the same particles, but on something else. For in them the variation of great parcels of matter alters not the identity: an oak growing from a plant to a great tree, and then lopped, is still the same oak; and a colt grown up to a horse, sometimes fat, sometimes lean, is all the while the same

horse: though, in both these cases, there may be a manifest change of the parts; so that truly they are not either of them the same masses of matter, though they be truly one of them the same oak, and the other the same horse. The reason whereof is, that, in these two cases — a mass of matter and a living body — identity is not applied to the same thing.

4. We must therefore consider wherein an oak differs from a mass of matter, and that seems to me to be in this, that the one is only the cohesion of particles of matter any how united, the other such a disposition of them as constitutes the parts of an oak; and such an organization of those parts as is fit to receive and distribute nourishment, so as to continue and frame the wood, bark, and leaves, &c., of an oak, in which consists the vegetable life. That being then one plant which has such an organization of parts in one coherent body, partaking of one common life, it continues to be the same plant as long as it partakes of the same life, though that life be communicated to new particles of matter vitally united to the living plant, in a like continued organization conformable to that sort of plants.

5. The case is not so much different in *brutes*.[1] ... Something we have like this in machines, and may serve to illustrate it. For example, what is a watch? It is plain it is nothing but a fit organization or construction of parts to a certain end, which, when a sufficient force is added to it, it is capable to attain. If we would suppose this machine one continued body, all whose organized parts were repaired, increased, or diminished by a constant addition or separation of insensible parts, with one common life, we should have something very much like the body of an animal; with this difference, That, in an animal the fitness of the organization, and the motion wherein life consists, begin together, the motion coming from within; but in machines the force coming sensibly from without, is often away when the organ is in order, and well fitted to receive it.

6. This also shows wherein the identity of the same *man*[2] consists; viz. in nothing but a participation of the same continued life, by constantly fleeting particles of matter, in succession vitally united to the same organized body. He that shall place the identity of man in anything else ... will find it hard to make an embryo, one of years, mad and sober, the same man, by any supposition, that will not make it possible for Seth, Ismael, Socrates, Pilate, St. Austin, and Caesar Borgia, to be the same man.[3] For if the identity of soul alone makes the same man; and there be nothing in the nature of matter why the same individual spirit may not be united to different bodies, it will be possible that those men, living in distant ages, and of different tempers, may have been the same man: which way of speaking must be from a very strange

---

1. Non-human animals.

2. Locke distinguishes the claim that A and B are the same *man* — i.e., the same human animal — from the claim that A and B are the same *person*. The point of this paragraph is to insist that even if we possess immaterial souls, the fact that A and B share the same soul is not enough to make them one and the same man.

3. Seth and Ismael (Ishmael): characters in the biblical book of Genesis. Socrates: Greek philosopher (c. 469–399 BCE). (Pontius) Pilate: judge at the trial of Jesus. St. Austin (Augustine of Hippo): Christian theologian (354–430). Caesar Borgia: Italian politician and cardinal (1475/6–1507).

use of the word man, applied to an idea out of which body and shape are excluded. And that way of speaking would agree yet worse with the notions of those philosophers who allow of transmigration, and are of opinion that the souls of men may, for their miscarriages, be detruded[4] into the bodies of beasts, as fit habitations, with organs suited to the satisfaction of their brutal inclinations. But yet I think nobody, could he be sure that the soul of Heliogabalus[5] were in one of his hogs, would yet say that hog were a man or Heliogabalus.

8. An animal is a living organized body; and consequently the same animal, as we have observed, is the same continued life communicated to different particles of matter, as they happen successively to be united to that organized living body. And whatever is talked of other definitions, ingenious observation puts it past doubt, that the idea in our minds, of which the sound *man* in our mouths is the sign, is nothing else but of an animal of such a certain form. Since I think I may be confident, that, whoever should see a creature of his own shape or make, though it had no more reason all its life than a cat or a parrot, would call him still a man; or whoever should hear a cat or a parrot discourse, reason, and philosophize, would call or think it nothing but a cat or a parrot; and say, the one was a dull irrational man, and the other a very intelligent rational parrot.

9. This being premised, to find wherein *personal identity* consists, we must consider what *person* stands for; which, I think, is a thinking intelligent being, that has reason and reflection, and can consider itself as itself, the same thinking thing, in different times and places; which it does only by that consciousness which is inseparable from thinking: it being impossible for any one to perceive without perceiving that he does perceive. When we see, hear, smell, taste, feel, meditate, or will anything, we know that we do so. Thus it is always as to our present sensations and perceptions: and by this every one is to himself that which he calls *self*: it not being considered, in this case, whether the same self be continued in the same or divers substances. For, since consciousness always accompanies thinking, and it is that which makes every one to be what he calls *self*, and thereby distinguishes himself from all other thinking things, in this alone consists personal identity, i.e. the sameness of a rational being: and as far as this consciousness can be extended backwards to any past action or thought, so far reaches the identity of that *person*; it is the same *self* now it was then; and it is by the same *self* with this present one that now reflects on it, that that action was done.

10. But it is further inquired, whether it be the same identical substance.[6] This few would think they had reason to doubt of, if these perceptions, with their consciousness, always remained present in the mind. . . . But that which seems to make the difficulty is this, that this consciousness being interrupted always by forgetfulness, there being no moment of our lives wherein we have the whole train of all our past actions before

---

4. Pushed.

5. Roman emperor for the period 218–222.

6. An animal persists through time even though the matter that composes it may change completely. The cub that exists in 1985 may be the same animal as the mature lion that exists in 1995 even though they have no material parts in common. In Locke's terminology, this is a case in which we have a persisting *animal* but no persisting **substance**. The point of this paragraph is to insist that a *person* may similarly persist even though no substance persists in it.

our eyes in one view, but even the best memories losing the sight of one part whilst they are viewing another; and we sometimes, and that the greatest part of our lives, not reflecting on our past selves, being intent on our present thoughts, and in sound sleep having no thoughts at all, or at least none with that consciousness which remarks our waking thoughts; I say, in all these cases, our consciousness being interrupted, and we losing the sight of our past selves, doubts are raised whether we are the same thinking thing, i.e. the same substance or no. Which, however reasonable or unreasonable, concerns not *personal identity* at all. The question being what makes the same *person*; and not whether it be the same identical substance, which always thinks in the same person: different substances, by the same consciousness (where they do partake in it) being united into one person, as well as different bodies by the same life are united into one animal, whose identity is preserved in that change of substances by the unity of one continued life. For, it being the same consciousness that makes a man be himself to himself, personal identity depends on that only, whether it be annexed solely to one individual substance, or can be continued in a succession of several substances. For as far as any intelligent being can repeat the idea of any past action with the same consciousness it had of it at first, and with the same consciousness it has of any present action; so far it is the same personal self. For it is by the consciousness it has of its present thoughts and actions, that it is self to itself now, and so will be the same self, as far as the same consciousness can extend to actions past or to come, and would be by distance of time, or change of substance, no more two persons, than a man be two men by wearing other clothes to-day than he did yesterday, with a long or a short sleep between: the same consciousness uniting those distant actions into the same person, whatever substances contributed to their production.

11. That this is so, we have some kind of evidence in our very bodies, all whose particles, whilst vitally united to this same thinking conscious self, so that we feel when they are touched, and are affected by, and conscious of good or harm that happens to them, as a part of ourselves; i.e. of our thinking conscious self. Thus, the limbs of his body are to every one a part of Himself; he sympathizes and is concerned for them. Cut off a hand, and thereby separate it from that consciousness he had of its heat, cold, and other affections, and it is then no longer a part of that which is himself, any more than the remotest part of matter. Thus, we see the substance whereof personal self consisted at one time may be varied at another, without the change of personal identity; there being no question about the same person, though the limbs which but now were a part of it, be cut off.

12. But the question is, Whether if the same substance which thinks be changed, it can be the same person; or, remaining the same, it can be different persons? And to this I answer: First, This can be no question at all to those who place thought in a purely material animal constitution, void of an immaterial substance.[7] For, whether their supposition be true or no, it is plain they conceive personal identity preserved

---

7. Locke alludes to a dispute over whether the thing that thinks in us is material or immaterial. Locke takes the latter view to be "more probable" (*Essay* II, xxvii.25) but insists that no matter how this dispute is resolved, A and B may be the same person even though the substance that thinks in A is distinct from the substance that thinks in B.

in something else than identity of substance; as animal identity is preserved in identity of life, and not of substance. And therefore those who place thinking in an immaterial substance only, before they can come to deal with these men, must show
why personal identity cannot be preserved in the change of immaterial substances,
or variety of particular immaterial substances, as well as animal identity is preserved
in the change of material substances.

13. As to the first part of the question, Whether, if the same thinking substance
(supposing immaterial substances only to think) be changed, it can be the same person? I answer, that cannot be resolved but by those who know what kind of substances they are that do think; and whether the consciousness of past actions can
be transferred from one thinking substance to another. . . . But yet, . . . , it must be
allowed, that, if the same consciousness can be transferred from one thinking substance to another, it will be possible that two thinking substances may make but one
person. For the same consciousness being preserved, whether in the same or different substances, the personal identity is preserved.

14. As to the second part of the question, Whether the same immaterial substance
remaining, there may be two distinct persons; which question seems to me to be
built on this, Whether the same immaterial being, being conscious of the action of
its past duration, may be wholly stripped of all the consciousness of its past existence,
and lose it beyond the power of ever retrieving it again: and so as it were beginning
a new account from a new period, have a consciousness that cannot reach beyond
this new state. . . . Suppose a Christian Platonist or a Pythagorean[8] should, upon God's
having ended all his works of creation the seventh day, think his soul hath existed
ever since; and should imagine it has revolved in several human bodies; as I once met
with one, who was persuaded his had been the soul of Socrates (how reasonably I will
not dispute); . . . would any one say, that he, being not conscious of any of Socrates's
actions or thoughts, could be the same person with Socrates? Let any one reflect upon
himself, and conclude that he has in himself an immaterial spirit, which is that which
thinks in him, and, in the constant change of his body keeps him the same: and is that
which he calls himself: let him also suppose it to be the same soul that was in Nestor
or Thersites,[9] at the siege of Troy, (for souls being, as far as we know anything of them,
in their nature indifferent to any parcel of matter, the supposition has no apparent
absurdity in it . . .): but he now having no consciousness of any of the actions either
of Nestor or Thersites, does or can he conceive himself the same person with either
of them? Can he be concerned in either of their actions? Attribute them to himself, or
think them his own, more than the actions of any other men that ever existed? So that
this consciousness, not reaching to any of the actions of either of those men, he is no
more one self with either of them than if the soul or immaterial spirit that now informs
him had been created, and began to exist, when it began to inform his present body;
though it were never so true, that the same spirit that informed Nestor's or Thersites'

8. The followers of Pythagoras (6th century BCE) were said to believe in the transmigration of souls, according to which a single thinking soul can, at death, move from one body to another. Many Christian
theologians follow Plato in endorsing the immortality and immateriality of the soul; however, the Church
has consistently rejected the Pythagorean doctrine of transmigration.

9. Greek mythological figures, both said by Homer to have participated in the siege of Troy.

body were numerically the same that now informs his. For this would no more make him the same person with Nestor, than if some of the particles of matter that were once a part of Nestor were now a part of this man; the same immaterial substance, without the same consciousness, no more making the same person, by being united to any body, than the same particle of matter, without consciousness, united to any body, makes the same person. But let him once find himself conscious of any of the actions of Nestor, he then finds himself the same person with Nestor.

16. [Thus] it is plain, consciousness, as far as ever it can be extended, should it be to ages past, unites existences and actions very remote in time into the same person, as well as it does the existences and actions of the immediately preceding moment: so that whatever has the consciousness of present and past actions, is the same person to whom they both belong. Had I the same consciousness that I saw the ark and Noah's flood, as that I saw an overflowing of the Thames[1] last winter, or as that I write now, I could no more doubt that I who write this now, that saw the Thames overflowed last winter, and that viewed the flood at the general deluge, was the same self, place that self in what substance you please, than that I who write this am the same myself now whilst I write (whether I consist of all the same substance, material or immaterial, or no) that I was yesterday. For as to this point of being the same self, it matters not whether this present self be made up of the same or other substances, I being as much concerned, and as justly accountable for any action that was done a thousand years since, appropriated to me now by this self-consciousness, as I am for what I did the last moment.

19. This may show us wherein personal identity consists: not in the identity of substance, but, as I have said, in the identity of consciousness, wherein if Socrates and the present mayor of Quinborough agree, they are the same person: if the same Socrates waking and sleeping do not partake of the same consciousness, Socrates waking and sleeping is not the same person. And to punish Socrates waking for what sleeping Socrates thought, and waking Socrates was never conscious of, would be no more of right, than to punish one twin for what his brother-twin did, whereof he knew nothing, because their outsides were so like, that they could not be distinguished; for such twins have been seen.

20. But yet possibly it will still be objected, suppose I wholly lose the memory of some parts of my life, beyond a possibility of retrieving them, so that perhaps I shall never be conscious of them again; yet am I not the same person that did those actions, had those thoughts that I once was conscious of, though I have now forgot them? To which I answer, that we must here take notice what the word *I* is applied to; which, in this case, is the man only. And the same man being presumed to be the same person, *I* is easily here supposed to stand also for the same person. But if it be possible for the same man to have distinct incommunicable consciousness at different times, it is past doubt the same man would at different times make different persons; which, we see, is the sense of mankind in the solemnest declaration of their opinions, human laws not punishing the mad man for the sober man's actions, nor the sober man for what the mad man did, thereby making them two persons: which is somewhat explained by our

---

1. River running through London.

way of speaking in English when we say such an one is "not himself," or is "beside himself"; in which phrases it is insinuated, as if those who now, or at least first used them, thought that self was changed; the selfsame person was no longer in that man.

22. But is not a man drunk and sober the same person? why else is he punished for the fact he commits when drunk, though he be never afterwards conscious of it? Just as much the same person as a man that walks, and does other things in his sleep, is the same person, and is answerable for any mischief he shall do in it. Human laws punish both, with a justice suitable to their way of knowledge; because, in these cases, they cannot distinguish certainly what is real, what counterfeit: and so the ignorance in drunkenness or sleep is not admitted as a plea. For, though punishment be annexed to personality, and personality to consciousness, and the drunkard perhaps be not conscious of what he did, yet human judicatures justly punish him; because the fact is proved against him, but want of consciousness cannot be proved for him. But in the Great Day,[2] wherein the secrets of all hearts shall be laid open, it may be reasonable to think, no one shall be made to answer for what he knows nothing of, but shall receive his doom,[3] his conscience accusing or excusing him.

26. *Person*, as I take it, is the name for this self. Wherever a man finds what he calls himself, there, I think, another may say is the same person. It is a forensic[4] term, appropriating actions and their merit; and so belongs only to intelligent agents, capable of a law, and happiness, and misery. This personality extends itself beyond present existence to what is past, only by consciousness, whereby it becomes concerned and accountable; owns and imputes to itself past actions, just upon the same ground and for the same reason as it does the present. All which is founded in a concern for happiness, the unavoidable concomitant of consciousness; that which is conscious of pleasure and pain, desiring that that self that is conscious should be happy. And therefore whatever past actions it cannot reconcile or appropriate to that present self by consciousness, it can be no more concerned in than if they had never been done: and to receive pleasure or pain, i.e. reward or punishment, on the account of any such action, is all one as to be made happy or miserable in its first being, without any demerit at all. For, supposing a man punished now for what he had done in another life, whereof he could be made to have no consciousness at all, what difference is there between that punishment and being created miserable? And therefore, conformable to this, the Apostle[5] tells us, that, at the Great Day, when every one shall "receive according to his doings, the secrets of all hearts shall be laid open." The sentence shall be justified by the consciousness all persons shall have, that they themselves, in what bodies soever they appear, or what substances soever that consciousness adheres to, are the same that committed those actions, and deserve that punishment for them.

2. The biblical day of judgment.

3. Judgment.

4. Pertaining to the law.

5. Paul the Apostle (c. 5–c. 67).

## TEST YOUR UNDERSTANDING

1. Suppose Charlie (a young colt in 1650) and Harry (an old horse in 1685) are the same horse. Explain why Locke thinks this shows that Charlie is not a "mass of matter."

2. Suppose person A (a teenager in 1650) and person B (middle-aged in 1685) are the same person. According to Locke, do A and B have to be the same *man*? ("Man" is used by Locke in the generic sense and may refer to either a man or a woman.) Explain your answer.

3. Suppose person A has an immaterial soul, and A gets attacked and eaten by bears. A's body is destroyed, but A's immaterial soul lives on. According to Locke, is it certain that person A has survived the bear attack? Explain your answer.

4. A man who commits a crime when drunk is punished for what he did when he sobers up. According to Locke, is the sober man the same person as the drunk man? Why does Locke think that the sober man is "justly" punished?

## NOTES AND QUESTIONS

1. In section 9, Locke gives an account of what personal identity consists in. Later, he argues that immaterial souls are irrelevant to personal identity. Explain Locke's account of personal identity and how he uses it to argue that immaterial souls are irrelevant. Is Locke's account of personal identity plausible?

2. In section 10 Locke claims that because consciousness is interrupted by sleep, you cannot be sure that any immaterial soul you had last night is the same as the one you have today: perhaps yesterday's soul has been switched out and replaced by today's. Here's a third-person version of his claim: you cannot be sure that any immaterial soul *I* had last night is the same as the one I have today. Use these claims to formulate an argument against the view that sameness of person consists in sameness of immaterial soul. Is the argument you have formulated persuasive?

3. All modern discussions of personal identity are in effect reactions to Locke's views in this chapter from his *Essay Concerning Human Understanding* (1689). (The chapter does not appear in the first edition of the *Essay*, but was added to the second edition.) As you will have discovered from reading the selection, Locke's views on personal identity are not especially clear. For discussion, see chapter 2 of Harold Noonan, *Personal Identity* (Routledge, 2003) and Galen Strawson, *Locke on Personal Identity: Consciousness and Concernment*, rev. ed. (Princeton University Press, 2014).

## Richard Swinburne (born 1934)

Swinburne is Emeritus Nolloth Professor of the Philosophy of the Christian Religion at the University of Oxford. His books include *The Coherence of Theism* (rev. ed. 1993), *Providence and the Problem of Evil* (1998), and most recently, *Mind, Brain, and Free Will* (2013).

# THE DUALIST THEORY
### from *Personal Identity*

There seems no contradiction in the supposition that a person might acquire a totally new body (including a completely new brain) — as many religious accounts of life after death claim that men do. To say that this body, sitting at the desk in my room, is my body is to say two things. First it is to say that I can move parts of this body (arms, legs, etc.), just like that, without having to do any other intentional action and that I can make a difference to other physical objects only by moving parts of this body. By holding the door handle and turning my hand, I open the door. By bending my leg and stretching it I kick the ball and make it move into the goal. But I do not turn my hand or bend my leg by doing some other intentional action; I just do these things. Secondly, it is to say that my knowledge of states of the world outside this body is derived from their effects on this body — I learn about the positions of physical objects by seeing them, and seeing them involves light rays reflected by them impinging on my eyes and setting up nervous impulses in my optic nerve. My body is the vehicle of my agency in the world and my knowledge of the world. But then is it not coherent to suppose that I might suddenly find that my present body no longer served this function, that I could no longer acquire information through these eyes or move these limbs, but might discover that another body served the same function? I might find myself moving other limbs and acquiring information through other eyes. Then I would have a totally new body. If that body, like my last body, was an occupant of the Earth, then we would have a case of reincarnation, as Eastern religions have understood that. If that body was an occupant of some distant planet or an environment which did not belong to the same space as our world, then we would have a case of resurrection as on the whole Western religions (Christianity, Judaism and Islam) have understood that.

This suggestion of a man acquiring a new body (with brain) may be more plausible, to someone who has difficulty in grasping it, by supposing the event to occur gradually. Suppose that one morning a man wakes up to find himself unable to control the right side of his body, including his right arm and leg. When he tries to move the right-side parts of his body, he finds that the corresponding left-side parts of his body move; and when he tries to move the left-side parts, the corresponding right-side parts of his wife's body move. His knowledge of the world comes to depend on stimuli to his left side and to his wife's right side (e.g., light rays stimulating his left eye and his wife's right eye). The bodies fuse to some extent physiologically as with Siamese twins, while the man's wife loses control of her right side. The focus of the man's control of and knowledge of the world is shifting. One may suppose the process completed as the man's control is shifted to the wife's body, while the wife loses control of it.

Equally coherent, I suggest, is the supposition that a person might become disembodied. A person has a body if there is one particular chunk of matter through which he has to operate on and learn about the world. But suppose that he finds himself able to operate on and learn about the world within some small finite region, without having to use one particular chunk of matter for this purpose. He might find himself with knowledge of the position of objects in a room (perhaps by having visual sensations, perhaps not), and able to move such objects just like that, in the ways in which we know about the positions of our limbs and can move them. But the room would not be, as it were, the person's body; for we may suppose that simply by choosing to do so he can gradually shift the focus of his knowledge and control, e.g., to the next room. The person would be in no way limited to operating and learning through one particular chunk of matter. Hence we may term him disembodied. The supposition that a person might become disembodied also seems coherent.

I have been arguing so far that it is coherent to suppose that a person could continue to exist with an entirely new body or with no body at all. . . . Could a person continue to exist without any apparent memory of his previous doings? Quite clearly, we do allow not merely the logical possibility, but the frequent actuality of amnesia — a person forgetting all or certain stretches of his past life. Despite Locke, many a person does forget much of what he has done. But, of course, we normally only suppose this to happen in cases where there is the normal bodily and brain continuity. Our grounds for supposing that a person forgets what he has done are that the evidence of bodily and brain continuity suggests that he was the previous person who did certain things, which he now cannot remember having done. And in the absence of both of the main kinds of evidence for personal identity, we would not be justified in supposing that personal identity held. . . . For that reason I cannot describe a case where we would have good reason to suppose that $P_2$ was identical with $P_1$, even though there was neither brain continuity nor memory continuity between them. However, only given verificationist dogma[1] is there any reason to suppose that the only things which are true are those of whose truth we can have evidence. . . . We can make sense of states of affairs being true, of which we can have no evidence that they are true. And among them surely is the supposition that the person who acquires another body loses not merely control of the old one, but memories of what he did with its aid. . . .

Those who hope to survive their death, despite the destruction of their body, will not necessarily be disturbed if they come to believe that they will then have no memory of their past life on Earth; they may just want to survive and have no interest in continuing to recall life on Earth. Again, apparently, there seems to be no contradiction involved in their belief. . . .

Not merely is it not logically necessary that a person have a body made of certain matter, or have certain apparent memories, if he is to be the person which he is; it is not even necessitated by laws of nature. For let us assume that natural laws dictated the course of evolution and the emergence of consciousness. In 4000 million BC the Earth was a cooling globe of inanimate atoms. Natural laws then, we assume, dictated how this globe would evolve, and so which arrangements of matter will be the bodies of conscious men, and just how apparent memories of conscious men depend on their brain states. My point now is that what natural laws in no way determine is which

---

1. Verificationism is the view that a statement is meaningful — and therefore capable of being true — only if it can in principle be supported by evidence. Swinburne argues against verificationism in Sydney Shoemaker and Richard Swinburne, *Personal Identity* (Blackwell, 1984), chapter 3.

animate body is yours and which is mine. Just the same arrangement of matter and just the same laws could have given to me the body (and so the apparent memories) which are now yours, and to you the body (and so, the apparent memories) which are now mine. It needs either God or chance to allocate bodies to persons; the most that natural laws determine is that bodies of a certain construction are the bodies of some person or other, who in consequence of this construction have certain apparent memories. Since the body which is presently yours (together with the associated apparent memories) could have been mine (logic and even natural laws allow), that shows that none of the matter of which my body is presently made (nor the apparent memories) is essential to my being the person I am. That must be determined by something else. . . .

I could just leave my positive theory at that — that personal identity is unanalyzable.[2] But it will, I hope, be useful to express it in another way, to bring out more clearly what it involves and to connect it with another whole tradition of philosophical thought.

[According to] Aristotle's account of the identity of substances: . . . a substance at one time is the same substance as a substance at an earlier time if and only if the later substance has the same form as, and continuity of matter . . . with, the earlier substance.[3] On this view a person is the same person as an earlier person if he has the same form as the earlier person (i.e., both are persons) and has continuity of matter with him (i.e., has the same body).

Certainly, to be the same person as an earlier person, a later person has to have the same form — i.e., has to be a person. If my arguments for the logical possibility of there being disembodied persons are correct, then the essential characteristics of a person constitute a narrower set than those which Aristotle would have included. My arguments suggest that all that a person needs to be a person are certain mental capacities — for having conscious experiences (e.g., thoughts or sensations) and performing intentional actions. Thought-experiments of the kind described earlier allow that a person might lose his body, but they describe his continuing to have conscious experiences and his performing or being able to perform intentional actions, i.e., to do actions which he means to do, bring about effects for some purpose.

Yet if my arguments are correct, showing that two persons can be the same, even if there is no continuity between their bodily matter, we must say that in the form stated the Aristotelian account of identity applies only to inanimate objects and plants and has no application to personal identity. We are then faced with a choice either of saying that the criteria of personal identity are different from those for other substances, or of trying to give a more general account than Aristotle's of the identity of substances which would cover both persons and other substances. It is possible to widen the Aristotelian account

2. To "**analyze**" personal identity would be to provide a general account of the following form:

$P_1$ is the same person as $P_2$ if and only if $P_1$ stands in relation R to $P_2$,

where the relation R is specified without using the word "person" or any synonym thereof. Swinburne maintains that no such account is possible.

3. According to Aristotle's theory as Swinburne understands it, each thing belongs to a specific kind — person, dog, oak — and the form of a thing is the set of properties and capacities that make it a thing of that kind.

so that we can do the latter. We have only to say that two substances are the same if and only if they have the same form and there is continuity of the stuff of which they are made, and allow that there may be kinds of stuff other than matter. I will call this account of substance identity the wider Aristotelian account. We may say that there is a stuff of another kind, immaterial stuff, and that persons are made of both normal bodily matter and this immaterial stuff but that it is the continuity of the latter which provides that continuity of stuff which is necessary for the identity of the person over time.

This is in essence the way of expressing the simple theory which is adopted by those who say that a person living on Earth consists of two parts — a material part, the body; and an immaterial part, the soul. The soul is the essential part of a person, and it is its continuing which constitutes the continuing of the person. While on Earth, the soul is linked to a body (by the body being the vehicle of the person's knowledge of and action upon the physical world). But, it is logically possible, the soul can be separated from the body and exist in a disembodied state (in the way described earlier) or linked to a new body. This way of expressing things has been used in many religious traditions down the centuries, for it is a very natural way of expressing what is involved in being a person once you allow that a person can survive the death of his body. Classical philosophical statements of it are to be found in Plato and, above all, in Descartes. I shall call this view classical dualism. . . .

The arguments which Descartes gave in support of his account of persons are among the arguments which I have given in favour of the simple theory and since they take for granted the wider Aristotelian framework, they yield classical dualism as a consequence. Thus Descartes argues:

> Just because I know certainly that I exist, and that meanwhile I do not remark that any other thing necessarily pertains to my nature or essence, excepting that I am a thinking thing, I rightly conclude that my essence consists solely in the fact that I am a thinking thing. And although possibly . . . I possess a body with which I am very intimately conjoined, yet because, on the one side, I have a clear and distinct idea of myself inasmuch as I am only a thinking and unextended thing, and as, on the other, I possess a distinct idea of body, inasmuch as it is only an extended and unthinking thing, it is certain that this I [that is to say, my soul by which I am what I am], is entirely and absolutely distinct from my body, and can exist without it. [Descartes, sixth Meditation].

Descartes is here saying that he can describe a thought-experiment in which he continues to exist although his body does not. I have also described such a thought-experiment and have argued, as Descartes in effect does, that it follows that his body is not logically necessary for his existence, that it is not an essential part of himself. Descartes can go on "thinking" (i.e., being conscious) and so existing without it. Now if we take the wider Aristotelian framework for granted that the continuing of a substance involves the continuing of some of the stuff of which it is made, and since the continuing existence of Descartes does not involve the continuing of bodily matter, it follows that there must now be as part of Descartes some other stuff, which he calls his soul, which forms the essential part of Descartes. . . .

So Descartes argues, and his argument seems to me correct—given the wider Aristotelian framework. If we are prepared to say that substances can be the same, even though none of the stuff (in a wide sense) of which they are made is the same, the conclusion does not follow. The wider Aristotelian framework provides a partial definition of "stuff" rather than a factual truth.

To say that a person has an immaterial soul is not to say that if you examine him closely enough under an acute enough microscope you will find some very rarefied constituent which has eluded the power of ordinary microscopes. It is just a way of expressing the point within a traditional framework of thought that persons can—it is logically possible—continue, when their bodies do not. It does, however, seem a very natural way of expressing the point—especially once we allow that persons can become disembodied. . . .

It does not follow from all this that a person's body is no part of him. Given that what we are trying to do is to elucidate the nature of those entities which we normally call "persons," we must say that arms and legs and all other parts of the living body are parts of the person. My arms and legs are parts of me. The crucial point that Descartes was making is that the body is only, contingently and possibly temporarily, part of the person; it is not an essential part. . . .

The other arguments which I have given for the "simple theory," e.g., that two embodied persons can be the same despite their being no bodily continuity between them, can also, like the argument of Descartes just discussed, if we assume the wider Aristotelian framework, be cast into the form of arguments for classical dualism. . . .

There is, however, one argument often put forward by classical dualists—their argument from the indivisibility of the soul to its natural immortality—from which I must dissociate myself. Before looking at this argument, it is necessary to face the problem of what it means to say that the soul continues to exist. Clearly the soul continues to exist if a person exercises his capacities for experience and action, by having experiences and performing actions. But can the soul continue to exist when the person does not exercise those capacities? Presumably it can. For we say that an unconscious person (who is neither having experiences or acting) is still a person. We say this on the grounds that natural processes (i.e., processes according with the laws of nature) will, or at any rate may, lead to his exercising his capacities again—e.g., through the end of normal sleep or through some medical or surgical intervention. Hence a person, and so his soul, if we talk thus, certainly exists while natural processes may lead to his exercising those capacities again. But what when the person is not exercising his capacities, and no natural processes (whether those operative in our present material universe or those operative in some new world to which the person has moved) will lead to his exercising his capacities? We could say that the person and so his soul still exists on the grounds that there is the logical possibility of his coming to life again. To my mind, the more natural alternative is to say that when ordinary natural processes cannot lead to his exercising his capacities again, a person and so his soul has ceased to exist; but there remains the logical possibility that he may come into existence again (perhaps through God causing him to exist again). One argument against taking the latter alternative is the argument that no substance can have two beginnings of existence. If a person really ceases to exist, then there is not even the logical possibility of his coming into existence again. It would follow that the mere logical possibility of the person coming into existence again has the consequence that a person once existent, is always existent (even when he has no capacity for experience and action). But this principle — that no substance can have two beginnings of existence — is one which I see no good reason for adopting; and if we do not adopt it, then we must say that souls cease to exist when there is no natural possibility of their exercising their capacities. But that does not prevent souls which have ceased to exist coming into existence again. This way of talking does give substantial content to claims that souls do or do not exist, when they are not exercising their capacities.

Now classical dualists assumed (in my view, on balance, correctly) that souls cannot be divided. But they often argued from this, that souls were indestructible, and hence immortal, or at any rate naturally immortal (i.e., immortal as a result of the operation of natural processes, and so immortal barring an act of God to stop those processes operating). That does not follow. Material bodies may lose essential properties without being divided — an oak tree may die and become fossilized without losing its shape. It does not follow from a soul's being indivisible that it cannot lose its capacity for experience and action — and so cease to be a soul. Although there is (I have been arguing) no logical necessity that a soul be linked to a body, it may be physically necessary that a soul be linked to one body if it is to have its essential properties (of capacity for experience and action) and so continue to exist.

## TEST YOUR UNDERSTANDING

1. Does Swinburne think that a person is an immaterial soul with no material parts?

2. Is Swinburne arguing that the soul is immortal?

3. Suppose person A and person B swap brains. A's brain goes into B's skull; B's brain goes into A's skull. Is person A now in B's old body? Explain how Swinburne would answer.

## NOTES AND QUESTIONS

1. What is "classical dualism"? Set out Swinburne's **argument** for it in the form of premises and conclusion. Is the argument **valid**? Is it **sound**?

2. The selection is from *Personal Identity* (Blackwell, 1984) in which Swinburne engages in a debate with Sydney Shoemaker, who holds a theory of personal identity similar to Derek Parfit's (see the following reading). If you want to explore Swinburne's view further, Shoemaker's objections to Swinburne's theory in that book would be a good place to start.

## Derek Parfit (born 1942)

Parfit is Emeritus Fellow in Philosophy at All Souls College, University of Oxford. In addition to *Reasons and Persons* (1984), from which the selections below are drawn, he is the author of the two-volume work *On What Matters* (2011) and numerous essays in moral philosophy.

# PERSONAL IDENTITY
### from *Reasons and Persons*

I enter the Teletransporter. I have been to Mars before, but only by the old method, a spaceship journey taking several weeks. This machine will send me at the speed of light. I merely have to press the green button. Like others, I am nervous. Will it work? I remind myself what I have been told to expect. When I press the button, I shall lose consciousness, and then wake up at what seems a moment later. In fact I shall have been unconscious for about an hour. The Scanner here on Earth will destroy my brain and body, while recording the exact states of all of my cells. It will then transmit this information by radio. Traveling at the speed of light, the message will take three minutes to reach the Replicator on Mars. This will then create, out of new matter, a brain and body exactly like mine. It will be in this body that I shall wake up.

Though I believe that this is what will happen, I still hesitate. But then I remember seeing my wife grin when, at breakfast today, I revealed my nervousness. As she reminded me, she has often been teletransported, and there is nothing wrong with *her*. I press the button. As predicted, I lose and seem at once to regain consciousness, but in a different cubicle. Examining my new body, I find no change at all. Even the cut on my upper lip, from this morning's shave, is still there.

Several years pass, during which I am often Teletransported. I am now back in the cubicle, ready for another trip to Mars. But this time, when I press the green button, I do not lose consciousness. There is a whirring sound, then silence. I leave the cubicle, and say to the attendant: "It's not working. What did I do wrong?"

"It's working," he replies, handing me a printed card. This reads: "The New Scanner records your blueprint without destroying your brain and body. We hope that you will welcome the opportunities which this technical advance offers."

The attendant tells me that I am one of the first people to use the New Scanner. He adds that, if I stay for an hour, I can use the Intercom to see and talk to myself on Mars.

"Wait a minute," I reply, "If I'm here I can't *also* be on Mars." Someone politely coughs, a white-coated man who asks to speak to me in private. We go to his office, where he tells me to sit down, and pauses. Then he says, "I'm afraid that we're having problems with the New Scanner. It records your blueprint just as accurately, as you will see when you talk to yourself on Mars. But it seems to be damaging the cardiac systems which it scans. Judging from the results so far, though you will be quite healthy on Mars, here on Earth you must expect cardiac failure within the next few days.". . .

# Simple Teletransportation and the Branch-Line Case

Simple Teletransportation, as just described, is a common feature in science fiction. And it is believed by some readers of this fiction merely to be the fastest way of traveling. They believe that my Replica *would* be *me*. Other science fiction readers, and some of the characters in this fiction, take a different view. They believe that when I press the green button, I die. My Replica is *someone else,* who has been made to be exactly like me.

This second view seems to be supported by the end of my story. The New Scanner does not destroy my brain and body. Besides gathering the information, it merely damages my heart. While I am in the cubicle, with the green button pressed, nothing seems to happen. I walk out, and learn that in a few days I shall die. I later talk, by two-way television, to my Replica on Mars. Let us continue the story. Since my Replica knows that I am about to die, he tries to console me with the same thoughts with which I recently tried to console a dying friend. It is sad to learn, on the receiving end, how unconsoling these thoughts are. My Replica then assures me that he will take up my life where I leave off. He loves my wife, and together they will care for my children. And he will finish the book that I am writing. Besides having all of my drafts, he has all of my intentions. I must admit that he can finish my book as well as I could. All these facts console me a little. Dying when I know that I shall have a Replica is not quite as bad as, simply, dying. Even so, I shall soon lose consciousness, forever.

In Simple Teletransportation, I do not co-exist with my Replica. This makes it easier to believe that this is a way of traveling, that my Replica *is* me. At the end of my story, my life and that of my Replica overlap. Call this the *Branch-Line Case.* In this case, I cannot hope to travel on the *Main Line,* waking up on Mars with forty years of life ahead. I shall remain on the Branch-Line, on Earth, which ends a few days later. Since I can talk to my Replica, it seems clear that he is *not* me. Though he is exactly like me, he is one person, and I am another. When I pinch myself, he feels nothing. When I have my heart attack, he will again feel nothing. And when I am dead he will live for another forty years.

If we believe that my Replica is not me, it is natural to assume that my prospect, on the Branch Line, is almost as bad as ordinary death. I shall deny this assumption. As I shall argue later, I ought to regard having a Replica as being about as good as ordinary survival. . . .

# Qualitative and Numerical Identity

There are two kinds of sameness, or identity. I and my Replica are *qualitatively identical,* or exactly alike. But we may not be *numerically identical,* or one and the same person. Similarly, two white billiard balls are not numerically but may be qualitatively identical. If I paint one of these balls red, it will not now be qualitatively identical to itself yesterday. But the red ball that I see now and the white ball that I painted red are numerically identical. They are one and the same ball.

We might say, of someone, "After his accident, he is no longer the same person." This is a claim about both kinds of identity. We claim that *he*, the same person, is *not* now the same person. This is not a contradiction. We merely mean that this person's character has changed. This numerically identical person is now qualitatively different.

When we are concerned about our future, it is our numerical identity that we are concerned about. I may believe that after my marriage, I shall not be the same person. But this does not make marriage death. However much I change, I shall still be alive if there will be some person living who is numerically identical with me.

The philosophical debate is about the nature both of persons and of personal identity over time. It will help to distinguish these questions:

1. What is the nature of a person?

2. What is it that makes a person at two different times one and the same person?

3. What is necessarily involved in the continued existence of each person over time?

The answer to (2) can take this form: "X today is one and the same person as Y at some past time *if and only if. . . .*" This answer states the *necessary and sufficient conditions* for personal identity over time. And the answer to (2) provides the answer to (3). Each person's continued existence has the *same* necessary and sufficient conditions.

In answering (2) and (3) we shall also partly answer (1). The necessary features of our continued existence depend upon our nature. And the simplest answer to (1) is that, to be a person, a being must be self-conscious, aware of its identity and its continued existence over time. . . .

## The Physical Criterion of Personal Identity

On one view, what makes me the same person over time is that I have the same brain and body. . . . I shall continue to exist if and only if this particular brain and body continue both to exist and to be the brain and body of a living person.

This is the simplest version of this view. There is a better version.

> *The Physical Criterion:* (1) What is necessary is not the continued existence of the whole body, but the continued existence of *enough* of the brain to be the brain of a living person. X today is one and the same person as Y at some past time if and only if (2) enough of Y's brain continued to exist, and is now X's brain, and (3) there does not exist a different person who also has enough of Y's brain. (4) Personal identity over time just consists in the holding of facts like (2) and (3).

(1) is clearly needed in certain actual cases. Some people continue to exist even though they lose much of their bodies, perhaps including their hearts and lungs if they are on heart-lung machines. The need for (3) will be clear later.

Those who believe in the Physical Criterion would reject Teletransportation. They would believe this to be a way not of traveling, but of dying. They would also reject, as inconceivable, reincarnation. They believe that someone cannot have a life after death, unless he lives this life in a resurrection of the very same, physically continuous body. . . .

# The Psychological Criterion

Some people believe in a kind of psychological continuity that resembles physical continuity. This involves the continued existence of a purely mental *entity* or thing, a soul, or spiritual substance. I shall return to this view. But I shall first explain another kind of psychological continuity. This is less like physical continuity, since it does not consist in the continued existence of some entity. But this other kind of psychological continuity involves only facts with which we are familiar.

What has been most discussed is the continuity of memory. This is because it is memory that makes most of us aware of our own continued existence over time. The exceptions are the people who are suffering from amnesia. Most amnesiacs lose only two sets of memories. They lose all of their memories of having particular past experiences — or, for short, their *experience memories*. They also lose some of their memories about facts, those that are about their own past lives. But they remember other facts, and they remember how to do different things, such as how to speak, or swim.

Locke suggested that experience memory provides the criterion of personal identity.[1] Though this is not, on its own, a plausible view, I believe that it can be part of such a view. I shall therefore try to answer Locke's critics.

Locke claimed that someone cannot have committed some crime unless he now remembers doing so. We can understand a reluctance to punish people for crimes that they cannot remember. But, taken as a view about what is involved in a person's continued existence, Locke's claim is clearly false. If it was true, it would not be possible for someone to forget any of the things that he once did, or any of the experiences that he once had. But this *is* possible. I cannot now remember putting on my shirt this morning.

There are several ways to extend the experience-memory criterion so as to cover such cases. I shall appeal to the concept of an overlapping chain of experience-memories. Let us say that, between X today and Y twenty years ago, there are *direct memory connections* if X can now remember having some of the experiences that Y had twenty years ago. On Locke's view, this makes X and Y one and the same person. Even if there are *no* such direct memory connections, there may be *continuity of memory* between X now and Y twenty years ago. This would be so if between X now and Y at that time there has been an overlapping chain of direct memories. In the case of most people who are over twenty-three, there would be such an overlapping

---

1.  See section 9 of Locke's "Of Identity and Diversity" (earlier in this chapter).

chain. In each day within the last twenty years, most of these people remembered some of their experiences on the previous day. On the revised version of Locke's view, some present person X is the same as some past person Y if there is between them continuity of memory.

This revision meets one objection to Locke's view. We should also revise the view so that it appeals to other facts. Besides direct memories, there are several other kinds of direct psychological connection. One such connection is that which holds between an intention and the later act in which this intention is carried out. Other such direct connections are those which hold when a belief, or a desire, or any other psychological feature, continues to be had.

I can now define two general relations:

*Psychological connectedness* is the holding of particular direct psychological connections.
*Psychological continuity* is the holding of overlapping chains of *strong* connectedness.

Of these two general relations, connectedness is more important both in theory and in practice. Connectedness can hold to any degree. Between X today and Y yesterday there might be several thousand direct psychological connections, or only a single connection. If there was only a single connection, X and Y would not be, on the revised Lockean view, the same person. For X and Y to be the same person, there must be over every day *enough* direct psychological connections. Since connectedness is a matter of degree, we cannot plausibly define precisely what counts as enough. But we can claim that there is enough connectedness if the number of connections, over any day, is *at least half* the number of direct connections that hold, over every day, in the lives of nearly every actual person. When there are enough direct connections, there is what I call *strong* connectedness.

This relation cannot be the criterion of personal identity. A relation F is *transitive* if it is true that, if X is F-related to Y, and Y is F-related to Z, X and Z *must* be F-related. Personal identity is a transitive relation. If Bertie was one and the same person as the philosopher Russell,[2] and Russell was one and the same person as the author of *Why I Am Not a Christian*, this author and Bertie must be one and the same person.

Strong connectedness is *not* a transitive relation. I am now strongly connected to myself yesterday, when I was strongly connected to myself two days ago, when I was strongly connected to myself three days ago, and so on. It does not follow that I am now strongly connected to myself twenty years ago. And this is not true. Between me now and myself twenty years ago there are many fewer than the number of direct psychological connections that hold over any day in the lives of nearly all adults. For example, while these adults have many memories of experiences that they had in the previous day, I have few memories of experiences that I had twenty years ago.

---

2. British philosopher Bertrand Russell (1872–1970).

By "the criterion of personal identity over time" I mean what this identity *necessarily involves or consists in*. Because identity is a transitive relation, the criterion of identity must be a transitive relation. Since strong connectedness is not transitive, it cannot be the criterion of identity. And I have just described a case in which this is shown. I am the same person as myself twenty years ago, though I am not now strongly connected to myself then.

Though a defender of Locke's view cannot appeal to psychological connectedness, he can appeal to psychological continuity, which *is* transitive. He can appeal to . . .

*The Psychological Criterion:* (1) There is *psychological continuity* if and only if there are overlapping chains of strong connectedness. X today is one and the same person as Y at some past time if and only if (2) X is psychologically continuous with Y, (3) this continuity has the right kind of cause, and (4) there does not exist a different person who is also psychologically continuous with Y. (5) Personal identity over time just consists in the holding of facts like (2) to (4).

As with the Physical Criterion, the need for (4) will be clear later. . . .


## What Happens When I Divide?

Suppose first that I am one of a pair of identical twins, and that both my body and my twin's brain have been fatally injured. Because of advances in neurosurgery, it is not inevitable that these injuries will cause us both to die. We have between us one healthy brain and one healthy body. Surgeons can put these together.

This could be done even with existing techniques. Just as my brain could be extracted, and kept alive by a connection with a heart-lung machine, it could be kept alive by a connection with the heart and lungs in my twin's body. The drawback, to-day, is that the nerves from my brain could not be connected with the nerves in my twin's body. My brain could survive if transplanted into his body, but the resulting person would be paralysed. . . .

Let us suppose, however, that surgeons are able to connect my brain to the nerves in my twin's body. The resulting person would have no paralysis, and would be completely healthy. Who would this person be?

This is not a difficult question. . . .

On all versions of the Psychological Criterion, the resulting person would be me. And most believers in the Physical Criterion could be persuaded that, in this case, this is true. As I have claimed, the Physical Criterion should require only the continued existence of *enough* of my brain to be the brain of a living person, provided that no one else has enough of this brain. This would make it me who would wake up, after the operation. And if my twin's body was just like mine, I might even fail to notice that I had a new body.

It is in fact true that one hemisphere is enough. There are many people who have survived, when a stroke or injury puts out of action one of their hemispheres. With his remaining hemisphere, such a person may need to re-learn certain things, such as adult speech, or how to control both hands. But this is possible. In my example I am assuming that, as may be true of certain actual people, both of my hemispheres have the full range of abilities. I could thus survive with either hemisphere, without any need for re-learning.

I shall now combine these last two claims. I would survive if my brain was successfully transplanted into my twin's body. And I could survive with only half my brain, the other half having been destroyed. Given these two facts, it seems clear that I would survive if half my brain was successfully transplanted into my twin's body, and the other half was destroyed.

What if the other half was *not* destroyed? This is [a case] in which a person, like an amoeba, divides. To simplify the case, I assume that I am one of three identical triplets. Consider

> *My Division.* My body is fatally injured, as are the brains of my two brothers. My brain is divided, and each half is successfully transplanted into the body of one of my brothers. Each of the resulting people believes that he is me, seems to remember living my life, has my character, and is in every other way psychologically continuous with me. And he has a body that is very like mine. . . .

It may help to state, in advance, what I believe this case to show. . . . The main conclusion to be drawn is that *personal identity is not what matters.*

It is natural to believe that our identity is what matters. Reconsider the Branch-Line Case, where I have talked to my Replica on Mars, and am about to die. Suppose we believe that I and my Replica are different people. It is then natural to assume that my prospect is almost as bad as ordinary death. In a few days, there will be no one living who will be me. It is natural to assume that *this* is what matters. In discussing My Division, I shall start by making this assumption.

In this case, each half of my brain will be successfully transplanted into the very similar body of one of my two brothers. Both of the resulting people will be fully psychologically continuous with me, as I am now. What happens to me?

There are only four possibilities: (1) I do not survive; (2) I survive as one of the two people; (3) I survive as the other; (4) I survive as both.

The objection to (1) is this. I would survive if my brain was successfully transplanted. And people have in fact survived with half their brains destroyed. Given these facts, it seems clear that I would survive if half my brain was successfully transplanted, and the other half was destroyed. So how could I fail to survive if the other half was also successfully transplanted? How could a double success be a failure?

Consider the next two possibilities. Perhaps one success is the maximum score. Perhaps I shall be one of the two resulting people. The objection here is that, in this case, each half of my brain is exactly similar, and so, to start with, is each resulting person. Given these facts, how can I survive as only one of the two people? What can make me one of them rather than the other?

These first three possibilities cannot be dismissed as incoherent. We can understand them. But, while we assume that identity is what matters, (1) is not plausible. It is not plausible that My Division is equivalent to death. Nor are (2) and (3) plausible. There remains the fourth possibility: that I survive as both of the resulting people. . . .

After I have had this operation, the two "products" each have all of the features of a person. They could live at opposite ends of the Earth. Suppose that they have poor memories, and that their appearance changes in different ways. After many years, they might meet again, and fail even to recognise each other. We might have to claim of such a pair, innocently playing tennis: "What you see out there is a single person, playing tennis with himself. In each half of his mind he mistakenly believes that he is playing tennis with someone else." If we are not yet Reductionists,[3] we believe that there is one true answer to the question whether these two tennis-players are a single person. Given what we mean by "person", the answer must be No. . . .

On the Reductionist View, the problem disappears. On this view, the claims that I have discussed do not describe different possibilities, any of which might be true, and one of which must be true. These claims are merely different descriptions of the same outcome. We know what this outcome is. There will be two future people, each of whom will have the body of one of my brothers, and will be fully psychologically continuous with me, because he has half of my brain. Knowing this, we know everything. I may ask, "But shall I be one of these two people, or the other, or neither?" But I should regard this as an empty question. Here is a similar question. In 1881 the French Socialist Party split. What happened? Did the French Socialist Party cease to exist, or did it continue to exist as one or other of the two new Parties? Given certain further details, this would be an empty question. Even if we have no answer to this question, we could know just what happened.

I must now distinguish two ways in which a question may be empty. About some questions we should claim both that they are empty, and that they have no answers. We could decide to *give* these questions answers. But . . . any possible answer would be arbitrary. . . .

There is another kind of case in which a question may be empty. In such a case, this question has an answer. The question is empty because it does not describe different possibilities, any one of which might be true, and one of which must be true. The question merely gives us different descriptions of the same outcome. We could know the full truth about this outcome without choosing one of these descriptions. But, if we do decide to give an answer to this empty question, one of these descriptions is better than the others. Since this is so, we can claim that this description is the answer to this question. And I claim that there is a best description of the case where I divide. The best description is that neither of the resulting people will be me. . . .

---

3. "Reductionism" is Parfit's name for the view that the facts of personal identity are wholly determined by more basic facts about bodily continuity, psychological continuity, and the like, and that when these facts fail to settle whether a future person Y is the same person as some present person X, then there is *simply no answer to the question* whether X and Y are the same person.

# What Matters When I Divide?

Some people would regard division as being as bad, or nearly as bad, as ordinary death. This reaction is irrational. We ought to regard division as being about as good as ordinary survival. As I have argued, the two "products" of this operation would be two different people. Consider my relation to each of these people. Does this relation fail to contain some vital element that is contained in ordinary survival? It seems clear that it does not. I would survive if I stood in this very same relation to only one of the resulting people. It is a fact that someone can survive even if half his brain is destroyed. And on reflection it was clear that I would survive if my whole brain was successfully transplanted into my brother's body. It was therefore clear that I would survive if half my brain was destroyed, and the other half was successfully transplanted into my brother's body. In the case that we are now considering, my relation to each of the resulting people thus contains everything that would be needed for me to survive as that person. It cannot be the *nature* of my relation to each of the resulting people that, in this case, causes it to fail to be survival. Nothing is *missing*. What is wrong can only be the duplication.

Suppose that I accept this, but still regard division as being nearly as bad as death. My reaction is now indefensible. I would be like someone who, when told of a drug that could double his years of life, regarded the taking of this drug as death. The only difference in the case of division is that the extra years are to run concurrently. This is an interesting difference. But it cannot mean that there are *no* years to run. We might say: "You will lose your identity. But there are at least two ways of doing this. Dying is one, dividing is another. To regard these as the same is to confuse two with zero. Double survival is not the same as ordinary survival. But this does not make it death. It is further away from death than ordinary survival."

The problem with double survival is that it does not fit the logic of identity. Like certain other Reductionists, I claim

> *Relation R* is what matters. R is psychological connectedness and/or psychological continuity, with the right kind of cause. . . .

In the imagined case where I divide, R takes a "branching" form. But personal identity cannot take a branching form. I and the two resulting people cannot be one and the same person. Since I cannot be identical with two different people, and it would be arbitrary to call one of these people me, we can best describe the case by saying neither of these people will be me.

Which is the relation that is important? Is what matters personal identity, or relation R? In ordinary cases we need not decide which of these is what matters, since these relations coincide. In the case of My Division these relations do not coincide. We must therefore decide which of the two is what matters.

If we believe that we are separately existing entities,[4] we could plausibly claim that identity is what matters. On this view, personal identity is a deep further fact. But we have sufficient evidence to reject this view. If we are Reductionists, we *cannot* plausibly claim that, of these two relations, it is identity that matters. On our view, the fact of personal identity just consists in the holding of relation R, when it takes a non-branching form. If personal identity just consists in this other relation, this other relation must be what matters.

It may be objected: "You are wrong to claim that there is nothing more to identity than relation R. As you have said, personal identity has one extra feature, not contained in relation R. Personal identity consists in R holding *uniquely* — holding between one present person and *only one* future person. Since there is something more to personal identity than to relation R, we can rationally claim that, of the two, it is identity which is what matters."

In answering this objection, it will help to use some abbreviations. Call personal identity *PI*. When some relation holds uniquely, or in a one-one form, call this fact *U*. The view that I accept can be stated with this formula:

$$PI = R + U$$

Most of us are convinced that PI matters, or has value. Assume that R may also have value. There are then four possibilities:

1. R without U has no value.

2. U enhances the value of R, but R has value even without U.

3. U makes no difference to the value of R.

4. U reduces the value of R (but not enough to eliminate this value, since R + U = PI, which has value).

Can the presence or absence of U make a great difference to the value of R? As I shall argue, this is not plausible. If I will be R-related to some future person, the presence or absence of U makes no difference to the intrinsic nature of my relation to this person. And what matters most must be the intrinsic nature of this relation.

Since this is so, R without U would still have most of its value. Adding U makes R = PI. If adding U does not greatly increase the value of R, R must be what fundamentally matters, and PI mostly matters just because of the presence of R. If U makes no difference to the value of R, PI matters only because of the presence of R. Since U can be plausibly claimed to make a small difference, PI may, compared with R, have some extra value. But this value would be much less than the intrinsic value of R. The extra value of PI is much less than the value that R would have in the absence of PI, when U fails to hold.

4. That is, entities whose persistence through time is not determined by the underlying facts of physical and psychological continuity.

If it were put forward on its own, it would be difficult to accept the view that personal identity is not what matters. But I believe that, when we consider the case of division, this difficulty disappears. When we see *why* neither resulting person will be me, I believe that, on reflection, we can also see that this does not matter, or matters only a little. . . .

In the case where I divide, though my relation to each of the resulting people cannot be called identity, it contains what fundamentally matters. When we deny identity here, we are not denying an important judgement. Since my relation to each of the resulting people is about as good as if it were identity, it carries most of the ordinary implications of identity. Even when the person in Jack's body cannot be called me, because the other transplant succeeds, he can just as much deserve punishment or reward for what I have done. So can the person in Bill's body. As Wiggins writes: "a malefactor could scarcely evade responsibility by contriving his own fission."[5] . . .

## Is the True View Believable?

I have now reviewed the main arguments for the Reductionist View. Do I find it impossible to believe this view?

What I find is this. I can believe this view at the intellectual or reflective level. I am convinced by the arguments in favour of this view. But I think it likely that, at some other level, I shall always have doubts.

My belief is firmest when I am considering some of these imagined cases. I am convinced that if I divided, it would be an empty question whether I would then be one, or the other, or neither of the resulting people. I believe that there is nothing that could make these different possibilities, any of which might be what would really happen. . . .

When I consider certain other cases, my conviction is less firm. One example is Teletransportation. I imagine that I am in the cubicle, about to press the green button. I might suddenly have doubts. I might be tempted to change my mind, and pay the larger fare of a space-ship journey.

I suspect that reviewing my arguments would never wholly remove my doubts. At the reflective or intellectual level, I would remain convinced that the Reductionist View is true. But at some lower level I would still be inclined to believe that there must always be a real difference between some future person's being me, and his being someone else. Something similar is true when I look through a window at the top of a sky-scraper. I know that I am in no danger. But looking down from this dizzying height, I am afraid. I would have a similar irrational fear if I was about to press the green button.

It may help to add these remarks. On the Reductionist View, my continued existence just involves physical and psychological continuity. On the Non-Reductionist

---

5. David Wiggins, "Locke, Butler and the Stream of Consciousness," in Amelie Rorty, ed., *The Identities of Persons* (University of California Press, 1976), p. 146. [Parfit's note.]

View, it involves a further fact. It is natural to believe in this further fact, and to believe that, compared with the continuities, it is a *deep* fact, and is the fact that really matters. When I fear that, in Teletransportation, I shall not get to Mars, my fear is that the abnormal cause may fail to produce this further fact. As I have argued, there is no such fact. What I fear will not happen, *never* happens. I want the person on Mars to be me in a specially intimate way in which no future person will ever be me. My continued existence never involves this deep further fact. What I fear will be missing is *always* missing. Even a spaceship journey would not produce the further fact in which I am inclined to believe.

When I come to see that my continued existence does not involve this further fact, I lose my reason for preferring a spaceship journey. But, judged from the standpoint of my earlier belief, this is not because Teletransportation is *about as good as* ordinary survival. It is because ordinary survival is *about as bad as,* or little better than, Teletransportation. *Ordinary survival is about as bad as being destroyed and having a Replica.*

By rehearsing arguments like these, I might do enough to reduce my fear. I might be able to bring myself to press the green button. But I expect that I would never completely lose my intuitive belief in the Non-Reductionist View. It is hard to be serenely confident in my Reductionist conclusions. It is hard to believe that personal identity is not what matters. If tomorrow someone will be in agony, it is hard to believe that it could be an empty question whether this agony will be felt by *me*. And it is hard to believe that, if I am about to lose consciousness, there may be no answer to the question "Am I about to die?"

Nagel[6] once claimed that it is psychologically impossible to believe the Reductionist View. Buddha claimed that though this is very hard, it is possible.[7] I find Buddha's claim to be true. After reviewing my arguments, I find that, at the reflective or intellectual level, though it is very hard to believe the Reductionist View, this is possible. My remaining doubts or fears seem to me irrational. Since I can believe this view, I assume that others can do so too. We can believe the truth about ourselves.

## TEST YOUR UNDERSTANDING

1. Which of the following pairs are (a) numerically **identical**, (b) not numerically identical but only qualitatively identical?

    (i)    The author of the *Essay Concerning Human Understanding*; John Locke.

    (ii)    Your copy of this book; your classmate's copy of this book.

    (iii)    2 + 3; 5.

6. American philosopher Thomas Nagel (1937–), author of selections in chapters 9, 14, and 18 of this anthology.

7. In an appendix to *Reasons and Persons* Parfit gives some quotations from Buddhist texts to support his claim that the Buddha was a Reductionist.

(iv) The teenager who played Harry Potter in the movies; the adult British actor Daniel Radcliffe.

(v) The can of Acme soup on the left of the supermarket shelf; the can of Acme soup on the right of the shelf.

2. Which of the following **relations** are transitive?

(i) Person x is exactly the same height as person y.

(ii) Number x > number y.

(iii) Person x loves person y.

(iv) Person x is almost the same height as person y.

(v) Number x = 2 + number y.

3. Parfit accepts a certain "criterion of personal identity." Which one?

4. According to Parfit, "relation R" does not fit the "logic of identity." Explain what he means.

5. Does Parfit think that teletransportation is a method of *transportation*, a way of getting you to Mars?

## NOTES AND QUESTIONS

1. Parfit takes the case of "My Division" to show that "personal identity is not what matters." What does he mean by this, and how is My Division supposed to show that it is true? Set out Parfit's **argument** in the form of premises and conclusion. Is the argument **valid**? Is it **sound**? Assuming that the conclusion of the argument is true, should we be less concerned about our own deaths, or the deaths of other people?

2. Parfit's views have been the subject of much discussion. For an introduction, see chapter 9 of Harold Noonan, *Personal Identity* (Routledge, 2003).

## Bernard Williams (1929–2003)

Bernard Williams was, at the time of his death, Monroe Deutsch Professor of Philosophy at the University of California, Berkeley. His books include *Descartes: The Project of Pure Inquiry* (1978), *Ethics and the Limits of Philosophy* (1985), and *Shame and Necessity* (1993). His early essays on personal indentity and the nature of the self are collected in *Problems of the Self* (1973), from which the selection below is drawn.

# THE SELF AND THE FUTURE

$S$uppose that there were some process to which two persons, $A$ and $B$, could be subjected as a result of which they might be said — question-beggingly — to have *exchanged bodies*. That is to say — less question-beggingly — there is a certain human body which is such that when previously we were confronted with it, we were confronted with person $A$, certain utterances coming from it were expressive of memories of the past experiences of $A$, certain movements of it partly constituted the actions of $A$ and were taken as expressive of the character of $A$, and so forth; but now, after the process is completed, utterances coming from this body are expressive of what seem to be just those memories which previously we identified as memories of the past experiences of $B$, its movements partly constitute actions expressive of the character of $B$, and so forth; and conversely with the other body. . . .

One radical way of securing that condition in the imagined exchange case is to suppose, that the brains of $A$ and of $B$ are transposed. We may not need so radical a condition. Thus suppose it were possible to extract information from a man's brain and store it in a device while his brain was repaired, or even renewed, the information then being replaced: it would seem exaggerated to insist that the resultant man could not possibly have the memories he had before the operation. With regard to our knowledge of our own past, we draw distinctions between merely recalling, being reminded, and learning again, and those distinctions correspond (roughly) to distinctions between no new input, partial new input, and total new input with regard to the information in question; and it seems clear that the information-parking case just imagined would not count as new input in the sense necessary and sufficient for "learning again." Hence we can imagine the case we are concerned with in terms of information extracted into such devices from $A$'s and $B$'s brains and replaced in the other brain; this is the sort of model which, I think not unfairly for the present argument, I shall have in mind.

We imagine the following. The process considered above exists; two persons can enter some machine, let us say, and emerge changed in the appropriate ways. If $A$ and $B$ are the persons who enter, let us call the persons who emerge the *A-body-person* and the *B-body-person*: the $A$-body-person is that person (whoever it is) with whom I am confronted when, after the experiment, I am confronted with that body which previously was $A$'s body — that is to say, that person who would naturally be taken for $A$ by someone who just saw this person, was familiar with $A$'s appearance before the experiment, and did not know about the happening of the experiment. A non-question-begging description of the experiment will leave it open which (if either) of the persons $A$ and $B$ the $A$-body-person is; the description of the experiment as "persons changing bodies" of course implies that the $A$-body-person is actually $B$.

We take two persons $A$ and $B$ who are going to have the process carried out on them. . . . We further announce that one of the two resultant persons, the

A-body-person and the B-body-person, is going after the experiment to be given $100,00, while the other is going to be tortured. We then ask each of A and B to choose which treatment should be dealt out to which of the persons who will emerge from the experiment, the choice to be made (if it can be) on selfish grounds.

Suppose that A chooses that the B-body-person should get the pleasant treatment and the A-body-person the unpleasant treatment; and B chooses conversely (this might indicate that they thought that "changing bodies" was indeed a good description of the outcome). The experimenter cannot act in accordance with both these sets of preferences, those expressed by A and those expressed by B. Hence there is one clear sense in which A and B cannot both get what they want: namely, that if the experimenter, before the experiment, announces to A and B that he intends to carry out the alternative (for example), of treating the B-body- person unpleasantly and the A-body-person pleasantly—then A can say rightly, "That's not the outcome I chose to happen," and B can say rightly, "That's just the outcome I chose to happen." So, evidently, A and B before the experiment can each come to know either that the outcome he chose will be that which will happen, or that the one he chose will not happen, and in that sense they can get or fail to get what they wanted. But is it also true that when the experimenter proceeds *after* the experiment to act in accordance with one of the preferences and not the other, then one of A and B will have got what he wanted, and the other not?

There seems very good ground for saying so. For suppose the experimenter, having elicited A's and B's preference, says nothing to A and B about what he will do; conducts the experiment; and then, for example, gives the unpleasant treatment to the B-body-person and the pleasant treatment to the A-body-person. Then the B-body-person will not only complain of the unpleasant treatment as such, but will complain (since he has A's memories) that that was not the outcome he chose, since he chose that the B-body-person should be well treated; and since A made his choice in selfish spirit, he may add that he precisely chose in that way because he did not want the unpleasant things to happen to *him*. The A-body-person meanwhile will express satisfaction both at the receipt of the $100,000, and also at the fact that the experimenter has chosen to act in the way that he, B, so wisely chose. These facts make a strong case for saying that the experimenter has brought it about that B did in the outcome get what he wanted and A did not. It is therefore a strong case for saying that the B-body-person really is A, and the A-body-person really is B; and therefore for saying that the process of the experiment really is that of changing bodies. . . . This seems to show that to care about what happens to me in the future is not necessarily to care about what happens to *this* body (the one I now have); and this in turn might be taken to show that in some sense of Descartes's obscure phrase, I and my body are "really distinct"[1] (though, of course, nothing in these considerations could support the idea that I could exist without a body at all). . . .

---

1. Descartes's *Meditation VI* (see p. 361 of this anthology) argues that mind and body are not merely "formally distinct"—distinguishable in thought—but also "really distinct," in the sense that each can exist without the other. Williams borrows Descartes's phrase, but explicitly rejects this understanding of it.

Let us now consider something apparently different. Someone in whose power I am tells me that I am going to be tortured tomorrow. I am frightened, and look forward to tomorrow in great apprehension. He adds that when the time comes, I shall not remember being told that this was going to happen to me, since shortly before the torture something else will be done to me which will make me forget the announcement. This certainly will not cheer me up, since I know perfectly well that I can forget things, and that there is such a thing as indeed being tortured unexpectedly because I had forgotten or been made to forget a prediction of the torture: that will still be a torture which, so long as I do know about the prediction, I look forward to in fear. He then adds that my forgetting the announcement will be only part of a larger process: when the moment of torture comes, I shall not remember any of the things I am now in a position to remember. This does not cheer me up, either, since I can readily conceive of being involved in an accident, for instance, as a result of which I wake up in a completely amnesiac state and also in great pain; that could certainly happen to me, I should not like it to happen to me, nor to know that it was going to happen to me. He now further adds that at the moment of torture I shall not only not remember the things I am now in a position to remember, but will have a different set of impressions of my past, quite different from the memories I now have. I do not think that this would cheer me up, either. For I can at least conceive the possibility, if not the concrete reality, of going completely mad, and thinking perhaps that I am George IV or somebody; and being told that something like that was going to happen to me would have no tendency to reduce the terror of being told authoritatively that I was going to be tortured, but would merely compound the horror. Nor do I see why I should be put into any better frame of mind by the person in charge adding lastly that the impressions of my past with which I shall be equipped on the eve of torture will exactly fit the past of another person now living, and that indeed I shall acquire these impressions by (for instance) information now in his brain being copied into mine. Fear, surely, would still be the proper reaction: and not because one did not know what was going to happen, but because in one vital respect at least one did know what was going to happen — torture, which one can indeed expect to happen to oneself, and to be preceded by certain mental derangements as well.

If this is right, the whole question seems now to be totally mysterious. For what we have just been through is of course merely one side, differently represented, of the transaction which we considered before; and it represents it as a perfectly hateful prospect, while the previous considerations represented it as something one should rationally, perhaps even cheerfully, choose out of the options there presented. It is differently presented, of course, and in two notable respects; but when we look at these two differences of presentation, can we really convince ourselves that the second presentation is wrong or misleading, thus leaving the road open to the first version which at the time seemed so convincing? Surely not.

The first difference is that in the second version the torture is throughout represented as going to happen to *me*: "you," the man in charge persistently says. Thus he is not very neutral. But should he have been neutral? Or, to put it another way, does his use of the second person have a merely emotional and rhetorical effect on me, making me afraid when further reflection would have shown that I had no reason to be? It is certainly not obviously so. The problem just is that through every step of his predictions I seem to be able to follow him successfully. And if I reflect on whether what he has said gives me grounds for fearing that I shall be tortured, I could consider that behind my fears lies some principle such as this: that my undergoing physical pain in the future is not excluded by any psychological state I may be in at the time, with the platitudinous exception of those psychological states which in themselves exclude experiencing pain, notably (if it is a psychological state) unconsciousness. In particular, what impressions I have about the past will not have any effect on whether I undergo the pain or not. This principle seems sound enough. . . .

I said that there were two notable differences between the second presentation of our situation and the first. The first difference, which we have just said something about, was that the man predicted the torture for *me*, a psychologically very changed "me." We have yet to find a reason for saying that he should not have done this, or that I really should be unable to follow him if he does; I seem to be able to follow him only too well. The second difference is that in this presentation he does not mention the other man, except in the somewhat incidental role of being the provenance of the impressions of the past I end up with. He does not mention him at all as someone who will end up with impressions of the past derived from me (and, incidentally, with $100,000 as well — a consideration which, in the frame of mind appropriate to this version, will merely make me jealous).

But why *should* he mention this man and what is going to happen to him? My selfish concern is to be told what is going to happen to me, and now I know: torture, preceded by changes of character, brain operations, changes in impressions of the past. The knowledge that one other person, or none, or many will be similarly mistreated may affect me in other ways, of sympathy, greater horror at the power of this tyrant, and so forth; but surely it cannot affect my expectations of torture? But — someone will say — this is to leave out exactly the feature which, as the first presentation of the case showed, makes all the difference: for it is to leave out the person who, as the first presentation showed, will be you. It is to leave out not merely a feature which should fundamentally affect your fears, it is to leave out the very person for whom you are fearful. So of course, the objector will say, this makes all the difference.

But can it? Consider the following series of cases. In each case we are to suppose that after what is described, A is, as before, to be tortured; we are also to suppose the person A is informed beforehand that just these things followed by the torture will happen to him:

(i)   *A* is subjected to an operation which produces total amnesia;

(ii)  amnesia is produced in *A*, and other interference leads to certain changes in his character;

(iii) changes in his character are produced, and at the same time certain illusory "memory" beliefs are induced in him; these are of a quite fictitious kind and do not fit the life of any actual person;

(iv)  the same as (*iii*), except that both the character traits and the "memory" impressions are designed to be appropriate to another actual person, *B*;

(v)  the same as (*iv*), except that the result is produced by putting the information into *A* from the brain of *B*, by a method which leaves *B* the same as he was before;

(vi)  the same happens to *A* as in (*v*), but *B* is not left the same, since a similar operation is conducted in the reverse direction.

I take it that no one is going to dispute that *A* has reasons, and fairly straightforward reasons, for fear of pain when the prospect is that of situation (*i*); there seems no conceivable reason why this should not extend to situation (*ii*), and the situation (*iii*) can surely introduce no difference of principle — it just seems a situation which for more than one reason we should have grounds for fearing, as suggested above. Situation (*iv*) at least introduces the person *B*, who was the focus of the objection we are now discussing. But it does not seem to introduce him in any way which makes a material difference; if I can expect pain through a transformation which involves new "memory"-impressions, it would seem a purely external fact, relative to that, that the "memory"-impressions had a model. . . .

But two things are to be noticed about this situation. First, if we concentrate on *A* and the *A*-body-person, we do not seem to have added anything which from the point of view of his fears makes any material difference; just as, in the move from (*iii*) to (*iv*), it made no relevant difference that the new "memory"-impressions which precede the pain had, as it happened, a model, so in the move from (*iv*) to (*v*) all we have added is that they have a model which is also their cause: and it is still difficult to see why that, to him looking forward, could possibly make the difference between expecting pain and not expecting pain. To illustrate that point from the case of character: if *A* is capable of expecting pain, he is capable of expecting pain preceded by a change in his dispositions — and to that expectation it can make no difference, whether that change in his dispositions is modeled on, or indeed indirectly caused by, the dispositions of some other person. If his fears can, as it were, reach through the change, it seems a mere trimming how the change is in fact induced. The second point about situation (*v*) is that if the crucial question for *A*'s fears with regard to what befalls the *A*-body-person is whether the *A*-body-person is or is not the person *B*, then that condition has not yet been satisfied in situation (*v*): for there we have an undisputed *B* in addition to the *A*-body-person, and certainly those two are not the same person.

But in situation (*vi*), we seemed to think, that is finally what he is. But if *A*'s original fears could reach through the expected changes in (*v*), as they did in (*iv*) and (*iii*), then certainly they can reach through in (*vi*). Indeed, from the point of view of *A*'s expectations and fears, there is less difference between (*vi*) and (*v*) than there is between (*v*) and (*iv*) or between (*iv*) and (*iii*). In those transitions, there were at least differences — though we could not see that they were really relevant differences — in the content and cause of what happened to him; in the present case there is absolutely no difference at all in what happens to him, the only difference being in what happens to someone else. If he can fear pain when (*v*) is predicted, why should he cease to when (*vi*) is?

I can see only one way of relevantly laying great weight on the transition from (*v*) to (*vi*); and this involves a considerable difficulty. This is to deny that, as I put it, the transition from (*v*) to (*vi*) involves merely the addition of something happening to *somebody else;* what rather it does, it will be said, is to involve the reintroduction of *A* himself, as the *B*-body-person; since he has reappeared in this form, it is for this person, and not for the unfortunate *A*-body-person, that *A* will have his expectations. This is to reassert, in effect, the viewpoint emphasized in our first presentation of the experiment. But this surely has the consequence that *A* should not have fears for the *A*-body-person who appeared in situation (*v*). For by the present argument, the *A*-body-person in (*vi*) is not *A*; the *B*-body-person is. But the *A*-body-person in (*v*) is, in character, history, everything, exactly the same as the *A*-body-person in (*vi*); so if the latter is not *A*, then neither is the former. . . . But no one else in (*v*) has any better claim to be *A*. So in (*v*), it seems, *A* just does not exist. This would certainly explain why *A* should have no fears for the state of things in (*v*) — though he might well have fears for the path to it. But it rather looked earlier as though he could well have fears for the state of things in (*v*). Let us grant, however, that that was an illusion, and that *A* really does not exist in (*v*); then does he exist in (*iv*), (*iii*), (*ii*), or (*i*)? It seems very difficult to deny it for (*i*) and (*ii*); are we perhaps to draw the line between (*iii*) and (*iv*)? . . .

Thus, to sum up, it looks as though there are two presentations of the imagined experiment and the choice associated with it, each of which carries conviction, and which lead to contrary conclusions. . . . Following from all that, I am not in the least clear which option it would be wise to take if one were presented with them before the experiment. I find that rather disturbing. . . .

I will end by suggesting one rather shaky way in which one might approach a resolution of the problem, using only the limited materials already available.

The apparently decisive arguments of the first presentation, which suggested that *A* should identify himself with the *B*-body-person, turned on the extreme neatness of the situation in satisfying, if any could, the description of "changing bodies." But this neatness is basically artificial; it is the product of the will of the experimenter to produce a situation which would naturally elicit, with minimum hesitation, that description. By the sorts of methods he employed, he could easily have left off earlier or gone on further. He could have stopped at situation (*v*), leaving *B* as he was; or he could have gone on and produced two persons each with *A*-like character and memories, as well as one or two with *B*-like characteristics. If he had done either of those, we should have been in yet greater difficulty about what to say; he just chose to make it as easy as possible for us to find something to say. Now if we had some model of ghostly persons in bodies, which were in some sense actually moved around by certain procedures, we could regard the neat experiment just as the *effective* experiment: the one method that really did result in the ghostly persons' changing places without being destroyed, dispersed, or whatever. But we cannot seriously use such a model. The experimenter has not in the sense of that model *induced* a change of bodies; he has rather produced the one situation out of a range of equally possible situations which we should be most disposed to call a change of bodies. As against this, the principle that one's fears can extend to future pain whatever psychological changes precede it seems positively straightforward. Perhaps, indeed, it is not; but we need to be shown what is wrong with it. Until we are shown what is wrong with it, we should perhaps decide that if we were the person *A* then, if we were to decide selfishly, we should pass the pain to the *B*-body-person. It would be risky: that there is room for the notion of a *risk* here is itself a major feature of the problem.

## TEST YOUR UNDERSTANDING

1. Explain what Williams means by saying that a certain description of "the experiment" is "question-begging."

2. Williams describes a second case, in which someone "tells me that I am going to be tortured tomorrow." How are the previous experiment and the second case related?

3. Williams describes a "series of cases," (i)–(vi), in response to an objection. What is that objection?

## NOTES AND QUESTIONS

1. Set out and evaluate Williams's suggestion at the end of "one rather shaky way" in which the problem could be solved. If you are *A* in the experiment, would you choose torture for the *A*-body-person or the *B*-body-person? Give reasons for your answer.

2. Williams's classic papers on personal identity and related topics are collected in his *Problems of the Self* (Cambridge University Press, 1976).

## ANALYZING THE ARGUMENTS

1. Locke's theory of personal identity is often taken to be something like this:

   *The Memory Criterion of personal identity*: Person A, who exists at $t_1$ = person B, who exists at $t_2$ **iff** B at $t_2$ can remember (some of) the experiences of A at $t_1$.

   The Scottish philosopher Thomas Reid (1710–1796) gave the following famous counterexample to the Memory Criterion:

   > An old general recalls taking a flag from the enemy as a young officer. When he was a young officer, he could remember being flogged as a boy. But now, when an old general, he can't remember this.

   Explain why this is a counterexample. (You may need to fill out some details of the case.) Parfit's Psychological Criterion is designed to evade Reid's objection to the Memory Criterion. Explain why it does so.

2. Preliminary definitions:

   A person P *survives* some event or happening E just in case P exists before E occurs, and when E is over, there exists some person who is (numerically) identical to P.

   *Teletransportation* is the process described by Parfit ("Personal Identity" in this chapter).

   *The Cartesian Criterion of personal identity*: Person A, who exists at time $t_1$ = person B, who exists at $t_2$, iff A's immaterial soul at $t_1$ = B's immaterial soul at time $t_2$.

   *The Bodily Criterion of personal identity*: Person A, who exists at $t_1$ = person B, who exists at $t_2$, iff A's body at $t_1$ = B's body at $t_2$.

   *The Brain Criterion of personal identity*: Person A, who exists at $t_1$ = person B, who exists at $t_2$, iff A's brain at $t_1$ = B's brain at $t_2$.

   *Exercise:* Consider the question:

   Does a person survive teletransportation?

   and say how proponents of the Cartesian, Body, Brain, and Parfit's Psychological criteria would answer. Try to imagine a real case in which you desperately need to get to Mars and are offered a choice between teletransportation and much more expensive and time-consuming journey by spaceship. Say which option you would choose and why. (Assume that teletransportation will certainly work as advertised, and in particular that there is no chance of inadvertent duplication.)

3. Were you once a four-week-old fetus in your mother's womb? How would Locke, Parfit, and Swinburne answer that question? How might Williams answer it? Give reasons for your own answer.

4. Parfit argues that in the case of My Division, I cease to exist, since the person who exists before the split is not identical to either of the people who exists afterward. This has been disputed by the American philosopher David Lewis (1941–2001). We are all familiar with cases in which two roads coincide in certain places while diverging

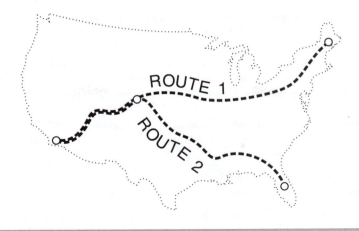

**Figure 1**

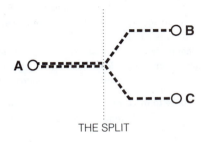

THE SPLIT

**Figure 2**

elsewhere. So consider two transcontinental highways, Route 1 and Route 2. The roads begin together in Los Angeles and coincide until Denver, at which point Route 1 heads off to Maine, while Route 2 heads off to Florida (fig. 1).

Someone who is crossing the road near Los Angeles may well think that he is only crossing one road, but in fact he's crossing two. The false impression is due to the fact that these two roads, while clearly *different*, nonetheless share an "initial segment." According to Lewis, just as roads are spread out in space, so people and other persisting objects are spread out in time. There is a part of you that stretches from your birth until your fifth birthday, and another (larger) part that stretches from your birth until your twelfth birthday. This is a controversial view, but suppose it's right. The case of My Division then looks like figure 2.

There are definitely two people at the end of the process, here called "B" and "C." But how many people were there at the start? Parfit assumes that there was only one—call him or her "A"—and argues that A ≠ B and A ≠ C, from which it follows that fission is a sort of death. Lewis denies this assumption. Just as there were two roads between

California and Denver that share an initial (spatial) segment, so there were two people prior to the division who share an initial (temporal) segment. If this is right, then it is a mistake to ask whether *the* person prior to the division survived as B or as C, just as it is a mistake to ask whether *the* road from Los Angeles to Denver continues on to Maine. This view allows us to say that division is sometimes a matter of genuine survival, in the sense that *everyone* who is present before the split is also present afterwards.

The view raises fascinating questions. For discussion, see Lewis's difficult but rewarding paper, "Survival and Identity," in his *Philosophical Papers,* vol. 1, (Cambridge University Press, 1983).

5. *The paradox of increase*. The selections focus on *personal* identity, but some puzzles arise even in the case of inanimate material things. Consider the *paradox of increase*:

> We have a tower T made out of five wooden blocks. You might think that we could make T taller by adding another block on the top. But we can't. After all, T and the five-block stack are identical. But when we add a new block on top, the five-block stack does not grow. It's still there, and it still contains five blocks. Adding a sixth block may bring a new object into existence: a six-block stack, which contains the original five-block stack as a part. But nothing has *grown* in this story. An old object has stayed the same, and a new object has come to be. But of course there is nothing special about towers made of wooden blocks. The case shows that *material objects cannot grow by acquiring new parts*. Every case that we might be tempted to describe in this way is really a matter of an old object remaining as it was, and a new object coming to be.

*Exercise:* Consider a response to this bizarre argument and say whether or not it succeeds. For discussion see Eric Olson, "The Paradox of Increase," *Monist* 89 (2006): 390–417.

# Part IV

# FROM METAPHYSICS TO ETHICS

# Do We Possess Free Will?

## A Question about Responsibility

In March of 2007 New York newspapers reported the brutal mugging of a 101-year-old woman in the lobby of her apartment building. As surveillance tapes reveal, the mugger held the door open for his victim, then followed her in, donned a ski mask, and beat her mercilessly for several minutes before fleeing with her purse.

This attack is not just a tragedy, as it might have been if the woman had been injured in a fall or mauled by an animal. It is a grotesque moral wrong and we blame the man who did it, which is to say that we hold him **morally responsible** for his act.

This is not a special case. The conviction that human beings are morally responsible for their behavior is deeply rooted in common sense. We take it for granted every day when we praise people for the good they do and blame people for the harm they cause. As a society we take it for granted when we punish people for their crimes. As we usually think, this is one of the most important differences between human beings and other animals. (It may be perfectly natural to get angry at your dog for tracking mud all over the house; but in a cool moment you know this makes no sense. He's just a dog, after all.) But if this is right, there must be something about us that explains it. And so we ask — not in a skeptical spirit but in a spirit of open-minded curiosity — *Why* are we morally responsible for what we do? What is it about *us* that makes us special in this regard?

## The Free Will Hypothesis

Think about the mugger in the moments just prior to the attack. There he is, holding the door open for his victim and watching her walk through. As he does this he is buffeted by biological and psychological forces of many kinds, including, we may suppose, a powerful *impulse* to attack. But if we think he is responsible for his act, we must think that he is capable of resisting this impulse — of "stepping back" and deciding for himself whether to act on it. This capacity is sometimes called **free will**—though this phrase is used in other ways as well. An act is free, on this conception, when the agent *could have done otherwise*. Before he acts, the free agent is in a certain psychological state: he has beliefs about his circumstances; he has desires, feelings, values; he has various physical capacities; and so on. In other animals this prior state *settles* what the animal will do (insofar as anything settles it). Holding all of these factors fixed, an animal has no real options. For human beings as we normally understand them, by contrast, while these factors may strongly incline a person to make one choice rather than another, it is ultimately *up to him* to choose. According to the free will hypothesis, that is why we are normally responsible for what we do, while other animals are not.

Let us put this cluster of commonsensical ideas under the microscope. It has several components.

1.  People are morally responsible for acts only if they act freely.

2.  People act freely only if they could have done otherwise.

3.  People could have done otherwise only if their choices were not determined by prior factors over which they had no control.

Taken together these entail:

4.  People are morally responsible for acts only if their choices were not determined by prior factors over which they had no control.

But we've said repeatedly that as we normally think,

5.  People *are* usually responsible for what they do.[1]

And so we have disclosed what might be called a *presupposition* of ordinary thought. If this commonsensical cluster of ideas is correct, then our practice of holding one another responsible—our practices of praise and blame, punishment and reward—take it for granted that

6.  Normal human choices are not determined by factors over which the agent had no control.

And now that we have isolated this presupposition, we must examine it. We may take it for granted as we go about our business. But is there any reason to believe that it is true?

## Doubts about Free Will

You might think that the claim is supported by introspection. Consider how it feels to make an ordinary choice. There you are, deciding whether to read the rest of this page or to take a break. Even if you're bored and really *want* to take

---

1. Why "usually"? Because we know that human beings are not always responsible for what they do. Someone who has been forced or hypnotized or tricked into acting badly is not responsible for what he does. **Proposition** (5) makes the commonsensical point that such excuses are not always available.

that break, it may seem obvious that nothing literally "forces" you one way or the other. So it's tempting to think that the *experience of conscious choice* confirms that our choices are not determined in advance.

In fact, however, introspective evidence shows no such thing. It may show that we are not normally *aware* of the factors that determine our choices. But our choices might still be determined by factors of which we are unaware. (When you see a flash of lightning you don't see what caused the flash, but that does not mean that nothing caused it!) But the opponent of (6) suspects that our choices are determined by factors of which we are unaware, and introspection can do nothing to exclude this possibility.

# Free Will and Divine Foreknowledge

Why might someone think that our choices are determined in this way? One venerable argument is theological. If God is eternal and all-knowing, then God always knew — from the beginning of time — that the mugger would attack the woman. So focus again on the moment just before the mugger's choice. It may seem to him (and to us) that he has two options: to attack or to walk away. But what he does not know is that before he was born God *predicted* that he would attack. This prediction is settled; it lies in the past and the mugger cannot do anything about it. To say that he is nonetheless capable of doing otherwise is to say that he is capable of *falsifying God's prediction*. And the trouble is that no one has that power. It is *impossible* for God to be mistaken, and so it is impossible for a person to act in a way that would cause God to have been mistaken.[2] If every human choice is foreseen by an infallible God, it follows that everything we do is settled in advance by a factor — God's prediction — that was in place before we were born. So if a free act must be an undetermined act, this theology entails that human freedom is an illusion. (See Nelson Pike, "Divine Omniscience and Voluntary Action," *Philosophical Review* 74, no.1 [1965].)

# Free Will and Physical Determinism

You can resist this argument by denying the existence of an eternal, all-knowing God. (You should consider whether there are other ways to resist it.) But a very different and wholly secular argument appears to lead to the same conclusion. From its origins in the seventeenth century, modern science has seemed to confirm the ancient speculation that the universe as a whole is a **deterministic** system in which the state of the cosmos at any one time is determined by its state at any

---

2. The view in question holds that it is part of God's **essence** to be infallible, just as it is part of the essence of a triangle to have three sides. No one can draw a four-sided triangle because four-sided triangles are impossible. Likewise, no one can falsify God's prediction because a mistaken God is impossible.

prior time, together with the laws of nature. On this view, the state of the universe at any point in the past — say, exactly 1 billion years ago — and the laws of nature together fix the state of the universe at every future time. If this view is correct, then given the past and the laws, absolutely everything that happens — every supernova, every mugging — is determined to occur just as it does.

It must be stressed that *physical determinism* of this sort is a scientific conjecture. The physics of Newton and his successors, including Einstein, was for the most part deterministic. But modern physics leaves open the possibility that the basic laws of nature assign *probabilities* to future occurrences without determining what will happen. Since physics is a work in progress, *no one knows at present whether physical determinism is true.* And this means that we should assume determinism (or its opposite) in our philosophy.

Instead we focus on the consequences of determinism. Suppose you wake up tomorrow to this headline:

SCIENTISTS DISCOVER, BEYOND DOUBT: UNIVERSE IS A DETERMINISTIC SYSTEM

What would this mean? It would mean that the motion of every particle, including the particles in our brains and bodies, was determined by the state of the universe a billion years ago together with the laws of nature. In particular it would mean that it was settled a billion years ago that the particles in the mugger's brain and body would do just what they did, and hence that he would do just what he did. And of course the same would be true of every human action. So if a free act must be an undetermined act, this sort of physics entails that human freedom is an illusion.

This argument should worry anyone who accepts determinism. But it should also worry anyone — and this should be all of us — who is genuinely uncertain about whether the laws of physics will turn out to be deterministic. For if the argument is cogent it shows that *for all we know at present,* human freedom is an illusion. And that is an unsettling thought. Think of the mugger again — or of anyone else whom you regard as obviously responsible for what he's done. If this line of thought is sound, you have no right to this confidence, since for all you know, the whole business was settled eons ago by factors over which the agent had no control.

## Free Will and Indeterminism

All of this may leave you hoping for a different headline. So imagine you wake up tomorrow to find this on the front page of the *New York Times*:

SCIENTISTS DISCOVER, BEYOND DOUBT: PHYSICAL UNIVERSE IS INDETERMINISTIC

Would this really be any better? Return to the moment just before the mugger's choice. His brain and body are in a certain state. Because the universe is indeterministic, this state does not determine his choice. Rather the laws of nature assign a certain probability to a decision to attack, and a certain (presumably lower) probability to a decision to walk away. Now a moment passes and he decides to attack. Why did he make *that* decision? If the process is genuinely indeterministic, this question may have no answer. When the choice was made, it was as if a coin was flipped in the mugger's head. His decision was a chance occurrence, a random fluctuation. And just as it is hard to see how a person can be responsible for a choice determined by factors beyond his control, it is hard to see how he can be responsible for a choice that simply *happens in him* as a result of random chance.

# The Dilemma of Determinism

Putting these pieces together, we face what is sometimes called the *dilemma of determinism:*

A. If determinism is true, we are not responsible, since our choices are determined by factors over which we have no control.

B. If indeterminism is true, we are not responsible, since every choice is a chance occurrence.

C. But either determinism is true or indeterminism is true.

D. Therefore, we are not morally responsible for what we do.

This is a profound problem. Common sense assures us that we are responsible because we are free to choose. The Dilemma tells us that we cannot be free, and that we are therefore not responsible. The only way to vindicate common sense is to find some flaw in the Dilemma. The selections below represent a range of strategies.

A. J. Ayer, Harry Frankfurt, P. F. Strawson, and Susan Wolf all reject (A). These writers are **compatibilists** who hold in various ways that we can be responsible for a choice even though that choice was determined in advance. Roderick Chisholm rejects (B), distinguishing mere chance occurrences, which have no cause, from genuine free choices, which are caused, not by prior events, but by "the agent himself."

Against all of this, Galen Strawson defends a version of the Dilemma, arguing that there is no credible account of human choice that would vindicate our commonsensical view of ourselves as free and responsible.

Some philosophers have suggested that even if human freedom is ultimately an illusion, the illusion is unshakeable in the sense that it is psychologically impossible for us to overcome it. To see what they may be getting at, try an experiment. Next time someone steals your parking space, try to persuade yourself that even though the act was selfish and obnoxious, it wasn't really the driver's fault, since no one is ever morally responsible for what he does. Next time you read a news story about a lying politician or a vicious murderer, try to tell yourself that your immediate reaction—that these people deserve blame and punishment—assumes an incoherent view of human action. Say to yourself, "For all I know, these acts are mere regrettable occurrences for which no one is responsible." The exercise will give you a vivid sense of what is at stake in this debate.

## Galen Strawson (born 1952)

Strawson is Professor of Philosophy at the University of Reading and at the University of Texas, Austin. His work ranges widely in the history of philosophy (*The Secret Connexion,* 1989), the philosophy of mind (*Mental Reality,* 1994), and metaphysics (*Selves: An Essay in Revisionary Metaphysics,* 2009).

# FREE WILL

## 1

You set off for a shop on the evening of a national holiday, intending to buy a cake with your last ten-dollar bill to supplement the preparations you've already made. There's one cake left in the shop and it costs ten dollars; everything is closing down. On the steps of the shop someone is shaking a box, collecting money for famine relief. You stop, and it seems clear to you that it is entirely up to you what you do next. It seems clear to you that you are truly, radically free to choose, in such a way that you will be ultimately morally responsible for whatever you do choose.

There is, however, an argument, which I will call the Basic Argument, that appears to show that we can never be truly or ultimately morally responsible for our actions. According to the Basic Argument, it makes no difference whether determinism is true or false.

The central idea can be quickly conveyed.

(A)  Nothing can be *causa sui* — nothing can be the cause of itself.

(B)  In order to be ultimately morally responsible for one's actions one would have to be *causa sui,* at least in certain crucial mental respects.

(C)  Therefore no one can be ultimately morally responsible.

We can expand it as follows.

(1)  Interested in free action, we're particularly interested in actions performed for a reason (as opposed to reflex actions or mindlessly habitual actions).

(2)  When one acts for a reason, what one does is a function of how one is, mentally speaking. (It's also a function of one's height, one's strength, one's place and time, and so on; but the mental factors are crucial when moral responsibility is in question.)

(3)  So if one is to be truly or ultimately responsible for how one acts, one must be truly or ultimately responsible for how one is, mentally speaking — at least in certain respects.

(4) But to be truly or ultimately responsible for how one is, in any mental respect, one must have brought it about that one is the way one is, in that respect. And it's not merely that one must have caused oneself to be the way one is, in that respect. One must also have consciously and explicitly chosen to be the way one is, in that respect, and one must have succeeded in bringing it about that one is that way.

(5) But one can't really be said to choose, in a conscious, reasoned fashion, to be the way one is in any respect at all, unless one already exists, mentally speaking, already equipped with some principles of choice, "P1" — preferences, values, ideals — in the light of which one chooses how to be.

(6) But then to be truly or ultimately responsible, on account of having chosen to be the way one is, in certain mental respects, one must be truly or ultimately responsible for one's having the principles of choice P1 in the light of which one chose how to be.

(7) But for this to be so one must have chosen P1, in a reasoned, conscious, intentional fashion.

(8) But for this to be so one must already have had some principles of choice P2, in the light of which one chose P1.

(9) And so on. Here we are setting out on a regress that we cannot stop. True or ultimate self-determination is impossible because it requires the actual completion of an infinite series of choices of principles of choice.

(10) So true or ultimate moral responsibility is impossible, because it requires true or ultimate self-determination, as noted in (3).

This may seem contrived, but essentially the same argument can be given in a more natural form. (1) It's undeniable that one is the way one is, initially, as a result of heredity and early experience, and it's undeniable that these are things for which one can't be held to be in any way responsible (morally or otherwise). (2) One can't at any later stage of life hope to accede to true or ultimate moral responsibility for the way one is by trying to change the way one already is as a result of heredity and previous experience. For (3) both the particular way in which one is moved to try to change oneself, and the degree of one's success in one's attempt to change, will be determined by how one already is as a result of heredity and previous experience. And (4) any further changes that one can bring about only after one has brought about certain initial changes will in turn be determined, via the initial changes, by heredity and previous experience. (5) This may not be the whole story; there may be some changes in the way one is that can't be traced to heredity and experience but rather to the influence of indeterministic or random factors. It is, however, absurd to suppose that indeterministic or random factors, for which one is obviously not responsible, can contribute in any way to one's being truly or ultimately morally responsible for how one is.

2

But what is this supposed "true" or "ultimate" moral responsibility? As I understand it, it's responsibility of such a kind that, if we have it, it means that it *makes sense* to suppose that it could be just to punish some of us with (eternal) torment in hell and reward others with (eternal) bliss in heaven. The stress on the words "makes sense" is important, for one certainly doesn't have to believe in any version of the story of heaven and hell in order to understand, or indeed believe in, the kind of true or ultimate moral responsibility that I'm using the story to illustrate. A less colorful way to convey the point, perhaps, is to say that true or ultimate responsibility exists if punishment and reward can be fair without having any sort of pragmatic justification.

One certainly doesn't have to refer to religious faith in order to describe the sorts of everyday situation that give rise to our belief in such responsibility. Choices like the one with which I began (the cake or the collection box) arise all the time, and constantly refresh our conviction about our responsibility. Even if one believes that determinism is true, in such a situation, and that one will in five minutes time be able to look back and say that what one did was determined, this doesn't seem to undermine one's sense of the absoluteness and inescapability of one's freedom, and of one's moral responsibility for one's choice. Even if one accepts the validity of the Basic Argument, which concludes that one cannot be in any way ultimately responsible for the way one is and decides, one's freedom and true moral responsibility seem, as one stands there, obvious and absolute.

Large and small, morally significant or morally neutral, such situations of choice occur regularly in human life. I think they lie at the heart of the experience of freedom and moral responsibility. They're the fundamental source of our inability to give up belief in true or ultimate moral responsibility. We may wonder why human beings experience these situations of choice as they do. It's an interesting question whether any cognitively sophisticated, rational, self-conscious agent must inevitably experience situations of choice in this way (MacKay 1960; Strawson 1986, 281–86). But they are the experiential rock on which the belief in ultimate moral responsibility is founded.

Most people who believe in ultimate moral responsibility take its existence for granted, and don't ever entertain the thought that one needs to be ultimately responsible for the way one *is* in order to be ultimately responsible for the way one *acts*. Some, however, reveal that they see its force. E. H. Carr states that "normal adult human beings are morally responsible for their own personality" (1961, 89). Sartre holds that "man is responsible for what he is" (1989, 29) and seeks to give an account of how we "choose ourselves" (1969, 440, 468, 503). In a later interview he judges his earlier assertions about freedom to be incautious, but still holds that "in the end one is always responsible for what is made of one" (1969). Kant puts it clearly when he claims that "man *himself* must make or have made himself into whatever, in a moral sense, whether good or evil, he is to become. Either condition must be an effect of his free choice; for otherwise he could not be held responsible for it and could therefore be *morally* neither good nor evil" (1960, 40). Since he is committed to belief in radical moral responsibility, Kant holds that such self-creation does indeed take place, and writes accordingly of "man's character, which he himself creates," and of "knowledge of oneself as a person who . . . is his own originator" (1956, 101). John Patten claims that "it is . . . self-evident that as we grow up each individual chooses whether to be good or bad"[1] (1992). Robert Kane, an eloquent recent defender of this view, writes as follows: "if . . . a choice issues from, and can be sufficiently explained by, an agent's character and motives (together with background conditions) then to be ultimately responsible for the choice, the agent must be at least in part responsible by virtue of choices or actions voluntarily performed in the past for having the character and motives he or she now has" (2009, 317–18). Christine Korsgaard agrees: "judgements of responsibility don't really make sense unless people create themselves" (2009, 20).

Most of us, as remarked, never follow this line of thought. It seems, though, that we do tend, in some vague and unexamined fashion, to think of ourselves as responsible for — answerable for — how we are. The point is somewhat delicate, for we don't ordinarily suppose that we have gone through some sort of active process of self-determination at some past time. It seems nevertheless that we do unreflectively experience ourselves, in many respects, rather as we might experience ourselves if we did believe that we had engaged in some such activity of self-determination; and we may well also think of others in this way.

Sometimes a part of one's character — a desire or tendency — may strike one as foreign or alien. But it can do this only against a background of character traits that aren't experienced as foreign, but are rather "identified" with. (It's only relative to such a background that a character trait can stand out as alien.) Some feel tormented by impulses that they experience as alien, but in many a sense of general identification with their character predominates, and this identification seems to carry within itself an implicit sense that one is, generally speaking, in control of, or at least answerable for, how one is (even, perhaps, for aspects of one's character that one doesn't like). So it is arguable that we find, semi-dormant in common thought, an implicit recognition of the idea that true or ultimate moral responsibility for what one does somehow involves responsibility for how one is. It seems that ordinary thought is ready to move this way under pressure.

There are also many aspects of our ordinary sense of ourselves as morally responsible free agents that we don't feel to be threatened in any way by the fact that we can't be ultimately responsible for how we are. We readily accept that we are products of our heredity and environment without feeling that this poses any threat to our freedom and moral responsibility at the time of action. It's very natural to feel that so long as one is fully consciously aware of oneself as able to choose in a situation of choice, then this is already entirely sufficient for one's radical freedom of choice—*whatever* else is or is not the case. It seems, then, that our ordinary conception of moral responsibility may contain mutually inconsistent elements. If this is so, it is a profoundly important fact; it would explain a great deal about the character of the philosophical debate about free will (Strawson 1986, §6.4). But these other elements in our ordinary notion of moral responsibility, important as they are, are not my present subject.

---

1. Quoted in *The Spectator*, April 17, 1992, p. 9. [Strawson's note.]

# 3

I want now to restate the Basic Argument in very loose—as it were conversational—terms. New forms of words allow for new forms of objection, but they may be helpful nonetheless.

> (1) You do what you do, in any situation in which you find yourself, because of the way you are.

So

> (2) To be truly morally responsible for what you do, you must be truly responsible for the way you are—at least in certain crucial mental respects.

Or:

> (1) When you act, what you do is a function of how you are.

(What you do won't count as an action at all unless it flows appropriately from your beliefs, preferences, and so on.) Hence

> (2) You have to get to have some responsibility for how you are in order to get to have some responsibility for what you intentionally do.

Once again I take the qualification about "certain mental respects" for granted. Obviously one isn't responsible for one's sex, basic body pattern, height, and so on. But if one weren't responsible for anything about oneself, how could one be responsible for what one did, given the truth of (1)? *This is the fundamental question,* and it seems clear that if one is going to be responsible for any aspect of oneself, it had better be some aspect of one's mental nature.

I take it that (1) is incontrovertible, and that it is (2) that must be resisted. For if (1) and (2) are conceded the case seems lost, because the full argument runs as follows.

> (1) You do what you do because of the way you are.

So

> (2) To be truly morally responsible for what you do, you must be truly responsible for the way you are—at least in certain crucial mental respects.

But

> (3) You can't be truly responsible for the way you are, so you can't be truly responsible for what you do.

Why can't you be truly responsible for the way you are? Because

> (4) To be truly responsible for the way you are, you must have intentionally brought it about that you are the way you are, and this is impossible.

Why is it impossible? Well, suppose it isn't. Suppose

(5) You have somehow intentionally brought it about that you are the way you now are, and that you have brought this about in such a way that you can now be said to be truly responsible for being the way you are now.

For this to be true

(6) You must already have had a certain nature N in the light of which you intentionally brought it about that you are as you now are.

But then

(7) For it to be true that you are truly responsible for how you now are, you must be truly responsible for having had the nature N in the light of which you intentionally brought it about that you are the way you now are.

So

(8) You must have intentionally brought it about that you had that nature N, in which case you must have existed already with a prior nature in the light of which you intentionally brought it about that you had the nature N in the light of which you intentionally brought it about that you are the way you now are. . . .

Here one is setting off on the regress. Nothing can be *causa sui* in the required way. Even if this attribute is allowed to belong (unintelligibly) to God, it can't plausibly be supposed to be possessed by ordinary finite human beings. "The *causa sui* is the best self-contradiction that has been conceived so far," as Nietzsche remarked in 1886:

> it is a sort of rape and perversion of logic. But the extravagant pride of man has managed to entangle itself profoundly and frightfully with just this nonsense. The desire for "freedom of the will" in the superlative metaphysical sense, which still holds sway, unfortunately, in the minds of the half-educated; the desire to bear the entire and ultimate responsibility for one's actions oneself, and to absolve God, the world, ancestors, chance, and society involves nothing less than to be precisely this *causa sui* and, with more than Baron Münchhausen's audacity, to pull oneself up into existence by the hair, out of the swamps of nothingness. (1966, *Beyond Good and Evil*, 21)

The rephrased argument is essentially exactly the same as before, although the first two steps are now more simply stated. Can the Basic Argument simply be dismissed? Is it really of no importance in the discussion of free will and moral responsibility, as some have claimed? (No and No.) Shouldn't any serious defence of free will and moral responsibility thoroughly acknowledge the respect in which the Basic Argument is valid before going on to try to give its own positive account of the nature of free will and moral responsibility? Doesn't the argument go to the heart of things if the heart of the free will debate is a concern about whether we can be truly morally responsible in the absolute way that we ordinarily suppose? (Yes and Yes.)

We are what we are, and we can't be thought to have made ourselves *in such a way* that we can be held to be free in our actions *in such a way* that we can be held to be morally responsible for our actions *in such a way* that any punishment or reward for our actions is ultimately just or fair. Punishments and rewards may seem deeply appropriate or intrinsically "fitting" to us; many of the various institutions of punishment and reward in human society appear to be practically indispensable in both their legal and non-legal forms. But if one takes the notion of justice that is central to our intellectual and cultural tradition seriously, then the consequence of the Basic Argument is that there is a fundamental sense in which no punishment or reward is ever just. It is exactly as just to punish or reward people for their actions as it is to punish or reward them for the (natural) color of their hair or the (natural) shape of their faces.

# 4

I have suggested that it is step (2) of the restated Basic Argument that must be rejected, and of course it can be rejected, because the phrases "truly responsible" and "truly morally responsible" can be defined in many ways. I'll sketch three sorts of response.

(I) The first response is *compatibilist*. Compatibilists say that one can be a free and morally responsible agent even if determinism is true. They claim that one can correctly be said to be truly responsible for what one does, when one acts, just so long as one isn't caused to act by any of a certain set of constraints (kleptomaniac impulses, obsessional neuroses, desires that are experienced as alien, post-hypnotic commands, threats, instances of *force majeure*, and so on). They don't impose any requirement that one should be truly responsible for how one is, so step (2) of the Basic Argument comes out as false. They think one can be fully morally responsible even if the way one is is totally determined by factors entirely outside one's control. They simply reject the Basic Argument. They know that the kind of responsibility ruled out by the Basic Argument is impossible, and conclude that it can't be the kind of responsibility that is really in question in human life, because we are indeed genuinely morally responsible agents. No theory that concludes otherwise can possibly be right, on their view.

(II) The second response is *libertarian*. *Incompatibilists* believe that freedom and moral responsibility are incompatible with determinism, and some incompatibilists are libertarians, who believe that we are free and morally responsible agents, and that determinism is therefore false. Robert Kane, for example, allows that we may act responsibly from a will already formed, but argues that the will must in this case be "'our own' free will by virtue of other past 'self-forming' choices or other actions that were undetermined and by which we made ourselves into the kinds of persons we are. . . . [T]hese undetermined self-forming actions (SFAs) occur at those difficult times of life when we are torn between competing visions of what we should do or become" (2009, 279). They paradigmatically involve a conflict between moral duty and non-moral desire, and it is essential that they involve indeterminism, on Kane's view, for this "screens off complete determination by influences of the past" (ibid., 279). He proposes that we are in such cases of "moral, prudential and practical struggle . . . truly 'making ourselves' in such a way that we are ultimately responsible for the outcome," and that this "making of ourselves" means that "we can be ultimately responsible for our present motives and character by virtue of past choices which helped to form them and for which we were ultimately responsible" (1989, 252).

Kane, then, accepts step (2) of the Basic Argument, and challenges step (3) instead. He accepts that we have to "make ourselves," and so be ultimately responsible for ourselves, in order to be morally responsible for what we do. But the old objection to libertarianism recurs. How can indeterminism help with moral responsibility? How can the occurrence of partly random or indeterministic events contribute to my being truly or ultimately morally responsible either for my actions or for my character? If my efforts of will shape my character in an admirable way, and are in so doing partly indeterministic in nature, while also being shaped (as Kane grants) by my already existing character, why am I not merely *lucky*?

(III) The third response begins by accepting that one can't be held to be ultimately responsible for one's character or personality or motivational structure. It accepts that this is so whether determinism is true or false. It then directly challenges step (2) of the Basic Argument. It appeals to a certain picture of the *self* in order to argue that one can be truly free and morally responsible in spite of the fact that one can't be held to be ultimately responsible for one's character or personality or motivational structure.

This picture can be set out as follows. One is free and truly morally responsible because one's self is, in a crucial sense, independent of one's character or personality or motivational structure — one's CPM, for short. Suppose one is in a situation which one experiences as a difficult choice between A, doing one's duty, and B, following one's non-moral desires. Given one's CPM, one responds in a certain way. One's desires and beliefs develop and interact and constitute reasons in favour both of A and of B, and one's CPM makes one tend towards either A or B. So far the problem is the same as ever: whatever one does, one will do what one does because of the way one's CPM is, and since one neither is nor can be ultimately responsible for the way one's CPM is, one can't be ultimately responsible for what one does.

Enter one's self, S. S is imagined to be in some way independent of one's CPM. S (i.e., one) considers the outputs of one's CPM and decides in the light of them, but it — S — incorporates a power of decision that is independent of one's CPM in such a way that one can after all count as truly and ultimately morally responsible in one's decisions and actions, even though one isn't ultimately responsible for one's CPM. The idea is that step (2) of the Basic Argument is false because of the existence of S (Campbell 1957).

The trouble with the picture is obvious. S (i.e., one) decides on the basis of the deliverances of one's CPM. But whatever S decides, it decides as it does because of the way it is (or because of the occurrence in the decision process of indeterministic factors for which it — i.e., one — can't be responsible, and which can't plausibly be thought to contribute to one's true moral responsibility). And this brings us back to where we started. To be a source of true or ultimate responsibility, S must be responsible for being the way it is. But this is impossible, for the reasons given in the Basic Argument. So while the story of S and CPM adds another layer to the description of the human decision process, it can't change the fact that human beings cannot be ultimately self-determining in such a way as to be ultimately morally responsible for how they are, and thus for how they decide and act.

In spite of all these difficulties, many (perhaps most) of us continue to believe that we are truly morally responsible agents in the strongest possible sense. Many feel that our capacity for fully explicit self-conscious deliberation in a situation of choice suffices — all by itself — to constitute us as such. All that is needed for true or ultimate responsibility, on this view, is that one is in the moment of action *fully self-consciously aware of oneself as an agent facing choices.*

The Basic Argument, however, appears to show that this is a mistake: however self-consciously aware we are as we deliberate and reason, every act and operation of our mind happens as it does as a result of features for which we are ultimately in no way responsible. Nevertheless the conviction that self-conscious awareness of one's situation can be a sufficient foundation of strong free will is very powerful. It runs deeper than rational argument, and it survives untouched, in the everyday conduct of life, even after the validity of the Basic Argument has been admitted.

REFERENCES

Campbell, C. A. 1957. "Has the Self Free Will?" In C. A. Campbell, *On Selfhood* and *Godhood*, Allen and Unwin, London.

Carr, E. H. 1961. *What Is History?*, Macmillan, London.

Kane, R. 1989. "Two Kinds of Incompatibilism," *Philosophy and Phenomenological Research* 50: 219-54.

Kane, R. 2009. "Free Will: New Directions for an Ancient Problem" in D. Pereboom, ed., *Free Will*, 2nd ed., Hackett, Indianapolis.

Kant, I. 1956. *Critique of Practical Reason*, trans. L. W. Beck, Bobbs-Merrill, Indianapolis.

Kant, I. 1960. *Religion within the Limits of Reason Alone*, trans. T. M. Greene and H. H. Hudson, Harper and Row, New York.

Korsgaard, C. 2009. *Self-Constitution: Agency, Identity, and Integrity*, Oxford University Press, Oxford.

Mackay, D. M. 1960. "On the Logic of Free Choice," *Mind* 69: 31–40.

Nietzsche, F. 1966. *Beyond Good and Evil*, trans., Walter Kaufmann, Random House, New York.

Sartre, J.-P., 1969. *Being and Nothingness,* trans. Hazel E. Barnes, Methuen, London.
Sartre, J.-P., 1989. *Existentialism and Humanism,* trans. Philip Mairet, Methuen, London.
Strawson, G. 1986. *Freedom and Belief,* Oxford University Press, Oxford.

## TEST YOUR UNDERSTANDING

1. Galen Strawson's conclusion is that we cannot be "truly and ultimately" responsible for what we do. Say what this means.

2. Explain the basis for Strawson's claim that "true or ultimate self-determination is impossible because it requires the actual completion of an infinite series of choices of principles of choice."

## NOTES AND QUESTIONS

1. Galen Strawson's argument depends crucially on what is sometimes called a *transfer principle:* a principle according to which we are only responsible for a choice if we are responsible for at least some of the prior facts that ground the choice. In Strawson's case, the principle maintains that we are morally responsible for an action only if we are morally responsible for the beliefs, desires, and values that led us to perform it, even if these prior mental states did not causally determine the act in question.

   But is this right? Suppose Jones kills Smith because he hates Smith and wants to see him dead. At trial the prosecutor says:

   > The defendant has hated Smith for years, but he is not on trial for hating Smith. The defendant is clearly a bad man, but he is not on trial for being a bad man. So it does not matter whether he is morally responsible for being the man he is. The defendant is on trial for killing Smith, and for this he has no excuse. No one made him kill Smith. He was not determined by prior causes to kill Smith. After all, many people in the defendant's circumstances were just as bad as he, and hated Smith just as much, but they did not kill Smith. The defendant alone acted on his hatred, and we seek to punish him for this act. His attorney, Professor Strawson, will tell you that since the choice was not determined by his prior mental states, the defendant is a "victim of random chance," and that it would therefore be a travesty to blame him. Nonsense. Chance did not make him act. Chance is not a force in our lives. To say that his choice occurred by "chance" is just to say that nothing forced him to choose. That is not an excuse! He is responsible.

   How might Strawson respond?

2. Galen Strawson's argument is developed in detail in *Freedom and Belief* (Oxford University Press, 1986; rev. ed. 2010).

## Roderick Chisholm (1916-1999)

Chisholm is the author of influential studies in metaphysics (*Person and Object*, 1976), epistemology (*The Foundations of Knowing*, 1982), and the philosophy of mind and language (*The First Person,* 1981). His collection of texts (*Realism and the Background of Phenomenology*, 1960) was an early effort to connect twentieth-century analytic philosophy with the tradition of European phenomenology.

# HUMAN FREEDOM AND THE SELF

> "A staff moves a stone, and is moved by a hand, which
> is moved by a man." Aristotle, *Physics.* 256a

1. The metaphysical problem of human freedom might be summarized in the following way: Human beings are responsible agents: but this fact appears to conflict with a deterministic view of human action (the view that every event that is involved in an act is caused by some other event): and it *also* appears to conflict with an indeterministic view of human action (the view that the act, or some event that is essential to the act, is not caused at all). To solve the problem, I believe, we must make somewhat far-reaching assumptions about the self or the agent — about the man who performs the act. . . .

2. Let us consider some deed, or misdeed, that may be attributed to a responsible agent: one man, say, shot another. If the man *was* responsible for what he did, then, I would urge, what was to happen at the time of the shooting was something that was entirely up to the man himself. There was a moment at which it was true, both that he could have fired the shot and also that he could have refrained from firing it. And if this is so, then, even though he did fire it, he could have done something else instead. (He didn't find himself firing the shot "against his will," as we say.) I think we can say, more generally, then, that if a man is responsible for a certain event or a certain state of affairs (in our example, the shooting of another man), then that event or state of affairs was brought about by some act of his, and the act was something that was in his power either to perform or not to perform.

But now if the act which he *did* perform was an act that was also in his power *not* to perform, then it could not have been caused or determined by any event that was not itself within his power either to bring about or not to bring about. For example, if what we say he did was really something that was brought about by a second man, one who forced his hand upon the trigger, say, or who, by means of hypnosis, compelled him to perform the act, then since the act was caused by the *second* man it was nothing that was within the power of the *first* man to prevent. And precisely the same thing is true, I think, if instead of referring to a second man who compelled the first one, we speak instead of the *desires* and *beliefs* which the first man happens to have had. For if what we say he did was really something that was brought about by his own beliefs and desires, if these beliefs and desires in the particular situation in which he happened to have found himself caused him to do just what it was that we say he did do, then, since *they* caused it, *he* was unable to do anything other than just what it was that he did do. It makes no difference whether the cause of the deed was internal or external; if the cause was some state or event for which the man himself was not responsible, then he was not responsible for what we have been mistakenly calling his act. . . . (It is true, of course, that if the man is responsible for the beliefs and desires that he happens to have, then he may also be responsible for the things they lead him to do. But the question now becomes: *is* he responsible for the beliefs and desires he happens to have? If he is, then there was a time when they were within his power either to acquire or not to acquire, and we are left, therefore, with our general point.) . . .

There is one standard objection to all of this and we should consider it briefly.

3. The objection takes the form of a stratagem — one designed to show that determinism (and divine providence) is consistent with human responsibility. The strategem is one that was used by Jonathan Edwards and by many philosophers in the present century, most notably, G. E. Moore.[1]

One proceeds as follows: The expression

(a) He could have done otherwise,

it is argued, means no more nor less than

(b) If he had chosen to do otherwise, then he would have done otherwise.

(In place of "chosen," one might say "tried," "set out," "decided," "undertaken," or "willed.") The truth of statement (b), it is then pointed out, is consistent with determinism (and with divine providence): for even if all of the man's actions were causally determined, the man could still be such that, *if* he had chosen otherwise, then he would have done otherwise. What the murderer saw, let us suppose, along with his beliefs and desires, *caused* him to fire the shot: yet he was such that *if,* just then, he had chosen or decided *not* to fire the shot, then he would not have fired it. All of this is certainly possible. . . . And therefore, the argument proceeds, if (b) is consistent with determinism, and if (a) and (b) say the same thing, then (a) is also consistent with determinism; hence we can say that the agent *could* have done otherwise even though he was caused to do what he did do; and therefore determinism and moral responsibility are compatible.

Is the argument sound? The conclusion follows from the premises, but the catch, I think, lies in the first premise — the one saying that statement (a) tells us no more nor less than what statement (b) tells us. For (b), it would seem, could be true while (a) is false. That is to say, our man might be such that, if he had chosen to do otherwise, then he would have done otherwise, and yet *also* such that he could not have done otherwise. Suppose, after all, that our murderer could not have *chosen,* or could not have *decided,* to do otherwise. Then the fact that he happens also to be a man such that, if he had chosen not to shoot he would not have shot, would make no difference. For if he could *not* have chosen *not* to shoot, then he could not have done anything other than just what it was that he did do. In a word: from our statement (b) above ("If he had chosen to do otherwise, then he would have done otherwise"), we cannot make an inference to (a) above ("He could have done otherwise") unless we can *also* assert:

(c) He could have chosen to do otherwise.

1. Jonathan Edwards, *Freedom of the Will* (Yale University Press, 1957): G. E. Moore, *Ethics* (Home University Library, 1912). ch. 6. [Chisholm's note.]

And therefore, if we must reject this third statement (c), then, even though we may be justified in asserting (b), we are not justified in asserting (a). If the man could not have chosen to do otherwise, then he would not have done otherwise — *even if* he was such that, if he *had* chosen to do otherwise, then he would have done otherwise.

The strategem in question, then, seems to me not to work, and I would say, therefore, that the ascription of responsibility conflicts with a deterministic view of action.

4. Perhaps there is less need to argue that the ascription of responsibility also conflicts with an indeterministic view of action — with the view that the act, or some event that is essential to the act, is not caused at all. If the act — the firing of the shot — was not caused at all, if it was fortuitous or capricious, happening so to speak out of the blue, then, presumably, no one — and nothing — was responsible for the act. Our conception of action, therefore, should be neither deterministic nor indeterministic. Is there any other possibility?

5. We must not say that every event involved in the act is caused by some other event; and we must not say that the act is something that is not caused at all. The possibility that remains, therefore, is this: We should say that at least one of the events that are involved in the act is caused, not by any other events, but by something else instead. And this something else can only be the agent — the man. If there is an event that is caused, not by other events, but by the man, then there are some events involved in the act that are not caused by other events. But if the event in question is caused by the man then it *is* caused and we are not committed to saying that there is something involved in the act that is not caused at all.

But this, of course, is a large consequence, implying something of considerable importance about the nature of the agent or the man.

6. If we consider only inanimate natural objects, we may say that causation, if it occurs, is a relation between *events* or *states of affairs.* The dam's breaking was an event that was caused by a set of other events — the dam being weak, the flood being strong, and so on. But if a man is responsible for a particular deed, then, if what I have said is true, there is some event, or set of events, that is caused, *not* by other events or states of affairs, but by the agent, whatever he may be.

I shall borrow a pair of medieval terms, using them, perhaps, in a way that is slightly different from that for which they were originally intended. I shall say that when one event or state of affairs (or set of events or states of affairs) causes some other event or state of affairs, then we have an instance of *transeunt* causation. And I shall say that when an *agent,* as distinguished from an event, causes an event or state of affairs, then we have an instance of *immanent* causation.

The nature of what is intended by the expression "immanent causation" may be illustrated by this sentence from Aristotle's *Physics*: "Thus, a staff moves a stone, and is moved by a hand, which is moved by a man." (VII, 5, 256a, 6–8) If the man was responsible, then we have in this illustration a number of instances of causation — most of them transeunt but at least one of them immanent. What the staff did to the stone was an instance of transeunt causation, and thus we may describe it as a relation between events: "the motion of the staff caused the motion of the stone."

And similarly for what the hand did to the staff: "the motion of the hand caused the motion of the staff." And, as we know from physiology, there are still other events which caused the motion of the hand. Hence we need not introduce the agent at this particular point, as Aristotle does — we *need* not, though we *may*. We *may* say that the hand was moved by the man, but we may *also* say that the motion of the hand was caused by the motion of certain muscles; and we may say that the motion of the muscles was caused by certain events that took place within the brain. But some event, and presumably one of those that took place within the brain, was caused by the agent and not by any other events. . . .

7. One may object, firstly: "If the *man* does anything, then, as Aristotle's remark suggests, what he does is to move the *hand*. But he certainly does not *do* anything to his brain — he may not even know that he *has* a brain. And if he doesn't do anything to the brain, and if the motion of the hand was caused by something that happened within the brain, then there is no point in appealing to 'immanent causation' as being something incompatible with 'transeunt causation' — for the whole thing, after all, is a matter of causal relations among events or states of affairs."

The answer to this objection, I think, is this: It is true that the agent does not *do* anything with his brain, or to his brain, in the sense in which he *does* something with his hand and does something to the staff. But from this it does not follow that the agent was not the immanent cause of something that happened within his brain.

We should note a useful distinction that has been proposed by Professor A. I. Melden — namely, the distinction between "making something A happen" and "doing A."[2] If I reach for the staff and pick it up, then one of the things that I *do* is just that — reach for the staff and pick it up. And if it is something that I do, then there is a very clear sense in which it may be said to be something that I know that I do. If you ask me, "Are you doing something, or trying to do something, with the staff?," I will have no difficulty in finding an answer. But in doing something with the staff, I also make various things happen which are not in this same sense things that I do: I will make various air-particles move; I will free a number of blades of grass from the pressure that had been upon them; and I may cause a shadow to move from one place to another. If these are merely things that I make happen, as distinguished from things that I do, then I may know nothing whatever about them; I may not have the slightest idea that, in moving the staff, I am bringing about any such thing as the motion of air-particles, shadows, and blades of grass.

We may say, in answer to the first objection, therefore, that it is true that our agent does nothing to his brain or with his brain; but from this it does not follow that the agent is not the immanent cause of some event within his brain; for the brain event may be something which, like the motion of the air-particles, he made happen in picking up the staff. . . .

The point is, in a word, that whenever a man does something A, then (by "immanent causation") he makes a certain cerebral event happen, and this cerebral event (by "transeunt causation") makes A happen.

2. A. I. Melden, *Free Action* (Routledge and Kegan Paul, 1961), especially ch. 3. Mr. Melden's own views, however, are quite the contrary of those that are proposed here. [Chisholm's note.]

8. The second objection is more difficult and concerns the very concept of "immanent causation," or causation by an agent, as this concept is to be interpreted here. The concept is subject to a difficulty which has long been associated with that of the prime mover unmoved. We have said that there must be some event A, presumably some cerebral event, which is caused not by any other event, but by the agent. Since A was not caused by any other event, then the agent himself cannot be said to have undergone any change or produced any other event (such as "an act of will" or the like) which brought A about. But if, when the agent made A happen, there was no event involved other than A itself, no event which could be described as *making* A happen, what did the agent's causation consist of? What, for example, is the difference between A's just happening, and the agents' *causing* A to happen? We cannot attribute the difference to any event that took place within the agent. And so far as the event A itself is concerned, there would seem to be no discernible difference. . . . Must we conclude, then, that there is no more to the man's action in causing event A than there is to the event A's happening by itself? . . .

The only answer, I think, can be this: that the difference between the man's causing A, on the one hand, and the event A just happening, on the other, lies in the fact that, in the first case but not the second, the event A *was* caused and was caused by the man. There was a brain event A; the agent did, in fact, cause the brain event; but there was nothing that he did to cause it.

This answer may not entirely satisfy and it will be likely to provoke the following question: "But what are you really *adding* to the assertion that A happened when you utter the words 'The agent *caused* A to happen'?" As soon as we have put the question this way, we see, I think, that whatever difficulty we may have encountered is one that may be traced to the concept of causation generally — whether "immanent" or "transeunt." . . .

For the problem, as we put it, referring just to "immanent causation," or causation by an agent, was this: "What is the difference between saying, of an event A, that A just happened and saying that someone caused A to happen?" The analogous problem, which holds for "transeunt causation," or causation by an event, is this: "What is the difference between saying, of two events A and B, that B happened and then A happened, and saying that B's happening was the *cause* of A's happening?" And the only answer that one can give is this — that in the one case the agent was the cause of A's happening and in the other case event B was the cause of A's happening. The nature of transeunt causation is no more clear than is that of immanent causation. . . .

11. If we are responsible, and if what I have been trying to say is true, then we have a prerogative which some would attribute only to God: each of us, when we act, is a prime mover unmoved. In doing what we do, we cause certain events to happen, and nothing — or no one — causes us to cause those events to happen.

12. If we are thus prime movers unmoved and if our actions, or those for which we are responsible, are not causally determined, then they are not causally determined by our *desires*. And this means that the relation between what we want or what we desire, on the one hand, and what it is that we do, on the other, is not as simple as most philosophers would have it.

We may distinguish between what we might call the "Hobbist approach" and what we might call the "Kantian approach" to this question. The Hobbist approach is the one that is generally accepted at the present time,[3] but the Kantian approach, I believe, is the one that is true. According to Hobbism, if we *know*, of some man, what his beliefs and desires happen to be and how strong they are, if we know what he feels certain of, what he desires more than anything else, and if we know the state of his body and what stimuli he is being subjected to, then we may *deduce*, logically, just what it is that he will do — or, more accurately, just what it is that he will try, set out, or undertake to do. . . . But according to the Kantian approach to our problem, and this is the one that I would take, there is no such logical connection between wanting and doing, nor need there even be a causal connection. No set of statements about a man's desires, beliefs, and stimulus situation at any time implies any statement telling us what the man will try, set out, or undertake to do at that time. As Reid[4] put it, though we may "reason from men's motives to their actions and, in many cases, with great probability," we can never do so "with absolute certainty."

This means that, in one very strict sense of the terms, there can be no science of man. If we think of science as a matter of finding out what laws happen to hold, and if the statement of a law tells us what kinds of events are caused by what other kinds of events, then there will be human actions which we cannot explain by subsuming them under any laws. We cannot say, "It is causally necessary that, given such and such desires and beliefs, and being subject to such and such stimuli, the agent will do so and so." For at times the agent, if he chooses, may rise above his desires and do something else instead.

But all of this is consistent with saying that, perhaps more often than not, our desires do exist under conditions such that those conditions necessitate us to act. And we may also say, with Leibniz,[5] that at other times our desires may "incline without necessitating."

13. Leibniz's phrase presents us with our final philosophical problem. What does it mean to say that a desire, or a motive, might "incline without necessitating"? There is a temptation, certainly, to say that "to incline" means to cause and that "not to necessitate" means not to cause, but obviously we cannot have it both ways. . . .

Let us consider a public official who has some moral scruples but who also, as one says, could be had. Because of the scruples that he does have, he would never take any positive steps to receive a bribe — he would not actively solicit one. But his morality has its limits and he is also such that, if we were to confront him with a *fait accompli* or to let him see what is about to happen ($10,000 in cash is being deposited behind the garage), then he would succumb and be unable to resist. The general situation is a familiar one and this is one reason that people pray to be delivered from temptation. (It also justifies Kant's remark: "And how many there are who may have led a long blameless life, who are only *fortunate* in having escaped so many

3. Chisholm's essay was first published in 1964.

4. Thomas Reid (1710–1796), Scottish philosopher famous for his defense of "common sense" against the skeptical arguments of David Hume and others. The quoted passage is from his *Essays on the Active Powers of the Human Mind* (1788).

5. Gottfried Wilhelm Leibniz (1646–1716), German philosopher and mathematician.

temptations."[6] Our relation to the misdeed that we contemplate may not be a matter simply of being able to bring it about or not to bring it about. As St. Anselm noted, there are at least four possibilities. We may illustrate them by reference to our public official and the event which is his receiving the bribe, in the following way: (i) he may be able to bring the event about himself (*facere esse*), in which case he would actively cause himself to receive the bribe; (ii) he may be able to refrain from bringing it about himself (*non facere esse*), in which case he would not himself do anything to insure that he receive the bribe; (iii) he may be able to do something to prevent the event from occurring (*facere non esse*), in which case he would make sure that the $10,000 was *not* left behind the garage; or (iv) he may be unable to do anything to prevent the event from occurring, in which case, though he may not solicit the bribe, he would allow himself to keep it. We have envisaged our official as a man who can resist the temptation to (i) but cannot resist the temptation to (iv): he can refrain from bringing the event about himself, but he cannot bring himself to do anything to prevent it.

Let us think of "inclination without necessitation," then, in such terms as these. First we may contrast the two propositions:

1. He can resist the temptation to do something in order to make A happen;

2. He can resist the temptation to allow A to happen (i.e. to do nothing to prevent A from happening).

We may suppose that the man has some desire to have A happen and thus has a motive for making A happen. His motive for making A happen, I suggest, is one that *necessitates* provided that, because of the motive, (1) is false; he cannot resist the temptation to do something in order to make A happen. His motive for making A happen is one that *inclines* provided that, because of the motive, (2) is false; like our public official, he cannot bring himself to do anything to prevent A from happening. And therefore we can say that this motive for making A happen is one that *inclines but does not necessitate* provided that, because of the motive, (1) is true and (2) is false; he can resist the temptation to make it happen but he cannot resist the temptation to allow it to happen.

## TEST YOUR UNDERSTANDING

1. Chisholm rejects G. E. Moore's suggestion that "He could have done otherwise" simply means "If he had chosen to do otherwise, he would have done otherwise." Explain the proposal and say why Chisholm rejects it.

2. Explain the distinction between *transeunt* and *immanent causation.*

3. Pick an ordinary free action and tell its story in Chisholm's way. Indicate the various causes it might have had and say exactly where in the story immanent causation does its work.

6. In the Preface to the *"Metaphysical Elements of Ethics,"* in *Kant's Critique of Practical Reason and Other Works on the Theory of Ethics,* ed. T. K. Abbott (Longman, 1959), p. 303. [Chisholm's note.]

## NOTES AND QUESTIONS

1. *Puzzles about agent causation.* According to Chisholm, a free choice is an event in the brain that is not caused by prior events, but rather by the agent himself. Chisholm calls this *immanent* causation, or sometimes **agent causation.** One of the main aims of Chisholm's essay is to suggest that agent causation is not more puzzling or mysterious than ordinary causation among events, but is this right?

   *The epistemological problem.* We can test claims of ordinary causation in many ways. If we want to know whether the mixture exploded *because it contained chemical X,* we can prepare a similar mixture that lacks X and see what happens. If it explodes in exactly the same way, that is good evidence that X was not a cause of the explosion. If it does not explode, that is evidence that X was indeed a cause. (For extensive discussion, see chapter 5 of this anthology.) How can we test claims of agent causation? Suppose we observe some event in Fred's brain—his choice to scratch his nose, for example. Suppose we can rule out the possibility that this event was caused by prior events. According to Chisholm, that leaves two possibilities: either the choice was caused by *Fred,* or it was a random occurrence with no determining cause at all. What evidence could possibly allow us to choose between these two hypotheses?

   *The metaphysical problem.* Chisholm tells us that human beings can cause events in their own brains. But are there any principled limits to this sort of causation? Suppose a radioactive atom in a box in front of you suddenly decays, and that careful investigation reveals that this event was not caused by prior events. Is it possible that this atom *caused itself to decay*? Is it possible that *you* caused it to decay? Are *rabbits* the agent-causes of their behavior? These possibilities sound absurd, but how can we exclude them? Until we can say *something* about the principles that govern agent causation, we cannot pretend to understand the notion.

   *Exercise:* Say how Chisholm might respond to these objections.

2. Chisholm's theory is presented and modified in *Person and Object* (Open Court, 1976). For a sympathetic defense, see Randolph Clarke, "Toward a Credible Agent-Causal Account of Free Will," *Noûs* 27, no.2 (1993).

## A. J. Ayer (1910–1989)

Ayer was one of the most distinguished representatives in the twentieth century of the British empiricist tradition of Locke, Hume, and Mill. His early manifesto, *Language, Truth and Logic* (1936), is a vigorous defense of the view that the claims of morality, religion, and metaphysics are mostly meaningless, since they are neither analytic (true simply in virtue of the meanings of words) nor empirically verifiable.

# FREEDOM AND NECESSITY

When I am said to have done something of my own free will it is implied that I could have acted otherwise; and it is only when it is believed that I could have acted otherwise that I am held to be morally responsible for what I have done. For a man is not thought to be morally responsible for an action that it was not in his power to avoid. But if human behavior is entirely governed by causal laws, it is not clear how any action that is done could ever have been avoided. It may be said of the agent that he would have acted otherwise if the causes of his action had been different, but they being what they were, it seems to follow that he was bound to act as he did. Now it is commonly assumed both that men are capable of acting freely, in the sense that is required to make them morally responsible, and that human behavior is entirely governed by causal laws: and it is the apparent conflict between these two assumptions that gives rise to the philosophical problem of the freedom of the will.

Confronted with this problem, many people will be inclined to agree with Dr. Johnson: "Sir, we *know* our will is free, and *there's* an end on't."[1] But, while this does very well for those who accept Dr. Johnson's premiss, it would hardly convince anyone who denied the freedom of the will. . . . What is evident, indeed, is that people often believe themselves to be acting freely; and it is to this "feeling" of freedom that some philosophers appeal when they wish, in the supposed interests of morality, to prove that not all human action is causally determined. But if these philosophers are right in their assumption that a man cannot be acting freely if his action is causally determined, then the fact that someone feels free to do, or not to do, a certain action does not prove that he really is so. It may prove that the agent does not himself know what it is that makes him act in one way rather than another: but from the fact a man is unaware of the causes of his action, it does not follow that no such causes exist.

So much may be allowed to the determinist; but his belief that all human actions are subservient to causal laws still remains to be justified. If, indeed, it is necessary that every event should have a cause, then the rule must apply to human behavior as much as to anything else. But why should it be supposed that every event must have a cause? The contrary is not unthinkable. Nor is the law of universal causation a necessary presupposition of scientific thought. The scientist may try to discover causal laws, and in many cases he succeeds; but sometimes he has to be content with statistical laws, and sometimes he comes upon events which, in the present state of his knowledge, he is not able to subsume under any law at all. In the case of these events he assumes that if he knew more he would be able to discover some law, whether causal or statistical, which would enable him to account for them. And this assumption cannot be disproved. For however far he may have carried his investigation, it is always open to him to carry it further; and it is always conceivable that if he

---

1. Samuel Johnson (1709–1784), English author and lexicographer. The famous remark is quoted in John Boswell's *Life of Samuel Johnson.*

carried it further he would discover the connection which had hitherto escaped him. Nevertheless, it is also conceivable that the events with which he is concerned are not systematically connected with any others: so that the reason why he does not discover the sort of laws that he requires is simply that they do not obtain.

Now in the case of human conduct the search for explanations has not in fact been altogether fruitless. Certain scientific laws have been established; and with the help of these laws we do make a number of successful predictions about the ways in which different people will behave. But these predictions do not always cover every detail. We may be able to predict that in certain circumstances a particular man will be angry, without being able to prescribe the precise form that the expression of his anger will take. We may be reasonably sure that he will shout, but not sure how loud his shout will be, or exactly what words he will use. And it is only a small proportion of human actions that we are able to forecast even so precisely as this. But that, it may be said, is because we have not carried our investigations very far. The science of psychology is still in its infancy and, as it is developed, not only will more human actions be explained, but the explanations will go into greater detail. The ideal of complete explanation may never in fact be attained: but it is theoretically attainable. Well, this may be so: and certainly it is impossible to show *a priori* that it is not so: but equally it cannot be shown that it is. This will not, however, discourage the scientist who, in the field of human behavior, as elsewhere, will continue to formulate theories and test them by the facts. And in this he is justified. For since he has no reason *a priori* to admit that there is a limit to what he can discover, the fact that he also cannot be sure that there is no limit does not make it unreasonable for him to devise theories, nor, having devised them, to try constantly to improve them.

But now suppose it to be claimed that, so far as men's actions are concerned, there is a limit: and that this limit is set by the fact of human freedom. An obvious objection is that in many cases in which a person feels himself be free to do, or not to do, a certain action, we are even now able to explain, in causal terms, why it is that he acts as he does. But it might be argued that even if men are sometimes mistaken in believing that they act freely, it does not follow that they are always so mistaken. For it is not always the case that when a man believes that he has acted freely we are in fact able to account for his action in causal terms. A determinist would say that we should be able to account for it if we had more knowledge of the circumstances, and had been able to discover the appropriate natural laws. But until those discoveries have been made, this remains only a pious hope. And may it not be true that, in some cases at least, the reason why we can give no causal explanation is that no causal explanation is available; and that this is because the agent's choice was literally free, as he himself felt it to be?

The answer is that this may indeed be true, inasmuch as it is open to anyone to hold that no explanation is possible until some explanation is actually found. But even so it does not give the moralist what he wants. For he is anxious to show that men are capable of acting freely in order to infer that they can be morally responsible for what they do. But if it is a matter of pure chance that a man should act in one way rather than another, he may be free but he can hardly be responsible. And indeed when a man's actions seem to us quite unpredictable, when, as we say, there is no knowing what he will do, we do not look upon him as a moral agent. We look upon him rather as a lunatic.

To this it may be objected that we are not dealing fairly with the moralist. For when he makes it a condition of my being morally responsible that I should act freely, he does not wish to imply that it is purely a matter of chance that I act as I do. What he wishes to imply is that my actions are the result of my own free choice: and it is because they are the result of my own free choice that I am held to be morally responsible for them.

But now we must ask how it is that I come to make my choice. Either it is an accident that I choose to act as I do or it is not. If it is an accident, then it is merely a matter of chance that I did not choose otherwise; and if it is merely a matter of chance that I did not choose otherwise, it is surely irrational to hold me morally responsible for choosing as I did. But if it is not an accident that I choose to do one thing rather than another, then presumably there is some causal explanation of my choice: and in that case we are led back to determinism.

Again, the objection may be raised that we are not doing justice to the moralist's case. His view is not that it is a matter of chance that I choose to act as I do, but rather that my choice depends upon my character. Nevertheless he holds that I can still be free in the sense that he requires; for it is I who am responsible for my character. But in what way am I responsible for my character? Only, surely, in the sense that there is a causal connection between what I do now and what I have done in the past. It is only this that justifies the statement that I have made myself what I am: and even so this is an over-simplification, since it takes no account of the external influences to which I have been subjected. But, ignoring the external influences, let us assume that it is in fact the case that I have made myself what I am. Then it is still legitimate to ask how it is that I have come to make myself one sort of person rather than another. And if it be answered that it is a matter of my strength of will, we can put the same question in another form by asking how it is that my will has the strength that it has and not some other degree of strength. Once more, either it is an accident or it is not. If it is an accident, then by the same argument as before, I am not morally responsible, and if it is not an accident we are led back to determinism.

Furthermore, to say that my actions proceed from my character or, more colloquially, that I act in character, is to say that my behavior is consistent and to that extent predictable: and since it is, above all, for the actions that I perform in character that I am held to be morally responsible, it looks as if the admission of moral responsibility, so far from being incompatible with determinism, tends rather to presuppose it. But how can this be so if it is a necessary condition of moral responsibility that the person who is held responsible should have acted freely? It seems that if we are to retain this idea of moral responsibility, we must either show that men can be held responsible for actions which they do not do freely, or else find some way of reconciling determinism with the freedom of the will.

Let it be granted . . . [that] when we speak of reconciling freedom with determinism we are using the word "freedom" in an ordinary sense. It still remains for us to make this usage clear: and perhaps the best way to make it clear is to show what it is that freedom, in this sense, is contrasted with. Now we began with the assumption that freedom is contrasted with causality, so that a man cannot be said to be acting freely if his action is causally determined. But this assumption has led us into difficulties and I now wish to suggest that it is mistaken. For it is not, I think, causality that freedom is to be contrasted with, but constraint. And while it is true that being constrained to do an action entails being caused to do it, I shall try to show that the converse does not hold. I shall try to show that from the fact that my action is causally determined it does not necessarily follow that I am constrained to do it: and this is equivalent to saying that it does not necessarily follow that I am not free.

If I am constrained, I do not act freely. But in what circumstance can I legitimately be said to be constrained? An obvious instance is the case in which I am compelled by another person to do what he wants. In a case of this sort the compulsion need not be such as to deprive one of the power of choice. It is not required that the other person should have hypnotized me, or that he should make it physically impossible for me to go against his will. It is enough that he should induce me to do what he wants by making it clear to me that, if I do not, he will bring about some situation that I regard as even more undesirable than the consequence of the action that he wishes me to do. Thus, if the man points a pistol at my head I may still choose to disobey him: but this does not prevent its being true that if I do fall in with his wishes he can legitimately be said to have compelled me. And if the circumstances are such that no reasonable person would be expected to choose the other alternative, then the action that I am made to do is not one for which I am held to be morally responsible.

A similar but somewhat different case is that in which another person has obtained a habitual ascendancy over me. Where this is so, there may be no question of my being induced to act as the other person wishes by being confronted with a still more disagreeable alternative: for if I am sufficiently under his influence this special stimulus will not be necessary. Nevertheless I do not act freely, for the reason that I have been deprived of the power of choice. And this means that I have acquired so strong a habit of obedience that I no longer go through any process of deciding whether or not to do what the other person wants. About other matters I may still deliberate; but as regards the fulfilment of this other person's wishes, my own deliberations have ceased to be a causal factor in my behaviour. And it is in this sense that I may be said to be constrained. It is not, however, necessary that such constraint should take the form of subservience to another person. A kleptomaniac is not a free agent, in respect of his stealing, because he does not go through any process of deciding whether or not to steal. Or rather, if he does go through such a process, it is irrelevant to his behavior. Whatever he resolved to do, he would steal all the same. And it is this that distinguishes him from the ordinary thief.

But now it may be asked whether there is any essential difference between these cases and those in which the agent is commonly thought to be free. No doubt the ordinary thief does go through a process of deciding whether or not to steal, and no doubt it does affect his behavior. If he resolved to refrain from stealing, he could carry his resolution out. But if it be allowed that his making or not making this resolution is causally determined, then how can he be any more free than the kleptomaniac? It may be that unlike the kleptomaniac he could refrain from stealing if he chose: but if there is a cause, or set of causes, which necessitate his choosing as he does, how can he be said to have the power of choice? Again, it may be true that no one now compels me to get up and walk across the room: but if my doing so can be causally explained in terms of my history or my environment, or whatever it may be, then how am I any more free than if some other person had compelled me? I do not have the feeling of constraint that I have when a pistol is manifestly pointed at my head; but the chains of causation by which I am bound are no less effective for being invisible.

The answer to this is that the cases I have mentioned as examples of constraint do differ from the others: and they differ just in the ways that I have tried to bring out. If I suffered from a compulsion neurosis, so that I got up and walked across the room, whether I wanted to or not, or if I did so because somebody else compelled me, then I should not be acting freely. But if I do it now, I shall be acting freely, just because these conditions do not obtain; and the fact that my action may nevertheless have a cause is, from this point of view, irrelevant. For it is not when my action has any cause at all, but only when it has a special sort of cause, that it is reckoned not to be free.

But here it may be objected that, even if this distinction corresponds to ordinary usage, it is still very irrational. For why should we distinguish, with regard to a person's freedom, between the operations of one sort of cause and those of another? Do not all causes equally necessitate? And is it not therefore arbitrary to say that a person is free when he is necessitated in one fashion but not when he is necessitated in another?

That all causes equally necessitate is indeed a tautology, if the word "necessitate" is taken merely as equivalent to "cause": but if, as the objection requires, it is taken as equivalent to constrain or compel, then I do not think that this proposition is true. For all that is needed for one event to be the cause of another is that, in the given circumstances, the event which is said to be the effect would not have occurred if it had not been for the occurrence of the event which is said to be the cause, or *vice versa*, according as causes are interpreted as necessary, or sufficient, conditions: and this fact is usually deducible from some causal law which states that whenever an event of the one kind occurs then, given suitable conditions, an event of the other kind will occur in a certain temporal or spatio-temporal relationship to it. In short, there is an invariable concomitance between the two classes of events; but there is no compulsion, in any but a metaphorical sense. Suppose, for example, that a psycho-analyst is able to account for some aspect of my behavior by referring it to some lesion that I suffered in my childhood. In that case, it may be said that my childhood experience, together with certain other events, necessitates my behaving as I do. But all that this involves is that it is found to be true in general that when people have had certain experiences as children, they subsequently behave in certain specifiable ways; and my case is just another instance of this general law. It is in this way indeed that my behavior is explained. But from the fact that my behavior is capable of being explained, in the sense that it can be subsumed under some natural law, it does not follow that I am acting under constraint.

If this is correct, to say that I could have acted otherwise is to say, first, that I should have acted otherwise if I had so chosen; secondly, that my action was voluntary in the sense in which the actions, say, of the kleptomaniac are not; and thirdly, that nobody compelled me to choose as I did: and these three conditions may very well be fulfilled. When they are fulfilled, I may be said to have acted freely. But this is not to say that it was a matter of chance that I acted as I did, or, in other words, that my action could not be explained. And that my actions should be capable of being explained is all that is required by the postulate of determinism.

If more than this seems to be required it is, I think, because the use of the very word "determinism" is in some degree misleading. For it tends to suggest that one event is somehow in the power of another, whereas the truth is merely that they are actually correlated. And the same applies to the use, in this context, of the word "necessity" and even of the word "cause" itself. Moreover, there are various reasons for this. One is the tendency to confuse causal with logical necessitation, and so to infer mistakenly that the effect is contained in the cause. Another is the uncritical use of a concept of force which is derived from primitive experiences of pushing and striking. A third is the survival of an animistic conception of causality, in which all causal relationships are modeled on the example of one person's exercising authority over another. As a result we tend to form an imaginative picture of an unhappy effect trying vainly to escape from the clutches of an overmastering cause. But, I repeat, the fact is simply that when an event of one type occurs, an event of another type occurs also, in a certain temporal or spatio-temporal relation to the first. The rest is only metaphor. And it is because of the metaphor, and not because of the fact, that we come to think that there is an antithesis between causality and freedom.

## TEST YOUR UNDERSTANDING

1. Ayer distinguishes between cases in which an agent is *constrained* to act as he does and cases in which the agent is merely *caused* to act as he does. Explain the distinction and say why it matters for Ayer's argument.

2. According to Ayer, what does it mean to say, "Jones could have acted otherwise"?

## NOTES AND QUESTIONS

1. *Ayer on causation.* According to Ayer, the free will problem dissolves when we realize that even if our actions are always *caused* by prior events, it does not follow that we are *compelled* to act as we do.

> That all causes equally necessitate is indeed a tautology, if the word "necessitate" is taken merely as equivalent to "cause": but if . . . it is taken as equivalent to "constrain" or "compel," then I do not think that this proposition is true.

As Ayer's contemporary readers would have understood, this proposal relies on a theory of causation due to David Hume.

[W]e may define a cause to be an object, followed by another, and where all objects similar to the first are followed by objects similar to the second. (Hume, *An Enquiry Concerning Human Understanding*, VII, p. 203 of this anthology.)

On this view, causes do not literally *force* their effects to occur: they simply precede their effects, and are linked to them by a general pattern or regularity. "The gunshot caused his death" simply means: "The shot preceded his death, and in general, when people are shot in this way, they tend to die shortly thereafter." Hume's theory is discussed at length in chapter 5 of this anthology.

2. *Causation and compulsion.* This view may help us to see that an action can be caused without being compelled. But it raises a question about whether actions are *ever* forced or compelled. Suppose Jones kills Smith only because he has been hypnotized and "programmed" to shoot when the clock strikes midnight. Suppose that hypnotism works as it does in the movies: it is a law of nature—an exceptionless regularity—that whenever someone is hypnotized in this way, he does exactly what he has been programmed to do. Jones is on trial and his lawyer argues that his client is not responsible, since he was compelled to act, to which the prosecutor responds, "That is no defense. We can agree that Jones was caused to act as he did, and that the cause was somewhat unusual. But causes do not compel, as Professor Ayer has taught us. So Jones was not compelled." How should Jones's lawyer respond?

## Harry Frankfurt (born 1929)

Frankfurt, Professor Emeritus of Philosophy at Princeton University, is the author of a seminal study of Descartes's philosophy (*Demons, Dreamers, and Madmen*, 1970) and the surprise best seller *On Bullshit* (2005). His papers on ethics, moral psychology, and political philosophy are collected in *The Importance of What We Care About* (1988) and *Necessity, Volition, and Love* (1999).

# ALTERNATE POSSIBILITIES AND MORAL RESPONSIBILITY

A dominant role in nearly all recent inquiries into the free-will problem has been played by a principle which I shall call "the principle of alternate possibilities." This principle states that a person is morally responsible for what he has done only if he could have done otherwise. Its exact meaning is a subject of controversy, particularly concerning whether someone who accepts it is thereby committed to believing that moral responsibility and determinism are incompatible. Practically no one, however, seems inclined to deny or even to question that the principle of alternate possibilities (construed in some way or other) is true. It has generally seemed so overwhelmingly plausible that some philosophers have even characterized it as an *a priori* truth. People whose accounts of free will or of moral responsibility are radically at odds evidently find in it a firm and convenient common ground upon which they can profitably take their opposing stands.

But the principle of alternate possibilities is false. A person may well be morally responsible for what he has done even though he could not have done otherwise. The principle's plausibility is an illusion, which can be made to vanish by bringing the relevant moral phenomena into sharper focus.

## I

In seeking illustrations of the principle of alternate possibilities, it is most natural to think of situations in which the same circumstances both bring it about that a person does something and make it impossible for him to avoid doing it. These include, for example, situations in which a person is coerced into doing something, or in which he is impelled to act by a hypnotic suggestion, or in which some inner compulsion drives him to do what he does. In situations of these kinds there are circumstances that make it impossible for the person to do otherwise, and these very circumstances also serve to bring it about that he does whatever it is that he does.

However, there may be circumstances that constitute sufficient conditions for a certain action to be performed by someone and that therefore make it impossible for the person to do otherwise, but that do not actually impel the person to act or in any way produce his action. A person may do something in circumstances that leave him no alternative to doing it, without these circumstances actually moving him or leading him to do it — without them playing any role, indeed, in bringing it about that he does what he does. . . .

## II

It is generally agreed that a person who has been coerced to do something did not do it freely and is not morally responsible for having done it. Now the doctrine that coercion and moral responsibility are mutually exclusive may appear to be no more than a somewhat particularized version of the principle of alternate possibilities. It is natural enough to say of a person who has been coerced to do something that he could not have done otherwise. And it may easily seem that being coerced deprives a person of freedom and of moral responsibility simply because it is a special case of being unable to do otherwise. The principle of alternate possibilities may in this way derive some credibility from its association with the very plausible proposition that moral responsibility is excluded by coercion.

It is not right, however, that it should do so. The fact that a person was coerced to act as he did may entail both that he could not have done otherwise and that he bears no moral responsibility for his action. But his lack of moral responsibility is not entailed by his having been unable to do otherwise. The doctrine that coercion excludes moral responsibility is not correctly understood, in other words, as a particularized version of the principle of alternate possibilities.

Let us suppose that someone is threatened convincingly with a penalty he finds unacceptable and that he then does what is required of him by the issuer of the threat. We can imagine details that would make it reasonable for us to think that the person was coerced to perform the action in question, that he could not have done otherwise, and that he bears no moral responsibility for having done what he did. But just what is it about situations of this kind that warrants the judgment that the threatened person is not morally responsible for his act?

This question may be approached by considering situations of the following kind. Jones decides for reasons of his own to do something, then someone threatens him with a very harsh penalty (so harsh that any reasonable person would submit to the threat) unless he does precisely that, and Jones does it. Will we hold Jones morally responsible for what he has done? I think this will depend on the roles we think were played, in leading him to act, by his original decision and by the threat.

One possibility is that $Jones_1$ is not a reasonable man: he is, rather, a man who does what he has once decided to do no matter what happens next and no matter what the cost. In that case, the threat actually exerted no effective force upon him. He acted without any regard to it, very much as if he were not aware that it had been made. If this is indeed the way it was, the situation did not involve coercion at all. The threat did not lead $Jones_1$ to do what he did. Nor was it in fact sufficient to have prevented him from doing otherwise: if his earlier decision had been to do something else, the threat would not have deterred him in the slightest. It seems evident that in these circumstances the fact that $Jones_1$ was threatened in no way reduces the moral responsibility he would otherwise bear for his act. This example, however, is not a counterexample either to the doctrine that coercion excuses or to the principle of alternate possibilities. For we have supposed that $Jones_1$ is a man upon whom the threat had no coercive effect and, hence, that it did not actually deprive him of alternatives to doing what he did.

Another possibility is that $Jones_2$ was stampeded by the threat. Given that threat, he would have performed that action regardless of what decision he had already made. The threat upset him so profoundly, moreover, that he completely forgot his own earlier decision and did what was demanded of him entirely because he was terrified of the penalty with which he was threatened. In this case, it is not relevant to his having performed the action that he had already decided on his own to perform it. When the chips were down he thought of nothing but the threat, and fear alone led him to act. The fact that at an earlier time Jones₂ had decided for his own reasons to act in just that way may be relevant to an evaluation of his character; he may bear full moral responsibility for having made that decision. But he can hardly be said to be morally responsible for his action. For he performed the action simply as a result of the coercion to which he was subjected. His earlier decision played no role in bringing it about that he did what he did, and it would therefore be gratuitous to assign it a role in the moral evaluation of his action.

Now consider a third possibility. Jones₃ was neither stampeded by the threat nor indifferent to it. The threat impressed him, as it would impress any reasonable man, and he would have submitted to it wholeheartedly if he had not already made a decision that coincided with the one demanded of him. In fact, however, he performed the action in question on the basis of the decision he had made before the threat was issued. When he acted, he was not actually motivated by the threat but solely by the considerations that had originally commended the action to him. It was not the threat that led him to act, though it would have done so if he had not already provided himself with a sufficient motive for performing the action in question.

No doubt it will be very difficult for anyone to know, in a case like this one, exactly what happened. Did Jones₃ perform the action because of the threat, or were his reasons for acting simply those which had already persuaded him to do so? Or did he act on the basis of two motives, each of which was sufficient for his action? It is not impossible, however, that the situation should be clearer than situations of this kind usually are. And suppose it is apparent to us that Jones₃ acted on the basis of his own decision and not because of the threat. Then I think we would be justified in regarding his moral responsibility for what he did as unaffected by the threat even though, since he would in any case have submitted to the threat, he could not have avoided doing what he did. It would be entirely reasonable for us to make the same judgment concerning his moral responsibility that we would have made if we had not known of the threat. For the threat did not in fact influence his performance of the action. He did what he did just as if the threat had not been made at all.

### III

The case of Jones₃ may appear at first glance to combine coercion and moral responsibility, and thus to provide a counterexample to the doctrine that coercion excuses. It is not really so certain that it does so, however, because it is unclear whether the example constitutes a genuine instance of coercion. Can we say of Jones₃ that he was coerced to do something, when he had already decided on his own to do it and when he did it entirely on the basis of that decision? Or would it be more correct to say that Jones₃ was not coerced to do what he did, even though he himself recognized that there was an irresistible force at work in virtue of which he had to do it? . . .

This murkiness, however, does not interfere with our drawing an important moral from an examination of the example. Suppose we decide to say that Jones₁ was *not* coerced. Our basis for saying this will clearly be that it is incorrect to regard a man as being coerced to do something unless he does it *because* of the coercive force exerted against him. The fact that an irresistible threat is made will not, then, entail that the person who receives it is coerced to do what he does. It will also be necessary that the threat is what actually accounts for his doing it. On the other hand, suppose we decide to say that Jones₃ *was* coerced. Then we will be bound to admit that being coerced does not exclude being morally responsible. And we will also surely be led to the view that coercion affects a person's moral responsibility only when the person acts as he does because he is coerced to do so — i.e., when the fact that he is coerced is what accounts for his action.

Whichever we decide to say, then, we will recognize that the doctrine that coercion excludes moral responsibility is not a particularized version of the principle of alternate possibilities. Situations in which a person who does something cannot do otherwise because he is subject to coercive power are either not instances of coercion at all, or they are situations in which the person may still be morally responsible for what he does if it is not because of the coercion that he does it. When we excuse a person who has been coerced, we do not excuse him because he was unable to do otherwise. . . .

# IV

The case of Jones₃ . . . may well seem to provide a decisive counterexample to the principle of alternate possibilities and thus to show that this principle is false. For the irresistibility of the threat to which Jones₃ is subjected might well be taken to mean that he cannot but perform the action he performs. And yet the threat, since Jones₃ performs the action without regard to it, does not reduce his moral responsibility for what he does.

The following objection will doubtless be raised against the suggestion that the case of Jones₃ is a counterexample to the principle of alternate possibilities. There is perhaps a sense in which Jones₃ cannot do otherwise than perform the action he performs, since he is a reasonable man and the threat he encounters is sufficient to move any reasonable man. But it is not this sense that is germane to the principle of alternate possibilities. His knowledge that he stands to suffer an intolerably harsh penalty does not mean that Jones₃, strictly speaking, *cannot* perform any action but the one he does perform. After all it is still open to him, and this is crucial, to defy the threat if he wishes to do so and to accept the penalty his action would bring down upon him. In the sense in which the principle of alternate possibilities employs the concept of "could have done otherwise," Jones$_3$'s inability to resist the threat does not mean that he cannot do otherwise than perform the action he performs. Hence the case of Jones$_3$ does not constitute an instance contrary to the principle.

... I believe that whatever force this objection may be thought to have can be deflected by altering the example in the following way.[1] Suppose someone — Black, let us say — wants Jones$_4$ to perform a certain action. Black is prepared to go to considerable lengths to get his way, but he prefers to avoid showing his hand unnecessarily. So he waits until Jones$_4$ is about to make up his mind what to do, and he does nothing unless it is clear to him (Black is an excellent judge of such things) that Jones$_4$ is going to decide to do something other than what he wants him to do. If it does become clear that Jones$_4$ is going to decide to do something else, Black takes effective steps to ensure that Jones$_4$ decides to do, and that he does do, what he wants him to do.[2] Whatever Jones$_4$'s initial preferences and inclinations, then, Black will have his way.

What steps will Black take, if he believes he must take steps, in order to ensure that Jones$_4$ decides and acts as he wishes? Anyone with a theory concerning what "could have done otherwise" means may answer this question for himself by describing whatever measures he would regard as sufficient to guarantee that, in the relevant sense, Jones$_4$ cannot do otherwise. Let Black pronounce a terrible threat, and in this way both force Jones$_4$ to perform the desired action and prevent him from performing a forbidden one. Let Black give Jones$_4$ a potion, or put him under hypnosis, and in some such way as these generate in Jones$_4$ an irresistible inner compulsion to perform the act Black wants performed and to avoid others. Or let Black manipulate the minute processes of Jones$_4$'s brain and nervous system in some more direct way, so that causal forces running in and out of his synapses and along the poor man's nerves determine that he chooses to act and that he does act in the one way and not in any other. Given any conditions under which it will be maintained that Jones$_4$ cannot do otherwise, in other words, let Black bring it about that those conditions prevail. The structure of the example is flexible enough, I think, to find a way around any charge of irrelevance by accommodating the doctrine on which the charge is based.[3]

1. After thinking up the example that I am about to develop, I learned that Robert Nozick, in lectures given several years ago, had formulated an example of the same general type and had proposed it as a counterexample to the principle of alternate possibilities. [Frankfurt's note.]

2. The assumption that Black can predict what Jones$_4$ will decide to do does not beg the question of determinism. We can imagine that Jones$_4$ has often confronted the alternatives — A and B — that he now confronts, and that his face has invariably twitched when he was about to decide to do A and never when he was about to decide to do B. Knowing this, and observing the twitch, Black would have a basis for prediction. This does, to be sure, suppose that there is some sort of causal relation between Jones$_4$'s state at the time of the twitch and his subsequent stares. But any plausible view of decision or of action will allow that reaching a decision and performing an action both involve earlier and later phases, with causal relations between them, and such that the earlier phases are not themselves part of the decision or of the action. The example does not require that these earlier phases be deterministically related to still earlier events. [Frankfurt's note.]

3. The example is also flexible enough to allow for the elimination of Black altogether. Anyone who thinks that the effectiveness of the example is undermined by its reliance on a human manipulator, who imposes his will on Jones$_4$, can substitute for Black a machine programmed to do what Black does. If this is still not good enough, forget both Black and the machine and suppose that their role is played by natural forces involving no will or design at all. [Frankfurt's note.]

Now suppose that Black never has to show his hand because Jones$_4$, for reasons of his own, decides to perform and does perform the very action Black wants him to perform. In that case, it seems clear, Jones$_4$ will bear precisely the same moral responsibility for what he does as he would have borne if Black had not been ready to take steps to ensure that he do it. It would be quite unreasonable to excuse Jones$_4$ for his action, or to withhold the praise to which it would normally entitle him, on the basis of the fact that he could not have done otherwise. This fact played no role at all in leading him to act as he did. He would have acted the same even if it had not been a fact. Indeed, everything happened just as it would have happened without Black's presence in the situation and without his readiness to intrude into it.

In this example there are sufficient conditions for Jones$_4$'s performing the action in question. What action he performs is not up to him. Of course it is in a way up to him whether he acts on his own or as a result of Black's intervention. That depends upon what action he himself is inclined to perform. But whether he finally acts on his own or as a result of Black's intervention, he performs the same action. He has no alternative but to do what Black wants him to do. If he does it on his own, however, his moral responsibility for doing it is not affected by the fact that Black was lurking in the background with sinister intent, since this intent never comes into play.

## V

The fact that a person could not have avoided doing something is a sufficient condition of his having done it. But, as some of my examples show, this fact may play no role whatever in the explanation of why he did it. It may not figure at all among the circumstances that actually brought it about that he did what he did, so that his action is to be accounted for on another basis entirely. Even though the person was unable to do otherwise, that is to say, it may not be the case that he acted as he did *because* he could not have done otherwise. Now if someone had no alternative to performing a certain action but did not perform it because he was unable to do otherwise, then he would have performed exactly the same action even if he *could* have done otherwise. The circumstances that made it impossible for him to do otherwise could have been subtracted from the situation without affecting what happened or why it happened in any way. Whatever it was that actually led the person to do what he did, or that made him do it, would have led him to do it or made him do it even if it had been possible for him to do something else instead.

Thus it would have made no difference, so far as concerns his action or how he came to perform it, if the circumstances that made it impossible for him to avoid performing it had not prevailed. The fact that he could not have done otherwise clearly provides no basis for supposing that he *might* have done otherwise if he had been able to do so. When a fact is in this way irrelevant to the problem of accounting for a person's action it seems quite gratuitous to assign it any weight in the assessment of his moral responsibility. Why should the fact be considered in reaching a moral judgment concerning the person when it does not help in any way to understand either what made him act as he did or what, in other circumstances, he might have done?

This, then, is why the principle of alternate possibilities is mistaken. It asserts that a person bears no moral responsibility — that is, he is to be excused — for having performed an action, if there were circumstances that made it impossible for him to avoid performing it. But there may be circumstances that make it impossible for a person to avoid performing some action without those circumstances in any way bringing it about that he performs that action. It would surely be no good for the person to refer to circumstances of this sort in an effort to absolve himself of moral responsibility for performing the action in question. For those circumstances, by hypothesis, actually had nothing to do with his having done what he did. He would have done precisely the same thing, and he would have been led or made in precisely the same way to do it, even if they had not prevailed.

We often do, to be sure, excuse people for what they have done when they tell us (and we believe them) that they could not have done otherwise. But this is because we assume that what they tell us serves to explain why they did what they did. We take it for granted that they are not being disingenuous, as a person would be who cited as an excuse the fact that he could not have avoided doing what he did but who knew full well that it was not at all because of this that he did it.

Suppose a person tells us that he did what he did because he was unable to do otherwise; or suppose he makes the similar statement that he did what he did because he had to do it. We do often accept statements like these (if we believe them) as valid excuses. . . . But I think that when we accept such statements as valid excuses it is because we assume that we are being told more than the statements strictly and literally convey. We understand the person who offers the excuse to mean that he did what he did *only because* he was unable to do otherwise, or *only because* he had to do it. And we understand him to mean, more particularly, that when he did what he did it was not because that was what he really wanted to do. The principle of alternate possibilities should thus be replaced, in my opinion, by the following principle: a person is not morally responsible for what he has done if he did it only because he could not have done otherwise. This principle does not appear to conflict with the view that moral responsibility is compatible with determinism.

## TEST YOUR UNDERSTANDING

1. State the principle of alternate possibilities (PAP).

2. Does Frankfurt think that the case of $Jones_3$ provides a counterexample to PAP?

3. Give a Frankfurt-style counterexample of your own to PAP modeled on the case of $Jones_4$.

## NOTES AND QUESTIONS

1. Jones$_4$ kills Smith for his own reasons, but if he had wavered at all in his deliberations, Black would have intervened (perhaps via mind control) to cause him to kill Smith. According to Frankfurt, this is a counterexample to the principle of alternate possibilities. But is this right? Consider the following puzzle for Frankfurt's view.

   Jones$_4$ has been convicted for Smith's murder, but just prior to sentencing he stands up to address the court:

   > I admit that I killed Smith for my own reasons and that no one made me do it. But tell me, your honor, what should I have done? Don't say that I should have walked away. You've heard all about Black. You know that I could not have walked away. In fact it was never in my power to do anything other than what I actually did, since if I had wavered even for a second, Black would have caused me to carry on with my plan. So now that you know the facts, you know that I did the best thing that I could possibly have done in the circumstances (because I did the only thing that I could have done). How can that be wrong? And if I didn't do anything wrong, how can you blame me?

   This little speech suggests an argument:

   (i)    X is blameworthy for A only if it was *wrong* for X to do A.

   (ii)   It was wrong for X to do A only if X *should* have done something else (say B) instead.

   (iii)  X should have done B only if X *could* have done B.

   (iv)   Given Black's presence, Jones could not have done anything other than what he actually did.

   (v)    So there is nothing else that Jones should have done.

   (vi)   So it was not wrong for Jones to kill Smith.

   (vii)  So Jones is not blameworthy for killing Smith.

   If the argument is sound, Frankfurt has not refuted PAP. (See David Wiederker, "Frankfurt on 'Ought Implies Can' and the Principle of Alternate Possibilities," *Analysis* 51 [1991].) How might Frankfurt respond?

2. Frankfurt's positive theory of freedom and responsibility is developed in *The Importance of What We Care About* (Cambridge University Press, 1988). His counterexamples to the Principle of Alternate Possibilities have generated an extensive literature. For two early responses, see Peter van Inwagen, "Ability and Responsibility," *Philosophical Review* 87, no. 2 (1978) and John M. Fischer, "Responsibility and Control," *Journal of Philosophy* 79, no. 1 (1982).

## Susan Wolf (born 1952)

Wolf, the Edna J. Koury Professor of Philosophy at the University of North Carolina, Chapel Hill, works mainly in ethics and moral psychology. Her most recent book is *Meaning in Life and Why It Matters* (2010).

# ASYMMETRICAL FREEDOM

In order for a person to be morally responsible, two conditions must be satisfied. First, he must be a free agent—an agent, that is, whose actions are under his own control. For if the actions he performs are not up to him to decide, he deserves no credit or discredit for doing what he does. Second, he must be a moral agent—an agent, that is, to whom moral claims apply. For if the actions he performs can be neither right nor wrong, then there is nothing to credit or discredit him with. I shall call the first condition, *the condition of freedom*, and the second, *the condition of value*. . . . In what follows, I shall argue that . . . the condition of freedom depends on the condition of value. . . .

I shall say that an agent's action is *psychologically determined* if his action is determined by his interests — that is, his values or desires — and his interests are determined by his heredity or environment. If all our actions are so determined, then the thesis of psychological determinism is true. . . .

Many people believe that if psychological determinism is true, the condition of freedom can never be satisfied. For if an agent's interests are determined by heredity and environment, they claim, it is not up to the agent to have the interests he has. And if his actions are determined by his interests as well, then he cannot but perform the actions he performs. In order for an agent to satisfy the condition of freedom, then, his actions must not be psychologically determined. Either his actions must not be determined by his interests, or his interests must not be determined by anything external to himself. They therefore conclude that the condition of freedom requires the absence of psychological determinism. . . .

Let us imagine, however, what an agent who satisfied this condition would have to be like. Consider first what it would mean for the agent's actions not to be determined by his interests — for the agent, in other words, to have the ability to act despite his interests. This would mean, I think, that the agent has the ability to act against everything he believes in and everything he cares about. It would mean, for example, that if the agent's son were inside a burning building, the agent could just stand there and watch the house go up in flames. Or that the agent, though he thinks his neighbor a fine and agreeable fellow, could just get up one day, ring the doorbell, and punch him in the nose. One might think such pieces of behavior should not be classified as actions at all — that they are rather more like spasms that the agent cannot control.

If they are actions, at least, they are very bizarre, and an agent who performed them would have to be insane. Indeed, one might think he would have to be insane if he had even the ability to perform them. . . .

So let us assume instead that his actions are determined by his interests, but that his interests are not determined by anything external to himself. Then of any of the interests he happens to have, it must be the case that he does not have to have them. Though perhaps he loves his wife, it must be possible for him not to love her. Though perhaps he cares about people in general, it must be possible for him not to care. This agent, moreover, could not have reasons for his interests — at least no reasons of the sort we normally have. He cannot love his wife, for example, because of the way his wife is — for the way his wife is is not up to him to decide. Such an agent, presumably, could not be much committed to anything; his interests must be something like a matter of whim. Such an agent must be able not to care about the lives of others, and, I suppose, he must be able not to care about his own life as well. An agent who didn't care about these things, one might think, would have to be crazy. And again, one might think he would have to be crazy if he had even the ability not to care.

In any case, it seems, if we require an agent to be psychologically undetermined, we cannot expect him to be a moral agent. For if we require that his actions not be determined by his interests, then *a fortiori* they cannot be determined by his moral interests. And if we require that his interests not be determined by anything else, then *a fortiori* they cannot be determined by his moral reasons.

When we imagine an agent who performs right actions, it seems, we imagine an agent who is rightly determined: whose actions, that is, are determined by the right sorts of interests, and whose interests are determined by the right sorts of reasons. But an agent who is not psychologically determined cannot perform actions that are right in this way. . . . So the satisfaction of the condition of freedom seems to rule out the satisfaction of the condition of value.

This suggests that the condition of freedom was previously stated too strongly. When we require that a responsible agent "could have done otherwise" we cannot mean that it was not determined that he did what he did. It has been proposed that "he could have done otherwise" should be analyzed as a conditional instead. For example, we might say that "he could have done otherwise" means that he would have done otherwise, if he had tried. . . .

Incompatibilists, however, will quickly point out that such an analysis is insufficient.[1] For an agent who would have done otherwise if he had tried cannot be blamed for his action if he could not have tried. The compatibilist might try to answer this objection with a new conditional analysis of "he could have tried." He might say, for example, that "he could have tried to do otherwise" be interpreted to mean he would have tried to do otherwise, if he had chosen. But the incompatibilist now has a new objection to make: namely, what if the agent could not have chosen?

---

1. Incompatibilism is the view that an action (or a choice) that has been determined by prior causes cannot be free. Its denial, **compatibilism**, is the view that it is possible for an act to be both free and determined.

It should be obvious that this debate might be carried on indefinitely with a proliferation of conditionals and a proliferation of objections. But if an agent is determined, no conditions one suggests will be conditions that an agent could have satisfied. . . .

We seem to think of ourselves one way when we are thinking about freedom, and to think of ourselves another way when we are thinking about morality. When we are thinking about the condition of freedom, our intuitions suggest that the incompatibilists are right. For they claim that an agent can be free only insofar as his actions are not psychologically determined. But when we are thinking about the condition of value, our intuitions suggest that the compatibilists are right. For they claim that an agent can be moral only insofar as his actions are psychologically determined. If our intuitions require that both these claims are right, then the concept of moral responsibility must be incoherent. For then a free agent can never be moral, and a moral agent can never be free.

In fact, however, I believe that philosophers have generally got our intuitions wrong. There is an asymmetry in our intuitions about freedom which has generally been overlooked. . . . What we need in order to be responsible beings, I shall argue, is a suitable combination of determination and indetermination.

When we try to call up our intuitions about freedom, a few stock cases come readily to mind. We think of the heroin addict and the kleptomaniac, of the victim of hypnosis, and the victim of a deprived childhood. These cases, I think, provide forceful support for our incompatibilist intuitions. For of the kleptomaniac it may well be true that he would have done otherwise if he had tried. The kleptomaniac is not responsible because he could not have tried. . . .

The victim of the deprived childhood who, say, embezzles some money, provides the most poignant example of all. For this agent is not coerced nor overcome by an irresistible impulse. . . . He acts on the basis of his choice, and he chooses on the basis of his reasons. If there is any explanation of why this agent is not responsible, it would seem that it must consist simply in the fact that his reasons are determined.

These examples are all peculiar, however, in that they are examples of people doing bad things. If the agents in these cases were responsible for their actions, this would justify the claim that they deserve to be blamed. We seldom look, on the other hand, at examples of agents whose actions are morally good. We rarely ask whether an agent is truly responsible if his being responsible would make him worthy of praise. . . .

When we ask whether an agent's action is deserving of praise, it seems we do not require that he could have done otherwise. If an agent does the right thing for just the right reasons, it seems absurd to ask whether he could have done the wrong. "I cannot tell a lie," "He couldn't hurt a fly" are not exemptions from praiseworthiness but testimonies to it. If a friend presents you with a gift and says "I couldn't resist," this suggests the strength of his friendship and not the weakness of his will. If one feels one "has no choice" but to speak out against injustice, one ought not to be upset about the depth of one's commitment. . . .

Of course, these phrases must be given an appropriate interpretation if they are to indicate that the agent is deserving of praise. "He couldn't hurt a fly" must allude to someone's gentleness — it would be perverse to say this of someone who was in an iron lung. It is not admirable in George Washington that he cannot tell a lie, if it is because he has a tendency to stutter that inhibits his attempts. "He could not have done otherwise" as it is used in the context of praise, then, must be taken to imply something like "because he was too good." An action is praiseworthy only if it is done for the right reasons. So it must be only in light of and because of these reasons that the praiseworthy agent "could not help" but do the right thing.

But when an agent does the right thing for the right reasons, the fact that, having the right reasons, he *must* do the right [thing] should surely not lessen the credit he deserves. For presumably the reason he cannot do otherwise is that his virtue is so sure or his moral commitment so strong. . . .

One might still be concerned that if his motives are determined, the man cannot be truly deserving of praise. If he cannot help but have a generous character, then the fact that he is generous is not up to him. If a man's motives are determined, one might think, then *he* cannot control them, so it cannot be to his credit if his motives turn out to be good. But whether a man is in control of his motives cannot be decided so simply. We must know not only whether his motives are determined, but how they are determined as well.

We can imagine, for example, a man with a generous mother who becomes generous as a means of securing her love. He would not have been generous had his mother been different. Had she not admired generosity, he would not have developed this trait. We can imagine further that once this man's character had been developed, he would never subject it to question or change. His character would remain unthinkingly rigid, carried over from a childhood over which he had no control. As he developed a tendency to be generous, let us say, he developed other tendencies — a tendency to brush his teeth twice a day, a tendency to avoid the company of Jews. The explanation for why he developed any one of these traits is more or less the same as the explanation for why he has developed any other. . . . These tendencies are all, for him, merely habits which he has never thought about breaking. Indeed, they are habits which, by hypothesis, it was determined he would never think about breaking. Such a man, perhaps, would not deserve credit for his generosity, for his generosity might be thought to be senseless and blind. But we can imagine a different picture in which no such claim is true, in which a generous character might be determined and yet under the agent's control.

We might start again with a man with a generous mother who starts to develop his generosity out of a desire for her love. But his reasons for developing a generous nature need not be his reasons for retaining it when he grows more mature. He may notice, for example, that his generous acts provide an independent pleasure, connected to the pleasure he gives the person on whom his generosity is bestowed. He may find that being generous promotes a positive fellow feeling and makes it easier for him to make friends than it would otherwise be. Moreover, he appreciates being the object of the generous acts of others, and he is hurt when others go to ungenerous extremes. All in all, his generosity seems to cohere with his other values. It fits in well with his ideals of how one ought to live.

Such a picture, I think, might be as determined as the former one. But it is compatible with the exercise of good sense and an open frame of mind. It is determined, because the agent does not create his new reasons for generosity any more than he created his old ones. He does not *decide* to feel an independent pleasure in performing acts of generosity, or decide that such acts will make it easier for him to make friends. He discovers that these are consequences of a generous nature — and if he is observant and perceptive, he cannot help but discover this. He does not choose to be the object of the generous acts of others, or to be the victim of less generous acts of less virtuous persons. Nor does he choose to be grateful to the one and hurt by the other. He cannot help but have these experiences — they are beyond his control. So it seems that what reasons he *has* for being generous depends on what reasons there *are*.

If the man's character is determined in this way, however, it seems absurd to say that it is not under his control. His character is determined on the basis of his reasons, and his reasons are determined by what reasons there are. What is not under his control, then, is that generosity be a virtue, and it is only because he realizes this that he remains a generous man. But one cannot say for *this* reason that his generosity is not praiseworthy. . . .

So it seems that an agent can be morally praiseworthy even though he is determined to perform the action he performs. But we have already seen that an agent cannot be morally blameworthy if he is determined to perform the action he performs. Determination, then, is compatible with an agent's responsibility for a good action, but incompatible with an agent's responsibility for a bad action. . . .

The condition of freedom, as it is expressed by the requirement that an agent could have done otherwise, thus appears to demand a conditional analysis after all. But the condition must be one that separates the good actions from the bad — the condition, that is, must be essentially value-laden. An analysis of the condition of freedom that might do the trick is:

He could have done otherwise if there had been good and sufficient reason.

where the "could have done otherwise" in the analysans[2] is not a conditional at all. For presumably an action is morally praiseworthy only if there are no good and sufficient reasons to do something else. And an action is morally blameworthy only if there are good and sufficient reasons to do something else. Thus, when an agent performs a good action, the condition of freedom is a counterfactual: though it is required that the agent would have been able to do otherwise *had there been* good and sufficient reason to do so, the situation in which the good-acting agent actually found himself is a situation in which there was no such reason. Thus, it is compatible with the satisfaction of the condition of freedom that the agent in this case could not actually have done other than what he actually did. When an agent performs a bad action, however, the condition of freedom is not a counterfactual.

---

2. In a philosophical **analysis**, the term or phrase to be defined is called the *analysandum* and the phrase in terms of which it is defined is called the *analysans*. Here the analysandum is "He acted freely" and the proposed analysans is "He could have done otherwise if there had been good and sufficient reason."

The bad-acting agent does what he does in the face of good and sufficient reasons to do otherwise. Thus the condition of freedom requires that the agent in this case could have done otherwise in just the situation in which he was actually placed. An agent, then, can be determined to perform a good action and still be morally praiseworthy. But if an agent is to be blameworthy, he must unconditionally have been able to do something else.

It may be easier to see how this analysis works, and how it differs from conditional analyses that were suggested before, if we turn back to the case in which these previous analyses failed — namely, the case of the victim of a deprived childhood.

We imagined a case, in particular, of a man who embezzled some money, fully aware of what he was doing. He was neither coerced nor overcome by an irresistible impulse, and he was in complete possession of normal adult faculties of reason and observation. Yet it seems he ought not to be blamed for committing his crime, for, from his point of view, one cannot reasonably expect him to see anything wrong with his action. We may suppose that in his childhood he was given no love — he was beaten by his father, neglected by his mother. And that the people to whom he was exposed when he was growing up gave him examples only of evil and selfishness. From his point of view, it is natural to conclude that respecting other people's property would be foolish. For presumably no one had ever respected his. . . .

In light of this, it seems that this man shouldn't be blamed for an action we know to be wrong. For if we had had his childhood, we wouldn't have known it either. Yet this agent seems to have as much control over his life as we are apt to have over ours: he would have done otherwise, if he had tried. He would have tried to do otherwise, if he had chosen. And he would have chosen to do otherwise, if he had had reason. It is because he couldn't have had reason that this agent should not be blamed.

Though this agent's childhood was different from ours, it would seem to be neither more nor less binding. The good fortune of our childhood is no more to our credit than the misfortune of his is to his blame. So if he is not free because of the childhood he had, then it would appear that we are not free either. Thus it seems no conditional analysis of freedom will do — for there is nothing internal to the agent which distinguishes him from us.

My analysis, however, proposes a condition that is not internal to the agent. And it allows us to state the relevant difference: namely that, whereas our childhoods fell within a range of normal decency, his was severely deprived. The consequence this has is that he, unlike us, could not have had reasons even though there were reasons around.[3] . . .

3. Wolf distinguishes the claim that *there is* a reason for Jones to be generous from the claim that Jones *has* a reason to be generous. The first claim concerns an objective matter of moral fact. *There is* a reason for Jones to be generous if the facts justify generous acts, whether Jones knows this or not. The second claim has a subjective condition. Jones *has* a reason to be generous when (a) there is a reason for him to be generous, and (b) Jones is aware of this reason and cares enough about the values that underlie it to be moved by it.

The goal, to put it bluntly, is the True and the Good. The freedom we want is the freedom to find it. But such a freedom requires not only that we, as agents, have the right sorts of abilities — the abilities, that is, to direct and govern our actions by our most fundamental selves.[4] It requires as well that the world cooperate in such a way that our most fundamental selves have the opportunity to develop into the selves they ought to be.

If the freedom necessary for moral responsibility is the freedom to be determined by the True and the Good, then obviously we cannot know whether we have such a freedom unless we know, on the one hand, that there *is* a True and a Good and, on the other, that there *are* capacities for finding them. As a consequence of this, the condition of freedom cannot be stated in purely metaphysical terms. . . .

More specifically, the condition of freedom cannot be stated in terms that are value-free. Thus, the problem of free will has been misrepresented insofar as it has been thought to be a purely metaphysical problem. And, perhaps, this is why the problem of free will has seemed for so long to be hopeless.

That the problem should have seemed to be a purely metaphysical problem is not, however, unnatural or surprising. For being determined by the True and the Good is very different from being determined by one's garden variety of causes, and I think it not unnatural to feel as if one rules out the other. For to be determined by the Good is not to be determined by the Past. And to do something because it is the right thing to do is not to do it because one has been taught to do it. One might think, then, that one can be determined only by one thing or the other. For if one is going to do whatever it is right to do, then it seems one will do it whether or not one has been taught. And if one is going to do whatever one has been taught to do, then it seems one will do it whether or not it is right. . . .

These two explanations do not necessarily compete, [however,] for they are explanations of different kinds. Consider, for example, the following situation: you ask me to name the capital of Nevada, and I reply "Carson City." We can explain why I give the answer I do give in either of the following ways: First, we can point out that when I was in the fifth grade I had to memorize the capitals of the fifty states. I was taught to believe that Carson City was the capital of Nevada, and was subsequently positively reinforced for doing so. Second, we can point out that Carson City *is* the capital of Nevada, and that this was, after all, what you wanted to know. So on the one hand, I gave my answer because I was taught. And on the other, I gave my answer because it was right.

Presumably, these explanations are not unrelated. For if Carson City were not the capital of Nevada, I would not have been taught that it was. . . .

Similarly, we can explain why a person acts justly in either of the following ways: First, we can point out that he was taught to act justly, and was subsequently positively reinforced for doing so. Second, we can point out that it is right to act justly,

4. Wolf alludes to a theory, due to Harry Frankfurt among others, according to which a free act is an act that is suitably determined by the agent's most fundamental preferences or values, even when those preferences or values are misguided. See Frankfurt, "Freedom of the Will and the Concept of a Person," *Journal of Philosophy* 68, no. 1 (1971): 5–20.

and go on to say why he knows this is so. Again, these explanations are likely to be related. For if it weren't right to act justly, the person may well not have been taught that it was. . . . Of course, the explanations of both kinds in this case will be more complex than the explanations in the previous case. But what is relevant here is that these explanations are compatible: that one can be determined by the Good and determined by the Past.

In order for an agent to be morally free, then, he must be capable of being determined by the Good. Determination by the Good is, as it were, the goal we need freedom to pursue. We need the freedom *to* have our actions determined by the Good, and the freedom to be or to become the sorts of persons whose actions will continue to be so determined. In light of this, it should be clear that no standard incompatibilist views about the conditions of moral responsibility can be right, for, according to these views, an agent is free only if he is the sort of agent whose actions are not causally determined at all. Thus, an agent's freedom would be incompatible with the realization of the goal for which freedom is required. The agent would be, in the words, though not in the spirit, of Sartre, "condemned to be free" — he could not both be free and realize a moral ideal.

Thus, views that offer conditional analyses of the ability to do otherwise, views that, like mine, take freedom to consist in the ability *to be determined* in a particular way, are generally compatibilist views. For insofar as an agent *is* determined in the right way, the agent can be said to be acting freely. Like the compatibilists, then, I am claiming that whether an agent is morally responsible depends not on whether but on how that agent is determined. My view differs from theirs only in what I take the satisfactory kind of determination to be.

However, since on my view the satisfactory kind of determination is determination by reasons that an agent ought to have, it will follow that an agent can be both determined and responsible only insofar as he performs actions that he ought to perform. If an agent performs a morally bad action, on the other hand, then his actions can't be determined in the appropriate way. So if an agent is ever to be responsible for a bad action, it must be the case that his action is not psychologically determined at all. According to my view, then, in order for both moral praise and moral blame to be justified, the thesis of psychological determinism must be false.

Is it plausible that this thesis is false? I think so. For though it appears that some of our actions are psychologically determined, it appears that others are not. . . .

Thus, one may have good reasons to go to graduate school and good reasons not to; good reasons to get married, and good reasons to stay single. Though we might want, in these cases, to choose on the basis of reasons, our reasons simply do not settle the matter for us. Other psychological events may be similarly undetermined, such as the chance occurrence of thoughts and ideas. One is just struck by an idea, but for no particular reason — one might as easily have had another idea or no idea at all. Or one simply forgets an appointment one has made, even though one was not particularly distracted by other things at the time. . . .

Let us turn, then, to instances of immoral behavior, and see what the right kind of indetermination would be. For indetermination, in this context, is indetermination among some number of fairly particular alternatives — and if one's alternatives are not of the appropriate kind, indetermination will not be sufficient to justify moral blame. It is not enough, for example, to know that a criminal who happened to rob a bank might as easily have chosen to hold up a liquor store instead. What we need to know, in particular, is that when an agent performs a wrong action, he could have performed the right action for the right reasons instead. That is, first, the agent could have had the interests that the agent ought to have had, and second, the agent could have acted on the interests on which he ought to have acted. . . .

There is, admittedly, some difficulty in establishing that an agent who performs a morally bad action satisfies the condition of freedom. It is hard to know whether an agent who did one thing could have done another instead. But presumably we decide such questions now on the basis of statistical evidence — and, if, in fact, these actions are not determined, this is the best method there can be. We decide, in other words, that an agent could have done otherwise if others in his situation have done otherwise, and these others are like him in all apparently relevant ways. Or we decide that an agent could have done otherwise if he himself has done otherwise in situations that are like this one in all apparently relevant ways.

It should be emphasized that the indetermination with which we are here concerned is indetermination only at the level of psychological explanation. Such indetermination is compatible with determination at other levels of explanation. In particular, a sub-psychological, or physiological, explanation of our behavior may yet be deterministic. Some feel that if this is the case, the nature of psychological explanations of our behavior cannot be relevant to the problem of free will. Though I am inclined to disagree with this view, I have neither the space nor the competence to argue this here. . . .

Seen from a certain perspective, this dealing out of praise and blame may seem unfair. In particular, we might think that if it is truly undetermined whether a given agent in a given situation will perform a good action or a bad one, then it must be a matter of chance that the agent ends up doing what he does. If the action is truly undetermined, then it is not determined by the agent himself. One might think that in this case the agent has no more control over the moral quality of his action than does anything else.

However, the fact that it is not determined whether the agent will perform a good action or a bad one does not imply that which action he performs can properly be regarded as a matter of chance. Of course, in some situations an agent might choose to make it a matter of chance. For example, an agent struggling with the decision between fulfilling a moral obligation and doing something immoral that he very much wants to do might ultimately decide to let the toss of a coin settle the matter for him. But, in normal cases, the way in which the agent makes a decision involves no statistical process or randomizing event. It appears that the claim that there is no complete explanation of why the agent who could have performed a better action performed a worse one or of why the agent who could have performed a worse action performed a better one rules out even the explanation that it was a matter of chance.

In order to have control over the moral quality of his actions, an agent must have certain requisite abilities — in particular, the abilities necessary to see and understand the reasons and interests he ought to see and understand and the abilities necessary to direct his actions in accordance with these reasons and interests. And if, furthermore, there is nothing that interferes with the agent's use of these abilities — that is, no determining cause that prevents him from using them and no statistical process that, as it were, takes out of his hands the control over whether or not he uses them — then it seems that these are all the abilities that the agent needs to have. But it is compatible with the agent's having these abilities and with there being no interferences to their use that it is not determined whether the agent will perform a good action or a bad one. The responsible agent who performs a bad action fails to exercise these abilities sufficiently, though there is no complete explanation of why he fails. The responsible agent who performs a good action does exercise these abilities — it may or may not be the case that it is determined that he exercise them.

## TEST YOUR UNDERSTANDING

1. What is it for an action to be *psychologically determined*?

2. Give an example of your own to illustrate Wolf's claim that you can be responsible for a good act even if you were psychologically determined to perform it.

3. Does Wolf believe that you can be responsible for a bad act that you were psychologically determined to perform?

## NOTES AND QUESTIONS

1. *Psychological vs. physical determinism.* Wolf discusses cases in which an agent is psychologically determined to act badly and concludes that in such cases the agent is not blameworthy. But what about an agent who is *physically*, but not psychologically, determined to act badly on some occasion? Describe such a case and address the question: Does Wolf's argument for the incompatibility of *psychological* determination and moral blameworthiness entail that someone who is *physically* determined to act badly is not blameworthy for his act?

2. *Praiseworthiness for one's unearned virtues.* Suppose Jane is a generous person who performs a generous act on some occasion, and who, when pressed to say why she did it, responds: "I had no choice; he needed my help and so I helped him." Suppose that Jane was determined to be generous by a good upbringing, and that having been so determined, she was determined to act as she did. For Wolf, this is a clear case of an act for which the agent deserves praise. Consider the following challenge to that view:

> If we are being clearheaded, we do not praise people who are lucky enough to be born beautiful or rich or talented. We praise these people only insofar as we think their achievements are due to hard work that they were not determined to perform. Jane's generosity is due in part to good genes and in

part to good luck. So she deserves no credit for it. And since it determined her to act, she deserves no special credit for that either. In general, just as people who are determined to act badly are victims of bad luck, so people who are determined to act well are beneficiaries of good luck. And the beneficiary of luck deserves no praise for what she does.

How should Wolf respond?

## P. F. Strawson (1919–2006)

Until his retirement in 1987, Strawson was the Waynflete Professor of Metaphysical Philosophy at the University of Oxford. His writings include seminal contributions to the philosophy of language ("On Referring," 1950), metaphysics (*Individuals*, 1959) and the interpretation of Kant's philosophy (*The Bounds of Sense*, 1966).

# FREEDOM AND RESENTMENT

1. Some philosophers say they do not know what the thesis of determinism is. Others say, or imply, that they do know what it is. Of these, some — the pessimists perhaps — hold that if the thesis is true, then the concepts of moral obligation and responsibility really have no application, and the practices of punishing and blaming, of expressing moral condemnation and approval, are really unjustified. Others — the optimists perhaps — hold that these concepts and practices in no way lose their *raison d'être* if the thesis of determinism is true. . . . If I am asked which of these parties I belong to, I must say it is the first of all, the party of those who do not know what the thesis of determinism is. But this does not stop me from having some sympathy with the others, and a wish to reconcile them. Should not ignorance, rationally, inhibit such sympathies? Well, of course, though darkling, one has some inkling — some notion of what sort of thing is being talked about. This lecture is intended as a move towards reconciliation; so it is likely to seem wrongheaded to everyone. . . .

2. . . . Some optimists about determinism point to the efficacy of the practices of punishment, and of moral condemnation and approval, in regulating behaviour in socially desirable ways. In the fact of their efficacy, they suggest, is an adequate basis for these practices; and this fact certainly does not show determinism to be false. To this the pessimists reply, all in a rush, that *just* punishment and *moral* condemnation imply moral guilt and guilt implies moral responsibility and moral responsibility implies freedom and freedom implies the falsity of determinism. And to this the optimists are wont to reply in turn that it is true that these practices require freedom in a sense, and the existence of freedom in this sense is one of the facts as we

know them. But what "freedom" means here is nothing but the absence of certain conditions the presence of which would make moral condemnation or punishment inappropriate. They have in mind conditions like compulsion by another, or innate incapacity, or insanity, or other less extreme forms of psychological disorder, or the existence of circumstances in which the making of any other choice would be morally inadmissible or would be too much to expect of any man. To this list they are constrained to add other factors which, without exactly being limitations of freedom, may also make moral condemnation or punishment inappropriate or mitigate their force: as some forms of ignorance, mistake, or accident. And the general reason why moral condemnation or punishment are inappropriate when these factors or conditions are present is held to be that the practices in question will be generally efficacious means of regulating behaviour in desirable ways only in cases where these factors are *not* present. Now the pessimist admits that the facts as we know them include the existence of freedom, the occurrence of cases of free action, in the negative sense which the optimist concedes; and admits, or rather insists, that the existence of freedom in this sense is compatible with the truth of determinism. Then what does the pessimist find missing? When he tries to answer this question, his language is apt to alternate between the very familiar and the very unfamiliar. Thus he may say, familiarly enough, that the man who is the subject of justified punishment, blame or moral condemnation must really *deserve* it; and then add, perhaps, that, in the case at least where he is blamed for a positive act rather than an omission, the condition of his really deserving blame is something that goes beyond the negative freedoms that the optimist concedes. It is, say, a genuinely free identification of the will with the act. And this is the condition that is incompatible with the truth of determinism.

The conventional, but conciliatory, optimist need not give up yet. He may say: Well, people often decide to do things, really intend to do what they do, know just what they're doing in doing it; the reasons they think they have for doing what they do, often really are their reasons and not their rationalizations. These facts, too, are included in the facts as we know them. If this is what you mean by freedom — by the identification of the will with the act — then freedom may again be conceded. But again the concession is compatible with the truth of the determinist thesis. For it would not follow from that thesis that nobody decides to do anything; that nobody ever does anything intentionally; that it is false that people sometimes know perfectly well what they are doing. I tried to define freedom negatively. You want to give it a more positive look. But it comes to the same thing. Nobody denies freedom in this sense, or these senses, and nobody claims that the existence of freedom in these senses shows determinism to be false.

But it is here that the lacuna in the optimistic story can be made to show. For the pessimist may be supposed to ask: But *why* does freedom in this sense justify blame, etc.? You turn towards me first the negative, and then the positive, faces of a freedom which nobody challenges. But the only reason you have given for the practices of moral condemnation and punishment in cases where this freedom is present is the efficacy of these practices in regulating behaviour in socially desirable ways. But this is not a sufficient basis, it is not even the right *sort* of basis, for these practices as we understand them.

Now my optimist, being the sort of man he is, is not likely to invoke an intuition of fittingness at this point. So he really has no more to say. And my pessimist, being the sort of man he is, has only one more thing to say; and that is that the admissibility of these practices, as we understand them, demands another kind of freedom, the kind that in turn demands the falsity of the thesis of determinism. But might we not induce the pessimist to give up saying this by giving the optimist something more to say?

3. I have mentioned punishing and moral condemnation and approval; and it is in connection with these practices or attitudes that the issue between optimists and pessimists . . . is felt to be particularly important. But it is not of these practices and attitudes that I propose, at first, to speak. These practices or attitudes permit, where they do not imply, a certain detachment from the actions or agents which are their objects. I want to speak, at least at first, of something else: of the non-detached attitudes and reactions of people directly involved in transactions with each other; of the attitudes and reactions of offended parties and beneficiaries; of such things as gratitude, resentment, forgiveness, love, and hurt feelings. . . .

What I have to say consists largely of commonplaces. So my language, like that of commonplaces generally, will be quite unscientific and imprecise. The central commonplace that I want to insist on is the very great importance that we attach to the attitudes and intentions towards us of other human beings, and the great extent to which our personal feelings and reactions depend upon, or involve, our beliefs about these attitudes and intentions. . . . If someone treads on my hand accidentally, while trying to help me, the pain may be no less acute than if he treads on it in contemptuous disregard of my existence or with a malevolent wish to injure me. But I shall generally feel in the second case a kind and degree of resentment that I shall not feel in the first. If someone's actions help me to some benefit I desire, then I am benefited in any case; but if he intended them so to benefit me because of his general goodwill towards me, I shall reasonably feel a gratitude which I should not feel at all if the benefit was an incidental consequence, unintended or even regretted by him, of some plan of action with a different aim. . . .

We should think of the many different kinds of relationship which we can have with other people — as sharers of a common interest; as members of the same family; as colleagues; as friends; as lovers; as chance parties to an enormous range of transactions and encounters. Then we should think, in each of these connections in turn, and in others, of the kind of importance we attach to the attitudes and intentions towards us of those who stand in these relationships to us, and of the kinds of *reactive* attitudes and feelings to which we ourselves are prone. In general, we demand some degree of goodwill or regard on the part of those who stand in these relationships to us, though the forms we require it to take vary widely in different connections. The range and intensity of our *reactive* attitudes towards goodwill, its absence or its opposite vary no less widely. I have mentioned, specifically, resentment and gratitude; and they are a usefully opposed pair. But, of course, there is a whole continuum of reactive attitude and feeling stretching on both sides of these and — the most comfortable area — in between them.

The object of these commonplaces is to try to keep before our minds something it is easy to forget when we are engaged in philosophy, especially in our cool, contemporary style, viz. what it is actually like to be involved in ordinary interpersonal relationships, ranging from the most intimate to the most casual.

4. It is one thing to ask about the general causes of these reactive attitudes I have alluded to; it is another to ask about the variations to which they are subject, the particular conditions in which they do or do not seem natural or reasonable or appropriate; and it is a third thing to ask what it would be like, what it is like, not to suffer them. I am not much concerned with the first question; but I am with the second; and perhaps even more with the third.

Let us consider, then, occasions for resentment: situations in which one person is offended or injured by the action of another and in which — in the absence of special considerations — the offended person might naturally or normally be expected to feel resentment. Then let us consider what sorts of special considerations might be expected to modify or mollify this feeling or remove it altogether. It needs no saying now how multifarious these considerations are. But, for my purpose, I think they can be roughly divided into two kinds. To the first group belong all those which might give occasion for the employment of such expressions as "He didn't mean to," "He hadn't realized," "He didn't know"; and also all those which might give occasion for the use of the phrase "He couldn't help it," when this is supported by such phrases as "He was pushed," "He had to do it," "It was the only way," "They left him no alternative," etc. Obviously these various pleas . . . differ from each other in striking and important ways. But for my present purpose they have something still more important in common. None of them invites us to suspend towards the agent, either at the time of his action or in general, our ordinary reactive attitudes. They do not invite us to view the *agent* as one in respect of whom these attitudes are in any way inappropriate. They invite us to view the *injury* as one in respect of which a particular one of these attitudes is inappropriate. . . .

The second group of considerations is very different. I shall take them in two subgroups of which the first is far less important than the second. In connection with the first subgroup we may think of such statements as "He wasn't himself," "He has been under very great strain recently," "He was acting under post-hypnotic suggestion"; in connection with the second, we may think of "He's only a child," "He's a hopeless schizophrenic," "His mind has been systematically perverted," "That's purely compulsive behaviour on his part." Such pleas as these do, as pleas of my first general group do not, invite us to suspend our ordinary reactive attitudes towards the agent, either at the time of his action or all the time. They do not invite us to see the agent's action in a way consistent with the full retention of ordinary inter-personal attitudes and merely inconsistent with one particular attitude. They invite us to view the agent himself in a different light from the light in which we should normally view one who has acted as he has acted.

The second and more important subgroup of cases allows that the circumstances were normal, but presents the agent as psychologically abnormal — or as morally undeveloped. The agent was himself; but he is warped or deranged, neurotic or just a child. When we see someone in such a light as this, all our reactive attitudes tend to be profoundly modified. I must deal here in crude dichotomies and ignore the ever-interesting and ever-illuminating varieties of case. What I want to contrast is the attitude (or range of attitudes) of involvement or participation in a human relationship, on the one hand, and what might be called the objective attitude (or range of attitudes) to another human being, on the other. Even in the same situation, I must add, they are not altogether *exclusive* of each other; but they are, profoundly, *opposed* to each other. To adopt the objective attitude to another human being is to see him, perhaps, as an object of social policy; as a subject for what, in a wide range of sense, might be called treatment; as something certainly to be taken account, perhaps precautionary account, of. . . . If your attitude towards someone is wholly objective, then though you may fight him, you cannot quarrel with him, and though you may talk to him, even negotiate with him, you cannot reason with him. You can at most pretend to quarrel, or to reason, with him. . . .

What I have called the participant reactive attitudes are essentially natural human reactions to the good or ill will or indifference of others towards us, as displayed in *their* attitudes and actions. The question we have to ask is: What effect would, or should, the acceptance of the truth of a general thesis of determinism have upon these reactive attitudes? More specifically, would, or should, the acceptance of the truth of the thesis lead to the decay or the repudiation of all such attitudes? Would, or should, it mean the end of gratitude, resentment, and forgiveness; of all reciprocated adult loves; of all the essentially *personal* antagonisms?

But how can I answer, or even pose, this question without knowing *exactly* what the thesis of determinism is? Well, there is one thing we do know; that if there is a coherent thesis of determinism, then there must be a sense of "determined" such that, if that thesis is true, then all behaviour whatever is determined in that sense. Remembering this, we can consider at least what possibilities lie formally open; and then perhaps we shall see that the question can be answered *without* knowing exactly what the thesis of determinism is. We can consider what possibilities lie open because we have already before us an account of the ways in which particular reactive attitudes, or reactive attitudes in general, may be, and, sometimes, we judge, should be, inhibited. Thus I considered earlier a group of considerations which tend to inhibit, and, we judge, should inhibit, resentment, in particular cases of an agent causing an injury, without inhibiting reactive attitudes in general towards that agent. Obviously this group of considerations cannot strictly bear upon our question; for that question concerns reactive attitudes in general. But resentment has a particular interest; so it is worth adding that it has never been claimed as a consequence of the truth of determinism that one or another of *these* considerations was operative in every case of an injury being caused by an agent; that it would follow from the truth of determinism that anyone who caused an injury *either* was quite simply ignorant of causing it *or* had acceptably overriding reasons for acquiescing reluctantly in causing it *or* . . . etc. The prevalence of this happy state of affairs would not be a consequence of the reign of universal determinism, but of the reign of universal goodwill. We cannot, then, find here the possibility of an affirmative answer to our question.

Next, I remarked that the participant attitude . . . tend[s] to give place, and it is judged by the civilized should give place, to objective attitudes, just in so far as the agent is seen as excluded from ordinary adult human relationships by deep-rooted psychological abnormality — or simply by being a child. But it cannot be a consequence of any thesis which is not itself self-contradictory that abnormality is the universal condition.

Now this dismissal might seem altogether too facile; and so, in a sense, it is. But . . . we can sometimes, and in part, . . . look on the normal (those we rate as "normal") in the objective way in which we have learned to look on certain classified cases of abnormality. And our question reduces to this: could, or should, the acceptance of the determinist thesis lead us always to look on everyone exclusively in this way? For this is the only condition worth considering under which the acceptance of determinism could lead to the decay or repudiation of participant reactive attitudes.

It does not seem to be self-contradictory to suppose that this might happen. So I suppose we must say that it is not absolutely inconceivable that it should happen. But I am strongly inclined to think that it is, for us as we are, practically inconceivable. The human commitment to participation in ordinary inter-personal relationships is, I think, too thoroughgoing and deeply rooted for us to take seriously the thought that a general theoretical conviction might so change our world that, in it, there were no longer any such things as inter-personal relationships as we normally understand them. . . .

5.  The reactive attitudes I have so far discussed are essentially reactions to the quality of others' wills towards us, as manifested in their behaviour: to their good or ill will or indifference or lack of concern. Thus resentment, or what I have called resentment, is a reaction to injury or indifference. The reactive attitudes I have now to discuss might be described as the sympathetic or vicarious or impersonal or disinterested or generalized analogues of the reactive attitudes I have already discussed. They are reactions to the qualities of others' wills, not towards ourselves, but towards others. Because of this impersonal or vicarious character, we give them different names. Thus one who experiences the vicarious analogue of resentment is said to be indignant or disapproving, or morally indignant or disapproving.

. . . The generalized or vicarious analogues of the personal reactive attitudes rest on, and reflect . . . the demand for the manifestation of a reasonable degree of goodwill or regard, on the part of others, not simply towards oneself, but towards all those on whose behalf moral indignation may be felt, i.e., as we now think, towards all men. . . .

Now, as of the personal reactive attitudes, so of their vicarious analogues, we must ask in what ways, and by what considerations, they tend to be inhibited. Both types of attitude involve, or express, a certain sort of demand for inter-personal regard. The fact of injury constitutes a prima facie appearance of this demand's being flouted or unfulfilled. We saw, in the case of resentment, how one class of considerations may show this appearance to be mere appearance, . . . without in any way tending to make us suspend our ordinary interpersonal attitudes to the agent. Considerations of this class operate in just the same way, for just the same reasons, in connection with moral disapprobation or indignation; they inhibit indignation without in any way inhibiting the sort of demand on the agent of which indignation can be an expression, the range of attitudes towards him to which it belongs.

But suppose we see the agent in a different light: as one whose picture of the world is an insane delusion; or as one whose behaviour, or a part of whose behaviour, is unintelligible to us, perhaps even to him, in terms of conscious purposes, and intelligible only in terms of unconscious purposes; or even, perhaps, as one wholly impervious to the self-reactive attitudes I spoke of, wholly lacking, as we say, in moral sense. Seeing an agent in such a light as this tends, I said, to inhibit resentment in a wholly different way. It tends to inhibit resentment because it tends to inhibit ordinary interpersonal attitudes in general, and the kind of demand and expectation which those attitudes involve; and tends to promote instead the purely objective view of the agent as one posing problems simply of intellectual understanding, management, treatment, and control. Again the parallel holds for those generalized or moral attitudes towards the agent which we are now concerned with. The same abnormal light which shows the agent to us as one in respect of whom the personal attitudes, the personal demand, are to be suspended, shows him to us also as one in respect of whom the impersonal attitudes, the generalized demand, are to be suspended. . . .

What concerns us now is to inquire, as previously in connection with the personal reactive attitudes, what relevance any general thesis of determinism might have to their vicarious analogues. The answers once more are parallel; though I shall take them in a slightly different order. First, we must note, as before, that when the suspension of such an attitude or such attitudes occurs in a particular case, it is *never* the consequence of the belief that the piece of behaviour in question was determined in a sense such that all behaviour *might* be, and, if determinism is true, all behaviour is, determined in that sense. For it is not a consequence of any general thesis of determinism which might be true that nobody knows what he's doing or that everybody's behaviour is unintelligible in terms of conscious purposes or that everybody lives in a world of delusion or that nobody has a moral sense, i.e. is susceptible of self-reactive attitudes, etc. In fact no such sense of "determined" as would be required for a general thesis of determinism is ever relevant to our actual suspensions of moral reactive attitudes. Second, suppose it granted, as I have already argued, that we cannot take seriously the thought that theoretical conviction of such a general thesis would lead to the total decay of the personal reactive attitudes. Can we then take seriously the thought that such a conviction . . . would nevertheless lead to the total decay or repudiation of the vicarious analogues of these attitudes? I think that the change in our social world which would leave us exposed to the personal reactive attitudes but not at all to their vicarious analogues, the generalization of abnormal egocentricity which this would entail, is perhaps even harder for us to envisage as a real possibility than the decay of both kinds of attitude together. . . . Finally, to the further question whether it would not be *rational*, given a general theoretical conviction of the truth of determinism, so to change our world that in it all these attitudes were wholly suspended, I must answer that one who presses this question has wholly failed to grasp the import of the preceding answer, the nature of the human commitment that is here involved: it is *useless* to ask whether it would not be rational for us to do what it is not in our nature to (be able to) do. . . .

6. Optimist and pessimist[, then,] misconstrue the facts in very different styles. But in a profound sense there is something in common to their misunderstandings. Both seek, in different ways, to over-intellectualize the facts. Inside the general structure or web of human attitudes and feelings of which I have been speaking, there is endless

room for modification, redirection, criticism, and justification. But questions of justification are internal to the structure or relate to modifications internal to it. The existence of the general framework of attitudes itself is something we are given with the fact of human society. As a whole, it neither calls for, nor permits, an external "rational" justification. Pessimist and optimist alike show themselves, in different ways, unable to accept this. . . .

## TEST YOUR UNDERSTANDING

1. P. F. Strawson sees the free will debate as a clash between "optimists" and "pessimists." State these positions.

2. What is a "reactive attitude"? Give examples and attempt a general characterization.

3. Why, according to Strawson, are we not blameworthy when we cause harm *by accident*?

## NOTES AND QUESTIONS

1. For P. F. Strawson, the urgent question that underlies the free will debate is whether certain emotions — guilt, resentment, admiration, etc. — are ever justified. According to Strawson, we can understand this question in two ways. We might be asking whether these emotions are justified by the standards we accept in daily life. Alternatively, we might be asking whether they are justified by some ideal standard, e.g., the standard that it would be *best* for us to adopt. Strawson's conclusion is that even if determinism is true, our normal reactions are often justified in both senses. Is he right?

2. Suppose a stranger cuts in front of you in line at the bank. He's not a child, he's not insane, and there is no emergency that would justify his rude behavior, so your first reaction is to blame him. You are then informed (say, by a scientist) that his action was determined by forces that were in place before he was born; and as soon as you learn this, you conclude that it would be unfair for you to blame him. This suggests that if determinism is true, our reactive emotions are not justified *by ordinary standards*. We fail to notice this in daily life only because we ignore the possibility of determinism. How might Strawson respond to this suggestion?

3. Strawson claims that if we were to abandon the negative reactive attitudes like guilt and resentment, certain immensely valuable forms of friendship and love would be impossible, and hence that the negative reactive attitudes must be justified by the standards that it would be *best* for us to adopt. But is this right? Can't we imagine a world in which people love their friends and family but never resent them and never feel guilty? Try to describe a world of this sort in some detail in order to assess Strawson's claim that the negative reactive attitudes are justified even by *ideal* standards.

## ANALYZING THE ARGUMENTS

1. Suppose that freedom and responsibility are mere illusions (perhaps for the reasons Galen Strawson gives). How should we respond to this discovery? How should it affect our relationships with other people? How should it affect our social practices, including the practice of criminal punishment?

2. Albert and Boris are convicted of assault and robbery in separate attacks on defenseless victims. When asked why, both say, "I wanted the money and I get a kick out of beating people up." According to prison psychiatrists, their psychological profiles are identical. Both are selfish and cruel, but neither is insane by legal standards. The only difference lies in the past. Albert is an ordinary criminal with an ordinary history. Boris, on the other hand, was a decent, law-abiding philosophy professor until quite recently, when his personality suddenly changed for the worse. A medical examination reveals that this change in personality is due to a small brain tumor. The tumor is inoperable and its effects are permanent but not life threatening. Is Boris responsible for his behavior? How might Ayer, P. F. Strawson, or Frankfurt approach the question?

3. It is widely agreed that people who suffer from serious mental illness (acute schizophrenia, advanced dementia) are not morally responsible for their behavior. What is the best explanation for this fact? (For discussion, see Susan Wolf, "Sanity and the Metaphysics of Responsibility," in Ferdinand David Schoeman, ed., *Responsibility, Character, and the Emotions: New Essays in Moral Psychology*, Cambridge University Press, 1987.)

4. Ernst is on trial for war crimes and his lawyer speaks in his defense:

   > Your honor, it is true that my client was a guard in a Nazi concentration camp, and that he participated in the extermination of many innocent people. But he was raised in a Nazi village by Nazi parents, and everything he was taught from earliest childhood led him to believe that his victims were not people, but animals whose lives meant nothing. He could not possibly have known his actions were wrong, so he is not responsible and should not be punished.

   What is the best response to this shocking argument?

5. Seymour has three drinks at a party, gets into his car, and drives home without incident. Chester has three drinks at the same party, gets into his car, and as he is driving home, hits a pedestrian in a crosswalk. Suppose that (a) Seymour and Chester were equally drunk and equally reckless, and (b) if Chester had not been drunk, he would not have hit the pedestrian. By ordinary standards, both are clearly blameworthy for driving drunk, a serious moral wrong. But Chester is also blameworthy for *killing a person*, and that is a *much* more serious moral wrong. So we blame Chester more intensely, and also punish him more severely. Is this view coherent? Consider the following argument:

   > The only difference between Chester and Seymour is that Chester happened to encounter a pedestrian. But Chester had no control over whether there would be a pedestrian in the crosswalk. From hi  point of view, this was just a matter of bad luck. (By the same token, Seymour had the good luck to encounter no one.) But we should not blame a person for what he cannot control. So we should not blame Chester for killing the pedestrian.

(For discussion, see Thomas Nagel, "Moral Luck," in his *Mortal Questions*, Cambridge University Press, 1979.)

6. Many of the arguments in this section turn on claims about what a person *could* have done. Many philosophers have been tempted by the following analysis of this idiom.

*The Conditional Analysis:* X *could* have done A if and only if X *would have done A if* X had tried.

Unfortunately, the analysis is incorrect.

*Austin's golfer:* Tiger Woods misses an easy putt. As the ball skids past the hole he says to himself: "I could have made that shot!" His claim is true. And yet the conditional, "If he had tried to make the putt, he would have made it," is clearly false. After all, he *did* try, and he failed. (See J. L. Austin, "Ifs and Cans," in his *Philosophical Papers*, Oxford University Press, 1961.)

*Paralyzed by fear:* Al is hiking when a snake crosses his path. If he tried to run away, he would succeed: he is not literally paralyzed and the path is clear. But he cannot run away. He is so terrified by snakes that he cannot bring himself to try.

Explain why these examples make trouble for the Conditional Analysis and consider how a proponent of the analysis might respond.

# 14

# Is Morality Objective?

## Morality in Life

Consider three hypothetical situations:

1. You clean up after your party and find your friend's wallet. It contains $100. She had told you she lost it while shopping. Because she is so confused, you are confident that you can keep it without her knowing. But you know you should not, and return the wallet to her.

2. Someone breaks into your apartment and steals your laptop. Luckily you are insured. Still, you are annoyed at the inconvenience of getting a new one. But beyond the annoyance, you are indignant. You have not merely been inconvenienced; you have been wronged.

3. You want to buy a shirt. But you learn that the company that made it is hiring people desperate for work who will accept $5/hour. Is it wrong to pay so little? The company did not put the people they are hiring in desperate circumstances. And the employees are better off taking the jobs than turning them down. But is the company exploiting vulnerabilities by paying so little? Are you complicit in the exploitation if you buy the shirt? You think about the issue and discuss it with friends. Maybe you decide that it is permissible to pay the low wage. Maybe you decide that they ought to pay more. In either case, you feel the force of the idea that you should not exploit vulnerability.

In each of these cases, you are concerned about what is right: about doing the right thing and about being treated rightly. That moral concern is part of our ordinary experience, woven into our thought, feeling, conversation, and action. It shows in your decision to return the wallet, your indignation at the person who has stolen your laptop, your pause before buying the shirt.

One aspect of that experience is that moral considerations, reasons, and requirements strike us as *objective*. Think about your friend's wallet. You ought to return it. That thought about what you ought to do—what anyone in your situation should do—does not strike you as an invention, or convention, or a matter of feeling and attitude. It is not like a local cultural rule against eating peas with a fork. You ought to do it, whatever your feelings, beliefs, and social and cultural circumstances happen to be. At least that is how it strikes you.

Sometimes, as in the case of buying the shirt, moral questions are complicated. *Are* you complicit in exploiting vulnerability when you buy it? Or are you helping someone who is willing to take a job and would be better off if he took it? These considerations pull you in different directions. You need to think about the issue, not simply apply a crisp rule. But even when the questions get complicated, the considerations, reasons, and requirements do not strike you as optional.

In life, then, moral considerations present themselves as objective. But are they what they seem to be?

J. L. Mackie says "no." "There are," he says, "no objective values." Mackie agrees that we *experience* moral requirements — like the requirement to return the wallet — as objective. The objectivist understanding, he says, has "a firm basis in ordinary thought, and even in the meanings of moral terms." But this understanding is in error. The truth about morality, Mackie argues, is a "skepticism" or "subjectivism" that denies the objectivity of moral considerations, reasons, and requirements.

# Philosophy and Life

Does it matter if morality is objective? The answer might seem obvious. If morality is not objective, then isn't it fine to do whatever you want? The answer is not so easy and is a subject of considerable philosophical disagreement.

To clarify the disagreement, let's distinguish *first-order* and *second-order* moral views. First-order moral views are claims, both specific and general, about what you ought to do: you ought to return the wallet; you ought to keep your promises; you ought to do what maximizes human welfare. Second-order moral views are claims about the nature of morality. The view that morality is objective is a second-order view, as is Mackie's moral skepticism. So, too, is Sharon Street's "mind-dependent" conception of value, according to which there are no truths about what is good or what is right that are independent of our attitudes.

One answer to the question about the importance of objectivity, then, is based on the claim that first-order and second-order views are completely independent from one another. Call this the *Independence Thesis*. According to the Independence Thesis, for example, moral subjectivism (a second-order view) has no implications for first-order moral views. Even if you are convinced of moral subjectivism, you should still think it is right to return the wallet and you should still return the wallet; you just should not think that that requirement is objective. Mackie endorses the Independence Thesis. Philosophy, he believes, teaches us that morality is not really objective. But when we close our philosophy books, we should go about our lives just as before.

Critics of the Independence Thesis (including Thomas Nagel and Street) deny that we can keep our first- and second-order views so neatly separated. Moral skepticism, they argue, undermines our first-order beliefs about what we ought to do.[1]

Suppose, for example, you believe that slavery is wrong. You take that to be an objective matter. Now imagine you are persuaded of the second-order view that the wrongness of slavery is not objective. You continue to think that slavery is wrong, but now you think, say, that the wrongness of slavery is a matter of attitude or social convention.

If, however, you think the wrongness is a matter of social convention, then don't you also think that if social conventions approved of slavery, then slavery would be permissible? But you started out thinking that slavery would still be wrong even if people (mistakenly) thought it was right: even if social conventions endorsed slavery. So your first-order conviction that it is wrong seems to be in tension with the second-order idea that its wrongness is a matter of social convention.

If the Independence Thesis is true, then skepticism about moral objectivity is an interesting intellectual challenge to our ordinary views about morality, though it does not have practical implications. If the Independence Thesis is wrong, then skepticism is consequential for how we should live.

So should we be skeptics about moral objectivity? Much of the philosophical debate about this question focuses on the merits of three arguments for skepticism — a *metaphysical argument*, a *motivational argument*, and an *argument from disagreement*.

# The Metaphysical Argument

You think that returning the wallet is right. But you find yourself wondering whether it is *really* right. Not that you think *keeping* the wallet is right. Instead, you wonder whether any action is *really* right or wrong. Rightness, you think, is not something in the world.

The world includes social conventions, religious texts, parental admonitions, social pressures, traditions, and personal attitudes instructing you to return the wallet. But when you scrutinize the world, you do not detect rightness anywhere. These doubts are *metaphysical* because they arise from a concern about whether rightness is among the constituents of the world. "Permissibility, rightness, wrongness, or blameworthiness," as R. Jay Wallace says, "do not seem to correspond to any objects or properties in the natural world."

---

1. For a vigorous rejection of the Independence Thesis, see Ronald Dworkin, *Justice for Hedgehogs* (Harvard University Press, 2011), part 1.

The problem is not that we have yet to locate rightness in the way that particle physicists had not located the Higgs particle until 2012. The physicists knew what they were looking for—a zero-spin particle that decays very fast into a variety of other particles—and how to look for it. The problem, according to the metaphysical argument, arises from the odd kind of property that *rightness* would need to be. It would have to be, Mackie says, a "to be-doneness" that is present in an action, that imposes a demand on us, and that we can recognize through our powers of intuition and perception. How could there be such "intrinsic to-be-doneness"? The property is too bizarre to take seriously. (Mackie calls this the "argument from queerness.") Because there is no such property of moral rightness, morality is not objective.

Critics of the metaphysical argument think it is founded on a misconception of moral rightness. They say that what makes it right to return the wallet is not a special property possessed by the act of returning the wallet. When I think that I ought to return the wallet, I am thinking that a kind of reasoning supports my returning it. Nagel describes the reasoning as "impersonal" practical reasoning. When I reason impersonally, I stand back from my desires and circumstances and ask not just about me, but about what "*one should* do—and that means not just what *I* should do but what *this person* should do. The same answer should be given by anyone to whom the data are presented." I reflect on the rightness of the action by considering what the balance of reasons supports, given the circumstances.

This conception of moral thought as an exercise in impersonal practical reasoning arguably defuses the metaphysical argument for skepticism. It does not, however, provide any *assurance* of objectivity. We could pursue impersonal reasoning and find that it does not give any definite answers to practical questions. What it does tell us is that moral objectivity depends on where we are led by practical reasoning, not on the results of a metaphysical expedition.

## Motivational Argument

Suppose you are tempted to keep the wallet. You pause, think about it, conclude that you ought to return it, and hand it over. How does this work? How does the thought that an action is right motivate you to do it? Can a thought alone have that practical effect?

The questions are prompted by the observation that thoughts alone do not typically issue in action. When you are thirsty and drink some water, you do not drink simply because you have the belief that your body needs water. There is a thirst: an *urge* or *impulse* or *desire* to drink. The belief that you need water alone does not suffice. Is that really right? Suppose your doctor tells you to drink even when you have no thirst. Still it is not the belief alone that results in drinking. There also needs to be a desire to be healthy.

Suppose it is the same with morality. When you decide to return the wallet, what really happens is that you have formed a desire to return the wallet: that—not the thought that it is right—explains why you return it. This line of thinking leads to the "subjectivism" about morality that Wallace explores. The subjectivist argues—in a more or less complicated way—that when I say "I ought to give back the wallet," what I am doing is revealing my desire to return the wallet. Having the conviction that I ought to return it is really a matter of having a desire to return it. That explains how morality motivates.

Is the subjectivist right in thinking that moral thought is really a matter of feelings and desires? Suppose the wallet left at my party belongs to a stranger. I wonder if I should return it. I need $100. I did not invite the stranger. I am annoyed that he came. He was a pain. All my feelings are negative. I don't want to give the wallet back. But I think that I ought to and that all my feelings are leading me astray. Can subjectivism make sense of this thought, which stands opposed to my feelings about returning the wallet? "The challenge," as Wallace says, "is to explain how we can achieve critical distance from our motivating attitudes, within a framework that understands moral thought essentially in terms of those attitudes."

These observations about "critical distance" may create troubles for the subjectivist criticism of moral objectivity. But they do not solve the puzzle about how morality motivates. One line of response urges that moral thoughts *do* motivate without depending on prior attitudes and desires, that I can be motivated to return the wallet simply by the thought that returning it is the right thing to do. Nagel and Wallace suggest this line of argument, pointing to parallels between moral motivation and the motivation to act in ways that promote our long-term happiness.

## Argument from Disagreement

In 1864, Abraham Lincoln wrote: "If slavery is not wrong, then nothing is wrong." Lincoln thought that slavery was objectively wrong. He did not simply think that he hated it or that his party or section of the country opposed it. But Lincoln knew well that this judgment was not universally embraced. Consider Aristotle. He was a deeply reflective person and he did not think that slavery is wrong.[2] This diversity of moral convictions may suggest problems for moral objectivity.

Perhaps moral judgments are like judgments of taste—about who is good looking, what food is delicious, and which colors make good companions. As Philippa Foot observes, "we find wide variations in [such] judgements between different cultures and different generations." In these cases, it is very tempting to think that the

---

2. In the first book of his *Politics*, Aristotle says that some people are by nature slaves. *Politics*, book I, chapter 5.

judgments are somehow relativistic. Broccoli is delicious to me but repellant to you, in something like the way that Bill is behind me but in front of you. There is no issue about whether broccoli is *really* delicious or repellant, any more than there is an issue about whether Bill is *really* in front or behind. The reason for that confidence is not merely that people disagree. We can see no way to argue that one judgment is right and the other is wrong: so much varies between distant cultures that we may have no basis for argument. But with judgments of taste—say, judgments of attractiveness—no trouble is created by the diversity of views because disagreement about attractiveness does not challenge our own standards.

With morality things seem different. Because we experience moral judgments as objective, we cannot simply allow that what is morally right in one place is not morally right in another place. For this reason, Mackie thinks that the relativity of moral judgments undercuts their objectivity. Diverse moral standards reflect different "ways of life," he says. They are not insights into what is morally required.

Nagel and Foot resist this step from disagreement to lack of objectivity. Writing in a **Kantian** spirit, Nagel says that facts about moral disagreement do not undermine impersonal moral reasoning; instead, they provide additional materials for such reasoning to wrestle with. Writing in an **Aristotelian** spirit, Foot begins with the thought that genuine moral requirements have some connection to what is good for people. Moreover, when it comes to the core elements of a good life, human beings share a great deal: "All need affection, the cooperation of others, a place in the community, and help in trouble. It isn't true to suppose that human beings can flourish without these things—being isolated, despised or embattled, or without courage or hope. We are not, therefore, simply expressing values that we happen to have if we think of some moral systems as good moral systems and others as bad." Rather, we are asserting that some moral systems are defensible by arguments based on what is good for human beings, and some are not. Lincoln knew well that some people disagreed with him about the morality of slavery. He thought they were wrong. In addition, he thought he could defend his view with forceful arguments.

So we should be cautious about jumping too quickly from observed disagreements to the relativist idea that what is right for them and what is right for us are different. Why, Foot asks, are we so sure that we know where our reflection on moral standards and human good might lead? The problem with "relativists, and subjectivists generally," she says, is that that they "are ready to make pronouncements about the later part of moral arguments, and moral reviews, without being able to trace the intermediate steps."

Though they draw on different philosophical traditions, Nagel and Foot converge here. We experience moral requirements as objective. But are they really objective? Nagel and Foot agree that we will not find the answer in second-order arguments about the nature of moral thought. The only way to answer this question, they think, is to do the hard work of substantive, first-order, moral reflection—to think about what you ought to do and see whether that thinking leads to compelling conclusions. If it does, then you have a strong case for moral objectivity.

## J. L. Mackie (1917–1981)

Mackie was born in Sydney, Australia. He taught in New Zealand, Australia, and England, and ended his teaching career as a fellow at University College, Oxford. A skeptically minded empiricist, Mackie made important contributions to metaphysics (*The Cement of the Universe*) and the philosophy of religion (*The Miracle of Theism*), as well as metaethics.

# THE SUBJECTIVITY OF VALUES
from *Ethics: Inventing Right and Wrong*

## 1. Moral Scepticism

There are no objective values. . . .

The claim that values are not objective, are not part of the fabric of the world, is meant to include not only moral goodness, which might be most naturally equated with moral value, but also other things that could be more loosely called moral values or disvalues — rightness and wrongness, duty, obligation, an action's being rotten and contemptible, and so on. It also includes non-moral values, notably aesthetic ones, beauty and various kinds of artistic merit. . . .

Since it is with moral values that I am primarily concerned, the view I am adopting may be called moral scepticism. But this name is likely to be misunderstood: "moral scepticism" might also be used as a name for either of two first order views, or perhaps for an incoherent mixture of the two. A moral sceptic might be the sort of person who says "All this talk of morality is tripe," who rejects morality and will take no notice of it. Such a person may be literally rejecting all moral judgements; he is more likely to be making moral judgements of his own, expressing a positive moral condemnation of all that conventionally passes for morality; or he may be confusing these two logically incompatible views, and saying that he rejects all morality, while he is in fact rejecting only a particular morality that is current in the society in which he has grown up. But I am not at present concerned with the merits or faults of such a position. These are first order moral views, positive or negative: the person who adopts either of them is taking a certain practical, normative, stand. By contrast, what I am discussing is a second order view, a view about the status of moral values and the nature of moral valuing, about where and how they fit into the world. These first and second order views are not merely distinct but completely independent: one could be a second order moral sceptic without being a first order one, or again the other way round. A man could hold strong moral views, and indeed ones whose content was thoroughly conventional, while believing that they were simply attitudes and policies with regard to conduct that he and other people held. Conversely, a man could reject all established morality while believing it to be an objective truth that it was evil or corrupt. . . .

# 2. Subjectivism

Another name often used, as an alternative to "moral scepticism," for the view I am discussing is "subjectivism." But this too has more than one meaning. Moral subjectivism too could be a first order, normative, view, namely that everyone really ought to do whatever he thinks he should. This plainly is a (systematic) first order view; on examination it soon ceases to be plausible, but that is beside the point, for it is quite independent of the second order thesis at present under consideration. What is more confusing is that different second order views compete for the name "subjectivism." Several of these are doctrines about the meaning of moral terms and moral statements. What is often called moral subjectivism is the doctrine that, for example, "This action is right" *means* "I approve of this action," or more generally that moral judgements are equivalent to reports of the speaker's own feelings or attitudes. But the view I am now discussing is to be distinguished in two vital respects from any such doctrine as this. First, what I have called moral scepticism is a negative doctrine, not a positive one: it says what there isn't, not what there is. It says that there do not exist entities or relations of a certain kind, objective values or requirements, which many people have believed to exist. Of course, the moral sceptic cannot leave it at that. If his position is to be at all plausible, he must give some account of how other people have fallen into what he regards as an error, and this account will have to include some positive suggestions about how values fail to be objective, about what has been mistaken for, or has led to false beliefs about, objective values. But this will be a development of his theory, not its core: its core is the negation. Secondly, what I have called moral scepticism is an ontological thesis, not a linguistic or conceptual one. It is not, like the other doctrine often called moral subjectivism, a view about the meanings of moral statements. . . .

The denial that there are objective values does not commit one to any particular view about what moral statements mean, and certainly not to the view that they are equivalent to subjective reports. . . .

# 4. Is Objectivity a Real Issue ?

The main tradition of European moral philosophy from Plato onwards has combined the view that moral values are objective with the recognition that moral judgements are partly prescriptive or directive or action-guiding. Values themselves have been seen as at once prescriptive and objective. In Plato's theory the Forms, and in particular the Form of the Good, are eternal, extra-mental, realities.[1] They are a very central structural element in the fabric of the world. But it is held also that just knowing them or "seeing" them will not merely tell men what to do but will ensure that they do it, overruling any contrary inclinations. The philosopher-kings in the *Republic* can, Plato thinks, be trusted with unchecked power because their education will have given them knowledge of the Forms. Being acquainted with the Forms of the Good and Justice and Beauty and the rest they will, by this knowledge alone, without any further motivation, be impelled to pursue and promote these ideals. Similarly, Kant believes that pure reason can by itself be practical, though he does not pretend to be able to explain how it can be so.[2] Again, Sidgwick argues that if there is to be a science of ethics — and he assumes that there can be, indeed he defines ethics as "the science of conduct" — what ought to be "must in another sense have objective existence: it must be an object of knowledge and as such the same for all minds"; but he says that the affirmations of this science "are also precepts," and he speaks of happiness as 'an end *absolutely* prescribed by reason.[3] [M]any philosophers have thus held that values are objectively prescriptive. . . .

## 7. The Claim to Objectivity

As I have said, the main tradition of European moral philosophy includes the. . . claim, that there are objective values of just the sort I have denied. I have referred already to Plato, Kant, and Sidgwick. Kant in particular holds that the categorical imperative[4] is not only categorical and imperative but objectively so: though a rational being gives the moral law to himself, the law that he thus makes is determinate and necessary. Aristotle begins the *Nicomachean Ethics* by saying that the good is that at which all things aim, and that ethics is part of a science which he calls "politics," whose goal is not knowledge but practice; yet he does not doubt that there can be

1. One of the central doctrines in Plato's philosophy is his "theory of forms." Consider the many things that are good, or the many things that are beautiful. According to the theory of forms, goodness itself ("the form of the good") is a single thing alongside the many good things; beauty itself ("the form of beauty") is a single thing alongside the many beautiful things.

2. Immanuel Kant (1724–1804) was a German philosopher, one of the most influential thinkers of the Enlightenment, and the author of the *Critique of Pure Reason*, the *Critique of Practical Reason*, and the *Critique of Judgment*. He explores the idea that "pure reason can by itself be practical" — that our conduct can be guided by reason itself — in his *Groundwork of the Metaphysics of Morals* and *Critique of Practical Reason*.

3. Mackie is here quoting from Henry Sidgwick's *Methods of Ethics*. Sidgwick (1838–1900) was an English moral philosopher. A classical utilitarian, he held that the standard of right conduct is the principle of utility: that conduct is right if and only if it produces the greatest sum of happiness.

4. According to the categorical imperative, which Kant presents in his *Groundwork of the Metaphysics of Morals*, we ought only to act on a rule that we could approve of everyone acting on.

*knowledge* of what is the good for man, nor, once he has identified this as well-being or happiness, *eudaimonia,* that it can be known, rationally determined, in what happiness consists; and it is plain that he thinks that this happiness is intrinsically desirable, not good simply because it is desired. . . .

Even the sentimentalist Hutcheson defines moral goodness as "some quality apprehended in actions, which procures approbation . . . , " while saying that the moral sense by which we perceive virtue and vice has been given to us (by the Author of nature) to direct our actions.[5] Hume indeed was on the other side, but he is still a witness to the dominance of the objectivist tradition, since he claims that when we "see that the distinction of vice and virtue is not founded merely on the relations of objects, nor is perceiv'd by reason," this "wou'd subvert all the vulgar systems of morality."[6] . . .

But this objectivism about values is not only a feature of the philosophical tradition. It has also a firm basis in ordinary thought, and even in the meanings of moral terms. . . .

Someone in a state of moral perplexity, wondering whether it would be wrong for him to engage, say, in research related to bacteriological warfare, wants to arrive at some judgement about this concrete case, his doing this work at this time in these actual circumstances. . . . The question is not, for example, whether he really wants to do this work, whether it will satisfy or dissatisfy him, whether he will in the long run have a pro-attitude towards it, or even whether this is an action of a sort that he can happily and sincerely recommend in all relevantly similar cases. Nor is he even wondering just whether to recommend such action in all relevantly similar cases. He wants to know whether this course of action would be wrong in itself. . . .

I conclude, then, that ordinary moral judgements include a claim to objectivity, an assumption that there are objective values in just the sense in which I am concerned to deny this. And I do not think it is going too far to say that this assumption has been incorporated in the basic, conventional, meanings of moral terms. Any analysis of the meanings of moral terms which omits this claim to objective, intrinsic, prescriptivity[7] is to that extent incomplete. . . .

If second order ethics were confined, then, to linguistic and conceptual analysis, it ought to conclude that moral values at least are objective: that they are so is part of what our ordinary moral statements mean: the traditional moral concepts of the ordinary man as well as of the main line of western philosophers are concepts of objective value.

---

5. Francis Hutcheson (1694–1746) was a Scottish philosopher who held that human beings use various "senses" to navigate the world, including (in addition to the five senses commonly known) a sense of beauty, a public sense, a sense of honor, a sense of the ridiculous, and, most important, the moral sense described here. Mackie here quotes from Hutcheson's 1725 essay *An Inquiry concerning Moral Good and Evil.*

6. David Hume (1711–1776) was a Scottish philosopher and a student of Hutcheson's. Mackie is quoting from *A Treatise of Human Nature* (1736). Selections from Hume's writings on morality are in chapters 15 and 16 of this anthology.

7. Moral claims are *prescriptive*: they call for certain kinds of conduct. When we say that telling the truth is the *right* thing to do, we mean not only that it is objectively right. We are prescribing truth-telling.

But it is precisely for this reason that linguistic and conceptual analysis is not enough. The claim to objectivity, however ingrained in our language and thought, is not self-validating. It can and should be questioned. But the denial of objective values will have to be put forward not as the result of an analytic approach, but as an "error theory," a theory that although most people in making moral judgements implicitly claim, among other things, to be pointing to something objectively prescriptive, these claims are all false. It is this that makes the name "moral scepticism" appropriate. . . .

Traditionally [this skeptical theory] has been supported by arguments of two main kinds, which I shall call the argument from relativity and the argument from queerness. . . .

# 8. The Argument from Relativity

The argument from relativity has as its premiss the well-known variation in moral codes from one society to another and from one period to another, and also the differences in moral beliefs between different groups and classes within a complex community. Such variation is in itself merely a truth of descriptive morality, a fact of anthropology which entails neither first order nor second order ethical views. Yet it may indirectly support second order subjectivism: radical differences between first order moral judgements make it difficult to treat those judgements as apprehensions of objective truths. But it is not the mere occurrence of disagreements that tells against the objectivity of values. Disagreement on questions in history or biology or cosmology does not show that there are no objective issues in these fields for investigators to disagree about. But such scientific disagreement results from speculative inferences or explanatory hypotheses based on inadequate evidence, and it is hardly plausible to interpret moral disagreement in the same way. Disagreement about moral codes seems to reflect people's adherence to and participation in different ways of life. The causal connection seems to be mainly that way round: it is that people approve of monogamy because they participate in a monogamous way of life rather than that they participate in a monogamous way of life because they approve of monogamy. Of course, the standards may be an idealization of the way of life from which they arise: the monogamy in which people participate may be less complete, less rigid, than that of which it leads them to approve. This is not to say that moral judgements are purely conventional. Of course there have been and are moral heretics and moral reformers, people who have turned against the established rules and practices of their own communities for moral reasons, and often for moral reasons that we would endorse. But this can usually be understood as the extension, in ways which, though new and unconventional, seemed to them to be required for consistency, of rules to which they already adhered as arising out of an existing way of life. In short, the argument from relativity has some force simply because the actual variations in the moral codes are more readily explained by the hypothesis that they reflect ways of life than by the hypothesis that they express perceptions, most of them seriously inadequate and badly distorted, of objective values.

But there is a well-known counter to this argument from relativity, namely to say that the items for which objective validity is in the first place to be claimed are not specific moral rules or codes but very general basic principles which are recognized at least implicitly to some extent in all society — such principles as provide the foundations of what Sidgwick has called different methods of ethics: the principle of universalizability, perhaps, or the rule that one ought to conform to the specific rules of any way of life in which one takes part, from which one profits, and on which one relies, or some utilitarian principle of doing what tends, or seems likely, to promote the general happiness. It is easy to show that such general principles, married with differing concrete circumstances, different existing social patterns or different preferences, will beget different specific moral rules; and there is some plausibility in the claim that the specific rules thus generated will vary from community to community or from group to group in close agreement with the actual variations in accepted codes.

The argument from relativity can be only partly countered in this way. To take this line the moral objectivist has to say that it is only in these principles that the objective moral character attaches immediately to its descriptively specified ground or subject: other moral judgements are objectively valid or true, but only derivatively and contingently — if things had been otherwise, quite different sorts of actions would have been right. And despite the prominence in recent philosophical ethics of universalization, utilitarian principles, and the like, these are very far from constituting the whole of what is actually affirmed as basic in ordinary moral thought. Much of this is concerned rather with what Hare calls "ideals" or, less kindly, "fanaticism."[8] That is, people judge that some things are good or right, and others are bad or wrong, not because — or at any rate not only because — they exemplify some general principle for which widespread implicit acceptance could be claimed, but because something about those things arouses certain responses immediately in them, though they would arouse radically and irresolvably different responses in others. "Moral sense" or "intuition" is an initially more plausible description of what supplies many of our basic moral judgements than "reason." With regard to all these starting points of moral thinking the argument from relativity remains in full force.

## 9. The Argument from Queerness

Even more important, however, and certainly more generally applicable, is the argument from queerness. This has two parts, one metaphysical, the other epistemological. If there were objective values, then they would be entities or qualities or relations of a very strange sort, utterly different from anything else in the universe. Correspondingly, if we were aware of them, it would have to be by some

---

8.  R. M. Hare (1919–2002) was an English moral philosopher, author of *The Language of Morals* (1952) and *Freedom and Reason* (1963).

special faculty of moral perception or intuition, utterly different from our ordinary ways of knowing everything else. These points were recognized by Moore[9] when he spoke of non-natural qualities, and by the intuitionists in their talk about a "faculty of moral intuition." Intuitionism has long been out of favour, and it is indeed easy to point out its implausibilities. What is not so often stressed, but is more important, is that the central thesis of intuitionism is one to which any objectivist view of values is in the end committed: intuitionism merely makes unpalatably plain what other forms of objectivism wrap up. Of course the suggestion that moral judgements are made or moral problems solved by just sitting down and having an ethical intuition is a travesty of actual moral thinking. But, however complex the real process, it will require (if it is to yield authoritatively prescriptive conclusions) some input of this distinctive sort, either premises or forms of argument or both. When we ask the awkward question, how we can be aware of this authoritative prescriptivity, of the truth of these distinctively ethical premises or of the cogency of this distinctively ethical pattern of reasoning, none of our ordinary accounts of sensory perception or introspection or the framing and confirming of explanatory hypotheses or inference or logical construction or conceptual analysis, or any combination of these, will provide a satisfactory answer; "a special sort of intuition" is a lame answer, but it is the one to which the clear-headed objectivist is compelled to resort. . . .

Plato's Forms give a dramatic picture of what objective values would have to be. The Form of the Good is such that knowledge of it provides the knower with both a direction and an overriding motive; something's being good both tells the person who knows this to pursue it and makes him pursue it. An objective good would be sought by anyone who was acquainted with it, not because of any contingent fact that this person, or every person, is so constituted that he desires this end, but just because the end has to-be-pursuedness somehow built into it. Similarly, if there were objective principles of right and wrong, any wrong (possible) course of action would have not-to-be-doneness somehow built into it. . . .

The need for an argument of this sort can be brought out by reflection on Hume's argument that "reason" — in which at this stage he includes all sorts of knowing as well as reasoning — can never be an "influencing motive of the will." Someone might object that Hume has argued unfairly from the lack of influencing power (not contingent upon desires) in ordinary objects of knowledge and ordinary reasoning, and might maintain that values differ from natural objects precisely in their power, when known, automatically to influence the will. To this Hume could, and would need to, reply that this objection involves the postulating of value-entities or value-features of quite a different order from anything else with which we are acquainted, and of a corresponding faculty with which to detect them. That is, he would have to supplement his explicit argument with what I have called the argument from queerness.

Another way of bringing out this queerness is to ask, about anything that is supposed to have some objective moral quality, how this is linked with its natural features.

---

9. G. E. Moore (1873–1958) was an English philosopher, author of *Principia Ethica* (1903).

What is the connection between the natural fact that an action is a piece of deliberate cruelty — say, causing pain just for fun — and the moral fact that it is wrong? It cannot be an entailment, a logical or semantic necessity. Yet it is not merely that the two features occur together. The wrongness must somehow be "consequential" or "supervenient"; it is wrong because it is a piece of deliberate cruelty. But just *what in the world* is signified by this "because"? And how do we know the relation that it signifies, if this is something more than such actions being socially condemned, and condemned by us too, perhaps through our having absorbed attitudes from our social environment? It is not even sufficient to postulate a faculty which "sees" the wrongness: something must be postulated which can see at once the natural features that constitute the cruelty, and the wrongness, and the mysterious consequential link between the two. . . .

It may be thought that the argument from queerness is given an unfair start if we thus relate it to what are admittedly among the wilder products of philosophical fancy — Platonic Forms, non-natural qualities, self-evident relations of fitness, faculties of intuition, and the like. Is it equally forceful if applied to the terms in which everyday moral judgements are more likely to be expressed — though still, as has been argued in Section 7, with a claim to objectivity — "you must do this," "you can't do that," "obligation," "unjust," "rotten," "disgraceful," "mean," or talk about good reasons for or against possible actions? Admittedly not; but that is because the objective prescriptivity, the element a claim for whose authoritativeness is embedded in ordinary moral thought and language, is not yet isolated in these forms of speech, but is presented along with relations to desires and feelings, reasoning about the means to desired ends, interpersonal demands, the injustice which consists in the violation of what are in the context the accepted standards of merit, the psychological constituents of meanness, and so on. There is nothing queer about any of these, and under cover of them the claim for moral authority may pass unnoticed. But if I am right in arguing that it is ordinarily there, and is therefore very likely to be incorporated almost automatically in philosophical accounts of ethics which systematize our ordinary thought even in such apparently innocent terms as these, it needs to be examined, and for this purpose it needs to be isolated and exposed as it is by the less cautious philosophical reconstructions. . . .

## TEST YOUR UNDERSTANDING

1. Which of the following alternatives best captures Mackie's account of moral subjectivism?

   (i)    Each of us has our own personal moral code.

   (ii)   There are no objective values.

   (iii)  We should each do whatever we wish.

   (iv)   Moral statements are expressions of attitudes.

2. What is the difference between a first-order moral view and a second-order moral view? Give two examples of each. Is Mackie's moral subjectivism a first-order view or a second-order view?

3. State in your own words the two parts of Mackie's "argument from queerness" (do not give the argument: just describe its two components).

## NOTES AND QUESTIONS

1. According to Mackie, the idea that values are *objectively prescriptive* is endorsed by many philosophers and by common sense. Explain what "objectively prescriptive" means. Does the claim that values are *objective* mean that values are objects that we interact with? If not that, then what does it mean? Consider two interpretations of *prescriptive*:

   (i) A moral statement is *prescriptive* if and only if a person who fully understands the statement is motivated to comply with it.

   (ii) A moral statement is *prescriptive* if and only if a person who fully understands the statement knows what kinds of conduct it requires of those to whom it applies.

   What is the difference between these interpretations? Which interpretation does Mackie rely on in his discussions of Plato, Kant, and Sidgwick?

2. Mackie's argument from relativity begins from the fact that moral beliefs vary across societies and across groups within a single society. This variation, he says, "may indirectly support second-order subjectivism."

   (i) Why is the support for subjectivism only indirect? Why doesn't moral disagreement lead directly to subjectivism?

   (ii) How exactly does the variation in moral views within and between societies (indirectly) support second-order subjectivism? (*Hint:* Focus on Mackie's contrast between explaining scientific and moral disagreement.) Is Mackie convincing on this point?

   Mackie considers a "well-known counter to the argument from relativity."

   (i) The counter draws on the distinction between specific moral rules and general principles. Give some examples of the distinction. How does this distinction provide the basis for a reply to the argument from relativity?

   (ii) How does Mackie respond to the counterargument?

   (iii) Consider a reply to Mackie's response. To make things more concrete, consider a **utilitarian** who thinks that the principle of utility is objectively valid. The utilitarian might say:

   You need to distinguish between making moral judgments and defending those judgments. When people make moral judgments, they often respond unreflectively to a specific situation. Their responses draw on a conventional moral code and strong feelings that have grown up around the code. They say things like "Don't break promises to your friends" and "Tell your parents the truth." But when they are called on to defend their judgments, they appeal to general principles—in particular, they try to show that the conventional moral code is the best way to promote overall happiness. So there is variation in morality across groups and societies. But the variation is explained, as the justifications suggest, by beliefs about how to apply the principle of utility in different situations.

What response is available to Mackie? For an argument along these lines, aiming to show that commonsense morality is implicitly utilitarian, see Henry Sidgwick, *Methods of Ethics* (Hackett, 1980), Book 4.

3. Mackie thinks that we erroneously believe that values are objectively prescriptive. He endorses an **error theory** about values, according to which people quite generally and persistently hold a mistaken belief about values. You find error theories in other areas of philosophy as well. Error theorists about causation think that people generally believe that causality is a real connection between events (one event *makes* the other happen), though there is no such real connection; error theorists about color think that people generally assume colors to be objectively present in objects, though colors are only a matter of how we respond to objects; error theorists about scientific unobservables (say, quarks) think that people generally believe that there are unobservable objects even though talk about unobservables is simply a way of predicting observations; error theorists about aesthetics think that beauty is only in the beholder's eyes, though we believe (mistakenly) that beauty is present in the world.

Because error theorists claim to have detected a pervasive and persistent mistake, they typically offer explanations of the roots of the error: a story about our *objectification errors* that explains how we have ended up projecting some feature of our thinking, feeling, talking, or interacting onto the world. In section 10 of "The Subjectivity of Values" (omitted from this reading), Mackie suggests some explanations of the objectification error he detects in moral philosophy and ordinary moral thought. One explanation begins with the fact that we sometimes want people to do something—say, keep a promise. Instead of saying "You should keep your promise because I want you to" or "You should keep your promise because we want you to," we just say: "You ought to keep your promise," or, more simply, "You promised." Morality thus involves "suppressing any explicit reference to demands."

    (i)   Why would we want to suppress any explicit reference to demands?

    (ii)  How could Mackie's explanation work if people are aware that moral claims are simply a shorthand for expressions of demands?

4. According to the (unhappily named) argument from queerness, objective values, if there were such, would need to be objects, or relations, or qualities unlike anything we are familiar with. What precisely makes objective values so unusual? Consider three answers:

(i)   Values are not in space-time.

(ii)  Values lead people who fully understand them to act.

(iii) Values instruct us about what to do.

Which answer does Mackie offer? Once you have settled on an interpretation of Mackie, consider whether he is right that commonsense morality assumes such odd things to exist.

## R. Jay Wallace (born 1957)

Wallace is a professor of philosophy at the University of California, Berkeley, where he holds the Judy Chandler Webb Distinguished Chair for Innovative Teaching and Research. He writes on moral philosophy, with a particular focus on moral psychology and practical reasoning.

# MORAL SUBJECTIVISM

Moral thought is commonly supposed to be a matter of subjective attitude, in a way that contrasts with thought about (say) mathematics or the natural world. If you judge that $12 \times 3 = 36$, or that the cat is sleeping on the bed, nobody is likely to conclude that that is just your opinion. Your thoughts seem to be about a subject matter that is prior to and independent of them, and in that respect objective. We might say that judgments of these kinds are answerable to independent facts of the matter, insofar as their correctness or incorrectness depends on how things are independently of the judgments being made.

With moral thought, by contrast, things are often taken to be otherwise. Consider the judgments that it is wrong to make insincere promises or to exploit the weak and vulnerable. It is widely believed that judgments of this kind are not answerable to a prior and independent subject matter, but are merely a matter of subjective opinion. This thought is the animating idea behind moral subjectivism. To a first approximation, subjectivism is the position that moral judgments — such as the judgment that lying promises are wrong — are not about a set of facts that are prior to and independent of them. Instead, the subjectivist maintains, they reflect the attitudes of the person who makes those judgments.[1]

1. The term "subjectivism" is sometimes used more narrowly in philosophical discussion, to refer to the view that moral judgments are about an agent's subjective states; the dispositionalist position discussed below is a subjectivist view in this more narrow sense. [Wallace's note.]

Two aspects of moral thought particularly encourage this subjectivist interpretation of it.[2] One concerns its subject matter. Moral judgments typically involve evaluative or normative concepts, as applied to persons and their actions. In moral thought we conclude that doing X would be permissible or required, right or wrong, and we judge that people are admirable or blameworthy in virtue of their character traits and the things they have done.[3] Concepts such as permissibility, rightness, wrongness, or blameworthiness, however, do not seem to correspond to any objects or properties in the natural world. Actions are not wrong, for instance, in the way the leaf of a tree might be green or oblong or bitter to the taste. We see that the eucalyptus leaf is green and oblong when we look at it, and we taste its bitterness when we put it in our mouth; these properties can affect our sense organs, in ways that make them potential objects of empirical investigation and scientific study. But the properties involved in moral thought do not in the same way seem to make a causal difference to our experiences. We don't, after all, have any special organs of perception or sensation that enable us to detect the wrongness of acts of lying.[4]

Considerations of this kind make it natural to suppose that the world is devoid of the evaluative and normative properties that moral thought apparently trades in. But if there are no evaluative and normative properties in the world, it seems to follow that moral thought cannot be understood in objective terms. It does not answer to a set of independent facts about the way things are in the world, since the world as we find it has no place for evaluative and normative objects and properties.

A second consideration that encourages the subjectivist interpretation concerns the effects of moral thought on action. One of the important ways we use moral concepts is in deliberation — the kind of systematic reflection we engage in when we attempt to get clear about what we ought to do.[5] In deliberation, we take it for granted that we could choose to act in a number of different ways (keeping a promise or breaking it, say), and we reflect on those alternatives, asking, among other things, whether they are morally permissible or required. The thoughts that figure in deliberative reflection are in this way practical in their subject matter: they are about what to do. But deliberation is practical in a very different sense as well. After reaching a conclusion about what they ought to do, those who engage in deliberation often act

2. A third aspect of moral thought that is sometimes cited in this connection is the fact of disagreement about what it is right or wrong to do. But this consideration strikes me as less significant than the other two, so I shall set it aside in what follows. [Wallace's note.]

3. Normative concepts are concepts that involve the ideas of a reason or a requirement, whereas evaluative concepts involve ideas of the good. Here I gloss over large issues about the relation between reasons and values. I also simply assume, throughout my discussion, that moral thought is a species of normative thought, concerning a special class of reasons or requirements. [Wallace's note.]

4. Note that this argument apparently also applies to mathematical thought, which similarly does not seem to be about objects and properties that we interact with causally. And yet, mathematical thought seems to be a paradigm of objectivity. Does this undermine the argument from metaphysics? [Wallace's note.]

5. Another important context in which normative thought figures is that of advice, where we reflect on the options that other people face, and try to arrive at conclusions about what they ought to do. In what follows I shall focus primarily on contexts of deliberation, in which agents reflect on their own options for action. But you should consider how the subjectivist approaches I sketch might be extended to apply to contexts of advice. [Wallace's note.]

on the verdict they have arrived at, choosing the option that deliberation has identified to be for the best.

Consider the members of a campus club who, after deliberation, decide that it is wrong to maintain their secret policy of excluding people from certain ethnic groups, even if doing so would be to their advantage. (Perhaps there are wealthy benefactors who will stop supporting the group if it becomes more inclusive in its membership.) Having arrived at this moral conclusion, the club members might adjust their policies accordingly, opening the club to people from all ethnic and cultural backgrounds, because they have come to see that that is the right thing to do. Moral thought might not have as much influence on action as we would like, but it is at least capable of moving people directly to act. It is thus practical not merely in its subject matter, but also in its effects.

This practical dimension of moral thought appears difficult to make sense of if we understand such thought in objectivist terms. The judgments that seem paradigmatically about a realm of independent objects and relations do not have this kind of influence on the will. The thought that fresh beets are available for sale in the local supermarket, for instance, does not on its own seem able to move us to action one way or another. To do so, it would need to combine with some distinct attitude on our part, such as a desire to have roast beets for dinner; if you hate beets, or are simply indifferent to them, then the true belief that you can buy some at the local supermarket will have no effect on your motivations whatsoever.[6] Moral thought, by contrast, seems capable of engaging the will directly, without the addition of attitudes that are extraneous to it. The conclusion that it is wrong to discriminate against members of certain ethnic groups, as we saw above, is already apt to move us to action by itself. It is natural to hypothesize that such conclusions must essentially involve the subject's desires or emotions, mobilizing the kinds of subjective attitudes that move us to act.

We might refer to these two lines of thought as the arguments from metaphysics and from motivation, respectively. They were both taken very seriously by David Hume, who was led by them to the subjectivist conclusion that morality "is more properly felt than judg'd of."[7] Hume meant by this that moral deliberation trades in attitudes of emotion or desire of the kind that move us to action, rather than judgments about an independent set of normative and evaluative facts. This conclusion is an extremely tempting one when we think about moral thought, and it contains at least a grain of truth. In the end, however, I don't believe that we should accept the Humean position. In support of this claim, I shall begin by considering a simple version of moral subjectivism, and then explore three different ways of refining the position. A particularly important theme will be the role of *critical reflection* in normative and moral thought: its role, that is, as a method of scrutinizing and improving our own subjective reactions. I shall argue that this is something the subjectivist cannot give an adequate account of.

Perhaps the simplest way to develop the subjectivist idea is to interpret it as a form of *expressivism*. This is a view in what is often called metaethics, the study of the meaning of the language that is used to express moral claims. Expressivists hold

---

6. Of course, you might have promised a friend that you would pick up some beets for him in the store. But then you will be led to act by the moral thought that you will wrong your friend if you fail to do what you promised, a thought that is also extraneous to your factual belief about the availability of the beets. [Wallace's note.]

7. David Hume, *A Treatise of Human Nature* (Oxford University Press, 1978), p. 470. [Wallace's note.]

that moral and other normative judgments are not in the business of representing a set of independent facts or relations. Their function is instead to give expression to practical attitudes of approval or disapproval, such as desires or intentions.[8] Moral language, on this approach, might be compared to the verbalizing that goes on at a football game or a rock concert, which does not even attempt to make claims about the way things are in the world, but rather gives expression to the spectators' attitudes toward the events they are observing. To say that it is wrong to exploit and mock the vulnerable, for instance, is to give voice to your disapproval of acting in this way; it expresses a desire that people should not perform actions of this kind, much as the lusty booing that takes place at the football stadium expresses the audience's disapproval of the botched play that just took place on the field.

This expressivist position does a good job of accommodating the considerations marshaled in the arguments from metaphysics and motivation. According to expressivism, moral and other normative assertions don't really say anything at all about the world, so we can make sense of such discourse without postulating any funny properties or states of affairs. The expressivist account also offers a nice explanation of the practical dimension of moral thought. If moral discourse is in the business of expressing the agent's desires, then we can immediately understand how it is that moral judgments can directly engage the will. The practical attitudes that moral discourse expresses guarantee that such motivations will be present whenever a moral judgment is endorsed.

The problem, however, is that the simple expressivist view seems to go too far in the direction of assimilating moral thought to the formation of such practical attitudes. If people can be motivated to act directly by their normative judgments, this connection can also break down. You might for instance think that it would be wrong to keep a wallet that you have found in the university library (rather than turning it in at the lost-and-found office), but give in to the temptation to keep the wallet when you realize how much money it contains. In cases of this kind, people act against their own moral judgments,[9] and the possibility of doing this suggests that moral judgments don't simply involve the expression of effective motivating attitudes.

Normative thought has an important critical dimension. It can be brought to bear on our own emotions and desires, including the motivations that lead us to act when we go astray by our own lights. This dimension of moral thought needs to be accounted for in an adequate development of the subjectivist position. The challenge is to explain how we can achieve critical distance from our motivating attitudes, within a framework that understands moral thought essentially in terms of such attitudes.

One way of responding to this challenge would be to modify the simple version of expressivism by restricting the class of subjective attitudes that moral and normative language is taken to express. In this spirit, normative discourse might

---

8. See, for example, Allan Gibbard, *Thinking How to Live* (Harvard University Press, 2003). [Wallace's note.]

9. The phenomenon of action against one's better judgment is often referred to as "akrasia" (from the ancient Greek) or "weakness of will." [Wallace's note.]

be supposed to give voice to our second-order attitudes, including above all the preferences we form about our first-order desires.[1] When you act against your better judgment concerning the permissibility of keeping the wallet, for example, you have a first-order desire to hang on to the money that the wallet contains. But you also form a distinct attitude about that desire, preferring that it should not prove effective in determining what you do. The subjectivist might say that it is second-order desires of this kind that it is the distinctive function of normative language to express. On the resulting picture, practical attitudes are subject to criticism by something outside themselves; but the standards for such critical assessment are fixed by further practical attitudes of the agent.[2]

A natural question to ask about this more sophisticated expressivism, however, concerns the standing of higher-order attitudes to constitute a basis for critical assessment. Suppose you form a second-order desire that your desire for money should not prevail in determining whether you keep the wallet you have found. This higher-order desire is an attitude of the same basic type as the first-order attitude that is its object; it is just another desire or preference that you are subject to. If there is a real issue about the credentials of the first-order attitude, it is hard to see how it can be resolved simply through the formation of further attitudes of the same basic kind. Won't those attitudes be prone to further iterations of skeptical undermining? You could, after all, step back from your second-order desire regarding the original temptation to keep the wallet, and call that desire into question in turn, forming a third-order desire to ignore the scruples of conscience. Nothing in the nature of your second-order preferences seems to block such critical questions from being raised about them.

The sophisticated expressivist might respond by noting that we generally don't extend the process of reflection to such extremes. We step back from our first-order attitudes to subject them to critical scrutiny, but we rarely take this process further, scrutinizing our second-order attitudes in turn. What matters, fundamentally, is that normative thought is a reflective process, in which we step back from our subjective attitudes and engage in reflection on them; this reflective character is what confers on higher-order attitudes their standing in situations of critical assessment. Higher-order attitudes function as standards of normative assessment, in other words, not because of their nature as desires, but because of the reflective procedures that lead to their formation.

This approach works, however, only in cases in which agents have actually undergone a course of reflection about their first-order desires. Prior to such reflection, the approach suggests, there are no standards for the critical assessment of our motivating

1. See, for example, Harry G. Frankfurt, "Freedom of the Will and the Concept of a Person," in his *The Importance of What We Care About* (Cambridge University Press, 1988), pp. 11–25. [Wallace's note.]

2. Since the higher-order attitudes that are expressed in normative discourse are themselves desires, this version of expressivism can explain the capacity of moral thought to engage the will. But it can also explain why normative thought sometimes fails to give rise to corresponding motivations, since the first-order desires the agent reflects on might be stronger than the second-order desires that normative language expresses. [Wallace's note.]

attitudes, and this is an awkward result. Suppose that in thinking about the question of whether to hang onto the wallet or turn it in at the lost-and-found office, you reach the conclusion that personal financial advantage is not a good reason to keep property that is not rightfully yours. In arriving at this conclusion, you will probably think that you are making a moral and normative discovery, about something that was true all along. It is not that your arriving at this conclusion somehow makes it the case that it is wrong to keep other people's property when it falls into your hands; rather, it was wrong even before you started thinking about the question. But how can the subjectivist make sense of this aspect of moral thought?

One possibility is to appeal to the agent's dispositions. What matters to the normative standing of a given first-order attitude, we might say, is not that the agent has actually endorsed or rejected it through critical reflection, but that the agent is disposed to endorse or reject it through such reflection (i.e., that she *would* endorse or reject the desire if she were to engage in critical reflection on it). Building on this idea, some philosophers have proposed a different way of developing the subjectivist approach, which we might call *dispositionalism*. The dispositionalist holds that normative discourse functions not to express our higher-order attitudes, but to make claims *about* the higher-order attitudes we would arrive at through rational reflection. To say that a lying promise is wrong, on this approach, is to say that one would desire that one not give in to the temptation to make a false promise, if one were to reflect rationally on the matter. When we affirm a normative claim of this kind, we might be expressing our practical attitudes, but we aren't *merely* doing that; we might also be making true statements about a normative subject matter.[3]

Dispositionalism seems to be an advance on expressivism in at least one important respect. It allows us to say that there are normative facts that moral discourse makes claims about, facts that are capable of being discovered when we engage in normative reflection. Moreover, it does this without violating the naturalistic metaphysical commitments of subjectivism. Thus, the normative facts that dispositionalism posits do not involve any weird nonnatural properties, of the kind that would be difficult to locate in the world that the natural sciences describe. Instead, they are facts about the attitudes of human agents, in particular facts about the dispositions of those agents to form higher-order attitudes through critical reflection. Your act of betraying a secret is wrong, on this approach, just in case the following conditional statement is true about you: that you would want yourself not to act on the temptation to betray the secret, if you were to reflect fully on the matter. Dispositional facts of this kind define standards for the normative assessment of the agent's practical attitudes, but the standards are in the relevant sense subjective; they are a matter, fundamentally, of the dispositions of the agents whom the standards regulate.

It is an open question, however, whether dispositionalism can really dispense with normative standards that are independent of the person whose attitudes are subject to assessment. To see this, let's go back to the motivational side of moral thought.

---

3. See, for example, Michael Smith, *The Moral Problem* (Blackwell, 1994). [Wallace's note.]

Suppose I have arrived at the conclusion that I would want myself to refrain from deception, if I were rational. The dispositionalist says: this judgment *just is* the moral judgment that it would be wrong for me to lie. As we have emphasized, however, moral judgments of this kind are supposed to provide standards not merely for the criticism of our practical attitudes, but for their control; they are practical not just in their subject matter, but in their effect, giving rise to new motivations. But how are judgments about our dispositions to desire things supposed to have this practical effect? The dispositionalist puts motivation into the content of moral judgments, construing them as claims about what we would desire if we were rational. One could form a judgment with this content, however, without having the desire that the judgment is about; how can the dispositionalist bridge this gap?

The natural answer is to appeal to rationality to do this job. That is, dispositionalists often propose the following principle of rationality (or some variant of it):

> It is irrational to judge that I would want myself to do X if I were rational, but to fail to have a desire to do X.

Applying this principle to the case at hand, we get that it would be irrational to judge that it would be wrong to tell a lie for personal advantage, but to fail to desire to act accordingly. Our responsiveness to this standard of rationality, the dispositionalist might then say, is what enables normative reflection to generate new desires. This suggestion is plausible, furthermore, because cases in which we fail to have desires that accord with our normative judgments seem to be paradigm cases of irrationality. If you really believe that you shouldn't lie to your teacher to get an extension on the paper, but you end up doing so anyway, then you are going astray by your own lights; what could be more irrational than that?[4] The problem, for the dispositionalist, is to explain where this principle of rationality comes from. It looks to be a substantive normative standard, one that is prior to and independent of the attitudes that are up for assessment. The postulation of normative standards that are in this way objective, however, violates the subjectivist's most basic metaphysical commitments.

Moral thought involves the application of rational standards, standards that are normative for the agent, in the sense that they properly regulate the agent's critical reflections. The challenge for the subjectivist, as we have now seen, is to make sense of this aspect of moral thought, without recourse to standards that are completely independent of the attitudes of the agents whose reflections they govern. *Constructivism* in moral philosophy can be understood as a response to this problem. On the constructivist view, practical attitudes are subject to scrutiny by reference to critical standards. But those standards are not independent of the attitudes to which they apply; rather, they appropriately govern the subject's deliberation precisely because the subject is already committed to complying with them.[5]

---

4. Thus, weakness of will is generally understood to be the most flagrant form of irrationality in action. [Wallace's note.]

5. An example of this kind of constructivist view is Christine M. Korsgaard, *The Sources of Normativity* (Cambridge University Press, 1996). [Wallace's note.]

Consider the instrumental principle, which tells us to choose the means that are necessary to achieve our ends. If you intend to go to medical school, for instance, and "Introduction to Organic Chemistry" is a prerequisite for admission to medical school, then the instrumental principle says that you should take the class; your intentions are subject to criticism if you fail to act in this way. But this is because your intention to go to medical school *already* involves a commitment to take the means that are necessary for the attainment of that end. Indeed, the intention to realize the end just is (in part) a commitment to take the necessary means, and hence to comply with the instrumental principle.[6] Constructivists generalize from this example, holding that all of the standards that govern our practical reflections are likewise standards that we are committed to complying with, in virtue of practical attitudes that we have already adopted.

The constructivist approach can be thought of as combining elements of expressivism and dispositionalism. It shares with the former an emphasis on the essential involvement of practical attitudes in the processes of normative and moral reflection. Such reflection takes as its starting point the intentions and desires that we already have, and it attempts to adjust and to refine them through critical thought. We go astray, on this approach, when we fail to live up to our own commitments — as the signers of the Declaration of Independence arguably did, for example, when they condoned practices of slavery while endorsing the principle that "all men are created equal."

Normative reflection can accordingly be understood as a process of figuring out what our commitments really entail, a process that can lead to normative *discoveries*, of the kind the dispositionalist was concerned to make room for. It might take some time for people to come to see that their own commitments (say, about human equality) have the consequence that some of their other attitudes and practices should be rejected or revised. The normative standards that govern the process of critical reflection are thus not restricted to standards whose consequences the agent already explicitly acknowledges. At the same time, the fact that those standards are anchored in the agent's own commitments sheds light on the practical effects of moral thought. For it is in the nature of commitments that they involve an orientation of the will, which moves us to act once we become clear about what the commitments really entail. People who are genuinely committed to the fundamental equality of all people will be moved to abandon and even to fight against practices such as slavery, once they finally face up to the fact that those practices cannot be reconciled with their own moral principles.

This approach represents a promising way of understanding the critical dimension of practical thought, if we accept the subjectivist idea that normative standards are never prior to and independent of the agents whose attitudes they regulate. But

---

6. Thus, if you realize that "Introduction to Organic Chemistry" is necessary to get into medical school, but you have resolved never to take the course, then it seems you have effectively abandoned your original intention to become a doctor. [Wallace's note.]

the resulting position shares with other forms of subjectivism some consequences that are difficult to accept. Most basically, the constructivist approach makes morality itself hostage to the commitments of the agents whose actions and attitudes are up for assessment. Whether or not it is wrong for me to break a promise or to keep the wallet I have found is ultimately a question of whether, like the Founding Fathers in the case of slavery, I am already committed to moral principles that would prohibit conduct of these kinds.

Kantians in ethics often accept this framework for thinking about moral standards, affirming a generalized constructivism about normativity. They contend that the most basic moral requirements — the moral law or the "categorical imperative"[7] — are universal principles of willing, insofar as they are ones that every agent is *necessarily* committed to complying with. If this claim could be defended, then morality would turn out to represent a set of universal normative constraints on rational agents. But the Kantian claim is exceptionally ambitious, and it has proven very difficult to give a clear and compelling account of the idea that rational agency involves an essential, built-in commitment to follow the moral law. If the Kantian is correct, then it ought to be possible to identify the concrete commitments that villains and scoundrels are betraying when they pursue their reprehensible ends. But does this seem plausible to you? (What is it in the attitudes of the fraudster or the terrorist — people like Bernie Madoff or Timothy McVeigh, say — that would commit them to the basic moral standards that they flout in their actual behavior?)

Those who wish to make sense of morality as a set of nonnegotiable critical standards may therefore need to question the subjectivist framework within which constructivism operates. Perhaps our practical attitudes are answerable to standards that are more robustly independent of the subjects of those attitudes. Before we can accept this objectivist approach, however, we will need to come up with convincing responses to the arguments from metaphysics and motivation canvassed above. Can we make sense of the idea that reality includes irreducibly normative facts and truths, about, for instance, the wrongness of deceptive promises or the impermissibility of exploitation and fraud? How can reflection about such facts and truths reliably give rise to new motivations to action, in the way that we have seen to be characteristic of practical deliberation? These questions continue to push some philosophers back to subjectivist ways of understanding morality, despite the serious difficulties that subjectivism faces in accounting for the critical dimension of normative thought.

7. The categorical imperative is Kant's candidate for the supreme principle of morality, the abstract principle from which our more specific moral duties can be derived. For different formulations of this principle, and Kant's argument that it represents a universal principle of rational willing, see Immanuel Kant, *Groundwork of the Metaphysics of Morals*, ed. and trans. by Mary Gregor (Cambridge University Press, 1997). [Wallace's note.]

## TEST YOUR UNDERSTANDING

1.  How does Wallace define "moral subjectivism"? Pick one of the following:

    (i)   Each of us has his or her own personal moral code;

    (ii)  There are no objective values;

    (iii) Individuals should do whatever they wish;

    (iv)  Moral statements are expressions of attitudes.

2.  Describe in your own words the two aspects of moral thought that encourage, Wallace thinks, a subjectivist interpretation of morality.

3.  Wallace distinguishes a few versions of subjectivism: **expressivism** (simpler and more complex), dispositionalism, and constructivism. What question is each trying to answer? In your own words, sketch what each version says about moral thought.

4.  Wallace says that subjectivism has trouble providing an adequate account of the place of "critical reflection" in moral thought. Briefly explain what he means by "critical reflection."

## NOTES AND QUESTIONS

1.  Sketch Wallace's simple version of expressivism and his more sophisticated version. Then answer these questions:

    (i)   How does the simple version address the metaphysical and motivational concerns that motivate subjectivism?

    (ii)  What problem does Wallace raise for the simple version?

    (iii) How does the more sophisticated version of expressivism respond to the specific challenge Wallace raises for the simpler version? (Do not just say how the sophisticated version is different. Explain how it handles the objection.)

    (iv)  To challenge the more sophisticated expressivist, who brings in second-order desires, Wallace says: "This higher-order desire is an attitude of the same basic type as the first-order attitude that is its object." What does he mean by "same basic type"? Suppose the sophisticated expressivist responds by saying: "No! It is a second-order desire, and that makes it a *different* type from the first-order desire." Is this response convincing?

    (v)   Are second-order desires a good way to understand the kind of critical reflection that Wallace says is so central to moral thought? Think of some examples of second-order desires and explain why they help or fail to help in understanding critical reflection.

2. State the dispositionalist view in your own words.

   (i)   How does dispositionalism respond to the troubles Wallace finds in expressivism?

   (ii)  Wallace says that dispositionalists appeal to a principle of rationality. What role does the principle play?

   (iii) Suppose I hear the dispositionalist theory and then think: "OK, I am tempted to cheat on my taxes. But I also think it is wrong to cheat on my taxes. And (as the dispositionalist says) what that means is that *if I thought rationally about the issue, I would desire not to give in to the temptation to cheat on my taxes.* And (as the dispositionalist says) I see that it is irrational for me to have that thought about what I *would* desire, but then not desire right now to resist the temptation. So I see that rationality requires that I desire now to resist the temptation to cheat. But I am unmoved because I do not care about being rational. What grip is rationality supposed to have on me?" How can the dispositionalist respond?

3. Suppose the constructivist argues as follows:

   > Acting rationally involves acting for a purpose. But acting for a purpose commits you to thinking that your purpose is worth achieving. And "worth achieving" means not simply that achieving the purpose is *important to you.* You are committed to its objective importance—to the idea that achieving the purpose has an importance that everyone should acknowledge. But if you are committed to the objective importance of your achieving your purposes, then you are committed to the objective importance of others' achieving their purposes: after all, what is so special about *you*? So as a rational agent, you are committed to acknowledging the importance of others achieving their purposes. So as a rational agent, you are committed to the core moral idea that the purposes of others are just as important as your purposes. Moreover, as Wallace says, "it is in the nature of commitments that they involve an orientation of the will, which moves us to act once we become clear about what the commitments really entail." So as a rational agent, you are committed to morality. And being committed to morality means both that you are intellectually committed to the importance of being a moral agent and that you are motivated by moral reasons.

   The point of this constructivist argument is to draw a tight connection between being a rational agent and being a moral agent. Does the argument provide a compelling response to Wallace's concerns about the ability of subjectivism to accommodate the normative character of moral thought as well as its *practical* nature—the motivational concern that animates subjectivism?

## Thomas Nagel (born 1937)

Nagel is Emeritus University Professor of Philosophy and Law at New York University. He has made influential contributions to ethics, political philosophy, epistemology, and philosophy of mind. His books include *The Possibility of Altruism* (1970), *The View from Nowhere* (1986), *Equality and Partiality* (1991), and *Mind and Cosmos* (2012).

# ETHICS
## from *The Last Word*

## I

Let me . . . turn to the question of whether moral reasoning is . . . fundamental and inescapable.[1] Unlike logical or arithmetical reasoning, it often fails to produce certainty, justified or unjustified. It is easily subject to distortion by morally irrelevant factors, social and personal, as well as outright error. It resembles empirical reason in not being reducible to a series of self-evident steps.

I take it for granted that the objectivity of moral reasoning does not depend on its having an external reference. There is no moral analogue of the external world — a universe of moral facts that impinge on us causally. Even if such a supposition made sense, it would not support the objectivity of moral reasoning. Science, which this kind of reifying realism[2] takes as its model, doesn't derive its objective validity from the fact that it starts from perception and other causal relations between us and the physical world. The real work comes after that, in the form of active scientific reasoning, without which no amount of causal impact on us by the external world would generate a belief in Newton's or Maxwell's or Einstein's theories, or the chemical theory of elements and compounds, or molecular biology.[3]

If we had rested content with the causal impact of the external world on us, we'd still be at the level of sense perception. We can regard our scientific beliefs as objectively true not because the external world causes us to have them but because we are able to *arrive at* those beliefs by methods that have a good claim to be reliable, by virtue of their success in selecting among rival hypotheses that survive the best criticisms and questions we can throw at them. Empirical confirmation plays a vital role in this process, but it cannot do so without theory.

Moral thought is concerned not with the description and explanation of what happens but with decisions and their justification. It is mainly because we have no comparably uncontroversial and well-developed methods for thinking about morality that a subjectivist position here is more credible than it is with regard

---

1. This discussion of the nature of moral objectivity comes from Thomas Nagel's *The Last Word*, chapter 6. Nagel proposes a common approach to objectivity in logic, science, and ethics in which the idea of *inescapability* plays a central role.

2. To reify is to treat as a thing. In morality, "reifying realism" is the view that moral objectivity requires moral objects or moral facts in the world that we interact with causally.

3. Sir Isaac Newton (1643–1727) was an English physicist and mathematician, whose law of gravity and three laws of motion dominated modern physics until the early twentieth century. James Clerk Maxwell (1831–1879) was a Scottish physicist who developed an integrated theory of electricity, magnetism, and light, expressed in Maxwell's equations. Albert Einstein (1879–1955) won the 1921 Nobel Prize in physics, and is best known for his special and general theories of relativity.

to science. But just as there was no guarantee at the beginnings of cosmological and scientific speculation that we humans had the capacity to arrive at objective truth beyond the deliverances of sense-perception — that in pursuing it we were doing anything more than spinning collective fantasies — so there can be no decision in advance as to whether we are or are not talking about a real subject when we reflect and argue about morality. The answer must come from the results themselves. Only the effort to reason about morality can show us whether it is possible — whether, in thinking about what to do and how to live, we can find methods, reasons, and principles whose validity does not have to be subjectively or relativistically qualified.

Since moral reasoning is a species of practical reasoning, its conclusions are desires, intentions, and actions, or feelings and convictions that can motivate desire, intention, and action. We want to know how to live, and why, and we want the answer in general terms, if possible. Hume famously believed that because a "passion" immune to rational assessment must underly every motive, there can be no such thing as specifically practical reason, nor specifically moral reason either.[4] That is false, because while "passions" are the source of some reasons, other passions or desires are themselves motivated and/or justified by reasons that do not depend on still more basic desires. And I would contend that either the question whether one should have a certain desire or the question whether, given that one has that desire, one should act on it, is always open to rational consideration.

The issue is whether the procedures of justification and criticism we employ in such reasoning, moral or merely practical, can be regarded finally as just something we do — a cultural or societal or even more broadly human collective practice, within which reasons come to an end. I believe that if we ask ourselves seriously how to respond to proposals for contextualization and relativistic detachment, they usually fail to convince. Although it is less clear than in some of the other areas we've discussed, attempts to get entirely outside of the object language of practical reasons, good and bad, right and wrong, and to see all such judgments as expressions of a contingent, nonobjective perspective will eventually collapse before the independent force of the first-order judgments themselves.[5]

---

4. David Hume (1711–1776), a Scottish philosopher and empiricist, said in his *Treatise of Human Nature* that reason can never be more than a "slave of the passions." For selections from Hume, see chapters 4, 5, 7, 15, and 17 of this anthology.

5. *First-order judgments* are such judgments as *Cruelty is wrong; Cecilia Bartoli sings beautifully;* and *I have a reason to show special attention to my friends.* They are judgments about the rightness of conduct, the goodness of states of affairs, and what a person has reason to do. First-order judgments are expressed in what Nagel calls an "object language" that uses the terms "reasons," "right," and "beautiful." *Second-order judgments* are judgments about those first-order judgments. Suppose, for example, I say: "When Kant says 'Cruelty is wrong,' he is simply expressing his negative feeling about cruelty." This statement of mine expresses a second-order judgment: it does not use the term "wrong" to criticize conduct, but tells us what it means to use that term. Moreover, because it talks about language, it is sometimes said to be in a metalanguage, rather than an object language.

## ||

Suppose someone says, for example, "You only believe in equal opportunity because you are a product of Western liberal society. If you had been brought up in a caste society or one in which the possibilities for men and women were radically unequal, you wouldn't have the moral convictions you have or accept as persuasive the moral arguments you now accept." The second, hypothetical sentence is probably true, but what about the first — specifically the "only"? In general, the fact that I wouldn't believe something if I hadn't learned it proves nothing about the status of the belief or its grounds. It may be impossible to explain the learning without invoking the content of the belief itself, and the reasons for its truth; and it may be clear that what I have learned is such that even if I hadn't learned it, it would still be true. The reason the genetic fallacy[6] is a fallacy is that the explanation of a belief can sometimes confirm it.

To have any content, a subjectivist position must say more than that my moral convictions are my moral convictions. That, after all, is something we can all agree on. A meaningful subjectivism must say that they are *just* my moral convictions — or those of my moral community. It must *qualify* ordinary moral judgments in some way, must give them a self-consciously first-person (singular or plural) reading. That is the only type of antiobjectivist view that is worth arguing against or that it is even possible to disagree with.

But I believe it is impossible to come to rest with the observation that a belief in equality of opportunity, and a wish to diminish inherited inequalities, are merely expressions of our cultural tradition. True or false, those beliefs are essentially objective in intent. Perhaps they are wrong, but that too would be a nonrelative judgment. Faced with the fact that such values have gained currency only recently and not universally, one still has to try to decide whether they are right — whether one ought to continue to hold them. That question is not displaced by the information of contingency: The question remains, at the level of moral content, whether I would have been in error if I had accepted as natural, and therefore justified, the inequalities of a caste society, or a fairly rigid class system, or the orthodox subordination of women. It can take in additional facts as material for reflection, but the question of the relevance of those facts is inevitably a moral question: Do these cultural and historical variations and their causes tend to show that I and others have less reason than we had supposed to favor equality of opportunity? Presentation of an array of historically and culturally conditioned attitudes, including my own, does not disarm first-order moral judgment but simply gives it something more to work on — including information about influences on the formation of my convictions that may lead me to change them. But the relevance of such information is itself a matter for moral reasoning — about what are and are not good grounds for moral belief.

---

6. The genetic fallacy is the mistake of thinking that an idea or practice can be supported or discredited by pointing to its origins.

When one is faced with these real variations in practice and conviction, the requirement to put oneself in everyone's shoes when assessing social institutions — some version of universalizability[7] — does not lose any of its persuasive force just because it is not universally recognized. It dominates the historical and anthropological data: Presented with the description of a traditional caste society, I have to ask myself whether its hereditary inequalities are justified, and there is no plausible alternative to considering the interests of all in trying to answer the question. If others feel differently, they must say why they find these cultural facts relevant — why they require some qualification to the objective moral claim. On both sides, it is a moral issue, and the only way to defend universalizability or equal opportunity against subjectivist qualification is by continuing the moral argument. It is a matter of understanding exactly what the subjectivist wants us to give up, and then asking whether the grounds for those judgments disappear in light of his observations.

In my opinion, someone who abandons or qualifies his basic methods of moral reasoning on historical or anthropological grounds alone is nearly as irrational as someone who abandons a mathematical belief on other than mathematical grounds. Even with all their uncertainties and liability to controversy and distortion, moral considerations occupy a position in the system of human thought that makes it illegitimate to subordinate them completely to anything else. Particular moral claims are constantly being discredited for all kinds of reasons, but moral considerations per se keep rising again to challenge in their own right any blanket attempt to displace, defuse, or subjectivize them.

This is an instance of the more general truth that the normative cannot be transcended by the descriptive.[8] The question "What should I do?" like the question "What should I believe?" is always in order. It is always possible to think about the question in normative terms, and the process is not rendered pointless by any fact of a different kind — any desire or emotion or feeling, any habit or practice or convention, any contingent cultural or social background. Such things may in fact guide our actions, but it is always possible to take their relation to action as an object of further normative reflection and ask, "How should I act, given that these things are true of me or of my situation?"

The type of thought that generates answers to this question is practical reason. But, further, it is always possible for the question to take a specifically moral form, since one of the successor questions to which it leads is, "What should anyone in my situation do?" — and consideration of that question leads in turn to questions about what everyone should do, not only in this situation but more generally.

Such universal questions don't always have to be raised, and there is good reason in general to develop a way of living that makes it usually unnecessary to raise them. But if they are raised, as they always can be, they require an answer of the appropriate

7. *Universalizability* is a matter of putting yourself in the situation of others, for example by asking whether you could approve of everyone doing what you are considering doing, or whether you could approve of your conduct if you looked at it through the eyes of others.

8. **Normative** statements are statements about how things ought to be. Descriptive statements are statements about how things are.

kind — even though the answer may be that in a case like this one may do as one likes. They cannot be ruled out of order by pointing to something more fundamental — psychological, cultural, or biological — that brings the request for justification to an end. Only a justification can bring the request for justifications to an end. Normative questions in general are not undercut or rendered idle by anything, even though particular normative answers may be. (Even when some putative justification is exposed as a rationalization, that implies that something else could be said about the justifiability or nonjustifiability of what was done.)

## III

The point of view to defeat, in a defense of the reality of practical and moral reason, is in essence the Humean one. Although Hume was wrong to say that reason was fit only to serve as the slave of the passions, it is nevertheless true that there are desires and sentiments prior to reason that it is not appropriate for reason to evaluate — that it must simply treat as part of the raw material on which its judgments operate. The question then arises how pervasive such brute motivational data are, and whether some of them cannot perhaps be identified as the true sources of those grounds of action which are usually described as reasons. . . .

If there is such a thing as practical reason, it does not simply dictate particular actions but, rather, governs the *relations* among actions, desires, and beliefs — just as theoretical reason governs the relations among beliefs and requires some specific material to work on. Prudential rationality, requiring uniformity in the weight accorded to desires and interests situated at different times in one's life, is an example — and the example about which Hume's skepticism is most implausible, when he says it is not contrary to reason "to prefer even my own acknowledged lesser good to my greater, and have a more ardent affection for the former than the latter."[9] Yet Hume's position always seems a possibility, because whenever such a consistency requirement or similar pattern has an influence on our decisions, it seems possible to represent this influence as the manifestation of a systematic second-order desire[1] or calm passion, which has such consistency as its object and without which we would not be susceptible to this type of "rational" motivation. Hume need then only claim that while such a desire (for the satisfaction of one's future interests) is quite common, to lack it is not contrary to reason, any more than to lack sexual desire is contrary to reason. The problem is to show how this misrepresents the facts.

---

9. *A Treatise of Human Nature*, book 2, part 3, sec. 3, ed. L. A. Selby-Bigge (Oxford University Press, 1888), p. 416. (See p. 653 of this anthology.)

1. *A second-order desire* is a desire about my desires. My desire to drink coffee is a *first-order desire;* my desire not to desire to drink coffee is a second-order desire, as is my desire that my future desires be satisfied.

The fundamental issue is about the order of explanation, for there is no point in denying that people have such second-order desires: the question is whether they are sources of motivation or simply the manifestation in our motives of the recognition of certain rational requirements. A parallel point could be made about theoretical reason. It is clear that the belief in modus ponens, for example, is not a rationally ungrounded *assumption* underlying our acceptance of deductive arguments that depend on modus ponens: Rather, it is simply a recognition of the validity of that form of argument.[2]

The question is whether something similar can be said of the "desire" for prudential consistency in the treatment of desires and interests located at different times, I think it can be and that if one tries instead to regard prudence as simply a desire among others, a desire one happens to have, the question of its appropriateness inevitably reappears as a normative question, and the answer can only be given in terms of the principle itself. The normative can't be displaced by the psychological.

If I think, for example, "What if I didn't care about what would happen to me in the future?" the appropriate reaction is not like what it would be to the supposition that I might not care about movies. True, I'd be missing something if I didn't care about movies, but there are many forms of art and entertainment, and we don't have to consume them all. Note that even this is a judgment of the *rational acceptability* of such variation — of there being no reason to regret it. The supposition that I might not care about my own future cannot be regarded with similar tolerance: It is the supposition of a real failure — the paradigm of something to be regretted — and my recognition of that failure does not reflect merely the antecedent presence in me of a contingent second-order desire. Rather, it reflects a judgment about what is and what is not relevant to the justification of action against a certain factual background.

Relevance and consistency both get a foothold when we adopt the standpoint of decision, based on the total circumstances, including our own condition. This standpoint introduces a subtle but profound gap between desire and action, into which the free exercise of reason enters. It forces us to the idea of the difference between doing the right thing and doing the wrong thing (here, without any specifically ethical meaning as yet) — given our total situation, *including* our desires. Once I see myself as the subject of certain desires, as well as the occupant of an objective situation, I still have to decide what to do, and that will include deciding what justificatory weight to give to those desires.

This step back, this opening of a slight space between inclination and decision, is the condition that permits the operation of reason with respect to belief as well as with respect to action, and that poses the demand for generalizable justification. The two kinds of reasoning are in this way parallel. It is only when, instead of simply being pushed along by impressions, memories, impulses, desires, or whatever, one

---

2. **Modus ponens** is a rule of inference. If we assume the premises (1) *If P, then Q* and (2) *P*, then *modus ponens* licenses us to infer the conclusion that *Q*. When Nagel says that we recognize the **validity** of this form of **argument**, he means that we recognize that if the premises are true, then the conclusion must be true as well.

stops to ask "What should I do?" or "What should I believe?" that reasoning becomes possible — and, having become possible, becomes necessary. Having stopped the direct operation of impulse by interposing the possibility of decision, one can get one's beliefs and actions into motion again only by thinking about what, in light of the circumstances, one should do.

The controversial but crucial point, here as everywhere in the discussion of this subject, is that the standpoint from which one assesses one's choices after this step back is not just first-personal. One is suddenly in the position of judging what one ought to do, against the background of all one's desires and beliefs, in a way that does not merely flow from those desires and beliefs but *operates* on them — by an assessment that should enable anyone else also to see what is the right thing for you to do against that background.

It is not enough to find some higher order desires that one happens to have, to settle the matter: such desires would have to be placed among the background conditions of decision along with everything else. Rather, even in the case of a purely self-interested choice, one is seeking the right answer. One is trying to decide what, given the inner and outer circumstances, *one should do* — and that means not just what *I* should do but what *this person* should do. The same answer should be given to that question by anyone to whom the data are presented, whether or not he is in your circumstances and shares your desires. That is what gives practical reason its generality.

The objection that has to be answered, here as elsewhere, is that this sense of unconditioned, nonrelative judgment is an illusion — that we cannot, merely by stepping back and taking ourselves as objects of contemplation, find a secure platform from which such judgment is possible. On this view whatever we do, after engaging in such an intellectual ritual, will still inevitably be a manifestation of our individual or social nature, not the deliverance of impersonal reason — for there is no such thing.

But I do not believe that such a conclusion can be established a priori,[3] and there is little reason to believe it could be established empirically. The subjectivist would have to show that all purportedly rational judgments about what people have reason to do are really expressions of rationally unmotivated desires or dispositions of the person making the judgment — desires or dispositions to which normative assessment has no application. The motivational explanation would have to have the effect of *displacing* the normative one — showing it to be superficial and deceptive. It would be necessary to make out the case about many actual judgments of this kind and to offer reasons to believe that something similar was true in all cases. Subjectivism involves a positive claim of empirical psychology.

Is it conceivable that such an argument could succeed? In a sense, it would have to be shown that all our supposed practical reasoning is, at the limit, a form of rationalization. But the defender of practical reason has a general response to all psychological claims of this type. Even when some of his actual reasonings are convincingly

---

3. **A priori** means "prior to, or independent of, experience." Mathematical knowledge is often said to be *a priori* because mathematical knowledge is based on proofs, which do not depend on experience. In contrast, **a posteriori** knowledge is knowledge that depends on experience.

analyzed away as the expression of merely parochial or personal inclinations, it will in general be reasonable for him to add this new information to the body of his beliefs about himself and then step back once more and ask, "What, in light of all this, do I have reason to do?" It is logically conceivable that the subjectivist's strategy might succeed by exhaustion; the rationalist might become so discouraged at the prospect of being once again undermined in his rational pretensions that he would give up trying to answer the recurrent normative question. But it is far more likely that the question will always be there, continuing to appear significant and to demand an answer. To give up would be nothing but moral laziness.

More important, as a matter of substance I do not think the subjectivist's project can be plausibly carried out. It is not possible to give a debunking psychological explanation of prudential rationality, at any rate. For suppose it is said, plausibly enough, that the disposition to provide for the future has survival value and that its implantation in us is the product of natural selection. As with any other instinct, we still have to decide whether acting on it is a good idea. With some biologically natural dispositions, both motivational and intellectual, there are good reasons to resist or limit their influence. That this does not seem the right reaction to prudential motives (except insofar as we limit them for moral reasons) shows that they cannot be regarded simply as desires that there is no reason to have. If they were, they wouldn't give us the kind of reasons for action that they clearly do. It will never be reasonable for the rationalist to concede that prudence is just a type of consistency in action that he happens, groundlessly, to care about, and that he would have no reason to care about if he didn't already.

The null hypothesis — that in this unconditional sense there are no reasons — is acceptable only if from the point of view of detached self-observation it is superior to the alternatives; and as elsewhere, I believe it fails that test.

## TEST YOUR UNDERSTANDING

1. Why does Nagel think that a subjectivist view about morality is more plausible than a subjectivist view about science?

2. According to Nagel, the right response to an awareness of slave and caste societies is to:

   (i)   Recognize that our convictions about equality of opportunity are just our way of thinking and acting, with no objective basis;

   (ii)  Dismiss the beliefs and practices of other societies as irrelevant to how we should think and act, because we can safely assume that we have learned from their mistakes and that we are right;

   (iii) Assume that other societies know something that we do not know; or

   (iv)  Consider whether the divergence in belief and practices gives us reasons to change our convictions about the importance of equal opportunity.

3. What does prudential rationality require of us?

4. Nagel considers the possibility that some of our actual practical reasonings "are convincingly analyzed away as the expression of merely parochial or personal inclinations." Give two examples of the kinds of analyses that Nagel has in mind.

## NOTES AND QUESTIONS

1. Nagel says that "attempts to get entirely outside of the object language of practical reasons, good and bad, right and wrong, and to see all such judgments as expressions of a contingent, nonobjective perspective will eventually collapse before the independent force of the first-order judgments themselves."

   (i)   Give three examples of first-order judgments of good and bad, right and wrong. (One example: Do not stick pins in babies.)

   (ii)  What does Nagel mean by the "independent force" of these judgments? Do you agree that your examples have "independent force"?

   (iii) Explain what it would mean to see these judgments "as expressions of a contingent perspective."

   (iv)  Why is Nagel so confident about the collapse of attempts to see these judgments as expressions of a contingent perspective? (Consider his example of the belief in equal opportunity.)

2. Explain in your own words the distinction Nagel draws between not caring about movies and not caring about your future. Suppose someone (inspired by Hume) says:

   > Yes, there is a difference. Most people, the vast majority, do in fact desire that things go well for themselves in the future: they have the second-order desire that their future desires be satisfied. In contrast, many more people are not enthusiastic about movies. But that is all there is to the distinction. Neither caring about movies nor having a second-order desire focused on future desires is required by reason. It is just a brute fact about us that we care about our future: perhaps a fact about us that is explained by evolution. If you don't care about your future, you are unusual, but not irrational.

   In response, Nagel says:

   (i)   "The fundamental issue is about the order of explanation."

   (ii)  A failure to be concerned about one's own future is a "real failure — the paradigm of something to be regretted."

   (iii) The point of view that one takes in judging that the future matters "is not just first-personal."

   Look at these passages and try to explain how these points, put together, form an argument against the view expressed in italics.

## Philippa Foot (1920–2010)

Foot was born in Owston Ferry, England. She taught at the University of Oxford and the University of California, Los Angeles, served as Vice Principal of Somerville College, and was a co-founder of Oxfam. A forceful critic of excessive abstraction in moral philosophy and a defender of moral naturalism, Foot emphasized throughout her work that moral argument is based "ultimately in facts about human life."

# MORAL RELATIVISM

It will be worth spending a little time considering what might be meant by calling certain types of judgements relativistic; and what relativism amounts to in those areas in which it seems to belong. I am thinking, for instance, of certain judgements of "taste," such as those asserting that some people but not others are good-looking, that some food or drink is appetising or delicious, or that certain colours go well together for furnishings or clothes. Here, it seems, we find wide variations in judgements between different cultures and different generations. One does not have to go as far as ancient Mexico to find a set of faces that we find ugly while supposing that they were once admired, and while we think Nureyev's a better looking face than Valentino's there was a time when the verdict would probably have gone the other way.[1] It is obvious that there is the same kind of disagreement about the palatability of food and drink; and combinations of colors once declared deplorable are now thought particularly good. The old rhyme said that "blue and green should never be seen," and black and brown were once seen as colours that killed each other as we should say that navy blue kills black.

The reason why such judgements seem undoubtedly relativistic is not, of course, that a wide variety of opinions exist, but rather that no one set of these opinions appears to have any more claim to truth than any other. But there is a problem here. For if the differences in the application of concepts such as "good-looking" are as great as this, why are we so confident that at different times or in different places the judgements are *about the same thing*? This difficulty must be taken seriously, and may lead us to cut down the number of judgements that we would count as certainly relativistic, even in the area of "taste." Perhaps some kind of relativism is true of many other judgements, but relativism is most obviously true where we need set no limit to the variations in the application of an expression, or rather no limits to its application within a given domain. This condition seems to be fulfilled for our examples, but it would not have been fulfilled had we been operating with concepts such as *prettiness,* or even *handsomeness.* It makes sense to speak of another society as thinking good-looking just the faces we think not good-looking, but not as thinking pretty just

---

1. Rudolph Valentino (1895–1926) was an Italian actor and silent film star in the 1920s. Rudolf Nureyev (1938–1993) was a ballet dancer from the Soviet Union; he defected to England in 1961.

the faces we think not pretty. The examples most suitable for the present purposes are those that are rather general, and this is why I suggested considering the good-looking, the good-tasting, and the good combinations of colours.

Let us suppose then that there are in different communities divergent sets of such judgements which we have no hope of reconciling, and that in this area we also have no thought of distinguishing the opinions of one group of people as right and those of the others as wrong. Shall we say that this is because the judgements describe reactions such as admiration and liking, and that reactions vary from place to place and time to time? This is not, in the area we are now discussing, the truth. To say that someone is good-looking is not to say that his looks are admired, any more than to say that someone is likeable is to say that he is well-liked. No doubt it is true that the concept *likeable* depends on reactions of liking. And no doubt it can operate as it does only on account of shared reactions of liking. Shared reactions are also necessary if the language of a particular community is to contain a word like "elegant," or if it is to be possible to say in it that certain colours go well together. But there is no reason to think that the judgements describe the reactions. One might as well think that "is red" means the same as "seems red to most people," forgetting that when asked if an object is red we look at it to see if it is red, and not in order to estimate the reaction that others will have to it. That one does not describe one's own reaction of admiration in saying that someone is good-looking is shown by the fact that one may admit a mistake. That one does not describe the reactions of others in one's community is shown by the fact that one may accuse them of mistake. Nor is this kind of language empty, the mere reiteration of the expression of one's own reaction. There is room here for the idea of showing, even if not of proving or demonstrating. An individual who makes some very idiosyncratic judgement may simply be ignored or told that he is out of his mind. But he may say something that his fellows find instructive, either with an explanation or without it. I do not want to attribute to any particular type of judgement one jot of (local) objectivity that does not really belong to it, or any method for bringing agreement that does not really go along with it. But distinctions are there to be made. It will not do for one of us to say that Charles Laughton got up as the Hunchback of Notre Dame[2] presented the appearance of a good-looking man; but Laughton's brother's suggestion that he was, in his own person, good-looking was a surprising but possible corrective idea. . . .

[This view] is certainly relativism. For the key concepts will work as they do work — with a kind of objectivity and the attribution of truth — only where there are shared reactions. Once this background is left behind it is impossible to speak of "right" and "wrong," "mistaken" and "correct," as we commonly do. And therefore it is empty to say of the judgements of another group whose reactions are very different from ours that their opinions are wrong. Our own discussions of these matters of "taste" implicitly invoke the standards set by our paradigms and our way of going on from them, and here we can speak of right and wrong. But if we are talking of the views of another

---

2. Charles Laughton (1899–1962) was an English-American actor who played Quasimodo in a 1939 film version of *The Hunchback of Notre Dame.*

society we shall speak of what is true by their standards and by our standards, without the slightest thought that our standards are "correct." If the ancient Mexicans admired the looks of someone whose head had been flattened, a proposition not *about* this admiration may have been true as spoken by them, though it is false as spoken by us.

We have, then, a version of relativism true of some judgements. . . . The question is whether moral assertions might similarly admit only of relative truth. It will probably be objected that this is impossible because moral judgements do not depend on local moral standards as our judgements of taste were thought to depend on local standards of taste. The thought behind this objection is that a challenge to a moral judgement or moral system can be made "out in the open" as it were, with no agreed method, formal or informal, for showing that the challenge is justified. The idea is that there can be disagreement, with each party thinking the other mistaken, even if there is in principle no way of settling the "dispute." It is therefore supposed that an individual can challenge the views of his own society not just in the way that we think it possible for someone to query some judgement of taste, but more radically. He is to be able to say anything he likes about what is morally good and bad, so long as he is consistent, and is to be taken seriously as a man of very eccentric taste would not be. It follows also that the members of one society may similarly challenge the moral view of another society. No common starting point is necessary, and nothing to back up an accusation of falsity or mistake.

Anyone taking this position will insist that moral assertions do not have merely relative truth. Local standards are supposed to be irrelevant, and there is to be no point at which a set of moral opinions inconsistent with one's own are to be admitted to have just as much truth. This is an argument that we should examine carefully; it is perhaps not as powerful as it looks.

The case against construing moral judgements as relativistic along the lines that fit judgements of taste has been made to depend, it seems, on some points of linguistic usage. It was thought crucial that we can say of the moral opinions of our own society, or of some other society, that they are "mistaken" or "false," and this was described in terms of a "challenge" to moral views that differ from our own. The question is whether "challenge" is the right description if words such as "true" and "false" are used as they are supposed to be used here; and in general whether it is important that these words are or are not so employed. It will be remembered that by our hypothesis talk of truth and falsity was to go on even in the absence of any kind of proving or showing, or any *possibility* of proving or showing, that one view rather than the other was in fact true. And this is, of course, a situation very different from that in which the vocabulary of "true" and "false" is used in discussing ordinary matters of fact, in everyday life or in science or history, or even literary criticism. Using Bernard Williams's terminology one might say that words such as "true" and "false" are not used "substantially" when used like this.[3] This is not, of course, to

3. Bernard Williams, "Consistency and Realism," *Aristotelian Society Supplementary Volume* (1966); idem, "The Truth in Relativism," *Proceedings of the Aristotelian Society,* New Series, 75 (1974–75): 215–28. [Foot's note.]

say that there is something wrong with the usage, but it does raise doubts about the weight that can be placed on it in discussions of relativism. The linguistic facts were appealed to in the attempt to show that moral judgements could not be relativistic as some judgements of taste seem to be. Yet if we suppose, as a kind of thought experiment, that the same linguistic possibilities exist in the case of these other judgements we see that their relativism is left unchanged. In this new situation it would be possible for an individual to reject as "false" everything that other members of his society said about good-looking faces, and such things, and it would be possible for one society so to describe the views of another society however far apart their judgements. The important point is that substantial truth would still belong only where common standards were in some sense presupposed; it would still be right to deny that there was any substantial truth belonging to the standards of any particular community.

According to the argument just presented relativism is true in a given area if in that area all *substantial* truth is truth relative to one or other of a set of possible standards. . . .

This account of relativism is gravely deficient in so far as it depends on the idea of substantial truth, and gives only merest indication of what this is. Nevertheless there is enough in what has been said about that, and in the comparison with judgements of taste, to make it possible to enquire further. . . .

I must now approach, with some trepidation, the extremely difficult question whether relativism is a correct theory of moral judgement.

Let me ask, first, whether we have the same reason to accept moral relativism as we had to accept relativism for our handpicked bunch of judgements of taste? This, it seems to me, we do not. For our starting point there was the thought that some rather general judgements of taste could be identified through any amount of variation in the application of the key concepts through the relevant domain. I myself have frequently argued that such variation cannot be postulated in the case of moral judgements, because the thought of moral goodness and badness cannot be held steady through any and every change in the codes of behaviour taught, and in their grounds.[4] From this it follows that not everything that anyone might want to call a "moral code" should properly be so described. . . .

I shall assume that even general moral terms such as "right" or "ought" are restricted, to a certain degree, in their extension, at least at the level of basic principles. It is not possible that there should be two moral codes the mirror images of each other, so that what was considered fundamentally right in one community would be considered wrong at the same level in the other. It seems that some considerations simply are and some are not evidence for particular moral assertions. Nevertheless it does not look as if a correct account of what it is to have a moral thought, or a moral attitude, or to teach a moral code, will suffice to dismiss relativism out of hand. Even if some moral judgements are perfectly objective, there may be others whose

---

4. See, e.g., P. R. Foot, "Moral Arguments," *Mind* 1958, and "Moral Beliefs," *Proceedings of the Aristotelian Society,* 1958–59. [Foot's note.]

truth or falsity is not easily decidable by criteria internal to the subject of moral-ity. We may suppose, I think, that it is clearly an objective moral fact that the Nazi treatment of the Jews was morally indefensible, given the facts and their knowledge of the facts. The Nazis' moral opinions had to be held on grounds either false or irrelevant or both, as on considerations about Germany's "historic mission," or on the thought that genocide could be a necessary form of self-defence. It was impos-sible, logically speaking, for them to argue that the killing of millions of innocent people did not need any moral justification, or that the extension of the German Reich was in itself a morally desirable end. Yet after such things have been said the problem of moral relativism is still with us. Even if the fact that it is morality that is in question gives us some guaranteed starting points for arguments about moral right or wrong, how much is this going to settle? Are there not some moral matters on which, even within our own society, disagreement may be irreducible? And is it not possible that some alien moral systems cannot be faulted by us on any objective principles, while our moral beliefs can also not be faulted by theirs? May there not be places where societies simply confront each other, with no rational method for settling their differences? . . .

[I]f some societies with divergent moral systems merely confront each other, having no use for the assertion that their own systems are true and the others false except to mark the system to which they adhere, then relativism is a true theory of morality. Yet at this point one may become uneasy about [the] reasons for say-ing that relativism is true. For it seems strange to suggest that there is any society whose values we can identify without being able to set them critically beside our own, and our own beside theirs. Some parts of the moral vocabulary do indeed seem unusable when we are considering very alien and distant communities. For instance it would be odd then to talk in terms of the permissible and the imper-missible, simply because language of this kind cannot venture very far from actual sets of permissions and prohibitions. But this does not mean that we cannot in any way judge the moral rules and values of societies very different in this respect from our own. Granted that it is wrong to assume identity of aim between peoples of different cultures; nevertheless there is a great deal that all men have in com-mon. All need affection, the cooperation of others, a place in a community, and help in trouble. It isn't true to suppose that human beings can flourish without these things — being isolated, despised or embattled, or without courage or hope. We are not, therefore, simply expressing values that we happen to have if we think of some moral systems as good moral systems and others as bad. Communities as well as individuals can live wisely or unwisely, and this is largely the result of their values and the codes of behavior that they teach. Looking at these societies, and critically also at our own, we surely have some idea of how things work out and why they work out as they do. We do not have to suppose it is just as good to promote pride of place and the desire to get an advantage over other men as it is to have an ideal of affection and respect. These things have different harvests, and unmistakably different connexions with human good.

No doubt it will be argued that even if all this is true it leaves moral relativism substantially intact, since objective evaluation of moral systems can go only a little way, and will come to an end before all the radical disagreements are resolved. One wonders, however, why people who say this kind of thing are so sure that they know where discussions will lead and therefore where they will end. It is, I think, a fault on the part of relativists, and subjectivists generally, that they are ready to make pronouncements about the later part of moral arguments, and moral reviews, without being able to trace the intermediate steps. Nor is it that they just do not bother to take the whole journey; for there are reasons why they are not able to. One of these has to do with conventions about moral philosophy, conventions that forbid the philosopher to fill chapters with descriptive material about human nature and human life. It isn't supposed to be part of his work to think in the somewhat discursive way that is suitable to reflections about the human heart, and the life of men in society. It is, of course, a kind of decency that keeps moral philosophers in the analytic tradition away from the pseudo-profundity that is found in some philosophies as well as in vulgar preachers. Yet it may be that they have to do this work, and do it properly, before they will know the truth about divergent moralities and values. And we have, after all, a rich tradition of history and literature on which to draw.

There is, however, another reason why moral philosophers tend to give only a sketch of the beginning and end of discussions of the values of different societies; and this has to do with a gap in our philosophical understanding. Perhaps it would be better to speak of a series of gaps, of which I shall give instances in the next few paragraphs. My thought is that there are some concepts which we do not understand well, and cannot employ competently in an argument, that are, unfortunately, essential to genuine discussions of the merits of different moral systems.

Let me give some examples of the kind of thing that I have in mind. I would suppose, for instance, that in some fundamental moral enquiries we might find ourselves appealing to the fact that human life is of value. But do we really understand this thought? Do we know what we mean by saying that *anything* has value, or even that we value it, as opposed to wanting it or being prepared to go to trouble to get it? I do not know of any philosopher living or dead who has been able to explain this idea. And then again we are likely to find ourselves talking about happiness, which is a most intractable concept. To realize that one does not understand it one has only to try to explain why, for instance, the contented life of someone on whom a prefrontal lobotomy has been performed is not the happy life, or why we would count someone as unfortunate rather than endowed with happiness if he were tricked into thinking he was successfully spending his life on important work when he was really just messing around. That we do not understand the concept of happiness is shown, once more, by the fact that we are inclined to think stupid thoughts about the idea of great happiness, as if it were simply extreme and prolonged euphoria. That great happiness depends on its objects is a surprising idea once we understand this, as it should be understood, as a conceptual not a causal matter. It seems that great happiness, unlike euphoria or even great pleasure, must come from something related to what is deep in human nature, and fundamental in human life, such as affection for children and friends, and the desire to work, and love of freedom and truth. But what do we mean by calling some things in human nature deep, and some things in life fundamental? In one way we know this, because we are able, for instance, to understand a man who says at the end of his life that he has wasted his time on "things that don't matter." But what are things that "matter" if they are not the trivial things on which we spend so much time? Clearly such questions are relevant to fundamental discussions of the moralities of other societies and our own. It is impossible to judge a society's morality if we cannot talk about its values, and we must be able to handle the thought of false values if we are to say what is wrong with a materialistic society such as ours. But what is it to have false values if it is not to think too highly of things that do not matter very much?

It seems, then, that we are all at sea with some of the ideas that we are bound to employ in any real discussion of divergent moralities. What we tend to do is to ignore these ideas, and pretend that the debate can be carried on in other terms. But why should this be supposed possible? With other, more jejune, concepts we shall get another discussion, and from it we cannot draw conclusions about how the first would end. Moving from one to the other we are merely guessing at results, and this is, I think, exactly what happens in many arguments about moral relativism. Personally I feel uncomfortable in these arguments, and perhaps this is because I am advancing opinions on the basis of a guess. The practical conclusion may be that we should not at the moment try to say whether moral relativism is true or false, but should start the work farther back.

## TEST YOUR UNDERSTANDING

1. What are some examples of judgments that Foot thinks are relativistic? Why does she think that the "most suitable" examples are "rather general"? Provide two or three other examples of judgments that are relativistic.

2. Foot sketches an argument for the thesis that "moral assertions do not have merely relative truth." She says that "we should examine [it] carefully." The argument, she says, "is perhaps not as powerful as it looks." What is the argument? How does it depend on "linguistic facts"?

3. Foot asks "whether we have the same reason to accept moral relativism as we had to accept relativism for our handpicked bunch of judgments of taste." What is her answer?

4. Foot gives two reasons why people (relativists and subjectivists in general) think "objective evaluation of moral systems can go only a little way, and will come to an end before all the radical disagreements are resolved." What are the two reasons?

## NOTES AND QUESTIONS

1. What does Foot think of the case against moral relativism that depends "on some points of linguistic usage"?

    (i)   What are the points of linguistic usage that are used against the moral relativist?

    (ii)  What does Foot have in mind by "substantial truth"? (She emphasizes that her characterization is not very precise, but thinks it is enough "to make it possible to enquire further.")

    (iii) How does the idea of substantial truth shape her subsequent response to moral relativism?

2. Foot says "It is not possible that there should be two moral codes the mirror image of each other, so that what was considered fundamentally right in one community would be considered wrong at the same level in the other." In making this statement, she contrasts the kinds of disagreement we can have about general judgments of taste with the kinds of disagreement we can have about moral judgments. For example, two communities can disagree completely about whether eating raw fish is delicious or distasteful, Bach's *Art of Fugue* is beautiful or boring, Charlie Chaplin brilliantly funny or silly, and James Joyce's *Ulysses* a work of incandescent brilliance or of tiresomely self-indulgent wordplay. In short, we face a genuine possibility of radical disagreements on judgments of taste. But consider the thought that it is wrong to prevent famines because death is good, or right to stick pins in people because pain is good. Those are not moral views that differ radically from ours; instead, they are not moral views at all. Because they are not moral views at all, the scope of moral disagreement is smaller than we might have supposed.

    (i)   Does Foot's point about the possibility of radical disagreement on judgments of taste work for all judgments of taste? (*Hint:* Consider her distinction between particular and general judgments.) Give two examples of judgments of taste that do not allow such radical disagreement. (*Hint:* Consider her examples of prettiness and handsomeness.)

    (ii)  Once we correctly understand what counts as a moral view, and the limits on moral disagreement that follow from this correct understanding, have we answered the moral relativist? What remains to be done?

3. "[T]here is a great deal that all [people] have in common. All need affection, the cooperation of others, a place in a community, and help in trouble. It isn't true to suppose that human beings can flourish without these things—being isolated, despise or embattled, or without courage or hope."

    (i)   Do you agree with these assertions? Which do you (dis)agree with?

    (ii)  Can you think of other things that people have in common?

    (iii) What role do these assertions play in Foot's assessment of relativism?

4. Foot says that we are "at sea with some of the ideas that we are bound to employ in any real discussion of divergent moralities." Her examples include the (related) ideas of having value, of happiness, and of genuinely mattering. Relativism is fueled, she thinks, in part by a neglect of these important ideas.

(i)   Why does a neglect of these ideas foster moral relativism?

(ii)  What is the thought that great happiness is extreme and prolonged euphoria a "stupid thought"? What does great happiness depend on that the euphoria theory overlooks? (Consider as well her two other examples of mistaken views of happiness.)

(iii) Suppose we accept that great happiness is not prolonged euphoria, but depends on devoting attention to things that matter. How would this help with a response to moral relativism?

## Sharon Street (born 1973)

Street is an associate professor of philosophy at New York University. She specializes in metaethics, and has a particular interest in understanding the relationship between natural science and norms.

# DOES ANYTHING REALLY MATTER OR DID WE JUST EVOLVE TO THINK SO?

Life is preferable to death. Health is better than sickness. We should care for our children, not harm them. Altruists are to be admired rather than condemned. Cheaters ought to be punished, not rewarded.

These and many other evaluative beliefs assail us with great emotional force. They strike us as self-evidently correct and command a high degree of consensus across time and cultures. It is tempting to suppose that they are recognitions of independent truths about what matters.

But what if we hold such values "just" because the mindless process of evolution by natural selection shaped us that way? What if the best scientific explanation of our deepest evaluative convictions is simply that these were the ones that it "paid" to have in the struggle to survive and reproduce? Would the truth of that explanation undermine our values? Or, rather, *should* it?

1.

Sometimes learning the causal origins of a belief can undermine it. Suppose a friend asks you who the twentieth president of the United States was, and an answer springs to mind. "Rutherford B. Hayes," you say, feeling pleased at your mastery of

U.S. history. Your friend bursts into laughter. "You really don't remember, do you?" she says. "That's one of the beliefs the hypnotist implanted in you!" Dismayed, you recall that last night you served as a volunteer in a hypnosis demonstration. Your confidence that Hayes was the twentieth president vanishes. With no other information currently at your disposal, you realize you have no idea whether Hayes was the twentieth president or not.

Other times, learning the causal origins of a belief can strengthen it. Suppose a man approaches you on the street, asking for directions, and you think to yourself, "This guy is up to no good." As you try to put your finger on it, however, there's nothing about him that you can pinpoint. The man is polite and personable. You worry that too many years in the city have made you grumpy and paranoid. Then it hits you: This is the murder suspect you saw profiled a few weeks ago on *America's Most Wanted*! Your belief that the man is up to no good reasserts itself with great force. As you reach nervously for your cell phone, you realize that although it took some moments for your conscious thought process to catch up, at some level your mind had immediately drawn the connection with the murder suspect you'd seen on TV.

These cases illustrate how learning new information about a belief's genealogy can bring about an adjustment in that belief — sometimes diminishing one's confidence in the belief, other times bolstering it. Moreover, notice: Not only do we think these adjustments in belief *would* take place; we think they *should* take place. We think, in other words, that suspending belief in the hypnosis case and increasing one's confidence in the *America's Most Wanted* case are *rationally appropriate* responses to the new information about these beliefs' origins.

Let's explore further why these responses seem rationally appropriate. In the first case, you learn that your belief that Hayes was the twentieth president has its origins in a causal process that as far as you know has nothing to do with whether Hayes was in fact the twentieth president. As far as you know, in other words, the hypnotist last night had no interest in implanting in you a true belief on the subject. When the answer "Hayes" first sprang to mind, it was natural to assume that the belief had its causal origins in your high school history class or some other reliable source. When you learn the belief's actual origin, however, you realize that you have no reason to regard your initial hunch as any guide to the truth on the matter. Moreover, as we have stipulated, you have no other relevant information currently at your disposal. It is therefore rational for you to suspend belief pending access to further information.

In the second case, in contrast, you learn that your belief was, initially without clear conscious awareness on your part, caused by facts directly relevant to the question whether the man was up to no good. Someone's having been profiled as a murder suspect on *America's Most Wanted*, after all, is a pretty good reason to think he is up to no good, and that turns out to be exactly the fact you were responding to when you formed the initial belief, though you didn't realize it at first. Upon discovering the *cause* of your initial hunch, you simultaneously discover what you recognize to be a good *reason* for it. It is therefore rational for you to increase your confidence in the belief accordingly.

# 2.

Can we draw any general lessons? Suppose one learns a new causal explanation of one's belief that P, where "P" stands for some proposition. When should that genealogical discovery diminish one's confidence in the belief, and when should it increase one's confidence? Our two cases suggest the following answer:

PRINCIPLE OF UNDERMINING VERSUS VINDICATING GENEALOGIES

*Undermining genealogy:* If the causal process that gave rise to one's belief that P is such that (as far as one knows) there is no reason to think that it would lead one to form true beliefs about the subject matter in question — and if (as far as one knows) there is no other good reason to believe that P — then one should suspend belief that P.

*Vindicating genealogy:* If, on the other hand, the causal process that gave rise to one's belief that P constitutes or otherwise reveals (what is, as far as one knows) a good reason to believe that P — a reason of which one was not previously aware — then (all else remaining the same) one should increase one's confidence that P.

Notice something important about this principle. According to it, genealogical information *by itself* implies nothing one way or another about whether we should continue to hold a given belief. Rather, in order validly to draw any conclusions about whether or how to adjust one's belief that P, one must assess the *rational significance* of the genealogical information, locating it in the context of a larger set of premises about *what counts as a good reason* for the belief that P. For example, "that I was hypnotized to think so" is not a good reason to think Hayes was the twentieth president, whereas "that my competent high school teacher said so" would be a good reason. Your belief that Hayes was the twentieth president is undermined because you learn that your initial hunch was based on no good reason, whereas your belief that the man is up to no good is vindicated because you learn that your initial hunch was based on a good reason.

# 3.

Armed with the above principle, let's turn now to what we might call our "evaluative hunches" and their genealogy. The theory of evolution by natural selection offers profound insight into the causal origins of our species' *most basic evaluative tendencies*, where by this I mean our tendencies to value certain very general types of things rather than others.

Consider, for example, the following evaluative claims:

(1)   The fact that something would promote one's survival is a reason to do it.

(2)   The fact that something would promote one's health is a reason to do it.

(3)   The fact that something would help one's child is a reason to do it.

(4)   The fact that someone is altruistic is a reason to admire, praise, and reward him or her.

(5)   The fact that someone has cheated (not holding up his or her end of a cooperative deal) is a reason to shun, condemn, and punish him or her.

The most basic evaluative impulses that are expressed by (1)–(5), while of course not universal, are overwhelmingly common among human beings across history and cultures. Versions of them are even evident in close biological relatives such as the chimpanzees. Why is that?

To sharpen the question, consider the following conceivable evaluative views:

(1′)   The fact that something would promote one's survival is a reason not to do it.

(2′)   The fact that something would promote one's health is a reason not to do it.

(3′)   The fact that something would help one's child is reason not to do it.

(4′)   The fact that someone is altruistic is a reason to dislike, condemn, and punish him or her.

(5′)   The fact that someone has cheated (not holding up his or her end of a cooperative deal) is a reason to seek out that person's cooperation again and praise and reward him or her.

Consider also even more bizarre possible evaluative views such as the following:

(6)   The good life is one devoted to screaming constantly.

(7)   One ought to do cartwheels every four seconds until one dies.

Why do human beings generally tend so strongly in the direction of values of the kind expressed by (1)–(5) as opposed to other conceivable values — for example, those expressed by (1′)–(5′), (6), and (7)? An evolutionary biological perspective sheds enormous light. For the theory of evolution by natural selection explains not only the existence of certain *physical* traits such as our lungs, eyes, and ears, but also the existence of certain *psychological* traits such as our devotion to our children and our enjoyment of food and sex.

Not every observable trait (whether physical or psychological) is an adaptation that can be explained by natural selection; the importance of this point cannot be overemphasized. But when it comes to the kinds of basic evaluative tendencies expressed by (1)–(5), a powerful evolutionary explanation of their widespread presence in the human population is in the offing. That explanation, very roughly, is that ancestors with a tendency toward values such as (1) through (5) would have tended to leave more descendants than others with a tendency toward values such as, say, (1′) through (5′) or (6) or (7). It is fairly obvious, for example, why a creature who thought its survival was a good thing and that its offspring deserved protection would tend to leave more descendants than a creature who thought its survival was a bad thing and that its offspring should be eliminated. It is also fairly obvious why a tendency to reward those who helped one and punish those who cheated one would have a better evolutionary "payoff" than the reverse.

Complications abound. The causes that have shaped human values are innumerable, and the suggestion that there are innate predispositions in the direction of some values rather than others does not imply that we — either as a species or as individuals — are genetically determined to hold any one particular value. On the contrary, above all we evolved to be flexible creatures — evaluatively incredibly malleable — and we are capable of holding any given value up for reflective scrutiny and rejecting it if we think rejection warranted. The point is rather that while it's often the diversity of human values that captures our attention, on another way of looking at things it's actually the *uniformity* that is striking. If we compare the evaluative views that human beings actually tend to hold with the universe of *conceivable* evaluative views, we see that these values fall within a relatively narrow range and consistently display a particular kind of content. And there appears to be a very good Darwinian explanation for that.

# 4.

Assume such an explanation can be borne out (and more on it below). Should this information about the genealogy of our values undermine them, as in the hypnotism case? Or might it somehow vindicate them, as in the *America's Most Wanted* case?

The Principle of Undermining versus Vindicating Genealogies tells us to focus on the following question: Is the causal process in question (here, evolution by natural selection) such that there is any reason to think that it would lead us to form true beliefs about the subject matter in question (here, evaluative truths about how to live)? If yes, then the evolutionary explanation of our most basic values may vindicate them. If no, then the evolutionary explanation of our most basic values may undermine them.

Immediately we hit complications, however. Unlike the case of "Who was the twentieth president?," where we are more or less clear on what would count as reliable means of arriving at true beliefs on the subject (allowing one's beliefs to be shaped by a hypnotist is not; listening to one's history teacher is), the nature of *this* subject matter — the subject matter of *what is valuable and how to live* — is itself a highly contested and puzzling question. Indeed, the nature of this subject matter is the focal point of the whole subfield of philosophy known as *metaethics*, which is riven with disagreement.

So how do we proceed? There are any number of competing metaethical views on the nature of value. It will be helpful to focus on one key distinction among these views, namely the contrast between *mind-independent* versus *mind-dependent* conceptions of value.

At issue between such conceptions is the question: Are things valuable ultimately *because we value them*, or are at least some things valuable in a way that is robustly *independent of our valuing them*? According to *mind-independent* conceptions, it's the latter: there are at least some things that possess their value in a way that is independent of the evaluative attitudes that we might happen to hold toward them, where by *evaluative attitudes* I mean mental states such as an agent's values, cares, desires, states of approval and disapproval, unreflective evaluative tendencies, and so on. According to *mind-dependent* conceptions, in contrast, there are *no* independent truths about what is valuable. Rather, if something is valuable, then this is ultimately in virtue of our evaluative attitudes toward the thing — such that if our evaluative attitudes were to change radically enough, so that it was no longer in any way implied by our own attitudes that the thing was valuable, it would thereby cease to *be* valuable. We all hold a mind-dependent view of *some* kinds of value. For example, we all agree that the value of chocolate ultimately depends on the fact that people like it. No one thinks that had human beings all found chocolate disgusting, we would have been missing an independent fact about chocolate's value. The question is whether *all* value is ultimately like that. The mind-dependent theorist says "yes"; the mind-independent theorist says "no."

# 5.

Our tools refined with this distinction, let's return to our question: *Is the causal process in question (here, evolution by natural selection) such that there is any reason to think that it would lead us to form true beliefs about the subject matter in question (here, evaluative truths)?* Since the nature of the subject matter is contested, let's try "plugging in" first one conception of value and then the other, and see what undermining or vindicating "results" we get. Start with a mind-independent conception of value. If we conceive of evaluative truths as robustly independent of our evaluative attitudes, is there any reason to think that evolutionary forces would have shaped us in such a way as to be reliable at detecting those truths?

You might think yes. After all, evolutionary forces seem to have made us reliable about a lot of things. We're pretty good at detecting objects and movement in our immediate environment, for example, and a great deal else. Why not think that evolutionary forces similarly made us skilled at detecting independent evaluative truths? On this line of thought, it somehow promoted reproductive success to grasp independent evaluative truths, and so ancestors with an ability to do so were selected for.

But this proposal fails. The suggestion is that *somehow* it promoted reproductive success to grasp the independent evaluative truth, but we haven't been told yet why or how, and until we've been told this, we have no explanation at all. *Why* would it promote reproductive success to detect the independent evaluative truth? In the case of predators, trees, or fires, it is obvious why it would promote reproductive success to detect them, for these things can kill you or injure you if you fail to notice them. What happens, though, if one fails to notice an independent evaluative truth about how to live? Well, one won't live in accordance with the independent evaluative truth about how to live, but that's not an answer with any explanatory power. It just leads to a repeat of the question: *Why* would it hurt reproductive success not to live in accordance with the independent evaluative truth about how to live?

Consider evaluative views (1) through (5) again. To explain why we evolved with a tendency to accept these views, there is no reason to suppose that these evaluative views are *true* and that it promoted reproductive success to recognize such truths. The best explanation is simpler: All we need to notice is that a creature who accepts these evaluative views — valuing its survival, health, and offspring, for example — will tend to look out for itself and its offspring and so will of course leave more descendants than a creature who, say, despises its own survival, health, and offspring. Truth and falsity have nothing to do with which values would proliferate and which would die out. Thus, if we assume a mind-independent conception of value, it's not at all clear why evolutionary forces would have shaped us to value those things that were, as a matter of independent fact, valuable. It seems that evolutionary forces would just push us to value those things such that valuing them motivated us to do things that promoted survival and reproduction.

It appears that if we conceive of evaluative truths as robustly mind-independent, there is no reason to think that our species arrived at its most basic evaluative assumptions in a way that is reliable with respect to those truths. The case of evolution and value would appear to be more like the hypnosis example, where the causal process that gave rise to the belief in question is not — as far as we can see anyway — one that we have any reason to suppose is a reliable means of arriving at true beliefs about the subject matter. It would seem that we should abandon all confidence in our values and conclude that they have been shaped in a way that bears no relation to the truth.

It cannot be exaggerated what a radical move this would be — to abandon all confidence in our values. To conclude that we are unreliable about the evaluative truth would be to accept *global evaluative skepticism* in the sense of a conviction that one has no idea how to live. Is it plausible, however, to think that when you wake up in the morning, you have no idea at all how to live? That as far as you know you haven't the slightest clue as to whether you should spend your life screaming constantly, doing cartwheels, or something else?

Recall, though: We arrived at this skeptical result only on a certain assumption about the nature of evaluative truths, namely that they are mind-independent. So maybe we're not forced to it. What happens if we plug in a mind-dependent conception of evaluative truths?

If a mind-dependent conception of value is right, then the evolutionary origins of our most basic evaluative "hunches" would seem to be no threat to the idea that we're at least somewhat reliable about the subject matter of how to live. For on a mind-dependent conception, it doesn't matter *what* the causal origins of our most basic evaluative convictions are: since what *is* valuable is ultimately just a function of whatever we start out taking to be valuable, on a mind-dependent conception, we are able simply to start wherever we start with no worry that those starting points are in some deep sense off-track. It's not exactly that our initial evaluative hunches are *vindicated*, on a mind-dependent view; it's rather that vindication turns out not to be an issue at the deepest level. That's because on a mind-dependent view, there is no question of missing something in the very end with one's evaluative attitudes; value is instead understood as something created or constructed by those attitudes.

# 6.

If the arguments of the previous section are correct, then whether we get an undermining result depends on the conception of value we plug in. A mind-independent conception of value, when coupled with the evolutionary genealogy, leads to global evaluative skepticism, whereas a mind-dependent conception has no such implication. Does this mean that we have to settle the issue of whether value is mind-independent or mind-dependent before we can know whether an evolutionary explanation of valuing is undermining or not?

I would argue not. Rather, I would argue that these very results — the undermining result if we assume a mind-independent conception, and the non-undermining result if we assume a mind-dependent conception — are actually what *settles* the debate between these two views of value, with the right conclusion being that the undermining result implied by the mind-independent conception is so implausible that it's the mind-independent conception that must be thrown out.

The evolutionary theory of our origins is overwhelmingly supported by our best science. Taking that as a fixed point, I suggest that it is much more plausible to think that a *mind-independent conception of value is false* than it is to think that *we have no idea how to live*, which is the conclusion that results if we pair a mind-independent conception of value with an evolutionary genealogy of valuing. Accepting this radical skeptical conclusion would involve nothing less than suspending all evaluative judgment, and either continuing to move about but regarding oneself as acting for no reason at all, or else sitting paralyzed where one is and just blinking in one's ignorance of how to go forward. Accepting the conclusion that value is mind-dependent, on the other hand, preserves many of our evaluative views — allowing us to see why we are reasonably reliable about matters of value — while at the same time allowing us to see ourselves as evolved creatures.

The suggestion is that in response to *this* genealogical investigation, we should — to the extent we started out with a conception of value as mind-independent — *revise our conception of the subject matter*. That move might seem odd. It's as though upon learning that your belief about Hayes had its origin in hypnosis, you find it *so implausible that you could be wrong about whether Hayes was the twentieth president* that you opt to change your conception of the subject matter, concluding that facts about who was the twentieth president are constituted by facts about who you *think* the twentieth president was, no matter what the source of your views, hypnotism included.

Obviously in that context, such a move would be absurd. But as always in philosophy, it's a question of what's most plausible all-things-considered. I claim that in the case of the evolutionary origins of valuing, the weakest link in the overall picture — the thing that must go — is a mind-independent conception of value.

We have been asking whether an evolutionary biological explanation of our values ought to undermine them. The answer I've suggested is "yes and no." The answer is "yes" to the extent *you started out thinking that there are mind-independent truths about value*. If that was your view going in, then I've suggested that you ought to abandon it and move to an mind-dependent conception. But once you adopt a *mind-dependent* conception of value — or if you already held such a view to begin with — then the answer is "no," evolutionary explanations of our values aren't undermining in the least.

Your *metaethical* view might need to change, in other words. But your most basic evaluative convictions — that life is preferable to death, that health is better than sickness, that we should care for our children, that altruism is admirable while cheating is to be condemned — all these deepest values should remain untouched by genealogical revelations. In answer to the title's question: Nothing "really" matters in the sense of mattering independently of the attitudes of living beings who *take* things to matter, but the nice fact is that living beings evolved, began taking things to matter, and thereby *made* things matter.

## TEST YOUR UNDERSTANDING

1. "Sometimes learning the causal origins of a belief can undermine it. . . . Other times, learning the causal origins of a belief can strengthen it." Street gives examples of both types of effect. Give an example of an undermining and a strengthening genealogy.

2. What is metaethics about? Why does Street think that we need to explore competing metaethical views in order to decide whether evolutionary explanations of our most basic values are undermining or vindicating?

3. State in your own words the distinction between mind-dependent and mind-independent conceptions of value. Which conception of value does Street think we should endorse?

4. Evaluate the truth or falsity of these two claims:

   (i)   Assuming a mind-independent conception of value, evolution provides an undermining genealogy of our basic evaluative tendencies.

   (ii)  Assuming a mind-dependent conception of value, evolution provides a vindicating genealogy of our basic evaluative tendencies. (In evaluating this claim, be sure to read the last paragraph of section 5 carefully).

## NOTES AND QUESTIONS

1. According to Street, "The theory of evolution by natural selection offers profound insight into the causal origins of our species' *most basic evaluative tendencies*."

   (i)   Pick two entries from Street's list of basic evaluative tendencies and provide a quick sketch of how the theory of evolution by natural selection explains them.

   (ii)  Think of an alternative explanation of our most basic evaluative tendencies. (The explanation need not be one that you find compelling: just another candidate.)

   (iii) Street thinks that the evolutionary explanation provides an undermining genealogy, if we accept a mind-independent conception of value. Is your alternative explanation also undermining, on the mind-independent conception of value?

2. If value is mind-dependent, then, Street argues, evolutionary explanations of our basic evaluative tendencies are not undermining (though they are not vindicating either). Why not? Suppose I say:

   *Mind-Dependence:* X is good for people generally if and only if people generally value X.

Is Mind-Dependence a plausible account of value? (Does it accurately state Street's account of mind-dependence?) Suppose we all think salt is good for us until we learn that it is unhealthy, thus not good: so we do now value it, but it is not good for us. Cases like this may have motivated Street not to endorse Mind-Dependence. She says that mind-dependent views make value "ultimately" a matter of "our evaluative attitudes." In this spirit, we might modify Mind-Dependence to something like:

   *Informed Mind-Dependence:* X is good for people generally if and only if people would value X if they were well informed about X and the consequences of having (using, pursuing) X.

Informed Mind-Dependence does connect value "ultimately" to our evaluative attitudes: being good is a matter of what we would value under idealized conditions. But it allows for some distance between our current values and what is good for us. Now though we may ask a question about Informed Mind-Dependence like the question that Street asks about mind-independent conceptions of value: Why should we suppose that evolutionary forces made us skilled at valuing what is good—that is, what we would value if we were well-informed?

Can you find a variant of Mind-Dependence that meets two requirements: (i) it presents a plausible condition on being a good thing (more plausible than Mind-Dependence); and (ii) evolutionary forces plausibly have made us good at grasping the condition (more plausibly than with Informed Mind-Dependence)?

## ANALYZING THE ARGUMENTS

1.  Mackie says, in effect, that the objectivity of morality does not matter to substantive morality. As he puts it, questions about objectivity are second-order questions, not first-order moral questions: the two are "completely independent." So moral subjectivism leaves morality itself untouched. Nagel says that efforts to stand outside morality and see morality as the expression of a non-objective perspective "collapse" under the weight of substantive moral judgments: when we actually reason about what morality requires, the idea that it is not objective gives way. So Mackie seems to disagree with Nagel about the connections between first-and second-order moral judgments. Street, in contrast, agrees with Nagel. She thinks that if we hold a mind-independent view of values—a second-order view—then evolutionary theory undermines our first-order values. So a second-order view has significant effects on first-order views.

    Is Mackie right? If you think, for example, that moral requirements are social conventions, does that affect the content of your first-order moral convictions? Consider specific moral requirements when you answer, focusing on requirements that you endorse.

2.  Foot thinks that philosophical discussions about moral objectivity need to look very different from the way they are ordinarily conducted. We need to pay much more attention to human nature, how people live together in society, and to the human heart. How would Wallace respond to this proposal? Are facts of the kind that Foot mentions relevant to responding to moral subjectivism, as Wallace describes it?

3.  When the great physicist Richard Feynman introduced quantum mechanics to undergraduates, he began his lecture by saying: "Things on a very small scale [including electrons, protons, neutrons, photons] behave like nothing that you have any direct experience about. They do not behave like waves, they do not behave like particles, they do not behave like clouds, or billiard balls, or weights on springs, or like anything that you have ever seen.... Because atomic behavior is so unlike ordinary experience, it is very difficult to get used to, and it appears peculiar and mysterious to everyone—both to the novice and to the experienced physicist."[1]

    Would Mackie respond to Feynman by saying: "Well, then we should not think that things on a small scale exist, because they are so odd, so 'utterly different from anything else in the universe.'" If not, why not?

    How would Wallace and Nagel respond to Feynman's point? Are they troubled about the thought that objective values are unlike anything else we are familiar with? Why, or why not?

4.  Consider the view that morality is objective because God set down fundamental moral laws that distinguish right from wrong. Moreover, God created us with the power to understand those laws, thus to grasp the difference between right and wrong. Describe how each of the views in this chapter would respond to these claims about the nature of moral objectivity.

1.  Richard Feynman, *The Feynman Lectures on Physics,* vol. 3 (Pearson, 2006), § 1-1.

# Part V

# ETHICS AND POLITICAL PHILOSOPHY

# 15

# Why Do What Is Right?

Suppose you find yourself in an uncomfortable situation. Your friend has told you that when funds are tight he regularly "borrows" money from the register at the retail store where you both work and then repays it when he gets his next paycheck. The manager noticed that some money went missing during yesterday's shift when your friend was working. The manager tells you that he suspects another worker who is an annoying, uncooperative thorn in everyone's side, but the manager says he does not want to fire anyone unfairly. He asks if you have any reason to suspect anyone else. If you lie, you could protect your friend and eliminate a minor nemesis from the workplace. If you tell the truth, you may lose your friend and your friend may lose his job. You know that morality requires you to tell the truth, or at least not to lie. But you also know that you could get away with lying and that it would benefit you and your friend if you lie.

You face a moral question: "Is telling the truth the right thing to do?" But even if you know the answer to that question—you know that the right thing is to tell the truth and not to permit an innocent person to be fired for theft—you also face a further, theoretical question: "Why *ought* I do the right thing when it would be so much better for me to lie?" On many occasions, doing the right thing comes at a personal cost, perhaps even a large one. We may be confident that telling the truth, repaying a debt, or helping those in need is what's morally right, but nevertheless wonder whether that means we must do it. Why not ignore your duty just this once, and enjoy a brief holiday from morality? And, as Plato's character Glaucon asks in *The Republic*, once you've raised this question, you can raise a more general question: "Why not extend this holiday even further and ignore morality altogether?" This chapter explores this skeptical question and some answers philosophers have given in response.

## Self-interested Reasons

In the moment when you feel tempted to shirk your duty, the most compelling answer to the question "Why should I do the right thing?" may be that doing the right thing is in your self-interest, narrowly considered. After all, behaving badly may court the disapproval of other people. It may even risk punishment. Conversely, acting well usually elicits others' approval and cooperation, and the good opinion of others can be useful to you. Further, in some religious traditions, acting well is a precondition of enjoying God's grace, whether in this life or a later, postmortem existence. Finally, doing the wrong thing could produce crushing guilt that will gnaw on your conscience.

Such self-interested reasons may help you resist temptation in the moment. Yet, many philosophers doubt that they provide *basic* reasons to do the right thing as such. Those who do the right thing to serve themselves, rather than others, may seem shallow and to have missed the point of acting morally. As Glaucon observes to Socrates, these self-interested considerations are really only reasons to *appear* to act morally, rather than reasons to do the right thing as such. Yet, even if one could act secretly and behave badly with impunity, suffering no adverse consequences from others, it still strikes us that we *ought* to behave well. "But God will know!" Perhaps, but even if God does not exist, we still have good reason not to harm others for fun, convenience, or mere personal benefit.

True, even without God or the sanctions of others, if you behaved immorally, *you* would still know what you did and you might not escape suffering from a guilty conscience. But that fact does not support the theory of self-interest. Although guilt is unpleasant and something one wishes to avoid, guilt is a justified reaction to the recognition that there is a prior, distinct good reason to do the right thing: a reason to which one has been irresponsibly insensitive. To make sense of the guilt we are prone to feel when we do the wrong thing, we need to locate that other, more fundamental reason.

## Care for Others

Perhaps we should do the right thing not primarily *because* it is in our self-interest, narrowly construed, but because we *care* about other people. As David Hume argues, we feel a natural sympathy for others and we have a "passion" for their welfare. Of course, if we care about others, we will *want* to do the right thing. In that sense, we will satisfy our interests and desires when we act morally. We may even derive a pleasant feeling of satisfaction when we fulfill those desires. But, if we do the right thing because we care about others, it would be misleading to think of this motive as the motive of self-interest.

Although the sympathetic person feels good when she helps others, she does not help *in order to* feel good or reap a personal benefit. She feels good as a consequence of an *independent* desire to promote the interests of *others*. That desire cannot be reduced to a form of narrow self-interest. Acting from care for others may, *as a side-effect*, promote the sympathetic person's own interest, but only because what serves her interests extends, by virtue of her concern for others, beyond the narrow sphere of herself.

Many philosophers agree that we are capable of acting directly from concern for others and that such direct concern is not selfish or self-interested. Still, some, like Immanuel Kant, contest the claim that concern for others offers the primary reason *why* we should behave morally. After all, even if one is not feeling particularly caring or sympathetic to others on a particular occasion, one *still* has reason to behave well and to refrain from immoral conduct. One's duty not to steal does not wax and wane depending on whether one actually cares about one's potential victim; so how could one's *reason* to do one's duty depend on things that may vary, such as one's mood or temperament? Moreover, sometimes one has duties whose satisfaction may constrain one's ability to advance the interests of those one actively cares about. For instance, one has a duty not to perjure oneself in court, even if telling the truth enhances the prosecution's case against a friend. Finally, it may well be that our natural sympathy runs out at a certain point: we may not care very much, or at all, about people in distant places, or about people who will exist only in the future; yet we still have powerful reasons not to wrong these people, for example, by destroying the environment in which they will live. So if we have moral reasons of this sort, they do not derive entirely from our felt concern for others.

## The Role of Reason

For these reasons, Kant concludes that neither our self-interest nor our sentiments can supply general grounds for doing what is right. His reasoning is as follows:

1. Our desires, interests and sentiments — including our concern for others — are contingent, as are their objects: they vary from person to person and from occasion to occasion.

2. Whether morality requires an action to be performed does not generally depend upon how the agent feels about that action or its effects. Two people with very different desires, interests, and sentiments can both be morally required to do the same thing, for the same reason, despite their different desires, interests, and sentiments.

3. On every occasion that morality requires us to perform an action, each of us has the same basic reason to perform that action.

4. Therefore, our basic reasons for acting morally do not derive from our contingent desires, interests, and sentiments.

On this view, self-interest and our sentiments may at most reinforce our basic reason to do what is right, which is to perform the right action primarily from what Kant calls "respect for the moral law." Respect for the moral law consists of the recognition that one always has an overriding reason to do one's duty for duty's sake and not just because doing one's duty happens, as a matter of fact, to correspond to what one happens to feel like doing. This respect for the moral law is required of us, Kant thinks, no matter how we happen to feel, and from this Kant concludes that it is required by reason itself. (Kant adds that our actions have moral worth only insofar as they are motivated by respect for the moral law. It is possible to do the right thing merely for selfish reasons, or from sympathy; but if you do, your action does not merit moral admiration.) Kant then argues that this recognition of the overriding reason to perform one's duty for duty's sake alone can guide us to identify the content of the moral law. That is, this recognition may help us discern what it is we ought to do (an argument he pursues more fully in a later chapter of his book, excerpted here in chapter 16).

# What Can Reason and Rationality Require?

As is emerging, the question of what reason we have to do the right thing connects closely to other profound questions about how our basic faculties of desire, sympathy, and reason relate to one another and to what we ought to do. Although Kant contends that morality binds us because we are rational agents, not because we are feeling creatures, Hume's sympathetic approach is driven by his skepticism that the faculty of reason could, by itself, motivate any action, much less moral action. His preliminary question, pursued in *A Treatise of Human Nature*, is whether reason or "passion" (by which he means feeling and sentiment) is the source of our motivation to do the right thing. He argues that reason cannot be the ultimate source of moral motivation (or the source of the contents of moral requirements either) because reason alone cannot motivate the will: it can only discover what exists, what properties things have, and how ideas and things relate to one another. To initiate and propel action, some sort of sentiment or passion is necessary. One must *care* about what one is bringing about. But reason cannot itself provoke such passions; it can only give them guidance. As Hume declares, "[R]eason is, and ought only to be the slave of the passions, and can never pretend to any other office than to serve and obey them."

Kant does not directly refute these arguments, but appeals to our moral experience as evidence that the Humean conception of the bounds of reason is overly cramped. We are familiar with the difference between conforming with the requirements of duty for self-interested reasons, conforming with duty out of sympathy, and conforming with duty for its own sake. The possibility of this last form of behavior seems essential to our understanding of moral worth. Our sense of conforming with duty for its own sake gives us grounds to believe that our faculty of reason is not just a "slave of the passions." It can supply us with "ends," and not just with information about the means to our ends, and can distinguish between permissible and impermissible means to our ends. Our faculty of reason, therefore, can supply us with grounds for acting morally.

Judith Jarvis Thomson supplies another perspective on the relation between one's concerns, rationality, and what one *ought* to do. Like Hume, she connects what it would be rational to do with what one cares about, although she denies that what it is rational to do just consists of that action that would in fact advance one's concerns. She argues that what it is *rational* for you to do is what would *appear* to advance what you care about, given the information in your possession. Thomson argues that rationality is a matter of what is in the mind and how well the mind grapples with what it is justified in believing. Consequently, she claims that what it is rational to do depends upon what would be most likely to advance one's concerns, relative to what one is justified in believing, even if one is ultimately mistaken about the facts. Suppose you aim to heal your sick child but mistakenly believe that he is allergic to penicillin. If this mistaken belief is justified, then it would not be rational in Thomson's sense to administer the drug. Yet, you *ought* to do it for two reasons. First, the penicillin would work and so you *ought* to do it because what one *ought* to do in order to advance one's concerns is what would in fact advance one's concerns. Second, she agrees with Kant that what one *ought* morally to do binds one to act whether it advances one's concerns or not. (Unlike Kant, she declines to claim that *rationality* demands the action). So, whether one cares to cure the child or not, one *ought* to give him the penicillin because it would cure him and parents owe it to their children to give them appropriate medical treatment, whether they are motivated by love and sympathy or not. Parents owe medical treatment to their children because children are dependent on their parents and parents have assumed obligations to look after them; justice therefore demands the administration of the penicillin. When justice demands a particular action, one ought to do it for the very reasons that explain why it is just to perform that action.

In Thomson's view, it may or may not be rational to do what justice or morality demands. Further, what justice or morality demands may or may not further one's deepest concerns or cares. But, she does not embrace the skeptical position we began with. She has no doubt that one *ought* to do the right thing. She thinks we go wrong by entertaining the skeptical question in the first place. If we know what the right thing to do is, we know automatically that there is a sufficient reason to do it. The reason to repay a debt to a friend in need is just whatever reason it is that repaying a debt is in fact the right thing to do. We may not be able to articulate that reason right away: that may require philosophical reflection. But if we know the act is right, we know that something about it makes it right, and that the features that make the act right also make it something one ought to do. The questions "What is the right thing to do?" and "Why *ought* I do the right thing?" are not, in her view, two distinct and separate questions; the answer to the latter is supplied by the very considerations that answer the former.

Consider again the case of your friend who steals from work and the manager who asks you if you know anything that would exonerate your unjustly suspected coworker. As you read the selections, imagine how the author would respond to the sincere questions: "I know that it would be morally wrong to lie, but does that mean I should tell the truth? Do I really have sufficient *reason* not to lie? What is that reason?"

## Plato (429–347 BCE)

Plato is one of the most important figures in Western philosophy. He founded the Academy in Athens, which was a major center of learning in classical Greece, where he taught Aristotle (384–322 BCE). Plato's works typically take the form of dialogues, and nearly all of them feature his teacher Socrates (469–399 BCE). In the following dialogue, Socrates discusses our reasons to act morally, or justly, with two of Plato's brothers, Glaucon and Adeimantus.

# THE REPUBLIC

# Book II

Glaucon: Socrates, do you want to seem to have persuaded us that it is better in every way to be just than unjust, or do you want truly to convince us of this?

Socrates: I want truly to convince you, if I can.

Glaucon: Tell me, do you think there is a kind of good we welcome, not because we desire what comes from it, but because we welcome it for its own sake — joy, for example, and all the harmless pleasures that have no results beyond the joy of having them?

Socrates: Certainly, I think there are such things.

Glaucon: And is there a kind of good we like for its own sake and also for the sake of what comes from it — knowing, for example, and seeing and being healthy? We welcome such things, I suppose, on both counts.

Socrates: Yes.

Glaucon: And do you also see a third kind of good, such as physical training, medical treatment when sick, medicine itself, and the other ways of making money? We'd say that these are onerous but beneficial to us, and we wouldn't choose them for their own sakes, but for the sake of the rewards and other things that come from them.

Socrates: There is also this third kind. But what of it?

Glaucon: Where do you put justice?

Socrates: I myself put it among the finest goods, as something to be valued by anyone who is going to be blessed with happiness, both because of itself and because of what comes from it.

Glaucon: That isn't most people's opinion. They'd say that justice belongs to the onerous kind, and is to be practiced for the sake of the rewards and popularity that
come from a reputation for justice, but is to be avoided because of itself as something burdensome.

Socrates: I know that's the general opinion. Thrasymachus[1] faulted justice on these
grounds a moment ago and praised injustice, but it seems that I'm a slow learner.

Glaucon: . . . I think that Thrasymachus gave up before he had to, charmed by you as
if he were a snake. But I'm not yet satisfied by the argument on either side. I want
to know what justice and injustice are and what power each itself has when it's by
itself in the soul. I want to leave out of account their rewards and what comes from
each of them. So, if you agree, I'll renew the argument of Thrasymachus. First, I'll
state what kind of thing people consider justice to be and what its origins are. Second, I'll argue that all who practice it do so unwillingly, as something necessary,
not as something good. Third, I'll argue that they have good reason to act as they
do, for the life of an unjust person is, they say, much better than that of a just one.

It isn't, Socrates, that I believe any of that myself. . . . But I've yet to hear anyone defend justice in the way I want, proving that it is better than injustice. I
want to hear it praised *by itself*, and I think that I'm most likely to hear this from
you. Therefore, I'm going to speak at length in praise of the unjust life, and in
doing so I'll show you the way I want to hear you praising justice and denounc-
ing injustice. . . .

[To start,] let's discuss the first subject I mentioned — what justice is and
what its origins are.

They say that to do injustice is naturally good and to suffer injustice bad, but
that the badness of suffering it so far exceeds the goodness of doing it that those
who have done and suffered injustice and tasted both, but who lack the power to
do it and avoid suffering it, decide that it is profitable to come to an agreement
with each other neither to do injustice nor to suffer it. As a result, they begin to
make laws and covenants, and what the law commands they call lawful and just.
This, they say, is the origin and essence of justice. It is intermediate between the
best and the worst. The best is to do injustice without paying the penalty; the
worst is to suffer it without being able to take revenge. Justice is a mean between
these two extremes. People value it not as a good but because they are too weak
to do injustice with impunity. Someone who has the power to do this, however,
and is a true man wouldn't make an agreement with anyone not to do injustice
in order not to suffer it. For him that would be madness. This is the nature of
justice, according to the argument, Socrates, and these are its natural origins.

We can see most clearly that those who practice justice do it unwillingly
and because they lack the power to do injustice, if in our thoughts we grant to
a just and an unjust person the freedom to do whatever they like. We can then
follow both of them and see where their desires would lead. And we'll catch
the just person red-handed travelling the same road as the unjust. The reason
for this is the desire to outdo others and get more and more. This is what

---

1. A Sophist (itinerant teacher) who appears earlier in the dialogue.

anyone's nature naturally pursues as good, but nature is forced by law into the perversion of treating fairness with respect.

The freedom I mentioned would be most easily realized if both people had the power they say the ancestor of Gyges of Lydia[2] possessed. The story goes that he was a shepherd in the service of the ruler of Lydia. There was a violent thunderstorm, and an earthquake broke open the ground and created a chasm at the place where he was tending his sheep. Seeing this, he was filled with amazement and went down into it. And there, . . . he saw a hollow bronze horse. There were windowlike openings in it, and, peeping in, he saw a corpse, which seemed to be of more than human size, wearing nothing but a gold ring on its finger. He took the ring and came out of the chasm. He wore the ring at the usual monthly meeting that reported to the king on the state of the flocks. And as he was sitting among the others, he happened to turn the setting of the ring towards himself to the inside of his hand. When he did this, he became invisible to those sitting near him, and they went on talking as if he had gone. He wondered at this, and, fingering the ring, he turned the setting outwards again and became visible. So he experimented with the ring to test whether it indeed had this power—and it did. If he turned the setting inward, he became invisible; if he turned it outward, he became visible again. When he realized this, he at once arranged to become one of the messengers sent to report to the king. And when he arrived there, he seduced the king's wife, attacked the king with her help, killed him, and took over the kingdom.

Let's suppose, then, that there were two such rings, one worn by a just and the other by an unjust person. Now, no one, it seems, would be so incorruptible that he would stay on the path of justice or stay away from other people's property, when he could take whatever he wanted from the marketplace with impunity, go into people's houses and have sex with anyone he wished, kill or release from prison anyone he wished, and do all the other things that would make him like a god among humans. Rather his actions would be in no way different from those of an unjust person, and both would follow the same path. This, some would say, is a great proof that one is never just willingly but only when compelled to be. No one believes justice to be a good when it is kept private, since, wherever either person thinks he can do injustice with impunity, he does it. Indeed, every man believes that injustice is far more profitable to himself than justice. And any exponent of this argument will say he's right, for someone who didn't want to do injustice, given this sort of opportunity, and who didn't touch other people's property would be thought wretched and stupid by everyone aware of the situation, though, of course, they'd praise him in public, deceiving each other for fear of suffering injustice. So much for my second topic.

As for the choice between the lives we're discussing, we'll be able to make a correct judgment about that only if we separate the most just and the most unjust. . . . Here's the separation I have in mind. We'll subtract nothing from the injustice of an unjust person and nothing from the justice of a just one, but we'll take

---

2. Lydia was an ancient kingdom located in what is now the western portion of Turkey.

each to be complete in his own way of life. First, therefore, we must suppose that an unjust person will act as clever craftsmen do: A first-rate captain or doctor, for example, knows the difference between what his craft can and can't do. He attempts the first but lets the second go by, and if he happens to slip, he can put things right. In the same way, an unjust person's successful attempts at injustice must remain undetected, if he is to be fully unjust. Anyone who is caught should be thought inept, for the extreme of injustice is to be believed to be just without being just. And our completely unjust person must be given complete injustice; nothing may be subtracted from it. We must allow that, while doing the greatest injustice, he has nonetheless provided himself with the greatest reputation for justice. If he happens to make a slip, he must be able to put it right. If any of his unjust activities should be discovered, he must be able to speak persuasively or to use force. And if force is needed, he must have the help of courage and strength and of the substantial wealth and friends with which he has provided himself.

Having hypothesized such a person, let's now in our argument put beside him a just man, who is simple and noble and who, as Aeschylus[3] says, doesn't want to be believed to be good but to be so. We must take away his reputation, for a reputation for justice would bring him honor and rewards, so that it wouldn't be clear whether he is just for the sake of justice itself or for the sake of those honors and rewards. We must strip him of everything except justice and make his situation the opposite of an unjust person's. Though he does no injustice, he must have the greatest reputation for it, so that he can be tested as regards justice unsoftened by his bad reputation and its effects. Let him stay like that unchanged until he dies — just, but all his life believed to be unjust. In this way, both will reach the extremes, the one of justice and the other of injustice, and we'll be able to judge which of them is happier.

Socrates: Glaucon, how vigorously you've scoured each of the men for our competition, just as you would a pair of statues for an art competition.

Glaucon: . . . Since the two are as I've described, in any case, it shouldn't be difficult to complete the account of the kind of life that awaits each of them. And if what I say sounds crude, Socrates, remember that it isn't I who speak but those who praise injustice at the expense of justice. They'll say that a just person in such circumstances will be whipped, stretched on a rack, chained, blinded with fire, and, at the end, when he has suffered every kind of evil, he'll be impaled, and will realize then that one shouldn't want to be just but to be believed to be just. Indeed, Aeschylus' words are far more correctly applied to unjust people than to just ones, for the supporters of injustice will say that a really unjust person, having a way of life based on the truth about things and not living in accordance with opinion, doesn't want simply to be believed to be unjust but actually to be so. . . . He rules his city because of his reputation for justice; he marries into any family he wishes; he gives his children in marriage to anyone he wishes; he has contracts and partnerships with anyone he wants; and besides benefiting himself

---

3. Aeschylus (525–456 BCE) was a famous Ancient Greek poet and playwright.

in all these ways, he profits because he has no scruples about doing injustice. In any contest, public or private, he's the winner and outdoes his enemies. And by outdoing them, he becomes wealthy, benefiting his friends and harming his enemies. . . .

Adeimantus: You surely don't think that the position has been adequately stated?

Socrates: Why not?

Adeimantus: The most important thing to say hasn't been said yet. . . .

Socrates: If Glaucon has omitted something, you must help him. Yet what he has said
     is enough to throw me to the canvas and make me unable to come to the aid
     of justice.

Adeimantus: Nonsense. . . . Hear what more I have to say, for we should also fully
     explore the arguments that are opposed to the ones Glaucon gave, the ones that
     praise justice and find fault with injustice, so that what I take to be his intention
     may be clearer.

When fathers speak to their sons, they say that one must be just, as do all the others who have charge of anyone. But they don't praise justice itself, only the high reputations it leads to and the consequences of being thought to be just, such as the public offices, marriages, and other things Glaucon listed. But they elaborate even further on the consequences of reputation. By bringing in the esteem of the gods, they are able to talk about the abundant good things that they themselves and the noble Hesiod and Homer[4] say that the gods give to the pious, for Hesiod says that the gods make the oak trees

> Bear acorns at the top and bees in the middle
> And make fleecy sheep heavy laden with wool

for the just, and tells of many other good things akin to these. And Homer is similar:

> When a good king, in his piety,
> Upholds justice, the black earth bears
> Wheat and barley for him, and his trees are heavy with fruit.
> His sheep bear lambs unfailingly, and the sea yields up its fish. . . .

Consider another form of argument about justice and injustice employed both by private individuals and by poets. All go on repeating with one voice that justice and moderation are fine things, but hard and onerous, while licentiousness and injustice are sweet and easy to acquire and are shameful only in opinion and law. They add that unjust deeds are for the most part more profitable than just ones, and, whether in public or private, they willingly honor vicious people who have wealth and other types of power and declare them to be happy. But

---

4. Hesiod and Homer were the two most important epic poets of Ancient Greece, both of whom lived at some point between 750 BCE and 650 BCE; the precise dates are unknown.

they dishonor and disregard the weak and the poor, even though they agree that they are better than the others. . . .

They say that the gods, too, assign misfortune and a bad life to many good people, and the opposite fate to their opposites. Begging priests and prophets frequent the doors of the rich and persuade them that they possess a god-given power founded on sacrifices and incantations. If the rich person or any of his ancestors has committed an injustice, they can fix it with pleasant rituals. Moreover, if he wishes to injure some enemy, then, at little expense, he'll be able to harm just and unjust alike, for by means of spells and enchantments they can persuade the gods to serve them. . . . And they persuade not only individuals but whole cities that the unjust deeds of the living or the dead can be absolved or purified through ritual sacrifices and pleasant games. These initiations, as they call them, free people from punishment hereafter, while a terrible fate awaits those who have not performed the rituals. . . .

Why, then, should we still choose justice over the greatest injustice? Many eminent authorities agree that, if we practice such injustice with a false façade, we'll do well at the hands of gods and humans, living and dying as we've a mind to. So, given all that has been said, Socrates, how is it possible for anyone of any power — whether of mind, wealth, body, or birth — to be willing to honor justice and not laugh aloud when he hears it praised? Indeed, if anyone can show that what we've said is false and has adequate knowledge that justice is best, he'll surely be full not of anger but of forgiveness for the unjust. He knows that, apart from someone of godlike character who is disgusted by injustice or one who has gained knowledge and avoids injustice for that reason, no one is just willingly. Through cowardice or old age or some other weakness, people do indeed object to injustice. But it's obvious that they do so only because they lack the power to do injustice, for the first of them to acquire it is the first to do as much injustice as he can. . . .

Socrates, of all of you who claim to praise justice, from the original heroes of old whose words survive, to the men of the present day, not one has ever blamed injustice or praised justice except by mentioning the reputations, honors, and rewards that are their consequences. No one has ever adequately described what each itself does of its own power by its presence in the soul of the person who possesses it, even if it remains hidden from gods and humans. No one, whether in poetry or in private conversations, has adequately argued that injustice is the worst thing a soul can have in it and that justice is the greatest good. If you had treated the subject in this way and persuaded us from youth, we wouldn't now be guarding against one another's injustices, but each would be his own best guardian, afraid that by doing injustice he'd be living with the worst thing possible. . . .

[I]t's because I want to hear the opposite from you that I speak with all the force I can muster. So don't merely give us a theoretical argument that justice is stronger than injustice, but tell us what each itself does, because of its own powers, to someone who possesses it, that makes injustice bad and justice good. Follow Glaucon's advice, and don't take reputations into account, for if you don't deprive justice and injustice of their true reputations and attach false ones to them, we'll say that you are not praising them but their reputations and that you're encouraging us to be unjust in secret. In that case, we'll say that you agree with Thrasymachus that justice is the good of another, the advantage of the stronger, while injustice is one's own advantage and profit, though not the advantage of the weaker.

You agree that justice is one of the greatest goods, the ones that are worth getting for the sake of what comes from them, but much more so for their own sake, such as seeing, hearing, knowing, being healthy, and all other goods that are fruitful by their own nature and not simply because of reputation. Therefore, praise justice as a good of that kind, explaining how—because of its very self—it benefits its possessors and how injustice harms them. Leave wages and reputations for others to praise.

Others would satisfy me if they praised justice and blamed injustice in that way, extolling the wages of one and denigrating those of the other. But you, unless you order me to be satisfied, wouldn't, for you've spent your whole life investigating this and nothing else. Don't, then, give us only a theoretical argument that justice is stronger than injustice, but show what effect each has because of itself on the person who has it—the one for good and the other for bad—whether it remains hidden from gods and human beings or not. . . .

Socrates: That's well said in my opinion, for you must indeed be affected by the divine if you're not convinced that injustice is better than justice and yet can speak on its behalf as you have done. And I believe that you really are unconvinced by your own words. I infer this from the way you live, for if I had only your words to go on, I wouldn't trust you.

## TEST YOUR UNDERSTANDING

1. Socrates and Glaucon identify three sorts of goods. What are they? Briefly give your own examples of each of the three sorts.

2. Which sort of good is justice, according to Socrates? (Remember that in this passage, "justice" encompasses all forms of morally correct conduct.) Briefly explain how Socrates's classification of "justice" supports his conclusion that "it is better in every way to be just rather than unjust."

## NOTES AND QUESTIONS

1. *Glaucon's predictions.* Suppose Glaucon's prediction is correct and that those who possess Gyges's ring would behave terribly. According to Glaucon, this shows that we have no foundational reason to behave well, but only a reason to *appear* to behave well. Why does he think this? Are you convinced? Can you think of an alternative explanation why others' knowledge of your behavior might affect your behavior? (*Hint:* Consider how groups like sports teams, Weight Watchers, and Alcoholics Anonymous are thought to help their members achieve their goals.)

2. *Adeimantus's challenge.* At the end of the selection, Adeimantus challenges Socrates to show that the life of justice "because of its very self ... benefits its possessors." That is, he asks Socrates to show that independent of any external reward, living justly has a good effect on the life of the just person. Some translations represent Adeimantus as demanding that Socrates show that the just life improves the *soul* of the just person. Suppose Socrates could show this. Would this supply a person with the right sort of reason to do the right thing?

Consider the following objection: "Showing that leading a moral life benefits you spiritually just offers a variation on an argument from self-interest. Meeting Adeimantus's challenge would still fail to show that we have non-self-interested reasons to be moral." Do you think this objection is persuasive?

## Judith Jarvis Thomson (born 1929)

Thomson was born in New York and is Professor Emeritus at Massachusetts Institute of Technology. She has made a number of field-defining contributions in moral theory, applied ethics, political philosophy, legal philosophy, and metaphysics. Her books include *Rights, Restitution and Risk* (1986), *The Realm of Rights* (1998), *Goodness and Advice* (2001) and *Normativity* (2006).

# WHY OUGHT WE DO WHAT IS RIGHT?

## 1

In Plato's *Republic*, two young men, Glaucon and Adeimantus, ask Socrates a question. Socrates is among those who praise justice — who, in particular, believe that if justice requires a person to ϕ, then the person ought to ϕ — and they ask him why. Thus suppose justice requires Alfred to pay Bert ten dollars. Glaucon and Adeimantus know that Socrates would say that Alfred therefore ought to pay Bert ten dollars, and they want to know why.

Notice that Glaucon and Adeimantus — from here on, "G&A" — are not asking Socrates what makes it the case that justice requires a person to do a thing. They assume that is clear enough, and let us for the time being agree. So, for example, suppose that Alfred borrowed ten dollars from Bert, and promised to repay him; suppose also that Bert relied on being paid by Alfred, and now needs the ten dollars, and that no one (not even Alfred) will suffer any hardship if Alfred repays Bert. Then we can surely assume that justice requires Alfred to repay Bert. What Socrates is to do is only to say why Alfred therefore ought to repay Bert.

## 2

G&A plainly think they are asking Socrates a hard question, and Socrates does too. But is it a hard question?

Suppose that justice requires a person to φ. Then the person's failing to φ would be unjust. And therefore defective. And therefore bad. And therefore wrong. But if wrong, then *a fortiori,* to be avoided. Thus the person ought not fail to φ. Therefore the person ought to φ.

Similarly for the requirements of generosity, kindness, loyalty, responsibility, and so on. Suppose it is instead generosity, kindness, loyalty, or responsibility that requires the person to φ. Then the person's failing to φ would be defective, therefore bad, therefore wrong. But if wrong, then *a fortiori,* to be avoided. Thus the person ought not fail to φ. Therefore the person ought to φ.

In short, if a virtue such as justice requires a person to φ, then the person acts rightly only if he or she φs. *A fortiori,* the person ought to φ.

That certainly looks easy! So why do G&A and Socrates think they are asking Socrates a hard question? And why would so many people agree with them? — for many people would. It is very likely that G&A and Socrates, and the many who would agree with them, would dig in their heels at those "*a fortiori*"s. Thus they would agree that if justice — or generosity, kindness, loyalty, responsibility, and so on — requires a person to φ, then the person will act rightly only if he or she φs. But they would ask why it should be thought to follow that the person *ought* to φ. We can expect them to say that the person might well ask "Why ought I do what is right?"

That G&A have that in mind emerges when they tell Socrates about a constraint on his answer.

They say people often praise justice to the young by pointing to the profits that (as people say) come to those who act justly, namely good reputations, honors, and rewards. But G&A say that won't do. For they say that those are the profits that come, not of acting justly, but of being thought to act justly. And they say that if that is all that their elders can say for justice, then the appropriate conclusion for the young to draw is not that they ought to act justly, but rather that they ought to seem to act justly.

However, Socrates believes that the young ought to act justly, and not merely to seem to act justly. Therefore, would he please tell G&A how justice profits its possessors "because of its very self" and not because of the public rewards it brings.

What emerges from G&A's imposing that constraint on Socrates's answer is that they assume the following:

*Ought Only If Profitable Thesis*: Alfred ought to φ only if he would profit by φ-ing.

They say that in the case of justice, the profit has to issue from what justice *is*. Presumably they would say that in the case of the other virtues, the profits have to have different sources — for example, what generosity *is* in the case of generosity. But for each there has to be *a* profit.

Socrates accepts their constraint on his answer to their question, so we can conclude that he too assumes the Ought Only If Profitable Thesis.

We can say about all three of them, then: they think that if a person asks "Why ought I do what is right?" there had better be an answer — an answer that explains why we would be warranted in replying "You'll profit if you do."

But what is the warrant? In what way exactly would Alfred profit by repaying Bert? We can therefore see why G&A and Socrates think that G&A's question is a hard one. For while the facts I supplied entitle us to assume that justice requires Alfred to repay Bert, it is far from obvious how they could be thought to guarantee that Alfred would profit if he repaid Bert.

3

But perhaps we should just reject G&A's question? For there is room for an objection to the Ought Only If Profitable Thesis: surely it can't be right to think that Alfred ought to repay Bert only if sheer selfishness would itself motivate him to do so!

There is room for defense of the Ought Only If Profitable Thesis against that objection to it. A defender might reply as follows.

> "You bring too constrained a notion of profit to bear on it.
>
> "People often obtain 'personal profits' by doing the things they do. Let us say that Alice obtains a personal profit by doing a thing if an outcome of her doing it is her getting something for herself, where she values her getting it for herself. Thus suppose Alice sold a short story she wrote, and thereby got some money for herself, where she valued her getting that money for herself. It follows that she obtained a personal profit by selling the short story.
>
> "Let us say that Alice obtains an 'impersonal profit' by doing a thing if an outcome of her doing it is her getting something for others, where she values her getting it for them. Thus suppose Alice sent a check to Oxfam, and thereby got some benefits for others, where she valued her getting those benefits for them; it follows that she obtained an impersonal profit by sending the check to Oxfam.
>
> "Three things are worth stress. First: people do not act only in order to bring about that they get something good for themselves; they often act in order to bring about that others get something good for those others.[1] We can certainly suppose that Alice got a personal profit by sending that check to Oxfam, for we can suppose that by sending that check she got something for herself that she valued her getting, namely the satisfaction that comes of helping others. But we can also suppose that it was not in order to get satisfaction for herself that she sent her check, rather that it was in order to get benefits for others.
>
> "Second: profits of both of those two kinds really are profits. What makes it the case that you obtain a profit by doing a thing is that your doing it has among

---

1. G&A say it is widely thought that people would always act unjustly if they could get away with it — as they could if, for example, they acquired the mythical Ring of Gyges, which enables its owner to become invisible whenever he wishes. But that is surely an excessively sour view of what people are like. Hume, for example, rejects it in the selection reprinted in this chapter. [Thomson's note.]

its outcomes something that you value — whether the outcome that you value is your getting something for yourself, or your getting something for others.

"Third: a person's act has many outcomes, some of which are personal or impersonal profits, and others of which are personal or impersonal losses. Suppose that another outcome of Alice's selling her story was gloom in her roommate, who also writes fiction but who has had no success with hers; and suppose also that Alice places a negative value on her roommate's feeling gloomy. Then Alice's selling her story produced at least one loss for her (an impersonal loss) as well as at least one profit for her (a personal profit). Let us say that a person profits *on balance* by φ-ing just in case the sum of the amounts of profit he or she obtains by φ-ing, minus the sum of the amounts of loss, is greater than that which he or she would have obtained by doing anything else that was open to him or her at the time. To ensure clarity, then, let us rewrite the Ought Only If Profitable Thesis as follows:

> *Ought Only If Profitable Thesis*: Alfred ought to φ only if he would profit on balance by φ-ing.

"So in sum, accepting the thesis does not require you to accept that Alfred ought to repay Bert only if sheer selfishness would itself motivate him to do so. If Alfred values Bert's relief from need more than he values keeping the ten dollars that he owes Bert, then he will profit on balance from giving it to Bert. But if Alfred were selfish, he wouldn't be motivated to give the ten dollars to Bert: that is because if he were selfish, he wouldn't value Bert's relief from need more than he values keeping the ten dollars that he owes Bert."

This reply may allay some of the mistrust with which we initially regarded the thesis. But we might wonder *why* we should agree that Alfred ought to repay Bert only if he would profit on balance by doing it. What has whether Alfred would profit got to do with whether he ought to repay Bert?

# 4

Many people would say that the answer to that question lies in the popular idea that there are tight connections first between what a person ought to do and what it would be rational for the person to do, and second between what it would be rational for the person to do and what it would profit the person to do. For suppose that

> *Ought Only If Rational Thesis*: Alfred ought to φ only if it would be rational for him to φ.

and

> *Rational Only If Profitable Thesis*: It would be rational for Alfred to φ only if he would profit on balance by φ-ing.

are true. They jointly entail

> *Ought Only If Profitable Thesis:* Alfred ought to φ only if he would profit
> on balance by φ-ing.

But those two premises seem very plausible.

Notice that if we accept the conclusion on the ground of those two premises, and someone asks us "Why ought I do what is right?" then we can say not only "You'll profit if you do" but also "Rationality requires you to."

# 5

But should we accept those two premises? I begin with the second, namely the Rational Only If Profitable Thesis.

Suppose that Alfred's child now has an infection that only penicillin cures. Alfred, however, justifiably believes that penicillin is poisonous. (He was told so by people he has every reason to trust.) So it would be rational for him to refuse to allow his child to be given penicillin. The thesis yields that it would therefore profit him on balance to refuse. But on the assumption that he greatly values his child's life, he would lose (rather than profit) if he refused. So the thesis won't do.

Another route to that conclusion is as follows. By hypothesis, Alfred would not profit by refusing. The thesis therefore yields that his refusing would not be rational — thus that his refusing would be irrational. But given what he justifiably believes, his refusing would not be irrational. Alfred's refusing would issue from his being ill-informed, not from his being irrational. So (again) the thesis won't do.

The explanation of the fact that the thesis won't do is the fact that rationality and irrationality are "in the head." They are not a function of what will or will not happen, or of whether a person has this or that piece of information; rather they are a function of how well or ill the person reasons from what he or she is justified in believing.

The fact that rationality is in the head lies behind a very familiar contemporary account of what rationality requires of a person.[2]

Suppose you justifiably believe that your options for action here and now are φ-ing, ψ-ing, and so on.

Next suppose you justifiably believe that if you φ, then the following outcomes may come about: $O_{\phi 1}$, $O_{\phi 2}$, and so on. Suppose further that you justifiably believe that if you φ, then the probability that outcome $O_{\phi 1}$ will come about is $P_{O\phi 1}$. Suppose also that you justifiably believe that the amount to which $O_{\phi 1}$ is valuable is $V_{O\phi 1}$. (Since you might justifiably believe that $O_{\phi 1}$ is of negative rather than positive value, $V_{O\phi 1}$ might be a negative number.) Then let us say that the expected value to you of $O_{\phi 1}$ is

---

2. Kant can be interpreted as offering a different account of what rationality requires of a person: on his view, what it requires is acting in accord with the Categorical Imperative. See the selection from Kant in this chapter. [Thomson's note.]

$P_{O\phi1}$ times $V_{O\phi1}$. Similarly, the expected value to you of $O_{\phi2}$ is $P_{O\phi2}$ times $V_{O\phi2}$. And so on. Then let us say that the expected value to you of your $\phi$-ing is the sum of the expected values to you of $O_{\phi1}$, $O_{\phi2}$, and so on.

Similarly, the expected value to you of your $\psi$-ing is the sum of the expected values to you of $O_{\psi1}$, $O_{\psi2}$, and so on. And so on for all of the options you justifiably believe you now have.

Finally, let us say that you maximize your expected value just in case you choose the act that has the greatest expected value to you.

According to the theory of rationality I referred to, that is exactly what rationality requires of you. Thus if your $\phi$-ing has the greatest expected value to you, then you maximize your expected value by $\phi$-ing; and what rationality requires you to do is therefore to $\phi$ — or anyway to try to $\phi$, if, as it might turn out, you were mistaken in thinking you could $\phi$.

That is a *very* plausible idea. So it is very plausible that we should reject the Rational Only If Profitable Thesis, and accept, instead:

*Rational Only If Maximizes Expected Value Thesis:* It would be rational for Alfred to $\phi$ only if he would maximize his expected value by $\phi$-ing.

This thesis yields (as an account of rationality should yield) that it would be irrational for Alfred to allow his child to be given penicillin.

# 6

Let us turn now to the first of the two premises of section 4, namely the Ought Only If Rational Thesis. Given the thesis about rationality that we reached in section 5, that first premise won't do. For the thesis about rationality yields that it would be irrational for Alfred to allow his child to be given penicillin. But he ought to. Alfred's mistakenly believing that penicillin is poisonous has no bearing on what he ought to do: what he ought to do turns on what would be best for his child — and by hypothesis, what would be best for his child is for it to be given penicillin.

Since Alfred justifiably believes that penicillin is poisonous, he will not be at fault, he will not be blameworthy, if he refuses to allow his child to be given penicillin. But he himself will agree that he ought to have allowed it to be given penicillin when he learns, after its death, that allowing this would have saved it.

So we must reject the Ought Only If Rational Thesis.

# 7

Having to give up the Ought Only If Rational Thesis may well seem unfortunate. But perhaps we can retain what made it seem plausible if we revise it. Let us take seriously the fact that the difficulty we looked at in the preceding section issued from Alfred's believing, falsely, that penicillin is poisonous. We might then think: the answer to the question of which act would maximize Alfred's expected value rested heavily on his having had that false belief. No wonder there was trouble for the Ought Only If Rational Thesis! Maximizing expected value is surely at the heart of rationality, but not where maximizing expected value is at the mercy of false beliefs.

So let us impose a constraint that makes false beliefs irrelevant. Imagine the following about Abigail. (i) Whenever she can do a thing, she knows she can. (ii) If she knows she can do a thing, she knows what outcomes her doing it would issue in. (iii) If an outcome that her doing a thing would issue in has value, positive or negative, then she knows that it has value, and how much. That is, she knows all the actual values of all the actual outcomes of her doing the thing. Call Abigail "Relevantly Well-Informed." *A fortiori*, she has no relevant false beliefs.

Hardly anybody is like Abigail in that respect. (Is anybody?) Alfred certainly isn't. But let us now ask what rationality would require of him if he were Relevantly Well-Informed. If he were, then he would not make the mistake about penicillin that he actually made, and rationality would require him to allow his child to be given penicillin. That, of course, is exactly what he ought to do.

More generally, we can retain a tight connection between rationality and what a person ought to do, while avoiding the difficulty that was made for that connection by mistaken beliefs, if we reject the Ought Only If Rational Thesis in favor of:

> *Revised Ought Only If Rational Thesis*: Alfred ought to φ only if it would be rational for him to φ if he were Relevantly Well-Informed.

Notice that if we accept the revised thesis, and someone asks "Why ought I do what is right?" then while we can't reply "Rationality requires you to," we can reply "Rationality requires you to if you are, or would require you to if you were, free of relevant false beliefs."

# 8

Here, then, is what we have replaced the two premises of section 4 with:

> *Rational Only If Maximizes Expected Value Thesis*: It would be rational for Alfred to φ only if he would maximize his expected value by φ-ing.

and

> *Revised Ought Only If Rational Thesis*: Alfred ought to φ only if it would be rational for him to φ if he were Relevantly Well-Informed.

These theses are weaker than the two premises of section 4, and they don't entail the Ought Only If Profitable Thesis. But they do entail something weaker, namely:

> *Revised Ought Only Profitable Thesis*: Alfred ought to φ only if he would profit on balance by φ-ing if he were Relevantly Well-Informed.

For suppose that Alfred ought to φ. Then from the Revised Ought Only If Rational Thesis we can conclude that it would be rational for him to φ if he were Relevantly Well-Informed. So suppose he is Relevantly Well-Informed; it follows that it would be rational for him to φ. Then from the Rational Only If Maximizes Expected Value Thesis we can conclude that he would maximize his expected value by φ-ing. Since he is (as we are supposing) Relevantly Well-Informed, maximizing his expected value is maximizing actual value. It follows that his φ-ing would actually issue in outcomes that he (rightly) thinks would have a higher value than those that his doing anything else would issue in. So he would profit on balance by φ-ing.

And we can suppose that the fact that Alfred ought to repay Bert makes no trouble for this thesis. For if Alfred were Relevantly Well-Informed, then we can suppose that he would (rightly) regard Bert's being relieved of his needs as having a higher value than his retaining the ten dollars that he owes Bert — higher enough for his repaying Bert to profit him on balance.

Moreover, we have yet another answer available if someone asks us "Why ought I do what is right?" We can reply "If you were free of relevant false beliefs, then it would profit you to do what is right."

9

But should we accept the Revised Ought Only If Profitable Thesis? Not unless we are prepared to accept:

> Alfred ought to φ only if the actual outcomes of his φ-ing would be of greater actual value than the actual outcomes of his doing any of the other things it is open to him to do at the time.

And there really is no good reason to accept *that* unless we accept a familiar moral theory, namely:

> *Consequentialism*: For it to be the case that a person ought to φ is for it to be the case that his or her φ-ing would maximize actual value.

Sympathetic attention to G&A's question "Why ought I do what justice requires?" led us by plausible-looking steps along an unusual route to Consequentialism.

There is a rich literature on Consequentialism — many people have written in support of it, many in objection to it.[3] A familiar kind of objection to it issues from considerations of justice. Suppose that Alfred's failing to repay Bert would issue in outcomes that have more value than the outcomes his doing anything else would have. A Consequentialist is therefore committed to the conclusion that Alfred ought not repay Bert.

---

3. See, for example, the selections in this volume by Mill and Scanlon in chapter 16, "How Do We Reason about What Is Right?" [Thomson's note.]

But many people think that since Alfred's repaying Bert is required by justice, he ought to repay Bert, despite the gain in value that would issue from his not doing so.[4]

More generally, the considerations that bear on whether a person ought to φ differ in the way they bear on that question. Some considerations would plainly be outcomes of the person's φ-ing, and they are thought by many people to bear by having higher or lower value. (Compare Bert's needs' being met if Alfred repays him what he owes him.) Others, however, are not plainly *outcomes* of the person's φ-ing. The person's φ-ing's being just — or generous, kind, loyal, or responsible — are among the ones that are not. How these bear on whether the person ought to φ is disputable. But it is a very plausible idea that they bear by straightforwardly entailing that the person ought to φ.

10

If we opt for that very plausible idea, then we are accepting that it is trivially true that if justice requires Alfred to repay Bert, then Alfred ought to repay Bert, and that G&A's question is not the hard question they thought it was.

They should have asked Socrates a different question: what makes it the case that justice requires Alfred to repay Bert? Alternatively put: what makes it the case that justice requires Alfred to repay Bert, given that if justice does require him to repay Bert, then it trivially follows that he ought to? For an answer to the question why justice requires Alfred to repay Bert should *itself* supply an answer to the question why Alfred ought to repay Bert.

And if a person is told that he or she ought to do a thing because doing it would be right, and therefore asks "Why ought I do what is right?" then we should reply "Because of whatever it is that makes your doing the thing *be* right." We should not be misled into thinking that anything more than that is called for.

## TEST YOUR UNDERSTANDING

1. What does Thomson mean by "rational"? Offer your own example in which what it is rational to do to further one's goals, in Thomson's sense of "rational," may fail to coincide with what one *ought* to do to further one's goals.

2. Toward the end of her essay, Thomson considers a case in which Alfred's repaying a debt to Bert would not promote the goals that Alfred cares about. Nevertheless, she concludes that Alfred ought to repay Bert. Briefly, explain why Thomson believes that Alfred ought to pay Bert even if it does not advance what Alfred most cares about.

---

4. A deeper objection to Consequentialism, and indeed, to much of what discussion of what G&A had in mind has led us to, is that it isn't clear what property we can be thought to be ascribing to an outcome of an act in saying of it that it "has value." [Thomson's note.]

## NOTES AND QUESTIONS

1. *Ought one do what it is irrational to do?* Thomson considers a two-premise **argument** for the conclusion that Alfred ought to repay a debt owed to Bert only if Alfred would profit by repaying Bert:

    (i) Alfred ought to repay Bert only if it would be rational for Alfred to repay Bert.

    (ii) It would be rational for Alfred to repay Bert only if Alfred would profit (on balance) by repaying Bert.

    Conclusion: Therefore, Alfred ought to repay Bert only if Alfred would profit (on balance) by repaying Bert.

    Thomson rejects both premises. She rejects the first premise because she contends that sometimes one ought to do something that it would be irrational to do. How is that possible? She rejects the second premise because it could be rational for Alfred to pay Bert with the aim of profiting from repayment even though Alfred might not in fact profit. How is that possible? Do you think either premise can be defended against her challenge? Would your defense involve using the terms "ought," "rational," and "irrational," in the same way that she does?

2. *Are we mistaken to ask the question "Why do what is right?"* Thomson argues that once one grasps the considerations in favor of an action that one ought, in fact, to perform, there is no sense in asking the further question why one *should* do what one ought to do. The reasons that make that action the right thing to do are the very same reasons that one ought to do it. It is a mistake to try to answer the question "Why do the action that is right?" as though it were a further question from the question "Why is that action the right action?"

    When philosophers claim that others have made a mistake, they often try to show *how* this mistake was made. It makes an argument more convincing to show where its opposition misstepped.

    *Exercise:* Explain how Thomson might be correct but yet some reasonable people might have mistakenly supposed that the question of whether an action is right and why one should perform it are separate questions. Your explanation should try to pinpoint the error in reasoning that leads Thomson's opponents astray.

## David Hume (1711–1776)

Hume was a Scottish philosopher, essayist, and historian, and a central figure in Western philosophy. His *Treatise of Human Nature* (1739), *An Enquiry Concerning Human Understanding* (1748), and *An Enquiry Concerning the Principles of Morals* (1751) have been very influential. (The two *Enquiries* revise material from the *Treatise*.) Many contemporary philosophical discussions in epistemology, metaphysics, and ethics are reactions to Hume's theories and arguments. Hume's *Dialogues Concerning Natural Religion* (published posthumously in 1779) is a classic attack on "design arguments" for the existence of God.

# OF THE PASSIONS
from *A Treatise of Human Nature, Book II*

## Section III. Of the Influencing Motives of the Will.

Nothing is more usual in philosophy, and even in common life, than to talk of the combat of passion and reason, to give the preference to reason, and to assert that men are only so far virtuous as they conform themselves to its dictates. Every rational creature, 'tis said, is oblig'd to regulate his actions by reason; and if any other motive or principle challenge the direction of his conduct, he ought to oppose it, 'till it be entirely subdu'd, or at least brought to a conformity with that superior principle. . . . In order to shew the fallacy of all this philosophy, I shall endeavour to prove *first*, that reason alone can never be a motive to any action of the will; and *secondly*, that it can never oppose passion in the direction of the will.

The understanding exerts itself after two different ways, as it judges from demonstration or probability; as it regards the abstract relations of our ideas, or those relations of objects, of which experience only gives us information.[1] I believe it scarce will be asserted, that the first species of reasoning alone is ever the cause of any action. As its proper province is the world of ideas, and as the will always places us in that of realities, demonstration and volition seem, upon that account, to be totally remov'd, from each other. Mathematics, indeed, are useful in all mechanical operations, and arithmetic in almost every art and profession: But 'tis not of themselves they have any influence. Mechanics are the art of regulating the motions of *bodies to some design'd end or purpose*; and the reason why we employ arithmetic in fixing the proportions of numbers, is only that we may discover the proportions of their influence and operation. A merchant is desirous of knowing the sum total of his accounts with any person: Why? but that he may learn what sum will have the same *effects* in paying his debt, and going to market, as all the particular articles taken together. Abstract or demonstrative reasoning, therefore, never influences any of our actions, but only as it directs our judgment concerning causes and effects; which leads us to the second operation of the understanding.

'Tis obvious, that when we have the prospect of pain or pleasure from any object, we feel a consequent emotion of aversion or propensity, and are carry'd to avoid or embrace what will give us this uneasiness or satisfaction. 'Tis also obvious, that this emotion rests not here, but making us cast our view on every side, comprehends whatever objects are connected with its original one by the relation of cause and effect. Here then reasoning takes place to discover this relation; and according as our reasoning

---

1. For Hume, "ideas" are those mental items that are images or copies of perceptions or what he calls "impressions." The category of impressions encompasses "sensations, passions, and emotions." The perception you have of black ink while reading this text is an impression; your thought about or recollection of that impression is, in Hume's terminology, an idea. "Relations of ideas" concern how different ideas relate to each other, e.g., they seem similar or distinct, one seems to lead to another, one seems to exclude another, or together, they number a certain amount.

varies, our actions receive a subsequent variation. But 'tis evident in this case, that the impulse arises not from reason, but is only directed by it. 'Tis from the prospect of pain or pleasure that the aversion or propensity arises towards any object: And these emotions extend themselves to the causes and effects of that object, as they are pointed out to us by reason and experience. It can never in the least concern us to know, that such objects are causes, and such others effects, if both the causes and effects be indifferent to us. Where the objects themselves do not affect us, their connexion can never give them any influence; and 'tis plain, that as reason is nothing but the discovery of this connexion, it cannot be by its means that the objects are able to affect us.

Since reason alone can never produce any action, or give rise to volition, I infer, that the same faculty is as incapable of preventing volition, or of disputing the preference with any passion or emotion. . . . Nothing can oppose or retard the impulse of passion, but a contrary impulse; and if this contrary impulse ever arises from reason, that latter faculty must have an original influence on the will, and must be able to cause, as well as hinder any act of volition. But if reason has no original influence, 'tis impossible it can withstand any principle, which has such an efficacy, or ever keep the mind in suspense a moment. Thus it appears, that the principle, which opposes our passion, cannot be the same with reason, and is only call'd so in an improper sense. We speak not strictly and philosophically when we talk of the combat of passion and of reason. Reason is, and ought only to be the slave of the passions, and can never pretend to any other office than to serve and obey them.

. . . When I am angry, I am actually possest with the passion, and in that emotion have no more a reference to any other object, than when I am thirsty, or sick, or more than five foot high. 'Tis impossible, therefore, that this passion can be oppos'd by, or be contradictory to truth and reason; since this contradiction consists in the disagreement of ideas, consider'd as copies, with those objects, which they represent.

. . . [A]s nothing can be contrary to truth or reason, except what has a reference to it, and as the judgments of our understanding only have this reference, it must follow, that passions can be contrary to reason only so far as they are *accompany'd* with some judgment or opinion. According to this principle, which is so obvious and natural, 'tis only in two senses, that any affection can be call'd unreasonable. First, When a passion, such as hope or fear, grief or joy, despair or security, is founded on the supposition of the existence of objects, which really do not exist. Secondly, When in exerting any passion in action, we chuse means insufficient for the design'd end, and deceive ourselves in our judgment of causes and effects. Where a passion is neither founded on false suppositions, nor chuses means insufficient for the end, the understanding can neither justify nor condemn it. 'Tis not contrary to reason to prefer the destruction of the whole world to the scratching of my finger. 'Tis not contrary to reason for me to chuse my total ruin, to prevent the least uneasiness of a . . . person wholly unknown to me. 'Tis as little contrary to reason to prefer even my own acknowledg'd lesser good to my greater, and have a more ardent affection for the former than the latter. A trivial good may, from certain circumstances, produce a desire superior to what arises from the greatest and most valuable enjoyment. . . . In short, a passion must be accompany'd with some false judgment, in order to its being unreasonable; and even then 'tis not the passion, properly speaking, which is unreasonable, but the judgment.

The consequences are evident. Since a passion can never, in any sense, be call'd unreasonable, but when founded on a false supposition, or when it chuses means insufficient for the design'd end, 'tis impossible, that reason and passion can ever oppose each other, or dispute for the government of the will and actions. . . .

# OF MORALS
from *A Treatise of Human Nature, Book III*

## Section I. Moral Distinctions not Deriv'd from Reason

If morality had naturally no influence on human passions and actions, 'twere in vain to take such pains to inculcate it; and nothing wou'd be more fruitless than that multitude of rules and precepts, with which all moralists abound. . . . [Morality] 'tis supposed to influence our passions and actions, and to go beyond the calm and indolent judgments of the understanding. And this is confirm'd by common experience, which informs us, that men are often govern'd by their duties, and are deter'd from some actions by the opinion of injustice, and impell'd to others by that of obligation.

Since morals, therefore, have an influence on the actions and affections, it follows, that they cannot be deriv'd from reason; and that because reason alone, as we have already prov'd, can never have any such influence. Morals excite passions, and produce or prevent actions. Reason of itself is utterly impotent in this particular. The rules of morality, therefore, are not conclusions of our reason.

Reason is the discovery of truth or falsehood. Truth or falsehood consists in an agreement or disagreement either to the *real* relations of ideas, or to *real* existence and matter of fact. Whatever, therefore, is not susceptible of this agreement or disagreement, is incapable of being true or false, and can never be an object of our reason. Now 'tis evident our passions, volitions, and actions, are not susceptible of any such agreement or disagreement; being original facts and realities, compleat in themselves, and implying no reference to other passions, volitions, and actions. 'Tis impossible, therefore, they can be pronounced either true or false, and be either contrary or conformable to reason.

. . . Actions may be laudable or blameable; but they cannot be reasonable or unreasonable: Laudable or blameable, therefore, are not the same with reasonable or unreasonable. The merit and demerit of actions frequently contradict, and sometimes control our natural propensities. But reason has no such influence. Moral distinctions, therefore, are not the offspring of reason. Reason is wholly inactive, and can never be the source of so active a principle as conscience, or a sense of morals.

. . . [R]eason, in a strict and philosophical sense, can have an influence on our conduct only after two ways: Either when it excites a passion by informing us of the existence of something which is a proper object of it; or when it discovers the connexion of causes and effects, so as to afford us means of exerting any passion. These are the only kinds of judgment, which can accompany our actions, or can be said to produce them in any manner; and it must be allow'd, that these judgments may often be false and erroneous. A person may be affected with passion, by supposing a pain or pleasure to lie in an object, which has no tendency to produce either of these sensations, or which produces the contrary to what is imagin'd. A person may also take false measures for the attaining his end, and may retard, by his foolish conduct, instead of forwarding the execution of any project. These false judgments may be thought to affect the passions and actions, which are connected with them, and may be said to render them unreasonable, in a figurative and improper way of speaking. But tho' this be acknowledg'd, 'tis easy to observe, that these errors are so far from being the source of all immorality, that they are commonly very innocent, and draw no manner of guilt upon the person who is so unfortunate as to fall into them. . . . No one can ever regard such errors as a defect in my moral character. . . .

Thus upon the whole, 'tis impossible, that the distinction betwixt moral good and evil, can be made by reason; since that distinction has an influence upon our actions, of which reason alone is incapable. . . .

. . . Take any action allow'd to be vicious: Wilful murder, for instance. Examine it in all lights, and see if you can find that matter of fact, or real existence, which you call *vice*. In which-ever way you take it, you find only certain passions, motives, volitions and thoughts. There is no other matter of fact in the case. The vice entirely escapes you, as long as you consider the object. You never can find it, till you turn your reflexion into your own breast, and find a sentiment of disapprobation, which arises in you, towards this action. Here is a matter of fact; but 'tis the object of feeling, not of reason. It lies in yourself, not in the object. So that when you pronounce any action or character to be vicious, you mean nothing, but that from the constitution of your nature you have a feeling or sentiment of blame from the contemplation of it. Vice and virtue, therefore, may be compar'd to sounds, colours, heat and cold, which, according to modern philosophy, are not qualities in objects, but perceptions in the mind: And this discovery in morals, like that other in physics, . . . has little or no influence on practice. Nothing can be more real, or concern us more, than our own sentiments of pleasure and uneasiness; and if these be favourable to virtue, and unfavourable to vice, no more can be requisite to the regulation of our conduct and behaviour.

I cannot forbear adding . . . an observation, which may, perhaps, be found of some importance. In every system of morality, which I have hitherto met with, . . . the author proceeds for some time in the ordinary way of reasoning, and establishes the being of a God, or makes observations concerning human affairs; when of a sudden I am surpriz'd to find, that instead of the usual copulations of propositions, *is*, and *is not*, I meet with no proposition that is not connected with an *ought*, or an *ought not*. This change is imperceptible; but is, however, of the last consequence. For as this *ought*, or *ought not*, expresses some new relation or affirmation, 'tis necessary that it shou'd be observ'd and explain'd; and at the same time that a reason should be given, for what seems altogether inconceivable, how this new relation can be a deduction from others, which are entirely different from it. . . .

# Section II: Moral Distinctions Deriv'd from a Moral Sense

Thus the course of the argument leads us to conclude, that since vice and virtue are not discoverable merely by reason, or the comparison of ideas, it must be by means of some impression or sentiment they occasion, that we are able to mark the difference betwixt them. . . . Morality, therefore, is more properly felt than judg'd of; tho' this feeling or sentiment is commonly so soft and gentle, that we are apt to confound it with an idea, according to our common custom of taking all things for the same, which have any near resemblance to each other.

. . . An action, or sentiment, or character is virtuous or vicious; why? because its view causes a pleasure or uneasiness of a particular kind. In giving a reason, therefore, for the pleasure or uneasiness, we sufficiently explain the vice or virtue. To have the sense of virtue, is nothing but to *feel* a satisfaction of a particular kind from the contemplation of a character. The very *feeling* constitutes our praise or admiration. . . .

No[t] every sentiment of pleasure or pain, which arises from characters and actions, of that *peculiar* kind, which makes us praise or condemn. The good qualities of an enemy are hurtful to us; but may still command our esteem and respect. 'Tis only when a character is considered in general, without reference to our particular interest, that it causes such a feeling or sentiment, as denominates it morally good or evil. 'Tis true, those sentiments, from interest and morals, are apt to be confounded, and naturally run into one another. It seldom happens, that we do not think an enemy vicious, and can distinguish betwixt his opposition to our interest and real villainy or baseness. But this hinders not, but that the sentiments are, in themselves, distinct.

. . . [I]f ever there was any thing, which cou'd be call'd natural . . . the sentiments of morality certainly may; since there never was any nation of the world, nor any single person in any nation, who was utterly depriv'd of them, and who never, in any instance, shew'd the least approbation or dislike of manners. These sentiments are so rooted in our constitution and temper, that without entirely confounding the human mind by disease or madness, 'tis impossible to extirpate and destroy them.

. . . [V]irtue is distinguished by the pleasure, and vice by the pain, that any action, sentiment or character gives us by the mere view and contemplation. . . .

## WHY UTILITY PLEASES
from *An Enquiry Concerning the Principles of Morals*

---

# Part I

It seems so natural a thought to ascribe to their utility the praise, which we bestow on the social virtues, that one would expect to meet with this principle everywhere in moral writers, as the chief foundation of their reasoning and enquiry. In common life, we may observe, that the circumstance of utility is always appealed to; nor is it supposed, that a greater eulogy can be given to any man, than to display his usefulness to the public, and enumerate the services, which he has performed to mankind and society. . . .

From the apparent usefulness of the social virtues, it has readily been inferred by sceptics, both ancient and modern, that all moral distinctions arise from education, and were, at first, invented, and afterwards encouraged, by the art of politicians, in order to render men tractable, and subdue their natural ferocity and selfishness, which incapacitated them for society. This principle, indeed, of precept and education, must so far be owned to have a powerful influence, that it may frequently increase or diminish, beyond their natural standard, the sentiments of approbation or dislike; and may even, in particular instances, create, without any natural principle, a new sentiment of this kind; as is evident in all superstitious practices and observances: But that *all* moral affection or dislike arises from this origin, will never surely be allowed by any judicious enquirer. Had nature made no such distinction, founded on the original constitution of the mind, the words, *honourable* and *shameful, lovely* and *odious, noble* and *despicable,* had never had place in any language; nor could politicians, had they invented these terms, ever have been able to render them intelligible, or make them convey any idea to the audience. . . .

The social virtues must, therefore, be allowed to have a natural beauty and amiableness, which, at first, antecedent to all precept or education, recommends them to the esteem of uninstructed mankind, and engages their affections. And as the public utility of these virtues is the chief circumstance, whence they derive their merit, it follows, that the end, which they have a tendency to promote, must be some way agreeable to us, and take hold of some natural affection. It must please, either from considerations of self-interest, or from more generous motives and regards.

It has often been asserted, that, as every man has a strong connexion with society, and perceives the impossibility of his solitary subsistence, he becomes, on that account, favourable to all those habits or principles, which promote order in society, and insure to him the quiet possession of so inestimable a blessing. As much as we value our own happiness and welfare, as much must we applaud the practice of justice and humanity, by which alone the social confederacy can be maintained, and every man reap the fruits of mutual protection and assistance.

This deduction of morals from self-love, or a regard to private interest, is an obvious thought, . . . yet, the voice of nature and experience seems plainly to oppose the selfish theory.

We frequently bestow praise on virtuous actions, performed in very distant ages and remote countries; where the utmost subtlety of imagination would not discover any appearance of self-interest, or find any connexion of our present happiness and security with events so widely separated from us.

A generous, a brave, a noble deed, performed by an adversary, commands our approbation; while in its consequences it may be acknowledged prejudicial to our particular interest.

Where private advantage concurs with general affection for virtue, we readily perceive and avow the mixture of these distinct sentiments, which have a very different feeling and influence on the mind. We praise, perhaps, with more alacrity, where the generous humane action contributes to our particular interest: But the topics of praise, which we insist on, are very wide of this circumstance. And we may attempt to bring over others to our sentiments, without endeavouring to convince them, that they reap any advantage from the actions which we recommend to their approbation and applause. . . .

Usefulness is agreeable, and engages our approbation. This is a matter of fact, confirmed by daily observation. But, *useful*? For what? For somebody's interest, surely. Whose interest then? Not our own only: For our approbation frequently extends farther. It must, therefore, be the interest of those, who are served by the character or action approved of; and these we may conclude, however remote, are not totally indifferent to us. By opening up this principle, we shall discover one great source of moral distinctions.

# Part II

Self-love is a principle in human nature of such extensive energy, and the interest of each individual is, in general, so closely connected with that of the community, that those philosophers were excusable, who fancied that all our concern for the public might be resolved into a concern for our own happiness and preservation. . . .

But notwithstanding this frequent confusion of interests, . . . we have found instances, in which private interest was separate from public; in which it was even contrary: And yet we observed the moral sentiment to continue, notwithstanding this disjunction of interests. And wherever these distinct interests sensibly concurred, we always found a sensible increase of the sentiment, and a more warm affection to virtue, and detestation of vice. . . . Compelled by these instances, we must renounce the theory, which accounts for every moral sentiment by the principle of self-love. We must adopt a more public affection, and allow, that the interests of society are not, even on their own account, entirely, indifferent to us. Usefulness is only a tendency to a certain end; and it is a contradiction in terms, that anything pleases as means to an end, where the end itself no wise affects us. If usefulness, therefore, be a source of moral sentiment, and if this usefulness be not always considered with a reference to self; it follows, that everything, which contributes to the happiness of society, recommends itself directly to our approbation and good-will. Here is a principle, which accounts, in great part, for the origin of morality: And what need we seek for abstruse and remote systems, when there occurs one so obvious and natural?[1]

---

1. It is needless to push our researches so far as to ask, why we have humanity or a fellow-feeling with others. It is sufficient, that this is experienced to be a principle in human nature. We must stop somewhere in our examination of causes; and there are, in every science, some general principles, beyond which we cannot hope to find any principle more general. No man is absolutely indifferent to the happiness and misery of others. The first has a natural tendency to give pleasure; the second, pain. This every one may find in himself. [Hume's note.]

Have we any difficulty to comprehend the force of humanity and benevolence? Or to conceive, that the very aspect of happiness, joy, prosperity, gives pleasure; that of pain, suffering, sorrow, communicates uneasiness? The human countenance, says Horace,[2] borrows smiles or tears from the human countenance. Reduce a person to solitude, and he loses all enjoyment, except either of the sensual or speculative kind; and that because the movements of his heart are not forwarded by correspondent movements in his fellow-creatures. The signs of sorrow and mourning, though arbitrary, affect us with melancholy; but the natural symptoms, tears and cries and groans, never fail to infuse compassion and uneasiness. And if the effects of misery touch us in so lively a manner; can we be supposed altogether insensible or indifferent towards its causes; when a malicious or treacherous character and behaviour are presented to us?

We enter, I shall suppose, into a convenient, warm, well-contrived apartment: We necessarily receive a pleasure from its very survey; because it presents us with the pleasing ideas of ease, satisfaction, and enjoyment. The hospitable, good-humoured, humane landlord appears. This circumstance surely must embellish the whole; nor can we easily forbear reflecting, with pleasure, on the satisfaction which results to every one from his intercourse and good-offices.

His whole family, by the freedom, ease, confidence, and calm enjoyment, diffused over their countenances, sufficiently express their happiness. I have a pleasing sympathy in the prospect of so much joy, and can never consider the source of it, without the most agreeable emotions.

He tells me, that an oppressive and powerful neighbour had attempted to dispossess him of his inheritance, and had long disturbed all his innocent and social pleasures. I feel an immediate indignation arise in me against such violence and injury.

But it is no wonder, he adds, that a private wrong should proceed from a man, who had enslaved provinces, depopulated cities, and made the field and scaffold stream with human blood. I am struck with horror at the prospect of so much misery, and am actuated by the strongest antipathy against its author.

In general, it is certain, that, wherever we go, whatever we reflect on or converse about, everything still presents us with the view of human happiness or misery, and excites in our breast a sympathetic movement of pleasure or uneasiness. In our serious occupations, in our careless amusements, this principle still exerts its active energy. . . .

Any recent event or piece of news, by which the fate of states, provinces, or many individuals is affected, is extremely interesting even to those whose welfare is not immediately engaged. Such intelligence is propagated with celerity, heard with avidity, and enquired into with attention and concern. The interest of society appears, on this occasion, to be in some degree the interest of each individual. The imagination is sure to be affected; though the passions excited may not always be so strong and steady as to have great influence on the conduct and behaviour.

The perusal of a history seems a calm entertainment; but would be no entertainment at all, did not our hearts beat with correspondent movements to those which are described by the historian. . . .

---

2. Quintus Horatius Flaccus (65–8 BCE), Roman poet.

The frivolousness of the subject too, we may observe, is not able to detach us entirely from what carries an image of human sentiment and affection.

When a person stutters, and pronounces with difficulty, we even sympathize with this trivial uneasiness, and suffer for him. . . .

If any man from a cold insensibility, or narrow selfishness of temper, is unaffected with the images of human happiness or misery, he must be equally indifferent to the images of vice and virtue: As, on the other hand, it is always found, that a warm concern for the interests of our species is attended with a delicate feeling of all moral distinctions; a strong resentment of injury done to men; a lively approbation of their welfare. In this particular, though great superiority is observable of one man above another; yet none are so entirely indifferent to the interest of their fellow-creatures, as to perceive no distinctions of moral good and evil, in consequence of the different tendencies of actions and principles. How, indeed, can we suppose it possible in any one, who wears a human heart, that if there be subjected to his censure, one character or system of conduct, which is beneficial, and another which is pernicious to his species or community, be will not so much as give a cool preference to the former, or ascribe to it the smallest merit or regard? Let us suppose such a person ever so selfish; let private interest have ingrossed ever so much his attention; yet in instances, where that is not concerned, he must unavoidably feel *some* propensity to the good of mankind, and make it an object of choice, if everything else be equal. Would any man, who is walking along, tread as willingly on another's gouty toes, whom he has no quarrel with, as on the hard flint and pavement? There is here surely a difference in the case. We surely take into consideration the happiness and misery of others, in weighing the several motives of action, and incline to the former, where no private regards draw us to seek our own promotion or advantage by the injury of our fellow-creatures. And if the principles of humanity are capable, in many instances, of influencing our actions, they must, at all times, have *some* authority over our sentiments, and give us a general approbation of what is useful to society, and blame of what is dangerous or pernicious. The degrees of these sentiments may be the subject of controversy; but the reality of their existence, one should think, must be admitted in every theory or system. . . .

Thus, in whatever light we take this subject, the merit, ascribed to the social virtues, appears still uniform, and arises chiefly from that regard, which the natural sentiment of benevolence engages us to pay to the interests of mankind and society. If we consider the principles of the human make, such as they appear to daily experience and observation, we must, *a priori*,[3] conclude it impossible for such a creature as man to be totally indifferent to the well or ill-being of his fellow-creatures, and not readily, of himself, to pronounce, where nothing gives him any particular bias, that what promotes their happiness is good, what tends to their misery is evil, without any farther regard or consideration. Here then are the faint rudiments, at least, or outlines, of a *general* distinction between actions; and in proportion as the humanity of the person is supposed to encrease,

---

3. For Hume, **a priori** means "without resort to evidence from our sensory experience but ascertainable through the operation of reason alone."

his connexion with those who are injured or benefited, and his lively conception of their misery or happiness; his consequent censure or approbation acquires proportionable vigour. There is no necessity, that a generous action, barely mentioned in an old history or remote gazette, should communicate any strong feelings of applause and admiration. Virtue, placed at such a distance, is like a fixed star, which, though to the eye of reason it may appear as luminous as the sun in his meridian, is so infinitely removed as to affect the senses, neither with light nor heat. Bring this virtue nearer, by our acquaintance or connexion with the persons, or even by an eloquent recital of the case; our hearts are immediately caught, our sympathy enlivened, and our cool approbation converted into the warmest sentiments of friendship and regard. These seem necessary and infallible consequences of the general principles of human nature, as discovered in common life and practice.

Again; reverse these views and reasonings: Consider the matter *a posteriori*;[4] and weighing the consequences, enquire if the merit of social virtue be not, in a great measure, derived from the feelings of humanity, with which it affects the spectators. It appears to be matter of fact, that the circumstance of *utility*, in all subjects, is a source of praise and approbation: That it is constantly appealed to in all moral decisions concerning the merit and demerit of actions: That it is the *sole* source of that high regard paid to justice, fidelity, honour, allegiance, and chastity: That it is inseparable from all the other social virtues, humanity, generosity, charity, affability, lenity, mercy, and moderation: And, in a word, that it is a foundation of the chief part of morals, which has a reference to mankind and our fellow-creatures.

It appears also, that, in our general approbation of characters and manners, the useful tendency of the social virtues moves us not by any regards to self-interest, but has an influence much more universal and extensive. It appears that a tendency to public good, and to the promoting of peace, harmony, and order in society, does always, by affecting the benevolent principles of our frame, engage us on the side of the social virtues. And it appears, as an additional confirmation, that these principles of humanity and sympathy enter so deeply into all our sentiments, and have so powerful an influence, as may enable them to excite the strongest censure and applause.

## TEST YOUR UNDERSTANDING

1.  Hume argues that reason is "but the slave of the passions." What are the two ways that Hume believes that reason can influence our behavior? According to Hume, could an insight of reason, on its own, propel me to quit smoking? If yes, what is that insight and how can it cause me to quit smoking? If not, what else would be necessary?

2.  Hume believes that moral distinctions, e.g., between judgments of good and evil, reflect our sentiments of approval and disapproval toward certain sorts of actions. Briefly explain what distinguishes moral judgments from judgments of self-interest, in his view. How do we know the two are not identical?

---

4. By **a posteriori**, Hume means "in light of the evidence presented to us by our empirical experience."

## NOTES AND QUESTIONS

1.  *Morality and the diversity of moral judgments.* Hume argues that moral distinctions between good and evil reflect the sentiments of approbation and disapprobation (i.e., approval and disapproval) we feel in contemplating certain sorts of actions. Does this mean that he believes that moral judgments are purely a matter of *individual* emotional reactions? Suppose that two people, X and Y, contemplate the same act of willful murder: X disapproves, and so judges the act bad, while Y approves and judges it good. Does Hume's view entail that these two judgments are both correct? How might Hume resist this conclusion?

2.  *Must evil action involve an error of reason?* Suppose Hitler knew all of the facts about the people he murdered and about the consequences of his actions, but he celebrated those consequences and chose to engage in his aggressive crusade of genocide and war because he approved of them. On Hume's view we cannot say that Hitler behaved unreasonably or contrary to reason. For some critics, this marks a stupefying defect in Hume's theory.

    Philippa Foot,[1] however, follows Hume on this point, arguing that the person

    > who rejects morality because he sees no reason to obey its rules can be convicted of villainy but not of inconsistency. Nor will his action necessarily be irrational. Irrational actions are those in which a man in some way defeats his own purposes, doing what is calculated to be disadvantageous or to frustrate his ends. Immorality does not *necessarily* involve any such thing.[2]

    Note that Foot appears to endorse Hume's view that what we have reason to do depends entirely on what we happen to want or care about. To say that someone acts contrary to reason, on this view, is to say that his action fails to promote his ends. So, we cannot say an informed, wholehearted mass murderer like Hitler was "irrational." But, with Hume, she insists that we can say he behaved wrongly and that he was a villain, even if he did not violate any dictates of reason. She and other Humeans do not regard their position as excluding their use of tough moral adjectives and condemnations.

    *Exercise:* Explain how Hume could claim that a fully informed Hitler was a villain who acted wrongly but did not act contrary to reason. Is this plausible? If we are able to charge Hitler, so described, with being an evil, villainous, brutal mass murderer, is there anything important missing from this condemnation? Why might it add an important dimension of criticism to be able to say, in addition, that he acted contrary to reason?

---

1.  Foot's famous article about relativism is excerpted on p. 677 of this anthology.
2.  Philippa Foot "Morality as a System of Hypothetical Imperatives," *Philosophical Review* 81, no. 3 (July, 1972): 305–316, p. 310. For another important modern article decoupling moral criticism from the criticism of irrationality, see Bernard Williams, "Internal and External Reasons," in his *Moral Luck* (Cambridge University Press, 1982). Later in her career, Philippa Foot advanced a different position from her 1972 article. She contended in *Natural Goodness* (Oxford University Press, 2003) that acting morally *is* an aspect of our rationality in virtue of our membership within the species of human beings who must live and cooperate with one another to thrive.

## Immanuel Kant (1724–1804)

Kant was a German philosopher of the Enlightenment whose work extolled the faculty of reason, exploring its powers and limitations. He was born in Königsberg and was a professor at the University of Königsberg. His work exerted and continues to exert a profound influence on the development of modern and contemporary philosophy in ethics, political philosophy, metaphysics, epistemology, the philosophy of mind and of psychology, aesthetics, and the philosophy of religion. His most famous books include *The Critique of Pure Reason* (1781), *Prolegomena to Any Future Metaphysics* (1783), *Groundwork of the Metaphysics of Morals* (1785), *The Critique of Practical Reason* (1788), *The Critique of Judgment* (1790), and *The Metaphysics of Morals* (1797).

# GROUNDWORK OF THE METAPHYSICS OF MORALS

## Preface

Everyone must admit that a law, if it is to hold morally, i.e. as the ground of an obligation, must carry with it absolute necessity; that the command: thou shalt not lie, does not just hold for human beings only, as if other rational beings did not have to heed it; and so with all remaining actual moral laws; hence that the ground of the obligation here must not be sought in the nature of the human being, or in the circumstances of the world in which he is placed, but a priori solely in concepts of pure reason, and that any other prescription that is founded on principles of mere experience — and even a prescription that is in some certain respect universal, in so far as it relies in the least part on empirical grounds, perhaps just for a motivating ground — can indeed be called a practical rule, but never a moral law. . . .

A metaphysics of morals is thus indispensably necessary, not merely on the grounds of speculation, for investigating the source of the practical principles that lie a priori in our reason, but because morals themselves remain subject to all sorts of corruption as long as we lack that guideline and supreme norm by which to judge them correctly. For in the case of what is to be morally good it is not enough that it *conform* with the moral law, but it must also be done *for its sake*; if not, that conformity is only very contingent and precarious, because the immoral ground will indeed now and then produce actions that conform with the law, but in many cases actions that are contrary to it. But now the moral law in its purity and genuineness . . . is to be sought nowhere else than in a pure philosophy; it (metaphysics) must thus come first, and without it there can be no moral philosophy at all; and that which mixes these pure principles in with empirical ones does not even deserve the name of a philosophy . . . much less that of a moral philosophy, since it even infringes on the purity of morals themselves by this intermingling and proceeds contrary to its own end. . . .

The present groundwork, however, is nothing more than the identification and corroboration of the *supreme principle of morality*. . . .

# First Section: Transition from Common to Philosophical Moral Rational Cognition

It is impossible to think of anything at all in the world, or indeed even beyond it, that could be taken to be good without limitation, except a good will. Understanding, wit, judgment, and whatever else the *talents* of the mind may be called, or confidence, resolve, and persistency of intent, as qualities of *temperament*, are no doubt in many respects good and desirable; but they can also be extremely evil and harmful if the will that is to make use of these gifts of nature, and whose distinctive constitution is therefore called *character*, is not good. It is just the same with *gift of fortune*. Power, riches, honor, even health, and the entire well-being and contentment with one's condition, under the name of *happiness*, inspire confidence and thereby quite often overconfidence as well, unless a good will is present to correct and make generally purposive their influence on the mind, and with it also the whole principle for acting; not to mention that a rational impartial spectator can nevermore take any delight in the sight of the uninterrupted prosperity of a being adorned with no feature of a pure and good will, and that a good will thus appears to constitute the indispensable condition even of the worthiness to be happy.

Some qualities are even conducive to this good will itself and can make its work much easier; but regardless of this they have no inner unconditional worth, but always presuppose a good will, which limits the high esteem in which they are otherwise tightly held, and makes it impermissible to take them for good per se. Moderation in affects and passions, self-control and sober deliberation are not only good in many respects, they even appear to constitute part of the *inner* worth of a person; but they are far from deserving to be declared good without limitation (however uncondition-ally they were praised by the ancients). For without principles of a good will they can become most evil, and the cold blood of a scoundrel makes him not only far more dangerous, but also immediately more loathsome in our eyes than he would have been taken to be without it.

A good will is good not because of what it effects, or accomplishes, not because of its fitness to attain some intended end, but good just by its willing, i.e. in itself and, considered by itself, it is to be esteemed beyond compare much higher than anything that could ever be brought about by it in favor of some inclination, and indeed, if you will, the sum of all inclinations. Even if by some particular disfavor of fate, or by the scanty endowment of a stepmotherly nature, this will should entirely lack the capacity to carry through its purpose; if despite its greatest striving it should still accomplish nothing, and only the good will were to remain (not, of course, as a mere wish, but as the summoning of all means that are within our control); then, like a jewel, it would still shine by itself, as something that has its full worth in itself. Usefulness or fruitlessness can neither add anything to this worth, nor take anything away from it. It would, as it were, be only the setting to enable us to handle it better in ordinary commerce, or to attract the attention of those who are not yet expert enough; but not to recommend it to experts, or to determine its worth.

Even so, in this idea of the absolute worth of a mere will, not taking into account any utility in its estimation, there is something so strange that, regardless of all the agreement with it even of common reason, a suspicion must yet arise that it might perhaps covertly be founded merely on some high-flown fantastication, and that we may have misunderstood Nature's purpose in assigning Reason to our will as its ruler. We shall therefore submit this idea to examination from this point of view.

In the natural predispositions of an organized being, i.e. one arranged purposively for life, we assume as a principle that no organ will be found in it for any end that is not also the most fitting for it and the most suitable. Now in a being that has reason and a will, if the actual end of Nature were its *preservation*, its *prosperity*, in a word its *happiness*, then she would have made very bad arrangements for this in appointing the creature's Reason as the accomplisher of this purpose. For all the actions that it has to perform with a view to this purpose, and the whole rule of its conduct, would be marked out for it far more accurately by instinct, and that end would thereby have been obtained much more reliably than can ever be done by reason; and if in addition reason should have been bestowed on the favored creature, it would have had to serve it only to contemplate the fortunate predisposition of its nature, to admire it, to rejoice in it, and to be grateful for it to the beneficent cause; but not to subject its desiderative faculty to that weak and deceptive guidance and meddle with Nature's purpose; in a word, Nature would have prevented Reason from striking out into *practical use*, and from having the impudence, with its feeble insights, to devise its own plan for happiness and for the means of achieving it. Nature herself would have taken over the choice not only of ends, but also of means, and as a wise precaution would have entrusted them both solely to instinct.

In actual fact, we do find that the more a cultivated reason engages with the purpose of enjoying life and with happiness, so much the further does a human being stray from true contentment; and from this there arises in many, and indeed in those who are most experienced in its use, if only they are sincere enough to admit it, a certain degree of *misology*, i.e. hatred of reason, since after calculating all the advantages they derive — I do not say from the invention of all the arts of common luxury, but even from the sciences (which in the end also appear to them to be a luxury of the understanding)—they still find that they have in fact just brought more hardship upon their shoulders than they have gained in happiness, and that because of this they eventually envy, rather than disdain, the more common run of people, who are closer to the guidance of mere natural instinct, and who do not allow their reason much influence on their behavior. And to that extent one must admit that the judgment of those who greatly moderate and even reduce below zero the vainglorious eulogies extolling the advantages that reason was supposed to obtain for us with regard to the happiness and contentment of life, is by no means sullen, or ungrateful to the kindliness of the government of the world; but that these judgments are covertly founded on the idea of another and far worthier purpose of their existence, to which, and not to happiness, reason is quite properly destined, and to which, as its supreme condition, the private purpose of a human being must therefore largely take second place.

For since reason is not sufficiently fit to guide the will reliably with regard to its objects and the satisfaction of all our needs (which in part it does itself multiply) — an end to which an implanted natural instinct would have led much more reliably — but reason as a practical faculty, i.e. as one that is meant to influence has yet been imparted to us, its true function must be to produce a *will that is good*, not for other purposes *as a means*, but good *in itself* — for which reason was absolutely necessary — since nature has everywhere else gone to work purposively in distributing its predispositions. Therefore this will need not, indeed, be the only and the entire good, but it must yet be the highest good, and the condition of everything else, even of all longing for happiness; in which case it is quite consistent with the wisdom of nature when one perceives that the cultivation of reason, which is required for the first and unconditional purpose, in many ways limits — at least in this life—the attainment of the second, namely of happiness, which is always conditional, indeed that it may reduce it to less than nothing without nature's proceeding unpurposively in this; because reason, which recognizes as its highest practical function the grounding of a good will, in attaining this purpose, is capable only of a contentment after its own kind, namely from fulfilling an end that again is determined only by reason, even if this should involve much infringement on the ends of inclination.

In order, then, to unravel the concept of a will to be highly esteemed in itself and good apart from any further purpose, as it already dwells in natural sound understanding and needs not so much to be taught as rather just to be brought to light, this concept that always comes first in estimating the entire worth of our actions and constitutes the condition of everything else: we shall inspect the concept of duty, which contains that of a good will, though under certain subjective limitations and hindrances, which, however, far from concealing it and making it unrecognizable, rather bring it out by contrast and make it shine forth all the more brightly.

I here pass over all actions already recognized as contrary to duty, even though they may be useful in this or that respect; for in their case there is no question whether they might have been done *from duty*, since they even conflict with it. I also set aside actions that actually conform with duty but to which human beings immediately have *no inclination*, but which they still perform, because they are impelled to do so by another inclination. For there it is easy to distinguish whether the action that conforms with duty was done *from duty* or from a self-serving purpose. It is much more difficult to notice this difference when an action conforms with duty and the subject has in addition an *immediate* inclination towards it. E.g. it certainly conforms with duty that a shopkeeper not overcharge his inexperienced customer, and where there is much commerce, a prudent merchant actually does not do this, but keeps a fixed general price for everyone, so that a child may buy from him just as well as everyone else. Thus one is served *honestly*; but this is not nearly enough for us to believe that the merchant proceeded in this way from duty and principles of honesty; his advantage required it; it cannot be assumed here that he had, besides, an immediate inclination towards his customers, so as from love, as it were, to give no one preference over another in the matter of price. Thus the action was done neither from duty, nor from immediate inclination, but merely for a self-interested purpose.

By contrast, to preserve one's life is one's duty and besides everyone has an immediate inclination to do so. But on account of this the often anxious care with which the greatest part of humanity attends to it has yet no inner worth, and their maxim no moral content. They preserve their lives *in conformity with duty*, but not *from duty*. By contrast, if adversities and hopeless grief have entirely taken away the taste for life; if the unfortunate man, strong of soul, more indignant about his fate than despondent or dejected, wishes for death, and yet preserves his life, without loving it, not from inclination, or fear, but from duty; then his maxim has a moral content.

To be beneficent where one can is one's duty, and besides there are many souls so attuned to compassion that, even without another motivating ground of vanity, or self-interest, they find an inner gratification in spreading joy around them, and can relish the contentment of others, in so far as it is their work. But I assert that in such a case an action of this kind — however much it conforms with duty, however amiable it may be — still has no true moral worth, but stands on the same footing as other inclinations, e.g. the inclination to honor, which if it fortunately lights upon what is in fact in the general interest and in conformity with duty, and hence honorable, deserves praise and encouragement, but not high esteem; for the maxim lacks moral content, namely to do such actions not from inclination, but *from duty*. Suppose, then, that the mind of that friend of humanity were beclouded by his own grief, which extinguishes all compassion for the fate of others; that he still had the means to benefit others in need, but the need of others did not touch him because he is sufficiently occupied with his own; and that now, as inclination no longer stimulates him to it, he were yet to tear himself out of this deadly insensibility, and to do the action without any inclination, solely from duty; not until then does it have its genuine moral worth. Still further: if nature had as such placed little sympathy in the heart of this or that man; if (otherwise honest) he were by temperament cold and indifferent to the sufferings of others, perhaps because he himself is equipped with the peculiar gift of patience and enduring strength towards his own, and presupposes, or even requires, the same in every other; if nature had not actually formed such a man (who would truly not be its worst product) to be a friend of humanity, would he not still find within himself a source from which to give himself a far higher worth than that of a good-natured temperament may be? Certainly! It is just there that the worth of character commences, which is moral and beyond all comparison the highest, namely that he be beneficent, not from inclination, but from duty.

To secure one's own happiness is one's duty (at least indirectly); for lack of contentment with one's condition, in the trouble of many worries and amidst unsatisfied needs, could easily become a great *temptation to transgress one's duties*. But, even without taking note of duty, all human beings have already of their own the most powerful and intimate inclination to happiness, as it is just in this idea that all inclinations unite in one sum. However, the prescription of happiness is predominantly such, that it greatly infringes on some inclinations and yet human beings can form no determinate and reliable concept of the sum of the satisfaction of all under the name of happiness; which is why it is not surprising that a single inclination — if determinate with regard to what it promises, and to the time its satisfaction can be obtained — can outweigh a wavering idea, and that a human being, e.g. someone suffering from gout of the foot, can choose to enjoy what he fancies and to suffer what he can since, according to his calculation, at least then he has not denied himself the enjoyment of the present moment because of perhaps groundless expectations of some good fortune that is meant to lie in health. But also in this case, if the universal inclination to happiness did not determine his will, if health, at least for him, did not enter into this calculation so necessarily, then here, as in all other cases, there still remains a law, namely to advance one's happiness, not from inclination, but from duty; and it is not until then that his conduct has its actual moral worth.

It is in this way, no doubt, that we are to understand the passages from Scripture that contain the command to love one's neighbor, even our enemy. For love as inclination cannot be commanded, but beneficence from duty itself — even if no inclination whatsoever impels us to it, indeed if natural and unconquerable aversion resists — is *practical* and not *pathological* love, which lies in the will and not in the propensity of sensation, in principles of action and not in melting compassion; and only the former can be commanded.

The second proposition is: an action from duty has its moral worth *not in the purpose* that is to be attained by it, but in the maxim according to which it is resolved upon, and thus it does not depend on the actuality of the object of the action, but merely on the *principle* of *willing* according to which — regardless of any object of the desiderative faculty — the action is done. That the purposes that we may have when we act, and their effects, as ends and incentives of the will, can bestow on actions no unconditional moral worth, is clear from what was previously said. In what, then, can this worth lie, if it is not to consist in the will with reference to their hoped-for effect? It can lie nowhere else *than in the principle of the will*, regardless of the ends that can be effected by such action; for the will stands halfway between its a priori principle, which is formal, and its a posteriori incentive, which is material, as it were at a crossroads, and since it must after all be determined by something, it will have to be determined by the formal principle of willing as such when an action is done from duty, as every material principle has been taken away from it.

The third proposition, as the conclusion from both previous ones, I would express as follows: *duty is the necessity of an action from respect for the law*. For the object as the effect of the action I have in mind I can indeed have *inclination*, but *never respect*, precisely because it is merely an effect and not activity of a will. Likewise, I cannot have respect for inclination as such, whether it is mine or that of another; I can at most in the first case approve of it, in the second at times love it myself, i.e. view it as favorable to my own advantage. Only what is connected with my will merely as ground, never as effect, what does not serve my inclination, but outweighs it, or at least excludes it entirely from calculations when we make a choice, hence the mere law by itself; can be an object of respect and thus a command. Now, an action from duty is to separate off entirely the influence of inclination, and with it every object of the will; thus nothing remains for the will that could determine it except, objectively, the *law* and, subjectively, *pure respect* for this practical law, and hence the maxim of complying with such a law, even if it infringes on all my inclinations.

Thus the moral worth of the action does not lie in the effect that is expected from it, nor therefore in any principle of action that needs to borrow its motivating ground from this expected effect. For all these effects (agreeableness of one's condition, indeed even advancement of the happiness of others) could also have been brought about by other causes, and thus there was, for this, no need of the will of a rational being; even so, in it alone can the highest and unconditional good be found. Nothing other than the *representation of the law* in itself — *which of course can take place only in a rational being* — in so far as it, not the hoped-for effect, is the determining ground of the will, can therefore constitute the pre-eminent good that we call moral, which is already present in the person himself who acts according to it, and is nor first to be expected from the effect.

But what kind of law can that possibly be, the representation of which — even without regard for the effect expected from it — must determine the will for it to be called good absolutely and without limitation? Since I have robbed the will of all impulses that could arise for it from following some particular law, nothing remains but as such the universal conformity of actions with law, which alone is to serve the will as its principle, i.e. I ought never to proceed except in such a way *that I could also will that my maxim should become a universal law*. Here, then, mere conformity with law as such (not founded on any law determined with a view to certain actions) is what serves the will as its principle, and must so serve it if duty is not to be as such an empty delusion and a chimerical concept; common human reason in its practical judging is actually in perfect agreement with this, and always has the envisaged principle before its eyes.

Let the question be, e.g., may I not, when I am in trouble, make a promise with the intention not to keep it? Here I easily discern the different meanings the question can have: whether it is prudent, or whether it conforms with duty to make a false promise. The former can no doubt quite often take place. I do see very well that it is not enough to extricate myself from the present predicament by means of this subterfuge, but that it requires careful deliberation whether this lie may not later give rise to much greater inconvenience for me than those from which I am now liberating myself; and — since with all my supposed *cunning* the consequences cannot be so easily foreseen that trust once lost might not be far more disadvantageous to me than any ill that I now mean to avoid — whether one might not act *more prudently* in this matter by proceeding according to a universal maxim, and by making it one's habit to promise nothing except with the intention of keeping it. But here it soon becomes clear to me that such a maxim will still only be founded on the dreaded consequences. Now, to be truthful from duty is something quite different from being truthful from dread of adverse consequences; as in the first case, the concept of the action in itself already contains a law for me, whereas in the second I must first look around elsewhere to see what effects on me this might involve. For if I deviate from the principle of duty, this is quite certainly evil; but if I defect from my maxim of prudence, that can sometimes be very advantageous to me, though it is of course safer to adhere to it. However, to instruct myself in the very quickest and yet undeceptive way with regard to responding to this problem — whether a lying promise conforms with duty — I ask myself: would I actually be content that my maxim (to extricate myself from a predicament by means of an untruthful promise) should hold as a universal law (for myself as well as for others), and would I be able to say to myself: everyone may make an untruthful promise when he finds himself in a predicament from which he can extricate himself in no other way? Then I soon become aware that I could indeed will the lie, but by no means a universal law to lie; for according to such a law there would actually be no promise at all, since it would be futile to pretend my will to others with regard to my future actions, who would not believe this pretense; or, if they rashly did so, would pay me back in like coin, and hence my maxim, as soon as it were made a universal law, would have to destroy itself.

I do not, therefore, need any wide-ranging acuteness to see what I have to do for my willing to be morally good. Inexperienced with regard to the course of the world, incapable of bracing myself for whatever might come to pass in it, I just ask myself: can you also will that your maxim become a universal law? If not, then it must be rejected, and that not because of some disadvantage to you, or to others, that might result, but because it cannot fit as a principle into a possible universal legislation, for which reason extracts from me immediate respect; and although I do not yet *see* on what it is founded (which the philosopher may investigate), at least I do understand this much: that it is an estimation of a worth that far outweighs any worth of what is extolled by inclination, and that the necessity of my actions from *pure* respect for the practical law is that which constitutes duty, to which every other motivating ground must give way, because it is the condition of a will good *in itself* whose worth surpasses everything.

Thus, then, we have progressed in the moral cognition of common human reason to reach its principle, which admittedly it does not think of as separated in this way in a universal form, but yet always actually has before its eyes and uses as the standard of its judging. Here it would be easy to show how, with this compass in hand, it is very well informed in all uses that occur, to distinguish what is good, what is evil, what conforms with duty or is contrary to it, if — without in the least teaching it anything new — one only . . . makes it aware of its own principle; and that there is thus no need of science and philosophy to know what one has to do in order to be honest and good, indeed even to be wise and virtuous. It should actually have been possible to presume all along that acquaintance with what it is incumbent upon everyone to do, and hence also to know, would be the affair of every human being, even the commonest. Here one cannot without admiration observe the great advantage the practical capacity to judge has over the theoretical in common human understanding. In the latter, when common reason dares to depart from the laws of experience and the perceptions of the senses, it falls into nothing but sundry incomprehensibilities and internal contradictions, or at least into a chaos of uncertainty, obscurity, and instability. But in practical matters the power of judging first begins to show itself to advantage just when common understanding excludes all sensuous incentives from practical laws. Then it even becomes subtle, whether it seeks to engage in legalistic quibbles with its conscience, or with other claims referring to what is to be called right, or seeks sincerely to determine the worth of actions for its own instruction; and, what is most important, in the latter case it stands just as good a chance of hitting the mark as a philosopher can ever expect; indeed it is almost more sure in this than even the latter, because he can have no other principle, but can easily confuse his judgment with a host of alien and irrelevant considerations and deflect it from the straight course. Accordingly, would it not be more advisable, in moral things, to leave it with the judgment of common reason, and at most to bring on philosophy to present the system of morals more completely and accessibly, and likewise its rules in a form more convenient for use (and still more for disputation), but not to let it lead common human understanding away from its fortunate simplicity for practical purposes, and by means of philosophy to put it on a new route of investigation and instruction?

Innocence is a glorious thing, but then again it is very sad that it is so hard to preserve and so easily seduced. Because of this even wisdom — which probably consists more in behavior than in knowledge elsewhere — yet needs science too, not in order to learn from it, but to obtain access and durability for its prescription. The human being feels within himself a powerful counterweight to all the commands of duty — which reason represents to him as so worthy of the highest respect — in his needs and inclinations, the entire satisfaction of which he sums up under the name of happiness. Now reason issues its prescriptions unrelentingly, yet without promising anything to the inclinations, and hence, as it were, with reproach and disrespect for those claims, which are so vehement and yet seem so reasonable (and will not be eliminated by any command). But from this there arises a *natural dialectic*,[1] i.e. a propensity to rationalize against those strict laws of duty, and to cast doubt on their validity, or at least their purity and strictness and, where possible, to make them better suited to our wishes and inclinations, i.e. fundamentally to corrupt them and deprive them of their entire dignity, something that in the end even common practical reason cannot endorse.

Thus *common human reason* is impelled to leave its sphere not by some need of speculation (which never comes over it as long as it is content to be mere sound reason), but rather on practical grounds, and to take a step into the field of a *practical philosophy*, in order to receive there intelligence and distinct instruction regarding the source of this principle and its correct determination in contrast with maxims based on need and inclination, so that it may escape from the predicament caused by mutual claims, and not run the risk of being deprived of all genuine moral principles because of the ambiguity into which it easily falls. Thus also in practical common reason, when

---

1. The term *dialectic* refers to the process of reasoning by which one examines opposing ideas to ascertain which, if any, have merit and whether their apparent conflict may be resolved.

it cultivates itself, a *dialectic* inadvertently unfolds that necessitates it to seek help in philosophy, just as happens to it in its theoretical use, and the one is therefore just as unlikely as the other to find rest anywhere but in a complete critique of our reason.

## TEST YOUR UNDERSTANDING

1. Kant believes that an act possesses "moral worth" when it involves doing the right thing for the right reasons. What sorts of motives and reasons for action does he eliminate as possible reasons (or "grounds") for morally worthy action?

2. Explain Kant's distinction between conforming with duty and acting from duty. Formulate an example of your own in which one conforms with duty but does not act from duty. Then, formulate an example of your own in which one acts from duty but yet fails to conform with duty.

3. Would an action performed from duty but that failed to conform with duty have moral worth in Kant's view? (*Hint:* Consider Kant's "second proposition.")

## NOTES AND QUESTIONS

1. Kant claims that the honest shopkeeper who acts from sympathy for his blind customer conforms with duty but does not perform a morally worthy action when he does not "upcharge" the customer. So too, it might seem that the son who visits his sick father in the hospital from filial love does not perform a morally worthy action, in Kant's sense. How should Kant respond to the objection that we admire the son who visits his father out of care and concern, but recoil at the son who does so only from a sense of duty?

   (*Hint:* Consider whether Kant's purpose in identifying the conditions of morally worthy actions is to argue that we *must* always perform morally worthy actions. Might he have another reason to draw our attention to them? Might there be middle ground between acting with indifference toward morality and acting in a morally praiseworthy way?)

   A sophisticated account of the relation between sympathetic motives and the motive of duty in Kant's work appears in Barbara Herman, "On the Value of Acting from the Motive of Duty," *Philosophical Review* 90, no. 3 (July 1981): 359–82.

2. Kant argues that the source of morality lies "**a priori** in our reason," and not in our particular interests or inclinations.

   *Exercise:* Explain how Kant's condemnation of the lying promise meets this standard. That is, explain how his argument for the wrongness of the lying promise does not depend upon the particular interests or inclinations of the promisor. Describe an alternative theory of the wrong of false promising that does not meet this standard, that is, a theory that appeals to the particular interests or inclinations of the promisor.

## ANALYZING THE ARGUMENTS

1. *The Gyges Ring: What sort of argument must we give to its possessor?*

   a. Hume's position is that we value morally good action because we approve of the motive of sympathy in ourselves and others that gives rise to such actions. How would you fashion this into a response to Glaucon and the possessor of Gyges's ring? Does Hume's view about the good of moral action fit into any of the categories of goods identified in Plato's *Republic*? In particular, does Hume's argument suggest that moral action is the sort of good we value for its consequences, and particularly for the good feeling it causes in us?

   b. Kant's position is, roughly, that acting immorally is contrary to reason or irrational. If his arguments are successful, should they satisfy Glaucon? Could Kant's argument be met with the further question, "Why ought I be rational?" Or is that further question nonsensical?

2. *Rationality, the emotions, and morality.*

   a. Thomson argues that what it is rational for a person to do depends, in part, upon what information that person has. As she puts it, "rationality is in the head." Other philosophers, like Hume, seem to take a different view of rationality. One point of contrast is that Hume seems to think that it can be contrary to reason to fail to take the appropriate means to one's ends, even if one is unaware of those facts that show those are the appropriate means; further, Hume thinks that a passion may be unreasonable when it is founded upon the presupposition that some object exists which in fact does not exist.

   *Exercise:* Give an example in which (1) the agent ought to do some act A; (2) according to Hume's theory, it would be contrary to reason for the person not to do A; but (3) according to Thomson's theory, it would be rational for the person to do A. Then consider whether it is a problem for Thomson's view that it might be irrational to do what one ought to do. Is it a problem for Hume's view that, if we accepted his view of rationality, it could be that performing a certain act would be contrary to reason even though all the evidence we possess suggests that we should perform it? That is, could it really be contrary to reason to act sensibly upon the evidence we have?

   b. Kant worries that motivations from inclination, including sympathy, are contingent and variable. The authority of morality is not contingent or variable; it does not depend on how we feel. We are *always* required to do the right thing as a matter of "absolute necessity." Hence, the correct motivation to do the right thing cannot stem from inclination.

   Consider the following reply by a Humean:

   Kant is concerned that not all rational beings necessarily, by virtue of their rationality, have sympathy. This should not concern us. Morality is a system of principles that regulate human beings and its demands are therefore tailored to human beings. All human beings have a natural disposition to care and feel sympathy for their fellow humans. Any human being lacking this capacity is defective.

We would not revise our principles of medicine or of anatomy just because they failed to apply to rational Martians. Why should we be troubled that our theories of moral motivation only fit human beings and not other sorts of rational creatures?

Is this reply persuasive? How should Kant respond?

3. *Self-interest.* Hume and Kant concur that morally worthy action—action that commands our moral approval—is not solely or dominantly motivated by self-interest. But what is it for an action to be "self-interested"? A simple view would say that an act is self-interested whenever the agent desires to perform it. But this would deprive the label "self-interested" of useful meaning. Someone who sacrifices his life for his friend in some sense *desires* to save his friend, but such acts are not self-interested in any useful sense.

*Exercise:* Provide an account of what makes an action self-interested that takes the form: An action is self-interested if and only if _____ .

A successful account should satisfy these conditions: (a) it should make sense that wholly self-interested acts do not merit moral approval, and (b) it should not follow from the fact that the agent wanted to act as he did, that his action was therefore self-interested.

4. *Moral motivation:* All the authors in this chapter agree that it is possible to do the morally right thing for the wrong reasons. A complete moral theory needs an account of what more is required for a person's action to be morally worthy.

*Exercise:* Provide an account of what makes an action morally worthy that takes the form: When an action merits moral admiration, it does so because _____ .

Then consider the following two questions:

a. Would any of the authors in this chapter agree with your account? Would any disagree with your account? How would you reply to the one(s) who might object to your view?

b. Is it a necessary feature of those actions that merit moral admiration that the action is in fact the morally right action? Suppose a strong swimmer walks by the shore of a lake and hears a number of bystanders cry out that they see a child drowning. The swimmer jumps in, swims out to save the child, and begins to haul the child to shore. But, in fact, the child is not drowning. The child and the bystanders are all actors practicing for an outdoor performance of a play. Rather than saving a child, the swimmer has interrupted a rehearsal. Is the swimmer's action morally worthy?

# 16

# How Do We Reason about What Is Right?

Suppose a friend starts smoking. I reasonably believe that if he continues, it will begin an addiction that risks his health and may cause him to die far earlier and more painfully than he would otherwise. May I hide his cigarettes and his pocket money to obstruct this nascent addiction? Or, does treating him with respect demand that I share my concerns but respect the decision he makes about his own habits?

I feel bound to do the morally right thing. But in many cases — as in this one — it is difficult to identify what the right thing to do is. Even when a moral decision is difficult, it seems inappropriate to flip a coin. It is an important part of acting morally that I *decide* how to act based on deliberation about the relevant reasons. So how do I reason about what is right?

## Top-down Approach

Some philosophers reason from the top down. They begin by identifying the fundamental elements and concepts of morality. These elements and **concepts**, in turn, suggest fundamental principles that may then be applied to hard and easy cases. That application will yield answers about what is the right thing to do and why it is right: why, for example, we should help others in need, refrain from theft, abjure violence, keep our promises, and tell the truth.

On the top-down approach, we might start by asking what morality is. One proposal is that morality consists of a body of principles that offer guidance about how one should regard and behave toward others — principles that express the *moral perspective*, rather than the prudential or aesthetic perspectives. Of course, how to characterize the moral perspective is a vexed matter, but some jumping-off points seem relatively uncontroversial.

From the moral perspective, it seems that:

A. Each of us matters, and it matters that each person's life goes well.[1]

B. No one is intrinsically more important than anyone else: everyone matters equally.

C. We cannot act merely to satisfy our own interests, desires, and aims. We must respect others by taking into account how our actions affect them in a manner that reflects their equal importance.

These ideas about the nature of the moral perspective suggest two questions that more specific moral views will answer in different ways:

1. *What is it for a human life to go well?* Unsurprisingly, there is heated debate about this matter. For example, **hedonists** claim that a life goes well when it contains as much pleasure and as little pain as possible. **Preference-satisfaction** theorists concur with hedonists that one should maximize (or bring about as much as possible of) what matters, but they contend that life goes well when one's preferences are maximally satisfied, whether or not that satisfaction always yields pleasure. Others, call them **autonomy** theorists, contend that a life goes well if one is respected and supported by others as a free and equal person, one has and exercises the opportunity to develop one's capacities, and one lives a well-considered life structured by choices made in response to good reasons. Or, perhaps, as some **objective list** theorists argue, a good life defies a simple formulaic summary, but features an amalgam of specific components such as being healthy over a reasonably long life, forming good relationships, having satisfying, stimulating work and projects, having access to the resources, abilities, and social freedom that facilitate a comfortable life free from coercion and vulnerability to exploitation, and having a sufficient education and knowledge to make informed, deliberate decisions and to understand and appreciate one's life, one's environment, and the other goods life offers.

2. *What does respecting the value and equal importance of others' lives involve?* Here again, there are divergent answers. **Consequentialists** contend that the morally correct action for me must reflect the implications of my actions on my own life exactly as much as but no more than their impact on others. The correct action to take is the one that yields the best consequences, impartially considered, of all the possible alternatives.

   *Non-consequentialists* contend there is a different way to respect the equal importance of others' lives. Respect for the equal importance of others' lives involves subjecting myself to the same rules that others should abide by.

---

1. What creatures constitute "us"? Only human beings? All possible rational agents? Do animals have moral standing? Any complete moral theory must confront these issues of scope. For reasons of space, this chapter concentrates on moral relations between people.

That is, I should act in ways that I also think others should (and may) act in relevantly similar circumstances. So it is permissible for me to pay more attention to myself and my loved ones in my daily transactions, as long as I do not ignore others' needs, treat others unfairly, or cause them serious harm.

Philosophers who adopt the top-down approach produce robust moral theories by developing more specific arguments about how we should answer these two questions.

# Utilitarianism

**Utilitarians** adopt the consequentialist view that the morally right action maximizes the best consequences available. They combine that claim with the view that a life goes well when it contains the maximum possible amount of **utility**, that is, as much net happiness (total happiness minus total unhappiness) as possible. John Stuart Mill, for example, argues that "between [an agent's] own happiness and that of others, utilitarianism requires him to be as strictly impartial as a disinterested and benevolent spectator." Hence, the utilitarian principle supplies the "one fundamental principle or law, at the root of all morality," namely that the morally right action is the action, from among all the alternatives, that would produce the most happiness, aggregating and giving equal weight to the effects on all people.[2]

In one sense, Mill affirms the traditional utilitarian answer to the question of what makes a life go well, namely the doctrine that all that is intrinsically valuable is pleasure and the absence of pain. His view is more nuanced, however, than simple, hedonistic interpretations of utility that treat all forms of equally intense pleasure as interchangeable and equally valuable. Mill regards the pleasures associated with the exercise of the "higher faculties," e.g., the pleasures associated with acquiring and appreciating knowledge, as "higher" than mere sensory pleasures. Pleasures, in Mill's view, may be ranked not merely by their intensity and duration, but by whether one sort is decidedly preferred over another by those who have experienced both.

Mill's utilitarianism provides guidance about how to reason about what is right. For example, his principle would direct us not to kill or injure others from revenge because the enormous costs in happiness to victims, to their associates, and to all of us who would fear that we might be victimized, would outweigh whatever gains one might achieve by acting on one's anger. The prohibitions on lying and

---

2. Some read Mill to claim that the morally right action is the action that conforms to *that rule* the universal adoption of which would maximize utility. This formulation is called *rule-utilitarianism* because it focuses on the *rule* of action that would maximize utility, rather than on the particular *act* that would maximize utility (as *act-utilitarians* do). Although this difference in formulation may matter in some contexts, it is unessential to the issues discussed here.

promise-breaking and the imperative to help would be similarly explained. Whether you should hide your friend's cigarettes would depend upon whether the happiness your friend would gain from a longer, healthier life and that you would gain from facilitating it would outweigh the unhappiness your intervention might cause, including the effects of the intrusion on your friend's own choices, his possible anger and estrangement from you, and the loss of revenue to the tobacco industry.

# Criticism of Utilitarianism

Utilitarianism faces fierce criticism. One line of criticism says that it gives the wrong reasons for why an action is right or wrong. For example, the moral prohibition on killing does not seem to hinge upon whether killing fails to maximize happiness. Even if it would make a killer and his enormous, rabid group of followers deliriously happy, that should not alter our opinion about the wrongness of killing an innocent person. Even if those facts were true, they would supply no reason whatsoever to contemplate murder. The happiness a killer derives from murder has no positive moral significance. It does not weigh against the victim's happiness but rather is morally objectionable in itself. Further, although we should help others in need, it is not evident that the reason is that we must always maximize happiness. The idea that we are obligated to maximize aggregate happiness (or good consequences otherwise construed) would, critics allege, place overwhelming demands on each of us to devote our entire lives and each of our actions to increasing the overall aggregate of global happiness, whether or not such actions ever contributed to our own lives. A maximization requirement would demand this dedication, even if it were incompatible with leading an autonomous life, pursuing important projects of personal concern, and developing meaningful personal relationships.

Critics of utilitarianism trace these concerns to fundamental differences about the basic components of a moral theory. Some focus critical attention on utilitarian answers to the first question: about what makes a life go well. They contest that all happiness, whether pleasure or preference satisfaction, is good. They argue, further, that there are more fundamental components of well-being that a person should prefer, whether she actually does or not, such as acting rationally and freely while leading a healthy life, pursuing rewarding work, and cultivating relationships with others.

Critics also contest the utilitarian answer to the second question. They reject the consequentialist proposition that we must always bring about the best consequences from an impartial point of view. Non-consequentialists stress the special relationship each of us has to our own lives and the need to treat ourselves and particular people as special to develop a unified and distinctively individual character, pursue projects in depth, and enjoy strong personal relationships. They contend that recognition of the equal moral importance of others from the impartial point of view is still consistent with giving special consideration to our own interests, loved ones, and projects. On their view, equality instead demands that we act in ways that could be *justified* to others, that we should accept if others acted in the same way, and that do not depend upon making an exception of ourselves.

# Non-Consequentialist Theories

Immanuel Kant and Thomas Scanlon offer prominent examples of non-consequentialist moral reasoning, driven by top-down considerations. Like Mill, Kant seeks to capture the foundations of morality through a fundamental principle. Kant concurs that as moral agents, we must act from a principle of impartiality that recognizes the equal moral status of all rational beings, but his argument about what impartiality demands emphasizes what principles of action we would affirm for everyone. Like a law of nature or a piece of legislation, the fundamental principle of morality should have universal, uniform, and mandatory application, irrespective of how we feel about the action or its consequences; in Kant's terms, it binds all rational agents *categorically*.

When I aim to act for a particular purpose, to be consistent with duty, my aim must be compatible with a system of lawlike rules. I must ask whether my *maxim*, the relevant description of my action in light of my purpose in performing it, *could possibly* operate as a principle of rational agency that could apply to, and be applied by, everyone who appropriately valued our status as rational, autonomous agents. In Kant's language, I must ask if my maxim could be *universalized*. In some cases, my maxim may not be universalizable because its universal application would undermine its own purpose, or because its universal application would conflict with the realization of other mandatory aims we have in light of the inestimable value of rational, autonomous agency. When my maxim is not universalizable, it reveals that my aim conflicts with my treating myself as one rational (valuable) agent among others, living in a community of equals governed by law.

Kant expresses this idea in different ways, the most important of which are these:

1.  The *universal law formulation* of the **categorical imperative**, which says that one should "act only in accordance with that maxim through which [one] can at the same time will that it become a universal law."

2.  The *humanity formulation* of the categorical imperative, which says that one should "[s]o act that you use humanity, whether in your own person or in the person of any other, always at the same time as an end, never merely as a means."

Scanlon puts forward another non-consequentialist theory called *contractualism*. He proposes that morality is best understood as fulfilling our need to justify our conduct to one another. If so, morality would not, as utilitarianism does, orient us toward aggregating the effects of actions on all parties, lumping them together. Instead, we must ask whether an action conforms to a rule of conduct that could not be reasonably rejected by any agent motivated to select rules of conduct that would govern all persons. Therefore, morality orients us toward thinking about who will be most badly affected by our actions and whether that impact may be adequately justified to those people.

Both of these non-consequentialist theories would direct me to interfere with my friend's smoking not because it would maximize happiness but only when either my maxim could be universalized, or when interference conforms to a rule that rational people would not reject. To assess whether these conditions are satisfied would lead us to ask specific questions about whether interference is compatible with respecting others' autonomous control over themselves and whether we would agree to rules that might protect our health but reduce our control over our own lives.

# Bottom-up Approach

Thus far, we have been investigating top-down moral theories that begin from fundamental moral precepts, connect those elements to moral principles, and then apply those principles to specific situations. Critics of this method doubt that our best reasoning proceeds from such a high level of abstraction. They think instead that we should launch our moral reasoning from more concrete and familiar locations, where our moral confidence is strongest: for example, from our convictions that we should help others in need, keep our promises, tell the truth, and refrain from injuring others (absent exigent threatening circumstances).

Writing in the Aristotelian tradition, Rosalind Hursthouse emphasizes character as the key to moral reasoning. Hursthouse contends that sound moral judgment does not involve deploying an all-purpose moral principle or theory. Rather, to reason about morality well, one must develop and exercise a virtuous character and imagine what the virtuous person would do in the specific circumstances. She argues that we have insight into what the virtues involve because we have experience and a sense of how to apply specific labels of virtue and vice through our linguistic practices that, themselves, represent generations of wisdom.

A related bottom-up approach leverages our moral confidence about familiar cases to identify preliminary hypotheses about what broader principles connect and explain them that may then be applied to resolve harder cases. One might hypothesize that our clear moral convictions embody a fundamental insight that we must support and respect others' autonomy. For example, we condemn violence because through violence we control and disable others, rather than enlist their rational, free support for our plans. We must help friends or strangers *in need*, to take another example, because conditions of *need* force people's energies solely on meeting urgent, nondiscretionary requirements rather than on making life choices based on plans that seem worthy and express their individuality. By contrast, when a stranger's ability to lead a free, independent life is secure and she merely wishes for our help, our strong responsibility to assist dissipates. If our fundamental moral obligation is to support and respect others' autonomous choices, rather than to promote their happiness at every turn, that suggests a different answer to our initial question: my obligation is to refrain from interfering forcibly with my friend's decision to smoke so long as his choice is autonomous, whether or not refraining maximizes happiness.

Bottom-up theorists not only generalize to principles from specific moral judgments, they also test possible principles against these judgments. For instance, we may challenge utilitarianism because it might dictate actions that seem plainly objectionable: e.g., it might demand incarcerating an innocent person to provide a scapegoat to mollify a massive, angry crowd.

John Rawls's method involves using concrete and abstract judgments in tandem, a hybrid of top-down and bottom-up approaches. Rawls regards "the nature of moral theory" as an effort to describe the foundations underlying our moral capacities and their application, just as the study of grammar describes the systematic rules underlying our fairly automatic application of our sense of grammar to the formation and recognition of well-formed sentences. To understand morality, we must understand our considered moral judgments about particular cases and identify unifying, rationally defensible principles that justify and illuminate these judgments. Rawls, a contractualist, conceives of these principles as those we would *choose* under fair conditions if we were choosing principles to regulate our interactions; so we must consider what constitutes fair choice conditions and whether our candidate principles would be chosen. If our principles and judgments conflict, then we must investigate whether the principles are flawed and need revision, or whether our judgments are mistaken assessments that upon reflection seem hasty, ill-considered, or to reflect an unreasonable favoring of one's own circumstances or interests. When the principles and our judgments harmonize, we occupy what Rawls calls a "**reflective equilibrium**," a theoretical position that provides a moral foundation for justifying, criticizing, and guiding conduct.

All ethical theories that use bottom-up approaches confront criticism about the use of our considered particular judgments about cases, otherwise referred to as **intuitions** or, in Elizabeth Harman's terms, "specific ethical claims." Our intuitions may merely reflect our upbringing, prejudices, or immediate gut reactions, rather than encapsulating sound reasoning. Further, different people's intuitions may conflict, suggesting that intuitions may not offer solid footing for a universal moral theory. Some intuitions must be mistaken, rendering them unreliable calibration points. Harman offers a rousing defense of the use of intuitions in moral reasoning against these doubts.

# Skepticism about Moral Reasoning

Friedrich Nietzsche provides a highly critical counterpoint to all these approaches, voicing skepticism about the widely shared presupposition that we can identify the content of morality through careful reasoning, whether top-down or bottom-up. Nietzsche not only strongly tilts against the substance of most modern moral thought, he also writes in a markedly different style. He used the epigrammatic form self-consciously, declaring "it is my ambition to say in ten sentences what everyone else says in a book—what everyone else does not say in a book."[3] Refreshing and stimulating to some while exasperating for others, his tone echoes the rebellious substance of his ideas.

Nietzsche contends that reasoning will not reveal morality's content because morality is a socially created set of rules designed to serve the interests of a particular group of people (of whom he is critical). Nietzsche champions the use of the **genealogical method**, a process of excavating the origins of conventional moral ideas to expose whose interests they serve, to discredit conventional moral principles. Among his surprising conclusions, *contra* Mill, is that pain and suffering are not morally special or particularly bad and that we do not have strong reasons to relieve others' suffering. Rather than investigating what respect for others requires, Nietzsche advocates fostering the greatest individual lives, lives akin to great works of art. As individuals, each of us should confront with unblinking honesty the truth about ourselves and endeavor to live joyfully and exuberantly.

## John Stuart Mill (1806–1873)

Mill was born in London, England. He was educated by his father, James Mill, a distinguished Scottish philosopher, political theorist, economist, and historian. A utilitarian, empiricist, and important public thinker, Mill was author of *Utilitarianism, Considerations on Representative Government, Principles of Political Economy, Subjection of Women, System of Logic, The Autobiography of John Stuart Mill,* and, most famously, *On Liberty.* Apart from his writings, Mill worked at the East India Company (1823–58), served as a Member of Parliament (1865–68), and was Lord Rector of the University of St. Andrews (1865–68).

# UTILITARIANISM

---

# Chapter 1: General Remarks

There ought either to be some one fundamental principle or law, at the root of all morality, or if there be several, there should be a determinate order of precedence among them; and the one principle, or the rule for deciding between the various principles when they conflict, ought to be self-evident. . . .

---

3. Friedrich Nietzsche, *Twilight of the Idols,* from *The Portable Nietzsche,* trans. Walter Kaufman (Viking Press, 1976), p. 556.

On the present occasion, I shall, without further discussion of other theories, attempt to contribute something towards the understanding and appreciation of the Utilitarian or Happiness theory. . . .

I shall offer some illustrations of the doctrine itself; with the view of showing more clearly what it is, distinguishing it from what it is not, and disposing of such of the practical objections to it as either originate in, or are closely connected with, mistaken interpretations of its meaning. . . .

# Chapter 2: What Utilitarianism Is

. . . The creed which accepts as the foundation of morals, Utility, or the Greatest Happiness Principle, holds that actions are right in proportion as they tend to promote happiness, wrong as they tend to produce the reverse of happiness. By happiness is intended pleasure, and the absence of pain; by unhappiness, pain, and the privation of pleasure. To give a clear view of the moral standard set up by the theory, much more requires to be said; in particular, what things it includes in the ideas of pain and pleasure; and to what extent this is left an open question. But these supplementary explanations do not affect the theory of life on which this theory of morality is grounded — namely, that pleasure, and freedom from pain, are the only things desirable as ends; and that all desirable things (which are as numerous in the utilitarian as in any other scheme) are desirable either for the pleasure inherent in themselves, or as means to the promotion of pleasure and the prevention of pain.

Now, such a theory of life excites in many minds . . . inveterate dislike. To suppose that life has (as they express it) no higher end than pleasure — no better and nobler object of desire and pursuit — they designate as utterly mean and grovelling; as a doctrine worthy only of swine, to whom the followers of Epicurus[1] were, at a very early period, contemptuously likened. . . .

The Epicureans have always answered, that it is not they, but their accusers, who represent human nature in a degrading light; since the accusation supposes human beings to be capable of no pleasures except those of which swine are capable. . . . Human beings have faculties more elevated than the animal appetites, and when once made conscious of them, do not regard anything as happiness which does not include their gratification. . . . There is no known Epicurean theory of life which does not assign to the pleasures of the intellect, of the feelings and imagination, and of the moral sentiments, a much higher value as pleasures than to those of mere sensation. . . .

If I am asked, what I mean by difference of quality in pleasures, or what makes one pleasure more valuable than another, merely as a pleasure, except its being greater in amount, there is but one possible answer. Of two pleasures, if there be one to which

---

1. Epicurus (341–270 BCE) was an Ancient Greek philosopher whose complete works have not survived. His fragments and the works of his followers suggest that he contended that a good life involved attaining pleasure and avoiding pain.

all or almost all who have experience of both give a decided preference, irrespective of any feeling of moral obligation to prefer it, that is the more desirable pleasure. If one of the two is, by those who are competently acquainted with both, placed so far above the other that they prefer it, even though knowing it to be attended with a greater amount of discontent, and would not resign it for any quantity of the other pleasure which their nature is capable of, we are justified in ascribing to the preferred enjoyment a superiority in quality, so far outweighing quantity as to render it, in comparison, of small account.

Now it is an unquestionable fact that those who are equally acquainted with, and equally capable of appreciating and enjoying, both, do give a most marked preference to the manner of existence which employs their higher faculties. Few human creatures would consent to be changed into any of the lower animals, for a promise of the fullest allowance of a beast's pleasures; no intelligent human being would consent to be a fool, no instructed person would be an ignoramus, no person of feeling and conscience would be selfish and base, even though they should be persuaded that the fool, the dunce, or the rascal is better satisfied with his lot than they are with theirs. They would not resign what they possess more than he for the most complete satisfaction of all the desires which they have in common with him. If they ever fancy they would, it is only in cases of unhappiness so extreme, that to escape from it they would exchange their lot for almost any other, however undesirable in their own eyes. A being of higher faculties requires more to make him happy, is capable probably of more acute suffering, and certainly accessible to it at more points, than one of an inferior type; but in spite of these liabilities, he can never really wish to sink into what he feels to be a lower grade of existence. . . .

Whoever supposes that this preference takes place at a sacrifice of happiness — that the superior being, in anything like equal circumstances, is not happier than the inferior — confounds the two very different ideas, of happiness, and content. It is indisputable that the being whose capacities of enjoyment are low, has the greatest chance of having them fully satisfied; and a highly endowed being will always feel that any happiness which he can look for, as the world is constituted, is imperfect. But he can learn to bear its imperfections, if they are at all bearable; and they will not make him envy the being who is indeed unconscious of the imperfections, but only because he feels not at all the good which those imperfections qualify. It is better to be a human being dissatisfied than a pig satisfied; better to be Socrates dissatisfied than a fool satisfied. And if the fool, or the pig, are a different opinion, it is because they only know their own side of the question. The other party to the comparison knows both sides. . . .

From this verdict of the only competent judges, I apprehend there can be no appeal. On a question which is the best worth having of two pleasures, . . . the judgment of those who are qualified by knowledge of both, or, if they differ, that of the majority among them, must be admitted as final. . . .

I have dwelt on this point, as being a necessary part of a perfectly just conception of Utility or Happiness, considered as the directive rule of human conduct. But it is by no means an indispensable condition to the acceptance of the utilitarian standard;

for that standard is not the agent's own greatest happiness, but the greatest amount of happiness altogether; and if it may possibly be doubted whether a noble character is always the happier for its nobleness, there can be no doubt that it makes other people happier, and that the world in general is immensely a gainer by it. Utilitarianism, therefore, could only attain its end by the general cultivation of nobleness of character, even if each individual were only benefited by the nobleness of others, and his own, so far as happiness is concerned, were a sheer deduction from the benefit. . . .

According to the Greatest Happiness Principle, as above explained, the ultimate end, with reference to and for the sake of which all other things are desirable (whether we are considering our own good or that of other people), is an existence exempt as far as possible from pain, and as rich as possible in enjoyments, both in point of quantity and quality; the test of quality, and the rule for measuring it against quantity, being the preference felt by those who in their opportunities of experience, to which must be added their habits of self-consciousness and self-observation, are best furnished with the means of comparison. This, being, according to the utilitarian opinion, the end of human action, is necessarily also the standard of morality; which may accordingly be defined, the rules and precepts for human conduct, by the observance of which an existence such as has been described might be, to the greatest extent possible, secured to all mankind; and not to them only, but, so far as the nature of things admits, to the whole sentient creation.

Against this doctrine, however, arises another class of objectors, who say that happiness, in any form, cannot be the rational purpose of human life and action; because, in the first place, it is unattainable. . . .

Something might still be said for the utilitarian theory; since utility includes not solely the pursuit of happiness, but the prevention or mitigation of unhappiness; and if the former aim be chimerical, there will be all the greater scope and more imperative need for the latter. . . . If by happiness be meant a continuity of highly pleasurable excitement, it is evident enough that this is impossible. A state of exalted pleasure lasts only moments, or in some cases, and with some intermissions, hours or days, and is the occasional brilliant flash of enjoyment, not its permanent and steady flame. Of this the philosophers who have taught that happiness is the end of life were as fully aware as those who taunt them. The happiness which they meant was not a life of rapture; but moments of such, in an existence made up of few and transitory pains, many and various pleasures, with a decided predominance of the active over the passive, and having as the foundation of the whole, not to expect more from life than it is capable of bestowing. A life thus composed, to those who have been fortunate enough to obtain it, has always appeared worthy of the name of happiness. . . .

. . . The main constituents of a satisfied life appear to be two, either of which by itself is often found sufficient for the purpose: tranquillity, and excitement. With much tranquillity, many find that they can be content with very little pleasure: with much excitement, many can reconcile themselves to a considerable quantity of pain. There is assuredly no inherent impossibility in enabling even the mass of mankind to unite both; since the two are so far from being incompatible that they are in natural alliance, the prolongation of either being a preparation for, and exciting a wish for, the other. . . . When people who are tolerably fortunate in their outward lot do not find in life sufficient enjoyment to make it valuable to them, the cause generally is, caring for nobody but themselves. To those who have neither public nor private affections, the excitements of life are much curtailed, and in any case dwindle in value as the time approaches when all selfish interests must be terminated by death: while those who leave after them objects of personal affection, and especially those who have also cultivated a fellow-feeling with the collective interests of mankind, retain as lively an interest in life on the eve of death as in the vigour of youth and health. Next to selfishness, the principal cause which makes life unsatisfactory is want of mental cultivation. A cultivated mind — I do not mean that of a philosopher, but any mind to which the fountains of knowledge have been opened, and which has been taught, in any tolerable degree, to exercise its faculties — finds sources of inexhaustible interest in all that surrounds it; in the objects of nature, the achievements of art, the imaginations of poetry, the incidents of history, the ways of mankind, past and present, and their prospects in the future. . . .

Now there is absolutely no reason in the nature of things why an amount of mental culture sufficient to give an intelligent interest in these objects of contemplation, should not be the inheritance of every one born in a civilised country. As little is there an inherent necessity that any human being should be a selfish egotist, devoid of every feeling or care but those which centre in his own miserable individuality. Something far superior to this is sufficiently common even now. . . . Genuine private affections and a sincere interest in the public good, are possible, though in unequal degrees, to every rightly brought up human being. In a world in which there is so much to interest, so much to enjoy, and so much also to correct and improve, every one who has this moderate amount of moral and intellectual requisites is capable of an existence which may be called enviable; and unless such a person, through bad laws, or subjection to the will of others, is denied the liberty to use the sources of happiness within his reach, he will not fail to find this enviable existence, if he escape the positive evils of life, the great sources of physical and mental suffering — such as indigence, disease, and the unkindness, worthlessness, or premature loss of objects of affection. . . . Most of the great positive evils of the world are in themselves removable, and will, if human affairs continue to improve, be in the end reduced within narrow limits. Poverty, in any sense implying suffering, may be completely extinguished by the wisdom of society, combined with the good sense and providence of individuals. Even that most intractable of enemies, disease, may be indefinitely reduced in dimensions by good physical and moral education, and proper control of noxious influences; while the progress of science holds out a promise for the future of still more direct conquests over this detestable foe. And every advance in that direction relieves us from some, not only of the chances which cut short our own lives, but, what concerns us still more, which deprive us of those in whom our happiness is wrapt up. As for vicissitudes of fortune, and other disappointments connected with worldly circumstances, these are principally the effect either of gross imprudence, of ill-regulated desires, or of bad or imperfect social institutions. . . .

Unquestionably it is possible to do without happiness; it is done involuntarily by nineteen-twentieths of mankind, even in those parts of our present world which are least deep in barbarism; and it often has to be done voluntarily by the hero or the martyr, for the sake of something which he prizes more than his individual happiness. But this something, what is it, unless the happiness of others or some of the requisites of happiness? It is noble to be capable of resigning entirely one's own portion of happiness, or chances of it: but, after all, this self-sacrifice must be for some end; it is not its own end; and if we are told that its end is not happiness, but virtue, which is better than happiness, I ask, would the sacrifice be made if the hero or martyr did not believe that it would earn for others immunity from similar sacrifices? Would it be made if he thought that his renunciation of happiness for himself would produce no fruit for any of his fellow creatures, but to make their lot like his, and place them also in the condition of persons who have renounced happiness? . . .

The utilitarian morality does recognise in human beings the power of sacrificing their own greatest good for the good of others. It only refuses to admit that the sacrifice is itself a good. A sacrifice which does not increase, or tend to increase, the sum total of happiness, it considers as wasted. . . .

The happiness which forms the utilitarian standard of what is right in conduct, is not the agent's own happiness, but that of all concerned. As between his own happiness and that of others, utilitarianism requires him to be as strictly impartial as a disinterested and benevolent spectator. In the golden rule of Jesus of Nazareth, we read the complete spirit of the ethics of utility. To do as you would be done by, and to love your neighbour as yourself, constitute the ideal perfection of utilitarian morality. As the means of making the nearest approach to this ideal, utility would enjoin, first, that laws and social arrangements should place the happiness, or (as speaking practically it may be called) the interest, of every individual, as nearly as possible in harmony with the interest of the whole; and secondly, that education and opinion, which have so vast a power over human character, should so use that power as to establish in the mind of every individual an indissoluble association between his own happiness and the good of the whole; especially between his own happiness and the practice of such modes of conduct, negative and positive, as regard for the universal happiness prescribes; so that not only he may be unable to conceive the possibility of happiness to himself, consistently with conduct opposed to the general good, but also that a direct impulse to promote the general good may be in every individual one of the habitual motives of action, and the sentiments connected therewith may fill a large and prominent place in every human being's sentient existence. . . .

[Some] objectors to utilitarianism . . . sometimes find fault with its standard as being too high for humanity. They say it is exacting too much to require that people shall always act from the inducement of promoting the general interests of society. But this is to mistake the very meaning of a standard of morals, and confound the rule of action with the motive of it. It is the business of ethics to tell us what are our duties, or by what test we may know them; but no system of ethics requires that the sole motive of all we do shall be a feeling of duty; on the contrary, ninety-nine hundredths of all our actions are done from other motives, and rightly so done, if the rule of duty does not condemn them. . . . He who saves a fellow creature from drowning does what is morally right, whether his motive be duty, or the hope of being paid for his trouble; he who betrays the friend that trusts him, is guilty of a crime, even if his object be to serve another friend to whom he is under greater obligations.

. . . It is a misapprehension of the utilitarian mode of thought, to conceive it as implying that people should fix their minds upon so wide a generality as the world, or society at large. The great majority of good actions are intended not for the benefit of the world, but for that of individuals, of which the good of the world is made up; and the thoughts of the most virtuous man need not on these occasions travel beyond the particular persons concerned, except so far as is necessary to assure himself that in benefiting them he is not violating the rights, that is, the legitimate and authorised expectations, of any one else. The multiplication of happiness is, according to the utilitarian ethics, the object of virtue: the occasions on which any person (except one in a thousand) has it in his power to do this on an extended scale, in other words to be a public benefactor, are but exceptional; and on these occasions alone is he called on to consider public utility; in every other case, private utility, the interest or happiness of some few persons, is all he has to attend to. Those alone the influence of whose actions extends to society in general, need concern themselves habitually about so large an object. In the case of abstinences indeed — of things which people forbear to do from moral considerations, though the consequences in the particular case might be beneficial — it would be unworthy of an intelligent agent not to be consciously aware that the action is of a class which, if practised generally, would be generally injurious, and that this is the ground of the obligation to abstain from it. . . .

The same considerations dispose of another reproach against the doctrine of utility, founded on a still grosser misconception of the purpose of a standard of morality, and of the very meaning of the words right and wrong. It is often affirmed that utilitarianism renders men cold and unsympathising; that it chills their moral feelings towards individuals; that it makes them regard only the dry and hard consideration of the consequences of actions, not taking into their moral estimate the qualities from which those actions emanate. If the assertion means that they do not allow their judgment respecting the rightness or wrongness of an action to be influenced by their opinion of the qualities of the person who does it, this is a complaint not against utilitarianism, but against having any standard of morality at all; for certainly no known ethical standard decides an action to be good or bad because it is done by a good or a bad man, still less because done by an amiable, a brave, or a benevolent man, or the contrary. These considerations are relevant, not to the estimation of actions, but of persons; and there is nothing in the utilitarian theory inconsistent with the fact that there are other things which interest us in persons besides the rightness and wrongness of their actions. . . . Utilitarians are quite aware . . . that a right action does not necessarily indicate a virtuous character, and that actions which are blamable, often proceed from qualities entitled to praise. When this is apparent in any particular case, it modifies their estimation, not certainly of the act, but of the agent. I grant that they are, notwithstanding, of opinion, that in the long run the best proof of a good character is good actions; and resolutely refuse to consider any mental disposition as good, of which the predominant tendency is to produce bad conduct. . . .

Utility is often summarily stigmatised as an immoral doctrine by giving it the name of Expediency, and taking advantage of the popular use of that term to contrast it with Principle. But the Expedient, in the sense in which it is opposed to the Right, generally means that which is expedient for the particular interest of the agent himself. . . . When it means anything better than this, it means that which is expedient for some immediate object, some temporary purpose, but which violates a rule whose observance is expedient in a much higher degree. The Expedient, in this sense, instead of being the same thing with the useful, is a branch of the hurtful. Thus, it would often be expedient, for the purpose of getting over some momentary embarrassment, or attaining some object immediately useful to ourselves or others, to tell a lie. But inasmuch as the cultivation in ourselves of a sensitive feeling on the subject of veracity, is one of the most useful, and the enfeeblement of that feeling one of the most hurtful, things to which our conduct can be instrumental; and inasmuch as any, even unintentional, deviation from truth, does that much towards weakening the trustworthiness of human assertion, which is not only the principal support of all present social well-being, but the insufficiency of which does more than any one thing that can be named to keep back civilisation, virtue, everything on which human happiness on the largest scale depends; we feel that the violation, for a present advantage, of a rule of such transcendant expediency, is not expedient, and that he who, for the sake of a convenience to himself or to some other individual, does what depends on him to deprive mankind of the good, and inflict upon them the evil, involved in the greater or less reliance which they can place in each other's word, acts the part of one of their worst enemies. Yet that even this rule, sacred as it is, admits of possible exceptions, is acknowledged by all moralists; the chief of which is when the withholding of some fact (as of information from a malefactor, or of bad news from a person dangerously ill) would save an individual (especially an individual other than oneself) from great and unmerited evil, and when the withholding can only be effected by denial. But in order that the exception may not extend itself beyond the need, and may have the least possible effect in weakening reliance on veracity, it ought to be recognised, and, if possible, its limits defined; and if the principle of utility is good for anything, it must be good for weighing these conflicting utilities against one another, and marking out the region within which one or the other preponderates.

. . . [Some object] that there is not time, previous to action, for calculating and weighing the effects of any line of conduct on the general happiness. This is exactly as if any one were to say that it is impossible to guide our conduct by Christianity, because there is not time, on every occasion on which anything has to be done, to read through the Old and New Testaments. The answer to the objection is, that there has been ample time, namely, the whole past duration of the human species. During all that time, mankind have been learning by experience the tendencies of actions; on which experience all the prudence, as well as all the morality of life, are dependent. People talk as if the commencement of this course of experience had hitherto been put off, and as if, at the moment when some man feels tempted to meddle with the property or life of another, he had to begin considering for the first time whether murder and theft are injurious to human happiness. . . .

[M]ankind must by this time have acquired positive beliefs as to the effects of some actions on their happiness; and the beliefs which have thus come down are the rules of morality for the multitude, and for the philosopher until he has succeeded in finding better. . . . The corollaries from the principle of utility, like the precepts of every practical art, admit of indefinite improvement. . . .

But to consider the rules of morality as improvable, is one thing; to pass over the intermediate generalisations entirely, and endeavour to test each individual action directly by the first principle, is another. It is a strange notion that the acknowledgment of a first principle is inconsistent with the admission of secondary ones. To inform a traveller respecting the place of his ultimate destination, is not to forbid the use of landmarks and direction-posts on the way. The proposition that happiness is the end and aim of morality, does not mean that no road ought to be laid down to that goal, or that persons going thither should not be advised to take one direction rather than another. . . . Nobody argues that the art of navigation is not founded on astronomy, because sailors cannot wait to calculate the Nautical Almanack.[2] Being rational creatures, they go to sea with it ready calculated; and all rational creatures go out upon the sea of life with their minds made up on the common questions of right and wrong, as well as on many of the far more difficult questions of wise and foolish. . . . Whatever we adopt as the fundamental principle of morality, we require subordinate principles to apply it by; the impossibility of doing without them, being common to all systems, can afford no argument against any one in particular. . . .

The remainder of the stock arguments against utilitarianism mostly consist in laying to its charge the common infirmities of human nature. . . . We are told that a utilitarian will be apt to make his own particular case an exception to moral rules, and, when under temptation, will see a utility in the breach of a rule, greater than he will see in its observance. But is utility the only creed which is able to furnish us with excuses for evil doing, and means of cheating our own conscience? They are afforded in abundance by all doctrines which recognise as a fact in morals the existence of conflicting considerations; which all doctrines do, that have been believed by sane persons. It is not the fault of any creed, but of the complicated nature of human affairs, that rules of conduct cannot be so framed as to require no exceptions, and that hardly any kind of action can safely be laid down as either always obligatory or always condemnable. There is no ethical creed which does not temper the rigidity of its laws, by giving a certain latitude, under the moral responsibility of the agent, for accommodation to peculiarities of circumstances; and under every creed, at the opening thus made, self-deception and dishonest casuistry[3] get in. There exists no moral system under which there do not arise unequivocal cases of conflicting obligation. . . . If utility is the ultimate source of moral obligations, utility may be invoked to decide between them when their demands are incompatible. Though the application of the standard may be difficult, it is better than none at all: while in other systems, the moral laws all claiming independent authority, there is no common umpire entitled to interfere between them; their claims to precedence one over another rest on little better than

2. To assist in navigation, a nautical almanac offers projections about the locations and distances of celestial bodies during a calendar year. The information could be calculated by sailors, *en route*, with difficulty, but Mill's point is that it is reasonable to rely on prior calculations.

3. Casuistry is the ethical evaluation of particular cases, with a sensitivity to their distinguishing details. The term "casuistry" is sometimes used pejoratively to suggest the use of specious reasoning to make distinctions, often to serve one's own purposes.

sophistry, and unless determined, as they generally are, by the unacknowledged influence of considerations of utility, afford a free scope for the action of personal desires and partialities. We must remember that only in these cases of conflict between secondary principles is it requisite that first principles should be appealed to.

## TEST YOUR UNDERSTANDING

1. For Mill, is it better to be "a human being dissatisfied than a pig satisfied"? Is it better to be "Socrates dissatisfied" or a satisfied fool?

2. For a utilitarian, happiness "forms the standard of what is right in conduct." Whose happiness counts?

3. Mill claims that utilitarianism tells us what our duties are, but not what our motives should be in performing them. What is his example of the difference between the "rule of action" and the "motive of action"? What objection to utilitarianism does he use this distinction to answer?

## NOTES AND QUESTIONS

1. *Mill on pleasure:* Mill responds to some critics of early forms of utilitarianism by rejecting *simple hedonism.* Mill does not equate "pleasure" with sensory experiences of pleasure. Moreover, he contends that not all pleasures are alike qualitatively, e.g., pleasure need not resemble the lovely feeling one gets when basking in the sun or enjoying an ice cream. Finally, he observes that not all pleasures are equally important. His more sophisticated view of pleasure may save his version of utilitarianism from the insult that it is a "doctrine worthy only of swine." Is his account open to the objection that one might fail to enjoy and even dislike what Mill counts as an episode of "pleasure"? Does that render his account of pleasure implausible and does it cast doubt upon his utilitarian theory?

2. *Is pleasure always good and is pain always bad?* Should we agree that pleasure and the absence of pain are always good? Consider the following criticisms: (a) The pleasure a sadist receives from contemplating another's (nonconsensual) suffering does not seem good in any way. (b) Further, the emotional pain of guilt that a criminal feels upon recognizing and regretting the wrong of her past actions is a good thing. Someone who has done something wrong but does not suffer painful pangs of guilt is defective and does not lead a better life.

3. *Pleasure is the only good.* Some critics agree with Mill that actions are right because of their consequences. They and Mill are *consequentialists.* Non-utilitarian consequentialists differ from Mill about how to characterize *which* consequences are valuable. They argue that pleasure is not the only good and that other individual and social

states are also ends (or intrinsically valuable things). For example, some contend that it is intrinsically desirable for individuals to have the status of an equal and for societies to manifest equal social relations; further, equality is desirable independent from its bringing pleasure (although it probably does). To take a different example, some believe that preserving art, architecture, history, and the environment are intrinsically desirable ends, independent of whether people gain pleasure from or prefer their preservation. Indeed, people *should* prefer their preservation. How might Mill respond? Would those responses persuade you?

4. *Harming innocents as a means to generating aggregate utility.* Consider the following three scenarios:

    (i)    A super-sized stadium full of sadists gathers to witness the nonconsensual, public flogging of an innocent child. Enough fervent sadists attend so that the aggregate utility, given their intense experiences of elation, would outweigh the disutility experienced by the victim and his sympathizers, even taking into account his absolutely awful pain, his feelings of betrayal, and subsequent trauma.

    (ii)   Suppose if a child is privately tortured, that upon hearing his screams, his parent will reveal secret information that will assist the government in trade negotiations and raise the nation's standard of living a small amount, thereby generating enough positive utility for citizens that would, in the aggregate, outweigh (numerically) the terrific disutility experienced by the solitary victim, his parents, and the torturer.

    (iii)  Suppose if a child is privately tortured, that his parent will reveal secret information that will prevent a terrorist bombing, save 1,000 innocent lives, and thereby generate more positive utility than the disutility experienced by the victim and his parent.

    Is utilitarianism vulnerable to the objections that (a) it would require the child be tortured in all of these cases and (b) if the utility produced were equal in quantity, that it would not regard these cases as different and would not be sensitive to the reasons why utility was produced?

5. The issues raised by these questions are crucial points of contention between consequentialists and some non-consequentialist critics who argue that, morally, we are sometimes *prohibited* from bringing about the best consequences. For instance, they claim that some courses of action are horrific in nature and must not be taken, even if they sometimes produce good consequences. Actions like torture, killing for sport, or scapegoating the innocent involve treating human beings in ways that are inconsistent with a core feature of morality: to show respect for each person. We must not treat any person with profound disrespect even if our purposes are otherwise good. This position represents an example of **deontology**, the view that, morally, there are certain sorts of actions we have duties to perform or to refrain from and these duties may be characterized by features other than the consequences they happen to bring about in particular circumstances. Some important discussions of the deontological criticism of utilitarianism may be found in Bernard Williams, "A Critique of Utilitarianism," in J.J.C. Smart and Bernard Williams, *Utilitarianism: For and Against* (Cambridge

University Press: 1975); Thomas Nagel, "War and Massacre," *Philosophy and Public Affairs* 1, no. 2 (1972): 123–44 (excerpted on p. 901 of this anthology); Samuel Scheffler, *The Rejection of Consequentialism*, rev. ed. (Oxford University Press, 1994); Frances Kamm, "Non-consequentialism, the Person as an End-in-Itself, and the Significance of Status," *Philosophy and Public Affairs* 21, no. 4 (1992): 354–89.

## Immanuel Kant (1724–1804)

Kant was a German philosopher of the Enlightenment whose work extolled the faculty of reason, exploring its powers and limitations. He was born in Königsberg and was a professor at the University of Königsberg. His work exerted and continues to exert a profound influence on the development of modern and contemporary philosophy in ethics, political philosophy, metaphysics, epistemology, the philosophy of mind and of psychology, aesthetics, and the philosophy of religion. His most famous books include *The Critique of Pure Reason* (1781), *Prolegomena to Any Future Metaphysics* (1783), *Groundwork of the Metaphysics of Morals* (1785), *The Critique of Practical Reason* (1788), *The Critique of Judgment* (1790), and *The Metaphysics of Morals* (1797).

# GROUNDWORK OF THE METAPHYSICS OF MORALS

## Second Section: Transition from Popular Moral Philosophy to the Metaphysics of Morals

Unless one wants to refuse the concept of morality all truth and reference to some possible object, one cannot deny that its law is so extensive in its significance that it must hold not merely for human beings but for all *rational beings as such*, not merely under contingent conditions and with exceptions, but with *absolute necessity*. . . . [I]t is clear that no experience can give occasion to infer even just the possibility of such apodictic laws.[1] For by what right can we bring what is perhaps valid only under the contingent conditions of humanity into unlimited respect, as a universal prescription for every rational nature?

Moreover, one could not give morality worse counsel than by seeking to borrow it from examples. For every example of it that is presented to me must itself first be judged according to principles of morality, whether it is actually worthy to serve as

---

1. That is, indisputable or certain laws.

an original example, i.e. as a model; but by no means can it furnish the concept of it at the outset. Even the Holy One of the Gospel must first be compared with our ideal of moral perfection before he is recognized as one. . . . Imitation has no place at all in moral matters; and examples serve for encouragement only, i.e. they put beyond doubt the feasibility of what the law commands, they make intuitive what the practical[2] rule expresses more generally, but they can never entitle us to set aside their true original, which lies in reason, and to go by examples.

. . . It is clear from what has been said that all moral concepts have their seat and origin completely a priori[3] in reason . . . that they cannot be abstracted from any empirical and hence merely contingent cognition; that their dignity to serve us as supreme practical principles lies just in this purity of their origin; that every time in adding anything empirical to them one takes away as much from their genuine influence and from the unlimited worth of actions; that it is not only a requirement of the greatest necessity for theoretical purposes, when only speculation counts, but also a matter of the greatest practical importance to draw its concepts and laws from pure reason, to set them forth pure and unmingled, indeed to determine the scope of this entire practical but pure rational cognition, i.e. the entire faculty of pure practical reason, and in so doing not . . . to make its principles dependent on the particular nature of human reason, but because moral laws are to hold for every rational being as such, already to derive them from the universal concept of a rational being as such. . . .

Every thing in nature works according to laws. Only a rational being has the capacity to act *according to the representation* of laws, i.e. according to principles, or a *will*. Since *reason* is required for deriving actions from laws, the will is nothing other than practical reason. If reason determines the will without fail, then the actions of such a being that are recognized as objectively necessary are also subjectively necessary; i.e. the will is a capacity to choose *only that* which reason, independently of inclination, recognizes as practically necessary, i.e. as good. If, however, reason all by itself does not sufficiently determine the will, if it is also subject to subjective conditions (to certain incentives) that are not always in agreement with the objective ones; in a word, if the will does not *in itself* completely conform with reason (as is actually the case with human beings), then actions objectively recognized as necessary are subjectively contingent, and the determination of such a will, in conformity with objective laws, is *necessitation*; i.e. the relation of objective laws to a will not altogether good is represented as the determination of the will of a rational being by grounds of reason, to which this will is not, however, according to its nature necessarily obedient.

The representation of an objective principle in so far as it is necessitating for a will is called a command (of reason), and the formula of the command is called imperative.

---

2. When Kant uses "practical," he is referring to principles, concepts, or reasoning relevant to action (as opposed merely to thought or reasoning independent of action).

3. Here, Kant means that moral concepts, moral principles, and their application can be known through consulting reason alone and one need not consult experience, our behavior, or our customs to know them. They apply to us and can be known merely by virtue of our being rational.

All imperatives are expressed by an *ought,* and by this indicate the relation of an objective law of reason to a will that according to its subjective constitution is not necessarily determined by it (a necessitation). They say that to do or to omit something would be good, but they say it to a will that does not always do something just because it is represented to it that it would be good to do it. Practically *good,* however, is what determines the will by means of representations of reason, hence not from subjective causes, but objectively, i.e. from grounds that are valid for every rational being, as such. It is distinguished from the *agreeable,* as that which influences the will only by means of sensation from merely subjective causes, which hold only for the senses of this or that one, and not as a principle of reason, which holds for everyone.

. . . Now, all *imperatives* command either *hypothetically,* or *categorically.* The former represent the practical necessity of a possible action as a means to achieving something else that one wants (or that at least is possible for one to want). The categorical imperative would be the one that represented an action as objectively necessary by itself, without reference to another end.

Because every practical law represents a possible action as good and hence, for a subject practically determinable by reason, as necessary, all imperatives are formulae for the determination of an action necessary according to the principle of a will that is good in some way. Now, if the action would be good merely as a means to *something else,* the imperative is *hypothetical*; if the action is represented as good *in itself,* hence as necessary in a will that in itself conforms to reason, as its principle, then it is *categorical.*

. . . Now, the skill in the choice of the means to one's own greatest well-being can be called prudence in the narrowest sense. Thus the imperative that refers to the choice of means to one's own happiness, i.e. the prescription of prudence, is still *hypothetical*; the action is not commanded per se, but just as a means to another purpose.

Finally, there is one imperative that — without presupposing as its condition any other purpose to be attained by a certain course of conduct — commands this conduct immediately. This imperative is categorical. It concerns not the matter of the action or what is to result from it, but the form and the principle from which it does itself follow; and the essential good in it consists in the disposition, let the result be what it may. This imperative may be called that of morality. . . .

Now the question arises: how are all these imperatives possible? . . . How an imperative of skill is possible probably requires no special discussion. Whoever wills the end also wills (in so far as reason has decisive influence on his actions) the indispensably necessary means to it that is in his control. As far as willing is concerned, this proposition is analytic; for in the willing of an object, as my effect, my causality is already thought, as an acting cause, i.e. the use of means, and the imperative already extracts the concept of actions necessary to this end from the concept of a willing of this end.

The imperatives of prudence would totally and entirely coincide with those of skill, and be equally analytic, if only it were so easy to provide a determinate concept of happiness. For here as well as there it would be said: whoever wills the end also wills (in conformity with reason necessarily) the only means to it that are in his control. But, unfortunately, the concept of happiness is so indeterminate a concept that, even though every human being wishes to achieve it, yet he can never say determinately and in agreement with himself what he actually wishes and wants. The cause of this is: that the elements that belong to the concept of happiness are one and all empirical, i.e. must be borrowed from experience. . . .

By contrast, the question of how the imperative of *morality* is possible is no doubt the only one in need of a solution, since it is not hypothetical at all, and thus the objectively represented necessity cannot rely on any presupposition, as in the case of the hypothetical imperatives. However, it is never to slip our attention in this matter that it cannot be made out *by any example,* and hence empirically, whether there is any such imperative at all; but to be dreaded that all imperatives that appear categorical may yet in some hidden way be hypothetical. E.g. when it is said that you ought not to make deceitful promises; and one assumes that the necessity of this omission is not merely giving counsel for avoiding some other ill, so that what is said would be: you ought not to make lying promises lest, if it comes to light, you are deprived of your credit; but that an action of this kind must be considered as by itself evil, thus that the imperative of the prohibition is categorical; one still cannot establish in any example with certainty that the will is here determined, without another incentive, merely by the law, even if it appears so; for it is always possible that fear of embarrassment, perhaps also an obscure dread of other dangers, may covertly influence the will. . . .

We shall thus have to investigate the possibility of a *categorical* imperative entirely a priori, since we do not here enjoy the advantage that its actuality is being given in experience, in which case its possibility would be necessary not for corroboration, but merely for explanation. For the time being, however, this much can be seen: that the categorical imperative alone expresses a practical law, and that the others can indeed one and all be called *principles* of the will, but not laws; since what it is necessary to do merely for attaining a discretionary purpose can be regarded as in itself contingent, and we can always be rid of the prescription if we give up the purpose, whereas the unconditional command leaves the will no free discretion with regard to the opposite, and hence alone carries with it that necessity which we demand for a law.

In the case of this categorical imperative or law of morality the ground of the difficulty (of insight into its possibility) is actually very great. It is an a priori synthetic practical proposition[4] and since gaining insight into the possibility of propositions of this kind causes so much difficulty in theoretical cognition, it can easily be inferred that in practical cognition there will be no less.

---

4. Here, Kant means that the concept of a categorical imperative is one that could be known without consulting experience but is **synthetic,** by which he means it is not a proposition true by definition.

With this problem, we shall first try to see whether the mere concept of a categorical imperative may perhaps also furnish its formula, which contains the proposition that alone can be a categorical imperative . . .

When I think of a *hypothetical* imperative as such I do not know in advance what it will contain, until I am given the condition. But when I think of a *categorical* imperative I know at once what it contains. For since besides the law the imperative contains only the necessity of the maxim[5] to conform with this law, whereas the law contains no condition to which it was limited, nothing is left but the universality of a law as such, with which the maxim of the action ought to conform, and it is this conformity alone that the imperative actually represents as necessary.

There is therefore only a single categorical imperative, and it is this: *act only according to that maxim through which you can at the same time will that it become a universal law.*

. . . Since the universality of the law according to which effects happen constitutes that which is actually called *nature* in the most general sense (according to its form), i.e. the existence of things in so far as it is determined according to universal laws, the universal imperative of duty could also be expressed as follows: *so act as if the maxim of your action were to become by your will a universal law of nature.*

We shall now enumerate some duties, according to their usual division, into duties to ourselves and to other human beings, into perfect and imperfect duties.

1) Someone who feels weary of life because of a series of ills that has grown to the point of hopelessness is still so far in possession of his reason that he can ask himself whether it is not perhaps contrary to a duty to oneself to take one's own life. Now he tries out: whether the maxim of his action could possibly become a universal law of nature. But his maxim is: from self-love I make it my principle to shorten my life if, when protracted any longer, it threatens more ill than it promises agreeableness. The only further question is whether this principle of self-love could become a universal law of nature. But then one soon sees that a nature whose law it were to destroy life itself by means of the same sensation the function of which it is to impel towards the advancement of life, would contradict itself and would thus not subsist as a nature, hence that maxim could not possibly take the place of a universal law of nature, and consequently conflicts entirely with the supreme principle of all duty.

2) Another sees himself pressured by need to borrow money. He knows full well that he will not be able to repay, but also sees that nothing will be lent to him unless he solemnly promises to repay it at a determinate time. He feels like making such a promise; but he still has enough conscience to ask himself: is it not impermissible and contrary to duty to help oneself out of need in such a way? Suppose that he still resolved to do so, his maxim of the action would go as follows: when I believe myself to be in need of money I shall borrow money, and promise to repay it, even

---

5. A *maxim* is the subjective principle of acting, and must be distinguished from the *objective* principle, namely the practical law. The former contains the practical rule determined by reason conformably with the conditions of the subject (often his ignorance or also his inclinations), and is therefore the principle in accordance with which the subject *acts*; but the law is the objective principle valid for every rational being, and the principle in accordance with which he *ought to act*, i.e., an imperative. [Kant's note.]

though I know that it will never happen. Now this principle of self-love, or of one's own benefit, is perhaps quite consistent with my whole future well-being, but the question now is: whether it is right? I therefore transform the imposition of self-love into a universal law, and arrange the question as follows: how things would stand if my maxim became a universal law. Now, I then see at once that it could never hold as a universal law of nature and harmonize with itself, but must necessarily contradict itself. For the universality of a law that everyone, once he believes himself to be in need, could promise whatever he fancies with the intention not to keep it, would make the promise and the end one may pursue with it itself impossible, as no one would believe he was being promised anything, but would laugh about any such utterance, as a vain pretense.

3) A third finds in himself a talent that by means of some cultivation could make him a useful human being in all sorts of respects. However, he sees himself in comfortable circumstances and prefers to give himself up to gratification rather than to make the effort to expand and improve his fortunate natural predispositions. Yet he still asks himself: whether his maxim of neglecting his natural gifts, besides its agreement with his propensity to amusement, also agrees with what one calls duty. Now he sees that a nature could indeed still subsist according to such a universal law, even if human beings . . . should let their talents rust and be intent on devoting their lives merely to idleness, amusement, procreation, in a word, to enjoyment; but he cannot possibly will that this become a universal law of nature, or as such be placed in us by natural instinct. For as a rational being he necessarily wills that all capacities in him be developed, because they serve him and are given to him for all sorts of possible purposes.

Yet a *fourth,* who is prospering while he sees that others have to struggle with great hardships (whom he could just as well help), thinks: what's it to me? May everyone be as happy as heaven wills, or as he can make himself, I shall take nothing away from him, not even envy him; I just do not feel like contributing anything to his well-being, or his assistance in need! Now, certainly, if such a way of thinking were to become a universal law of nature, the human race could very well subsist, and no doubt still better than when everyone chatters about compassion and benevolence, even develops the zeal to perform such actions occasionally, but also cheats wherever he can, sells out the right of human beings, or infringes it in some other way. But even though it is possible that a universal law of nature could very well subsist according to that maxim, it is still impossible to will that such a principle hold everywhere as a law of nature. For a will that resolved upon this would conflict with itself, as many cases can yet come to pass in which one needs the love and compassion of others, and in which, by such a law of nature sprung from his own will, he would rob himself of all hope of the assistance he wishes for himself.

These, then, are some of the many actual duties, or at least of what we take to be such, whose division can clearly be seen from the one principle stated above. One must *be able to will* that a maxim of our action become a universal law: this is as such the canon of judging it morally. Some actions are such that their maxim cannot even be *thought* without contradiction as a universal law of nature; let alone that one could *will* that it *should* become such. In the case of others that inner impossibility is indeed not to be found, but it is still impossible to *will* that their maxim be elevated to the universality of a law of nature, because such a will would contradict itself. It is easy to see that the first conflicts with strict or narrower (unrelenting) duty, the second only with wider (meritorious) duty, and thus that all duties, as far as the kind of obligation (not the object of their action) is concerned, have by these examples been set out completely in their dependence on the one principle.

If we now attend to ourselves in every transgression of a duty, we find that we actually do not will that our maxim should become a universal law, since that is impossible for us, but that its opposite should rather generally remain a law; we just take the liberty of making an *exception* to it for ourselves, or (just for this once) to the advantage of our inclination. Consequently, if we considered everything from one and the same point of view, namely that of reason, we would find a contradiction in our own will, namely that a certain principle be objectively necessary as a universal law and yet subjectively should not hold universally, but allow of exceptions.

We have thus established at least this much, that if duty is a concept that is to contain significance and actual legislation for our actions it can be expressed only in categorical imperatives, but by no means in hypothetical ones; likewise we have—and this is already a lot—presented distinctly and determined for every use the content of the categorical imperative, which would have to contain the principle of all duty (if there were such a thing at all).

. . . [One] must put the thought right out of one's mind that the reality of this principle can be derived from some *particular property of human nature.* For duty is to be practical unconditional necessity of action; it must thus hold for all rational beings (to which an imperative can at all apply), and *only in virtue of this* be a law also for every human will. By contrast, whatever is derived from the special natural predisposition of humanity, from certain feelings and propensity, and indeed even, possibly, from a special tendency peculiar to human reason, and would not have to hold necessarily for the will of every rational being—that can indeed yield a maxim for us, but not a law, a subjective principle on which propensity and inclination would fain have us act, but not an objective principle on which we would be *instructed* to act even if every propensity, inclination and natural arrangement of ours were against it. . . .

The will is thought as a capacity to determine itself to action *in conformity with the representation of certain laws.* And such a capacity can be found only in rational beings. Now, what serves the will as the objective ground of its self-determination is the *end,* and this, if it is given by mere reason, must hold equally for all rational beings. By contrast, what contains merely the ground of the possibility of an action the effect of which is an end is called the *means.* The subjective ground of desiring is the *incentive,* the objective ground of willing the *motivating ground;* hence the difference between subjective ends, which rest on incentives, and objective ones, which depend on motivating grounds that hold for every rational being. Practical principles are *formal* if they abstract from all subjective ends; they are *material* if they have these, and hence certain incentives, at their foundation. The ends that a rational being intends at its discretion as *effects* of its actions (material ends) are one and all only relative; for merely their relation to a particular kind of desiderative faculty of the subject gives them their worth, which can therefore furnish no universal principles that are valid as well as necessary for all rational beings, or for all willing, i.e. practical laws. That is why all these relative ends are the ground of hypothetical imperatives only.

But suppose there were something *the existence of which in itself* has an absolute worth, that, as an *end in itself,* could be a ground of determinate laws, then the ground of a possible categorical imperative, i.e. of a practical law, would lie in it, and only in it alone.

Now I say: a human being and generally every rational being *exists* as an end in itself, *not merely as a means* for the discretionary use for this or that will, but must in all its actions, whether directed towards itself or also to other rational beings, always be considered *at the same time as an end.* All objects of inclinations have a conditional worth only; for if the inclinations, and the needs founded on them, did not exist, their object would be without worth. But the inclinations themselves, as sources of need, are so far from having an absolute worth—so as to make one wish for them as such—that to be entirely free from them must rather be the universal wish of every rational being. Therefore the worth of any object *to be acquired* by our action is always conditional. Beings whose existence rests not indeed on our will but on nature, if they are non-rational beings, still have only a relative worth, as means, and are therefore called *things,* whereas rational beings are called *persons,* because their nature already marks them out as ends in themselves, i.e. as something that may not be used merely as a means, and hence to that extent limits all choice (and is an object of respect). These are therefore not merely subjective ends, the existence of which, as the effect of our action, has a worth *for us;* but rather *objective ends,* i.e. entities whose existence in itself is an end, an end such that no other end can be put in its place, for which they would do service *merely* as means, because without it nothing whatsoever of *absolute worth* could be found; but if all worth were conditional, and hence contingent, then for reason no supreme practical principle could be found at all.

If, then, there is to be a supreme practical principle and, with regard to the human will, a categorical imperative, it must be such that, from the representation of what is necessarily an end for everyone, because it is an *end in itself,* it constitutes an *objective* principle of the will, and hence can serve as a universal practical law. The ground of this principle is: *a rational nature exists as an end in itself.* That is how a human being by necessity represents his own existence; to that extent it is thus a *subjective* principle of human actions. But every other rational being also represents its existence in this way, as a consequence of just the same rational ground that also holds for me; thus it is at the same time an *objective* principle from which, as a supreme practical ground, it must be possible to derive all laws of the will. The practical imperative will thus be the following: *So act that you use humanity, in your own person as well as in the person of any other, always at the same time as an end, never merely as a means.* Let us try to see whether this can be done.

To keep to the previous examples:

*First,* according to the concept of necessary duty to oneself, someone who is contemplating self-murder will ask himself whether his action can be consistent with the idea of humanity, *as an end in itself.* If to escape from a troublesome condition he destroys himself, he makes use of a person, merely as *a means*, to preserving a bearable condition up to the end of life. But a human being is not a thing, hence not something that can be used *merely* as a means, but must in all his actions always be considered as an end in itself. Thus the human being in my own person is not at my disposal, so as to maim, to corrupt, or to kill him. . . .

*Secondly*, as far as necessary or owed duty to others is concerned, someone who has it in mind to make a lying promise to others will see at once that he wants to make use of another human being *merely as a means*, who does not at the same time contain in himself the end. For the one I want to use for my purposes by such a promise cannot possibly agree to my way of proceeding with him and thus himself contain the end of this action. This conflict with the principle of other human beings can be seen more distinctly if one introduces examples of attacks on the freedom and property of others. For then it is clear that the transgressor of the rights of human beings is disposed to make use of the person of others merely as a means, without taking into consideration that, as rational beings, they are always to be esteemed at the same time as ends, i.e. only as beings who must, of just the same action, also be able to contain in themselves the end.

*Thirdly*, with regard to contingent (meritorious) duty to oneself it is not enough that the action not conflict with humanity in our person, as an end in itself, it must also *harmonize with it.* Now there are in humanity predispositions to greater perfection, which belong to the end of nature with regard to humanity in our subject; to neglect these would perhaps be consistent with the *preservation* of humanity, as an end in itself, but not with the *advancement* of this end.

*Fourthly*, as concerns meritorious duty to others, the natural end that all human beings have is their own happiness. Now, humanity could indeed subsist if no one contributed anything to the happiness of others while not intentionally detracting anything from it; but this is still only a negative and not positive agreement with *humanity, as an end in itself,* if everyone does not also try, as far as he can, to advance the ends of others. For if that representation is to have its *full* effect in me, the ends of a subject that is an end in itself must, as much as possible, also be *my* ends.

This principle of humanity and of every rational nature as such, *as an end in itself* (which is the supreme limiting condition of the freedom of actions of every human being) is not borrowed from experience, first, because of its universality, as it aims at all rational beings as such, and about that no experience is sufficient to determine anything; secondly, because in it humanity is represented not as an end of human beings (subjectively), i.e. as an object that by itself one actually makes one's end, but as an objective end that, whatever ends we may have, as a law is to constitute the supreme limiting condition of all subjective ends, and hence must arise from pure reason. For the ground of all practical legislation lies *objectively in the rule* and the form of universality, which (according to the first principle) makes it capable of being a law (or perhaps a law of nature), *subjectively,* however, *in the end*; the subject of all ends, however, is every rational being, as an end in itself (according to the second principle): from this now follows the third practical principle of the will, as the supreme condition of its harmony with universal practical reason, the idea *of the will of every rational being as a universally legislating will.*

According to this principle, all maxims are rejected that are not consistent with the will's own universal legislation. Thus the will is not just subject to the law, but subject in such a way that it must also be viewed *as self-legislating,* and just on account of this as subject to the law (of which it can consider itself the author) in the first place. . . .

Now, if we look back on all the efforts that have ever been undertaken to detect the principle of morality to this day, it is no wonder why one and all they had to fail. One saw the human being bound to laws by his duty, but it did not occur to anyone that he is subject *only to his own* and yet *universal legislation,* and that he is only obligated to act in conformity with his own will which is, however, universally legislating according to its natural end. For if one thought of him just as subject to a law (whichever it may be), it had to carry with it some interest as stimulation or constraint, because it did not as a law arise from *his* will, which instead was necessitated by *something else,* in conformity with a law, to act in a certain way. Because of this entirely necessary conclusion, however, all the labor of finding a supreme ground of duty was irretrievably lost. For one never got duty, but the necessity of an action from a certain interest, be it one's own interest or that of another. But then the imperative always had to be conditional, and could not be fit to be a moral command at all. I shall therefore call this principle the principle of the autonomy of the will, in opposition to every other, which I accordingly count as heteronomy.[6]

The concept of every rational being that must consider itself as universally legislating through all the maxims of its will, so as to judge itself and its actions from this point of view, leads to a very fruitful concept attached to it, namely that *of a kingdom of ends.*

By a *kingdom,* however, I understand the systematic union of several rational beings through common laws. Now, since laws determine ends according to their universal validity, it is possible — if one abstracts from the personal differences among rational beings, and likewise from all content of their private ends — to conceive a whole of all ends (of rational beings as ends in themselves, as well as the ends of its own that each of them may set for itself) in systematic connection, i.e. a kingdom of ends, which is possible according to the above principles.

For all rational beings stand under the *law* that each of them is to treat itself and all others *never merely as a means,* but always *at the same time as an end in itself.* But by this there arises a systematic union of rational beings through common objective laws, i.e. a kingdom, which — because what these laws have as their purpose is precisely the reference of these beings to one another, as ends and means—can be called a kingdom of ends (of course only an ideal).

The above three ways of representing the principle of morality are fundamentally only so many formulae of the selfsame law, one of which of itself unites the other two within it. . . .

We can now end where we set out from at the beginning, namely with the concept of an unconditionally good will. A *will is absolutely good* that cannot be evil, hence whose maxim, if made a universal law, can never conflict with itself. This principle

6. By "heteronomy," Kant refers to a force or impulse external to one's rational will.

is therefore also its supreme law: act always on that maxim the universality of which as a law you can will at the same time; this is the only condition under which a will can never be in conflict with itself, and such an imperative is categorical. Since the validity of the will, as a universal law for possible actions, has an analogy with the universal connection of the existence of things according to universal laws, which is what is formal in nature as such, the categorical imperative can also be expressed as follows: *act according to maxims that can at the same time have as their object them-selves as universal laws of nature.* Such, then, is the formula of an absolutely good will.

A rational nature is distinguished from the others by this, that it sets itself an end. . . .

## TEST YOUR UNDERSTANDING

1. How does a categorical imperative differ from a hypothetical imperative? Identify one of Kant's examples of a hypothetical imperative and supply one of your own.

2. A maxim is a description of the morally relevant features of an action, along with one's morally relevant reasons for acting in that way. In Kant's example of the false promise, the would-be promisor's maxim is "when I believe myself to be in need of money I shall borrow money and promise to repay it, even though I know that this will never happen." Can you identify the maxims in his other examples?

3. What is the humanity formulation of the categorical imperative and why does Kant regard this principle as a categorical imperative? In your own words, can you briefly explain why this principle might deem as wrong offering a false promise? Refusing to help others?

## NOTES AND QUESTIONS

1. *Contradiction in the conception.* A maxim may fail the categorical imperative test if its universalization would yield a *contradiction in the conception* (of its universaliza-tion). That means that it would not be *possible* for the maxim to operate as a universal law and succeed in accomplishing its purpose. We are to ask whether everyone could act in similar circumstances as the maxim directs and for this fact to be known or understood (or, "public"). In Kant's most famous example, the maxim "When in need of money but without the ability to repay, to get funds, one requests a loan and prom-ises to repay without the intention of repaying" fails this test. If everyone in those circumstances offered false promises when they were in financial need, the ability of a promise to persuade someone to give you a loan would no longer succeed because the recipient of the promise would have no reason to believe that the promisor would repay. This failure shows that the success of one's action depends upon making an exception for oneself and concealing morally relevant features of one's circumstances (one's inability to repay) and one's intention to renege. That shows that one is not act-ing on universal reasons that could be shared and implemented by all rational agents.

*Exercise:* Kant's other case involving a failure through a contradiction in the conception is his example of suicide. Can you describe in your own words what the maxim is and how its universalization purportedly fails? Given this argument, would Kant disapprove of a person who chose to end his life because his mental capacities were deteriorating and he foresaw that he would soon fail to reason and behave well?

2. *Contradiction in the will.* A maxim may also fail the universalization test by revealing a contradiction in the will. In such cases, the maxim could possibly be universalized but its universalization would be inconsistent with another end that we must have. Take Kant's example of the person who, while flourishing, refuses to show regard for others and to help others in need to suit his own convenience. There is no contradiction in the conception here. It would be possible for all those flourishing to ignore the needs of others to suit their own convenience. (The consequences for others would be awful, but not inconceivable.) He argues that there is a contradiction in the will, however, because one's maxim contradicts another maxim that one must have as a matter of respect for one's self. Out of respect for the value of one's own life, one must will that one would seek help from others if one were in need of help. But that maxim's satisfaction would conflict with the universalization of the wealthy person's maxim to decline to aid those in need. Hence, the maxim to decline aid to others contradicts another maxim that person must affirm. So, there is a contradiction in the will.

*Exercise:* Consider Kant's example of a person who for pleasure and convenience decides to let her talents lie fallow. Her maxim purportedly fails the contradiction in the will test. Can you describe how Kant's argument is meant to work?

3. *Differences and specialization.* Some actions are permissible to perform, although we could not survive if everyone behaved the same way. For instance, it seems permissible that some of us grow wheat but do not dig wells, and that others of us do not engage in agriculture at all, although it is essential that some people do so. Is Kant's idea that one's maxim must be universalizable consistent with these examples? Can you say how?

4. *Market exchange and never treating humanity as a means only.* Suppose I enter a shop and I give the shopkeeper money in exchange for milk. I do not ask the shopkeeper how she is, or what her interests are. I interact with her only to get the milk I need and then I leave. Do I treat her unacceptably as a mere means to my nutrition and not as an end in herself?

# Thomas M. Scanlon (born 1940)

Scanlon is Alford Professor of Natural Religion, Moral Philosophy, and Civil Polity at Harvard University. A leading philosopher in the areas of moral, political, and legal philosophy, he is best known for his development of the moral theory of contractualism. He has published many significant articles and books, including *What We Owe to Each Other* (1998), *The Difficulty of Tolerance* (2003), and *Moral Dimensions: Permissibility, Meaning, and Blame* (2008).

# CONTRACTUALISM AND UTILITARIANISM

Utilitarianism occupies a central place in the moral philosophy of our time. It is not the view which most people hold; certainly there are very few who would claim to be act utilitarians.[1] But for a much wider range of people it is the view towards which they find themselves pressed when they try to give a theoretical account of their moral beliefs. Within moral philosophy it represents a position one must struggle against if one wishes to avoid it. . . .

The wide appeal of utilitarianism is due, I think, to philosophical considerations of a more or less sophisticated kind which pull us in a quite different direction than our first-order moral beliefs.[2] In particular, utilitarianism derives much of its appeal from alleged difficulties about the foundations of rival views. What a successful alternative to utilitarianism must do, first and foremost, is to sap this source of strength by providing a clear account of the foundations of non-utilitarian moral reasoning. . . . I will put forward a version of contractualism which, I will argue, offers [such an account].

I

Given any candidate for the role of subject matter of morality we must explain why anyone should care about it. . . .

[W]hat must an adequate philosophical theory of morality say about moral motivation? It need not, I think, show that the moral truth gives anyone who knows it a reason to act which appeals to that person's present desires or to the advancement of his or her interests. I find it entirely intelligible that moral requirement might correctly apply to a person even though that person had no reason of either of these kinds for complying with it. . . . But what an adequate moral philosophy must do, I think, is to make clearer to us the nature of the reasons that morality does provide, at least to those who are concerned with it. A philosophical theory of morality must offer an account of these reasons that is, on the one hand, compatible with its account of moral truth and moral reasoning and, on the other, supported by a plausible analysis of moral experience. A satisfactory moral philosophy will not leave concern with morality as a simple special preference, like a fetish or a special taste, which some people just happen to have. It must make it understandable why moral reasons

---

1. *Act utilitarianism* is the moral view that the best act is that which produces the most overall utility. It is contrasted with *rule utilitarianism*, which holds that the best act is the one in conformance with the rule whose general observance would produce the most overall utility.

2. *First-order moral beliefs* are beliefs about what actions one should or should not perform, e.g., one should keep one's promises, help those in need, and refrain from gratuitous violence. *Second-order moral beliefs* are beliefs about our moral beliefs, e.g., that moral beliefs are objective (or purely subjective) or that moral beliefs give us reasons to act in ways they suggest.

are ones that people can take seriously, and why they strike those who are moved by them as reasons of a special stringency and inescapability. . . .

While a philosophical characterisation of morality makes a kind of claim that differs from a first-order moral judgement, this does not mean that a philosophical theory of morality will be neutral between competing normative doctrines. The adoption of a philosophical thesis about the nature of morality will almost always have some effect on the plausibility of particular moral claims, but philosophical theories of morality vary widely in the extent and directness of their normative implications. At one extreme is intuitionism, understood as the philosophical thesis that morality is concerned with certain non-natural properties.[3] Rightness, for example, is held by Ross[4] to be the property of "fittingness" or "moral suitability."

Intuitionism holds that we can identify occurrences of these properties, and that we can recognise as self-evident certain general truths about them, but that they cannot be further analysed or explained in terms of other notions. So understood, intuitionism is in principle compatible with a wide variety of normative positions. One could, for example, be an intuitionistic utilitarian or an intuitionistic believer in moral rights, depending on the general truths about the property of moral rightness which one took to be self-evident.

The other extreme is represented by philosophical utilitarianism. The term "utilitarianism" is generally used to refer to a family of specific normative doctrines — doctrines which might be held on the basis of a number of different philosophical theses about the nature of morality. In this sense of the term one might, for example, be a utilitarian on intuitionist or on contractualist grounds. But what I will call "philosophical utilitarianism" is a particular philosophical thesis about the subject matter of morality, namely the thesis that the only fundamental moral facts are facts about individual well-being. I believe that . . . the attractiveness of philosophical utilitarianism accounts for the widespread influence of utilitarian principles.

It seems evident to people that there is such a thing as individuals being made better or worse off. Such facts have an obvious motivational force; it is quite understandable that people should be moved by them in much the way that they are supposed to be moved by moral considerations. Further, these facts are clearly relevant to morality as we now understand it. Claims about individual well-being are one class of valid starting points for moral argument. But many people find it much harder to see how there could be any other, independent starting points. Substantive moral requirements independent of individual well-being strike people as intuitionist in an objectionable sense. They would represent "moral facts" of a kind it would be difficult to explain. There is no problem about recognising it as a fact that a certain act is, say, an instance of lying or of promise breaking. And a utilitarian can acknowledge that such facts as these often have (derivative) moral significance: they are morally significant because of their consequences for individual well-being. The problems, and the charge of "intuitionism,"

---

3. A *non-natural property* is a feature or trait that cannot be reduced to natural properties such as needs, wants, or pleasures.

4. W. D. Ross (1877–1971) was a Scottish philosopher who taught at the University of Oxford. He is best known for his book *The Right and the Good* (1930), which defended an intuitionist position.

arise when it is claimed that such acts are wrong in a sense that is not reducible to the fact that they decrease individual well-being. How could this independent property of moral wrongness be understood in a way that would give it the kind of importance and motivational force which moral considerations have been taken to have? If one accepts the idea that there are no moral properties having this kind of intrinsic significance, then philosophical utilitarianism may seem to be the only tenable account of morality. And once philosophical utilitarianism is accepted, some form of normative utilitarianism seems to be forced on us as the correct first-order moral theory. . . .

[For] if all that counts morally is the well-being of individuals, no one of whom is singled out as counting for more than the others, and if all that matters in the case of each individual is the degree to which his or her well-being is affected, then it would seem to follow that the basis of moral appraisal is the goal of maximising the *sum* of individual well-being. . . .

## II

If what I have said about the appeal of utilitarianism is correct, then what a rival theory must do is to provide an alternative to philosophical utilitarianism as a conception of the subject matter of morality. This is what the theory which I shall call contractualism seeks to do. Even if it succeeds in this, . . . [t]he possibility will remain that normative utilitarianism can be established on other grounds, for example as the normative outcome of contractualism itself. But one direct and, I think, influential argument for normative utilitarianism will have been set aside.

To give an example of what I mean by contractualism, a contractualist account of the nature of moral wrongness might be stated as follows.

An act is wrong if its performance under the circumstances would be disallowed by any system of rules for the general regulation of behaviour which no one could reasonably reject as a basis for informed, unforced general agreement.

This is intended as a characterisation of the kind of property which moral wrongness is. . . .

The idea of "informed agreement" is meant to exclude agreement based on superstition or false belief about the consequences of actions, even if these beliefs are ones which it would be reasonable for the person in question to have. The intended force of the qualification "reasonably," on the other hand, is to exclude rejections that would be unreasonable *given* the aim of finding principles which could be the basis of informed, unforced general agreement. Given this aim, it would be unreasonable, for example, to reject a principle because it imposed a burden on you when every alternative principle would impose much greater burdens on others. . . .

The requirement that the hypothetical agreement which is the subject of moral argument be unforced is meant not only to rule out coercion, but also to exclude being forced to accept an agreement by being in a weak bargaining position, for example because others are able to hold out longer and hence to insist on better terms. Moral argument abstracts from such considerations. The only relevant pressure for agreement comes from the desire to find and agree on principles which no one who had this desire could reasonably reject. According to contractualism, moral argument concerns the possibility of agreement among persons who are all moved by this desire, and moved by it to the same degree. But this counter-factual assumption characterises only the agreement with which morality is concerned, not the world to which moral principles are to apply. Those who are concerned with morality look for principles for application to their imperfect world which they could not reasonably reject, and which others in this world, who are not now moved by the desire for agreement, could not reasonably reject should they come to be so moved. . . .

It seems likely that many non-equivalent sets of principles will pass the test of non-rejectability. This is suggested, for example, by the fact that there are many different ways of defining important duties, no one of which is more or less "rejectable" than the others. There are, for example, many different systems of agreement-making and many different ways of assigning responsibility to care for others. It does not follow, however, that any action allowed by at least one of these sets of principles cannot be morally wrong according to contractualism. If it is important for us to have *some* duty of a given kind (some duty of fidelity to agreements, or some duty of mutual aid) of which there are many morally acceptable forms, then one of these forms needs to be established by convention. In a setting in which one of these forms *is* conventionally established, acts disallowed by it will be wrong in the sense of the definition given. For, given the need for such conventions, one thing that could not be generally agreed to would be a set of principles allowing one to disregard conventionally established (and morally acceptable) definitions of important duties. This dependence on convention introduces a degree of cultural relativity into contractualist morality. In addition, what a person can reasonably reject will depend on the aims and conditions that are important in his life, and these will also depend on the society in which he lives. The definition given above allows for variation of both of these kinds by making the wrongness of an action depend on the circumstances in which it is performed. . . .

## III

I have so far said little about the normative content of contractualism. For all I have said, the act utilitarian formula might turn out to be a theorem of contractualism. I do not think that this is the case, but my main thesis is that whatever the normative implications of contractualism may be it still has distinctive content as a philosophical thesis about the nature of morality. This content — the difference, for example, between being a utilitarian because the utilitarian formula is the basis of general agreement and being a utilitarian on other grounds — is shown most clearly in the answer that a contractualist gives to the question of who should motivate us morally.

Philosophical utilitarianism is a plausible view partly because the facts which it identifies as fundamental to morality—facts about individual well-being—have obvious motivational force. Moral facts can motivate us, on this view, because of our sympathetic identification with the good of others. But as we move from philosophical utilitarianism to a specific utilitarian formula as the standard of right action, the form of motivation that utilitarianism appeals to becomes more abstract. If classical utilitarianism is the correct normative doctrine then the natural source of moral motivation will be a tendency to be moved by changes in aggregate well-being, however these may be composed. We must be moved in the same way by an aggregate gain of the same magnitude whether it is obtained by relieving the acute suffering of a few people or by bringing tiny benefits to a vast number, perhaps at the expense of moderate discomfort for a few. This is very different from sympathy of the familiar kind toward particular individuals, but a utilitarian may argue that this more abstract desire is what natural sympathy becomes when it is corrected by rational reflection. This desire has the same content as sympathy—it is a concern for the good of others—but it is not partial or selective in its choice of objects.

Leaving aside the psychological plausibility of this even-handed sympathy, how good a candidate is it for the role of moral motivation? Certainly sympathy of the usual kind is one of the many motives that can sometimes impel one to do the right thing. It may be the dominant motive, for example, when I run to the aid of a suffering child. But when I feel convinced by Peter Singer's article on famine,[5] and find myself crushed by the recognition of what seems a clear moral requirement, there is something else at work. In addition to the thought of how much good I could do for people in drought-stricken lands, I am overwhelmed by the further, seemingly distinct thought that it would be wrong for me to fail to aid them when I could do so at so little cost to myself. A utilitarian may respond that his account of moral motivation cannot be faulted for not capturing this aspect of moral experience, since it is just a reflection of our non-utilitarian moral upbringing. Moreover, it must be groundless. For what kind of fact could this supposed further fact of moral wrongness be, and how could it give us a further, special reason for acting? The question for contractualism, then, is whether it can provide a satisfactory answer to this challenge.

According to contractualism, the source of motivation that is directly triggered by the belief that an action is wrong is the desire to be able to justify one's actions to others on grounds they could not reasonably reject. I find this an extremely plausible account of moral motivation—a better account of at least my moral experience than the natural utilitarian alternative—and it seems to me to constitute a strong point for the contractualist view. We all might like to be in actual agreement with the people around us, but the desire which contractualism identifies as basic to morality does not lead us simply to conform to the standards accepted by others whatever these may be. The desire to be able to justify one's actions to others on grounds they could not reasonably reject will be satisfied when we know that there is adequate justification for our action even though others in fact refuse to accept it (perhaps because they have no interest in finding principles which we and others could not reasonably reject). . . .

---

5. Excerpted on p. 865 of this anthology.

One rough test of whether you regard a justification as sufficient is whether you would accept that justification if you were in another person's position. This connection between the idea of "changing places" and the motivation which underlies morality explains the frequent occurrence of "Golden Rule" arguments within different systems of morality and in the teachings of various religions. But the thought experiment of changing places is only a rough guide; the fundamental question is what would it be unreasonable to reject as a basis for informed, unforced, general agreement. . . .

[I]t seems to me that the desire to be able to justify one's actions (and institutions) on grounds one takes to be acceptable is quite strong in most people. People are willing to go to considerable lengths, involving quite heavy sacrifices, in order to avoid admitting the unjustifiability of their actions and institutions. The notorious insufficiency of moral motivation as a way of getting people to do the right thing is not due to simple weakness of the underlying motive, but rather to the fact that it is easily deflected by self-interest and self-deception. . . .

# IV

It seems unlikely that act utilitarianism will be a theorem of the version of contractualism which I have described. The positive moral significance of individual interests is a direct reflection of the contractualist requirement that actions be defensible to each person on grounds he could not reasonably reject. But it is a long step from here to the conclusion that each individual must agree to deliberate always from the point of view of maximum aggregate benefit and to accept justifications appealing to this consideration alone. . . .

The fundamental question here is whether the principles to which contractualism leads must be ones whose general adoption (either ideally or under some more realistic conditions) would promote maximum aggregate well-being. It has seemed to many that this must be the case. To indicate why I do not agree I will consider one of the best known arguments for this conclusion and explain why I do not think it is successful. . . .

The argument I will consider . . . proceeds via an interpretation of the contractualist notion of acceptance. . . . To think of a principle as a candidate for unanimous agreement I must think of it not merely as acceptable to *me* (perhaps in virtue of my particular position, my tastes, etc.) but as acceptable to others as well. To be relevant, my judgement that the principle is acceptable must be impartial. What does this mean? To judge impartially that a principle is acceptable is, one might say, to judge that it is one which you would have reason to accept no matter who you were. That is, and here is the interpretation, to judge that it is a principle which it would be rational to accept if you did not know which person's position you occupied and believed that you had an equal chance of being in any of these positions. . . .

[C]onsider the possibility that the distribution with the highest average utility, call it *A*, might involve extremely low utility levels for some people, levels much lower than the minimum anyone would enjoy under a more equal distribution.

Suppose that *A* is a principle which it would be rational for a self-interested chooser with an equal chance of being in anyone's position to select. Does it follow that no one could reasonably reject *A*? It seems evident that this does not follow. Suppose that the situation of those who would fare worst under *A*, call them the Losers, is extremely bad, and that there is an alternative to *A*, call it *E*, under which no one's situation would be nearly as bad as this. Prima facie, the losers would seem to have a reasonable ground for complaint against *A*. Their objection may be rebutted, by appeal to the sacrifices that would be imposed on some other individual by the selection of *E* rather than *A*. But the mere fact that *A* yields higher average utility, which might be due to the fact that many people do very slightly better under *A* than under *E* while a very few do much worse, does not settle the matter.

Under contractualism, when we consider a principle our attention is naturally directed first to those who would do worst under it. This is because if anyone has reasonable grounds for objecting to the principle it is *likely* to be them. It does not follow, however, that contractualism always requires us to select the principle under which the expectations of the worse off are highest. The reasonableness of the Losers' objection to *A* is not established simply by the fact that they are worse off under *A* and no-one would be this badly off under *E*. The force of their complaint depends also on the fact that their position under *A* is, in absolute terms, very bad, and would be significantly better under *E*. This complaint must be weighed against those of individuals who would do worse under *E*. The question to be asked is, is it unreasonable for someone to refuse to put up with the Losers' situation under *A* in order that someone else should be able to enjoy the benefits which he would have to give up under *E*? As the supposed situation of the Loser under *A* becomes better, or his gain under *E* smaller in relation to the sacrifices required to produce it, his case is weakened.

One noteworthy feature of contractualist argument as I have presented it is that it is non-aggregative: what are compared are individual gains, losses, and levels of welfare....

I have described this version of contractualism only in outline.... I hope that I have said enough to indicate its appeal as a philosophical theory of morality and as an account of moral motivation.

## TEST YOUR UNDERSTANDING

1.  What is philosophical utilitarianism? How does it differ from utilitarianism, understood as a "first-order moral theory"?

2.  How does contractualism differ from philosophical utilitarianism? (*Hint:* Does it suggest that facts about individual well-being are not fundamental moral facts, or does it suggest that there may be other fundamental moral facts than facts about individual well-being?)

3.  How does Scanlon think the utilitarian would represent the relevant motivation for helping children suffering in a famine? How does he think the contractualist would represent the relevant motivation?

## NOTES AND QUESTIONS

1. *Aggregation, utilitarianism, and contractualism:* Scanlon characterizes utilitarianism as a theory oriented around maximum aggregate benefit. What does this mean? Why does Scanlon believe that a contractualist account of what makes an action wrong is unlikely to produce a set of rules that aggregate in the way utilitarianism does?

   *Exercise:* Generate two examples of actions that utilitarianism might favor but would be disallowed by a system of rules produced by the contractualist framework. Do these examples lend support to the utilitarian view or the contractualist view?

2. *What counts as justifying one's action to others?* Scanlon describes the underlying motivation behind contractualism as the desire to justify one's actions to others. How does ensuring that one acts according to principles no one could reasonably reject satisfy that desire?

   *Exercise:* Consider the following objection:

   > Whether your action is justified or not depends just on whether it produces maximum aggregate utility among the entire population. If it does, then it is justified. If it does not, then either your action treats some people as though they matter more than others, fails to reflect the significance of different degrees of utility, or reflects the incorrect judgment that some things matter morally other than their effect on human well-being.

   How might Scanlon respond?

## Rosalind Hursthouse (born 1943)

Hursthouse is a New Zealand philosopher who taught for many years at the Open University in England and is now a professor at the University of Auckland. A famous exponent of virtue ethics, she is the author of *Beginning Lives* (1987), *On Virtue Ethics* (1999), and *Ethics, Humans, and Other Animals* (2013).

# VIRTUE ETHICS

In Book 6 of the *Nicomachean Ethics*, Aristotle introduced a difficult concept into moral philosophy. Taking one of the many Greek terms for knowledge, *phronesis*, he gave it his own special sense. *Phronesis* is the knowledge that enables its possessor to make correct moral decisions about what to do — to reason correctly about what is right; we translate it as (moral or practical) wisdom. He writes as though some people, albeit not many, actually have it, and as if you either have it or you do not. Nowadays we tend to take it as the concept of an ideal to which we can aspire and possess to a greater or lesser degree.

Modern moral philosophy lost sight of the concept until it was enthusiastically revived by virtue ethics, in which the question "How should we reason about what is right?" becomes inseparable from the question "What is *phronesis*?" What *does* a person who possesses it know that enables her to do this reasoning so well? And since that amounts to the question "What is wisdom?" it is very hard to answer. I am just going to discuss two aspects of it and the knowledge each involves, each derived from something Aristotle says about it.

The first is that you can't have *phronesis* without being truly virtuous, that is, a morally good person. This is what makes "moral wisdom" a good translation — we do not think that the Hitlers of this world have moral wisdom, only people we think are morally good. What follows? Well, it follows that the correct decisions about what it is right to do which the person with *phronesis* reaches are the decisions of a truly virtuous person. We all know that we still have a fair way to go before we become as good as that, so we cannot reason in exactly the way this ideal person does. How can we best approximate that reasoning?

According to modern virtue ethics, we should not reason about what to do in terms of what will maximise the best consequences, and not in terms of what will be in accordance with correct moral principles such as "Do not lie" or "Keep promises," but in terms of *what a virtuous agent would do in the circumstances*. This is in some ways very straightforward, in other ways very difficult. The difficulty is inevitable whatever account we give of how to reason about what to do. We all know that life presents us with situations in which it is agonisingly difficult, if not impossible, to know what it is right to do. But we will start with what is straightforward.

Of course, thinking in terms of "what a virtuous agent would do" does not look immediately straightforward because the word "virtue" is hardly common usage nowadays. But, oddly enough, everyone still has the concept. Google "virtues" and you find 1.6 million pages, many of them with lists of the virtues and vices. Although we might disagree (I certainly do) with some of the examples, and a few of them will sound old-fashioned to most people, they are comprehensible. We can see that the virtues listed are all supposed to be character traits that we praise and admire people for having because they constitute being a morally good person. (Web material is often a bit careless: I have seen beauty and health listed as virtues, but they cannot be because they are not character traits and hence not virtues.) Note that, although "vice" still does have a common usage, it connotes something more evil than "moral fault" or "defect," but when we speak of "the virtues and vices" in this context, "vice" is shorthand for "vice *or* moral defect.")

So we are to think of "the virtuous agent" as someone who has the virtues, that is, as someone who *is*, through and through, all the way down, benevolent (or "charitable" in the original sense), courageous, generous, honest, just, kind, loyal, responsible, and trustworthy, for example. And, having the virtues, the virtuous agent acts accordingly, characteristically or typically doing what *is* benevolent, courageous, generous, honest, just, kind, loyal, responsible, and trustworthy, and not what is malevolent, cowardly, mean, dishonest, unjust, unkind, disloyal, irresponsible, or untrustworthy.

Terms for the virtues and vices generate adjectives that describe both people *and* actions. Consequently, virtue ethics offers an enormous number of moral rules for action guidance. *Every* virtue generates a prescription — do what is benevolent, etc., and *every* vice a prohibition — do not do what is malevolent, etc. Let's call these the "v-rules" (for "virtue- and vice-rules"). So the straightforward way to think about what to do in terms of what the virtuous agent would do is, initially, to think in terms of the v-rules. And that, often, is indeed very straightforward. Is it right not to go to my friend's birthday party when I have promised to because something more enjoyable has turned up? No, because it would be untrustworthy, disloyal, inconsiderate, selfish, and (on some construals of justice) unjust. Is it right to take her a birthday present — yes, it would be mean (in the sense of "stingy" or "ungenerous") not to. Is it right to take my dog for a walk every day? Yes, it is benevolent, kind, and responsible to do so, and callous, unkind, and irresponsible not to.

Now one might say "But these examples are so obvious that no-one needs to reason about them!" True — though it is in relation to such obvious examples that we first acquire the virtue and vice vocabulary and thereby learn to identify morally relevant features of actions which ethical theories other than virtue ethics ignore at their peril. For instance, some moral philosophers say we should reason about what is right in such a way that there turns out to be nothing wrong with breaking my promise to my friend (if I can deceive him successfully later about why I didn't turn up). Other philosophers say we should reason about what is right in such a way that it turns out not to be true that I ought to give my dog regular exercise (because I do not have any moral duties to animals). And some insist that our reasoning in these examples should be impartial and make no reference to *my* friend or *my* dog.

Here is an interesting thing about the v-rules. They are not invented or discovered by moral philosophers or peculiar to religious doctrine. They are simply created by the words — the available virtue and vice words — in ordinary language, and the ordinary use of these words is extraordinarily subtle and nuanced, heavily dependent on features of the conversation in which they occur. Hence the importance of thinking about what it is right to do in terms of what the virtuous agent would do *in the circumstances.* Suppose we tweak one of the obvious examples above a bit.

Is it right to break my promise to turn up to the school play my daughter is in, because, on my way to it, I see an old woman being threatened by a mugger? Of course — it would be cowardly, irresponsible, and callous not to stop to help, and, in *these* circumstances, not disloyal or inconsiderate or selfish to break the promise.

Would it be untrustworthy? Well, if so, the example illustrates something that it is easy to forget when we are thinking about that unfamiliar concept "the virtuous agent." It is natural to assume that the virtuous person would never do what is dishonest, such as lying, or untrustworthy, such as breaking a promise, or disloyal, such as letting a friend down; that the compassionate would never intentionally cause anyone great suffering. But as soon as we think of certain examples, we realise that that's a mistake. In *some* circumstances, they *do* do such things. They do not do them typically or willingly or cheerily (as people who are dishonest, untrustworthy, disloyal, etc. do); they regret that circumstances have made it necessary; and afterwards they look around for ways to make up for what circumstances have compelled them to do, but they do *do* them — and it is no poor reflection on their virtue.

Consult your own understanding of what it means to be a trustworthy and loyal person. You have a friend you think is both, so when he fails to keep his promise to come to your birthday party you are surprised. If you really believe he is trustworthy and loyal, will you not expect that he must have had a good reason for breaking it? And when he rings up the next day to apologise and explain about the mugger, will you not find your expectation confirmed?

We understand that even the trustworthy and loyal may do such things as break promises because we understand the virtue and vice words — we grasp what is involved in having the individual virtues and thereby the sorts of reasons for which, in particular circumstances, people with those character traits do the things they do. Even quite small children can come to understand that trustworthy people do not always keep their promises. Although they begin by saying, in tearful outrage, "But you *promised!*" they learn that their parents, and others, can be good, trustworthy people despite their occasional defaulting (assuming that they are being brought up by fairly decent parents who do not default improperly and who take time to explain the defaults). So in the straightforward cases, even quite a young child can see that the circumstances in which a promise is broken can give a good person compelling reason to break it.

Similarly, small children often do not understand why their parents hush their tactless remarks. "But it's the *truth!*" they say. "He *is* fat." But, as they begin to acquire good manners, tact, considerateness, kindness, they learn that, just as trustworthy people sometimes break their word, honest people do not always volunteer the truth. Think of the sort of person who says "I speak as I find" and "I believe in calling a spade a spade" and whose word you dread when they say (as they typically do) "I hope you won't mind my saying this BUT . . . ." I would not describe such a person as having the virtue of honesty, but, instead, as being brutally frank or candid. Candour is not a true virtue, because being an honest person is not incompatible with being a discreet, tactful, considerate, kind person.

Is honesty compatible with being a con man? No. Is it compatible with being a magician? Yes, even though deception is a magician's trade. Is it compatible with being "economical with the truth"? In some circumstances yes, in others no — when, for example, parsimony with the truth involves being phoney, sneaky, manipulative, or hypocritical.

How do we know all of this? Because a great deal of our moral knowledge — our understanding of which *particular* actions, done in the very circumstances in which they are done, are what a virtuous person would do or would not do — is, unconsciously, stored in our ordinary virtue and vice words. We started to acquire the knowledge as we learnt to use the words, and, as we get older and more experienced, we learn to use them with greater nuance and subtlety. And this is the beginning of practical wisdom — an understanding, applicable in particular circumstances, of what is involved in being an honest, trustworthy, considerate, . . . virtuous person. So here is a large part of what the person with *phronesis* knows — he really knows, as we begin to know as we grow up, what is involved in having the virtues, and this knowledge is part of what enables him to reason correctly about what it is right to do.

Consider another example. When I was very small, I thought my mother was being mean and unkind when she made me go to bed early (I was a sickly child, and often convalescent); but as I grew older, I realised this was not so. If I had known the words, I would have said she was being responsible and loving, and "doing me a kindness" by sending me to bed. And later I learnt the point of the expression "being cruel to be kind."

With this expression, we begin to enter the territory of difficult cases. As we saw, following the prescriptions "Do what is honest" and "Do not do what is dishonest" does not demand one tells the rude, inconsiderate, or unkind truth. In many circumstances you can look for a nicer truth to tell, or remain discreetly silent. But there are other circumstances in which virtuous agents have to tell the truth. Honest and responsible judges on talent shows faced with aspirants who lack talent, people breaking off relationships that are going nowhere, doctors with patients whose tests show they are in urgent need of a somewhat risky operation, professors with mature students who dream of becoming philosophers but are not capable of postgraduate study, tell the truth and cause those on the receiving end bitter grief. Have they done what is honest but unkind or cruel or callous?

I deny that characterisation. In all these cases (in most of the circumstances in which they occur), I would say one does the recipients no kindness in concealing the truth from them. It is a shattering truth they need to know, and, in those circumstances, the only way to do what is kind is to convey it in a considerate and sensitive way. Judges of talent shows who make the audience laugh at the talentless are being cruel, and doctors and professors who just state the truth baldly without easing the recipient into a dawning realisation of what it is going to be are being insensitive and inconsiderate. (Breaking off relationships is *really* tricky. I read of someone who did it cruelly with the intention of making her partner hate her, because she thought that would make it easier for him, and I can imagine circumstances in which that would be the kindest way to do it.)

You may notice that the reasoning in the paragraph above involves a judgement about "the sort of truth that one does people no kindness in concealing, because they need to know it." What sort of truth is that? Truths that are about something important, the sort of thing that really matters in life? But then, what is "important," and what "really matters" in that way? If you have no idea, and could not understand the above paragraph, then I cannot help you. I have to rely on your knowledgeable uptake. In so doing, I am relying on your having some moral wisdom.

Now we can see why Aristotle, making the first point about *phronesis* I mentioned above, says that it is impossible without virtue. Someone who isn't at all concerned about doing what is right but only in having a good time or exercising power or making a lot of money is not going to be at all interested in acquiring the virtues, and hence will not develop an understanding of them, and his ideas of what is important or really matters in life (lots of pleasure or power or money) are going to be quite different from those of someone who is (at least fairly) virtuous. Someone who is concerned but has been corrupted by a bad upbringing or an immoral culture will have a distorted idea of the virtues and some terrible ideas about what is important and thereby reason incorrectly again and again. (Think of how corrupting racism has been and still is. Racists who are conscientious about not breaking promises, or lying, to members of their own race will cheerfully do it to those against whom they are bigoted and not think that they, or their fellow members, show themselves to be dishonest or untrustworthy in doing so. They think what race someone is is a really important thing about them, and that "keeping those people in their place" really matters in life.)

So here is another large part of what people with *phronesis* know (which is inseparable from their knowledge of what is involved in the virtues); such people know what is truly important in life, what matters, what is worthwhile. That knowledge too is part of what enables the person with *phronesis* to reason correctly about what it is right to do.

The second thing Aristotle says about *phronesis* is that it comes only with age and experience. This is what makes "practical wisdom" a good translation — we do not think of the young and inexperienced as having practical wisdom, however good they are, only those who can draw on a rich experience of life. So what difference does experience make to reasoning correctly about what to do?

When we are reasoning about what to do, aiming for a correct moral decision which we will then act upon, we are always trying to find what it would be right to do *in these circumstances*, in *this* situation. But if we are to succeed, we need to get "the situation" right; if we make a mistake about it, taking it to be thus and so when it isn't, we will reach a correct decision only by happy accident. Only through age and experience, learning from our own and others' mistakes, do we become good at knowing what "the situation" is.

The inexperienced frequently make mistakes about, for example, what other people are feeling. Taking the smiling front at face value, they do not see that the other person is hurt, or uncertain, angry, frightened, or worried; or they see shiftiness or arrogance where the more experienced see embarrassment. Often "the situation" is not something right in front of you, but you have to ask around to find out what is going on; the inexperienced are not expert at assessing the reliability of what other people say. Sometimes they are too gullible in accepting someone else's account, instead of thinking "But he *couldn't* know all that" or "That's the sort of thing people often make mistakes, or conceal the truth, about"; sometimes they are too incredulous, unable to recognise someone else's expertise or sincerity. And so they misjudge the situation. Sometimes they don't even recognise the situation for what it is. (This frequently happens when we encounter other cultures, which is why one should be circumspect as a tourist and try to gain some secondhand experience from books of what might be offensive before one travels.) When we do not get the situation right, we cannot reason correctly about what it is right to do in *it*. But the person with *phronesis* does reason correctly. So she has the sort of knowledge, born of experience, which enables her not to make these sorts of mistakes; this knowledge we call, in general terms, knowledge of people or human nature.

Getting the situation right, and reaching a correct decision about what to do in a general way, still isn't enough for the virtuous agent. Suppose I am right that a person urgently needs to understand he is in a life-threatening situation, or that this other person needs help, or that this one has been insulted, or that we are all in danger. Suppose I correctly decide that I must tell the truth, must help, must right the wrong of the insult, must risk myself getting us out of the danger. But *how?* The devil is in the details, and if I lack experience I may well make the wrong decision about *how* to do what is right, and hence wind up not doing it at all. Again, the person with *phronesis* does reason correctly. So again, she has the sort of knowledge, born of experience, which enables her not to make these sorts of mistakes. She possesses a sort of general know-how about what works and what doesn't in life.

This practical knowledge — both of people and of what works and doesn't — is in *part* worldly knowledge which successfully cunning and wicked people have too; you can't be an effective con man or tyrant without it. But part of it is knowledge that can only be gained by the virtuous; the wicked do not, for example, know what love and trust can do for people and wouldn't know how to set about using that knowledge if they had it.

There is more to the knowledge someone with *phronesis* has than that which I have sketched above, but I will leave the topic here and conclude with the third thing Aristotle says about *phronesis*. It is that you can't have *perfect* virtue without it. And we have just seen why. Insofar as we lack *phronesis* we mess things up, notwithstanding our virtuous intentions. We intend to convey the truth but blurt it out so brutally that the other person can't take it in; we intend to help, but we harm; we intend to right a wrong but we compound it; we intend to save the day and we make things worse. We don't reason correctly about what to do. So we do not do what a perfectly virtuous agent would do.

Looking back, we see that you can't have *phronesis* without having virtue and you can't have virtue without having *phronesis*. "They" turn out to be the same thing viewed from different aspects, two sides of the same coin. "It" is what we need to develop and improve if we are to reason correctly about what is right. Moral philosophers' theories may help us on the way, but there is no shortcut to virtue, and hence none to *phronesis*.

## TEST YOUR UNDERSTANDING

1. What is a virtue and what is a vice? Give an example of each. Why does Hursthouse deny that beauty and health are virtues?

2. Does Hursthouse think the virtuous person would ever break a promise? If he did, would that make him untrustworthy?

3. How do we come to learn what the virtues are and what the virtuous person would do?

## NOTES AND QUESTIONS

1. *What if the virtuous person is uncertain?* Is it possible on Hursthouse's view for a virtuous person to be uncertain about what to do in difficult circumstances? Shouldn't moral philosophy be able to offer him more specific counsel than to tell him that he should act as the virtuous person would act? How do you think Hursthouse might respond to this complaint?

2. *Is virtue ethics circular?* How do you think Hursthouse would answer the following objection?

   To know what the virtuous person would do, we need to know what the right thing to do is. We don't have any clear, independent sense of what virtuous people do other than knowing that they regularly do the right thing. So, it is not helpful when one is uncertain about what to do to direct us to consider what the virtuous person would do.

## John Rawls (1921–2002)

After receiving his PhD from Princeton University in 1950, Rawls taught at Princeton, Cornell University, and the Massachusetts Institute of Technology before joining the Harvard University faculty in 1962. At his retirement from Harvard in 1991, he was James Conant Bryant University Professor. Rawls wrote three powerful and influential books of political philosophy: *A Theory of Justice* (1971), *Political Liberalism* (1993), and *The Law of Peoples* (1999).

# A THEORY OF JUSTICE

Editor's note: *Rawls's aim in* A Theory of Justice *is to identify and argue for principles of justice. Although his focus is on principles of justice, the methodology he describes for making arguments and evaluating provisional conclusions about justice have been thought, by many, to apply to moral judgments and moral theory more generally. For instance, in different ways, both Thomas Scanlon's selection and Elizabeth Harman's selection in this section draw inspiration from Rawls's methodology. Many have been influenced by his contractualist way of thinking about the content of appropriate normative principles. Others who eschew contractualism still deploy the idea of testing provisional principles against considered judgments to arrive at a reflective equilibrium.*

*In an earlier passage, Rawls suggests that to reason about what justice requires, we may start by asking what principles of mutual governance we would agree to in a fair* "initial situation," that is, a circumstance of mutual agreement that would be equal, free from bias, and uncoerced. In particular, Rawls proposes that we consider what principles we would choose to govern our interactions if we reasoned as though we wore "a veil of ignorance" and did not know those features about us that might bias our choices in favor of ourselves, such as our identity, our class position, our individual characteristics, and our projects and goals. He calls this hypothetical situation of choice featuring the veil of ignorance "the original position." Conceptualizing the correct principles of justice as those we would select in a fair choice situation he calls "the contract approach." After imagining what principles we would choose in the original position, he recommends that we subject those principles and this conception of a fair context of choice to critical evaluation. In what follows, Rawls explains how we should critically evaluate these preliminary principles of justice and introduces the idea of a "reflective equilibrium."

---

# 4. The Original Position and Justification

One should not be misled ... by the somewhat unusual conditions which characterize the original position. The idea here is simply to make vivid to ourselves the restrictions that it seems reasonable to impose on arguments for principles of justice, and therefore on these principles themselves. Thus it seems reasonable and generally acceptable that no one should be advantaged or disadvantaged by natural fortune or social circumstances in the choice of principles. It also seems widely agreed that it should be impossible to tailor principles to the circumstances of one's own case. We should insure further that particular inclinations and aspirations, and persons' conceptions of their good do not affect the principles adopted. The aim is to rule out those principles that it would be rational to propose for acceptance, however little the chance of success, only if one knew certain things that are irrelevant from the standpoint of justice. For example, if a man knew that he was wealthy, he might find it rational to advance the principle that various taxes for welfare measures be counted unjust; if he knew that he was poor, he would most likely propose the contrary principle. To represent the desired restrictions one imagines a situation in which everyone is deprived of this sort of information. One excludes the knowledge of those contingencies which sets men at odds and allows them to be guided by their prejudices. In this manner the veil of ignorance is arrived at in a natural way. This concept should cause no difficulty if we keep in mind the constraints on arguments that it is meant to express. At any time we can enter the original position, so to speak, simply by following a certain procedure, namely, by arguing for principles of justice in accordance with these restrictions.

It seems reasonable to suppose that the parties in the original position are equal. That is, all have the same rights in the procedure for choosing principles; each can make proposals, submit reasons for their acceptance, and so on. Obviously the purpose of these conditions is to represent equality between human beings as moral persons, as creatures having a conception of their good and capable of a sense of justice. The basis of equality is taken to be similarity in these two respects. Systems of ends are not ranked in value; and each man is presumed to have the requisite ability to understand and to act upon whatever principles are adopted. Together with the veil of ignorance, these conditions define the principles of justice as those which rational persons concerned to advance their interests would consent to as equals when none are known to be advantaged or disadvantaged by social and natural contingencies.

There is, however, another side to justifying a particular description of the original position. This is to see if the principles which would be chosen match our considered convictions of justice or extend them in an acceptable way. We can note whether applying these principles would lead us to make the same judgments about the basic structure of society which we now make intuitively and in which we have the greatest confidence; or whether, in cases where our present judgments are in doubt and given with hesitation, these principles offer a resolution which we can affirm on reflection. There are questions which we feel sure must be answered in a certain way. For example, we are confident that religious intolerance and racial discrimination are unjust. We think that we have examined these things with care and have reached what we believe is an impartial judgment not likely to be distorted by an excessive attention to our own interests. These convictions are provisional fixed points which we presume any conception of justice must fit. But we have much less assurance as to what is the correct distribution of wealth and authority. Here we may be looking for a way to remove our doubts. We can check an interpretation of the initial situation, then, by the capacity of its principles to accommodate our firmest convictions and to provide guidance where guidance is needed.

In searching for the most favored description of this situation we work from both ends. We begin by describing it so that it represents generally shared and preferably weak conditions. We then see if these conditions are strong enough to yield a significant set of principles. If not, we look for further premises equally reasonable. But if so, and these principles match our considered convictions of justice, then so far well and good. But presumably there will be discrepancies. In this case we have a choice. We can either modify the account of the initial situation or we can revise our existing judgments, for even the judgments we take provisionally as fixed points are liable to revision. By going back and forth, sometimes altering the conditions of the contractual circumstances, at others withdrawing our judgments and conforming them to principle, I assume that eventually we shall find a description of the initial situation that both expresses reasonable conditions and yields principles which match our considered judgments duly pruned and adjusted. This state of affairs I refer to as reflective equilibrium. It is an equilibrium because at last our principles and judgments coincide; and it is reflective since we know to what principles our judgments conform and the premises of their derivation. At the moment everything is in order. But this equilibrium is not necessarily stable. It is liable to be upset by further examination of the conditions which should be imposed on the contractual situation and by particular cases which may lead us to revise our judgments. Yet for the time being we have done what we can to render coherent and to justify our convictions of social justice.

. . . I do not claim for the principles of justice proposed that they are necessary truths or derivable from such truths. A conception of justice cannot be deduced from self-evident premises or conditions on principles; instead, its justification is a matter of the mutual support of many considerations, of everything fitting together into one coherent view.

A final comment. We shall want to say that certain principles of justice are justified because they would be agreed to in an initial situation of equality. I have emphasized that this original position is purely hypothetical. It is natural to ask why, if this agreement is never actually entered into, we should take any interest in these principles, moral or otherwise. The answer is that the conditions embodied in the description of the original position are ones that we do in fact accept. Or if we do not, then perhaps we can be persuaded to do so by philosophical reflection. Each aspect of the contractual situation can be given supporting grounds. Thus what we shall do is to collect together into one conception a number of conditions on principles that we are ready upon due consideration to recognize as reasonable. These constraints express what we are prepared to regard as limits on fair terms of social cooperation. One way to look at the idea of the original position, therefore, is to see it as an expository device which sums up the meaning of these conditions and helps us to extract their consequences. On the other hand, this conception is also an intuitive notion that suggests its own elaboration, so that led on by it we are drawn to define more clearly the standpoint from which we can best interpret moral relationships. . . .

# 9. Some Remarks about Moral Theory

It seems desirable at this point, in order to prevent misunderstanding, to discuss briefly the nature of moral theory. I shall do this by explaining in more detail the concept of a considered judgment in reflective equilibrium and the reasons for introducing it.

Let us assume that each person beyond a certain age and possessed of the requisite intellectual capacity develops a sense of justice under normal social circumstances. We acquire a skill in judging things to be just and unjust, and in supporting these judgments by reasons. Moreover, we ordinarily have some desire to act in accord with these pronouncements and expect a similar desire on the part of others. Clearly this moral capacity is extraordinarily complex. To see this it suffices to note the potentially infinite number and variety of judgments that we are prepared to make. The fact that we often do not know what to say, and sometimes find our minds unsettled, does not detract from the complexity of the capacity we have.

Now one may think of moral philosophy at first (and I stress the provisional nature of this view) as the attempt to describe our moral capacity; or, in the present case, one may regard a theory of justice as describing our sense of justice. This enterprise is very difficult. For by such a description is not meant simply a list of the judgments on institutions and actions that we are prepared to render, accompanied with supporting reasons when these are offered. Rather, what is required is a formulation of a set of principles which, when conjoined to our beliefs and knowledge of the circumstances, would lead us to make these judgments with their supporting reasons were we to apply these principles conscientiously and intelligently. A conception of justice characterizes our moral sensibility when the everyday judgments we do make are in accordance with its principles. These principles can serve as part of the premises of an argument which arrives at the matching judgments. We do not understand our sense of justice until we know in some systematic way covering a wide range of cases what these principles are. Only a deceptive familiarity with our everyday judgments and our natural readiness to make them could conceal the fact that characterizing our moral capacities is an intricate task. The principles which describe them must be presumed to have a complex structure, and the concepts involved will require serious study.

A useful comparison here is with the problem of describing the sense of grammaticalness that we have for the sentences of our native language.[1] In this case the aim is to characterize the ability to recognize well-formed sentences by formulating clearly expressed principles which make the same discriminations as the native speaker. This is a difficult undertaking which, although still unfinished, is known to require theoretical constructions that far outrun the ad hoc precepts of our explicit grammatical knowledge.[2] A similar situation presumably holds in moral philosophy. There is no reason to assume that our sense of justice can be adequately characterized by familiar common sense precepts, or derived from the more obvious learning principles. A correct account of moral capacities will certainly involve principles and theoretical constructions which go much beyond the norms and standards cited in everyday life. . . .

So far, though, I have not said anything about considered judgments. Now, as already suggested, they enter as those judgments in which our moral capacities are most likely to be displayed without distortion. Thus in deciding which of our judgments to take into account we may reasonably select some and exclude others. For example, we can discard those judgments made with hesitation, or in which we have little confidence. Similarly, those given when we are upset or frightened, or when we stand to gain one way or the other can be left aside. All these judgments are likely to be erroneous or to be influenced by an excessive attention to our own interests. Considered judgments are simply those rendered under conditions favorable to the exercise of the sense of justice, and therefore in circumstances where the more common excuses and explanations for making a mistake do not obtain. The person making the judgment is presumed, then, to have the ability, the opportunity, and the desire to reach a correct decision (or at least, not the desire not to). Moreover, the criteria that identify these judgments are not arbitrary. They are, in fact, similar to those that single out considered judgments of any kind. And once we regard the sense of justice as a mental capacity, as involving the exercise of thought, the relevant judgments are those given under conditions favorable for deliberation and judgment in general.

1. See Noam Chomsky, *Aspects of the Theory of Syntax* (MIT Press, 1965), pp. 3–9. [Rawls's note.]

2. By "ad hoc precepts," Rawls means something like highly specific rules tailored to the particular situation at hand.

I now turn to the notion of reflective equilibrium. The need for this idea arises as follows. . . . In describing our sense of justice an allowance must be made for the likelihood that considered judgments are no doubt subject to certain irregularities and distortions despite the fact that they are rendered under favorable circumstances. When a person is presented with an intuitively appealing account of his sense of justice (one, say, which embodies various reasonable and natural presumptions), he may well revise his judgments to conform to its principles even though the theory does not fit his existing judgments exactly. He is especially likely to do this if he can find an explanation for the deviations which undermines his confidence in his original judgments and if the conception presented yields a judgment which he finds he can now accept. From the standpoint of moral philosophy, the best account of a person's sense of justice is not the one which fits his judgments prior to his examining any conception of justice, but rather the one which matches his judgments in reflective equilibrium. As we have seen, this state is one reached after a person has weighed various proposed conceptions and he has either revised his judgments to accord with one of them or held fast to his initial convictions (and the corresponding conception).

The notion of reflective equilibrium introduces some complications that call for comment. For one thing, it is a notion characteristic of the study of principles which govern actions shaped by self-examination. Moral philosophy is Socratic: we may want to change our present considered judgments once their regulative principles[3] are brought to light. And we may want to do this even though these principles are a perfect fit. A knowledge of these principles may suggest further reflections that lead us to revise our judgments. . . .

There are, however, several interpretations of reflective equilibrium. For the notion varies depending upon whether one is to be presented with only those descriptions which more or less match one's existing judgments except for minor discrepancies, or whether one is to be presented with all possible descriptions to which one might plausibly conform one's judgments together with all relevant philosophical arguments for them. In the first case we would be describing a person's sense of justice more or less as it is although allowing for the smoothing out of certain irregularities; in the second case a person's sense of justice may or may not undergo a radical shift. Clearly it is the second kind of reflective equilibrium that one is concerned with in moral philosophy. To be sure, it is doubtful whether one can ever reach this state. For even if the idea of all possible descriptions and of all philosophically relevant arguments is well-defined (which is questionable), we cannot examine each of them. The most we can do is to study the conceptions of justice known to us through the tradition of moral philosophy and any further ones that occur to us, and then to consider these. . . .

This explanation of reflective equilibrium suggests straightaway a number of further questions. For example, does a reflective equilibrium (in the sense of the philosophical ideal) exist? If so, is it unique? Even if it is unique, can it be reached? Perhaps the

---

3. By "regulative principles," Rawls means those justificatory principles that support and justify our specific considered judgments. In calling moral philosophy "Socratic," Rawls means that our understanding and articulation of moral philosophy will evolve as we come to a deeper understanding of the connections between and implications of particular judgments and their foundations.

judgments from which we begin, or the course of reflection itself (or both), affect the resting point, if any, that we eventually achieve. It would be useless, however, to speculate about these matters here. They are far beyond our reach. I shall not even ask whether the principles that characterize one person's considered judgments are the same as those that characterize another's. I shall take for granted that these principles are either approximately the same for persons whose judgments are in reflective equilibrium, or if not, that their judgments divide along a few main lines represented by the family of traditional doctrines discussed. (Indeed, one person may find himself torn between opposing conceptions at the same time.) If men's conceptions of justice finally turn out to differ, the ways in which they do so is a matter of first importance. Of course we cannot know how these conceptions vary, or even whether they do, until we have a better account of their structure. . . . [I]f we should be able to characterize one (educated) person's sense of justice, we would have a good beginning toward a theory of justice. We may suppose that everyone has in himself the whole form of a moral conception. . . .

A theory of justice is subject to the same rules of method as other theories. Definitions and analyses of meaning do not have a special place: definition is but one device used in setting up the general structure of theory. Once the whole framework is worked out, definitions have no distinct status and stand or fall with the theory itself. In any case, it is obviously impossible to develop a substantive theory of justice founded solely on truths of logic and definition. The analysis of moral concepts and the a priori,[4] however traditionally understood, is too slender a basis. Moral philosophy must be free to use contingent assumptions and general facts as it pleases. There is no other way to give an account of our considered judgments in reflective equilibrium. . . .

I wish, then, to stress the central place of the study of our substantive moral conceptions. But the corollary to recognizing their complexity is accepting the fact that our present theories are primitive and have grave defects. We need to be tolerant of simplifications if they reveal and approximate the general outlines of our judgments. Objections by way of counterexamples are to be made with care, since these may tell us only what we know already, namely that our theory is wrong somewhere. The important thing is to find out how often and how far it is wrong. All theories are presumably mistaken in places. The real question at any given time is which of the views already proposed is the best approximation overall. . . .

## TEST YOUR UNDERSTANDING

1. Rawls contends we should identify some of our considered moral judgments and formulate "a set of principles which, when conjoined to our beliefs and knowledge of the circumstances, would lead us to make these judgments with their supporting reasons were we to apply these principles conscientiously and intelligently." Once we have a

---

4. Rawls means that which can be known without reference to our experience and to contingent facts about us.

"rough draft" of those principles, we should test to see if they are both consistent with and explain the full range of our considered judgments. Rawls's procedure, therefore, depends heavily upon these considered judgments.

Produce two examples of moral judgments that might qualify as considered judgments. Produce two examples of moral judgments that might not qualify as considered judgments and explain why they would not qualify.

2. Why does Rawls use the term "reflective equilibrium"? Why "reflective"? Why "equilibrium"?

## NOTES AND QUESTIONS

1. Rawls's methodology depends heavily on one's considered moral judgments. But what if a person's considered moral judgments are all wrong, each and every one of them? Does that possibility pose a difficulty for Rawls's proposed methodology? Is there a superior alternative?

2. We often disagree about moral matters and have differing considered moral judgments. Does that mean that, using Rawls's methodology, we might arrive at different moral theories? Discuss whether it might be *possible* for us to begin with different considered judgments yet converge upon the same moral theory, i.e., whether we could arrive at the same reflective equilibrium point.

## Elizabeth Harman (born 1975)

Harman is a Professor of Philosophy at Princeton University. She specializes in moral philosophy and is especially well known for her work on harm and the ethics of procreation.

# IS IT REASONABLE TO "RELY ON INTUITIONS" IN ETHICS?

Some philosophers argue for ethical conclusions by relying on specific ethical claims about described cases. I will discuss and defend this practice. It is often described as "relying on intuitions," though I will argue that this description is deeply misleading.

Ethical arguments can usefully rely on specific ethical claims about described cases in at least three ways. First, a specific ethical claim can be offered as a *counterexample* to a more general ethical claim. Second, a specific ethical claim can be used to motivate or *support* a more general ethical claim; for example, an author might argue that if a specific ethical claim is true, then it must be true *because* a more general ethical claim is true, and so the more general ethical claim must be true. Third, a specific ethical claim may be used in an argument for another specific ethical claim. There are many ways such an argument might proceed. For example, it might proceed via argument for a more general ethical claim, or it might proceed by claiming that there are no morally significant differences between the two cases in question that could warrant different verdicts about the cases.

It will be helpful to have in mind some examples of the type of argument I am discussing. In "Famine, Affluence, and Morality," Peter Singer argues that each of us ought to give a lot of money (much more than people typically give) to famine relief.[1] His argument relies on the claim that if a man is walking by a drowning child, and he is the only person in a position to save the child, but saving the child would involve getting his suit muddy, then he ought to save the child. This specific ethical claim is used to *support* the general claim that if one can prevent something bad from happening without sacrificing anything of comparable moral importance, then one should do so, which Singer then uses to support his conclusion about famine relief. Judith Jarvis Thomson's paper "A Defense of Abortion" argues for the claim that ordinary abortions are permissible even if early fetuses have the full moral status of persons.[2] Her argument crucially depends on the claim that if a man wakes up in a hospital, perfectly healthy himself but with his kidneys being used to keep a famous violinist alive, and if the violinist will die unless the man stays in the hospital for nine months, then it is permissible for the man to detach himself and leave the hospital, causing the violinist's death. She uses this claim as a *counterexample* to the general claim that it is never permissible to violate a right to life merely in order to have control of one's body. Both Singer's and Thomson's papers argue *from one specific ethical claim to another*.

Why might it be thought to be unreasonable to rely on specific claims about described cases in ethics? It is sometimes pointed out that not everyone agrees on these specific claims. Indeed, sometimes survey data is produced to *prove* that there is disagreement about the specific claims.[3] This complaint may simply misunderstand what is going on when people rely on specific claims about described cases in ethics, and in philosophy more generally. Such arguments have as a premise *a certain claim about the case*. They do not have as a premise *a claim that everyone agrees with a certain claim about the case*.

---

1. Peter Singer, "Famine, Affluence, and Morality," *Philosophy and Public Affairs* 1 (1972): 229–43. Excerpted in chapter 18 of this volume. [Harman's note.]

2. Judith Jarvis Thomson, "A Defense of Abortion," *Philosophy and Public Affairs* 1 (1971): 47–66. Excerpted in chapter 18 of this volume. [Harman's note.]

3. See Joshua D. Greene, "The Secret Joke of Kant's Soul," in *Moral Psychology*, vol. 3: *The Neuroscience of Morality: Emotion, Disease, and Development*, ed. W. Sinnott-Armstrong (MIT Press, 2007), which makes a more complicated argument than the one I go on to discuss; see Selim Berker, "The Normative Insignificance of Neuroscience," *Philosophy and Public Affairs* 37, no. 4 (2009): 293–329, for a critique of Greene. [Harman's note.]

It might be thought that philosophical arguments should not have any premises about which there is disagreement. But having such premises is in the very nature of philosophical arguments, and certainly ethical arguments. Many moral philosophy papers begin by assuming Kantianism, utilitarianism, consequentialism, or virtue ethics and proceeding from there. The arguments these papers offer are not bad arguments simply because they have deeply controversial assumptions. In ethics, and in philosophy more generally, there is quite a lot of disagreement. Arguments often have substantive premises with which some people agree and some people disagree. Two things happen when someone puts forward such an argument. Those who believe the premises are invited to follow the line of reasoning outlined, and to believe the conclusion of the argument. Those who do not believe the premises are invited to follow a related line of reasoning, to a weaker conclusion: they are invited to believe that *if* those premises are true, *then* the argument's conclusion is true. Thus, a paper that argues from particular premises is not interesting only to those who believe the paper's premises; it has something to say to *everyone*. And the weaker conclusion (that if the premises are true then the conclusion is true) may be interesting to someone even if he does not believe the argument's premises. For example, if one of the premises is (or is implied by) a view that he thinks is false, and that he wants to convince others is false, then the paper may help him in this project by showing further implausible commitments of the rival view. Or to return to our prior examples, Singer intends his 1972 paper to convince his readers of his conclusion. But some readers may become convinced of the weaker conditional: if it is morally obligatory to save a drowning child right in front of one, at the cost of getting one's suit muddy, then it is morally obligatory to give lots of money away regularly to prevent remote children from starving. These readers may believe this conditional and be moved to employ modus tollens rather than modus ponens: because we are not morally obligated to give lots of money away, they conclude that a man who can save a drowning child only at the cost of muddying his suit is not obligated to do so.

Similarly, someone who lacks a clear belief about whether it is permissible, in Thomson's violinist case, for the man in the hospital to unplug himself, may nevertheless find himself persuaded by Thomson's argument to believe that if the man's unplugging himself is permissible, then abortion of a fetus with full moral status is permissible. This person thereby comes to believe something about the relationship between the obligations to be a good Samaritan who helps others at significant cost to himself, on the one hand, and the obligation not to abort on the other: if the first obligation does not exist, then the second does not either.

Disagreement does pose another worry, which cannot be so easily dismissed. The fact that there is disagreement over a certain premise may seem to give those who believe the premise sufficient reason to doubt their judgment, so that they should cease to believe the premise.[4] This is an *epistemological worry*, that is, a worry about whether *belief* in the premise of an argument is justified; it is not a worry about

---

4. Jonathan Weinberg, Shaun Nichols, and Stephen Stich, "Normativity and Epistemic Intuitions," *Philosophical Topics* 29, no. 1/2 (2001): 429–60. [Harman's note.]

whether the premise is true. Epistemological worries pose the most serious kind of challenge to the practice I am defending. I now turn to three sorts of epistemological worries: the first arises from the fact of disagreement; the second arises from a concern that mere intuitive seemings cannot justify beliefs; and the third arises from a concern that some described cases are too far-fetched.

I will begin with the worry arising from disagreement.

Suppose that Anne believes a particular specific ethical claim, about the following case. A train is heading for five innocent people caught on the tracks, all of whom will die if they are hit. A person is standing on a bridge over the tracks. She can push a large fat man, who is next to her, off the bridge onto the track. His body would stop the train, preventing it from hitting the five. (Her own smaller body would not stop the train; if she jumped, she would die along with the five.) Anne believes it would be wrong for the woman to push the fat man off the bridge, to save the five. Suppose that Anne learns that there is disagreement about this case. In surveys, while many people agree with Anne, many disagree with her.[5] Furthermore, the disagreement is not just among people considering the case for the first time. Even among people who have thought long and hard about this case, there is disagreement.

Upon learning this, Anne may find herself in a situation in which apparent *epistemic peers* disagree with her. That is, Anne may expect that other ordinary people would be roughly as good as she is at discerning the moral truth about a described case if they have the same evidence she does; and she may take others to have the same evidence she has. It may seem that in this situation, Anne would be unreasonable in continuing to believe that it would be wrong to push the fat man. After all, she has no particular reason to think she is better at responding to the shared evidence than other people; but she would have to have such a reason to trust her own judgment more than others'.

The view I have just outlined holds that when one faces disagreement from an epistemic peer, one should suspend judgment about the disputed claim, because one has no independent reason to take one's own judgment to be better. This view might be supported by the claim that when Anne confronts disagreement, the only thing that grounds her belief is *the fact that she has judged the claim to be true;* the question then seems to become whether she believes her judgment is better than those she disagrees with. This claim is not true, however. Independently of the fact of disagreement (and prior to Anne's learning of the disagreement), Anne's belief was either justified or not. If it was justified, there were some factors which made it justified. Those factors remain after Anne hears of the disagreement; what is under dispute is whether they are still sufficient to justify her belief, that is, whether they are undermined by the fact of disagreement. On the view I endorse, these factors *do* make it reasonable for Anne to continue to hold her belief; *they* furthermore justify her belief that others, in this case, are in error: she concludes they are in error because they think it is permissible to push the fat man, which is false. (The fact that she judged the claim to be true plays no justifying role in her continuing to believe the claim.) On the other hand, if Anne's belief was not initially justified, then it is still not

---

5. Greene, 2007. [Harman's note.]

justified after she learns of the disagreement. But the fact of disagreement does not make it unjustified; it was independently unjustified.

I have endorsed a stark view on which disagreement poses no skeptical threat at all.[6] If one's beliefs are justified, learning that some others disagree should not at all undermine one's beliefs. I might instead have endorsed a more concessive view, according to which the fact that some others disagree with one makes it reasonable to be *less certain* of a belief one holds, but does not require one to suspend belief.[7] Both this more concessive view and the stark view I favor vindicate Anne in continuing to believe it is wrong to push the fat man, even in the face of disagreement.[8]

Let's turn to the second epistemological worry. This worry arises out of two claims. First, all specific ethical beliefs are formed on the basis of an intuitive seeming — on the basis of a claim's seeming to be true, but not for any other reason, that is, not on the basis of any evidence other than the claim's seeming to be true. Second, it is unreasonable to form specific ethical beliefs on the basis of intuitive seemings.

Is it true that all specific ethical beliefs are formed on the basis of intuitive seemings? No. Some specific ethical beliefs are formed on the basis of explicit reasoning *from ethical theories,* despite the believer's finding their negations intuitive. For example, a consequentialist may believe it is permissible to push the fat man off the bridge despite finding it intuitive that it is impermissible.

We might revise the worry's first claim to this: if a specific ethical belief is one that a person simply finds himself with upon reading a description of a case, then it was formed on the basis of an intuitive seeming — on the basis of the claim's seeming to be true, but not for any other reason. The worry's second claim remains the same, that it is unreasonable to form specific ethical beliefs on the basis of intuitive seemings. The worry's conclusion becomes the more limited claim that *in cases where a belief was formed in this way,* the belief is not a reasonable belief and so not a reasonable basis for an inference to a new belief. (The worry in this form applies to an argument as read by some readers but not as read by others.)

Is it true that if a reader simply finds himself with an ethical belief about a case upon reading a description of the case, then the belief must have been formed on the basis of an intuitive seeming — on the basis of the claim's seeming to be true, but not for any other reason? Surely not. The belief may have been implicitly inferred from other ethical commitments the person has;[9] this may have happened without the person's realizing it, or he may be *unsure* whether this has happened.

No *general* account will accurately describe what happens in all instances in which people read descriptions of cases and then find themselves with beliefs about the cases. Sometimes people have pre-existing beliefs about the cases. (For example,

6. Thomas Kelly, "The Epistemic Significance of Disagreement," in *Oxford Studies in Epistemology,* vol. 1, ed. John Hawthorne and Tamar Gendler Szabo (Oxford University Press, 2005), 167–96. [Harman's note.]

7. Thomas Kelly, "Peer Disagreement and Higher Order Evidence," in *Disagreement,* ed. Richard Feldman and Ted Warfield (Oxford University Press, 2010). [Harman's note.]

8. For a defense of the view that Anne would not be reasonable to continue to hold her belief, see Adam Elga, "Reflection and Disagreement." *Noûs* 41, no. 3 (2007): 478–502. [Harman's note.]

9. F. M. Kamm, "Introduction," in *Creation and Abortion* (Oxford University Press, 1992). [Harman's note.]

some people already believe that a stranger walking by a drowning child should save the child, before reading Singer's description of that case.) Sometimes people infer particular beliefs about the cases from more general beliefs they already have. Or they make explicit a particular belief they already implicitly had.

Consider the famous example of the doctor who cuts up an innocent healthy person to save five people dying of organ failure. It regularly happens that people hear this case described for the first time. They often react by believing that what the doctor does is wrong. Though they have never heard the case described, they do not *newly believe* that what the doctor does is wrong; they either already implicitly believed it or were already implicitly committed to it.

These points show that someone may simply find herself with a particular belief, upon hearing a case described, without it being true that her belief was formed on the basis of an intuitive seeming — on the basis of the claim's seeming true to her, and nothing else. We should not assume that, most of the time, beliefs about described cases are formed on the basis of intuitive seemings.

Indeed, intuitive seemings may play *no role* in the epistemology of specific ethical beliefs, as they actually occur. But if intuitive seemings do play a role, this may not be problematic. We might have the view that intuitive seemings *can* justify beliefs. We might hold that intuitive seemings justify beliefs in the same way that perceptual seemings justify beliefs. This claim could be elaborated in several different ways. One view holds that a person's intuitive seemings justify beliefs if her intuitive seemings are reliable;[1] this is an analogue of a reliabilist story about perceptual justification. Another view would hold that intuitive seemings justify beliefs simply because of their content: that it seems to you that p is true is in itself a reason to believe that p is true; this is an analogue of the "dogmatic" view of perceptual justification offered by James Pryor.[2]

We are now in a position to see why the practice I am defending — the making of ethical arguments that rely on specific ethical claims about described cases — should not be described as "relying on intuitions" in doing ethics. At least two mistakes are present in that description. First — as I mentioned early in this paper — there is a conflation of two very different practices: relying on certain claims that may in fact be intuitive, on the one hand, and relying on the claim *that* these claims are intuitive, on the other hand. Philosophical arguments of the type I am defending (and of the type often criticized for "relying on intuitions") do not rely on any claims about intuition; they rely on specific moral claims themselves. Second, there is an assumption that whenever we believe specific moral claims about described cases, we believe them simply because they are intuitive; as I've just argued, this is not true.

The third epistemological worry is sometimes voiced as follows: "Some described cases are too odd, too complicated, or involve too much science fiction for us to have reasonable beliefs about the cases." If this worry is meant to apply to all uses of claims about described cases, it is false. Singer's case, of the man and the drowning child, is neither odd, nor complicated, nor involving science fiction. Thomson's case

1.  George Bealer, "A Theory of the A Priori," *Philosophical Perspectives* 13 (1999): 29–55. [Harman's note.]

2.  James Pryor, "The Skeptic and the Dogmatist," *Noûs* 34, no. 4 (2000): 517–49. [Harman's note.]

involves some *fiction*: she supposes that medical records have shown that the man in the hospital, attached to the violinist, is the only person who can help; she supposes that he has been kidnapped and attached; and she supposes that one person's kidneys can be used to restore another person to health across nine months. But none of these suppositions is very far removed from the actual world: donor databases for bone marrow transplants sometimes reveal to someone that he is the only person who can save a stranger's life, organs are sometimes stolen from healthy people, and in order to donate kidneys or parts of livers, people sometimes endure serious health risks and hospital stays to restore others to health. The case of the woman on the bridge with the fat man is not very complicated. The case of the doctor who cuts up his healthy patient to save five patients with organ failure is also quite simple. Neither of these two cases involves any science fiction.

Sometimes people complain that particular described cases are too odd, too complicated, or involve too much science fiction as a way of explaining why they themselves are unmoved by the arguments that rely on claims about these cases: they find that they *lack* beliefs about the cases, or that they lack stable, confident beliefs about the cases. This fact, that *some people* lack beliefs about the claims in question, does not show that everyone lacks such beliefs. The arguments may nevertheless be perfectly good arguments that appeal to claims believed by some people but not by everyone.

It is a *much stronger* claim that some particular described cases are so odd, so complicated, or involve so much science fiction that *no one* could reasonably have a justified belief about the cases. This claim is not true about any of the four described cases I have just mentioned. Indeed, each case is such that we could come upon a similar case in real life. Would the case be too odd for us to judge whether the agent had acted permissibly? Surely not.[3]

I will briefly mention a final concern. This concern maintains that our general ethical beliefs are better grounded, or more reliable, than our specific ethical beliefs about cases, such that we should always do ethics by proceeding *from* the general to the specific, and never vice versa.[4] Kantians and utilitarians often believe this is the correct view of the epistemology of ethics. There are many different reasons that might be offered for this view. But none of the three epistemological worries I have discussed can support this view. As for the first worry, I conjecture that if we were to conduct surveys of people's beliefs in general ethical claims, we would find substantial disagreement. Consideration of disagreement will not tell in favor of general ethical claims over specific ethical claims. As for the second worry, whether intuitive seemings can be a source of justified beliefs favors neither specific nor general ethical claims. The third worry might seem to favor general claims. Whereas some specific ethical claims are about cases that may be odd or complicated, nothing corresponding holds of general ethical claims: being general,

---

3. Timothy Williamson, "Thought Experiments," chapter 6 in *The Philosophy of Philosophy* (Blackwell, 2007). [Harman's note.]

4. Peter Singer, "Ethics and Intuitions," *The Journal of Ethics* 9 (2005): 331–52; R. M. Hare, "Rawls' *A Theory of Justice*: Part I," *Philosophical Quarterly* 23 (1973): 144–55. [Harman's note.]

they are not focused on anything odd or complicated. But the third worry, properly understood, simply presses the point that some specific ethical claims are such that some people will be unsure what to make of them. The same is true of general ethical claims.

# Conclusion

I have defended the making of arguments for ethical conclusions on the basis of specific ethical claims about described cases. I have argued that three objections to this practice fail.[5]

Where does this leave someone who wants to pursue ethical questions by reading philosophy papers? Suppose you read a paper that argues for an ethical conclusion on the basis of specific ethical claims about described cases.

If you believe the specific ethical claims the paper relies on, then the paper is offering you an argument for its conclusion, which you might well reasonably rely on in coming to believe the conclusion.

If you do not believe a specific ethical claim the paper relies on, either because you believe it is false or because you are unsure what to make of it, then the paper is not in a position to convince you of its conclusion. You may, however, find it interesting whether the weaker conditional is true — that if its premises are true, then its conclusion is true — and the paper may reasonably convince you of this claim. You may also find it interesting that this paper may convince others; you may want to engage with the paper as an argument addressed to others, perhaps showing (to those who believe the premises) that the premises do not really imply the conclusion.

When is a philosophy paper that relies on specific ethical claims criticizable for relying on such claims? No paper is criticizable simply for being *a paper that relies on some specific ethical claims about described cases* — some papers do so and are excellent, compelling, important philosophy papers.[6] If a paper relies on claims that are only believed by some people, it is still a contribution for being of interest to those people (and it is also of interest to everyone as offering a claim about what follows from certain other claims). But a paper might rely on specific ethical claims such that no one is in a position to form a justified belief about those claims. Such a paper is less interesting because it provides no interesting argument for its conclusion; but it may still be interesting as arguing that if its premises are true, then its conclusion is true.

5. For two very different defenses of reliance of specific ethical claims, see Kamm, 1992 and the final section of Tamar Szabo Gendler, "Philosophical Thought Experiments, Intuitions, and Cognitive Equilibrium," *Midwest Studies in Philosophy* 31 (2007): 68–89. [Harman's note.]

6. Thomson, 1971; Singer, 1972; Michael Tooley, "Abortion and Infanticide," *Philosophy and Public Affairs* 2 (1972): 37–65; James Rachels, "Active and Passive Euthanasia," *New England Journal of Medicine* 292 (1975): 78–80; Susan Wolf, "Asymmetrical Freedom," *Journal of Philosophy* 77, no. 3 (1980): 151–166; Derek Parfit, "Part Three: Personal Identity," *Reasons and Persons* (Oxford University Press, 1982); Seana Shiffrin, "Wrongful Life, Procreative Responsibility, and the Significance of Harm," *Legal Theory* 5 (1999): 117–48; and Frances Kamm, "Terrorism and Several Moral Distinctions," *Legal Theory* 12, no. 1 (2006): 19–69. [Harman's note.]

## TEST YOUR UNDERSTANDING

1. What, in Harman's view, is a "specific ethical claim"? What are the three main uses she identifies of specific ethical claims in ethical arguments? Produce two examples of your own of a specific ethical claim and show how they can be used in these three ways.

2. Harman argues for the validity of relying on specific ethical claims in ethical deliberation, despite the fact that we sometimes have differing moral reactions to cases. Explain why she believes that this variation does not impugn the enterprise of using specific ethical claims to support our ethical conclusions.

3. Why does Harman contend that it might be valuable for you to consider an ethical argument that is premised on a specific ethical claim that you reject?

## NOTES AND QUESTIONS

1. *Does disagreement make any difference?* Harman argues that if you discover that someone whose judgment you respect deeply disagrees with you about an ethical issue, the mere fact of disagreement does not itself give you reason to doubt your own view. If it is reasonable to continue to hold fast to your position, does the discovery of difference give you any reason to think, reason, or do *anything* differently? If so, what? Or, is the discovery of this different judgment more of a mere curiosity like discovering that your best friend strangely does not care for chocolate?

2. *Strange cases:* Harman responds to the criticism that we should not rely too heavily on conclusions drawn from strange cases. Might we have the opposite concern and worry that our reactions to highly familiar cases, e.g., our sense that it is morally permissible to spend money on going to the movies rather than giving it to charity, reflect ingrained social biases, habitual reactions, and self-serving rationalizations? Perhaps introducing fictional elements into the cases we consider might improve our reasoning. Harman briefly discusses Judith Jarvis Thomson's famous violinist example. How might consideration of the violinist's plight help to address some of the potential hazards of familiarity?

3. *Two Distinctions:* Harman draws two important, but subtle, distinctions. The first is the distinction between

   1a. Claiming that a particular behavior is permissible

   and

   1b. Claiming that everyone agrees that a particular behavior is permissible.

   The second is the distinction between

   2a. Relying on an ethical claim that may in fact be intuitive and

  2b.  Relying on the claim *that* an ethical claim is intuitive.

*Exercise:* Explain these two distinctions in your own words and offer examples. (*Hint:* Often, one way to see a distinction more clearly is to ask what evidence you would offer if someone asked "Why do you think that?" If you would give different evidence for different contentions, that helps you see the difference between them.)

## Friedrich Nietzsche (1844–1900)

Nietzsche was a German philosopher and classical philologist who taught at the University of Basel. Most famous for his works on aesthetics, moral philosophy, philosophy of religion, and philosophy of science, Nietzsche is well known for his cutting criticism of systematic philosophy and his unusual argumentative style that makes heavy use of metaphor, poetry, and aphorism. His numerous books include *The Birth of Tragedy* (1872), *The Gay Science* (1882), *Thus Spoke Zarathustra* (1885), *Beyond Good and Evil* (1887), *On the Genealogy of Morals* (1887), and *Ecce Homo* (1888).

# ON THE GENEALOGY OF MORALS

## 6

We need a *critique* of moral values, *the value of these values themselves must first be called in question* — and for that there is needed a knowledge of the conditions and circumstances in which they grew, under which they evolved and changed (morality as consequence, as symptom, as mask, as tartufferie,[1] as illness, as misunderstanding; but also morality as cause, as remedy, as stimulant, as restraint, as poison), a knowledge of a kind that has never yet existed or even been desired. One has taken the *value* of these "values" as given, as factual, as beyond all question; one has hitherto never doubted or hesitated in the slightest degree in supposing "the good man" to be of greater value than "the evil man," of greater value in the sense of furthering the advancement and prosperity of man in general (the future of man included). But what if the reverse were true? What if a symptom of regression were inherent in the "good," likewise a danger, a seduction, a poison, a narcotic, through

---

1. By "tartufferie," Nietzsche means "hypocrisy." The term was coined for the main character in *Tartuffe* by the French playwright Molière (1622–1673): Tartuffe falsely but convincingly appears to be a religiously pious person and gains power because of that appearance.

which the present was possibly living *at the expense of the future*? . . . So that precisely morality would be to blame if the *highest power and splendor* actually possible to the type man was never in fact attained? . . .

# BEYOND GOOD AND EVIL

---

## 257

Every enhancement of the type "man" has so far been the work of an aristocratic society—and it will be so again and again—a society that believes in the long ladder of an order of rank and differences in value between man and man, and that needs slavery in some sense or other. Without that *pathos of distance* which grows out of the ingrained difference between strata—when the ruling caste constantly looks afar and looks down upon subjects and instruments and just as constantly practices obedience and command, keeping down and keeping at a distance—that other, more mysterious pathos could not have grown up either—the craving for an ever new widening of distances within the soul itself the development of ever higher, rarer, more remote, further-stretching, more comprehensive states—in brief, simply the enhancement of the type "man," the continual "self-overcoming of man," to use a moral formula in a supra-moral sense.

To be sure, one should not yield to humanitarian illusions about the origins of an aristocratic society (and thus of the presupposition of this enhancement of the type "man"): truth is hard. Let us admit to ourselves, without trying to be considerate, how every higher culture on earth so far has *begun*. Human beings whose nature was still natural, barbarians in every terrible sense of the word, men of prey who were still in possession of unbroken strength of will and lust for power, hurled themselves upon weaker, more civilized, more peaceful races, perhaps traders or cattle raisers, or upon mellow old cultures whose last vitality was even then flaring up in splendid fireworks of spirit and corruption. . . .

## 258

Corruption as the expression of a threatening anarchy among the instincts and of the fact that the foundation of the affects, which is called "life," has been shaken: corruption is something totally different depending on the organism in which it appears. When, for example, an aristocracy, like that of France at the beginning of the Revolution,[1]

---

1. Nietzsche refers to the French Revolution (1789–1799) in which a popular movement inspired by egalitarian ideals overthrew an entrenched monarchy and its supportive aristocracy.

throws away its privileges with a sublime disgust and sacrifices itself to an extravagance of its own moral feelings, that is corruption; it was really only the last act of that centuries-old corruption which had led them to surrender, step by step, their governmental prerogatives, demoting themselves to a mere *function* of the monarchy (finally even to a mere ornament and showpiece). The essential characteristic of a good and healthy aristocracy, however, is that it experiences itself *not* as a function (whether of the monarchy or the commonwealth) but as their *meaning* and highest justification — that it therefore accepts with a good conscience the sacrifice of untold human beings who, *for its sake*, must be reduced and lowered to incomplete human beings, to slaves, to instruments. Their fundamental faith simply has to be that society must *not* exist for society's sake but only as the foundation and scaffolding on which a choice type of being is able to raise itself to its higher task and to a higher state of *being* — comparable to those sun-seeking vines of Java . . . that so long and so often enclasp an oak tree with their tendrils until eventually, high above it but supported by it, they can unfold their crowns in the open light and display their happiness.

# 259

Refraining mutually from injury, violence, and exploitation and placing one's will on a par with that of someone else — this may become, in a certain rough sense, good manners among individuals if the appropriate conditions are present (namely, if these men are actually similar in strength and value standards and belong together in *one* body). But as soon as this principle is extended, and possibly even accepted as the *fundamental principle of society,* it immediately proves to be what it really is — a will to the *denial* of life, a principle of disintegration and decay.

Here we must beware of superficiality and get to the bottom of the matter, resisting all sentimental weakness: life itself is *essentially* appropriation, injury, overpowering of what is alien and weaker; suppression, hardness, imposition of one's own forms, incorporation and at least, at its mildest, exploitation. . . .

Even the body within which individuals treat each other as equals, as suggested before — and this happens in every healthy aristocracy — if it is a living and not a dying body, has to do to other bodies what the individuals within it refrain from doing to each other: it will have to be an incarnate will to power, it will strive to grow, spread, seize, become predominant — not from any morality or immorality but because it is living and because life simply is will to power. . . . [E]verywhere people are now raving, even under scientific disguises, about coming conditions of society in which "the exploitative aspect" will be removed — which sounds to me as if they promised to invent a way of life that would dispense with all organic functions. "Exploitation" does not belong to a corrupt or imperfect and primitive society: it belongs to the essence of what lives, as a basic organic function; it is a consequence of the will to power, which is after all the will of life. . . .

# 260

Wandering through the many subtler and coarser moralities which have so far been prevalent on earth, or still are prevalent, I found that certain features recurred regularly together and were closely associated — until I finally discovered two basic types and one basic difference.

There are *master morality* and *slave morality*—I add immediately that in all the higher and more mixed cultures there also appear attempts at mediation between these two moralities, and yet more often the interpenetration and mutual misunderstanding of both, and at times they occur directly alongside each other — even in the same human being, within a *single* soul. The moral discrimination of values has originated either among a ruling group whose consciousness of its difference from the ruled group was accompanied by delight — or among the ruled, the slaves and dependents of every degree.

In the first case, when the ruling group determines what is "good," the exalted, proud states of the soul are experienced as conferring distinction and determining the order of rank. The noble human being separates from himself those in whom the opposite of such exalted, proud states finds expression: he despises them. It should be noted immediately that in this first type of morality the opposition of "good" and "bad" means approximately the same as "noble" and "contemptible." (The opposition of "good" and "*evil*" has a different origin.) One feels contempt for the cowardly, the anxious, the petty, those latent on narrow utility; also for the suspicious with their unfree glances, those who humble themselves, the doglike people who allow themselves to be maltreated, the begging flatterers, above all the liars: it is part of the fundamental faith of all aristocrats that the common people lie. "We truthful ones" — thus the nobility of ancient Greece referred to itself.

It is obvious that moral designations were everywhere first applied to *human beings* and only later, derivatively, to actions. Therefore it is a gross mistake when historians of morality start from such questions as: why was the compassionate act praised? The noble type of man experiences *itself* as determining values; it does not need approval; it judges, "what is harmful to me is harmful in itself"; it knows itself to be that which first accords honor to things; it is *value-creating*. Everything it knows as part of itself it honors: such a morality is self-glorification. In the foreground there is the feeling of fullness, of power that seeks to overflow, the happiness of high tension, the consciousness of wealth that would give and bestow: the noble human being, too, helps the unfortunate, but not, or almost not, from pity, but prompted more by an urge begotten by excess of power. The noble human being honors himself as one who is powerful, also as one who has power over himself, who knows how to speak and be silent, who delights in being severe and hard with himself and respects all severity and hardness. . . . Such a type of man is actually proud of the fact that he is *not* made for pity. . . . Noble and courageous human beings who think that way are furthest removed from that morality which finds the distinction of morality precisely in pity, or in acting for others, or in *désintéressement*;[2] faith in oneself, pride in oneself, a fundamental hostility and irony against "selflessness" belong just as definitely to noble morality as does a slight disdain and caution regarding compassionate feelings and a "warm heart."

---

2. A French word meaning "disinterestedness" or "unselfishness."

... A morality of the ruling group, however, is most alien and embarrassing to the present taste in the severity of its principle that one has duties only to one's peers; that against beings of a lower rank, against everything alien, one may behave as one pleases or "as the heart desires," and in any case "beyond good and evil" — here pity and like feelings may find their place. The capacity for, and the duty of, long gratitude and long revenge — both only among one's peers — refinement in repaying, the sophisticated concept of friendship, a certain necessity for having enemies (as it were, as drainage ditches for the affects of envy, quarrelsomeness, exuberance — at bottom, in order to be capable of being good friends): all these are typical characteristics of noble morality which, as suggested, is not the morality of "modern ideas" and therefore is hard to empathize with today....

It is different with the second type of morality, *slave morality*. Suppose the violated, oppressed, suffering, unfree, who are uncertain of themselves and weary, moralize: what will their moral valuations have in common? Probably, a pessimistic suspicion about the whole condition of man will find expression, perhaps a condemnation of man along with his condition. The slave's eye is not favorable to the virtues of the powerful: he is skeptical and suspicious, *subtly* suspicious, of all the "good" that is honored there — he would like to persuade himself that even their happiness is not genuine. Conversely, those qualities are brought out and flooded with light which serve to ease existence for those who suffer: here pity, the complaisant and obliging hand, the warm heart, patience, industry, humility, and friendliness are honored — for here these are the most useful qualities and almost the only means for enduring the pressure of existence. Slave morality is essentially a morality of utility.

Here is the place for the origin of that famous opposition of "good" and "evil": into evil one's feelings project power and dangerousness, a certain terribleness, subtlety, and strength that does not permit contempt to develop. According to slave morality, those who are "evil" thus inspire fear; according to master morality it is precisely those who are "good" that inspire, and wish to inspire, fear, while the "bad" are felt to be contemptible.

The opposition reaches its climax when, as a logical consequence of slave morality, a touch of disdain is associated also with the "good" of this morality — this may be slight and benevolent — because the good human being has to be *undangerous* in the slaves' way of thinking: he is good-natured, easy to deceive, a little stupid perhaps.... Wherever slave morality becomes preponderant, language tends to bring the words "good" and "stupid" closer together.

One last fundamental difference: the longing for *freedom*, the instinct for happiness and the subtleties of the feeling of freedom belong just as necessarily to slave morality and morals as artful and enthusiastic reverence and devotion are the regular symptom of an aristocratic way of thinking and evaluating.

This makes plain why love *as passion* — which is our European specialty — simply must be of noble origin: as is well known, its invention must be credited to the Provençal knight-poets, those magnificent and inventive human beings of the "*gai saber*[3] [Gay Science] to whom Europe owes so many things and almost owes itself. —

---

3. This term refers to the art and technique of fourteenth-century troubadours, who combined music, dance, and poetry.

# 261

Among the things that may be hardest to understand for a noble human being is vanity: he will be tempted to deny it, where another type of human being could not find it more palpable. The problem for him is to imagine people who seek to create a good opinion of themselves which they do not have of themselves — and thus also do not "deserve" — and who nevertheless end up *believing* this good opinion themselves. This strikes him half as such bad taste and lack of self-respect, and half as so baroquely irrational, that he would like to consider vanity as exceptional, and in most cases when it is spoken of he doubts it.

He will say, for example: "I may be mistaken about my value and nevertheless demand that my value, exactly as I define it, should be acknowledged by others as well — but this is no vanity (but conceit or, more frequently, what is called 'humility' or 'modesty')." Or: "For many reasons I may take pleasure in the good opinion of others: perhaps because I honor and love them and all their pleasures give me pleasure; perhaps also because their good opinion confirms and strengthens my faith in my own good opinion; perhaps because the good opinion of others, even in cases where I do not share it, is still useful to me or promises to become so — but all that is not vanity."

The noble human being must force himself, with the aid of history, to recognize that, since time immemorial, in all somehow dependent social strata the common man *was* only what he was *considered*: not at all used to positing values himself, he also attached no other value to himself than his masters attached to him (it is the characteristic *right of masters* to create values).

It may be understood as the consequence of an immense atavism that even now the ordinary man still always *waits* for an opinion about himself and then instinctively submits to that — but by no means only a "good" opinion; also a bad and unfair one (consider, for example, the great majority of the self-estimates and self-underestimates that believing women accept from their father-confessors, and believing Christians quite generally from their church).

In accordance with the slowly arising democratic order of things (and its cause, the intermarriage of masters and slaves), the originally noble and rare urge to ascribe value to oneself on one's own and to "think well" of oneself will actually be encouraged and spread more and more now; but it is always opposed by an older, ampler, and more deeply ingrained propensity — and in the phenomenon of "vanity" this older propensity masters the younger one. The vain person is delighted by *every* good opinion he hears of himself (quite apart from all considerations of its utility, and also apart from truth or falsehood), just as every bad opinion of him pains him: for he submits to both, he *feels* subjected to them in accordance with that oldest instinct of submission that breaks out in him.

It is "the slave" in the blood of the vain person, a residue of the slave's craftiness — and how much "slave" is still residual in woman, for example! — that seeks to *seduce* him to good opinions about himself; it is also the slave who afterwards immediately prostrates himself before these opinions as if he had not called them forth. . . .

# 293

A man who says, "I like this, I take this for my own and want to protect it and defend it against anybody"; a man who is able to manage something, to carry out a resolution, to remain faithful to a thought, to hold a woman, to punish and prostrate one who presumed too much; a man who has his wrath and his sword and to whom the weak, the suffering, the hard pressed, and the animals, too, like to come and belong by nature, in short a man who is by nature a *master* — when such a man has pity, well, *this* pity has value. But what good is the pity of those who suffer. Or those who, worse, *preach* pity.

Almost everywhere in Europe today we find a pathological sensitivity and receptivity to pain; also a repulsive incontinence in lamentation, an increase in tenderness that would use religion and philosophical bric-a-brac to deck itself out as something higher — there is a veritable cult of suffering. . . .

This newest kind of bad taste should be exorcized vigorously and thoroughly. . . .

# THE GAY SCIENCE

---

# 290

*One thing is needful.* — To "give style" to one's character — a great and rare art! It is practiced by those who survey all the strengths and weaknesses of their nature and then fit them into an artistic plan until every one of them appears as art and reason and even weaknesses delight the eye. Here a large mass of second nature has been added; there a piece of original nature has been removed — both times through long practice and daily work at it. Here the ugly that could not be removed is concealed; there it has been reinterpreted and made sublime. . . . In the end, when the work is finished, it becomes evident how the constraint of a single taste governed and formed everything large and small. Whether this taste was good or bad is less important than one might suppose, if only it was a single taste!

It will be the strong and domineering natures that enjoy their finest gaiety in such constraint and perfection under a law of their own; the passion of their tremendous will relents in the face of all stylized nature, of all conquered and serving nature. Even when they have to build palaces and design gardens they demur at giving nature freedom.

Conversely, it is the weak characters without power over themselves that *hate* the constraint of style. They feel that if this bitter and evil constraint were imposed upon them they would be demeaned; they become slaves as soon as they serve; they hate to serve. Such spirits — and they may be of the first rank — are always out to shape and interpret their environment as *free* nature: wild, arbitrary, fantastic, disorderly, and surprising. And they are well advised because it is only in this way that they can give pleasure to themselves. For one thing is needful: that a human being should *attain* satisfaction with himself, whether it be by means of this or that poetry and art; only then is a human being at all tolerable to behold. Whoever is dissatisfied with himself is continually ready for revenge, and we others will be his victims, if only by having to endure his ugly sight. . . .

# 301

*The fancy of the contemplatives.* — What distinguishes the higher human beings from the lower is that the former see and hear immeasurably more, and see and hear thoughtfully — and precisely this distinguishes human beings from animals, and the higher animals from the lower. For anyone who grows up into the heights of humanity the world becomes ever fuller; ever more fishhooks are cast in his direction to capture his interest; the number of things that stimulate him grows constantly, as does the number of different kinds of pleasure and displeasure: The higher human being always becomes at the same time happier and unhappier. But he can never shake off a *delusion*: He fancies that he is a *spectator* and *listener* who has been placed before the great visual and acoustic spectacle that is life; he calls his own nature *contemplative* and overlooks that he himself is really the poet who keeps creating this life. . . . We who think and feel at the same time are those who really continually *fashion* something that had not been there before: the whole eternally growing world of valuations, colors, accents, perspectives, scales, affirmations, and negations. This poem that we have invented is continually studied by the so-called practical human beings (our actors) who learn their roles and translate everything into flesh and actuality, into the everyday. Whatever has *value* in our world now does not have value in itself, according to its nature — nature is always value-less, but has been *given* value at some time, as a present — and it was *we* who gave and bestowed it. Only we have created the world *that concerns man*! — But precisely this knowledge we lack, and when we occasionally catch it for a fleeting moment we always forget it again immediately. . . .

# 304

*By doing we forego.* — At bottom I abhor all those moralities which say: "Do not do this! Renounce! Overcome yourself!" But I am well disposed toward those moralities which goad me to do something and do it again, from morning till evening, and then to dream of it at night, and to think of nothing except doing this *well,* as well as *I* alone can do it. When one lives like that, one thing after another that simply does not belong to such a life drops off. . . . He may not even notice that it takes its leave; for his eye is riveted to his goal — forward, not sideward, backward, downward. What we do should determine what we forego; by doing we forego. . . . But I do not wish to strive with open eyes for my own impoverishment; I do not like negative virtues — virtues whose very essence it is to negate and deny oneself something. . . .

## 338

*The will to suffer and those who feel pity.* — Is it good for you yourselves to be above all full of pity? And is it good for those who suffer? But let us leave the first question unanswered for a moment.

Our personal and profoundest suffering is incomprehensible and inaccessible to almost everyone; here we remain hidden from our neighbor, even if we eat from one pot. But whenever people *notice* that we suffer, they interpret our suffering superficially. It is the very essence of the emotion of pity that it strips away from the suffering of others whatever is distinctively personal. Our "benefactors" are, more than our enemies, people who make our worth and will smaller. When people try to benefit someone in distress, the intellectual frivolity with which those moved by pity assume the role of fate is for the most part outrageous; one simply knows nothing of the whole inner sequence and intricacies that are distress for *me* or for *you*. The whole economy of my soul and the balance effected by "distress," the way new springs and needs break open, the way in which old wounds are healing, the way whole periods of the past are shed — all such things that may be involved in distress are of no concern to our dear pitying friends; they wish to *help* and have no thought of the personal necessity of distress, although terrors, deprivations, impoverishments, midnights, adventures, risks, and blunders are as necessary for me and for you as are their opposites. It never occurs to them that, to put it mystically, the path to one's own heaven always leads through the voluptuousness of one's own hell. No, the "religion of pity" (or "the heart") commands them to help, and they believe that they have helped most when they have helped most quickly.

If you, who adhere to this religion, have the same attitude toward yourselves that you have toward your fellow men; if you refuse to let your own suffering lie upon you even for an hour and if you constantly try to prevent and forestall all possible distress way ahead of time; if you experience suffering and displeasure as evil, hateful, worthy of annihilation, and as a defect of existence, then it is clear that besides your religion of pity you also harbor another religion in your heart that is perhaps the mother of the religion of pity: the *religion of comfortableness.* How little you know of human *happiness,* you comfortable and benevolent people, for happiness and unhappiness are sisters and even twins that either grow up together or, as in your case, *remain small* together. But now back to the first question!

How is it at all possible to keep to one's own way? Constantly, some clamor or other calls us aside; rarely does our eye behold anything that does not require us to drop our own preoccupation instantly to help. I know, there are a hundred decent and praiseworthy ways of losing *my own way,* and they are truly highly "moral"! Indeed, those who now preach the morality of pity even take the view that precisely this and only this is moral — to lose one's *own* way in order to come to the assistance of a neighbor. I know just as certainly that I only need to expose myself to the sight of some genuine distress and am lost. . . . All such arousing of pity and calling for help is secretly seductive, for our "own way" is too hard and demanding and too remote from the love and gratitude of others, and we do not really mind escaping from it — and from our very own conscience — to flee into the conscience of the others and into the lovely temple of the "religion of pity."

... I do not want to remain silent about my morality which says to me: Live in seclusion so that you *can* live for yourself. Live in *ignorance* about what seems most important to your age. And the clamor of today, the noise of wars and revolutions should be a mere murmur for you. You will also wish to help—but only those whose distress you *understand* entirely because they share with you one suffering and one hope—your friends—and only in the manner in which you help yourself. I want to make them bolder, more persevering, simpler, gayer. I want to teach them what is understood by so few today, least of all by these preachers of pity: *to share not suffering but joy*.

## TEST YOUR UNDERSTANDING

1. Nietzsche recommends that we undertake a genealogy of morals, an investigation into "the conditions and circumstances in which [contemporary moral beliefs] ... grew." Does his narrative of those conditions and circumstances reinforce his confidence in those beliefs or sow doubts about them?

2. Nietzsche suggests that learning the historical source of an idea, practice, or a belief, and particularly that an idea, practice, or belief may serve someone's interests, may cast doubt upon the truth of that idea or belief. Identify one example in his text of an idea whose truth should be doubted because of its historical source. Can you produce an example from your own experience in which learning the source of an idea or whose interest it serves casts doubt upon its plausibility?

3. Does Nietzsche believe we should strive to reduce pain and suffering and to achieve the social conditions of equality?

## NOTES AND QUESTIONS

1. *Recasting epigrams into claims and arguments.* Nietzsche pursues a number of provocative **metaethical** and substantive claims that it may be helpful to separate and restate into more contemporary, straightforward language. Interpretation of Nietzsche is notoriously controversial. Do you agree that Nietzsche makes the claims outlined below?

   N1. To understand and evaluate our normative beliefs, we need to understand the sociological history of those beliefs. We must pursue a **genealogy of morals**. That is, to understand and evaluate normative principles and to use normative concepts (such as "good," "bad," and "evil"), we need to understand why people began to believe in those principles and to use those concepts. [GM 6]

   N2. Values are created and constructed, not discovered, by people. [GS 301]

   N3. Pursuing a genealogy of morals reveals that the values constructed by people were norms that served (a conception of) their interests.

   N4. "Bad" and "evil" are not synonymous. The paired concepts of "good" and "bad" arise from aristocratic culture, within which "good" represents a celebration of the traits of the strong. "Bad" represents their absence and a corresponding contempt for their absence. The quite contrary paired concepts of "good" and "evil" emanate from "slave morality," the values constructed by "the weak," reflecting their resentment toward their oppression. The morality of "good" and "evil" was constructed to serve the interests of the weak by representing the natural actions of the strong as wrong and by duping the strong to suppress their will to live and their natural instincts to dominate. The resentment of the weak leads them to champion selflessness and altruism not because those traits are good in themselves, but because celebrating them serves the interests of the weak, who are at risk for being the casualties of the strong. [BGE 259, 260]

N5. Most modern ethical theories presuppose some form of moral egalitarianism, the view that each person matters equally and should be treated equally. But, such egalitarianism is unnatural and stifles the life spirit. An appreciation of the differences between people and a hierarchical social system in which some dominate others are crucial conditions for particular individuals achieving the best that humanity is capable of. [BGE 257, 258, 259, 260]

N6. The values we endorse should not emanate from destructive and reactive character traits like resentment, guilt, and pity. We, especially we "higher human beings," should value the positive, joyful expression of the individual, and seek to express ourselves fully. [BGE 260; GS 290, 301, 338]

N7. A moral theory that stresses meeting the needs of others and advances such prohibitions as *do not harm others* or *do not take more than your share* is constraining and self-denying. It fails because it does not articulate what, positively, each of us should pursue to achieve our fullest personal expression. [BGE 259; GS 304, 338]

N8. Ethical views that emphasize the prevention and alleviation of pain and suffering are mistaken. Suffering is often essential to achieving excellence within a human life and therefore, real happiness. [GS 338]

2. Many of Nietzsche's claims will understandably strike modern readers as highly offensive, especially his claims about "higher" and "lower" human beings and the "need for slavery." Is it possible to reconstruct the crux of his argument while eliminating these offensive premises? Could one accept his metaethical position (e.g., claims N1 and N2 above) but reject his anti-egalitarianism? Could one argue for his substantive claims N6, N7 and N8 while rejecting his anti-egalitarianism in N4 and N5?

3. How do you think Nietzsche might respond to the following criticism of his genealogical method?

Initially, I formed the belief not to cross the street without looking because my parents instructed me to do so and I wished to obey them. Of course, that I wished to obey my parents is not the *real* reason to look before crossing. I learned the multiplication tables first by being told they were true. I only later came to understand *why* 6 times 7 is 42. Generally, how and why I first came to believe something often differs from the best reason to believe that thing.

Explain the objection and craft a reply on behalf of Nietzsche.

## ANALYZING THE ARGUMENTS

1. *The value of beneficence.* Most moral theories have, at their center, an argument about why we should help others in need. Nietzsche, however, calls into question whether we should attempt to relieve and prevent others' pain. Further, he argues that the imperatives to help others and to constrain the pursuit of our self-interest emanate from resentment by people who are frustrated with themselves and resent the success of others. Finding themselves at a disadvantage, they produce a moral code that condemns the strength and success of others.

    *Exercise:* Summarize, briefly, the positive arguments for helping others in need that Mill, Kant, Scanlon, and Hursthouse offer. How do their arguments differ? Do any of these arguments address Nietzsche's skepticism?

2. *When do numbers count?* Utilitarians contend that impartial respect for all requires that we aggregate the effects of our actions on everyone and select the action with the best outcome. Many criticize aggregative methods because they would be open to the implication that we should kill an innocent young person in order to harvest her organs to save six people in need of organ transplants. The case is meant to exemplify that aggregative methods entail the sacrifice of important interests of individuals when they conflict with the interests of the many. But many utilitarians criticize alternative theories as having difficulty explaining why if you could either save one drowning person or five drowning people, but not all six, you should not flip a coin or save the one. Rather, the numbers count. You should aggregate and save the five.

    *Exercise:* Explain how the non-utilitarian theorists you have read (Kant, Scanlon, and Hursthouse) would handle the organ transplant problem and the problem of the drowning victims. Do their theories suggest we should never consider how many people we could help, or is their criticism of forced organ harvesting more subtle?

3. *Using examples in moral reasoning.* Kant declares that no one "could give worse advice to morality than by wanting to derive it from examples."

    *Exercise:* Describe Kant's argument for this position. Explain how his argument is consistent with his use of examples. Consider whether the approaches of Harman, Hursthouse, or Rawls are guilty of giving this advice and are vulnerable to Kant's criticism. How might they defend their methodology against his concerns?

4. *Outcomes versus explanation.* Often, moral theories will converge regarding what they recommend, but offer different reasons for their recommendations. For example, utilitarians may forswear violence to express anger because peaceful methods maximize utility while violence causes pain and trauma, whereas non-utilitarians may argue that violence is wrong because it shows disrespect for the autonomy and the rational capacities of the victim or because it violates rules that rational parties would not reasonably reject to govern their interactions.

    *Exercise:* Consider the objection that utilitarian theories fail reliably to condemn lying for personal convenience.

a. Formulate this objection as an objection that utilitarianism recommends the wrong action.

b. Now imagine that the utilitarian can show that, as a matter of fact, because of how the facts about utility turn out, utilitarianism would condemn lying in all the same circumstances as a Kantian. Reformulate the objection that utilitarianism does not reliable condemn lying for personal convenience as an objection that utilitarianism offers the *wrong* reasons for condemning lying for personal convenience.

c. Now formulate an objection by the utilitarian that contends that the Kantian offers the wrong reasons for condemning lying.

d. Finally, explain why, even when disputants concur about *what to do,* philosophers think it matters that an alternate moral theory offers *the wrong reason* for doing the right thing. What is at stake in getting the explanation right, as opposed to just producing the correct moral recommendation?

5. *Terminology.* Philosophers often use similar terms in different ways and different terms for similar things. Good philosophical reading and writing demands that one keep careful track of these uses and be able to account for their relationship to each other. Sometimes when similar terms are used in different ways, it is helpful to generate a new term to forestall further confusion.

*Exercise:* Scanlon discusses a view called "intuitionism." Harman discusses "ethical intuitions" and "specific ethical claims." Rawls discusses "considered judgments." Are they all discussing the same thing, or are there major or minor differences between them? Which term or terms do you prefer, and why?

# 17

# Do Your Intentions Matter?

Suppose Betsy promises her friend Alfred that she will meet him at the local café at 10 AM tomorrow morning to help him decipher a tricky philosophical text, one she studied last term. Later that night, she starts playing the new version of *World of Warcraft* and cannot tear herself away. After her all-nighter, she stumbles into the café for coffee the next morning, having forgotten all about Alfred. To her surprise and embarrassment, she encounters Alfred, who immediately peppers Betsy with questions about Thomas Aquinas.

Betsy showed up at the appointed place and time, but only by accident, and not because she meant to keep her promise. This everyday case raises some interesting philosophical questions. Betsy was morally required to keep her promise. Did she do what she was required to do? Did she *keep* her promise if she only accidentally fulfilled its terms? That is, does keeping a promise merely involve performing the *action* one agreed to perform, or does it also require that one *intends* to perform the action *because* of the commitment?

Consider another example. Suppose Betsy donates to a charity for earthquake victims, but not because she cares about their plight. Betsy hopes to impress her employer, who is collecting donations, and to make her employer think they share a commitment to a cause. This case differs somewhat from her accidentally fulfilling a promise. The accidentally fulfilled coffee date might be thought to lack the full value of the deliberately fulfilled promise. After all, part of the point of a promise is that one's deliberation about one's future action is supposed to be guided by the fact of one's commitment. By contrast, in the donation case, although Betsy's purpose is only to benefit herself, her selfishly motivated donation helps others just as much as an altruistically motivated donation would. If the value of donations lies in the effective assistance others receive, perhaps it does not matter morally *why* she donates.

Yet, in another respect, the donation case and the promise case seem similar. The selfishly motivated donation case is still troubling, even if the earthquake victims are helped. Something seems awry when an otherwise good action is performed for a selfish, deceitful motive, rather than from an appreciation of the goodness of the action itself. In that respect, Betsy's behavior in the promise case may seem better than in the donation case. In the promise case, the problem is that Betsy forgot, but she did not have a poor motive like using others' suffering as an occasion for professional advancement.

Although something seems problematic in both cases, it is tricky to identify exactly *what*. For instance, does Betsy's selfishness make the donation *itself* morally impermissible, or does it make the donation *process* morally wrongful in some other way? Perhaps, one may think, these cases reveal something troubling not about her action per se but rather about her character. Maybe we should say that although she performs the right actions, *she* is selfish and morally careless. Moreover, although we may agree that selfish purposes do not provide morally exemplary reasons for donating, we may wonder, what is the exemplary reason for donating that Betsy lacks? Is it that she should care about people in need and *want* to help them, or is it that helping people in need, when one can, is one's duty and that her action should be the product of her sense of duty? Similarly, we may think that even if accidentally showing up counts as a way of keeping the promise, nonetheless it is a shabby, defective way to do so. Does its defect lie in a failure to be motivated by her duty as a promisor, by her failure to care enough about Alfred's need for help, or both? Larger questions lurk right under the surface of these cases, such as whether we should admire the person who gives from compassion as much as (or even more than) the person who gives from a sense of duty. Which motive, benevolence or a sense of duty, is morally foundational?

These kinds of questions about the significance of good, poor, and absent intentions have been a focal point of moral philosophy for centuries. We might divide them into two main categories. First, are a person's intentions relevant to the assessment of the moral character of her action? That is, when, if ever, does a person's intention in acting serve as a central component of the moral characterization of her action, helping to make that action right or wrong or permissible or impermissible? Or, should we deny that a person's intentions are a component of the moral nature of her actions and instead insist that her intentions mainly figure in the assessment of her character? The second category of questions asks *which* intention the morally motivated agent should have. When one acts morally, should one be acting from duty, from benevolent care and concern, or from some other motive?

# If Intentions Matter, How Do They Matter?

By examining our practices of praise and blame as well as our expectations of others, David Hume offers answers to both categories of questions. He contends that our fundamental moral evaluations center on a person's motive in acting. If a person aims at a good action but is somehow incapacitated by external circumstances, we would still praise her. For example, if Betsy sets out to keep her promise to Alfred but does not reach the café because she is caught in a traffic accident, her action is without fault. Alfred has no grounds to criticize her. The thought *is* what counts.

Hume contends that we value actions predominantly *because* they are the outward expressions of this underlying praiseworthy motive. So, for Hume, it isn't merely that intentions matter. Intentions are the central components of moral actions. Indeed, Hume believes that it is the good intention of a person that *makes* her action a good one. Actions are the external manifestations of a person's intentions, and we value them insofar as they express a person's underlying good intention.

Hume's objective is to identify the good motive that we esteem so highly because he thinks it is the key to understanding what actions are the right actions and why. Although one might think it is the motive of duty, that is, the sense that *that action must (morally) be done*, Hume offers a famous argument that that motive of duty cannot be the primary or first virtuous motive. Hume claims the motive of duty must depend upon there having been a prior virtuous motive that renders certain actions good ones. Why? Well, the motive of duty presupposes that there are, already, actions that morally *must* be performed; the motive of duty responds to the imperative that they must be done. What are those actions and what makes them morally important? As we have just seen, Hume contends that the value, or virtue, of an action does not stem from any external properties of that action. Rather, Hume claims that actions are morally good because they are the products of a good motive. What is that underlying motive? It cannot be the motive of duty, he thinks, because we would then have a vicious circle, for we would be saying that the motive of duty aims at good actions. Which actions are those? The very ones picked out by the motive of duty. That reply would be circular.

To avoid this circle, Hume argues that good actions must be the product of a different motive than the motive of duty. This other motive must itself be a morally good motive, that is, a motive we morally esteem. Further, because this motive is an alternative to the motive of duty, this alternative motive must orient us toward particular actions as choice-worthy for reasons other than that the action is a morally good one. For Hume, an action becomes morally good only (logically) after and because the motive that produces it is morally estimable.

So what is this alternative motive? Hume argues that the primary moral motive is the motive of benevolence. We morally esteem those actions that emanate from care and concern for others, which involve desires to help others for their sake. Helping actions, for example, are morally good because they are characteristic expressions of the motive of care.

Hume does not deny that we can act from the motive of duty. He just believes that the motive of duty is subordinate to the motive of benevolence. The motive of duty is a lesser substitute for the real thing, the motive of benevolence, when we happen not to feel care and concern. So, those who find themselves lacking a sympathetic motive on occasion may be spurred to perform good actions from the motive of duty. But the purely dutiful agent only knows what actions to perform, i.e., what actions are good, because those actions are the general product of the more foundational motive of benevolence. Our dutiful agent may lack an active feeling of concern for others, but she knows what the benevolent agent would do; the merely dutiful agent would not know what action to perform without knowledge of what those whose foundational motive of benevolence is active would do. Hence, Hume claims that benevolence lies at the basis of the distinction between morally good and bad actions, even though in some individual cases where a person happens to be devoid of care and sympathy, a good action may not be animated by benevolence but, instead, by the motive of duty.

Hume's claim that good actions are, standardly, actions motivated by benevolence may seem subject to a counterexample. Many actions required by justice, such as respecting property and keeping promises, are often owed to people in circumstances that would not and should not evoke care or concern by even the most benevolent person. Think of a very poor person repaying a debt to a billionaire who does not need the money. That action does not seem plausibly motivated by benevolence, but only by duty. Hume concedes that individual instances of justice may be motivated by a sense of duty. Still, the underlying social rules that create and define those duties are founded on motives such as benevolence and self-interest because just actions, taken together as a system, promote the interests of others and of oneself. Thus, Hume contends that morally admirable motives have a direct and indirect influence in delineating which actions are the just ones to perform and that, even in the case of justice, the foundational, primary moral motive is still benevolence.

# Doctrine of Double Effect

G.E.M. Anscombe, like Hume, regards the motives of the moral agent as crucial to the moral qualities of an action. Her focus is not, however, on the moral motive of benevolence but, rather, on the difference motives make in a concrete case. Specifically, she argues that the decisions by President Truman in World War II to drop atomic bombs on the cities of Hiroshima and Nagasaki were deeply morally wrong. Although Truman's motive was to end the war, his decisions were wrong because he aimed to kill innocent people as a means to ending the war more quickly. In Anscombe's view, it is always impermissible to intend to kill innocent civilians, no matter what good result might follow.

To support this judgment, Anscombe defends a specific application of the idea that one's intention in acting may determine that action's moral status, by advancing what is widely considered a classic articulation of the **doctrine of double effect**. Anscombe, Thomas Scanlon, and Barbara Herman all characterize it slightly differently, but essentially, the doctrine of double effect distinguishes between intentionally harming innocents from causing foreseen but unintended harm to them. The former is impermissible and the latter is, sometimes, permissible. Specifically, the doctrine declares one may not intend to harm innocent people as an end or a means to an end; yet, sometimes, it may be morally permissible to bring equally harmful consequences to innocents as a foreseeable, unintended side effect of one's otherwise permissible activity, if the good that one intends is proportionate to or greater than any harmful side effects.

Anscombe invokes this idea to distinguish between permissible and impermissible acts in war. She contends that to *intend* to kill an innocent person as a means to accomplishing a good end is always murder and always wrong, even if one's end is to save the lives of other innocent people. The mere killing of innocents is not always wrong, for sometimes that is an unavoidable by-product of a permissible aim. What is always wrong is to *intend* to kill the innocent. That intention involves embracing evil as though it were worthwhile, just because of its consequences. It may be permissible to bomb an enemy's munitions plant to stall their weapons production, even if predictable but unwanted civilian deaths ensue as a side effect. But it would be wrong to bomb a village with the very purpose of killing the same number of innocent civilians in order to break the enemy's morale. One may never make the deaths of civilians one's animating aim of action.

## Reasons, Not Intentions

Scanlon rejects Anscombe's general thesis that a person's intention matters to the permissibility of an action because that thesis entails that the exact same physical action with the exact same consequences could be permissible in one case if the actor's intention is a good one but impermissible in another case if that actor's intention is a poor one. To Scanlon, it seems that either bombing a munitions factory in war is permissible or not, depending upon the external qualities of the action and its consequences, including whether bombing is likely to bring significant military advantage and minimal harm to noncombatants. It doesn't make sense, he thinks, to judge that such bombing would be permissible if the pilot deeply regrets the accidental civilian deaths but impermissible if the pilot privately relishes them. Scanlon contends that whether an action is morally permissible or impermissible does not hinge upon the intentions or reasons any particular person actually *has* when acting. Instead, whether an action is permissible or impermissible depends upon what reasons she *should* act on, under the circumstances.

Of course, Scanlon agrees that we often do care about a person's intentions when assessing her behavior. Hence, we should distinguish whether an action is permissible from whether the agent acts in a blameworthy way. If Bob aims to kill someone by stabbing pins in a doll, that does not make using a doll as a pin cushion itself impermissible. The *action* of sticking a pin into a stuffed cotton sack is itself harmless, whatever Bob's beliefs and intentions. There is no moral reason to forbear from using a doll this way, although Bob's intentions reveal he has a wretched character and is blameworthy. On the other hand, if Juan, while looking for sugar, absent-mindedly picks up a bottle of arsenic, fails to read the label, and spoons it into his friend's coffee, Juan has done something impermissible. There is every reason in the world not to feed someone arsenic and to pay attention when feeding friends. Juan did not act with a poor intention and did not mean to hurt his friend; he is certainly not blameworthy for murder or its attempt, though perhaps he is blameworthy for negligence, since he should have paid more attention. Because giving arsenic to a person can be fatal, that action is impermissible regardless of a person's intentions.

So, Scanlon agrees that a person's bad intention may matter in making the action's meaning to others disrespectful; in showing *her* (though not her action) to be blameworthy and worthy of criticism; in making bad consequences more likely; or, perhaps, by making her actions deceptive because others would naturally assume her intention to be good. Betsy's not mentioning to Albert that she'd forgotten the appointment might be deceptive because he assumed she'd remembered; here, Scanlon would contend that her failure to fess up, not her absent-mindedness, is the real reason Betsy behaves impermissibly. In short, a poor intention may be morally significant in myriad ways, but usually it cannot render an otherwise permissible action impermissible. In other words, one can do the right thing yet have bad intentions or misguided motives.

# A Kantian Defense of the Relevance of Intentions

Barbara Herman disagrees with Scanlon. She defends the central importance of a person's intentions in assessing whether her action, and not merely her character, is morally right or morally wrong. Herman writes in the **Kantian** tradition, a tradition that agrees with Hume that the central feature of moral action is the agent's reason for performing the action. Kantians agree with Hume on the first category of questions—about whether intentions matter to the moral character of actions. The Kantian tradition diverges from Hume, however, with respect to the second category of questions—about what intentions are morally central, because Kantians regard the motive of duty and not the motive of benevolence as the foundational moral motive.

It may be helpful to read Herman's piece as advancing three main points in critical response to Scanlon. First, she argues that views like Scanlon's mistakenly emphasize moral permissibility and moral impermissibility, suggesting that these concepts are the exclusive barometers of an action's moral rightness or wrongness. Consider a burglar who stakes out a house but changes her plan upon noticing a security camera. She complies with the law against theft only to avoid arrest. She does nothing impermissible, but her intention is not to treat others' property and their privacy with respect. The would-be burglar does the required thing, intentionally, but not *because* one should do the right thing, only because it is expedient. In Herman's view, she acts wrongly, albeit permissibly. The fact that one's actions happen to coincide with the actions specified by a moral principle sometimes suffices to make one's actions morally permissible. But that correspondence is insufficient to make an action morally right. Something crucial is missing. Whether an action is morally right depends on whether a person adheres to the moral principles that apply to her. Adhering to a moral principle requires being aware of the principle *and* intending to be guided by it.

Second, Herman argues that focusing on moral prohibitions, such as the prohibition against killing, may misleadingly lend support to the idea that the external qualities of an action determine its moral character. When one instead considers positive moral requirements, like keeping a promise or telling the truth, one errs in focusing only on an action's external qualities. The value of truth-telling depends upon the agent's telling the truth *because the agent believes what she says*. An agent who accidentally lets the truth slip out does not comply with the duty of truth-telling. The person who tries to deceive her interlocutor, but accidentally tells the truth, has acted impermissibly. One's intention to tell the truth (or keep one's promise) is a crucial component of fulfilling the relevant duty.

Third, Herman recommends drawing an analogy to theoretical reasoning. The student who accidentally guesses the answer to a mathematics problem but does not know how to do the proof gives the correct answer but has not solved the problem or demonstrated knowledge; a teacher would reasonably fail to give that answer credit. Why think of morality differently? In mathematics, the right answer requires proper reasoning to the correct solution; likewise, Herman claims, the morally right action requires proper reasoning to the correct action.

## David Hume (1711–1776)

Hume was a Scottish philosopher, essayist, and historian, and a central figure in Western philosophy. His *A Treatise of Human Nature* (1739), *An Enquiry Concerning Human Understanding* (1748), and *An Enquiry Concerning the Principles of Morals* (1751) have been very influential. (The two *Enquiries* revise material in the *Treatise*.) Many contemporary philosophical discussions in epistemology, metaphysics, and ethics are reactions to Hume's theories and arguments. Hume's *Dialogues Concerning Natural Religion* (published posthumously in 1779) is a classic attack on "design arguments" for the existence of God.

# OF JUSTICE AND INJUSTICE
### from *A Treatise of Human Nature*

## Section I. Justice, Whether a Natural or Artificial Virtue?

I have already hinted, that our sense of every kind of virtue is not natural; but that there are some virtues, that produce pleasure and approbation by means of an artifice or contrivance, which arises from the circumstances and necessities of mankind. Of this kind I assert *justice*[1] to be. . . .

'Tis evident, that when we praise any actions, we regard only the motives that produced them, and consider the actions as signs or indications of certain principles in the mind and temper. The external performance has no merit. We must look within to find the moral quality. This we cannot do directly; and therefore fix our attention on actions, as on external signs. But these actions are still considered as signs; and the ultimate object of our praise and approbation is the motive, that produc'd them.

After the same manner, when we require any action, or blame a person for not performing it, we always suppose, that one in that situation shou'd be influenc'd by the proper motive of that action, and we esteem it vicious in him to be regardless of it. If we find, upon enquiry, that the virtuous motive was still powerful over his breast, tho' check'd in its operation by some circumstances unknown to us, we retract our blame, and have the same esteem for him, as if he had actually perform'd the action, which we require of him.

It appears, therefore, that all virtuous actions derive their merit only from virtuous motives, and are consider'd merely as signs of those motives. From this principle I conclude, that the first virtuous motive, which bestows a merit on any action, can never be a regard to the virtue of that action, but must be some other natural motive or principle. To suppose, that the mere regard to the virtue of the action, may be the first motive, which produc'd the action, and render'd it virtuous, is to reason in a circle. Before we can have such a regard, the action must be really virtuous; and this virtue must be deriv'd from some virtuous motive: And consequently the virtuous motive must be different from the regard to the virtue of the action. A virtuous motive is requisite to render an action virtuous. An action must be virtuous, before we can have a regard to its virtue. Some virtuous motive, therefore, must be antecedent to that regard.

. . . We blame a father for neglecting his child. Why? because it shews a want of natural affection, which is the duty of every parent. Were not natural affection a duty, the care of children cou'd not be a duty; and 'twere impossible we cou'd have the duty

---

1. By "justice," Hume primarily has in mind respect for others' property, including refraining from theft, paying wages, and repaying debt.

in our eye in the attention we give to our offspring. In this case, therefore, all men suppose a motive to the action distinct from a sense of duty.

Here is a man, that does many benevolent actions; relieves the distress'd, comforts the afflicted, and extends his bounty even to the greatest strangers. No character can be more amiable and virtuous. We regard these actions as proofs of the greatest humanity. This humanity bestows a merit on the actions. A regard to this merit is, therefore, a secondary consideration, and deriv'd from the antecedent principle of humanity, which is meritorious and laudable.

In short, it may be establish'd as an undoubted maxim, *that no action can be virtuous, or morally good, unless there be in human nature some motive to produce it, distinct from the sense of its morality.*

But may not the sense of morality or duty produce an action, without any other motive? I answer, It may: But this is no objection to the present doctrine. When any virtuous motive or principle is common in human nature, a person, who feels his heart devoid of that principle, may hate himself upon that account, and may perform the action without the motive, from a certain sense of duty, in order to acquire by practice, that virtuous principle, or at least, to disguise to himself, as much as possible, his want of it. A man that really feels no gratitude in his temper, is still pleas'd to perform grateful actions, and thinks he has, by that means, fulfill'd his duty. Actions are at first only consider'd as signs of motives: But 'tis usual, in this case, as in all others, to fix our attention on the signs, and neglect, in some measure, the thing signify'd. But tho', on some occasions, a person may perform an action merely out of regard to its moral obligation, yet still this supposes in human nature some distinct principles, which are capable of producing the action, and whose moral beauty renders the action meritorious.

Now to apply all this to the present case; I suppose a person to have lent me a sum of money, on condition that it be restor'd in a few days; and also suppose, that after the expiration of the term agreed on, he demands the sum: I ask, *What reason or motive have I to restore the money?* It will, perhaps, be said, that my regard to justice, and abhorrence of villainy and knavery, are sufficient reasons for me, if I have the least grain of honesty, or sense of duty and obligation. And this answer, no doubt, is just and satisfactory to man in his civiliz'd state, and when train'd up according to a certain discipline and education. But in his rude and more *natural* condition, if you are pleas'd to call such a condition natural, this answer wou'd be rejected as perfectly unintelligible and sophistical. For one in that situation wou'd immediately ask you, *Wherein consists this honesty and justice, which you find in restoring a loan, and abstaining from the property of others?* It does not surely lie in the external action. It must, therefore, be plac'd in the motive, from which the external action is deriv'd. This motive can never be a regard to the honesty of the action. For 'tis a plain fallacy to say, that a virtuous motive is requisite to render an action honest, and at the same time that a regard to the honesty is the motive of the action. We can never have a regard to the virtue of an action, unless the action be antecedently virtuous. No action can be virtuous, but so far as it proceeds from a virtuous motive. A virtuous motive, therefore, must precede the regard to the virtue; and 'tis impossible, that the virtuous motive and the regard to the virtue can be the same.

'Tis requisite, then, to find some motive to acts of justice and honesty, distinct from our regard to the honesty; and in this lies the great difficulty. For shou'd we say, that a concern for our private interest or reputation is the legitimate motive to all honest actions; it wou'd follow, that wherever that concern ceases, honesty can no longer have place. But 'tis certain, that self-love, when it acts at its liberty, instead of engaging us to honest actions, is the source of all injustice and violence; nor can a man ever correct those vices, without correcting and restraining the *natural* movements of that appetite.

But shou'd it be affirm'd, that the reason or motive of such actions is the *regard to publick interest,* to which nothing is more contrary than examples of injustice and dishonesty; shou'd this be said, I wou'd propose the three following considerations, as worthy of our attention. *First,* public interest is not naturally attach'd to the observation of the rules of justice; but is only connected with it, after an artificial convention for the establishment of these rules, as shall be shewn more at large hereafter. *Secondly,* if we suppose, that the loan was secret, and that it is necessary for the interest of the person, that the money be restor'd in the same manner (as when the lender wou'd conceal his riches) in that case the example ceases, and the public is no longer interested in the actions of the borrower; tho' I suppose there is no moralist, who will affirm, that the duty and obligation ceases. *Thirdly,* experience sufficiently proves, that men, in the ordinary conduct of life, look not so far as the public interest, when they pay their creditors, perform their promises, and abstain from theft, and robbery, and injustice of every kind. That is a motive too remote and too sublime to affect the generality of mankind, and operate with any force in actions so contrary to private interest as are frequently those of justice and common honesty.

In general, it may be affirm'd, that there is no such passion in human minds, as the love of mankind, merely as such, independent of personal qualities, of services, or of relation to ourself. 'Tis true, there is no human, and indeed no sensible, creature, whose happiness or misery does not, in some measure, affect us, when brought near to us, and represented in lively colours: But this proceeds merely from sympathy, and is no proof of such an universal affection to mankind, since this concern extends itself beyond our own species. . . .

If public benevolence, therefore, or a regard to the interests of mankind, cannot be the original motive to justice, much less can *private benevolence,* or a *regard to the interests of the party concern'd,* be this motive. For what if he be my enemy, and has given me just cause to hate him? What if he be a vicious man, and deserves the hatred of all mankind? What if he be a miser, and can make no use of what I wou'd deprive him of? What if he be a profligate debauchee, and wou'd rather receive harm than benefit from large possessions? What if I be in necessity, and have urgent motives to acquire something to my family? In all these cases, the original motive to justice wou'd fail; and consequently the justice itself, and along with it all property, right, and obligation.

. . . A man's property is suppos'd to be fenc'd against every mortal, in every possible case. But private benevolence towards the proprietor is, and ought to be, weaker in some persons, than in others: And in many, or indeed in most persons, must absolutely fail. Private benevolence, therefore, is not the original motive of justice.

From all this it follows, that we have naturally no real or universal motive for observing the laws of equity,[2] but the very equity and merit of that observance; and as no action can be equitable or meritorious, where it cannot arise from some separate motive, there is here an evident sophistry and reasoning in a circle. Unless, therefore, we will allow, that nature has establish'd a sophistry, and render'd it necessary and unavoidable, we must allow, that the sense of justice and injustice is not deriv'd from nature, but arises artificially, tho' necessarily from education, and human conventions. . . .

. . . [W]hen I deny justice to be a natural virtue, I make use of the word, *natural*, only as oppos'd to *artificial*. In another sense of the word; as no principle of the human mind is more natural than a sense of virtue; so no virtue is more natural than justice. Mankind is an inventive species; and where an invention is obvious and absolutely necessary, it may as properly be said to be natural as any thing that proceeds immediately from original principles, without the intervention of thought or reflexion. Tho' the rules of justice be *artificial*, they are not *arbitrary*. . . .

## Section II: Of the Origin of Justice and Property

. . . [J]ustice takes its rise from human conventions; and that these are intended as a remedy to some inconveniences, which proceed from the concurrence of certain *qualities* of the human mind with the *situation* of external objects. The qualities of the mind are *selfishness* and *limited generosity*: And the situation of external objects is their *easy change*, join'd to their *scarcity* in comparison of the wants and desires of men. . . .

[I]f every man had a tender regard for another, or if nature supplied abundantly all our wants and desires, that the jealousy of interest, which justice supposes, could no longer have place; nor would there be any occasion for those distinctions and limits of property and possession, which at present are in use among mankind. Encrease to a sufficient degree the benevolence of men, or the bounty of nature, and you render justice useless, by supplying its place with much nobler virtues, and more valuable blessings. The selfishness of men is animated by the few possessions we have, in proportion to our wants; and 'tis to restrain this selfishness, that men have been oblig'd to separate themselves from the community, and to distinguish betwixt their own goods and those of others.

. . . [W]hen there is such a plenty of any thing as satisfies all the desires of men, . . . the distinction of property is entirely lost, and every thing remains in common. This we may observe with regard to air and water, tho' the most valuable of all external objects; and may easily conclude, that if men were supplied with every thing in the same abundance, or if *every one* had the same affection and tender regard for *every one* as for himself; justice and injustice would be equally unknown among mankind.

2. Hume uses "equity" here to mean "justice."

... '[T]is only from the selfishness and confin'd generosity of men, along with the scanty provision nature has made for his wants, that justice derives its origin. . . .

We come now to the question . . . *Why we annex the idea of virtue to justice, and of vice to injustice?* . . .

After men have found by experience, that their selfishness and confin'd generosity, acting at their liberty, totally incapacitate them for society; and at the same time have observ'd, that society is necessary to the satisfaction of those very passions, they are naturally induc'd to lay themselves under the restraint of such rules, as may render their commerce more safe and commodious. To the imposition then, and observance of these rules, both in general, and in every particular instance, they are at first, mov'd only by a regard to interest; and this motive, on the first formation of society, is sufficiently strong and forcible. But when society has become numerous, and has encreas'd to a tribe or nation, this interest is more remote; nor do men so readily perceive, that disorder and confusion follow upon every breach of these rules, as in a more narrow and contracted society. But tho' in our own actions we may frequently lose sight of that interest, which we have in maintaining order, and may follow a lesser and more present interest, we never fail to observe the prejudice we receive, either mediately or immediately, from the injustice of others; as not being in that case either blinded by passion, or byass'd by any contrary temptation. Nay when the injustice is so distant from us, as no way to affect our interest, it still displeases us; because we consider it as prejudicial to human society, and pernicious to every one that approaches the person guilty of it. We partake of their uneasiness by *sympathy*; and as every thing, which gives uneasiness in human actions, upon the general survey, is call'd Vice, and whatever produces satisfaction, in the same manner, is denominated Virtue; this is the reason why the sense of moral good and evil follows upon justice and injustice. And tho' this sense, in the present case, be deriv'd only from contemplating the actions of others, yet we fail not to extend it even to our own actions. The *general rule* reaches beyond those instances, from which it arose; while at the same time we naturally *sympathize* with others in the sentiments they entertain of us. *Thus self-interest is the original motive to the establishment of justice: but a* sympathy *with public interest is the source of the* moral approbation, *which attends that virtue*. . . .

## TEST YOUR UNDERSTANDING

1. Why does Hume think our practices of praise and blame are evidence for the view that one's "external performance has no merit"? What part of a morally good action does have merit, in his view?

2. Consider *just* actions, such as refraining from theft and paying one's debts. Why does Hume think they pose potential **counterexamples** to his claim that the motive of duty cannot be the original moral motive?

3. What are the two original motives that Hume believes underwrite the system of justice, which in turn supply the motive of duty with its object?

## NOTES AND QUESTIONS

1. *Is a person's motive the only relevant feature of a moral action?* Hume contends that, fundamentally, what we value about moral action is the underlying motive of the agent, that is, the person who performs the action. Do you agree that the agent's motive for performing an action is what matters morally? Is it the *only* thing that matters? Why shouldn't we think that the action's *results* or *consequences* also matter morally?

   Consider the following example: If your child were drowning, would you care why the lifeguard saved him or simply *that* she saved him? Explain how this example might be construed as a counterexample to Hume's claim. How do you think he might respond to this argument? (*Hint:* If a sudden, violent earthquake were to slosh a drowning child out of a pool, would we deem the earthquake morally good or morally praiseworthy? Why not?)

2. *Is benevolence always a welcome motive?* Hume suggests that what we value most are actions motivated by benevolence and caring. Can you think of actions that are morally correct and morally praiseworthy but are not motivated by benevolence? Can you think of circumstances in which you would prefer not to be the object of another's benevolence? Would such examples pose a challenge to Hume's argument? How do you think he might respond?

3. *Hume's circle.* Hume contends that the "motive of duty" cannot be the original and only moral motive because, on its own, it would have no object. One way of thinking about this complaint is that if people were motivated only by duty, they would not know which actions were required by duty. Can you explain why he thinks the motive of duty, on its own, lacks an object? How might other motives supply the motive of duty with an object?

## G.E.M. Anscombe (1919–2001)

Anscombe was a British analytical philosopher who taught at Somerville College, the University of Oxford, and also served as Professor of Philosophy at Cambridge University. She is the author of *Intention* (1957), widely considered a classic in the fields of philosophy of mind and action, and wrote many other important works in moral philosophy, the philosophy of action, the philosophy of mind, the philosophy of language, and logic. She is also considered one of the most important Catholic philosophers of the twentieth century.

# MR TRUMAN'S DEGREE[1]

## I

In 1939, on the outbreak of war, the President of the United States asked for assurances from the belligerent nations that civil populations would not be attacked.

In 1945, when the Japanese enemy was known by him to have made two attempts towards a negotiated peace, the President of the United States gave the order for dropping an atom bomb on a Japanese city; three days later a second bomb, of a different type, was dropped on another city. No ultimatum was delivered before the second bomb was dropped.

Set side by side, these events provide enough of a contrast to provoke enquiry. Evidently development has taken place; one would like to see its course plotted. It is not, I think, difficult to give an intelligible account:

(1) The British Government gave President Roosevelt the required assurance with a reservation which meant "If the Germans do it we shall do it too." You don't promise to abide by the Queensberry Rules[2] even if your opponent abandons them.

(2) The only condition for ending the war was announced to be unconditional surrender. Apart from the "liberation of the subject peoples," the objectives were vague in character. Now the demand for unconditional surrender was mixed up with a determination to make no peace with Hitler's government. In view of the character of Hitler's regime that attitude was very intelligible. Nevertheless some people have doubts about it now. It is suggested that defeat of itself would have resulted in the rapid discredit and downfall of that government. On this I can form no strong opinion. The important question to my mind is whether the intention of making no peace with Hitler's government necessarily entailed the objective of unconditional surrender. If, as may not be impossible, we could have formulated a pretty definite objective, a rough outline of the terms which we were willing to make with Germany, while at the same time indicating that we would not make terms with Hitler's government, then the question of the wisdom of this latter demand seems to me a minor one; but if not, then that settles it. It was the insistence on unconditional surrender that was the root of all evil. The connection between such a demand and the need to use the most ferocious methods of warfare will be obvious. And in itself the proposal of an unlimited objective in war is stupid and barbarous.

(3) The Germans did a good deal of indiscriminate bombing in this country. It is impossible for an uninformed person to know how much, in its first beginnings, was due to indifference on the part of pilots to using their loads only on military targets,

---

1. © M C Gormally. Professor Anscombe published this essay in a privately printed pamphlet to explain her opposition to Oxford University's decision to confer an honorary doctorate to President Truman in 1956.

2. The Queensberry Rules are a traditional set of boxing rules that restrict boxers from "no-holds-barred" fighting.

and how much to actual policy on the part of those who sent them. Nor do I know what we were doing in the same line at the time. . . .

(4) For some time before war broke out, and more intensely afterwards, there was propaganda in this country on the subject of the "indivisibility" of modern war. The civilian population, we were told, is really as much combatant as the fighting forces. The military strength of a nation includes its whole economic and social strength. Therefore the distinction between the people engaged in prosecuting the war and the population at large is unreal. There is no such thing as a non-participator; you cannot buy a postage stamp or any taxed article, or grow a potato or cook a meal, without contributing to the "war effort." War indeed is a "ghastly evil," but once it has broken out no one can "contract out" of it. "Wrong" indeed must be being done if war is waged, but you cannot help being involved in it. There was a doctrine of "collective responsibility" with a lugubriously elevated moral tone about it. The upshot was that it was senseless to draw any line between legitimate and illegitimate objects of attack. . . . I am not sure how children and the aged fitted into this story: probably they cheered the soldiers and munitions workers up.

(5) The Japanese attacked Pearl Harbour and there was war between America and Japan. Some American (Republican) historians now claim that the acknowledged fact that the American Government knew an attack was impending some hours before it occurred, but did not alert the people in local command, can only be explained by a purpose of arousing the passions of American people. However that may be, those passions were suitably aroused and the war was entered on with the same vague and hence limitless objectives; and once more unconditional surrender was the only condition on which the war was going to end.

(6) Then came the great change: we adopted the system of "area bombing" as opposed to "target bombing." This differed from even big raids on cities, such as had previously taken place in the course of the war, by being far more extensive and devastating and much less random; the whole of a city area would be systematically plotted out and dotted with bombs. "Attila was a Sissy," as the *Chicago Tribune* headed an article on this subject.

(7) In 1945, at the Potsdam conference[3] in July, Stalin informed the American and British statesmen that he had received two requests from the Japanese to act as a mediator with a view to ending the war. He had refused. The Allies agreed on the "general principle" — marvellous phrase! — of using the new type of weapon that America now possessed. The Japanese were given a chance in the form of the Potsdam Declaration, calling for unconditional surrender in face of overwhelming force soon to be arrayed against them. The historian of the Survey of International Affairs considers that this phrase was rendered meaningless by the statement of a series of terms; but of these the ones incorporating the Allies' demands were mostly of so vague and sweeping a nature as to be rather a declaration of what unconditional surrender would be like than to constitute conditions. It seems to be generally agreed that the Japanese were desperate enough to have accepted the Declaration but for

3. Meeting (in Potsdam, Germany) of the Soviet Union, United Kingdom, and United States following Nazi Germany's unconditional surrender on May 8, 1945, to establish the postwar order.

their loyalty to their Emperor:[4] the "terms" would certainly have permitted the Allies to get rid of him if they chose. The Japanese refused the Declaration. In consequence, the bombs were dropped on Hiroshima and Nagasaki. The decision to use them on people was Mr Truman's.

For men to choose to kill the innocent as a means to their ends is always murder, and murder is one of the worst of human actions. So the prohibition on deliberately killing prisoners of war or the civilian population is not like the Queensberry Rules: its force does not depend on its promulgation as part of positive law, written down, agreed upon, and adhered to by the parties concerned.

When I say that to choose to kill the innocent as a means to one's ends is murder, I am saying what would generally be accepted as correct. But I shall be asked for my definition of "the innocent," I will give it, but later. Here, it is not necessary; for with Hiroshima and Nagasaki we are not confronted with a borderline case. In the bombing of these cities it was certainly decided to kill the innocent as a means to an end. And a very large number of them, all at once, without warning, without the interstices of escape or the chance to take shelter, which existed even in the "area bombings" of the German cities. . . .

I have been accused of being "high-minded." I must be saying "You may not do evil that good may come," which is a disagreeably high-minded doctrine. The action was necessary, or at any rate it was thought by competent, expert military opinion to be necessary; it probably saved more lives than it sacrificed; it had a good result, it ended the war. Come now: if you had to choose between boiling one baby and letting some frightful disaster befall a thousand people — or a million people, if a thousand is not enough — what would you do? Are you going to strike an attitude and say "You may not do evil that good may come"? (People who never hear such arguments will hardly believe they take place, and will pass this rapidly by.)

"It pretty certainly saved a huge number of lives." Given the conditions, I agree. That is to say, if those bombs had not been dropped the Allies would have had to invade Japan to achieve their aim, and they would have done so. Very many soldiers on both sides would have been killed; the Japanese, it is said — and it may well be true — would have massacred the prisoners of war; and large numbers of their civilian population would have been killed by "ordinary" bombing.

I do not dispute it. Given the conditions, that was probably what was averted by that action. But what were the conditions? The unlimited objective, the fixation on unconditional surrender. The disregard of the fact that the Japanese were desirous of negotiating peace. The character of the Potsdam Declaration — their "chance." I will not suggest, as some would like to do, that there was an exultant itch to use the new weapons, but it seems plausible to think that the consciousness of the possession of such instruments had its effect on the manner in which the Japanese were offered their "chance." . . .

---

4. Emperor Hirohito (1901–1989) ruled Japan from 1926 until his death.

## ||

Choosing to kill the innocent as a means to your ends is always murder. Naturally, killing the innocent as an end in itself is murder too; but that is no more than a possible future development for us: in our part of the globe it is a practice that has so far been confined to the Nazis. I intend my formulation to be taken strictly; each term in it is necessary. For killing the innocent, even if you know as a matter of statistical certainty that the things you do involve it, is not necessarily murder. I mean that if you attack a lot of military targets, such as munitions factories and naval dockyards, as carefully as you can, you will be certain to kill a number of innocent people; but that is not murder. On the other hand, unscrupulousness in considering the possibilities turns it into murder. I here print as a case in point a letter which I received lately from Holland:

> We read in our paper about your opposition to Truman. I do not like him either, but do you know that in the war the English bombed the dykes of our province Zeeland,[5] an island where nobody could escape anywhere to. Where the whole population was drowned, children, women, farmers working in the field, all the cattle, everything, hundreds and hundreds, and we were your allies! Nobody ever speaks about that. Perhaps it were well to know this. Or, to remember.

That was to trap some fleeing German military. I think my correspondent has something.

It may be impossible to take the thing (or people) you want to destroy as your target; it may be possible to attack it only by taking as the object of your attack what includes large numbers of innocent people. Then you cannot very well say they died by accident. Here your action is murder.

"But where will you draw the line? It is impossible to draw an exact line." This is a common and absurd argument against drawing any line; it may be very difficult, and there are obviously borderline cases. But we have fallen into the way of drawing no line, and offering as justifications what an uncaptive mind will find only a bad joke. Wherever the line is, certain things are certainly well to one side or the other of it.

Now who are "the innocent" in war? They are all those who are not fighting and not engaged in supplying those who are with the means of fighting. A farmer growing wheat which may be eaten by the troops is not "supplying them with the means of fighting." Over this, too, the line may be difficult to draw. But that does not mean that no line should be drawn, or that, even if one is in doubt just where to draw the line, one cannot be crystal clear that this or that is well over the line.

"But the people fighting are probably conscripts! In that case they are just as innocent as anyone else." "Innocent" here is not a term referring to personal responsibility at all. It means rather "not harming." But the people fighting are "harming," so they can be attacked; but if they surrender they become in this sense innocent and so may

5. Province of the Netherlands consisting of a number of islands.

not be maltreated or killed. Nor is there ground for trying them on a criminal charge; not, indeed, because a man has no personal responsibility for fighting, but because they were not the subjects of the state whose prisoners they are.

There is an argument which I know from experience it is necessary to forestall at this point, though I think it is visibly captious. It is this: on my theory, would it not follow that a soldier can only be killed when he is actually attacking? Then, for example, it would be impossible to attack a sleeping camp. The answer is that "what someone is doing" can refer either to what he is doing at the moment or to his role in a situation. A soldier under arms is "harming" in the latter sense even if he is asleep. But it is true that the enemy should not be attacked more ferociously than is necessary to put them *hors de combat*.[6]

These conceptions are distinct and intelligible ones. . . . Anyone can see that they are good, and we pay tribute to them by our moral indignation when our enemies violate them. . . .

It is characteristic of nowadays to talk with horror of killing rather than of murder, and hence, since in war you have committed yourself to killing — for example "accepted an evil" — not to mind whom you kill. This seems largely to be the work of the devil; but I also suspect that it is in part an effect of the existence of pacifism, as a doctrine which many people respect though they would not adopt it. This effect would not exist if people had a distinct notion of what makes pacifism a false doctrine.

It therefore seems to me important to show that for one human being deliberately to kill another is not inevitably wrong. I may seem to be wasting my time, as most people do reject pacifism. But it is nevertheless important to argue the point because if one does so one sees that there are pretty severe restrictions on legitimate killing. Of course, people accept this within the state, but when it comes to war they have the idea that any restrictions are something like the Queensberry Rules — instead of making the difference between being guilty and not guilty of murder.

I will not discuss the self-defence of a private person. If he kills the man who attacks him or someone else, it ought to be accidental. To aim at killing, even when one is defending oneself, is murderous. . . .

But the state actually has the authority to order deliberate killing in order to protect its people or to put frightful injustices right. (For example, the plight of the Jews under Hitler would have been a reasonable cause of war.) The reason for this is pretty simple: it stands out most clearly if we first consider the state's right to order such killing within its confines. I am not referring to the death penalty, but to what happens when there is rioting or when violent malefactors have to be caught. Rioters can sometimes only be restrained, or malefactors seized, by force. Law without force is ineffectual, and human beings without laws miserable (though we, who have too many and too changeable laws, may easily not feel this very distinctly). So much is indeed fairly obvious, though the more peaceful the society the less obvious it is that

---

6. "Outside the fight" (French), referring to soldiers who are unable to continue in battle because they are wounded, ill, without equipment, and so on.

the force in the hands of the servants of the law has to be force up to the point of killing. It would become perfectly obvious any time there was rioting or gangsterism which had to be dealt with by the servants of the law fighting. . . .

Now, this is also the ground of the state's right to order people to fight external enemies who are unjustly attacking them or something of theirs. The right to order to fight for the sake of other people's wrongs, to put right something affecting people who are not actually under the protection of the state, is a rather more dubious thing obviously, but it exists because of the common sympathy of human beings whereby one feels for one's neighbour if he is attacked. So in an attenuated sense it can be said that something that belongs to, or concerns, one is attacked if anybody is unjustly attacked or maltreated.

Pacifism, then, is a false doctrine. Now, no doubt, it is bad just for that reason, because it is always bad to have a false conscience. In this way the doctrine that it is a bad act to lay a bet is bad: it is all right to bet what it is all right to risk or drop in the sea. But I want to maintain that pacifism is a harmful doctrine in a far stronger sense than this. Even the prevalence of the idea that it was wrong to bet would have no particularly bad consequences; a false doctrine which merely forbids what is not actually bad need not encourage people in anything bad. But with pacifism it is quite otherwise. It is a factor in that loss of the conception of murder which is my chief interest in this pamphlet.

I have very often heard people say something like this: "It is all very well to say 'Don't do evil that good may come.' But *war* is evil. We all know that. Now, of course, it is possible to be an Absolute Pacifist. I can respect that, but I can't be one myself, and most other people won't be either. So we have to accept the evil. It is not that we do not see the evil. And once you are in for it, you have to go the whole hog."

This is much as if I were defrauding someone, and when someone tried to stop me I said: "Absolute honesty! I respect that. But of course absolute honesty really means having no property at all . . ." Having offered the sacrifice of a few sighs and tears to absolute honesty, I go on as before.

The correct answer to the statement that "war is evil" is that it is bad — for example a misfortune — to be at war. And no doubt if two nations are at war at least one is unjust. But that does not show that it is wrong to fight or that if one does fight one can also commit murder.

Naturally my claim that pacifism is a very harmful doctrine is contingent on its being a false one. If it were a true doctrine, its encouragement of this nonsensical "hypocrisy of the ideal standard" would not count against it. But given that it is false, I am inclined to think it is also very bad, unusually so for an idea which seems as it were to err on the noble side.

When I consider the history of events from 1939 to 1945, I am not surprised that Mr Truman is made the recipient of honours. But when I consider his actions by themselves, I am surprised again.

Some people actually praise the bombings and commend the stockpiling of atomic weapons on the ground that they are so horrible that nations will be afraid ever again to make war. "We have made a covenant with death, and with hell we are at an agreement." There does not seem to be good ground for such a hope for any long period of time. . . .

Protests by people who have not power are a waste of time. I was not seizing an opportunity to make a "gesture of protest" at atomic bombs; I vehemently object to *our* action in offering Mr Truman honours, because one can share in the guilt of a bad action by praise and flattery, as also by defending it.

## TEST YOUR UNDERSTANDING

1. What motive does Anscombe argue President Truman had in deciding to bomb Hiroshima and Nagasaki? Why is his motive a reason to condemn his action?

2. Anscombe argues that it may sometimes be permissible to bomb a munitions factory, even if some civilians will be killed as a side effect. Assuming that the good to be achieved would be substantial and very few civilians would be killed, what motive would make this action acceptable, in her view? What motive would make a bombing with the same number of civilian casualties unacceptable, in her view?

3. Why does Anscombe believe that farmers are "innocents" but that involuntarily conscripted soldiers opposed to the war effort are not "innocents"?

## NOTES AND QUESTIONS

1. *Whose motive matters?* Anscombe's essay represents a famous defense of the **doctrine of double effect,** the view that one may not intend to harm innocents as an end or means to an end, but it may be permissible to cause harm to innocents as a foreseen but unintended side effect of one's otherwise permissible activity, if the good that one intends is proportionate to or greater than these side effects. This doctrine emphasizes the moral importance of the motive that gives rise to an action. Now consider actions that involve coordination between different people with different reasons for acting. Whose motive is relevant for assessing the morality of the action?

    Suppose, for example, that a nation is fighting a just war of self-defense against a belligerent neighbor. An air force captain of the beleaguered nation instructs a pilot to drop bombs on a munitions factory when the factory is closed. The captain's aim is to destroy an important source of weapons, thereby reducing the military power of the attackers. By bombing when the factory is closed, the captain hopes not to kill anyone, although she knows a few innocents may die if they happen to be near the factory when it is bombed. Suppose the pilot thinks that the belligerent nation has an oversupply of weapons so that eliminating the factory will make no difference to the war effort, but that the killing of the few civilians who happen to be near the factory during the bombing *will* make a difference because it will help to lower morale and to feed political sentiment to end the war.

So, in this case, does the captain's motive satisfy Anscombe's constraints? Does the pilot's motive? As described, the pilot drops the bomb and thereby follows the captain's order, but the pilot hopes to kill innocent people. In that case, is the pilot's action murder? Whose motive matters here: the captain's motive or the pilot's motive? (*Hint:* Note that Anscombe's essay focuses on President Truman. Why do you think she discusses Truman and not Paul Tibbets and Charles Sweeney, the pilots who flew the planes that dropped the bombs at Hiroshima and Nagasaki?)

2. *What is one's motive?* Anscombe argues that President Truman's motive was to kill innocent civilians to overwhelm the Japanese and thereby to end the war. Thus, in her view, President Truman engaged in mass murder because his motive was to kill innocents as a means to his end of bringing the war to a close (on his terms of unconditional surrender). Suppose Truman read Anscombe's essay and objected that he did not seek the *deaths* of those civilians as a means to his end at all. Of course, he knew that they would die if the bombs were dropped, but their deaths as such were not what he sought. Rather, he sought the *convincing appearance* of massive civilian deaths to generate the emperor's belief that the millions had died at the hands of an irrepressible and indefatigable foe. That they actually died was not his aim at all, although it was foreseen. If the appearance of their deaths could have been generated without their actually dying, he would have preferred it. Therefore, their deaths were not intended. He might argue that his intention is not significantly different from the bomber who targets the naval shipyard to disrupt a military supply chain but who knows that the deaths of innocents walking in the neighborhood are a predictable but unwanted side effect of the bombing. Their deaths are anticipated side effects of destroying the shipyard, but the mission would be as successful if they did not die.

Evaluate Truman's potential reply. Must we accept Truman's description of his own intention as accurate? Is it plausible to say that the person who bombs a city to convince a military opponent that further resistance is hopeless merely intends to induce the appearance of massive civilian deaths but does not intend their deaths? Why or why not? Is this case analogous to or dissimilar from the case of the accidental, but foreseeable, deaths of innocents when bombing a dockyard?

## Thomas M. Scanlon (born 1940)

Scanlon is Alford Professor of Natural Religion, Moral Philosophy, and Civil Polity at Harvard University. A leading philosopher in the areas of moral, political, and legal philosophy, he is best known for his development of the moral theory of contractualism. He has published many significant articles and books, including *What We Owe to Each Other* (1998), *The Difficulty of Tolerance* (2003), and *Moral Dimensions: Permissibility, Meaning, and Blame* (2008).

# WHEN DO INTENTIONS MATTER TO PERMISSIBILITY?

Does the permissibility of an action depend on the agent's intentions in performing it? It seems obvious that an agent's intentions can make a moral difference. For example, there is a clear moral difference between injuring a person intentionally and doing so inadvertently. But in order to assess the significance of this fact we need to consider more carefully what kind of moral significance is involved, and what is meant by "intention."

"Intention" is commonly used in wider and narrower senses. When we say that a person did something intentionally, one thing we may mean is simply that it was something that he or she was aware of doing, or realized was likely to be a consequence of his or her action. This is the sense of "intentionally" that is opposed to "unintentionally." To say that you did something unintentionally is to claim that it was something you did not realize you were doing. But "intention" is also used in a narrower sense. To ask a person what her intention was in doing a certain thing is to ask her what her aim was in doing it, and what plan guided her action.

Knowing whether an agent acted intentionally also tells us something about the agent's view of the reasons bearing on his or her action. Whether an agent acted intentionally is in the first instance a matter of what the agent believed about the likely consequences of her action. It is also true that if an agent does something intentionally in this wider sense — if she is aware of a particular aspect of her situation such as that the room's acoustics are such that her action will cause a loud noise — then even if she does not take this aspect of what she is doing to provide a reason for so acting, she at least does not (insofar as she is not acting irrationally) take it to constitute a sufficient reason not to act in that way.

When I said above that it matters morally whether a person causes harm intentionally or inadvertently, what I meant was that it makes a moral difference whether the person was aware that her action was likely to cause harm. But this moral difference need not be a difference in the moral permissibility of the action. What matters to the action's moral permissibility is not what the agent was aware of or believed but what he or she should have believed, under the circumstances. It is impermissible to act in a way that one should have seen was likely to cause unjustified harm, whether one sees this or not. And when an agent believes that his action is likely to be harmful, if the action is impermissible what makes it so is not the agent's belief but, rather, the fact that there was, under the circumstances, good reason to believe that this harm was likely to occur. If someone believes, for no good reason, that his friend will die if he himself does not eat oatmeal for breakfast every morning, this does not make it impermissible for him to fail to eat his oatmeal.

Even when acting with clueless negligence and acting with full knowledge that one's action is likely to be harmful are both impermissible, there is still a moral difference between these actions. The difference is not in permissibility, but in what I call *meaning*: the significance of an action for the agent's relations with others. Failing to consider whether one's action is likely to harm others, and doing what one knows to be harmful, involve different kinds of fault — different forms of culpable failure to take the interests of others into account in the right way.

Consider now "intention" in the narrower sense. If an agent (unjustifiably) takes the fact that his action is likely to harm someone as counting in favor of that action, this indicates a third kind of faulty attitude. An agent is open to a different kind of moral criticism for doing something that is likely to harm someone because she wants to harm this person than she would be for failure to pay due attention to whether her action is likely to cause harm, or for acting in disregard of the fact that it is likely to do this. These differences in meaning and blameworthiness remain even when all three actions are impermissible.

So differences in intention, or in whether an agent is doing something intentionally or unintentionally, can "make a moral difference" without making a difference in permissibility. It does not follow, however, that the permissibility of an action never depends on the agent's intentions, or, more broadly, on what the agent saw as reasons for so acting. One reason it may not follow is that the likely consequences of an action can depend on the reasons that the agent will be governed by as he or she carries it out. For example, whether my driving a car is likely to cause harm will depend on whether, as I drive, I will be exercising due care not to cause harm: that is, whether I will be on the lookout for possible harmful consequences, and see them as things I have reason to avoid. If I would not have these attitudes, then my driving may be unacceptably risky, and therefore impermissible. Cases like this, in which an agent's intention to avoid causing harm make it more likely that he or she will not cause harm, are instances of what I will call the *predictive* significance of intent.

The next question is whether an agent's intention in acting can make a difference to the permissibility of an action in ways other than by affecting the likely consequences of that action. For example, there seems to be an important moral difference, in war, between, on the one hand, attacking a military target in a way that can be foreseen to lead to a certain number of civilian casualties, and, on the other, killing the same number of civilians in order to demoralize the population or discourage them from aiding the enemy. Since these two lines of action — tactical bombing and terror bombing — are expected to kill the same number of people, the difference between them seems to lie in the fact that in the latter case, but not the former, those who carry out the attack intend to kill the civilians. They are not merely aware that this will probably be the effect of what they are doing; they are aiming at it, as a means to their end.

More generally, many people are inclined to accept the Principle of Double Effect, which holds that although it can be permissible to do something that one can foresee will lead to the deaths of innocent people when doing this is necessary to achieve some greater good, it is always impermissible to aim at the deaths of innocent people, either as one's ultimate end or as one's chosen means to some greater good.

This principle is controversial, but it is appealing because it seems to offer the best explanation of the distinction between terror bombing and tactical bombing, and also to explain other cases such as the following:

> *Rescue I*: As I am driving home, I receive a phone call telling me that a car is stalled along a seldom-traveled road that I could easily take. The car is delivering medicine to someone who will die unless he receives it within the next few hours. I could easily take that road and restart the stalled car.

Clearly I should do so.

> *Rescue II*: This is the same as the previous case except that I am also told that along yet another road I could take there is a stalled car that was taking medicine to five people in equally urgent need. There is not enough time for me to go to the aid of both cars.

Clearly in this case it is at least permissible for me to aid the second car, so as to save five rather than only one.

> *Rescue/Transplant*: This is the same as *Rescue I* except that I know that there are five people in urgent need of transplants who will be saved using the organs of the patient awaiting the medicine, if he dies very soon, as he will if I do not go to the aid of the stalled car.

If it is impermissible to refrain from aiding the car in *Rescue I*, then it is impermissible in this case as well. But it is permissible in *Rescue II*. As before, the Principle of Double Effect provides an explanation: in *Rescue/Transplant*, but not *Rescue II*, I would be intending that the one person should die, as a means to saving the five.

But the Principle of Double Effect is not needed in order to explain the difference between these cases, or the difference between the bombing cases, and the most plausible explanations of these cases do not turn on the agents' intentions.

Our thinking about the bombing cases is shaped by certain assumptions about the principles governing the conduct of war. These principles are often formulated in terms of what that agent can *intend*, but they are better understood as having something like the following form, which makes no reference to intent:

> In war, one is sometimes permitted to use destructive and potentially deadly force of a kind that would normally be prohibited. But such force is permitted only when its use is very likely to bring some military advantage, such as destroying enemy combatants or war-making materials, and it is permitted only if expected harm to noncombatants is minimized, and only if this harm is "proportional" to the importance of the military advantage to be gained.

This statement of the principle is only approximate. There are difficult questions about how the idea of a "military advantage" and the distinction between combatants and noncombatants are to be understood, and how the significance of these ideas is to be defended. I do not mean to ignore or minimize these problems, but they are problems that any view of these matters must face. My point is that there is no need, in addition, to appeal to the significance of intent in order to explain cases like the ones we have considered.

The proposed bombing of the munitions plant is permissible only if the destruction of the plant constitutes a military advantage in the relevant sense, and only if the conditions just listed are fulfilled: only if harm to noncombatants is minimized and the expected harm is "proportional." If there is no munitions plant, but a bombing raid that would kill the same number of noncombatants would hasten the end of war by undermining morale, this raid (a pure case of "terror bombing") would not be permissible. It is impermissible because it can be expected to kill noncombatants, and the circumstances are not such as to provide a justification for doing this under the principle just stated. The death of noncombatants is not rendered a "military advantage" by the fact that it would shorten the war by undermining public morale. So the fact that it would do this does not bring the case under the exception, just described, to the prohibition against doing what there is good reason to believe will cause loss of life.

As I have said, there are well-known difficulties about how the idea of a military advantage and the distinction between combatants and noncombatants are to be understood and defended. But on a plausible understanding of these ideas, the principle I have stated would rule out the nuclear bombing of Hiroshima and Nagasaki at the end of World War II, as well as the fire bombing of Tokyo and, earlier, of Dresden. There is no need to appeal to the agents' intentions in order to explain these cases.

On the view I am proposing, it remains true that a person acts wrongly if she intends to kill noncombatants in order to shorten the war by undermining morale (and has no further justification for her action). Such a person has an intention that she should abandon. But this truth should not be taken to suggest that intention has a fundamental role in determining the impermissibility of this action, in the way claimed by the Principle of Double Effect. The intention is wrongful because the act intended is wrongful, and the act is wrongful because of its likely consequences, not (fundamentally) because of this intention.

In the rescue and transplant cases, it was assumed that it is impermissible simply to take a living person's organs, even if this would benefit others, but that once a person is dead his or her organs are available for use to save others. Like the distinction between combatants and noncombatants, this assumption might be questioned, but it was presupposed in the examples as I presented them. The assumption that the person's organs would be available for transplant to save the five if, but only if, he was dead, is what forces on us the question of whether the possibility of saving others in this way justifies an exception to the general principle that requires us to save the person in *Rescue I*.

Once the question is posed in this way, however, we can see clearly why this does not justify such an exception. The general form of the question is this: as long as a person is alive, we have an obligation to him not to do X. If he were to die, and we were thus freed from this obligation, we could accomplish some good by doing X. Does this good therefore justify an exception to the principle requiring us to save the person (or a principle that would forbid killing him)? It would be absurd to think that it does, that is to say, that the fact that a person's death would release us from some obligation to him can count in favor of killing him, or against saving him. This absurdity does not itself depend on the idea that an individual has a special claim to his or her organs, although that is the particular moral claim that is at issue in the case we are discussing. The same absurdity could arise with respect to any underlying moral claim.

No similar absurdity is involved in *Rescue II*. In that case the principle in question incorporates an exception allowing us not to save a person if we could instead save a greater number and we do not have time or resources to do both. We would be permitted, and able to, save the greater number even if the other person's life were not in jeopardy. So *Rescue II* and *Rescue/Transplant* do differ in that in the latter case, but not the former, the death of the one is seen as required in order for us to save the five (morally required, in order to make this permissible, not causally required, in order to bring it about). In this respect the explanation I have offered has some similarity with the Principle of Double Effect. But in my explanation this difference has nothing to do with the intentions of the agents involved.

Like a terror bomber, an agent who took the possibility of saving the five in *Rescue/Transplant* as sufficient reason not to save the one would be making a moral mistake: he or she would be taking something to be a good moral reason that is not in fact such a reason, and would have an intention (a plan) that he or she ought to abandon. But this intention is not what makes the agent's action impermissible. The action is impermissible, and the intention mistaken, because, for the reasons I have outlined, the prospect of saving five by means of transplant does not justify an exception to the duty to save the one.

If the Principle of Double Effect is mistaken, why should it seem plausible to many people? The tendency to think that the agent's intention makes a fundamental difference to the permissibility of an action in these cases may result from a failure to distinguish between the deliberative use of a principle, in which it specifies the considerations that count for or against an action, and the critical use of a principle as a standard for assessing the way in which an agent went about deciding what to do. An assessment of the latter kind will always depend on what the agent *saw* as reasons for or against an action. The deliberative use of a principle identifies the considerations that *are* reasons for or against an action, such as the harm it is likely to cause, or the fact that the agent has promised to do it. These need not be facts about the agent's beliefs.

It is easy to confuse these two forms of assessment. We might say, for example, that what I did was wrong because I took the fact that it was more fun to watch a soap opera as a reason not to pick you up at the airport, as I had promised to do. But what would make this action wrong would be the fact that I promised to pick you up, and had no sufficient reason not to keep this promise. I was in error in taking the pleasure of watching television as a sufficient reason, but the fact that this was my reason is not what made my action wrong. The failure to distinguish between these two forms of assessment may lend plausibility to the Principle of Double Effect, by making it seem that an agent's particular reason for acting is what makes his action wrong when it does not in fact do so.

It is also possible that supporters of the Principle of Double Effect may not be thinking of this principle as a criterion of permissibility in the sense I am concerned with, but rather as a criterion for assessing the moral goodness of an action, which may well depend on an agent's intention, or on the reasons he or she acted from. If so, then the disagreement about the Principle of Double Effect is not about which actions fall within a certain moral category (the permissible) but about which moral category we should be concerned with (permissibility or goodness).

There certainly are cases in which the permissibility of an action depends on the agent's reasons for so acting, albeit in a less fundamental way than the Doctrine of Double Effect would suggest. One class of such cases includes ones in which the meaning of an action depends on the agent's reasons for engaging in it, and it is impermissible to mislead others about this meaning, or to fail to disclose this meaning. In what I will call *expression* cases, actions involve presenting oneself as being moved by certain reasons. When I call a sick relative and inquire about her health, for example, I may present myself as being moved by affectionate concern for her welfare. Suppose, however, that I am not moved by this reason at all. I might telephone the relative and inquire about her health just to curry favor with my wealthy grandfather, or simply to get my mother to stop nagging me about it. This may not make it impermissible for me to call. Perhaps a call from me would do so much to cheer the person up that I should make the call, despite the fact that it would be hypocritical. But the fact that I would be misrepresenting the reason for which I was calling at least counts against the action, and could do so decisively in the absence of other considerations to the contrary.

Something similar is true in a wider range of what might be called *expectation* cases. These are cases in which someone enters into a certain relation with an agent—a conversation, perhaps, or some form of cooperation—only because he or she assumes (perhaps without the agent's having done anything to encourage this assumption) that the agent has certain intentions, or is moved by certain reasons and not others. In these cases, an agent's intentions, and the reasons by which he or she is moved, are relevant to the permissibility of the agent's action. But they are relevant only in a derivative way, as a consequence of a more basic moral requirement not to mislead others or take advantage of their mistaken beliefs about one's intentions. So the question remains whether there are cases in which facts about an agent's reasons for acting are relevant to permissibility in a more fundamental way.

One class of cases in which the significance of an agent's reasons for acting is not derivative in this way is what I will call *threat* cases. There are many things to be said about the morality of threats, but in the important class of cases I have in mind a threat is wrong because it would be wrong to carry out the threat—that is to say, wrong to do the thing one has threatened to do *because the victim refused to comply.* In the case of some threats, such as the familiar "Your money or your life!" example, the condition I have italicized plays no role. Killing the victim would be wrong independent of the holdup person's reasons for doing it. But in other cases these reasons matter to the permissibility of the threatened action. Suppose, for example, that a hiring officer who has only one job to fill has sufficient reason to hire any one of several candidates, so there is no candidate whom it would be wrong not to hire. Still, it would be wrong for the hiring officer to refuse to hire a candidate because he or she would not have sex with the officer (or would not pay a bribe, or agree to do household chores). And it would consequently be wrong to threaten to do this.

The explanation of this wrong is that, first, an acceptable principle governing such cases must give the hiring officer authority to decide whom to hire. (This may be justified by considerations of the efficiency of the firm or, in the case of a single proprietor, perhaps by his or her property rights.) But a principle that permitted the hiring officer to make this decision for reasons of the kind just mentioned would give him or her an unacceptable form of control over the lives of job candidates. So such decisions are impermissible. The relevance of the agent's reasons in this case is not derivative in the way that it is in expression and expectation cases. All it depends on is the victims' having sufficient grounds for objecting to the principle permitting hiring decisions to be made for such reasons. When there are grounds for rejecting such a principle, the reasons a hiring agent acted on can make his or her action impermissible.

I have argued that we should reject the Principle of Double Effect as a criterion of permissibility, and I have identified a mistake (confusing the deliberative and the critical uses of a principle) that may lead one to conclude that intention is relevant to permissibility when in fact it is not. But I have also identified a number of ways in which an agent's intentions or, more broadly, his or her reasons for acting, can be relevant to the permissibility of an action. These include cases in which these factors have predictive significance, expression and expectation cases, and threat cases. There may be other cases beyond these. But morally objectionable reasons do not always render an action impermissible. Suppose I see a person drowning, and I could easily save him. He is someone I hate, and I would like to see him dead, but I do not want him to die *now* because his estate would go to a person with whom I am locked in a bitter electoral contest, and would provide her with much more money to spend on her campaign. If I save the man for this reason, seeing no other reason to do it, I have acted badly but not, I would say, impermissibly. There is such a thing as doing the right (permissible) thing for the wrong (that is to say, morally objectionable) reasons.

## TEST YOUR UNDERSTANDING

1. Scanlon argues that a person's poor intentions in acting do not, generally, make a difference to the permissibility of her action. They do, however, reflect on the action's meaning, the person's praiseworthiness or blameworthiness, and the person's character. Consider Scanlon's example of the person who (strangely) believes she must eat oatmeal every morning to save her friend's life. Suppose, one day, in a rage with her friend, she declines to eat her oatmeal in an attempt to cause her friend's death. Explain how Scanlon would analyze this case. What is her intention? Given her intention, is the action of eating toast instead of oatmeal permissible? What is the action's meaning? What does this action show about the person's character?

2. Scanlon identifies four categories of cases in which a person's intentions are relevant to the permissibility of her action. Identify these cases and give an example falling into each category. Scanlon draws a distinction between derivative cases and non-derivative cases. What is this distinction? Give an example of each type.

## NOTES AND QUESTIONS

1.  *Scanlon's opposition to terror-bombing.* Scanlon contends that the wrongness of terror bombing may be explained without referring to the intent of the bomber and, therefore, without invoking the doctrine of double effect. What is his alternative explanation and how does it differ from arguments that appeal to intention? How might Scanlon respond to someone who objects that Scanlon's account has no principled way of distinguishing between strategic bombing and terror bombing if the number of civilian casualties is the same? Does Scanlon have a good reason for thinking that a reduction in enemy morale is not a military advantage?

2.  *Scanlon's criticism of the doctrine of double effect.* Philosophers who criticize widespread views often try to provide charitable explanations for their opponents' views for (at least) two related reasons. First, if you can give an account of *how and why* a person made a mistake, that person may find it easier to reject the flawed reasoning if she can see exactly where the mistake occurs. Second, if you can explain how people *reasonably* came to an incorrect position and show their mistake, you may dispel the lingering and tempting sense that because lots of intelligent people have held the view, they must have had a good reason, and thus there must be something right about it.

    Scanlon offers an explanation for why his opponents have been attracted to the **doctrine of double effect,** a principle he claims is misguided. What is his explanation, and is it persuasive? For a fuller elaboration of his critique and his positive theory, see T. M. Scanlon, *Moral Dimensions: Permissibility, Meaning, Blame* (Belknap Press, 2008).

3.  *The disunity of action and character.* It seems possible on Scanlon's view that a person could have a terrible moral character, yet always do the morally permissible thing. It also seems possible, on his view, that a person could have a wonderful moral character, yet always perform the morally impermissible action. Can you see why? Do these possibilities create a problem for his view? Should a moral theory classify the permissibility of actions and the goodness of agents in such different ways that these categories operate that distinctly?

## Barbara Herman (born 1945)

Herman is Griffin Professor of Philosophy at the University of California, Los Angeles. A leading philosopher in moral and political philosophy, she is most famous for her nuanced work on moral psychology and her sophisticated interpretations and defenses of Kantian moral theory. She has published many influential articles and books, including *The Practice of Moral Judgment* (1993) and *Moral Literacy* (2007).

# IMPERMISSIBILITY AND WRONGNESS

There is now widespread agreement that rightness and wrongness are about our actions and their effects, not about our motives or intentions. If one wanted to argue that Robin Hood wasn't wrong in taking from the rich to feed the poor, his good motives wouldn't be what made it so. Motives and intentions are separate from the action, part of its history, and so should figure in the appraisal of agents (the way they come to act), not of actions (what is done). I think there is reason to doubt that this view of rightness and wrongness (call it the "acts-not-motives view") can be correct.

In recent versions of the acts-not-motives view, the central norm of wrongness in action is taken to be impermissibility. If a proposed action is impermissible, it may not be done; if it is permissible, then it may be done, even if there are better things an agent could have done instead. On the acts-not-motives view, an otherwise permissible action is not made wrong by a "bad" motive or intention, and only rarely (if ever) do motive and intention even partly explain an action's impermissibility.

Impermissibility is, I believe, a thin moral notion, best taken as a mark or sign of moral wrongness, not capturing what wrongness is. There are purposes for which its thinness is an advantage: e.g., in taking some actions off the table entirely (dismembering one to save five, terrorizing civilians as a wartime strategy), in regions of moral regulation where a clear and strict rule is what is wanted. The problem with the acts-not-motives view is not with the category of impermissibility, or with the idea that wrongness *can* sometimes attach to actions without regard to intention or motive. What should be resisted is the acts-not-motives view's generalization from contexts where the exclusion of motives *is* appropriate, to a broader view about what moral wrongness of action is. If we reverse the order and investigate moral wrongness first, we will be better able to see the reasons to include motive and intention in an account of morally wrong action (and, of course, right action as well).

1. Impermissibility tends to move to the center of attention when we think the first moral question about action is "What may I do?" when faced with alternatives whose moral availability is in doubt. I could stand in line for the next two hours and miss seeing an old friend, or falsely claim an emergency to elicit immediate service. It is impermissible to make the false claim. Why? In these circumstances, making a false claim would violate moral principle—be it a rule about what everyone is permitted to do, or about an appropriate balance of benefits and burdens, or about fairness. When a principle of this kind introduces the feature that makes us judge an action wrong, call it the "wrong-maker," it is no surprise that the verdict about what may or may not be done is, in almost all cases, motive- and intention-independent: neither item is involved in the explanation of wrongness.

Here's the kind of example often used to support the acts-not-motives view. Suppose moral principle requires saving a threatened life. Someone does the saving, but he is motivated by desire for fame or reward or because he has nasty plans that involve the victim later. Since despite (or even because of) his selfish motives, he does what is required, he *does* nothing wrong. That we cannot reasonably say that he should not have acted as he did — not saved the life — is a sign that the fault we find in his character or goals is not transmitted to his action. The action that should have been done was done.

But now add an example from Derek Parfit.[1] Parfit asks us to imagine a coffee-ordering gangster, thuggishly motivated to do whatever it takes to make the world conform to his will. He is ready to cause all kinds of mayhem if anyone crosses him, and regards the barista as he would a potentially recalcitrant soda machine that he will lash out at if it balks at dispensing his drink. But he is not crossed; the coffee is ordered and delivered; the easiest thing to do is pay, and so he does. Both Parfit and the acts-not-motives view conclude that since that act is one that satisfies moral principle (paying for purchases, say), nothing untoward has happened. We have a nasty guy you wouldn't want to have around, but for all that, unless and until he does something forbidden, the moral problem is all a matter of potential and probabilities — of bad motives, not bad action.

I think we should hold that, to the contrary, the gangster's action is morally wrong: not wrong in that he paid for the coffee, but wrong nonetheless. He did something he should not have done.

One might challenge the conclusion that nothing bad happened. The barista was surely put at risk in ways he ought not to have been. If we imagine that the danger is evident, it would be odd to say that nothing wrong occurred if you escape harm only by avoiding eye contact or placating or doing whatever is needed to avoid setting off those around you who are primed for easy violence. Making it safely through a minefield is not a walk in the park. (Note that the issue here is not predictive: that acting with such a nasty attitude is likely to cause harm and so wrong. There is a wrong to the agent who made it through unharmed.) But let us leave this response aside. The question I want to press is whether it is true that the gangster's action *in handing over the money* conforms to, or does not violate, moral principle.

What might lead one to think that the gangster's action does conform to moral principle? Both the movement of things and the behaviors of animals and persons blindly conform to natural laws. Actions of persons can conform to (or at least not violate) positive law without their knowing or caring that it does. When, without paying attention, someone drives 39 mph in a 40 mph zone, she drives just below the speed limit and lawfully. But what about when, not remembering a promise I have made, I show up, doing what I promised, but for some other reason. Have I kept my promise? I think not. Suppose a doctor in an emergency room acts on a private rule under which he treats the patient to his left, or the white patient, or the cute patient. Perhaps he has never treated the "wrong" patient. He is surely doing something wrong nevertheless. Is he conforming or not conforming to the triage rule in an emergency room to attend first to those with greatest need who can be saved?

1. Derek Parfit, *On What Matters* (Oxford University Press, 2011), pp. 87–88. [Herman's note.]

Whichever is true, it's an interesting question whether, if there were moral police around, they should stop the doctor from this action. The sickest patient is being taken care of, even if only by happenstance. As with the gangster and the selfish life-saver, why not conclude: no harm, no foul? A moral advisor would counsel reform about *the way* decisions are being made. And normally, insofar as we care about reliably getting the right thing done, we avoid such agents if we can. But here and now, no morally wrong action was done.

There are important differences in the cases. The gangster chooses to pay for his coffee; the self-serving agent intends to save a life: each intends to do the thing morality requires even if neither their intention nor their motive is a moral one. By contrast, in the triage and promise cases, the fact that the act chosen is the act that morally must be done is a pure accident. It is not clear how the acts-not-motives view can keep these cases separate. If it cannot require that the agent be motivated or intend to do the right thing as a condition of an action's rightness, it is not clear it can require the agent to intend the action under any special description (*as* a paying-for-services or *as* a promise-keeping). Whenever an agent acts intentionally, she acts under some description; conformity to or violation of moral principle is, except in special cases, about actions and effects in the external world. It is just this fact that I think we should find puzzling. How could external conformity be enough? In none of these cases is the beneficial or according-to-principle action or outcome the result of anything working right.

The paradigm case for the acts-not-motives view is a moral requirement that we *not* do something. We succeed in omitting a prohibited action if we do something else. If there are only two possible choices for action and one is prohibited, then the other must be permitted. Prohibitions give moral space the structure of a game board: so long as we do not step on the blue squares or a square that anyone has been on before, we're fine. To the agent "playing," why the square is not available makes no difference, and that it's not available need not figure in her mind for a move to be prohibited (suppose a siren goes off if there's a misstep). The picture looks even stranger for positive moral requirements: promising, truth-telling, rescue. Then the fact that it's not a blue square is not enough. The player should be on the right square for the right reason (to put someone in checkmate, for example). It should seem odd that the prohibition pattern dominates our account of moral wrongness.

In many versions of the acts-not-motives view one catches sight of something like a sleight-of-thought. Behind what appears to be an account of wrongness or impermissibility that makes no substantive moral claims, there is a hidden assumption about moral content: namely, that moral wrongness is about action as it produces effects, either singly, or as a function of what would happen if we all acted on some principle. That is, in thinking about the permissibility of an action, we are to look to the resulting distribution of burdens and benefits, asking who should bear what costs for which goods. Morality tells us which effects or pattern of effects we may and which we may not cause by our actions, given our options. If what matters to (im)permissibility is solely the effects of actions, neither motives nor intentions could be candidate wrong-makers. But this result is not then a function of a content-neutral feature of moral requirement or obligation: something that appears to be neutral is in fact a substantive view about what matters morally in action.

Tracing out the role of the Doctrine of Double Effect (DDE)[2] in arguments for the acts-not-motives view reveals just this kind of move. DDE came about as a way to distinguish two types of good-producing actions — one where producing the good had a collateral but unintended cost, the other where the good came about by morally forbidden means. DDE did this by locating the moral difference in the agent's intention.[3] As an account of the permissibility of a certain set of cases, DDE, and so an intention-dependent argument for permissibility that relies on it, fails if there is a better account of the cases. Acts-not-motives accounts get to the same results by appeal to patterns of consequences: whether some have a claim not to be harmed for the sake of the goods in question (e.g., killing civilians to lower enemy morale vs. seeing their deaths as a collateral effect of legitimate combat). Once the cases are described in this way, as a distributive issue across goods and independent moral claims, the intention to bring about one of the patterns could not be the wrong-maker — it's the pattern of consequences that matters.

It is not at all clear that such arguments accurately capture the problem DDE was aiming to account for by bringing intention in.[4] DDE is not meant to be a primary moral principle but something like a principle of exceptions. Where an action-kind is normally morally prohibited (e.g., causing deaths in the pursuit of a good end), DDE may permit an exception in some cases if the relevant actor has the right intention. This makes sense, since the exemption that comes with an exception is only available if the agent has the right intention. For similar reasons, we wouldn't call it self-defense if A kills B without knowing (or caring?) that B is launching a lethal attack against him.

2. If what is presented as a content-neutral feature of wrongness in fact depends on a specific kind of case and a substantive view about what makes an action wrong, we might not arrive at the acts-not-motives view if we began by looking at other kinds of cases and a different account of wrongness. The idea is not to eliminate impermissibility as a category of moral assessment, but to assign it a more limited place in an account of the moral wrongness of actions. As an alternative, I want to look at a Kant-inspired account of motive and of action assessment that shifts focus from the axis of avoiding impermissibility onto the more complicated requirements of getting it right about duty and obligation.

---

2. Other discussions of the DDE appear in the introduction to this chapter, and in readings by Anscombe and Scanlon (this chapter), and Nagel and Rawls (chapter 18). [Herman's note.]

3. According to DDE, an agent may perform an action that will produce both good and harmful effects if the good effects significantly outweigh the harms, and the agent merely foresees but does not intend the harm, either for itself or as a means to the good effects. [Herman's note.]

4. Warren Quinn explored this question in "Actions, Intentions, and Consequences: The Doctrine of Double Effect" reprinted in his *Morality and Action* (Cambridge University Press, 1993), chapter 8. [Herman's note.]

The acts-not-motives view assumes that wrongness in action is about producing a comparatively deficient configuration of interests and claims: one should have produced a better balance of effects (as some moral principle directs). By contrast, on a Kantian view, morality may require that we do and avoid more complicated things. For example, what I am to do is: "having promised, show up"; "recognizing he is in need, extend a hand." But also I must avoid: "having promised, show up only if it's to my advantage," and "recognizing need, help on condition that I benefit." The emphasis is on an agent's subjective principle, her maxim, what we might describe as the instrumental and evaluative representation of a possible action that moves her.

On the acts-not-motives view, motives range across appetites, instincts, habits, inclinations; they reach to emotions and passions. Their objects can be primitive (food) or complex (justice). The motive itself remains somewhat murky; it is a force that inclines or disposes an agent to activity. A moral motive is a kind of attachment to morality, a disposition to do what morality requires. No such motive could contribute to the rightness of the action; its job is to orient the agent's activity to rightness.

For Kant, however, "motive" is a general term for the way an agent exercises its causality. Some motives are opaque forces. Others involve reasoning and evaluative capacities. We are capable of being moved, of coming to act, from a recognition that something is required of us. A moral requirement—that one help the needy or promise honestly—then functions as a premise of practical reasoning. Reasoning from premise to action is not a cognitive exercise that attracts a motive (or not), but is itself what moves us. A Kantian moral motive is then not a form of attachment to a principle, but the agent's principle of reasoning, her maxim, in acting. Since the same act—a bit of effect-producing causality—can come from different maxims, it can be wrong to x if x-ing comes via one maxim and not wrong to x if its source is a different maxim. So here, the wrong-maker is a difference of motive.

There is nothing in itself odd about the idea of two doings that are externally or behaviorally the same, yet not the same action. In addition to actions that merely "look" the same (homonymous actions—inspecting and spying, for example), there are "as if" actions: imitations, pretendings, theatrical performances. "I promise" in a theatrical performance does not obligate, though in the theatrical fiction one character intelligibly holds another to what he promised. Promises between thieves might be regarded by the parties as promises, but if what's promised is immoral, there is no obligation, and so no real promise. If, having spotted a highway patrol car, I slow down to 65 mph, my driving at the speed limit for the few minutes I'm under surveillance is not driving-at-the-speed-limit, though for purposes of avoiding a ticket, it is just as good.

So why not say that the coffee-buyings of the ordinary customer and the gangster are not the same doings because their reasoning, their maxims, is different? The acts-not-motives view regards the action of the morally motivated customer as the right action plus a good motive. We might instead regard the gangster's action as the right action or outcome, minus something. It reproduces the dutiful action's external form, but it's a kind of simulation, not the real thing. As a simulation it is good enough for some purposes. But even to be a simulation, there must be something that has what it lacks.

There are other regions of rationally governed activity where we hold that a right outcome is not enough, not the real thing. An unjustified true belief is of course true and a belief, but it is also *qua* belief (that is, strictly) incorrect or wrong or defective. The flaw is a fact about the belief, not about the agent (though it may imply something about the agent). The route to the belief, by evidence or testimony, or by astrology or need, determines the belief's epistemic status, whether appropriate to hold or not. (Only, perhaps, for bare perceptual beliefs is mere correspondence to reality sufficient to make them *correct* beliefs). An accidentally true belief can do some of the work of a well-founded one, but not all (in scientific reasoning about counterfactuals, for example, but also in simpler cases: my belief that there will not be an earthquake tomorrow may be true, but if I believe it because I think earthquakes only happen when it is sunny, I may well be unprepared for the "big one" during the rainy season).

The acts-not-motives view encourages thinking about moral choice in terms of act-outcome pairs. It tends to be a complaint-centered view of morality: for an agent faced with a pair of possible actions, her question is whether someone affected would have grounds to object to her doing one rather than the other. The framework for choice on a Kantian view isn't directly about options but about the duties and obligations that bear. These duties and obligations place demands on agents' reasoning, laying out connections between moral premises and possible actions that follow. One duty will tell us that an action-type, deceit, for example, is not available as a means to an agent reasoning from self-interest ("because I want it" is a powerful premise; duties and obligations in this way constrain that premise's authority). Another duty will require that certain premises figure in our choices: where needs of others are acute and we can safely help, their needs, and not our convenience, should be our first premise in reasoning to action. In like manner we understand that making a promise involves taking on a premise in future reasoning to action.

The basic moral requirement thus involves our motives — that we reason correctly in choosing. When we don't, we are in error about our action, even if we do the very deed correct reasoning would have us do. Were we talking about Humean motives, the murky pressures, dispositions, and states of mind, it would be strange to talk about a requirement on motives: we lack the kind of control over these states that would permit morality's direct rule. But Kantian motives, or the ones morality cares about, are composed of the elements of reasoning. Whatever our disposition, we can be held to standards of correct reasoning. If P is the premise that obligation requires in our circumstances, and we know that it is, we are able to reason from P. This is no less true in the sphere of action than belief. That we are vulnerable to mistake and corruptions of reasoning does not imply that correctness in reasoning was out of reach: we can reason as we should, and therefore can be obligated to do so.

3. That we could be so obligated doesn't explain why morality should require correct reasoning over and above correct action. Consider the requirement to help others in need. Some persons are naturally and directly moved to promote the well-being of others: motivated by feelings of care or concern, they offer advice or a helping

hand, sometimes risking a great deal to prevent harms. The Kantian view will say that such actions simulate beneficence, a duty which also aims to promote the well-being of others. The beneficent and the natural motive do not generate actions from the same premises; the maxims are different; the agents' understanding of the needs they are responding to is different, even if the thing done to help is the same. Motivated by natural sympathy, we aim to relieve pain and suffering as such. The duty of beneficence aims to alleviate pain and suffering as or because they impede our good functioning (suppose).[5] Of course, given the nature of our vulnerabilities, it's no surprise that a sympathetic temperament can often stand in for beneficence. But the simulation can separate from the duty in cases where sympathy directs us to alleviate varieties of pain we should not ease (such as the pain of guilt, or the pain that is part of learning).

From the point of view of a victim in the moment, it makes little difference how the action is motivated or from what reasoning it issues. He gets what he needs equally well from the real thing or a simulation. No reason for regrets; no ground for complaint. But this point of view is highly selective. The agent whose helping action flows from moral premises is oriented in her acting to getting it right about help and what helping may involve. This includes both helping in the right way (e.g., in a way that does not produce dependence), and managing the aftermath: taking further steps, if needed, and negotiating the complexities of gratitude. None of this is found in the simulation, and it (partly) explains why morality requires more.

Where morality is present to us in duties and obligations, the hard question is often not a decision between options, but determining whether our circumstances warrant making an exception to a duty or obligation that applies. We know there is a duty about truth-telling that prohibits lying to promote our purposes. But in a case where the point or value of truth-telling is subverted (say, where telling the truth will enable wrongdoing), there is a question about whether the prohibition on lying might be canceled or suspended. Likewise, a duty to respect the physical space persons are in — we may not just push each other out of the way — can yield an exception in a medical emergency because in that case, it is the frantic push and not courtesy that does the work of the duty (enabling free action and choice).[6] However, unless the exception is recognized and the action taken in its light, it does no justificatory work. If we lie to protect a friend, or shove because we always regard ourselves as entitled, what we do is wrong.

Making an exception requires an exercise of deliberative authority. The agent whose reasoning is faulty — who does not have and act from a correct practical grasp of the moral terrain — is not competent to act contrary to the rule of duty that applies. Morality requires more of us than avoiding an unhappy outcome; we can act, but only if we get it right, and that is possible only when motive and intention express the authority of the agent's reasoning.

---

5. Learning the ins and outs of the duty of beneficence is one of the ways that we come to grasp the special needs of our kind of agency. [Herman's note.]

6. Describing the duty as a "duty to respect" rather than as a "duty not to interfere" captures this. [Herman's note.]

If we generalized from this result, we would conclude that the standard of correctness of an action includes the deliberative route by which the agent came to perform it. Just as weighing evidence is not an attitude one might or might not have about correct belief-formation, the work of the moral motive is not a special attitude one might or might not have towards morally required action. In acting from the correct motive, we get it right about what morality requires of action.[7]

On the Kantian alternative, several features of the acts-not-motives view remain in place. We often have moral reason not to be concerned about motive or intention: we want the drowning person saved; no one should kill one to save two. Some actions cannot be taken for any reason, and many actions are simply not available for the pursuit of our interests. We shouldn't need to deliberate to avoid cheating and shoplifting, or brutality to children. However, even though, as competent agents, there are things we know without thinking about them, moral reasoning is correctly imputed to us and retrievable. Whatever we do, it is not, strictly speaking, a morally correct action unless motive and intention are correct, unless, that is, we have acted on the right maxim.

When we correct a child who does the right thing to get a reward or to avoid the disapproval of her parents, we are in effect telling her that what she's done is not enough: she's gotten only part of the way there. It's a lesson not unlike others where we nudge children past rote performances and towards thinking out their actions for themselves. We want them to take possession of the activity and its standards of correctness so that they can, with authority, do the right thing.

On the acts-not-motives view, taking morality into our system of motives is a way to become morally reliable and to have our relations with others marked by moral concern, not just rectitude. On the alternative or Kantian view, we don't grasp what morality requires unless we come to conformity with moral principle in the right way, from the inside, in the way we deliberate and reason to action.

## TEST YOUR UNDERSTANDING

1. Herman challenges the **inference** from "Action A is morally wrong" to the conclusion "Therefore, action A is impermissible." Explain, using one of her examples, how an action may be permissible, yet wrong. Then, generate an example of your own.

2. Herman suggests there is an analogy between mathematical reasoning and moral reasoning. Correctly solving a mathematical problem requires (a) correct reasoning and (b) for that correct reasoning to yield the correct answer. In light of the analogy she draws, how does she think the following should be completed? Performing the right action requires: (a) _____ and (b) _____.

---

7. A fuller account of this interpretive claim can be found in my "Reasoning to Obligation," *Inquiry* 49, no. 1 (2006): 44–61. [Herman's note.]

## NOTES AND QUESTIONS

1. *Moral wrong versus moral impermissibility.* Herman claims that the coffee-ordering gangster behaves wrongly, if not impermissibly. What do you think the difference is between behaving wrongly and behaving impermissibly? Why do you think she insists that the gangster acts wrongly and not merely that he has a bad character? Can you think of an example of a person with a good character who behaves permissibly yet wrongly in her sense?

2. *Morality as advice.* Consider the following objection:

   The main function of moral reasoning is to give us guidance about how to behave — about what actions to perform and what actions to forgo. A moral judgment offers advice about what to do. But you can only advise someone to perform a particular action. You cannot advise someone to perform a particular action *for a particular reason.* You do not choose which reasons strike you as valid and which reasons motivate you to act. Reasons are not matters of choice. So a moral theory that insists that having a particular reason is an essential feature of a right action must be mistaken because it cannot yield useful advice.

   How might Herman respond? Should she challenge the advice-centered conception of morality or the claim that reasons are not matters of choice, or both?

## ANALYZING THE ARGUMENTS

1. Scanlon argues that an agent's poor intentions in acting do not, generally, make a difference to the permissibility of the action, but they do make a difference for the action's *meaning*. Can you offer some additional examples of what an action's meaning is in Scanlon's sense? Does this idea correspond to or differ from Herman's sense that an action may be wrong, even if permissible?

2. Herman argues that when you promise to meet a friend for lunch at a particular restaurant, forget all about the promise, but then just happen to wander into that restaurant at the right time, you have not really kept the promise at all. Keeping a promise requires both performing a certain action and performing it in light of the fact that one promised. Do you agree? Do all morally required actions have this structure, or is promising special? How might this example be thought to pose a challenge to Scanlon's position? Can he convincingly answer this challenge?

3. According to the **doctrine of double effect,** it matters whether one intends to harm an innocent as a means or an end, or whether that harm is merely foreseen. This raises the question: what is it to intend to harm an innocent as a means or an end? One simple answer runs as follows:

> For A to intend to harm an innocent person B as a means or as an end is for A to want B to suffer harm and to decide to act in a way that will cause B harm.

But consider the following cases:

*Orders*: A is a soldier who, privately, hates her fellow soldier B. She wants B to suffer and frequently fantasizes about B getting a painful comeuppance, but she would never act on that desire. Based on faulty, but credible, information, A's commander orders A to arrest B and confine B in an uncomfortable jail where B will suffer. A decides to follow the orders because they are her commander's orders.

*Faulty Weapon*: A is a soldier who enjoys violence and wishes to wound a civilian, B, for pleasure. A picks up her gun, knowing that there is only one round in the six-round chamber, spins the chamber so that there is only a one-in-six chance that she will wound B, and pulls the trigger.

*Reluctant Warrior*: A, a reluctant soldier, has read Anscombe's article and disagrees with Anscombe. She is horrified by war and believes it is never justified. She further believes that any action that will hasten the end of a war and minimize deaths is permissible. She becomes convinced that, in a particular war, terror-bombing the enemy leader's home village will eviscerate the leader's morale and result in immediate and fair peace negotiations with fewer civilian casualties than any other method. She decides to initiate and undertake the terror bombing but does so reluctantly. She does not want anyone to die and she hopes that somehow, the parties will enter peace negotiations without her having to take this terrible step.

*Exercise:* Explain why the examples appear to pose a problem for the simple definition. Discuss whether there are convincing replies to the purported counterexamples or whether the definition should be modified, and if so, how.

4. The doctrine of double effect surfaces not only in discussions about the ethics of war, but in other important contexts, such as end-of-life care. For example, some opponents of assisted suicide argue that it is permissible for a doctor to give a suffering patient medication in order to relieve his pain, even though it may increase the risk of the patient's death as a side effect. Yet they claim it is impermissible for a doctor to give a suffering patient lethal medication that will cause his death as a means of relieving the patient's pain. Can you explain how this reasoning resembles the reasoning used by proponents of the doctrine of double effect? Does it make a difference in the assisted suicide case that the recipient of the medication that may cause death *requests* it from the doctor? Could one agree with Anscombe's judgments about permissible and impermissible conduct in war but disagree with this reasoning about assisted suicide?

Some justices of the U.S. Supreme Court invoked the doctrine of double effect in justifying a state's prohibition on assisted suicide; see *Vacco v. Quill*, 521 U.S. 793 (1997). Criticism of that use may be found in Judith Jarvis Thomson, "Physician-Assisted Suicide: Two Arguments," *Ethics*, 109, no. 3 (1999): 497–518, especially pp. 507–18, and in Allison McIntyre, "The Double Life of Double Effect," *Theoretical Medicine and Bioethics* 25, no. 1 (2004): 61–74.

# 18

# What Is the Right Thing to Do?

You may hope that studying ethics will provide answers about what to do when you confront difficult problems in your own life. Some challenging problems arise rather frequently, such as whether it is permissible to break a rule that others regularly flout (e.g., whether to cheat on an exam) and how much help, and what sort, we must offer others in need. Other questions arise more episodically in our personal lives, but confront us regularly as political issues. These include issues such as whether we may assist terminal, long-suffering patients with suicide, whether abortion is permissible, and what, if anything, should limit our conduct during war.

Many of these questions are agonizing and carry life-and-death consequences. Most involve the fundamental problem of when, whether as individuals or as a collective, we may pursue our self-interest and how much we should subordinate and sacrifice to serve other people or values. Given these emotionally provocative features, it is unsurprising that some feel torn and uncertain about these questions. Others have strong but diverging responses that render conflicts over these matters seemingly intractable. The ambition of philosophy is to lend clarity and structure to our investigation of these questions so we may resolve them, as individuals, and to facilitate greater agreement, or at least, mutual understanding, among one another.

Some wonder, however, *how* philosophical analysis could help. The general principles and broad arguments that philosophy contemplates may not seem to apply squarely to the complex particularities of the real-life situation. Moreover, one might worry that these issues turn upon matters of ultimate preference or personal conscience. Philosophical arguments resonate for us, the skeptic may worry, only when and because they reflect our pre-formed biases; they cannot alter our gut reactions. Therefore, they cannot resolve disagreements between people with different starting points.

Applied ethicists resist such skepticism. They insist that philosophical arguments can alter and improve our understanding of difficult questions such as those concerning abortion and our conduct in war. How? Ethicists deploy three main techniques to gain traction on these problems and to bridge any gaps between large, general principles and quite specific situations: the use of simplifying examples, the use of analogies, and the introduction and refinement of plausible mid-level, topic-specific principles to unify a set of cases — techniques you will see used by the authors in this chapter.

# Simplifying Examples

When analyzing the ethics of complex situations, ethicists often begin with examples that are simpler or about which our judgments are clearer. Such cases also allow disputants to identify common ground and articulate justifications for their positions, facilitating engagement and reasoned discussion rather than mere exchanges of difference. From there, ethicists add complicating features to the case, one by one, to see which complications make a difference and where our disagreements emerge. Further, our confident judgments about easier cases may serve as leverage to force us to think more deeply about hard cases, to understand how our judgments relate to each other, and to adjust our judgments when we uncover a tension in our network of judgments.

For example, a philosopher considering whether it is ethical to facilitate the death of a suffering, terminally ill, and consenting patient might begin with our judgments about three clearer cases:

1. *Healthy Patient:* It seems morally wrong to help a healthy person with a bright future die if she asks for our assistance, especially if her reasons for seeking death involve minor, temporary, or soluble problems.

2. *Suffering, Non-consenting Patient:* It seems morally wrong to facilitate the death of a terminally ill, long-suffering patient who refuses consent.

3. *Pain Relief:* It seems not only permissible but morally imperative to administer pain relief to a severely suffering patient who consents, even if the pain relief induces long periods of unconsciousness and carries, as a side effect, a higher risk of death.

These three lodestars suggest that neither a patient's consent nor a patient's terminal status, by itself, is a sufficient condition for permissibly assisting another's death. Now complicate the case. Suppose a patient is both terminally ill *and* consents. Do these two factors, when combined, make a difference and render the assistance permissible? We might answer that question by asking why assisting the *Healthy Patient* seems impermissible. If assisting the *Healthy Patient*'s suicide seems impermissible because we must never contribute to a death, then one might ask whether that reason squares with our judgments in the *Pain Relief* case.

The *Pain Relief* case suggests that we may relieve the pain of a suffering person, even if that action risks death; thus, if we lose the risk, we may permissibly, if unintentionally, contribute to a death. This judgment introduces further questions: first, whether it makes a moral difference whether a death is facilitated intentionally or occurs as a mere side effect of an otherwise permissible act, and second, whether it matters if the death was certain or merely made more likely. If neither difference is significant, then we must either reject our judgment in the *Pain Relief* case or conclude that sometimes we may permissibly contribute to a person's death, in which case there must be a different justification of the *Healthy Patient* case. Perhaps the better justification of the *Healthy Patient case* is that it is wrong to assist a patient's death when a non-lethal way to alleviate her suffering is available. That justification is compatible with our judgment in the *Pain Relief* case.

Considering simple cases moves us quickly beyond our gut reactions to giving justifications and identifying what factors require further consideration. In the example just rehearsed, starting with simple cases reveals the limits and power of consent; the need to consider whether the patient's terminal status and suffering make a moral difference; the need to consider whether intent matters; and whether it matters if the death is certain or merely risked.

# Analogies

A second, related technique deploys analogies to introduce some intellectual distance from any exaggerated emotional reactions, preconceived notions, or rigid judgments. Applied ethicists examine cases that are different but structurally similar to the problem under consideration, and assess whether those analogical cases illuminate the case at hand or meaningfully differ. Sometimes, this technique shows that ethical disagreements turn on verifiable empirical facts, or that a person's judgments are in strong tension with each other.

For instance, to analyze the permissibility of cheating in an environment where cheating is rampant, one might start with analogous cases, some where the absence of reciprocity matters and others where it does not.

4. *Charades:* Suppose, in a game of charades, each team agrees the game is better when the parties do not act out individual letters to spell words. Each team pledges to *try* not to spell out words. Still, if one team resorts to the technique in a moment of desperation, then it seems permissible for the rival team to start spelling words when they wish.

5. *Vandalism:* Suppose vandalizing another person's home is a common response to an unresolved conflict or insult within one's neighborhood. It is still impermissible for you to vandalize the home of a person with whom you have a serious conflict, despite the fact that others do it.

Reciprocity or its absence matters in the *Charades* case but not in the *Vandalism* case. The next philosophical step would be to ask why the cases differ and whether cheating is more like the *Charades* case or more like the *Vandalism* case. Notably, in the *Charades* case, others' decisions not to abide by the rule change the meaning of one's own observance of the rule. Refraining from spelling would put one at a competitive disadvantage, given that the others do spell. In the *Charades* case, the expectation that one respect the rule seems conditioned on the voluntary compliance of others. In the *Vandalism* case, by contrast, the point of resolving conflict peacefully rather than aggressively is not diminished in one's own case by others' vandalism; the reason one should not vandalize has nothing to do with others' behavior.

Which case does cheating resemble? If a test is meant to develop one's capacities and assess one's knowledge, then the point of one's honest efforts is not diminished by others' dishonesty. The closer analogy may be the *Vandalism* case. On the other hand, if one's performance is evaluated on a curve, others' dishonesty may distort the results, making it more like the *Charades* case. Still, unlike the *Charades* case, cheating would not merely impact those who do not comply with the rule but would adversely affect other students; cheating would also represent a breach of trust with the professor and would deprive the cheater of a learning experience. These additional facts render salient that there are alternative measures of response to others' cheating, such as alerting the professor and seeking a different test.

# Crafting Plausible Principles

A third technique is to propose a potential, plausible principle to justify and unify a range of relevant, related cases that might shed light on the problem at hand. Then, one identifies some implications that principles would have in other cases to assess the principle's power and to uncover any flaws with the principle. Sometimes, dissatisfaction with the proposed principle is just as helpful as its endorsement. By articulating our reservations about a principle or its implications, we inch closer toward grasping what really matters and understanding the crux of our differences.

Suppose we return to the problem about assisted suicide. We might first formulate the following principle as underlying the resistance to assisted suicide:

(P) One may never intentionally facilitate another person's death.

Then, we would attempt to assess why this principle might be true and search for any clear counterexamples to it. Although respect for the value of life and the autonomy of persons might motivate endorsement of (P), there are some significant counterexamples to (P). As both Thomas Nagel and John Rawls agree, one may cause another person's death if it is necessary to defend oneself; further, soldiers may permissibly cause enemy soldiers' deaths during declared wars, at least if the wars are just, and they may help other soldiers do so. These counter-examples might then place pressure on the position that (P) justifies the conclusion that assisted suicide is wrong. If one may facilitate others' deaths, even when they resist death and do not consent, wouldn't it seem as though it must also be permissible to facilitate the death of a person who elects death for good reasons?

The critic of assisted suicide must either:

A. Defend a plausible principle that condemns consensual assisted suicide but that allows one to kill an involuntary victim in self-defense or in combat. To defend this principle, she must articulate a morally relevant difference between the cases of assisted suicide, on the one hand, and self-defense and combat, on the other.

Or,

B. Concede that our willingness to cause deaths in self-defense and in war must also be mistaken, and then defend those judgments.

Thus, triangulating from a mid-level principle and identifying counterexamples quickly helps us map some of the broader moral terrain in which the issue of assisted suicide is situated.

All three techniques are used by ethicists to help clarify thoughts about responsibilities to address global famine, the permissibility of abortion, and the ethics of conduct in war. Each of these issues raises hard problems about when and how much we should take steps to prevent the deaths of strangers and when we may, if ever, permissibly cause death. The chapter aims to introduce you to some nuances of the competing arguments about these issues and to demonstrate how philosophical arguments may deepen your understanding of debates about which you may already have some familiarity.

# Famine

None of us, at least not as individuals, caused the life-threatening circumstances faced by the poor in countries where food is scarce and terrible diseases are rampant. Nevertheless, it seems difficult to deny that, if we are able to help people in danger of losing their lives at a small cost to ourselves, we should. As Peter Singer emphasizes, advancing a simplifying example, if we see a child drowning in a lake or choking on a bone, we should put aside what we are doing and save the endangered life, even when the interruption is inconvenient and our clothes get dirty.

These straightforward ideas have profound, personally challenging implications when one considers the magnitude of global poverty. The World Health Organization estimates that *nearly a billion* people are significantly undernourished.

Must each of us, personally, give as much as we *possibly* can to address this problem, even if this means forgoing many of the expenditures that most of our family and peers make (e.g., expenditures on clothes, music, films, restaurants, and electronics)?

Singer contends that yes, we are obliged to give as much as possible.

Singer argues, first, that human suffering and premature deaths from hunger are terrible and preventable. Second, if we can prevent significantly bad events without sacrificing something comparably important, we should. Why? He proposes that our duty to save a drowning child stems from the **utilitarian** principle. In every case, each of us must act to generate the best consequences possible in terms of promoting happiness and reducing suffering, without regard for who enjoys the benefits and who endures the costs. Third, the lack of proximity of suffering people diminishes neither the significance of their suffering nor our obligation. Fourth, the fact that others may fail to help does not justify our own failure to help, because our help on its own would still save lives. Because most of us have more resources than famine victims and giving very generously would not make us worse off than the desperately poor, we should give *a lot*. Singer's somber conclusion is that we are each obligated to do *a very great deal* to help alleviate global poverty, even if substantial giving would considerably reduce our standard of living.

Onora O'Neill concurs with Singer that we have strong obligations to contribute to famine relief but gives a different argument that has different implications. O'Neill advances three major criticisms of the utilitarian approach. First, the utilitarian approach is predicated on contested empirical predictions that direct forms of famine relief will yield better overall, long-term consequences than the alternatives. It is unclear whether direct aid works to the long-term benefit of the poor, or instead increases detrimental forms of dependence. In the face of this empirical uncertainty, the utilitarian cannot make a determinate recommendation about what to do. But, surely, O'Neill says, we ought to do something to relieve present suffering. Second, a utilitarian might recommend ignoring those presently in need if giving help might contribute to overpopulation that could engender greater forms of poverty; this objectionably ignores the humanity of currently suffering people and treats their suffering as a (tragic) means to achieve a better overall outcome. Third, the utilitarian wrongly focuses on overall consequences assessed in terms of happiness. Our true obligations are not to maximize happiness but to ensure that each person may lead an autonomous life.

O'Neill contends that we must treat each person, not as a mere means, but as an end-in-herself, by respecting what makes people morally valuable, namely, their rational capacities to lead self-determining lives. Hence, we may not use coercion to achieve our own purposes; we should protect others from coercive treatment, and we should act to ensure that each person has access to the conditions and resources necessary for living as an autonomous being. Concretely, we may not allow some to die now to ease resource pressure later; and our famine relief efforts should be focused not on maximizing happiness but on enabling recipients to become independent and self-sufficient.

# Abortion

Although the morality of famine relief is a markedly different topic than the morality of abortion, the underlying philosophical issues helpfully overlap. Don Marquis asks whether the deaths occasioned by abortion should concern us as much as the deaths food shortages impose, given that the former concerns beings who lack the developed personalities and lives that victims of famine possess. Judith Jarvis Thomson's article shows that getting clear on the moral permissibility of abortion requires thinking through how much one person may be expected to give to another, a topic continuous with the philosophical questions presented by famine relief.

Marquis argues that "the overwhelming majority of deliberate abortions are seriously immoral." He diagnoses the central dispute in the abortion debate as turning on the highly contested question of whether it matters that embryos and fetuses lack full personalities and rich lives already in progress. Marquis suggests we step back to a simplifying case and consider why it is wrong to kill where we are *certain* that killing is wrong, to see if that reason applies to killing fetuses and embryos. Killing an adult, he claims, is not primarily wrong because it ends experiences that the adult actually values; for it is surely wrong to kill severely depressed adults, even if they do not currently value their lives. Killing an adult is wrong because it deprives that adult of the loss of a *future* in which to pursue the activities, projects, and relationships that make life valuable. Toddlers, fetuses, and embryos, if they are not killed, also have long futures ahead of them in which they may engage in such valuable pursuits. Even if those pursuits are not yet fully determinate, the deprivation of those opportunities represents a tremendous loss that Marquis contends it would be wrong to impose unless there are much stronger reasons to the contrary.

By sharp contrast, Thomson argues that abortion may be permissible even if an embryo or fetus is a person with a "right to life" whose death matters just as much as an adult's. She contends that a reasonable, morally decent person could be within her rights to refuse to bear the heavy burdens and risks to health of pregnancy and childbirth, even if another person needed those efforts to live. Although we may owe some sorts of assistance to one another and some women find this form of assistance extremely rewarding, we do not owe it to any particular person to make such extraordinary efforts and to take such major risks on their behalf. Further, we may extricate ourselves from shouldering these burdens if we have not voluntarily undertaken them. Thomson makes this argument through the use of powerful, creative analogies. Her justly famous examples are best encountered for the first time in the original text, so they will not be summarized here.

# War

As Marquis's and Thomson's articles demonstrate, abortion presents difficult moral issues partly because we are uncertain how to think about lives that have not fully begun and that are entirely dependent on particular individual's bodily support. The final set of readings about war changes gears. It addresses some ethical issues about killing those whose lives are fully in progress and who are not dependent on others, but rather who are enmeshed in hostile political conflicts.

Pacifists condemn war as always impermissible because war necessarily involves deliberate killing to resolve conflict and the inevitable deaths of innocent people. Nagel and Rawls both reject this pacifist view as well as the opposite view that anything is fair game in war. Their enterprise is to articulate and defend plausible principles that occupy this middle ground.

Rawls advances three main contentions. First, a primary mission of a just society is to avoid war. War may only be engaged in for purposes of self-defense and not to gain territory or resources. The advancement of human rights should be pursued through economic and educational missions to encourage and persuade "outlaw" states to treat their citizens and other states humanely, which in turn would reduce the risk of war. Second, even in justified wars of self-defense, war must be conducted in a way that renders a lasting peace available. Therefore, some forms of conduct are impermissible. Civilians may not be targeted because they are not responsible for the aggression giving rise to war. Soldiers' human rights must be respected both because that is what it is to have a right and because respecting the enemy's rights underscores the significance of such rights and educates one's enemy about the nature of the peaceful relations toward which everyone should aim. Third, the protected status of civilians as immune from legitimate attack admits to an exception where rare conditions constituting a "supreme emergency" obtain.

Nagel's parallel case against civilian killings and torture of combatants emphasizes moral principles, rather than political principles of justice and statecraft. Even if it would end a war more quickly and spare the loss of lives, Nagel argues that it is impermissible, without exception, deliberately to kill civilians, medical personnel, and prisoners of war, and impermissible, without exception, to torture or maim even permissible targets of aggression. Why? Morality demands that we treat all people with respect. Respect demands that hostile treatment be justified by something *about that person* meriting that form of hostility. Targeting the innocent violates this principle. So does targeting nonaggressive features of combatants, such as their needs and vulnerabilities as *humans*. One may forcefully impede an aggressor from her aggressive activity. It is quite another matter to starve, blind, or torture a combatant prisoner of war; such actions involve hostility to features about her with which no one could have a justified quarrel.

## Peter Singer (born 1946)

Singer is an Australian philosopher who teaches at Princeton University and the University of Melbourne. Famous for his sustained defense of utilitarianism and his application of utilitarian principles to the issues concerning global poverty, the treatment of animals, and end-of-life decision making, his books include *Animal Liberation* (1975), *Practical Ethics* (1979), *Rethinking Life and Death* (1994), and *The Life You Can Save: Acting Now to End World Poverty* (2009).

# FAMINE, AFFLUENCE, AND MORALITY

As I write this, in November 1971, people are dying in East Bengal from lack of food, shelter, and medical care. The suffering and death that are occurring there now are not inevitable, not unavoidable in any fatalistic sense of the term. Constant poverty, a cyclone, and a civil war have turned at least nine million people into destitute refugees; nevertheless, it is not beyond the capacity of the richer nations to give enough assistance to reduce any further suffering to very small proportions. The decisions and actions of human beings can prevent this kind of suffering. Unfortunately, human beings have not made the necessary decisions. At the individual level, people have, with very few exceptions, not responded to the situation in any significant way. Generally speaking, people have not given large sums to relief funds; they have not written to their parliamentary representatives demanding increased government assistance; they have not demonstrated in the streets, held symbolic fasts, or done anything else directed toward providing the refugees with the means to satisfy their essential needs. At the government level, no government has given the sort of massive aid that would enable the refugees to survive for more than a few days. . . .

So far as it concerns us here, there is nothing unique about this situation except its magnitude.[1] The Bengal emergency is just the latest and most acute of a series of major emergencies in various parts of the world, arising both from natural and from man-made causes. There are also many parts of the world in which people die from malnutrition and lack of food independent of any special emergency. . . .

What are the moral implications of a situation like this? In what follows, I shall argue that the way people in relatively affluent countries react to a situation like that in Bengal cannot be justified; indeed, the whole way we look at moral issues — our

1. As Singer later wrote in a revised version of the essay: "The crisis in Bangladesh that spurred me to write the above article is now of historical interest only, but the world food crisis is, if anything, still more serious. . . . [P]oor people are still starving in several countries, and malnutrition remains very widespread. The need for assistance is . . . just as great as when I first wrote, and we can be sure that without it there will, again, be major famines. The contrast between poverty and affluence that I wrote about is also as great as it was then. . . . So the case for aid, on both a personal and a governmental level, remains as great now as it was in 1971."

moral conceptual scheme — needs to be altered, and with it, the way of life that has come to be taken for granted in our society. . . .

I begin with the assumption that suffering and death from lack of food, shelter, and medical care are bad. . . .

My next point is this: if it is in our power to prevent something bad from happening, without thereby sacrificing anything of comparable moral importance, we ought, morally, to do it. By "without sacrificing anything of comparable moral importance" I mean without causing anything else comparably bad to happen, or doing something that is wrong in itself, or failing to promote some moral good, comparable in significance to the bad thing that we can prevent. This principle seems... uncontroversial. . . . It requires us only to prevent what is bad, and not to promote what is good, and it requires this of us only when we can do it without sacrificing anything that is, from the moral point of view, comparably important. I could even, as far as the application of my argument to the Bengal emergency is concerned, qualify the point so as to make it: if it is in our power to prevent something very bad from happening, without thereby sacrificing anything morally significant, we ought, morally, to do it. An application of this principle would be as follows: if I am walking past a shallow pond and see a child drowning in it, I ought to wade in and pull the child out. This will mean getting my clothes muddy, but this is insignificant, while the death of the child would presumably be a very bad thing.

The uncontroversial appearance of the principle just stated is deceptive. If it were acted upon, even in its qualified form, our lives, our society, and our world would be fundamentally changed. For the principle takes, firstly, no account of proximity or distance. It makes no moral difference whether the person I can help is a neighbor's child ten yards from me or a Bengali whose name I shall never know, ten thousand miles away. Secondly, the principle makes no distinction between cases in which I am the only person who could possibly do anything and cases in which I am just one among millions in the same position.

I do not think I need to say much in defense of the refusal to take proximity and distance into account. The fact that a person is physically near to us, so that we have personal contact with him, may make it more likely that we *shall* assist him, but this does not show that we *ought* to help him rather than another who happens to be further away. If we accept any principle of impartiality, universalizability,[2] equality, or whatever, we cannot discriminate against someone merely because he is far away from us (or we are far away from him). Admittedly, it is possible that we are in a better position to judge what needs to be done to help a person near to us than one far away, and perhaps also to provide the assistance we judge to be necessary. If this were the case, it would be a reason for helping those near to us first. This may once have been a justification for being more concerned with the poor in one's own town than with famine victims in India. Unfortunately for those who like to keep their moral responsibilities limited, instant communication and swift transportation have

---

2. The principle of universalizability roughly requires that I act only in ways that I believe others, similarly situated, should act (even if our situations and roles were reversed).

changed the situation. From the moral point of view, the development of the world into a "global village" has made an important, though still unrecognized, difference to our moral situation. . . .

There may be a greater need to defend the second implication of my principle — that the fact that there are millions of other people in the same position, in respect to the Bengali refugees, as I am, does not make the situation significantly different from a situation in which I am the only person who can prevent something very bad from occurring. Again, of course, I admit that there is a psychological difference between the cases; one feels less guilty about doing nothing if one can point to others, similarly placed, who have also done nothing. Yet this can make no real difference to our moral obligations Should I consider that I am less obliged to pull the drowning child out of the pond if on looking around I see other people, no further away than I am, who have also noticed the child but are doing nothing? One has only to ask this question to see the absurdity of the view that numbers lessen obligation. . . .

The view that numbers do make a difference can be made plausible if stated in this way: if everyone in circumstances like mine gave £5 to the Bengal Relief Fund, there would be enough to provide food, shelter, and medical care for the refugees; there is no reason why I should give more than anyone else in the same circumstances as I am; therefore I have no obligation to give more than £5. Each premise in this argument is true, and the argument looks sound.[3] It may convince us, unless we notice that it is based on a hypothetical premise, although the conclusion is not stated hypothetically. The argument would be sound if the conclusion were: if everyone in circumstances like mine were to give £5, I would have no obligation to give more than £5. If the conclusion were so stated, however, it would be obvious that the argument has no bearing on a situation in which it is not the case that everyone else gives £5. This, of course, is the actual situation. It is more or less certain that not everyone in circumstances like mine will give £5. So there will not be enough to provide the needed food, shelter, and medical care. Therefore by giving more than £5 I will prevent more suffering than I would if I gave just £5. . . .

If my argument so far has been sound, neither our distance from a preventable evil nor the number of other people who, in respect to that evil, are in the same situation as we are, lessens our obligation to mitigate or prevent that evil. I shall therefore take as established the principle I asserted earlier. As I have already said, I need to assert it only in its qualified form: if it is in our power to prevent something very bad from happening, without thereby sacrificing anything else morally significant, we ought, morally, to do it.

The outcome of this argument is that our traditional moral categories are upset. The traditional distinction between duty and charity cannot be drawn, or at least, not in the place we normally draw it. Giving money to the Bengal Relief Fund is regarded as an act of charity in our society. The bodies which collect money are

---

3. A **sound** argument is an **argument** with true premises and that arrives at a conclusion that logically follows from the premises.

known as "charities." These organizations see themselves in this way — if you send them a check, you will be thanked for your "generosity." Because giving money is regarded as an act of charity, it is not thought that there is anything wrong with not giving. The charitable man may be praised, but the man who is not charitable is not condemned. People do not feel in any way ashamed or guilty about spending money on new clothes or a new car instead of giving it to famine relief. (Indeed, the alternative does not occur to them.) This way of looking at the matter cannot be justified. When we buy new clothes not to keep ourselves warm but to look "well-dressed" we are not providing for any important need. We would not be sacrificing anything significant if we were to continue to wear our old clothes, and give the money to famine relief. By doing so, we would be preventing another person from starving. It follows from what I have said earlier that we ought to give money away, rather than spend it on clothes which we do not need to keep us warm. To do so is not charitable, or generous. Nor is it the kind of act which philosophers and theologians have called "supererogatory" — an act which it would be good to do, but not wrong not to do. On the contrary, we ought to give the money away, and it is wrong not to do so.

I am not maintaining that there are no acts which are charitable, or that there are no acts which it would be good to do but not wrong not to do. It may be possible to redraw the distinction between duty and charity in some other place. All I am arguing here is that the present way of drawing the distinction, which makes it an act of charity for a man living at the level of affluence which most people in the "developed nations" enjoy to give money to save someone else from starvation, cannot be supported. . . .

One objection to the position I have taken might be simply that it is too drastic a revision of our moral scheme. . . . Most people reserve their moral condemnation for those who violate some moral norm, such as the norm against taking another person's property. They do not condemn those who indulge in luxury instead of giving to famine relief. But given that I did not set out to present a morally neutral description of the way people make moral judgments, the way people do in fact judge has nothing to do with the validity of my conclusion. My conclusion follows from the principle which I advanced earlier, and unless that principle is rejected, or the arguments shown to be unsound, I think the conclusion must stand, however strange it appears.

It might, nevertheless, be interesting to consider why our society, and most other societies, do judge differently from the way I have suggested they should. In a well-known article, J. O. Urmson suggests that the imperatives of duty, which tell us what we must do, as distinct from what it would be good to do but not wrong not to do, function so as to prohibit behavior that is intolerable if men are to live together in society. This may explain the origin and continued existence of the present division between acts of duty and acts of charity. Moral attitudes are shaped by the needs of society, and no doubt society needs people who will observe the rules that make social existence tolerable. From the point of view of a particular society, it is essential to prevent violations of norms against killing, stealing, and so on. It is quite inessential, however, to help people outside one's own society.

If this is an explanation of our common distinction between duty and supererogation, however, it is not a justification of it. The moral point of view requires us to look beyond the interests of our own society. Previously, as I have already mentioned, this may hardly have been feasible, but it is quite feasible now. From the moral point of view, the prevention of the starvation of millions of people outside our society must be considered at least as pressing as the upholding of property norms within our society.

It has been argued by some writers, among them Sidgwick[4] and Urmson, that we need to have a basic moral code which is not too far beyond the capacities of the ordinary man, for otherwise there will be a general breakdown of compliance with the moral code. Crudely stated, this argument suggests that if we tell people that they ought to refrain from murder and give everything they do not really need to famine relief, they will do neither, whereas if we tell them that they ought to refrain from murder and that it is good to give to famine relief but not wrong not to do so, they will at least refrain from murder. The issue here is: Where should we drawn the line between conduct that is required and conduct that is good although not required, so as to get the best possible result? This would seem to be an empirical question, although a very difficult one. One objection to the Sidgwick-Urmson line of argument is that it takes insufficient account of the effect that moral standards can have on the decisions we make. Given a society in which a wealthy man who gives five percent of his income to famine relief is regarded as most generous, it is not surprising that a proposal that we all ought to give away half our incomes will be thought to be absurdly unrealistic. In a society which held that no man should have more than enough while others have less than they need, such a proposal might seem narrow-minded. What it is possible for a man to do and what he is likely to do are both, I think, very greatly influenced by what people around him are doing and expecting him to do. In any case, the possibility that by spreading the idea that we ought to be doing very much more than we are to relieve famine we shall bring about a general breakdown of moral behavior seems remote. . . . Finally, it should be emphasized that these considerations are relevant only to the issue of what we should require from others, and not to what we ourselves ought to do. . . .

It is sometimes said that overseas aid should be a government responsibility, and that therefore one ought not to give to privately run charities. Giving privately, it is said, allows the government and the noncontributing members of society to escape their responsibilities.

This argument seems to assume that the more people there are who give to privately organized famine relief funds, the less likely it is that the government will take over full responsibility for such aid. This assumption is unsupported, and does not strike me as at all plausible. . . .

4. Henry Sidgwick (1838–1900) was a famous utilitarian.

I do not, of course, want to dispute the contention that governments of affluent nations should be giving many times the amount of genuine, no-strings-attached aid that they are giving now. I agree, too, that giving privately is not enough, and that we ought to be campaigning actively for entirely new standards for both public and private contributions to famine relief. . . .

Another, more serious reason for not giving to famine relief funds is that until there is effective population control, relieving famine merely postpones starvation. If we save the Bengal refugees now, others, perhaps the children of these refugees, will face starvation in a few years' time. . . .

I accept that the earth cannot support indefinitely a population rising at the present rate. This certainly poses a problem for anyone who thinks it important to prevent famine. Again, however, one could accept the argument without drawing the conclusion that it absolves one from any obligation to do anything to prevent famine. The conclusion that should be drawn is that the best means of preventing famine, in the long run, is population control. It would then follow from the position reached earlier that one ought to be doing all one can to promote population control (unless one held that all forms of population control were wrong in themselves, or would have significantly bad consequences). . . .

A third point raised by the conclusion reached earlier relates to the question of just how much we all ought to be giving away. One possibility is that we ought to give until we reach the level of marginal utility — that is, the level at which, by giving more, I would cause as much suffering to myself or my dependents as I would relieve by my gift. This would mean, of course, that one would reduce oneself to very near the material circumstances of a Bengali refugee. It will be recalled that earlier I put forward both a strong and a moderate version of the principle of preventing bad occurrences. The strong version, which required us to prevent bad things from happening unless in doing so we would be sacrificing something of comparable moral significance, does seem to require reducing ourselves to the level of marginal utility. I should also say that the strong version seems to me to be the correct one. I proposed the more moderate version — that we should prevent bad occurrences unless, to do so, we had to sacrifice something morally significant — only in order to show that even on this surely undeniable principle a great change in our way of life is required. On the more moderate principle, it may not follow that we ought to reduce ourselves to the level of marginal utility, for one might hold that to reduce oneself and one's family to this level is to cause something significantly bad to happen. Whether this is so I shall not discuss, since, as I have said, I can see no good reason for holding the moderate version of the principle rather than the strong version. Even if we accepted the principle only in its moderate form, however, it should be clear that we would have to give away enough to ensure that the consumer society, dependent as it is on people spending on trivia rather than giving to famine relief, would slow down and perhaps disappear entirely. There are several reasons why this would be desirable in itself. The value and necessity of economic growth are now being questioned not only by conservationists, but by economists as well. There is no doubt, too, that the consumer society has had a distorting effect on the goals and purposes of its members.

## TEST YOUR UNDERSTANDING

1. Singer argues both from an initial principle and then from a qualified version of that principle. What are the two principles and how do they differ? Does the qualified principle yield different conclusions?

2. Singer begins his essay contending that "the whole way we look at moral issues — our moral conceptual scheme — needs to be altered." What perspective on famine relief does he think must be altered? Which moral concepts are commonly used, but misapplied, in this context?

3. How does Singer respond to the objection that international famine relief is the responsibility of governments, not private citizens?

## NOTES AND QUESTIONS

1. *The personal costs of beneficence.* Would following Singer's recommendations demand that one make major changes in the nature of one's close relationships to family members and friends? If so, would this demand provide a reason to doubt his position? An extended discussion of this question can be found in Garrett Cullity, *The Moral Demands of Affluence* (Oxford University Press, 2004).

2. *Does the starting point matter?* Singer's argument begins by asking you to imagine that while on a walk, you see a child drowning in a pond. Call this the *Single Child Case.* Singer's argument draws upon your reaction that you should save the child, even if it ruins your clothes and disrupts your day. Singer then applies that judgment to other, similar cases.

   Suppose instead that we began with a modified example, the *Series Case.* Suppose that as soon as you save the one child and you walk on, within seconds, you immediately encounter another drowning child, and thereafter another and another yet. This happens day after day. Do you have a strong sense that you should stop and help every child in the *Series Case,* even though engaging in these rescue efforts means that you will never reach your destination and the life you had planned will be utterly disrupted?

   *Exercise:* Discuss whether your judgment that you should help in the *Series Case* is as confident as your judgment that you must help in the *Single Child Case,* and what, if anything, could justify any varying reactions to these examples. Would a different reaction to the cases cast any doubt on Singer's use of the *Single Child Case* as a starting point?

3. *Is the cause of famine relevant?* Singer does not specify the cause of the drowning child's predicament. These details do not seem to matter. Whether the child fell by accident or was pushed by another child seems irrelevant to one's obligation to aid. Is the cause of famine also irrelevant to one's duty to contribute to famine relief?

*Exercise:* With respect to one's obligation to contribute to famine relief, discuss whether it matters if famines are caused by unpredictable weather catastrophes or by institutional failures of the victims' governments, such as corruption or failures of planning.

4. *Is reciprocity relevant?* If bystanders lingered nearby and watched the child as she was drowning, their presence would not diminish or extinguish your obligation to save the child. So, too, Singer argues that the fact that other citizens do not give to famine relief does not excuse you from giving. Do others' failures to act make *any* sort of difference?

   *Exercise:* Discuss whether the failure of your peers and fellow citizens to contribute to famine relief heightens or diminishes your obligation to contribute. Should you give more because it is important that someone make up the difference for their failure, as with rescuing the child, or is it unfair for you to make sacrifices if others do not also give? (Are both **disjuncts** true?)

   A longer discussion of the obligations we may incur from others' failures to help appears in Liam Murphy, *Moral Demands in Non-Ideal Theory* (Oxford University Press, 2003).

5. *What to do?* Many people feel moved but overwhelmed after reading Singer's arguments, and want to know more about what sort of help would be effective. Two sites that attempt to identify charities that efficiently put donations to use include www.givingwhatwecan.org and www.givewell.org. Some difficult problems associated with identifying effective modes of assistance are canvassed in a forum in the *Boston Review*. See Abhijit Vinayak Banerjee, "Making Aid Work," and the replies by distinguished commentators: https://bostonreview.net/banerjee-making-aid-work (2006). Worries about the effectiveness of international aid and a call for more political, institutional solutions appear in Angus Deaton, "How to Help Those Left Behind," chapter 7 in his *The Great Escape: Health, Wealth and the Origins of Inequality* (Princeton University Press, 2013).

## Onora O'Neill (born 1941)

O'Neill is a British philosopher and politician. She was born in Ireland, educated in England and the United States, taught at Barnard College and the University of Essex, was Principal of Newnham College, and is now Emeritus Professor of Newnham College, University of Cambridge. A member of the House of Lords, she chairs the Equality and Human Rights Commission in Great Britain. Well known for her defense of Kantian ethics and its application to issues of poverty and bioethics, her books include *Acting on Principle* (1975), *Faces of Hunger: An Essay on Poverty, Development and Justice* (1986), *Constructions of Reason: Exploration of Kant's Practical Philosophy* (1989), *Bounds of Justice* (2000), and *Autonomy and Trust in Bioethics* (2002).

# THE MORAL PERPLEXITIES OF FAMINE AND WORLD HUNGER

Through history millions have died of sheer starvation and of malnutrition or from illnesses that they might have survived with better food. Whenever there were such deaths, nearby survivors may have realized that they could help prevent some deaths and may have done so, or wondered whether to do so. But nobody sought to prevent faraway deaths. Distance made an important difference; with few exceptions there was nothing to be done for the victims of faraway famines.

In a global economy things are different. Food from areas with agricultural surplus (nowadays mainly North America, Australia, and western Europe) can be distributed to the starving in Bangladesh or Somalia. Longer-term policies that affect economic development, fertility levels, and agricultural productivity may hasten or postpone far-off famines or make them more or less severe. Consequently we can now ask whether we ought to do some of these newly possible actions. Ought we (or others) to try to distribute food or aid, to control fertility, or to further economic development? Who should foot the bills and suffer the other costs? To whom (if anyone) should aid be given and to whom should it be denied? How much hardship or sacrifice, if any, is demanded of those who have the means to help? . . .

I will try in this essay to show how certain moral theories *can* help us think about some questions about famine and also to use considerations about famine to show some of the strengths and limitations of these theories. . . .

## Utilitarian Approaches to Famine Questions

. . . No disagreement over famine and world hunger could be more fundamental than one between (1) those who think that either individual citizens or social groups in the developed world are morally required to take an active part in trying to reduce and end the poverty of the Third World and (2) those who think that they are morally required not to do so. Yet utilitarian arguments have been offered for both conclusions.[1] . . .

One well-known utilitarian dispute about famine has been between the basically Malthusian[2] perspective of Garrett Hardin[3] and the more optimistic, developmentalist

---

1. O'Neill refers to the moral theory of utilitarianism, according to which the morally right (and obligatory) action to perform is that action that will produce the most happiness, taking into account all of those affected, whether positively or negatively and whether directly or indirectly.

2. Thomas Malthus (1766–1834) was a British economist who argued that historically, famine, among other disasters, has kept population size in check.

3. Garrett Hardin (1915–2003) was an American ecologist whose research focused on the problems associated with overpopulation.

perspectives of other utilitarian writers. For the latter position I shall draw particularly on Peter Singer's influential article, "Famine, Affluence, and Morality."[4]

Hardin's argument may be summarized as follows: the citizens of developed countries are like the passengers of a lifeboat around which other, desperate people are swimming. Those in the lifeboats can rescue some of the drowning. But if the affluent rescue some of the starving, this will — unlike many lifeboat rescues — have bad consequences. It will mean that the affluent world will then have a smaller safety margin. While this might in the short run be outweighed by the added happiness and benefit of those who have been rescued, the longer-run effects are grim. The rescued will assume that they are secure; they will multiply, and next time that similar dangers arise they will be more numerous and rescue will not be possible. It is better, from a utilitarian point of view, to lose some lives now than to lose more lives later. So it would be morally wrong to rescue those who are desperate, and the starving must be left to starve.

Hardin's use of the lifeboat analogy has often been criticized. . . . Those in the boats may be entitled to their seats, and they have no options except to stay put or to give up everything. The affluent are in a different position. They may risk little in trying to help the hungry, they may lack clear title to all that they have (perhaps, for example, some of it has been acquired by unjust exploitation of parts of the Third World), and there are many ways in which they can give up something without sacrificing everything. Hardin does not take these points seriously because he thinks that the longer-term balancing of beneficial and harmful results of attempting to help the Third World point the other way. . . . He writes:

> If poor countries received no food aid from outside, the rate of their population growth would be periodically checked by crop failures and famines. But if they can always draw on a world food bank in time of need, their population can continue to grow unchecked, and so will their "need" for aid. In the short run a world food bank may diminish that need, but in the long run it actually increases the need without limit.[5]

From this perspective it follows that the prosperous ought, if they are utilitarians, to leave the starving to themselves to die or survive as best they may.

Singer's utilitarianism, by contrast, leads to interventionist conclusions. He starts from the standard utilitarian assumption that "if it is in our power to prevent something bad from happening, without thereby sacrificing anything of comparable moral importance, we ought, morally, to do it." He then points out that contributions to famine relief, even if they amount to a large proportion of our income — say 50 percent — do not sacrifice anything of moral importance comparable to that of the famine they relieve. . . . So he concludes that the prosperous, even the modestly

---

4. Excerpted earlier in this chapter.

5. Garrett Hardin, "Lifeboat Ethics: The Case against Helping the Poor," in W. Aiken and H. La Follette, *World Hunger and Moral Obligation* (Prentice-Hall, 1977), p. 17. [O'Neill's note.]

prosperous, ought to help feed the hungry and to give up their affluence until they have so reduced their own standard of living that any further giving would sacrifice "something of comparable moral importance."

Singer's position . . . has been challenged from within the famine-relief movement itself. Tony Jackson, an Oxfam food aid consultant, has argued in *Against the Grain* that giving food doesn't always benefit the starving.[6]

Food aid commonly takes two forms. . . . [G]overnment-to-government food aid, which Third World governments obtain from food surplus countries and sell in their own countries, . . . may do more to support a government that is failing to address needs than it does to meet those needs. The second form of food aid, so-called project food aid, is mostly channeled through the World Food Programme and various voluntary agencies. This food aid represents the very sort of action to relieve the greatest suffering that Peter Singer advocates on utilitarian grounds. . . .

Jackson disagrees with Singer . . . because he thinks that providing food aid — even project food aid, which is intended to get the food where it is needed — has been shown to harm the needy. Project food aid competes with local food production, depriving vulnerable farmers of their living and driving them into the cities. Third World food production is then decreased rather than increased. Moreover, the food that is given often fails to reach those whose need is greatest and is diverted by others. . . . In some cases food-aid dependence is institutionalized and development hindered rather than helped. Apart from genuine short-term emergencies, such as the plight of refugees or results of sudden natural catastrophes, the provision of food aid often does more to benefit the prosperous farmers of the developed world, whose surplus is bought at subsidized prices, than it does to help the Third World. So the enormous international effort that goes into providing food aid preempts other and possibly more effective moves. . . .

The radically different policy conclusions reached by different utilitarian arguments about famine policy raise sharp dilemmas. . . .

It is not surprising that utilitarians disagree over famine and development policies. For utilitarians, it is *results* and not *principles* or *intentions* that count. . . .

If we are to work out the consequences of alternative available actions and policies, as utilitarianism demands, we shall repeatedly find ourselves confronted with impossible calculations. While accepting that precision is not generally possible or required in these matters, we cannot dispense with some accurate way of listing available options and the general character of the results of each. But our capacity to make accurate, if imprecise, judgments is on the whole restricted to matters that are relatively close at hand. We lack the sort of social science that provides an exhaustive list of available options or gives a generally accurate account of the long-term and overall likely results of each. Yet problems of world hunger, possible famine, and future population and resource growth cannot be considered without attending to the longer-term global results of available courses of action. If utilitarians lack a

---

6. Oxfam is a nonprofit organization that works around the world to relieve hunger and poverty.

science of society and have only a limited ability to foresee results, they may have no general way to decide whether a proposed action or policy is morally required, forbidden, or neither. . . .

Utilitarianism is an appealing theory for anyone who wants to deliberate morally about famine problems. Its scope is comprehensive and it offers a pattern of reasoning which, if we could get appropriate information, would give us accurate and precise resolution of moral problems. . . . [But] the ambitious character of utilitarian thinking in the abstract is not sustained in determinate contexts. Where such reasoning is silent, we may have to look in other directions. . . .

## Kantian Approaches to Some Famine Problems

The second moral theory whose scope and determinacy in dealing with famine problems I shall consider was developed by the German philosopher Immanuel Kant (1724–1804).[7] . . .

Kant does not . . . try to generate a set of precise rules defining human obligations in all possible circumstances; instead, he attempts to provide a set of *principles of obligation* that can be used as the starting points for moral reasoning in actual contexts of action. The primary focus of Kantian ethics is, then, on *action* rather than *results*, as in utilitarian thinking. . . . [T]o know *what* sort of action is required (or forbidden) in which circumstances, we should not look just at the expected results of action . . . but, in the first instance, at the nature of the proposed actions themselves.

[T]he famous Categorical Imperative plays the same role in Kantian thinking that the Greatest Happiness Principle plays in utilitarian thought.

One . . . formulation . . . of the Categorical Imperative . . . is *The Formula of the End in Itself.* . . .

> Act in such a way that you always treat humanity, whether in your own person or in the person of any other, never simply as a means but always at the same time as an end.[8]

To understand this principle we need in the first place to understand what Kant means by the term *maxim*. The maxim of an act or policy or activity is the *underlying principle* of the act, policy or activity, by which other, more superficial aspects of action are guided. . . .

It is helpful to think of some examples of maxims that might be used to guide action in contexts where poverty and the risk of famine are issues. Somebody who

---

7. Some of Kant's work is excerpted in chapters 15 and 16 of this volume.

8. Kant, *Groundwork for the Metaphysic of Morals,* trans, H. J. Paton as *The Moral Law* (Hutcheson, 1953), p. 430 (Prussian Academy pagination). [O'Neill's note.]

contributes to famine-relief work or advocates development might have an underlying principle such as, "Try to help reduce the risk or severity of world hunger." This commitment might be reflected in varied surface action in varied situations. In one context a gift of money might be relevant; in another some political activity such as lobbying for or against certain types of aid and trade might express the same underlying commitment. Sometimes superficial aspects of action may seem at variance with the underlying maxim they in fact express. For example, if there is reason to think that indiscriminate food aid damages the agricultural economy of the area to which food is given, then the maxim of seeking to relieve famine might be expressed in action aimed at limiting the extent of food aid. More lavish use of food aid might *seem* to treat the needy more generously, but if in fact it will damage their medium- or long-term economic prospects, then it is not (contrary to superficial appearances) aimed at improving and securing their access to subsistence. On a Kantian theory, the basis for judging action should be its *fundamental* principle or policy, and superficially similar acts may be judged morally very different. Regulating food aid in order to drive up prices and profit from them is one matter; regulating food aid in order to enable local farmers to sell their crops and to stay in the business of growing food quite another.

When we want to work out whether a proposed act or policy is morally required we should not, on Kant's view, try to find out whether it would produce more happiness than other available acts. Rather we should see whether the act or policy is required by, or ruled out by, or merely compatible with maxims that avoid using others as mere means and maxims that treat others as ends in themselves. These two aspects of Kantian duty can each be spelled out and shown to have determinate implications for acts and policies that may affect the risk and course of famines.

## Using Others As Mere Means

We use others as *mere means* if what we do reflects some maxim *to which they could not in principle consent*. Kant does not suggest that there is anything wrong about using someone as a means. Evidently every cooperative scheme of action does this. A government that agrees to provide free or subsidized food to famine-relief agencies both uses and is used by the agencies; a peasant who sells food in a local market both uses and is used by those who buy it. In such examples each party to the transaction can and does consent to take part in that transaction. Kant would say that the parties to such transactions use one another but do not use one another as *mere* means. Each party assumes that the other has its own maxims of action and is not just a thing or prop to be used or manipulated.

But there are other cases where one party to an arrangement or transaction not only uses the other but does so in ways that could only be done on the basis of a fundamental principle or maxim to which the other could not in principle consent.

If a false promise is given, the party that accepts the promise is not just used but used as a mere means, because it is *impossible* for consent to be given to the fundamental principle or project of deception that must guide every false promise, whatever its surface character. . . . In false promising the deceived party becomes, as it were, a prop or tool — a *mere* means — in the false promisor's scheme. . . .

Another standard way of using others as mere means is by coercing them. Coercers, like deceivers, standardly don't give others the possibility of dissenting from what they propose to do. . . . Here any "consent" given is spurious because there was no option *but* to consent. If a rich or powerful landowner or nation threatens a poorer or more vulnerable person, group, or nation with some intolerable difficulty unless a concession is made, the more vulnerable party is denied a genuine choice between consent and dissent. . . . Maxims of coercion may threaten physical force, seizure of possessions, destruction of opportunities, or any other harm that the coerced party is thought to be unable to absorb without grave injury or danger. A moneylender in a Third World village who threatens not to make or renew an indispensable loan, without which survival until the next harvest would be impossible, uses the peasant as mere means. The peasant does not have the possibility of genuinely consenting to the "offer he can't refuse." . . .

To avoid unjust action it is not enough to observe the outward forms of free agreement and cooperation; it is also essential to see that the weaker party to any arrangement has a genuine option to refuse the fundamental character of the proposal.

## Treating Others as Ends in Themselves

For Kant . . . justice is only one part of duty. We may fail in our duty, even when we don't use anyone as mere means (by deception or coercion), if we fail to treat others as "ends in themselves." To treat others as "Ends in Themselves" we must not only avoid using them as mere means but also treat them as rational and autonomous beings with their own maxims. If human beings were *wholly* rational and autonomous then, on a Kantian view, duty would require only that they not use one another as mere means. But, as Kant repeatedly stressed, but later Kantians have often forgotten, human beings are *finite* rational beings. They are finite in several ways.

First, human beings are not ideal rational calculators. We *standardly* have neither a complete list of the actions possible in a given situation nor more than a partial view of their likely consequences. In addition, abilities to assess and to use available information are usually quite limited.

Second, these cognitive limitations are *standardly* complemented by limited autonomy. Human action is limited not only by various sorts of physical barrier and inability but by further sorts of (mutual or asymmetrical) dependence. To treat one another as ends in themselves such beings have to base their action on principles that do not undermine but rather sustain and extend one another's capacities for autonomous action. A central requirement for doing so is to share and support one another's ends and activities at least to some extent. Since finite rational beings cannot generally achieve their aims without some help and support from others, a general refusal of help and support amounts to failure to treat others as rational and autonomous beings, that is as ends in themselves. Hence Kantian principles require us not only to act justly, that is in accordance with maxims that don't coerce or deceive others, but also to avoid manipulation and to lend some support to others' plans and activities. Since famine, great poverty and powerlessness all undercut the possibility of autonomous action, and the requirement of treating others as ends in themselves demands that Kantians standardly act to support the possibility of autonomous action where it is most vulnerable, Kantians are required to do what they can to avert, reduce, and remedy famine. On a Kantian view, beneficence is as indispensable as justice in human lives.

## Justice to the Vulnerable in Kantian Thinking

For Kantians, justice requires action that conforms (at least outwardly) to what could be done in a given situation while acting on maxims neither of deception nor of coercion. Since anyone hungry or destitute is more than usually vulnerable to deception and coercion, the possibilities and temptations to injustice are then especially strong. . . .

Where shortage of food is being dealt with by a reasonably fair rationing scheme, any mode of cheating to get more than one's allocated share involves using some others and is unjust. Equally, taking advantage of others' desperation to profiteer — for example, selling food at colossal prices or making loans on the security of others' future livelihood, when these are "offers they can't refuse" — constitutes coercion and so uses others as mere means and is unjust. Transactions that have the outward form of normal commercial dealing may be coercive when one party is desperate. Equally, forms of corruption that work by deception — such as bribing officials to gain special benefits from development schemes, or deceiving others about their entitlements — use others unjustly. . . .

[O]nce we remember the limitations of human rationality and autonomy, and the particular ways in which they are limited for those living close to the margins of subsistence, we can see that mere conformity to ordinary standards of commercial honesty and political bargaining is not enough for justice toward the destitute. If international agreements themselves can constitute "offers that cannot be refused" by the government of a poor country, or if the concessions required for investment by a transnational corporation or a development project reflect the desperation of recipients rather than an appropriate contribution to the project, then (however benevolent the motives of some parties) the weaker party to such agreements is used by the stronger. . . .

# Beneficence to the Vulnerable in Kantian Thinking

In Kantian moral reasoning, the basis for beneficent action is that we cannot, without it, treat others of limited rationality and autonomy as ends in themselves. This is not to say that Kantian beneficence won't make others happier, for it will do so whenever they would be happier if (more) capable of autonomous action, but that happiness secured by purely paternalistic means, or at the cost (for example) of manipulating others' desires, will not count as beneficent in the Kantian picture. Clearly the vulnerable position of those who lack the very means of life, and their severely curtailed possibilities for autonomous action, offer many different ways in which it might be possible for others to act beneficently. Where the means of life are meager, almost any material or organizational advance may help extend possibilities for autonomy. Individual or institutional action that aims to advance economic or social development can proceed on many routes. The provision of clean water, of improved agricultural techniques, of better grain storage systems, or of adequate means of local transport may all help transform material prospects. Equally, help in the development of new forms of social organization — whether peasant self-help groups, urban cooperatives, medical and contraceptive services, or improvements in education or in the position of women — may help to extend possibilities for autonomous action. . . . [W]here some activity helps secure possibilities for autonomous action for more people, or is likely to achieve a permanent improvement in the position of the most vulnerable, or is one that can be done with more reliable success, this provides reason for furthering that project rather than alternatives.

Clearly the alleviation of need must rank far ahead of the furthering of happiness in the Kantian picture. I might make my friends very happy by throwing extravagant parties: but this would probably not increase anybody's possibility for autonomous action to any great extent. But the sorts of development-oriented changes that have just been mentioned may *transform* the possibilities for action of some. Since famine and the risk of famine are always and evidently highly damaging to human autonomy, any action that helps avoid or reduce famine must have a strong claim on any Kantian who is thinking through what beneficence requires. . . .

[W]herever we find ourselves, our duties are not, on the Kantian picture, limited to those close at hand. Duties of justice arise whenever there is some involvement between parties — and in the modern world this is never lacking. Duties of beneficence arise whenever destitution puts the possibility of autonomous action in question for the more vulnerable. When famines were not only far away, but nothing could be done to relieve them, beneficence or charity may well have begun — and stayed — at home. In a global village, the moral significance of distance has shrunk, and we may be able to affect the capacities for autonomous action of those who are far away.

# The Scope of Kantian Deliberations about Famine and Hunger

. . . Kantian moral reasoning . . . does not propose a process of moral reasoning that can (in principle) rank *all* possible actions or all possible institutional arrangements from the happiness-maximizing "right" action or institution downward. It aims rather to offer a pattern of reasoning by which we can identify whether *proposed action or institutional arrangements* would be just or unjust, beneficent or lacking in beneficence. While *some* knowledge of causal connections is needed for Kantian reasoning, it is far less sensitive than is utilitarian reasoning to gaps in our causal knowledge. . . .

[T]he Kantian picture of beneficence . . . judges beneficence by its overall contribution to the prospects for human autonomy and not by the quantity of happiness expected to result. . . . For utilitarians, paternalistic imposition of, for example, certain forms of aid and development assistance need not be wrong and may even be required. But for Kantians, whose beneficence should secure others' possibilities for autonomous action, the case for paternalistic imposition of aid or development projects without the recipients' involvement must always be questionable.

In terms of some categories in which development projects are discussed, utilitarian reasoning may well endorse "top-down" aid and development projects which override whatever capacities for autonomous choice and action the poor of a certain area now have in the hopes of securing a happier future. If the calculations work out in a certain way, utilitarians may even think a "generation of sacrifice" — or of forced labor or of imposed population-control policies not only permissible but mandated. In their darkest Malthusian moments some utilitarians have thought that average happiness might best be maximized not by improving the lot of the poor but by minimizing their numbers, and so have advocated policies of "benign neglect" of the poorest and most desperate. Kantian patterns of reasoning are likely to endorse less global and less autonomy-overriding aid and development projects; they are not likely to endorse neglect or abandoning of those who are most vulnerable and lacking in autonomy. If the aim of beneficence is to keep or put others in a position to act for themselves, then emphasis must be placed on "bottom-up" projects, which from the start draw on, foster, and establish indigenous capacities and practices of self-help and local action.

# Utilitarian and Kantian Moral Reasoning

In the contrasting utilitarian and Kantian pictures of moral reasoning and of their implications in famine situations we can also discern two sharply contrasting pictures of the value of human life.

Utilitarians, since they value happiness above all, aim to achieve the happiest possible world. If . . . happiness is the supreme value, then anything may and ought to be sacrificed for the sake of a greater happiness. . . .

[W]e can see that on a utilitarian view lives must be sacrificed to build a happier world if this is the most efficient way to do so, whether or not those who lose their lives are willing. There is nothing wrong with using another as mere means, provided that the end in view is a happier result than could have been achieved any other way, taking account of the misery the means may have caused. In utilitarian thinking, persons are not ends in themselves. Their special moral status, such as it is, derives from their being means to the production of happiness. . . .

Kantians reach different conclusions about human life. They see it as valuable because humans have considerable (but still quite incomplete) capacities for autonomous action. . . .

The fundamental idea behind the Categorical Imperative is that the actions of a plurality of rational beings can be mutually consistent. A minimal condition for their mutual consistency is that each, in acting autonomously, not preclude others' autonomous action. This requirement can be spelled out, as in the formula of the end in itself, by insisting that each avoid action which the other could not freely join in (hence avoid deception and coercion) and that each seek to secure others' capacities for autonomous action. What this actually takes will, as we have seen, vary with circumstances. But it is clear enough that the partial autonomy of human beings is undermined by life-threatening and destroying circumstances, such as famine and destitution. Hence a fundamental Kantian commitment must be to preserve life in two senses. First, others must not be deprived of life. . . . Second, others' lives must be preserved in forms that offer them sufficient physical energy, psychological space, and social security for action. Partial autonomy is vulnerable autonomy, and in human life psychological and social as well as material needs must be met if any but the most meager possibility of autonomous action is to be preserved. Kantians are therefore committed to the preservation not only of biological but of biographical life. To act in the typical ways humans are capable of we must not only be alive, but have a life to lead.

On a Kantian view, we may justifiably — even nobly — risk or sacrifice our lives for others. When we do so, we act autonomously, and nobody uses us as a mere means. But we cannot justly use others (nor they us) as mere means in a scheme that could only be based on some deception or on coercion. Nor may we refuse others the help they need to sustain the very possibility of autonomous action. . . .

Where others' possibilities for autonomous action are eroded by poverty and malnutrition, the necessary action must clearly include moves to change the picture. But these moves will not meet Kantian requirements if they provide merely calories and basic medicine. The action must also seek to enable those who begin to be adequately fed to act autonomously. It must therefore aim at least at minimal security and subsistence. Hence the changes that Kantians argue or work for must always be oriented to development plans that create enough economic self-sufficiency and social security for independence in action to be feasible and sustainable.

## TEST YOUR UNDERSTANDING

1. O'Neill criticizes the **utilitarian** approach to famine because its recommendations are overly indeterminate. That is, they hinge upon too many facts that are difficult to ascertain and that remain in dispute. What factual disputes render the utilitarian approach indeterminate, and why does she regard this indeterminacy as a flaw?

2. Explain how O'Neill's approach is more oriented around "principles and intentions" than "results." Give an example of how her **Kantian** approach differs from the utilitarian approach to global poverty.

## NOTES AND QUESTIONS

1. *Why end hunger?* O'Neill argues that the primary reason to promote famine relief is to enable others' **autonomy** and help them avoid coercion. Perhaps surprisingly, she does not think the main reason to promote famine relief is to relieve the physical suffering associated with hunger.

   Consider the following objection to O'Neill's account:

   > What motivates you to eat when you are hungry is not that satisfying your hunger will help you resist coercion, but rather that hunger is uncomfortable, that your body needs nutrients, and that eating is pleasurable. Doesn't that suggest that the reasons we should enable others to eat are the same reasons we aim to satisfy our own hunger?

   Explain this objection in your own words and then consider how O'Neill should respond to it.

2. *The plural pronoun.* Most of O'Neill's essay uses the plural pronoun "we." That is, she mainly discusses what "we" should do and not what each of us should do to contribute to famine relief. One might take this as a stylistic writing choice, or one might interpret it as a more conscious decision, signaling that global poverty is a problem we share and must solve together. Is there anything about O'Neill's arguments that supports the idea that collective solutions coordinated and spearheaded by institutions and governments are more appropriate than aggregating individual efforts? Are there principled reasons to aim one's efforts toward political change and political solutions in addition to, or instead of, individual efforts at direct relief, or, in deciding what to do as an individual, should one just try to assess what actions will be most effective?

## Judith Jarvis Thomson (born 1929)

Thomson was born in New York and is Professor Emeritus at the Massachusetts Institute of Technology. She has made a number of field-defining contributions in moral theory, applied ethics, political philosophy, legal philosophy, and metaphysics. Her books include *Rights, Restitution and Risk* (1986), *The Realm of Rights* (1998), *Goodness and Advice* (2001), and *Normativity* (2006).

# A DEFENSE OF ABORTION

---

Most opposition to abortion relies on the premise that the fetus is a human being, a person, from the moment of conception. . . .

How, precisely, are we supposed to get from there to the conclusion that abortion is morally impermissible? . . .

Something like this, I take it. Every person has a right to life. So the fetus has a right to life. No doubt the mother has a right to decide what shall happen in and to her body; everyone would grant that. But surely a person's right to life is stronger and more stringent than the mother's right to decide what happens in and to her body, and so outweighs it. So the fetus may not be killed; an abortion may not be performed.

It sounds plausible. But now let me ask you to imagine this. You wake up in the morning and find yourself back to back in bed with an unconscious violinist. A famous unconscious violinist. He has been found to have a fatal kidney ailment, and the Society of Music Lovers has canvassed all the available medical records and found that you alone have the right blood type to help. They have therefore kidnapped you, and last night the violinist's circulatory system was plugged into yours, so that your kidneys can be used to extract poisons from his blood as well as your own. The director of the hospital now tells you, "Look, we're sorry the Society of Music Lovers did this to you — we would never have permitted it if we had known. But still, they did it, and the violinist now is plugged into you. To unplug you would be to kill him. But never mind, it's only for nine months. By then he will have recovered from his ailment, and can safely be unplugged from you." Is it morally incumbent on you to accede to this situation? No doubt it would be very nice of you if you did, a great kindness. But do you *have* to accede to it? What if it were not nine months, but nine years? Or longer still? What if the director of the hospital says, "Tough luck, I agree, but you've now got to stay in bed, with the violinist plugged into you, for the rest of your life. Because remember this. All persons have a right to life, and violinists are persons. Granted you have a right to decide what happens in and to your body, but a person's right to life outweighs your right to decide what happens in and to your body. So you cannot ever be unplugged from him." I imagine you would regard this as outrageous, which suggests that something really is wrong with that plausible-sounding argument I mentioned a moment ago.

In this case, of course, you were kidnapped; you didn't volunteer for the operation that plugged the violinist into your kidneys. Can those who oppose abortion on the ground I mentioned make an exception for a pregnancy due to rape? Certainly. They can say that persons have a right to life only if they didn't come into existence because of rape; or they can say that all persons have a right to life, but that some have less of a right to life than others, in particular, that those who came into existence because of rape have less. But these statements have a rather unpleasant sound. Surely the question of whether you have a right to life at all, or how much of it you have, shouldn't turn on the question of whether or not you are the product of a rape. And in fact the people who oppose abortion on the ground I mentioned do not make this distinction, and hence do not make an exception in case of rape.

Nor do they make an exception for a case in which the mother has to spend the nine months of her pregnancy in bed. They would agree that would be a great pity, and hard on the mother; but all the same, all persons have a right to life, the fetus is a person, and so on. . . .

Some won't even make an exception for a case in which continuation of the pregnancy is likely to shorten the mother's life; they regard abortion as impermissible even to save the mother's life. Such cases are nowadays very rare, and many opponents of abortion do not accept this extreme view. All the same, it is a good place to begin: a number of points of interest come out in respect to it.

1. Let us call the view that abortion is impermissible even to save the mother's life "the extreme view." I want to suggest first that it does not issue from the argument I mentioned earlier without the addition of some fairly powerful premises. Suppose a woman has become pregnant, and now learns that she has a cardiac condition such that she will die if she carries the baby to term. What may be done for her? The fetus, being a person, has a right to life, but as the mother is a person too, so has she a right to life. Presumably they have an equal right to life. How is it supposed to come out that an abortion may not be performed? If mother and child have an equal right to life, shouldn't we perhaps flip a coin? Or should we add to the mother's right to life her right to decide what happens in and to her body, which everybody seems to be ready to grant — the sum of her rights now outweighing the fetus' right to life?

The most familiar argument here is the following. We are told that performing the abortion would be directly killing the child, whereas doing nothing would not be killing the mother, but only letting her die. Moreover, in killing the child, one would be killing an innocent person, for the child has committed no crime, and is not aiming at his mother's death. And then there are a variety of ways in which this might be continued. (1) But as directly killing an innocent person is always and absolutely impermissible, an abortion may not be performed. Or, (2) as directly killing an innocent person is murder, and murder is always and absolutely impermissible, an abortion may not be performed. Or, (3) as one's duty to refrain from directly killing an innocent person is more stringent than one's duty to keep a person from dying, an abortion may not be performed. Or, (4) if one's only options are directly killing an innocent person or letting a person die, one must prefer letting the person die, and thus an abortion may not be performed.

Some people seem to have thought that these are not further premises which must be added if the conclusion is to be reached, but that they follow from the very fact that an innocent person has a right to life. But this seems to me to be a mistake, and perhaps the simplest way to show this is to bring out that while we must certainly grant that innocent persons have a right to life, the theses in (1) through (4) are all false. Take (2), for example. If directly killing an innocent person is murder, and thus is impermissible, then the mother's directly killing the innocent person inside her is murder, and thus is impermissible. But it cannot seriously be thought to be murder if the mother performs an abortion on herself to save her life. It cannot seriously be said that she *must* refrain, that she *must* sit passively by and wait for her death. Let us look again at the case of you and the violinist. There you are, in bed with the violinist, and the director of the hospital says to you, "It's all most distressing, and I deeply sympathize, but you see this is putting an additional strain on your kidneys, and you'll be dead within the month. But you *have* to stay where you are all the same. Because unplugging you would be directly killing an innocent violinist, and that's murder, and that's impermissible." If anything in the world is true, it is that you do not commit murder, you do not do what is impermissible, if you reach around to your back and unplug yourself from that violinist to save your life.

The main focus of attention in writings on abortion has been on what a third party may or may not do in answer to a request from a woman for an abortion. This is in a way understandable. Things being as they are, there isn't much a woman can safely do to abort herself. So the question asked is what a third party may do, and what the mother may do, if it is mentioned at all, is deduced, almost as an afterthought, from what it is concluded that third parties may do. But it seems to me that to treat the matter in this way is to refuse to grant to the mother that very status of person which is so firmly insisted on for the fetus. For we cannot simply read off what a person may do from what a third party may do. Suppose you find yourself trapped in a tiny house with a growing child. I mean a very tiny house, and a rapidly growing child — you are already up against the wall of the house and in a few minutes you'll be crushed to death. The child on the other hand won't be crushed to death; if nothing is done to stop him from growing he'll be hurt, but in the end he'll simply burst open the house and walk out a free man. Now I could well understand it if a bystander were to say, "There's nothing we can do for you. We cannot choose between your life and his, we cannot be the ones to decide who is to live, we cannot intervene." But it cannot be concluded that you too can do nothing, that you cannot attack it to save your life. However innocent the child may be, you do not have to wait passively while it crushes you to death. Perhaps a pregnant woman is vaguely felt to have the status of house, to which we don't allow the right of self-defense. But if the woman houses the child, it should be remembered that she is a person who houses it.

I should perhaps stop to say explicitly that I am not claiming that people have a right to do anything whatever to save their lives. I think, rather, that there are drastic limits to the right of self-defense. If someone threatens you with death unless you torture someone else to death, I think you have not the right, even to save your life, to do so. But the case under consideration here is very different. In our case there are only two people involved, one whose life is threatened, and one who threatens it. Both are innocent: the one who is threatened is not threatened because of any fault, the one who threatens does not threaten because of any fault. For this reason we may feel that we bystanders cannot intervene. But the person threatened can.

In sum, a woman surely can defend her life against the threat to it posed by the unborn child, even if doing so involves its death. And this shows not merely that the theses in (1) through (4) are false; it shows also that the extreme view of abortion is false. . . .

2. The extreme view could of course be weakened to say that while abortion is permissible to save the mother's life, it may not be performed by a third party, but only by the mother herself. But this cannot be right either. For what we have to keep in mind is that the mother and the unborn child are not like two tenants in a small house which has, by an unfortunate mistake, been rented to both: the mother *owns* the house. The fact that she does adds to the offensiveness of deducing that the mother can do nothing from the supposition that third parties can do nothing. But it does more than this. . . . Certainly it lets us see that a third party who says "I cannot choose between you" is fooling himself if he thinks this is impartiality. If Jones has found and fastened on a certain coat, which he needs to keep him from freezing, but which Smith also needs to keep him from freezing, then it is not impartiality that says "I cannot choose between you" when Smith owns the coat. Women have said again and again "This body is *my* body!" and they have reason to feel angry, reason to feel that it has been like shouting into the wind. . . .

3. Where the mother's life is not at stake, the argument I mentioned at the outset seems to have a much stronger pull. "Everyone has a right to life, so the unborn person has a right to life." And isn't the child's right to life weightier than anything other than the mother's own right to life, which she might put forward as ground for an abortion?

This argument treats the right to life as if it were unproblematic. It is not, and this seems to me to be precisely the source of the mistake.

For we should now, at long last, ask what it comes to, to have a right to life. In some views having a right to life includes having a right to be given at least the bare minimum one needs for continued life. But suppose that what in fact *is* the bare minimum a man needs for continued life is something he has no right at all to be given? If I am sick unto death, and the only thing that will save my life is the touch of Henry Fonda's cool hand on my fevered brow,[1] then all the same, I have no right to be given the touch of Henry Fonda's cool hand on my fevered brow. It would be frightfully nice of him to fly in from the West Coast to provide it. It would be less nice, though no doubt well meant, if my friends flew out to the West Coast and carried Henry Fonda back with them. But I have no right at all against anybody that he should do this for me. Or again, to return to the story I told earlier, the fact that for continued life that violinist needs the continued use of your kidneys does not establish that he has a right to be given the continued use of your kidneys. He certainly has no right against you that *you* should give him continued use of your kidneys. For nobody has any right to use your kidneys unless you give him such a right; and nobody has the right against you that you shall give him this right — if you do allow him to go on using your kidneys, this is a kindness on your part, and not something he can claim from you as his due. Nor has he any right against anybody else that *they* should give him continued use of your kidneys. Certainly he had no right against the Society of Music Lovers that they should plug him into you in the first place. And if you now start to unplug yourself,

---

1. Henry Fonda (1905–1982) was a serious actor and, for some, a heartthrob. A contemporary analog might be Denzel Washington.

having learned that you will otherwise have to spend nine years in bed with him, there is nobody in the world who must try to prevent you, in order to see to it that he is given something he has a right to be given.

Some people are rather stricter about the right to life. In their view, it does not include the right to be given anything, but amounts to, and only to, the right not to be killed by anybody. But here a related difficulty arises . . . [D]oes he have a right against everybody that they shall refrain from unplugging you from him? To refrain from doing this is to allow him to continue to use your kidneys. . . . [T]he violinist has no right against you that *you* shall allow him to continue to use your kidneys. As I said, if you do allow him to use them, it is a kindness on your part, and not something you owe him.

. . . I am not arguing that people do not have a right to life. I am arguing only that having a right to life does not guarantee having either a right to be given the use of or a right to be allowed continued use of another person's body — even if one needs it for life itself. . . .

4. In the most ordinary sort of case, to deprive someone of what he has a right to is to treat him unjustly. Suppose a boy and his small brother are jointly given a box of chocolates for Christmas. If the older boy takes the box and refuses to give his brother any of the chocolates, he is unjust to him, for the brother has been given a right to half of them. But suppose that, having learned that otherwise it means nine years in bed with that violinist, you unplug yourself from him. You surely are not being unjust to him, for you gave him no right to use your kidneys, and no one else can have given him any such right. But we have to notice that in unplugging yourself, you are killing him; and violinists, like everybody else, have a right to life, and thus in the view we were considering just now, the right not to be killed. So here you do what he supposedly has a right you shall not do, but you do not act unjustly to him in doing it.

The emendation which may be made at this point is this: the right to life consists not in the right not to be killed, but rather in the right not to be killed unjustly. This runs a risk of circularity, but never mind: it would enable us to square the fact that the violinist has a right to life with the fact that you do not act unjustly toward him in unplugging yourself, thereby killing him. For if you do not kill him unjustly, you do not violate his right to life, and so it is no wonder you do him no injustice.

But if this emendation is accepted, the gap in the argument against abortion stares us plainly in the face: it is by no means enough to show that the fetus is a person, and to remind us that all persons have a right to life — we need to be shown also that killing the fetus violates its right to life, i.e., that abortion is unjust killing. And is it?

I suppose we may take it as a datum that in a case of pregnancy due to rape the mother has not given the unborn person a right to the use of her body for food and shelter. Indeed, in what pregnancy could it be supposed that the mother has given the unborn person such a right? It is not as if there were unborn persons drifting about the world, to whom a woman who wants a child says "I invite you in."

But it might be argued that there are other ways one can have acquired a right to the use of another person's body than by having been invited to use it by that person.

Suppose a woman voluntarily indulges in intercourse, knowing of the chance it will issue in pregnancy, and then she does become pregnant; is she not in part responsible for the presence, in fact the very existence, of the unborn person inside her? No doubt she did not invite it in. But doesn't her partial responsibility for its being there itself give it a right to the use of her body? If so, then her aborting it would be more like the boy's taking away the chocolates, and less like your unplugging yourself from the violinist — doing so would be depriving it of what it does have a right to, and thus would be doing it an injustice.

And then, too, it might be asked whether or not she can kill it even to save her own life: If she voluntarily called it into existence, how can she now kill it, even in self-defense? . . .

And we should also notice that it is not at all plain that this argument really does go even as far as it purports to. For there are cases and cases, and the details make a difference. If the room is stuffy, and I therefore open a window to air it, and a burglar climbs in, it would be absurd to say "Ah, now he can stay, she's given him a right to the use of her house — for she is partially responsible for his presence there, having voluntarily done what enabled him to get in, in full knowledge that there are such things as burglars, and that burglars burgle." It would be still more absurd to say this if I had had bars installed outside my windows, precisely to prevent burglars from getting in, and a burglar got in only because of a defect in the bars. It remains equally absurd if we imagine it is not a burglar who climbs in, but an innocent person who blunders or falls in. Again, suppose it were like this: people-seeds drift about in the air like pollen, and if you open your windows, one may drift in and take root in your carpets or upholstery. You don't want children, so you fix up your windows with fine mesh screens, the very best you can buy. As can happen, however, and on very, very rare occasions does happen, one of the screens is defective; and a seed drifts in and takes root. Does the person-plant who now develops have a right to the use of your house? Surely not — despite the fact that you voluntarily opened your windows, you knowingly kept carpets and upholstered furniture, and you knew that screens were sometimes defective. Someone may argue that you are responsible for its rooting, that it does have a right to your house, because after all you *could* have lived out your life with bare floors and furniture, or with sealed windows and doors. But this won't do — for by the same token anyone can avoid a pregnancy due to rape by having a hysterectomy, or anyway by never leaving home without a (reliable!) army. . . .

5. There is room for yet another argument here, however. We surely must all grant that there may be cases in which it would be morally indecent to detach a person from your body at the cost of his life. Suppose you learn that what the violinist needs is not nine years of your life, but only one hour: all you need do to save his life is to spend one hour in that bed with him. Suppose also that letting him use your kidneys for that one hour would not affect your health in the slightest. Admittedly you were kidnapped. Admittedly you did not give anyone permission to plug him into you. Nevertheless it seems to me plain you *ought* to allow him to use your kidneys for that hour — it would be indecent to refuse.

Again, suppose pregnancy lasted only an hour, and constituted no threat to life or health. And suppose that a woman becomes pregnant as a result of rape. Admittedly she did not voluntarily do anything to bring about the existence of a child. Admittedly she did nothing at all which would give the unborn person a right to the use of her body. All the same it might well be said, as in the newly emended violinist story, that she *ought* to allow it to remain for that hour — that it would be indecent in her to refuse.

Now some people are inclined to use the term "right" in such a way that it follows from the fact that you ought to allow a person to use your body for the hour he needs, that he has a right to use your body for the hour he needs, even though he has not been given that right by any person or act. They may say that it follows also that if you refuse, you act unjustly toward him. This use of the term is perhaps so common that it cannot be called wrong; nevertheless it seems to me to be an unfortunate loosening of what we would do better to keep a tight rein on. Suppose that box of chocolates I mentioned earlier had not been given to both boys jointly, but was given only to the older boy. There he sits, stolidly eating his way through the box, his small brother watching enviously. Here we are likely to say "You ought not to be so mean. You ought to give your brother some of those chocolates." My own view is that it just does not follow from the truth of this that the brother has any right to any of the chocolates. If the boy refuses to give his brother any, he is greedy, stingy, callous — but not unjust. I suppose that the people I have in mind will say it does follow that the brother has a right to some of the chocolates, and thus that the boy does act unjustly if he refuses to give his brother any. But the effect of saying this is to obscure what we should keep distinct, namely the difference between the boy's refusal in this case and the boy's refusal in the earlier case, in which the box was given to both boys jointly, and in which the small brother thus had what was from any point of view clear title to half. . . .

So my own view is that even though you ought to let the violinist use your kidneys for the one hour he needs, we should not conclude that he has a right to do so — we should say that if you refuse, you are, like the boy who owns all the chocolates and will give none away, self-centered and callous, indecent in fact, but not unjust. And similarly, that even supposing a case in which a woman pregnant due to rape ought to allow the unborn person to use her body for the hour he needs, we should not conclude that he has a right to do so; we should conclude that she is self-centered, callous, indecent, but not unjust, if she refuses. The complaints are no less grave; they are just different. However, there is no need to insist on this point. If anyone does wish to deduce "he has a right" from "you ought," then all the same he must surely grant that there are cases in which it is not morally required of you that you allow that violinist to use your kidneys, and in which he does not have a right to use them, and in which you do not do him an injustice if you refuse. And so also for mother and unborn child. Except in such cases as the unborn person has a right to demand it — and we were leaving open the possibility that there may be such cases — nobody is morally *required* to make large sacrifices, of health, of all other interests and concerns, of all other duties and commitments, for nine years, or even for nine months, in order to keep another person alive. . . .

[W]hile I am arguing for the permissibility of abortion in some cases, I am not arguing for the right to secure the death of the unborn child. It is easy to confuse these two things in that up to a certain point in the life of the fetus it is not able to survive outside the mother's body; hence removing it from her body guarantees its death. But they are importantly different. I have argued that you are not morally required to spend nine months in bed, sustaining the life of that violinist; but to say this is by no means to say that if, when you unplug yourself, there is a miracle and he survives, you then have a right to turn round and slit his throat. You may detach yourself even if this costs him his life; you have no right to be guaranteed his death, by some other means, if unplugging yourself does not kill him. . . .

At this place, however, it should be remembered that we have only been pretending throughout that the fetus is a human being from the moment of conception. A very early abortion is surely not the killing of a person, and so is not dealt with by anything I have said here.

## TEST YOUR UNDERSTANDING

1. Assuming that an embryo or fetus has a "right to life," does it follow that abortion is wrong? In Thomson's view, what missing **premise** or missing premises would have to be defended for that conclusion to follow? Why does she regard it as doubtful that that defense could be supplied?

2. What is the "people-seeds" example and how does it address the observation that much sexual intercourse is consensual?

## NOTES AND QUESTIONS

1. *Emergency assistance.* Consider the following example offered by John Martin Fischer:[1]

   Suppose you have planned for many years to take a trip to a very remote place in the Himalaya mountains. You have secured a cabin in an extremely remote and inaccessible place in the mountains. You wish to be alone; you have enough supplies for yourself, and also have some extras in case of an emergency. Unfortunately, a very evil man has kidnapped an innocent person and brought him to die in the desolate mountain country near your cabin. The innocent person wanders for hours and finally happens upon your cabin. . . . You can radio for help, but because of the remoteness and inaccessibility of your cabin and the relatively primitive technology of the country in which it is located, the rescue party will require nine months to reach your cabin. Thus, you are faced with a

1. Fischer's case and his analysis of it appear in John Martin Fischer, "Abortion and Self-Determination," *Journal of Social Philosophy* 22 (1991): 5–11.

choice. You can let the innocent stranger into your cabin and provide food and shelter until the rescue party arrives in nine months, or you can forcibly prevent him from entering your cabin (or staying there) and thus cause his death (or perhaps allow him to die). It is evident that he will die unless you allow him to stay in the cabin.

Fischer argues that it seems that, morally, you must allow the stranger in the cabin. He then contends that this judgment casts doubt upon Thomson's claim about the violinist and, therefore, her conclusion about the moral permissibility of abortion.

*Exercise:* Consider how Thomson might reply to this objection. Is Fischer correct that you must allow the stranger in the cabin? If so, is the cabin case analogous to the violinist case, or are there important distinctions between them?

2. *Intentional conception and consensual attachment.* Thomson's main examples all involve people who are burdened without consenting to those burdens. The violinist is attached without one's consent. The people-seeds that take root in one's home are not sought or wanted. Is this a crucial feature of her argument?

*Exercise:* Suppose the argument, as Thomson presented it, is successful. Now consider a modified case similar to one introduced by Frances Kamm. As in the original case, you are the only person who could help the violinist. You consider attachment but you are concerned that the burdens may prove too great. So, on a trial basis, you permit the violinist to be attached but discover, after experiencing the burdens, that they are too constricting, painful, and taxing. In that case, would it be wrong to detach yourself?

Frances Kamm's extensive analysis of the case appears in F. M. Kamm, *Creation and Abortion* (Oxford University Press, 1992).

## Don Marquis (born 1935)

Marquis is a professor of philosophy at the University of Kansas. He is widely known for his articles in applied ethics on topics concerning procreation, death, and end-of-life decisions.

# WHY ABORTION IS IMMORAL

This essay sets out an argument that purports to show, as well as any argument in ethics can show, that abortion is, except possibly in rare cases, seriously immoral, that it is in the same moral category as killing an innocent adult human being.

The argument is based on a major assumption. Many of the most insightful and careful writers on the ethics of abortion . . . believe that whether or not abortion is morally permissible stands or falls on whether or not a fetus is the sort of being whose life it is seriously wrong to end. The argument of this essay will assume, but not argue, that they are correct.

Also, this essay will neglect issues of great importance to a complete ethics of abortion. Some anti-abortionists will allow that certain abortions, such as abortion before implantation or abortion when the life of a woman is threatened by a pregnancy or abortion after rape, may be morally permissible. This essay will not explore the casuistry of these hard cases. The purpose of this essay is to develop a general argument for the claim that the overwhelming majority of deliberate abortions are seriously immoral.

A sketch of standard anti-abortion and pro-choice arguments exhibits how those arguments possess certain symmetries that explain why partisans of those positions are so convinced of the correctness of their own positions, why they are not successful in convincing their opponents, and why, to others, this issue seems to be unresolvable. An analysis of the nature of this standoff suggests a strategy for surmounting it.

Consider the way a typical anti-abortionist argues. She will argue or assert that life is present from the moment of conception or that fetuses look like babies or that fetuses possess a characteristic such as a genetic code that is both necessary and sufficient for being human. Anti-abortionists seem to believe that (1) the truth of all of these claims is quite obvious, and (2) establishing any of these claims is sufficient to show that abortion is morally akin to murder.

A standard pro-choice strategy exhibits similarities. The pro-choicer will argue or assert that fetuses are not persons or that fetuses are not rational agents or that fetuses are not social beings. Pro-choicers seem to believe that (1) the truth of any of these claims is quite obvious, and (2) establishing any of these claims is sufficient to show that an abortion is not a wrongful killing.

In fact, both the pro-choice and the anti-abortion claims do seem to be true, although the "it looks like a baby" claim is more difficult to establish the earlier the pregnancy. We seem to have a standoff. How can it be resolved?

As everyone who has taken a bit of logic knows, if any of these arguments concerning abortion is a good argument, it requires not only some claim characterizing fetuses, but also some general moral principle that ties a characteristic of fetuses to having or not having the right to life or to some other moral characteristic that will generate the obligation or the lack of obligation not to end the life of a fetus. Accordingly, the arguments of the anti-abortionist and the pro-choicer need a bit of filling in to be regarded as adequate.

Note what each partisan will say. The anti-abortionist will claim that her position is supported by such generally accepted moral principles as "It is always prima facie seriously wrong to take a human life" or "It is always prima facie seriously wrong to end the life of a baby." Since these are generally accepted moral principles, her position is certainly not obviously wrong. The pro-choicer will claim that her position is supported by such plausible moral principles as "Being a person is what gives an individual intrinsic moral worth" or "It is only seriously prima facie wrong to take the life of a member of the human community." Since these are generally accepted moral principles, the pro-choice position is certainly not obviously wrong. Unfortunately, we have again arrived at a standoff.

Now, how might one deal with this standoff? The standard approach is to try to show how the moral principles of one's opponent lose their plausibility under analysis. It is easy to see how this is possible. On the one hand, the anti-abortionist will defend a moral principle concerning the wrongness of killing which tends to be broad in scope in order that even fetuses at an early stage of pregnancy will fall under it. The problem with broad principles is that they often embrace too much. In this particular instance, the principle "It is always prima facie wrong to take a human life" seems to entail that it is wrong to end the existence of a living human cancer-cell culture, on the grounds that the culture is both living and human. Therefore, it seems that the anti-abortionist's favored principle is too broad.

On the other hand, the pro-choicer wants to find a moral principle concerning the wrongness of killing which tends to be narrow in scope in order that fetuses will *not* fall under it. The problem with narrow principles is that they often do not embrace enough. Hence, the needed principles such as "It is prima facie seriously wrong to kill only persons" or "It is prima facie wrong to kill only rational agents" do not explain why it is wrong to kill infants or young children or the severely retarded or even perhaps the severely mentally ill. Therefore, we seem again to have a standoff. The anti-abortionist charges, not unreasonably, that pro-choice principles concerning killing are too narrow to be acceptable; the pro-choicer charges, not unreasonably, that anti-abortionist principles concerning killing are too broad to be acceptable.

Attempts by both sides to patch up the difficulties in their positions run into further difficulties. The anti-abortionist will try to remove the problem in her position by reformulating her principle concerning killing in terms of human beings. Now we end up with: "It is always prima facie seriously wrong to end the life of a human being." This principle has the advantage of avoiding the problem of the human cancer-cell culture counterexample. But this advantage is purchased at a high price. For although it is clear that a fetus is both human and alive, it is not at all clear that a fetus is a human *being*. There is at least something to be said for the view that something becomes a human being only after a process of development, and that therefore first trimester fetuses and perhaps all fetuses are not yet human beings. . . .

The pro-choicer fares no better. She may attempt to find reasons why killing in-fants, young children, and the severely retarded is wrong which are independent of her major principle that is supposed to explain the wrongness of taking human life, but which will not also make abortion immoral. This is no easy task. Appeals to social utility will seem satisfactory only to those who resolve not to think of the enormous difficulties with a utilitarian account of the wrongness of killing and the significant social costs of preserving the lives of the unproductive.[1] A pro-choice strategy that extends the definition of "person" to infants or even to young children seems just as arbitrary as an anti-abortion strategy that extends the definition of "human being" to fetuses. Again, we find symmetries in the two positions and we arrive at a standoff. . . .

There is a way out of this apparent dialectical quandary. . . .

A necessary condition of resolving the abortion controversy is a more theoretical account of the wrongness of killing. After all, if we merely believe, but do not understand, why killing adult human beings such as ourselves is wrong, how could we conceivably show that abortion is either immoral or permissible?

In order to develop such an account, we can start from the following unproblematic assumption concerning our own case: it is wrong to kill *us*. Why is it wrong? Some answers can be easily eliminated. It might be said that what makes killing us wrong is that a killing brutalizes the one who kills. But the brutalization consists of being inured to the performance of an act that is hideously immoral; hence, the brutalization does not explain the immorality. It might be said that what makes killing us wrong is the great loss others would experience due to our absence. Although such hubris is understandable, such an explanation does not account for the wrongness of killing hermits, or those whose lives are relatively independent and whose friends find it easy to make new friends.

A more obvious answer is better. What primarily makes killing wrong is neither its effect on the murderer nor its effect on the victim's friends and relatives, but its effect on the victim. The loss of one's life is one of the greatest losses one can suffer. The loss of one's life deprives one of all the experiences, activities, projects, and enjoyments that would otherwise have constituted one's future. Therefore, killing someone is wrong, primarily because the killing inflicts (one of) the greatest possible losses on the victim. To describe this as the loss of life can be misleading, however. The change in my biological state does not by itself make killing me wrong. The effect of the loss of my biological life is the loss to me of all those activities, projects, experiences, and enjoyments which would otherwise have constituted my future personal life. These activities, projects, experiences, and enjoyments are either valuable for their own sakes or are means to something else that is valuable for its own sake. Some parts

---

1. Marquis here is referring to a criticism leveled against ethical theorists, roughly labeled **utilitarians**, who attempt to explain and justify moral norms by referring to what would bring about the greatest amount of human well-being overall or what would best promote people's interests overall. They tend to demonstrate that one course of action is morally required by showing that, lumping together the effects on everyone, that course of action fulfills a greater amount of people's interests and preferences and frustrates fewer people's interests and preferences, adjusting for intensity, than any alternative course of action. Some have criticized utilitarians as being unable to explain directly, in terms of the victim's interests, why killing is wrong. After all, killing extinguishes the victim and, as a result, there is no longer a live person whose interests are frustrated, as those interests were extinguished along with the victim. This problem is thought to be particularly severe with respect to why we should save — and forbear from killing — people who will be severely disabled, given how expensive their needs are and that, if they die, they will not suffer the frustration of their interests.

of my future are not valued by me now, but will come to be valued by me as I grow older and as my values and capacities change. When I am killed, I am deprived both of what I now value which would have been part of my future personal life, but also what I would come to value. Therefore, when I die, I am deprived of all of the value of my future. Inflicting this loss on me is ultimately what makes killing me wrong. This being the case, it would seem that what makes killing *any* adult human being prima facie seriously wrong is the loss of his or her future. . . .

The claim that what makes killing wrong is the loss of the victim's future is directly supported by two considerations. In the first place, this theory explains why we regard killing as one of the worst of crimes. Killing is especially wrong, because it deprives the victim of more than perhaps any other crime. In the second place, people with AIDS or cancer who know they are dying believe, of course, that dying is a very bad thing for them.[2] They believe that the loss of a future to them that they would otherwise have experienced is what makes their premature death a very bad thing for them. . . .

[T]he claim that the loss of one's future is the wrong-making feature of one's being killed does not entail, as sanctity of human life theories do, that active euthanasia is wrong. Persons who are severely and incurably ill, who face a future of pain and despair, and who wish to die will not have suffered a loss if they are killed. It is, strictly speaking, the value of a human's future which makes killing wrong in this theory. This being so, killing does not necessarily wrong some persons who are sick and dying. Of course, there may be other reasons for a prohibition of active euthanasia, but that is another matter. Sanctity-of-human-life theories seem to hold that active euthanasia is seriously wrong even in an individual case where there seems to be good reason for it independently of public policy considerations. This consequence is most implausible, and it is a plus for the claim that the loss of a future of value is what makes killing wrong that it does not share this consequence. . . .

[T]he account of the wrongness of killing defended in this essay does straightforwardly entail that it is prima facie seriously wrong to kill children and infants, for we do presume that they have futures of value. Since we do believe that it is wrong to kill defenseless little babies, it is important that a theory of the wrongness of killing easily account for this. Personhood theories of the wrongness of killing, on the other hand, cannot straightforwardly account for the wrongness of killing infants and young children. . . .

The claim that the primary wrong-making feature of a killing is the loss to the victim of the value of its future has obvious consequences for the ethics of abortion. The future of a standard fetus includes a set of experiences, projects, activities, and such which are identical with the futures of adult human beings and are identical with the futures of young children. Since the reason that is sufficient to explain why it is wrong to kill human beings after the time of birth is a reason that also applies to fetuses, it follows that abortion is prima facie seriously morally wrong. . . .

---

2. At the time Marquis wrote, there were no effective treatments for HIV infection, and infected patients in the West rapidly deteriorated (as most do now in Africa, where treatments are financially prohibitive).

Of course, this value of a future-like-ours argument, if sound, shows only that abortion is prima facie wrong, not that it is wrong in any and all circumstances. Since the loss of the future to a standard fetus, if killed, is, however, at least as great a loss as the loss of the future to a standard adult human being who is killed, abortion, like ordinary killing, could be justified only by the most compelling reasons. The loss of one's life is almost the greatest misfortune that can happen to one. Presumably abortion could be justified in some circumstances, only if the loss consequent on failing to abort would be at least as great. Accordingly, morally permissible abortions will be rare indeed unless, perhaps, they occur so early in pregnancy that a fetus is not yet definitely an individual. Hence, this argument should be taken as showing that abortion is presumptively very seriously wrong, where the presumption is very strong — as strong as the presumption that killing another adult human being is wrong. . . .

One way to overturn the value of a future-like-ours argument would be to find some account of the wrongness of killing which is at least as intelligible and which has different implications for the ethics of abortion. Two rival accounts possess at least some degree of plausibility. One account is based on the obvious fact that people value the experience of living and wish for that valuable experience to continue. Therefore, it might be said, what makes killing wrong is the discontinuation of that experience for the victim. Let us call this the *discontinuation account*. Another rival account is based upon the obvious fact that people strongly desire to continue to live. This suggests that what makes killing us so wrong is that it interferes with the fulfillment of a strong and fundamental desire, the fulfillment of which is necessary for the fulfillment of any other desires we might have. Let us call this the *desire account*. . . .

One problem with the desire account is that we do regard it as seriously wrong to kill persons who have little desire to live or who have no desire to live or, indeed, have a desire not to live. We believe it is seriously wrong to kill the unconscious, the sleeping, those who are tired of life, and those who are suicidal. The value-of-a-human-future account renders standard morality intelligible in these cases; these cases appear to be incompatible with the desire account.

The desire account is subject to a deeper difficulty. We desire life, because we value the goods of this life. The goodness of life is not secondary to our desire for it. If this were not so, the pain of one's own premature death could be done away with merely by an appropriate alteration in the configuration of one's desires. This is absurd. Hence, it would seem that it is the loss of the goods of one's future, not the interference with the fulfillment of a strong desire to live, which accounts ultimately for the wrongness of killing. . . .

The discontinuation account looks more promising as an account of the wrongness of killing. It seems just as intelligible as the value of a future-like-ours account, but it does not justify an anti-abortion position. Obviously, if it is the continuation of one's activities, experiences, and projects, the loss of which makes killing wrong, then it is not wrong to kill fetuses for that reason, for fetuses do not have experiences, activities, and projects to be continued or discontinued. Accordingly, the discontinuation account does not have the anti-abortion consequences that the value of a future-like-ours account has. Yet, it seems as intelligible as the value of a future-like-ours account, for when we think of what would be wrong with our being killed, it does seem as if it is the discontinuation of what makes our lives worthwhile which makes killing us wrong.

Is the discontinuation account just as good an account as the value of a future-like-ours account? The discontinuation account will not be adequate at all, if it does not refer to the *value* of the experience that may be discontinued. One does not want the discontinuation account to make it wrong to kill a patient who begs for death and who is in severe pain that cannot be relieved short of killing. (I leave open the question of whether it is wrong for other reasons.) Accordingly, the discontinuation account must be more than a bare discontinuation account. It must make some reference to the positive value of the patient's experiences. But, by the same token, the value of a future-like-ours account cannot be a bare future account either. Just having a future surely does not itself rule out killing the above patient. This account must make some reference to the value of the patient's future experiences and projects also. Hence, both accounts involve the value of experiences, projects, and activities. So far we still have symmetry between the accounts.

The symmetry fades, however, when we focus on the time period of the value of the experiences, etc., which has moral consequences. Although both accounts leave open the possibility that the patient in our example may be killed, this possibility is left open only in virtue of the utterly bleak future for the patient. It makes no difference whether the patient's immediate past contains intolerable pain, or consists in being in a coma (which we can imagine is a situation of indifference), or consists in a life of value. If the patient's future is a future of value, we want our account to make it wrong to kill the patient. If the patient's future is intolerable, whatever his or her immediate past, we want our account to allow killing the patient. Obviously, then, it is the value of that patient's future which is doing the work in rendering the morality of killing the patient intelligible.

This being the case, it seems clear that whether one has immediate past experiences or not does no work in the explanation of what makes killing wrong. The addition the discontinuation account makes to the value of a human future account is otiose. Its addition to the value-of-a-future account plays no role at all in rendering intelligible the wrongness of killing. Therefore, it can be discarded with the discontinuation account of which it is a part. . . .

In this essay, it has been argued that the correct ethic of the wrongness of killing can be extended to fetal life and used to show that there is a strong presumption that any abortion is morally impermissible. If the ethic of killing adopted here entails, however, that contraception is also seriously immoral, then there would appear to be a difficulty with the analysis of this essay.

But this analysis does not entail that contraception is wrong. Of course, contraception prevents the actualization of a possible future of value. Hence, it follows from the claim that futures of value should be maximized that contraception is prima facie immoral. This obligation to maximize does not exist, however; furthermore, nothing in the ethics of killing in this paper entails that it does. The ethics of killing in this essay would entail that contraception is wrong only if something were denied a human future of value by contraception. Nothing at all is denied such a future by contraception, however.

Candidates for a subject of harm by contraception fall into four categories: (1) some sperm or other, (2) some ovum or other, (3) a sperm and an ovum separately, and (4) a sperm and an ovum together. Assigning the harm to some sperm is utterly arbitrary, for no reason can be given for making a sperm the subject of harm rather than an ovum. Assigning the harm to some ovum is utterly arbitrary, for no reason can be given for making an ovum the subject of harm rather than a sperm. One might attempt to avoid these problems by insisting that contraception deprives both the sperm and the ovum separately of a valuable future like ours. On this alternative, too many futures are lost. Contraception was supposed to be wrong, because it deprived us of one future of value, not two. One might attempt to avoid this problem by holding that contraception deprives the combination of sperm and ovum of a valuable future like ours. But here the definite article misleads. At the time of contraception, there are hundreds of millions of sperm, one (released) ovum and millions of possible combinations of all of these. There is no actual combination at all. Is the subject of the loss to be a merely possible combination? Which one? This alternative does not yield an actual subject of harm either. Accordingly, the immorality of contraception is not entailed by the loss of a future-like-ours argument simply because there is no nonarbitrarily identifiable subject of the loss in the case of contraception.

The purpose of this essay has been to set out an argument for the serious presumptive wrongness of abortion subject to the assumption that the moral permissibility of abortion stands or falls on the moral status of the fetus. Since a fetus possesses a property, the possession of which in adult human beings is sufficient to make killing an adult human being wrong, abortion is wrong. This way of dealing with the problem of abortion seems superior to other approaches to the ethics of abortion, because it rests on an ethics of killing which is close to self-evident, because the crucial morally relevant property clearly applies to fetuses, and because the argument avoids the usual equivocations on "human life," "human being," or "person." The argument rests neither on religious claims nor on Papal dogma. It is not subject to the objection of "speciesism." Its soundness is compatible with the moral permissibility of euthanasia and contraception. It deals with our intuitions concerning young children.

Finally, this analysis can be viewed as resolving a standard problem — indeed, *the* standard problem — concerning the ethics of abortion. Clearly, it is wrong to kill adult human beings. Clearly, it is not wrong to end the life of some arbitrarily chosen single human cell. Fetuses seem to be like arbitrarily chosen human cells in some respects and like adult humans in other respects. The problem of the ethics of abortion is the problem of determining the fetal property that settles this moral controversy. The thesis of this essay is that the problem of the ethics of abortion, so understood, is solvable.

## TEST YOUR UNDERSTANDING

1. Contraception prevents the creation of an embryo. Thereby, a potential person who would emerge from the embryo does not enjoy the future she might have had, had her creation not been prevented. Nevertheless, Marquis distinguishes between the moral status of abortion and that of contraception. Explain the distinction he draws in your own words.

2. Why does Marquis believe that the morality of abortion depends less on whether in light of an embryo's or fetus's characteristics it is a human being or closely resembles a baby, and more on facts about the potential future of a fetus or embryo?

## NOTES AND QUESTIONS

1. *Does having a personality matter?* Don Marquis argues that a fetus who dies and an adult who dies prematurely are harmed in the same way. Both are deprived of their future and, in particular, enjoying life's goods and opportunities.

   Consider the following objection to his argument:

   > We regard the deaths of adults and children as tragedies because they have distinctive personalities, interests, desires, and characteristics that make their lives worth living. The death of an adult or a child eliminates the future of that distinctive, individual personality and the pursuit of its development and projects. The death of a fetus differs because the fetus does not yet have any distinctively individual features.

   Explain this objection and consider how Marquis might respond.

2. *The significance of potential.* Don Marquis's argument for the "serious presumptive wrongness of abortion" appeals to the fact that "a fetus possesses a property" such that killing it would be wrong. Namely, the fetus has the potential for a valuable future if it is not killed.

   What if kittens could have valuable futures analogous to that of adults? Michael Tooley offered the following thought experiment in his essay "Abortion and Infanticide," *Philosophy & Public Affairs* 2 (Autumn, 1972): 37–65:

   > Suppose at some future time a chemical were to be discovered which when injected into the brain of a kitten would cause the kitten to develop into a cat possessing a brain of the sort possessed by humans, and consequently into a cat having all the psychological capabilities characteristic of adult humans. Such cats would be able to think, to use language, and so on.

   *Exercise:* Consider the objection that Marquis's argument implausibly suggests that failing to inject the kitten is "seriously morally wrong" because it would deprive the kitten of the sort of valuable future that we think it is wrong to deprive adults of. Consider the related objection that Marquis's argument suggests if such a chemical were available: killing the kitten instead of injecting it would be comparable to killing an adult human being, for both actions would deprive a being of a valuable future that she could enjoy. How might Marquis respond to these objections?

## Thomas Nagel (born 1937)

Nagel is Emeritus University Professor of Philosophy and Law at New York University. He has made influential contributions to ethics, political philosophy, epistemology, and philosophy of mind. His books include *The Possibility of Altruism* (1970), *The View from Nowhere* (1986), *Equality and Partiality* (1991), and *Mind and Cosmos* (2012).

# WAR AND MASSACRE

I wish to argue that certain [moral] restrictions [on the conduct of war] are neither arbitrary nor merely conventional, and that their validity does not depend simply on their usefulness. There is, in other words, a moral basis for the rules of war. . . .

## I

I propose to discuss the most general moral problem raised by the conduct of warfare: the problem of means and ends. In one view, there are limits on what may be done even in the service of an end worth pursuing — and even when adherence to the restriction may be very costly. A person who acknowledges the force of such restrictions can find himself in acute moral dilemmas. He may believe, for example, that by torturing a prisoner he can obtain information necessary to prevent a disaster, or that by obliterating one village with bombs he can halt a campaign of terrorism. If he believes that the gains from a certain measure will clearly outweigh its costs, yet still suspects that he ought not to adopt it, then he is in a dilemma produced by the conflict between two disparate categories of moral reason: categories that may be called *utilitarian* and *absolutist*.

Utilitarianism gives primacy to a concern with what will *happen*. Absolutism gives primacy to a concern with what one is *doing*. The conflict between them arises because the alternatives we face are rarely just choices between *total outcomes*: they are also choices between alternative pathways or measures to be taken. . . .

## II

Utilitarianism says that one should try, either individually or through institutions, to maximize good and minimize evil . . . and that if faced with the possibility of preventing a great evil by producing a lesser, one should choose the lesser evil. There are certainly problems about the formulation of utilitarianism, and much has been written about it, but its intent is morally transparent. Nevertheless, despite the addition of various refinements, it continues to leave large portions of ethics unaccounted for. I do not suggest that some form of absolutism can account for them all, only that an examination of absolutism will lead us to see the complexity, and perhaps the incoherence, of our moral ideas.

Utilitarianism certainly justifies *some* restrictions on the conduct of warfare. There are strong utilitarian reasons for adhering to any limitation which seems natural to most people — particularly if the limitation is widely accepted already. An exceptional measure which seems to be justified by its results in a particular conflict may create a precedent with disastrous long-term effects. It may even be argued that war involves violence on such a scale that it is never justified on utilitarian grounds — the consequences of refusing to go to war will never be as bad as the war itself would be, even if atrocities were not committed. . . . But I shall not consider these arguments, for my concern is with reasons of a different kind, which may remain when reasons of utility and interest fail. . . .

In the final analysis, I believe that the dilemma cannot always be resolved. While not every conflict between absolutism and utilitarianism creates an insoluble dilemma, and while it is certainly right to adhere to absolutist restrictions unless the utilitarian considerations favoring violation are overpoweringly weighty and extremely certain — nevertheless, when that special condition is met, it may become impossible to adhere to an absolutist position. What I shall offer, therefore, is a somewhat qualified defense of absolutism. I believe it underlies a valid and fundamental type of moral judgment—which cannot be reduced to or overridden by other principles. And while there may be other principles just as fundamental, it is particularly important not to lose confidence in our absolutist intuitions, for they are often the only barrier before the abyss of utilitarian apologetics for large-scale murder.

## III

One absolutist position that creates no problems of interpretation is pacifism: the view that one may not kill another person under any circumstances, no matter what good would be achieved or evil averted thereby. The type of absolutist position that I am going to discuss is different. Pacifism draws the conflict with utilitarian considerations very starkly. But there are other views according to which violence may be undertaken, even on a large scale, in a clearly just cause, so long as certain absolute restrictions on the character and direction of that violence are observed. The line is drawn somewhat closer to the bone, but it exists.

The philosopher who has done most to advance contemporary philosophical discussion of such a view, and to explain it to those unfamiliar with its extensive treatment in Roman Catholic moral theology, is G.E.M. Anscombe. In 1958 Miss Anscombe published a pamphlet entitled *Mr. Truman's Degree* on the occasion of the award by Oxford University of an honorary doctorate to Harry Truman.[1] The pamphlet explained why she had opposed the decision to award that degree, recounted the story of her unsuccessful opposition, and offered some reflections on the history of Truman's decision to drop atom bombs on Hiroshima and Nagasaki, and on the difference between murder and allowable killing in warfare. . . .

The policy of attacking the civilian population in order to induce an enemy to surrender, or to damage his morale, seems to have been widely accepted in the civilized world, and seems to be accepted still, at least if the stakes are high enough. It gives evidence of a moral conviction that the deliberate killing of noncombatants — women, children, old people — is permissible if enough can be gained by it. This follows from the more general position that any means can in principle be justified if it leads to a sufficiently worthy end. Such an attitude is evident not only in the more spectacular current weapons systems but also in the day-to-day conduct of the nonglobal war in Indochina:[2] the indiscriminate destructiveness of antipersonnel weapons, napalm, and aerial bombardment; cruelty to prisoners; massive relocation of civilians; destruction of crops; and so forth. An absolutist position opposes to this the view that certain acts cannot be justified no matter what the consequences. Among those acts is murder — the deliberate killing of the harmless: civilians, prisoners of war, and medical personnel. . . .

Many people feel, without being able to say much more about it, that something has gone seriously wrong when certain measures are admitted into consideration in the first place. The fundamental mistake is made there, rather than at the point where the overall benefit of some monstrous measure is judged to outweigh its disadvantages, and it is adopted. An account of absolutism might help us to understand this. If it is not allowable to *do* certain things, such as killing unarmed prisoners or civilians, then no argument about what will happen if one doesn't do them can show that doing them would be all right.

Absolutism does not, of course, require one to ignore the consequences of one's acts. It operates as a limitation on utilitarian reasoning, not as a substitute for it. An absolutist can be expected to try to maximize good and minimize evil, so long as this does not require him to transgress an absolute prohibition like that against murder. But when such a conflict occurs, the prohibition takes complete precedence over any consideration of consequences. Some of the results of this view are clear enough. It requires us to forgo certain potentially useful military measures, such as the slaughter of hostages and prisoners or indiscriminate attempts to reduce the enemy civilian population by starvation, epidemic infectious diseases like anthrax and bubonic plague, or mass incineration. It means that we cannot deliberate on whether such measures are justified by the fact that they will avert still greater evils, for as intentional measures they cannot be justified in terms of any consequences whatever. . . .

1. Excerpted on p. 829 of this anthology.

2. Here, and throughout the essay, Nagel refers to the events and policies of the United States in the Vietnam War (1955–75).

# IV

[T]here remain a few relatively technical matters which are best discussed at this point.

First, it is important to specify as clearly as possible the kind of thing to which absolutist prohibitions can apply. We must take seriously the proviso that they concern what we deliberately do to people. There could not, for example, without incoherence, be an absolute prohibition against *bringing about* the death of an innocent person. For one may find oneself in a situation in which, no matter what one does, some innocent people will die as a result. I do not mean just that there are cases in which someone will die no matter what one does, because one is not in a position to affect the outcome one way or the other. That, it is to be hoped, is one's relation to the deaths of most innocent people. I have in mind, rather, a case in which someone is bound to die, but who it is will depend on what one does. Sometimes these situations have natural causes, as when too few resources (medicine, lifeboats) are available to rescue everyone threatened with a certain catastrophe. . . . Whatever one does in cases such as these, some innocent people will die as a result. If the absolutist prohibition forbade doing what would result in the deaths of innocent people, it would have the consequence that in such cases nothing one could do would be morally permissible.

This problem is avoided, however, because what absolutism forbids is *doing* certain things to people, rather than bringing about certain *results*. Not everything that happens to others as a result of what one does is something that one has *done* to them. Catholic moral theology seeks to make this distinction precise in a doctrine known as the law of double effect, which asserts that there is a morally relevant distinction between bringing about the death of an innocent person deliberately, either as an end in itself or as a means, and bringing it about as a side effect of something else one does deliberately. In the latter case, even if the outcome is foreseen, it is not murder, and does not fall under the absolute prohibition, though of course it may still be wrong for other reasons (reasons of utility, for example).[3] Briefly, the principle states that one is sometimes permitted knowingly to bring about as a side effect of one's actions something which it would be absolutely impermissible to bring about deliberately as an end or as a means. In application to war or revolution, the law of double effect permits a certain amount of civilian carnage as a side effect of bombing munitions plants or attacking enemy soldiers. And even this is permissible only if the cost is not too great to be justified by one's objectives.

However, despite its importance and its usefulness in accounting for certain plausible moral judgments, . . . the law of double effect . . . is not always clear, so that it introduces uncertainty where there need not be uncertainty.

In Indochina, for example, there is a great deal of aerial bombardment, strafing, spraying of napalm, and employment of pellet- or needle-spraying antipersonnel weapons against rural villages in which guerrillas are suspected to be hiding, or from

---

3. The **doctrine of double effect** is also discussed by G.E.M. Anscombe, Thomas Scanlon, and Barbara Herman in the selections in chapter 17 and by John Rawls in the next selection in this chapter.

which small-arms fire has been received. The majority of those killed and wounded in these aerial attacks are reported to be women and children, even when some combatants are caught as well. However, the government regards these civilian casualties as a regrettable side effect of what is a legitimate attack against an armed enemy.

It might be thought easy to dismiss this as sophistry: if one bombs, burns, or strafes a village containing a hundred people, twenty of whom one believes to be guerrillas, so that by killing most of them one will be statistically likely to kill most of the guerrillas, then isn't one's attack on the group of one hundred a *means* of destroying the guerrillas, pure and simple? . . .

The difficulty is that this argument depends on one particular description of the act, and the reply might be that the means used against the guerrillas is not: killing everybody in the village — but rather: obliteration bombing of the *area* in which the twenty guerrillas are known to be located. If there are civilians in the area as well, they will be killed as a side effect of such action.

Because of casuistical problems like this, I prefer to stay with the original, unanalyzed distinction between what one does to people and what merely happens to them as a result of what one does. . . . It is clear that by bombing the village one slaughters and maims the civilians in it. Whereas by giving the only available medicine to one of two sufferers from a disease, one does not kill the other, even if he dies as a result.

The second technical point[:] . . . [t]he absolutist focus on actions rather than outcomes does not merely introduce a new, outstanding item into the catalogue of evils. That is, it does not say that the worst thing in the world is the deliberate murder of an innocent person. For if that were all, then one could presumably justify one such murder on the ground that it would prevent several others, or ten thousand on the ground that they would prevent a hundred thousand more. . . . But if this is allowable, then there is no absolute prohibition against murder after all. Absolutism requires that we *avoid* murder at all costs, not that we *prevent* it at all costs.

Finally, let me remark on a frequent criticism of absolutism that depends on a misunderstanding. It is sometimes suggested that such prohibitions depend on a kind of moral self-interest, a primary obligation to preserve one's own moral purity, to keep one's hands clean no matter what happens to the rest of the world. If this were the position, it might be exposed to the charge of self-indulgence. After all, what gives one man a right to put the purity of his soul or the cleanness of his hands above the lives or welfare of large numbers of other people? . . .

But there are two confusions behind the view that moral self-interest underlies moral absolutism. First, it is a confusion to suggest that the need to preserve one's moral purity might be the *source* of an obligation. For if by committing murder one sacrifices one's moral purity or integrity, that can only be because there is *already* something wrong with murder. The general reason against committing murder cannot therefore be merely that it makes one an immoral person. Secondly, the notion that one might sacrifice one's moral integrity justifiably, in the service of a sufficiently worthy end, is an incoherent notion. For if one were justified in making such a sacrifice . . . then one would not be sacrificing one's moral integrity by adopting that course: one would be preserving it. . . .

# V

It is easier to dispose of false explanations of absolutism than to produce a true one. A positive account of the matter must begin with the observation that war, conflict, and aggression are relations between persons. . . . A man's acts usually affect more people than he deals with directly, and those effects must naturally be considered in his decisions. But if there are special principles governing the manner in which he should *treat* people, that will require special attention to the particular persons toward whom the act is directed, rather than just to its total effect.

Absolutist restrictions in warfare appear to be of two types: restrictions on the class of persons at whom aggression or violence may be directed and restrictions on the manner of attack, given that the object falls within that class. These can be combined, however, under the principle that hostile treatment of any person must be justified in terms of something *about that person* which makes the treatment appropriate. Hostility is a personal relation, and it must be suited to its target. One consequence of this condition will be that certain persons may not be subjected to hostile treatment in war at all, since nothing about them justifies such treatment. Others will be proper objects of hostility only in certain circumstances, or when they are engaged in certain pursuits. And the appropriate manner and extent of hostile treatment will depend on what is justified by the particular case.

A coherent view of this type will hold that extremely hostile behavior toward another is compatible with treating him as a person — even perhaps as an end in himself. . . . If hostile, aggressive, or combative treatment of others always violated the condition that they be treated as human beings, it would be difficult to make further distinctions on that score *within* the class of hostile actions. That point of view, on the level of international relations, leads to the position that if complete pacifism is not accepted, no holds need be barred at all, and we may slaughter and massacre to our hearts' content, if it seems advisable.

But the fact is that ordinary people do not believe this about conflicts, physical or otherwise, between individuals, and there is no more reason why it should be true of conflicts between nations. There seems to be a perfectly natural conception of the distinction between fighting clean and fighting dirty. To fight dirty is to direct one's hostility or aggression not at its proper object, but at a peripheral target which may be more vulnerable, and through which the proper object can be attacked indirectly. This applies in a fist fight, an election campaign, a duel, or a philosophical argument. If the concept is general enough to apply to all these matters, it should apply to war — both to the conduct of individual soldiers and to the conduct of nations.

Suppose that you are a candidate for public office, convinced that the election of your opponent would be a disaster, that he is an unscrupulous demagogue who will serve a narrow range of interests and seriously infringe the rights of those who disagree with him; and suppose you are convinced that you cannot defeat him by conventional means. Now imagine that various unconventional means present themselves as possibilities: you possess information about his sex life which would scandalize the electorate if made public; or you learn that his wife is an alcoholic or that in his youth he was associated for a brief period with a proscribed political party, and you believe that this information could be used to blackmail him into withdrawing his candidacy; or you can have a team of your supporters flatten the tires of a crucial subset of his supporters on election day; or you are in a position to stuff the ballot boxes; or, more simply, you can have him assassinated. What is wrong with these methods, given that they will achieve an overwhelmingly desirable result?

There are, of course, many things wrong with them: some are against the law; some infringe the procedures of an electoral process to which you are presumably committed by taking part in it; very importantly, some may backfire, and it is in the interest of all political candidates to adhere to an unspoken agreement not to allow certain personal matters to intrude into a campaign. But that is not all. We have in addition the feeling that these measures, these methods of attack are *irrelevant* to the issue between you and your opponent, that in taking them up you would not be directing yourself to that which makes him an object of your opposition. You would be directing your attack not at the true target of your hostility, but at peripheral targets that happen to be vulnerable.

The same is true of a fight or argument outside the framework of any system of regulations or law. In an altercation with a taxi driver over an excessive fare, it is inappropriate to taunt him about his accent, flatten one of his tires, or smear chewing gum on his windshield; and it remains inappropriate even if he casts aspersions on your race, politics, or religion, or dumps the contents of your suitcase into the street.

The[se] . . . restrictions . . . all derive from a single principle: that hostility or aggression should be directed at its true object. This means both that it should be directed at the person or persons who provoke it and that it should aim more specifically at what is provocative about them. The second condition will determine what form the hostility may appropriately take. . . .

[T]he idea is difficult to state. I believe it is roughly this: whatever one does to another person intentionally must be aimed at him as a subject, with the intention that he receive it as a subject. It should manifest an attitude to *him* rather than just to the situation, and he should be able to recognize it and identify himself as its object. The procedures by which such an attitude is manifested need not be addressed to the person directly. Surgery, for example, is not a form of personal confrontation but part of a medical treatment that can be offered to a patient face to face and received by him as a response to his needs and the natural outcome of an attitude toward *him*.

Hostile treatment, unlike surgery, is already addressed *to* a person, and does not take its interpersonal meaning from a wider context. But hostile acts can serve as the expression or implementation of only a limited range of attitudes to the person who is attacked. Those attitudes in turn have as objects certain real or presumed characteristics or activities of the person which are thought to justify them. When this background is absent, hostile or aggressive behavior can no longer be intended for the reception of the victim as a subject. Instead it takes on the character of a purely bureaucratic operation. This occurs when one attacks someone who is not the true object of one's hostility — the true object may be someone else, who can be attacked through the victim; or one may not be manifesting a hostile attitude toward anyone, but merely using the easiest available path to some desired goal. One finds oneself not facing or addressing the victim at all, but operating on him — without the larger context of personal interaction that surrounds a surgical operation.

If absolutism is to defend its claim to priority over considerations of utility, it must hold that the maintenance of a direct interpersonal response to the people one deals with is a requirement which no advantages can justify one in abandoning. The requirement is absolute only if it rules out any calculation of what would justify its violation. [T]here may be circumstances so extreme that they render an absolutist position untenable. One may find then that one has no choice but to do something terrible. . . .

VI

I have said that there are two types of absolutist restrictions on the conduct of war: those that limit the legitimate targets of hostility and those that limit its character, even when the target is acceptable. I shall say something about each of these. . . .

First let us see how it implies that attacks on some people are allowed, but not attacks on others. It may seem paradoxical to assert that to fire a machine gun at someone who is throwing hand grenades at your emplacement is to treat him as a human being. Yet the relation with him is direct and straightforward. The attack is aimed specifically against the threat presented by a dangerous adversary, and not against a peripheral target through which he happens to be vulnerable but which has nothing to do with that threat. For example, you might stop him by machine-gunning his wife and children, who are standing nearby, thus distracting him from his aim of blowing you up and enabling you to capture him. But if his wife and children are not threatening your life, that would be to treat them as means with a vengeance.

This, however, is just Hiroshima on a smaller scale. One objection to weapons of mass annihilation — nuclear, thermonuclear, biological, or chemical — is that their indiscriminateness disqualifies them as direct instruments for the expression of hostile relations. In attacking the civilian population, one treats neither the military enemy nor the civilians with that minimal respect which is owed to them as human beings. This is clearly true of the direct attack on people who present no threat at all. But it is also true of the character of the attack on those who are threatening you, viz., the government and military forces of the enemy. Your aggression is directed against an area of vulnerability quite distinct from any threat presented by them which you may be justified in meeting. You are taking aim at them through the mundane life and survival of their countrymen, instead of aiming at the destruction of their military capacity. . . .

This . . . also helps us to understand the importance of the distinction between combatants and noncombatants. . . . According to an absolutist position, deliberate killing of the innocent is murder, and in warfare the role of the innocent is filled by noncombatants. . . .

In the absolutist position, the operative notion of innocence is not moral innocence, and it is not opposed to moral guilt. If it were, then we would be justified in killing a wicked but noncombatant hairdresser in an enemy city who supported the evil policies of his government, and unjustified in killing a morally pure conscript who was driving a tank toward us with the profoundest regrets and nothing but love in his heart. But moral innocence has very little to do with it, for in the definition of murder "innocent" means "currently harmless," and it is opposed not to "guilty" but to "doing harm." . . . [I]n war we may often be justified in killing people who do not deserve to die, and unjustified in killing people who do deserve to die, if anyone does.

So we must distinguish combatants from noncombatants on the basis of their immediate threat or harmfulness. . . . Children are not combatants even though they may join the armed forces if they are allowed to grow up. Women are not combatants just because they bear children or offer comfort to the soldiers. More problematic are the supporting personnel, whether in or out of uniform, from drivers of munitions trucks and army cooks to civilian munitions workers and farmers. I believe they can be plausibly classified by applying the condition that the prosecution of conflict must direct itself to the cause of danger, and not to what is peripheral. The threat presented by an army and its members does not consist merely in the fact that they are men, but in the fact that they are armed and are using their arms in the pursuit of certain objectives. Contributions to their arms and logistics are contributions to this threat; contributions to their mere existence as men are not. It is therefore wrong to direct an attack against those who merely serve the combatants' needs as human beings, such as farmers and food suppliers, even though survival as a human being is a necessary condition of efficient functioning as a soldier.

This brings us to the second group of restrictions: those that limit what may be done even to combatants. . . .

One provision of the rules of war which is universally recognized . . . is the special status of medical personnel and the wounded in warfare. It might be more efficient to shoot medical officers on sight and to let the enemy wounded die rather than be patched up to fight another day. But someone with medical insignia is supposed to be left alone and permitted to tend and retrieve the wounded. I believe this is because medical attention is a species of attention to completely general human needs, not specifically the needs of a combat soldier, and our conflict with the soldier is not with his existence as a human being.

By extending the application of this idea, one can justify prohibitions against certain particularly cruel weapons: starvation, poisoning, infectious diseases (supposing they could be inflicted on combatants only), weapons designed to maim or disfigure or torture the opponent rather than merely to stop him. It is not, I think, mere casuistry to claim that such weapons attack the men, not the soldiers. . . .

Finally, the same condition of appropriateness to the true object of hostility should limit the scope of attacks on an enemy country: its economy, agriculture, transportation system, and so forth. Even if the parties to a military conflict are considered to be not armies or governments but entire nations (which is usually a grave error), that does not justify one nation in warring against every aspect or element of another nation. That is not justified in a conflict between individuals, and nations are even more complex than individuals, so the same reasons apply. Like a human being, a nation is engaged in countless other pursuits while waging war, and it is not in those respects that it is an enemy. . . .

# VII

Having described the elements of the absolutist position, we must now return to the conflict between it and utilitarianism. Even if certain types of dirty tactics become acceptable when the stakes are high enough, the most serious of the prohibited acts, like murder and torture, are not just supposed to require unusually strong justification. They are supposed *never* to be done, because no quantity of resulting benefit is thought capable of *justifying* such treatment of a person.

The fact remains that when an absolutist knows or believes that the utilitarian cost of refusing to adopt a prohibited course will be very high, he may hold to his refusal to adopt it, but he will find it difficult to feel that a moral dilemma has been satisfactorily resolved. The same may be true of someone who rejects an absolutist requirement and adopts instead the course yielding the most acceptable consequences. In either case, it is possible to feel that one has acted for reasons insufficient to justify violation of the opposing principle. . . .

There may exist principles, not yet codified, which would enable us to resolve such dilemmas. But then again there may not. We must face the pessimistic alternative that these two forms of moral intuition are not capable of being brought together into a single, coherent moral system, and that the world can present us with situations in which there is no honorable or moral course for a man to take, no course free of guilt and responsibility for evil.

## TEST YOUR UNDERSTANDING

1. What is the moral distinction, for Nagel, between killing enemy soldiers who are aiming guns at your platoon and destroying the medical supply of an enemy platoon so the enemy soldiers cannot recover from your platoon's debilitating attack?

2. Why are soldiers permissible objects of military attack but not the farmers who produce food that supply the troops?

## NOTES AND QUESTIONS

1. *Trade-offs.* Nagel's absolutism prohibits a soldier from torturing an enemy soldier because torture "attacks the man, not the soldier." Suppose, however, that one knew that if one tortured one particular soldier, one could gain the information that would permit one to prevent an enemy plan to capture and torture hundreds of other people. Would Nagel endorse torture of one person to prevent the torture of hundreds of others? Why or why not?

2. *Nonlethal force as a substitute for appropriate hostility.* Nagel argues that one may respond to a hostile aggressor with hostile responsive action that aims to impede or end the aggression. Further, one is entitled to use lethal force to do so, if the aggression is serious enough and if lesser means will not suffice to impede the aggression. So, one may kill soldiers in self-defense, but one may not, he says, interrupt food or medical supplies to enemy soldiers, because one's dispute is not with their human needs but only with their aggressive action.

    Consider the following objection:

    You say that denying food or medical supplies to enemy soldiers is disrespectful of their humanity. But, suppose doing so only rendered them ravenous and sick. Isn't that outcome better and more respectful of their humanity than killing them?

    How should Nagel respond?

## John Rawls (1921–2002)

After receiving his PhD from Princeton University in 1950, Rawls taught at Princeton, Cornell University, and the Massachusetts Institute of Technology, before joining the Harvard University faculty in 1962. At his retirement from Harvard in 1991, he was James Conant Bryant University Professor. Rawls wrote three powerful and influential books of political philosophy: *A Theory of Justice* (1971), *Political Liberalism* (1993), and *The Law of Peoples* (1999).

# ON THE KILLING OF CIVILIANS IN WARTIME
## from *The Law of Peoples*

*Editor's note: This excerpt is from a book by John Rawls that advances a theory of the principles of international justice. Reading the excerpt will be easier if you know a little about Rawls's terminology and methodology. The book's focus is on how "well-ordered peoples" would govern their relations with each other, that is, on what rules those societies of people motivated to cooperate and to comply with rules of international justice would choose to follow in their mutual relations. In thinking about what rules "well-ordered peoples" would, if reasonable, choose, Rawls means* *to situate his theory in the "**social contract**" tradition, an approach to political philosophy that understands the principles of political philosophy as those that parties have or would agree to. By "well-ordered peoples," he means to refer to societies that aim to follow the rules of international justice and are either constitutional liberal democracies or "decent" societies that, although they do not fully subscribe to liberal, constitutional rights or implement a democratic structure of government, nonetheless respect basic human rights, apply minimal standards of domestic justice toward their members, and allow for political participation and input by citizens. Rawls aims to provide a "political conception" of these principles of justice, by which he means a conception that people with quite different beliefs about ethics, religion, and morality could agree to with respect to their political interactions. Rawls hopes that an "overlapping consensus" around this "political conception" could be built by people who regard these political principles as just and not merely as an expedient compromise, even while they retain quite different comprehensive normative views about how each is to lead his or her life. Rawls calls his proposed theory of the principles of international justice that well-ordered people would reasonably agree to "The Law of Peoples," and occasionally, "political liberalism."*

*In this part of the book, Rawls discusses what constraints justice places on the conduct of well-ordered peoples, should they find themselves at war with what he calls "outlaw" states, by which he means political regimes that are unwilling to comply with "The Law of Peoples."*

---

Well-ordered peoples do not initiate war against one another; they go to war only when they sincerely and reasonably believe that their safety and security are seriously endangered by the expansionist policies of outlaw states. . . .

When a liberal society engages in war in self-defense, it does so to protect and preserve the basic freedoms of its citizens and its constitutionally democratic political institutions. Indeed, a liberal society cannot justly require its citizens to fight in order to gain economic wealth or to acquire natural resources, much less to win power and empire. (When a society pursues these interests, it no longer honors the Law of Peoples, and it becomes an outlaw state.) To trespass on citizens' liberty by conscription, or other such practices in raising armed forces, may only be done on a liberal political conception for the sake of liberty itself, that is, as necessary to defend liberal democratic institutions and civil society's many religious and nonreligious traditions and forms of life. . . .

Their defense is, however, only their first and most urgent task. Their long-run aim is to bring all societies eventually to honor the Law of Peoples and to become full members in good standing of the society of well-ordered peoples. Human rights would thus be secured everywhere. How to bring all societies to this goal is a question of foreign policy; it calls for political wisdom, and success depends in part on luck. . . .

For well-ordered peoples to achieve this long-run aim, they should establish new institutions and practices to serve as a kind of confederative center and public forum for their common opinion and policy toward non-well-ordered regimes. . . . This confederative center may be used both to formulate and to express the opinion of the well-ordered societies. There they may expose to public view the unjust and cruel institutions of oppressive and expansionist regimes and their violations of human rights. Even outlaw regimes are not altogether indifferent to this kind of criticism. . . . Gradually over time, then, well-ordered peoples may pressure the outlaw regimes to change their ways; but by itself this pressure is unlikely to be effective. It may need to be backed up by the firm denial of economic and other assistance, or the refusal to admit outlaw regimes as members in good standing in mutually beneficial cooperative practices. . . .

Let us now take up the principles restricting the conduct of war — *jus in bello*. I begin by setting forth six principles and assumptions familiar from traditional thought on the subject:

(i)   The aim of a just war waged by a just well-ordered people is a just and lasting peace among peoples, and especially with the people's present enemy.

(ii)   Well-ordered peoples do not wage war against each other, but only against non-well-ordered states whose expansionist aims threaten the security and free institutions of well-ordered regimes and bring about the war.

(iii)   In the conduct of war, well-ordered peoples must carefully distinguish three groups: the outlaw state's leaders and officials, its soldiers, and its civilian population. The reason why a well-ordered people must distinguish between an outlaw state's leaders and officials and its civilian population is as follows: since the outlaw state is not well-ordered, the civilian members of the society cannot be those who organized and brought on the war. This was done by the leaders and officials, assisted by other elites who control and staff the state apparatus. They are responsible; they willed the war; and, for doing that, they are criminals. But the civilian population, often kept in ignorance and swayed by state propaganda, is not responsible. This is so even if some civilians knew better yet were enthusiastic for the war. No matter what the initial circumstances of war . . . it is the leaders, and not the common civilians, of nations who finally initiate the war. In view of these principles, both the fire-bombing of Tokyo and other Japanese cities in the spring of 1945 and the atomic bombing of Hiroshima and Nagasaki, all primarily attacks on civilian populations, were very grave wrongs, as they are now widely, though not generally, seen to have been.

As for soldiers of the outlaw state, leaving aside the upper ranks of an officer class, they, like civilians, are not responsible for their state's war. For soldiers are often conscripted and in other ways forced into war; they are coercively indoctrinated in martial virtues; and their patriotism is often cruelly exploited. The reason why they may be attacked directly is not that they are responsible for the war, but that well-ordered peoples have no other choice. They cannot defend themselves in any other way, and defend themselves they must.

(iv) Well-ordered peoples must respect, so far as possible, the human rights of the members of the other side, both civilians and soldiers, for two reasons. One is simply that the enemy, like all others, has these rights by the Law of Peoples. The other reason is to teach enemy soldiers and civilians the content of those rights by the example set in the treatment they receive. In this way the meaning and significance of human rights are best brought home to them.

(v) Continuing the thought of teaching the content of human rights, the next principle is that well-ordered peoples are by their actions and proclamations, when feasible, to foreshadow during a war both the kind of peace they aim for and the kind of relations they seek. By doing so, they show in an open way the nature of their aims and the kind of people they are. These last duties fall largely on the leaders and officials of the governments of well-ordered peoples, since only they are in the position to speak for the whole people and to act as this principle requires. . . . The way a war is fought and the deeds done in ending it live on in the historical memory of societies and may or may not set the stage for future war. It is always the duty of statesmanship to take this longer view.

(vi) Finally, practical means-end reasoning must always have a restricted role in judging the appropriateness of an action or policy. This mode of thought — whether carried on by utilitarian reasoning, or by cost-benefit analysis, or by weighing national interests, or by other possible ways — must always be framed within and strictly limited by the preceding principles and assumptions.

[T]he fourth and fifth principles of the conduct of war are binding especially on statesmen as great leaders of peoples. For they are in the most effective position to represent their people's aims and obligations. But who is the statesman? There is no office of statesman, as there is of president, or chancellor, or prime minister. Rather, the statesman is an ideal, like that of the truthful or virtuous individual. Statesmen are presidents or prime ministers or other high officials who, through their exemplary performance and leadership in their office, manifest strength, wisdom, and courage. They guide their people in turbulent and dangerous times. . . .

The statesman sees deeper and further than most others and grasps what needs to be done. The statesman must get it right, or nearly so, and then hold fast from this vantage. . . . Statesmen may have their own interests when they hold office, yet they must be selfless in their judgments and assessments of their society's fundamental interests and must not be swayed, especially in war, by passions of vindictiveness.

Above all, statesmen are to hold fast to the aim of gaining a just peace, and they are to avoid the things that make achieving such a peace more difficult. In this regard, they must assure that the proclamations made on behalf of their people make clear that once peace is securely reestablished, the enemy society is to be granted an autonomous well-ordered regime of its own. . . .

The [supreme emergency] exemption allows us to set aside — in certain special circumstances — the strict status of civilians that normally prevents their being directly attacked in war. We must proceed here with caution. Were there times during World War II when Britain could properly have held that civilians' strict status was suspended, and thus could have bombed Hamburg or Berlin? Possibly, but only if it was sure that the bombing would have done some substantial good; such action cannot be justified by a doubtful marginal gain. When Britain was alone and had no other means to break Germany's superior power, the bombing of German cities was arguably justifiable. This period extended, at the least, from the fall of France in June 1940 until Russia had clearly beaten off the first German assault in the summer and fall of 1941 and showed that it would be able to fight Germany until the end. It could be argued that this period extended further until the summer and fall of 1942 or even through the Battle of Stalingrad (which ended with German surrender in February 1943). But the bombing of Dresden in February 1945 was clearly too late.

Whether the supreme emergency exemption applies depends upon certain circumstances, about which judgments will sometimes differ. Britain's bombing of Germany until the end of 1941 or 1942 could be justified because Germany could not be allowed to win the war, and this for two basic reasons. First, Nazism portended incalculable moral and political evil for civilized life everywhere. Second, the nature and history of constitutional democracy and its place in European history were at stake. Churchill really did not exaggerate when he said to the House of Commons on the day France capitulated that, "if we fail [to stand up to Hitler], the whole world including the United States . . . will sink into a new Dark Age." This kind of threat, in sum, justifies invoking the supreme emergency exemption, on behalf not only of constitutional democracies, but of all well-ordered societies.

The peculiar evil of Nazism needs to be understood. It was characteristic of Hitler that he recognized no possibility at all of a political relationship with his enemies. They were always to be cowed by terror and brutality, and ruled by force. From the beginning, the campaign against Russia was to be a war of destruction and even at times extermination of Slavic peoples, with the original inhabitants remaining, if at all, only as serfs. . . .

It is clear, however, that the supreme emergency exemption never held at any time for the United States in its war with Japan. The United States was not justified in fire-bombing Japanese cities; and during the discussion among allied leaders in June and July 1945 prior to the use of the atomic bomb on Hiroshima and Nagasaki, the weight of practical means-end reasoning carried the day, overwhelming the qualms of those who felt that limits were being crossed.

Dropping the bombs, it was claimed, was justified in order to hasten the end of the war. It is clear that Truman[1] and most other allied leaders thought it would do that and thereby save the lives of American soldiers. Japanese lives, military and civilian,

---

1. Harry S. Truman, the president of the United States at the end of World War II, ordered the nuclear bombing of Nagasaki and Hiroshima.

presumably counted for less. Moreover, dropping the bombs, it was reasoned, would give the Emperor and the Japanese leaders a way to save face,[2] an important matter given Japanese military samurai culture.[3] Some scholars also believe the bombs were dropped in order to impress Russia with American power and make Russian leaders more agreeable to American demands.

The failure of all these reasons to justify violations of the principles for the conduct of war is evident. What caused this failure of statesmanship on the part of allied leaders? Truman once described the Japanese as beasts and said they should be treated as such, yet how foolish it sounds now to call the Germans and the Japanese as a whole barbarians and beasts. The Nazis and Tojo militarists,[4] yes, but they are not the German and Japanese people. Churchill ascribed his failure of judgment in bombing Dresden to the passion and intensity of the conflict. But it is a duty of statesmanship to prevent such feelings, as natural and inevitable as they may be, from altering the course a well-ordered people should follow in striving for peace. The statesman understands that relations with the present enemy have special importance: war must be openly and publicly conducted in ways that prepare the enemy people for how they will be treated and that make a lasting and amicable peace possible. The fears or fantasies on the part of the enemy people that they will be subject to revenge and retaliation must be put to rest. Difficult though it may be, the present enemy must be seen as a future associate in a shared and just peace.

Another failure of statesmanship was in not considering negotiations with the Japanese before any drastic steps such as the fire-bombing of Japanese cities in the spring of 1945 and the bombing of Hiroshima and Nagasaki were taken. I believe this route could have been effective and avoided further casualties. An invasion was unnecessary by August 6, as the war was effectively over. But whether that is true or not makes no difference. As a liberal democratic people, the United States owed the Japanese people an offer of negotiations in order to end the war. . . .

It is clear that the bombings of Hiroshima and Nagasaki and the fire-bombing of Japanese cities were great wrongs of the kind that the duties of statesmanship require political leaders to avoid; yet it is equally clear that an articulate expression of the principles of just war, if introduced at that time, would not have altered the outcome. For it was simply too late: by that time the bombing of civilians had become an accepted practice of war. Reflections on just war would have fallen on deaf ears. For this reason, these questions must be carefully considered in advance of conflict.

---

2. To save face is a complicated sociological concept; it centrally involves preserving one's sense of the respect and deference that one is entitled to receive from others.

3. The samurai were the warrior class (especially, its upper echelons) of preindustrial Japan. They followed a strict code of conduct that prized honor above all else. This code influenced the Japanese military through World War II.

4. Hideki Tojo was the Japanese prime minister during most of World War II. His term as prime minister is associated with militaristic and nationalist indoctrination in the national education system and with totalitarian policies. After the war ended, Tojo was tried for war crimes and executed by the International Military Tribunal for the Far East.

Similarly, the grounds of constitutional democracy and the basis of its rights and duties need to be continually discussed in all the many associations of civil society as part of citizens' understanding and education prior to taking part in political life. These matters need to be part of the political culture; they should not dominate the day-to-day contents of ordinary politics, but must be presupposed and operating in the background. At the time of the World War II bombings, there was not sufficient prior grasp of the great importance of the principles of just war for the expression of them to have blocked the handy appeal to practical means-end reasoning. This reasoning justifies too much, too quickly, and provides a way for the dominant forces in government to quiet any bothersome moral scruples. If the principles of war are not put forward before that time, they simply become more considerations to be balanced in the scales. These principles must be in place well in advance of war and widely understood by citizens generally. The failure of statesmanship rests in part on and is compounded by the failure of the public political culture — including its military's culture and its doctrine of war — to respect the principles of just war.

Two nihilist doctrines of war are to be repudiated absolutely. One is expressed by Sherman's remark, "War is hell," with the implication that anything goes to get it over with as soon as possible.[5] The other holds that we are all guilty, so we stand on the same level and cannot rightly blame or be blamed. These doctrines — if they deserve this title — both superficially deny all reasonable distinctions; their moral emptiness is manifest in the fact that just and decent civilized societies — their institutions and laws, their civil life, background culture, and mores — depend always on making significant moral and political distinctions. Certainly war is a kind of hell; but why should that mean that normative distinctions cease to hold? Granted also that sometimes all or nearly all may be to some degree guilty; but that does not mean that all are equally so. In short, there is never a time when we are excused from the fine-grained distinctions of moral and political principles and graduated restraints. . . .

The Law of Peoples is both similar to and different from the familiar Christian natural law doctrine of just war. They are similar in that both imply that universal peace among nations is possible if all peoples act according to either the Christian natural law doctrine *or* the Law of Peoples. . . .

However, it is important here to take a step back and to see where the essential difference lies in how they are conceived. The natural law is thought to be part of the law of God that can be known through the natural powers of reason by our study of the structure of the world. As God has supreme authority over all creation, this law is binding for all humankind as members of one community. . . . By contrast, the Law of Peoples falls within the domain of the political as a political conception. . . . Both views support the right to war in self-defense; but the content of the principles for the conduct of war is not in all ways the same.

---

5. William Tecumseh Sherman was a Union general in the Civil War, best known for a campaign of total devastation in Georgia toward the end of the war that involved the destruction of infrastructure, crops, and civilian homes. Sherman is associated with the doctrine of "total war" to which Rawls alludes. The remark, however, was delivered in an address at a military academy in 1879, urging cadets to suppress their desire to put their skills into action.

This last remark is illustrated by the Catholic doctrine of double-effect. It agrees with the principles of the Law of Peoples for the conduct of war that civilians are not to be directly attacked. Both views agree also that the fire-bombing of Japan in the spring and summer of 1945 and the bombing of Hiroshima and Nagasaki were great wrongs. Yet they differ in that the principles for the conduct of war in the social contract conception include the supreme emergency exemption, but the doctrine of double-effect does not. The doctrine of double-effect forbids civilian casualties except insofar as they are the unintended and indirect result of a legitimate attack on a military target. Resting on the divine command that the innocent must never be killed, this doctrine says that one must never act with the intention of attacking the enemy state by the means of taking the innocent lives of its civilians. Political liberalism allows the supreme emergency exemption; the Catholic doctrine rejects it, saying that we must have faith and adhere to God's command. This is intelligible doctrine but is contrary to the duties of the statesman in political liberalism.

The statesman is a central figure in considering the conduct of war, and must be prepared to wage a just war in defense of liberal democratic regimes. Indeed, citizens expect those who seek the office of president or prime minister to do so, and it would violate a fundamental political understanding, at least in the absence of a clear public declaration prior to election, to refuse to do so for religious, philosophical, or moral reasons. Quakers, who oppose all war, can join an overlapping consensus on a constitutional regime, but they cannot always endorse a democracy's particular decisions — here, to engage in a war of self-defense — even when those decisions are reasonable in the light of its political values. This indicates that they could not in good faith, in the absence of special circumstances, seek the highest offices in a liberal democratic regime. The statesman must look to the political world, and must, in extreme cases, be able to distinguish between the interests of the well-ordered regime he or she serves and the dictates of the religious, philosophical, or moral doctrine that he or she personally lives by.

## TEST YOUR UNDERSTANDING

1. In Rawls's view, is it permissible to attack an "outlaw state" because it violates the human rights of its own citizens? What conditions, if any, would make a military attack on such a state consistent with justice?

2. Rawls argues that in war, well-ordered peoples must distinguish among three groups of people in an outlaw state. What are the three groups, and what is the significance of the distinction among them?

3. What is the "supreme emergency" exception and what is Rawls's example of a case that would constitute a "supreme emergency"? From this example, can you identify some of the characteristics of a supreme emergency that distinguish it from more "standard" conditions of war?

## NOTES AND QUESTIONS

1. Rawls argues for certain rules governing the conduct of war, in part, to instruct one's enemy about human rights, both in wartime and in peacetime. Consider the following objection:

   > Observing these rules *during war* may pose a danger to one's own soldiers. During war, the moral instruction that Rawls champions should take place not through our actions but through proclamations and speech. Even if actions and omissions represent an important form of moral education, we should wait to enact them until after our soldiers are out of harm's way, once the war is over.

   How might Rawls respond? Why do you think he believes this form of teaching must happen through behavior, by example, during wartime? Is his position plausible?

2. Rawls argues that the Law of Peoples closely resembles the **doctrine of double effect** but differs in that the former is a political doctrine and the latter is a religious doctrine for some and a moral doctrine for others. He claims that without "clear public declaration prior to election," it would violate a "fundamental political understanding" for a political leader to follow the doctrine of double effect rather than the Law of Peoples, when they diverge.

   *Exercise:* Identify the major respect in which the practical recommendations of the doctrine of double effect and the Law of Peoples would diverge with respect to the treatment of civilians in war. Formulate an argument in favor of Rawls's contention that absent a preelection disclosure to the contrary, the Law of Peoples, not the doctrine of double effect, governs political leaders in light of the office they occupy. Consider how Rawls might respond to the following objection: "The doctrine of double effect shows more respect for and is more protective of innocent civilians than the Law of Peoples. It should be the default position for leaders to follow, absent a preelection disclosure to the contrary that the candidate intends to implement the Law of Peoples instead."

## ANALYZING THE ARGUMENTS

1. *Three techniques of argumentation.* As the introduction to this chapter discussed, to make headway on difficult ethical problems, applied ethicists commonly use three techniques: the use of simplifying examples, the use of analogies, and the attempt to identify and test hypotheses about what mid-level principles might govern the situation.

   *Exercise:* Can you identify where these techniques are used in the assigned selections? Which did you find the most successful, and why?

2. *Proximity and obligation.* Singer and O'Neill share the conviction that our physical distance from people in need does not intrinsically diminish the strength of our duties to them. Why do they think our lack of proximity is not morally significant? Given their positions, could either of them agree with the claim that we have some obligations to our neighbors and compatriots that we do not have to others in foreign countries? What reasons could they appeal to support or reject that claim?

3. *Thomson and famine relief.* Does Thomson's position that you are not required to give life-sustaining support to the violinist have implications for the question of whether you are required to give support to innocents in danger of dying from hunger and other threats occasioned by poverty? Consider whether there are morally important differences between these cases. Could Singer agree with Thomson about the violinist but still insist that we must give all we can to famine relief?

4. *The harm of abortion.* If Marquis's analysis of how an embryo or fetus is harmed by abortion is right, does it follow that Thomson's conclusions are wrong? If so, which ones? If she is right, does it follow that Marquis's conclusions are wrong? If so, which ones?

5. *Does it matter whether abortion is a denial of support or a killing?* Thomson's argument for the permissibility of abortion conceives of abortion as fundamentally a removal of support that one is not required to give; when the support is removed, the embryo or fetus may, regrettably, die. When Marquis analyzes abortion, he describes it as a form of killing. Do these conceptions of abortion importantly differ, or are they merely varying ways of saying the same thing? If Thomson's argument is right, does it matter for the morality of abortion whether the method of abortion involves removing the fetus from the woman's body (resulting in its death) or directly killing the fetus and then removing it from the pregnant woman's body?

6. *War: same conclusions, different reasoning.* Nagel and Rawls agree about many conclusions, but the arguments they give for those conclusions differ in some respects.

   a. *Distinguishing soldiers from civilians:* Consider, for example, their reasons for why, during war, civilian populations should not be the targets of military attack, and why soldiers may be the targets of such attack. Identify the differences between their arguments for this position and the differences between their conclusions. Are their arguments largely compatible or largely incompatible? Which position do you find more plausible?

   b. *Treating the enemy with dignity.* Both Rawls and Nagel stress that even when one's participation in a war is justified, it is crucial that one should not treat one's opponents as enemies in all respects, and one should not regard the hostile relationship as permanent. What arguments in their essays justify this shared conviction? Do they arrive at this conclusion for the same reason?

7. *Nagel, Thomson, and abortion.* Consider the following argument:

> Nagel argues that hostile acts, to be morally permissible, must be directed at those whose behavior merits a hostile response. Embryos and fetuses lack consciousness and have not engaged in any behavior that merits a hostile response. Abortion is a hostile activity. Therefore, if Nagel is right about the principles governing our behavior in war, then Thomson must be incorrect that abortion is morally permissible.

Consider how Thomson might reply.

8. *The interests of others.* Many issues in applied ethics involve the question of when one may pursue one's own interests and concerns and when the interests and concerns of others, as one's moral equals, make moral claims on and against one's activity. It seems clear that one need not sacrifice *all* of one's own interests to advance those of others. It also seems clear that one may not single-mindedly attend to one's own interests without considering and responding to some needs of others. Identifying a plausible moral principle that gives adequate weight to oneself as well as to the interests of others proves challenging.

Consider this candidate principle that attempts to strike a plausible balance:

> *Ethical Harm Principle:* One may always permissibly act to advance one's own interests if and only if so acting would not cause harm to others.

Despite its initial attractiveness, some **counterexamples** suggest it gives both too much and too little weight to the interests of others.

> *Competition and Self-Defense:* It seems permissible to apply for admission to college or for employment even when one's successful application will entail another person's failure to secure a spot. Further, it seems permissible to defend oneself against a person posing a threat to one's life, even when defending oneself will impose harm to the threat.

> *Drowning Child:* It is not always permissible to advance one's own interests rather than to help another person in need, even when one is not the cause of the other's peril. It is wrong to continue on one's way to work rather than to rescue a drowning child, even though one's going to work is not what would cause the child harm; the child's inability to swim to safety and the slippery banks of the pond would be what causes the child to drown.

> *Neighbor:* It seems impermissible to ignore the request of an elderly neighbor for help when he is struggling with heavy, cumbersome packages, even when helping involves interrupting one's homework and the neighbor will not suffer harm if one ignores him; he will simply have to make more trips from the car to the house.

Explain why these examples appear to pose a challenge to the *Ethical Harm Principle.* Consider how a proponent of the principle might respond. (*Note:* One response is to modify the principle to avoid the counterexamples. Another is to argue that the cases do not really pose counterexamples.)

# 19

# How Can the State Be Justified?

## Justifying the State

Imagine living in a place with lots of other people but without a state. Perhaps the state never existed. Or perhaps it existed but has now disappeared. Don't worry about the past. Just imagine that, however you ended up there, you are now living with others in a stateless condition.

What does it mean to live without a state? Let's say that we have a state where a collection of people all live under a single political authority. A political authority makes and enforces rules of conduct (laws) in a territory. So I am asking you to imagine living without a common authority making and enforcing rules. Imagine yourself in what some philosophers have called a **state of nature**. Anthropologists have written about stateless societies. But don't think of a state of nature as a primitive condition. Think of it, simply, as a situation—say, in your community—with no political authority. (The exercise is *hard*, but try it before you keep reading.)

One important feature of a state of nature is that there are no laws and no enforcement of public standards of conduct. You have to decide whether to keep your agreement to compensate me for the couch I delivered to you yesterday, whether to keep your hands off my shoes and food, and which shoes and food are yours and which are mine. You have to decide whether my decision to walk close to you represents a threat, and if it is, how to respond. You have to decide, as does everyone else.

Thomas Hobbes proposes this remarkable thought experiment in his *Leviathan*. Part of what is so remarkable is that he thought he knew what life would be like in the state of nature. In a world without authority, a world without public standards and enforcers, a world in which we each must rely on our own judgment and our powers, we would face, Hobbes says, a war of all against all. Not that we might. Not that we could. But that we would.

In the absence of a political authority, Hobbes thinks, human beings cannot live together in peace.

How do we get from that conclusion to a justification for the state? Assume, as Hobbes does, that a justification for the state is an argument directed to each individual who is subject to the state's authority — an argument designed to show that each of us, despite our many differences in interests, values, and circumstances, has sufficient reason to accept a common political authority. Variants on this idea of justification run through the **social contract** tradition in political philosophy.

Now, each of us arguably has very strong reasons to desire peace. And not just to desire it, but to act in ways that flow from that desire. We each have a very strong reason because, whatever else we care about, we care about living a happy life. But in a state of war, our lives would be, as Hobbes famously says in *Leviathan*, "solitary, poor, nasty, brutish, and short." And even more than we care about continuing to live, we fear violent death. To be sure, we sometimes celebrate violent death in the service of a great cause. But what could be worse than a violent death that serves no cause, a violent death that results simply from a lack of basic protections?

So a state of nature would be a state of war. And war is terrible for each of us. Because war is so terrible, we each have very good reason to seek peace. But how?

Suppose that we each acknowledge a common political authority—a **sovereign**, in Hobbes's terms — as having the right to rule. That authority makes and enforces public standards for conduct. You no longer need to rely solely on your own judgment of what is acceptable, or of what is yours and what is mine. You no longer need to rely solely on your own capacity to protect yourself from people who may aggress against you, if only to protect themselves from what they judge to be your suspicious intentions. For these reasons, the authority can keep the peace, from which it follows that we each have sufficient reason to accept the authority of a state.

That, in essence, is Hobbes's contractual justification of the state.

This rationale for the state may seem too quick. The state of nature may be awful, but states can be awful, too. Even at their most benign, states deploy coercive tools to enforce the laws. And they are not always at their most benign. Political authorities may repress some groups of people; they may lead the state into destructive, adventurous wars; they may invade the homes and imprison the bodies of subjects.

These concerns about abuses of political authority seem especially troubling for the kind of sovereign that Hobbes defended. He argued for an **absolute sovereign**, a political authority with unlimited rule-making and rule-enforcing power. Only such an authority would suffice to keep the peace. The resulting restrictions on individual conduct, however unattractive, are needed to avoid the worst possible situation: a state of nature with what "is worst of all, continual fear and danger of violent death."

So the state is justified, according to Hobbes, because each us has a compelling reason to accept the state's authority in exchange for the personal safety and the possibility of happiness that come with peace.

# Anarchist Arguments

Anarchists reject this line of thought. Anarchists oppose the state. Not that they favor war and human calamity. Instead, they find fault with Hobbes's argument.

One kind of anarchist accepts the contractualist idea of justification but argues that Hobbes overstates the dangers in a state of nature and underplays the dangers in a state. Drawing on a mix of theoretical argument about human cooperation and historical evidence from stateless societies, they say that, even in the absence of a political authority, people are more capable than Hobbes thought. Moreover, even if a state of nature is dangerous, power is so easily abused that a state, which monopolizes the use of force, imposes greater dangers than we would face in a state of nature. And to the extent that we *do* face dangers, we have ways to address them without creating the greater dangers of a state. We can protect ourselves individually, or band together with others for self-defense, or we can hire other people to protect us. The result of such hirings will be a market in protection services, not a monopolist who extracts payments for protective services throughout the territory.

The anarchist may acknowledge that political authority will benefit *some* people. Still, it could be a bad bet for many, perhaps for most. So this first variety of anarchist might agree with Hobbes's contractual idea: that a justification needs to show that *each* person subject to the state has sufficient reason to accept its authority. But the anarchist who thinks a state of nature need not be so bad and that the state is a source of much misery rejects Hobbes's claim that each of us individually has a strong reason to accept the authority of the state.

A variant on this first kind of anarchism says that Hobbes's story about the absence of political authority is too general. Under some conditions—say, of deep social division—states may be needed to keep the peace. But in other conditions, states are not needed. Karl Marx[1] held a view of this kind. He thought that the state was needed in much of human history to serve the interests of a dominant social class—slave owners, or feudal lords, or capitalists—against the interests of subordinate social classes—slaves, or serfs, or wage laborers. But in a future classless society, without deep conflicts between social classes, the state would wither away.

A second variety of anarchist, suggested by David Lyons, argues against the state from **utilitarian** premises. Utilitarians think that what is right is what produces the greatest sum of happiness. So they think that the state is justified if and only if the presence of the state yields a greater sum of human happiness than its absence. For utilitarians, then, a justification of the state does not need to show that each person has sufficient reason to accept the authority of the state. Utilitarians do not accept the contractualist idea of justification, with its focus on reasons for individuals. If some people do well in a state and others do not, the state is justified if and only if the gains for some outweigh the losses to others.

1. Karl Marx (1818–1883) was a German philosopher, historian, and revolutionary activist. His most notable publications are *The Communist Manifesto* (1848) and *Capital* (1867–1894).

For the utilitarian, then, the justification of the state is a complex empirical question. Utilitarian anarchists would argue that the benefits of the state for some are outweighed by the greater losses to others.

A third variety of anarchists goes further. These anarchists think the state is not simply a bad bet. They say that states, virtually of necessity, violate our rights. We have rights to personal security and to basic liberty, they say. Moreover, we each have a right to protect these rights, and perhaps to protect the rights of others as well. John Locke, whose doctrine of **natural rights** in his *Two Treatises of Government* inspires this third anarchist argument, based these rights to protect other rights on what he called the "executive right of the law of nature"—a right we each have to protect ourselves and others from aggression. We can exercise our executive right by hiring someone to protect us, if we wish. But we can also reserve that right and exercise it ourselves.

Because we have a basic right to enforce our own rights (and the rights of others), what matters to the justification of the state is not simply that each of us has sufficient *reason* to accept the authority of a state, nor simply that it protects our other rights (to personal security and basic liberty). Instead, what matters is that we actually *agree* to hire someone to protect us. You may have reason to hire me to paint your house: the house desperately needs a fresh coat of paint. But unless you actually hire me—unless you actually consent—I am not justified in painting your house, no matter how much you may benefit. And I am certainly not justified in painting your house and sending you the bill. Similarly, these rights-based anarchists say, unless we each individually consent to the state's authority, it is impermissible for a state to claim authority over us. In his discussion of rights-based justifications for the state, John Simmons observes that this approach, with its focus on actual consent, may well lead us to anarchist conclusions because most political societies are simply not consensual associations.

# Limited Authority

Hobbes justifies a Leviathan state. The anarchist denies that the state is justified. A third view is that a state with limited political authority can be justified. Hobbes is right: we need political authorities to provide basic protections. But we also need to ensure that they do not abuse their authority. The way to provide this assurance might be with such institutions as a constitution, rule of law, separation of powers, and democratic monitoring of the exercise of power. These political institutions help ensure that the authority we establish to keep the peace also protects our basic rights and interests better than if we are left to our own devices.

Utilitarian premises are one possible source of argument for such limits. A utilitarian justification for limited political authority would say that we get a greater sum of happiness from limited authority than from the unconditional authority of Hobbes's Leviathan state. (Lyons explores this line of argument, too.)

A more familiar argument for a state with limited authority is based on the **contractualist** idea of justification. According to the contractualist argument for limited authority, we do not have good reason to submit to an unlimited authority. Even if the state of nature is dangerous, unconditional authority can be dangerous, too; so we may be violating our obligations to ourselves and to others if we accept an authority without proper limits. In his classical statement of the contractualist argument for limited authority, Locke asked: why should we protect ourselves from wily polecats and foxes by putting ourselves in the hands of a very powerful lion—a lion "made licentious by impunity"?

A Hobbesian understands the temptation to tie the hands of authorities. But the Hobbesian argues that such limits defeat the purpose of having a state. If we tie the hands of the authorities, what will happen when domestic or foreign dangers emerge? Tying the hands of the authority threatens a return to a state of nature, with all its terrible troubles.

## Authority and Self-Government

Contractualist justifications for unlimited and limited authority both present a picture of the state as founded on an exchange. They think that we have sufficient reason to accept authority because, in return, we get greater security to our person, our goods, our lives, our rights. In exchange for these protections, we give obedience to the rules that authorities make. Contractualists disagree about the kinds of protections and the extent of the obedience. But they agree that we sacrifice something we value when we have a state: our right to govern ourselves.

It is hard to see an alternative. If we need to live by common rules, then each of us must accept governance by authorities who make the rules. Restrictions on our freedom appear to be the cost of political authority. How could it be otherwise?

It could be otherwise if we could live together under an authority that makes the rules but which is not a third-party rule maker and enforcer. Suppose instead that *we* are the authority. Imagine that the authority is a body of equals. Members of the body—citizens—act as a group to make rules for everyone. They make the rules for themselves and make them in the service of their common good.

An authority of that kind would solve what Jean-Jacques Rousseau describes, in *The Social Contract,* as the basic political problem: to find a way of living together that protects the person and the goods of each associate, while at the same time enabling each person to "remain as free as before." We need a common authority—Rousseau is not an anarchist—because our personal safety and well-being depend on shared, public rules that are enforced. But freedom is essential to our nature: "to renounce one's freedom is to renounce one's quality as a man, the rights of humanity, and even its duties." Because freedom cannot be alienated, we need to find a way to ensure security and opportunity that does not demand submission to the judgment and will of others.

Rousseau thinks we can achieve a state of this kind if, but only if, we treat one another as equal members of the sovereign authority and share a concern with others about the common good of our society. When that shared point of view lies at the basis of the laws, we each "follow the law one has prescribed to oneself." We achieve a kind of **autonomy**, which Rousseau calls "moral freedom."

In presenting his case, Rousseau relies on a version of the contractualist idea of justification. Political authority is justified by showing that each person subject to it has sufficient reason for accepting it. But the reason for being part of a common authority directed to the common good is not to pay a price in obedience for a compensating benefit in protection. The state is not based on an exchange. The reason for accepting political authority is that an equal share in political authority is how we express our nature as free.

# The Best Life

The idea of a state as a self-governing community—a collection of citizens who express their free nature by ruling themselves—takes us some distance from Hobbes's justification of the state, with its emphasis on advancing our interests in life and happiness. But does the Rousseauean rationale for the state, focused on expressing our nature as free persons, accurately represent the greatest good that comes from a self-governing community of citizens? Aristotle suggests not. He offers a different account of what is at stake, and a very different justification for the state, commonly described as **perfectionist**. "Our conclusion," he says," is that "political society exists for the sake of noble actions, and not of living together."

Neither the contractualist nor utilitarian justifications of the state draw on an idea of virtuous, noble actions. Perfectionists do, because they think of political philosophy as an extension of ethics, which is centrally concerned with better and worse—more or less virtuous, noble—ways to live a human life. "The true student of politics," Aristotle says in his *Nicomachean Ethics*, "is thought to have studied virtue above all things; for he wishes to make his fellow citizens good and obedient to the laws."

The best way to live, Aristotle argues, involves the virtuous exercise of our distinctive human powers of reasoning and deliberative judgment. The state is a "body of citizens" who govern themselves by playing a role in "deliberative or judicial administration." And the great good that comes from having a state is that it provides an occasion and venue for the virtuous exercise of those human powers. Though the state may "come into existence for the sake of the bare needs of life," Aristotle says, it continues to exist not simply to sustain life but "for the sake of the good life."

Rousseau does not justify the state in terms of its contribution to human virtue. But this should not obscure a deep point of convergence between the Rousseauean and Aristotelian views. For them, the justification of the state does not depend on the Hobbesian idea that the state of nature would be a disaster. Suppose instead that it would be a world of relative peace and material sufficiency. Still, the state would be justified as the only condition in which we can achieve a larger human good—a free community of equals, on Rousseau's view; the virtuous exercise of human powers, on Aristotle's. For them, the state is not the price we pay to avoid calamity. Instead, it enables us to do something of great value together that we cannot possibly do on our own.

## Aristotle (384–322 BCE)

Aristotle was born in Stagira and joined Plato's Academy when he was eighteen. A philosopher of extraordinary intellectual reach, he wrote remarkable and remarkably influential treatises on all areas of philosophy and science. His writings on logic, metaphysics, rhetoric, ethics, and politics continue to have a profound impact on philosophical discussion.

# POLITICS

---

# Book I

1. Every state[1] is a community of some kind, and every community is established with a view to some good; for everyone always acts in order to obtain that which they think good. But, if all communities aim at some good, the state or political community, which is the highest of all, and which embraces all the rest, aims at good in a greater degree than any other, and at the highest good. . . .

2. He who considers things in their first growth and origin, whether a state or anything else, will obtain the clearest view of them. In the first place there must be a union of those who cannot exist without each other; namely, of male and female, that the race may continue (and this is a union which is formed, not of choice, but because, in common with other animals and with plants, mankind have a natural desire to leave behind them an image of themselves), and of natural ruler and subject, that both may be preserved. For that which can foresee by the exercise of mind is by nature lord and master, and that which can with its body give effect to such foresight is a subject, and by nature a slave; hence master and slave have the same interest. . . .

---

1. Aristotle's term is *polis*, which is sometimes translated as "city." When he discusses "states," he is thinking of Athens, Sparta, Thebes, Corinth, and other Greek city-states, which were all relatively small political units by modern standards. In the fifth century BCE some 250,000 people, including citizens, women, and slaves, lived, for example, in Athens, which was among the largest.

Out of these two relationships the first thing to arise is the family, and Hesiod[2] is right when he says,

First house and wife and an ox for the plough,

for the ox is the poor man's slave. The family is the association established by nature for the supply of men's everyday wants. . . . But when several families are united, and the association aims at something more than the supply of daily needs, the first society to be formed is the village. And the most natural form of the village appears to be that of a colony from the family, composed of the children and grandchildren, who are said to be "suckled with the same milk." . . .

When several villages are united in a single complete community, large enough to be nearly or quite self-sufficing, the state comes into existence, originating in the bare needs of life, and continuing in existence for the sake of a good life. And therefore, if the earlier forms of society are natural, so is the state, for it is the end of them, and the nature of a thing is its end. For what each thing is when fully developed, we call its nature, whether we are speaking of a man, a horse, or a family. Besides, the final cause and end of a thing is the best, and to be self-sufficing is the end and the best.

Hence it is evident that the state is a creation of nature, and that man is by nature a political animal. And he who by nature and not by mere accident is without a state, is either a bad man or above humanity; he is like the

Tribeless, lawless, heartless one,

whom Homer[3] denounces — the natural outcast is forthwith a lover of war; he may be compared to an isolated piece at draughts.

Now, that man is more of a political animal than bees or any other gregarious animals is evident. Nature, as we often say, makes nothing in vain, and man is the only animal who has the gift of speech. And whereas mere voice is but an indication of pleasure or pain, and is therefore found in other animals (for their nature attains to the perception of pleasure and pain and the intimation of them to one another, and no further), the power of speech is intended to set forth the expedient and inexpedient, and therefore likewise the just and the unjust. And it is a characteristic of man that he alone has any sense of good and evil, of just and unjust, and the like, and the association of living beings who have this sense makes a family and a state. . . .

The proof that the state is a creation of nature and prior to the individual is that the individual, when isolated, is not self-sufficing; and therefore he is like a part in relation

2. Hesiod was a Greek poet of the eighth century BCE. This quotation is taken from his poem *Works and Days* (ll. 405–13), which offers practical advice about daily life. He is also the author of *Theogony,* a mythic account of the origin of the universe.

3. Homer is the name conventionally used for the Greek epic poet or poets, probably of the eighth century BCE, responsible for bringing the *Iliad* and *Odyssey* into written form. This quotation is taken from *Iliad* IX.63. The Achaeans are in danger of losing the Trojan War and Nestor, a prominent Achaean elder, advises Agamemnon, the Achaean king, to reconcile with Achilles, the leading warrior.

to the whole. But he who is unable to live in society, or who has no need because he is sufficient for himself, must be either a beast or a god: he is no part of a state. A social instinct is implanted in all men by nature, and yet he who first founded the state was the greatest of benefactors. For man, when perfected, is the best of animals, but, when separated from law and justice, he is the worst of all; since armed injustice is the more dangerous, and he is equipped at birth with arms, meant to be used by intelligence and excellence, which he may use for the worst ends. That is why, if he has not excellence, he is the most unholy and the most savage of animals, and the most full of lust and glut-tony. But justice is the bond of men in states; for the administration of justice, which is the determination of what is just, is the principle of order in political society. . . .

# Book III

1. He who would inquire into the essence and attributes of various kinds of govern-ment must first of all determine what a state is. . . . [A] state is composite, like any other whole made up of many parts — these are the citizens, who compose it. It is evident, therefore, that we must begin by asking, Who is the citizen, and what is the meaning of the term? . . . The citizen whom we are seeking to define is a citizen in the strictest sense, . . . and his special characteristic is that he shares in the administration of jus-tice, and in offices. Now of offices some are discontinuous, and the same persons are not allowed to hold them twice, or can only hold them after a fixed interval; others have no limit of time — for example, the office of juryman or member of the assem-bly.[4] It may, indeed, be argued that these are not magistrates at all, and that their functions give them no share in the government. Bur surely it is ridiculous to say that those who have the supreme power do not govern. Let us not dwell further upon this, which is a purely verbal question; what we want is a common term including both juryman and member of the assembly. Let us, for the sake of distinction, call it "indefinite office," and we will assume that those who share in such office are citizens. This is the most comprehensive definition of a citizen, and best suits all those who are generally so called.

But . . . governments differ in kind, and some of them are prior and others are posterior; those which are faulty or perverted are necessarily posterior to those which are perfect. (What we mean by perversion will be hereafter explained.) The citizen then of necessity differs under each form of government; and our definition[5] is best

---

4. At the height of its democratic period, Athens distributed the functions of juryman and assembly mem-ber widely to free adult men (as many as 8,000 citizens would sometimes attend the assembly). This wide distribution to free adult men, without special election or appointment or qualification, is what Aristotle has in mind by an "indefinite office."

5. Aristotle is referring to the definition he stated in the previous paragraph, where he said that citizens are those who share in an *indefinite office*, with no time limit. He is emphasizing that in nondemocratic regimes the responsibilities of juror (judging) and lawmaker (deliberating) are magisterial positions, or "definite offices."

adapted to the citizen of a democracy; but not necessarily to other states. For in some states [unlike democracies] the people are not acknowledged, nor have they any regular assembly, but only extraordinary ones; and law-suits are distributed by sections among the magistrates. At Lacedaemon, for instance, the Ephors determine suits about contracts, which they distribute among themselves, while the elders are judges of homicide, and other causes are decided by other magistrates.... We may, indeed, modify our definition of the citizen so as to include these states. In them it is the holder of a definite, not an indefinite office, who is juryman and member of the assembly, and to some or all such holders of definite offices is reserved the right of deliberating or judging about some things or about all things. The conception of the citizen now begins to clear up.

He who has the power to take part in the deliberative or judicial administration of any state is said by us to be a citizen of that state,[6] and, speaking generally, a state is a body of citizens sufficing for the purposes of life....

4. There is a point nearly allied to the preceding [discussion of who a citizen is]: Whether the excellence of a good man and a good citizen is the same or not. But before entering on this discussion, we must certainly first obtain some general notion of the excellence of the citizen. Like the sailor, the citizen is a member of a community. Now, sailors have different functions, for one of them is a rower, another a pilot, and a third a look-out man, a fourth is described by some similar term; and while the precise definition of each individual's excellence applies exclusively to him, there is, at the same time, a common definition applicable to them all. For they have all of them a common object, which is safety in navigation. Similarly, one citizen differs from another, but the salvation of the community is the common business of them all. This community is the constitution; the excellence of the citizen must therefore be relative to the constitution of which he is a member. If, then, there are many forms of government, it is evident that there is not one single excellence of the good citizen which is perfect excellence. But we say that the good man is he who has one single excellence which is perfect excellence. Hence it is evident that the good citizen need not of necessity possess the excellence which makes a good man.

The same question may also be approached by another road, from a consideration of the best constitution. If the state cannot be entirely composed of good men, and yet each citizen is expected to do his own business well, and must therefore have excellence, still, inasmuch as all the citizens cannot be alike, the excellence of the citizen and of the good man cannot coincide. All must have the excellence of the good citizen—thus, and thus only, can the state be perfect; but they will not have the excellence of a good man, unless we assume that in the good state all the citizens must be good....

But will there then be no case in which the excellence of the good citizen and the excellence of the good man coincide? To this we answer that the good *ruler* is a good and wise man, but the citizen need not be wise....

---

6. Having first defined a citizen as someone with an indefinite office, a definition most suited to democracy, now Aristotle corrects the definition to cover a broader range of regimes, democratic and nondemocratic: a citizen, he says, is anyone with authority to judge or deliberate.

If the excellence of a good ruler is the same as that of a good man, and we assume further that the subject is a citizen as well as the ruler, the excellence of the good citizen and the excellence of the good man cannot be absolutely the same, although in some cases they may; for the excellence of a ruler differs from that of a citizen. It was the sense of this difference which made Jason[7] say that "he felt hungry when he was not a tyrant," meaning that he could not endure to live in a private station. But, on the other hand, it may be argued that men are praised for knowing both how to rule and how to obey, and he is said to be a citizen of excellence who is able to do both well. Now if we suppose the excellence of a good man to be that which rules, and the excellence of the citizen to include ruling and obeying, it cannot be said that they are equally worthy of praise. Since, then, it is sometimes thought that the ruler and the ruled must learn different things and not the same, but that the citizen must know and share in them both, the inference is obvious. There is, indeed, the rule of a master, which is concerned with menial offices — the master need not know how to perform these, but may employ others in the execution of them: the other would be degrading; and by the other I mean the power actually to do menial duties, which vary much in character and are executed by various classes of slaves, such, for example, as handicraftsmen, who, as their name signifies, live by the labour of their hands — under these the mechanic is included. Hence in ancient times, and among some nations, the working classes had no share in the government — a privilege which they only acquired under extreme democracy. Certainly the good man and the statesman and the good citizen ought not to learn the crafts of inferiors except for their own occasional use; if they habitually practise them, there will cease to be a distinction between master and slave.

But there is a rule of another kind, which is exercised over freemen and equals by birth — a constitutional rule, which the ruler must learn by obeying, as he would learn the duties of a general of cavalry by being under the orders of a general of cavalry, or the duties of a general of infantry by being under the orders of a general of infantry, and by having had the command of a regiment and of a company. It has been well said that he who has never learned to obey cannot be a good commander. The excellence of the two is not the same, but the good citizen ought to be capable of both; he should know how to govern like a freeman, and how to obey like a freeman — these are the excellences of a citizen. And, although the temperance and justice of a ruler are distinct from those of a subject, the excellence of a good man will include both; for the excellence of the good man who is free and also a subject, e.g. his justice, will not be one but will comprise distinct kinds, the one qualifying him to rule, the other to obey, and differing as the temperance and courage of men and women differ. For a man would be thought a coward if he had no more courage than a courageous woman, and a woman would be thought loquacious if

---

7. Jason of Pherae was a tyrant, a *tagos* (a special office, like "great khan," held occasionally by charismatic leaders who exercised extraordinary power and commanded large armies) who ruled Thessaly 380–370 BCE.

she imposed no more restraint on her conversation than the good man; and indeed their part in the management of the household is different, for the duty of the one is to acquire, and of the other to preserve. Practical wisdom is the only excellence peculiar to the ruler: it would seem that all other excellences must equally belong to ruler and subject. The excellence of the subject is certainly not wisdom, but only true opinion; he may be compared to the maker of the flute, while his master is like the flute-player or user of the flute.

From these considerations may be gathered the answer to the question, whether the excellence of the good man is the same as that of the good citizen, or different, and how far the same, and how far different. . . .

6. Having determined these questions, we have next to consider whether there is only one form of government or many, and if many, what they are, and how many, and what are the differences between them.

A constitution is the arrangement of magistracies in a state, especially of the highest of all. The government is everywhere sovereign in the state, and the constitution is in fact the government. For example, in democracies the people are supreme, but in oligarchies, the few; and, therefore, we say that these two constitutions also are different: and so in other cases.

First, let us consider what is the purpose of a state, and how many forms of rule there are by which human society is regulated. . . .

The rule of a master, although the slave by nature and the master by nature have in reality the same interests, is nevertheless exercised primarily with a view to the interest of the master, but accidentally considers the slave, since, if the slave perish, the rule of the master perishes with him. On the other hand, the government of a wife and children and of a household, which we have called household management, is exercised in the first instance for the good of the governed or for the common good of both parties, but essentially for the good of the governed, as we see to be the case in medicine, gymnastic, and the arts in general, which are only accidentally concerned with the good of the artists themselves. For there is no reason why the trainer may not sometimes practise gymnastics, and the helmsman is always one of the crew. The trainer or the helmsman considers the good of those committed to his care. But, when he is one of the persons taken care of, he accidentally participates in the advantage, for the helmsman is also a sailor, and the trainer becomes one of those in training. And so in politics: when the state is framed upon the principle of equality and likeness, the citizens think that they ought to hold office by turns. Formerly, as is natural, everyone would take his turn of service; and then again, somebody else would look after his interest, just as he, while in office, had looked after theirs. But nowadays, for the sake of the advantage which is to be gained from the public revenues and from office, men want to be always in office. One might imagine that the rulers, being sickly, were only kept in health while they continued in office; in that case we may be sure that they would be hunting after places. The conclusion is evident: that governments which have a regard to the common interest are constituted in accordance with strict principles of justice, and are therefore true forms; but those which regard only the interest of the rulers are all defective and perverted forms, for they are despotic, whereas a state is a community of freemen.[8] . . .

9. [To understand what justice and the true forms are, let] us begin by considering the common definitions of oligarchy and democracy, and what is oligarchical and democratic justice. For all men cling to justice of some kind, but their conceptions are imperfect and they do not express the whole idea. . . . [I]f men met and associated out of regard to wealth only, their share in the state would be proportioned to their property, and the oligarchical doctrine would then seem to carry the day. It would not be just that he who paid one mina should have the same share of a hundred minae, whether of the principal or of the profits, as he who paid the remaining ninety-nine. But a state exists for the sake of a good life, and not for the sake of life only: if life only were the object, slaves and brute animals might form a state, but they cannot, for they have no share in happiness or in a life based on choice. Nor does a state exist for the sake of alliance and security from injustice, nor yet for the sake of exchange and mutual intercourse; for then the Tyrrhenians and the Carthaginians, and all who have commercial treaties with one another, would be the citizens of one state. True, they have agreements about imports, and engagements that they will do no wrong to one another, and written articles of alliance. But there are no magistracies common to the contracting parties; different states have each their own magistracies. Nor does one state take care that the citizens of the other are such as they ought to be, nor see that those who come under the terms of the treaty do no wrong or wickedness at all, but only that they do no injustice to one another. Whereas, those who care for good government take into consideration political excellence and defect. Whence it may be further inferred that excellence must be the care of a state which is truly so called, and not merely enjoys the name: for without this end the community becomes a mere alliance which differs only in place from alliances of which the members live apart; and law is only a convention, "a surety to one another of justice," as the sophist Lycophron[9] says, and has no real power to make the citizens good and just. . . .

Again, if men dwelt at a distance from one another, but not so far off as to have no intercourse, and there were laws among them that they should not wrong each other in their exchanges, neither would this be a state. Let us suppose that one man is a carpenter, another a farmer, another a shoemaker, and so on, and that their number is ten thousand: nevertheless, if they have nothing in common but exchange, alliance, and the like, that would not constitute a state. Why is this? Surely not because they are at a distance from one another; for even supposing that such a community

---

8. A state is a community that aims at the highest good. When the government exercises power for the benefit of the rulers, not for the common good, we have a "perverted form," not a true government and constitution, because a government is supposed to guide the community to the common good.

9. Lycophron was a Greek Sophist. The Sophists were itinerant teachers who claimed to be able to teach students (for a fee) the correct way to manage one's own affairs and the affairs of the state.

were to meet in one place, but that each man had a house of his own, which was in a manner his state, and that they made alliance with one another, but only against evil-doers; still an accurate thinker would not deem this to be a state, if their intercourse with one another was of the same character after as before their union. It is clear then that a state is not a mere society, having a common place, established for the prevention of mutual crime and for the sake of exchange. These are conditions without which a state cannot exist; but all of them together do not constitute a state, which is a community of families and aggregations of families in well-being, for the sake of a perfect and self-suffing life. Such a community can only be established among those who live in the same place and intermarry. Hence there arise in cities family connexions, brotherhoods, common sacrifices, amusements which draw men together. But these are created by friendship, for to choose to live together is friendship. The end of the state is the good life, and these are the means towards it. And the state is the union of families and villages in a perfect and self-suffing life, by which we mean a happy and honourable life.

Our conclusion, then, is that political society exists for the sake of noble actions, and not of living together. Hence they who contribute most to such a society have a greater share in it than those who have the same or a greater freedom or nobility of birth but are inferior to them in political excellence; or than those who exceed them in wealth but are surpassed by them in excellence. . . .

## TEST YOUR UNDERSTANDING

1. What is Aristotle's "proof" that the state is a "creation of nature"?

2. What is the chief characteristic of a citizen "in the strictest sense"?

3. Does a state exist for the sake of living together peacefully and comfortably or for the sake of noble actions? What do you think Aristotle means by "noble actions"? Give some examples.

## NOTES AND QUESTIONS

1. Much of the Aristotle selection comes from Book III of his *Politics*, in which Aristotle presents a general account of *constitutions*. A constitution is the way a political society is organized, how it makes decisions. It is "the arrangement of magistracies in a state, especially the highest of all" (section 6). Aristotle's account is not focused exclusively on laws and formal institutions of decision making but on who effectively exercises the ruling power, and for what purposes (by whom and for whom). Thus, Aristotle classifies constitutions on two dimensions:

(i)   What are the purposes for which political rule is exercised? In particular, is the constitution "true" or "perverse"? In true constitutions, rule is exercised for the common good; in perverse (corrupt) constitutions, rule is exercised for the benefit of rulers.

(ii)  Who exercises the ruling power? In particular, is supreme authority in the hands of one, a few, or many? Typically, when a few govern, it is the few rich; when it is many, it is the poor.

Putting the two dimensions together, then, we have a six-fold classification of constitutions. The true constitutions are kingship (one), aristocracy (few), and, simply, a constitution (many). The perverse constitutions are tyranny, oligarchy, and democracy. Here, democracy is rule by the many for the benefit of the "needy," not for the "common good of all."

The overall structure of the *Politics*, then, is as follows: in Book I Aristotle presents a general account of the distinction between the household and polity, as different human communities, and discusses different kinds of rule (master over slave; man over wife and children; citizens over one another). Book II discusses and criticizes previous views of the best constitution, as well as a few actual constitutions that were widely thought to be well governed. Book III presents a general account of constitutions and citizenship. In Books IV–VI, Aristotle discusses actual constitutions, with a particular focus on democracy and oligarchy, and revolutions. In the final books, he considers the ideal form of state, including discussion of size, location, social structure, and education, as well as the larger purposes that politics serves.

Bear these points about constitutions and their differences in mind as you consider Aristotle's discussion of the relationship between the good man and the good citizen. This issue is fundamental for Aristotle because he thinks of politics as continuous with ethics, which is centrally concerned with the human good. (See Aristotle, *Nicomachean Ethics*, trans. Terence Irwin [Hackett, 1985], Book X, chapter 9.) He starts by raising the issue of "Whether the excellence of a good man and a good citizen is the same or not" (Book III, chapter 7). Drawing on the sketch provided above of types of constitutions, reconstruct Aristotle's argument for the conclusion that "the good citizen need not of necessity possess the excellence which makes a good man." How does that argument differ from the arguments in the subsequent paragraphs, beginning with "The same question. . . ." and then with "But will there be no case . . . "? Aristotle ends this section by saying "From these considerations may be gathered the answer to the question, whether the excellence of the good man is the same as that of the good citizen, or different, and how far the same, and how far different." What is the answer?

2.  In his discussion of "oligarchical and democratic justice" (Book III, chapter 9), Aristotle says that "all men cling to justice of some kind, but their conceptions are imperfect and they do not express the whole idea." This comment is very important. Aristotle is asserting that people are misled in politics not simply because they are indifferent to justice, but because they misunderstand what justice requires. Correspondingly, it is important not simply that people pay attention to justice, but that they have reasonable ideas about justice.

How does Aristotle apply this point about imperfect and partial ideas of justice in his criticism of oligarchical justice, beginning with "if men met and associated out of regard to wealth only . . ."? Drawing on the example Aristotle discusses, try to formulate the view of the proponent of oligarchical justice. What is the fundamental mistake of the proponent of oligarchical justice? (The trick is to see how the fundamental mistake reflects a broad misconception of the nature of the state, of its central purpose.)

## Thomas Hobbes (1588–1679)

Hobbes was born in Malmesbury, England. He wrote on a wide range of philosophical, scientific, and historical topics. But Hobbes is known principally for his contributions to political philosophy. His *Leviathan* (1651) is perhaps the most influential work of modern political philosophy. Though most political philosophers have rejected his absolutist conclusions, Hobbes's argument for the state, his defense of sovereignty, and his contractual reasoning continue to exercise considerable influence on political thought.

# LEVIATHAN

## Chapter XIII: Of the Natural Condition of Mankind, as Concerning Their Felicity, and Misery

Nature hath made men so equal in the faculties of body and mind as that, though there be found one man sometimes manifestly stronger in body or of quicker mind than another, yet when all is reckoned together the difference between man and man is not so considerable as that one man can thereupon claim to himself any benefit to which another may not pretend as well as he. For as to the strength of body, the weakest has strength enough to kill the strongest, either by secret machination, or by confederacy with others that are in the same danger with himself.

And as to the faculties of the mind — setting aside the arts grounded upon words, and especially that skill of proceeding upon general and infallible rules called science (which very few have, and but in few things), as being not a native faculty (born with us), nor attained (as prudence) while we look after somewhat else — I find yet a greater equality amongst men than that of strength. For prudence is but experience, which equal time equally bestows on all men in those things they equally apply themselves unto. That which may perhaps make such equality incredible is but a vain conceit of one's own wisdom, which almost all men think they have in a greater degree than the vulgar, that is, than all men but themselves and a few others whom, by fame or for concurring with themselves, they approve. . . .

From this equality of ability ariseth equality of hope in the attaining of our ends. And therefore, if any two men desire the same thing, which nevertheless they cannot both enjoy, they become enemies; and in the way to their end, which is principally their own conservation, and sometimes their delectation only, endeavour to destroy or subdue one another. And from hence it comes to pass that, where an invader hath no more to fear than another man's single power, if one plant, sow, build, or possess a convenient seat, others may probably be expected to come prepared with forces united, to dispossess and deprive him, not only of the fruit of his labour, but also of his life or liberty. And the invader again is in the like danger of another.

And from this diffidence[1] of one another, there is no way for any man to secure himself so reasonable as anticipation, that is, by force or wiles to master the persons of all men he can, so long till he see no other power great enough to endanger him. And this is no more than his own conservation requireth, and is generally allowed. Also, because there be some that taking pleasure in contemplating their own power in the acts of conquest, which they pursue farther than their security requires, if others (that otherwise would be glad to be at case within modest bounds) should not by invasion increase their power, they would not be able, long time, by standing only on their defence, to subsist. And by consequence, such augmentation of dominion over men being necessary to a man's conservation, it ought to be allowed him.

Again, men have no pleasure, but on the contrary a great deal of grief, in keeping company where there is no power able to over-awe them all. For every man looketh that his companion should value him at the same rate he sets upon himself, and upon all signs of contempt, or undervaluing, naturally endeavours, as far as he dares (which amongst them that have no common power to keep them in quiet, is far enough to make them destroy each other), to extort a greater value from his contemners, by damage, and from others, by the example.

So that in the nature of man we find three principal causes of quarrel: first, competition; secondly, diffidence; thirdly, glory.

The first maketh men invade for gain; the second, for safety; and the third, for reputation. The first use violence to make themselves masters of other men's persons, wives, children, and cattle; the second, to defend them; the third, for trifles, as a word, a smile, a different opinion, and any other sign of undervalue, either direct in their persons, or by reflection in their kindred, their friends, their nation, their profession, or their name.

Hereby it is manifest that during the time men live without a common power to keep them all in awe, they are in that condition which is called war, and such a war as is of every man against every man. For WAR consisteth not in battle only, or the act of fighting, but in a tract of time wherein the will to contend by battle is sufficiently known. And therefore, the notion of *time* is to be considered in the nature of war, as it is in the nature of weather. For as the nature of foul weather lieth not in a shower or two of rain, but in an inclination thereto of many days together, so the nature of war consisteth not in actual fighting, but in the known disposition thereto during all the time there is no assurance to the contrary. All other time is PEACE.

1. "Diffidence," in its archaic usage, means "distrust."

Whatsoever therefore is consequent to a time of war, where every man is enemy to every man, the same is consequent to the time wherein men live without other security than what their own strength and their own invention shall furnish them withal. In such condition there is no place for industry, because the fruit thereof is uncertain, and consequently, no culture of the earth, no navigation, nor use of the commodities that may be imported by sea, no commodious building, no instruments of moving and removing such things as require much force, no knowledge of the face of the earth, no account of time, no arts, no letters, no society, and which is worst of all, continual fear and danger of violent death, and the life of man, solitary, poor, nasty, brutish, and short.

It may seem strange, to some man that has not well weighed these things, that nature should thus dissociate, and render men apt to invade and destroy one another. And he may, therefore, not trusting to this inference made from the passions, desire perhaps to have the same confirmed by experience. Let him therefore consider with himself—when taking a journey, he arms himself, and seeks to go well accompanied; when going to sleep, he locks his doors; when even in his house, he locks his chests; and this when he knows there be laws, and public officers, armed, to revenge all injuries shall be done him—what opinion he has of his fellow subjects, when he rides armed; of his fellow citizens, when he locks his doors; and of his children and servants, when he locks his chests. Does he not there as much accuse mankind by his actions, as I do by my words? . . .

To this war of every man against every man, this also is consequent: that nothing can be unjust. The notions of right and wrong, justice and injustice, have there no place. Where there is no common power, there is no law; where no law, no injustice. Force and fraud are in war the two cardinal virtues. Justice and injustice are none of the faculties neither of the body, nor mind. If they were, they might be in a man that were alone in the world, as well as his senses and passions. They are qualities that relate to men in society, not in solitude. It is consequent also to the same condition that there be no propriety, no dominion, no *mine* and *thine* distinct, but only that to be every man's that he can get, and for so long as he can keep it. And thus much for the ill condition which man by mere nature is actually placed in, though with a possibility to come out of it, consisting partly in the passions, partly in his reason.

# Chapter XVII: Of the Causes, Generation, and Definition of a Commonwealth

The final cause, end, or design of men (who naturally love liberty and dominion over others) in the introduction of that restraint upon themselves in which we see them live in commonwealths is the foresight of their own preservation, and of a more contented life thereby; that is to say, of getting themselves out from that miserable condition of war, which is necessarily consequent (as hath been shown [ch. xiii]) to the natural passions of men, when there is no visible power to keep them in awe. . . .

[B]e there never so great a multitude, yet if their actions be directed according to their particular judgments and particular appetites, they can expect thereby no defence, nor protection, neither against a common enemy, nor against the injuries of one another. For being distracted in opinions concerning the best use and application of their strength, they do not help, but hinder one another, and reduce their strength by mutual opposition to nothing; whereby they are easily, not only subdued by a very few that agree together, but also when there is no common enemy, they make war upon each other, for their particular interests. For if we could suppose a great multitude of men to consent in the observation of justice and other laws of nature[2] without a common power to keep them all in awe, we might as well suppose all mankind to do the same; and then there neither would be, nor need to be, any civil government or commonwealth at all, because there would be peace without subjection.

The only way to erect such a common power as may be able to defend them from the invasion of foreigners and the injuries of one another, and thereby to secure them in such sort as that by their own industry, and by the fruits of the earth, they may nourish themselves and live contentedly, is to confer all their power and strength upon one man, or upon one assembly of men, that may reduce all their wills, by plurality of voices, unto one will, which is as much as to say, to appoint one man or assembly of men to bear their person, and every one to own and acknowledge himself to be author of whatsoever he that so beareth their person shall act or cause to be acted, in those things which concern the common peace and safety, and therein to submit their wills, every one to his will, and their judgments, to his judgment. This is more than consent, or concord; it is a real unity of them all, in one and the same person, made by covenant of every man with every man, in such manner as if every man should say to every man *I authorise and give up my right of governing myself to this man, or to this assembly of men, on this condition, that thou give up thy right to him, and authorize all his actions in like manner.* This done, the multitude so united in one person is called a COMMONWEALTH, in Latin CIVITAS. This is the generation of that great LEVIATHAN[3] or rather (to speak more reverently) of that *Mortal God* to which we owe, under the *Immortal God,* our peace and defence. For by this authority, given him by every particular man in the commonwealth, he hath the use of so much power and strength conferred on him that by terror thereof he is enabled to conform the wills of them all to peace at home and mutual aid against their enemies abroad. And in him consisteth the essence of the commonwealth, which (to define it) is *one person, of whose acts a great multitude, by mutual covenants one with another, have made themselves every one the author, to the end he may use the strength and means of them all, as he shall think expedient, for their peace and common defence.*

And he that carrieth this person is called SOVEREIGN, and said to have *Sovereign Power;* and every one besides, his SUBJECT. . . .

2. Natural laws, for Hobbes, are rules of peaceful cooperation that can be discovered by reason. Justice — which is, Hobbes says, a matter of keeping valid agreements — is among those requirements of natural law. Hobbes discusses these issues in detail in *Leviathan,* chapters 14 and 15.

3. In the Old Testament, Book of Job 41:33–34, Leviathan is the great whale, about whom God says: "Upon earth there is not his like, who is made without fear. He beholdeth all high *things*: he *is* a king over all the children of pride."

# Chapter XVIII: Of the Rights of Sovereigns by Institution

A *commonwealth* is said to be *instituted,* when a *multitude* of men do agree and *covenant, every one with every one,* that to whatsoever *man* or *assembly of men* shall be given by the major part the *right* to *present* the person of them all (that is to say, to be their *representative*) every one, as well he that *voted for it* as he that *voted against it,* shall *authorize* all the actions and judgments of that man or assembly of men, in the same manner as if they were his own, to the end, to live peaceably amongst themselves and be protected against other men.

From this institution of a commonwealth are derived all the *rights* and *faculties* of him, or them, on whom the sovereign power is conferred by the consent of the people assembled.

First, because they covenant, it is to be understood they are not obliged by former covenant to anything repugnant hereunto. And consequently they that have already instituted a commonwealth, being thereby bound by covenant to own the actions and judgments of one, cannot lawfully make a new covenant amongst themselves to be obedient to any other, in any thing whatsoever, without his permission. And therefore, they that are subjects to a monarch cannot without his leave cast off monarchy and return to the confusion of a disunited multitude, nor transfer their person from him that beareth it to another man, or other assembly of men; for they are bound, every man to every man, to own, and be reputed author of, all that he that already is their sovereign shall do and judge fit to be done; so that, any one man dissenting, all the rest should break their covenant made to that man, which is injustice. And they have also every man given the sovereignty to him that beareth their person; and therefore if they depose him, they take from him that which is his own, and so again it is injustice. . . .

Secondly, because the right of bearing the person of them all is given to him they make sovereign by covenant only of one to another, and not of him to any of them, there can happen no breach of covenant on the part of the sovereign; and consequently none of his subjects, by any pretence of forfeiture, can be freed from his subjection.

That he which is made sovereign maketh no covenant with his subjects beforehand is manifest, because either he must make it with the whole multitude, as one party to the covenant, or he must make a several covenant with every man. With the whole, as one party, it is impossible, because as yet they are not one person; and if he make so many several covenants as there be men, those covenants after he hath the sovereignty are void, because what act soever can be pretended by any one of them for breach thereof is the act both of himself and of all the rest, because done in the person and by the right of every one of them in particular.

Besides, if any one (or more) of them pretend a breach of the covenant made by the sovereign at his institution, and others (or one other) of his subjects (or himself alone) pretend there was no such breach, there is in this case no judge to decide the controversy; it returns therefore to the sword again; and every man recovereth the right of protecting himself by his own strength, contrary to the design they had in the institution. . . .

Thirdly, because the major part hath by consenting voices declared a sovereign, he that dissented must now consent with the rest, that is, be contented to avow all the actions he shall do, or else justly be destroyed by the rest. For if he voluntarily entered into the congregation of them that were assembled, he sufficiently declared thereby his will (and therefore tacitly covenanted) to stand to what the major part should ordain; and therefore, if he refuse to stand thereto, or make protestation against any of their decrees, he does contrary to his covenant, and therefore unjustly. And whether he be of the congregation or not, and whether his consent be asked or not, he must either submit to their decrees or be left in the condition of war he was in before, wherein he might without injustice be destroyed by any man whatsoever.

Fourthly, because every subject is by this institution author of all the actions and judgments of the sovereign instituted, it follows that, whatsoever he doth, it can be no injury to any of his subjects, nor ought he to be by any of them accused of injustice. For he that doth anything by authority from another doth therein no injury to him by whose authority he acteth; but by this institution of a commonwealth every particular man is author of all the sovereign doth; and consequently he that complaineth of injury from his sovereign complaineth of that whereof he himself is author, and therefore ought not to accuse any man but himself; no nor himself of injury, because to do injury to one's self is impossible. It is true that they that have sovereign power may commit iniquity, but not injustice, or injury in the proper signification.

Fifthly, and consequently to that which was said last, no man that hath sovereign power can justly be put to death, or otherwise in any manner by his subjects punished. For seeing every subject is author of the actions of his sovereign, he punisheth another for the actions committed by himself.

And because the end of this institution is the peace and defence of them all, and whosoever has right to the end has right to the means, it belongeth of right to whatsoever man or assembly that hath the sovereignty, to be judge both of the means of peace and defence, and also of the hindrances and disturbances of the same, and to do whatsoever he shall think necessary to be done, both beforehand (for the preserving of peace and security, by prevention of discord at home and hostility from abroad) and, when peace and security are lost, for the recovery of the same. And therefore,

Sixthly, it is annexed to the sovereignty to be judge of what opinions and doctrines are averse, and what conducing, to peace; and consequently, on what occasions, how far, and what men are to be trusted withal, in speaking to multitudes of people, and who shall examine the doctrines of all books before they be published. For the actions of men proceed from their opinions, and in the well-governing of opinions consisteth the well-governing of men's actions, in order to their peace and concord. And though in matter of doctrine nothing ought to be regarded but the truth, yet this is not repugnant to regulating of the same by peace. For doctrine repugnant to peace can no more be true than peace and concord can be against the law of nature. . . .

Seventhly, is annexed to the sovereignty the whole power of prescribing the rules whereby every man may know what goods he may enjoy, and what actions he may do, without being molested by any of his fellow-subjects; and this is it men call *propriety*. For before constitution of sovereign power (as hath already been shown) all men had right to all things, which necessarily causeth war; and therefore, this propriety, being necessary to peace, and depending on sovereign power, is the act of that power, in order to the public peace. . . .

Eighthly, is annexed to the sovereiguty the right of judicature, that is to say, of hearing and deciding all controversies which may arise concerning law (either civil or natural) or concerning fact. For without the decision of controversies there is no protection of one subject against the injuries of another, the laws concerning *meum* and *tuum* are in vain, and to every man remaineth, from the natural and necessary appetite of his own conservation, the right of protecting himself by his private strength, which is the condition of war, and contrary to the end for which every commonwealth is instituted.

Ninthly, is annexed to the sovereignty the right of making war and peace with other nations and commonwealths, that is to say, of judging when it is for the public good, and how great forces are to be assembled, armed, and paid for that end, and to levy money upon the subjects to defray the expenses thereof. For the power by which the people are to be defended consisteth in their armies; and the strength of an army, in the union of their strength under one command; which command the sovereign instituted therefore hath, because the command of the *militia,* without other institution, maketh him that hath it sovereign. And therefore, whosoever is made general of an army, he that hath the sovereign power is always generalissimo. . . .

These are the rights which make the essence of sovereignty, and which are the marks whereby a man may discern in what man, or assembly of men, the sovereign power is placed and resideth. For these are incommunicable and inseparable. The power to coin money, to dispose of the estate and persons of infant heirs, to have preemption in markets, and all other statute prerogatives may be transferred by the sovereign, and yet the power to protect his subjects be retained. But if he transfer the *militia,* he retains the judicature in vain, for want of execution of the laws; or if he grant away the power of raising money, the *militia* is in vain; or if he give away the government of doctrines, men will be frighted into rebellion with the fear of spirits. And so if we consider any one of the said rights, we shall presently see, that the holding of all the rest will produce no effect, in the conservation of peace and justice, the end for which all commonwealths are instituted.

But a man may here object that the condition of subjects is very miserable, as being obnoxious to the lusts and other irregular passions of him or them that have so unlimited a power in their hands. And commonly, they that live under a monarch think it the fault of monarchy, and they that live under the government of democracy or other sovereign assembly attribute all the inconvenience to that form of commonwealth (whereas the power in all forms, if they be perfect enough to protect them, is the same), not considering that the estate of man can never be without some incommodity or other, and that the greatest that in any form of government can possibly happen to the people in general is scarce sensible,[4] in respect of the miseries

---

4. "Scarce sensible" literally means "barely noticeable." In the context, Hobbes is saying that the worst things that can happen under any form of government are hardly comparable to the horrors of the state of nature.

and horrible calamities that accompany a civil war (or that dissolute condition of masterless men, without subjection to laws and a coercive power to tie their hands from rapine and revenge), nor considering that the greatest pressure of sovereign governors proceedeth not from any delight or profit they can expect in the damage or weakening of their subjects (in whose vigour consisteth their own strength and glory), but in the restiveness of themselves that, unwillingly contributing to their own defence, make it necessary for their governors to draw from them what they can in time of peace, that they may have means on any emergent occasion, or sudden need, to resist or take advantage on their enemies. For all men are by nature provided of notable multiplying glasses (that is their passions and self-love), through which every little payment appeareth a great grievance, but are destitute of those prospective glasses (namely moral and civil science), to see afar off the miseries that hang over them, and cannot without such payments be avoided.

## TEST YOUR UNDERSTANDING

1. Hobbes's discussion of the state of nature explores "three principal causes of quarrel" (chapter 13). State the three principal causes in your own words.

2. What do people need to do to "erect . . . a common power as may be able to defend them from the invasion of foreigners and the injuries of one another" (chapter 17)?

3. What are some of the "rights and faculties" of the sovereign? Describe six of the rights, in familiar language.

## NOTES AND QUESTIONS

1. Hobbes begins his account of the state of nature by discussing certain kinds of equality. In what ways does he think human beings are equal? Do you find what he says plausible? Why does equality of "prudence," in particular, matter to his subsequent argument?

   For discussion, see Kinch Hoekstra, "Hobbesian Equality," in *Hobbes Today: Insights for the 21st Century*, ed. S. A. Lloyd (Cambridge University Press, 2012).

2. According to Hobbes, "when men live without a common power to keep them all in awe, they are in that condition which is called war, and such a war as is of every man against every man." Hobbes is saying that *without a strong power over everyone, people will be in a state of war*. Present a **valid argument**, starting from premises that you believe Hobbes endorses in chapter 13, for the italicized conclusion. Your reconstruction will need to include definitions of "common power" and "war."

   As a helpful starting point on this issue, see Jean Hampton, *Hobbes and the Social Contract Tradition* (Cambridge University Press, 1988).

3. If people care a great deal about self-preservation and peace, why are they unable, in the absence of a common power, to avoid conflict? And how is a sovereign able to resolve the conflicts and keep the peace? For example, suppose people end up in a

state of war because they do not trust each other. To ensure peace, does the state need to get them to trust each other? How does it manage that? Suppose they end up in a state of war because some people think they are better than others. To ensure peace, does the state need them to stop thinking that? What else can the sovereign do?

4. The only way to achieve a stable peace, Hobbes says, is by creating a "real unity . . . in one and the same person." What is this "real unity"? How is it created? (You will need to think hard about Hobbes's understanding of a sovereign, and his idea of authorizing the sovereign.) Real unity is supposed to be different from "consent and concord." How so?

5. Hobbes gives us a detailed list of the rights that belong to the sovereign. Does the sovereign need all of these rights to keep the peace? Which rights do you think are not really needed? Why?

## Jean-Jacques Rousseau (1712–1778)

Rousseau was born in Geneva. He was a philosopher, composer, and novelist, whose writings exercised considerable impact on the French Revolution. Rousseau's *Confessions* shaped modern conventions of autobiography; his *Emile* remains an important work on education; his two *Discourses — On the Arts and Sciences* and *On Inequality —* are foundational works for the critique of modern culture, and his *Social Contract* is an essential contribution to modern democratic thought. Rousseau exercised a profound influence on Immanuel Kant, who once described him as the Newton of the moral world.

# THE SOCIAL CONTRACT

## Book I, Chapter One: Subject of this First Book

Man is born free, and everywhere he is in chains. One believes himself the others' master, and yet is more a slave than they. How did this change come about? I do not know. What can make it legitimate? I believe I can solve this question. . . .

## Chapter Three: The Right of the Stronger

The stronger is never strong enough to be forever master, unless he transforms his force into right, and obedience into duty. Hence the right of the stronger; a right which is apparently understood ironically, and in principle really established. But will no one ever explain this word to us? Force is a physical power. I fail to see what morality can result from its effects. To yield to force is an act of necessity, not of will; at most it is an act of prudence. In what sense can it become a duty?

Let us assume this alleged right for a moment. I say that it can only result in an unintelligible muddle. For once force makes right, the effect changes together with the cause; every force that overcomes the first, inherits its right. Once one can disobey with impunity, one can do so legitimately, and since the stronger is always right, one need only make sure to be the stronger. But what is a right that perishes when force ceases? If one has to obey by force, one need not obey by duty, and if one is no longer forced to obey, one is no longer obliged to do so. Clearly, then, this word "right" adds nothing to force; it means nothing at all here. . . .

Let us agree, then, that force does not make right, and that one is only obliged to obey legitimate powers. Thus my original question keeps coming back.

# Chapter Four: Of Slavery

Since no man has a natural authority over his fellow-man, and since force produces no right, conventions remain as the basis of all legitimate authority among men.

If, says Grotius, an individual can alienate his freedom, and enslave himself to a master, why could not a whole people alienate its freedom and subject itself to a king?[1] There are quite a few ambiguous words here which call for explanation, but let us confine ourselves to the word *alienate*. To alienate is to give or to sell. Now, a man who enslaves himself to another does not give himself, he sells himself, at the very least for his subsistence: but a people, what does it sell itself for? A king, far from furnishing his subjects' subsistence, takes his own entirely from them, and according to Rabelais[2] a king does not live modestly. Do the subjects then give their persons on condition that their goods will be taken as well? I do not see what they have left to preserve.

The despot, it will be said, guarantees civil tranquility for his subjects. All right; but what does it profit them if the wars his ambition brings on them, if his insatiable greed, the harassment by his administration cause them more distress than their own dissension would have done? What does it profit them if this very tranquility is one of their miseries? Life is also tranquil in dungeons; is that enough to feel well in them? The Greeks imprisoned in the Cyclops's cave[3] lived there tranquilly, while awaiting their turn to be devoured. . . .

---

1. Hugo Grotius (1583–1645) was a Dutch jurist and one of the founders of international law. Rousseau is here referring to Grotius's *The Rights of War and Peace,* book 1, chapter 3, section 8, paragraph 1.

2. Rabelais (1494–1553) was a French humanist and the author of *Gargantua and Pantagruel,* a series of fantastical novels concerning the adventures of two giants. The book also includes extended meditations on contemporary social, political, and religious issues.

3. In Homer's *Odyssey,* book 9, Odysseus and twelve of his men are trapped in the cave of Polyphemus, a Cyclops. Polyphemus plans to eat them all, but they escape because of an ingenious plan devised by Odysseus.

To renounce one's freedom is to renounce one's quality as man, the rights of humanity, and even its duties. There can be no possible compensation for someone who renounces everything. Such a renunciation is incompatible with the nature of man, and to deprive one's will of all freedom is to deprive one's actions of all morality. Finally, a convention that stipulates absolute authority on one side, and unlimited obedience on the other, is vain and contradictory. Is it not clear that one is under no obligation toward a person from whom one has the right to demand everything, and does not this condition alone, without equivalent and without exchange, nullify the act? For what right can my slave have against me, since everything he has belongs to me, and his right being mine, this right of mine against myself is an utterly meaningless expression? . . .

## Chapter Five: That One Always Has to Go Back to a First Convention

Even if I were to grant everything I have thus far refuted, the abettors of despotism would be no better off. There will always be a great difference between subjugating a multitude and ruling a society. When scattered men, regardless of their number, are successively enslaved to a single man, I see in this nothing but a master and slaves, I do not see in it a people and its chief; it is, if you will, an aggregation, but not an association; there is here neither public good, nor body politic. That man, even if he had enslaved half the world, still remains nothing but a private individual; his interest, separate from that of the others, still remains nothing but a private interest. When this same man dies, his empire is left behind scattered and without a bond, like an oak dissolves and collapses into a heap of ashes on being consumed by fire.

A people, says Grotius, can give itself to a king. So that according to Grotius a people is a people before giving itself to a king. That very gift is a civil act, it presupposes a public deliberation. Hence before examining the act by which a people elects a king, it would be well to examine the act by which a people is a people. For this act, being necessarily prior to the other, is the true foundation of society.

Indeed, if there were no prior convention, then, unless the election were unanimous, why would the minority be obliged to submit to the choice of the majority, and why would a hundred who want a master have the right to vote on behalf of ten who do not want one? The law of majority rule is itself something established by convention, and presupposes unanimity at least once.

## Chapter Six: Of the Social Pact

I assume men having reached the point where the obstacles that interfere with their preservation in the state of nature prevail by their resistance over the forces which each individual can muster to maintain himself in that state. Then that primitive state can no longer subsist, and humankind would perish if it did not change its way of being.

Now, since men cannot engender new forces, but only unite and direct those that exist, they are left with no other means of self-preservation than to form, by aggregation, a sum of forces that might prevail over those obstacles' resistance, to set them in motion by a single impetus, and make them act in concert.

This sum of forces can only arise from the cooperation of many: but since each man's force and freedom are his primary instruments of self-preservation, how can he commit them without harming himself, and without neglecting the cares he owes himself? This difficulty, in relation to my subject, can be stated in the following terms.

"To find a form of association that will defend and protect the person and goods of each associate with the full common force, and by means of which each, uniting with all, nevertheless obey only himself and remain as free as before." This is the fundamental problem to which the social contract provides the solution.

The clauses of this contract are so completely determined by the nature of the act that the slightest modification would render them null and void; so that although they may never have been formally stated, they are everywhere the same, everywhere tacitly admitted and recognized; until, the social compact having been violated, everyone is thereupon restored to his original rights and resumes his natural freedom while losing the conventional freedom for which he renounced it.

These clauses, rightly understood, all come down to just one, namely the total alienation of each associate with all of his rights to the whole community: For, in the first place, since each gives himself entirely, the condition is equal for all, and since the condition is equal for all, no one has any interest in making it burdensome to the rest.

Moreover, since the alienation is made without reservation, the union is as perfect as it can be, and no associate has anything further to claim: For if individuals were left some rights, then, since there would be no common superior who might adjudicate between them and the public, each, being judge in his own case on some issue, would soon claim to be so on all, the state of nature would subsist and the association necessarily become tyrannical or empty.

Finally, each, by giving himself to all, gives himself to no one, and since there is no associate over whom one does not acquire the same right as one grants him over oneself, one gains the equivalent of all one loses, and more force to preserve what one has.

If, then, one sets aside everything that is not of the essence of the social compact, one finds that it can be reduced to the following terms: *Each of us puts his person and his full power in common under the supreme direction of the general will; and in a body we receive each member as an indivisible part of the whole.*

At once, in place of the private person of each contracting party, this act of association produces a moral and collective body made up of as many members as the assembly has voices, and which receives by this same act its unity, its common *self*, its life and its will. The public person thus formed by the union of all the others formerly assumed the name *City* and now assumes that of *Republic* or of *body politic*, which its members call *State* when it is passive, *Sovereign* when active, *Power* when comparing it to similar bodies. As for the associates, they collectively assume the name *people* and individually call themselves *Citizens* as participants in the sovereign authority, and *Subjects* as subjected to the laws of the State. But these terms are often confused and mistaken for one another; it is enough to be able to distinguish them where they are used in their precise sense.

## Chapter Seven: Of the Sovereign

This formula shows that the act of association involves a reciprocal engagement between the public and private individuals, and that each individual, by contracting, so to speak, with himself, finds himself engaged in a two-fold relation: namely, as member of the Sovereign toward private individuals, and as a member of the State toward the Sovereign. But here the maxim of civil right, that no one is bound by engagements toward himself, does not apply; for there is a great difference between assuming an obligation toward oneself, and assuming a responsibility toward a whole of which one is a part.

It should also be noted that the public deliberation which can obligate all subjects toward the Sovereign because of the two different relations in terms of which each subject is viewed cannot, for the opposite reason, obligate the Sovereign toward itself, and that it is therefore contrary to the nature of the body politic for the Sovereign to impose on itself a law which it cannot break. Since the Sovereign can consider itself only in terms of one and the same relation, it is then in the same situation as a private individual contracting with himself: which shows that there is not, nor can there be, any kind of fundamental law that is obligatory for the body of the people, not even the social contract. This does not mean that this body cannot perfectly well enter into engagements with others about anything that does not detract from this contract; for with regard to foreigners it becomes a simple being, an individual.

But the body politic or Sovereign, since it owes its being solely to the sanctity of the contract, can never obligate itself, even toward another, to anything that detracts from that original act, such as to alienate any part of itself or to subject itself to another Sovereign. To violate the act by which it exists would be to annihilate itself, and what is nothing produces nothing.

As soon as this multitude is thus united in one body, one cannot injure one of the members without attacking the body, and still less can one injure the body without the members being affected. Thus duty and interest alike obligate the contracting parties to help one another, and the same men must strive to combine in this two-fold relation all the advantages attendant on it.

Now the Sovereign, since it is formed entirely of the individuals who make it up, has not and cannot have any interests contrary to theirs; consequently the Sovereign power has no need of a guarantor toward the subjects, because it is impossible for the body to want to harm all of its members, and we shall see later that it cannot harm any one of them in particular. The Sovereign, by the mere fact that it is, is always everything it ought to be.

But this is not the case regarding the subjects' relations to the Sovereign, and notwithstanding the common interest, the Sovereign would have no guarantee of the subjects' engagements if it did not find means to ensure their fidelity.

Indeed each individual may, as a man, have a particular will contrary to or different from the general will he has as a Citizen. His particular interest may speak to him quite differently from the common interest; his absolute and naturally independent existence may lead him to look upon what he owes to the common cause as a gratuitous contribution, the loss of which will harm others less than its payment burdens him and, by considering the moral person that constitutes the State as a being of reason because it is not a man, he would enjoy the rights of a citizen without being willing to fulfill the duties of a subject; an injustice, the progress of which would cause the ruin of the body politic.

Hence for the social compact not to be an empty formula, it tacitly includes the following engagement which alone can give force to the rest, that whoever refuses to obey the general will shall be constrained to do so by the entire body: which means nothing other than that he shall be forced to be free; for this is the condition which, by giving each Citizen to the Fatherland, guarantees him against all personal dependence; the condition which is the device and makes for the operation of the political machine, and alone renders legitimate civil engagements which would otherwise be absurd, tyrannical, and liable to the most enormous abuses.

# Chapter Eight: Of the Civil State

This transition from the state of nature to the civil state produces a most remarkable change in man by substituting justice for instinct in his conduct, and endowing his actions with the morality they previously lacked. Only then, when the voice of duty succeeds physical impulsion and right succeeds appetite, does man, who until then had looked only to himself, see himself forced to act on other principles, and to consult his reason before listening to his inclinations. Although in this state he deprives himself of several advantages he has from nature, he gains such great advantages in return, his faculties are exercised and developed, his ideas enlarged, his sentiments ennobled, his entire soul is elevated to such an extent, that if the abuses of this new condition did not often degrade him to beneath the condition he has left, he should ceaselessly bless the happy moment which wrested him from it forever, and out of a stupid and bounded animal made an intelligent being and a man.

Let us reduce this entire balance to terms easy to compare. What man loses by the social contract is his natural freedom and an unlimited right to everything that tempts him and he can reach; what he gains is civil freedom and property in everything he possesses. In order not to be mistaken about these compensations, one has to distinguish clearly between natural freedom which has no other bounds than the individual's forces, and civil freedom which is limited by the general will, and between possession which is merely the effect of force or the right of the first occupant, and property which can only be founded on a positive title.

To the preceding one might add to the credit of the civil state moral freedom, which alone makes man truly the master of himself; for the impulsion of mere appetite is slavery, and obedience to the law one has prescribed to oneself is freedom. But I have already said too much on this topic, and the philosophical meaning of the word *freedom* is not my subject here.

. . . I shall close this book with a comment that should serve as the basis of the entire social system; it is that the fundamental pact, rather than destroying natural equality, on the contrary substitutes a moral and legitimate equality for whatever physical inequality nature may have placed between men, and that while they may be unequal in force or in genius, they all become equal by convention and by right.[4]

# Book II, Chapter Four: Of the Limits of Sovereign Power

All the services a Citizen can render the State, he owes to it as soon as the Sovereign requires them; but the Sovereign, for its part, cannot burden the subjects with any shackles that are useless to the community; it cannot even will to do so: for under the law of reason nothing is done without cause, any more than under the law of nature.

The commitments which bind us to the social body are obligatory only because they are mutual, and their nature is such that in fulfilling them one cannot work for others without also working for oneself. Why is the general will always upright, and why do all consistently will each one's happiness, if not because there is no one who does not appropriate the word *each* to himself, and think of himself as he votes for all? Which proves that the equality of right and the notion of justice which it produces follows from each one's preference for himself and hence from the nature of man; that the general will, to be truly such, must be so in its object as well as in its essence, that it must issue from all in order to apply to all, and that it loses its natural rectitude when it tends toward some individual and determinate object; for then, judging what is foreign to us, we have no true principle of equity to guide us. . . .

---

4. Under bad governments, this equality is only apparent and illusory: it serves only to keep the pauper in his poverty and the rich man in the position he has usurped. In fact, laws are always of use to those who possess and harmful to those who have nothing: from which it follows that the social state is advantageous to men only when all have something and none too much. [Rousseau's note.]

In view of this, one has to understand that what generalizes the will is not so much the number of voices, as it is the common interest which unites them: for in this institution, everyone necessarily submits to the conditions which he imposes on others; an admirable agreement between interest and justice which confers on common deliberations a character of equity that is seen to vanish in the discussion of any particular affair, for want of a common interest which unites and identifies the rule of the judge with that of the party.

From whatever side one traces one's way back to the principle, one always reaches the same conclusion: namely, that the social pact establishes among the Citizens an equality such that all commit themselves under the same conditions and must all enjoy the same rights. Thus by the nature of the pact every act of sovereignty, that is to say every genuine act of the general will, either obligates or favors all Citizens equally, so that the Sovereign knows only the body of the nation and does not single out any one of those who make it up. What, then, is, properly, an act of sovereignty? It is not a convention of the superior with the inferior, but a convention of the body with each one of its members: A convention which is legitimate because it is based on the social contract, equitable because it is common to all, and secure because the public force and the supreme power are its guarantors. So long as subjects are subjected only to conventions such as these, they obey no one, but only their own will; and to ask how far the respective rights of Sovereign and Citizens extend is to ask how far the Citizens can commit themselves to one another, each to all, and all to each.

From this it is apparent that the Sovereign power, absolute, sacred, and inviolable though it is, does not and cannot exceed the limits of the general conventions, and that everyone may fully dispose of such of his goods and freedom as are left him by these conventions: so that it is never right for the Sovereign to burden one subject more than another, because it then turns into a particular affair, and its power is no longer competent.

These distinctions once admitted, it is so [evidently] false that the social contract involves any genuine renunciation on the part of individuals, that, . . . as a result of the contract their situation really proves to be preferable to what it had been before, and that instead of an alienation they have only made an advantageous exchange of an uncertain and precarious way of being in favor of a more secure and better one, of natural independence in favor of freedom, of the power to harm others in favor of their own security, and of their force which others could overwhelm in favor of right made invincible by the social union. Their very life which they have dedicated to the State is constantly protected by it, and when they risk it for its defense, what are they doing but returning to it what they have received from it? What are they doing that they would not have done more frequently and at greater peril in the state of nature, when, waging inevitable fights, they would be defending the means of preserving their lives by risking them? All have to fight for the fatherland if need be, it is true, but then no one ever has to fight for himself. Isn't it nevertheless a gain to risk for the sake of what gives us security just a part of what we would have to risk for our own sakes if we were deprived of this security?

## TEST YOUR UNDERSTANDING

1. What does Rousseau tell us is "the fundamental problem to which the social contract provides the solution"? State the problem in your own words.

2. Rousseau distinguishes among natural freedom, civil freedom, and moral freedom. What does he mean by "moral freedom"? How is moral freedom different from natural and civil freedom?

3. In a remark on the general will, Rousseau says that "what generalizes the will is not so much the number of voices, as it is the common interest which unites them." What kind of common interest does he think unites people? (Go back to his statement of the fundamental problem, discussed in question 1, above.)

## NOTES AND QUESTIONS

1. In the social compact, Rousseau says, "each of us puts his person and his full power in common under the supreme direction of the general will." We agree to follow the general will, not simply our own particular will, which may be at odds with the general will. As you read the selection, you saw that understanding the general will is essential to understanding Rousseau's conception of the state. As you also saw, it is hard to understand. Rousseau writes beautifully, but also telegraphically. And he was enthusiastic about apparently paradoxical ways of putting things.

    In understanding the general will, then, it helps to bear in mind some of the claims that Rousseau makes about how the general will is justified, how it is expressed, and what its content is:

    a. The social compact is a mutual agreement to follow the general will.

    b. In making a social compact, we aim to protect our person and goods, and to remain as free as we were before.

    c. "What generalizes the will is not so much the number of voices, as it is the common interest which unites them" (Book II, chapter 4).

    d. The general will is directed to the common good.

    e. Sovereignty is the exercise of the general will.

    f. Acts of sovereignty (exercises of the general will) are not directives from superior to inferior but agreements of citizens with one another.

    g. Law is the declaration of the general will.

    h. An act of the general will "obligates or favors all citizens equally."

    i. In complying with the general will, we are morally free, which means that we give the law to ourselves.

    The challenge is to combine these pieces in a coherent and sensible way. One line of interpretation proceeds as follows: in the social compact, we agree to live together in a society in which the general will is the highest authority. In such a society, citizens share an idea of and a commitment to acting for the common good. For example, when they conduct political discussion, they all appeal to an idea of the common good. Acting for the common good consists, more specifically, in protecting the basic, common interests of each citizen, including interests in the protection of the person and goods of each. So acting for the common good requires showing equal concern for each citizen. Citizens act for the common good by making general laws. What makes the laws general is that they benefit all and impose obligations on all. Because the citizens share an idea of their common good and make laws that express that understanding, they act freely — they are "as free as before" — when they comply with the laws. More particularly, they achieve the moral freedom that consists in giving the law to yourself. For further elaboration of this line of interpretation, see Joshua Cohen, *Rousseau: A Free Community of Equals* (Oxford University Press, 2010).

In light of these comments on the general will, consider a few of Rousseau's statements and respond to the associated questions:

(i) The social compact involves no "genuine renunciation on the part of individuals" (Book II, chapter 4). How does he develop that idea of "no genuine renunciation" in the rest of the sentence?

(ii) The sovereign cannot "burden the subjects with any shackles that are useless to the community" (Book II, chapter 4). Why not? How does the idea of the general will support this conclusion?

(iii) "Whoever refuses to obey the general will shall be constrained to do so by the entire body: which means nothing other than that he shall be forced to be free" (Book I, chapter 8). What is Rousseau saying? Does it make sense? Is the idea that punishment forces people to be free? Is the idea that punishment *treats people as free* by holding them responsible for violating laws that are aimed at advancing the common good?

2. Rousseau was remarkably odd and remarkably talented. In a wonderful biography, Leo Damrosch says:

> In a series of amazingly original books, of which *The Social Contract* is the best known, he developed a political theory that deeply influenced the American Founding Fathers and the French revolutionaries, helped to invent modern anthropology, and advanced a concept of education that remains challenging and inspiring to this day. His *Confessions* virtually created the genre of autobiography as we know it, tracing lifelong patterns of feeling to formative experiences and finding a deep unity of the self beneath apparent contradictions; modern psychology owes him an immense debt. Rousseau achieved all that without ever attending school. And there is much else: *Le devin du village*, a comic opera admired by Gluck and the very young Mozart, performed 400 times (including at Fontainebleau and the Paris Opera, the first performance after the fall of the Bastille); a less successful play, *Narcissus, or the Self-Lover*, which was performed by the Comédie-Française in 1752; and *Julie, or the New Heloïse*, one of the most popular novels of the eighteenth century.

See Leo Damrosch, *Jean-Jacques Rousseau: Restless Genius* (Houghton-Mifflin, 2005).

## A. John Simmons (born 1950)

Simmons is Commonwealth Professor of Philosophy and a professor of law at the University of Virginia. A political philosopher, Simmons has written influential books on individual rights, political obligation, and political legitimacy. He is best known for his views about the importance of consent as a basis of political obligation and his skepticism that most people have consented in ways that establish obligations.

# RIGHTS-BASED JUSTIFICATIONS FOR THE STATE

## I. Rights

Rights are a familiar feature of our practical lives. We demand legal rights to practice our religions or be free of negligent injury; we declare support for the human rights of the victims of totalitarian regimes; and we acquire rights by joining such voluntary associations as sororities or unions. In these and countless other cases, we make *claims* to rights.

The rights we claim fall into two broad categories. Rights in the first category — call them "conventional rights" — are defined or created by social practices (including rules and laws). Our conventional rights include legal rights, as well as rights conferred on us by our positions or roles in our businesses, churches, clubs, etc. Conventional rights vary widely across place and time, since practices differ so widely across social groups and change over time within them. Thus, women won the right to vote in the United States in 1920, and 18-year-olds in 1971. In both cases, we have extensions of conventional rights.

Rights in the second category — call them "moral rights" — are not conferred by our social practices. Many of our conventional rights are conceived as enforcing or securing such moral rights: laws against murder, for example, secure a moral right not to be killed, a right that is not created by law but that the law protects. Moreover, we claim such moral rights even when our existing practices violate them: abolitionists, for example, condemned slavery for violating a moral right not to be enslaved. The languages of "natural rights" (most popular in the 17th–19th centuries) and of "human rights" (more popular since) have typically been employed to make claims about the moral rights that persons possess independent of political and legal practices.

Sometimes we attempt to *justify* institutions or practices — to justify the state, for example — by appealing to rights, as when we say that a state is legitimate because it has a special right to rule or because it protects the rights of the governed. Such arguments naturally appeal to *moral* rights: our social practices could hardly justify themselves simply by creating new conventional rights of the relevant sort. But how should we understand the moral rights that figure in such justifications?

Rights usually provide their holders with a range of options and impose corresponding restraints on the actions of others. For example, my right to freedom of speech gives me the options to speak or not, in private or in public, and also imposes duties on others not to silence me in certain ways. Some have found it helpful to think of persons' rights as defining a kind of "walled space" around them, the "walls" representing the restraints on others' actions and the "space" representing the range of the rightholders' permissible options. The walls and space are obviously not physical, since people violate others' rights with alarming ease and frequency. Instead, we must imagine moral (or legal) analogues of physical space.

Thinking of rights as walled spaces helps to highlight certain of the principal functions of rights. First, our rights function not only to bar self-serving aggression against us by other individuals, but also to bar certain ways of pursuing valuable group or social ends. Good ends — including the utilitarian end of social happiness — can sometimes be most efficiently pursued by bad means, including the sacrifice or exploitation of particular individuals. Rights are a bar on such pursuits, and the spatial picture represents these restrictions both by the walls and by the space within them. The wall is the boundary to society, and the space within represents a person's range of permissible options, that she need not choose to act always in a way that best promotes good ends; her space permits her sometimes to look out for herself or for her own values.

Second, the wall in the "walled space" characterization reminds us that rights make possible certain ways of regarding persons and their moral importance that would be impossible in a world without rights. In particular, in a world without rights (walls) we could not demand certain things (including others' actions) as *owed* to us; we would have to rely instead on others' good will to provide (or to respect) these things. Nor would it be possible without rights to think of people as possessing real dignity and independence, but only instead as valuable parts of some larger (e.g., social or religious) scheme. The "wall" of my rights pulls others up short, requiring them to respect my "space" in the world, to treat me as a being who *has* a space.

The "walled space" metaphor is also, however, misleading in certain ways. First, the metaphor may misleadingly suggest that all our rights must be "defensive" or *negative* — rights not to be directly harmed or interfered with. But while many of our most important rights *are* "negative," we also have "*positive* rights," rights that others act for our benefit, beyond their duties of forbearance. For example, we have positive rights that others fulfill their promises and provide reparation for injuries. Moreover, many moral theories hold that we have positive moral rights to rescue in emergencies or to a just redistribution of societal or global wealth.

Second, the term "right" is commonly used (in both law and morality) to designate a number of different types of relations, not all of which can be even approximately represented by thinking of "walled spaces." Consider, for example, the contrast between "claim rights" and "liberty rights." A claim right is a right that *correlates* with another's duty to respect the right (by acting or forbearing). With liberty rights there are no such correlative duties on others. Instead, the assertion of a liberty right to act entails only that there is no duty on the rightholder *not* to so act: when I have a liberty right to do something, it is permissible (or "alright") for me to do it. Each of us has, for example, a liberty right to pick up (and perhaps thereby establish a *claim* right in) the unowned gold nugget in the wilderness. But each person's right is here *competitive with* the rights of others: neither of us has any correlative duty to permit the other to pick it up first. In such cases, the "walled space" metaphor for rights seems particularly inapt.

# II. Rights-Based Justifications

Rights-based justifications for the state explain the state's authority or legitimacy in terms of the state's special relationship to the rights of individuals. Such justifications have an especially natural place in the social contract tradition in political philosophy. According to social contractarians, for a (or the) state to be justified, it must be the subject of an actual, a possible, or a hypothetical contract or agreement among the subjects of that state. In each of the three great strands of social contract thought — the political philosophies of Hobbes, Locke, and Kant — we can see a different way of bringing the idea of individual rights to bear on a justification for the state.

Hobbes's *Leviathan*, for instance, argues for a "sovereign" — with an absolute (unlimited) right to rule over the state's subjects. The sovereign gets that absolute authority by the continued possession of a right that everyone else — all the subjects of the sovereign — contractually renounces. In authorizing the sovereign person (or assembly, whichever governs) to exercise his (its) own right unhindered, the subjects agree with one another not to oppose his (its) will.

Hobbes begins with the idea that all persons are moral equals in their possession of the "right of nature," their "right to every thing." In a state of nature, with no political authority, life is so perilous that persons are seldom able to (safely) act peaceably. They are consequently entitled to use all the "advantages of war" against others in whatever ways they judge will enhance their personal security. (Notice that, because all possess competitively this same right of aggression, the right of nature cannot be understood as a claim right, correlating with others' duties of restraint; it must be understood instead as a mere liberty right, thus not as a wall.) Political society begins when each subject lays down this right to make war on others, either "voluntarily" (out of the desire to no longer live in a miserable state of nature) or at the point of a sword. The sovereign person (or body), however, retains the right of nature and thus remains at liberty to act as he (or she, or it) judges best. That is because the sovereign is not a party to the contract between subjects that makes him sovereign, but only the beneficiary of that agreement; so the sovereign's resulting authority is absolute. What justifies this absolute dominion (ideally, in Hobbes's view, rule by a monarch) is its sovereign's continued possession of the moral (liberty) right to use force against his subjects.

An idea of rights, then, plays a central role in Hobbes's justification of the state. Everyone starts with a right to everything, including the use of force against others. Subjects relinquish this right in forming the state; the sovereign retains the right. The result is the sovereign's moral "monopoly" on the use of force within the state.

Locke's *Second Treatise of Government* presents a superficially similar emphasis on individual rights and the sovereign monopoly on force as essential elements in justifying the state. But in the Lockean social contract, the rights with which persons are understood to begin are (mostly transferable) moral claim rights which correlate with the moral duties of others to respect those rights, not the competitive liberties of the Hobbesian state of nature; and the rights of authorities are not individual rights retained from their pre-political condition, but are *composed from* portions of all citizens' pre-political endowment of moral rights; individuals construct an authority by entrusting some of their rights to the state.

More specifically, persons naturally possess both a right to govern their own lives (within the bounds of moral duty), free from the interference of others, and a right to enforce the natural (moral) law according to their own conscientious interpretation of its requirements. This latter right to punish moral wrongdoers is wielded by private individuals in the state of nature. This exercise of the right to punish by private individuals is a source of "inconvenience" and potential conflict. The need to centralize this executive right in the hands of a neutral judge (to adjudicate disputes between individuals) is thus the key to the justification of the Lockean state. In any legitimate political society each person subject to the coercive powers of the state must have conveyed to the state, by contract or consent, his or her private executive right (in addition to other rights necessary for a viable polity). The state thus receives a "composite" right — composed of the separate rights of each subject — to make and enforce law on behalf of all citizens, a right that correlates with the contractually undertaken political obligations of those members. The state's legislative and executive rights, still limited by the requirements of natural law and by the peoples' purposes in entrusting them to the state, are what justifies any state activities within these prescribed limits.

Kant, like Locke, begins with the idea of natural equality and a basic right to freedom. The right to freedom is the one natural ("original") "innate" right, a right that each person possesses "in virtue of his humanity": a right to the maximum freedom from constraint by others that is consistent with every individual possessing that freedom. But Kant's right to freedom (unlike Locke's) cannot possibly be fully realized and respected except in a civil society under coercive law. Most rights in the lawless state of nature (where reasonable disagreement about their nature and extent is possible) are merely "provisional" and can only be made real or conclusive by legal enforcement. So Kant's innate right to freedom requires, then, that other persons join together to leave the state of nature and create (or sustain) political institutions that are capable of fully satisfying that right (by establishing a constitution and legal system that can guarantee our natural equality and independence). Each person is correlatively obligated to accept membership in a state with such institutions. The state is justified, on this account, because it is necessary for realizing our one innate moral right. In short, Locke argues that leaving the state of nature is advisable but morally optional for each person; Kant argues that doing so is morally obligatory.

Each of these three strands of social contract thought continues to have its adherents. But contemporary Hobbesians and Kantians seldom present their justifications of the state as rights-based. Contemporary Hobbesians draw on Hobbes's idea of the justified state as a rational choice for all. Hobbes argued that the choice of a strong, stable state, one that was unlikely to slide back into the horrors of the state of nature, is a choice that only a "fool" would reject. Only someone seduced by the prospect of immediate advantage or confused about the likely consequences of continuing to make war on others would choose the liberty of a state of nature over the peaceful security of political society. But if the state is a rational choice for all, this may seem sufficient by itself to explain why the state is justified in making and coercively enforcing law. If so, there seems little need to appeal to ideas about rights. Contemporary Hobbesians have mostly chosen to try to develop this rational choice side of Hobbes's arguments.

Similarly, contemporary Kantians have also displaced the idea of rights from the core of the state's justification. Putting aside Kant's claims about innate, pre-political rights, they emphasize instead a variant of Kant's test for the legitimacy of particular laws: that enacted laws are legitimate just in case they could have been consented to by the people who are subject to them. Contemporary Kantian political philosophers (most famously John Rawls) have argued that just political and legal institutions are those that would have been selected by persons choosing terms of cooperation in a fair original position of choice. State coercion, then, is legitimate or justified when it is used in accordance with rules which all reasonable citizens could be expected to endorse. No further justification, in terms of the realization of innate rights, is required.

It is thus primarily contemporary representatives of the Lockean strain in social contract thought who have continued to emphasize rights-based justifications of the state. Lockeans disagree significantly with one another, however, on the kinds of moral rights with which we are naturally endowed, thus as well on the details of their arguments about the state's legitimacy. The heart of one kind of defensible Lockean theory is presented below.

# III. Lockean Political Philosophy

Persons are, as Locke argued, naturally free and equal. We are not, of course, all equals in strength or intelligence, nor do all of us actually enjoy political freedom. But once our rationality and socialization progress to the point that we can appreciate basic moral demands of nonaggression and mutual assistance and are capable of conforming our actions to those demands, persons enjoy the *moral* freedom and equality to which each is born. Each person is equally subject to those demands of morality, and each enjoys the correlative rights to govern his or her own life within moral bounds. Each person is, in consequence, naturally free of the authority of others to command conduct. So *political authority* must be produced in ways that are consistent with our natural freedom and equality, typically by the voluntary (i.e., self-governing) choices of persons.

These Lockean claims of natural freedom and equality are much less controversial now than when Locke asserted them. Most of us are inclined to agree that enslaving or aggressing against morally innocent persons would be a wrong to them, even in a nonpolitical, nonlegal context. Different moral theories mostly converge on these basic Lockean claims. Locke himself argued both that these basic moral rights and duties can be inferred from the relation of persons to their Creator and that they are required simply by the nature of persons — a nature that includes the capacity and motivation to set ends and pursue life plans of their own. But the same conclusions appear to be derivable from other premises. Whether as creatures of God or as ends-in-themselves, persons are not mere things, morally available to be *used* for the purposes of others.

The more controversial step, for the Lockean, is the next one. Respect for our natural moral freedom and equality requires that political societies secure from each person subjected to the coercive powers of the state his or her own free consent to that subjection. Absent such consent, the state (and its employment of coercive power) is illegitimate (at least with respect to those non-consenters). We are under no moral duty to be members of a state, not even the state in which we were born or raised. To be sure, it is typically in our interest to accept membership in states whose powers are appropriately limited, or to work to create states with such a character. But only our own genuine, binding consent can subject us to any state's authority.

The Kantian denies that any such consent is needed: justice requires that we support the states in which we find ourselves because we have an obligation to respect everyone's basic right to freedom and can only discharge that obligation through subjection to political authority. The Lockean replies in two ways. First, perhaps persons can fully respect the freedom of others even in a state of nature, simply by refraining from aggression and offering morally required assistance. But second (and more important), such Kantian appeals to justice cannot really convincingly explain why particular persons or groups should be placed under the authority of particular states — for example, "Turkish" Kurds under Turkish political authority. Of course, we are *treated* as subjects of particular states simply as a matter of our (good or bad) luck in our births, but no plausible moral principle supports such treatment. Political custom and international law declare persons born in a particular territory to be subjects of the state controlling that territory. But that declaration is morally uninteresting, especially when we remember that the territorial boundaries (and the customs and laws) at issue were produced by bloody conquest, forceful seizure, decimation of aboriginal populations, political compromise, and collusion among the powerful. Only blind conservatism — not any good reason — recommends that we accept such declarations of subjection as authoritative. If we would respect a person's natural freedom and equality, we surely should not simply assign him or her by birth to the obligations of membership imposed by a state that claims him as its own, any more than we should randomly select some other state and ship him off for subjection there (even if we pay for his passage). We respect a person's rights to freedom and equality only by respecting that person's own free choice of membership — or, for that matter, that person's choice of *non*-membership. Subjection or non-subjection according to individual consent: that is the only way to take seriously each person's basic moral nature.

Beyond this requirement of individual consent, a good Lockean state also provides protection for our rights that is superior to what we could reasonably hope for with no state at all. It is not rational to accept membership in a state that does not provide such protections for rights. To accomplish this superior protection, the state must place legislative and coercive rights in impartial and adequately powerful hands. But to constitute an improvement for each person over the state of nature, this centralized power must be limited by the same moral constraints that naturally govern individual conduct (along with any further limits imposed by the people in entrusting their rights to governing agencies). Otherwise, the rights of some might be sacrificed to provide superior protection for the rights of others. Even in a state with suitably limited authority, achieved perhaps through a rule of law and a separation of legislative and executive powers, the actual security of our rights requires constant vigilance and preparation for united action by the people whose rights are at stake (thus Locke defended a right of popular revolution). But no state can expect better guardianship of individual rights than one in which each has freely joined herself to the society, establishing in that society clear limits on and a clear purpose for the entrusted powers of government.

Lockean political morality thus emphasizes two distinct dimensions in its assessment of the state. It locates the state's justification in the state's potential for superior protection of our rights; and it also argues that even a state that protects rights only has authority over (or legitimacy with respect to) those particular persons who have freely consented to its authority. This Lockean position does not necessarily morally endorse all — or any — existing states. Many existing states will fail to constitute genuine improvements (in securing our rights) over the state of nature; others will fail to be legitimated by the consent of their subjects.

Because of the importance of individual consent as a basis of legitimate authority, the Lockean insists that we think seriously about what, in the behavior of typical citizens of typical states, might plausibly be counted as a suitably free act of binding political consent. Locke himself suggested that mere continued residence in or use of the state's territories constitutes consent. But that seems a clearly inadequate indication that a person accepts authority and acknowledges an obligation to obey. Indeed, given the typical course of most persons' political lives, it is hard to see just how we could credibly portray their societies as consensual associations of the requisite sort to satisfy Lockean standards for legitimacy. A fully developed Lockean political morality, while providing us with clear standards for good and legitimate states, may thus still point us toward skeptical, anarchistic conclusions about the moral authority of existing states. Perhaps those states cannot legitimately claim authority over us; perhaps they cannot insist that in coercing our compliance they are simply enforcing our obligation to obey.

## TEST YOUR UNDERSTANDING

1.  What is the main difference between conventional rights and moral rights?

2.  Simmons mentions that some people have found it helpful to think of rights "as defining a kind of 'walled space'" around individuals. What are the benefits and disadvantages, according to Simmons, of thinking of rights as "walled spaces"?

3.  The Lockean says that only our free consent can "subject us to any state's authority." The Kantian says no such consent is required. What are the two Lockean responses to this Kantian view?

4.  Hobbes says that each person has a "right to every thing." When Hobbes says this, is he thinking of rights as walled spaces?

## NOTES AND QUESTIONS

1.  Simmons distinguishes the role of rights in the Hobbesian, Lockean, and Kantian arguments for a state. Sketch the main differences in the role of rights in these three theories. What do they think a right *is*? What rights do they think people have? Why does Kant think that we have an obligation to be members of a state?

2.  Locke, as Simmons describes him, thinks that the case for a legitimate state has two distinct dimensions: a state's justification requires that it be good at protecting rights *and* that the people over whom it exercises authority consent to that authority. Why is the second requirement important? Imagine a state ruled by a benevolent political party that provides strong protections of individual rights to association, speech, and fair trials but whose citizens have not consented to the state's authority. If rights are of such great importance, why isn't it enough to ensure that the rights are securely protected?

3.  For Locke's own view, see John Locke, *Two Treatises of Government* and *A Letter Concerning Toleration*, ed. Ian Shapiro (Yale University Press, 2003).

## David Lyons (born 1935)

Lyons is a professor of philosophy and of law at Boston University. He has written on utilitarian theories of morality, law, and politics, and on racial inequality and resistance in American history.

# THE UTILITARIAN JUSTIFICATION
# OF THE STATE

A state claims the right to control a defined territory and the people who live there. It does not gently guide the conduct of those people; it lays down rules of conduct and imposes penalties for violating those rules. These coercively enforced social controls deprive individuals of their liberty (with threats and prisons), their resources (with fines), even their lives (with capital punishment).

Punishments and coercive threats against liberty, resources, and life — all essential features of the state — adversely affect our welfare. For this reason, they present a special problem for a utilitarian justification of the state. Utilitarianism is the view that our actions and institutions are justified when (and only when) they produce the greatest sum of welfare for all who are affected: what matters fundamentally for the utilitarian are consequences for welfare, not that rights are protected or that individuals get what they deserve. So when social arrangements undermine any person's welfare, they require justification. To a utilitarian, dedicated to the promotion of welfare, punishment, even for terrible wrongdoing, can be justified only if it promotes welfare indirectly — by preventing worse harms. As the great utilitarian Jeremy Bentham said: "All punishment being in itself evil, upon the principle of utility, if it ought at all to be admitted, it ought only to be admitted in as far as it promises to exclude some greater evil."[1] To succeed, then, a utilitarian justification of the state must show that its coercive social controls advance welfare, despite their inevitable costs.

Utilitarian reasoning assumes that we can attribute welfare benefits and welfare costs to individual acts and social systems. It assumes in particular that we can calculate (or at least reasonably estimate) such benefits and costs for each person who is affected, that we can compare the welfare levels of different people, and that we can add together the net benefits or costs for each person in order to determine the overall or general utility of the social arrangements. A utilitarian appraisal of slavery, for example, requires that we determine the benefits and costs that would result from slavery for everyone affected by it, including slaves, masters, and others; that we then consider the same for the alternatives to slavery; and that finally we add up the benefits and subtract the costs caused by slavery and its alternatives. The right system is the one with the greatest net balance of benefits over costs.

A utilitarian justification of states, then, must show first that states are better than no social organization at all, that their coercive controls always secure welfare benefits that exceed the welfare costs of creating, maintaining, and applying instruments of control, such as police, courts, and prisons. Then second, it must show that states advance welfare more than non-coercive forms of social organization.

---

1. *The Principles of Morals and Legislation* (Macmillan, 1948), p. 170. Bentham (1748–1832) was a British philosopher and legal theorist. He is widely regarded as the founder of utilitarianism. [Lyons's note.]

To assess the utilitarian case, we'll first review why coercive social controls are thought to be needed. Then we'll consider three challenges to a utilitarian justification of states: that their coercive power can be used to implement policies that undermine rather than advance the general welfare; that there may be feasible alternatives to states' coercive rule; and that utilitarian evaluations neglect some crucial moral issues.

# The Perceived Need for Coercive Social Controls

The general need for social control — coercive or otherwise — is thought to arise because each of us has wants and needs that may be frustrated by other persons as well as by our own imprudent decisions. We need nourishment and food reserves because there are times when food would not otherwise be available. We need the protection that is provided by shelter and clothing and access to resources such as tools and raw materials. Because we need such material possessions, it is important to make them secure. The problem is that in looking out for ourselves and those we care about, we may disregard the interests of others, to their detriment. If we want food, for example, we may try to take some from the food reserves of other persons. Such unsociable conduct can be self-defeating, for it may provoke retaliation by those whose welfare we have threatened; moreover, it generates mistrust, discourages reliance on others, and hinders mutually beneficial cooperation.

If each of us has to protect ourselves from encroachments by others, we will be obliged to expend some of our limited resources in unproductive ways. We are better off, then, when social controls — norms, rules, traditions — effectively discourage unsociable behavior and secure our persons, possessions, and freedom, and the possibility of useful collaboration with others. Thus social controls can serve our most basic interests and promote our welfare to a very significant degree.

Many theorists believe that coercion is needed to enforce social controls, because non-coercive efforts to persuade us to comply with norms, rules, traditions, and appeals to a sense of moral decency will not suffice. The threat of punishment is needed to convince us to respect others' persons and property, and to keep the promises we have made to them. (And when threats fail, punishments must be carried out, otherwise the threats are not credible.) Coercion may also be used to discourage *free-riding* — when a person breaks the rules in order to get extra benefits for him- or herself, while taking advantage of others' compliance with the rules (for example, a person uses water, beyond his or her allotted share, during a water shortage, thus exploiting the self-restraint of others, who take only their share). When free-riding becomes widespread, it undermines the useful coordination, and everyone suffers. And coercion may be used paternalistically, to dissuade us from practices that undermine our own welfare.

The utilitarian accepts that such coercion imposes welfare costs, but may reason that the costs are justified by the greater welfare benefits they purchase, including security, freedom from fear, increased liberty, the ability to plan with others and to rely on others' commitments, and the benefits that other projects can generate.

Thomas Hobbes suggested that we might reasonably settle for the bare minimum that coercive controls can secure. He argued that in the absence of centralized coercive social controls, human life is "solitary, poor, nasty, brutish, and short." Hobbes held, in effect, that life under a state, *however oppressive the state might be*, is preferable to life without its coercive controls. Although Hobbes did not reason from utilitarian premises, he thus suggested a utilitarian justification of the state. But utilitarians have been less pessimistic than Hobbes, and have held that coercively enforced policies can advance the general welfare beyond the bare minimum of life and security of goods. States can levy taxes to promote projects, ranging from public utilities to museums, that ease and enrich our lives.

How should the rules be enforced? Specifically, who should impose coercion? A single person cannot enforce social rules, for each of us is physically vulnerable and no one is powerful enough to impose his or her will on others. To administer coercive social controls, some members of a community must work together. Experience shows that enforcement can be achieved by a minority of the members — even a small minority.

But the possibility of enforcement by a small minority leads to the first difficulty for a utilitarian justification of the state.

## Misuse of States' Coercive Power

Once coercive controls are established, they may be used to serve the aims and perceived interests of an influential minority at others' expense. Their use can enhance the general welfare or destroy it, for coercively enforced public policies need not be humane or beneficent.

This concern is supported by our collective experience. Many states have enforced oppressive class structures, including serfdom, peonage, and slavery, which are extremely unlikely to promote the general welfare.

Consider the United States. From its formal beginning in 1789 until 1865, it incorporated the brutally oppressive system of chattel slavery, which served the interests of some members of the community at a terrible price for others. Not long after slavery was abolished, it was replaced by the brutally oppressive system known as Jim Crow, which was maintained until the 1960s. Those systems of racial subordination, which together lasted nearly two centuries, depended on coercive social controls. If alternative social arrangements that would have better promoted the general welfare were feasible — as critics of slavery and Jim Crow maintained — then the U.S. federal state was not justifiable in utilitarian terms.

Moreover, states do not confine their activities within their political borders. State systems of coercive control have often been used to conscript members of their own communities in order to wage aggressive war, acquire territory, and create colonial empires. These facts are especially important from a utilitarian perspective, which demands that we give full consideration to the interests of *all* who are affected — that we may not discount the interests of any persons, wherever they may live, whatever their complexion, convictions, or culture.

To appreciate this point, it is essential not to confuse the utilitarian's general welfare criterion with the notion that a government should promote the interests of *its own* community. Such a "national interest" criterion means that a government may properly ignore the welfare of outsiders (except when the interests of the communities happen to converge). By contrast, utilitarianism requires that we treat *everyone, everywhere*, as full-fledged members of the *moral* community.

Some utilitarians may argue that this emphasis on universalism overlooks "indirect" utilitarian reasoning. Such reasoning is employed when we evaluate the conduct of an individual who helps administer coercive social controls not by the welfare benefits and costs of that conduct taken by itself. Instead, we judge the conduct by the system's rules, and then evaluate the rules in terms of the welfare effects of the system as a whole. For example, we say that a judge does the right thing when the judge acts impartially in a trial; and then we evaluate requirements of impartial judging in terms of the overall welfare benefits of a legal system that includes impartial judges. By analogous reasoning, it may be held that the people of the world are better off if each government dedicates itself to promoting the welfare of its own subjects (or at least gives greater weight to their interests than to the interests of others) than if it tries to give equal consideration to the interests of all.

That might be true, but it needs to be shown, not merely asserted; it needs empirical support. In any case, even if governments are justified in giving extra weight to the interests of citizens, a utilitarian theorist who seeks to justify the state must count the interests of all concerned equally, and not confine attention to those within a particular state.

While utilitarianism requires that everyone's interests be given full consideration, however, it is *not* committed, as a matter of principle, to political, economic, or social equality. As we have noted, utilitarianism can condone social "trade-offs," in which burdens are imposed on some persons for the sake of other persons' greater benefits — provided the arrangements maximize utility.

What seems to follow is that utilitarianism condemns, on its own terms, many states and many kinds of states. But states vary greatly, and the social systems they support change over time in relevant ways. A democratic South Africa is much more likely to promote the general welfare than South Africa under *apartheid*. Some states enforce rigid class structures (slavery, serfdom, caste) while others embrace freedom and social mobility, and a given state's policies can vary greatly over time (slavery and serfdom can be abolished; social and economic opportunities can become more widely distributed). Some states control their societies' resources and productive capabilities, while others promote private ownership and private arrangements, and a particular state can change such policies substantially over time. Some states control markets tightly, some try to maintain competition, while others condone concentrations of wealth and power, and these practices likewise change within given states from one era to another. As laws, policies, and circumstances vary and change, so do states' impact on welfare. Given the changes to which public policies are susceptible, a particular state's utilitarian merits are likely to vary over time.

The utilitarian defense of a particular regime thus requires a detailed empirical argument. Other theories, which justify the state in terms of universal consent, or the protection of individual rights, or preserving peace, or satisfying democratic principles, are much easier to apply. Utilitarianism requires much more complex support, including the consideration of alternatives.

## Feasible Alternatives

A utilitarian justification of states needs to compare the welfare benefits (and costs) of states with the welfare benefits (and costs) of feasible alternatives. Consider actual states first (we'll consider states in general later). Given the enormous suffering and loss of life caused by Germany's role in World War II and the Holocaust, it seems reasonable to suppose that the Nazi state compares unfavorably with feasible alternatives. This assumes, of course, that the development and maintenance of the Nazi state was not inevitable but resulted from human actions to which there were alternatives.

The feasibility of alternatives to a given state might vary over its lifetime, as ideas and attitudes towards government and specific institutions change. Consider the United States once again. In the late eighteenth century, anti-slavery sentiment was growing not only in the North but also in the Upper South, including Virginia. This is why Lower South states, such as South Carolina, sought constitutional protections for slavery. Given the new republic's resources, compensated emancipation might have been a politically feasible project, and it is arguable that the United States could have been founded without supporting slavery. If so, a United States without slavery from the start was a feasible alternative to the slavery-friendly republic that was actually founded. When slave-based enterprises came to dominate the U.S. economy in the nineteenth century, however, it became vastly more difficult to reduce the federal government's support for slavery. A slave-free republic might still have been feasible, but it would have been much more difficult to achieve. By the end of the Civil War, however, history shows that a slave-free alternative became feasible, though perhaps only at great cost.[2]

The problem of feasible alternatives applies not only to individual states but to states in general. There may be genuine alternatives to states as such if non-coercive social controls can be effective. Are they a real possibility, or only a figment of the utopian imagination?

Many theorists believe that social systems cannot persist without coercively enforced social controls, and thus that non-coercive social arrangements are not feasible alternatives. But it is difficult to judge, for we have had little experience of societies without coercive social controls, and it is not clear that their rarity reflects

---

2. Recall that utilitarian theory requires us to consider the costs as well as the benefits of realizing alternatives. But what counts as a feasible alternative is not entirely clear. One might assume, somewhat vaguely, that a feasible alternative must be a type of state that is imaginable by some members of the given society, and that it must be sustainable under the general circumstances. It is unclear how to make this more precise, as well as what other conditions should be understood to limit the class of feasible alternatives. [Lyons's note.]

their impracticality. From early on, we have been encouraged to regard states with their coercive social controls as natural and necessary. Is this a reasonable assumption? Are non-coercive systems not feasible?

We should be careful here. As coercive social controls are needed by those who wish to impose and maintain exploitative social systems and who possess the resources to influence prevailing attitudes, skepticism is appropriate. Consider some other assumptions that people have long been encouraged to make, such as the need for war, for colonizing other peoples, for enslaving others, and for taking their land. Given our historical experience, we cannot accept such views uncritically. We know better.

In fact, we also know that humans have sometimes lived in well-functioning societies *without* centralized systems of coercive control. Many Native American nations, for example, did not traditionally employ systems of coercive social controls like those with which we are familiar. It is not that they lacked standards of conduct or failed to uphold their standards. On the contrary, social control was maintained by procedures aimed at reconciliation rather than punishment or retribution.

Are those practices relevant to contemporary societies? It is true that many Native American communities were small by contemporary standards; it is also true, however, that some Native American communities encompassed populations with many thousands of members.

We do not yet know how capable humans are to live cooperatively, under non-coercive social control, and under what conditions centralized coercive systems might be required. Until we understand our human capabilities better, we should hesitate to suppose that human society requires coercive social controls or that they are justified by their contribution to human welfare.

## Moral Limits of Utilitarian Justifications

We have so far been considering utilitarianism on its own terms, and exploring the distinctively utilitarian approach to justifying the state. It is time to place the issue in a wider perspective, and ask about whether utilitarianism is a compelling outlook on political morality.

Recall that utilitarianism can tolerate social trade-offs — that it is capable, at least in principle, of condoning social arrangements that impose large burdens on some for the sake of a greater sum of benefits for others. As we have noted, it is doubtful that utilitarianism does in fact support such exploitative systems as chattel slavery in the United States, because it is doubtful that the welfare benefits to the beneficiaries more than compensate for the welfare costs to those who suffer.[3] One might still wonder, however, whether utilitarianism views the matter properly. For it implies

---

3. But the utilitarian must view a system like slavery to be *justified* on the ground that (as might have been the case in ancient Rome) there were no feasible alternatives. [Lyons's note.]

that serfdom, peonage, slavery, and other systems that subordinate some for the sake of others *would be morally justifiable* if the benefits were great enough or the beneficiaries were numerous enough. Suppose for example that a relatively small number of very productive slaves are employed in mines. Then the benefits may be very great and the burdens relatively small. Still, the slavery seems wrong.

One explanation of this moral perception is provided by the idea of human rights—the idea that each of us has some unconditional rights, the existence of which does not depend on social recognition or enforcement.

Consider the role of entrenched rights within political systems in which most public officials are elected by popular vote. Many such systems limit majority rule by recognizing a limited class of rights, belonging to individuals, that are legally enforceable and not easily repealed: for example, rights of expression, association, and conscience. This type of constitutional arrangement reflects the moral conviction that, contrary to what utilitarianism says, certain interests of individuals are not subject to social trade-offs—even if the enforcement of those rights is unwelcome, inconvenient, or costly to the majority.

Freedom of expression is a good example. Its constitutional protection represents the idea that expression may not be restricted even if many people are upset by what is said and the general welfare would be improved by silencing dissenters. The abolition of slavery is an even better example. We do not need to calculate welfare effects to recognize that allowing some people to treat others as fungible property unacceptably violates the dignity and independence of those who are enslaved.

A reasonable understanding of this priority given to a limited set of legal rights is that morality requires us to respect each individual, and that utilitarianism does not adequately capture the kind of respect that is owed to each person. The utilitarian does say that we must take the interests of each into consideration in a calculus of social costs and benefits. But the practice of entrenching rights suggests that morality also requires that certain interests of individuals may not be encroached upon in order to advance the general welfare. We may think of this practice in terms of the dignity of the individual and the respect that each person is due. If so, any acceptable answer to the question of whether a state is justified must consider not only its welfare effects, as utilitarianism insists, but also whether it treats each individual with dignity and respect.

Utilitarian theorists have disagreed about the idea of universal human rights. Utilitarian theory denies the existence of fundamental moral rights that are not subordinate to the calculus of welfare benefits and costs, and most utilitarian theorists have rejected the idea of moral rights. But utilitarianism leaves room for two ways of trying to accommodate a limited set of important rights, thus blunting the force of the criticism of utilitarianism for putting all human interests into a social calculus of costs and benefits.

Some utilitarian theorists, such as John Stuart Mill,[4] have embraced the idea of moral rights by arguing that the recognition and enforcement of some rights promotes the general welfare. Given that view, Mill could defend the constitutional

---

4. John Stuart Mill (1806–1873) was born in London, England. He was a utilitarian and a leading public thinker. In chapter 5 of his *Utilitarianism* (1863), Mill discusses the place of rights in utilitarianism. [Lyons's note.]

entrenchment of a limited set of moral rights. Moral rights aside, other utilitarian theorists claim that some interests of individuals are so crucial to individual welfare in any circumstances we are likely to confront that the calculus of welfare benefits and costs directly justifies the constitutional protection of some individual rights. Like other indirect utilitarian claims, each of these requires complex empirical support. If that support were forthcoming, utilitarianism — as a general moral framework, and as a way to think about whether, in particular, we ought to have a state with its coercive powers — would go a long way toward overcoming a significant objection.

## TEST YOUR UNDERSTANDING

1. What is utilitarianism?

2. Why is there a "perceived need for coercive social controls"?

3. What does Lyons mean by an "oppressive social structure"? What are some of his examples of states that have "enforced oppressive social structures"?

4. Lyons mentions three challenges to a utilitarian justification of states. State the three challenges in your own words.

## NOTES AND QUESTIONS

1. Lyons thinks that we should be more cautious than we are in assuming that human societies require coercive social controls. Do you think there could be a decent human society on a large scale (say, at least as large as Iceland, whose population is now 320,000) without coercive social controls? How would the society deal with people who injure one another? How would it resolve disagreements (for example, disagreements about who owns what)? How would it ensure that the resolutions are followed? How does Lyons's article speak to these issues?

2. Punishment, Lyons says, is an essential feature of the state. Moreover, punishment adversely affects the welfare of people who are punished. Because of the adverse impact, utilitarians favor punishment only when it prevents "worse harms" in the future. So part of the utilitarian case for having a state is that punishment is needed to prevent worse harms from occurring. Punishment in itself is a bad thing: it is justified (when it is justified) only by its good consequences.

   Utilitarians thus reject a *retributive* theory of punishment. For the retributivist, unlike the utilitarian, the rationale for punishment is not to create a better future: you punish people because they have done something wrong, and punishment is the appropriate or fitting response to wrongdoing. The rationale of punishment is backward looking, not forward looking. Kant, who held a retributive view, said:

> Even if a civil society were to be dissolved by with the consent of all its members (e.g., if a people inhabiting an island decided to separate and disperse throughout the whole world), the last murderer remaining in prison would first have to be executed so that each has done to him what his deeds deserve, and blood guilt does not cling to the people for not having insisted upon this punishment; for otherwise the people can be regarded as collaborators in this public violation of justice.[1]

(Many retributivists have opposed capital punishment. The point of quoting the passage from Kant is not to get you thinking about capital punishment, but to illustrate the idea that a crime should not be punished because punishment is fitting, not because it has good effects.)

Suppose you hold a retributive view of punishment: you think that wrongdoing should be punished because punishment is fitting, and not just because of the beneficial effects of punishment (say, because it will deter future crime). How would this shape your ideas about why there should be a state? Is it easier to justify a state if you think that punishment is needed simply because there is wrongdoing, not because of a calculation of the future consequences of punishment?

3. Utilitarianism, Lyons says, requires much more "detailed empirical argument" in evaluating a particular regime than alternative theories that "justify the state in terms of universal consent, or the protection of individual rights, or preserving peace, or satisfying democratic principles." What kind of empirical argument is needed for the utilitarian evaluation? Consider, for example, the kind of empirical argument you would need to make to show that a democratic system is better for overall human welfare than a more authoritarian regime.

Is Lyons's contrast between utilitarianism and alternative justifications of the state convincing? Suppose you think that a state like the one that Hobbes describes—an authoritarian state—is justified because it is better equipped than alternatives to keep the peace or to protect individual rights. That is, suppose you think that a very strong state is more likely to keep the peace than a less strong state; or suppose you think that a very strong state is better at protecting individual rights than any alternative kind of state. So you do not offer a utilitarian justification. Can you then rely on a less "detailed empirical argument" for the state than the utilitarian needs to provide?

---

1. Immanuel Kant, *The Metaphysics of Morals*, trans. Mary Gregor, in Immanuel Kant, *Practical Philosophy* (Cambridge University Press, 1996), p. 474.

## ANALYZING THE ARGUMENTS

1.  Aristotle famously says, "Man is by nature a political animal." What does that assertion mean? What reasons does Aristotle offer in support of it? A good way to approach this question is by asking whether Hobbes and Rousseau agree that we are by nature political animals. Consider two pairs of questions: (i) Does either Hobbes or Rousseau think it is possible to live outside the state? Does Aristotle think that it is possible? (ii) Does either Hobbes or Rousseau think it is possible to live a decent or good human life outside the state? Does Aristotle think it is possible?

    Once you have an interpretation of Aristotle's idea, ask yourself whether you think that people are, by their nature, political animals.

2.  This section provides you with five ideas about how to justify the existence of a state. Thus, the state is said to be needed for the purpose of:

    (i)   keeping the peace

    (ii)  promoting the general happiness

    (iii) protecting rights

    (iv)  achieving moral **autonomy**

    (v)   living a good and noble life by realizing our political natures

    How precisely do these ideas differ? Think of circumstances in which they lead to similar conclusions, and then think of circumstances in which they give conflicting results: in which protecting rights thwarts peace, or encouraging good and noble lives gets in the way of the general happiness. Which view seems most promising in view of these potential conflicts?

3.  If an anarchist friend asks you why you are not an anarchist, how, in light of what you have read, would you answer? (If you are an anarchist, how would you respond to the arguments in these selections?)

# 20

# What Is the
# Value of Liberty?

According to its preamble, the U.S. Constitution aims, among other things, to "insure domestic tranquility, provide for the common defense, promote the general welfare, and secure the blessings of liberty to ourselves and our posterity." Domestic peace, common defense, and the general welfare are all pretty uncontroversial. But what exactly are the blessings of liberty? And why are they important?

One thing is clear: most of us value liberty. As Mary Prince—a woman born into slavery in Bermuda in 1788 and freed in England in 1832—says in her autobiography, "to be free is very sweet."[1] While we do not share Prince's experience of enslavement, most of us share her sentiment about freedom's sweetness. We do not wish to be told how (or whether) to worship, with whom to associate, or what to say or do.

At the same time, however, the value of liberty is puzzling. Why shouldn't a state—responsible for security and public safety—have the authority to restrict liberty, when restrictions help to accomplish its purposes? In his defense of absolute authority, Thomas Hobbes argues that it should. (See the selection from Hobbes in chapter 19 of this anthology.) Individuals form a state, he says, by agreeing to submit their wills and judgments to the will and judgment of the political authority on all matters "which concern the common peace and safety." The political authority also is responsible for deciding which matters bear on peace and safety. So the political authority might decide that *any* doctrine or conduct threatens peace and safety—in other words, that it endangers national security. When that happens, the political authority becomes the arbiter of thought, speech, and conduct.

If you find freedom sweet, then you will find this demand for extreme deference to authority deeply troubling. The challenge is to provide a compelling response.

---

1. Mary Prince, *A History of Mary Prince: A West Indian Slave*, in Henry Louis Gates, ed., *The Classic Slave Narratives* (Signet, 1987), p. 214.

# Limiting Authority

Among the many kinds of liberty that we value—freedom to think, to speak, to associate—religious liberty has played a particularly prominent role in philosophical argument and political life. That prominence is understandable in part because religious beliefs are such a commanding force in many peoples' lives. Those beliefs provide a basic orientation in life, a foundation for judgments of right and wrong, how best to live, and what gives larger significance to life's ordinary activities.

Religious liberty is also a central topic because religious convictions can fuel social division and destructive political conflict: Protestants and Catholics in early modern Europe, Sunnis and Shiites in contemporary Syria and Iraq, Hindus and Muslims in India. A state, responsible for ensuring social peace and promoting the general welfare, may be tempted to respond by promoting greater religious uniformity. If we accept efforts of states to encourage, through schools and public symbols, a common national identity—as Americans, or Kenyans, or Germans, or Indians—because a sense of belonging is important for peaceful and productive social cooperation, why not a common religious identity as well?

John Locke's *Letter Concerning Toleration* presents the classical case against using the state's power to establish religious uniformity. In particular, Locke rejects the idea that the state has the authority to decide which religious view is right and to make laws founded on a religious conception. To be sure, Locke's defense of toleration has important limits. Locke does not favor toleration for Catholics or atheists. Atheists, he thinks, cannot be trusted as cooperating members of society: "Promises, covenants, and oaths, which are the bonds of human society, can have no hold upon an atheist. The taking away of God, though but even in thought, dissolves all." Catholics are not to be tolerated, Locke says, because they owe allegiance to the pope, in effect a competing political authority. Atheists and Catholics are thus denied toleration not because their beliefs are false or religiously divisive but because their views are socially disruptive. Despite these limits, Locke's argument has been influential and controversial.

One of the chief Lockean arguments for religious toleration begins from the proposition that a person's salvation depends on his or her religious beliefs, not simply on correct outward behavior. But the distinctive instruments of the state—laws and penalties—can have no impact on beliefs. "It is only light and evidence that can work a change in men's opinions; which light can in no manner proceed from corporal sufferings, or any other outward penalties." So the state should not try to coerce beliefs because force is bound to fail: the corporal sufferings and other outward penalties would serve no good purpose. This argument does not reject using penalties to change minds, if penalties might be effective. It says only that they are not effective.

Locke also suggests a **contractualist** argument for the same conclusion. The contract tradition justifies political authority by arguing that a state could (or would) be unanimously agreed to by people subject to its authority. The same contractual agreement that justifies the existence of political authority also can set limits on the use of authority. Thus Locke says that political authorities cannot have authority over religious beliefs in part because they *cannot get that authority from the people*. They cannot get it from the people because religion is so fundamental — so much at the core of individual convictions about what to think and how to live — that individuals cannot willingly yield control over it to any other person, much less to an authority.[2] So individuals must reject a proposed social contract that does not respect their religious liberty.

This contract strategy is neither confined to John Locke nor limited to religious liberty. John Rawls's social contract theory, for example, includes rights to religious liberty, and to freedom of speech and political liberty.[3] The list of liberties is more expansive than Locke's, but the strategy of argument is broadly similar. A contract view sets limits on authority by arguing that individual interests in some areas of belief and conduct are so fundamental — so nonnegotiable — that individuals cannot entrust their beliefs and conduct in these areas to others. If people can only rationally endorse a political order that leaves certain fundamental matters in their own hands, then the contract theorist's condition of unanimous agreement requires protecting those liberties from political authority.

# Utilitarianism and Liberty

**Utilitarians** reject the contractualist's test of unanimous agreement. They hold that the right actions, rules, and institutions are those that maximize the sum of human happiness. So even if an interest is fundamental, it can be overridden by a sufficiently large sum of benefits to others. If enough people would be happier in a world of religious uniformity, for example, then utilitarianism requires such uniformity, even at the cost of denying religious liberty to a minority. For this reason, many critics of utilitarianism have argued that the principle of utility is not a promising basis for defending liberty. But the classical utilitarians, Jeremy Bentham and John Stuart Mill, both found powerful resources within utilitarianism for defending liberty.

Consider an argument that Bentham offers against "morals legislation" in his Introduction to the *Principles of Morals and Legislation*.[4] Morals legislation punishes conduct with criminal sanctions. The conduct is punished *because it is wrong or sinful*, not because it causes harm to other people. In a 1991 Supreme Court case, Justice Antonin Scalia wrote in a concurring opinion: "Our society prohibits, and all human societies have prohibited, certain activities not because they harm others but because they are considered, in the traditional phrase, '*contra bonos mores*,'

2. John Rawls suggests a similar line of argument in *A Theory of Justice* (Harvard University Press, 1999), p. 181.

3. The right interpretation of Rousseau's view is more controversial. For discussion, see Joshua Cohen, *Rousseau: A Free Community of Equals* (Oxford University Press, 2010).

4. Jeremy Bentham, *The Principles of Morals and Legislation* (Macmillan, 1948), pp. 315–21. Bentham (1748–1832) is widely regarded as the founder of utilitarianism.

*i.e.,* immoral." And he mentions "sadomasochism, cockfighting, bestiality, suicide, drug use, prostitution, and sodomy" as areas in which legal regulation is justified by "traditional moral belief."[5] Historically, as Scalia's comments suggest, much of morals legislation has focused on issues of sexuality. Thus, laws against same-sex sexual activity—laws that have been the historical norm, not the exception—have traditionally been justified by moral reasons, not by reasons of harm to others.

Because he was a utilitarian, Bentham thought that criminal punishment should be decided on the basis of a calculation of costs in pain and benefits in pleasure. In particular, we should not impose criminal punishments when costs outweigh benefits. Punishments clearly impose pains. When there is not sufficient gain in pleasure, the punishments are "unprofitable." Bentham thought that morals laws belong in the unprofitable category. Because the conduct is not harmful to others, the benefits of stopping it cannot be that great. But the pains are very clear. So Bentham concluded that these are not "fit objects for the legislator to control." Unlike Locke, Bentham does not make the case for liberty depend on an especially important class of human interests. Nor does he follow the contractual approach of requiring unanimous agreement. But he does think that some liberties should be protected because the benefits of abridging them are smaller than the costs.

Mill's *On Liberty* offers a more complex utilitarian case for religious liberty, as well as liberty of thought, expression, and association, and the liberty of choosing a way of life. He defines the rightful scope of authority with "one simple principle," commonly called the **harm principle**, which says, "the only purpose for which power can be rightfully exercised over any member of a civilized community, against his will, is to prevent harm to others. His own good, either physical or moral, is not a sufficient warrant."[6] Harm to others is, in short, a necessary condition for justifying compulsion and control. The harm principle applies equally to democratic and aristocratic power. And it applies to power exercised through informal social sanctions, which put people under heavy pressure to conform, as well as to power exercised by the state through laws. Mill thinks that this informal pressure to conform threatens to establish a "social tyranny," which is especially dangerous because it "leaves fewer means of escape, penetrating much more deeply into the details of life, and enslaving the soul itself."[7]

Mill's defense of the harm principle is based on his utilitarianism. But his utilitarian calculus is different from Bentham's, and his case for liberty reflects a deeper exploration than Bentham's of "the greater good of human freedom," and the grave costs of limiting liberty. The most fundamental human interests, Mill thinks, are in "higher-quality pleasures" (see the introduction to chapter 16 and the selection from Mill's *Utilitarianism* in this anthology). These pleasures, preferred by experienced and well-informed judges, involve the development and exercise of our distinctively human capacities: perception, judgment, reasoning,

---

5. *Barnes v. Glen Theatre, Inc.,* 501 US 560 (1991), 575.

6. Mill, *On Liberty,* chapter 1, paragraph 9.

7. Mill, *On Liberty,* chapter 1, paragraph 5.

imagination, and moral and aesthetic evaluation. Following the harm principle, then, promotes the sum of human happiness because it provides favorable conditions for pursuing our fundamental interest in using our human capacities, thus for the qualitatively better human pleasures.

One link between liberty and the higher quality pleasures is that we exercise our capacities when we make choices about how to live. Making those choices is an important human good because it requires using our distinctively human powers: "He who chooses his plan for himself, employs all his faculties." Second, liberty enables us to explore alternative ways to live, observe the paths tried by others, and make informed judgments about the way that is best suited to each of us individually, rather than relying on custom and convention. Third, the protection of liberty fosters the vigorous challenge to received ideas that is essential for broader social and political progress.

Mill expected, then, that liberty would foster human diversity, and he understood that that would make some people uncomfortable and unsettle common convictions. But comfort is not a higher quality pleasure. Mill's utilitarian case for liberty, then, is that the "higher quality" human pleasures are best served by following the harm principle, and that those pleasures outweigh the costs in discomfort and inconvenience. Mill is not a contractualist, so he does not require unanimous agreement regarding the scope of authority. But as Locke assigned a special importance to the interest in salvation, Mill assigns a special importance to our interest in exercising our human powers. His case for liberty, then, turns on the idea that a society that embraces the harm principle will foster that interest.

Amartya Sen's theory of human rights shares this emphasis on a class of fundamental interests. Human rights—rights to be free of torture, slavery, extreme destitution, and religious intolerance, for example—are moral entitlements of all human beings. But what else are we all entitled to? The way to identify our human rights, Sen argues, is through ethical reasoning, not through legal argument. The reasoning aims to identify freedoms—like freedoms from torture, slavery, extreme destitution, and religious intolerance—that are important, that people share an interest in, and that can be protected and promoted through concerted action.

The Lockean and Millian arguments for liberty, and Sen's account of human rights, converge in identifying a class of especially important human interests that have a kind of priority over other interests. If there are such interests, and if liberty bears a close connection to the pursuit and advancement of those interests, then the case for liberty—whether contractualist or utilitarian—is well launched.

# A Skeptic

Patrick Devlin rejects the views of Bentham and Mill. Devlin wrote "Morals and the Criminal Law" in response to the Wolfenden Report: a 1957 British government report that proposed to decriminalize "homosexual behaviour between consenting adults in private." Devlin rejected the conclusions of the report, and defended morals laws on the basis of three central claims: (1) societies have the right to protect themselves from disintegration; (2) without a common morality — "shared ideas on politics, morals, and ethics" — a society disintegrates; and (3) enforcing a common morality through criminal law is necessary to preserving that common morality. It follows that a society has the right to enforce common morality through criminal law. Public morality speaks, for example, on issues about marriage, Devlin says, by embracing the values of monogamy and fidelity. Weaken the common sensibilities on those values and the institution would be "gravely threatened."

Devlin is not indifferent to the value of liberty but rejects hard and fast rules that define its scope and limits. We need to decide, in particular cases, whether we are faced with "a vice so abominable that its mere presence is an offence." When we are, punishment is permissible. For it may well be needed to reinforce the shared political, moral, and ethical ideas that enable us to live together. Devlin does not present his case for enforcement in utilitarian terms. But it can easily be reconstructed along those lines. He thinks that Bentham and Mill both underestimate the cost of eliminating morals laws because of their singular focus on injuries to individuals and corresponding neglect of damage to society. Devlin thinks that those laws help to forestall the erosion of shared moral ideas. If that erosion would produce social disintegration, then the decrease in pleasure and increase in pain would be very great.

A striking element of Mill's view may help to locate more precisely his disagreement with Devlin. In the opening chapter of *On Liberty*, Mill says that his principle applies only to "human beings in the maturity of their faculties," and that we may "leave out of consideration those backward states of society in which the race itself may be considered as in its nonage."[8] The harm principle "has no application to any state of things anterior to the time when mankind have become capable of being improved by free and equal discussion. Until then, there is nothing for them but implicit obedience to an Akbar or a Charlemagne, if they are so fortunate as to find one."[9] Mill's view, then, is that utilitarianism supports liberty when and only when people can be improved by discussion. When they can, utilitarianism recommends efforts at improvement through discussion and persuasion rather than coercion.

Perhaps, then, Devlin emphasizes the enforcement of shared moral ideas for the same reason that Hobbes emphasizes the importance of authority: because he doubts our capacity to listen to reason — to be improved by free and equal discussion. Mill, in contrast, thinks that we can afford the liberty and resulting diversity that worry Hobbes and Devlin, once the distinctive human capacity for improvement through discussion is in place.

---

8. *Nonage:* Period of immaturity.

9. Mill, *On Liberty*, chapter 1, paragraph 10.

## John Locke (1632–1704)

Locke was an English philosopher and medical doctor. His greatest work is *An Essay Concerning Human Understanding* (1689), which is about the limits of human knowledge. His *Two Treatises of Government* (1689) and *A Letter Concerning Toleration* (1689), both published anonymously, made important contributions to political philosophy. The second *Treatise* gives a theory of legitimate government in terms of natural rights and the social contract. Locke's political views influenced the Founding Fathers of the United States, in particular Thomas Jefferson.

# A LETTER CONCERNING TOLERATION

The toleration of those that differ from others in matters of religion, is so agreeable to the Gospel of Jesus Christ, and to the genuine reason of mankind, that it seems monstrous for men to be so blind, as not to perceive the necessity and advantage of it, in so clear a light. I will not here tax the pride and ambition of some, the passion and uncharitable zeal of others. These are faults from which human affairs can perhaps scarce ever be perfectly freed; but yet such as nobody will bear the plain imputation of, without covering them with some specious colour; and so pretend to commendation, whilst they are carried away by their own irregular passions. But, however, that some may not colour their spirit of persecution and unchristian cruelty with a pretence of care of the public weal, and observation of the laws, and that others, under pretence of religion, may not seek impunity for their libertinism and licentiousness; in a word, that none may impose either upon himself or others, by the pretences of loyalty and obedience to the prince, or of tenderness and sincerity in the worship of God; I esteem it above all things necessary to distinguish exactly the business of civil government from that of religion, and to settle the just bounds that lie between the one and the other. If this be not done, there can be no end put to the controversies that will be always arising between those that have, or at least pretend to have, on the one side a concernment for the interest of men's souls, and, on the other side, a care of the commonwealth.

The commonwealth seems to me to be a society of men constituted only for the procuring, preserving, and advancing their own civil interests.

Civil interest I call life, liberty, health, and indolency of body; and the possession of outward things, such as money, lands, houses, furniture, and the like.

It is the duty of the civil magistrate, by the impartial execution of equal laws, to secure unto all the people in general, and to every one of his subjects in particular, the just possession of these things belonging to this life. If any one presume to violate the laws of public justice and equity, established for the preservation of these things, his presumption is to be checked by the fear of punishment; consisting in the deprivation or diminution of those civil interests, or goods, which otherwise he might and ought to enjoy. But seeing no man does willingly suffer himself to be punished by the deprivation of any part of his goods, and much less of his liberty or life, therefore is the magistrate armed with the force and strength of all his subjects, in order to the punishment of those that violate any other man's rights.

Now that the whole jurisdiction of the magistrate reaches only to these civil concernments; and that all civil power, right, and dominion, is bounded and confined to the only care of promoting these things; and that it neither can nor ought in any manner to be extended to the salvation of souls; these following considerations seem unto me abundantly to demonstrate.

First, Because the care of souls is not committed to the civil magistrate, any more than to other men. It is not committed unto him, I say, by God; because it appears not that God has ever given any such authority to one man over another, as to compel any one to his religion. Nor can any power be vested in the magistrate by the consent of the people; because no man can so far abandon the care of his own salvation as blindly to leave it to the choice of any other, whether prince or subject, to prescribe to him what faith or worship he shall embrace. For no man can, if he would, conform his faith to the dictates of another. All the life and power of true religion consists in the inward and full persuasion of the mind; and faith is not faith without believing. Whatever profession we make, to whatever outward worship we conform, if we are not fully satisfied in our own mind that the one is true, and the other well-pleasing unto God, such profession and such practice, far from being any furtherance, are indeed great obstacles to our salvation. For in this manner, instead of expiating other sins by the exercise of religion, I say, in offering thus unto God Almighty such a worship as we esteem to be displeasing unto him, we add unto the number of our other sins, those also of hypocrisy, and contempt of his Divine Majesty.

In the second place. The care of souls cannot belong to the civil magistrate, because his power consists only in outward force: but true and saving religion consists in the inward persuasion of the mind, without which nothing can be acceptable to God. And such is the nature of the understanding, that it cannot be compelled to the belief of any thing by outward force. Confiscation of estate, imprisonment, torments, nothing of that nature can have any such efficacy as to make men change the inward judgment that they have framed of things.

It may indeed be alleged that the magistrate may make use of arguments, and thereby draw the heterodox into the way of truth, and procure their salvation. I grant it; but this is common to him with other men. In teaching, instructing, and redressing the erroneous by reason, he may certainly do what becomes any good man to do. Magistracy does not oblige him to put off either humanity or Christianity. But it is one thing to persuade, another to command; one thing to press with arguments, another with penalties. This the civil power alone has a right to do; to the other, good-will is authority enough. Every man has commission to admonish, exhort, convince another of error, and by reasoning to draw him into truth; but to give laws, receive obedience, and compel with the sword, belongs to none but the magistrate. And upon this ground I affirm, that the magistrate's power extends not to the establishing of any articles of faith, or forms of worship, by the force of his laws. For laws are of no force at all without penalties, and penalties in this case are absolutely impertinent; because they are not proper to convince the mind. Neither the profession of any articles of faith, nor the conformity to any outward form of worship, as has been already said, can be available to the salvation of souls, unless the truth of the one, and the acceptableness of the other unto God, be thoroughly believed by those that so profess and practise. But penalties are no ways capable to produce such belief. It is only light and evidence that can work a change in men's opinions; and that light can in no manner proceed from corporal sufferings, or any other outward penalties.

In the third place. The care of the salvation of men's souls cannot belong to the magistrate; because, though the rigour of laws and the force of penalties were capable to convince and change men's minds, yet would not that help at all to the salvation of their souls. For, there being but one truth, one way to heaven; what hopes is there that more men would be led into it, if they had no other rule to follow but the religion of the court, and were put under a necessity to quit the light of their own reason, to oppose the dictates of their own consciences, and blindly to resign up themselves to the will of their governors, and to the religion, which either ignorance, ambition, or superstition had chanced to establish in the countries where they were born? In the variety and contradiction of opinions in religion, wherein the princes of the world are as much divided as in their secular interests, the narrow way would be much straitened; one country alone would be in the right, and all the rest of the world put under an obligation of following their princes in the ways that lead to destruction: and that which heightens the absurdity, and very ill suits the notion of a Deity, men would owe their eternal happiness or misery to the places of their nativity.

These considerations, to omit many others that might have been urged to the same purpose, seem unto me sufficient to conclude, that all the power of civil government relates only to men's civil interests, is confined to the care of the things of this world, and hath nothing to do with the world to come.

## TEST YOUR UNDERSTANDING

1. In his case for religious toleration, Locke says that "civil power" should be confined to protecting and advancing civil interests and should not extend to the "salvation of souls." He gives three reasons for this conclusion. State each of the three reasons in a sentence or two.

2. A key premise in Locke's **argument** is that "the understanding . . . cannot be compelled to the belief of anything by outward force." Provide some examples that illustrate, in your judgment, Locke's idea that our beliefs cannot be changed by the use of force.

## NOTES AND QUESTIONS

1.  Locke's defense of religious toleration turns partly on the thesis that you cannot change people's beliefs by using force against them. Call this thesis *Limits of Force*:

    > *Limits of Force*: A person's beliefs cannot be changed by threats or applications of force against the person.

    Assume for the sake of argument that *Limits of Force* is true. How strong a case for religious toleration results?

    Two considerations suggest that *Limits of Force* does not yield a strong case. First, even if a state that aims to establish religious uniformity cannot change religious beliefs directly, it might try to ensure uniformity by using force to prohibit religious practices — say, the Eucharist or adult baptism. Because of the prohibitions, other people do not see the practices and are therefore less likely to follow them.

    Second, the state might use force against religious dissenters not for the purpose of changing the minds of *dissenters* but for the purpose of dissuading others (perhaps children) who might otherwise be tempted to follow the dissenting group. In his history of religious toleration, Perez Zagorin discusses this second consideration, which he calls the "pedagogy of fear": *How the Idea of Religious Toleration Came to the West* (Princeton University Press, 2005).

    Suppose your commitment to toleration is based on *Limits of Force*. Can you think of ways to respond to these two arguments, and to produce a stronger argument for toleration?

2.  Consider Locke's third argument for religious toleration. Even if "the rigor of laws and the force of penalties" were able to change people's minds, still, he says, political officials still should not use those instruments to promote religious uniformity. The argument turns on the idea that, while the religious convictions of the "princes of the world" are diverse, there is "but one truth." Reconstruct Locke's argument. Do you find his case compelling?

3.  Locke's argument focuses on religious toleration. He aims "to distinguish exactly the business of civil government from that of religion and settle the just bounds that lie between the one and the other." But if you consider Locke's second argument, which draws on the *Limits of Force* thesis, it is not clear why it is limited to *religious* toleration. If the state should be *religiously* tolerant because minds cannot be changed by force, then should it be equally tolerant of *all beliefs*? How, if at all, do Locke's arguments bear specifically on *religious* toleration?

## John Stuart Mill (1806–1873)

Mill was born in London, England. He was educated by his father, James Mill, a distinguished Scottish philosopher, political theorist, economist, and historian. A utilitarian, empiricist, and important public thinker, Mill was the author of *Utilitarianism, Considerations on Representative Government, Principles of Political Economy, Subjection of Women, System of Logic, The Autobiography of John Stuart Mill*, and, most famously,

*On Liberty*. Apart from his writings, Mill worked at the East India Company (1823–58), served as a Member of Parliament (1865–68), and was Lord Rector of the University of St. Andrews (1865–68).

# ON LIBERTY

---

# Chapter I: Introductory

The object of this essay is to assert one very simple principle, as entitled to govern absolutely the dealings of society with the individual in the way of compulsion and control, whether the means used be physical force in the form of legal penalties or the moral coercion of public opinion. That principle is that the sole end for which mankind are warranted, individually or collectively, in interfering with the liberty of action of any of their number is self-protection. That the only purpose for which power can be rightfully exercised over any member of a civilized community, against his will, is to prevent harm to others. His own good, either physical or moral, is not a sufficient warrant. He cannot rightfully be compelled to do or forbear because it will be better for him to do so, because it will make him happier, because, in the opinions of others, to do so would be wise or even right. These are good reasons for remonstrating with him, or reasoning with him, or persuading him, or entreating him, but not for compelling him or visiting him with any evil in case he do otherwise. To justify that, the conduct from which it is desired to deter him must be calculated to produce evil to someone else. The only part of the conduct of anyone for which he is amenable to society is that which concerns others. In the part which merely concerns himself, his independence is, of right, absolute. Over himself, over his own body and mind, the individual is sovereign.

It is, perhaps, hardly necessary to say that this doctrine is meant to apply only to human beings in the maturity of their faculties. We are not speaking of children or of young persons below the age which the law may fix as that of manhood or womanhood. Those who are still in a state to require being taken care of by others must be protected against their own actions as well as against external injury. For the same reason we may leave out of consideration those backward states of society in which the race itself may be considered as in its nonage.[1] . . . Liberty, as a principle, has no application to any state of things anterior to the time when mankind have become capable of being improved by free and equal discussion. Until then, there is nothing for them but implicit obedience to an Akbar[2] or

---

1. "Its nonage" means "its period of immaturity." Mill is here assuming that there is a period in human history in which people are not, in his words, "capable of being improved by free and equal discussion."

2. Abū al-Fath Jalāl al-Dīn Muhammad Akbar (1542–1605) was Moghul emperor of India, 1556–1605. Apart from leading a vast expansion and administrative centralization of the empire, Akbar the Great is associated with support for the arts and religious toleration.

a Charlemagne[3] if they·are so fortunate as to find one. But as soon as mankind have attained the capacity of being guided to their own improvement by conviction or persuasion (a period long since reached in all nations with whom we need here concern ourselves), compulsion, either in the direct form or in that of pains and penalties for noncompliance, is no longer admissible as a means to their own good, and justifiable only for the security of others.

It is proper to state that I forego any advantage which could be derived to my argument from the idea of abstract right as a thing independent of utility. I regard utility as the ultimate appeal on all ethical questions; but it must be utility in the largest sense, grounded on the permanent interests of man as a progressive being. Those interests, I contend, authorize the subjection of individual spontaneity to external control only in respect to those actions of each which concern the interest of other people. If anyone does an act *hurtful* to others, there is a *prima facie* case for punishing him by law or, where legal penalties are not safely applicable, by general disapprobation. There are also many positive acts for the benefit of others which he may rightfully be compelled to perform, such as to give evidence in a court of justice, to bear his fair share in the common defense or in any other joint work necessary to the interest of the society of which he enjoys the protection, and to perform certain acts of individual beneficence, such as saving a fellow creature's life or interposing to protect the defenseless against ill usage — things which whenever it is obviously a man's duty to do he may rightfully be made responsible to society for not doing. . . .

But there is a sphere of action in which society, as distinguished from the individual, has, if any, only an indirect interest: comprehending all that portion of a person's life and conduct which affects only himself or, if it also affects others, only with their free, voluntary, and undeceived consent and participation. When I say only himself, I mean directly and in the first instance; for whatever affects himself may affect others through himself: and the objection which may be grounded on this contingency will receive consideration in the sequel. This, then, is the appropriate region of human liberty. It comprises, first, the inward domain of consciousness, demanding liberty of conscience in the most comprehensive sense, liberty of thought and feeling, absolute freedom of opinion and sentiment on all subjects, practical or speculative, scientific, moral, or theological. The liberty of expressing and publishing opinions may seem to fall under a different principle, since it belongs to that part of the conduct of an individual which concerns other people, but, being almost of as much importance as the liberty of thought itself and resting in great part on the same reasons, is practically inseparable from it. Secondly, the principle requires liberty of tastes and pursuits, of framing the plan of our life to suit our own character, of doing as we like, subject to such consequences as may follow, without impediment from our fellow creatures, so long as what we do does not harm them, even though they should think our conduct foolish, perverse, or wrong. Thirdly, from this liberty of each individual follows the

3. Charlemagne (742–814) was King of the Franks (768–814) and crowned Holy Roman Emperor in 800 by Pope Leo II. He is associated with the "Carolingian Renaissance," comprising economic and legal reforms as well as a revival of the arts in the eighth and ninth centuries.

liberty, within the same limits, of combination among individuals; freedom to unite for any purpose not involving harm to others: the persons combining being supposed to be of full age and not forced or deceived.

No society in which these liberties are not, on the whole, respected is free, whatever may be its form of government; and none is completely free in which they do not exist absolute and unqualified. The only freedom which deserves the name is that of pursuing our own good in our own way, so long as we do not attempt to deprive others of theirs or impede their efforts to obtain it. Each is the proper guardian of his own health, whether bodily *or* mental and spiritual. Mankind are greater gainers by suffering each other to live as seems good to themselves than by compelling each to live as seems good to the rest. . . .

# Chapter III: Of Individuality, as One of the Elements of Well-Being

[In Chapter Two I have presented] the reasons which make it imperative that human beings should be free to form opinions and to express their opinions without reserve; and such the baneful consequences to the intellectual, and through that to the moral nature of man, unless this liberty is either conceded or asserted in spite of prohibition; let us next examine whether the same reasons do not require that men should be free to act upon their opinions — to carry these out in their lives without hindrance, either physical or moral, from their fellow men, so long as it is at their own risk and peril. This last proviso is of course indispensable. No one pretends that actions should be as free as opinions. . . . Acts, of whatever kind, which without justifiable cause do harm to others may be, and in the more important cases absolutely require to be, controlled by the unfavorable sentiments, and, when needful, by the active interference of mankind. The liberty of the individual must be thus far limited; he must not make himself a nuisance to other people. But if he refrains from molesting others in what concerns them, and merely acts according to his own inclination and judgment in things which concern himself, the same reasons which show that opinion should be free prove also that he should be allowed, without molestation, to carry his opinions into practice at his own cost. . . . As it is useful that while mankind are imperfect there should be different opinions, so it is that there should be different experiments of living; that free scope should be given to varieties of character, short of injury to others; and that the worth of different modes of life should be proved practically, when anyone thinks fit to try them. It is desirable, in short, that in things which do not primarily concern others individuality should assert itself. Where not the person's own character but the traditions or customs of other people are the rule of conduct, there is wanting one of the principal ingredients of human happiness, and quite the chief ingredient of individual and social progress.

In maintaining this principle, the greatest difficulty to be encountered does not lie in the appreciation of means toward an acknowledged end, but in the indifference of persons in general to the end itself. If it were felt that the free development of individuality is one of the leading essentials of well-being; that it is not only a co-ordinate element with all that is designated by the terms civilization, instruction, education, culture, but is itself a necessary part and condition of all those things, there would be no danger that liberty should be undervalued, and the adjustment of the boundaries between it and social control would present no extraordinary difficulty. But the evil is that individual spontaneity is hardly recognized by the common modes of thinking as having any intrinsic worth, or deserving any regard on its own account. . . . Few persons, out of Germany, even comprehend the meaning of the doctrine which Wilhelm von Humboldt,[4] so eminent both as a *savant* and as a politician, made the text of a treatise — that "the end of man, or that which is prescribed by the eternal or immutable dictates of reason, and not suggested by vague and transient desires, is the highest and most harmonious development of his powers to a complete and consistent whole"; that, therefore, the object "toward which every human being must ceaselessly direct his efforts, and on which especially those who design to influence their fellow men must ever keep their eyes, is the individuality of power and development"; that for this there are two requisites, "freedom, and variety of situations"; and that from the union of these arise "individual vigor and manifold diversity," which combine themselves in "originality."[5]

Little, however, as people are accustomed to a doctrine like that of von Humboldt, and surprising as it may be to them to find so high a value attached to individuality, the question, one must nevertheless think, can only be one of degree. No one's idea of excellence in conduct is that people should do absolutely nothing but copy one another. No one would assert that people ought not to put into their mode of life, and into the conduct of their concerns, any impress whatever of their own judgment or of their own individual character. On the other hand, it would be absurd to pretend that people ought to live as if nothing whatever had been known in the world before they came into it; as if experience had as yet done nothing toward showing that one mode of existence, or of conduct, is preferable to another. Nobody denies that people should be so taught and trained in youth as to know and benefit by the ascertained results of human experience. But it is the privilege and proper condition of a human being, arrived at the maturity of his faculties, to use and interpret experience in his own way. It is for him to find out what part of recorded experience is properly applicable to his own circumstances and character. The traditions and customs of other people are, to a certain extent, evidence of what their experience has taught *them* — presumptive evidence, and as such, have a claim to his deference: but, in the

---

4. Baron von Humboldt (1767–1835) was a philosopher, linguist, and public official. His book *On the Limits of State Action* forcefully defended liberty on the basis of its contribution to the development of individual capacities.

5. *The Sphere and Duties of Government* [*The Limits of State Action*], from the German of Baron Wilhelm von Humboldt, pp. 11, 13. [Mill's note.]

first place, their experience may be too narrow, or they may have not interpreted it rightly. Secondly, their interpretation of experience may be correct, but unsuitable to him. Customs are made for customary circumstances and customary characters; and his circumstances or his character may be uncustomary. Thirdly, though the customs be both good as customs and suitable to him, yet to conform to custom merely *as* custom does not educate or develop in him any of the qualities which are the distinctive endowment of a human being. The human faculties of perception, judgment, discriminative feeling, mental activity, and even moral preference are exercised only in making a choice. He who does anything because it is the custom makes no choice. He gains no practice either in discerning or in desiring what is best. The mental and moral, like the muscular, powers are improved only by being used. The faculties are called into no exercise by doing a thing merely because others do it, no more than by believing a thing only because others believe it. If the grounds of an opinion are not conclusive to the person's own reason, his reason cannot be strengthened, but is likely to be weakened, by his adopting it: and if the inducements to an act are not such as are consentaneous to his own feelings and character (where affection, or the rights of others, are not concerned), it is so much done toward rendering his feelings and character inert and torpid instead of active and energetic.

He who lets the world, or his own portion of it, choose his plan of life for him has no need of any other faculty than the ape-like one of imitation. He who chooses his plan for himself employs all his faculties. He must use observation to see, reasoning and judgment to foresee, activity to gather materials for decision, discrimination to decide, and when he has decided, firmness and self-control to hold to his deliberate decision. And these qualities he requires and exercises exactly in proportion as the part of his conduct which he determines according to his own judgment and feelings is a large one. It is possible that he might be guided in some good path, and kept out of harm's way, without any of these things. But what will be his comparative worth as a human being? . . .

It will probably be conceded that it is desirable people should exercise their understandings, and that an intelligent following of custom, or even occasionally an intelligent deviation from custom, is better than a blind and simply mechanical adhesion to it. To a certain extent it is admitted that our understanding should be our own; but there is not the same willingness to admit that our desires and impulses should be our own likewise, or that to possess impulses of our own, and of any strength, is anything but a peril and a snare. Yet desires and impulses are as much a part of a perfect human being as beliefs and restraints; and strong impulses are only perilous when not properly balanced, when one set of aims and inclinations is developed into strength, while others, which ought to coexist with them, remain weak and inactive. It is not because men's desires are strong that they act ill; it is because their consciences are weak. There is no natural connection between strong impulses and a weak conscience. The natural connection is the other way. To say that one person's desires and feelings are stronger and more various than those of another is merely to say that he has more of the raw material of human nature and is therefore capable, perhaps of more evil, but certainly of more good. Strong impulses are but another name for energy. Energy may be turned to bad uses; but more good may always be made of an energetic nature than of an indolent and impassive one.... Whoever thinks that individuality of desires and impulses should not be encouraged to unfold itself must maintain that society has no need of strong natures — is not the better for containing many persons who have much character — and that a high general average of energy is not desirable. ...

In our times, from the highest class of society down to the lowest, everyone lives as under the eye of a hostile and dreaded censorship. Not only in what concerns others, but in what concerns only themselves, the individual or the family do not ask themselves, what do I prefer? or, what would suit my character and disposition? or, what would allow the best and highest in me to have fair play and enable it to grow and thrive? They ask themselves, what is suitable to my position? what is usually done by persons of my station and pecuniary circumstances? or (worse still) what is usually done by persons of a station and circumstances superior to mine? I do not mean that they choose what is customary in preference to what suits their own inclination. It does not occur to them to have any inclination except for what is customary. Thus the mind itself is bowed to the yoke: even in what people do for pleasure, conformity is the first thing thought of; they like in crowds; they exercise choice only among things commonly done; peculiarity of taste, eccentricity of conduct are shunned equally with crimes, until by dint of not following their own nature they have no nature to follow: their human capacities are withered and starved; they become incapable of any strong wishes or native pleasures, and are generally without either opinions or feelings of home growth, or properly their own. Now is this, or is it not, the desirable condition of human nature?

It is so, on the Calvinistic theory.[6] According to that, the one great offense of man is self-will. All the good of which humanity is capable is comprised in obedience. You have no choice; thus you must do, and no otherwise: "Whatever is not a duty is a sin." Human nature being radically corrupt, there is no redemption for anyone until human nature is killed within him. To one holding this theory of life, crushing out any of the human faculties, capacities, and susceptibilities is no evil: man needs no capacity but that of surrendering himself to the will of God. ...

Many persons, no doubt, sincerely think that human beings thus cramped and dwarfed are as their Maker designed them to be, just as many have thought that trees are a much finer thing when clipped into pollards, or cut out into figures of animals, than as nature made them. But if it be any part of religion to believe that man was made by a good Being, it is more consistent with that faith to believe that this Being gave all human faculties that they might be cultivated and unfolded, not

---

6. Calvinism is the theological system associated with John Calvin (1509–1564), a leading figure in the Protestant Reformation, and with the Reformed churches. The central ideas in Calvinism are the total depravity of human nature (that everything we do is tainted by sin), and predestination. According to predestination, God makes an unconditional choice about who will be saved (unconditional election); Christ's death atoned exclusively for the sins of those whom God had chosen; those who have been predestined to salvation cannot fail to be saved (irresistible grace); and they cannot lose their salvation (perseverance of the saints).

rooted out and consumed, and that he takes delight in every nearer approach made by his creatures to the ideal conception embodied in them, every increase in any of their capabilities of comprehension, of action, or of enjoyment. There is a different type of human excellence from the Calvinistic: a conception of humanity as having its nature bestowed on it for other purposes than merely to be abnegated. "Pagan self-assertion" is one of the elements of human worth, as well as "Christian self-denial." There is a Greek ideal of self-development, which the Platonic and Christian ideal of self-government blends with, but does not supersede. It may be better to be a John Knox[7] than an Alcibiades;[8] but it is better to be a Pericles than either; nor would a Pericles,[9] if we had one in these days, be without anything good which belonged to John Knox.

It is not by wearing down into uniformity all that is individual in themselves, but by cultivating it and calling it forth, within the limits imposed by the rights and interests of others, that human beings become a noble and beautiful object of contemplation. . . . As much compression as is necessary to prevent the stronger specimens of human nature from encroaching on the rights of others cannot be dispensed with; but for this there is ample compensation even in the point of view of human development. The means of development which the individual loses by being prevented from gratifying his inclinations to the injury of others are chiefly obtained at the expense of the development of other people. And even to himself there is a full equivalent in the better development of the social part of his nature, rendered possible by the restraint put upon the selfish part. To be held to rigid rules of justice for the sake of others develops the feelings and capacities which have the good of others for their object. But to be restrained in things not affecting their good, by their mere displeasure, develops nothing valuable except such force of character as may unfold itself in resisting the restraint. If acquiesced in, it dulls and blunts the whole nature.

Having said that the individuality is the same thing with development, and that it is only the cultivation of individuality which produces, or can produce, well-developed human beings, I might here close the argument; for what more or better can be said of any condition of human affairs than that it brings human beings themselves nearer to the best thing they can be? Or what worse can be said of any obstruction to good than that it prevents this? Doubtless, however, these considerations will not suffice to convince those who most need convincing; and it is necessary further to show that these developed human beings are of some use to the undeveloped — to point out to those who do not desire liberty, and would not avail themselves of it, that

---

7. John Knox (1510–1572), a Scottish clergyman, was a central figure in the Protestant Reformation and a founder of Presbyterianism. Knox was closely associated with Calvin, and brought Calvinism to Scotland.

8. Alcibiades was an Athenian politician and a general in the Peloponnesian War. He is a central character in Plato's *Symposium*.

9. Pericles (495–429 BCE) was a leading political and military figure in Athens, described by Thucydides as "the first citizen of Athens," and widely credited with fostering Athenian democracy.

they may be in some intelligible manner rewarded for allowing other people to make use of it without hindrance.[1]

## TEST YOUR UNDERSTANDING

1. Mill says that the aim of *On Liberty* is to "assert one very simple principle." State the principle in your own words. Give two examples of conduct that should not be regulated according to Mill's liberty principle.

2. According to Mill, "individuality is the same thing with development," and "it is only the cultivation of individuality that produces, or can produce, well developed human beings." Why is individuality needed for being well developed? Try to describe a life that is well developed but that is pretty traditional, thus lacking in individuality.

3. Mill says "it may be better to be a John Knox than an Alcibiades; but it is better to be a Pericles than either." Explain how Mill's examples (Knox, Alcibiades, Pericles) illustrate his point, made earlier in the paragraph, about the "Greek ideal of self-development" and the "Platonic and Christian ideal of self-government."

## NOTES AND QUESTIONS

1. Mill says that if a person is acting against his own best interests, we have reason for "remonstrating with him, or reasoning with him, or persuading him, or entreating him, but not for compelling him or visiting him with any evil in case he do otherwise." Think of an example of a person (perhaps a friend) who has acted against his or her best interests: say, the person has started drinking heavily. How would you draw the distinction between actions that Mill thinks are acceptable — remonstrating, reasoning, persuading, or entreating — and actions Mill says are unacceptable — compelling him or "visiting him with any evil"? Suppose you know that your friend is very sensitive, and will sink into depression if you encourage him to stop drinking. If you nevertheless encourage him, and he sinks into depression, have you entreated him or have you visited an evil on him? Or suppose the person is very susceptible to your influence, or dependent on you for a grade or a salary.

---

1. In the rest of chapter 3 of *On Liberty*, Mill tries to make this further case: that human development, which is fostered by protecting individual liberty, is also a great benefit for those who choose not to develop their own powers, and live in more conventional ways. Individuals who do not choose to develop their own powers, Mill says, might "learn something" from those who do; moreover, we all benefit, he argues, from the economic, social, political progress that results from the choices of "developed human beings."

When there is a relation of dependence, can you provide encouragement that does not come across as a threat? Try to state a general principle that draws a line between the compulsion Mill rejects and the persuasion he allows. Does the distinction help you decide what you should do in these cases?

2.  Mill claims that he defends his principle on the basis of "utility," not on the basis of "abstract right as a thing independent of utility." Critics of **utilitarianism** have argued that the principle of utility does not provide a strong case in favor of liberties. The principle of utility says that the right acts and institutions are the ones that maximize the sum of happiness. But, the critics say, if you can make enough people happy by enslaving other people, or requiring religious conformity, or demanding compliance with customs and conventions, then utilitarianism must endorse limits on liberty. Or they say that utilitarians are too quick to favor restrictions on freedom of speech or assembly in the name of national security. How might Mill respond to these concerns? Why does he think that the principle of utility supports the liberty principle?

3.  One line of argument for liberty that Mill uses is that liberty is important for individuality and that individuality is the "same thing with development." He goes on to say that "developed human beings are of some use to the undeveloped." Is that a good case for extending liberties to all? In answering, you should think about four questions:

    (i)   Why is liberty important for individuality?

    (ii)  Why is individuality so closely related to the development of human powers? (Mill gives three reasons in the paragraph that begins: "Little, however, as people are accustomed to . . .")

    (iii) In what ways are "developed human beings" of use "to the undeveloped"?

    (iv)  Would the results be better, in terms of the sum of happiness, if liberties were available only to people who would use the liberties to become "well-developed"?

4.  For a helpful discussion of utilitarianism (including Mill's version of utilitarianism), and the troubles it may have with liberty, see John Rawls, *A Theory of Justice* (Harvard University Press, 1999), pp. 19–24, 184–85.

## Patrick Devlin (1905–1992)

Devlin was born in Kent, England. A commercial lawyer and judge — the youngest High Court judge appointed in the twentieth century — Devlin became a member of the House of Lords in 1961. He wrote "Morals and the Criminal Law" in criticism of the Wolfenden Report (1957), which called for the abolition of British laws that criminalized homosexuality. He subsequently changed his mind, and in 1965 signed a letter that urged the implementation of the reforms recommended by the Wolfenden Report.

# MORALS AND THE CRIMINAL LAW[1]

What is the connexion between crime and sin and to what extent, if at all, should the criminal law of England concern itself with the enforcement of morals and punish sin or immorality as such? . . .

I think it is clear that the criminal law as we know it is based upon moral principle. In a number of crimes its function is simply to enforce a moral principle and nothing else. The law, both criminal and civil, claims to be able to speak about morality and immorality generally. Where does it get its authority to do this and how does it settle the moral principles which it enforces? Undoubtedly, as a matter of history, it derived both from Christian teaching. But I think that the strict logician is right when he says that the law can no longer rely on doctrines in which citizens are entitled to disbelieve. It is necessary therefore to look for some other source. . . .

I have framed three interrogatories addressed to myself to answer:

1. Has society the right to pass judgement at all on matters of morals? Ought there, in other words, to be a public morality, or are morals always a matter for private judgement?

2. If society has the right to pass judgement, has it also the right to use the weapon of the law to enforce it?

3. If so, ought it to use that weapon in all cases or only in some; and if only in some, on what principles should it distinguish?

I shall begin with the first interrogatory and consider what is meant by the right of society to pass a moral judgement, that is, a judgement about what is good and what is evil. The fact that a majority of people may disapprove of a practice does not of itself make it a matter for society as a whole. Nine men out of ten may disapprove of what the tenth man is doing and still say that it is not their business. There is a case for a collective judgement (as distinct from a large number of individual opinions which sensible people may even refrain from pronouncing at all if it is upon somebody else's private affairs) only if society is affected. Without a collective judgement there can be no case at all for intervention. Let me take as an illustration the Englishman's attitude to religion as it is now and as it has been in the past. His attitude now is that a man's religion is his private affair; he may think of another man's religion that it is right or wrong, true or untrue, but not that it is good or bad. In earlier times that was not so; a man was denied the right to practise what was thought of as heresy, and heresy was thought of as destructive of society. . . .

1. Lord Devlin's essay was written in response to "The Report of the Departmental Committee on Homosexual Offences and Prostitution" (commonly known as the Wolfenden Report). The Wolfenden Report, released in Britain on September 4, 1957, recommended that "homosexual behaviour between consenting adults in private should no longer be a criminal offence."

This view — that there is such a thing as public morality — can . . . be justified by *a priori* argument. What makes a society of any sort is community of ideas, not only political ideas but also ideas about the way its members should behave and govern their lives; these latter ideas are its morals. Every society has a moral structure as well as a political one: or rather, since that might suggest two independent systems, I should say that the structure of every society is made up both of politics and morals. Take, for example, the institution of marriage. Whether a man should be allowed to take more than one wife is something about which every society has to make up its mind one way or the other. In England we believe in the Christian idea of marriage and therefore adopt monogamy as a moral principle. Consequently the Christian institution of marriage has become the basis of family life and so part of the structure of our society. It is there not because it is Christian. It has got there because it is Christian, but it remains there because it is built into the house in which we live and could not be removed without bringing it down. The great majority of those who live in this country accept it because it is the Christian idea of marriage and for them the only true one. But a non-Christian is bound by it, not because it is part of Christianity but because, rightly or wrongly, it has been adopted by the society in which he lives. . . .

We see this more clearly if we think of ideas or institutions that are purely political. Society cannot tolerate rebellion; it will not allow argument about the rightness of the cause. Historians a century later may say that the rebels were right and the Government was wrong and a percipient and conscientious subject of the State may think so at the time. But it is not a matter which can be left to individual judgement.

The institution of marriage is a good example for my purpose because it bridges the division, if there is one, between politics and morals. Marriage is part of the structure of our society and it is also the basis of a moral code which condemns fornication and adultery. The institution of marriage would be gravely threatened if individual judgements were permitted about the morality of adultery; on these points there must be a public morality. But public morality is not to be confined to those moral principles which support institutions such as marriage. People do not think of monogamy as something which has to be supported because our society has chosen to organize itself upon it; they think of it as something that is good in itself and offering a good way of life and that it is for that reason that our society has adopted it. I return to the statement that I have already made, that society means a community of ideas; without shared ideas on politics, morals, and ethics no society can exist. Each one of us has ideas about what is good and what is evil; they cannot be kept private from the society in which we live. If men and women try to create a society in which there is no fundamental agreement about good and evil they will fail; if, having based it on common agreement, the agreement goes, the society will disintegrate. For society is not something that is kept together physically; it is held by the invisible bonds of common thought. If the bonds were too far relaxed the members would drift apart. A common morality is part of the bondage. The bondage is part of the price of society; and mankind, which needs society, must pay its price. . . .

[T]he answer to the first question determines the way in which the second should be approached and may indeed very nearly dictate the answer to the second question. If society has no right to make judgements on morals, the law must find some special justification for entering the field of morality: if homosexuality and prostitution are not in themselves wrong, then the onus is very clearly on the lawgiver who wants to frame a law against certain aspects of them to justify the exceptional treatment. But if society has the right to make a judgement and has it on the basis that a recognized morality is as necessary to society as, say, a recognized government, then society may use the law to preserve morality in the same way as it uses it to safeguard anything else that is essential to its existence. If therefore the first proposition is securely established with all its implications, society has a prima facie right to legislate against immorality as such. . . .

. . . [Devlin presents a Wolfenden Committee objection to the view he just presented, and now he responds]: I think that it is not possible to set theoretical limits to the power of the State to legislate against immorality. It is not possible to settle in advance exceptions to the general rule or to define inflexibly areas of morality into which the law is in no circumstances to be allowed to enter. Society is entitled by means of its laws to protect itself from dangers, whether from within or without. Here again I think that the political parallel is legitimate. The law of treason is directed against aiding the king's enemies and against sedition from within. The justification for this is that established government is necessary for the existence of society and therefore its safety against violent overthrow must be secured. But an established morality is as necessary as good government to the welfare of society. Societies disintegrate from within more frequently than they are broken up by external pressures. There is disintegration when no common morality is observed and history shows that the loosening of moral bonds is often the first stage of disintegration, so that society is justified in taking the same steps to preserve its moral code as it does to preserve its government and other essential institutions. The suppression of vice is as much the law's business as the suppression of subversive activities; it is no more possible to define a sphere of private morality than it is to define one of private subversive activity. . . . You may argue that if a man's sins affect only himself it cannot be the concern of society. If he chooses to get drunk every night in the privacy of his own home, is any one except himself the worse for it? But suppose a quarter or a half of the population got drunk every night, what sort of society would it be? You cannot set a theoretical limit to the number of people who can get drunk before society is entitled to legislate against drunkenness. The same may be said of gambling. . . .

In what circumstances the State should exercise its power is the third of the interrogatories I have framed. But before I get to it I must raise a point which might have been brought up in any one of the three. How are the moral judgements of society to be ascertained? By leaving it until now, I can ask it in the more limited form that is now sufficient for my purpose. How is the law-maker to ascertain the moral judgements of society? It is surely not enough that they should be reached by the opinion of the majority; it would be too much to require the individual assent of every citizen. English law has evolved and regularly uses a standard which does not depend on the counting of heads. It is that of the reasonable man. He is not to be confused with the rational man. He is not expected to reason about anything and his judgement may be largely a matter of feeling. It is the viewpoint of the man in the street — or to use an archaism familiar to all lawyers — the man in the Clapham omnibus.[2] He might also be called the right-minded man. For my purpose I should like to call him the man in the jury box, for the moral judgement of society must be something about which any twelve men or women drawn at random might after discussion be expected to be unanimous. . . .

Immorality then, for the purpose of the law, is what every right-minded person is presumed to consider to be immoral. Any immorality is capable of affecting society injuriously and in effect to a greater or lesser extent it usually does; this is what gives the law its *locus standi*.[3] It cannot be shut out. But — and this brings me to the third question — the individual has a *locus standi* too; he cannot be expected to surrender to the judgement of society the whole conduct of his life. It is the old and familiar question of striking a balance between the rights and interests of society and those of the individual. This is something which the law is constantly doing in matters large and small. To take a very down-to-earth example, let me consider the right of the individual whose house adjoins the highway to have access to it; that means in these days the right to have vehicles stationary in the highway, sometimes for a considerable time if there is a lot of loading or unloading. There are many cases in which the courts have had to balance the private right of access against the public right to use the highway without obstruction. It cannot be done by carving up the highway into public and private areas. It is done by recognizing that each have rights over the whole; that if each were to exercise their rights to the full, they would come into conflict; and therefore that the rights of each must be curtailed so as to ensure as far as possible that the essential needs of each are safeguarded.

I do not think that one can talk sensibly of a public and private morality any more than one can of a public or private highway. Morality is a sphere in which there is a public interest and a private interest, often in conflict, and the problem is to reconcile the two. This does not mean that it is impossible to put forward any general statements about how in our society the balance ought to be struck. Such statements cannot of their nature be rigid or precise; they would not be designed to circumscribe the operation of the law-making power but to guide those who have to apply it. . . .

I believe that most people would agree upon the chief of these elastic principles. There must be toleration of the maximum individual freedom that is consistent with the integrity of society. . . . [This toleration] is not confined to thought and speech;

---

2. "Man in the Clapham omnibus" is a nineteenth-century British phrase that refers to an intelligent but unremarkable person. It was used to generate a basis of comparison in court cases — what would the man in the Clapham omnibus have done in this situation? — or to make claims about public opinion. "Clapham" is a London suburb and "omnibus" is a (now archaic) term for a public bus.

3. *Locus standi* is the right to bring a legal action (what is commonly called "standing"). Devlin is not using the term literally here. He means that both the individual and society have substantial interests at stake in the issue under consideration about the legal enforcement of morality, not that they have a right to bring legal action.

it extends to action, as is shown by the recognition of the right to conscientious objection in war-time; this example shows also that conscience will be respected even in times of national danger. The principle appears to me to be peculiarly appropriate to all questions of morals. Nothing should be punished by the law that does not lie beyond the limits of tolerance. It is not nearly enough to say that a majority dislike a practice; there must be a real feeling of reprobation. Those who are dissatisfied with the present law on homosexuality often say that the opponents of reform are swayed simply by disgust. If that were so it would be wrong, but I do not think one can ignore disgust if it is deeply felt and not manufactured. Its presence is a good indication that the bounds of toleration are being reached. Not everything is to be tolerated. No society can do without intolerance, indignation, and disgust, they are the forces behind the moral law, and indeed it can be argued that if they or something like them are not present, the feelings of society cannot be weighty enough to deprive the individual of freedom of choice. I suppose that there is hardly anyone nowadays who would not be disgusted by the thought of deliberate cruelty to animals. No one proposes to relegate that or any other form of sadism to the realm of private morality or to allow it to be practised in public or in private. It would be possible no doubt to point out that until a comparatively short while ago nobody thought very much of cruelty to animals and also that pity and kindliness and the unwillingness to inflict pain are virtues more generally esteemed now than they have ever been in the past. But matters of this sort are not determined by rational argument. Every moral judgement, unless it claims a divine source, is simply a feeling that no right-minded man could behave in any other way without admitting that he was doing wrong. It is the power of a common sense and not the power of reason that is behind the judgements of society. But before a society can put a practice beyond the limits of tolerance there must be a deliberate judgement that the practice is injurious to society. There is, for example, a general abhorrence of homosexuality. We should ask ourselves in the first instance whether, looking at it calmly and dispassionately, we regard it as a vice so abominable that its mere presence is an offence. If that is the genuine feeling of the society in which we live, I do not see how society can be denied the right to eradicate it. Our feeling may not be so intense as that. We may feel about it that, if confined, it is tolerable, but that if it spread it might be gravely injurious; it is in this way that most societies look upon fornication, seeing it as a natural weakness which must be kept within bounds but which cannot be rooted out. It becomes then a question of balance, the danger to society in one scale and the extent of the restriction in the other. . . .

This then is how I believe my third interrogatory should be answered — not by the formulation of hard and fast rules, but by a judgement in each case taking into account the sort of factors I have been mentioning. The line that divides the criminal law from the moral is not determinable by the application of any clear-cut principle. It is like a line that divides land and sea, a coastline of irregularities and indentations. There are gaps and promontories, such as adultery and fornication, which the law has for centuries left substantially untouched. Adultery of the sort that breaks up marriage seems to me to be just as harmful to the social fabric as homosexuality or bigamy. The only ground for putting it outside the criminal law is that a law which made it a crime would be too difficult to enforce; it is too generally regarded as a human weakness not suitably punished by imprisonment. All that the law can do with fornication is to act against its worst manifestations; there is a general abhorrence of the commercialization of vice, and that sentiment gives strength to the law against brothels and immoral earnings. There is no logic to be found in this. The boundary between the criminal law and the moral law is fixed by balancing in the case of each particular crime the pros and cons of legal enforcement in accordance with the sort of considerations I have been outlining. The fact that adultery, fornication, and lesbianism are untouched by the criminal law does not prove that homosexuality ought not to be touched. The error of jurisprudence in the Wolfenden Report is caused by the search for some single principle to explain the division between crime and sin. The Report finds it in the principle that the criminal law exists for the protection of individuals; on this principle fornication in private between consenting adults is outside the law and thus it becomes logically indefensible to bring homosexuality between consenting adults in private within it. But the true principle is that the law exists for the protection of society. It does not discharge its function by protecting the individual from injury, annoyance, corruption, and exploitation; the law must protect also the institutions and the community of ideas, political and moral, without which people cannot live together. Society cannot ignore the morality of the individual any more than it can his loyalty; it flourishes on both and without either it dies. . . .

I return now to the main thread of my argument and summarize it. Society cannot live without morals. Its morals are those standards of conduct which the reasonable man approves. A rational man, who is also a good man, may have other standards. If he has no standards at all he is not a good man and need not be further considered. If he has standards, they may be very different; he may, for example, not disapprove of homosexuality or abortion. In that case he will not share in the common morality; but that should not make him deny that it is a social necessity. A rebel may be rational in thinking that he is right but he is irrational if he thinks that society can leave him free to rebel.

## TEST YOUR UNDERSTANDING

1. State the three questions that Devlin addresses in his essay.

2. Devlin asks whether it is proper to punish "immorality as such." What does he mean by "immorality as such"?

3. To illustrate his idea that every society has a "moral structure," Devlin considers the institution of marriage. How does the institution of marriage illustrate Devlin's point about "moral structure"?

4. According to Devlin, society will "disintegrate" without a set of "shared ideas on politics, morals, and ethics." What does he mean by "disintegrate"?

## NOTES AND QUESTIONS

1. Devlin thinks both that a society has the right to pass judgment on moral issues and that it has the right to use the law to enforce its moral judgments. He argues for the latter right on the basis of the former. In fact, he says that the right to pass judgment "very nearly dictate[s]" the right to use the law to enforce the judgments. Reconstruct Devlin's argument for the right to use the law to enforce moral judgments.

   Before beginning the reconstruction, it will help to address two prior questions: (i) How does society "pass judgment" on a moral issue? (How would you know what a society's judgment is?) (ii) Why does a society have a right to pass judgment on a moral issue?

2. Consider three proposed **sufficient conditions** for a right to enforcement, all of which are suggested by Devlin's essay:

   (i)   Society has a right to enforce moral judgments when there is a realistic concern about social "disintegration."

   (ii)  Society has a right to enforce moral judgments when enforcement is required by the "integrity of society."

   (iii) Society has a right to enforce moral judgments when a practice provokes a "real feeling of reprobation."

   Do these three conditions come to the same thing? For example, in the United States in the 1950s, there appears to have been, in many parts of the country, a real feeling of reprobation about interracial marriage. (In 1958, 72 percent of Southern whites — and more than 40 percent of Northern whites — supported a *legal ban* on interracial marriage.) That feeling of reprobation, assuming it existed, would have provided good reason for a legal ban based on condition (iii). What about conditions (i) and (ii)?

   Does Devlin think that a society ought to enforce all the moral judgments it has a right to enforce? (Review his discussion of the third question.) Which of its moral judgments should a society enforce?

3. For discussion of Devlin's views, see H. L. A. Hart, *Law, Liberty, and Morality* (Stanford University Press, 1963); Ronald Dworkin, "Lord Devlin and the Enforcement of Morals," *Yale Law Journal* 75, no. 6 (1966): 986–1005; and Gerald Dworkin, "Devlin Was Right: Law and the Enforcement of Morality," *William and Mary Law Review* 40 (1999): 927–46.

## Amartya Sen (born 1933)

Sen was born in Santiniketan, West Bengal, India. An economist and philosopher, he is currently Thomas W. Lamont University Professor at Harvard University. He has written on a vast range of subjects, including social choice theory, welfare economics, economic development, justice, famines, democracy, rationality, poverty, inequality, and human capabilities. His books include *The Idea of Justice* (2010), *Poverty and Famines* (1981), *Development as*

*Freedom* (1999), *Inequality Reexamined* (1995), *Identity and Violence* (2007), and *Collective Choice and Social Welfare* (1990). Sen was awarded the Nobel Memorial Prize in Economic Sciences in 1998.

# ELEMENTS OF A THEORY OF HUMAN RIGHTS

## I. The Need for a Theory

Few concepts are as frequently invoked in contemporary political discussions as human rights. There is something deeply attractive in the idea that every person anywhere in the world, irrespective of citizenship or territorial legislation, has some basic rights, which others should respect. The moral appeal of human rights has been used for a variety of purposes, from resisting torture and arbitrary incarceration to demanding the end of hunger and of medical neglect.

At the same time, the central idea of human rights as something that people have, and have even without any specific legislation, is seen by many as foundationally dubious and lacking in cogency. A recurrent question is, Where do these rights come from? It is not usually disputed that the invoking of human rights can be politically powerful. Rather, the worries relate to what is taken to be the "softness" (some would say "mushiness") of the conceptual grounding of human rights. . . .

Human rights activists are often quite impatient with such critiques. The invoking of human rights tends to come mostly from those who are concerned with changing the world rather than interpreting it (to use a classic distinction made famous, oddly enough, by that overarching theorist, Karl Marx). It is not hard to understand their unwillingness to spend time trying to provide conceptual justification, given the great urgency to respond to terrible deprivations around the world. This proactive stance has had its practical rewards, since it has allowed immediate use of the colossal appeal of the idea of human rights to confront intense oppression or great misery, without having to wait for the theoretical air to clear. However, the conceptual doubts must also be satisfactorily addressed, if the idea of human rights is to command reasoned loyalty and to establish a secure intellectual standing. It is critically important to see the relationship between the force and appeal of human rights, on the one hand, and their reasoned justification and scrutinized use, on the other.

There is, thus, need for some theory and also for some defense of any proposed theory. The object of this article is to do just that, and to consider, in that context, the justification of the general idea of human rights and also of the includability of economic and social rights within the broad class of human rights. For such a theory to be viable it is necessary to clarify what kind of a claim is made by a declaration of human rights, and how such a claim can be defended, and furthermore how the diverse criticisms of the coherence, cogency and legitimacy of human rights (including economic and social rights) can be adequately addressed. . . .

# III. Human Rights: Ethics and Law

What kind of an assertion does a declaration of human rights make? I would submit that proclamations of human rights are to be seen as articulations of ethical demands. They are, in this respect, comparable with pronouncements in utilitarian ethics, even though their respective substantive contents are, obviously, very different. . . .

A pronouncement of human rights includes an assertion of the importance of the corresponding freedoms — the freedoms that are identified and privileged in the formulation of the rights in question — and is indeed motivated by that importance. For example, the human right of not being tortured springs from the importance of freedom from torture for all. But it includes, furthermore, an affirmation of the need for others to consider what they can reasonably do to secure the freedom from torture for any person. For a would-be torturer, the demand is obviously quite straightforward, to wit, to refrain and desist. The demand takes the clear form of what Immanuel Kant called a perfect obligation.[1] However, for others too (that is, those other than the would-be torturers) there are responsibilities, even though they are less specific and come in the general form of "imperfect obligations" (to invoke another Kantian concept). The perfectly specified demand not to torture anyone is supplemented by the more general, and less exactly specified, requirement to consider the ways and means through which torture can be prevented and then to decide what one should, thus, reasonably do. . . .

An ethical understanding of human rights goes . . . against seeing them as legal demands (and against taking them to be, as in Bentham's view, legal *pretensions*[2]), but also differs from a law-centered approach to human rights that sees them as if they are basically *grounds* for law, almost "laws in waiting." Ethical and legal rights do, of course, have motivational connections. In a rightly celebrated article "Are There Any Natural Rights"? Herbert Hart has argued that people "speak of their moral rights mainly when advocating their incorporation in a legal system." He added that the concept of a right "belongs to that branch of morality which is

---

1. Kant distinguishes perfect from imperfect duties. Intuitively, a perfect duty requires a specific action of an agent, whereas an imperfect duty leaves an agent with more discretion. For example, if I promise to be in my office at 3 PM, I have a duty to be there then: the duties associated with promising are perfect. In contrast, the duty of beneficence, a duty to help others in need, leaves me more discretion about when to help, whom to help, and precisely how much help to provide: the duty of beneficence is thus imperfect. See, for example, Kant, *Groundwork of the Metaphysics of Morals,* in Immanuel Kant, *Practical Philosophy,* translated and edited by Mary J. Gregor (Cambridge University Press, 1996), p. 73n. [Sen's note.]

2. The English legal and political theorist Jeremy Bentham (1748–1832) was a leading utilitarian and a sharp critic of the idea of natural rights. Bentham said that "natural rights are nonsense," and that "imprescriptible natural rights" are "nonsense on stilts." All rights, he argued, are creatures of law, and all laws are commands of a sovereign authority: to say that a person has a right to free speech, for example, is to say that the law protects the person's speaking. If a natural right is a right that is, in some way, prior to law, a right that people have even without a legal system, then there are no such rights: indeed, the very idea, Bentham thought, makes no sense. See Jeremy Bentham, *Anarchical Fallacies,* in *The Works of Jeremy Bentham,* volume 2 (Edinburgh, 1838–1843), pp. 491–534. [Sen's note.]

specifically concerned to determine when one person's freedom may be limited by another's and so to determine what actions may appropriately be made the subject of coercive legal rules.[3] Whereas Bentham saw rights as a "child of law," Hart's view takes the form, in effect, of seeing some natural rights as *parents* of law: they motivate and inspire specific legislations. Although Hart does not make any reference whatever to human rights in his article, the reasoning about the role of natural rights as inspiration for legislation can be seen to apply to the concept of human rights as well.

There can, in fact, be little doubt that the idea of moral rights can serve, and has often served in practice, as the basis of new legislation. . . .

However, to acknowledge that such a connection exists is not the same as taking the relevance of human rights to lie *exclusively* in determining what should "appropriately be made the subject of coercive legal rules." It is important to see that the idea of human rights can be, and is, actually used in several other ways as well. . . . For example, monitoring and other activist support, provided by such organizations as Human Rights Watch or Amnesty International or Oxfam or Médecins Sans Frontières, can themselves help to advance the effective reach of acknowledged human rights. In many contexts, legislation may not, in fact, be involved.

## IV. Rights, Freedoms and Social Influence

Why are human rights important? Since declarations of human rights are ethical affirmations of the need to pay appropriate attention to the significance of freedoms incorporated in the formulation of human rights (as was discussed in the last section), an appropriate starting point must be the importance of freedoms of human beings to be so recognized. . . .

Freedoms can vary in importance and also in terms of the extent to which they can be influenced by social help. For a freedom to count as a part of the evaluative system of human rights, it clearly must be important enough to justify requiring that others should be ready to pay substantial attention to decide what they can reasonably do to advance it. It also has to satisfy a condition of plausibility that others could make a material difference through taking such an interest.

There have to be some "threshold conditions" of (i) importance and (ii) social influenceability for a freedom to figure within the interpersonal and interactive spectrum of human rights. . . .

The threshold conditions may prevent, for a variety of reasons, particular freedoms from being an appropriate subject matter of human rights. To illustrate, it is not

3. H.L.A. Hart, "Are There Any Natural Rights"? *Philosophical Review* 64 (1955), reprinted in *Theories of Rights*, ed. Jeremy Waldron (Oxford University Press, 1984), p. 79. [Sen's note.]

hard to argue that some importance should be attached to all four of the following freedoms:

1. a person's freedom not to be assaulted;

2. her freedom to receive medical care for a serious health problem;

3. her freedom not to be called up regularly by her neighbors whom she detests;

4. her freedom to achieve tranquillity.

However, even though all four may be important in one way or another, it is not altogether implausible to argue that the first (freedom not to be assaulted) is a good subject matter for a human right, and so is the second (freedom to receive necessary medical care), but the third (freedom not to be called up by detested neighbors) is not, in general, important enough to cross the threshold of social significance to qualify as a human right. Also, the fourth, while quite possibly extremely important for the person, is too inward-looking — and too hard to be influenced by others — to be a good subject matter for human rights. The exclusion of a "right to tranquillity" relates not to any skepticism about the possible importance of tranquillity and the significance of a person's being free to achieve it, but to the difficulty of guaranteeing it through social help. . . .

## V. Processes, Opportunities and Capabilities

I turn now to a closer scrutiny of the contents of freedom and its multiple features. I have argued elsewhere that "opportunity" and "process" are two aspects of freedom that require distinction, with the importance of each deserving specific acknowledgment. An example can help to bring out the *separate* (though not necessarily independent) relevance of both *substantive opportunities* and *freedom of processes*.

Consider an adult person, let us call her Rima, who decides that she would like to go out in the evening. To take care of some considerations that are not central to the issues involved here (but which could make the discussion more complex), it is assumed that there are no particular safety risks involved in her going out, and that she has critically reflected on this decision and judged that going out would be the sensible, indeed the ideal, thing to do. Now consider the threat of a violation of this freedom if some authoritarian guardians of society decide that she must not go out in the evening ("it is most unseemly"), and if they force her, in one way or another, to stay indoors. To see that there are two distinct issues involved in this one violation, consider an alternative case in which the authoritarian bosses decide that she must — absolutely *must* — go out ("you are expelled for the evening: just obey"). There is clearly a violation of freedom here even though Rima is being forced to do exactly what she would have chosen to do anyway, and this is readily seen when we compare the two alternatives "choosing freely to go out" and "being forced to go out." The latter involves an immediate violation of the *process aspect* of Rima's freedom, since an action is being forced on her (even though it is an action she would have freely chosen also).

The opportunity aspect may also be affected, since a plausible accounting of opportunities can include having options and it can inter alia include valuing free choice. However, the violation of the opportunity aspect would be more substantial and manifest if she were not only forced to do something chosen by another, but in fact, forced to do something she herself would not otherwise choose to do. The comparison between "being forced to go out" (when she would have gone out anyway, if free) and, say, "being forced to polish the shoes of others at home" (not her favorite activity) brings out this contrast, which is primarily one of the opportunity aspect, rather than the process aspect. In being forced to stay home and polish the shoes of others, Rima loses freedom in two different ways, related respectively to (1) being forced with no freedom of choice, and (2) being obliged in particular to do something she would not choose to do.

Both processes and opportunities can figure in human rights. A denial of "due process" in being, say, imprisoned without a proper trial can be the subject matter of human rights (no matter what the outcome of the fair trial might be), and so can be the denial of the opportunity of medical treatment, or the opportunity of living without the danger of being assaulted (going beyond the exact process through which these opportunities are made real). . . .

## VIII. Economic and Social Rights

I turn now to criticisms that have been particularly aimed against extending the idea of human rights to include economic and social rights, such as the right not to be hungry, or the right to basic education or to medical attention. Even though these rights did not figure in the classic presentations of rights of human beings in, say, the U.S. Declaration of Independence, or French "rights of man," they are very much a part of the contemporary domain of what Cass Sunstein calls the "rights revolution.[4] The legitimacy of including these claims within the general class of human rights has been challenged through two specific lines of reproach, which I shall call, respectively, the *institutionalization critique* and the *feasibility critique.*

The institutionalization critique, which is aimed particularly at economic and social rights, relates to the general issue of the exact correspondence between authentic rights and precisely formulated correlate duties. Such a correspondence, it is argued,

---

4. Cass Sunstein, *After the Rights Revolution: Reconceiving the Regulatory State* (Harvard University Press, 1990). [Sen's note.]

would exist only when a right is institutionalized. Onora O'Neill has presented this line of criticism with force:

> Unfortunately much writing and rhetoric on rights heedlessly proclaims univer-
> sal rights to goods and services, and in particular "welfare rights," as well as to
> other social, economic and cultural rights that are prominent in international
> Charters and Declarations, without showing what connects each presumed
> right-holder to some specific obligation-bearer(s), which leaves the content
> of these supposed rights wholly obscure. . . . Some advocates of universal eco-
> nomic, social and cultural rights go no further than to emphasize that they *can*
> be institutionalized, which is true. But the point of difference is that they *must* be
> institutionalized: if they are not there is no right.[5]

In responding to this significant criticism, we have to invoke the understanding, already discussed, that obligations can be both perfect and imperfect. Even the classical "first generational" rights, like freedom from assault, can be seen as yielding imperfect obligations on others. . . . Depending on institutional possibilities, economic and social rights may similarly call for both perfect and imperfect obligations. There is a large area of fruitful public discussion and possibly effective pressure, concerning what the society and the state, even an impoverished one, can do to prevent violations of certain basic economic or social rights (associated with, say, the prevalence of famines, or chronic undernourishment, or absence of medical care).

Indeed, the supportive activities of social organizations are often aimed precisely at institutional change, and these activities can be seen as part of imperfect obligations that individuals and groups have in a society where basic human rights are violated. Onora O'Neill is right to emphasize the importance of institutions for the realization of "welfare rights" (and even for economic and social rights in general), but the ethical significance of these rights provide good grounds for seeking realization through institutional expansion and reform. This can be helped through a variety of approaches, including demanding and agitating for appropriate legislation, and the supplementation of legal demands by political recognition and social monitoring. To deny the ethical status of these claims would be to ignore the reasoning that motivates these constructive activities.

The *feasibility critique* proceeds from the argument that even with the best of efforts, it may not be feasible to arrange the realization of many of the alleged economic and social rights for all. This would have been only an empirical observation (of some interest of its own), but it is made into an allegedly powerful criticism of the acceptance of these claimed rights on the basis of the presumption, largely undefended, that recognized human rights must, of necessity, be wholly accomplishable. If this presumption were accepted that would have the effect of immediately putting many so-called economic and social rights outside the domain of possible human rights, especially in the poorer societies.

5. Onora O'Neill, *Towards Justice and Virtue* (Cambridge University Press, 1996), pp. 131–32. See also her *Bounds of Justice* (Cambridge University Press, 2000). [Sen's note.]

Maurice Cranston puts the argument thus:

> The traditional political and civil rights are not difficult to institute. For the most part, they require governments, and other people generally, to leave a man alone. . . . The problems posed by claims to economic and social rights, however, are of another order altogether. How can governments of those parts of Asia, Africa, and South America, where industrialization has hardly begun, be reasonably called upon to provide social security and holidays with pay for millions of people who inhabit those places and multiply so swiftly.[6]

In assessing this line of rejection, we have to ask: why should complete feasibility be a condition of cogency of human rights when the objective is to work towards enhancing their actual realization, if necessary through expanding their feasibility? The understanding that some rights are not fully realized, and may not even be fully *realizable* under present circumstances, does not, in itself, entail anything like the conclusion that these are, therefore, not rights at all. Rather, that understanding suggests the need to work towards changing the prevailing circumstances to make the unrealized rights realizable, and ultimately, realized.

It is also worth noting in this context that the question of feasibility is not confined to economic and social rights only; it is a much more widespread problem. Even for liberties and autonomies, to guarantee that a person is "left alone," which Cranston seems to think is simple to guarantee, has never been particularly easy. . . .

# IX. The Reach of Public Reasoning

How can we judge the acceptability of claims to human rights and assess the challenges they may face? How would such a disputation — or a defense — proceed? I would argue that like the assessment of other ethical claims, there must be some test of open and informed scrutiny, and it is to such a scrutiny that we have to look in order to proceed to a disavowal or an affirmation. The status of these ethical claims must be dependent ultimately on their survivability in unobstructed discussion. In this sense, the viability of human rights is linked with what John Rawls has called "public reasoning" and its role in "ethical objectivity."[7]

Indeed, the connection between public reasoning and the formulation and use of human rights is extremely important to understand. Any general plausibility that these ethical claims, or their denials, have is dependent, on this theory, on their survival and flourishing when they encounter unobstructed discussion and scrutiny, along with adequately wide informational availability. The force of a claim for a human right would be seriously undermined if it were possible to show that they are unlikely to survive open public scrutiny. . . .

6. Maurice Cranston, "Are There Any Human Rights?" *Daedalus* (1983): 13. [Sen's note.]

7. John Rawls, *A Theory of Justice* (Harvard University Press, 1971), and *Political Liberalism* (Columbia University Press, 1993), esp. pp. 110–13. [Sen's note.]

However, it is important not to confine the domain of public reasoning to a given society only, especially in the case of human rights, in view of the inescapably non-parochial nature of these rights, which are meant to apply to all human beings. . . .

There does, of course, exist considerable variation in the balance of manifest opinions and observed preconceptions in different countries and different societies. These opinions and beliefs often reflect, as Adam Smith noted in a powerfully illuminating analysis, strong influence of existing *practices* in different parts of the world, along with a lack of broader intellectual engagement. The need for open scrutiny, with unrestrained access to information (including that about practices elsewhere in the world, and the experiences there), is particularly great because of these connections. Which is precisely why Adam Smith's insistence on the necessity of viewing actions and practices from a "certain distance" is so important for substantive ethics in general and the understanding of human rights in particular.

In a chapter entitled "On the Influence of Custom and Fashion upon the Sentiments of Moral Approbation and Disapprobation," Smith illustrated his contention:

> . . . the murder of new-born infants was a practice allowed of in almost all the states of Greece, even among the polite and civilized Athenians; and whenever the circumstances of the parent rendered it inconvenient to bring up the child, to abandon it to hunger, or to wild beasts, was regarded without blame or censure. . . . Uninterrupted custom had by this time so thoroughly authorized the practice, that not only the loose maxims of the world tolerated this barbarous prerogative, but even the doctrine of philosophers, which ought to have been more just and accurate, was led away by the established custom, and upon this, as upon many other occasions, instead of censuring, supported the horrible abuse, by far-fetched considerations of public utility. Aristotle talks of it as of what the magistrates ought upon many occasions to encourage. Plato is of the same opinion, and, with all that love of mankind which seems to animate all his writings, no where marks this practice with disapprobation.[8]

What are taken to be perfectly "normal" and "sensible" in an insulated society may not be able to survive a broad-based and less limited examination once the parochial gut reactions are replaced by critical scrutiny, including an awareness of variations of practices and norms across the world.

Scrutiny from a distance may have something to offer in the assessment of practices as different from each other as the stoning of adulterous women in Taliban's Afghanistan and the abounding use of capital punishment (sometimes with mass jubilation) in parts of the United States. This is the kind of issue that made Smith insist that "the eyes of the rest of mankind" must be invoked to understand whether "a punishment appears equitable." Ultimately, the discipline of critical moral scrutiny requires, among other things, "endeavouring to view [our sentiments and beliefs] with the eyes of other people, or as other people are likely to view them."

---

8. Adam Smith, *The Theory of Moral Sentiments* (rev. ed., 1790, V.2.15; republished, Clarendon Press, 1976), p. 210. [Sen's note.]

The need for interactions across the borders can be as important in rich societies as they are in poorer ones. The point to note here is not so much whether we are *permitted* to make cross-boundary scrutiny, but that the discipline of critical assessment of moral sentiments, no matter how locally established they are, *demands* that such scrutiny be undertaken.

## TEST YOUR UNDERSTANDING

1. What is Sen's view about the relationship between human rights and law? In your answer, distinguish Sen's view from Bentham's and Hart's (as Sen represents them).

2. Sen distinguishes the freedom not to be assaulted, to receive medical care, not to be called by neighbors you detest, and to achieve tranquility. What is the point of these four examples?

3. What is the point of Sen's example of Rima? What distinction is the example supposed to illustrate?

## NOTES AND QUESTIONS

1. According to Sen, freedoms must meet "some threshold conditions of (i) importance and (ii) social influenceability . . . to figure within the interpersonal and interactive spectrum of human rights." What does he mean by "importance"? By "social influenceability"? How does Sen apply these two threshold conditions to the four freedoms listed in section 4?

2. In his discussion of social and economic rights, Sen discusses the "institutionalization critique" and the "feasibility critique." Both critiques aim to raise troubles for the idea that there are social and economic rights. While they accept that there are political and civil rights, they oppose "extending the idea of human rights to include economic and social rights." State the distinction between economic and social rights and civil and political rights, and give some examples to illustrate the distinction. Then formulate each of the two critiques as an argument that leads to the conclusion that there are no social or economic rights. (Be sure that the arguments do not lead to the conclusion that there are no human rights at all. Remember, the proponents of the institutionalization and feasibility critiques are trying to distinguish civil and political rights, which are genuine human rights, from economic and social rights, which are not.) Does Sen provide an effective reply to these critiques? Which premises in the arguments you have reconstructed would Sen reject?

   As background, you should review the Universal Declaration of Human Rights (www.un.org/en/documents/udhr/), the International Covenant on Civil and Political Rights (www.ohchr.org/en/professionalinterest/pages/ccpr.aspx), and the International Covenant on Social, Economic, and Cultural Rights (www.ohchr.org/EN/ProfessionalInterest/Pages/CESCR.aspx).

## ANALYZING THE ARGUMENTS

1. Mill says that his principle of liberty

    > has no application to any state of things anterior to the time when mankind have become capable of being improved by free and equal discussion.... But as soon as mankind have attained the capacity of being guided to their own improvement by conviction or persuasion (a period long since reached in all nations with whom we need here concern ourselves), compulsion, either in the direct form or in that of pains and penalties for noncompliance, is no longer admissible as a means to their own good, and justifiable only for the security of others.

    What role does this assumption—that the people Mill is thinking about can be "guided to their own improvement by conviction or persuasion"—play in Mill's defense of the liberty principle? Do you think that people are capable of being improved by free and equal discussion? Does Devlin think that people can be improved through free and equal discussion? Locke? Sen?

2. Sen says that *public reasoning* is the way to evaluate human rights claims. Beginning from that idea, get together with three other students from your course. Take Sen's four examples of freedom (from section 4), and discuss his application of the *importance* and *social influenceability* conditions to those examples. Be sure that you have a common understanding of the conditions. Then have each student in the group extend Sen's list by coming up with two additional examples of freedoms (for example, freedom from illiteracy, freedom from traffic, freedom from dust, freedom from annoying questions). Take the pool of examples—Sen's four examples plus two from each of the four students in the group—and discuss whether each example meets Sen's conditions of importance and social influenceability. How much agreement do you find in the group? If you do not all agree on the examples, does that raise troubles for Sen's theory of human rights?

    As a final step in the exercise, consider whether your discussion has met the standards of unobstructed critical scrutiny that Sen describes in the last part of his paper. Have you achieved "an awareness of variations of practices and norms across the world"? If not, how might you do that?

3. In chapter 4 of *On Liberty* (not included in this chapter), Mill discusses a series of examples that are designed to show that his liberty principle is not directed against "imaginary evils," but against "serious and practical" problems. In one example, he describes a majority Muslim country in which people find the consumption of pork "really revolting." Nevertheless, he thinks that it is wrong to prohibit the consumption of pork. In a second example, he says that the "sincere feelings" of Spanish Catholics condemn married clergy "as not only irreligious, but unchaste, indecent, gross, disgusting." Still, he thinks it is wrong to prohibit those marriages. The prohibitions are wrong because neither the Muslim majority nor the Spanish Catholics are *harmed* by the conduct. Neither the consumption of pork nor married clergy "concern the interests of others."

    Suppose a critic says that Mill is wrong in both cases. According to the critic:

*Mill's Critic:* The Muslims are *harmed* by the pork consumption and the Spanish Catholics are *harmed by* the married clergy. It is not simply that they think the conduct is impious or wrong. The Muslims are *revolted* and the Spanish Catholics are *disgusted*. In both cases the negative feelings, as Mill acknowledges, are sincere and strongly felt. Why are these not cases of harm? Why are the interests of others not at stake? Because revulsion and disgust are mental, not physical? That response will not do, for two reasons. First, think what happens when you find something *really revolting:* the impact *is* partly physical. When you find something really revolting, you might wretch or feel queasy or nauseated. Second, even if the reaction is mental, you may still have been harmed. If you tell parents, falsely, that their child has died, and they are grief-stricken and despondent, you have harmed them. The harms are no less real because they are mental.

Consider the following Millian response:

*Millian Response:* Person A does not harm person B when B has undesirable feelings — say, strong revulsion — because A has done something that offends of B's religious or moral convictions. After all, A does not harm B simply because A violates B's religious or moral standards: that is the core of Mill's liberty principle. By extension, then, A does not harm B when A's conduct results in B's undesirable feelings, *if* the undesirable feelings exist because of B's religious or moral convictions: if, that is, the feelings would not exist if the convictions were different.

Is the Millian Response compelling? If not, can you find a more forceful reply?

To explore these issues further, see Joel Feinberg, *The Moral Limits of the Criminal Law: Offence to Others* (Oxford University Press, 1988).

4. Consider a world in which most countries establish religious or moral uniformity by actively restricting liberty internally, but in which national borders are pretty easy to cross. As a result, most people are perfectly happy with the restrictions on liberty that apply to them. Is there anything wrong with this world? How might a proponent of liberty object? Are the objections convincing?

# 21

# Does Justice Require Equality?

## The Problem

In the United States today, economic inequality is as great as at any time on record. The income share for the top 1 percent is now around 21 percent; and 7.7 percent of all income flows to the top 0.1 percent. The distribution of wealth — housing, stocks, and other assets — is even more unequal than the income distribution.

To be sure, economic inequality can be defined in many ways. Suppose John, Jean, and June have $100, $52, and $1, respectively. Now Jean loses $51, so they have $100, $1, and $1. If you measure inequality by the ratio of top income to bottom income, it remains the same, 100:1. But if you measure inequality by how far people in general are from the average income, it grows when Jean loses her money.[1] These different understandings are of considerable interest. But on any understanding, economic inequality has been growing in the United States. That much is largely undisputed. Judgments about the *justness* of economic inequalities are, in contrast, matters of intense and longstanding disagreement.

According to one familiar outlook, economic inequality is an inevitable consequence of protecting liberty. Proponents say that individual differences — in family background and culture, native abilities and acquired skills, personal aspirations and sheer good luck — mean that some people in a free society are bound to do better — perhaps much better — in income and health than others. Preventing or mitigating those inequalities, they say, requires overriding individual choices. That, they say, deprives people of what they are entitled to — for their efforts or contributions or for the simple fact of having been chosen by someone else as the recipient of a benefit. And that, they say, is wrong, an unjust deprivation of liberty.

An alternative outlook, also familiar, says that current inequalities reward people who had the undeserved good fortune to have been born rich, or endowed with

---

1. See Amartya Sen, *On Economic Inequality* (Oxford University Press, 1997).

some scarce, high-priced skill, or located in the right place (say, Silicon Valley) at the right time (say, 1994). An economic system, proponents say, is not a talent contest to reward the gifted, or a race that goes to the swift. It should be designed, they say, as a fair system that ensures reasonable conditions for all. Mitigating inequalities, they say, is required by justice, ultimately by the equal importance of each human life.

These disagreements about the justness of economic equalities mix philosophical with empirical judgments. Economists, sociologists, and political scientists debate the empirical issues: about the effects of taxes and transfers on incentives to work and invest, or the consequences for democracy of increased inequality. Philosophical discussions about justice and economic inequality need to be attentive to these empirical arguments. But the distinctive contribution of philosophy lies elsewhere, in articulating the values that are at stake.

# Philosophical Egalitarianism

Utilitarian thinkers in the nineteenth century offered a reason for being concerned about economic inequality. **Utilitarianism** is the view that the right action (or policy or institution) is the action (or policy or institution) that produces the greatest sum of happiness. Assume now that each individual gets some additional happiness from each additional dollar that comes his or her way, but the increase in happiness declines as the person gets richer. So your 101st dollar gives you more added happiness than does your 201st, which adds more than your 1001st. This is called "declining marginal utility." If marginal utility declines, then, all else equal, a greater sum of utility would be generated by shifting resources from someone with more—say, Warren Buffett—to someone with fewer—say, a bus driver or nurse. Buffett will lose a little happiness when he loses a dollar; but that loss will be more than compensated by the greater increase in happiness for the bus driver or nurse.[2]

But all else is not equal. The utilitarian case for equality needs to take incentives into account. Suppose Warren Buffett will not invest as much if his last dollar is taxed at a high rate. Then, to prevent damaging effects on longer-term growth and standards of living, we will need to be careful not to set the tax rate too high.

Some philosophical egalitarians think that the case for mitigating economic inequalities on grounds of justice is not as dependent as the utilitarian supposes on the facts about declining marginal utility and responsiveness to incentives. According to one important line of philosophical-egalitarian argument, certain kinds of inequalities are unjust because they are objectionably *unfair*. They are unfair because they are based on treating equal persons in indefensibly different ways.

---

2. Harry Frankfurt sketches and criticizes the utilitarian argument in his contribution in this chapter.

That is the core idea in Rawls's theory of "justice as fairness." Rawls presents an account of what justice requires by developing a theory about fair terms of social cooperation. Part of that theory — its most strikingly egalitarian part — is the **difference principle**. According to this principle, our default distribution of resources should be equal. Inequalities in income and wealth are just only if they are needed to maximize the income and wealth of people in the least advantaged social group. Fair inequalities cover training costs for developing socially valuable skills and provide incentives to encourage people to use their resources and talents for the benefit of all. According to the difference principle, then, the reason for accepting inequalities is not to ensure that people receive what they deserve or to reward contributions or efforts. It is to improve the circumstances of the least advantaged group (say, people in the bottom 20 percent of the income distribution).

The rationale for the difference principle lies in the idea of fairness. To see how, it will help to step back and consider the idea of **equality of opportunity**. Some kind of equality of opportunity is widely agreed to be a requirement of justice. Consider laws that restrict social mobility, as in a caste structure or a system of racial apartheid. They are unjust because, as Martha Nussbaum observes, human lives are of equal importance. Given that equal importance, laws are unfair — they treat equal persons in indefensibly different ways — if they prevent some people from pursuing socially valued opportunities that others are able to pursue.

Justice as fairness embraces this requirement that laws not establish unequal opportunities. But it adds a more demanding requirement of equal opportunity: the idea that people from different social backgrounds have equal chances to attain desirable social positions. More specifically, *equality of fair opportunity* says that equally talented and equally motivated people should have equal chances to attain socially desirable positions. It is unfair when Albert has greater chances than Alice simply because he comes from a wealthier family with the resources to support his aspirations. Thus, as Rawls puts it, "Chances to acquire cultural knowledge and skills should not depend upon one's class position, and so the school system, whether public or private, should be designed to even out class barriers." Nussbaum suggests that an equal opportunity requirement of this kind lies at the heart of justice.

It is unfair for Albert to do better than Alice as a result of his class background, because Albert's advantage means that the society permits the accidents of social background to play a large role in shaping the course of our lives. But — returning now to the difference principle — suppose that Albert does better than Alice because of a natural talent: he has the steady hand needed to be a surgeon or the mathematical aptitude required of a financial analyst. Albert is not advantaged by social background but by something comparably accidental: the talents he happens to be born with, for which he is not responsible, and which he did nothing to deserve. But "there is no more reason to permit the distribution of income and wealth to be settled by the distribution of natural assets than by historical and social fortune." The difference principle, with its requirement that inequalities work to the benefit of the least advantaged, is Rawls's proposal about how to address this unfair dependence of a person's opportunities to gain resources on the contingencies of native endowments.

According to justice as fairness, considerations of fairness provide a rationale for both the equality of fair opportunity principle and the difference principle. It is unfair for Albert to have greater opportunities than Alice because of the contingencies of their social backgrounds, and unfair, too, when the resources at his command are greater simply because of the talents he happens to possess. When the two principles are joined, the result is that many familiar inequalities turn out to be unjust. They reflect a society that treats equal persons in indefensibly different ways.

You may be puzzled by the description of *justice as fairness* as a kind of egalitarianism. After all, neither the opportunity principle nor the difference principle condemns all inequalities of income and wealth as unjust. To the contrary: if a very large incentive is needed to motivate a talented person to do something that contributes a small bit to the benefit of the least advantaged, that large incentive is justified. If you are looking for an egalitarianism that condemns all inequalities, you are unlikely to find it. Equality, Jonathan Wolff observes, is "sometimes associated with uniformity: sameness of income, consumption, or standard of living. Yet equality as uniformity seems to ignore human diversity of tastes and effort, as well as ignoring the requirements of a complex economy in which differences in rewards are needed both for incentives and informational purposes." What makes justice as fairness egalitarian, then, is its claim that inequalities require a special justification—focused on the least advantaged—if they are to be consistent with fair treatment for equal persons. "We can grant that all human beings have fundamentally equal worth," Nussbaum says, "without granting that one person should always get the same reward as another."

To be sure, some views are more egalitarian than Rawls's. The difference principle, as he understands it, permits *incentive inequalities*. Suppose now that Albert could become a doctor and do a great deal for people's health. But Albert is willing to be a doctor only if he makes ten times the average income. If he makes less than that, he would prefer to write indifferent literary fiction. You might think it is clear that he should get the high salary. As a practical matter, that seems right. But is it just? Albert could perfectly well be a doctor for a smaller reward. He is simply unwilling to. Is he taking unfair advantage of scarce medical talent?

Reactions differ. Some people think that justice is a matter of laws and policies: it is about the rules of social cooperation. Getting Albert to act differently, they say, is not a matter for law and policy: the challenge comes from his preferences and values, which we need to accept as given when we are thinking about justice. Others think that Albert is making an unjust demand. To be sure, the problem does not lie in laws and policies but in his preferences and values. Nevertheless, they say, he is extracting unfair advantages that offend against justice.

# Distributions or Relationships?

The case for justice as fairness is partly an argument about a just distribution of resources. Wolff is troubled by an exclusive focus on resource distribution. He distinguishes two strands of thought about justice and equality. One, commonly referred to as "luck egalitarianism," is animated by the idea that one person should not fare better or worse than another because of conditions for which he or she is not responsible. For the luck egalitarian, the central challenge in a theory of justice is not to describe fair terms of social cooperation, but to ensure that inequalities reflect choice, not mere chance. So it is acceptable for Barbara to be better off than Bill because she decided to get specialized medical training or to work long hours, while Bill—who could have done the same if he wanted to—decided instead to try to be a great poet. But it is not acceptable for Barbara to be better off because she could afford training that Bill could not afford.

The second strand of egalitarianism, which Wolff traces to the British socialist R. H. Tawney, is concerned with relationships. The leading question is not who has more, but whether people relate to one another as equals, or see one another instead as belonging to fundamentally different social groups. The relational egalitarian objects directly to "deep social division, intensified by snobbery and servility." For then, "it is as if society is composed of two (or more) societies, attending different schools, accessing different types of health care, enjoying different types of leisure, and meeting only when one class performs services for the other. Tawney's goal is not in the first instance to ensure an egalitarian distribution of resources, but to create a society where people can live together as equals." The relational egalitarian is sometimes critical of economic inequalities, because they may undermine egalitarian relationships. But the principal concern is to protect against subordination and servility, not to mitigate differences. (Wolff does not mention justice as fairness, though the emphasis on fair cooperation among equals appears to place justice as fairness in the second tradition.)

To crystallize the difference between these views, consider a world composed of two entirely separate islands. The residents of one island are much richer than the residents of the other. The relational egalitarian will not see an injustice that requires remedy, because the residents are not related at all. Nor will justice as fairness, with its emphasis on the rules and conditions of fair social cooperation, because the islands are not cooperating, whether fairly or unfairly. The luck egalitarian, in contrast, will be concerned if, for example, the different standards of living reflect differences in the resource endowment of the two islands. That inequality is unjust because it does not reflect any choices for which people on the islands are responsible, but the different resources available to them.

# Against Equality

Concerns about distributive fairness — for example, the idea that we need some special justification for departures from equality — focus typically on how some people are doing *relative* to how others are doing. Is that focus reasonable?

Suppose you have decided to open a small restaurant. The restaurant's success matters a great deal to you. Not that you care if it grows — you are not hoping to start a chain — but you want it to last. You think good food is important, enjoy the company, have an intense aversion to working for other people, and would like to support your family through income from the business. You know that some people make lots more than you; you know that some make less. But that does not matter to you. What matters is that you are doing something you value, and that you have sufficient resources to sustain the business, to ensure that your kids have decent clothes, decent food, and a good education, and to spend time with people whose company you enjoy.

If that is what matters to you, then you may regard a social concern with equality as a bad thing. A concern with equality is a concern with how you are faring relative to others. And that concern may strike you as a tempting distraction from what really matters, which is that you have what you need to pursue your aspirations with some prospect of success.

Harry Frankfurt offers such skepticism about a concern with equality. "With respect to the distribution of economic assets, what *is* important from the point of view of morality is not that everyone should have *the same* but that each should have *enough*. If everyone had enough, it would be of no moral consequence whether some had more than others. I shall refer to this alternative to egalitarianism — namely, that what is morally important with respect to money is for everyone to have enough — as 'the doctrine of sufficiency.'" According to the doctrine of sufficiency, justice requires that each person have enough (sufficiency is necessary for justice); relative positions, in contrast, make no inherent difference to justice. The qualification "inherent" is important. Economic inequalities may, as Wolff emphasizes, have bad consequences for social relationships or political equality. Still, the inequalities in and of themselves are not an appropriate focus of political morality.

Frankfurt's focus on sufficiency resonates with popular ideas about the importance of a social safety net that ensures that each person has enough. A focus on a safety net, however, is usually associated with the idea that demanding more than that from others is demanding too much: that you are not entitled, as a matter of justice, to more than a safety net. Frankfurt's focus is different. Worrying about inequality as such is ethically misguided, he argues, because inequality is a matter of relative positions, of who is doing better and who is doing worse. But concerns about relative positions betray a distorted view of what matters in life. What matters — as in the case of the small-restaurant owner — is having a sense of what is worth doing and sufficient resources to do it. Nothing of genuine interest in a good human life turns directly on where you stand relative to others in the distribution of income and wealth. The focus on equality thus "contributes to the moral disorientation and shallowness of our time."

# Libertarianism

Robert Nozick's libertarian criticisms of egalitarianism are fundamentally different from Frankfurt's. Libertarians do not agree that justice requires sufficiency. The sufficiency theory is an example of what Nozick calls a "patterned theory" of justice. According to a patterned theory, you can tell whether a distribution is just simply by looking at it. In the case of the sufficiency doctrine, you ask whether each person has "enough." You do not need to know anything about how the distribution came about.

Nozick's historical-entitlement approach to justice condemns any effort to require that the distribution fit a pattern—whether of equality, sufficiency, merit or contribution, or maximizing happiness. The problem with patterns is that they are at odds with liberty. "Liberty," Nozick says, "upsets patterns." Establish any pattern, and free choices will upend it.

What matters for distributive justice is exclusively the history of transactions. If we examine transactions one by one, and find that each transaction is acceptable—in each case, people exchange something they own for something owned by others—then the outcome is just, whatever it turns out to be. The results may be more equal or less equal, but whatever they are, they are just because they emerge from a history of individually just transactions, in which individuals choose who they will transact with and what the terms of the transaction will be. Distributive justice is nothing more (and nothing less) than the historical product of individually just transactions.

For justice as fairness, the result of implementing this view is a pervasively unfair society, riddled with morally arbitrary inequalities, calling for remedy through law and public policy. The luck egalitarian will find all kinds of troubling inequalities with no connection to individual choices. The relational egalitarian will expect to find patterns of subordination and deference. The libertarian will see the implications of individual freedom and reject efforts to correct inequalities as an unjust abridgement of human liberty.

## John Rawls (1921–2002)

Rawls was born in Baltimore, Maryland. After receiving his PhD from Princeton University in 1950, he taught at Princeton, Cornell University, and the Massachusetts Institute of Technology, before joining the Harvard University faculty in 1962. At his retirement from Harvard in 1991, he was James Conant Bryant University Professor. Rawls wrote three powerful and influential books of political philosophy: *A Theory of Justice* (1971), *Political Liberalism* (1993), and *The Law of Peoples* (1999).

# TWO PRINCIPLES OF JUSTICE
## from *A Theory of Justice*

I shall now state in a provisional form the two principles of justice that I believe would be agreed to in the original position.[1] The first formulation of these principles is tentative. As we go on I shall consider several formulations and approximate step by step the final statement to be given much later. I believe that doing this allows the exposition to proceed in a natural way.

The first statement of the two principles reads as follows.

First: each person is to have an equal right to the most extensive scheme of equal basic liberties compatible with a similar scheme of liberties for others.

Second: social and economic inequalities are to be arranged so that they are both (a) reasonably expected to be to everyone's advantage, and (b) attached to positions and offices open to all.

There are two ambiguous phrases in the second principle, namely "everyone's advantage" and "open to all." Determining their sense more exactly will lead to a second formulation of the principle in § 13.[2] . . .

These principles primarily apply . . . to the basic structure of society and govern the assignment of rights and duties and regulate the distribution of social and economic advantages. . . . [I]t is essential to observe that the basic liberties are given by a list of such liberties. Important among these are political liberty (the right to vote and to hold public office) and freedom of speech and assembly; liberty of conscience and freedom of thought; freedom of the person, which includes freedom from psychological oppression and physical assault and dismemberment (integrity of the person); the right to hold personal property and freedom from arbitrary arrest and seizure as defined by the concept of the rule of law. These liberties are to be equal by the first principle.

The second principle applies, in the first approximation, to the distribution of income and wealth and to the design of organizations that make use of differences in authority and responsibility. While the distribution of wealth and income need not be equal, it must be to everyone's advantage, and at the same time, positions of authority and responsibility must be accessible to all. . . .

---

1. The *original position* is a hypothetical situation in which individuals choose the standards of justice for their society. Rawls proposes that we make this choice behind a "veil of ignorance," which keeps us from knowing our class, race, gender, religion, or any other features that distinguish us from other persons. In chapter 3 of *A Theory of Justice* (which comprises sections 20–30), Rawls argues that the two principles of justice he will state would be selected in the original position.

2. Rawls is here referring us to section 13 of *A Theory of Justice*.

# 12. Interpretations of the Second Principle

I have already mentioned that since the phrases "everyone's advantage" and "equally open to all" are ambiguous, both parts of the second principle have two natural senses. Because these senses are independent of one another, the principle has four possible meanings. Assuming that the first principle of equal liberty has the same sense throughout, we then have four interpretations of the two principles. These are indicated in the table below.

| | "Everyone's advantage" | |
| "Equally open" | Principle of efficiency | Difference principle |
| --- | --- | --- |
| Equality as careers open to talents | System of Natural Liberty | Natural Aristocracy |
| Equality as equality of fair opportunity | Liberal Equality | Democratic Equality |

... In working out justice as fairness, we must decide which interpretation is to be preferred. I shall adopt that of democratic equality, explaining in the next section what this notion means. . . .

The first interpretation . . . I shall refer to as the system of natural liberty. In this rendering the first part of the second principle is understood as the principle of efficiency adjusted so as to apply to institutions or, in this case, to the basic structure of society,[3] and the second part is understood as an open social system in which, to use the traditional phrase, careers are open to talents. I assume in all interpretations that the first principle of equal liberty is satisfied and that the economy is roughly a free market system, although the means of production may or may not be privately owned. The system of natural liberty asserts, then, that a basic structure satisfying the principle of efficiency and in which positions are open to those able and willing to strive for them will lead to a just distribution. Assigning rights and duties in this way is thought to give a scheme which allocates wealth and income authority and responsibility, in a fair way whatever this allocation turns out to be. . . .

The system of natural liberty selects an efficient distribution roughly as follows. Let us suppose that we know from economic theory that under the standard assumptions defining a competitive market economy, income and wealth will be distributed in an efficient way, and that the particular efficient distribution which results in any period of time is determined by the initial distribution of assets, that is, by the initial distribution of income and wealth, and of natural talents and abilities. With each initial distribution, a definite efficient outcome is arrived at. Thus it turns out that if we are to accept the outcome as just, and not merely as efficient, we must accept the basis upon which over time the initial distribution of assets is determined.

---

3. According to the *principle of efficiency*, a basic structure is efficient when, roughly speaking, any change of rules that benefits some people makes other people less well off.

In the system of natural liberty the initial distribution is regulated by the arrangements implicit in the conception of careers open to talents (as earlier defined). These arrangements presuppose a background of equal liberty (as specified by the first principle) and a free market economy. They require a formal equality of opportunity in that all have at least the same legal rights of access to all advantaged social positions. But since there is no effort to preserve an equality, or similarity, of social conditions, except insofar as this is necessary to preserve the requisite background institutions, the initial distribution of assets for any period of time is strongly influenced by natural and social contingencies. The existing distribution of income and wealth, say, is the cumulative effect of prior distributions of natural assets — that is, natural talents and abilities — as these have been developed or left unrealized, and their use favored or disfavored over time by social circumstances and such chance contingencies as accident and good fortune. Intuitively, the most obvious injustice of the system of natural liberty is that it permits distributive shares to be improperly influenced by these factors so arbitrary from a moral point of view.

The liberal interpretation, as I shall refer to it, tries to correct for this by adding to the requirement of careers open to talents the further condition of the principle of fair equality of opportunity. The thought here is that positions are to be not only open in a formal sense, but that all should have a fair chance to attain them. Offhand it is not clear what is meant, but we might say that those with similar abilities and skills should have similar life chances. More specifically, assuming that there is a distribution of natural assets, those who are at the same level of talent and ability, and have the same willingness to use them, should have the same prospects of success regardless of their initial place in the social system. In all sectors of society there should be roughly equal prospects of culture and achievement for everyone similarly motivated and endowed. The expectations of those with the same abilities and aspirations should not be affected by their social class.

The liberal interpretation of the two principles seeks, then, to mitigate the influence of social contingencies and natural fortune on distributive shares. To accomplish this end it is necessary to impose further basic structural conditions on the social system. Free market arrangements must be set within a framework of political and legal institutions which regulates the overall trends of economic events and preserves the social conditions necessary for fair equality of opportunity. The elements of this framework are familiar enough, though it may be worthwhile to recall the importance of preventing excessive accumulations of property and wealth and of maintaining equal opportunities of education for all. Chances to acquire cultural knowledge and skills should not depend upon one's class position, and so the school system, whether public or private, should be designed to even out class barriers.

While the liberal conception seems clearly preferable to the system of natural liberty, intuitively it still appears defective. For one thing, even if it works to perfection in eliminating the influence of social contingencies, it still permits the distribution of wealth and income to be determined by the natural distribution of abilities and talents. Within the limits allowed by the background arrangements, distributive shares are decided by the outcome of the natural lottery; and this outcome is arbitrary from a moral perspective. There is no more reason to permit the distribution of income and wealth to be settled by the distribution of natural assets than by historical and social fortune. Furthermore, the principle of fair opportunity can be only imperfectly carried out, at least as long as some form of the family exists. The extent to which natural capacities develop and reach fruition is affected by all kinds of social conditions and class attitudes. Even the willingness to make an effort, to try, and so to be deserving in the ordinary sense is itself dependent upon happy family and social circumstances. It is impossible in practice to secure equal chances of achievement and culture for those similarly endowed, and therefore we may want to adopt a principle which recognizes this fact and also mitigates the arbitrary effects of the natural lottery itself. That the liberal conception fails to do this encourages one to look for another interpretation of the two principles of justice. . . .

## 13. Democratic Equality and the Difference Principle

The democratic interpretation, as the table suggests, is arrived at by combining the principle of fair equality of opportunity with the difference principle. This principle removes the indeterminateness of the principle of efficiency by singling out a particular position from which the social and economic inequalities of the basic structure are to be judged. Assuming the framework of institutions required by equal liberty and fair equality of opportunity, the higher expectations of those better situated are just if and only if they work as part of a scheme which improves the expectations of the least advantaged members of society. The intuitive idea is that the social order is not to establish and secure the more attractive prospects of those better off unless doing so is to the advantage of those less fortunate. . . .

To illustrate the difference principle, consider the distribution of income among social classes. Let us suppose that the various income groups correlate with representative individuals by reference to whose expectations we can judge the distribution. Now those starting out as members of the entrepreneurial class in property-owning democracy, say, have a better prospect than those who begin in the class of unskilled laborers. It seems likely that this will be true even when the social injustices which now exist are removed. What, then, can possibly justify this kind of initial inequality in life prospects? According to the difference principle, it is justifiable only if the difference in expectation is to the advantage of the representative man who is worse off, in this case the representative unskilled worker. The inequality in expectation is permissible only if lowering it would make the working class even more worse off. Supposedly, given the rider in the second principle concerning open positions, and the principle of liberty generally, the greater expectations allowed to entrepreneurs encourages them to do things which raise the prospects of laboring class. Their better prospects act as incentives so that the economic process is more efficient, innovation proceeds at a faster pace, and so on. I shall not consider how far these things are true.

The point is that something of this kind must be argued if these inequalities are to satisfy by the difference principle. . . .

Thus . . . the outcome of the last several sections is that the second principle reads as follows:

> Social and economic inequalities are to be arranged so that they are both (a) to the greatest expected benefit of the least advantaged and (b) attached to offices and positions open to all under conditions of fair equality of opportunity. . . .

# 17. The Tendency to Equality

I wish to conclude this discussion of the two principles by explaining the sense in which they express an egalitarian conception of justice. . . .

First we may observe that the difference principle gives some weight to the considerations singled out by the principle of redress. This is the principle that undeserved inequalities call for redress; and since inequalities of birth and natural endowment are undeserved, these inequalities are to be somehow compensated for. Thus the principle holds that in order to treat all persons equally, to provide genuine equality of opportunity, society must give more attention to those with fewer native assets and to those born into the less favorable social positions. The idea is to redress the bias of contingencies in the direction of equality. In pursuit of this principle greater resources might be spent on the education of the less rather than the more intelligent, at least over a certain time of life, say the earlier years of school. . . .

[A]lthough the difference principle is not the same as that of redress, it does achieve some of the intent of the latter principle. It transforms the aims of the basic structure so that the total scheme of institutions no longer emphasizes social efficiency and technocratic values. The difference principle represents, in effect, an agreement to regard the distribution of natural talents as in some respects a common asset and to share in the greater social and economic benefits made possible by the complementarities of this distribution. Those who have been favored by nature, whoever they are, may gain from their good fortune only on terms that improve the situation of those who have lost out. The naturally advantaged are not to gain merely because they are more gifted, but only to cover the costs of training and education and for using their endowments in ways that help the less fortunate as well. No one deserves his greater natural capacity nor merits a more favorable starting place in society. But, of course, this is no reason to ignore, much less to eliminate these distinctions. Instead, the basic structure can be arranged so that these contingencies work for the good of the least fortunate. Thus we are led to the difference principle if we wish to set up the social system so that no one gains or loses from his arbitrary place in the distribution of natural assets or his initial position in society without giving or receiving compensating advantages in return.

In view of these remarks we may reject the contention that the ordering of institutions is always defective because the distribution of natural talents and the contingencies of social circumstance are unjust, and this injustice must inevitably carry over to human arrangements. Occasionally this reflection is offered as an excuse for ignoring injustice, as if the refusal to acquiesce in injustice is on a par with being unable to accept death. The natural distribution is neither just nor unjust; nor is it unjust that persons are born into society at some particular position. These are simply natural facts. What is just and unjust is the way that institutions deal with these facts. Aristocratic and caste societies are unjust because they make these contingencies the ascriptive basis for belonging to more or less enclosed and privileged social classes. The basic structure of these societies incorporates the arbitrariness found in nature. But there is no necessity for men to resign themselves to these contingencies. The social system is not an unchangeable order beyond human control but a pattern of human action. In justice as fairness men agree to avail themselves of the accidents of nature and social circumstance only when doing so is for the common benefit. The two principles are a fair way of meeting the arbitrariness of fortune; and while no doubt imperfect in other ways, the institutions which satisfy these principles are just.

A further point is that the difference principle expresses a conception of reciprocity. It is a principle of mutual benefit. At first sight, however, it may appear unfairly biased towards the least favored. . . .

One may object that those better situated deserve the greater advantages they could acquire for themselves under other schemes of cooperation whether or not these advantages are gained in ways that benefit others. Now it is true that given a just system of cooperation as a framework of public rules, and the expectations set up by it, those who, with the prospect of improving their condition, have done what the system announces it will reward are entitled to have their expectations met. In this sense the more fortunate have title to their better situation; their claims are legitimate expectations established by social institutions and the community is obligated to fulfill them. But this sense of desert is that of entitlement. It presupposes the existence of an ongoing cooperative scheme and is irrelevant to the question whether this scheme itself is to be designed in accordance with the difference principle or some other criterion.

Thus it is incorrect that individuals with greater natural endowments and the superior character that has made their development possible have a right to a cooperative scheme that enables them to obtain even further benefits in ways that do not contribute to the advantages of others. We do not deserve our place in the distribution of native endowments, any more than we deserve our initial starting place in society. That we deserve the superior character that enables us to make the effort to cultivate our abilities is also problematic; for such character depends in good part upon fortunate family and social circumstances in early life for which we can claim no credit. The notion of desert does not apply here. To be sure, the more advantaged have a right to their natural assets, as does everyone else; this right is covered by the first principle under the basic liberty protecting the integrity of the person. And so the more advantaged are entitled to whatever they can acquire in accordance with the rules of a fair system of social cooperation. Our problem is how this scheme, the basic structure of society, is to be designed. From a suitably general standpoint, the difference principle appears acceptable to both the more advantaged and the less advantaged individual. Of course, none of this is strictly speaking an argument for the principle. . . . But these intuitive considerations help to clarify the principle and the sense in which it is egalitarian. . . .

A further merit of the difference principle is that it provides an interpretation of the principle of fraternity. In comparison with liberty and equality, the idea of fraternity has had a lesser place in democratic theory, It is thought to be less specifically a political concept, not in itself defining any of the democratic rights but conveying instead certain attitudes of mind and forms of conduct without which we would lose sight of the values expressed by these rights. Or closely related to this, fraternity is held to represent a certain equality of social esteem manifest in various public conventions and in the absence of manners of deference and servility. No doubt fraternity does imply these things, as well as a sense of civic friendship and social solidarity, but so understood it expresses no definite requirement. We have yet to find a principle of justice that matches the underlying idea. The difference principle, however, does seem to correspond to a natural meaning of fraternity: namely, to the idea of not wanting to have greater advantages unless this is to the benefit of others who are less well off. The family, in its ideal conception and often in practice, is one place where the principle of maximizing the sum of advantages is rejected. Members of a family commonly do not wish to gain unless they can do so in ways that further the interests of the rest. Now wanting to act on the difference principle has precisely this consequence. Those better circumstanced are willing to have their greater advantages only under a scheme in which this works out for the benefit of the less fortunate. . . .

[Thus] we can associate the traditional ideas of liberty, equality, and fraternity with the democratic interpretation of the two principles of justice as follows: liberty corresponds to the first principle, equality to the idea of equality in the first principle together with equality of fair opportunity, and fraternity to the difference principle. . . .

# 77. The Basis of Equality

I now turn to the basis of equality, the features of human beings in virtue of which they are to be treated in accordance with the principles of justice. Our conduct toward animals is not regulated by these principles, or so it is generally believed. On what grounds then do we distinguish between mankind and other living things and regard the constraints of justice as holding only in our relations to human persons? . . .

The natural answer seems to be that it is precisely the moral persons who are entitled to equal justice. Moral persons are distinguished by two features: first they are capable of having (and are assumed to have) a conception of their good (as expressed by a rational plan of life); and second they are capable of having (and are assumed to acquire) a sense of justice, a normally effective desire to apply and to act upon the principles of justice, at least to a certain minimum degree. We use the characterization of the persons in the original position to single out the kind of beings to whom the principles chosen apply. After all, the parties are thought of as adopting these criteria to regulate their common institutions and their conduct toward one another; and the description of their nature enters into the reasoning by which these principles are selected. Thus equal justice is owed to those who have the capacity to take part in and to act in accordance with the public understanding of the initial situation. One should observe that moral personality is here defined as a potentiality that is ordinarily realized in due course. It is this potentiality which brings the claims of justice into play. I shall return to this point below.

We see, then, that the capacity for moral personality is a sufficient condition for being entitled to equal justice. Nothing beyond the essential minimum is required. Whether moral personality is also a necessary condition I shall leave aside. I assume that the capacity for a sense of justice is possessed by the overwhelming majority of mankind, and therefore this question does not raise a serious practical problem. That moral personality suffices to make one a subject of claims is the essential thing. We cannot go far wrong in supposing that the sufficient condition is always satisfied. Even if the capacity were necessary, it would be unwise in practice to withhold justice on this ground. The risk to just institutions would be too great.

It should be stressed that the sufficient condition for equal justice, the capacity for moral personality, is not at all stringent. When someone lacks the requisite potentiality either from birth or accident, this is regarded as a defect or deprivation. There is no race or recognized group of human beings that lacks this attribute. Only scattered individuals are without this capacity, or its realization to the minimum degree, and the failure to realize it is the consequence of unjust and impoverished social circumstances, or fortuitous contingencies. Furthermore, while individuals presumably have varying capacities for a sense of justice, this fact is not a reason for depriving those with a lesser capacity of the full protection of justice. Once a certain minimum is met, a person is entitled to equal liberty on a par with everyone else. . . .

## TEST YOUR UNDERSTANDING

1. Formulate, in your own words, the two components of Rawls's second principle of justice, which he calls *fair equality of opportunity* and the *difference principle*.

2. What are the key differences between *natural liberty, liberal equality*, and *democratic equality*?

3. What are the connections between Rawls's principles of justice and the values of liberty, equality, and fraternity?

4. What is a "sense of justice"? Does Rawls think it is unusual for people to have a sense of justice?

# NOTES AND QUESTIONS

1.  "The social system," Rawls says, "is not an unchangeable order beyond human control but a pattern of human action." What does this mean? Why is it important to his theory of justice as fairness?

2.  Rawls's case for *democratic equality* proceeds in two steps: he provides reasons for preferring liberal equality to natural liberty, and then reasons for preferring democratic equality to liberal equality. The argument is complicated, influential, and important: it needs to be read closely.

    In motivating the move from natural liberty to liberal equality, Rawls says: "the most obvious injustice of the system of natural liberty is that it permits distributive shares to be improperly influenced by these factors so arbitrary from a moral point of view." To understand this criticism of natural liberty, you will need to answer these questions:

    (i)   What is the system of natural liberty?

    (ii)  What "factors" is Rawls referring to?

    (iii) How, in the system of natural liberty, do the factors he has in mind influence distributive shares? (In answering this question, put aside whether the influence is "improper" or not.)

    (iv)  What makes these factors "so arbitrary from a moral point of view"?

    (v)   Why (if at all) is it objectionable for factors that are arbitrary from a moral point of view to influence distributive shares?

    In motivating the move from liberal equality to democratic equality, Rawls says that in a system of liberal equality "distributive shares are decided by the outcome of the natural lottery; and this outcome is arbitrary from a moral perspective. There is no more reason to permit the distribution of income and wealth to be settled by the distribution of natural assets than by historical and social fortune." To understand the criticism of liberal equality, you will need to answer these questions:

    (i)   What is the system of liberal equality?

    (ii)  What "natural assets" is Rawls referring to?

    (iii) How, in the system of liberal equality, does the distribution of natural assets influence distributive shares?

    (iv)  Why is the distribution of natural assets "arbitrary from a moral perspective"?

    (v)   Is there "no more reason to permit the distribution of income and wealth to be settled by the distribution of natural assets than by historical and social fortune"?

3.  Adam Smith uses the phrase "system of natural liberty" in *An Inquiry into the Nature and Causes of the Wealth of Nations*, ed. Edwin Cannan (London, 1904), Book 4, chapter 9. Smith says:

    All systems either of preference or of restraint, therefore, being thus completely taken away, the obvious and simple system of natural liberty establishes itself of its own accord. Every man, as long as he does not violate the laws of justice, is left perfectly free to pursue his own interest his own way, and to bring both his industry and capital into competition with those of any other man, or order of men.... According to the system of natural liberty, the sovereign has only three duties to attend to ... first, the duty of protecting the society from violence and invasion of other independent societies; secondly, the duty of protecting, as far as possible, every member of the society from the injustice or oppression of every other member of it, or the duty of establishing an exact administration of justice; and, thirdly, the duty of erecting and maintaining certain public works and certain public institutions which it can never be for the interest of any individual, or small number of individuals, to erect and maintain; because the profit could never repay the expence to any individual or small number of individuals, though it may frequently do much more than repay it to a great society.

Rawls does not refer to Smith's use of the phrase, but their uses closely overlap, especially in the characterization of the responsibilities of government (of "the sovereign," in Smith's terms). See James Buchanan, "The Justice of Natural Liberty," *Journal of Legal Studies* (January 1976): 1–16.

4. According to Rawls's difference principle, social and economic inequalities are fully just (part of a perfectly just scheme) only if they work to the greatest expected advantage of the least advantaged. How can an inequality make the least advantaged better off? (To answer, you will need to bear in mind that Rawls is assuming that the size of the economic pie is not fixed: it can be increased in ways that make everyone better off.) Provide an example of an inequality that contributes maximally to the expected advantage of the least advantaged. Provide an example of an inequality that does not contribute to the expected advantage of the least advantaged.

Rawls's own examples of inequalities that can work to the advantage of the least advantaged focus on *incentives*. For criticism of incentive inequalities, see G. A. Cohen, *If You Are an Egalitarian, How Come You Are So Rich?* (Harvard University Press, 2001), pp. 117–47.

5. The selection from Rawls in this anthology does not include the most famous argument in A *Theory of Justice* for his two principles of justice. That argument uses the device of a **social contract**. Rawls argues that people would unanimously agree to his two principles in a hypothetical situation—he calls it the *original position*—in which people come together to choose principles of justice for their own society. The most striking feature of the original position is that the parties make their choice of principles under a *veil of ignorance*. In particular, they do not know their social class, race, gender, religion, moral convictions, talents, or goals in life. The idea is that these characteristics are not relevant to the choice of principles of justice. So we are to put them behind the veil of ignorance to keep them from shaping our decision. The parties in the original position do know, however, that they represent the interests of a free and equal moral person who has a conception of the good (without knowing what that conception is), an interest in being able to choose and revise that conception, and an interest in forming and acting on a sense of justice.

The intuitive reasoning, then, proceeds as follows. You are asked to choose, under conditions of ignorance, principles of justice for your society. You do not know which person you will be, but you have to live with the principles you choose: you have no recourse for a bad decision. So you want to be sure — if you can — that your situation is (roughly) acceptable whatever it turns out to be. Because of the veil of ignorance, you want to be sure that the society is acceptable from the point of view of each person, *because you may be that person*. In particular, you want to be sure that it will be acceptable even if you land in the lowest social position, where it is least likely to be acceptable. So you try to make sure that the minimum position is as good as it can be. And, Rawls argues, this is the assurance — the strong protection against great risks — that the two principles provide: they ensure that social arrangements are acceptable to each member of society. If you choose the two principles in the original position, in effect you provide protection against luck, or inheritance, or talent not working out well, since you ensure that the minimum is as high as possible.

See John Rawls, *A Theory of Justice*, chapter 3, esp. sections 26, 29. For an especially illuminating criticism of Rawls's argument, see John Harsanyi, "Can the Maximin Principle Serve as the Basis for Morality? A Critique of John Rawls's Theory," in *Essays on Ethics, Social Behavior, and Scientific Explanation* (Reidel, 1976), chapter 4.

## Harry Frankfurt (born 1929)

Frankfurt is professor emeritus of philosophy at Princeton University. After receiving his PhD at Johns Hopkins University (1954), Frankfurt taught at Rockefeller University and Yale University before moving to Princeton. Frankfurt has written on Descartes, freedom of the will, and the nature and importance of love and care. Frankfurt is best known for his 2005 book *On Bullshit* (originally published as a paper in 1986), which explains what bullshit is and deplores its cultural proliferation.

# EQUALITY AS A MORAL IDEAL

First man: "How are your children"?
Second man: "Compared to what"?

|

Economic egalitarianism is, as I shall construe it, the doctrine that it is desirable for everyone to have the same amounts of income and of wealth (for short, "money"). Hardly anyone would deny that there are situations in which it makes sense to tolerate deviations from this standard. It goes without saying, after all, that preventing or correcting such deviations may involve costs which — whether measured in economic terms or in terms of noneconomic considerations — are by any reasonable measure unacceptable. Nonetheless, many people believe that economic equality has considerable moral value in itself. For this reason they often urge that efforts to approach the egalitarian ideal should be accorded — with all due consideration for the possible effects of such efforts in obstructing or in conducing to the achievement of other goods — a significant priority.

In my opinion, this is a mistake. Economic equality is not, as such, of particular moral importance. With respect to the distribution of economic assets, what *is* important from the point of view of morality is not that everyone should have *the same* but that each should have *enough*. If everyone had enough, it would be of no moral consequence whether some had more than others. I shall refer to this alternative to egalitarianism — namely, that what is morally important with respect to money is for everyone to have enough — as "the doctrine of sufficiency."

The fact that economic equality is not in its own right a morally compelling social ideal is in no way, of course, a reason for regarding it as undesirable. My claim that equality in itself lacks moral importance does not entail that equality is to be avoided. . . .

But despite the fact that an egalitarian distribution would not necessarily be objectionable, the error of believing that there are powerful moral reasons for caring about equality is far from innocuous. In fact, this belief tends to do significant harm. . . .

To the extent that people are preoccupied with equality for its own sake, their readiness to be satisfied with any particular level of income or wealth is guided not by their own interests and needs but just by the magnitude of the economic benefits that are at the disposal of others. In this way egalitarianism distracts people from measuring the requirements to which their individual natures and their personal circumstances give rise. It encourages them instead to insist upon a level of economic support that is determined by a calculation in which the particular features of their own lives are irrelevant. How sizable the economic assets of others are has nothing much to do, after all, with what kind of person someone is. A concern for economic equality, construed as desirable in itself, tends to divert a person's attention away from endeavoring to discover — within his experience of himself and of his life — what he himself really cares about and what will actually satisfy him, although this is the most basic and the most decisive task upon which an intelligent selection of economic goals depends. Exaggerating the moral importance of economic equality is harmful, in other words, because it is alienating. . . .

The mistaken belief that economic equality is important in itself leads people to detach the problem of formulating their economic ambitions from the problem of understanding what is most fundamentally significant to them. It influences them to take too seriously, as though it were a matter of great moral concern, a question that is inherently rather insignificant and not directly to the point, namely, how their economic status compares with the economic status of others. In this way the doctrine of equality contributes to the moral disorientation and shallowness of our time. . . .

## II

There are a number of ways of attempting to establish the thesis that economic equality is important. Sometimes it is urged that the prevalence of fraternal relationships among the members of a society is a desirable goal and that equality is indispensable to it. Or it may be maintained that inequalities in the distribution of economic benefits are to be avoided because they lead invariably to undesirable discrepancies of other kinds — for example, in social status, in political influence, or in the abilities of people to make effective use of their various opportunities and entitlements. In both of these arguments, economic equality is endorsed because of its supposed importance in creating or preserving certain noneconomic conditions. Such considerations may well provide convincing reasons for recommending equality as a desirable social good or even for preferring egalitarianism as a policy over the alternatives to it. But both arguments construe equality as valuable derivatively, in virtue of its contingent connections to other things. In neither argument is there an attribution to equality of any unequivocally inherent moral value.

A rather different kind of argument for economic equality, which comes closer to construing the value of equality as independent of contingencies, is based upon the principle of diminishing marginal utility. According to this argument, equality is desirable because an egalitarian distribution of economic assets maximizes their aggregate utility. The argument presupposes: ($a$) for each individual the utility of money invariably diminishes at the margin and ($b$) with respect to money, or with respect to the things money can buy, the utility functions of all individuals are the same. In other words, the utility provided by or derivable from an $n$th dollar is the same for everyone, and it is less than the utility for anyone of dollar ($n - 1$). Unless $b$ were true, a rich man might obtain greater utility than a poor man from an extra dollar. In that case an egalitarian distribution of economic goods would not maximize aggregate utility even if $a$ were true. But given both $a$ and $b$, it follows that a marginal dollar always brings less utility to a rich person than to one who is less rich. And this entails that total utility must increase when inequality is reduced by giving a dollar to someone poorer than the person from whom it is taken.

In fact, however, both $a$ and $b$ are false. Suppose it is conceded, for the sake of the argument, that the maximization of aggregate utility is in its own right a morally important social goal. Even so, it cannot legitimately be inferred that an egalitarian distribution of money must therefore have similar moral importance. For in virtue of the falsity of $a$ and $b$, the argument linking economic equality to the maximization of aggregate utility is unsound.

So far as concerns $b$, it is evident that the utility functions for money of different individuals are not even approximately alike. Some people suffer from physical, mental, or emotional weaknesses or incapacities that limit the satisfactions they are able to obtain. Moreover, even apart from the effects of specific disabilities, some people simply enjoy things more than other people do. Everyone knows that there are, at any given level of expenditure, large differences in the quantities of utility that different spenders derive.

So far as concerns *a*, there are good reasons against expecting any consistent diminution in the marginal utility of money. The fact that the marginal utilities of certain goods do indeed tend to diminish is not a principle of reason. It is a psychological generalization, which is accounted for by such considerations as that people often tend after a time to become satiated with what they have been consuming and that the senses characteristically lose their freshness after repetitive stimulation. It is common knowledge that experiences of many kinds become increasingly routine and unrewarding as they are repeated.

It is questionable, however, whether this provides any reason at all for expecting a diminution in the marginal utility of *money* — that is, of anything that functions as a generic instrument of exchange. Even if the utility of everything money can buy were inevitably to diminish at the margin, the utility of money itself might nonetheless exhibit a different pattern. It is quite possible that money would be exempt from the phenomenon of unrelenting marginal decline because of its limitlessly protean versatility. . . . For there may always remain for [a person], no matter how tired he has become of what he has been doing, untried goods to be bought and fresh new pleasures to be enjoyed.

There are in any event many things of which people do not, from the very outset, immediately begin to tire. From certain goods, they actually derive more utility after sustained consumption than they derive at first. This is the situation whenever appreciating or enjoying or otherwise benefiting from something depends upon repeated trials, which serve as a kind of "warming up" process: for instance, when relatively little significant gratification is obtained from the item or experience in question until the individual has acquired a special taste for it, has become addicted to it, or has begun in some other way to relate or respond to it profitably. The capacity for obtaining gratification is then smaller at earlier points in the sequence of consumption than at later points. In such cases marginal utility does not decline; it increases. Perhaps it is true of everything, without exception, that a person will ultimately lose interest in it. But even if in every utility curve there is a point at which the curve begins a steady and irreversible decline, it cannot be assumed that every segment of the curve has a downward slope. . . .

# IV

The preceding discussion has established that an egalitarian distribution may fail to maximize aggregate utility. It can also easily be shown that, in virtue of the incidence of utility thresholds, there are conditions under which an egalitarian distribution actually minimizes aggregate utility. Thus, suppose that there is enough of a certain resource (e.g., food or medicine) to enable some but not all members of a population to survive. Let us say that the size of the population is ten, that a person needs at least five units of the resource in question to live, and that forty units are available. If any members of this population are to survive, some must have more than others. An equal distribution, which gives each person four units, leads to the worst possible outcome, namely, everyone dies. Surely in this case it would be morally grotesque to insist upon equality! Nor would it be reasonable to maintain that, under the conditions specified, it is justifiable for some to be better off only when this is in the interests of the worst off. If the available resources are used to save eight people, the justification for doing this is manifestly not that it somehow benefits the two members of the population who are left to die. . . .

# VI

The fundamental error of egalitarianism lies in supposing that it is morally important whether one person has less than another regardless of how much either of them has. This error is due in part to the false assumption that someone who is economically worse off has more important unsatisfied needs than someone who is better off. In fact the morally significant needs of both individuals may be fully satisfied or equally unsatisfied. Whether one person has more money than another is a wholly extrinsic matter. It has to do with a relationship between the respective economic assets of the two people, which is not only independent of the amounts of their assets and of the amounts of satisfaction they can derive from them but also independent of the attitudes of these people toward those levels of assets and of satisfaction. The economic comparison implies nothing concerning whether either of the people compared has any morally important unsatisfied needs at all nor concerning whether either is content with what he has. . . .

In most societies the people who are economically at the bottom are indeed extremely poor, and they do, as a matter of fact, have urgent needs. But this relationship between low economic status and urgent need is wholly contingent. It can be established only on the basis of empirical data. There is no necessary conceptual connection between a person's relative economic position and whether he has needs of any degree of urgency.

It is possible for those who are worse off not to have more urgent needs or claims than those who are better off because it is possible for them to have no urgent needs or claims at all. The notion of "urgency" has to do with what is *important*. Trivial needs or interests, which have no significant bearing upon the quality of a person's life or upon his readiness to be content with it, cannot properly be construed as being urgent to any degree whatever or as supporting the sort of morally demanding claims to which genuine urgency gives rise. From the fact that a person is at the bottom of some economic order, moreover, it cannot even be inferred that he has *any* unsatisfied needs or claims. After all, it is possible for conditions at the bottom to be quite good; the fact that they are the worst does not in itself entail that they are bad or that they are in any way incompatible with richly fulfilling and enjoyable lives. . . .

# VII

What does it mean, in the present context, for a person to have enough? One thing it might mean is that any more would be too much: a larger amount would make the person's life unpleasant, or it would be harmful or in some other way unwelcome. This is often what people have in mind when they say such things as "I've had enough!" or "Enough of that!" The idea conveyed by statements like these is that *a limit has been reached,* beyond which it is not desirable to proceed. On the other hand, the assertion that a person has enough may entail only that *a certain requirement or standard has been met,* with no implication that a larger quantity would be bad. This is often what a person intends when he says something like "That should be enough." Statements such as this one characterize the indicated amount as sufficient while leaving open the possibility that a larger amount might also be acceptable.

In the doctrine of sufficiency the use of the notion of "enough" pertains to *meeting a standard* rather than to *reaching a limit.* To say that a person has enough money means that he is content, or that it is reasonable for him to be content, with having no more money than he has. And to say this is, in turn, to say something like the following: the person does not (or cannot reasonably) regard whatever (if anything) is unsatisfying or distressing about his life as due to his having too little money. In other words, if a person is (or ought reasonably to be) content with the amount of money he has, then insofar as he is or has reason to be unhappy with the way his life is going, he does not (or cannot reasonably) suppose that money would — either as a sufficient or as a necessary condition — enable him to become (or to have reason to be) significantly less unhappy with it.

It is essential to understand that having enough money differs from merely having enough to get along or enough to make life marginally tolerable. People are not generally content with living on the brink. The point of the doctrine of sufficiency is not that the only morally important distributional consideration with respect to money is whether people have enough to avoid economic misery. A person who might naturally and appropriately be said to have just barely enough does not, by the standard invoked in the doctrine of sufficiency, have enough at all.

There are two distinct kinds of circumstances in which the amount of money a person has is enough — that is, in which more money will not enable him to become significantly less unhappy. On the one hand, it may be that the person is suffering no substantial distress or dissatisfaction with his life. On the other hand, it may be that although the person is unhappy about how his life is going, the difficulties that account for his unhappiness would not be alleviated by more money. Circumstances of this second kind obtain when what is wrong with the person's life has to do with noneconomic goods such as love, a sense that life is meaningful, satisfaction with one's own character, and so on. These are goods that money cannot buy; moreover, they are goods for which none of the things money can buy are even approximately adequate substitutes. ....

It is possible that someone who is content with the amount of money he has might also be content with an even larger amount of money. Since having enough money does not mean being at a limit beyond which more money would necessarily be undesirable, it would be a mistake to assume that for a person who already has enough the marginal utility of money must be either negative or zero. Although this person is by hypothesis not distressed about his life in virtue of any lack of things which more money would enable him to obtain, nonetheless it remains possible that he would enjoy having some of those things. They would not make him less unhappy, nor would they in any way alter his attitude toward his life or the degree of his contentment with it, but they might bring him pleasure. If that is so, then his life would in this respect be better with more money than without it. The marginal utility for him of money would accordingly remain positive. . . .

But how can all this be compatible with saying that the person is content with what he has? What *does* contentment with a given amount of money preclude, if it does not preclude being willing or being pleased or preferring to have more money or even being ready to make sacrifices for more? It precludes his having an *active interest* in getting more. A contented person regards having more money as *inessential* to his being satisfied with his life. The fact that he is content is quite consistent with his recognizing that his economic circumstances could be improved and that his life might as a consequence become better than it is. But this possibility is not important to him. He is simply not much interested in being better off, so far as money goes, than he is. His attention and interest are not vividly engaged by the benefits which would be available to him if he had more money. He is just not very responsive to their appeal. They do not arouse in him any particularly eager or restless concern, although he acknowledges that he would enjoy additional benefits if they were provided to him.

In any event, let us suppose that the level of satisfaction that his present economic circumstances enable him to attain is high enough to meet his expectations of life. This is not fundamentally a matter of how much utility or satisfaction his various activities and experiences provide. Rather, it is most decisively a matter of his attitude toward being provided with that much. The satisfying experiences a person has are one thing. Whether he is satisfied that his life includes just those satisfactions is another. Although it is possible that other feasible circumstances would provide him with greater amounts of satisfaction, it may be that he is wholly satisfied with the amounts of satisfaction that he now enjoys. Even if he knows that he could obtain a greater quantity of satisfaction overall, he does not experience the uneasiness or the ambition that would incline him to seek it. Some people feel that their lives are good enough, and it is not important to them whether their lives are as good as possible. . . .

It may seem that there can be no reasonable basis for accepting less satisfaction when one could have more, that therefore rationality itself entails maximizing, and, hence, that a person who refuses to maximize the quantity of satisfaction in his life is not being rational. Such a person cannot, of course, offer it as his reason for declining to pursue greater satisfaction that the costs of this pursuit are too high; for if that were his reason then, clearly, he would be attempting to maximize satisfaction after all. But what other good reason could he possibly have for passing up an opportunity for more satisfaction? In fact, he may have a very good reason for this: namely, *that he is satisfied with the amount of satisfaction he already has.*

He might still be open to criticism on the grounds that he *should not* be satisfied—that it is somehow unreasonable, or unseemly, or in some other mode wrong for him to be satisfied with less satisfaction than he could have. On what basis, however, could *this* criticism be justified? Is there some decisive reason for insisting that a person ought to be so hard to satisfy? Suppose that a man deeply and happily loves a woman who is altogether worthy. We do not ordinarily criticize the man in such a case just because we think he might have done even better. Moreover, our sense that it would be inappropriate to criticize him for that reason need not be due simply to a belief that holding out for a more desirable or worthier woman might end up costing him more than it would be worth. Rather, it may reflect our recognition that the desire to be happy or content or satisfied with life is a desire for a satisfactory amount of satisfaction and is not inherently tantamount to a desire that the quantity of satisfaction be maximized. . . .

Contentment may be a function of excessive dullness or diffidence. The fact that a person is free both of resentment and of ambition may be due to his having a slavish character or to his vitality being muffled by a kind of negligent lassitude. It is possible for someone to be content merely, as it were, by default. But a person who is content with resources providing less utility than he could have may not be irresponsible or indolent or deficient in imagination. On the contrary, his decision to be content with those resources—in other words, to adopt an attitude of willing acceptance toward the fact that he has just that much—may be based upon a conscientiously intelligent and penetrating evaluation of the circumstances of his life.

## TEST YOUR UNDERSTANDING

1. Frankfurt offers "the doctrine of sufficiency" as an alternative to egalitarianism. Provide a brief statement of the doctrine of sufficiency.

2. According to Frankfurt, the belief that equality has support from important moral reasons "tends to do significant harm." What are the harms that Frankfurt describes? Which word best describes the harms?

   (i)   political

   (ii)  ethical

   (iii) legal

   (iv)  economic

3. Review the **utilitarian argument** for equality that Frankfurt discusses. What are the main premises in the argument? What are Frankfurt's criticisms of those premises?

4. Frankfurt distinguishes two ways we might understand the notion of "enough" in the doctrine of sufficiency. What are the two ways? Which does he offer as the right way?

## NOTES AND QUESTIONS

1. "There is no necessary conceptual connection between a person's relative economic position and whether he has needs of any degree of urgency." Explain what this statement means and how Frankfurt defends it. Why does he say "no necessary conceptual connection"? (*Hint:* Look at the previous three sentences in the paragraph.) What does he mean by "urgency"?

2. The main idea in Frankfurt's "doctrine of sufficiency" is that, when it comes to the economic assets, "each should have *enough.*" According to the doctrine, "If everyone had enough, it would be of no moral consequence whether some had more than others." A simple formulation of the doctrine of sufficiency, then, says:

   *Sufficiency*: A distribution of economic resources is morally right if and only if each person has enough.

   According to *Sufficiency*, then, changes in the distribution of resources make no moral difference, so long as each person has enough. When some people do not have enough, the situation calls for remedy. The plausibility of *Sufficiency* depends on how we understand what is *enough*. Frankfurt offers the following account (focused on having enough *money*, which is the concern of this article):

   *Enough*: A person has enough money if and only if the person will not become significantly less unhappy by having more money.

   A person, for example, has enough money if he or she is "suffering no substantial distress or dissatisfaction with his life." More money cannot alleviate this person's unhappiness because the person has no unhappiness to be alleviated.

   Consider, however, the case of Joseph. Joseph is satisfied with his life—he suffers no substantial distress or dissatisfaction—even though he is extremely poor. He is satisfied because he is accustomed from birth to having very little. Having little, he wants little and thinks he does not deserve to have more. He has what are called *adaptive* preferences: his preferences and sense of entitlement have *adapted* to his condition of extreme poverty. Suppose, now, that if Joseph had more money, his preferences would change: perhaps because he is now able to do more, he develops a desire to travel, to see more of his country or more of the larger world. Looking back, Joseph might say that when he was satisfied, he did not have enough money and that it was morally objectionable that he did not have more. He did not have enough because he lacked the resources needed to imagine different ways to live and decide which way is best.

   Do adaptive preferences raise a serious problem for *Enough*? Do they raise troubles for *Sufficiency*? Can you modify *Enough* so that *Sufficiency* can handle the difficulty presented by Joseph?

   For discussion of adaptive preferences, see Jon Elster, *Sour Grapes: Studies in the Subversion of Rationality* (Cambridge University Press, 1983); Amartya Sen, *Development as Freedom* (Oxford University Press, 1999); and Martha Nussbaum, *Women and Human Development* (Oxford University Press, 2000).

3. It follows from *Enough* that a person who has enough may still be very unhappy: that is true when the unhappiness cannot be addressed by more money. But if more money

will make a person significantly less unhappy, then the person does not have enough. And if someone does not have enough, then *Sufficiency* tells us that something is not morally right.

Consider now the case of Albert, who has very ambitious goals. He wants to travel often and comfortably, eat at the best restaurants, pilot his own jet, have a large wine cellar with a large stock of the best wines, contribute large amounts of support to worthy causes, have a large family, ensure that all his children attend great schools, have lovely homes in all the places he travels, each filled with Impressionist paintings, and have an opera company on call to perform for him in his personal opera house. Albert already has considerable wealth (let's say he is in the top 0.1 percent in wealth). But because his wealth is not nearly sufficient to achieve his ambitious goals, he retains a very "active interest" (to use Frankfurt's term) in having more. So he is unhappy, and money can help.

Do we need to modify *Enough* or *Sufficiency* to respond to Albert? As stated, *Enough* implies that Albert does not have enough. And then *Sufficiency* tells us that something is morally wrong. Is it morally wrong that Albert does not have what he needs to fulfill his very ambitious goals? If it is not morally wrong, then we need to modify *Enough* so that Albert has enough, despite his discontentment. Or do we need to modify *Sufficiency* so that there is not something morally wrong whenever some people have less than enough? If we modify *Sufficiency*, we give up on Frankfurt's central idea: that everyone is entitled to have enough. So consider some modifications in *Enough* that address the challenge presented by Albert. As a starting point, consider the passages in which Frankfurt says that a person has enough when the person "is (*or ought reasonably to be*) content with the amount of money he has" (emphasis added). Will it help to reformulate *Enough*?

> *Enough*\*: A person has enough money if and only if the person will not reasonably become significantly less unhappy by having more money.

What makes Albert unreasonable? Do you think Albert is unreasonable? If you do, would you say he is unreasonable because he has a misguided idea of what a good life is, or because he is demanding too much of other people?

Albert is an example of a person with *expensive tastes*. For discussion of the problem of expensive tastes, see G. A. Cohen, "Expensive Taste Rides Again," in *Dworkin and His Critics*, ed. Justine Burley (Blackwell, 1994), pp. 3–29, and the response by Dworkin to Cohen in that same volume.

4. Frankfurt's doctrine of sufficiency has been the subject of considerable discussion, and has been codified as *sufficientarianism*—a view of distributive justice distinct from *egalitarianism* and *prioritarianism*. For a critical exploration of Frankfurt's view and some of the surrounding literature on sufficientarianism, see Paula Casal, "Why Sufficiency Is Not Enough," *Ethics* 117 (January 2007): 296–326. On the three –isms, see the entries in the *Stanford Encyclopedia of Philosophy* on "Equality" (http://plato .stanford.edu/entries/equality/) and on "Justice and Bad Luck" (http://plato.stanford .edu/entries/justice-bad-luck/).

5. In this paper, Frankfurt focuses attention on equality of money. In a later paper, he says that his case for sufficiency applies with equal force to "all egalitarian doctrines." "In rejecting equality as a moral ideal," Frankfurt says, "I intend the scope of my rejection to be entirely unlimited." So it does not matter if the focus is money, or

opportunity, or rights, or liberties, or respect. In each case, equality is not an appropriate concern. See "The Moral Irrelevance of Equality," *Public Affairs Quarterly* 14, no. 2 (April 2000): 87–103.

How does Frankfurt's central objection to a concern with *economic* equality lead to this completely general conclusion about all forms of equality? His central objection cannot be that "there are goods that money cannot buy." That would not lead to the general conclusion. So what does lead to the general conclusion? (*Hint:* Review Frankfurt's reasons, stated early in the article, for thinking that a concern for equality is harmful.)

## Martha Nussbaum (born 1947)

Nussbaum is Ernst Freund Distinguished Service Professor of Law and Ethics at the University of Chicago, with appointments in the philosophy department, the law school, and the divinity school. She received her PhD from Harvard University in 1975 and taught at Harvard and Brown University before moving to the University of Chicago. Nussbaum has written on an extraordinary range of subjects, including political philosophy, ethics, ancient philosophy, American constitutional law, human emotions, literature, music, Indian religion and politics, feminism, and humanistic education. Her books include *The Fragility of Goodness* (2013, second edition), *Sex and Social Justice* (1998), *Women and Human Development* (2000), *Frontiers of Justice* (2006), *Not for Profit: Why Democracy Needs the Humanities* (2012), and *Political Emotions: Why Love Matters for Justice* (2013). In 2003, she cofounded the Human Development and Capability Association.

# POLITICAL EQUALITY

Equality is a cherished political value in modern democracies. It is often associated with the idea of human worth or dignity, and also with questions of political entitlements and rights (including the right to vote, the right to education, and many others). The U. S. Declaration of Independence states, "We hold these truths to be self-evident, that all men are created equal, that they are endowed by their Creator with certain unalienable rights, that among these are life, liberty, and the pursuit of happiness." Most modern constitutions the world over contain similar appeals to human equality.

Such appeals are resonant, but it is not terribly clear what they mean. That all human beings are already equal? (Equal in what respect? Surely not in current resources and opportunities. In basic powers and capacities? In worth or dignity? And how, if at all, might that dignity be related to basic powers and capacities?) That all human beings are such that they ought to be treated equally? (Again, equally in what respect?

In respect and self-respect? In political rights and liberties? In economic opportunity? In economic achievement?) And why should human beings be treated equally? Because they are in some other sense already equal?

And who are the human beings who are or ought to be equal? The U. S. founders by and large did not believe that slaves or women were or should be equal: that view was achieved only gradually and with much struggle. South Africa and India, by contrast, assert human equality in their founding documents, announcing the end of an era of racial and caste-based hierarchy. Does any nation, however, fully commit itself to the view that human beings with profound cognitive disabilities are or should be equal? (Are such people given equal voting rights? Equal rights to education?) Despite much recent progress, debates continue in most nations.

Finally, is it only human beings, and not other animals, who are equal and who have the right to "life, liberty, and the pursuit of happiness"? If so, we might want to be told what is special about human beings that allows them the right to establish dominion over other forms of life.

These thorny and intricate questions have not been given any final answer in political philosophy, but tracing the paths among the different types and conceptions of political equality at least helps us think better about our alternatives. First we must understand what it means to think of equality as a distinctively political value. Then, addressing the basis of human equality, we will see why a "minimalist" account is attractive; in the light of this account, the community of equals ranges widely. We can then understand why equality of the relevant kind has wide-ranging political and social implications.

# I. Political and Comprehensive

Equality is a political value: a value enshrined in the basic political principles of nations and in their founding documents, and connected with ideas of political entitlement (including both political and civil rights, such as the right to vote, and social and economic rights, such as the right to education, or a right to social security). Equality is also, however, an ethical value, meaning one that people use in the nonpolitical aspects of their lives. Even when we are not thinking about political matters at all, we often talk of the equal worth of people, demanding that others respect it. For example, people condemn racism and sexism, even when they are found within the private sphere or in the bosom of the family, because they insult human equality. Such ethical conceptions of human equality are often rooted in some more comprehensive religious or ethical view, which covers all aspects of life, and not simply politics. The Christian doctrine of the equality of all souls in the eyes of God, for example, has been a major source of ethical equality principles.

But all modern nations contain many different religious and nonreligious views that guide the lives of their members. It therefore seems inappropriate, even disrespectful, to build political principles on any particular religious or metaphysical conception. That seems like a demand that everyone convert to that religion or meta-physical conception, if they want to enjoy full citizen status. (Even the Declaration's reference to a creator God now strikes many people as too sectarian, in a nation containing believers and nonbelievers, and in which even many believers do not ac-cept the idea that God created the world.) So the political value of equality should be articulated in a way that does not rely on such divisive or sectarian ideas, ideas that many citizens could not accept without converting. If I live in a Christian nation, I should not feel pressured to convert to Christianity by the role Christian language plays in public debate.

If many of a nation's people belong to a religion that teaches a doctrine of human equality, that may certainly be helpful in leading them to accept that everyone is entitled to equal rights. (In the United States, for example, Christian views helped buttress the new nation's political ideals.) But such widespread doctrines of equality are not necessary for the acceptance of a specifically political ideal. When Mahatma Gandhi asked all Indians to accept the political idea of human equality as the foun-dation of the new Indian nation, he was not relying on the traditions of the majority religion. Hinduism had long taught the unequal worth of human beings, including the idea of untouchability—a doctrine that the Indian constitution outlawed from the start, because it was incompatible with the political ideal. Despite the fact that many Indians continued to believe privately in human inequality, they accepted po-litical equality — perhaps because their long experience of domination by the British had shown them its worth. Similarly, many people all over the world have not built the equality of women into their overall views of human life, but they can often ac-cept the idea that women are equal for the purpose of framing political entitlements and responsibilities.

Our topic is political equality, not ethical or social equality. Sometimes, then, the best answer to disputed questions about the basis of human equality may be, "Answer them in your own way. So long as you accept the political ideal, nothing more need be said." Often, however, philosophers (and political leaders) have felt that more needs to be said, even to ground political principles. Following some of the major answers and the connections they suggest will help us think — even if we may conclude that some familiar replies (such as the Christian language of the Declaration) are too sec-tarian for political life in a pluralistic society. The ideas that are good guides may be slight variants on the more problematic ones: simply by omitting the Declaration's reference to a creator God we have a view that all Americans can probably accept.

## II. The Basis of Human Equality

What does it mean to assert that human beings are equal? We might begin by un-derstanding what people who make such claims are reacting against. Feudalism, for example, involved a belief that nature has placed people in different social condi-tions, that these differences are fixed and immutable, part of people's very nature as human beings, constituting immutably distinct subspecies, and that political differences are rightly grounded on those differences of human worth and status. The Indian caste hierarchy was founded upon similar beliefs — as were American views of racial hierarchy. To assert, against this, that human beings are equal is, most fundamentally, to assert that all human beings have a worth or dignity that is basically equal, and that they are not inherently, naturally, ranked above and below one another in a hierarchical ordering. The hierarchies we observe are the creation of social forces.

How might one defend such a view, in a world in which human beings, as we encounter them, are already profoundly affected by entrenched social hierarchies?

Some philosophers have thought it important to point out that human beings are all roughly similar in their innate physical and mental powers. Thomas Hobbes, for example, points out that in the "state of nature," meaning a situation without organized political society, people will soon recognize that their powers are pretty similar, since even the physically weakest could kill the strongest by stealth. Adam Smith,[1] similarly, said that the differences we observe between a philosopher and a street porter are not grounded in innate characteristics, but, instead, in social differences: differences, for example, of nutrition, education, and opportunity. Such claims are important because they are true, and because they remind us of the enormous power of social differences in our world. Class differences affect people's height, strength, health, cognitive development, emotions, and expectations, in such a way that in many eras people of different classes, races, or genders believed that they were really different subspecies of human beings.

It is not clear, however, that this is the right way to defend the political claim of equal worth or dignity. For one thing, it encourages us to believe that marked or life-long disabilities, physical and mental, diminish a person's worth as a human being, something that seems both incorrect and repugnant.

Other philosophers (beginning with the ancient Greek Stoics) have thought that the source of our equal worth lies in our power of ethical choice. Even though people may vary to some degree in their ethical skill and virtue, they said, all possess in sufficient measure the ability to rank and evaluate goals and to act in accordance with that ranking, and this sufficient degree of ethical capacity is enough to make them of fully equal worth, wherever they are placed in society (male or female, free or slave, rich or poor). In contemporary philosophy, John Rawls espouses a similar view in *A Theory of Justice*. This way of thinking about the source of equality is much more attractive than the way that alludes to equal physical and intellectual powers, since moral capacity does appear to be a source of worth or dignity, and people of very unequal intellectual development may have it in comparable measure; and yet many will think that it does not make quite enough room for equal respect for people with profound cognitive disabilities. Many of these people may not be able to evaluate and rank goals. But does this mean that we owe them

---

1. Adam Smith (1723–1790), a leading Scottish moral philosopher and economist, was the author of *The Theory of Moral Sentiments* (1759) and *The Wealth of Nations* (1776).

unequal respect and concern, or that it is fine to place "normal" human beings hierarchically above them?

At this point, many people will want to point to some further fact about human beings, such as their relationship to God or their possession of a soul, that makes them equal regardless of their powers, whether physical or moral. This type of reply, however, is more suited to personal ethical choice than to political choice, where we have said that we want to avoid sectarian answers.

We could try, instead, what we might call a thinner or more "minimalist" answer: so long as a living creature is of the human species (born of human parents) and possesses some degree of agency or striving and some consciousness, that being is, for political purposes, the full equal of all other humans in worth and dignity. This reply will include people with profound disabilities, but it may not include people in a persistent vegetative state, or fetuses, or anencephalic infants. It will therefore be controversial, since believers in the soul believe that all these creatures have souls and are full equals of people who have consciousness and agency. Political principles will need to wrestle with the special difficulty of such cases, in a country in which political principles ought to be nonsectarian. Nonetheless, the fact that a view cannot solve all our problems in the most difficult cases is not a strong argument against it. Political life poses many hard questions, and sometimes lines must simply be drawn in the best way one can.

If we give the minimalist answer, we have to face the fact that we are ascribing to bare species membership (plus striving and minimal awareness) a political significance that is hard to defend, in a world in which members of other species also have striving and awareness. Why should the fact that creature A is born of two human parents give this creature priority over creature B, who might have very similar physical and mental powers but be born of two chimpanzee or two elephant parents? Isn't the preference for the human species itself a kind of sectarian reply, in a world in which many people believe in the underlying kinship of all life and the worth and dignity of other species?

This question has all too rarely been faced by political philosophy, and more rarely still by real-life politics. One reason for this silence is that most assume that the basis of human equality, whatever it is, resides in some property or properties that raise us above "the beasts." Most of the history of Western philosophy encourages this thought, although Hinduism and Buddhism do not. But the idea of a "ladder of nature," humans occupying the top rung, has little to commend it as a political doctrine. There are many capacities in which at least some animals surpass human beings: strength, speed, spatial perception, auditory sensitivity, sensory memory. If we now say, "But they don't have moral rationality," we may possibly be right, but we tip our hand: we are according to that property a decisive political importance, without any convincing argument. And if we have already taken the minimalist position, thus including people with profound cognitive disabilities as full equals, we cannot take this route without inconsistency. So the political idea of equality seems threatened with either an arbitrary species-ism or a repugnant denial of equal worth to some human beings.

We can respond to this dilemma by saying that for some purposes (cruelty, pain, desperate material conditions) the species boundary is not relevant: laws should protect all creatures from these assaults on their dignity. For others (voting, religious freedom), the species boundary is relevant because these things are good within one species community (the human) but not in another one (the chimp or elephant community). For a human with cognitive disabilities to be denied the equal right to vote is an offense to her human dignity; to deny the vote to a chimp with similar cognitive powers is not a similar offense, because voting is a good within the human community and not the chimp community.

# III. Who Is Equal?

Seeing how difficult and potentially divisive the question about the basis of equal worth turns out to be, we might wonder whether we are not better off trying not to answer this question at all, at least in the political realm. When we look at history, however, we can see that we can never quite avoid it, because we always have to answer the question "Who is equal"? in order to give a good political argument for our political arrangements. And to do that in a politically productive way, we must at the very least rule out some unsatisfactory answers.

Why shouldn't we say that people whose skin color differs from our own are political unequals, fit for subordination? We need to have something to say, and we usually say that skin color is not relevant to political entitlement because it does not render people inherently different in basic human worth. Why shouldn't we say that women are unequal to men, fit to be ruled by men? Such views were long held, and some still hold them, so we need to have something to say. Typically, we say that the biological accidents of gender do not affect a person's fundamentally equal human worth: human worth resides elsewhere. Well then, where does it reside? The negative reply prompts a search for some type of positive answer, however vague. Again, why have most societies decided that it is wrong to deem people with physical and mental disabilities politically unequal, lacking equal political entitlements? Well, because they have come to the conclusion that a child with Down syndrome, for example, is of equal worth with a professor of philosophy — even though, unlike Smith's street porter, the child's differences from the philosopher cannot plausibly be said to be entirely due to mere social arrangements. We have come to believe, that is, that the basis of human equality lies elsewhere — in a dignity in which the child and the philosopher equally share.

We should probably continue to offer such negative answers without definitively articulating a positive theory of the basis of equality, apart from the vague minimalist account suggested, given the difficulty of going further in a nonsectarian way. We have to remain prepared, however, to respond to challenges and offer some account of why the hierarchies we assail are unjustified.

# IV. Equality and Entitlement

When the framers of the Declaration of Independence affirmed the equal worth of human beings (really, of white males), they did so in order to demonstrate the wrong-fulness of Britain's arbitrary rule over the colonies. The thought of equal worth is typically connected to ideas of political obligation. How?

First, we need the view that material and institutional conditions matter deeply for human life. The Stoics affirmed the equal worth of human beings, but derived no political conclusions from this thought, because they thought that conditions such as wealth and poverty, political voice and lack of voice, even freedom and slavery, make no difference at all to human beings. The source of our equal worth and dignity is safe within, in our moral capacity, and nothing the world does to it can remove or even damage it.

The Stoic idea is deep. In part we should and do believe it: we don't think that peo-ple become less valuable as human beings, or lose their basic human dignity, when they lose political rights, or honor, or money, or freedom. And yet, unlike the Stoics, we typically believe that these conditions matter profoundly, and that certain forms of life insult or offend human dignity. Think of rape: we don't think that a woman who has been raped has lost her human dignity, but we do think that something deep has happened to her that cuts to the very heart of her dignity, or violates it. In a sim-ilar way, we often think that respect for equal human worth requires at least protect-ing people from the direst conditions, those that most deeply assail human dignity.

Second, we need a conception of the job of government, and the U. S. founders had one: governments are "instituted among men" in order "to secure these rights," namely the basic entitlements to "life, liberty, and the pursuit of happiness," entitle-ments grounded in human beings' equal worth. In other words, according to this widely shared view, government exists to provide at least minimum threshold con-ditions that enable a life that is worthy of our basic human equality. Human dignity itself is inalienable, as are the rights grounded upon it; but the conduct of George III was an insult to it. A government that behaves like this can rightly be rejected.

This idea is vague and intuitive. Where does it lead us? In most modern nations, it has led to the thought that it is unacceptable for governments to give citizens less than fully equal religious freedom, voting rights, freedom of speech, freedom of as-sociation, and other key civil and political liberties. To give one person only half a vote is seen, plausibly, as an insult to the person's equal human dignity. This group of political rights has a particularly intimate connection with human dignity, since these rights seem to lie at the heart of a person's role as a free and equal citizen. Few today would question this conclusion, although it is often not fully honored in prac-tice. (Equal voting rights for people with extreme cognitive disabilities will require not only assistance at the polls, but, in some cases, forms of surrogacy that are not yet accepted.)

The payoff of equality for questions of material entitlement is far more disputed. There is widespread agreement that respect for human equality at least requires that government prevent people from living in desperate conditions, because that type of extreme poverty does seem like an assault on human dignity, because it stops people from developing and unfolding their human powers. (Adam Smith said that children sent to work in factories instead of being able to go to school were being "mutilated and deformed.") Beyond this, however, there is dispute. Some believe that the equal worth of human beings requires full-scale equality in educational provisions, in health care, and at least a rough equality in income and wealth. The U. S. founders were closer to that idea than is commonly supposed. James Madison, the primary architect of the U. S. Constitution, wrote that the new government should prevent "an immoderate, and especially an unmerited, accumulation of riches," and should do so "by the silent operation of laws, which, without violating the rights of property, reduce extreme wealth to a state of mediocrity [i.e., a middle level] and raise extreme indigence toward a state of comfort." Like Thomas Paine and other framers, then, he favored strongly redistributive policies aimed at achieving greater economic equality. But the United States has never given economic and social entitlements the status of constitutional rights. Even to the extent that such entitlements have been protected in legislation, it is typically an ample threshold level of provision that is sought, rather than complete equality. Other modern nations, such as India, South Africa, and the nations of Europe, have done much more to connect the thought of equal human worth to definite ideas of substantial equality in economic entitlement. At the very least, they believe, respect for human equality requires an ample social minimum, plus considerable diminution of inequalities between rich and poor, through redistributive taxation and a wide range of social welfare programs. Even issues that seem like matters of private personal choice, like the choice to take a rewarding vacation, or the choice to enjoy a peaceful day at home, depend in many ways on government policies: maximum hours laws, bans on child labor, prohibitions on domestic violence, and so forth. The closer we look, the more we can see the need for government to establish legal protections for human equality in every area of life.

On the other hand, too much government intrusion into material arrangements may allow too little room for incentives to work hard and to achieve. We can grant that all human beings have fundamentally equal worth without granting that one person should always get the same reward as another. A good teacher will not give the same grades to students regardless of their effort, even though she believes them equal in human worth. Similarly, a just society should preserve a decent space for effort and rewards for effort, while providing all with a decent minimum. And a society that would require all parents to spend the same amount on the education of all children would also be too intrusive, diminishing parents' incentives to achieve — although a decent society should certainly guarantee far more educational equality than most modern societies have managed to attain, particularly given the importance of education for all future opportunities.

Here material entitlements look very different from political entitlements: being a slacker should not remove a person's right to vote, or a person's equal freedom of religion. We may be satisfied by "enough" education, where some inequalities remain, but we should not be satisfied by "enough" votes, where some groups have more votes than others.


# V. Equality as Goal: Equality of What?

Suppose we have decided that in some areas of social and economic life (health care, education, employment), respect for people as equals requires pursuing equality (or, at least, greater equality) as a political goal. Suppose, that is, we are aiming at making people who are already equals in some underlying sense equal (or more nearly equal) in material living conditions. What is the best way of thinking about that goal? What sort of equality should we be aiming at? We now need to make the concept of equality as political goal more precise.

A first appealing thought is that satisfaction is what we want to equalize — how pleased people feel about their lives. Satisfaction, however, is notoriously malleable and elusive. We know that people can get used to a bad state of affairs, avoiding constant frustration by defining their goals down. So they might feel satisfied in a rather bad condition. Many women did not demand equal political and economic rights, for example, before a process of consciousness raising made them aware of their situation.

Another idea we might try out is that people should be equal (or more nearly equal) in the amount of resources (income and wealth) that they control. That sort of equality is what redistributive policies of taxation typically support, and this makes a good deal of sense, because giving people all-purpose resources allows them freedom to choose how to use them. In a society without any entrenched hierarchies, it may well be the best sort of equality to focus on. But when a society contains longstanding hierarchies, giving members of the dominant and subordinate groups exactly the same amount of resources may not be enough. Getting people out of marginalization and low social status into a position of reasonable equality may require spending more on them. Many developing countries, for example, find that they must spend more to educate girls than boys, because girls face obstacles to education (in their families, their villages) that boys do not.

One might then conclude that the right sort of equality to focus on is equality of what some philosophers call "capabilities": substantial opportunities to choose and act. Income and wealth are sometimes good proxies for these freedoms and opportunities, but where they are not, we should focus on opportunity itself. Philosophers who think this way do not insist that full equality of "capability" is the right goal in every area: in some (for example, housing), an ample social minimum may be enough. Still, a focus on "capabilities," or substantial opportunities, provides a very attractive way of linking the idea of human freedom and choice with the idea that meaningful freedoms involve a background of government action ensuring substantial opportunity.

## TEST YOUR UNDERSTANDING

1. How does Nussbaum complete the following sentence?

   *To say that all human beings are equal is to say that*

   (i)   all human beings have similar physical and mental powers.

   (ii)  all human beings have a power of ethical choice.

   (iii) all human beings have equal dignity.

   (iv)  all human beings are born of human parents.

2. What is the Stoic view about equal dignity? Does Nussbaum think we should accept it? What parts of the Stoic position does she agree with? What parts does she disagree with?

3. Why it is hard to avoid the question about the basis of equal worth?

4. Why does Nussbaum think that the capability view is better than alternative answers to the question *"equality of what?"*

## NOTES AND QUESTIONS

1. Nussbaum asks: Why do all human beings have a "worth or dignity that is basically equal"? Formulate the answers she considers in your own words. What problems does she identify in the views she associated with Hobbes and with the Stoics? How does her "minimalist" answer avoid those problems?

   Nussbaum worries that the minimalist view avoids a "repugnant denial of equal worth to some human beings" at the cost of endorsing an "arbitrary species-ism." Explain what she means by "arbitrary species-ism." How does she answer the charge of arbitrary species-ism? Is the answer convincing?

2. Explain the difference between treating equality as an ethical value and as a political value. Why does Nussbaum think it is important to treat equality as a political value?

   (i)  In support of the political conception of equality, she says it is wrong "to build political principles on any particular religious or metaphysical conception." To do this, she says, is tantamount to "a demand that everyone convert to that religion or metaphysical conception, if they want to enjoy full citizen status." But if the possession of full political and civil rights in a country is not dependent on converting (say, not dependent in England on being a member of the Anglican Church), what does it mean to say that there is a demand to convert as a condition of full citizen status?

   (ii) If equality is treated as a political value without deeper moral or religious moorings, does that make equality seem arbitrary?

   As background for Nussbaum's account of equality as a political value, see John Rawls, *Political Liberalism*, second edition (Columbia University Press, 2005). Rawls emphasizes the importance, under conditions of religious, moral, and philosophical pluralism, of formulating a political conception of justice that can be endorsed by people with different fundamental convictions.

## Jonathan Wolff (born 1959)

Wolff is a professor of philosophy at University College London. He writes on political philosophy and on issues at the intersection between philosophy and public policy. Among his books are *Robert Nozick: Property, Justice, and the Minimal State* (Polity Press, 1991), *Ethics and Public Policy: A Philosophical Inquiry* (2011), and *The Human Right to Health* (2013).

# EQUALITY AS A BASIC DEMAND OF JUSTICE

## Introduction

Equality occupies an awkward place in political philosophy. On the one hand it is all too easy to argue for equality. For who now would defend, say, racial or sexual inequality? Of course, it is possible to criticize various ideas about the means for achieving equality — for example, quota systems or affirmative action — but that is different from rejecting equality itself. Indeed, virtually every theorist accepts that political philosophy must begin from the assumption that all humans are moral equals, in contrast to earlier times in which it was taken for granted that men, rather than women, or white people, rather than those of other skin colors, were moral superiors. In this sense, then, we are all egalitarians now.

In another sense, however, none of us are egalitarians now, and perhaps never were. For equality is also sometimes associated with uniformity: sameness of income, consumption, or standard of living. Yet equality as uniformity seems to ignore human diversity of tastes and effort, as well as ignoring the requirements of a complex economy in which differences in rewards are needed both for incentives and informational purposes. Although models of a fully equalized society have been proposed, they find few supporters, even as depictions of an ideal. In particular it is often argued that complete equality is incompatible with recognizing any form of individual responsibility.

# Distributional and Relational Equality

In one sense, then, almost all of us are egalitarians; and in another virtually none of us are. But there is, of course, deep controversy about the ideal of equality, and neither the idea we accept nor the one we reject can explain what is at stake. To understand that controversy, we need to describe a conception of equality — I will call it a "substantive idea of equality" — that goes beyond the common ground of moral equality accepted in contemporary liberal theory but avoids an unattractive ideal of demoralizing uniformity. In fact, there are several such conceptions — several competing substantive ideas of equality — and we can best appreciate the value of equality by considering the relative merits of some of these competing ideas.

One substantive idea of equality takes its lead from the work of Ronald Dworkin, who is particularly concerned to develop a theory that is true to the motivating ideas of equality, yet at the same time finds space for individual responsibility.[1] Dworkin's theory — he calls it "equality of resources" — is built around a distinction between what he calls "option luck" and "brute luck." Dworkin suggests that if one is born of low talent or intelligence, or disabled, then one has poor brute luck, and egalitarian justice requires compensation — extra "external resources" to make up for a lack of "internal resources." However, if two people have the same talents and abilities and one chooses to work hard and take risks while the other takes it easy and plays safe, then this is a matter of differential option luck, and any resulting disparities in life fortunes are perfectly just, and, indeed, compatible with equality. This view has been called "luck egalitarianism" because it aims to equalize the effects of brute luck on the distribution of material resources.

Luck egalitarianism is one member of a family of egalitarian views, all of which focus on the distribution of resources, and see the demands of equality principally in terms of how resources are distributed. But in its single-minded concern to ensure a fair distribution of resources, luck egalitarianism — like other kinds of distributive egalitarianism — leaves out some essential elements of the egalitarian ideal: its concern with the nature of social relations, and particularly with the ideal of people relating to one another as equals.

The English socialist R. H. Tawney, writing in 1931, provides an outline of a *relational* egalitarian alternative to distributive egalitarianism.[2] Instead of formulating a precise principle of equality, he provides examples of gross inequalities and how they reproduce over generations. He sets out figures showing the different health prospects of people of different social and economic classes, and even the differential nutritional value of the food they eat. He illustrates his case with examples such as that of British high court judges, almost all of whom, at the time he was writing, had

---

1. Ronald Dworkin, " What Is Equality? Part 1: Equality of Welfare," *Philosophy and Public Affairs* 10 (1981a), 185–246; Ronald Dworkin, "What Is Equality? Part 2: Equality of Resources," *Philosophy and Public Affairs* 10 (1981b), 283–345. [Wolff's note.]

2. R. H. Tawney, *Equality* (George Allen & Unwin, 1931). [Wolff's note.]

been educated at a small number of elite schools. The thread running through Tawney's examples is a concern about deep social division, intensified by snobbery and servility. It is as if society is composed of two (or more) societies, attending different schools, accessing different types of health care, enjoying different types of leisure, and meeting only when one class performs services for the other. Tawney's goal is not in the first instance to ensure an egalitarian distribution of resources, but to create a society where people can live together as equals.

To understand the distinction between the distributive and relational approaches, consider someone who from birth has suffered from a mobility problem that makes it very difficult, or even impossible, to find employment given the way the workplace and public transport systems are constructed. According to the distributive egalitarian view, to be disabled in this way is an undoubted misfortune. Compensation in the form of extra resources will be owed from other members of society, certainly to make up for difficulties in earning a decent living, and also, depending on the details of the theory, for the disability itself. On this view redistribution is owed because of the unfairness of being socially disadvantaged as a result of having been born disabled.

Relational egalitarians will approach the issue a different way. At bottom, they may suggest, the difficulty that people with disabilities face is not an unfair share of resources — although this may well also be the case — but a form of social exclusion. Rather than accept that people with disabilities cannot work, and provide them with compensation, what we must do instead is to rethink urban and workplace design to make the world more accommodating for everyone. Furthermore, we should examine ourselves for prejudicial assumptions. And, indeed, many societies are encouraging such programs both by means of new building codes and accessibility requirements, and supporting activities giving positive images of people with disabilities, such as the Paralympics. Such measures try to ensure that everyone is equally regarded as entitled to a worthwhile place in society, and not merely a fair share of resources.

Naturally it can be asked whether the two approaches are really so far apart. Dworkin focuses on the egalitarian distribution of resources, Tawney on a society where all are regarded as equals. These ideas are conceptually distinct, but in practice are very likely to be connected. For example, it has recently been argued that among countries at similar levels of economic development there is a very clear correlation between income inequality and a whole host of social problems, such as crime, drug addiction, and poor health. In the light of these facts it seems plausible that achieving income equality and overcoming social division go hand in hand. Furthermore, both views are concerned with fairness: in the first case fairness with respect to the distribution of resources, and in the second fairness with respect to social, economic, and perhaps political opportunity, as well as overcoming serious unfairness in the distribution of resources.

There are several reservations, however, about attempting to minimize the difference in this way. While relational egalitarians are certainly concerned about inequalities in resource distribution, their focus is different, and while they will regard gross income inequalities as highly problematic, this does not mean that they would regard the pursuit of income equality as worthwhile. In common with other earlier socialists, such as the poet and artist William Morris, Tawney, for example, is sympathetic to a strain in socialist thought that diagnoses an obsession with ownership and consumption as a symptom of a misguided bourgeois, consumerist mentality. William Morris argues that to live a good life is to be healthy and active in body and mind, to have a worthwhile occupation, and to live in a world of beauty.[3] Tawney would at least agree that a concentration on material wealth will be a distraction from what is truly important in life, including not only the cultivation of the mind but also of one's relations with others. While distributive egalitarians appear to imply that material goods are so important that they should be distributed according to precise principles of justice, relational egalitarians regard a focus on material goods as a form of pathology, at least beyond a certain level. There are two reasons for this. First, material wealth is not the most important thing in life. Second, the pursuit of material wealth may well be corrosive of what is more important: relating to others as equals.

Indeed it can also be argued that in some cases a concern for fine-grained accounting for justice, making sure that everyone has exactly their fair share, could stand in the way of creating the open, generous, and accommodating relations that characterize an egalitarian society. For a trivial example, think of those who insist that everyone pay exactly his or her fare share of a restaurant bill. No doubt this is better than a situation in which some deliberately try to underpay, but surely not as good as a situation in which, for the sake of friendship, no one even wants to know who has done relatively well or badly. Justice is important, but it is not everything. The general point is that precise accounting can undercut valuable social relations. There are therefore two related contrasts in play: first, between a concentration on the distribution of resources and a concern for equality of social standing; and second, between a strict and a rather looser notion of fairness, in the name of protecting valuable social relations.

## Relational Equality and the Capability View

The relational view captures an important aspect of what is so often valued in the egalitarian ideal. Yet how exactly to formulate the relational view in detail is problematic. As we have seen, relational egalitarians oppose hierarchy and favor inclusion, but specifying a model of an equal society requires much greater theoretical precision. The first issue must be to provide an account of what makes a human life go well or badly, at least insofar as this can be a legitimate subject of government concern. Relational egalitarians accept that human well-being is a complicated

---

3. William Morris, "How We Live and How We Might Live" (1884) www.marxists.org/archive/morris/works/1884/hwl/hwl.htm. [Wolff's note.]

matter. Individual well-being cannot be reduced to the possession of income and wealth. But at the same time, it could not be seriously proposed that all that matters is whether others treat and regard you as an equal. Other people's attitudes to you will not stop you from starving or preserve your health, unless backed up with considerable action. Hence the relational view appears to require a complex account of human well-being, including "material" as well as "relational" elements.

Many of those who endorse a version of the relational view have found Amartya Sen's "capability theory" very helpful.[4] Capability theory concentrates not on the level of resources people have, or even the subjective satisfaction that they derive from those resources, but rather on what they can "do or be" with them: what, in other words, they are capable of. We have already seen, in effect, an illustration of the distinction between resources and capabilities by means of the example of someone who suffers from physical disability. Increasing a person's income and wealth may be a relatively ineffective way of improving his or her capabilities if the physical and social world remains unwelcoming. This was a reason, we saw, for concentrating on such things as urban and workplace design, to increase the capabilities of disabled people even without increasing their individual resources.

It is also important to explore the distinction between capability theory and subjective satisfaction theories. To be sure, increasing an individual's capabilities may typically also increase his or her satisfaction. Yet capability theorists have often pointed to examples of people who have a high subjective satisfaction but low capability. The "happy slave" is a standard example, but it is also true that studies have also shown that people with very significant physical disabilities often report levels of satisfaction similar to those of the general population. It is possible to "adapt" one's preferences to one's situation. However, what matters, according to the capability view, is not how happy people are, but whether they have the capabilities to be included in society as equals, with others. Indeed, on a theory requiring equal subjective satisfactions, if people with physical disabilities report similar levels of satisfaction to others then nothing further needs to be done. By contrast, capability theory aims to equalize capabilities, even if this could lead to inequalities in subjective satisfaction.

Well-being, according to capability theory, needs to be considered in a multidimensional way. Those who lack mobility, or access to education, or a safe environment, or health, need a very specific form of action to improve their lives, often requiring the provision of various common or public services. Hence the capability approach, with its insistence that a fulfilling life involves a range of goods, not all of which can be substituted for each other, depends on a rich and realistic account of well-being. However, it is one thing to say that well-being is multidimensional; it is quite another to say what the dimensions are. Amartya Sen has always refused to give a definitive list of capabilities, arguing that what is important will vary in place and

---

4. Amartya Sen, "Equality of What?," in S. McMurrin (ed.), *Tanner Lectures on Human Values* (Cambridge University Press, 1980), pp. 195–220; Amartya Sen, *Development as Freedom* (Oxford University Press, 1999); Amartya Sen, *The Idea of Justice* (Harvard University Press, 2009). [Wolff's note.]

time, and so needs to be worked out as part of the democratic process, rather than legislated by the philosopher. Martha Nussbaum, in contrast, believes it is possible to enumerate core capabilities for purposes of cross-cultural comparisons. These she lists as: life; bodily health; bodily integrity; senses, imagination, and thought; emotions; practical reason; affiliation; relations to other species; play; and control over one's environment (political and material).[5]

How one decides whether the list of capabilities is correct is an interesting question, and theorists have devised alternative lists, using interviews and surveys in addition to philosophical analysis. But it is worth noting that several elements on Nussbaum's list show why the capability approach is particularly helpful for the relational approach to equality. Most obviously we can note the importance of affiliation, and of emotions, which will often depend on the nature of one's connection to others. Other elements, such as control over one's environment, bodily integrity, and play, however, also contain reference to how one interacts with others as part of individual well-being. At the same time material and individual elements of well-being, such as health and nutrition, are not neglected.

It is important, however, to add a further element to capability theory. Consider Sen's example of the people of the Sundarban. This is the habitat of the Royal Bengal tiger, which is protected by a hunting ban. The area also produces honey in natural beehives. The local people are honey collectors. Every year some fifty or more of them are killed by tigers. Note too that even those who are not attacked by tigers suffer a form of disadvantage through the risk and insecurity they suffer. Generally, then, an individual is worse off if his or her enjoyment of any good is insecure and under threat. Acknowledging that vulnerability can itself make people badly off, we should modify capability theory so that what matters is not just the enjoyment of capabilities but their security over time.

## Capability Theory and Equality

Capability theory provides a realistic account of human well-being, even if it must remain, to some degree, open-ended and contested. Such realism is, of course, a great strength, but it comes at a cost. For the more complex an account of well-being, the harder it will be to say when equality has been achieved. In consequence it becomes easier to understand why resource-based theories of equality can be so attractive. At least we know how to measure money and can come to a view about the degree of equality or inequality in a society. This is much harder on a capability view. Where two people have very different capabilities, it may be very difficult to come to a clear determination of which person is better off. The idea of "equalizing capabilities" may seem daunting, not only in practice, but even in the theoretical task of saying what this would mean. This has become known as the "indexing problem": how do we "index" capabilities in order to tell whether one person is better off than another?

5. Martha Nussbaum, *Women and Human Development* (Cambridge University Press, 2000). [Wolff's note.]

But even if we can solve the indexing problem, it is unclear that the goal of equalizing capabilities is attractive, without substantial modification. For like all theories of equality it is affected by the "leveling-down" objection. The easiest way of equalizing capabilities may well be to destroy them all, so that everyone has an equal amount: none. The natural response is to argue that although equality is important it is not the only thing that is important. Most theorists of equality argue that, in practice, equality should be replaced either with a notion of "priority to the worst off" or "sufficiency for all" to avoid the leveling-down problem. On such views there are at least two values to be balanced: one is equality, the other human well-being, which should not always be sacrificed for the sake of equality.

A further difficulty, however, is that, even ignoring the leveling-down problem, arguing for "equality of capabilities" seems to come perilously close simply to a version of distributive equality. If so, it then seems an inappropriate way of formulating the relational egalitarian idea, which was intended to contrast with distributive equality.

One possible way of dealing with the three problems identified above — the "indexing problem," the "leveling-down" objection, and the possibility of collapse into distributional equality — is to argue that society ought to provide each individual with a high level of enjoyment of each capability taken one by one, and not try to come to an assessment of whether the overall situation is equal or unequal. This approach certainly has appeal. So, for example, it may be plausible to argue that each person should enjoy a high level of health or control over their environment, whatever else is true of them. As an ideal this is certainly attractive, even inspiring, and it is reasonable to suppose that if we have achieved such an ideal we could safely say that we have also achieved the goal of a society of equals. The difficulty we face, however, is that even the wealthiest societies are some way off from achieving anything like this goal, and accordingly, for practical purposes capability theory needs to grapple with the non-ideal circumstances of the real world. And indeed, even with infinite resources it may not be possible to achieve good health, or emotional well-being, for all.

To put the point graphically: if our political leaders became convinced that they should take on the goal of achieving relational equality by means of adopting the capability approach, what should they do in the coming months and years to begin this task? From the point of view of equality the urgent task seems to be to identify the worst off and try to take steps so their lives will be improved. But now our problem comes to this. How do we define the worst off?

The most natural suggestion would be to try to come to some sort of overall score for each person or group. But how should the different categories be weighted? Should we give the same "score" to someone who has low capability for play as someone who has low capability for bodily health? If not, how do we decide on the relevant weights? It seems clear that there is no uncontroversial answer to the question of relative weightings, and, therefore, it seems, no clear answer to the question of how to rank individuals in terms of their capability achievement, and therefore no way of identifying the worst off.

However, this difficulty may not be as severe as it appears. In many, if not all, societies it is reasonable to suppose that disadvantage "clusters" in the sense that those who do badly on one capability are at least at risk of doing badly on others. Low performance in one capability is often associated with low, or vulnerable, enjoyment of others. So, for example, it has been noted that those with low control over their environment, poor affiliation, or under risk of attack (low capability for bodily integrity) have greater chance of poor health and lower life expectancy. If disadvantage does cluster in this way, as appears to be the case, then it is possible to identify the worst off in society without having to give scores. The worst off are those who suffer from relatively low, or highly insecure, capabilities over a range of important capabilities. And it is to these people the government should give their highest priority. Ideally, governments should aim to "decluster disadvantage": to make it very hard to say who in society is worst off.[6]

## Egalitarian Social Policy

How is government to move us closer to a society of equals by declustering disadvantage? Here we turn from political philosophy to social policy, and social science. But it is important to keep in mind that different dimensions of advantage and disadvantage often stand in causal relations. This, indeed, is why disadvantage tends to cluster. Accordingly governments have special reason to give particular attention to what we can call "corrosive disadvantages": disadvantages that are likely to lead to other problems. It is likely, for example, that drug addiction is corrosive in this sense: addiction is likely to lead to a breakdown in personal relations (loss of affiliation) and to dependency (loss of control over one's environment), and can be a threat to life, bodily health, emotional well-being, and play. The goal for governments, then, is to try to prevent people from forming such corrosive disadvantages, which lead to a downward spiral.

It is also important to attempt to identify, and encourage, "upward spirals," what can also be called "fertile functionings" (the opposite of corrosive disadvantages). Finding interventions that spread their benefits for the individual, and possibly for society too, is the holy grail of social policy. Naturally these can be very hard to find, but it is sometimes thought that high-quality early education is fertile in this sense, in that it will have beneficial effects throughout one's future life. It also seems plausible that affiliation is fertile, for people with strong, supportive social networks may reap benefits through better health, life expectancy, and emotional well-being. However, these are social-scientific claims that need to be tested by the methods of social science, rather than philosophical speculation, which can so often fail us when tested by experience.

## Conclusion

Relational equality, underpinned by the "secure capability" view of well-being, is an interpretation of the idea of equality. Unlike luck egalitarianism and other forms of distributional equality, it has a broad conception of human well-being, seeing

6. Jonathan Wolff and Avner de-Shalit, *Disadvantage* (Oxford University Press, 2007). [Wolff's note.]

resources, up to a certain point, as simply a means to a good life, but beyond that of little importance. Similar remarks apply to fairness. Gross unfairness can undermine a society of equals. But then, so can an obsessive concern to ensure everyone receives exactly a fair share. While distributional equality supposes that there is some thing of which everyone should have an equal share, relational equality, in contrast, proposes that each of us should be able to take our place as a member of a society where everyone has the capability to function as an equal, and this is how each person regards each other.

## TEST YOUR UNDERSTANDING

1. "In one sense, then, almost all of us are egalitarians; and in another virtually none of us are." Explain what Wolff has in mind. In what sense of "egalitarian" are virtually all of us egalitarians? In what sense are virtually none of us egalitarians?

2. What are the alternatives to the capability theory of well-being? Briefly state the objections of the capability theorist to the alternative theories.

## NOTES AND QUESTIONS

1. Provide a brief statement of the distributive and relational conceptions of equality. What are the essential differences?

   Consider three differences between the views (each suggested by Wolff):

   (i)   Distributive views focus on resources, relational views on how people relate to each other.

   (ii)  Distributive views are concerned with fairness, relational views with social inclusion.

   (iii) Distributive views aim at a precise accounting of equality, relational views at an attentiveness to social complexity.

   Use the example of the disabled person—who has a problem with mobility that makes it hard to find employment—to interpret the differences between the two conceptions. Which of the three distinctions is most fundamental?

   Suppose a defender of the distributive view says:

   > The distinction you are drawing is misleading. I am concerned about how people relate to each other: ensuring that people have the resources they are entitled to *is* a way to relate to them. Moreover, I am concerned with social inclusion: ensuring that people have a fair share of resources *is* a kind of social inclusion. And finally, I do not deny social complexity. I just think that we should leave the navigation of social complexity in the hands of individuals.

The social/political job is to ensure that they have the resources they are entitled to as they approach that navigation.

How might Wolff respond?

2. For discussion of the *relational* approach to equality endorsed by Wolff, see Elizabeth Anderson, "What Is the Point of Equality?" *Ethics* 109 (1999): 287–333; Samuel Scheffler, "What is Egalitarianism?" *Philosophy and Public Affairs* 31 (2003): 6–35.

3. The relational egalitarian needs an account of when a human life goes well or badly, and many relational egalitarians, Wolff says, are drawn to a "capability theory." According to a capability theory:

   (i) Person A is *better off* than person B if and only if A has greater capabilities than B.

   (ii) A has *greater capabilities* than B if and only if a wider range of activities or "functionings" is available to A than to B.

   The capability theorist compares well-being by comparing capabilities, rather than by comparing resources or satisfactions.

   For discussions of the capability approach, see Amartya Sen, *Inequality Reexamined* (Harvard University Press, 1995), and Martha Nussbaum, *Women and Human Development* (Cambridge University Press, 2000). Nussbaum also sketches the idea of capabilities in her contribution in this chapter.

   Although Wolff favors the capability approach, he rejects the idea that justice requires equalizing capabilities.

   (i) What are the troubles with the idea of equalizing capabilities?

   (ii) How does the idea that disadvantages form clusters help to address the troubles Wolff identifies with equalizing capabilities?

4. According to the relational egalitarian view, Wolff says, each of us is entitled to "the capability to function as an equal." What is the force of "as an equal"? Wolff does not, for example, think that we are entitled to equal capabilities. Why not say, then, that each of us should have the capability to live a decent life, with access to resources and relationships that are important for living well? Is anything added by saying that "relational equality . . . is an interpretation of the idea of equality"?

## Robert Nozick (1938–2002)

Nozick was born in Brooklyn, New York. He received his PhD at Princeton University (1963) and taught at Harvard University 1969–2002. Best known for his early work in political philosophy, *Anarchy, State and Utopia* (1974), Nozick had remarkably broad interests, and made original contributions to philosophical discussions of personal identity, knowledge, objectivity, the meaning of life, and rationality. He was the author of *Philosophical Explanations* (1983), *The Examined Life* (1990), *The Nature of Rationality* (1993), *Socratic Puzzles* (1999), and *Invariances* (2001).

# DISTRIBUTIVE JUSTICE
## from *Anarchy, State, and Utopia*

The term "distributive justice" is not a neutral one. Hearing the term "distribution," most people presume that some thing or mechanism uses some principle or criterion to give out a supply of things. Into this process of distributing shares some error may have crept. So it is an open question, at least, whether *redistribution* should take place; whether we should do again what has already been done once, though poorly. However, we are not in the position of children who have been given portions of pie by someone who now makes last minute adjustments to rectify careless cutting. There is no *central* distribution, no person or group entitled to control all the resources, jointly deciding how they are to be doled out. What each person gets, he gets from others who give to him in exchange for something, or as a gift. In a free society, diverse persons control different resources, and new holdings arise out of the voluntary exchanges and actions of persons. There is no more a distributing or distribution of shares than there is a distributing of mates in a society in which persons choose whom they shall marry. . . .

## The Entitlement Theory

The subject of justice in holdings consists of three major topics. The first is the *original acquisition of holdings,* the appropriation of unheld things. This includes the issues of how unheld things may come to be held, the process, or processes, by which unheld things may come to be held, the things that may come to be held by these processes, the extent of what comes to be held by a particular process, and so on. We shall refer to the complicated truth about this topic, which we shall not formulate here, as the principle of justice in acquisition. The second topic concerns the *transfer of holdings* from one person to mother. By what processes may a person transfer holdings to another? How may a person acquire a holding from another who holds it? Under this topic come general descriptions of voluntary exchange, and gift and (on the other hand) fraud, as well as reference to particular conventional details fixed upon in a given society. The complicated truth about this subject (with placeholders for conventional details) we shall call the principle of justice in transfer. (And we shall suppose it also includes principles governing how a person may divest himself of a holding, passing it into an unheld state.)

If the world were wholly just, the following inductive definition[1] would exhaustively cover the subject of justice in holdings.

---

1. An inductive definition defines an object by reference to itself. For example, an inductive definition of *natural number* says: 0 is a natural number; and every number you get by adding 1 to a natural number is a natural number. Nozick's definition is inductive because a person is entitled to something if they get it according to principles of justice in transfer *from someone who is entitled to it.*

1. A person who acquires a holding in accordance with the principle of justice in acquisition is entitled to that holding.

2. A person who acquires a holding in accordance with the principle of justice in transfer, from someone else entitled to the holding, is entitled to the holding.

3. No one is entitled to a holding except by (repeated) applications of 1 and 2.

The complete principle of distributive justice would say simply that a distribution is just if everyone is entitled to the holdings they possess under the distribution. . . .

Not all actual situations are generated in accordance with the two principles of justice in holdings: the principle of justice in acquisition and the principle of justice in transfer. Some people steal from others, or defraud them, or enslave them, seizing their product and preventing them from living as they choose, or forcibly exclude others from competing in exchanges. None of these are permissible modes of transition from one situation to another. And some persons acquire holdings by means not sanctioned by the principle of justice in acquisition. The existence of past injustice (previous violations of the first two principles of justice in holdings) raises the third major topic under justice in holdings: the rectification of injustice in holdings. If past injustice has shaped present holdings in various ways, some identifiable and some not, what now, if anything, ought to be done to rectify these injustices? . . .

The general outlines of the theory of justice in holdings are that the holdings of a person are just if he is entitled to them by the principles of justice in acquisition and transfer, or by the principle of rectification of injustice (as specified by the first two principles). If each person's holdings are just, then the total set (distribution) of holdings is just. To turn these general outlines into a specific theory we would have to specify the details of each of the three principles of justice in holdings: the principle of acquisition of holdings, the principle of transfer of holdings, and the principle of rectification of violations of the first two principles. I shall not attempt that task here. . . .

## Historical Principles and End-Result Principles

The general outlines of the entitlement theory illuminate the nature and defects of other conceptions of distributive justice. The entitlement theory of justice in distribution is *historical*; whether a distribution is just depends upon how it came about. In contrast, *current time-slice principles* of justice hold that the justice of a distribution is determined by how things are distributed (who has what) as judged by some *structural* principle(s) of just distribution. A utilitarian who judges between any two distributions by seeing which has the greater sum of utility and, if the sums tie, applies some fixed equality criterion to choose the more equal distribution, would hold a current time-slice principle of justice. As would someone who had a fixed schedule of trade-offs between the sum of happiness and equality. According to a current time-slice principle, all that needs to be looked at, in judging the justice of a distribution, is who ends up with what; in comparing any two distributions one need look only at the matrix presenting the distributions. No further information need be fed into a principle of justice. . . .

Henceforth, we shall refer to such unhistorical principles of distributive justice, including the current time-slice principles, as *end-result principles* or *end-state principles*.

In contrast to end-result principles of justice, *historical principles* of justice hold that past circumstances or actions of people can create differential entitlements or differential deserts to things. An injustice can be worked by moving from one distribution to another structurally identical one, for the second, in profile the same, may violate people's entitlements or deserts; it may not fit the actual history.

# Patterning

The entitlement principles of justice in holdings that we have sketched are historical principles of justice. To better understand their precise character, we shall distinguish them from another subclass of the historical principles. Consider, as an example, the principle of distribution according to moral merit. This principle requires that total distributive shares vary directly with moral merit; no person should have a greater share than anyone whose moral merit is greater. (If moral merit could be not merely ordered but measured on an interval or ratio scale, stronger principles could be formulated.) Or consider the principle that results by substituting "usefulness to society" for "moral merit" in the previous principle. Or instead of "distribute according to moral merit," or "distribute according to usefulness to society," we might consider "distribute according to the weighted sum of moral merit, usefulness to society, and need," with the weights of the different dimensions equal. Let us call a principle of distribution *patterned* if it specifies that a distribution is to vary along with some natural dimension, weighted sum of natural dimensions, or lexicographic ordering of natural dimensions. And let us say a distribution is patterned if it accords with some patterned principle. . . . The principle of distribution in accordance with moral merit is a patterned historical principle, which specifies a patterned distribution. "Distribute according to I.Q." is a patterned principle that looks to information not contained in distributional matrices. It is not historical, however, in that it does not look to any past actions creating differential entitlements to evaluate a distribution; it requires only distributional matrices whose columns are labeled by I.Q. scores. The distribution in a society, however, may be composed of such simple patterned distributions, without itself being simply patterned. Different sectors may operate different patterns, or some combination of patterns may operate in different proportions across a society. A distribution composed in this manner, from a small number of patterned distributions, we also shall term "patterned." And we extend the use of "pattern" to include the overall designs put forth by combinations of end-state principles.

Almost every suggested principle of distributive justice is patterned: to each according to his moral merit, or needs, or marginal product,[2] or how hard he tries, or the weighted sum of the foregoing, and so on. The principle of entitlement we have sketched is not patterned. There is no one natural dimension or weighted sum or combination of a small number of natural dimensions that yields the distributions generated in accordance with the principle of entitlement. The set of holdings that results when some persons receive their marginal products, others win at gambling, others receive a share of their mate's income, others receive gifts from foundations, others receive interest on loans, others receive gifts from admirers, others receive returns on investment, others make for themselves much of what they have, others find things, and so on, will not be patterned. . . .

To think that the task of a theory of distributive justice is to fill in the blank in "to each according to his _____" is to be predisposed to search for a pattern; and the separate treatment of "from each according to his _____" treats production and distribution as two separate and independent issues. On an entitlement view these are *not* two separate questions. Whoever makes something, having bought or contracted for all other held resources used in the process (transferring some of his holdings for these cooperating factors), is entitled to it. The situation is *not* one of something's getting made, and there being an open question of who is to get it. Things come into the world already attached to people having entitlements over them. From the point of view of the historical entitlement conception of justice in holdings, those who start afresh to complete "to each according to his _____" treat objects as if they appeared from nowhere, out of nothing. A complete theory of justice might cover this limit case as well; perhaps here is a use for the usual conceptions of distributive justice.[3]

So entrenched are maxims of the usual form that perhaps we should present the entitlement conception as a competitor. Ignoring acquisition and rectification, we might say:

> From each according to what he chooses to do, to each according to what he makes for himself (perhaps with the contracted aid of others) and what others choose to do for him and choose to give him of what they've been given previously (under this maxim) and haven't yet expended or transferred.

This, the discerning reader will have noticed, has its defects as a slogan. So as a summary and great simplification (and not as a maxim with any independent meaning) we have:

> *From each as they choose, to each as they are chosen.*

---

2. In economics, the marginal product is the extra output produced by one additional unit of input.

3. The "usual conceptions" include distribution according to need, or effort, or contribution. Nozick's point is that these conceptions, unlike his historical entitlement view, may be appropriate in deciding how to distribute goods that appear from nowhere, that were not made by people working with things they own.

# How Liberty Upsets Patterns

It is not clear how those holding alternative conceptions of distributive justice can reject the entitlement conception of justice in holdings. For suppose a distribution favored by one of these nonentitlement conceptions is realized. Let us suppose it is your favorite one and let us call this distribution $D_1$; perhaps everyone has an equal share, perhaps shares vary in accordance with some dimension you treasure. Now suppose that Wilt Chamberlain is greatly in demand by basketball teams, being a great gate attraction.[4] (Also suppose contracts run only for a year, with players being free agents.) He signs the following sort of contract with a team: In each home game, twenty-five cents from the price of each ticket of admission goes to him. (We ignore the question of whether he is "gouging" the owners, letting them look out for themselves.) The season starts, and people cheerfully attend his team's games; they buy their tickets, each time dropping a separate twenty-five cents of their admission price into a special box with Chamberlain's name on it. They are excited about seeing him play; it is worth the total admission price to them. Let us suppose that in one season one million persons attend his home games, and Wilt Chamberlain winds up with \$250,000, a much larger sum than the average income and larger even than anyone else has. Is he entitled to this income? Is this new distribution $D_2$, unjust? If so, why? There is *no* question about whether each of the people was entitled to the control over the resources they held in $D_1$; because that was the distribution (your favorite) that (for the purposes of argument) we assumed was acceptable. Each of these persons *chose* to give twenty-five cents of their money to Chamberlain. They could have spent it on going to the movies, or on candy bars, or on copies of *Dissent* magazine, or of *Monthly Review*.[5] But they all, at least one million of them, converged on giving it to Wilt Chamberlain in exchange for watching him play basketball. If $D_1$ was a just distribution, and people voluntarily moved from it to $D_2$, transferring parts of their shares they were given under $D_1$ (what was it for if not to do something with?), isn't $D_2$ also just? If the people were entitled to dispose of the resources to which they were entitled (under $D_1$), didn't this include their being entitled to give it to, or exchange it with, Wilt Chamberlain? Can anyone else complain on grounds of justice? Each other person already has his legitimate share under $D_1$. Under $D_1$, there is nothing that anyone has that anyone else has a claim of justice against. After someone transfers something to Wilt Chamberlain, third parties *still* have their legitimate shares; *their* shares are not changed. By what process could such a transfer among two persons give rise to a legitimate claim of distributive justice on a portion of what was transferred, by a third party who had no claim of justice on any holding of the others *before* the transfer? To cut off objections irrelevant here, we might imagine the exchanges occurring in a socialist society,

---

4. Wilt Chamberlain (1936–1999) was one of the greatest basketball players of all time, and when Nozick wrote his book, he was playing center for the Los Angeles Lakers. Chamberlain once scored 100 points in a single game, and was named Most Valuable Player four times.

5. *Dissent* and *Monthly Review* are both American political magazines, on the political left.

after hours. After playing whatever basketball he does in his daily work, or doing whatever other daily work he does, Wilt Chamberlain decides to put in *overtime* to earn additional money. . . .

The general point illustrated by the Wilt Chamberlain example . . . is that no end-state principle or distributional patterned principle of justice can be continuously realized without continuous interference with people's lives. Any favored pattern would be transformed into one unfavored by the principle, by people choosing to act in various ways; for example, by people exchanging goods and services with other people, or giving things to other people, things the transferrers are entitled to under the favored distributional pattern. To maintain a pattern one must either continually interfere to stop people from transferring resources as they wish to, or continually (or periodically) interfere to take from some persons resources that others for some reason chose to transfer to them. (But if some time limit is to be set on how long people may keep resources others voluntarily transfer to them, why let them keep these resources for *any* period of time? Why not have immediate confiscation?) . . .

## Redistribution and Property Rights

Patterned principles of distributive justice necessitate *redistributive* activities. The likelihood is small that any actual freely-arrived-at set of holdings fits a given pattern; and the likelihood is nil that it will continue to fit the pattern as people exchange and give. From the point of view of an entitlement theory, redistribution is a serious matter indeed, involving, as it does, the violation of people's rights. (An exception is those takings that fall under the principle of the rectification of injustices.) From other points of view, also, it is serious.

Taxation of earnings from labor is on a par with forced labor. Some persons find this claim obviously true: taking the earnings of *n* hours labor is like taking *n* hours from the person; it is like forcing the person to work *n* hours for another's purpose. Others find the claim absurd. But even these, *if* they object to forced labor, would oppose forcing unemployed hippies to work for the benefit of the needy. And they would also object to forcing each person to work five extra hours each week for the benefit of the needy. But a system that takes five hours' wages in taxes does not seem to them like one that forces someone to work five hours, since it offers the person forced a wider range of choice in activities than does taxation in kind with the particular labor specified. . . . Furthermore, people envisage a system with something like a proportional tax on everything above the amount necessary for basic needs. Some think this does not force someone to work extra hours, since there is no fixed number of extra hours he is forced to work, and since he can avoid the tax entirely by earning only enough to cover his basic needs. This is a very uncharacteristic view of forcing for those who *also* think people are forced to do something *whenever* the alternatives they face are considerably worse. However, *neither* view is correct. The fact that others intentionally intervene, in violation of a side constraint against aggression, to threaten force to limit the alternatives, in this case to paying taxes or (presumably the worse alternative) bare subsistence, makes the taxation system one of forced labor and distinguishes it from other cases of limited choices which are not forcings. . . .

What sort of right over others does a legally institutionalized end-state pattern give one? The central core of the notion of a property right in *X*, relative to which other parts of the notion are to be explained, is the right to determine what shall be done with *X*; the right to choose which of the constrained set of options concerning *X* shall be realized or attempted. The constraints are set by other principles or laws operating in the society; in our theory, by the Lockean rights people possess (under the minimal state).[6] My property rights in my knife allow me to leave it where I will, but not in your chest. I may choose which of the acceptable options involving the knife is to be realized. This notion of property helps us to understand why earlier theorists spoke of people as having property in themselves and their labor. They viewed each person as having a right to decide what would become of himself and what he would do, and as having a right to reap the benefits of what he did. . . .

When end-result principles of distributive justice are built into the legal structure of a society, they (as do most patterned principles) give each citizen an enforceable claim to some portion of the total social product; that is, to some portion of the sum total of the individually and jointly made products. This total product is produced by individuals laboring, using means of production others have saved to bring into existence, by people organizing production or creating means to produce new things or things in a new way. It is on this batch of individual activities that patterned distributional principles give each individual an enforceable claim. Each person has a claim to the activities and the products of other persons, independently of whether the other persons enter into particular relationships that give rise to these claims, and independently of whether they voluntarily take these claims upon themselves, in charity or in exchange for something.

Whether it is done through taxation on wages or on wages over a certain amount, or through seizure of profits, or through there being a big *social pot* so that it's not clear what's coming from where and what's going where, patterned principles of distributive justice involve appropriating the actions of other persons. Seizing the results of someone's labor is equivalent to seizing hours from him and directing him to carry on various activities. If people force you to do certain work, or unrewarded work, for a certain period of time, they decide what you are to do and what purposes your work is to serve apart from your decisions. This process whereby they take this decision from you makes them a *part-owner* of you; it gives them a property right in you. Just as having such partial control and power of decision, by right, over an animal or inanimate object would be to have a property right in it.

---

6. Lockean rights are the individual rights that the English philosopher John Locke (1632–1704) emphasizes in his *Second Treatise of Government*. They are rights we would have even if there were no government, including rights to life, liberty, and possessions. The minimal state is a state whose functions are limited to the protection of these basic individual rights.

End-state and most patterned principles of distributive justice institute (partial) ownership by others of people and their actions and labor. These principles involve a shift from the classical liberals' notion of self-ownership to a notion of (partial) property rights in *other* people.

## TEST YOUR UNDERSTANDING

1. According to Nozick, what types of principle does a theory of justice in holdings require? (Nozick does not attempt to state actual principles, but he does distinguish a few types of principle that are needed.)

2. State the difference between *end-state* principles and *historical* principles of justice. Give an example of each. Within the category of historical principles, sketch the difference between *patterned* and *unpatterned* principles. Give an example of each.

## NOTES AND QUESTIONS

1. What is the point of the Wilt Chamberlain example? Review Nozick's presentation of it and then consider four variants of the case. In each case, assume (following Nozick's presentation) that the status quo distribution fits a distributional pattern:

> *No Taxation 1*: Each person who attends a basketball game is required, as part of the admission fee, to drop $10 into a Wilt Chamberlain box. At the end of the season, the Chamberlain box has accumulated $10 million. Everything in the box is handed to Chamberlain as a supplement to his salary, with no taxes on this income.
>
> *No Taxation 2*: Each person who attends a basketball game is required to put $5 into a Wilt Chamberlain box and is given the option of also putting $5 into a Literacy Program box. Attendance is the same as in *No Taxation 1*. At the end of the season, the Chamberlain box has $5 million, which he receives without taxation, and the Literacy Program box has nothing. Chamberlain then gives his $5 million to the literacy program.
>
> *Taxation 1*: A tax rate of 50 percent is announced before the basketball season starts, and it is announced that the revenues will be spent on funding a literacy program. Chamberlain decides not to play, and so no money is put in the Wilt Chamberlain box. Attendance is 20% lower than it would have been, and everyone keeps their $10.
>
> *Taxation 2*: A tax rate of 50 percent is announced before the season starts, and it is announced that the revenues will be spent on a literacy program. Chamberlain plays and each person who attends drops $10 into the Wilt Chamberlain box. Once more, $10 million is accumulated in the box. Chamberlain gets $5 million and the $5 million in taxes goes to the literacy program.

(i) In *Taxation 1* and *Taxation 2*, do we have an intrusion on liberty? Whose liberty is burdened? (Notice that in *Taxation 2*, people willingly pay and Chamberlain willingly plays.)

(ii) How should we think about the use of the money to support the literacy program? Does that spending benefit the liberty of the people who receive the training?

(iii) Nozick says "liberty upsets patterns." In which of the four cases has liberty upset the previous pattern?

2. Nozick says "taxation on earnings from labor is on a par with forced labor." To illustrate: suppose James works 40 hours each week as a lawyer. Assume that it is illegitimate for the law to require James to spend eight of those hours (20 percent of his time) working at a school. (Do you think this assumption is correct, that it is illegitimate?) How, then, could it be legitimate to tax 20 percent of his earnings to support the school? "Seizing the results of someone's labor," Nozick says, "is equivalent to seizing hours from him and directing him to carry on various activities."

   Is Nozick right about this deep connection between taxation and forced labor? List some possible distinctions between being taxed to support the school and being required to work in the school. (Think about your own reactions to being taxed as distinct from being required to work in the school.) After you have a list, review Nozick's discussion of taxation and forced labor to see how it addresses the apparent differences. Is he right that the distinctions do not make a moral difference?

3. Nozick says that patterned conceptions are in conflict with the "classical liberal's notion of self-ownership." Patterned conceptions "institute (partial) ownership by others of people and their actions and labor." Nozick's idea is that each of us belongs fully to him- or herself; none belongs at all to humanity or to our state, church, community, race, ethnicity, or nation, nor to those who brought us into existence, whether the makers be biological parents or God. Because we fully own ourselves, we can sell ourselves into slavery if we wish to, or submit to unlimited political authority. Moreover, we are entitled to everything we can get other people to pay for the use of our talents.

   For discussion of the idea of self-ownership in Nozick's theory, see G. A. Cohen, *Self-Ownership, Freedom, and Equality* (Cambridge University Press, 1995), chapters 3 and 4.

4. The place of self-ownership in classical liberalism is a complex issue. John Locke is widely agreed to be a classical liberal, and Nozick presents some of his ideas as having a Lockean inspiration. In chapter 5 of his *Second Treatise of Government*, Locke suggests the idea of self-ownership when he says that each of us "has a property in his own person." See John Locke, *Two Treatises of Government* and *A Letter Concerning Toleration*, ed. Ian Shapiro (Yale University Press, 2003), §27 of *Two Treatises*. But Locke's position is founded on natural obligations based on natural laws established by God. Those natural laws qualify the rights we have in our own persons in two ways, each of which distinguishes Locke from Nozick. First, the natural laws limit what we are permitted to do to ourselves. We are not permitted, for example, to kill ourselves, enslave ourselves, or submit to an absolute political authority. We are not permitted to because the natural laws limit our authority over

ourselves: "A man cannot subject himself to the arbitrary power of another, but only so much as the law of nature gave him for the preservation of himself and the rest of mankind, this is all he doth or can give up to the commonwealth" (*Second Treatise*, §135). Second, the natural laws require us to assist others in certain cases, and not simply to care for ourselves: "when [a person's] own preservation comes not in competition, ought he, as much as he can, to preserve the rest of mankind" (*Second Treatise*, §6).

For an illuminating discussion of Locke's theory of rights and natural obligations, see A. John Simmons, *The Lockean Theory of Rights* (Princeton University Press, 1992).

# ANALYZING THE ARGUMENTS

1. Rawls describes several ways in which his principles of justice "express an egalitarian conception of justice." Restate the points in your own words. Does an "egalitarian" conception of justice say that all inequalities are unjust? If an egalitarian conception does not condemn all inequalities as unjust, what exactly makes it *egalitarian*? How would Rawls answer this question? What about Nussbaum and Wolff?

2. The idea of a patterned conception of distributive justice plays a central role in Nozick's discussion of distributive justice and his criticisms of egalitarian views of distributive justice. His entitlement conception is not patterned, whereas most other conceptions are patterned, he says. Review Nozick's definition of patterned conceptions. (Be sure to understand the differences between patterned conceptions and end-state conceptions of justice.) Is Rawls's conception of justice a patterned conception? What about Frankfurt's sufficiency doctrine? Does Wolff endorse patterned principles? Nussbaum? Do Nozick's criticisms of patterned views apply with equal force to all of these views?

3. Wolff mentions (and seems to endorse) the view that "a concentration on material wealth will be a distraction from what is truly important in life, including not only the cultivation of the mind but also one's relations with others." And he suggests that this view has led some egalitarians away from a focus on "the pursuit of income equality." How close is this view to Frankfurt's view that a focus on equality—on where you stand relative to others—is a harmful distraction from what matters and "contributes to the moral disorientation and shallowness of our time"? Wolff's point is that material resources are less important than people sometimes think, and that in relating to one another as equals, we should pay less attention to differences in material resources. Is Frankfurt concerned by excessive attention to material resources or excessive attention to equality?

   Do you think that a concentration on material resources is a distraction from what is truly important in life?

4. In his discussion of the basis of equality, of "the features of human beings in virtue of which we are to be treated in accordance with the principles of justice," Rawls asks: "On what grounds . . . do we distinguish between mankind and other living things and regard the constraints of justice as holding only in our relations to human persons"? Rawls's answer—his account of the basis of equality—provides a **sufficient condition** for being owed justice.

   (i) What is Rawls's proposed sufficient condition? Would there be troubles if Rawls treated the condition as also necessary? Reformulate Rawls's proposed condition as both necessary and sufficient for being owed justice. Does the answer seem any less plausible?

   (ii) Rawls says that the sufficient condition is "not at all stringent." Formulate a more stringent and a less stringent condition. Are either of the proposed conditions more plausible?

   (iii) Rawls says that we do best to assume that the sufficient condition is "always satisfied." What does he mean? And why is that the best thing to do?

Do you agree with Rawls that considerations of justice apply only to our "relations to human persons"? Do you think he has given a good explanation why?

Nussbaum expresses some reservations about Rawls's account of the basis of equality and offers her more "minimalist" account as an alternative. What precisely is the difference between Rawls's view and Nussbaum's minimalist view? What are her reservations? In addressing these issues, it will help to consider the following questions:

(i)   Does Nussbaum think that Rawls is offering a necessary condition for being owed justice?

(ii)  Does Nussbaum think that Rawls's condition is too stringent? In what ways is it too stringent?

(iii) When Rawls says that we do best to assume that his sufficient condition is "always satisfied," does he mean that we should assume it to be satisfied in the cases that Nussbaum is concerned about?

Is Nussbaum's minimalist answer more compelling than Rawls's answer to the question about the basis of equality?

# A Brief Guide to Logic
# and Argumentation

When a philosopher tackles a question, her aim is not just to answer it. Her aim is to provide an argument for her answer and so to present her audience with reasons for believing what she believes. When you read a philosophical text, your main job is to identify and assess the author's arguments. When you write a philosophy paper, your main job is to offer arguments of your own. And because philosophy is an especially reflective discipline — every question *about* philosophy is a philosophical question — philosophers have turned their attention to this phenomenon. What is an argument? What is a *good* argument? How can we tell whether an argument is a good one? The aim of this brief guide is to introduce some of the tools that philosophers have developed for answering these questions. But be warned: Some of what follows is controversial, and many of the most important questions in this area remain wide open. It may be unsettling to discover that even at this elementary stage philosophy raises questions that centuries of reflection have not resolved. But that is the nature of the subject, and you might as well get used to it.

## 1. What Is an Argument?

An **argument** is a sequence of statements. The last claim in the sequence is the **conclusion**. This is the claim that the argument seeks to establish or support. An argument will usually include one or more **premises**: statements that are simply asserted without proof in the context of the present argument but which may be supported by arguments given elsewhere. Consider, for example, the following argument for the existence of God:

## ARGUMENT A

(1)  The Bible says that God exists.

(2)  Whatever the Bible says is true.

(3)  Therefore, God exists.

Here the premises are (1) and (2), and statement (3) is the conclusion.

Now, anyone who propounds this argument will probably realize that his premises are controversial, so he may seek to defend them by independent arguments. In defense of (2) he may argue:

## ARGUMENT B

(4)  The Bible has predicted many historical events that have come to pass.

(5)  Therefore, whatever the Bible says is true.

These two arguments may be combined:

## ARGUMENT C

(6)  The Bible has predicted many historical events that have come to pass.

(7)  Therefore, whatever the Bible says is true.

(8)  The Bible says that God exists.

(9)  Therefore, God exists.

Here the premises are (6) and (8). Statement (7) is now an **intermediate conclusion**, supported by premise (6), and the conclusion of the argument as a whole is (9), which is in turn supported by (7) and (8). It can be useful to make all of this explicit by writing the argument out as follows:

## ARGUMENT C, ANNOTATED

(6)  The Bible has predicted many historical events that
     have come to pass.                                      [premise]

(7)  Therefore, whatever the Bible says is true              [from (6)]

(8)  The Bible says that God exists.                                [premise]

(9)  Therefore, God exists.                                        [from (7),(8)]

All of this is trivial when the arguments are simple and neatly packaged. But when you are reading a philosophical text with an eye toward identifying the author's argument, it is extraordinarily important (and often quite difficult) to distinguish the author's premises — the propositions she takes for granted as a starting point — from her conclusions. Why is this important? If a statement is meant as a conclusion, then it is fair to criticize the author if she has failed to give a reason for accepting it. If, on the other hand, a statement is a premise, then this sort of criticism would not be fair. Every argument must start somewhere. So you should not object to an argument simply on the ground that the author has not proved her premises. Of course you can object in other ways. As we will see, it is perfectly fair to reject an argument when its premises are false or implausible, or defective in some other way. The point is rather simply this: Since every argument must have premises, *it is not a flaw in an argument that the author has not argued for her premises.*

> *Rules of thumb:* If a sentence begins with "hence" or "therefore" or "so," that is a clue that it functions as a conclusion. If a sentence begins with "Let us assume that . . . " or "It seem perfectly obvious that . . . " or "Only a fool would deny that . . . ," this is a clue that it functions as a premise.

*Exercise:* Consider the following passage. What are the premises? What is the main conclusion?

> Everyone knows that people are usually responsible for what they do. But you're only responsible for an action if your choice to perform it was a free choice, and a choice is only free if it was not determined in advance. So we must have free will, and that means that some of our choices are not determined in advance.

# 2. Validity

An argument is **valid** if and only if it is *absolutely impossible* for its premises to be true and its conclusion false. In our examples, Argument A is clearly valid. If the premises are true — if the Bible is infallible, and if the Bible says that God exists — then God must certainly exist. There is no possible situation — no possible world — in which the premises of the argument are true and the conclusion false. Argument B, by contrast, is clearly **invalid**. It is easy to imagine a circumstance in which the Bible makes many correct predictions about historical events while remaining fallible on other matters. When an argument is valid, we say that the premises **entail** or **imply** the conclusion, or, equivalently, that the conclusion **follows from** the premises.

This concept of validity is a technical one, and some of its applications may strike you as odd. Consider:

ARGUMENT D

> All philosophers are criminals.
> All criminals are short.
> Therefore, all philosophers are short.

ARGUMENT E

> God exists.
> Therefore, God exists.

ARGUMENT F

> The moon is green.
> The moon is not green.
> Therefore, God exists.

It is easy to see that Argument D is valid. The premises are *false*, but that's irrelevant. They *could* have been true, and any possible circumstance in which they *are* true is one in which the conclusion is also true. Argument E is also valid. Since the premise and the conclusion are identical, it is clearly impossible for the one to be true and the other false. To see that Argument F is valid, note that it is obviously impossible for its premises to be true together — the moon cannot be both green and not green! But this means that it is impossible for the premises to be true and the conclusion false, and that is exactly our definition of validity.

As the examples show, a valid argument can be a *lousy* argument. Still, validity is an important property of arguments. Some disciplines — notably, mathematics — insist on valid arguments at every stage. In these areas, a good argument must be a **proof**, and a proof is a valid argument from premises known to be true. Philosophy, like most disciplines, does not insist on proof. Yet philosophers often aspire to produce valid arguments for their conclusions, and there is a good reason for this. Begin by noting that it is always possible to turn an invalid argument, or an argument whose validity is uncertain, into a valid argument by adding premises. Suppose a philosopher offers the following argument:

ARGUMENT G

> I can imagine existing without my body. (I can imagine my feet slowly and painlessly disappearing, then my knees, then my legs... As my body disappears, I lose all sensation. As my head disappears, everything goes black and silent because my eyes and ears have disappeared, but still I'm thinking about these strange events, and because I'm thinking, I must exist.)

> Therefore, I am not my body.

It may be hard to say whether this is a valid argument, but we can easily turn it into an argument whose validity is beyond dispute:

ARGUMENT H

> I can imagine existing without my body.
> If I can imagine X existing without Y, then X is not Y.
> Therefore, I am not my body.

A philosopher who offers Argument G as a proof that human beings are not identical to their bodies probably has Argument H in mind. She is probably tacitly *assuming* the premise that is missing in G but that H makes explicit. For philosophical purposes, it is often important to make these tacit assumptions explicit so that we can subject them to the bright light of scrutiny. *When you reconstruct the argument implicit in a philosophical text, you should set yourself the task of producing a valid argument for the author's conclusion from the author's stated premises, supplying any missing premises that might be necessary for this purpose, so long as they are premises that the author might have accepted.* If there are many ways to do this, you will find yourself with several competing interpretations of the argument. If there is only one sensible way of doing this (as with Argument G), you will have identified the author's tacit assumptions. This is often a valuable step in your effort to assess the argument.

*Exercise:* Spot the valid argument(s):

[i]   If abortion is permissible, infanticide is permissible.
      Infanticide is not permissible.
      Therefore, abortion is not permissible.

[ii]  It is wrong to experiment on a human subject without consent.
      Dr. X experimented on Mr. Z.
      Mr. Z consented to this experiment.
      Therefore, it was not wrong for Dr. X to experiment on Mr. Z.

[iii]   I will not survive my death.
        My body will survive my death.
        Therefore, I am not my body.

[iv]    Geoffrey is a giraffe.
        If X is a giraffe, then X's parents were giraffes.
        Therefore, all of Geoffrey's ancestors were giraffes.

*Exercise:* The following arguments are not valid as they stand. Supply missing premises to make them valid.

[v]     Every event has a cause.
        No event causes itself.
        Therefore, the universe has no beginning in time.

[vi]    It is illegal to keep a tiger as a pet in New York City.
        Jones lives in New York City.
        Therefore, it would be wrong for Jones to keep a tiger as a pet.

[vii]   The sun has risen every day for the past 4 billion years.
        Therefore, the sun will rise tomorrow.

> *Check your understanding.* Some statements express **necessary truths**: truths that could not possibly have been false under any circumstances. The truths of pure mathematics are the best examples. There is no possible circumstance in which $2 + 3 \neq 5$, so "$2 + 3 = 5$" is a necessary truth. With this in mind, show that an argument whose conclusion is a necessary truth is automatically a valid argument.

# 3. Soundness

A valid philosophical argument is a fine thing. But if the premises are false, it cannot be a good argument. Good arguments, after all, provide us with reasons for accepting their conclusions, and an argument with false premises cannot do that. Recall argument D:

ARGUMENT D

(1)  All philosophers are criminals.

(2)  All criminals are short.

(3)  Therefore, all philosophers are short

The argument is perfectly valid, but it obviously fails to establish its conclusion.

This means that when you evaluate a philosophical argument, it is never enough to show that the author's conclusions follow from her premises. You must also ask whether the premises are true. A valid argument with true premises is called a **sound** argument.

> *Check your understanding.* Use the definitions of soundness and validity to show that if an argument is sound, its conclusion must be true.

# 4.  How to Reconstruct an Argument: An Example.

One of the most important skills a philosopher can acquire is the ability to extract an explicit argument from a dense block of prose. There is no recipe for doing this: it is an art. Here we work through an example to illustrate one way of proceeding.

*Assignment:* Identify and assess the argument in the following passage.

> We see that things which lack intelligence, such as natural bodies, act for an end, and this is evident from their acting always, or nearly always, in the same way, so as to obtain the best result. Hence it is plain that not fortuitously, but designedly, do they achieve their end. Now whatever lacks intelligence cannot move towards an end, unless it be directed by some being endowed with knowledge and intelligence, as the arrow is shot to its mark by the archer. Therefore some intelligent beings exist by whom all natural things are directed to their end. (Thomas Aquinas, *Summa Theologica*, Part I, question 2, article 3)

## STEP 1: IDENTIFY THE CONCLUSION

When you seen an argument like this, your first job is to identify the main conclusion. Unsurprisingly, this will usually come at the end, though many writers will tell you at the start what the conclusion of the argument is going to be. (This is very helpful to the reader, and you should always do it in your own writing.) In this case, the main conclusion is helpfully marked by an explicit "therefore."

(Main Conclusion)    Some intelligent being exists by whom all natural things are directed to their end.

## STEP 2: INTERPRET THE CONCLUSION

Now that you have identified the conclusion, your next job is to understand it. This can be difficult, especially when the text is old and the language unfamiliar.

What is it for a being to be *intelligent*? What is a *natural* thing? In this case, the most pressing issue is to understand what it means for a natural thing to be "directed towards an end." As the context makes clear, a natural thing is anything that is not a person or an artifact — an animal or a plant, or perhaps a rock. What is it for such a thing to have an "end"? This is in fact a profound question, but to a first approximation, the end of a thing is its purpose or function. The *end* of the heart is to pump blood; the *end* of a worker bee is to supply food for the queen, and so on. The conclusion of the argument, reformulated in more familiar terms, is therefore this:

> (Main conclusion, reformulated)
>
> There is an intelligent being that ensures that natural objects perform their functions.

This illustrates a general point: When you analyze an argument, you are not required to employ the author's original words in every case. It is sometimes useful to supply more familiar words and grammatical constructions, provided they represent a plausible interpretation of the author's meaning. In this case, we have replaced Aquinas's talk of "ends" with talk of "functions."

### STEP 3: RECONSTRUCT THE ARGUMENT

Your next job is to reconstruct the argument for the main conclusion. What are the premises from which Aquinas argues? You might think that the first sentence states a premise: "We see that things which lack intelligence ... act for an end". But as we read on, it becomes clear that this is, in fact, an intermediate conclusion. The first sentence, taken as a whole, is itself an argument.

> Unintelligent things always or nearly always act in the same way, so as to achieve the best result. [premise]
> Therefore, unintelligent things perform a function.

This is an interesting argument, but the connection between the premise and the conclusion is obscure. As it stands, the argument is not clearly valid. But we can render it valid by interpolating an unstated premise:

(1) Unintelligent things always or nearly always act in the same way, so as to achieve the best result.

(2) If a thing always or nearly always acts in a certain way, so as to achieve the best result, then that thing performs a function.

(3) Therefore, unintelligent things perform a function.

This shows the value of making unstated premises fully explicit. The unstated premise (2) contains an important idea. The function of the heart is to pump blood. How do we know? Because hearts almost always pump blood, and this is a benefit to the organism as a whole. In general, when we see a natural thing acting in a way that provides a benefit, we infer that its function (or one of its functions) is to provide that benefit. The second premise makes this assumption explicit.

When we turn to the next sentence, we have a puzzle. "Hence it is plain that not fortuitously, but designedly, do they achieve their result." This sentence begins with "hence," so we naturally assume that it is supposed to be a conclusion supported by what precedes it. If we pursue this interpretation, the argument will look like this:

(1) Unintelligent things always or nearly always act in the same way, so as to achieve the best result. [premise]

(2) If a thing always or nearly always acts in a certain way, so as to achieve the best result, then that thing performs a function. [premise]

(3) Therefore, unintelligent things perform a function. [from (1) and (2)]

Therefore, unintelligent things perform their functions by design (and not by accident). [from ?]

The puzzle is that nothing in the argument appears to support this new conclusion. Why shouldn't natural beings perform their functions by accident rather than by design? Nothing in the text speaks to this question, and so it may be unclear whether Aquinas means this to be a new premise or an intermediate conclusion supported by what comes before.

Again, we can interpolate an unstated premise that will render the argument valid. Aquinas apparently finds it obvious that if a thing has a function, it must have been designed to perform that function. If this is right, then the complete argument up to this point runs as follows:

(1) Unintelligent things always or nearly always act in the same way, so as to achieve the best result. [premise]

(2) If a thing always or nearly always acts in a certain way, so as to achieve the best result, then that thing performs a function. [premise]

(3) Therefore, unintelligent things perform a function. [intermediate conclusion, from (1) and (2)]

(4) If a thing performs a function, it does so by design. [implicit premise]

(5) Therefore, unintelligent things perform their functions by design. [intermediate conclusion, from (3) and (4)]

The remainder of the argument is now straightforward. The next sentence states another premise.

(6) If an unintelligent thing performs a function by design, then there exists an intelligent being that ensures that it performs this function. [premise]

And from this, Aquinas moves directly to his main conclusion:

(7) Therefore, there exists an intelligent being that ensures that natural objects perform their functions. [conclusion, from (5) and (6)]

*What just happened?* We took a dense philosophical text and we turned it into an explicit argument. Along the way, we did our best to make the author's unspoken premises explicit and to understand what they might mean. The result is a **reconstruction** of the original argument.


STEP 4

We are now in a position to assess the argument as we have reconstructed it. We have two questions to ask: Is it valid, and are the premises true?

Taking the second question first, we twenty-first-century philosophers will have doubts about premise (1) — Do *most* natural things really act so as to achieve the "best result"? — and also about premise (6). The heart of an animal performs a function. Must it have been designed by an intelligent being for that purpose? Certainly not; natural selection can do the job even if no intelligence is involved. So the premises of the argument are certainly open to question.

But even if we waive this objection and suppose that the premises are true, there is a further problem. The conclusion (7) claims that there is a *single* intelligent being that ensures that natural things perform their functions. But the premises only require that each natural thing be directed toward its end by some intelligent being or other. To see the difference, note that it is one thing to say that every clock has a designer, and another to say that there is a single master-designer who is responsible for every clock. This means that we can accept Aquinas's premises and much of his reasoning without accepting his main conclusion. Even if every natural thing was designed by an intelligent being, it does not follow a single intelligent being designed them all. Verdict: *Aquinas's argument, as we have reconstructed it, is not valid.*

This brings up a very important point. We have given a reasonably careful reconstruction of Aquinas's argument, but despite our best efforts, the argument as we have reconstructed it is clearly *bad*. Now of course no one is perfect: good philosophers sometimes give bad arguments. But when you have produced a reconstruction of an argument by a good philosopher and the result is an argument that is clearly flawed, that is a sign that you may have misunderstood the original argument. The philosophers represented in this collection are all good philosophers, so you should approach their arguments with this in mind: *Before you dismiss an argument on the basis of your reconstruction of it, you should be sure that your reconstruction is the most charitable interpretation you can find.* A charitable reconstruction will present the argument in its best light. It may still involve mistakes, but they will not be gross and obvious mistakes. The most convincing way to object to a philosophical argument is to take the time to identify the best possible version of it, and then to show that *this* version of the argument is still no good.

*Exercise:* Provide a reconstruction of Aquinas's argument that does not commit the logical error mentioned above in the transition from (6) to (7).

# 5. Formal Validity

Consider:

ARGUMENT H

Every number is an abstract object.
Abstract objects are not located in space.
So numbers are not located in space.

This is a concrete argument with a specific subject matter. It is about numbers, spatial location, and so on. But we can abstract from these specific features of the argument in order to focus on its *form*. One way to do this is to replace all of the subject-specific terms in the argument with **schematic letters**, leaving only the logical skeleton of the argument in place. In the case of argument H, this yields the following **schematic argument**.

Every F is a G.
Gs are not H.
So Fs are not H.

Once we have identified this schematic argument, it is easy to produce other arguments that exhibit the same form but concern an entirely unrelated subject matter. For example:

ARGUMENT I

Every whale is a mammal.
Mammals do not lay eggs.
So whales do not lay eggs.

In this case it is clear not just that our original argument is valid but that any argument generated from it in this way must be valid. (The second premise in

Argument I is false, as every platypus knows. But that does not prevent the argument from being valid. If that puzzles you, review the definition of validity.) When an argument is an instance of a scheme all of whose instances are valid, the argument is said to be **formally valid**.

Note: An argument can be valid without being formally valid. Consider:

ARGUMENT J

> Every crayon in the box is scarlet.
> So every crayon in the box is red.

The underlying form of this argument is:

> Every F is G.
> So every F is H.

And it is obvious that many arguments of this form will not be valid. (Exercise: Give an example.) Of course, we can make Argument J formally valid by adding the premise, "If a thing is scarlet, then it is red." As we have emphasized, this is always worth doing when you are analyzing a philosophical argument. And yet, the original argument is valid as it stands, since it is absolutely impossible for the premise to be true and the conclusion false.

    **Formal logic** is the study of formally valid arguments. It aims to catalog the vast array of formally valid arguments and to provide general principles for determining whether any given argument has this feature. Formal logic is an intricate, highly developed subject at the intersection of philosophy and mathematics, and it can be extraordinarily useful for the student of philosophy. Here we list some examples of formally valid arguments along with their traditional names. In what follows the schematic letters P, Q and R stand for complete declarative sentences. For your amusement, we also include the standard symbolic representations of these forms of inference. Here '$\rightarrow$' means 'if ... then'; '$\sim$' means 'it is not the case that'; and '$\lor$' means 'or.'

*modus ponens*

| | |
|---|---|
| If P then Q | $P \rightarrow Q$ |
| P | P |
| —— | —— |
| Q | Q |

*modus tollens*

| | |
|---|---|
| If P then Q | $P \rightarrow Q$ |
| It is not the case that Q | $\sim Q$ |
| —— | —— |
| It is not the case that P | $\sim P$ |

*disjunctive syllogism*

| Either P or Q | $P \lor Q$ |
| It is not the case that P | $\sim P$ |
| --- | --- |
| Q | Q |

*hypothetical syllogism*

| If P then Q | $P \rightarrow Q$ |
| If Q then R | $Q \rightarrow R$ |
| --- | --- |
| If P then R | $P \rightarrow R$ |

*contraposition*

| If P then Q | | $P \rightarrow Q$ |
| --- | --- | --- |
| If it is not the case that Q, then it is not the case that P | | $\sim Q \rightarrow \sim P$ |

All of this may seem obvious, but it can sometimes be quite tricky to determine whether an argument is formally valid. Consider:

> A person is responsible for a choice only if it is a free choice.
> Every human choice is either caused or uncaused.
> If a choice is caused, then it is caused either by prior events, or by the agent himself.
> If a choice is caused by prior events, then it is not free.
> If a choice is uncaused, it is not free.
> So a choice is free only if it is caused by the agent himself
> But no choice is caused by the agent himself.
> So there is no such thing as a free choice.
> So no one is ever responsible for his choices.

Is this a valid argument? You could stare it for a while, and you might find yourself persuaded one way or the other. Or you could take a logic class and learn enough formal logic to settle the matter conclusively once and for all. One of the great advantages of formal logic is that it permits us to *prove* that an argument of this sort is valid by breaking it down into steps, each of which is indisputably an instance of a valid form.

# 6. A Puzzle about Formal Logic

Apart from its utility as a tool, formal logic is a source of philosophical perplexity in its own right. Imagine a long row of colored squares on the wall in front of you. The leftmost square — square 1 — is bright red; the rightmost square — square 1000 — is bright yellow. The squares in between run from red on the left through orange in the middle to yellow on the right. But there are so many of them that they satisfy the following condition:

(1) Square $n$ and square $n + 1$ are indistinguishable by ordinary means.

If you had a measuring device you might discover that they differ slightly in color, but you can't tell them apart just by looking, no matter how hard you try. (If you don't think this is possible, get out your paint set and play around. It is easy to produce a sequence of colored patches running from red to yellow that satisfies this condition.)

We now note what appears to be an obvious fact:

(2) If two things are indistinguishable by ordinary means, then if one of them is red, so is the other.

If someone shows you a red rose and tells you, "I've got another rose that's indistinguishable from this one, but it it's not red," you would know immediately that he was lying. It's built in to our concept of *red* that if two objects look just alike to the naked eye in broad daylight, then either both are red or neither is.

From these two premises, it follows by modus ponens that

(3) If square $n$ is red, then so is square $n + 1$.

But now we're in trouble. For we can reason as follows:

(4) Square 1 is red                                         [premise]

(5) If square 1 is red, then square 2 is red               [3]

(6) So square 2 is red                                      [4, 5, modus ponens]

(7) If square 2 is red, then square 3 is red               [3]

(8) So square 3 is red                                      [6, 7, modus ponens]

$\cdot$
$\cdot$
$\cdot$

(1002) So square 999 is red                                [1000, 1001, modus ponens]

(1003) If square 999 is red, then square 1000 is red       [3]

(1004) So square 1000 is red.                              [1002, 1003, modus ponens]

But this is nuts. It was built in to our description of the situation that square 1000 is not red; it is bright yellow!

What's gone wrong? If you look closely you will see that this argument has only three premises. Two of them are stipulated as part of our description of the situation: Square 1 is red, and adjacent squares are indistinguishable by ordinary means. The other premise is (2), the claim that there cannot be two indistinguishable things, one of which is red, the other not. The argument uses only one rule of inference: modus ponens. And this leaves us with only two responses to the paradox: Either (2) is false and there is a sharp cutoff between red and "not red" somewhere in our series, or modus ponens is not a valid rule of inference after all. What is the best response? The problem is called the **sorites paradox** (pronounced saw-*rye*-tees), and it remains unsolved.


# 7. What Makes an Argument Good?

We have seen (§2) that valid arguments can be lousy arguments. The same goes for sound arguments. The question of God's existence is the most important question in the philosophy of religion. But it is easy to produce a sound argument that settles it:


ARGUMENTS K AND L

> **K:** God exists.
>    Therefore, God exists.
> **L:** God does not exist.
>    Therefore, God does not exist.

These arguments are both formally valid, and one of them has true premises. That means that *one of them is sound*. But neither of these arguments is a contribution to philosophy, and neither could possibly provide a reason for believing its conclusion. Why not?

The obvious answer is that these arguments are defective because they are **circular** — their conclusions are included among their premises — and that is certainly a defect. This might tempt us to say that an argument is good if and only if it is sound and noncircular. But this is not quite right. Consider:


ARGUMENT M

> God knows when you will die.
> Therefore, God exists.

This argument may be sound, and the premise is clearly *different* from the conclusion, so it is not circular. And yet it is perfectly useless for establishing its conclusion. One way to bring this out is to note that anyone who doubts the conclusion will *automatically* doubt the premise. We cannot imagine a reasonable person *coming to believe* that God exists by first believing that God knows when she will die, and then *inferring* the existence of God. If she believes the premise, she must *already* believe the conclusion.

This shows something important. In a good argument, the premises must be credible *independently* of the conclusion. It must be possible for someone who has not already accepted the conclusion to accept the premise first, and to do so reasonably. This point is sometimes put by saying that a good argument must not **beg the question**. Imagine that you are arguing with someone who doubts your conclusion. Now ask: Could this person reasonably accept my premises if he has not already accepted my conclusion? If not, then the argument is bad in this distinctive way.

It is worth stressing, however, that this idea is not completely clear. Suppose you have read about the platypus but you are not sure that such things exist. (For all you know, the platypus may be extinct like the dodo, or legendary like the hippogriff.) A friend may set you straight as follows:

ARGUMENT N

> That thing in the bushes is a platypus.
> So platypuses exist.

This is a valid argument, and if it is sound — if your friend really is pointing to a platypus — it might give you an excellent reason for accepting its conclusion. Argument N is thus a good argument: it does not beg the question.

Now suppose that you have been impressed by Descartes' famous suggestion that for all you know, there is no external world at all, and in particular that for all you know, you are a disembodied spirit whose experiences are hallucinations produced in your minds by a malicious demon.[1] At this stage you are in the market for an argument to show that the material world — the world of rocks and trees and houses — really exists. Trying to be helpful, I hold up a rock and say:

ARGUMENT O

> This rock in my hand is a material object.
> So material objects exist.

Argument O has exactly the same form as argument N. Both are valid, and both may be sound. And yet it has seemed to many (though not to all) that given the context

---

1. René Descartes, "Meditation I: What May be Called Into Doubt," in his *Meditations on First Philosophy*, reprinted in chapter 7 of this anthology.

in which it has been given, Argument O begs the question. If you want to prove the existence of the material world to someone who doubts it, you can't just hold up a rock and say "Voilà!" Your interlocutor, after all, will not believe the rock is real.[2]

What is the difference between these two "proofs"? This is a difficult question. It is often easy to tell in practice when an argument begs the question — when it *presupposes* what it seeks to prove. But it is quite hard to provide a general rule for determining when an argument begs the question in this sense. This is one point at which our understanding of the contrast between good and bad arguments is incomplete.

# 8. Non-Demonstrative Arguments

So far we have been discussing valid arguments and asking, in effect: What is the difference between a good valid argument and a bad one? We have seen that a good valid argument must be sound, and that it must not beg the question. And there is no doubt that philosophers have often sought to provide arguments of just this sort. But it would be a grave mistake to suppose that every worthwhile argument must fit this description.

Consider:

ARGUMENTS P, Q, R, AND S

    **P:**   Everyone who has drunk hemlock has died soon afterwards
         ∴ If I drink this hemlock, I will die

    **Q:**  Despite years of looking, no one has ever seen a unicorn
         ∴ Unicorns do not exist

    **R:**  The cheese in the cupboard is disappearing
        We hear scratching sounds in the cupboard late at night
        There is a suspicious mouse-sized hole in the back of the cupboard.
         ∴ A mouse has come to live with us.

    **S:**   It's normally wrong to kill a person.
        The bartender is a person.
         ∴ It would be wrong to kill the bartender.

By ordinary standards, these are all excellent arguments. If you are trying to give me reason to believe that unicorns don't exist, or that I will die if I drink the hemlock, or that a mouse has infiltrated the kitchen, or that I shouldn't kill the bartender,

---

2. Samuel Johnson (1709–1784) disagreed. As his biographer reports:
   After we came out of the church, we stood talking for some time together of Bishop Berkeley's ingenious sophistry to prove the nonexistence of matter, and that every thing in the universe is merely ideal. I observed, that though we are satisfied his doctrine is not true, it is impossible to refute it. I never shall forget the alacrity with which Johnson answered, striking his foot with mighty force against a large stone, till he rebounded from it — "I refute it *thus.*" James Boswell, *Life of Johnson*, ed. G. B. Hill, Oxford University Press, 1935, v. 1, p.471.

these arguments ought to do the trick. But of course *these arguments are not valid*. In each case, it is logically possible for the premises to be true and the conclusion false. Unicorns may be very good at hiding. I may be a biological freak immune to hemlock. The evidence in the kitchen may be a hoax cooked up by my roommates as a joke. The bartender might be a dangerous fiend who will destroy the world unless I shoot him, and so on.

Arguments like P, Q, R, and S are called **non-demonstrative** arguments. (A **demonstration** is a valid proof; and since these arguments are not valid, they are not demonstrations.) A good non-demonstrative argument must have true premises, and it must not beg the question. But how do we distinguish a good non-demonstrative argument from a bad one? We have a developed theory of validity for demonstrative arguments, namely, formal logic. When it comes to non-demonstrative arguments, however, we have nothing comparable. The problem of formulating a general account of good non-demonstrative reasoning is one of the great open problems in philosophy. We cannot solve it here, but we can introduce some terminology that may be helpful.

Some non-demonstrative arguments exhibit a common form.

**Inductive arguments** take as premises a series of observations that exhibit a pattern, and then conclude that that the pattern holds as a general rule. Argument P is a very simple inductive argument. Its form appears to be this:

In the past, events of type A have always been followed by events of type B.
Therefore, in the future, events of type A will be followed by events of type B.

But it would be a mistake to suppose that every argument of this form is a good one. Consider:

In the past, every time a presidential election has been held in the United States, the winning candidate has been a man.
Therefore, in the future, every time a presidential election is held in the United States, the winning candidate will be a man.

As of 2015, the premise of this argument is true; but it would be silly to conclude that there will never be a female president on this basis. Philosophers have long hoped that there might be some sort of formal test for distinguishing the good inductive arguments from the bad ones, but that turns out to be impossible. (See Nelson Goodman's "New Riddle of Induction," reprinted in Chapter 4 of this volume.) The theory of statistical inference is an attempt to characterize the good inductive inferences in mathematical terms.

**Abductive argument** — also called **inference to the best explanation** — begins from some collection of settled facts, and then reasons backwards from these facts to the hypothesis that would best explain them. Arguments Q and R are abductive arguments. Their general form is roughly this:

Certain facts are observed. (The cheese is disappearing, etc.; no one has ever found a unicorn despite years of looking.)

The best explanation for these facts is H. (There is a mouse in the kitchen; there are no unicorns.)

H is a good explanation (and not merely the best of a bad lot).

Therefore, H is (probably) true.

Many of the arguments that one finds in the natural sciences are abductive. Whenever the scientist defends a theory about unobserved objects or events by appeal to evidence, the argument takes roughly this form. (Think about the chemist's case for molecules, or Darwin's case for evolution.) A theory of abductive argument will tell us what it is for a hypothesis to constitute the *best* explanation of the data, and it will identify the conditions under which it is reasonable to infer the truth of best explanation. This part of the theory of argumentation is even less well developed than the theory of inductive argument, and remains an active area of research.

Argument S is neither inductive nor abductive. Indeed, there is no standard name for arguments of this sort. Their general form is roughly this:

Normally, P.

∴ P.

We know that cats normally have four legs; so if we are told that Felix is a cat, it is reasonable to infer that Felix has four legs — unless, of course, we have special information about Felix that would suggest that he might be an exception. Argument of this sort may be especially important in ethics. Some writers hold that the general principles of ethics — unlike the laws of physics and mathematics — are not exceptionless rules but, rather, powerful but imperfect generalizations: rules that hold for the most part, but which tolerate exceptions. If that is so — and this is highly controversial — whenever we apply an ethical principle to a case in order to derive a verdict about how to act, our inference is of this nameless non-demonstrative form.

# 9. Some General Remarks on Argumentation in Philosophy

In some areas of inquiry — mathematics is the best example — the only good arguments are valid arguments. Suppose I want to argue for Goldbach's Conjecture: Every even number greater than 2 is the sum of two prime numbers.

If I have a lot of time on my hands, I might begin by checking some examples.

$$4 = 2 + 2 \quad \checkmark$$
$$6 = 3 + 3 \quad \checkmark$$
$$8 = 3 + 5 \quad \checkmark$$
$$10 = 3 + 7 \quad \checkmark$$

Impressed by the pattern but getting bored, I might program a computer to check some more examples, and if I do I can easily verify that

(#) Every even number between 2 and 10 billion is the sum of two prime numbers.

And yet it would be a mistake by mathematical standards to treat this as an argument for Goldbach's Conjecture. It is always *possible* that some even number I have not checked provides a counterexample. The inference from (#) to Goldbach's Conjecture is not valid, and in mathematics the only good arguments are valid arguments.

Philosophy grew up with mathematics, and philosophers have sometimes held themselves to a similar standard, insisting that the only good philosophical arguments are (non–question begging) valid arguments from true premises. (Indeed, they have often insisted on valid arguments from *indisputably* true premises.) This remains the gold standard for argument in philosophy. Interesting arguments of this sort are often possible, and when they are possible, they are desirable. When you reconstruct the arguments of the philosophers for the purposes of evaluating them, or when you give arguments of your own, it often makes sense to try for arguments of this sort.

And yet it is a mistake to suppose that philosophical arguments are only good when they are valid. As we have noted, the arguments that serve us well in science and in ordinary life—the arguments that persuade us that atoms and molecules exist, or that it would be wrong to kill the bartender—are often non-demonstrative in character. There is no good reason to hold philosophy to a higher standard. But, of course, this leaves us in a difficult position, since as we have stressed, there is no accepted account of when a non-demonstrative argument is a good one.

# Some Guidelines For Writing Philosophy Papers

Writing a good philosophy paper is a lot like writing a good paper in history, political science, literature, or biology. Yes, philosophy papers are a little different in that they require a particularly careful use of language and a particularly close examination of ideas and arguments. Still, a good philosophy paper is basically a good paper that happens to be about philosophy. So the guidelines we sketch here apply with equal force in other courses as well.

Generally speaking, a philosophy paper presents an argument in support of a thesis. Here are some examples of philosophical theses (as you will see, some are very broad and some are much narrower):

- Numbers are real.

- We cannot know that there are objects outside the mind.

- Van Inwagen's argument for the incompatibility of free will and determinism is unpersuasive.

- The best interpretation of Hume's theory of causation is as follows. (Here you supply your own interpretation of Hume's theory.)

- Moral convictions are nothing more than strongly held feelings.

- The ontological proof of God's existence is flawed because (here you state what you see as the principal flaw).

Although philosophy papers require careful, abstract, critical reasoning, they also have a personal side. You are saying what you think and trying to defend it. When you do that, you expose your ideas—thus yourself—to criticism. The only way to learn from writing a paper is to accept that vulnerability, be as clear as you can about what you think, and make the best case for your views. You can try to protect your ideas by obscuring them with a blur of words, but that defeats the purpose.

Writing a paper—with this blend of abstract reasoning and personal conviction—is best approached in a social way, as if you were in a dialogue with another person. So you should write with a particular reader in mind: a friend, or a student in another class who wonders what you are working on. Write the paper as if you were directing your argument to this particular person. Your reader can, of course, only read your paper, not your mind. So you need to tell him or her what you are aiming to show in the paper, to consider where he or she will need some more explanation, to ask yourself where your reader might have some doubts about what you are saying, to articulate those doubts for your reader, and to try to answer them.

More specifically,

1. **State the main thesis** of your paper at the beginning, preferably in the opening paragraph. It is not bad to say something like: "I will argue that . . . ." (Although in some fields, using the first-person pronoun is frowned on, in philosophy it is encouraged: it is a straightforward method of conveying your perspective.) If you do not have a thesis, then get one. You are not expected to remain above the fray. Take a position!

2. **Take seriously the philosophers you are discussing.** The philosophers you are reading are not fools, even if their views or arguments are incorrect. Keep in mind that the readings in your course are the product of sustained reflection. The authors often distributed drafts of their manuscripts to other people who disagreed with them, and then tried to incorporate responses to objections. Their views may not be right, or fully coherent, or nice. But you can safely assume that they have greater depth and coherence than a first reading might suggest.

   A first step toward taking a philosopher seriously is to make your criticisms and points of agreement explicit, rather than simply expressing your approval or disapproval of what you have read. Suppose, for example, you think that David Hume's views on causation are wrong. Before you start writing a paper, you will first need to clarify your disagreement with Hume. Are you disputing his assumptions, or the reasoning that leads from his assumptions to his conclusion? Then try to "argue against yourself": how would Hume respond to your criticism? This means that you will need to get "inside" his view and develop a sense of its internal integrity.

3. **Keep the writing focused.** Do not pad your paper with digressions from the main topic. For example, suppose you are examining Hobbes's argument that in a state of nature, with no political authority, we would all be at war with one another. You will need to explain why he thinks we need an authority to keep us from fighting each other. You should *not* also discuss his views on monarchy. Confine yourself to the aspects of Hobbes's view that are of immediate relevance to your thesis.

4. **Avoid sweeping generalities.** Forget such profundities as: "Since Plato, philosophers have sought out the meaning of justice," or "For millennia, human beings have searched for truth." (What about: "Man is born free, but is everywhere in chains"? If you are Jean-Jacques Rousseau, you are allowed to violate our guidelines.) By distracting from your point, such remarks subtract substance. Moreover, they suggest that you are unsure of what to say and are looking to fill space. So just get right to the point.

5. **Write clearly.** Philosophical ideas are often abstract and subtle, which makes it is easy to get lost. You should therefore write short sentences, avoid very long paragraphs, and be sure to signal transitions. If a sentence occupies more than (say) five lines, find a way to divide it up; similarly if a paragraph goes on for more than 20 lines. If your paper falls into sections, make sure to include a sentence or two of connective tissue between them. Assume that your reader is unfamiliar with philosophical vocabulary, which means that you will need to explain the philosophical terms in your paper. If possible, define them. At the very least, give examples of how the terms are used. Note that writing philosophy does not require esoteric words, or long words, or newly invented words. Nor do you need to strive to use different words to express the same concept within the same paragraph or page: indeed, it is helpful if you stick with the same term. Your papers need to focus readers' attention on the ideas you wish to express, not on the words you have chosen to express those ideas. As George Orwell (the author of *1984*) wrote, "Good prose is like a windowpane." Bad writing is a smudge on the window.

6. **Support assertions.** When you attribute a position to someone, provide some evidence for the attribution by citing relevant passages. You need not include quotations. As a general rule, you should only quote a passage if the passage plays an important role in your paper (say, it is a passage that you will want to be able to refer back to at various points in the argument), or if you think that there is some controversy about whether the philosopher held the view you are attributing to him or her. Your paper should not string together lots of quotations.

7. **Do not confuse philosophy with a debate team.** The point in a philosophy paper is not to win a competition but to isolate the truth of the matter. One good argument, explored in depth, beats three or four quick and dirty ones. Indeed, the best philosophy papers identify objections to the author's thesis and state those objections in the strongest way possible. Try to do this. It is an intellectual virtue to admit where the weaknesses of your argument lie rather than to pretend that your position faces no difficulties.

8. **Leave time for substantial revision and rethinking.** After you have written your first draft, put it aside for an hour or a day and then reread it for clarity, organization, and soundness. Does each argument contribute to the overall

position? Is it directly germane to your thesis? Are the arguments presented in a logical order? Could someone unfamiliar with the ideas or arguments you are discussing follow what you are saying? Edit your paper accordingly. If in the course of your revisions you find that you cannot respond to one of the objections that you have raised to your thesis, change your thesis and start over. The aim is not to defend your first thoughts on the topic but to defend your *considered* views, and these may well change during the process of writing. Expect to rewrite your paper more than once.

9. As part of your editing process, **read your paper aloud.** If it does not *sound* right, it will not read right. Rewrite any part of it that sounds unclear or weak in argumentation.

# Glossary

**A posteriori**  Dependent upon experience. Person $S$ knows $p$ a posteriori (or *empirically*) iff S's knowledge of $p$ depends upon her experience. Smith's knowledge that Shakespeare died in 1616 is a posteriori, whether she knows it first hand (as an eyewitness) or on the basis of testimony. (In the latter case, her knowledge depends on her experience of the testimony.) A **proposition** is a posteriori iff it can only be known a posteriori. An **argument** is a posteriori iff it contains at least one a posteriori premise. The **Design argument** is an a posteriori argument for the existence of God.

See also **a priori**.

**A priori**  Prior to, or independent of, experience. Person $S$ knows $p$ a priori (or *nonempirically*) iff S's knowledge of $p$ does not depend on his experience. Our knowledge of logic and pure mathematics is widely (though not universally) held to be a priori. A **proposition** is a priori iff it can be known a priori. An **argument** is a priori iff all of its premises are a priori.

**Abduction**  See **inference to the best explanation**.

**Absolute sovereign**  See **sovereign**.

**Abstract object**  An object that does not exist in space and lacks causal powers. The existence of abstract objects is controversial, but possible examples include mathematical objects like the number 17, fictional characters like Spiderman, abstract **types** like the Greek letter "$\alpha$" (as distinct from the concrete inscription of the letter on this page of your copy of this book), and **propositions** like the proposition that snow is white.

**Accident**  See **essence**.

**Actual world**  See **possible world**.

**Agent causation**  Sometimes called "immanent causation"; an irreducible causal relation between an agent and an **event**, as when Jones directly causes an event in his mind or brain. The existence of agent causation is controversial. Agent causation contrasts with *event causation* (also called "transeunt causation"), the uncontroversial sort of causal relation in which an event is caused by prior events.

Most statements which seem to cite an agent (or an object) as a cause are really shorthand for claims of event causation. Instead of saying that *the rock* caused the window to break one could have said more long-windedly that an event involving the rock—e.g., the *collision of the rock with the window*—caused the window to break. Proponents of agent causation hold that in certain special cases there is no shorthand of this sort. To say that John caused his arm to move isn't to say that an event involving John caused the movement, but that John himself was the cause.

**Agnosticism**  In the philosophy of religion, the view that we cannot know whether God exists and should therefore suspend judgment about God's existence. More generally, a person is *agnostic* about a topic if and only if he or she adopts a principled suspense of judgment on that topic. ("Pauline is agnostic about the existence of abstract objects.")

**Analogical argument**  An **argument** of the form:

P1. *A* resembles *B* in so-and-so respects
P2. *B* has property *F*
Therefore
C. *A* has property *F*

**Analysandum, analysans**  See **analysis**.

**Analysis**  To analyze a word or a **concept** is to define it in more basic terms. For example, "triangle" can be analyzed as "plane figure with three interior angles." The word or concept to be analyzed (for example, "triangle") is the *analysandum*; the proposed definition (for example, "plane figure with three interior angles") is the *analysans*. Philosophical analyses are standardly formulated as general **biconditionals**, e.g.,

*X* is a triangle iff *X* is a plane figure with three interior angles
*S* knows *p* iff *S* believes *p*, *S*'s belief is **justified**, and *p* is true

"Analysis" can denote either the process of analyzing words or concepts ("Philosophical analysis is difficult") or the product of this process ("Jill's analysis of the concept *knowledge* was influential").

**Analytic and Synthetic**  A sentence is analytic iff it is "true solely in virtue of its meaning," or "true by definition" or "true by virtue of linguistic convention."

Alternatively, a sentence is analytic iff any competent speaker of the language is in a position to recognize its truth simply by virtue of being a competent speaker.

Examples are controversial (on either understanding of "analytic"), but possibilities include:

An even number is divisible by 2.
Red is a color.
Nothing can be red and green all over.
If *a* is taller than *b*, then *b* is shorter than *a*.

A true sentence that is not analytic is *synthetic*.

**Antecedent**  See **conditional**.

**Argument**  In logic, a list or sequence of **propositions** or *statements*: $p_1, \ldots p_n, c$. (Alternatively, a list of *sentences*: "$P_1$," ... "$P_n$," "$C$.") $p_1, \ldots p_n$ are the **premises** and *c* is the *conclusion*. See also **soundness and validity**.

**Argument from evil**  Sometimes called the *problem of evil* or the *argument from suffering*. An argument against the existence of God that proceeds from the premise that some people and animals suffer unnecessarily. A simple version:

P1. If God exists, then God is omnipotent and perfectly good.
P2. A perfectly good being would prevent unnecessary suffering if it could.
P3. An omnipotent being could prevent unnecessary suffering.

Therefore:

C1. If God exists, there is no unnecessary suffering.

P4. There is unnecessary suffering.

Therefore:

C2. God does not exist.

The argument is sometimes presented as a **proof** that there is no God. In more recent versions, the existence of apparently unnecessary suffering is adduced as powerful *evidence* that there is no God. An attempted answer to the argument from evil is a *theodicy*.

**Aristotelian** Resembling the views of Aristotle (384–322 BC). *Aristotelian ethics* is an approach to ethical theory that focuses on the question: What is the best human life?, explores the virtues that are required for living the best human life, and — in some formulations — connects the notion of the best human life with an account of human nature.

**Aristotelian logic** A system of logic due to Aristotle (384–322 BC) and his followers which attempts a complete catalogue of valid arguments. Aristotelian logic assumes that every assertion contains two terms, a subject "$S$" and a predicate "$P$," which may be either particular ("Socrates") or general "human being." An assertion either affirms or denies that the predicate holds of the subject. Assertions are therefore of the form:

Every $S$ is $P$

Some $S$ is $P$

No $S$ is $P$

Not every $S$ is $P$

Aristotelian logic aims to reduce all valid arguments to sequences of *syllogisms*: two premise arguments involving assertions of this sort, where the premises must have at least one term in common. For example

No human being is immortal

Every sailor is a human being

Therefore:

No sailor is immortal

The great achievement in this tradition is a complete catalog of the various forms of valid syllogism, and a set of techniques for reducing arguments to sequences of syllogisms. The limits of Aristotelian logic were clear by the 14th century. For example, the following argument is valid, though not representable as a valid Aristotelian syllogism:

Every horse is an animal

Therefore:

The head of a horse is the head of an animal

Modern logic is developed on rather different principles.

**Atheism** The view that there are no gods.

**Autonomy** Literally, *self-rule*. In ethics, the capacity of rational agents to act on reflectively endorsed reasons or principles, and not simply in response to non-rational impulses, desires or feelings.

In political philosophy, the capacity of individuals to determine how they will live. *Private autonomy* is the capacity to determine the course of one's own life. *Public autonomy* is the capacity to decide, along with the others, the basic rules and regulations of public order. A political system designed to promote autonomy will involve limits on coercive interference; but it may also involve of legal rules designed to ensure that individual choices are not driven by need or by the domination of others, e.g., a system of public assistance funded by taxes.

**Axiom** Broadly, an assumption; a claim taken for granted without proof or argument. More narrowly, one of a class of privileged statements in the presentation of a formal theory. Classically, an axiom is a proposition that "neither needs nor admits of proof," but which is nonetheless clearly true. For example, "Every natural number has a successor," is an axiom in the standard theory of arithmetic. In modern mathematics it is common to present a theory by specifying its axioms, and then to study the theory without regard to the truth of its axioms. The **theorems** of a theory are the *logical consequences* (see **entailment**) of its axioms.

## B

**Basic belief and knowledge** A belief in *p* is *basic* for a person *S* iff *S* believes *p* but has no reasons or evidence (distinct from *p* itself) that supports *p*. A belief in *p* is **properly basic** for *S* iff it is basic for *S* and **justified**. Properly basic **propositions** are those we are justified in believing without further evidence. A belief in *p* is *basic knowledge* for *S* iff it is basic for *S* and *S* knows *p*.

**Begging the question and circular arguments** An **argument** is *circular* iff if its conclusion is also one of its premises. The simplest form of such an argument "*P*, therefore *P*." Note that there is need be no *logical* flaw in a circular argument: "*P*, therefore *P*" is **valid**, and may well be **sound**. The problem is that circular arguments cannot justify their conclusions, and so cannot provide a rational basis for accepting their conclusions. Circular arguments are unpersuasive because they *beg the question*: anyone who does not already believe the conclusion will not believe one of the premises. More generally, an argument begs the question against person *S* iff *S* regards the justification of a premise of the argument as resting on the truth of the conclusion.

Note that a **cogent** argument may sometimes beg the question against certain people. Consider:

P1: Radiocarbon dating shows these bones to be 60,000 years old.
Therefore:
C: The Earth is more than 6,000 years old and young-Earth creationism is false.

This argument may beg the question against a biblical literalist who maintains that P1 depends for its justification on the assumption that young-Earth creationism is false; and yet the argument is cogent in the sense that a reasonable person might come to accept the conclusion on the basis of it.

More controversially, some philosophers hold that the following argument is cogent.

P1: I have a hand
Therefore:
C: At least one material object exists.

Yet this argument begs the question against a **skeptic** who doubts the existence of the material world.

**Behaviorism** In psychology, the view that the proper object of psychological study is behavior, and that explanations of behavior that appeal to internal states and processes are to be avoided. In the philosophy of mind, the view that **mental states** are **dispositions** to behave in such-and-such ways. *Analytical behaviorism* is the view that mental state **concepts** can be **analyzed** in terms of behavior.

**Biconditional** A statement of the form "*P* if and only if *Q*" or some related form, either in a natural language or a formal logical language. Usually written in symbolic logic as "$P \leftrightarrow Q$".

**Burden of proof** In law, the burden of proof lies with the party who must prove his case if he is to prevail. (The term is also sometimes used to refer to the standard of certainty with which one's case must be proved if one is to prevail.) More generally, the burden of proof in a debate or controversy lies with the party who must provide positive evidence for his view if it is to be accepted.

## C

**Categorical Imperative** In **Kantian** moral philosophy, an imperative of the form "Do A in circumstances C" is categorical iff it is binding on all rational agents regardless of their particular desires, plans or commitments. The phrase is sometimes used for basic principles of ethics that Kant himself deemed categorical, for example:

> Act only in accordance with that maxim through which you can at the same time will that it become a universal law. (Kant's "Formula of Universal Law")
> So act that you use humanity, whether in your own person or in the person of any other, always at the same time as an end, never merely as a means. (Kant's "Formula of Humanity")

**Circular argument** See **begging the question and circular arguments**.

**Classical foundationalism** See **foundationalism**.

**Closure principle** In epistemology, a principle affirming that knowledge or **justified belief** is "closed" under some form of **entailment**. For example:

> If *S* knows *p*, and *p* entails *q*, then *S* knows *q*.

or

> If *S* is justified in believing *p*, and *S* knows that *p* entails *q*, then S is justified in believing *q*.

**Cogent argument** An **argument** that genuinely establishes its conclusion. Alternatively, an argument whose premises provide good, though perhaps inconclusive, grounds for accepting its conclusion.

**Compatibilism** The view that **free will** is compatible with **determinism**. Alternatively, the view that **moral responsibility** is compatible with determinism.

**Concept** The meaning of a word or phrase. "Cat" (in English) and "gato" (in Spanish) both mean *cat*: that is, they both express the concept *cat*. Alternatively, concepts are symbols in the brain — perhaps words in some neural language — that are used in thinking.

**Conceptual analysis** See **analysis**.

**Conditional** A sentence of the form "If $P$, then $Q$", or some related form, either in a natural language or a formal logical language. "$P$" is the *antecedent* of the conditional and "$Q$" the *consequent*. Some important varieties of conditionals include:

> **Material conditional**: in symbolic logic, usually written as "$P \supset Q$" or "$P \rightarrow Q$". By definition, the material conditional is false when its antecedent is true and its consequent is false, and true in all other cases, even when the antecedent and consequent are entirely unrelated. For example, the following material conditionals are true:
>
> > $2 + 2 = 4 \supset$ Albany is the capital of New York
> > $2 + 2 = 5 \supset$ the moon is made of cheese
> > $2 + 2 = 5 \supset$ Albany is the capital of New York
>
> whereas the following is false:
>
> > $2 + 2 = 4 \supset$ the moon is made of cheese
>
> **Counterfactual conditional**: A sentence of the form "If it were that $P$, it would be that $Q$" or "If it had been that $P$, it would have been that $Q$."
>
> **Indicative conditional**: A natural language sentence of the form "If $P$, then $Q$" where "$P$" and "$Q$" are in the indicative mood, e.g., "If Bob is not in his office, he's at home." Some philosophers hold that indicative conditionals are material conditionals. But consider:
>
> > If Ronald Reagan was a spy, no one knew it.
> > If Ronald Reagan was a spy, he was a spy for the Martians.
>
> The corresponding material conditionals (e.g. "Ronald Reagan was a spy $\supset$ no one knew it") are both true, since their antecedents are false and that is enough to render a material conditional true. But the first conditional seems true and the second false. This suggests that indicative conditionals are not material conditionals.

**Conjunction** A sentence of the form "$P$ and $Q$," or some related form either in a natural language or a formal logical language. In symbolic logic, usually written as "$P$ & $Q$" or "$P \wedge Q$." By definition, "$P$ & $Q$" is true iff both *conjuncts* — "$P$" and "$Q$" — are true.

**Consequent** See **conditional**.

**Consequentialism** The view that the moral rightness of an act depends entirely on the (actual or expected) value of its consequences. Historically, the most important form of consequentialism is **utilitarianism**, but the general framework permits a variety of alternatives.

**Consistency** A set of sentences (or **propositions**) is consistent iff it possible for all of the sentences (or propositions) in the set to be true together. For example, the set {"John is happy," "John is rich"} is consistent, since it is possible for someone to be both happy and rich. By contrast, the set {"John is rich," "John is not rich"} is not consistent since it is impossible for the two sentences to be true together.

**Constructivism** In moral philosophy, the view that the truth of a moral claim is determined, not by its conformity to mind-independent reality, but rather by the fact that it would be accepted by members of some (perhaps idealized) individual or group after informed reflection.

**Content (of a mental state)** Some **mental states**, for example *believing that grass is green*, appear to involve **relations** to **propositions** — in this cases, the proposition that grass is green. (See **propositional attitudes**.) When a mental state involves a relation to a proposition, the proposition is called the "content" of the state, or sometimes its *representational* or *intentional* content. Thus the content of the state of believing that grass is green is the proposition that grass is green.

**Contextualism** In epistemology, the view that the truth or falsity of a **propositional knowledge** attribution — a statement of the form "S knows *p*" — depends on the context in which the sentence is uttered. Suppose a student is asked, "Who wrote *Hamlet*?" and answers "Shakespeare." Now consider two utterances of "The student *knows* that Shakespeare wrote *Hamlet*," one made by her English teacher in an ordinary classroom context, the other made by a scholar during the course of a heated academic debate about whether Shakespeare really wrote the plays attributed to him. According to the contextualist, the first utterance may be true and the second false: the student's belief may count as knowledge *by ordinary standards*, but not by the more demanding standards of scholarly debate.

**Contingent proposition** See **possibility and necessity**.

**Contractualism** Broadly, the view that moral principles are justified by an actual or hypothetical agreement by members of a society, usually conceived as being forged under fair conditions of choice.

More narrowly, the view that an act is morally right because it is permitted by principles that informed, reasonable people would accept (or would not reject) for the purposes of regulating their conduct in society. See **Social Contract Theory**.

**Contrapositive** The contrapositive of a **conditional**, "If *P* then *Q*," is the conditional, "If not-*Q*, then not-*P*."

**Converse of a relation** See **relation**.

**Cosmic (or cosmological) fine-tuning argument** A version of the **design argument** for the existence of God based on the alleged fact that if the numerical constants in the fundamental laws of nature had been slightly different, there would have been no organized matter and hence no life anywhere in the universe. This premise is sometimes put as the claim that the basic laws of nature appear "fine tuned" to support the existence of life.

**Cosmological argument** An argument for the existence of God that begins from a manifest fact about the natural world — e.g., the fact that objects are in motion — and then argues that this fact entails the existence of an **entity** that differs from ordinary objects in fundamental respects: an uncaused cause, or a first mover. Every version of the cosmological argument exploits general principles about causation and explanation, e.g., the principle that whatever comes to be comes to be from something else. A simple version:

P1. Some object *X* has come into existence.
P2. Whenever an object comes into existence, its existence is caused by something else.
Therefore:
C1. *X*'s existence is caused by something else, *Y*.
Therefore (from P2 and C1):

C2. If $Y$ has come into existence, then its existence was caused by something else, $Z$.

P3. This sequence of causes cannot go on forever or loop round in a circle. Therefore:

C3. There must be at least one object that has not come into existence.

Cosmological arguments rarely purport to establish the existence of the God of Christianity, Islam, etc. Rather they purport to show that there must be at least one being that differs from ordinary objects (and resembles God) in fundamental metaphysical respects.

**Counterexample** A particular case that refutes a general claim. The discovery of a black swan refutes the general claim that all swans are white and is thus a counterexample to that claim. If the general claim is supposed to be only *contingently* true, as in the example just given, the particular case must actually obtain. If the general claim is meant to be a *necessary* truth, as is common in philosophy, then it can be refuted by a merely *possible* counterexample. (See **possibility and necessity**.) Thus if a philosopher claims that, necessarily, an act is free only if the agent could have acted differently, her claim can be refuted by describing a merely possible case in which an agent acts freely but could not have acted differently.

**Counterfactual conditional** See **conditional**.

**Counterfactual dependence** An event $e_2$ counterfactually depends on an event $e_1$ iff $e_2$ would not have occurred if $e_1$ had not occurred.

**Criterion of personal identity** A general specification of the conditions under which a person existing at one time is **numerically identical** to (the very same person as) a person existing at another time. A criterion of personal identity is often given by a principle of the form:

Person $A$ who exists at $t_1$ = Person $B$ who exists at $t_2$ iff $A$ stands in relation $R$ to $B$,

where R is specified without using the word "person" or any synonym thereof. For example,

Person $A$ at $t_1$ = Person $B$ at $t_2$ iff $A$'s soul at $t_1$ = $B$'s soul at $t_2$.

or

Person $A$ at $t_1$ = Person $B$ at $t_2$ iff at $t_1$, $B$ can remember some experience $A$ had at $t_1$

**D**

**Decision theory** Also *rational choice theory*. The effort to state general principles that specify which option a rational agent should choose in any given situation as a function of the agent's preferences or **utilities** and her degrees of confidence.

**Demarcation problem** The problem of drawing the boundary between science and pseudoscience.

**Demonstrative argument** See **proof**.

**Demonstrative certainty.** For David Hume and other early modern philosophers, a proposition is demonstratively certain iff it can be known with certainty, but only on the basis of a **proof**.

Demonstrative certainty contrasts with **intuitive certainty**, the certainty of a proposition that can be known without proof or reasoning. For example, the Pythagorean Theorem (that the square of the length of the hypotenuse of a right triangle is equal to the sum of the squares of the other two sides) is (at best) demonstratively certain, whereas "1 = 1" might be intuitively certain.

**Deontology** Originally, the part of ethics concerned with duty and obligation. In contemporary usage, the term is normally reserved for non-consequentialist theories of right action, and more specifically for theories according to which the basic principles of ethics consist in highly general non-consequentialist rules of conduct. In this contemporary sense, deontology is an alternative to **consequentialism**, but also to **virtue ethics** and to *particularism*, the view that there are no general rules that specify the conditions under which an act is right.

**Design arguments** Arguments for the existence of God that begins with the premise that nature exhibits marks of purpose or "apparent design." Design arguments sometimes point to objects that are particularly well suited for certain purposes: the eye for seeing, the hand for grasping. In other cases they point to general marks of design — ordered complexity — whose underlying purpose may not be evident. Design arguments typically proceed by **inference to the best explanation**:

P1. The natural world exhibits such-and-such signs of apparent design.
P2. The best explanation of this apparent design posits a supernatural being.
Therefore:
C: A supernatural being exists.

**Determinism** Roughly, the thesis that the state of the universe at any one time determines the state of the universe at all future times. In older treatments, determinism is formulated as the claim that every event is determined (or necessitated) by prior causes. In contemporary treatments, determinism is often defined as the thesis that:

For any time $t$, the complete state of the universe at $t$ and the laws of nature together entail the state of the universe at every later time.

*Indeterminism*, the negation of determinism, is the thesis that the laws of nature and the state of the universe at $t$ do not in general determine the state of the universe at later times, and so leave room for genuine randomness or chance.

**Difference Principle** In the political philosophy of John Rawls (1921–2002), a principle of justice according to which social and economic inequalities are just only if they arise under a system of rules that works for the maximum benefit of the least well-off members of society.

**Disjunction** A sentence of the form "*P* or *Q*," or some related form either in a natural language or a formal logical language. In symbolic logic, usually written as "$P \vee Q$." By definition, "$P \vee Q$" is true iff at least one *disjunct* — "*P*" or "*Q*" — is true.

**Disposition** In metaphysics, the tendency, power, or propensity of an object to behave in certain ways under certain conditions. Thus, fragility is a disposition (or a dispositional **property**), since it consists in the tendency to break when struck or dropped.

**Doctrine of double effect**  In ethics, a principle governing actions that have both good and bad effects, according to which the permissibility of the act depends on whether the bad effect is intended or merely foreseen. Ethicists dispute how it should be formulated (and whether it is correct). One version of the principle states:

> It is permissible to perform an action that foreseeably has both good and bad effects iff:
>
> a. the act itself (apart from its consequences) is not intrinsically immoral;
> b. the agent does not intend the bad effect, either as a means or as an end;
> c. the good effect is not produced by means of the bad effect;
> d. the value of the good effect is sufficiently great to warrant causing the bad effect.

It is also sometimes referred to as the *principle* of double effect or the *law* of double effect.

**Dominance reasoning**  In **decision theory**, a rule according to which it is rational to choose the *dominant act* when one exists. In a choice between actions A and B, action A *dominates* B when the **utility** of A is at least as great as the utility of B however things turn out, and greater in at least one case. For example, in a choice between an act A that pays $5 if it rains and $10 if it does not rain, and another act B that pays $4 if it rains and $10 if it does not rain, A is the dominant option, since A is better than B in one case and at least as good in every other. Dominance reasoning instructs the agent to choose option A in this situation. Note: In many decision problems there is no dominant act, in which case dominance reasoning is not available.

**Doxastic voluntarism**  The view that our beliefs are sometimes under our direct voluntary control.

**Dualism**  In the philosophy of mind, dualism comes in two varieties.

> **Substance dualism:** the view that there are two fundamentally distinct kinds of **substance**: thinking things and material (or physical) things. This was famously defended by René Descartes (1596–1650), so is often called *Cartesian* dualism. Descartes also held that a thinking thing and its associated material body causally interact, and this is sometimes called Cartesian *interactionism*.
>
> **Property dualism:** the view that there are two fundamentally distinct kinds of **property**: mental properties (e.g., the property of being in pain) and physical properties (e.g., the property of having a brain with such-and-such neural firing pattern).
>
> Dualists reject **physicalism**.

## E

**Efficient cause**  See **four causes**.

**Eliminativism**  In the philosophy of mind, the view no one has ever been in any **mental state** (or in a mental state of a certain kind), and that mentalistic vocabulary should ultimately be eliminated from scientific psychology.

For example, eliminativism about belief is the view that no one has ever believed anything, and so psychologists should not use the word "belief" any more than biologists should use "Bigfoot." More generally, eliminativism about *F*s —also sometimes called an **error theory** about *F*s —is the view that there are no *F*s, or that nothing has the property of being *F*. Thus *color eliminativism* is the view that nothing is colored — roses are not red (or any other color), violets are not blue (or any other color), and so on.

**Empirical** See **a posteriori**.

**Empiricism** Roughly, the view that all (substantive) knowledge derives from experience, or is **a posteriori**. **Concept** empiricism is the view that all *concepts* are either acquired from experience or "composed from" concepts that are acquired from experience (as the concept *unicorn* is said to be composed from concepts like *horse* and *horn*). **Epistemological** empiricism is view that all **synthetic** knowledge is *a posteriori*. Empiricists typically deny the existence of innate knowledge and the existence of a faculty of Reason that yields substantive, a priori knowledge of reality. Prominent empiricists include David Hume (1711–76) and John Stuart Mill (1806–73).

**Entailment** Proposition *p entails* proposition *q* iff it is *absolutely impossible* for *p* to be true and *q* false. Equivalently: *p* entails *q* when as a matter of *absolute necessity*, if *p* true then so is q. (See **necessity and possibility**.) Synonyms: *p implies q*; *p necessitates q*; *q* is a *consequence* of *p*. Alternatively: sentence *"P"* entails sentence *"Q"* if and only if it is absolutely impossible for *"P"* to be true and *"Q"* false.

The terminology of *"logical* entailment" and *"logical* consequence" is used more narrowly, and specifically for sentences: *"P"* logically entails *"Q"* iff *"Q"* follows from *"P"* by formal logic alone, or alternatively, iff the argument from the premise *"P"* to the conclusion *"Q"* is *formally valid*. (See **soundness and validity**.)

**Entity** A maximally general term designed to apply to anything whatsoever. Ordinary physical objects are entities. But so are immaterial souls (if they exist), mathematical objects (if they exist), events, properties, relations, facts, propositions, and so on.

**Enumerative induction** See **induction**.

**Epiphenomenalism** In the philosophy of mind, the view that a person's psychology or mental life never has any physical effects (although it may have physical causes): wanting pizza never causes the ingestion of pizza, intending to go the lecture never causes attendance at the lecture, and so on. Sometimes more specifically, the view that **qualia** never have physical effects. According to the qualia epiphenomenalist, the distinctive qualia associated with pain do not cause what we naively regard as the physical manifestations of pain — wincing, etc. Rather, physical changes in the brain cause both distinctive pain qualia and these physical manifestations.

**Epistemic rationality** See **practical vs. theoretical rationality**.

**Epistemology** Literally, the theory of knowledge. More commonly, the part of philosophy that studies knowledge, rational belief and the principles governing the rational revision of belief.

**Equality of Opportunity** The requirement that people have equal chances of attaining social desirable positions or other goods. A more formal idea of equality of opportunity requires that people not face legal obstacles to attaining social desirable positions. A more substantive idea of equal opportunity, expressed in John Rawls's (1921–2002) idea of *fair equality of opportunity*, requires that people who are equally able and equally motivated have equal chances of attaining desirable social positions.

**Error theory** The view that our claims about some topic (e.g., color, ethics, mathematics) are completely mistaken because they involve a fundamental error about what the world is like. An error theoretic view of ethics holds that ethical claims are systematically false because *nothing* is right or wrong. (Alternatively, it might be held that ethical claims are meaningless, and so don't even manage to be false.) An error theoretic view of color holds that color claims ("This rose is red," etc.) are systematically false because, despite appearances, nothing is colored. (See **eliminativism**.)

Alternatively, a theory that explains *why* we are prone to systematic metaphysical error in some area; for example, an account of why we think objects are colored when in fact nothing is.

**Essence and accident**  The *essential properties* of an object are the properties that it cannot possibly fail to possess, or equivalently: the properties the object possesses in every **possible world** in which it exists. Alternatively, an essential property is a property an object possess *by its very nature*, or *simply in virtue of being the thing that it is*. A property that is not essential is **accidental**. Examples are controversial, but plausible examples include: Gold is essentially a metal, but only accidentally rare; Socrates is essentially human, but only accidentally wise.

**Event**  A happening or occurrence, like a baseball game, a lecture, a wedding, a war, or a flash of lightning.

**Expected utility**  See **utility**.

**Expressivism**  The view that moral statements like "Stealing is wrong" do not express beliefs, which are capable of being true or false, but rather serve to express states of mind that are not capable of truth or falsity. According to the expressivist, a sincere utterance of "Stealing is wrong" does not ascribe a moral property, wrongness, to certain acts. Rather it expresses the speaker's *disapproval* of stealing, or her *intention* not to steal, or some similar state that can be characterized without invoking moral properties, and which cannot be assessed as true or false.

**Extension**  The extension of a word or concept is the set of things to which the word or concept applies. For example, the extension of the concept *horse* is the set of horses. The extension of the phrase "man with nine fingers" is the set of nine-fingered men. Terms with the same extension are *co-extensional* or *co-extensive*. Note: co-extensional terms can be **contingently** co-extensional. So if, as a matter of fact, every philosopher is a genius and every genius is a philosopher, then "philosopher" and "genius" have the same extension, despite the fact that there could have been a philosopher who is not a genius and vice versa.

**Externalism and internalism about justification**  In epistemology, *internalism* is (roughly) the view that when a person has a **justified belief**, the facts in virtue of which the belief is justified must be accessible to the subject. *Externalism*, the denial of internalism, is the view that a belief may be justified in virtue of facts that lie beyond the subject's ken. One simple form of internalism holds that a belief is justified in virtue of facts about the subject's conscious experiences, assumed to be accessible to the subject. One simple form of externalism (called *reliablism*) holds that a belief is justified in virtue of facts about the reliability of the causal process that produced the belief, regardless of whether the subject is in a position to know about this process or its reliability.

**Externalism and internalism about the mind**  In the philosophy of mind, *internalism* is the view that all **mental states** are *intrinsic* states. (See **extrinsic and intrinsic**.) Equivalently, internalism is the view that if two people are perfect duplicates, exactly alike "from the skin in," they must have exactly the same mental states—the same beliefs, desires, intentions, sensory experiences, and so on. *Externalism*, the denial of internalism, is the view that some mental states involve the subject's relation to his or her environment, and are thus *extrinsic*. According to an externalist, two people who are identical from the skin in may nevertheless have different beliefs because of differences in their respective environments.

**Extrinsic and Intrinsic** An *intrinsic* **property** is a property a thing possess "on its own," regardless of its relations to other things. Alternatively, an intrinsic property is a property with respect to which *perfect duplicates* cannot differ. (A "perfect duplicate" of a certain dollar bill, say, is an atom-for-atom replica of the dollar bill, indistinguishable from the original by the most powerful microscopes.) For example, the property of being round is intrinsic, since, any perfect duplicate of a round thing must be round. A property is *extrinsic* iff it is not intrinsic. For example, the property of *being made in the USA* is extrinsic, since there could be a pair of perfect duplicates — perhaps two copies of this book — one made in the USA, the other made elsewhere.

## F

**Fact** A truth, a true **proposition**. That the Earth is round is a fact; equivalently, that the Earth is round is true, or is a true proposition.

Alternatively, a fact is something "in virtue of which" a true proposition is true. It is controversial whether there are facts in this alternative sense, but if there are, then they are not true propositions — instead, they "make" true propositions true, or "ground" the truth of propositions.

**Falsificationism** Narrowly, the view that a theory counts as genuinely scientific only if it can in principle be falsified — that is, shown to be false. More broadly, the view that science proceeds by framing theories and then seeking to falsify them by means of observation and experiment, retaining only those theories that have survived many such tests.

**Final cause** See **four causes.**

**Finite and infinite** Literally, "limited" and "unlimited."

Traditionally, a *finite quantity* is a quantity that can be exceeded or increased. For example, if an object weighs 5 grams, then its mass is finite, since it is possible for an object to weigh more than 5 grams. An infinite quantity, by contrast, cannot possibly be exceeded. To say that God's wisdom and mercy are infinite is to say that that nothing could possibly have been wiser or more merciful than God. An **entity** is infinite (in some respect) iff some feature of it is infinite. To say that space is infinite, for example, is to say that it its size or volume could not possibly be exceeded or increased.

The words are used somewhat differently in mathematics. According to one definition, a set is infinite when the addition of a new member results in a set with the same size as the original. (Two sets are the same size iff they can be placed in one-one correspondence; i.e., iff there is a mapping that associates each member of the first with exactly one member of the second, and vice versa.) The set of positive whole numbers {1, 2, 3, . . .} is infinite, since the result of adding a new member to the set — say, 0 — yields a set {0, 1, 2, 3, . . .} that is the same size as the original. To see that these two sets are the same size, note that they can be placed in one-one correspondence as follows:

It is a striking fact about infinite sets that some infinite sets are larger than others. For example, the set of real numbers, or points on a line, is larger than the set of whole numbers, though both are infinite. Indeed, for every infinite set, there is a larger infinite set. A set may therefore be infinite in the mathematical sense without being infinite in the traditional sense (unsurpassably large).

**Formal cause**  See **four causes**.

**Formal validity**  See **soundness and validity**.

**Foundationalism**  In epistemology, the view that whenever a person $S$ knows some **proposition** $p$, $S$'s knowledge of $p$ is either **basic**—independent of his knowledge of other facts—or grounded in his basic knowledge. Alternatively, the view that whenever $S$ is **justified** in believing $p$, $S$'s justification for $p$ is either basic—independent of his other beliefs—or grounded in his basic justified beliefs. **Classical foundationalism** is the view that whenever S is justified in holding a non-basic belief, his justification ultimately derives from basic beliefs that are known with perfect certainty.

**Four causes**  Aristotle (384–322 B.C.E.) distinguishes four kinds of cause (or explanatory principle):

> The **material cause** of a thing is the matter that composes it. The material cause of the statue might be a certain quantity of bronze.

> The **formal cause** of a thing is the distinctive arrangement of parts that makes it the thing it is and which persists so long as the thing persists, even though its matter changes. The formal cause of a statue is its shape.

> The **efficient cause** of an object is the entity or process whose activity brings it into being. The formal cause of the statue is the sculptor, or some capacity of the sculptor, whose activity brings the statue into existence.

> The **final cause** of a thing is "that for the sake of which" it exists. The final cause of the statue might be aesthetic contemplation. The final cause of exercise is health.

Contemporary uses of "cause" do not correspond neatly to any of Aristotle's causes, although "efficient cause" comes closest.

**Free will**  Roughly, the power to choose or to act without certain forms of determination or constraint; alternatively, the power of an agent to control or determine her own choices. Some writers define a free choice as a choice that is not determined in any way by prior causes. Other writers define a free choice as a choice that is not *forced* or *substantially constrained,* but which may nonetheless be caused. Free will is usually understood to be a distinctively human capacity. A dog playing in an open field may be free to *act* as he likes, because nothing gets in the way of his acting as he likes; but his choices are determined by his impulses, over which he has no control. A being with free will, by contrast, would possess the capacity to "step back" from his impulses in order to determine for himself whether to act on them.

**Function**  In logic and mathematics, a mapping from one collection—the *domain*—to another—the *range*—that associates each item in the domain with at most one item in the range. Thus *heart of x* is a function from (say) the set of animals (the domain) to the set of organs (the range), since it associates each animal with at most one organ, its heart. By contrast *kidney of x* is not a function, since many animals have more than one kidney. Thus $x^2$ is a function (from real numbers to real numbers) since every real number has just one square, whereas as $\sqrt{x}$ is not a function, since positive real numbers always have two square roots.

**Functionalism** In the philosophy of mind, the view that **mental states** are defined by their causes and effects, including their causal relations to other mental states. Thus a functionalist might define *being in pain* as a state that is typically caused by damage to the body, and which typically causes certain behavior (e.g., wincing) and also certain other mental states, including the belief that one is in pain and the desire to change one's state. Functionalism is opposed to **dualism**, the **identity theory** and also to **behaviorism**, according to which mental states can be defined in terms of their environmental causes and behavioral effects, without mentioning their relations to other mental states.

## G

**Genealogical method** A method developed by Friedrich Nietzsche (1844–1900) for casting doubt on a social arrangement or a set of values (e.g., Christian morality) by examining the psychological and historical factors that that gave rise to it. More generally, a genealogy explains a concept or practice by tracing it back to its origins. A genealogy in this more general sense need not cast doubt on the concept or practice.

**God of the gaps** A pejorative term for versions of the **Design argument** that proceed by pointing to "gaps," that is, to facts that current science cannot explain (e.g., the origin of life) and then insisting that these facts require a supernatural explanation.

## H

**Hard problem of consciousness** An expression introduced by David Chalmers (1966–). The problem of explaining why certain physical states (e.g., states of the brain) are associated with certain conscious states, or with conscious states of any kind. Even if we had a complete account of the *neural correlates of consciousness*, the physical states that in fact underlie conscious states, the hard problem would still arise, since it would remain to say *why* these physical states give rise to conscious experience as they do.

**Harm principle** In political philosophy, the claim, due to John Stuart Mill (1806–1873), that a law that limits the freedom of citizens can only by justified if it is serves to prevent harm to others. The principle precludes purely *paternalistic* laws that are designed to prevent individuals from harming themselves; certain forms of *morals legislation*, designed to deter conduct that may be wrong in itself but which does not cause harm to others; and perfectionist regulations, designed to foster human excellence.

**Hedonism** The view (sometimes called "ethical hedonism") that pleasure is the only intrinsic good, i.e., the only thing worth pursuing for its own sake. Alternatively, the view that a person's level of well-being is determined by the nature, quantity, and distribution of her pains and pleasures.

**Humanity, formula of** See **categorical imperative**.

## I

**Idealism** In metaphysics, the view that reality as a whole is in some sense mental or mind-dependent.

**Identity** Objects $A$ and $B$ are **numerically identical** iff they are one and the same thing: $A = B$. Mark Twain and Samuel Clemens are numerically identical, as are $2^2$ and 4. If $A$ and $B$ are numerically identical then the plural "are" is misleading: "they" are not two things, but one. Objects are **qualitatively identical** iff they are alike in all **intrinsic** respects; equivalently, iff they are perfect duplicates of one another. Numerically identical objects are alike in absolutely every respect. Qualitatively identical objects are alike in some respects — size, shape, chemical composition — though different in others: e.g., location, monetary value, etc.

**Identity theory (of mind)** The view that every **mental state** is *numerically identical* (see **identity**) to a physical state, e.g. the state of having a brain with such-and-such neural firing pattern.

**Iff** Abbreviation for "if and only if." See also **biconditional**.

**Incompatibilism** See **compatibilism**.

**Induction** A form of **argument** in which the premise describes a pattern or regularity in the observed data and the conclusion extends that regularity to cases that have not yet been examined. The simplest *inductive rule* is the rule of **enumerative induction**:

> P1. Every observed $F$ is $G$
> Therefore:
> C: Every $F$ is $G$

or more cautiously:

> C*: The next $F$ we examine will be $G$

More sophisticated inductive rules specify the conditions under which statistics gleaned from observation ("95% of $F$s are $G$") support generalizations and predictions about unexamined cases.

**Inference** See **reasoning and inference**.

**Inference to the best explanation** Also called **abduction**. A form of argument in which the fact that some hypothesis $H$ is the best available explanation of the evidence is taken to support the conclusion that $H$ is true. In one version:

> P1. $H$ is the best available explanation for some fact $F$
> P2. $H$ is a good explanation of $F$ (and not just the best of a bad lot)
> Therefore:
> C: $H$ is true.

**Intentional content** See **content (of a mental state)**.

**Internalism about the mind** See **externalism and internalism about the mind**.

**Internalism about justification** See **externalism and internalism about justification**.

**Intrinsic** See **extrinsic and intrinsic**.

**Intuition** A confident immediate judgment, often about a specific, hypothetical case, offered in support of a philosophical claim. For example, a philosopher may object to the view that we should always act so as to maximize happiness by citing the "intuition" that it would be wrong to kill John, an innocent person, in order to extract his organs for transplant into James, Joan, Jim, Jack, and Jane, even if this would increase the amount of happiness in the universe.

**Intuitive certainty** See **demonstrative certainty**.

**Invalid** See **soundness and validity**.

## J

**Justified belief**  *S* is justified in believing *p* iff *S*'s belief is "rightly held," e.g., *S* believes *p* on the basis of sufficient reasons or evidence for *p*, or adequate grounds. A belief can be true and yet unjustified, as when one makes a lucky guess. Also, a belief can justified but not true, as when one comes to believe that Jones is guilty on the basis of compelling but misleading evidence. (Some philosophers dispute this last claim because they hold that a belief in *p* is is only "rightly held" if one knows *p*. Since one can only know *p* if *p* is true, it follows that no false belief is justified.)

## K

**Kantian**  Resembling the views of Immanuel Kant (1724–1804). *Kantian ethics* is a tradition in moral theory that seeks to articulate general **deontological** principles that apply to all rational agents. In epistemology, *Kantian Humility* is the view that we cannot know the **intrinsic** properties of things. Ascribed to Kant by Rae Langton (1961–).

**Knowledge argument**  A controversial argument against **physicalism** in the philosophy of mind due to Frank Jackson (1943–). Suppose Mary is an expert color scientist who knows all the physical facts, but who has been raised in a black and white environment and so has never seen red. When she sees a red thing for the first time, she learns a new fact. "I never knew that *that's* what it's like to see red!," we can imagine her saying. But she knew all the physical facts in advance. Hence (the Knowledge argument concludes) physicalism is false.

## L

**Lawlike statement**  A statement or **proposition** that is suited, by its form and subject matter, to be a *law of nature*, for example:

> Water boils at 100°C
> Water boils at 50°C
> $e = mc^2$
> $e = mc^3$

Any statement that is in fact a law—e.g., the first and third of the above examples—is lawlike. But so are various false statements are not laws but which might have been laws had the world been different—e.g., the second and fourth examples. Laws that have some tacit "all things equal" qualification, like the first example (water doesn't boil at 100°C on the summit of Everest) are *ceteris paribus* laws. Lawlike statements are supposed to be general in scope, and not to refer to particular individuals. (Thus the proposition that it snowed yesterday and the proposition that Fred is eating lunch are not lawlike, even if they are true.) Beyond this, there are no clear tests to distinguish lawlike statements from the rest.

**Leibniz's Law**  A principle of metaphysics central to the philosophy of Gottfried Leibniz (1646–1716) according to which objects *A* and *B* are **numerically identical** if and only if every **property** of *A* is a property of *B*, and vice versa. So formulated, the principle combines two principles:

> *The indiscernibility of identicals*: If *A* = *B*, then every property of *A* is a property of *B*, and vice versa.
> *The identity of indiscernibles*: If every property of *A* is a property of *B*, and vice versa, then *A* = *B*.

The indiscernibility of identicals is relatively uncontroversial. The identity of indiscernibles is also uncontroversial if properties like *being identical to A* are allowed to count as properties. The principle is highly controversial, however, if only qualitative, *intrinsic* properties are allowed to count. So interpreted the principle entails that no two snowflakes are exactly alike in shape, composition, etc., which may be true in fact, but is certainly not a law of metaphysics.

**Libertarianism** In metaphysics, the view that human beings possess free will of a sort that is incompatible with determinism.

In political philosophy, the view that the government is justified in restricting the liberty of individuals only for a very narrow set of purposes: e.g., preventing violence, protecting private property and enforcing contracts. On one formulation, libertarianism is the view that liberty may be restricted only to better protect liberty itself.

**Logical consequence** See **entailment**.

## M

**Material cause** See **four causes**.

**Materialism** In metaphysics, view that the world is wholly material or physical. The term derives from a period in which the physical sciences focused exclusively on the properties of matter. Since modern physics recognizes many things that would not ordinarily be classified as *material*—e.g., spacetime and the various fields that pervade it—philosophers now often prefer to speak of **physicalism** (see that entry for a more precise characterization of the view). Materialism is incompatible with the existence of disembodied minds and God as traditionally conceived. It is often held to preclude the existence of **abstract objects.**

**Mental state** A psychological or mental condition or **property**, e.g. *believing that it's sunny, wanting to go swimming, hoping for rain, being angry, having a headache, seeming to see a tomato*. Some philosophers would add states of knowing (e.g. *knowing that it's sunny*) and seeing (e.g. *seeing a tomato*) to this list. Philosophers sympathetic to *internalism* (see **externalism and internalism about the mind**) resist this, on the grounds that knowing and seeing involve relations to the external environment.

**Meta-ethics** The part of philosophy concerned with the **metaphysics and epistemology** of ethics and with the linguistic function of ethical language. Meta-ethics asks, for example, whether ethical statements aim to describe a domain of ethical facts, and if so, whether those facts obtain objectively, independently of our beliefs about them. It asks whether moral words like "right" and "wrong" pick out moral properties, and if so, whether they can be defined in more fundamental (non-moral) terms. Meta-ethics asks whether ethical knowledge is possible, and in particular, whether it requires a special capacity for moral intuition. Meta-ethics is sometimes contrasted with *normative ethics*, which comprises both *ethical theory*—the effort to formulate and justifiy general moral principles—and *applied ethics*, the effort to solve relatively concrete moral problems.

**Metaphysics** The part of philosophy concerned with the nature and structure of reality. Contrasted with, e.g., **epistemology**, the part of philosophy concerned with our knowledge of reality.

**Mind-body problem** The problem of describing the relation between our mental lives and the physical aspects of our brains, bodies, and environments.

**Modus ponens and modus tollens** Forms of formally valid argument (see **soundness and validity**):

| | |
|---|---|
| Modus Ponens: | If *P* then *Q* |
| | *P* |
| | Therefore: |
| | *Q* |
| Modus Tollens: | If *P* then *Q* |
| | Not-*Q* |
| | Therefore |
| | not-*P* |

**Moorean shift (G.E. Moore shift)** A strategy for rebutting philosophical **arguments** whose conclusions clash with commonsense, named for the British philosopher G. E. Moore (1873 – 1958). The strategy is available whenever a premise of the argument is a non-obvious philosophical thesis. In such cases, the Moorean shift consists in treating the argument not as a proof of its conclusion, but rather as a refutation of the philosophical premise. The underlying idea is that given a clash between a philosophical thesis and a core commitment of common sense — sometimes called a *Moorean fact* — the rational option is to retain the common sense commitment and give up the philosophical thesis. For examples, suppose a philosopher argues that you cannot know that you have a body because (a) you can only know this sort of thing if you can prove it from premises about your experience, and (b) your experiences are consistent with the hypothesis that you do not have a body. The Moorean shift is to say: "Since I certainly *do* know that I have a body, at least one of your philosophical assumptions (a) and (b) must be mistaken."

**Moral realism** The view that moral statements describe a domain of moral facts, at least some of which obtain independently of our moral beliefs and practices.

**Moral responsibility** A person is morally responsible for an action iff she is properly held accountable for it, or praised or blamed on the basis of it.

## N

**Natural rights** Rights that human beings possess independently of law, government, or any other human convention or institution, e.g., the right to self-defense.

**Natural theology** The effort to establish principles of religion by scientific means, without appeal to revelation or religious experience. Proponents of natural theology typically invoke the **cosmological argument** and/or the **design argument** to establish the existence of a deity and at least some of its key attributes. The **cosmological fine-tuning argument** is a recent innovation in natural theology.

**Necessary and sufficient conditions** Being *G* is a *necessary condition* for being *F* iff it is impossible for a thing to be *F* without being *G*. Being *G* is a *sufficient condition* for being *F* iff it is impossible for a thing to be *G* without being *F*. For example, being a poodle is sufficient for being a dog, and being a dog is necessary for being a poodle. One of the chief aims of philosophical **analysis** is to supply non-trivial necessary and sufficient conditions for the application of important words and concepts. An analysis of "knowledge," for example, will supply a set of conditions for the truth of "*S* knows *p*" that are *individually necessary* and *jointly sufficient*.

**Necessity and possibility** A proposition *p* is *necessary* (or *necessarily true*) iff *p* could not possibly have been false; *p* is *possible* (or *possibly true*) iff *p* could have been true; p is *impossible* iff its **negation**, not-p, is necessary; p is *contingent* iff both p and not-p are possible; p is *contingently true* iff p is both contingent and true.

Another explanation appeals to **possible worlds**: a proposition is possible iff there is a possible world in which it is true; a proposition is necessary iff it is true in all possible worlds. An impossible proposition is true in no possible world, and a contingent proposition is true in some possible worlds but not in others.

A *necessary being* is a being that could not have failed to exist, or a being that exists in every possible world. Putative examples include God and the objects of pure mathematics, e.g., numbers. A *contingent being* is a being that exists in some possible worlds but not in others. It is widely thought that ordinary objects — mountains, people — are contingent beings, though some philosophers deny this.

Philosophers distinguish several varieties of necessity and possibility. For example:

A proposition is *absolutely* or *metaphysically* necessary if there is no possible world of any sort in which it is false. (Similarly, a proposition is *absolutely* or *metaphysically* impossible if there is no possible world of any sort in which it is true.) Examples are controversial, but the truths of pure logic and mathematics are widely regarded as metaphysically necessary, as are **analytic** truths (e.g., "Hexagons are six-sided") and truths about the **essential properties** of things, e.g., "Gold is a metal."

A proposition is *nomologically* or *physically necessary* iff it holds in every possible world in which the laws of nature hold. Thus it is nomologically necessary that massive bodies attract, even though there are could have been a world without gravity in which massive bodies do not attract. A proposition is *physically possible* iff it is consistent with the laws of physics.

A proposition is *mathematically* necessary iff it is a logical consequence of the truths of mathematics and *logically* necessary iff it is a consequence of the laws of logic. Thus it is *mathematically impossible* to tile a rectangle with 17 square tiles and *logically impossible* for an object to be both square and not square at the same time.

**Negation**  A sentence of the form "It is not the case that *P*," or some related form either in a natural language or a formal logical language. In symbolic logic, usually written as "*~P*." By definition, "*~P*" is true iff "*P*" is false.

The negation of a **proposition** p, *not-p*, is a proposition that, necessarily, is true iff p is false.

**Non-demonstrative argument (or inference)**  See **proof.**

**Normativity**  Narrowly, a normative statement is a statement about how things ought to be, or about a person ought to think or act. More broadly, a normative statement is a statement that evaluates or applies a standard. Normative statements in the broad sense include claims about what is good or desirable, claims about virtue and vice, and claims to the effect that an action or mental state is rational or reasonable or justified. Normative statements are contrasted with *descriptive* (better: *non-normative*) statements. Thus the claim that John *is* eating his vegetables is descriptive; the claim that he *ought* to eat them is normative.

## O

**Object** Sometimes used broadly, as interchangeable with "**entity**." On a narrower usage, an object is a **particular** that is not an **event**: on this usage, Barack Obama, Jupiter and (more controversially) the number 17, are objects while Obama's second inauguration and the First World War are not.

**Objective list theory** The view that there are many fundamental goods—things worth pursuing for their own sake, e.g., knowledge, pleasure, friendship, love, etc. Alternatively, the view that an agent's level of utility or well-being depends on many such factors. Objective list theories typically add that at least some fundamental goods or determinants of well-being concern the agent's relations to the world (e.g., knowledge, friendship) and not just her *intrinsic* **mental states** (e.g., pleasure). (See **extrinsic and intrinsic**.) The plurality of goods are given by a *list* because the objective list theorist believes that there is no unifying explanation of what goes on the list.

**Occam's razor** A methodological principle of parsimony in theorizing, often rendered by the slogan "entities are not to be multiplied beyond necessity," sometimes misattributed to William of Occam (or Ockham) (c. 1287–1347). More generally, the view that when all else is equal, it is reasonable to prefer a simple theory to a more complex one.

**Omnibenevolent** Perfectly good; morally flawless.

**Omnipotent** All-powerful; capable of performing any act, or bringing about any (possible) state of affairs.

**Omniscient** All-knowing. An omniscient being knows every true **proposition** and has no false beliefs.

**Ontological argument** An **a priori** argument for the existence of God which seeks to show that a correct account of God's nature (alternatively, a correct account of the concept *God*) entails that God exists. A simple version:

P1. God is, by definition, an absolutely perfect being.
P2. Existence is a perfection. (Just as a perfect being must be omniscient and omnipotent, so a perfect being must exist.)
Therefore:
C. God exists

The premises are meant to be acceptable to the *atheist* (the proponent of **atheism**) who must understand the word "God" if she is to deny that God exists. The argument as a whole is designed to show that just as it is incoherent to deny that God is wise, it is likewise incoherent to deny that God exists. The most widely discussed versions of the argument are due to Anselm of Canterbury (c. 1033–1109).

**Ontology** The study of being. Ontology seeks to clarify the sense (or senses) in which a thing may be said to be, or to exist, and to provide an account of the most basic categories of being. The *ontology of a theory* is the set of **entities** that exist according to the theory. The ontology of the Standard Model of particle physics, for example, includes quarks. A theorist is *ontologically committed* to Fs iff her views **entail** that Fs exist. So physicists who accept the Standard Model are ontologically committed to quarks.

**P**

**Paradox** An apparently **valid argument** with apparently true premises, but with an apparently false conclusion. Faced with a paradox, you have three options: deny one of the premises, deny the validity of the argument, or accept the conclusion. A famous and ancient paradox is the *paradox of the heap*:

> P1. 0 grains of sand do not make a heap.
> P2. For all numbers n, if n grains of sand do not make a heap, then n + 1 grains of sand do not make a heap.

> These two (apparently true) premises (apparently) **entail** that 1 grain does not make a heap, that 2 grains do not make a heap, and so on..., hence:

> C. No number of grains of sand, no matter how large, make a heap.

To *solve* the paradox is to make a compelling philosophical case either for rejecting one of the premises or for denying the validity of the argument.

**Particulars and universals** A *particular* is an individual, non-repeatable **object** or **event**, e.g., you, your **token** copy of this book, or your first philosophy lecture. A universal is an item that is (typically) capable of being repeated or multiply instantiated, e.g. the **property** of being human (instantiated by you, but also by Socrates); the **relation** of being *smaller than* (instantiated by Woody Allen and Charles Barkley, but also by the moon and the sun); the *Norton Introduction to Philosophy*, understood as a **type** with many tokens; and so on. The word "universal" is sometimes used more narrowly to refer to properties and relations but not to types.

**Pascal's wager** An argument due to Blaise Pascal (1623–62) which seeks to show that we have conclusive reasons of self-interest to believe that God exists, even if there is no evidence whatsoever for God's existence. The argument assumes that if there is a God, he rewards believers with infinite happiness. It then treats the decision whether to believe in God as a gamble in which one wagers one's earthly life for the prospect of gaining this infinite happiness. The argument assumes a framework for evaluating gambles that resembles modern **decision theory**. The key feature of the framework is the assumption that a gamble is rational iff and its **expected utility** is at least as great as than that of any alternative open to the agent. The argument crucially involves the claim that the expected utility of belief in God is infinite, whereas the expected value of disbelief is finite, even if God's existence is improbable.

**Perfectionism** An ethical outlook that characterizes the human good in terms of certain kinds of excellences à excellence, say, artistic or scientific. According to an *ethical perfectionist*, the best human life is not necessarily the most pleasurable life or the life a person most wants to lead, but a life that achieves these excellences. A *moral perfectionist* holds that the right way to live is the way that achieves these excellences: not simply that it would be good to achieve them but that we ought to achieve them. In politics, perfectionists hold that the right laws and policies foster the excellences that are components of the best human lives.

**Persistence** In metaphysics, an object is said to persist through an interval of time iff it exists at every moment in the interval. A leaf that turns from green to red persists through the change iff there is a single item that exists at each moment of the process. Some philosophers hold that what we call "change" is really a process in which one object (e.g., the green leaf) is replaced by another (the red leaf). If this is right in general then strictly speaking nothing persists through change.

**Personal knowledge** The sort of knowledge we attribute when we say, e.g., that Fred knows Mary, or that Alice knows London well. See also **procedural knowledge** and **propositional knowledge.**

**Phenomenal character** See **qualia.**

**Phenomenal consciousness** A term introduced by Ned Block (1942–). A **mental state** is phenomenally conscious iff there is "something that it is like" to be in that state; that is, iff the mental state has **qualia.** A phenomenally conscious *creature* is a creature who is in a phenomenally conscious state. The states of *feeling pain,* or *seeing green,* or *tasting sweetness,* are (at least typically) phenomenally conscious. The states of *believing that there are canals on Mars,* or *wanting to go to graduate school,* are (at least typically) not phenomenally conscious. We don't know what it's like to perceive insects by bat echolocation (and perhaps we could never know), but if there *is* something it is like to perceive in that way, then bats are often phenomenally conscious.

**Phenomenology** The study of the objects and structures of consciousness, as they seem from the first-person perspective. Sometimes used in a strict sense for an approach to philosophy pioneered by Edmund Husserl (1859–1938). In contemporary philosophy of mind, used for any attempt to characterize how things appear to us in perception or reflection.

**Physical possibility** See **possibility and necessity.**

**Physicalism** Also known as **materialism.** The view that the world is entirely physical: every **object** a physical object, every **property** a physical property, etc. Sometimes given a (weaker) formulation as a **supervenience** thesis: all the **facts** supervene on, or are determined by, the physical facts (roughly, facts expressible in the language of a complete physics). This version of physicalism can also be put as the thesis that any **minimal physical duplicate** of the actual world is a perfect duplicate of the actual world. (A minimal physical duplicate of the actual world is a possible world that exactly resembles the actual world in every physical respect, and which contains nothing more than is needed to be a physical duplicate of it.)

Physicalism can be restricted to a particular phenomenon: *physicalism about color* is the view that the colors are physical properties, or that the color facts supervene on the physical facts. *Physicalism about the mind* (opposed to **dualism**) is the view that **mental states** are physical states, or that mental facts supervene on the physical facts.

**Possible world** A maximally specific way things could have been. Picturesquely, a novel or story that (a) *could have been true* and (b) is *complete* in the sense that for every **proposition** *p,* either *p* or its **negation** is true according to the story. The *actual world* is the maximally specific way things in fact *are.* See also **necessity and possibility.**

**Possibility** See **necessity and possibility.**

**Practical vs. theoretical rationality** Practical rationality is the sort of rationality that governs choice and action; *theoretical* or *epistemic rationality* is the sort of rationality that governs the revision of belief in response to evidence. (See **theoretical vs. practical reasons for belief.**)

Note: We can ask whether it would practically rational to form or hold a belief. For example, **Pascal's Wager** is designed to show that it is in your interest to believe that God exists even if you have no evidence for God's existence. Some writers therefore hold that our beliefs are governed both by the requirements of theoretical rationality and by the (perhaps conflicting) requirements of practical rationality.

**Pragmatist theory of truth**  Roughly, the view that a **proposition** is true iff it would be useful for practical and scientific purposes to believe it. Associated with William James (1842–1910).

**Predicate**  A linguistic expression that combines with a proper name, or a sequence of proper names, to yield a complete sentence. So, for example, "... is tall" and "... loves ..." are predicates, since they yield complete sentences when the blanks are filled in by names. Sometimes we omit the copula, "is," and say that "tall" by itself qualifies as a predicate.

**Preference satisfaction theory**  In ethics, the view that a person's utility or well-being is determined by the extent to which her preferences are satisfied. An alternative to **hedonism** and the **objective list theory**.

**Premise**  See **argument**.

**Primary and secondary qualities**  A distinction drawn in several ways by philosophers in the early modern period, notably John Locke (1632–1704). *Primary* qualities are qualities (**properties**) possessed by bodies independently of our experience of them and which figure in a correct scientific account of their behavior. Examples include size, mass, and motion. *Secondary* qualities, by contrast, are not possessed by bodies independently of our experience of them, but rather consist in **dispositions** to produce certain sorts of experiences in us, or perhaps in features *of our experiences* that we mistakenly locate in external objects. On this way of using the terminology, it is a controversial thesis that colors (for example) are secondary qualities. Alternatively, secondary qualities are sometimes defined by means of a list including color, taste and odor, and excluding size, weight and motion. In this sense, everyone agrees that colors are secondary qualities.

**Problem of induction**  Inductive **reasoning** assumes that the objects we have examined constitute a representative sample of the domain under investigation, or equivalently, that the unexamined parts of the domain resemble the examined parts in relevant respects. Taken narrowly, the problem of induction is the problem of showing how this assumption can be justified. Some philosophers distinguish the **descriptive problem of induction**, which seeks to an explicit formulation of the principles that guide our inductive reasoning, from the **normative problem of induction**: the problem of showing that these principles are justified.

**Procedural knowledge**  The sort of knowledge we attribute when we say, e.g., that John knows how to ride a bicycle, or that Samantha knows how fix the toaster. See also **personal knowledge** and **propositional knowledge**.

**Proof**  A *valid* **argument** that establishes its conclusion with certainty. Alternatively, a *formally valid* argument whose premises are true (or are known to be true). (See **soundness and validity**.) Also known as a *demonstrative argument*. A cogent argument that is not a proof is a *non-demonstrative* argument.

   In formal logic, a proof in a formal system is an argument whose premises are **axioms** or **theorems** of the system and whose conclusion follows from the premises according to the rules of the system.

**Projectable property** A **property** suitable for use in **inductive** reasoning. The fact that every dog so far examined has been found to be warm-blooded gives us reason to believe that all dogs are warm-blooded. The property of *being warm blooded* is thus projectable. By contrast, the fact that every dog so far examined has been *observed before the year 2100* gives us no reason to believe that all dogs (past, present and future) have this feature. So the property of *being observed before 2100* is not projectable.

**Properly basic belief** See **basic belief and knowledge**.

**Property** A *feature* or *attribute*. Properties are often denoted by abstract nouns, e.g., "whiteness," "wisdom," or by complex noun phrases like "(the property of) weighing 2 grams." Unlike **particulars**, properties have *instances*. Many properties have multiple instances — the many white things are all instances of whiteness. But there may be properties with only one instance (*being John Malkovich*) or with no instances at all (*the property of being a round square*). Some philosophers hold that properties literally exist *in* the items that possess them; others hold that properties do not exist in space, and are therefore **abstract objects**.

**Proposition** When a French speaker utters the sentence "La neige est blanche" and a German speaker utters "Schnee ist weiß" they have used different words to make the *same* claim or statement, namely *that snow is white*. The content of this shared claim or statement is called a *proposition*, the proposition that snow is white. Propositions can be assessed for truth or falsity: the proposition that snow is white is true, the proposition that snow is purple is false. Propositions are commonly taken to play a number of roles in metaphysics and the philosophy of mind and language. They are said to be:

> the primary bearers of truth and falsity: when a sentence is true, that is because the proposition it expresses is true. When a belief is true, that is because the proposition that is its **content** à content is true.

> the meanings of (declarative) sentences: "La neige est blanche" and "Schnee ist weiß" both have the same meaning, the proposition *that snow is white*.

> the contents of **propositional attitudes** like belief and hope: Carlos believes/hopes *that it will rain*.

> the objects of certain linguistic acts: Marcus asserted/denied/implied *that Lisa is a lawyer*.

> **facts**, when true: *that the Earth is round* is a fact.

It is a matter of controversy whether one kind of thing can play all of these roles.

**Propositional attitude** A mental state that consists in a relation between a person and a proposition. If Alfred believes that the Pope is infallible, then Alfred bears a certain relation — the belief relation — to a certain proposition: the proposition that the Pope is infallible. If Elizabeth hopes that the Pope is infallible, then Elizabeth bears a different relation — the hope relation — to the same proposition. Believing and hoping are thus propositional attitudes: relations to — or attitudes towards — propositions. Wanting is commonly taken to be another example, but this is not as clear, because the most natural ways of ascribing wants do not employ a "that-clause," e.g., "Alfred wants pizza."

**Propositional knowledge** *Factual* knowledge, knowledge that something is the case; the sort of knowledge we attribute when we say, e.g., that Eleanor knows that Sue is a philosopher. See also **personal knowledge**" and **procedural knowledge**.

**Psycho-physical laws** Laws governing the relation between **mental states** and physical states. (See also **lawlike statement**.)

## Q

**Qualia** From Latin, "of what kind"; singular: *quale*. *Seeing green* is a **phenomenally conscious mental state**, and so are *seeing pink, being in pain*, and *tasting bitterness*. However, they are quite different states, in the sense that what it's like to see green is quite different from (e.g.) what it's like to taste bitterness. Put in the terminology of "qualia," *seeing green* and *tasting bitterness* have different qualia.

In this broad sense of "qualia," only an **eliminativist** about phenomenal consciousness would deny that mental states have qualia. But there is a narrower sense of the term, according to which qualia are (in addition) *non-physical* **properties** of mental states. In this narrow sense, **physicalists** deny that mental states have qualia.

In yet another sense of the term, qualia are perceptual qualities or properties, e.g., colors and tastes. In this sense, qualia are not properties of mental states, but (putative) properties of things in our environment, like cucumbers and coffee.

**Quantifier** Expressions like "all," "some," "many," "few," and "at least one" which serve to express claims about quantities of things, e.g. "All/some/many/few students attended the lecture." "All" and "every" are **universal quantifiers**, written in symbolic logic as "$\forall$." Statements like "All professors are wise" are **universally quantified statements** or **universal generalizations**. "Some" and "at least one" are **existential quantifiers**, written in symbolic logic as "$\exists$". Philosophers (but not linguists) often classify "there is . . ." and "there are . . ." as existential quantifiers, on the ground that "There are talking dogs" is equivalent to "Some dogs talk."

## R

**Reasoning and inference** The psychological process of forming new beliefs on the basis of other beliefs (or suppositions). For example, a detective may form the belief that the butler committed the murder on the basis of her beliefs that the butler had means, motive, and opportunity, or she may form the belief that the butler did it after supposing that the gardener did, and seeing that that supposition or assumption lead to absurdity, leaving the butler as the sole remaining suspect.

Reasoning is often divided into **theoretical reasoning** (*inference*, or reasoning as explained above) and **practical reasoning**, which results in an intention or decision to do something.

**Reductio ad absurdum** A form of **argument** in which a **proposition** *p* is established by showing that its **negation**, not-*p*, **entails** a contradiction or some other manifestly absurd conclusion.

**Reductionism** In the philosophy of science, reductionism about a domain of inquiry (e.g., psychology, biology, economics) is the view that every **concept** in the domain can be **analyzed** or defined in terms drawn from a more fundamental science (often physics). The term is sometimes used more broadly for the view that facts in one area (e.g., psychology) can be explained in more fundamental terms, and so amount nothing "over and above" these more basic facts.

In the philosophy of personal **identity**, reductionism is the view that the facts about the facts about personal identity over time are fully determined by facts that can be stated without reference to personal identity, e.g., facts about the physical and psychological relations that hold between persons existing at different times.

**Reflective equilibrium** A method for inquiry in ethics and other areas that begins from our firmly held "considered judgments" about particular cases and candidate general principles. It then assesses whether our general principles are consistent with our judgments about cases and whether the principles explain and illuminate these judgments. Where there is a conflict, the investigator is to revise either the principles or judgments until the two harmonize and the principles helpfully explain and entail a set of considered judgments we regard as reasonable. Proponents of the method hold that when a stable view of this sort (an equilibrium) has been achieved (through reflection), we are justified in accepting it even if we have no independent evidence for its correctness.

"Reflective equilibrium" sometimes denotes the process of harmonizing one's particular judgments and general principles and sometimes denotes the product of this process, that is, the equilibrium point that is sought.

**Regularity theory of causation** The view that causation is to be analyzed in terms of general regularities. In one version:

**Event** $C$ causes event $E$ iff

> $C$ is an event of kind $F$
> $E$ is an event of kind $G$

and

> Throughout the universe, events of kind $F$ are always followed by events of kind $G$.

**Relation** A relation is a **universal** instantiated by two or more entities or *terms*. Thus ... *is taller than* ... is a *two-place relation* (also called a *binary relation*), since it relates two terms — John is taller than Sam — whereas ... *is between* ... *and* ... is a *three-place relation*, since it relates three terms: Chicago is between New York and San Francisco. (A more expansive definition counts **properties** as one-place relations.) The terms of a relation are its *relata*.

> A binary relation $R$ is *reflexive* iff every object bears $R$ to itself. Examples: **numerical identity**, sameness of height, weight, color.

> A binary relation $R$ is *symmetric* iff whenever $x$ bears $R$ to $y$, $y$ bears $R$ to $x$. Examples: ... *is married to* ..., ... *lives next door to* ...

> A binary relation $R$ is *transitive* iff whenever $x$ bears $R$ to $y$ and $y$ bears $R$ to $z$, $x$ bears $R$ to $z$. Examples: ... *is taller than* ...; *is exactly the same color as* ...

> A binary relation $R$ is an *equivalence relation* iff R is reflexive, symmetric, and transitive. Examples: ... *is the same height as* ...... *is parallel to* ...

The *converse* of a binary relation $R$ is the relation R* such that $x$ bears $R$ to $y$ iff $y$ bears $R*$ to $x$. Example:... *is shorter than...* is the converse of... *is taller than....*

**Reliabilism**  See **externalism and internalism about justification.**
**Representational content**  See **content (of a mental state).**
**Rule utilitarianism**  See **utilitarianism.**


**S**

**Secondary quality**  See **primary and secondary qualities.**

**Self-evident proposition**  A proposition that can be known immediately, without further reasoning, by anyone who grasps it. Putative examples include basic logical principles (e.g., if a= b then b= a), basic mathematical principles (e.g., between any two points exactly one straight line can be drawn), and basic moral principles (e.g., evil is to be avoided). According to the American Declaration of Independence, it is a self-evident truth that all men are created equal.

**Sense data**  The *sense datum theory* holds that in sensory experience one is immediately or directly aware of *sense data*—patches of color, sounds, odors—that invariably *are* as they *appear.* If you look at the mountains in the distance and they look purple, the *mountains* need not be purple. However, according to the sense datum theory, you *are* aware of a something that *really is* purple, namely a purple *sense datum.* If there is such a thing, it is not a physical object, since there need be no purple physical object in the vicinity. Some versions of the theory hold that sense data are cannot exist unperceived; others hold that they are entirely mind-independent.

**Skeptical hypothesis**  Arguments for **skepticism** often proceed by describing a hypothetical scenario—a skeptical hypothesis—that is alleged to be consistent with our evidence, but in which our beliefs would be radically and systematically mistaken. Famous examples include the *dream hypothesis*, according to which you are currently dreaming; the *brain in a vat hypothesis*, according to which you are a disembodied brain whose sensory receptors are being stimulated by a supercomputer; and the *no past hypothesis* (due to Bertrand Russell [1872–1970]), according to which the physical universe was created five minutes ago with all of the traces of an apparent "past" in place.

**Skepticism** (also spelled "scepticism")  The view that nothing is known about a certain subject matter, or that we do not have **justified** beliefs about it. **Global skepticism** is the view that there is no knowledge (or justified belief) at all. **Local skepticisms** are (at least to some extent) selective, e.g., *moral* skepticism is the view that we have no moral knowledge; *inductive* skepticism the view that **inductive arguments** are never **cogent**; *external world* skepticism is the view that we have no knowledge of our environment.

**Social contract theory**  An approach to political philosophy according to which political arrangements are justified iff they could (or, in some formulations would) have been rationally agreed to by all who are subject to them. Social contract theories are typically hypothetical: they do not claim that people have *actually* agreed to political arrangements, but rather that they would agree under certain conditions—some kind of initial situation—suited to assessing political arrangements. Social contract theorists include Thomas Hobbes (1588–1679), John Locke (1632–1704), Jean-Jacques Rousseau (1712–1778), and John Rawls (1921–2002).

**Solipsism** The view that there is only one conscious subject, and that reality as a whole exists (or can be known to exist) only insofar as this subject is conscious of it.

**Soundness and validity** An **argument** is *valid* iff it is absolutely impossible for the premises to be true and the conclusion false. For example:

> P1. The book on the table is scarlet.
> Therefore
> C. The book on the table is red.

An argument is *formally valid* iff every argument that shares its *form* is valid. Thus the argument just given is not formally valid, but

> P1. Simon is a philosopher
> P2. All philosophers are subtle
> Therefore
> C. Simon is subtle.

is a formally valid argument because it is an instance of the valid form:

> P1. $A$ is $F$
> P2. All $F$s are $G$
> Therefore
> C. $A$ is $G$

A *sound* argument is a *valid* argument with true premises.

> P1. If a number is even then it is divisible by 2.
> P2. 8 is even
> Therefore
> C. 8 is divisible by 2.

**Sovereign** The supreme authority in a territory. In a monarchy, the monarch is sovereign; in a democracy, the people are sovereign. Though the sovereign is the supreme authority, the sovereign's authority need not be unlimited or unconditional. Sovereign authority may be subject to a constitution that defines how the authority is to be exercised and what its limits are. A sovereign whose authority is not limited in this way is *absolute*.

**State of Nature** In political philosophy, the condition of human beings living outside of a state, not subject to any political authority.

**Stuff** In metaphysics, a category that includes *water, plastic* and other items allegedly denoted by (some) *mass nouns*, common nouns that have no plural and cannot be modifed by numerical adjectives (like "seven"). Thus "rice" (no plural) is a mass noun, while "chair" is a *count* noun. Many nouns occur in both mass and count forms: there is *some hair* in the soup (mass occurrence of "hair"); there are *three hairs* in the soup (count occurrence).

**Subjectivism** In ethics, the view that moral statements are to be analyzed as statements about the subjective mental states of the speaker or some group to which the speaker belongs. Thus the subjectivist might claim that "Stealing is wrong" simply means: "I disapprove of stealing" or "Stealing is prohibited by the moral system that my culture accepts." Subjectivism is to be contrasted with **expressivism,** the view that moral statements *express* (but do not describe) the speaker's mental states. Analogy: Someone who says "Ouch!" expresses his pain; someone who says "I am in pain" describes his pain.

**Substance** Roughly, an independently existing **entity**. Traditional metaphysics draws a distinction between substances, which exist *in themselves*, and beings of other sorts, which exist only *in* substances, or as modifications of substances. Thus an animal might be a substance, whereas its various **properties**, the species to which it belongs, and its shape, would not be substances. Alternatively, the word is sometimes used for the basic or fundamental entities: items that exist, but not in virtue of the existence of other things. When the word is used in this way, even though Socrates exists and exemplifies various properties, he is not a substance because he exists in virtue of the arrangement of the atoms (or subatomic particles) that compose him. On a view of this sort, elementary particles might qualify as substances.

**Sufficient condition** See **necessary and sufficient conditions.**

**Supererogatory** Relating to the performance of morally good actions that go beyond the demands of duty.

**Supervenience** A relation between one class of facts—the **higher-level** or **supervenient** facts—and a class of more fundamental facts—the **supervenience base**—according to which the higher-level facts are fixed or determined by facts in the base. Thus the biological facts plausibly supervene on the physical facts in the following sense: two situations that are exactly alike in every physical respect—down to the last atom—must also be alike in every biological respect. More generally, the B-facts supervene on the A-facts iff the B-facts cannot differ unless the A-facts also differ. ("No B-difference without an A-difference.") Supervenience claims are common in philosophy. For example, it is widely held that the moral facts supervene on the purely descriptive, non-moral facts in the following strong sense: If two actions differ in some moral respect (the one good, the other bad, say), then they must also differ in some non-moral respect. Many philosophical doctrines are framed as supervenience theses. Thus **physicalism** is sometimes formulated as the thesis that all of the facts supervene on the physical facts.

**Symmetric relation** See **relation.**

**Synthetic statement** See **analytic and synthetic.**

## T

**Theism** The view that at least one god exists.

**Theodicy** A response to the **argument from evil** that seeks to show that evil and suffering in the world are compatible with the existence of a perfect God.

**Theoretical (or epistemic) rationality.** A **theoretical** (or **epistemic**) **reason** for believing that $p$ is a fact that supports the conclusion that $p$ is true. A **practical** (or **pragmatic**) reason for believing that $p$ is a reason for thinking that it would be good or beneficial to believe that $p$ regardless of whether $p$ is true. Thus the fact that the pavement is wet is a theoretical reason to believe that it has rained, while the fact you will be happier if you believe that God exists is a practical, though not an epistemic, reason to believe that God exists.

See also **practical rationality.**

**Tokens** See **types and tokens.**

**Types and tokens**

In metaphysics, a *type* is a kind or category of which there may be many concrete instances or examples or *tokens*. Thus a particular inscription of the sentence

The cat sat on the mat

will contain five word types — "the," "cat," "sat," "on" and "mat" — but six word *tokens*: one token each of "cat," "sat," "on" and "mat," but two distinct tokens of "the." The tokens of a given type are unrepeatable individuals, whereas the types themselves are **universals**.

Another example: the particular copy of the *Norton Introduction to Philosophy* you are currently holding is one of many *tokens* of a single *type*, the only book edited by Rosen, Byrne, Cohen, and Shiffrin.

**U**

**Undermining evidence** Evidence that weakens the force of evidence previously obtained.

**Uniformity of Nature** John Stuart Mill's (1806–73) name for the principle that allegedly underlies inductive reasoning. In David Hume's (1711–76) rough formulation, it is the assumption that *the future will resemble the past*, or more generally: "If, in a large sample, all observed *F*s are *G*, then (probably) all *F*s are *G*." The principle is sometimes put as the thesis that nature is governed by laws (or regularities) that hold in all times and places.

**Universal law, formula of** See **categorical imperative**.

**Universals** See **particulars and universals**.

**Utilitarianism** A form of **consequentialism** according to which an act is morally right if and only if it would produce more net happiness (or pleasure) overall than any other act open to the agent (**act utilitarianism**). Alternatively, the view that an act is right iff it is permitted by a set of rules general compliance with which would maximize happiness (**rule utilitarianism**).

**Utility** In **ethics,** a term that refers to the well-being of a person that plays an especially important role in **utilitarianism**. Different theories measure utility in different ways. Some, like **hedonism,** focus exclusively on a person's mental states, often placing great emphasis on the duration and intensity of pleasures and pains. Other theories, such as **preference-satisfaction** theories and **objective list** theories, assess a person's utility in terms both of her mental states and aspects of her objective circumstances.

In **decision theory**, a measure of an agent's preferences for different outcomes: the utility of *A* for an agent is greater than the utility of *B* for that agent if and only if the agent prefers *A* to *B*. The decision-theoretic utility of an outcome is a subjective matter. It is not a function of the outcome's moral value, or its real objective value, or its value to society. It is determined entirely by an agent's desire for the outcome, or by his preference for it over other outcomes. In economics it is sometimes assumed, with many caveats, that the utility you attach to an outcome can be measured by determining how much you would be willing to pay to bring it about.

The **expected utility** of an action is the sum of the utilities of the various outcomes the act might produce, each weighted by the probability that the action will produce that outcome. For example, if an action (say, bringing one's umbrella) has a utility of 10 if it rains and a utility of 2 if it does not, then the expected utility of the act is

(10 × the probability that it will rain) + (2 × the probability that it will not rain)

**V**

**Validity** See **soundness and validity.**

**Virtue ethics** The view that ethics is mainly concerned with describing various virtues of character and promoting their cultivation. The view is sometimes understood as an alternative to **consequentialism** and **deontology**, according to which the right action is identified, not as the act with the best consequences or the act that conforms to authoritative rules, but rather with the act that a virtuous agent would perform in the agent's circumstances.

**W**

**Warrant** In epistemology, sometimes used loosely as a synonym for "evidence" or "justification." Alternatively, following Alvin Plantinga (1932–), a technical term for whatever must be added to true belief to yield knowledge.

**Z**

**Zombies** In the philosophy of mind, hypothetical creatures exactly like human beings in all physical and biological respects but who are never **phenomenally conscious.** If there could have been zombies then **physicalism** is false.

# Credits

60–61, 61–64, 65, 66–68, 68–69, 70–71, 72–75, 75–76, 77–80, 80–81, 81–82, Cambridge, Mass.: Harvard University Press, Copyright © 1979, 1983 by Nelson Goodman.

C.L. Hardin: "Are 'Scientific' Objects Colored?" from *Mind*, New Series, Vol. 93, No. 372, Oct. 1984, pp. 491–500. By permission of Oxford University Press on behalf of the Mind Association.

Gilbert Harman: From "Evidence One Does Not Possess" from *Thought*. © 1973 Princeton University Press, 2001 renewed PUP. Reprinted by permission of Princeton University Press.

——: "The Inference to the Best Explanation" from *The Philosophical Review*, Vol. 74, No. 1. (Jan., 1965), pp. 88–95.

Thomas Hobbes: "Leviathan" from *Leviathan*, with selected variants from the Latin edition of 1668. Edited by Edwin Curley. Copyright © 1994 by Hackett Publishing Company, Inc. Reprinted by permission of Hackett Publishing Company, Inc. All rights reserved.

David Hume: From "Of the Idea of Necessary Connection," from *Enquiry Concerning Human Understanding and Concerning the Principles of Morals, 2ⁿᵈ Edition*, edited by Selby-Bigge and revised by Nidditch (1975) 5875w from pp. 60–79, 212–232. By permission of Oxford University Press.

——: "Of Justice and Injustice" from *A Treatise of Human Nature, 2e*, by Hume, edited by Selby-Bigge, revised by Nidditch (1978) 5490w from pp. 413–418, 455–501. By permission of Oxford University Press.

——: "Of the Passions" and "Of Morals" from *A Treatise of Human Nature, 2e*, by Hume, edited by Selby-Bigge, revised by Nidditch (1978) 5490w from pp. 413–418, 455–501. By permission of Oxford University Press.

Alec Hyslop and Frank Jackson: "The Analogical Inference to Other Minds" from *American Philosophical Quarterly*, Vol. 9, No. 2, April 1972, excerpts totaling about 7 pages from pp. 168–176. Reprinted by permission of American Philosophical Quarterly.

Frank Jackson: "Epiphenomenal Qualia" from *The Philosophical Quarterly*, April 1982, 32 (127): 127–136. Reprinted by permission of Oxford University Press.

——: "Postscript on Qualia" from *Mind, Method and Conditionals: Selected Essays*. Copyright © 1998 Frank Jackson. Reproduced by permission of Taylor & Francis Books UK.

Immanuel Kant: "Groundwork for the Metaphysics of Morals I" and "Groundwork for the Metaphysics of Morals II" from *Groundwork for the Metaphysics of Morals*, By Immanuel Kant, Translated and Edited by Mary Gregor, 1997, excerpts totaling about 12 pages, 5300 words, from pp. 1–18.

Saul Kripke: "Other Minds" from *Wittgenstein on rules and private language: an elementary exposition* by Kripke, Saul A. Reproduced with permission of Blackwell Pubs (UK) (B) in the format Book via Copyright Clearance Center.

John Locke: From *Essay Concerning Human Understanding*, by Locke, edited by Nidditch (1975) pp. 132–143. By permission of Oxford University Press.

J.L. Mackie: "The Subjectivity of Values," *Ethics: Inventing Right and Wrong*, 1977, pp. 15–42. Copyright © 1977 J.L. Mackie. Reproduced by permission of Penguin Books Ltd.

Don Marquis: "Why Abortion is Immoral" from *The Journal of Philosophy*, Vol. 86, No. 4, April 1989. Reprinted by permission of *The Journal of Philosophy*.

# Name Index

Page numbers in *italic* refer to reading selections.